WOMEN IN HIGHER EDUCATION
A FEMINIST PERSPECTIVE

Second Edition

Edited by

Judith Glazer-Raymo
Long Island University

Barbara K. Townsend
University of Missouri-Columbia

Becky Ropers-Huilman
Louisiana State University

ASHE Reader Series
James Ratcliff, Series Editor

Cover Art: "2 Priory Walk," by Jennifer Bartlett

Copyright © 1993 by Ginn Press.
Copyright © 2000 by Pearson Custom Publishing.
All rights reserved.

This copyright covers material written expressly for this volume by the editor/s as well as the compilation itself. It does not cover the individual selections herein that first appeared elsewhere. Permission to reprint these has been obtained by Pearson Custom Publishing for this edition only. Further reproduction by any means, electronic or mechanical, including photocopying and recording, or by any information storage or retrieval system, must be arranged with the individual copyright holders noted.

Printed in the United States of America

10 9 8 7 6 5 4 3 2 1

Please visit our web site at www.pearsoncustom.com

ISBN 0-536-60974-8

BA 992198

PEARSON CUSTOM PUBLISHING
75 Arlington Street, Suite 300, Boston, MA 02116
A Pearson Education Company

WOMEN IN AMERICAN HIGHER EDUCATION: A FEMINIST PERSPECTIVE
ASHE READER SERIES

Judith Glazer-Raymo, Barbara K. Townsend,
and Becky Ropers-Huilman, Editors

Contents

Acknowledgments vii

Introduction ix

Part I. Context: historical, social, and institutional

Chapter 1. Toward a woman-centered university. 3
  —*Adrienne Rich*

Chapter 2. Priorities, patterns, and principles. 16
  —*Elizabeth Tidball, Charles Tidball, Daryl Smith
  & Lisa Wolf-Wendel*

Chapter 3. Schemas that explain behavior. 22
  —*Virginia Valian*

Chapter 4. Coming to voice, coming to power:
  Black feminist thought as critical social theory. 34
  —*Patricia Hill Collins*

Chapter 5. Feminism & antifeminism: From civil rights to culture wars ... 53
  —*Moira Ferguson, Ketu H. Katrak, & Valerie Miner*

Chapter 6. Feminism, postmodernism, and theoretical developments 72
  —*Imelda Whelehan*

Part II. Feminist theoretical and research perspectives

A. Theory and research methods

Chapter 7. Methods, practice, and epistemology:
  The debate about feminism and research. 89
  —*Mary Maynard*

Chapter 8. Two feminists in search of an interview practice. 101
  —*Leslie R. Bloom*

Chapter 9. Dis-stance and other stances: Negotiations of power
  inside feminist research. 117
  —*Michelle Fine*

B. Feminist policy studies

Chapter 10. Policy analysis for postsecondary education:
   Feminist and critical perspectives.................... 133
   —Estela Bensimon & Catherine Marshall

Chapter 11. Analyzing backlash: Feminist standpoint theory
   as analytical tool.................................... 148
   —Mary Hawkesworth

Chapter 12. Affirmative action and the status of women
   in the academy....................................... 170
   — Judith S. Glazer

Chapter 13. Gender equity in collegiate sports:
   The role of athletic associations..................... 181
   —Lisa C. Hutchens & Barbara K. Townsend

Chapter 14. Cruel environments: Sexual abuse and harassment
   in the academy....................................... 192
   —Linda Serra Hagedorn

Chapter 15. Texts and repression: Hazards for feminists
   in the academy....................................... 221
   —Dorothy Smith

Part III. Women as academic leaders, faculty and students

A. Women leaders

Chapter 16. The leadership challenge for women college presidents 243
   — Margaret Jablonski

Chapter 17. Women and the community college presidency:
   Challenges and possibilities.......................... 252
   — Deborah DiCroce

Chapter 18. Asian women leaders of higher education.............. 259
   — Lori M. Ideta & Joanne E. Cooper

Chapter 19. How deans of women became men 270
   — Robert A. Schwartz

B. Women faculty

Chapter 20. Research, teaching, and service:
   Why shouldn't women's work count?.................... 285
   — Shelley M. Park

Chapter 21. (En)gender(ing) socialization 309
   — William G. Tierney & Estela Mara Bensimon

Chapter 22. Feminists at work: Collaborative relations
   among women faculty.................................. 326
   — Cynthia Sullivan Dickens & Mary Ann D. Sagaria

Chapter 23. For colored girls who have considered suicide
when the academy's not enough: Reflections
of an African American woman scholar.................341
—Gloria Ladson-Billings

Chapter 24. Who is your mother? Red roots of white feminism.........353
— Paula Gunn Allen

Chapter 25. A woman out of control: Deconstructing sexism
and racism in the university......................360
—Roxana Ng

C. Women students

Chapter 26. Of gentlemen and role models......................373
—Lani Guinier

Chapter 27. Detour from nowhere: The remarkable journey
of a re-entry community college woman.................379
—Sandria Rodriguez

Chapter 28. Black and female: Reflections on graduate school.........386
—bell hooks

Chapter 29. Dis/connecting literacy and sexuality:
Speaking the unspeakable in the classroom..............391
—Kathleen Rockhill

Chapter 30. Lessons from a young feminist collective................408
—Tiya Miles

Part IV. Comparative and international perspectives

Chapter 31. Multicultural and global feminism.....................415
—Rosemarie Putnam Tong

Chapter 32. Internationalizing the core curriculum..................439
— Patrice McDermott

Chapter 33. Trends in the gender gap in higher education...........446
— Suzanne Stiver Lie & Lynda Malik

Chapter 34. Women academic leaders in a Latin American university:
Reconciling the paradoxes of professional lives...........453
— Susan B. Twombly

Chapter 35. Academic feminism: Living the contradictions............472
— Sue Middleton

Part V. Feminist pedagogy and curriculum transformation.

Chapter 36. Challenging the traditional curriculum 487
— Marilyn Jacoby Boxer

Chapter 37. Writing everybody in..............................507
— Myrna Goldenberg & Barbara Stout

Chapter 38. Lesbian instructor comes out: The personal is pedagogy 516
— Janet Wright

Chapter 39. Knowledge as bait: Feminism, voice,
              and the pedagogical unconscious 526
    — Laurie Finke
Chapter 40. Gender and race in the classroom:
              Teaching way out of line 540
    — Lana F. Rakow
Chapter 41. Scholarship on the other side:
              Power and caring in feminist education 546
    — Becky Ropers-Huilman

Part VI. Selective bibliography 561

Acknowledgments

The development of this reader has been a collaborative process involving the expertise of several colleagues in the Association for the Study of Higher Education. The co-editors acknowledge the support of Lori Bittker, Series Editor of Pearson Publishing, who recognized the need for a revised edition and who urged us to prepare a new anthology. We also thank the members of the ASHE Editorial Board led by Bruce Jones and Kassie Freeman who enthusiastically endorsed our initial proposal and who have supported us throughout the entire process. We thank Monisa Shackelford for working with the editors in preparing the selective bibliography. And finally, we extend our appreciation to the members of the Advisory Board for this reader who shared their syllabi, offered suggestions, and commented on our selections. The following scholars participated in this process:

Ana Martinez-Aleman	Boston College
Estela Mara Bensimon	University of Southern California
James Davis	University of Delaware
Jennifer Grant Haworth	Loyola University
Carol Hollenshead	University of Michigan
Lisa Lattuca	Loyola University
Mikyong M. Kim	University of Missouri-Columbia
Kathryn Moore	Michigan State University
Robert Schwartz	Florida State University
Mary Anne D. Sagaria	Ohio State University
Sheila Slaughter	University of Arizona
Frances K. Stage	New York University
Carolyn Thompson	University of Missouri-Kansas City
Caroline Sotello Turner	University of Minnesota
Susan Twombly	University of Kansas
Lisa Wolf-Wendel	University of Kansas
Kelly Ward	Oklahoma State University

Introduction

This millennium edition of WOMEN IN AMERICAN HIGHER EDUCATION: A FEMINIST PERSPECTIVE incorporates contemporary scholarship on women faculty, students, and administrators, framing their lives within theoretical, historical, and cultural contexts, and focusing almost entirely on research findings published in the final decade of the twentieth century. It follows an earlier edition that incorporated 'classic' essays and groundbreaking studies about women in post-secondary education (see Glazer, Bensimon, & Townsend, 1993). In compiling this anthology of state-of-the-art scholarly research on women in the academy, the editors surveyed numerous publications from the United States and other English-speaking nations, i.e., the United Kingdom, Australia, and Canada. As a result, readers will find three new sections that reflect the significance of feminist research methods, the growth of feminist scholarship in policy analysis, and the burgeoning field of global feminism. The aim has been to present research that is explicitly feminist in epistemology and to enlighten and motivate women scholars to pursue this line of research. We have sought to be inclusive of the diversity of feminist perspectives as expressed by historians, sociologists, psychologists, political scientists, lawyers, and educators.

The rationale for producing an anthology devoted to scholarship by and about women in higher education arises from a number of factors. Women have made many advances during the past three decades, largely the result of legislative mandates and judicial decisions that led institutions to equalize opportunities and encourage women's progress as students, faculty, and academic leaders. Paradoxically, more subtle but intractable barriers continue to thwart women's advancement. Having crossed the threshold into the twenty-first century, they find it difficult to attain seniority in high-status professional fields and professorial ranks, particularly in major research universities. A deterrent to women's participation in leadership positions also emerges as the result of changes in institutional missions and purposes. One can only speculate on the impact for women of distance learning, privatization, and multinational universities. Long-standing traditions through which previous generations of academics have benefited are now being eroded with the rapid growth of non-tenure track and part-time positions, the decline in commitment to affirmative action and equal opportunity regardless of need or ability, and the efforts to decouple faculty tenure, job security, and academic freedom.

Higher education enjoyed a 60% increase in higher education enrolments between 1970 and 1995, from 8.6 million to 14.3 million, fueled largely by access being granted to women as part-time students and in male-dominated professional fields, and by the expansion of community colleges. By 1984, they were the majority of bachelor's and master's degree recipients; by 1999, they were making rapid progress toward parity with men as first professional and doctoral degree holders. Undoubtedly, there were sufficient numbers of women in the Ph.D. pipeline to populate Rich's "woman-centered university." But disparities have proven persistent for women faculty and administrators, particularly at senior ranks and in prestigious research universities. By 1994, women comprised slightly more than a third (34.6%) of full-time faculty compared to 24 percent in 1975 (an increase of only 10.6 percent) (Snyder, Hoffman & Geddes, 1998). However, instead of gaining in power and influence within the professoriate, they predominate in entry-level and non-tenure track positions, and are 54.2 percent of all lecturers and 50.4 percent of all instructors. Women presidents also have a difficult mountain to climb: 22 women are presidents of doctoral-granting universities and they are only 19 percent of all college presidents, mainly in community colleges, four-year colleges, and denominational and women's colleges (Ross & Green, 1998).

Organization of the reader

The forty-one selections contained in this reader articulate a variety of feminist perspectives in the extensive literature on women in higher education. The editors reviewed hundreds of articles and books, aided in this process by the recommendations of a national advisory board of feminist scholars. The objective has been to present an anthology that is inclusive and representative of contemporary feminist scholarship at the dawn of the twenty-first century. In making these selections, the editors have been mindful of the diversity of interests and approaches to the study of women in higher education. Some topics proved elusive in the search for examples of published research. Book length, dates of publication, and ease of availability from other sources also governed the final choices. The American focus of the reader notwithstanding, Part IV on global feminism incorporates exemplary international scholarship produced by feminists in the U.S. and other countries.

The intended audience is faculty and students engaged in the study of higher education and those pursuing coursework in women's studies, gender studies, and policy studies. It will also be of interest to those seeking materials to supplement classroom texts in educational research, psychology, sociology, and education. It is further designed as a resource to women and men concerned with the status of women in their organizations and as a reference work that extends knowledge about problems and concerns of women faculty, students, and administrators. An extensive bibliography gives supplementary sources of interest to scholars and practitioners. Several selections in this book reflect the emphasis that feminists have placed on biographical and autobiographical methods in researching women's lives and recording their experiences.

WOMEN IN AMERICAN HIGHER EDUCATION has been organized to facilitate its use as both a teaching and a reference tool. It is divided into five parts: Part I directs the reader's attention to the contexts in which women's participation in higher education has been channeled, particularly since the passage of Title IX, Title VII, and various executive orders. Part II, Theoretical and Research Perspectives, elucidates the meanings of feminism for higher education, its applications for conducting scholarly research, and the impact of both theory and research on feminist policy analyses. Part III focuses attention on research about the constituent groups of women who contribute to the life of the university as students, faculty, and professional staff. The linkages between gender, race, and sexual orientation are discussed in several essays that demonstrate the diversity of women's experiences and viewpoints. Part IV introduces readers to aspects of multicultural feminism and global feminism based on research conducted in Latin American, Australian, and European cultures. Finally, the essays in Part V take the reader into the classroom, reflecting on the problems and the promise of pedagogical content knowledge when experienced from a feminist perspective. It is within this context of change—yielding both optimism and concern—that we present this text.

Part I

Historical, cultural, and psychological contexts

The reader begins, most appropriately, with a classic essay by Adrienne Rich in which she proposes the transformation of research universities from male-dominated institutions to centers where "women shape the philosophy and the decision making though men may choose to study there." We have included this essay, first published in 1975, to place in historical perspective the goals and the realities of change in American higher education. The seventies were a time of great optimism about women's future prospects as academic leaders, following the promulgation of Title IX and Title VII regulations on college and university campuses, the inauguration of women's studies programs, the transformation of selective men's colleges and universities into coeducational institutions and the growth of community colleges. (Glazer-Raymo, 1999).

In their essay, Tidball, Tidball, Smith, and Wendel-Wolf review the positive role played by women's colleges in the past half-century and their unique contribution in the education and advancement of women students and faculty. The authors assert that principles and practices developed in the women's colleges in the past 50 years present a heritage of normative values that can empower, encourage, and support women in contemporary society. The complexity of feminist ideologies concerns several authors in this reader, evidence that feminist scholarship has evolved from a predominant focus on issues of equality and a numerical assessment of women's status to more diverse perspectives. For example, Virginia Valian, a psychology professor, focuses her attention on the psychology of women, asking what research tells us about the scarcity of women faculty and professionals in the upper echelons of status fields. She proposes the existence of "schemas" or stereotypes that serve as mental constructs in defining the professional roles and appropriate behavior of women and men. She observes that it is the interaction of these roles with gender stereotypes that must be evaluated to understand the persistent clash of normative values and gendered behavior. Patricia Hills Collins, a sociologist, applies schema analysis to a critical review of the progress made by Black feminists in finding their voices and coming to power on their own terms, pointing out emphatically the need to understand and address the differences between the Black feminist experience and the experience of White women, Asian-American women, Latina women, and sexual minorities. The multiplicity of feminist and anti-feminist voices now threatening the viability of the women's movement is put into a historical context by Ferguson, Katrak, and Miner. Their essay reveals the complexity of feminist ideologies from the perspectives of White, Latina, African-American, and Native American women, observing that the multidimensionality of the academic "culture wars" can be seen in the conservative rhetoric of opponents to women's studies, ethnic studies, gay and lesbian studies, and other multidisciplinary diversity programs. Finally, Imelda Whelehan's essay, written from the perspective of a European feminist, raises theoretical questions about the nature of gender identity politics so evident in the current debate between poststructuralists, postmodernists, and liberal feminists. Recognizing that the category of 'woman' does not connote a common identity, she questions whether the feminist postmodern arguments supporting gender differences will ultimately lead to a return to gender neutrality as the dominant stance. In affirming feminism's heterogeneity, she suggests that diversity and conflict in feminist circles should guide us to a "heterotopia" rather than a replication of the past.

Part II

Feminist theoretical and research perspectives

In an essay on theory as liberatory practice, bell hooks observed that feminist theory can be confining but it can also be liberating when it is linked to feminist practice, the social activism that arises from a need to change our social world (1994). What does it mean to research women's lives from a feminist perspective? How can feminist theory inform policy and practice in higher education? In noting that a considerable body of feminist research addresses these questions, Mary Maynard emphasizes the need to critically examine the entire process. We ascribe to the view expressed by Maynard that "there is no one methodological approach or research practice specific to feminism . . . since feminism embraces a number of theoretical positions and perspectives." Rather than declaim on different types of feminist theory, Maynard engages in a comparative analysis of multiple perspectives, identifying three major related concerns confronting feminists engaged in empirical social research: the role of women's experience, the importance of race and diversity, and the question of objectivity. Feminist method, she argues, must go beyond experience to address racism, classism, heterosexism, and disableism. It needs to be rigorous, relevant, and intellectually compelling. For doctoral students or faculty learning how to conduct research from a feminist perspective, the experiences of other scholars can be enlightening and reassuring. Thus, an essay by Leslie Bloom moves beyond Maynard's critique of feminist methodology to report on her experiences as a neophyte interviewer. She reflects on the process of asking good questions, engaging in conversations, and recording life histories. For Bloom and many other feminist scholars, ethnographic interviewing proves the pivotal focus of feminist methodology, particularly the ability to record and analyze personal narratives. But what happens when ideological objectives help frame research questions? What impact does this have on feminist methodology? Michelle Fine responds by exploring the importance of activist feminist research that is participatory and that links theoretical, practical, and political goals in conducting social change research. In the process, she also explores the difficult conflicts and the many contradictions that arise in collaborative and participatory studies.

Feminist policy studies

The epistemological foundations of feminist theory and feminist research methodology have been derived largely from liberal, socialist, radical, psychoanalytic, poststructuralist, and postmodern ideologies. More recently, in their use of feminism as critique, feminist scholars deconstruct and redefine the rationale and gender-neutral methods traditionally applied in the policy sciences. Bensimon and Marshall advocate the use of critical feminist policy analysis to reveal the shortcomings of gender and race-neutral evaluation techniques. Feminist policy analyses have evolved from critiques of discriminatory practices and incremental policy modifications replicating traditional social science techniques to assertions that conventional approaches used to describe and explain the policy cycle are gendered. They have moved further to stress the centrality of women's role in shaping and evaluating public policies and in promoting progressive policymaking. Three essays follow this theoretical analysis by Bensimon and Marshall. First, Mary Hawkesworth questions Sandra Harding's construct of feminist standpoint epistemology, particularly what she views as its subjectivity. She suggests, however, that it can be a useful heuristic device for studying policy problems and then sets out to demonstrate how this can be done. Hawkesworth applies standpoint theory to a feminist policy analysis of the decisions to abolish affirmative action and to reform welfare. To emphasize the subjective nature of standpoint theory, Hawkesworth adopts four distinct points-of-view or standpoints in her critique: liberal, socialist, black, and postmodern. She concludes that "by engaging competing theoretical frameworks, feminist standpoint theory enables women to explore uncharted territory in policy research, raise questions about conventional standards of evidence, models of explanation, and theoretical suppositions."

Judith Glazer adopts a critical feminist perspective in her analysis of mechanisms, including affirmative action, that have been employed in the past 25 years to improve the position of women in higher education. She traces the history of campus commissions on the status of women from the early seventies when anti-bias laws and regulations were promulgated, the historic, political, and symbolic functions played by the commissions and the reasons why, after being initiated with great fanfare, their vitality eroded by the mid-1980s. In this case, a liberal feminist strategy could not overcome the social backlash against women. Nor could it piece together in a meaningful way the conflicting and fragmented objectives of diverse constituencies in the postmodern university. The centerpiece of debate in determining compliance with anti-bias regulations has been resource allocation for women and men's athletics. Lisa Hutchens and Barbara Townsend adopt a liberal feminist perspective in tracing the NCAA's pivotal role in this debate. As the authors point out, Supreme Court decisions (most recently in 1992 in *Cohen v. Brown University*) have added another dimension to the policy process, with a major impact on athletics expenditures as well as on employment, sexual harassment, affirmative action, and academic freedom. The fourth set of policies covered in this section focus on sexual harassment in higher education. Linda Hagedorn's in-depth review of the literature on this important topic and her analysis of 50 policy statements, help to frame her assertion that current policies are inadequate on many campuses and that strategies are needed to eliminate gender inequities which perpetuate hostile environments and lead to charges of sexual harassment and abuse. Finally, a case study of sexual harassment in a Canadian university, conducted by Dorothy Smith, demonstrates the use of feminist methodology in investigating complex claims and counterclaims arising from a series of incidents in one department of political science of a research university. As the originator of feminist standpoint theory (1978), Smith's step-by-step analysis provides a valuable tool for understanding the complexity of adjudicating sexual harassment claims and their eventual impact on the larger organization.

Part III
Women as academic leaders, faculty, and students

Women administrators. The Wall Street Journal coined the phrase "glass ceiling" in 1986 to describe the barriers that thwarted women's upward mobility into the senior ranks of corporate America. This phrase has become a metaphor to characterize how the policies and practices impeding women's professional advancement are embedded in all institutions, including colleges and universities. Margaret Jablonski discusses the leadership challenge for women college presidents, examining the leadership styles of seven of these women, and raising questions about whether women lead differently than men. Not surprisingly, she found a significant gap between the numerous models of leadership espoused in the literature, the role expectations that boards of trustees and faculty had regarding women presidents, and the realities of their actual situations. Deborah DeCroce offers a first-person account of the experiences of a two-year college president. She suggests that women in her position have the opportunity to break down gender stereotypes, initiate dialogues about gender, race, sexual orientation, and related issues, and in general become more active players in the public policy arena. Another kind of gender stereotype, this time linked to issues of race and class, is discussed by Lori Ideta and Joanne Cooper in their essay on Asian-American women leaders in higher education. The difficulties of balancing personal and professional worlds runs through the stories told by Asian women as they relate their experiences with gender and race stereotypes in the academic workplace. The subtleties of sex discrimination are also revealed in Robert Schwartz's historical account of deans of women in American higher education. In this case, by 1950, deans of women became the "inevitable victims of the pervasive hostility that greeted women in general on campus." As a result, from the 1950s to the 1990s, the position of deans of men assumed greater administrative visibility and status, being expanded and elevated into student personnel leadership positions that were gender-neutral but male-dominated. Although student services positions now attract a high percentage of women, men continue to outrank women in the leadership roles of chief student personnel officers, deans of students, and vice presidents for student services.

Women faculty. In the past decade, increased attention has been given by scholars to the work of women faculty in all its complexity. Selecting from the many articles and books published in this decade has been a difficult task. The essays included in this section provide an overview of women in the professoriate, structuring their research questions within feminist frames of analysis. Beginning with an overview of the status of women faculty in academia at the close of the twentieth century, Shelley Park examines the adverse impact of gender hierarchies and roles on women's ability to earn tenure or promotion. Acknowledging the unequal weight given to the three dominant criteria—research, teaching, and service-she applies alternative criteria that expand on the notion of the scholarship of teaching as the basis for evaluating faculty work. What happens when women faculty are further differentiated by race, sexual orientation, and social class, is revealed by William Tierney and Estela Bensimon in their ethnographic study of junior faculty. They provide the reader with a vivid picture of the impact of gender inequities on women faculty in relation to both the socialization and professionalization processes. Cynthia Dickens and Mary Ann Sagaria also conducted extensive interviews to learn more about the interaction between feminist ideology, faculty collaboration, and faculty scholarship among women faculty in a research university. In their consideration of the range of ideologies implicit in contemporary feminist thought, they raise critical issues about the importance of shared personal values as the basis for establishing collaborative relationships. An autobiographical essay by Gloria Ladson-Billings discloses the dilemmas of an African-American scholar and public intellectual whose scholarship is "politically grounded and culturally significant." She draws on the work of Collins, citing the latter's belief that "knowledge claims must be grounded in individual character, values, and ethics," and that "not only what is said but who says it gives meaning and interpretation to knowledge claims." Ladson-Billings' scholarship is also analogous to Michelle Fine's notion of the researcher as social activist, seeking a system that is diverse, inclusive, and just. The connections between gender and race are also emphasized in an autobiographical essay by Paula Gunn Allen, a Native American feminist. She questions public attitudes that ignore the historical tradition of these women as "intellectual movers and shakers in the United States, Britain, and Europe," describing the Iroquois federal system as evidence that feminist notions of power may actually stem from tribal sources. Finally, Roxana Ng speaks from the perspective of an Asian-American feminist teaching courses on ethnic group and race relations. In commenting on the dynamics of faculty-student interactions in her classroom, she draws attention to how sexism and racism operate to disempower feminist and other minority teachers, affecting her authority and the extent to which she can be effective in challenging institutional norms and values.

Women college students. Women have been in the majority of students for almost two decades but, as Tierney and Bensimon pointed out in their interviews with women faculty, the socialization process frequently fails to take into account the diversity of their interests, experiences, and needs. Lani Guinier raises this issue in her analysis of how women law students are socialized by their professors to think and act like gentlemen in order to succeed in their chosen profession. As a law professor, she contemplates her role as an African-American feminist in adopting pedagogical approaches that break down the barriers between teacher and student and transform the law school from a male-dominated workplace into one that is more female-friendly. The antithesis of women law students in elite graduate programs is the story of a re-entry older woman student in a suburban community college. Sandria Rodriguez feels that this woman's story is not unique and that it cries out for sustained efforts on the part of faculty and staff in no longer marginalizing women with low incomes, few resources, and minority backgrounds. Bell hooks recalls what it was like for her as an African-American graduate student in a predominantly white university, admonishing Black women to overcome their passivity and to actively resist their marginalized and invisible status. Kathleen Rockhill echoes hooks' assertiveness, raising questions about the proclivity of teachers to overlook how class, race, ethnicity, age, physical ability, gender, and the sexuality of the learner enter into the challenges posed for literacy. She argues for more learner-centered approaches that confront, rather than ignore, the social location of the student. Finally, an undergraduate voice is heard when Tiya Miles relates her personal experience as a student involved in a failed effort of women undergraduates to publish a feminist magazine. In writing about this painful episode as a learning exercise, she reflects on the intersections of racism, classism, and sexism in students' thinking, and how they allowed issues of race and social class to affect this enterprise.

Part IV

Comparative and international feminist perspectives

The globalization of higher education is being facilitated by access to the Internet and electronic journals. Feminists have taken advantage of these trends to initiate dialogues on a range of topics of interest and concern to women in industrialized and developing countries. In her analyses of multicultural feminism and global feminism, Rosemarie Tong provides an introduction to feminist frameworks for conducting international and comparative studies. She focuses on gender, race, and social class in discussing the economic, political, and cultural aspects of global feminism and the challenges for women's scholarship. Patrice McDermott focuses on the issues that arise when women's studies programs are reconceptualized to be more inclusive, global, and multicultural. She and Tong both contend that postcolonial feminism and activism raise questions about western feminist thought and, in effect, redefine the boundaries of women's studies programs. A European perspective is provided by Lie and Malik in their discussion of "the global gender gap in higher education," one that is intensified by significant inequities in wealth, rank, and power in national higher education systems. Even though institutionalized discrimination may be declining in democratic nations, they found little evidence in the 17 countries they studied that men are ready to share power and privilege on an equal basis with women colleagues.

Two institutional studies disclose the diversity of viewpoints among women faculty and administrators in a Latin American and a New Zealand university. Interviews with women faculty in a Latin American university enable Susan Twombly to explore women's career paths and "the relationship between machismo and institutional culture" in women's professional careers. The overriding theme of this essay is women's acceptance of the complexity of their lives as a "series of negotiations and attempts to reconcile contradictions." An autobiographical essay by Sue Middleton, who teaches at the University of Waikato in New Zealand, notes the frustrations and problems she encountered in weaving her personal pedagogies into basic women's studies and education courses. Her work provides a transition to the next part of this reader and a discussion of feminist pedagogy and curriculum transformation.

Part V

Feminist Pedagogy and Curriculum Transformation

Over the past three decades, feminist educators have fostered many substantive changes in both the content and process of the higher education curriculum. Administrators, students, and faculty concerned with the goals of equal opportunity for all underrepresented groups have joined them. Marilyn Boxer's historical research on the origins and development of women's studies appropriately begins this section, describing how curriculum transformation has been, and can be, accomplished in colleges and universities. Paired with an essay by Myrna Goldenberg and Barbara Stout, Boxer's work emphasizes the importance of curricular content and pedagogy for the educational experience. Further, these essays provide both theoretical underpinnings and specific guidelines for accomplishing this transformation in universities and colleges and among diverse populations of students. Another theme of these selections relates to the identities and intentions of faculty members as they attempt to participate in this transformation through the use of feminist pedagogy. First, Janet Wright's article conveys how a lesbian faculty member, in attempting to enact feminist pedagogy, used her own identity as a tool for teaching and learning. She raises questions about when and how an instructor's identity is relevant to students' learning. Through the use of students' reactions to her disclosure, she describes how a teacher's identity can be effectively used as a teaching tool. Next, Laurie Finke uses psychoanalytic theory to reflect on the motivations of students and teachers in feminist classrooms. She illustrates the complexities of terms such as 'resistance' and 'voice,' concepts that are often used in discussions of feminist teaching. Lana Rakow also focuses on the concept of resistance, suggesting that until the broader context supporting specific social interactions is changed, those wishing to bring issues related to race and gender into their classrooms in a meaningful way will continue to meet active resistance from students. Finally, through Becky Ropers-Huilman's analysis of her transition from feminist student to feminist teacher, she points out the ways in which the structures of higher education support relations of power and caring that both impede and facilitate student learning.

The Nature of Research on Women in Higher Education

Taken collectively, the selections in this book present a multidisciplinary look at women in higher education. In some of the selections, a specific disciplinary lens is used. For example, Smith uses a sociological lens to examine sexual harassment in a political science department within a Canadian university. Similarly, Rich writes as a poet and literary critic in giving her vision of what research universities could become if freed from male domination. Valian provides another example in her use of the lens of psychology to present how gender schemas or stereotypes limit the advancement of women in the major professions.

The majority of selections have been written by researchers whose field of study is explicitly a multidisciplinary field, the field of higher education. Thus Glazer examines affirmative action in the academy from the multidisciplinary perspective of a scholar in higher education, as do Ideta and Cooper in their narratives of Asian-American higher education leaders, and Schwartz in his historical examination of deans of women. The interdisciplinarity of the curriculum as envisioned by feminist scholars and teachers has proven more difficult to achieve in practice and feminists continue to write mainly from their disciplinary perspectives. In addition to the fact that women's studies faculty tend to be drawn from departments in the humanities and the social sciences rather than to form autonomous units, and that the journals in which they publish are also disciplinary, women's studies programs are now competing for resources with gender studies, gay and lesbian studies, ethnic studies, and cultural studies programs.

The heterogeneity of feminism is exemplified in the variety of feminist perspectives presented and advocated. Some of the authors are explicit in their standpoint. For example, Collins and Ladson-Billings write from an overt, black feminist perspective. Bensimon and Marshall, Glazer, and Hawkesworth each use feminist critical policy analysis to critique and shed new light on social justice and educational policies. An implicit liberal standpoint is seen in DiCroce's discussion of how she can use her presidential position to improve gender and race relations in her college, and in Hutchens and Townsend's look at gender equity in college sports.

Several authors explicitly foreground their own racial or ethnic identity in their analysis of women's position in higher education. Thus Allen writes as a Native American woman scholar, Ng as an Asian-American feminist, and Collins, hooks, and Ladson-Billings as African-American feminists. Other authors write from their own experience within a particular role in the academy. Thus Miles writes as a student, DiCroce as a college president, Middleton as a women's studies and education professor, and Twombly as an American women in a Latin American culture.

The diversity of feminist and disciplinary perspectives represented in these selections may point the way for faculty and students in graduate programs focusing on the study of high education to rethink the current structure and content of these programs. For example, what happens when critical feminist perspectives are applied to traditional organizational theorizing? Are existing courses sufficiently inclusive of the diversity of students, faculty, and administrators now participating in academe? Do programmatic teaching practices and expectations accommodate the needs of all students, including women and people of color? Do classroom and administrative practices reflect an overt heterosexual bias? What research agenda for higher education might be articulated by a white, liberal feminist? By a feminist of color? These are just some of the questions that need to be addressed if higher education as a field of study is to incorporate not only a feminist perspective but also perspectives drawn from gender studies and ethnic studies.

Suggestions on using this reader as a teaching text

Several essays in this reader offer rich resources for teaching in higher education environments. Further, these selections reflect commonly held views on what is important to think about in considering the topic of this reader in more than a superficial way. As discussed throughout the literature on feminist teaching and curriculum transformation, content and pedagogy go hand in hand. With this in mind, we offer a few beliefs and approaches that may be useful to teachers and students wishing to engage with this text, recognizing that each context may call for different interactions.

Feminist educators typically draw on multiple methods and approaches in teaching and learning. They are interested in engaging in rich interactions, supported by the discipline and by their work as faculty. As such, they are sensitive to context and how students are experiencing their classrooms, and may change approaches depending on their perceptions of those experiences. Still, some general guidelines may provide beginning points for structuring teaching and learning interactions.

First, feminist education values student and faculty experiences as sources of knowing. Faculty members can encourage students to reflect on the ways in which their personal experiences are portrayed in, or negated by, the texts reviewed in class. What is missing? What is over-represented? Why does this portrayal matter? Through asking students to engage in deep reflection on the course texts in relation to their personal lives, feminist educators support students? beliefs in their own abilities as knowledge-producers. This process can lead to a critical evaluation of curricular materials as well, for example, asking students to engage in journal-writing as a means of reflecting on and analyzing course material through their own experiences. Further, students could be asked to write (or find) a selection that they think should have been in this reader, thereby fostering their own participation in the curriculum transformation described in several selections.

Second, feminist education values disciplinary and interdisciplinary knowledge as well as experiential knowledge. Feminist and other scholars have generated a great deal of rigorous and important scholarship. Feminist teachers tend to value the knowledge coming from that scholarship. In fact, because none of us are free from the ways in which our life experiences influence what we are able to perceive, feminist education relies on many, possibly contradictory, viewpoints on a given topic. We have attempted to include many different perspectives in this volume, and hope that readers will supplement these readings with others.

Third, feminist education recognizes that gender is not the only defining or influencing identity that affects how teachers and students interact. Gender is indeed a salient characteristic that has dramatic effects on a wide variety of social interactions. Yet, feminists recognize that other identities such as race, social class, disability, and sexual orientation, work together to shape social opportunities and interactions. As such, students cannot be seen as a unified body that will all read and interpret the texts in the same ways. One of the ways feminist educators can recognize the diversity that exists in every classroom is to use a variety of pedagogical practices and assessment or evaluation strategies. For example, students might be given a choice as to how they will demonstrate their knowledge of the course material. Other teachers ask for regular feedback from students about the ways in which the course is and isn't working for them. This feedback can be identifiable or anonymous, given in groups or by individuals, and used to rethink the teaching and learning interactions that are constructed. Also important are teachers' attempts to ensure that course objectives are met through using texts and material that reflect a wide range of identities.

Fourth, feminist education recognizes power hierarchies between teachers and learners. While the identities described above certainly affect teaching and learning interactions, there is another identity that is uniquely present in classrooms—that of teacher and student. While there are ways to mitigate the negative effects of the power dynamic that these roles establish, it is dangerous for students, as Ropers-Huilman points out in this volume, if teachers ever try to forget those roles. Feminist educators tend to be wary of the misuse of power because of its role in the oppression of women and others currently and throughout history. Still, they also recognize that institutional power can be useful in challenging beliefs that are harmful to teaching and learning interactions. As such, while feminist teachers may attempt to share their power with students, they also recognize that there are times when sharing power does not have the intended effects. In trying to negotiate power relations in their classes, some feminist teachers purposefully remain silent during rich discussions, opening space for others to communicate. They may ask students to grade each other's work or to provide a reflective analysis of their own work. They may further choose to discuss in class the ways in which they, as teachers, are consciously and subconsciously using power to shape the class structure and conversations in subtle and yet meaningful ways. Through the resulting analysis of power, students and teachers become more aware of its presence and more able to recognize its effects. For further discussion of power in feminist classrooms, see the selections by Finke, Ropers-Huilman, hooks, Middleton and Rakow in this volume.

Finally, feminist education recognizes the role of educating for social change. Many feminist scholars, including Fine, hooks, and Ladson-Billings, see their work in the academy as either supporting or constituting their activism. They want their work to make a difference in a significant and positive way. Through feminist content or interactions in higher education classrooms, students may be encouraged to view the world with a critical eye, better understanding the ways in which gender relations shape social possibilities. To facilitate this interaction, some educators may ask students to engage in the transformation of theory to practice in a forum of their choice. Students can be asked to apply knowledge derived from classroom experiences to conduct social action projects based on in-class learning. For an excellent discussion of the possibilities and complexities of this work, see Mimi Orner's (1996) work on "Teaching for the moment: Intervention projects as situated pedagogy."

As discussed in several of the articles in this reader, feminist transformation of the academy can be challenging and uncertain. This is true when considering feminist teaching as well. Questions for further discussion, perhaps in a classroom setting, might include: How does (or can) feminist education embrace the wide spectrum of diversity that exists in our society? How is feminist education limited and supported by its location in higher education institutions? These questions, and many others provoked by the readings in this volume, provide beginning points for potentially rich discussions about the roles of women in higher education.

To begin a conversation across institutional boundaries, it may be useful for women teaching higher education courses to share their syllabi. A website initiated as a joint venture of the American Educational Research Association-Division J (Postsecondary Education) and the Association for the Study of Higher Education is located at the University of California at Los Angeles. The editors and advisory board encourage readers to add their syllabi for women in higher education and related courses to this website, enabling women faculty to access them in preparing future courses. It can be accessed by following a link from ERIC higher education site [www.gwu.edu/-eriche), AERA Division J (aera.net/divisions/j), or UCLA Graduate School of Education and Information Studies (*www.gseis.ucla.edu*).]

References

Glazer, J.S., Bensimon, E.M., Townsend, B.K. (1993). *Women in higher education: A feminist perspective*. Needham Hts.: Ginn Press.

Glazer-Raymo, J. (1999). *Shattering the myths: Women in academe*. Baltimore: Johns Hopkins University Press.

hooks, bell. (1994). *Teaching to transgress; Education as the practice of freedom*. London: Routledge.

Orner, M. (1996). Teaching for the moment: Intervention projects as situated pedagogy. *Theory into practice*, 35 (2): 72–78.

Ross, M. and Green, M. (1998). *The American college president*. Washington, D.C.: American Council on Education.

Snyder, T., Hoffman, C. & Geddes, C. (Eds.). (1998). *Digest of educational statistics*. Washington, D.C. National Center for Educational Statistics, Office of Educational Reseach and Improvement.

Part I

Context: Historical, Social and Institutional

Chapter 1

Toward a Woman-Centered University
(1973–74)

Adrienne Rich

II

The early feminists, the women intellectuals of the past, along with educated men, assumed that the intellectual structure as well as the contents of the education available to men was viable: that is, enduring, universal, a discipline civilizing to the mind and sensitizing to the spirit. Its claims for both humanism and objectivity went unquestioned. One of the few voices to question this was that of Virginia Woolf, in her still little-read and extraordinary *Three Guineas*, an essay connecting war and fascism directly with the patriarchal system, and with the exclusion of women from learning and power. Far more radical in its vision than the more famous *A Room of One's Own*, it does not simply protest this exclusion but questions the very nature of the professions as practiced by men, the very quality of the intellectual heritage protected by the university.

> The questions that we have to ask and to answer about that [academic] procession during this moment of transition are so important that they may well change the lives of all men and women forever. For we have to ask ourselves, here and now, do we wish to join that procession, or don't we? On what terms shall we join that procession? Above all, where is it leading us, the procession of educated men? ... Let us never cease from thinking,—what is this "civilization" in which we find ourselves? What are these ceremonies and why should we take part in them? What are these professions and why should we make money out of them? Where in short is it leading us, the procession of the sons of educated men?[1]

The major educational question for the nineteenth and earlier twentieth centuries was whether the given educational structure and contents should be made available to women. In the nineteenth century the issue to be resolved was whether a woman's mind and body were intended by "nature" to grapple with intellectual training. In the first sixty years of our own century the "problem" seemed to be that education was "wasted" on women who married, had families, and effectively retired from intellectual life. These issues, of course, though they had to be argued, really veiled (as the question of "standards" veils the issue of nonwhite participation in higher education) the core of politics and social power. Why women gave up their careers after marriage, why even among the unmarried or childless so few were found in the front ranks of intellectual life were questions that opened up only when women began to ask them and to explore the answers.

Until the 1960s, the university continued to be seen as privileged enclave, somehow more defensible than other privileged enclaves, criticized if at all for being too idealistic, too little in

---

Reprinted from *On Lies, Secrets and Silence: Selected Prose, 1966–1978*, by Adrienne Rich, 1979. Copyright © 1979 W. W. Norton & Company.

touch with the uses and abuses of power; and romanticized as a place where knowledge is loved for its own sake, every opinion has an open-minded hearing, "the dwelling place of permanent values ... of beauty, of righteousness, of freedom," as the Brandeis University bulletin intones. The radical student critique—black and white—of the sixties readily put its finger on the facts underlying this fiction: racism of the academy and its curriculum, its responsiveness to pressures of vested interest, political, economic, and military; the use of the academy as a base for research into weapons and social control and as a machinery for perpetuating the power of white, middle-class men. Today the question is no longer whether women (or non-whites) are intellectually and "by nature" equipped for higher education, but whether this male-created, male-dominated structure is really capable of serving the humanism and freedom it professes.

Woolf suggested that women entering the professions must bring with them the education—unofficial, unpaid for, unvalued by society—of their female experience, if they are not to become part of the dehumanizing forces of competition, money lust, the lure of personal fame and individual aggrandizement, and of "unreal loyalties." In other words, we must choose what we will accept and what we will reject of institutions already structured and defined by patriarchal values. Today, more crucial even than the number of teaching jobs open to women—crucial as that continues to be—is the process of deciding "on what terms we shall join that procession." Woolf, for all the charges of lack of class consciousness thrown at her, was in fact extremely conscious of the evils of exclusivity and elitism. She had to a marked degree the female knowledge of what it means to be kept outside, alienated from power and knowledge, and of how subtly a place "inside" corrupts even liberal spirits.

> ... the professions have a certain undeniable effect upon the professors. They make the people who practice them possessive, jealous of any infringement of their rights, and highly combative if anyone dares dispute them.... Therefore this guinea, which is to help you help women to enter the professions, has this condition as a first condition attached to it. You shall swear that you will do all in your power to insist that any woman who enters any profession shall in no way hinder any other human being, whether man or woman, white or black, provided that he or she is qualified to enter that profession, from entering it; but shall do all in her power to help them.[2]

What present-day radical feminists have come to recognize, is that in order to become a force against elitism and exclusivity we must learn to place each other and ourselves first, not to hinder other human beings, but to tap the kinds of power and knowledge that exist—buried, diffused, misnamed, sometimes misdirected—within women.[3] At this point we need the university, with its libraries, laboratories, archives, collections, and some—but not all—of the kinds of trained thinking and expertise it has to offer. We need to consciously and critically select what is genuinely viable and what we can use from the masculine intellectual tradition, as we possess ourselves of the knowledge, skills, and perspectives that can refine our goal of self-determination with discipline and wisdom. (Certainly we do *not* need the university to continue replicating the tradition that has excluded us, or to become "amateur males.") The university is by no means the only place where this work will be carried on; nor, obviously, can the university become more woman-centered and less elitist while the society remains androcentric.

III

There are two ways in which a woman's integrity is likely to be undermined by the process of university education. This education is, of course, yet another stage in the process of her entire education, from her earliest glimpses of television at home to the tracking and acculturating toward "femininity" that became emphatic in high school. But when a woman is admitted to higher education—particularly graduate school—it is often made to sound as if she enters a sexually neutral world of "disinterested" and "universal" perspectives. It is assumed that coeducation means the equal education, side by side, of women and men. Nothing could be further from the truth; and nothing could more effectively seal a woman's sense of her secondary value in a man-centered world than her experience as a "privileged" woman in the university—if she knows how to interpret what she lives daily.

In terms of the *content* of her education, there is no discipline that does not obscure or devalue the history and experience of women as a group. What Otto Rank said of psychology has to be said of every other discipline, including the "neutral" sciences: it is "not only man-made . . . but masculine in its mentality."[4] Will it seem, in forty years, astonishing that a book should have been written in 1946 with the title *Woman as Force in History*? The title does not seem bizarre to us now. Outside of women's studies, though liberal male professors may introduce material about women into their courses, we live with textbooks, research studies, scholarly sources, and lectures that treat women as a subspecies, mentioned only as peripheral to the history of men. In every discipline where we *are* considered, women are perceived as the objects rather than the originators of inquiry, thus primarily through male eyes, thus as a special category. That the true business of civilization has been in the hands of men is the lesson absorbed by every student of the traditional sources. How this came to be, and the process that kept it so, may well be the most important question for the self-understanding and survival of the human species; but the extent to which civilization has been built on the bodies and services of women—unacknowledged, unpaid, and unprotected in the main—is a subject apparently unfit for scholarly decency. The witch persecutions of the fourteenth through seventeenth centuries, for example, involved one of the great historic struggles—a class struggle and a struggle for knowledge—between the illiterate but practiced female healer and the beginnings of an aristocratic nouveau science, between the powerful patriarchal Church and enormous numbers of peasant women, between the pragmatic experience of the wise-woman and the superstitious practices of the early male medical profession.[5] The phenomena of woman-fear and woman-hatred illuminated by those centuries of genocide are with us still; certainly a history of psychology or history of science that was not hopelessly one-sided would have to confront and examine this period and its consequences. Like the history of slave revolts, the history of women's resistance to domination awaits discovery by the offspring of the dominated. The chronicles, systems, and investigations of the humanities and the sciences are in fact a collection of half-truths and lacunae that have worked enormous damage to the ability of the sexes to understand themselves and one another.

If this is changing within the rubric of women's studies, it is doing so in the face of prejudice, contempt, and outright obstruction. If it is true that the culture recognized and transmitted by the university has been predominantly white Western culture, it is also true that within black and Third World studies the emphasis is still predominantly masculine, and the female perspective needs to be fought for and defended there as in the academy at large.

I have been talking about the content of the university curriculum, that is, the mainstream of the curriculum. Women in colleges where a women's studies program already exists, or where feminist courses are beginning to be taught, still are often made to feel that the "real" curriculum is the male-centered one; that women's studies are (like Third World studies) a "fad"; that feminist teachers are "unscholarly," "unprofessional," or "dykes." But the content of courses and programs is only the more concrete form of undermining experienced by the woman student. More invisible, less amenable to change by committee proposal or fiat, is the hierarchical image, the structure of relationships, even the style of discourse, including assumptions about theory and practice, ends and means, process and goal.

The university is above all a hierarchy. At the top is a small cluster of highly paid and prestigious persons, chiefly men, whose careers entail the services of a very large base of ill-paid or unpaid persons, chiefly women: wives, research assistants, secretaries, teaching assistants, cleaning women, waitresses in the faculty club, lower-echelon administrators, and women students who are used in various ways to gratify the ego. Each of these groups of women sees itself as distinct from the others, as having different interests and a different destiny. The student may become a research assistant, mistress, or even wife; the wife may act as secretary or personal typist for her husband, or take a job as lecturer or minor administrator; the graduate student may, if she demonstrates unusual brilliance and carefully follows the rules, rise higher into the pyramid, where she loses her identification with teaching fellows, as the wife forgets her identification with the student or secretary she may once have been. The waitress or cleaning woman has no such mobility, and it is rare for other women in the university, beyond a few socially aware or feminist students, to support her if she is on strike or unjustly fired. Each woman in the university is defined by her relationship to the men in power instead of her relationship to other women up and down the scale.

Now, this fragmentation among women is merely a replication of the fragmentation from each other that we undergo in the society outside; in accepting the premise that advancement and security—even the chance to do one's best work—lie in propitiating and identifying with men who have some power, we have always found ourselves in competition with each other and blinded to our common struggles. This fragmentation and the invisible demoralization it generates work constantly against the intellectual and emotional energies of the woman student.

The hidden assumptions on which the university is built comprise more than simply a class system. In a curious and insidious way the "work" of a few men—especially in the more scholarly and prestigious institutions—becomes a sacred value in whose name emotional and economic exploitation of women is taken for granted. The distinguished professor may understandably like comfort and even luxury and his ego requires not merely a wife and secretary but an au pair girl, teaching assistant, programmer, and student mistress; but the justification for all this service is the almost religious concept of "his work." (Those few women who rise to the top of their professions seem in general to get along with less, to get their work done along with the cooking, personal laundry, and mending without the support of a retinue.) In other words, the structure of the man-centered university constantly reaffirms *the use of women as means* to the end of male "work"—meaning male careers and professors of military science or behavioral psychology. In its very structure, then, the university encourages women to continue perceiving themselves as means and not as ends—as indeed their whole socialization has done.

It is sometimes pointed out that because the majority of women working in the university are in lower-status positions, the woman student has few if any "role models" she can identify with in the form of women professors or even high-ranking administrators. She therefore can conceive of her own future only in terms of limited ambitions. But it should be one of the goals of a woman-centered university to do away with the pyramid itself, insofar as it is based on sex, age, color, class, and other irrelevant distinctions. I will take this up again further on.

IV

For reasons both complex and painful, the "exceptional" woman who receives status and tenure in the university has often been less than supportive to young women beginning their own careers. She has for her own survival learned to vote against other women, absorb the masculine adversary style of discourse, and carefully avoid any style or method that could be condemned as "irrational" or "emotionally charged." She chooses for investigation subjects as remote as possible from her self-interest as a woman,[6] or if women are the objects of her investigation, she manages to write about them as if they belonged to a distant tribe. The kinds of personal knowledge and reflection that might illuminate the study of, say, death fantasies during pregnancy, or the recurrent figure of the Beautiful Dead Woman in male art, or that might lead to research on a method of birth control comparable with other developments in medicine and technology—such are ruled out lest she appear "unscholarly" or "subjective." (It is a grotesque fact that the professional literature available on the female orgasm and on lesbianism is almost entirely by male researchers.) Of course, the advent of feminist studies has been rapidly changing this scene, and will continue to change it. But again, the usually younger feminist scholar-teacher is in most places untenured and struggling, and the style and concerns of masculine scholarship still represent the mainstream.

The mental hospital and the psychotherapeutic situation have been described as replicating the situation of women in the patriarchal family.[7] The university is likewise a replica of the patriarchal family. The male teacher may have a genuinely "fatherly" relation to his gifted student-daughter, and many intellectual women have been encouraged and trained by their gifted fathers, or gifted male teachers. But it is the *absence* of the brilliant and creative mother, or woman teacher, that is finally of more significance than the presence of the brilliant and creative male. Like the father's favorite daughter in the patriarchal family, the promising woman student comes to identify with her male scholar-teacher more strongly than with her sisters. He may well be in a position to give her more, in terms of influence, training, and emotional gratification, than any academic woman on the scene. In a double sense, he confirms her suspicion that she is "exceptional." If she succeeds, it is partly that she has succeeded in pleasing *him*, winning his masculine interest and attention. The eroticism of the father-daughter relationship resonates here, and romance and flirtation are invisibly present even where there is no actual seduction. Alice Rossi has pointed out the potential undermining of a woman's self-confidence when she is engaged in an actual sexual alliance with her mentor: how can she be sure that his praise is not a form of seduction, that her recommendations were not won in bed?[8] And not infrequently the professor marries his gifted woman student and secures her for life as a brain as well as a body, the critic and editor of his books, "without whom . . .," as the dedications all say. A woman-centered university would be a place in which the much-distorted mother-daughter relationship could find a new model: where women of maturer attainments in every field would provide intellectual guidance along with concern for the wholeness of their young women students, an older woman's sympathy and unique knowledge of the processes younger women were going through, along with the power to give concrete assistance and support. Under such circumstances it is likely that far less eroticism would glamorize the male teacher, and the woman student could use whatever he had to offer her without needing to identify with him or adopt his perspective for her own.[9]

V

I have tried to show that the androcentric university not only undermines and exploits women but forces men who wish to succeed in it further into the cul-de-sac of one-sided masculinity. In this it is simply a microcosm of society. Virginia Woolf was a forerunner of contemporary feminist analysts in criticizing the drive for goals without consideration of means and process, the glorification of competition, the confusion between human beings and objects as products of this one-sided masculinity of culture; and in this century we have seen culture brought low and discredited because of them. Without pretending that we can in our present stage of understanding and of mystification through language define crisply and forever what is "masculine" and what is "feminine," we can at least say that the above corruption and confusions are products of a male-dominated history.

The world as a whole is rapidly becoming Westernized. In no culture more than in Western culture is the failure of ideas like "industrialization" and "development" more evident; for without famine, without authentic scarcity, without the naked struggle to stay alive, and with the apparent "freedom" of unveiled and literate women, the condition of woman has remained that of a nonadult, a person whose exploitation—physical, economic, or psychic— is accepted *no matter to what class she belongs*. A society that treats any group of adults as nonadult—that is, unfit to assume utmost responsibility in society and unfit for doing the work of their choice—will end by treating most of its citizens as patriarchal society has treated children—that is, lying to them and using force, overt or manipulative, to control them.

I want to suggest two categories of women's needs that would, if genuinely met, change the nature of the university and to some extent the community outside the university, and I am suggesting further that these needs of women are congruent with the humanizing of the community-at-large. The first category includes both the content of education and the style in which it is treated. The second includes institutionalized obstacles that effectively screen out large numbers of able women from full or partial engagement in higher education.

First, as to curriculum: As the hitherto "invisible" and marginal agent in culture, whose native culture has been effectively denied, women need a reorganization of knowledge, of perspectives and analytical tools that can help us know our foremothers, evaluate our present historical, political, and personal situation, and take ourselves seriously as agents in the creation of a more balanced culture. Some feminists foresee this culture as based on female primacy, others as "androgynous"; whatever it is to become, women will have the primary hand in its shaping. This does not and need not mean that the entire apparatus of masculine intellectual achievement should be scrapped, or that women should simply turn the whole apparatus inside out and substitute "she" for "he." Some of the structures will be seen as unhealthy for human occupation even while their grandeur in its own day can be appreciated; like old and condemned buildings, we may want to photograph these for posterity and tear them down; some may be reconstructed along different lines; some we may continue to live and use. But a radical reinvention of subject, lines of inquiry, and method will be required. As Mary Daly has written:

> The tyranny of methodolatry hinders new discoveries. It prevents us from raising questions never asked before and from being illuminated by ideas that do not fit into pre-established boxes and forms.... Under patriarchy, Method has wiped out women's questions so totally that even women have not been able to hear and formulate our own questions to meet our own experiences.

Daly also calls for "breaking down the barriers between technical knowledge and the deep realm of intuitive knowledge which some theologians call ontological reason."[10] In fact, it is in the realm of the apparently unimpeachable sciences that the greatest modifications and revaluations will undoubtedly occur. It may well be in this domain that has proved least hospitable or attractive to women—theoretical science—that the impact of feminism and of woman-centered culture will have the most revolutionary impact. It was a woman, Simone Weil, who wrote, in the early thirties:

> ... the technicians are ignorant of the theoretical basis of the knowledge which they employ. The scientists in their turn not only remain out of touch with technical problems but in addition are cut off from that over-all vision which is the very essence of theoretical culture. One could count on one's fingers the numbers of scientists in the entire world who have a general idea of the history and development of their own particular science; there is not one who is really competent as regards sciences other than his own....[11]

A more recent writer points out the historical origins for the scientist's claim to neutrality, his [sic] assertion of normative freedom, and his "conscious rejection and ignorance of the subjective and the a-rational in human activity."[12] He suggests that every attempt to bring public and social sanctions to bear on the scientist's designs has hitherto met with defeat and that every attempt to extend the boundaries of accepted epistemology, including psychoanalysis, has been labeled "pseudoscience." (He fails, however, to mention the healing and midwifery of wisewomen that were even more violently driven underground. Mendelsohn's article, in fact, though it is concerned with the return of science to the service of human needs, and though it was delivered as a lecture to a Radcliffe Institute symposium on women, never touches on the connection between the masculinization of the sciences and their elitism, indifference to values, and rigidity of method.) He ends, however, by calling for certain kinds of change in the procedures and priorities of the science that can be applied by extension to the entire body of knowledge and method that the university has adopted for its province:

> A reconstructed science would value truth, but also compassion. It would have an inbuilt ethic that would defend both being and living; that is, knowledge that would be non-violent, non-coercive, non-exploitative, non-manipulative... that would renounce finally the Faustian quest to achieve the limits of the universe or total knowledge, that would work to construct models that would be more explanatory and more inclusive—science practiced among and derived from the public. What if we were to say that we would not undertake to develop what could not be understood and publicly

absorbed, that we were intent on building a science not confined to academies and institutions.[13]

Certainly a major change will be along the lines already seen in women's studies: a breakdown of traditional departments and "disciplines," of that fragmentation of knowledge that weakens thought and permits the secure ignorance of the specialist to protect him from responsibility for the applications of his theories. It is difficult to imagine a woman-centered curriculum where quantitative method and technical reason would continue to be allowed to become means for the reduction of human lives, and where specialization would continue to be used as an escape from wholeness.[14]

It has been almost a given of women's courses that style and content are inseparable. A style has evolved in the classroom, more dialogic, more exploratory, less given to pseudo-objectivity, than the traditional mode. A couple of examples of the feminist approach are quoted below. The first comes from a description of an applied psychology course on discrimination against women, taught at the University of Wales in Cardiff:

> A "personal style" was adopted. By this I mean a style of communication which avoided such constructions as "it is said," "it is thought," "it is considered." In short, I acknowledged the subjective element by not avoiding the use of the personal pronoun. This style is more appropriate to a nonexploitative, non-patriarchal interaction between students and teacher. It is conducive to a greater degree of academic rigour.... It seems to me that the form of many communications in academia, both written and verbal, is such as to not only obscure the influence of the personal or subjective but also to give the impression of divine origin—a mystification composed of sybilline statements—from beings supposedly emptied of the "dross" of self. Additionally I believe that a "personal style" probably encourages greater creativeness. Further, it seems to me, that, when teaching, such a style encourages the active involvement of all concerned. It is opposed to any form of alienation. It seems particularly appropriate that women's studies counteract the misleading tendency in academe to camouflage the influence of the subject.

The second example comes from the actual syllabus handed to students in a course, "The Education of Women in Historical Perspective."

> I am teaching this course because I believe that education is the key to social change. Despite the generally conservative role that formal institutions play in society, philosophers, statesmen and parents have looked to schools for improving the *status quo*. Access to school has been used as a method of social control, as have curriculum and teaching methods. The schools can become vehicles for indoctrination, for oppression, as well as for healthy stimulation of individual and societal freedom; the line between 'education' and indoctrination is difficult to define, but essential to look for.
>
> ... I look at issues historically; that has been my training, and my primary interest. I have trouble with the twentieth century, far preferring the puzzle of the nineteenth. In women's education, this was when the biggest changes took place, when education for women was a revolutionary question. However, we may be in the midst of another revolutionary time, and an understanding of the past is essential for appreciation of the contemporary scene. History can be a delightful escape into a world where there is a finite number of questions.... This course is my attempt to escape from my ostrich tendencies, to understand my own role in the present movement.
>
> I want to stress this problem of bias because scholarship is supposed to be as bias-free as possible. We will look at all questions and issues from as many sides as we can think of; but I am inescapably a feminist.... You must question my assumptions, my sources, my information; that is part of learning to learn, You should also question your own assumptions. Skepticism about oneself is essential to continued growth and a balanced perspective.[15]

The underlying mode of the feminist teaching style is thus by nature antihierarchical.

VI

I have described the university as a hierarchy built on exploitation. To become truly educated and self-aware, against the current of patriarchal education, a woman must be able to discover and explore her root connection with *all women*. Her previous education has taught her only of her prescribed relationships with men, or "Women beware women." Any genuine attempt to fill this need would become a force for the dehierarchizing of the university. For it would have to involve all women in the institution, simultaneously, as students and as teachers, besides drawing on the special experience of nonacademic women, both within and outside the university—the grandmothers, the high-school dropouts, the professionals, the artists, the political women, the housewives. And it would involve them at an organic level, not as interesting exhibits or specimens.

There is one crucial hub around which all the above revolves—one need that is primary if women are to assume any real equality in the academic world, one challenge that the university today, like the society around it, evades with every trick in its possession. This is the issue of childcare. The welfare mother badgered to get out and work, the cafeteria worker whose child wears a latchkey, the student or assistant professor constantly uncertain about the source and quality of the next baby-sitter, all have this at stake; all are constantly forced to improvise or to give up in the struggle to fill this social vacuum. Full-time mothering is a peculiar and late-arrived social phenomenon and is assumed to be the "normal" mode of childrearing in the United States; but fulltime mothering, even by choice, is not an option for the majority of women. There is no improvisation of childcare—even if it be the child's own father who "generously" agrees to share the chores—that can begin to substitute for an excellent, dependable, nonsexist, imaginative system of care, cheap enough for all, and extending identical opportunities to the children of the poorest and the highest-paid women on the campus.

Alice Rossi has described some of the possibilities and practical solutions to this question in her "Equality between the Sexes: An Immodest Proposal,"[16] and much of what I am going to say here will merely develop what she earlier sketched out. Perhaps I shall say it with a greater sense of urgency, because even in the years since her essay was written, the struggle over childcare and the need for it have become more clear-cut. Attention to how children are to be cared for and socialized can be seen as a kind of test of the "humanism" of the university, which has hitherto been so responsive to the masters of war. In the past the university has *used* children, in its special kindergartens and laboratory schools, as guinea pigs for tests and new methods, just as it has used the community around it for such purposes.

The degree to which patriarchal society has neglected the problem of childcare is in some ways reflective of its need to restrict the lives of women. Even in "revolutionary" socialist societies, where women are a needed sector of the labor force, and where state-supported collective childcare exists, the centers are staffed by women and women bear the ultimate responsibility for children. This may not in itself be undesirable; but the relegation of this responsibility to women reflects a reactionary thinking about sexual roles rather than a conscious decision made in the light of a feminist analysis. In both China and the Soviet Union the grandmother is an important adjunct to collective day care; the grandfather goes unmentioned in this role.[17] In the United States, the rapid increase in single-parent families and female heads of households does not alter the fact that, as of today, the fantasy of the family as consisting of a breadwinning father, a homemaking mother, and children is the model on which most social constructs are based. School holidays and lunch and coming-home hours, for example, often reflect the assumption that there is a nonworking mother whose major responsibility is to be there when the children come home. Even within the women's movement, childcare for women who wish to be politically or culturally active is sometimes a neglected priority in the arranging of conferences and workshops.

It is difficult to imagine, unless one has lived it, the personal division, endless improvising, and creative and intellectual holding back that for most women accompany the attempt to combine the emotional and physical demands of parenthood and the challenges of work. To assume one can naturally combine these has been a male privilege everywhere in the world. For women, the energy expended in both the conflict and the improvisation has held many back from starting a professional career and has been a heavy liability to careers once begun. The few exceptions in this country have been personal solutions; for the majority of mothers no such options exist.

Since this essay is concerned, not with an ideal future but with some paths toward it, I am assuming that within the foreseeable future few if any adequate community children's centers will be available, certainly on the scale and of the excellence we need. Until such exist in every community, it will be necessary for any university concerned with shifting its androcentric imbalance to provide them. But again, they cannot be merely token custodial units, or testing grounds run by the university for its own experimental ends. The kind of childcare I am going to describe would be designed first of all in the interests of the children and mothers it serves.

(1) Childcare would be available for children of all students, staff, and faculty, with additional places for community children, at a subsidized rate that would make it effectively open to all. This is an absolutely necessary, though not sufficient, condition for the kinds of change we envision.

(2) Childcare would be of the highest quality, no merely custodial center would be tolerated. The early nurture and education of the children would be as flexible and imaginative as possible. There would be a conscious counterthrust against the sex-role programming of patriarchal society.

(3) The centers would be staffed, under experienced and qualified directorship, by women and men who have chosen and been trained for this kind of work. They would be assisted by several kinds of people:

   (a) College students, female and male, who want experience in early education or just want to spend time with children. (Several experienced baby-sitters could work with several times the number of children they ordinarily "sit" with in private homes, and with more expert supervision.)

   (b) High-school students similar to the college students in (a).

   (c) Older women and men from the community—"grandparents" with special qualifications, informal and formal.

   (d) Parents who want to share their children's lives on a part-time basis during the working day.

   (e) Apprentices from graduate programs in education, pediatrics, psychology, the arts, etc.

The children would thus be in contact with a wide range of women and men, of different ages, as "nurturant" figures from an early age. The core staff of the centers should be as sexually balanced and as permanent as possible.

I am aware that some feminists, including some lesbian mothers, might prefer to see the nurture and acculturation of young children entirely in the hands of women—not as an acting out of traditional roles, but as a cultural and political choice. I tend, however, to agree with Michelle Rosaldo when she writes:

> ... American society is ... organized in a way that creates and exploits a radical distance between private and public, domestic and social female ... this conflict is at the core of the contemporary rethinking of sex roles.... If the public world is to open its doors to more than an elite among women, the nature of work itself will have to be altered, and the asymmetry between work and the home reduced. For this we must ... bring men into the sphere of domestic concerns and responsibilities.[18]

(4) There should be flexibility enough to allow parents to, say, take their children to the university museum or for lunch in the cafeteria if they so desire. Nursing mothers should be able to come and feed their babies.

(5) A well-baby clinic, with both medical and dental care, should be regularly provided for all the children as a service of the centers. A referral service for mothers with physical or psychic problems should be available.

(6) There should be opportunities for staff and parents of the centers to discuss, in small groups, ideas of childrearing, criticisms of the running of the center, and

ways in which it can better serve its clients.

While excellent universal early childhood care should be a major priority in any reasonably humane society, the primary and moving impulse behind the children's center would be to help equalize the position of women.[19]

VII

The notion of the "full-time" student has penalized both women and the poor. The student with a full-time job and a full-time academic program is obviously more handicapped than the student who can afford to go to college without working. Many women—married, divorced, or single mothers—have the equivalent of an unpaid full-time job at home and are discouraged from considering advanced study. Until universal and excellent childcare is developed these women are handicapped in undertaking a full-time program. Sometimes only a year or so of part-time study would make the difference between continuing their education and dropping out, or between real achievement and a frantic attempt to muddle through.[20]

But in a university not dedicated primarily to reduplicating the old pyramid, two other groups will need the availability of part-time study. Women faculty should make it one of their special concerns that staff and community women be brought into the educational process. All staff—women and men—should have paid time off for auditing or taking courses for credit, as well as access to libraries and to academic counseling. Community women must be taken seriously as potential users of the university. Many of these women have suffered from the burdens of both race and sex; tracked into the nonacademic stream in high school, carrying the responsibilities of early marriages and large families, they have worked hard both within and outside the home and yet have often been dismissed in the most offhand stereotyping both by the radical male left and by male "liberals."

Whether invisible as scrubwomen or cafeteria workers, or vaguely perceived as shoppers in the local supermarket or mothers pushing prams in the community, these women are also becoming increasingly awake to expectations they have been denied.[21] The working women employed by the university and the women of its local community both have claims upon the resources it so jealously guards. They should be able to look to a nonelitist university for several kinds of resources: a women's health center, with birth-control and abortion counseling, Pap tests, pamphlets and talks on women's health problems; a rape crisis center; an adult education program in which women at first too shy or uncertain to enroll for college classes might test their interests and abilities (this might include remedial reading and writing, math, women's history, basic economics, current events, community organizing workshops, poetry and art workshops, etc.); a woman-staffed women's psychological counseling center with both group and individual counseling; a law clinic. A large university should be prepared to integrate services contributed to such centers with the other academic commitments of any faculty member willing and qualified to work in them. And, undoubtedly, a great deal of reciprocal education would be going on as women of very different backgrounds and shades of opinion began to meet, hold discussions, and discover their common ground.

I can anticipate one response to these recommendations, partly because it has been leveled at me in conversation, partly because I have leveled it at myself. The university cannot, it may be argued, become all to each, it cannot serve the education of young adults, train future specialists, provide a conduit for research and scholarship, and do all these other things you are suggesting. I have, I confess, thought long and hard on that side of the question. Part of my final resolution comes from the fact that we are talking about a process involving simultaneous changes both in society "out there" and in the university, and that when the local or national community becomes able to develop strong and responsive centers such as I have been describing for all its citizens, the burden would not have to fall on the university. Ideally, I imagine a very indistinct line between "university" and "community" instead of the familiar city-on-a-hill frowning down on its neighbors, or the wrought-iron gates by which town and gown have traditionally defined their relationship. For centuries women were by definition people of the town, not of the gown, and still, there are many more of us "down there."

Moreover, the university in contemporary America has not been at such pains to refrain from providing services to *certain* communities: consulting for industry and government, conducting classified military research, acting as a recruitment center for the military-industrial and intelligence communities. What I am really suggesting is that it change its focus but still continue its involvement outside the ivy—or graffiti—covered walls. Instead of serving such distant and faceless masters as the "challenge of Sputnik," Cold War "channeling," or the Air Force, a university responsive to women's needs would serve the needs of the human, visible community in which it sits—the neighborhood, the city, the rural county, its true environment. In a sense the solution I am proposing is anarchistic: that the university should address itself to the microcosms of national problems and issues that exist locally, and that it should do so with the greatest possible sense that it will not simply be giving, but be receiving, because academe has a great deal to learn from women and from other unprivileged people.

I have described the kinds of ad hoc teaching that might take place under university auspices. As a research institution, it should organize its resources around problems specific to its community, for example, adult literacy; public health; safer, cheaper, and simpler birth control; drug addiction; community action; geriatrics and the sociology and psychology of aging and death; the history and problems of women and those of people in nonwhite, non-middle-class cultures; urban (or rural) adolescence, public architecture; child development and pediatrics; urban engineering with the advice and consent of the engineered; folk medicine; the psychology, architecture, economics, and diet of prisons; union history; the economics of the small farmer—the possibilities would vary from place to place. The "community" is probably a misleading term. In fact, most large urban universities have many communities. The "community" around Columbia University, for example, is not simply black and Puerto Rican, but white middle-class, poor and aged, Jewish, Japanese, Cuban, etc. A sympathetic and concerned relationship with all these groups would involve members of the university in an extremely rich cluster of problems. And the nature of much research (and its usefulness) might be improved if it were conceived as research *for*, rather than *on*, human beings.

VIII

I have been trying to think of a celebrated literary utopia written by a woman. The few contenders would be contemporary: Monique Wittig's *Les Guerilléres*, but that is really a vision of epic struggle, or Elizabeth Gould Davis's early chapters in *The First Sex*, but those are largely based on Bachofen. Shulamith Firestone noted the absence of a female utopia in *The Dialectic of Sex* and proceeded, in the last chapter, to invent her own. These thoughts occur because any vision of things-other-than-as-they-are tends to meet with the charge of "utopianism," so much power has the way-things-are to denude and impoverish the imagination. Even minds practiced in criticism of the status quo resist a vision so apparently unnerving as that which foresees an end to male privilege and a changed relationship between the sexes. The university I have been trying to imagine does not seem to me utopian, though the problems and contradictions to be faced in its actual transformation are of course real and severe. For a long time, academic feminists, like all feminists, are going to have to take personal risks—of confronting their own realities, of speaking their minds, of being fired or ignored when they do so, of becoming stereotyped as "man-haters" when they evince a primary loyalty to women. They will also encounter opposition from successful women who have been the token "exceptions." This opposition—this female misogyny—is a leftover of a very ancient competitiveness and self-hatred forced on women by patriarchal culture. What is now required of the fortunate exceptional women are the modesty and courage to see why and how they have been fortunate at the expense of other women, and to begin to acknowledge their community with them. As one of them has written:

> The first responsibility of a "liberated" woman is to lead the fullest, freest and most imaginative life she can. The second responsibility is her solidarity with other women. She may live and work and make

love with men. But she has no right to represent her situation as simpler, or less suspect, or less full of compromises than it really is. Her good relations with men must not be bought at the price of betraying her sisters.[22]

To this I would add that from a truly feminist point of view these two responsibilities are inseparable.

I am curious to see what corresponding risks and self-confrontations men of intelligence and goodwill will be ready to undergo on behalf of women. It is one thing to have a single "exceptional" woman as your wife, daughter, friend, or protégé, or to long for a humanization of society by women; another to face each feminist issue—academic, social, personal—as it appears and to evade none. Many women have felt publicly betrayed time and again by men on whose good faith and comradeship they had been relying on account of private conversations. I know that academic men are now hardpressed for jobs and must fear the competition of women entering the university in greater numbers and with greater self-confidence. But masculine resistance to women's claims for full humanity is far more ancient, deeply rooted, and irrational than this year's job market. Misogyny should itself become a central subject of inquiry rather than continue as a desperate clinging to old, destructive fears and privileges. It will be interesting to see how many men are prepared to give more than rhetorical support today to the sex from which they have, for centuries, demanded and accepted so much.

If a truly universal excellent network of childcare can begin to develop, if women in sufficient numbers pervade the university at all levels—from community programs through college and professional schools to all ranks of teaching and administration—if older, more established faculty women begin to get in touch with their (always, I am convinced) latent feminism, if even a few men come forward willing to think through and support feminist issues beyond their own immediate self-interest, there is a strong chance that in our own time we would begin to see some true "universality" of values emerging from the inadequate and distorted corpus of patriarchal knowledge. This will mean not a renaissance but a *nascence*, partaking of some inheritances from the past but working imaginatively far beyond them.

It is likely that in the immediate future various alternatives will be explored. Women's studies programs, where they are staffed by feminists, will serve as a focus for feminist values even in a patriarchal context. Even where staffed largely by tokenists, their very existence will make possible some rising consciousness in students. Already, alternate feminist institutes are arising to challenge the curriculum of established institutions.[23] Feminists may use the man-centered university as a base and resource while doing research and writing books and articles whose influence will be felt far beyond the academy. Consciously woman-centered universities—in which women shape the philosophy and the decision making though men may choose to study and teach there—may evolve from existing institutions. Whatever the forms it may take, the process of women's repossession of ourselves is irreversible. Within and without academe, the rise in women's expectations has gone far beyond the middle class and has released an incalculable new energy—not merely for changing institutions but for human redefinition; not merely for equal rights but for a new kind of being.

Notes

1. Virginia Woolf, *Three Guineas* (New York: Harcourt Brace, 1966) pp. 62–63; first published 1938.
2. Ibid., p. 66.
3. The urge to leap across feminism to "human liberation" is a tragic and dangerous mistake. It deflects us from our real sources of vision, recycles us back into old definitions and structures, and continues to serve the purposes of patriarchy, which will use "women's lib," as it contemptuously phrases it, only to buy more time for itself—as both capitalism and socialism are now doing. Feminism is a criticism and subversion of *all* patriarchal thought and institutions—not merely those currently seen as reactionary and tyrannical.
4. Otto Rank, *Beyond Psychology* (New York: Dover, 1958), p. 37.
5. B. Ehrenreich and D. English, *Witches, Midwives and Nurses: A History of Women Healers* (Old Westbury, N.Y.: Feminist Press, 1973).
6. 'Until recently, most academic women have avoided women's subjects like the plague; to do otherwise was to diminish their chances of being considered serious contenders in traditionally male fields" (Barbara Sicherman,

"The Invisible Woman," in *Women in Higher Education*) Washington, D.C.: American Council on Education, 1972], p. 76). Leffler, et al. op. cit., pp. 12–13) suggest that although more recently a reverse trend is seen among "academic feminists," they "rarely research new topics or develop new ideas on the gender problem. Rather, they tend to trail in the movement's wake... (without acknowledging movement inspiration, naturally)."

7. Phyllis Chesler, *Women and Madness* (New York: Doubleday, 1972), p. 35.
8. Alice S. Rossi, "Looking Ahead: Summary and Prospects," in Rossi and Ann Calderwood, eds., *Academic Women on the Move* (New York: Russell Sage, 1973), ch. 21.
9. For the other side of the coin—exclusion of women from the protégé system on a sexual basis—see American Sociological Association, *The Status of Women in Sociology* (Washington, D.C.: 1973), pp. 26–28. On both sides of the coin, dependency on the male teacher is the rule.
10. Mary Daly, *Beyond God the Father* (Boston: Beacon, 1973), pp. 11–12; 39.
11. Richard Rees, *Simone Weil: A Sketch for a Portrait* (London: Oxford, 1966), pp. 20–21.
12. Everett Mendelsohn, "A Human Reconstruction of Science," prepared for "Women: Recourse for a Changing World," Radcliffe Institute Symposium, 1972; *Boston University Journal*, vol. 21, no. 2, spring 1973, p. 48.
13. Ibid., p. 52.
14. Mina P. Shaughnessy has written of the failures of measurement to account for actual events in the teaching process: "In how many countless and unconscious ways do we capitulate to the demand for numbers?... In how many ways has the need for numbers forced us to violate the language itself, ripping it from the web of discourse in order to count those things that can be caught in the net of numbers?" ("Open Admissions and the Disadvantaged Teacher," keynote speech at the Conference on College Composition and Communication, New Orleans, April 1973 [unpublished]).
15. Deborah Rosenfelt, ed., Female Studies, vol. 7 (Old Westbury, N.Y.: Feminist Press, 1973), pp. 10; 187.
16. In Robert J. Lifton, ed., *The Woman in America* (Boston: Beacon, 1968), pp. 121–24.
17. Ruth Sidel (*Women and Child-Care in China* [New York: Hill & Wang, 1972], p. 25) reports of China: "All nursery and kindergarten teachers are women. There seems to be no effort to recruit men into fields in which they would be working with small children. And there seems to be no concern for breaking down the traditional sex roles in professions such as teaching and nursing, both of which are virtually all female." See also Toni Blankern, "Preschool Collectives in the Soviet Union," in Pamela Roby, ed., *Child Care: Who Cares?* (New York: Basic Books, 1973), pp. 386–97.
18. In M. Rosaldo and L. Lamphere, eds., *Woman, Culture and Society* (Stanford, Calif.: Stanford University, 1974), p. 42.
19. See Simmons and Chayes, "University Day Care," and Hagen, "Child Care and Women's Liberation," in Roby, op. cit. Obviously, day care is both an educational and a political issue and can evoke different ideas of goal and quality from different groups. For example, the heterosexual mother and the lesbian mother may each see quite different objectives for the kind of center in which she would want to place her child. (See *Ain't I a Woman*, double issue on childcare, spring 1973.) These differences will undoubtedly emerge and have to be worked through, sometimes painfully; but I agree with Cross and MacEwen (in Roby, p. 295) that it must be the parents (I would say particularly the mothers) who establish goals for the center and that the university should be seen purely as a provider of space and funding.
20. K. Patricia Cross ("The Woman Student," in *Women in Higher Education*, op. cit., p. 49 ff) observes furthermore that "mature women constitute a significant segment of the [new student] population" and asserts the need for a recognition of American mobility (in which the wife is uprooted by the husband's career) through systems of transferable credits and credit-by-examination.
21. A *New York Times Magazine* article carried a series of transcribed conversations with middle-aged, mostly blue-collar, second-generation Italian and Jewish women in East Flatbush, all in their forties and members of a consciousness-raising group, all concerned with changing and expanding their lives now that their children are grown up. One recalls 'how hard I fought for my girls to go to college." The author comments that "two main concerns spurred their interest in feminism: the feeling that society in general, and their husbands in particular, no longer viewed them as sexually interesting... and the realization that they were 'out of a job' in the same sense as a middle-aged man who is fired by his employer of 20 years." (Susan Jacoby, "What Do I Do for the Next Twenty Years?" *New York Times Magazine*, June 17, 1973.)
22. Susan Sontag, "The Third World of Women," *Partisan Review*, vol. 40, no. 2, 1973, p. 206.
23. A.R., 1978: For example, the Feminist Studio Workshop in Los Angeles, the Sagaris Institute, Maiden Rock Institute in Minnesota, the projected Feminist Art Institute in New York.

CHAPTER 2

PRIORITIES, PATTERNS, AND PRINCIPLES

ELIZABETH TIDBALL, CHARLES TIDBALL, DARYL SMITH AND LISA WOLF-WENDEL

It is never too late to be what you might have become.
—Mary Ann Evans (1819-80)

Many things have become apparent as the chapters of this book have unfolded. Among them is an increasingly clear appreciation of the challenge that arises from attempts to communicate what has been learned from many divergent sources to readers coming from widely different experiences and perspectives. In this effort, the overarching goal has been to provide at least the essence of what it means for institutions of higher education to take women seriously. The issues are far greater than the simple sum of their separate parts. The effort of finding, collecting, and presenting the available material surrounding taking women seriously speaks to the very theme of this book. That is, if women *were* being taken seriously, it would not have been so difficult to produce relevant material on institutions that do so, bringing it forth for edification and action. Indeed, it would probably already have been accomplished many times over. But it has not—which says something important about the status of women in American higher education.

It is hoped that this book will change that for its readers and for all among whom they have influence. For *everyone* has a stake in the education of women. This is because women of all backgrounds constitute the largest untapped source of talent in our nation, and educated women the surest hope for the development of a humane, equitable, and productive society. Women's colleges offer the clearest and most complete vision of what education for women can be and should be so that the gifts of women can be duly received and incorporated into the ongoing life of the larger community (M. E. Tidball 1980b, 12).

Priorities

First Women

Acquiring an appreciation of the contexts in which the higher education of women has taken place, and especially in which women's colleges have been active, provides a framework within which to appreciate the considerable contributions of these institutions. The founders of women's colleges cited as exemplars stand before us to this day with their courage, their vision, and their enormously hard work. By whatever criteria—young Elisabeth Oesterlein's barefoot walk from Penn-

---

Reprinted from *Taking Women Seriously: Lessons and Legacies for Educating the Majority*, by M. Elizabeth Tidball, Daryl G. Smith, Charles S. Tidball and Lisa E. Wolf-Lendel, 1999. Copyright © 1999 American Council on Education and The Onyx Press.

sylvania to North Carolina, Mary Lyon's tireless search for the pennies and dollars that would ensure an endowment for her school before it opened, Mother Guerin's harsh voyage from France to the wilderness of southern Indiana, Susan Mills's venturesome experiment in the far west, Sophia Packard and Harriet Giles's exploration of education for southern black women, and Indiana Fletcher Williams's legacy on behalf of her beloved daughter—all of these women dedicated their lives and their persuasive energies to their unshakable belief that women were educable and that the country and the world would be the better when they were given the full benefit of higher education opportunities. These defining stories must continue to be told, else meanings located in the originating events are lost, and with that, the impetus necessary for future generations to take women seriously.

Reaching Out

The priorities of these pioneering women clearly materialized through their perspicacity and foresight: the fruits of their labors resulted not only in quality education for millions of women in women's colleges, but also in the establishment of hundreds of women's colleges both in the United States and abroad that continue to serve as institutional models of places that take women seriously. Like a pebble dropped into a pond, the work of these early founders in behalf of women has generated ripples of benefit not only to those who attended the early women's colleges, but to *all* women wherever they may participate in higher learning.

Women's colleges such as Cedar Crest, Wellesley, and Immaculata, along with the Women's College Coalition, have been among the institutions that have taken leadership in developing conferences, workshops, and symposia to increase understanding of what works for women in *any* higher education setting, and to recommend courses of action that will make taking women seriously possible. All women's colleges have regularly appreciated that, for women students to benefit optimally from the higher education environment, it is mandatory that there be a multitude of women faculty and administrators, trustees, and guests—women of a variety of backgrounds and lifestyles, some struggling and some secure in their identity—all taken seriously. Furthermore, *all* women are viewed as important to the education enterprise, and *all* are accorded respect, justice, and colleagueship. These priorities are consistent with the findings of human resource studies that regularly demonstrate that in order to flourish, even outstanding talent requires training, direction, provision for a sphere of action, and rewards (Committee on the Education and Employment of Women in Science and Engineering 1983, 1.1).

Going Public

Attempts to encourage educators to appreciate the vital role played by women's colleges included portions of the Carnegie Commission on Higher Education's *Opportunities for Women in Higher Education*. Its editors wrote:

> These accomplishments of the graduates of women's colleges are worthy of emphasis, not only as they bear on decisions of women's colleges... but also—and far more significantly in terms of potential influence—as they suggest how changes in policies and faculty attitudes in coeducational institutions could affect the accomplishments of their women students. (Carnegie Commission on Higher Education 1973, 74)

Yet even with this endorsement from so respected an institution as the Carnegie Commission, little attention or action resulted. Women and the encouragement of their talents have not merited a high priority in most environments. Still, what was known in women's colleges was now before the higher education community.

Shortly after the Carnegie report, the president of Wellesley College, in an invited response to the Department of Health, Education, and Welfare, stated:

> Unfortunately, the proposed Title IX guidelines read as if both sexes had suffered past discrimination in equal measure. This is not so. It has not been *men* who have been excluded from participation in, denied the benefits of, or subjected to discrimination in society. It has been *women*. The talents and resources of women are being lost to society. (Newell 1974)

The response to this statement, presented by the president of Brigham Young University before the U.S. Congress as the delegated representative of the higher education community, was an opposing view carrying the implication that all collegiate institutions supported his stand (Jamison 1975). Apparently, women were not to receive high priority, much less be taken seriously, except by other women.

Voicing her dismay at the continued negative ambiance on campuses around the country, Florence Howe noted, "Residence on the campuses of old and distinguished coeducational or formerly male colleges has convinced me anew of the maleness of higher education; of what I can only call at best the continued *toleration* of women, as faculty, administrators or students.... I am talking about the general tenor of campus life" (Howe 1984, 233). So it is that the communication of fact or even firsthand experience has not regularly merited positive action on behalf of women in higher education. Indeed, the communication of fact has frequently resulted in apathy if not antagonism.

How difficult it is to write of these things without voicing a complaint! Yet to omit them is to fail to bring forth the great contrast between institutions that take women seriously and those that do not. It is a matter of reordering priorities, a matter of restructuring the foundations, a matter of reformulating board bylaws—or whatever else it takes to bring women truly and fully into the mainstream of institutional life. Forthrightly acknowledging the struggles may be painful to note—and even more painful to see—but by doing so, by taking women seriously, a new and enlightened beginning for all people can ensue.

Patterns

So many patterns, so many insights, emerge from the examination and analysis of the most recent decades of American higher education. Formidable increases in the sheer number of individuals participating in collegiate education, along with enormous societal perturbations, have had significant impacts on all social institutions. Among those most vulnerable to the wide shifts in the patterns of national life have been small, independent colleges, and among the small colleges, some institutions particularly affected by change have been those whose first priority is the education of women. That so many women's colleges have continued to serve as models of what works for women is thus truly a significant accomplishment.

Patterns of Reorganization

In order for women's colleges to continue their role as foremost educators of women, it was necessary for them first to break with the patterns of collegiate education common to most small colleges before the middle of the 1960s: small, residential, liberal arts, and church-related being the most frequent characteristics. Only relatively few remain that way. Identifying the most essential characteristics of each institution in its role as a college for women became a top priority. Missions were reevaluated and reformed, collaborative efforts for governance were instigated, and new ways of reaching out not only to traditional but also nontraditional publics and potential participants were devised.

These activities were undertaken by virtually all women's colleges. Impressively diverse results emerged that nonetheless all retained at the core the basic mission of taking women seriously. A new consciousness developed in which the importance of women on faculties and among administrators and trustees was reaffirmed. The significance of women faculty to women students was realized, and the roles and value of men faculty at women's colleges discovered and celebrated (M. E. Tidball 1976a).

Although there was no longer a standard institutional organization for most women's colleges (as there had been in an earlier era), there were instead the adaptations to the sea changes in American society and higher education. These led not only to significant renewal and refreshment, but to a realization that the patterns basic to taking women seriously remained. Only the outward conventionalities were abandoned or reframed with a new understanding and intentionally.

For women's colleges, there emerged not only the revitalized residential, liberal arts college, in which the definition of liberal arts had been reformed to include such studies as computer science, but also many new shapes and emphases. Especially among the Roman Catholic colleges, there was an enhancement of the mission to serve the underserved, now seen as women of color, women from the inner city, single mothers, women workers who could not attend during customary classroom hours, and women with particular career-related requirements that could be met only by collegiate level studies. Many women's colleges also opened their doors to men for nonresidential classes during evenings and weekends. Virtually all women's colleges established academic programs for "returning" women, that is, women older than 22. The many new forms and the increased diversity of options for the education of women nonetheless continued to be based on the imperative to take women seriously.

Patterns of Research

At quite another level, along with conventional research methodologies, new tools were developed and applied to questions of what works for women. Principal among these were the disaggregation of data by sex and by institution type in order to study the situation for women apart from men, in all categories of institutions, in all constituencies of institutional life, and in terms of institutional productivities of achieving graduates. In these efforts, data repeatedly demonstrate that the environment of women's colleges is reliably associated with positive outcomes for women, testifying to the assertion that "wisdom ... begins with the will to disaggregate, seeking to give proper weight to settings that make a difference" (Clark 1987, v).

Some of these outcomes relate to individual students, such as increased aspirations, overall satisfaction with campus life, involvement in extracurricular activities, opportunities for leadership, and enhanced self-confidence and self-esteem. Other outcomes refer to post-college accomplishments; in these, women's colleges regularly produce the largest proportion of women career achievers and participants in graduate and medical education. Not only is the productivity of women's colleges disproportionately greater than their selectivity in admissions, but it is also consistently greater for women than that of any other category of higher education institution.

It must be added that the great outpouring of research that investigates environments for the education of women has regularly felt constrained to make use of definitions and endpoints that have traditionally been assigned by men to be the kinds of results that count. For example, measuring institutional productivity, as a highly quantitative and objective approach, was devised in part in response to critics' objections to "anecdotal" evidence; however, as a methodology outside the traditional realms of social science research, it has regularly been suspect. Alternatively, interrogation of survey databases based on respondents' opinions and attitudes has grown with ever-increasing complex statistical methods of analysis, in spite of the subjectivity of the original input material; yet these have been the reigning methods of sociological/psychological research with which one has had to comply in order to be heard at all. More recently, as research that seeks to understand what works for women has begun to gain some credibility, case studies are appearing as a formal means of gathering evidence; time will tell how acceptable case studies will prove to be. Regardless, researchers interested in learning what works for women continue to explore many routes to that end, even though their findings have often met with a not insignificant degree of disapprobation.

What has emerged from these prototypical attempts to gain an understanding of what is essential for the education of women is not a singular "best way" to do research to produce a "scientific answer." Rather, it is the recurrence of a theme regardless of the setting, or the type of investigation, or the institution in which the work was accomplished, that provides the kind of evidential material that bespeaks truth. Thus from these multiple perspectives has emerged a common theme, and that theme is the extraordinary contribution of women's colleges to the participation of women in a multiplicity of national and international leadership roles (M. E. Tidball 1998).

Patterns of Productivity

Other patterns that have become apparent from the new research are those associated with the doctoral field participation of women compared with that of men, participation distributions that are consistently different from each other, regardless of the type of baccalaureate institution from which the doctorate recipients graduated. Further, the large majority of college environments are more nurturing of men than of women. This becomes clear by studying patterns for both women and men from the same institutions. The men proceed more frequently to substantive postcollegiate accomplishments than do the women, even when the graduates come from the most productive institutions in the Country.

These differences in patterns of productivity raise a warning to coeducational institutions that they still have much to incorporate into their environments if they would truly take women seriously. Only by recognizing the existence of different productivity patterns for women and men is the way opened to learning the underlying reasons and devising ways and means for ameliorating any inequities they may signal (M. E. Tidball, 1993).

Discovering Wholeness

In all, these several patterns at different levels call to mind characteristics of chaos theory, in which the power of consistency among different scales leads at last to an appreciation of the importance of the whole (Gleick 1987, 115). Here are the different scales, all of which repeat the same theme of taking women seriously, albeit in differing ways, making it possible to identify a principle that applies universally (Ferris 1988, 385). Here there is a certain underlying consistency, even if it is not immediately apparent to the casual observer. What goes on in the boardroom with respect to women—the priorities of trustees and search committee members, the approach to hiring at all levels, and the criteria set for student admissions and staff qualifications—is intimately related to how and what professors teach and students learn. It is intimately related to how faculty see themselves in terms of competencies and self-respect, and how students develop self-confidence and self-esteem. It is intimately related to alumnae loyalty and the establishment of life-long friendships and support networks. Analogously, what goes on in the classroom, in the residence halls, on the playing fields, and what goes on in the alumnae association, and what goes on in the development office and the budget office, all contribute to outcomes for every member of the community. That is, in order to understand what is happening with respect to institutions that take women seriously, one must not imagine that there is any one way to meet the challenge. Rather, one must consider the *whole*, the totality of the interrelated functions and groups of individuals whose actions, beliefs, and energies are combined and interwoven in a multicolored tapestry that is incontrovertibly committed to taking women seriously.

Principles

Priorities and patterns lead unerringly to identifying the principles upon which the education of women is to be built by all institutions that would join the effort to educate women. Clearly the task is neither simple to devise nor straightforward to implement. Women's colleges—by virtue of their long history in dealing with the education of women, and most important, their creative adaptation to larger changes in the society and higher education across many eras of national life—are the natural institutional models of what works for women. But like women as individuals, they are regularly overlooked—invisible and inaudible—because they are but a small proportion of the higher education community. Not only are women's colleges a small proportion, but most are also small in size as individual institutions. Thus, they are doubly disadvantaged in a society in which large, if not largest, is beautiful as well as best, and in which institutions are measured and promoted by whatever they offer that can be counted and recorded in college guides and popular magazines.

Yet what works for women resides within the *wholeness* of the environment, originating from a mission in which women are taken seriously (M. E. Tidball 1996). It has to do with creating a community in which women have a clear sense of ownership, knowing that they make a difference and knowing that they matter and that they truly belong and always will. What is essential is not to be found in quantifiable categories except for that which has heretofore not been quantified by those who assess the value of various institutions, namely, to what extent is there a *critical mass of women*

Table 1

Institutional Characteristics Related to Taking Women Seriously

Essential

Visionary leadership committed to the education of women
Critical mass of women in all constituencies
Belief in women's capacities and high expectations
Places and spaces for women's voices to be heard
Opportunities for women's leadership in all aspects of institutional life
Celebration of traditions and institutional history
High degree of trust and responsibility
Active and empowering alumnae association

Nonessential

High selectivity in admissions
Large endowment
High faculty compensation
High proportion of faculty Ph.D.s
Extensive library holdings
Conformist student behaviors

as trustees, administrators, faculty, staff, students, graduates, guests, and friends.

In Table 1, two lists summarize what is and is not essential for taking women seriously. The nonessentials are all most certainly important aspects of institutional definition, and each can and does contribute in a positive way to the overall capabilities of an institution. For example, no one would belittle the potential importance of a large endowment. But having a large endowment is not *essential* to taking women seriously.

What has emerged from the writing of this book is that the essentials for taking women seriously are to be found in the vision of the leaders of an institution who know that what is most important are those characteristics that form the infrastructure upon which a thriving community of women is built. That is to say, the majority of those things that are most important, most essential, for the education of women are not countable. Examples of these include high expectations for excellence in all dimensions of community life; a wealth of spaces and places where women's voices are heard; personal responsibility as exemplified in the operation of an honor code, along with a large measure of trust and responsibility; the celebration of traditions and institutional history that tie the present to the originating events, thereby assuring a future with depth and meaning; and an ethic of service that grows from a larger purpose beyond self.

It is for all these reasons—the priorities and patterns that have illuminated the principles—that the principles, in turn, lead to infinite possibilities. These possibilities are not only for the education of women as full participants in national and international life, but for the education of men as well. Surely men, too, can benefit from the truths unmasked through the study of what works for women (M. E. Tidball 1984).

As a result of gaining a closer understanding of the context in which women's colleges have been founded, have grown and, most importantly, have adapted to the changing scene all around them; as a result of reviewing research relevant to institutional support for women and discovering that all approaches lead to a common end that points to women's colleges; and as a result of bringing forth for others those characteristics of women's colleges that lend themselves to serving as models for educational environments that support all participants; a new opportunity to enliven, enrich, and extend the educational community has been created. Further, beyond that new community there is now a revitalized opportunity for educators in all settings and in all constituencies to be key contributors to the development and expression of an equitable and humane society.

CHAPTER 3

SCHEMAS THAT EXPLAIN BEHAVIOR

VIRGINIA VALIAN

In chapters 2 and 3 we saw that adults—men and women alike—systematically misperceive and misevaluate children in terms of their expectations about sex differences. In chapters 4 and 5 we saw the limits of hormonal explanations of sex differences. As I will show in chapter 7, adults similarly misperceive and misevaluate each other, often underrating women and overrating men. Those misperceptions set up expectations that are at least partially fulfilled (as described in chapter 8). In this chapter I present a cognitive explanation of the distortions humans impose on reality. The notion of a schema introduced in chapter 1 plays a central role in the explanation.

Schemas are hypotheses that we use to interpret social events. Because our implicit hypotheses about males and females include expectations about their professional competence, they bias our interpretation of people's performance. To oversimplify, we expect men to do well and see their behavior in the rosy light of our positive expectations. Conversely, we expect women to do less well and judge their actual performance in the darker light of our negative expectations.

How Schemas Affect Perceptions, Interpretations, and Expectations

A schema is a mental construct that, as the name suggests, contains in schematic or abbreviated form someone's concept about an individual or event, or a group of people or events. It includes the person's or group's main characteristics, from the perceiver's point of view, and the relationship among those features. (See Fiske & Taylor 1991, for a fuller explication of schemas.) The term *schema* is broader and more neutral than the term *stereotype*, which tends to connote an inaccurate and negative view of a social group. Schemas may be accurate or inaccurate, and they may be positive, negative, or neutral.

At the most basic level, our schemas of individuals allow us to recognize people at a glance—even when they change their clothing, facial expressions, or hairstyle. But schemas also play a more important role. They are cognitive frameworks that help us perceive and categorize new individuals and provide explanations of people's actions; they also give rise to expectations about others' future actions. Schemas are thus a form of hypothesis, a small-scale intuitive hypothesis. Without schemas, our world would consist of millions of unrelated individuals and events; we would be unable to form any generalizations. They are a cognitive necessity for making sense of the social world of everyday life. Schemas may contain errors, but they are indispensable.

The schemas most relevant to human perceptions of women's and men's professional competence are *role schemas*, such as those of lawyer, professor, father, woman (Fiske & Taylor 1991). As

---

Reprinted from *Why So Slow?: The Advancement of Women*, by Virginia Valian, 1998. Copyright © 1998 MIT Press.

the mixed list suggests, some roles are professional (lawyer and professor), others refer to a person's family role (father), and yet others refer to the role someone plays in society as a whole (woman). It can be argued that a status—such as being a woman—should not be termed a role; but the exact classification is not important. What is important is that we not only have schemas or conceptions about people based on professional roles—including both what we think they should do to properly fill their roles and what we think they typically do—but we also have schemas based on people's place in society. (Sometimes, of course, people's different roles conflict.)

An example of a schema illustrating these is a college student's schema of a professor. All students have a conception of what professors are like, a conception that becomes more detailed through their undergraduate years. The schema gives rise to certain expectations: such as that the professor will have a solid understanding of his or her subject, will attend all class sessions, will be on time, will be prepared, will give homework assignments and examinations that reflect the course material, will grade fairly, will be in the office during posted office hours, and so on.

The student's schema of professor does not contain all the features of the professor's own schema of professor, which probably also includes conducting research and fulfilling various administrative functions. No matter how full the student's schema may be, the professor's is considerably fuller, due to his or her greater knowledge of the profession. Nevertheless, the student's schema does allow the student to predict the general outline of a professor's behavior. Even though some of the predictions may be inaccurate, the student is still farther ahead, with the schema, than she or he would be by treating each professor as a new individual unrelated to all other professors.

Schemas also allow observers to interpret behaviors. A student who hears a professor describe the spring day the clocks changed without her realizing it and the odd succession of events that ensued—from "early" closing of restaurants to movies starting off-schedule—will be amused by this evidence of an absentminded professor who kept supplying increasingly elaborate explanations for a day gone haywire. The student is unlikely to conclude that the professor is an idiot. A schema rules out some interpretations and makes others more likely.

Finally, perhaps most important, schemas fill in gaps when evidence is lacking or ambiguous. Even a professor whose behavior is blatantly at variance with the schema may for some time be perceived as consistent with it. A professor who is not present during office hours, for example, may be seen as having an emergency that prevented him or her from meeting that obligation. The student's first thought is not that the professor is too lazy to come in. The schema has produced the expectation that the professor will meet his or her pedagogical obligations, and the professor is perceived in the light of the schema. The failure to show up will be attributed to external causes, especially if the professor is later apologetic and produces a plausible excuse.

On the other hand, if the professor continues to skip office hours and makes no or only the most casual apology, the student will have more solid evidence that that professor does not fit the schema: that professor is a bad professor. But the schema for professor does not change; instead, the professor is perceived as an exception to the schema, a "subtype," the irresponsible professor.

In general, when observers receive information about an individual that contradicts their schema, they handle the information in one of two ways. They can ignore it by supplying a different interpretation of it. For example, the professor is not irresponsible; the absence is due to reasons beyond his or her control. Or the contradictory information can be treated as exceptional; the professor then falls into the subtype of bad professor. Almost never is the schema itself changed. The student still expects other professors to behave responsibly, knowledgeably, and fairly.

If a schema is reasonably accurate and based on a large sample, it is completely appropriate to treat the exception as a special category, a subtype. People should not change their beliefs about an entire group because of the behavior of one individual. The exception *should* be treated as an exception. The problem with social schemas is that observers can receive a great deal of information that is discrepant with the schema without altering it.

Our schemas constitute informal hypotheses, and we ourselves are informal scientists doing informal experiments. Just as scientists sometimes make errors because they interpret their data in the light of their working hypothesis, we as informal scientists can make similar mistakes. Cognitive and social psychologists and sociologists who specialize in the study of science have explored a phenomenon called *confirmation bias* (see initial work by Wason 1960). The term refers to the human tendency to seek information that confirms a hypothesis and to discount information that does not. When the information is not clearly contradictory but is ambiguous, people see no compelling reason to discard a hypothesis.

Once a hypothesis is firmly in place—especially a social hypothesis—it is very difficult to dislodge, no matter how much disconfirming evidence comes in (see Ross, Lepper, & Hubbard 1975, on *belief perseverance* and discussion in Nisbett & Ross 1980). People hang onto a hypothesis until they have a new one to replace it, ignoring contradictory evidence, or labeling the evidence as an exception that the otherwise-good hypothesis does not seem to handle. This phenomenon is now almost a truism of the history of science (see Kuhn 1962, esp. pp. 77ff.). Often, the process of looking for confirming evidence is very helpful; it allows us to build up the hypotheses we need to make sense out of our world, and it lessens the likelihood that we will abandon a successful hypothesis too early.

Schemas thus serve a number of functions. They give rise to expectations. They interpret behavior in ways that are consistent with the schema rather than inconsistent with it. They supply explanations where data are missing or ambiguous. They direct the search for new information. They make subtyping a likely way of handling exceptions.

The student's schema for professor is relatively benign (if *my* schema of the student's schema is correct). Some role schemas, however, have a negative character. The schema for politician, for example, has a negative cast, as does the schema for used-car salesperson.

The schema for used-car salesperson includes being deceitful, manipulative, crafty, and untruthful. It provides a good example of how individuals who do not fit the schema can be misperceived. A used-car salesperson who is honest, truthful, helpful, and sincere may be perceived, instead, as particularly clever, devious, and wily. In fact, it is hard to imagine anything a used-car salesperson could do to be seen even as an exception to the schema. The nature of this schema is such that any action or demeanor can be perceived as consistent with it: any behavior, no matter how straightforward it appears to be on the surface, can be interpreted as manipulative and crafty.

Schemas are thus extremely powerful shapers of our interpretations—and misinterpretations—of others' behaviors and motives. Although the student's schema of a professor, as I outlined it, is reasonably accurate, role schemas can be inaccurate—even if they include accurate elements—in three different ways: they may portray characteristics as more extreme than they actually are; they can give more weight to positive characteristics than to negative ones (or the reverse); and they can fail to indicate how much variability there is in the possession of a characteristic (Judd & Park 1993). Our schema of used-car salespeople may be inaccurate in all three ways. First, we may exaggerate their untrustworthiness, perhaps because of a single bad experience in the past. Second, we may pay more attention to their negative characteristics, such as venality, than to their positive features, such as knowledge of cars. Third, we may think that all used-car salespeople are alike, perhaps because we have had relatively few experiences and base our opinion on a small sample.

Sex Differences

There are hundreds of observable sex differences that we, as intuitive scientists, try to explain. Our hypotheses are an attempt to make sense of the data the environment provides us with. As we form our conceptions of what it means to be male or female, we do not consider where the sex differences came from or the actual extent of those differences. Even if the differences arise from cultural conventions, and even if they mask underlying similarities, they become for us hallmarks of sex differences. When I was thirteen years old I was allowed to place a waxy, pinkish-red compound on my lips. If asked, I would have agreed that application of this compound was a cultural convention. Nonetheless, it would have seemed laughable and faintly repugnant to me to see my male classmates doing the same thing. The convention seemed right and fitting, despite the fact that male and female lips are by nature exactly the same range of colors.

The data on which we base our gender schemas come from numerous sources. First, men and women look different. Some of the differences we see are given by nature, some are determined by nature but manipulated by culture, and some are purely cultural in origin. Besides genital differences, some of the "natural" differences are size, body shape, and amount of body hair.

Body hair is an example of a natural trait affected by cultural norms. Women naturally have much less chest, back, and facial hair than men. The norm in U.S. culture diminishes the difference in facial hair: men shave. In two other regions—the legs and armpits—there is high overlap between the sexes in amount of hair, although women have less than men. Here, American culture exaggerates the difference: most women shave or otherwise remove the hair in these areas. Finally, women naturally have more hair on their heads than men do, another difference that the cultural norm exaggerates. In the area of body hair, then, there exist several basic differences between American males and females; the culture exaggerates some, thereby presenting observers with misleading data about the "typical" male and the "typical" female. The sexes are actually physically more similar than our culturally conditioned observations would suggest.

Other purely conventional sex differences in U.S. culture are visible in the realm of dress. Mature males and females dress very differently, in everything from height of shoe heels to amount and type of facial decoration. With an effort of will one can abstract away the superficially imposed differences and notice how much overlap there is, for example, in the facial structure of males and females, especially older people. But it takes an effort of will, precisely because our perceptions are mediated by our gender schemas. Our observations are responsive to apparel, the wearing of metal, stone, and glass ornaments, and facial decoration. That is the purpose of such cultural conventions; they add information that the raw material does not convey.

Men and women also sound different. As we noted in chapter 4, voice pitch is a natural difference that is culturally manipulated; differences in pitch are only partially accounted for by anatomical differences (Sachs, Lieberman, & Erikson 1973). Sex differences in voice pitch are greater in North America than they are in Europe (McConnell-Ginet 1983), and smaller in England than in Japan (Loveday 1981). Although pitch is a subtle difference, it is one people readily recognize. When asked about men's and women's voices, Americans estimated that 73 percent of men had deep voices but that only 30 percent of women did (Deaux & Lewis 1984).

In pitch as in other superficial traits, observers usually do not know what the underlying facts are. Such knowledge requires access to information about large numbers of people from a variety of cultures and to facts about anatomy that most observers do not have.

Men and women also act differently in a number of ways. Here are a few random examples of such differences. Men have a much higher threshold for crying than women do. Mixed-sex couples in restaurants tend to occupy different seats, with the woman sitting with her back against the wall and the man facing the wall. In automobiles, the woman rides in the passenger seat and the man sits in the driver's seat. Men take showers and women take baths. Such behavioral differences are strong and ubiquitous. Although the differences are purely cultural, they have powerful effects. When I take the "man's" seat in a restaurant I feel faintly uncomfortable if my companion is male. I am transgressing an unspoken code.

Finally, there are personality differences in the way men and women see themselves. Men portray themselves as acting as an independent, effective agent more than women do, and as more task-oriented, and instrumental (Spence & Helmreich 1978; Spence & Sawin 1985). Women see themselves as more expressive and communal and more interested in people than men do. Most people of both sexes believe they have each attribute to some degree. That is quite reasonable, since the attributes are not mutually exclusive. One could have all of the traits, or none of them, and one could possess each of them to different degrees at different times. Men, however, do report one cluster of traits more often than women do; and women report a different cluster more often than men do. Those two clusters appear to form the core of our gender schemas; they capture the differences we see as essential to the natures of males and females.

A quantitative review of studies of personality characteristics conducted between 1940 and 1992 shows several enduring and sizable sex differences (Feingold 1994). It confirms that men consistently see themselves as an initiator of action more than women do, and that women see themselves as communal more than men do. Males also portray themselves as more assertive than females do. Females portray themselves as more anxious, more trusting, and more nurturant, than males do. Gender schemas are alive and well, and have moderated only slightly over the years. Sex differences in personality have changed less than sex differences in cognition.

Who's Normal? Who's Better?

Males tend to be perceived as the norm against which females are measured, not only in male-dominated areas like business but also in gender-neutral areas like citizenship. One study illustrates how pervasive this assumption is. When male and female college students were asked to imagine a typical American voter and were then asked questions about that person, about 75 percent of the students envisioned the voter as male (Miller, Taylor, & Buck 1991). As is usually the case, there were no differences between the male and female students; both tended to see the male as the norm. A man is a better example of a voter than a woman is.

In another question, the students were told of a fictitious difference in voting patterns between men and women and asked to account for it. For example, students were told that 8 percent more men than women had voted in the past several presidential elections. In the 1996 presidential elections there was a real gender gap: men showed less of a preference for Clinton than women did.

One possible way of explaining a difference would be to attribute characteristics to each sex that might affect their voting. For example, men are concerned about X and therefore vote for candidate Jones, who promises to do something about X; or women are concerned about Y and therefore vote for Smith, who promises to do something about Y. That form of explanation takes neither group as the norm. Each group's voting pattern gets attention and requires explanation. The students' explanations did not take that form.

A second possible way of explaining a difference is to take one group as the norm, the group whose behavior needs no explanation. When one group—say, in this case, men—is the norm, the other group's behavior—in this case, women's—needs explaining. If that is the case, then an explanation will refer to women's characteristics rather than men's. That is what the students did in this study (Miller et al. 1991). They saw the women's behavior as the deviant pattern that required explanation. They thus explained sex differences in voting in terms of how women are different from men, rather than in terms of how men are different from women, or in terms of how each group has particular characteristics that result in the observed differences.

Men exemplify the normal in other ways as well. It is more acceptable for a female to adopt masculine characteristics than for a male to adopt feminine ones. As in childhood, so in adulthood. A woman may wear pants but a man may not wear a skirt. A woman with a low-pitched voice is more acceptable than a man with a high-pitched one.

Such latitude for women is not, however, without its limits. When Ann Hopkins was being evaluated for partnership at the accounting firm Price Waterhouse, her evaluators criticized her for not wearing make-up and said she needed to go to charm school. Despite her outstanding performance, she was denied partnership. She clearly suffered because she had too few feminine characteristics and too many masculine ones. Of course, a man with too few masculine characteristics and too many feminine ones would probably not have been hired in the first place. The basis of the asymmetry appears to be the higher value placed by the culture as a whole on masculine traits compared to feminine ones.

I was reminded of this in class one day when I commented on a Halloween party I had attended. A couple had dressed their nine-month-old son in a dress and bonnet. I brought up the example in a discussion of the subtle differences in treatment of boys and girls that could affect later sex differences. The infant was very uncomfortable in the dress; its full skirt kept getting caught between his legs, and the snug fit of the bodice prevented him from moving his arms freely. His plight made me notice for the first time how constricting baby girls' clothing is. As one of the major differences observed between girls and boys is level of activity (as reviewed in chapter 4), I speculated in class that sex differences in infants' clothing could exaggerate that difference by restricting girls' freedom of movement.

The class, however, paid no attention to my speculation. They could not get beyond the idea of dressing a baby boy as a baby girl. One female student said, "When you described it, my first reaction was that it was cruel." Cruel not because the dress limited the child's movements, nor because he would suffer any lasting harm from spending a few hours in girls' clothing, but cruel because a boy was being made into a girl—and thus devalued. Dressing a girl as a boy, the same student said, would not have seemed cruel, just odd. The student's comment does not exhaust what the students found so shocking about the Halloween example, but it does illustrate the extent to which our culture values masculinity and how extreme reactions to dress violations can be.

Ten years later, in the late summer of 1995, I see a young man on the street in London wearing a slightly A-line skirt, which I later realize is the skirt of a dress. It comes down to just below his calves. He is wearing moccasins with no socks. I mentally salute him for his courage. As I discreetly watch him, I see him give a tug in an effort to align the skirt better. Like the baby boy, the young man finds the dress uncomfortable. I think of how often we see women tug, pull, align, and straighten their clothes. Women's garments demand that the wearer pay attention to them, whether the wearer is male or female.

What, in a situation like this, is the norm? Should we explain why men do not wear clothing that requires frequent attention, why women do, or both? Our everyday actions speak for us. Masculine clothing, except for the symbolic tie, defines the norm.

Origins of Gender Schemas

The hundreds of sex differences we observe every day could be the basis of our gender schemas; that is, our conceptions of the sexes might be the direct result of our observations. Or, alternatively, most of the sex differences we observe could be the result of gender schemas. That dichotomy, however, oversimplifies the possibilities. A more complex possibility is that a small number of intrinsic differences are the basis for gender schemas. The schemas, then, operate quasiindependently to elaborate and produce further differences between the sexes.

Yet another hypothesis is that gender schemas are based, not on intrinsic sex differences, but on the sexual division of labor. Eagly (1987) suggests that the typical social roles played by women and men call for the characteristics that we have come to associate with each sex. Because men have tended to occupy positions that, for competent performance, require characteristics like agency, independence, instrumentality, and task-orientation, we transfer the requirements of the roles to the personalities of the people who occupy them. We therefore see men as independent agents, task-oriented, and so on. Similarly, because women have tended to occupy positions that require nurturance and expressiveness, we have come to think of them as possessing the characteristics required to be a parent and homemaker.

There are at least two ways to interpret Eagly's hypothesis. The first one would argue that the cognitive and personality traits of the two sexes are identical but that we perceive males and females differently because they hold different jobs. A more plausible possibility, given the data, is that men and women develop the characteristics needed to fill certain roles at the expense of other characteristics, which are not needed. Although everyone might have the same intrinsic potential characteristics, some would predominate and others recede, depending on the role the person assumed. Thus, on Eagly's hypothesis, both actual sex differences and perceived sex differences could arise from the fact that men occupy certain roles and women others. The role differentiation could have originated in the absence of any intrinsic personality or cognitive differences between the sexes.

A weak spot of Eagly's (1987) intriguing hypothesis is the assumption that different roles genuinely require different personality characteristics along the divisions represented by gender schemas. Some roles, such as professor, therapist, minister, and doctor, could be seen as requiring nurturance, communality, and expressiveness as much as instrumentality and agency—and indeed the roles of professor and doctor are so perceived (Conway, Pizzamiglio, & Mount 1996). Yet those roles are primarily filled by men and were filled almost solely by men until the 1970s. Other roles, such as housekeeper, social worker, or nursery school teacher, could be seen as demanding instrumentality and the ability to act as an independent agent as much as nurturance and expressiveness. Yet those roles are still primarily filled by women. We might see still other roles, such as assembly-line worker, as calling for neither masculine nor feminine traits.

If, contrary to Eagly's assumption, most jobs require both masculine and feminine characteristics, the aspects of a job that are seen as primary should change over time, depending on the sex of the people occupying it (Reskin & Roos 1990). That prediction is borne out by the history of jobs ranging from bartending to bank work. For example, in 1917 there was a shortage of male bank workers. Low-level banking jobs were then described by banks as suitable for women because women were neat, tactful, and intuitive. During the Depression, a surplus of males led banks to redefine the same jobs as unsuitable for women, on the grounds that the banking public would not want women to handle their money. During World War II, jobs as tellers were again seen as suitable for women, on the grounds that women were good at dealing with the public (Reskin & Roos 1990). Jobs, it seems, can change their gender at employers' will.

World War II provides another example of how rapidly jobs can be redefined. In the United States and Britain, jobs previously held only by men, such as work in munitions plants, were increasingly held by women. Because only men were allowed to fill combat positions in the armed services, their departure left civilian jobs unoccupied. Suddenly, women found that they could rivet and solder and carry large pieces of metal. After the war, the jobs and the women who carried them out changed again, just as suddenly, so that returning male veterans could reoccupy the "masculine" positions they had left.

If many sex-segregated occupations do not genuinely require personality or cognitive traits that are differentially distributed between the sexes, our notions of masculinity and femininity cannot derive solely from the jobs males and females typically hold. The plasticity in how work is defined suggests instead that our conceptions of what characteristics different jobs require are shaped by our conceptions of the people who occupy them. If a job is predominantly held by women, we see it as a feminine job, emphasize the feminine characteristics it requires and, correspondingly, devalue the job. If a job is predominantly held by men, we see it as a masculine job, emphasize its masculine characteristics, and, correspondingly, value it more highly.

The occupation of physician is perhaps the best example of how people's conception of a profession is shaped by their conception of the people practicing it. In the United States, physicians have been largely male, and the occupation is both prestigious and lucrative. The average young male M.D. earned $155,000 a year in 1991 (Baker 1996). In Russia, where physicians are largely female, the occupation is neither prestigious nor lucrative. Eagly's assumption that most occupations require either "male" or "female" characteristics thus seems less than fully tenable.

A somewhat different hypothesis is Hoffman and Hurst's (1990) proposal that our gender schemas are an attempt to justify a pre-existing sexual division of labor. They argue that even if sex segregation was initially completely fortuitous, once it exists it requires rationalization. People expect jobs to be filled by different groups in proportion to their representation in the total population. If, instead, there is an imbalance in some occupations or roles, people will search for an explanation of the unequal division—in short, for a rationalization. Their explanation would attribute different internal characteristics to members of different groups: people from group X are highly represented in a particular position because they have a particular set of characteristics; group Y members are not highly represented because they lack those characteristics.

Hoffman and Hurst thus differ from Eagly in an important respect. Jobs do not create actual sex differences. Instead, jobs create gender schemas via the sexual division of labor. Still, they are similar to Eagly in taking job differentiation as the basis for gender schemas. They both hypothesize that the jobs men and women happen to fill at some point are seen, after the fact, as requiring certain traits, and that those traits are the foundation for gender schemas. Thus, Hoffman and Hurst's proposal has a weak spot similar to Eagly's. If the jobs occupied by men do not really require agency, aggressiveness, instrumentality, and task-orientation more than the jobs occupied by women, or if the jobs performed by women do not really require nurturance, communality, and expressiveness more than the jobs performed by men, something else must explain why we perceive men and women in those terms.

The discussion thus far has ignored what may be the most distinctive role occupied by women, motherhood. Although motherhood requires masculine as well as feminine traits, the trait most often associated with it is nurturance. That is probably because mothers physically nurture their children, and physical cues are disproportionately important in the formation of schemas. Motherhood may thus provide the missing link in the explanation of gender schemas. The cognitive analysis I propose combines Hoffman and Hurst's (1990) rationalization theory with the facts that only women can be mothers and that nurturance is a preeminent physical trait of mothers. *One* set of sexually differentiated activities, giving birth to and physically nursing infants, qualitatively separates the sexes; it lays the foundation for gender schemas and dominates conceptions of women among both men and women. The act of physical nurturance is extrapolated to the personality realm, so that we—both women and men—see women not only as literally nurturing but also as metaphorically nurturing.

My own hypothesis about the origin of gender schemas views the components of schema development as cognitively based: we apply the same reasoning to our social world as we do to our physical world, and we make mistakes in both. In the case of gender schemas, we make a mistake right at the beginning, by using physical nurturance as a metaphor for psychological nurturance. It is, I would argue, our beliefs in sex differences, based on our perception of a single difference, that create and amplify other sex differences.

Some evidence that people's thought processes fit my description comes from a passage in Parsons and Bales (1955). The authors are trying to explain the historical development of the sexual division of labor and sex differences. They express explicitly a line of reasoning that, I suggest, people implicitly adopt as intuitive social scientists. My concern here is not with the correctness of their account, which has been criticized from many points of view, but with its relevance to the way we form gender schemas.

> The fundamental explanation of the allocation of the roles between the biological sexes lies in the fact that the bearing and early nursing of children establish a strong presumptive primacy of the relation of the mother to the small child and this in turn establishes a presumption that the man, who is exempted from these biological functions, should specialize in the alternative instrumental direction.

The use of the terms *presumptive* and *presumption* shows that Parsons and Bales realize there is no logical connection between the premise that women give birth and nurse their infants and the conclusion that men and women have different societal roles. They suggest, as my proposal does, that people leap metaphorically over that logical chasm.

Parsons and Bales's use of the term *presumption* also makes it clear that no logic forces men into specializing in an "alternative instrumental direction." Being instrumental is not an alternative to being nurturant; nor do people have to specialize at all. Male and female schemas are not mutually contradictory, inconsistent, or incompatible. A single individual can possess all of the socially desirable masculine and feminine traits or none of them; data from rating scales show that some individuals do possess many traits of both types, while others possess only a few of each (Spence, Deaux, and Helmreich 1985).

Yet, as Parsons and Bales (1955) indicate, we do contrast instrumental to nurturant and often see so strong a contrast between them that we cannot see how one person could be both. As social beings, we tend to perceive the genders as alternatives to each other, as occupying opposite and contrasting ends of a continuum. The familiar term, the *opposite sex*, appears in scientific articles as well as in everyday speech, even though the sexes are not opposite but are much more alike than they are different.

Parsons and Bales also describe men as "exempted from" childbirth and nursing, as if these functions were like military service—an activity most people would avoid if they could only get a deferment! Another reflection of our everyday thinking is implicit in their references to the two persons in the passage as "mother" and "man." The woman is defined by her role vis-à-vis another person, but the father is defined by his sex.

I have drawn on Eagly's (1987) and Hoffman and Hurst's (1990) theorizing to suggest that the sexual division of one particular labor—the bearing and nursing of infants—leads people to develop gender schemas, the core of which is women's metaphorical nurturance. I am proposing that nonconscious hypothesizing and reasoning about the sexes along the lines of the passage from Parsons and Bales cause us to jump to conclusions that do not follow from the premises.

Hypothesis-formation is a natural and desirable cognitive activity, whether the domain is the physical world or the social world. It helps explain our world and guide our behavior. But the naturalness of hypothesis-construction does not guarantee the truth of the hypotheses we construct. The notion of a flat earth is a notable example of a natural concept, a concept most people's experiences seem to verify. People need very special data or specific instruction to discover that the flat-world hypothesis is false. The naturalness of a concept and its apparent fit with everyday experience is independent of its truth. Gender schemas, I suggest, are similar to a belief that the earth is flat.

An important difference between the two beliefs, however, is that no matter how deeply we believe the earth to be flat we cannot make it so. But beliefs about human nature can create evidence that superficially appears to confirm false beliefs. The cultural elaboration of gender schemas can lead, in turn, to the creation of real sex differences. Cultural expectations and practices that amplify existing differences can create other differences out of whole cloth. Even though the social world is not infinitely malleable, it is much more malleable than the physical world, which makes detecting our errors more difficult.

According to my analysis, even if we were to wipe the slate clean and start over today, we would recreate gender schemas and a sexual division of labor. The "presumptive primacy" of childbirth and nursing would be the grist for our cognitive mill. Without access to informative data or instruction to counter our natural logical leaps, we would form the same hypotheses about sex differences and recreate differences that would appear to confirm the hypotheses. Our uncorrected errors of reasoning would further entrench our false beliefs.

Entrenching Gender Schemas

There are three processes that work together to entrench gender schemas in our minds and social practices. The first, as the passage from Parsons and Bales illustrates, is the exceptional responsiveness of gender schemas to physical differences (Deaux 1987). If people look consistently different, we conclude that they are different. Males and females do look different, even though we have created many of those differences. We also want people to look different if our concept of them is that they are different. (The neighbors are always surprised to learn that the ordinary-looking person who lives next door is a murderer.) So males should look masculine and females should look feminine. We view people as odd if they fail to conform to gender norms. It is as if we need to be physically reassured about an individual's gender identity and can tolerate the crossing of gender lines in personality and intellect more easily if the person adheres to our physical gender conventions.

Another mechanism that entrenches gender schemas is our tendency to reason from extreme examples. We are prone to interpret extreme examples as an indication that a trait is more common than it actually is (Fiske & Taylor 1991). Some time ago, I taught a class in which one of the students was a recent immigrant from Israel. He was an exceptionally intelligent and diligent person who participated actively in class. I was impressed by the way he compensated for his unfamiliarity with English by looking up every unknown word in a dictionary. I soon found myself concluding that Israeli students in general were hard workers. The reasoning underlying my conclusion seems to be that if a behavior that extreme can occur in one person, it must be present to some degree in the group as a whole. An Israeli graduate student whom I later spoke to laughed at my schema. In Israel, she said, college students didn't work particularly hard. If there was any truth to my schema, it only applied to Israeli students who were studying in the United States.

In the domain of sex differences, we apply the same kind of reasoning. The existence of a few hyperfeminine-looking and hypermasculine-looking individuals contributes to our seeing the sexes as more different than they genuinely are. Moreover, because we tend to generalize from physical differences to differences in other domains, hyperstereotypic individuals help create a continuum, not just for physical differences, but for our conceptions of difference in general. The hyperstereotypic individuals at the poles act like metaphorical magnets, subjectively pulling males and females apart.

A third mechanism that entrenches gender schemas is our tendency to see the sexes as dichotomous and see gender traits as mutually exclusive. It is not just that we are primed to notice traits that are consistent with a male or female schema, but also that we tend *not* to see traits that are inconsistent—because they "belong" elsewhere. We tend not to perceive women's instrumentality, because it is already spoken for by men. We cannot simply add it to our conception of women, because it is already part of our conception of men.

The combination of these three processes thus results in a constant validation and reconfirmation of our gender schemas. The first process, the tendency to generalize from physical cues to cognitive and personality traits, leads us to see the innumerable small but consistent behavioral differences between men and women as confirmation that men and women are different. The second process is our tendency to translate extreme values into evidence of typicality. We see a few hyperstereotypic examples, and they lead us to distort the average tendency. The third process, our tendency to view the sexes dichotomously, makes us more sensitive to traits that are consistent with a given gender role and less sensitive to inconsistent traits.

Schema Interactions and Schema Clashes

Thus far we have looked at the role schemas for professions and gender schemas separately. To consider the issue of how women are evaluated, however, we need to know how schemas interact, since one or more schemas can be simultaneously active.

Consider, for example, a student encountering a female professor and a male professor. In addition to perceiving each person as a professor, the student will perceive them as female or male. As mentioned above, physical cues that signal age, ethnic group, and sex are among the first characteristics observers notice about a person and are the most likely to activate associated schemas (Fiske & Taylor 1991). Whether the student responds to each professor in terms of the professorial role, the gender role, or both, will vary, depending on what is at issue.

For certain expectations—for example, fair grading—the professor role, not the gender role, dictates behavior. Because gender schemas do not suggest greater fairness on the part of either sex, gender is irrelevant. In a situation where one schema gives rise to an expectation that is not relevant to the other, the first schema will completely determine expectations. The reverse situation can also arise; the gender schema is more important than the professor schema when the gender schema produces an expectation that the professor schema does not. The schema for professor, for example, includes nothing about receptivity to student requests for extensions on homework; some professors are receptive and others are not. In deciding whom to approach with a request to turn in a paper late, a student may rely on other schemas, such as gender. Since the gender schema for women presents them as nurturant, the student will, all other things being equal, prefer to approach a female professor than a male professor.

But what happens when schemas clash because they are associated with contradictory expectations? When this happens, interesting problems with highly emotionally charged overtones can arise. When schemas clash, something has to give. The more central a schema is to a person's beliefs, the more painful the clash will be.

Take, for example, the roles of executioner or military combatant. Each seems antithetical to the role of woman, whose schema has nurturance at its core. The debate over military women in combat is as intense as it is because the roles of killer and nurturer are in such apparent contradiction. When two schemas are in conflict, both cannot survive intact. Either the schema for women or the schema for military combatants must change fundamentally. Yet both schemas resist change. We see nurturance as an essential immutable trait of women. It would be difficult instead to see women as having no defining trait, but as sometimes nurturant and sometimes willing and able to kill. Similarly, we see military combatants as essentially masculine. It would be difficult to see the role as gender-neutral.

Discussions about women in the military first focused on their competence. That discussion too was a clash of schemas. Women could not be competent, even in noncombat roles, because the schema for military life demanded traits that were not only masculine but hypermasculine. There now appears to be general agreement at the high-command level that women are as capable as men, even though they have nothing like equal rank status. Apparently, some schema change—or at least the possibility of a subtype, military woman—is possible.

Military discussion then shifted to the "real" issue, the issue that underlay the doubts expressed about women's competence, namely that being physically aggressive to the point of killing another person is incompatible with being a woman. What is really at stake is our conceptions about what it means to be female or male. To preserve those false conceptions, women who want combat status are denied it.

The other contemporary debate about military life—the role of homosexuals—has focused on homosexual males. It too is related to gender schemas. There have been two principal negative reactions: the fear, expressed primarily by the military high command, that a lack of cohesion would result if openly homosexual men served in the military; and a fear, expressed primarily by the rank and file, of a predatory sexuality on the part of homosexual men—with heterosexual men as the prey. From a gender schema perspective, the two fears are related; both concern the self-schema of heterosexual men in the military.

Cohesion, a psychological concept, refers to the ability of a group of people to act as a unit because of their trust and confidence in one another. Why should the presence of people known to be homosexual threaten the cohesion of a military unit? The frankness with which some heterosexual men have expressed their fears of sexual victimization by homosexual men suggests part of the answer.

Their fear reveals an implicit schema of heterosexual relationships in which men are victimizers and women are victims (a schema that is veridical—in most abusive heterosexual relations the male is the predator). Sex and victimization are inextricably entwined in this schema. When extended to include all sexual relationships, it suggests that to be the object of another's sexual attention is to be that person's potential victim, a serious problem if one is not the physically stronger party. Another man's sexual attention leads to that possibility and is thus tantamount to being demasculinized (Kimmel 1995). The military reaction to the open inclusion of homosexual men reveals the strength of heterosexual men's fears of demasculinization. Data on sexual predation, however, show that most male-male sexual abuse is perpetrated by heterosexuals, not homosexuals (Herek 1993). Heterosexual males use sexual assault—in prisons, for example—to assert power over other men.

There is another way in which open inclusion of homosexual men in the military would challenge the male schema. Like giving combat status to women, it would drive a wedge between military life and a culture of hypermasculinity in which discipline, courage, camaraderie, maleness, and heterosexuality are tightly interwoven. Detaching discipline, courage, and camaraderie from sex or sexual orientation would simultaneously undo both a long-standing gender schema and a long-standing military schema.

That the debate has involved heterosexual

males' self-schemas rather than military competence is confirmed by the policy implemented in 1993 that homosexuals should neither be asked about their sexual orientation nor reveal it. "Don't ask, don't tell, don't pursue" would be an unthinkable policy if there were any actual performance issues at stake. The policy is a tacit acknowledgment that homosexuals and heterosexuals perform equally well. The problem the policy "solves" is the schema problem. It allows heterosexual males in the military brass and in Congress who cannot tolerate the breakdown of two particular schemas to retain them despite their inaccuracy.

In 1870 the University of Michigan allowed women to enter its medical school but deemed it necessary to erect walls in classrooms so that women would not hear certain lecture material in the presence of men (Bonner 1992). Whose embarrassment was being safeguarded against is not clear. In time, in certain classrooms, the walls were replaced by curtains. In other classrooms the "wall" was simply a red line on the floor, in symbolic obeisance to irrelevant differences. "Don't-ask-don't-tell-don't-pursue" is the late-twentieth-century's red line on the floor, a tribute to the power of gender schemas.

CHAPTER 4

COMING TO VOICE, COMING TO POWER: BLACK FEMINIST THOUGHT AS CRITICAL SOCIAL THEORY

PATRICIA HILL COLLINS

Although many experiences have shaped my own understanding of the relationship between knowledge and power, one event stands out as pivotal. In 1970, I taught an experimental course called "The Black Woman" at the Martin Luther King Jr. Middle School in Dorchester, Massachusetts. The school itself resembled a prison—iron grates encased all of its windows, external doors lacking handles barred entry from the outside, and a stick-carrying assistant principal patrolled its interior hallways, routinely demanding hall passes from everyone, including unknown teachers like me. Despite this setting, my class of energetic eighth-grade Black girls remained full of questions. Since I had so few answers, I searched one of Harvard University's libraries for material on African-American Women. I was stunned to find virtually nothing. Could it be, I wondered, that the absence of materials by and/or about Black women meant that our lives really were of little value? Or was something perhaps wrong with the library?

As Black feminist critic Mae Henderson points out, "It is not that black women... have had nothing to say, but rather that they have had no say" (1989, 24). Henderson's statement speaks to the importance that social theories produced by elites can have in maintaining social inequality (Van Dijk 1993). Designed to represent the interests of those privileged by hierarchical power relations of race, economic class, gender, sexuality, and nationality, elite discourses present a view of social reality that elevates the ideas and actions of highly educated White men as normative and superior. Thus, elite discourses measure everyone else's accomplishments in light of how much they deviate from this ideal. For example, social theories portraying Black people as intellectually inferior, criminally inclined, and sexually deviant emerged in conjunction with systems of political and economic exploitation such as slavery, de facto and de jure segregation, colonialism, and apartheid (Jones 1973; Said 1978; Richards 1980; Gould 1981; Delgado 1984; Gilman 1985; Asante 1987; McKee 1993). Similarly, theories of women's seemingly more emotional and less rational nature have long buttressed social arrangements designed to keep women ill educated and relegated to so-called helping professions (Keller 1985; Harding 1986, 1991; Fraser 1989; Smith 1990a, 1990b). These two traditions combine in shaping Black women's images and the discriminatory treatment condoned by those images (Collins 1990; Morton 1991; Jewell 1993; Mullings 1994). Racist and sexist assumptions that permeate much Western knowledge fail to wither away when the political arrangements that created them change. Instead they live on, having a life of their own (Minnich 1990; Torgovnick 1990). In this interpretive context, Black girls such as my eighth graders at Martin Luther King Jr. Middle School, the many African-American women whom I have known,

---

Reprinted from *Fighting Words: Black Women and the Search for Justice*, by Patricia Hill Collins, 1998. Copyright © 1998 University of Minnesota Press.

taught, and learned from over the years, and many other groups labeled as Others have long had "no say" in determining the knowledge included in the American national "library" and, in turn, in holding the power that the "library's" knowledge defends.

Given the significance of elite discourses in maintaining power relations, knowledge produced by, for, and/or in behalf of African-American women becomes vitally important in resisting oppression (Fanon 1963; Cabral 1973). Such oppositional knowledge typically aims to foster Black women's opposition to oppression and their search for justice. Since oppression applies to group relationships under unjust power relations, justice, as a construct, requires group-based or structural changes. For Black women as a collectivity, emancipation, liberation, or empowerment as a group rests on two interrelated goals. One is the goal of self-definition, or the power to name one's own reality. Self-determination, or aiming for the power to decide one's own destiny, is the second fundamental goal. Ideally, oppositional knowledge developed by, for, and/or in defense of African-American women should foster the group's self-definition and self-determination.

Historically, Black women's community work was organized in specific ways to foster these dual objectives. Based on the metaphor "lifting as we climb," the diverse patterns that such work took matched the contours of Black civil society. "Lifting as we climb" provided a certain analysis and prescription of Black civil society. Just as the shifting patterns of Black social organization require changes in Black feminist thought, the appearance of new slogans and metaphors applied to Black feminist thought highlights potential changes to this critical social theory. Metaphors provide interpretive frameworks that guide social meaning and serve as mental maps for understanding the world (Stepan 1990). Reflecting theoretical moves from more familiar to relatively unknown terrains, metaphors work by showing how a set of relations that seems evident in one sphere might illuminate thinking and action in other spheres. As Mary E. John observes, metaphors, "like other rhetorical devices, are tropical rather than logical instruments, which means that, depending upon their contexts and effective histories, they work *strategically*" (1996, 89; emphasis in original).

Given their significance, metaphors can provide suggestive road maps for thinking through new directions in Black feminist thought. In the 1970s, Black women encountered the feminist slogan "the personal is political," which, in part, operated as a metaphor in organizing feminist ideas and actions paralleling that of "lifting as we climb." As originally used, the phrase "the personal is political" pointed out how politics permeated everyday life. It also prescribed how actions in everyday life were important in challenging structural power relations. Consciousness-raising emerged as central to "the personal is political," because through it, individual women learned to see their individual lives in political terms (Sarachild 1978). Even though the slogan valorized individual experience or "voice," it linked such experiences to larger systems of structural power.

Since the 1970s, the phrase "coming to voice" has increasingly replaced the earlier feminist slogan "the personal is political." On the surface, this shift of replacing both "lifting as we climb" and "the personal is political" with a new metaphor seems to continue longstanding themes in Black feminist thought. If "voice" references the collective quest for self-definition and self-determination, Black women's searching for a "voice" in the United States is certainly not new. Anna Julia Cooper's 1892 volume of essays, which provided the first book-length treatment of race, class, and gender in Black women's thought, is entitled *A Voice from the South*. As a leader in the Black women's club movement, Cooper certainly knew that breathing life into "lifting as we climb" required that Black women gain a collective voice. However, since the phrase "coming to voice" emerged in a different political context, it shares with and diverges from the earlier "lifting as we climb" and "the personal is political" in some significant ways.

In the context of the new politics of containment, "coming to voice" provides a potentially useful, albeit limited, metaphor for African-American women's political activism. As Black feminist theorist bell hooks (1990) points out, its three interrelated components—breaking silence about oppression, developing self-reflexive speech, and confronting or "talking back" to elite discourses—remain essential for Black women's journey from objectification to full human subjectivity. Hooks's term *self-reflexive speech* refers to dialogues among individual women who share their individual angles of vision. In a sense, it emphasizes the process of crafting a group-based point of view. In contrast, I prefer the term *self-defined standpoint*, because it ties Black women's speech communities much more closely to institutionalized power relations. Under current social conditions of racial segregation and sophisticated surveillance whereby Black women's voices are routinely stripped of their oppositional power, "voice" is not enough. Given the challenges facing contemporary Black feminist thought as critical social theory, what are the contributions and limitations of "coming to voice" as a metaphor for Black women's political activism?

Breaking Silence

Breaking silence enables individual African-American women to reclaim humanity in a system that gains part of its strength by objectifying Black women. Works by Black women writers such as Toni Morrison's *The Bluest Eye* (1970), Ntozake Shange's *for colored girls who have considered suicide/when the rainbow is enuf* (1975), and Alice Walker's *The Color Purple* (1982) broke silence about a series of painful issues confronting African-American women. For example, *The Bluest Eye* examines how images of Black women prove disastrous to Black girls. The latter two works explore how Black women claim subjectivity by refusing to be silenced—in Shange's choreopoem, by talking to one another; and in Walker's prizewinning volume, through the words of one Black girl who writes to God. But breaking silence is not just a literary tactic designed to heal Black women's victimization. For the most part, breaking silence can be a triumphant process in lived experience. Shirley Chisholm's autobiography, *Unbought and Unbossed* (1970), constitutes a lone voice within U.S. electoral politics of one woman who broke silence. Individuals like Chisholm who break silence lay the foundation for a collective group voice.

The benefits gained by individuals from oppressed groups who finally break silence explain, in part, why people do it. In *Crossing the Boundary: Black Women Survive Incest*, Melba Wilson discusses the importance that breaking silence can have for Black women survivors of childhood sexual assault. Wilson's advice remains instructive for oppressed groups in general: "There is no more righteous use of our anger than in directing it against those who have abused us; those who would abuse us and our children; or those who expect us to remain silent about our abuse" (1993, 200). By speaking out, formerly victimized individuals not only reclaim their humanity, they simultaneously empower themselves by giving new meaning to their own particular experiences. Racism, poverty, sexism, and heterosexism all harm their victims. For individuals, healing from this harm by making one's experiences and point of view public remains one of the most fundamental contributions of breaking silence.

Also important is the type of speech that individual Black women invoke in breaking silence. Like Black women's giving testimonials that often disrupt Public truths about them, when Black women valorize their own concrete experiences, they claim the authority of experience. Even though Black women's autobiographical writings historically have remained largely unpublished and private, Black women wrote them anyway, because such writings challenged prevailing interpretations of Black women's experience (Braxton 1989; Franklin 1995). By invoking the authority of lived experience, African-American women confronted seemingly universal scientific truths by citing examples from their own experiences. The purpose was not simply to insert the missing experiences into prevailing wisdom. Instead, when effectively done, claiming the authority of concrete experiences used wisdom to challenge legitimated knowledge. Thus, breaking silence by claiming the authority of individual lived Black female experience offered an effective challenge to elite discourses claiming the authority of science.

Understanding the significance of breaking silence by invoking the authority of experience requires examining how knowledge is constructed within unjust power relations. Domination, whether of race, class, gender, sexuality, or nationality, produces public and private knowledges on both sides of power relations (Scott 1990). The public discourses of academia, government bureaucracies, the press, the courts, and popular culture constitute one type of knowledge (Van Dijk 1993). Controlled by elite groups, these public discourses typically count as legitimated knowledge—the knowledge included in the library—and these are the discourses that silence Black women. For example, consider the significance of the "mammy" image in shaping public discourse about Black women workers (Morton 1991; Jewell 1993). Mammy remains so fundamental to perceptions of Black women in serving or helping professions that, to keep their jobs, many Black women must give command performances rivaling that of Hattie McDaniel in *Gone with the Wind* (Rollins 1985; Dill 1988a). Even Black women professionals find ourselves doing "mammy work" in our jobs, work in which we care for everyone else, often at the expense of our own careers or personal well-being (Omolade 1994).

A second type of knowledge exists, the collective secret knowledge generated by groups on either side of power that are shared in private when the other side's surveillance seems absent. For oppressed groups, such knowledge typically remains "hidden" because revealing it weakens its purpose of assisting those groups in dealing with oppression. African-American women's everyday theorizing constitutes such knowledge. In contrast to the public transcript about mammy, very different discussions about domestic work, secretarial work, and corporate mammy work can be heard when Black women talk to one another outside the surveillance of the public sphere. In these private spaces, domestic workers, clerical workers, and "mammified" Black women professionals can transform into nonsubservient, decidedly unmammylike mothers, aunts, sisters, and grandmothers (Rollins 1985; Dill 1988a). Drawing on traditional African-American cultures of resistance, conversations around the kitchen table become classrooms of learning about how to deal with oppression. Ironically, in fulfilling the emotional labor of caring for Whites, males, and/or the affluent, these same mammy workers gain access to their private, usually hidden knowledge. Thus, access to both public and hidden knowledge on both sides of power positions African-American women and other similarly situated groups to develop distinctive standpoints on hierarchical power relations.

Silencing occurs when Black women are restrained from confronting racism, sexism, and elitism in public transcripts because doing so remains dangerous. When individual Black women do break silence in situations of profoundly unequal power—from that of the secretary who finally tells off her boss, to that of Anita Hill's public accusations of sexual harassment against Clarence Thomas—breaking silence represents less a *discovery* of these unequal power relations than a *breaking through* into the public arena of what oppressed groups have long expressed in private. Publicly articulating rage typically constitutes less a revelation about oppression than a discovery of voice.

For African-American women as individuals, breaking silence thus represents a moment of insubordination in relations of power, of saying *in public* what had been said many times before to each other around the kitchen table, in church, at the hairdresser, or at those all-Black women's tables in student dining halls. Breaking silence in hierarchical power relations also generates retaliation from elite groups. As James Scott notes, "A direct, blatant insult delivered before an audience is, in effect, a dare. If it is not beaten back, it will fundamentally alter those relations. Even if it is beaten back and driven underground, something irrevocable has nonetheless occurred. It is now public knowledge that relations of subordination, however immovable in practice, are not entirely legitimate" (1990, 215).

Much of the public voice that Black women gained in the 1980s represents such a dare. Because individual African-American women broke silence in multiple arenas, Black women's collective voice is now public and known. Such voice challenges the legitimacy of public transcripts claiming Black female inferiority. Because it represents profound public insubordination, this newly public voice was bound to generate new forms of suppression dedicated to resilencing African-American women.

African-American women as a collectivity are no longer silenced in the same way, in that Black women's public voice has gained much legitimacy. The 1980s and 1990s witnessed an explosion of works by and about Black women, designed to reclaim and highlight Black women's humanity. If I went to the library today in search of materials, I would find substantially more work by and about Black women in the United States. Events such as Toni Morrison's winning the 1993 Nobel Prize for Literature (the first time a Black woman and a Black American was afforded such an honor), and the 1995 release of the movie *Waiting to Exhale*, based on Terry McMillan's enormously popular novel, speak to the increased visibility granted African-American women's ideas. Moreover, White women and Black men, among others, routinely acknowledge the contributions of Black women's ideas to their own work (Caraway 1991; Awkward 1995). These trends suggest that Black women's intellectual production has achieved some legitimacy. As theorist Ann DuCille points out, Black women academics "stand in the midst of the 'dramatically *charged* field'—the traffic jam—that black feminist studies has become" (1994, 593). This heightened visibility bears little resemblance to the past. Then, Black women were virtually invisible, whereas now, Black women's visibility constitutes a "traffic jam." The question is not whether opposition to Black women's breaking silence will emerge, but rather what form it will take.

In the context of a new politics of containment in which visibility can bring increased surveillance, breaking silence by claiming the authority of experience has less oppositional impact than in the past. During the heady days of the 1970s and 1980s, a critical mass of Black women acquired access to outlets for expressing their ideas. Then, breaking silence meant criticizing, in public, scientific and other academic "truths" that presented the experiences of White men as representative of all human experience. Such knowledge was characterized by a false universalism unused to open dissent. Closely linked to power relations, false universal perspectives reflected the efforts of a small group of people to exclude the majority of humankind from both education and the making of what we call knowledge. These few defined themselves not only as the inclusive kind of human but also as the norm for humanity and as the ideal human. "It is very strange to maintain that one small group of people is simultaneously the essence, the inclusive term, the norm, *and* the ideal for all," philosopher Elizabeth Minnich wryly observes (1990, 39), but that is exactly what paradigms positing the universality of elite White male experiences do. Moreover, the logic of color blindness and tolerance instituted in the 1980s aggravated this situation. In a context in which to talk of race at all meant that one was racist, it became even more difficult to tackle false universalism concerning race (Frankenberg 1993).

False universal perspectives could persist only in situations that either excluded Black women as agents of knowledge in their own behalf, or controlled via tactics of surveillance those Black women who were included. When confronted with an intellectual context grounded in false universalism, breaking silence by using Black women's concrete experiences constituted one effective strategy of resistance. For example, social-science claims that Black women were bad mothers could be countered with "That's not my experience or that of most Black women I know." When strategically deployed, using concrete experiences revealed that what science often presented as universal and true was not so at all. Concrete experience effectively destabilized seemingly scientific categories when such categories appeared unable to explain Black women's experiences and when Black women refused to accept the authority of those categories to explain their lives.

In situations when simply presenting Black female experiences decenters the false universalism accorded to elite White male experience, public acts of insubordination such as breaking silence can remain highly effective. Still, in hegemonic conditions in which dissent is more often absorbed than responded to, and in which Black women can become "fixed" in the public eye, the strategy of breaking silence may be rendered less effective (Winant 1994). In particular, whereas breaking silence within an identity politics grounded in concrete experiences has merit for *individuals*, as a *group* politic it contains the seeds of its own limitations. One such seed concerns the propensity of identity politics to be harnessed to the needs of the state. In describing the development of multiculturalism in Great Britain, Floya Anthias and Nira Yuval-Davis observe that "multiculturalism constructs society as composed of a hegemonic, homogeneous majority, and small unmeltable minorities with their own essentially different communities and cultures which have to be understood, accepted, and basically left alone" (1992, 38). Such approaches construct minority collectivities as basically homogeneous within themselves, speaking with a unified voice, and essentially different from one another. Over time, historically situated differences between oppressed groups become collapsed into and trivialized within an identity politics of unmeltable minorities characterized by essential differences. The power of the seemingly homogeneous majority remains intact, whereas the groups on the bottom compete with one another to receive increasingly smaller portions of the fixed segment of societal resources reserved for them. What begins as legitimate political protest by Black people and other similarly situated groups can degenerate into notions of "difference" that don't make any difference at all (Hall 1992).

Not only does this state recasting of difference weaken group-based identity politics, it also dovetails with a distributive paradigm of justice that ignores structural oppression. Iris Marion Young (1990) notes that the distributive paradigm of social justice tends to focus on the allocation of material goods, such as resources, income, wealth, or the distribution of social positions, especially jobs. This emphasis ignores structural and institutional factors that determine distributive outcomes. Within this logic, social justice becomes reconfigured as "rights" that are distributed to "authentic" minority groups. Stated differently, justice becomes conceptualized as a bundle of static things, often in scarce supply, that are distributed to the most worthy. When coupled with state absorption and co-optation of identity politics, adhering to this model of justice leads to some unfortunate consequences.

One such consequence concerns competition among many groups to break silence in order to compete for social rewards distributed by the state. In the United States, African-American women have not been the only ones to "break silence." Many groups now do the same. Thus, current power relations are much more complex than the popular conception that White men operate as a homogeneous elite using sophisticated strategies of control against a conglomeration of disadvantaged groups allied in uncomplicated solidarity. Notions of an unproblematic unity among African-Americans, Asian-Americans, immigrant groups, White women, and sexual minorities, among others, seem obsolete. When power is diffused throughout a social system, groups police one another to maintain their place in the pecking order (Foucault 1979; 1980a; 1980b). Just as African-American women interact with many groups that do not uniformly share Black women's efforts to foster justice, Black women's knowledge or collective voice interconnects with many others. Some remain dominant to Black feminist thought in some sense, whereas others are subordinate to it. In this situation in which multiple groups deploy strategies of control against one another, the process becomes one not just of breaking silence in response to one dominant group but of breaking silence with many different groups simultaneously. This climate of multiple "voices" greatly shifts the terms of the debate. Dialogues among the formerly silenced and their silencers seem simplistic. Instead, adversarial debates among multiple voices, all shouting to be heard, seem more common. Everyone wants to talk—few wish to listen.

An overemphasis on authenticity constitutes another unfortunate consequence of relying too heavily on brokering collective voice in an assumed marketplace of ideas with an eye toward achieving justice. Within a cacophony of group voices that break silence, different groups vie for center stage, often striving to be the most oppressed or the most different. Since experiences in a sense speak for themselves, individual qualifications to represent a group voice rest on being deemed an "authentic" representative of the essentially different minority group. Specifically, claiming that only African-American women can invoke the authority of experience to adequately depict "the Black woman's experience" creates a new form of silencing that, in effect, restricts Black women merely to breaking silence in a narrow box of authenticity. When combined with a parallel strategy of locating a person who looks the part, whose external appearance symbolizes essential difference, the limitations of breaking silence within this reformulated identity politics become magnified. In this setting, the actual ideas of the individual matter less than the person's seemingly authentic performance as a member of the affected, "different" group. This notion of authenticity became clear to me at a public lecture that I delivered on Black feminism at a large state university in the Northeast. One student was disappointed in my talk. When I asked why, the student revealed that he had expected me to look more like his image of a Black feminist. Where were my dreadlocks and African attire? Why wasn't I visibly angry, chastising White people for centuries of oppression? In brief, to him, because I had not "walked the walk and talked the talk," I was less authentic and thereby less credible.

Within assumptions of an essentialized identity politics recast within a distributive paradigm of social justice, examples such as these illustrate how the *person* is distilled to his or her *image* and becomes a commodity exchanged in the marketplace of ideas. African-American gay filmmaker and cultural critic Marlon Riggs's observations on the reception he received for his work on Black gay subjectivity satirize this form of appropriation: "Can we talk? But of course we can, queer diva darling, if you abide by the rules of the dominant discourse, which means, in short, you must ultimately sing somebody else's tune to be heard. That somebody is, of course, most often in part responsible for the historic gag in your communal mouth.... My mouth moves, but you hear your own words. What nature of ventriloquism is this?" (1992, 101-3). Ironically, performances of authentic difference—in Riggs's example, that of an authentic gay Black man—can be just as exclusionary as false universalism.

Adhering to these ideas regarding identity politics within a distributive paradigm of justice results in another unfortunate consequence. Ironically, because individual African-American women so often explore Black women's collective voice via narrative forms, their work can be appropriated and commodified by all sorts of people who build careers and profit from Black women's pain. As Ann DuCille observes, the current explosion of interest in Black women as literary and historical subjects "increasingly marginalizes both the black women critics and scholars in question and their black feminist 'daughters' who would further develop those fields" (1994, 596). As a result, the works of Black women writers are appropriated, analyzed, and returned in a form virtually unrecognizable to their creators (Christian 1988). Moreover, since appropriation and co-optation can take many forms, it is often difficult to distinguish between the treatment of Black feminist thought by thinkers such as Manning Marable (1983), Elizabeth Spelman (1988), Charles Lemert (1993), and Michael Awkward (1995), among others, from that of other scholars who merely insert individual Black women's narratives into long-standing reactionary frameworks. Fostered by the increasing significance of mass media, images, and culture in shaping our view of the political, Black women's texts can be used to give the illusion of actual political, economic, and social change. Describing how the works of Black women writers are used by dominant groups, Black feminist literary critic Hazel Carby contends, "For White suburbia, as well as for White middle-class students in universities, these texts are becoming a way of gaining knowledge of the 'other,' a knowledge that appears to satisfy and replace the desire to challenge existing frameworks of segregation" (1992, 197). In this sense, in a society that has retained many of its historical practices of apartheid in housing and education, Black Cultural texts have become fictional substitutes for the lack of any sustained social or political relationships with Black people.

This treatment of Black women's texts enables members of privileged groups who cannot deal with *actual people* who are constructed as different under hierarchical power relations to substitute the *idea* of difference for conflict-ridden interpersonal contact. This constitutes a new form of White privilege, one whereby White students may know more about Black women's commodified texts than actual Black women who are barred from the classroom. Unwittingly, the reliance of Black feminist thought on individual Black women's "voices" reinforces this tendency. Because many of the texts are "fictional" and "narrative," or because the visual images present a simultaneous closeness and distance, consumers of books and visual media can engage Black women's experiences with racism, sexism, and class exploitation without making any tangible changes in their own lives. Moreover, when individual Black women aim to break silence about the concrete experiences of their lives, often for reasons of self-empowerment, their narratives remain vulnerable to appropriation for other ends. When dissent becomes incorporated within the terms of elite discourse in this fashion, Black feminist thought is robbed of its oppositional potential.

Within this slippery terrain of a false universalism that coexists with an increasingly co-opted identity politics, breaking silence in some settings may be oppositional yet in others it may not. The efficacy of breaking silence thus greatly depends on its strategic use as one form of resistance suitable in certain social contexts. As the examples of Anita Hill and Lani Guinier suggest, under a new politics of containment wherein Black women can be highly visible yet rendered powerless, breaking silence may not work. Healing the internalized oppression of individual victims is not necessarily the same thing as challenging the conditions that created their victimization. In conditions of hegemony, even the righteous anger of the oppressed can be incorporated into a toothless identity politics in which difference becomes a hot commodity. In this new terrain, breaking silence may appear to confront power relations when in actuality it participates in their manufacture.

Developing a Black Women's Standpoint

Black women in the United States are at a decision point that in many ways mirrors that of other groups who recently "broke silence" and gained a collective group "voice." Building on pathbreaking works by Toni Cade Bambara, Ntozake Shange, Angela Davis, Toni Morrison, June Jordan, Alice Walker, and Audre Lorde, among others, African-American women scholar-activists in the 1980s and 1990s developed a public "voice" (Collins 1990). However, although this collective voice has achieved a visibility unthinkable in the past, it operates in a greatly changed political and intellectual context. Reflecting the encroaching influence of the marketplace on all aspects of life, capitalist market relations have transformed Black women's writing into a hot commodity.

Beginning with the growth of capitalism in Europe in the 1600s and its export in conjunction with colonialism, slavery, and imperialism to people of color in Africa, Asia, and the Americas, notions of the commodification and ownership of property, ideas, and even people have been deeply woven into the very fabric of American society (Cox 1948; Baran and Sweezy 1966; Greenberg 1980; Marable 1983). In the United States, racial segregation and capitalist market relations go hand in hand. For example, by condoning slavery, the Constitution of the United States granted priority to property rights above human rights and thus laid the foundation for the subordinated status of African-Americans, Native Americans, women, and other American citizens (Bell 1987, 34–35). As critical legal theorist Patricia Williams observes, "Money ... signals a certain type of relationship. So perhaps it is not just money that is the problem, but the relationship it signals" (1991, 31). Human relationships are profoundly affected by the increasing commodification of all aspects of our lives, observes African-American philosopher Cornel West, "Respect goes to the person with the gun; that's what market forces lead to" (hooks and West 1991, 52).

In a capitalist political economy such as the United States, the exchange of commodities increasingly dominates all areas of life. This process fosters an intellectual climate in which everything—from bottled water to sexuality to actual people—becomes transformed into exchange values quantified for circulation in the marketplace (Jameson 1984; San Juan 1992, 73). As intellectual property, ideas, including Black feminist ones, have not been immune from this encroaching commodification. The synergistic relationship between commodified knowledge and commodified people is illustrated in Derrick Bell's analysis of how the racial composition of a law school's student population affects its perceived prestige (1987). If a school seems to have too many Blacks, it is perceived as not being as good as one that seems more White. In this case, knowledge becomes inseparable from the container in which it is packaged, namely, Black and White bodies, and the value of the knowledge is judged in relationship to its package.

In this context of commodification, knowledge validated by upper-middle- and upper-class White men becomes transformed into cultural capital that is systematically used to place people into niches within hierarchical power relations. Within these relations, Black feminist thought faces the danger of becoming just another commodified knowledge stripped of its critical edge. Initially, because it allowed African-American women access to one another's ideas, entering public space via books, movies, and print media proved invigorating. Thus, market relations initially facilitated Black feminist thought. Publishers put *The Bluest Eye* in the hands of many African-American women who had heard neither of Toni Morrison nor of Black women writers. However, in increasingly competitive global markets, anything that sells will be sold, regardless of the consequences. Black women's "voices" of all sorts now flood the market. And as with other commodities exchanged in capitalist markets, surplus cheapens value. Moreover, the fad of today can become the nostalgic memory of tomorrow.

Despite a host of important social issues that face African-American women as a collectivity, Black women's collective voice seems to be turning away from the types of concerns that traditionally preoccupied Black women who engaged in community work. This may reflect the recent success of Black feminist thought as a commodity in the academic marketplace. When the audience for Black feminist thought no longer is dominated by African-American women, market forces certainly will influence the content of Black women's "voice."

Given the high rates of poverty (Brewer 1988), poor health (Nsiah-Jefferson 1989; Avery 1994), restricted educational opportunities (Sands 1993), employment discrimination (Glenn 1985; Jones 1985; Amott and Matthaei 1991), violence (Arnold 1993; Wilson 1993), and other social problems confronting Black women in the United States as a group, this trend is unfortunate. Historically, influenced by the importance of Black women's community work to Black civil society, Black women scholar-activists' intellectual production reflected a group standpoint that fused theory and activism. Moreover, because African-American women confronted more than institutionalized racism, this Black women's standpoint addressed multiple forms of oppression. As Pauli Murray points out in her 1970 essay "The Liberation of Black Women," "Traditionally, racism and sexism in the United States have shared some common origins, displayed similar manifestations, reinforced one another, and are so deeply intertwined in the country's institutions that the successful outcome of the struggle against racism will depend in large part on the simultaneous elimination of all discrimination based on sex" (Murray 1995, 186). Building on the work of Murray, Toni Cade Bambara (1970), Shirley Chisholm (1970), and others, African-American women scholar-activists in the 1980s called for a new approach to analyzing Black womanhood. Claiming that African-American women's experiences are shaped not just by race but also by gender, social class, and sexuality, groundbreaking works by Angela Davis (1981), the Combahee River Collective (1982), and Audre Lorde (1984), among others, explored interconnections among systems of oppression. Subsequent works such as Deborah King's important essay "Multiple Jeopardy, Multiple Consciousness: The Context of Black Feminist Ideology" (1988) further explored this interconnected relationship, applying terms such as *matrix of domination* (Collins 1990) and *intersectionality* (Crenshaw 1991) to the connections among systems of oppression.

Redefining Black women's resistance also preoccupied African-American women scholar-activists in the 1970s and 1980s. If Black women's oppression in the United States was multiply defined, then Black women's legacy of struggle against multiple oppressions merited an equally complex analysis. Written while she was in jail awaiting trial on charges for which she was ultimately acquitted, Angela Davis's groundbreaking essay "Reflections on the Black Woman's Role in the Community of Slaves" (1971) suggested that the theme of Black women's resistance to American slavery be reconsidered:

> Even as she [the female slave] was suffering under her unique oppression as female, she was thrust by the force of circumstances into the center of the slave community. She was, therefore, essential to the *survival* of the community. Not all people have survived enslavement; hence her survival-oriented activities were themselves a form of resistance. Survival, moreover, was the prerequisite of all higher levels of struggle. (Davis 1995, 205)

Following Davis's leadership, Black women intellectuals in the 1980s explored the multifaceted contours of Black women's resistance. Cheryl Townsend Gilkes's article "'Holding Back the Ocean with a Broom': Black Women and Community Work," published in La Frances Rodgers-Rose's highly influential edited volume *The Black Woman* (1980), signaled interest in seeing Black women not as objects of history but as historical agents. Much of the excellent scholarship produced by Darlene Clark Hine, Paula Giddings, Elsa Barkley Brown, and other African-American women historians in the 1980s and 1990s, as well as work by Doris Wilkinson, Jacqueline Johnson Jackson, Leith Mullings, Bonnie Thornton Dill, and many other social scientists, explored this legacy of struggle—its successes, obstacles, and defeats (see, e.g., Crawford et al. 1990; Barnett 1993; Higginbotham 1993; and Guy-Sheftall 1995). All aimed to generate a historical and contemporary "voice" for Black women as agents of knowledge. Through their scholarship, African-American women theorists of the 1970s and 1980s identified core themes concerning work, family, controlling images, motherhood, and sexual politics that formed the foundation for Black feminist thought that ensued in the 1980s and 1990s (Collins 1990).

Despite this legacy of a Black women's intellectual tradition nurtured by Black women's community work, recent Black feminist thought neglects many of the social issues affecting Black civil society. Instead, increasingly preoccupied with issues of individual and group identity, its gaze has turned increasingly inward. On one level, current interest in whether Black women's intellectual production should be named "womanism" or "Black feminism" mirrors the current preoccupation with questions of individual identity within academia. In this light, questions of what to name a Black women's standpoint constitute yet another minor academic debate. On another level, however, naming practices reflect a concern with crafting a Black women's standpoint that is sensitive to differences among Black women yet grounded in solidarity. In this sense, the question whether to call a Black women's standpoint womanism or Black feminism forces a rethinking of long-standing notions of racial solidarity that have been so central to Black women's community work. Thus, trying to name a Black women's standpoint not only demonstrates the heterogeneity among Black women but also highlights the ongoing and contested functions of self-definition in developing adequate political analyses of current social conditions.

In her acclaimed volume of essays *In Search of Our Mothers' Gardens*, Alice Walker introduced four meanings of the term *womanist*. According to Walker's first definition, a womanist is "a black feminist or feminist of color" (1983, xi). Thus, on some basic level, Walker uses the two terms virtually interchangeably. Like Walker, many African-American women see little difference between the two, since both support a common agenda of Black women's self-definition and self-determination. As Barbara Omolade points out, "Black feminism is sometimes referred to as womanism because both are concerned with struggles against sexism and racism by Black women who are themselves part of the Black community's efforts to achieve equity and liberty" (1994, xx). Despite similar beliefs expressed by African-American women who define themselves as Black feminists, as womanists, as both, or in some cases as neither, increasing attention seems devoted to delineating the differences, if any, between groups naming themselves womanists or Black feminists. The name given to Black women's collective standpoint seems to matter, but why?

Womanism

Alice Walker's multiple definitions of the term *womanist* shed light on the issue of why many African-American women prefer the term *womanism* to *Black feminism*. Walker offers two seemingly contradictory meanings of *womanist*. On the one hand, Walker clearly sees womanism as rooted in Black women's particular history of racial and gender oppression in the United States. Taking the term from "You acting womanish," the southern Black folk expression of mothers to female children, Walker suggests that Black women's concrete history fosters a womanist worldview accessible primarily and perhaps exclusively to African-American women. Womanish girls acted in outrageous, courageous, and willful ways, using attributes that freed them from the conventions long limiting White women. Womanish girls wanted to know more and in greater depth than what was considered good for them. They were responsible, in charge, and serious (1983, xi).

On the other hand, Walker aspires to a universal meaning of *womanist* that transcends particular histories, including that of African-

American women. Walker sees womanists as being "traditionally universalist," a philosophy invoked by her metaphor of the garden, where room exists for all flowers to bloom equally and differently. Despite this disclaimer, Walker implies that African-American women are somehow superior to White women because of their Black folk tradition. Defining *womanish* as the opposite of the "frivolous, irresponsible, not serious" *girlish* (1983, xi), Walker constructs Black women's experiences in opposition to those of White women. This meaning presents womanism as different from and superior to feminism, a difference allegedly stemming from Black and White women's different histories within American racism. Walker's much cited phrase. "Womanist is to feminist as purple to lavender" (xii) clearly seems designed to set up this type of comparison—Black women are womanist, whereas White women remain merely feminist.

This usage sits squarely in Black nationalist traditions premised on the belief that Blacks and Whites cannot function as equals while inhabiting the same territory or participating in the same social institutions (Van Deburg 1992). Since Black nationalist philosophies posit that Whites as a group have a vested interest in continuing a system of institutionalized racism, they typically see little use for African-American integration or assimilation into a system predicated on Black subjugation. Black nationalist approaches also support a Black moral superiority over Whites because of Black suffering (Pinkney 1976; Moses 1978).

Walker's use of the term *womanist* promises to African-American women who operate within these Black nationalist assumptions yet see the need to address women's issues within African-American communities a partial reconciliation of two seemingly incompatible philosophies. Although womanism raises the issue of gender, it simultaneously offers a distance from the "enemy," in this case, Whites generally and White women in particular. Because of its seeming endorsement of racial separatism, this interpretation of womanism offers a vocabulary for addressing gender issues within African-American communities without violating norms of racial solidarity of Black civil society. Geneva Smitherman's understanding of womanism taps this meaning. For Smitherman, a womanist refers to an "African-American woman who is rooted in the Black community and committed to the development of herself and the entire community" (1996, 104). This usage provides Smitherman and others continuity with earlier generations of "race women" who worked on behalf of Black civil society.

This use of womanism sidesteps an issue central to many White feminists, namely, finding ways to foster interracial cooperation among women. African-American women who embrace Black nationalist philosophies typically express little interest in working with White women—in fact, White women are defined as part of the problem (see, e.g., Welsing 1991). Moreover, womanism appears to provide an avenue for fostering stronger relationships between Black women and Black men in the United States, another very important issue for African-American women regardless of their political perspective. Again, Walker's definition provides guidance when she notes that womanists are "committed to survival and wholeness of entire people, male *and* female" (1983, xi). Many Black women in the United States view feminism as a movement that, at best, is exclusively for women and, at worst, is dedicated to attacking or eliminating men. Shirley Williams takes this view when she notes that in contrast to feminism, "womanist inquiry . . . assumes that it can talk both effectively and productively about men" (1990, 70). Womanism seemingly supplies a way for Black women to address gender oppression without attacking Black men.

Walker also presents a visionary meaning for womanism that dovetails with Black civil society's norms concerning the centrality of moral, ethical principles to Black political struggle. As part of her second definition of *womanist*, Walker has a Black girl pose the question "Mama, why are we brown, pink, and yellow, and our cousins are white, beige, and black?" (1983, xi). The response, "The colored race is just like a flower garden, with every color flower represented" (xi), both criticizes colorism within African-American communities and broadens the notion of humanity to make all people "people of color." Reading this passage as a metaphor, womanism thus furnishes a vision wherein women and men of different colors coexist like flowers in a garden yet retain their cultural distinctiveness and integrity.

This meaning of womanism also invokes another major political tradition within African-American politics, namely, a pluralist version of Black empowerment (Van Deburg 1992). Pluralism views society as being composed of various ethnic and interest groups, all of whom compete for goods and services. Equity lies in providing equal opportunities rights, and respect to all groups. By retaining Black cultural distinctiveness and integrity, pluralism offers a modified version of racial integration premised not on individual assimilation but on group integration. Clearly rejecting what they perceive as the limited vision of feminism projected by North American White women, many Black women theorists have been attracted to the joining of pluralism and racial integration in this interpretation of Walker's womanism. Black women theologians, in particular, illustrate this use (Cannon 1988; Townes 1993; Sanders 1995). As an ethical system, womanism is always in the making—it is not a closed, fixed system of ideas but one that continually evolves through its rejection of all forms of oppression and its commitment to social justice.

Walker's definition thus manages to invoke three important yet seemingly contradictory philosophies that frame Black social and political thought in the United States. By claiming a moral and epistemological superiority for Black women because of their suffering under racial and gender oppression, Walker invokes Black nationalism. Through the metaphor of the garden, she embraces pluralism, and her claims that Black women are "traditionally universalist" call up integration and assimilation (Van Deburg 1992). Just as Black nationalism and racial integration coexist in uneasy partnership, with pluralism occupying the contested terrain between the two, Walker's definition of womanism demonstrates comparable tensions. By both grounding womanism in the concrete experiences of African-American women and generalizing about the potential for realizing a humanist vision of community via the experiences of African-American women, Walker depicts the potential for oppressed people to possess a moral vision and a standpoint on society that grows from their situation of oppression. This standpoint also emerges as an incipient foundation for a more humanistic, just society. Overall, these uses of Walker's term *womanist* create conceptual space to explore philosophical differences that exist among African-American women.

One particularly significant feature of African-American women's use of *womanist* concerns the part of Walker's definition that remains neglected. A troublesome line for many Black women who self-define as womanists precedes the often cited passage "committed to survival and wholeness of entire people, male *and* female." Just before Walker offers this admonition that womanists, by definition, are committed to wholeness, she states that a womanist is also "a woman who loves other women, sexually and/or nonsexually" (1983, xi). The relative silence of womanists on this dimension of womanism speaks to many African-American women's continued ambivalence in dealing with the links between race, gender, and sexuality, in this case, the "taboo" sexuality of lesbianism. In her essay "The Truth That Never Hurts: Black Lesbians in Fiction in the 1980s" (1990), Black feminist critic, Barbara Smith points out that African-American women have yet to come to terms with homophobia in African-American communities. Smith applauds the growth of Black women's fiction in the 1980s but also observes that within Black feminist intellectual production, Black lesbians continue to be ignored. Despite the fact that some of the most prominent and powerful Black women thinkers claimed by both womanists and Black feminists were and are lesbians, this precept often remains unacknowledged in the work of African-American writers. In the same way that many people read the Bible, carefully selecting the parts that agree with their worldview and rejecting the rest, many people engage in selective readings of Walker's womanism.

Another significant feature of African-American women's multiple uses of womanism concerns the potential for a slippage between the real and the ideal. To me, there is a distinction between describing Black women's responses to racial and gender oppression in the United States as womanist, and using *womanism* as a visionary term delineating an ethical or ideal vision of humanity for all people. Identifying the liberatory *potential* within Black women's communities that emerges from concrete, historical experiences differs from claiming that these same communities have already *arrived* at this ideal, "womanist" end point. Refusing to distinguish carefully between these two meanings of womanism thus collapses the historically real and the future ideal into one privileged position for African-American women in the present. Taking this position is reminiscent of the response of some Black women to the admittedly narrow feminist agenda forwarded by White women in the early 1970s. Those Black women proclaimed that they were already "liberated," although this was far from the truth.

Black Feminism

African-American women who use the term *Black feminism* also attach varying interpretations to this term. According to Black feminist theorist and activist Pearl Cleage, feminism is "the belief that women are full human beings capable of participation and leadership in the full range of human activities—intellectual, political, social, sexual, spiritual and economic" (1993, 28). In its broadest sense, feminism constitutes both an ideology and a global political movement that confronts sexism, a social relationship in which men as a collectivity have authority over women as a collectivity.

Globally, a feminist agenda encompasses several major areas. First and foremost, the economic status of women and issues associated with women's poverty, such as educational opportunities for girls, industrial development, employment policies, prostitution, and inheritance laws concerning property, constitute important women's issues globally. Political rights for women, such as the right to vote, to assemble, to travel in public, and to hold office, as well as the rights of political prisoners, and basic human rights violations against women, such as rape and torture, constitute a second area of concern. A third area of global attention consists of marital and family issues, such as marriage and divorce laws, child custody policies, and domestic labor. Women's health and survival issues, such as reproductive rights, pregnancy, sexuality, and AIDS constitute another area of global feminist concern. This broad global feminist agenda finds varying expressions in different regions of the world and among diverse populations.

Using the term *Black feminism* positions African-American women to examine how the particular constellation of issues affecting Black women in the United States are part of issues of women's emancipation struggles globally (Davis 1989; James and Busia 1994). In the context of feminism as a global political movement for women's rights and emancipation, the feminism that African-American women encounter in the United States represents a narrow segment refracted through the binary thinking of American racial politics. Because the media in the United States portray feminism as a for-Whites-only movement and because many White women have accepted racially segregated institutions of all types, including feminist organizations, feminism is often viewed by American Blacks and Whites as the cultural property of White women (Caraway 1991). Despite considerable ideological heterogeneity that operates within the term *feminism*, unfortunately racial segregation in the United States and the hegemonic ideologies that accompany it typically obscure this plurality.

Despite their erasure in the media, many African-American women have long struggled against this exclusionary American feminism and have participated in what appear to be for-Whites-only feminist activities. In some cases, Black women have directly challenged the assumptions guiding feminist organizations controlled by White women in order to generate more inclusive feminist agendas (see, e.g., Matthews 1989 and Poster 1995). At other times, even though Black women's past and present participation in feminist organizations remains largely invisible—for example, Pauli Murray made many contributions as a founding member of the National Organization for Women—African-American women have participated in women's organizations. In still other cases, Black women have combined allegedly divergent political agendas. For example, Pearl Cleage observes that Black feminist politics and Black nationalist politics need not be contradictory: "I don't think you can be a true Black Nationalist, dedicated to the freedom of Black people being a feminist, Black *people* being made up of both men and *women*, after all, and feminism being nothing more or less than a belief in the political, social and legal equality of women" (1993, 180).

In the United States, the term *Black feminism* also disrupts the racism inherent in presenting feminism as a for-Whites-only ideology and political movement. Inserting the adjective *Black* challenges the assumed Whiteness of feminism and disrupts the false universal of this term for both White and Black American women. Since many White women think that Black women lack feminist consciousness, the term *Black feminist* both highlights the contradictions underlying the assumed Whiteness of feminism and reminds White women that they are neither the only nor the normative "feminists." Because it challenges Black women to confront their own views on sexism and women's oppression, the term Black feminism also makes many African-American women uncomfortable. Even though they may support global feminist ideas, large numbers of African-American women reject the term *feminism* because of its perceived association with Whiteness. They are not alone in this rejection, since women of color globally have questioned the association of the term *feminism* with Western domination. Within this context, many Black women in the United States see feminism as operating exclusively within the term *White American* and perceive its opposite as being *Black American*. When given these two narrow and false choices, Black women routinely choose "race" and let the lesser question of "gender" go. In this situation, those Black women who identify with feminism must be recoded as either non-Black or less authentically Black.

The term *Black feminist* also disrupts a long-standing and largely unquestioned reliance on racial solidarity in Black civil society (Dyson 1993). Using family rhetoric that views Black family, community, race, and nation as a series of nested boxes, each gaining meaning from the other, certain rules apply to all levels of this "family" organization (Gilroy 1992). Just as families have internal, naturalized hierarchies that give, for example, older siblings authority over younger ones or males over females, groups defining themselves as racial families invoke similar rules (Collins forthcoming 1998b). Within African-American communities, one such rule is that Black women will support Black men no matter what, an unwritten family rule that was manipulated quite successfully during the Clarence Thomas confirmation hearings. Even if Anita Hill was harassed by Clarence Thomas, many proclaimed in barbershops and beauty parlors, she should have kept her mouth shut and not "aired dirty laundry." Even though Thomas recast the life of his own sister through the framework of an unworthy welfare queen, Black women should have kept their collective mouths shut in deference to rules of racial solidarity (McKay 1992). By counseling Black women not to remain silent in the face of abuse no matter who does it, Black feminism comes into conflict with codes of silence such as these.

Several difficulties accompany the use of the term *Black feminism*. One involves balancing the genuine concerns of African-American women against continual pressures to absorb and recast such interests within White feminist frameworks. For example, gaining quality educations, jobs, and health care remains a strong focal point in the feminism of African-American women. Yet within some academic feminist circles, the emphasis on individualism, individual subjectivity, and personal advocacy implied in the politics of postmodernism (see chapter 4) saps Black feminism of its critical edge as a group-based, critical social theory. Contemporary Black women thinkers' efforts to explicate a long-standing African-American women's intellectual tradition bearing the label "Black feminism" can attract the attention of White women advancing different feminist agendas. Issues raised by Black women that are not seen as explicitly "feminist" ones (i.e., issues that do not affect only women) receive much less sanction. Even well-meaning White feminists can inadvertently consume the limited resources of African-American women who claim Black feminism. The constant drumbeat of supporting White women in their efforts to foster an antiracist feminism diverts Black women's energy away from addressing social issues facing African-American communities. Because Black feminism appears to be so well received by White women, in the context of the segregated racial politics of the United States, some African-American women quite rightly suspect its motives.

Another difficulty with Black feminism concerns the direct conflict between Black feminism and selected elements of Black religious traditions in the United States. Given the significance of Christianity for African-American women (see, e.g., Gilkes 1985 and Higginbotham 1993), any social movement that criticizes such a fundamental element of Black civil society will remain suspect. Moreover, the visibility of White lesbians within North American feminism overall directly conflicts with many Black women's article of faith that homosexuality is a sin. Although individual African-American women may be accepting of gays, lesbians, and bisexuals as individuals, especially if such individuals are African-American, Black women as a collectivity have distanced themselves from social movements perceived as requiring acceptance of homosexuality. Feminism in the United States appears to be one such movement. As one African-American female student queried, "Why do I have to accept lesbianism in order to support Black feminism?" The association of feminism with lesbianism remains a problematic one for many Black women. Reducing Black lesbians to their sexuality, one that chooses women over men, reconfigures Black lesbians as enemies of Black men. This reduction not only constitutes a serious misreading of Black lesbianism—African-American lesbians have fathers, brothers, and sons of their own and are often embedded in a series of relationships as complex as those of their Black heterosexual counterparts—it simultaneously diverts attention away from more important issues (Lorde 1984). One might ask, who ultimately benefits when the presence of Black lesbians in any Black social movement leads to its rejection by African-Americans?

The theme of lesbianism and its association with feminism in the minds of many African-Americans also overlaps with another concern of many African-American women, namely, their commitment to African-American men. Sensitive to the specific issues confronting Black men generally (see, e.g., Madhubuti 1990a and Dyson 1993) and, as mothers, Black sons in particular (see, e.g., Golden 1995), Black women in the United States routinely reject philosophies and social movements that portray Black men as adversaries or enemies. Thus, another difficulty confronting Black feminism concerns its perceived separatism—many African-Americans define Black feminism as being exclusively for Black women and as rejecting Black men. In explaining her preference for *womanism*, Shirley Williams notes, "One of the most disturbing aspects of current black feminist criticism [is] its separatism—its tendency to see not only a *distinct* black female culture but to see that culture as a separate cultural form having more in common with white female experience than with the facticity of Afro-American life" (1990, 70). Geneva Smitherman offers a similar criticism. In response to a press conference of Black women intellectuals who denounced the alleged sexism of the 1995 Million Man March in Washington, D.C., Smitherman notes, "Black women must be wary of the seductive feminist trap. White males hold the power in this society, not Black ones. . . . To launch an attack against the first mass-based, sorely needed, long overdue, positive effort by Black men on the grounds of sexism is to engage in a misguided, retrogressive brand of feminism" (1996, 105). Smitherman's criticism cannot be dismissed as the ideas of a woman who lacks feminist consciousness. Involved for years as a community activist and scholar in Detroit, Smitherman knows firsthand what is happening to Black youth in inner cities. Until White and Black feminists show some concern for those issues, they are likely to have little support from Smitherman and other self-defined womanists.

Williams and Smitherman offer a valid criticism of Black feminism in the United States, one that, in my mind, must be addressed if Black feminism is to avoid the danger of becoming increasingly separated from African-American women's experiences and interests. It also speaks to the larger issue of the continuing difficulty of positioning Black feminism between Black nationalism and North American White feminism. In effect, Black feminism must come to terms with a White feminist agenda incapable of seeing its own racism, as well as a Black nationalist one resistant to grappling with its own sexism (White 1990). Finding a place that accommodates these seemingly contradictory agendas remains elusive (Christian 1989b).

Talking Back

Whatever African-American women choose to name a Black women's standpoint, womanism and Black feminism encounter the issues confronted by any knowledge that aims to "talk back" to knowledge, with more power. The chapters in part II investigate these issues in greater detail, but here I want to highlight one significant issue raised by the womanism/Black feminism analysis that is germane to this process of talking back. Articulating a Black women's standpoint under the new politics of containment confronts one fundamentally new challenge: how can Black feminist thought foster group unity while recognizing Black women's heterogeneous experiences? Ironically, the new public space provided by the successes of Black women scholar-activists in the 1980s and 1990s revealed differences among African-American women as individuals. Differences of sexuality, economic class, nationality, religion, region of country, and citizenship status all generate a substantial heterogeneity among Black women in the United States that is increasingly played out in public arenas. At this point, whether African-American women can fashion a singular "voice" about the Black *woman's* position remains less an issue than how Black women's knowledges collectively construct, affirm, and maintain a dynamic Black *women's* self-defined standpoint.

In essence, the discussion of whether to name Black women's intellectual production womanism or Black feminism participates in a larger discussion about the significance of difference for group self-definition. An identity politics that valorizes differences certainly helped create the conditions that allowed Black women to challenge the limitations imposed by racial solidarity. In particular, questioning notions of Black solidarity built on Black women's sacrifices has been beneficial. However, it is one thing to revitalize a politics organized around "lifting as we climb" by attending to difference among African-American women. It is quite another to replace that politics with one emphasizing different "voices," if not difference itself, as the theoretical anchor applied to Black women's experiences.

To me, overemphasizing differences among Black women while rarely, if ever, situating analyses in a context of Black women's distinctive group-based oppression in the United-States is, at best, politically naive. If such neglect of social structure is also intentional, at worst, it is also dangerous. Regardless of current academic fashions, I suspect that African-American women benefit much less from critical social theories organized around difference than do other groups. Take, for example, feminist theories and political movements controlled by middle-class and affluent White feminists in the United States. Within contemporary U.S. feminism, a well-intentioned effort to explore differences among women in order to build a multiracial, multicultural feminist movement has been under way for some time. Exploding the category "woman" aims to create space for new alliances among individual women across historical markers of difference. Such efforts at coalition building remain worthwhile, and I can see how White women who have had limited contact with Black women benefit from struggling with their own privilege, let alone how benefits might accrue to a women's movement that appears to tolerate difference. However, I am left wondering whether a similar politics organized around differences *among* African-American women would deliver comparable results and newfound freedoms for Black women as a group.

Although a politics organized around difference may expand the freedom of individuals already positioned to benefit from such emphases, African-American women as a group operate in a different political context. White women as a group can claim a legal history that respects their individuality and privacy, however regulated by domestic relations. This expectation of privacy is still denied large numbers of African-American women. Eliminating Black feminist thought as an expression of group-based knowledge and replacing it with a politics organized around difference may inadvertently foster a weakening of Black women's ability to resist injustice as a collectivity. The true irony here is that, like Black women's suffering that occurs in plain sight while the structural racial segregation that causes such suffering remains hidden, Black women's intellectual production that becomes overly preoccupied with differences among Black women may experience a similar fate. It may slowly disappear, all the while remaining in plain sight, with Black women as a collectivity left wondering what happened.

I suspect that the time has come to balance this issue of dialogues *between* African-American women and members of other groups with one of thinking through what types of themes beyond those of naming should permeate dialogues *among* Black women. In one sense, contemporary Black feminism, womanism, or whatever we or others in the academy name it in the future is a mature discourse. Since it has "come to voice," it now faces new issues. Because Black women's intellectual production now finds its way to Black women of all sorts, as well as to many other women and men who benefit from its ideas, its legitimation has been beneficial. However, under commodity relations, Black women are encouraged to sell their voices, and the more different they are from one another, the better. Novelty, rather than a continuation of long-standing concerns, becomes the selling point.

To recognize this process, one need only contrast Heidi Safia Mirza's edited volume *Black British Feminism* (1997) with the increasing specialization that characterizes Black feminist thought in the United States. Though its themes differ, the volume reminds me of works such as Toni Cade Bambara's *The Black Woman* (1970), Gloria Hull et al.'s edited volume *All the Women Are White, All the Blacks Are Men, But Some of Us Are Brave* (1982), Barbara Smith's *Home Girls: A Black Feminist Anthology* (1983), and other comparable anthologies reflecting dialogues among Black women in the United States in earlier periods. *Black British Feminism* manages to weave together diverse perspectives of Black British women to talk back to a public largely unaware that Black British women have a voice. As a foundational document, the volume contains an enthusiasm and excitement about coming to voice in a British context that has silenced this visible yet invisible minority. Within this volume of Black British women who self-define as "Black" (no small feat in that context), one sees a rich dialogue among established intellectuals such as Hazel Carby, KumKum Bhavnani, and Ann Phoenix, as well as emerging thinkers such as Debbie Weekes, Tracey Reynolds, and Jayne Ifekwunigwe that presents a collective yet far from uniform voice. In part, this freedom to explore multiple dimensions of Black women's experiences from diverse perspectives reflects the significance of distinctive migration patterns to the United Kingdom and the distinctive meaning of *Black* in Britain. In the United States, racial segregation established more stringent and more limiting boundaries on lived Black experience, with corresponding effects on Black critical discourse (Wallace 1990).

Trying to name a Black women's standpoint certainly constitutes an important activity. However, whatever a Black women's intellectual tradition is called remains less important than, first, maintaining dialogues among Black women that are attentive to *both* heterogeneity among African-American women *and* shared concerns arising from a common social location in U.S. market and power relations; and, second, using this continually evolving knowledge to engage other critical social theories. So much of Black women's intellectual production is now filtered through an array of different speech communities, many of which serve important gatekeeping functions, that doing intellectual work in this climate necessarily changes the thought itself. The cost of visibility lies in the very real threat of having one's voice annexed in support of other agendas. I am reminded of a conversation I had with a Black female graduate student at a prestigious university who shared with me her interest in studying questions of Black women's knowledge and power relations. Although her decision to attend graduate school resulted from her deep interest in Black women's critical social theory, she quickly was told by potential committee members that since they had little interest in her topic, she would have to work on something more "marketable." The very interest that got her to school now had to be abandoned to gain the legitimacy to one day revisit this topic.

This woman's situation is far from unique. Many aspiring and established Black women intellectuals now create ideas for dissertation committees, tenure committees, journals, and the popular press—outlets that are all targeted to a liberal White public segmented into constituencies most receptive to the given intellectual. Writing to mainstream audiences to gain access to the public that one truly wants to reach is important and, far too often, necessary. However, as Zora Neale Hurston's continual struggles with her White patrons illustrates, visibility can exact high costs. Moreover, with the erosion of institutions of African-American civil society, much of this newer work remains unmediated. Many Black women doing intellectual work no longer encounter the heterogeneity of Black women's experiences in the everyday social interactions of Black civil society. As a result, although they are held accountable for what they say by a larger White public, even if their work deals with Black women, many see little reason to be accountable to Black civil society. Take, for example, the top four platform issues listed on the Web page of the organizers of the 1997 Million Woman March. The women who assembled in Philadelphia wanted the following: a probe into the Central Intelligence Agency's relationship to the influx of drugs in African-American communities; the development of Black independent schools; new mechanisms that would help Black women when they leave the penal system; and better health care services, with greater emphasis on preventive and therapeutic treatment. Other platform issues included support for Black women who want to become professionals, taking steps to curb homelessness and gentrification of urban neighborhoods, and increased support for all Black elderly. Many African-American women doing intellectual work certainly examine these issues, as do Black women activists. Yet none of these platform issues occupies a prominent place in contemporary Black feminist thought. Where is the book presenting a Black feminist analysis of African-American women and the drug industry? Where can we find a womanist treatment of Black independent schools? Without diligently attending to how the demands of the so-called universal audience and marketplace forces affect oppositional scholarship, Black women intellectuals, especially those deemed "public intellectuals," may lose their critical edge.

Although fostering dialogues among Black women in the here and now is important, of greater significance is reconceptualizing Black women's intellectual work as engaging in dialogues across time. The significance of writing books, making films, recording music, and producing other forms of cultural production lies in their power to foster dialogues among a diverse array of current and future readers, viewers, and listeners. I for one am immensely grateful that early-twentieth-century Black club women such as Anna Julia Cooper, Ida Wells Barnett, and others took the time to record their ideas. Their written record allows me to talk with them about patterns of injustice characterizing Black women's collective group history. Some of the most important ideas in Black women's intellectual history come from this sense of writing across time, of having dialogues with women who grapple with questions of injustice in unfamiliar social settings. Without listening to those who have come before, how can Black women prepare an intellectual and political space for Black women who will confront future, reconfigured injustices? Keeping a tradition alive differs from the popular conception of performing certain rites and rituals repeatedly and letting those rituals serve as tradition. Keeping a tradition alive lies in recognizing that African-American women will continue to confront a series of ongoing challenges stemming from systemic injustice. Although these challenges may be organized differently across time and place—the experiences of early-twentieth-century Black club Women, Black women in the early 1970s, and contemporary Black British feminists cannot be collapsed into one another without doing serious damage—they share a commonality. When it comes to Black women in the United States and Black women globally, unfortunately, this commonality constitutes searching for justice.

Currently, no infrastructure exists for the type of rich dialogue that I envision. Instead, like all African-Americans in the United States, Black women intellectuals remain under surveillance in racially segregated marketplace relations. Fostering dialogues among Black women across these complexities requires building new institutional locations that will continue to raise these questions across time. It also means legitimating one another's work despite bona fide differences emerging from the richly textured heterogeneity among Black women. Black women intellectuals would do well to remember that having the space to engage in dialogues of self-definition illustrated by the luxury of struggling over a name remains the privilege of only a select few. Twenty years from now, terms such as *womanism* and *Black feminism* may have little meaning, especially in the absence of actual social institutions dedicated to investigating Black women's critical social theory.

Overall, coming to voice in the public sphere without simultaneously coming to power in the social institutions that constitute it does little to challenge the injustices confronting African-American women as a collectivity. In this sense, those Black women teachers and administrators who publish little but who hold positions of power and authority in higher education, school districts, publishing avenues, and the media may have far greater impact on Black women's intellectual production than do a handful of handpicked academics. Without this type of structural power, Black women's position of having "no say" in determining the knowledge included in the American national "library" and, in turn, the power that the "library's" knowledge defends will persist. Including a few more books on Black women in the library or a few safe Black women's "voices" in the curriculum represents a step in the right direction. Those fortunate individual African-American women like me who find our work published and read certainly gain individual benefit from our politics. Although I like to think that our work makes a difference to more than just us, our loved ones, and a few empathetic colleagues, I also recognize how our work can be used toward quite different ends. Changing both the books in the library and the overall organization of the library requires far more than my or any other individual's coming to voice. After so many years of being silenced, individual voices like mine can provide comfort, if not inspiration, to individuals from many groups who, like African-American women, have been similarly silenced. I also know that, lacking a collective voice, individual voices like mine will become fainter until, one day, many may forget that we ever spoke at all.

CHAPTER 5

FEMINISM AND ANTIFEMINISM: FROM CIVIL RIGHTS TO CULTURE WARS

MOIRA FERGUSON, KETU H. KATRAK, AND VALERIE MINER

Any academic discipline or social movement that speaks for women, minorities, and the disadvantaged in North American culture is perceived as threatening to a conservative mainstream. The feminist movement and women's studies were born out of the activist energies of the 1960s student movements and the struggle for civil rights. Feminism, even as an academic discipline, remains committed to social change, and continues to grapple with the integral, often complex, links between theory and practice. This activist impulse, which remains a strong undercurrent through different waves of feminisms, is scorned by conservative upholders of "objective" scholarly endeavors. One aspect of feminism's activist impulse and its alliance with other oppressed groups brings its goals into conjunction with those of ethnic and multicultural studies. The eighties and nineties have witnessed antifeminist and antiethnic attacks by adherents of a Western, canonical tradition of humanistic learning. Let us back up for a moment and contextualize these remarks.

"The sixties" has become a cliché and catchword for an era of radical change that began with civil rights and ended with the bombing of Haiphong Harbor. The explosion in print and in television viewing brought the social upheaval into U.S. households.

African Americans, Anglo women, Native Americans, and Hispanics pushed for redress of their grievances; movements variously designated as Civil Rights, Women's Liberation, Wounded Knee, and La Raza spread like wildfire. This emergence of the Civil Rights Movement, Chicana, Native American, and Asian activism and the New Left occurred almost simultaneously, with women involved in all of them. This participation would sharpen female political skills, raise self-awareness, and lead to a new phase of the Women's Movement.

Throughout the decade, the number of divorced women rose from 1,858,000 in 1960 to 3,004,000 in 1970 (Linden-Ward, ix–xxii). Women aged 55 to 64 divorced two hundred percent more than they did before 1960. Black women joined the labor force in greater numbers, more black marriages disintegrated, more black women headed households; concurrently, Daniel Moynihan created the mythology of the black matriarch.[1] Despite this collectivity of issues and demands, however, these movements advanced in fits and starts.

Five years after Rosa Parks's historical refusal to surrender her bus seat, four black students sat at a Woolworth's lunch counter in North Carolina. In Muriel Rukeyser's prophetic phrase, the world was "split open" ("The Poem as Mask," 3).

With the founding of the Student Non-Violent Coordinating Committee (SNCC) in 1960, on a basis of radical equality, Southern black students began to react to racist attitudes and policies with nonviolent tactics, such as the celebrated sit-ins and freedom rides. Everyone's opinion was consid-

---

Reprinted from *Anti-Feminism in the Academy*. Edited by V. Clark, S. N. Garner, H. Higgonet, and K. H. Ketrak 1996. Copyright © 1996 Routledge (US).

ered equally in making decisions, and meetings did not end until consensus was reached. Though frustrating at times, this lack of hierarchy and structure generated a keen sense of community and idyllic democracy. Young, black women played a large part in SNCC, organizing voter registration and fighting segregation in the Southern states. Rubye Doris Smith Robinson was just one woman who held a central position in SNCC. Many young, black women, however, objected to the fact that the majority of positions of power were given to men, while women were relied upon to do the cleaning, cooking, and clerical work.

Black women, moreover, held influential positions in the churches during the Southern Civil Rights Movement, a fact that provided the backbone for the movement. Young volunteers learned to turn to these women for strength and inspiration. Fannie Lou Hamer was fifty-two years old when she got involved in politics; before that she had not known that African Americans could register to vote. She and her husband lost their jobs because they were determined to utilize that right, and she worked continuously thereafter for the Civil Rights Movement. Sara Evans comments:

> She organized citizenship schools and voter registration projects, endured brutal beatings in jail, and founded the Mississippi Freedom Democratic party to challenge the all-white political structure in that state. Young black and white volunteers recalled the transforming power of women like Fannie Lou Hamer singing gospel hymns, organizing their communities, risking and suffering for freedom with indomitable pride and dignity. (Evans, *Born*, 271)

Other female leaders, such as Ella Baker, Septima Clark, and Dorothy Cotton, were involved in Martin Luther King, Jr.'s Southern Christian Leadership Conference (SCLC). In 1964. SNCC recruited hundreds of white student volunteers, many from the North, to participate in Freedom Summer, a mass voter registration drive in the deep South. The presence of white students drew the attention of the media as well as the government to the movement. Part of this reaction was due to hegemonic white society's protective attitudes toward young, white women. Basing their goals on an ideal of "beloved community," white and black students worked together to organize and teach in freedom schools, run libraries, canvass for voter registration, and generally raise political awareness among black communities in the South. The idea of radical equality, argued by former members of SNCC, influenced the goals of the Women's Liberation Movement.

Yet, despite SNCCs egalitarian platform and the involvement of black women in discussions of equality, tensions developed, often sexual and racial. Women frequently felt discriminated against within its ranks, with gender divisions in assignments a particular sore point later on. Black and white women did virtually all the typing and clerical work for SNCC, as well as the housework around the freedom house. But while these experiences reinforced stereotypical roles for women, other assignments—door-to-door voter registration and allied fieldwork—developed women's organizational and leadership skills.

This division of labor provoked intense discussion within the movement. At a staff retreat in November 1964, a paper entitled "Women in the Movement" was anonymously distributed. The authors, later revealed as Mary King and Casey Hayden, discussed various incidents in which women in SNCC had been discriminated against. Flora Davis calls this paper "the first blow struck for women's liberation," but the women were actually more concerned with patching up the existing movement than creating a new one (75).

By February 1965, SNCC had grown disillusioned with white membership and the disorder of the movement. (Many white students had stayed on after summer of 1964 to become SNCC staff members.) Black members argued that SNCC should be black-dominated, black-led, and more structured. Black nationalism became a key issue, with the male-led Black Panther Party forming in 1965. Many whites in SNCC agreed that their presence was causing dissension. King and Hayden wrote a memo to other women in the movement, later published in *Liberation*, questioning sex-stereotyped roles. Many women began to question their participation in male-dominated and male-led organizations.

Such discrimination, furthermore, inspired a number of black women to become involved in the renewed struggle for women's rights that began in the late 1960s and early 1970s. They included Dorothy Height, president of the National Council of Negro Women, lawyer Pauli Murray, union leaders Aileen Hernandez and Addie Wyatt, Representative Shirley Chisholm, and Fannie Lou Hamer. Florynce Kennedy, who formed the Media Workshop in 1966, an organization that dealt with racism in the media and advertising, also participated in protests waged by the National Organization of Women against sexism in the *New York Times* and Colgate-Palmolive. She organized protests supporting H. Rap Brown in Cambridge, Maryland in 1966, becoming involved in the Black Power movement as well (Kennedy, 53–58). The links between feminism and ethnicities continued to grow. Women of different ethnic groups, inspired by feminist ideals, took stands that enabled links to be made between gender and race.

Native American women, also faced with challenges of poverty and cultural genocide, were no exception. In 1970, the annual median Native American income was $5,832, compared to a national median of $9,540 (Linden-Ward, 65–66). Ada Deer, of the Menominee tribe, for example, speaks of the years 1961 to 1973 as a "political, economic, and cultural disaster for the Menominee.... Just a few people had the power to make decisions" (Katz, 149).[2] Spiritually and culturally as well as politically based, the American Indian Movement (AIM) was born in 1968. Old traditions of female leadership reemerged, with women such as Mary Ellen Crow Dog (Brave Bird) inspired by these activities to speak her mind. (At Wounded Knee, in South Dakota, at the uprising in 1973, women like Madonnah Thunder Hawk and Gladys Bissonette appeared among the negotiators.)[3] Bissonette and Ellen Moves Camp named that movement: "Go ahead and make your stand at Wounded Knee. If you men won't do it, you can stay here and talk for all eternity and we women will do it" (Crow Dog, 80. See also 124, 189).

Many women participated at Wounded Knee, with Crow Dog recalling their response to a white volunteer nurse who ventured to criticize this of women: "We told her ... we had other priorities." By the seventies, Native American women had formed Women of All the Red Nations. For African-American and Native American women, civil rights and cultural identity became priorities. Beginning in the sixties, that is, women across boundaries of race and class struggled against a patriarchal system, but within that system, while feminism still assumed certain normative privileges.

These priorities were also critical for Hispanic females, inflected with specifically feminist demands. Although many women worked in the Chicano movement along with men, activities such as the 1969 Chicano Liberation Conference, Women's Caucus, the 1971 National Chicano Conference, and the formation of Concilio Mujeres, Concilio Femenil, and the National Chicana Institute and the National Chicana Foundation also took place. In broader terms, in Martha Cotera's narrative about Chicana participation:

> It began with the Kennedy campaign in the 1960's, continued with social and economic issues in the mid-sixties, and then on to reform in the educational system in the late sixties. Further on, we moved into political participation in 1970 and to the founding of the Raza Unida Party. (*Chicana Feminist*, 17)

One major strategy of Chicanas nationally was to fill important elected positions in Texas; among them was Virginia Musquiz, one of the founders of Raza Unida in Texas and possibly the first Texas Chicana to run for a legislative seat (Cotera, *Profile*, 107–108). Other distinguished Chicanas include Jovita Gonzalez, an anthropologist and writer, and Emma Tenayuca Brooks and Manuela Solis Sager, labor leaders and activists from the area around San Antonio (Cotera, *Chicana Feminist*, 14). Student organizations were formed, such as UMAS (United Mexican American Students), which later changed its name to MECHA (Movimiento Estudiantil Chicano e de Azlan). Women also played a large part in Labor organizations such as the United Farm Workers, Cesar Chavez's unique organization that concentrated on the needs of the Mexican-American workers and community. Jesse Lopez de la Cruz, who began working with Chavez in 1962, joined the United Farm Workers in 1967, and committed herself to the task of bringing women into the union. Dolores Huerta, vice president of the union and chief negotiator, began working with Chavez in 1960 (Mirandé & Enríquez, *La Chicana* 233–234). In Sacramento, she went to head a legislative program, "lobbying for benefits like old-age pensions for noncitizens, the right to register voters door to door, the right to take driver's examinations in Spanish, and disability insurance for farm workers" (Mirandé & Enríquez, *La Chicana* 233).

In the student organizations, Chicanas often commented that they felt discriminated against by men in the movement; female leadership was discouraged, and women were relegated to subordinate positions. Due to the discrepancy between what Chicanas saw as the agenda of Anglo feminism and their own agenda, however, Chicanas were not willing to attach themselves to the ethnocentric, white, Women's Movement. The women's caucus at the 1969 Chicano Youth Conference held in Denver, Colorado, emerged with this resolution: "We have come to the consensus that we do not want to be liberated." Yet within two years, the First National Chicana Conference was held in Houston, Texas.

The predominant student organization in the North during the 1960s was Students for a Democratic Society, known as SDS. Prior to the Vietnam War, much of SDS's energy was spent on a project to educate and empower the Northern poor, in much the same way as the SNCC organized indigent black people in the South. Beyond that, with the United States's increasing involvement in Vietnam, particularly after February 1965, student groups concentrated on protesting the war and the draft. Many campuses held all-night sit-ins, educating anyone who would listen about the conflict in Vietnam. Draft resistance was a major concern. On April 17, 1965, SDS organized a march in Washington protesting the Vietnam War, thus locating themselves in the forefront of the antiwar movement.

From its inception, male intellectuals had dominated Students for a Democratic Society as leaders and theorists. Unlike female participants in SNCC, SDS women felt neither welcome nor treated equally. Women undertook menial, everyday tasks in order to support the movement, but rarely spoke publicly on the organization's behalf. Additionally, the New Left's involvement in the draft resistance movement tended to downplay female activists; since women could not be drafted, men felt that they were risking less. Gradually, women's workshops began to appear at SDS conferences and conventions; many simply discussed ways in which women could support the draft resistance movement, but others dealt seriously with women's dissatisfaction and inequality in the movement. Classes for and about women began to be offered in freedom schools and universities across the country.

On another front were older, professional women reacting to the lack of legislation concerning women's issues, concerns that harkened back to the old struggle for the Equal Rights Amendment (ERA). (This struggle is still a legislative battle, not a *fait accompli*.) In December 1961, President Kennedy established the President's Commission on the Status of Women (PCSW), with Eleanor Roosevelt as chairwoman.[4] While that first commission was preparing its report for President Kennedy in 1963, the publication of *The Feminine Mystique* by Betty Friedan identified white, middle-class, female unrest and traditional assumptions that women should be happy to forgo careers to work at home raising their children. Friedan highlighted the contradiction between the image of women, what was expected of them, and their material/psychological reality.

Commission concerns about the quality of women's lives generated more recognition of the need for a national organization. With Betty Friedan as president, the National Organization for Women (NOW) held its founding conference in Washington, D.C. on October 29 and 30, 1966. At its second annual conference in November 1967, NOW's decision to take a public stand on the ERA and abortion alienated a number of members. On the other hand, the announced agenda also attracted new members.

On the issue of class, the Women's Equity Action League (WEAL), founded in 1968 partly in response to NOW's decision to adopt such a broad agenda, wanted to concentrate more on discrimination against women in jobs and education. Many groups followed suit in forming single-issue organizations; abortion, women's health care, discriminatory law, including the fight to pass Title VII in the Civil Rights Act, were issues in the forefront.

In the academy, activism proceeded apace. Women's studies programs in colleges and universities rapidly grew. In the fall of 1969, according to Davis, there were only seventeen courses offered in this country that directly concerned women. In 1970 that number had risen to over one hundred. By 1971, almost a hundred colleges around the country offered a one-credit course or more. One door was formally opening to a fundamental change in the traditional academy that stressed interdisciplinary studies and the link between activism and scholarship.

But the split that had been developing in the white movement became undeniable by 1968 to 1969. In the summer of 1967, a group of women in Chicago's Students for a Democratic Society formed a splinter group, out of which, in 1969, New York Radical Women and the Redstockings eventually emerged (Fritz, 25–27). In the same year, 1969, an offshoot of New York Radical Women—WITCH—burned voter registration cards at the counterinaugural demonstration. The complex background to the split partly involved controversies over homophobia and class.

Let us back up for a moment to connect the two different strands: first, the sixties offered new avenues for struggle, and inspired many lesbians to come to renewed self-definitions despite historical hostility and employment and housing discrimination. Many lesbian feminists were movement leaders. Prior to the sixties, Del Martin and Phyllis Lyon had formed the Daughters of Bilitis, publishing *The Ladder* from 1956 to 1972—"the voice of the lesbian in America" (Damon, 298). Antihomosexual laws, however, remained on the books in major cities and states, and official harassment was common (Longauex y Vasquez, 382).

According to Leah Fritz, at the beginning of the Women's Movement lesbians remained outside or closeted within it:

> In NOW and most of the early radical groups, however, lesbianism was a forbidden subject or barely tolerated as an aberration. The *right* of lesbians to exist within some groups was acknowledged, but their *need* for specific recognition and approval was ignored. To NOW, lesbians were an embarrassment; to Marxists, they were a "problem" caused by capitalism; to heterosexual radical feminists, they were invisible. (32)

Martha Shelley alludes to the difficulties when she spoke about picketing the Miss America pageant in 1968: "the most terrible epithet heaped on our straight sisters was 'lesbians'" (308). The gay-straight split became a deeply controversial issue. With her lesbian conspiracy notions, Betty Friedan fanned the flames of the debate.

Second, socialist feminists differed with radical feminists over origins: the former viewed patriarchy as stemming from the division of society into classes; radical feminists, on the other hand, stressed female autonomy. The principal enemies were denoted as capitalism and patriarchy, respectively (Deckard, 455). Thus by 1968 the radical feminist movement was taking shape; socialist feminist groups sometimes functioned autonomously, sometimes collectively within the parent "left" group.

Women's liberation and consciousness-raising groups were forming around the country (Echols, 5). Over the past three decades, cross-class and cross-race feminists have experienced both disaffection and solidarity. Ideological debates about which oppression to "privilege"—class, race, sexual preference, or gender—became urgent and ubiquitous. Myths about a collective, politically unified left and "womanhood" were finally and visibly exploding. The New Left and the Women's Liberation Movement had parted company. The baiting that ensued is now legendary.

* * *

If the 1960s in the U.S. were a decade of recognizing the contradictions between women's competence and their power, between American progressives' ideas about equality among men and their inequitable treatment of men of color and women, the sixties also provided the momentum for what is popularly known as "second-wave feminism." Questions were raised in those years. The seventies offered a time for trying out answers—in the bedroom, the kitchen, the public workplace, the community, and the national political arena. Some answers were more successful than others, but just as important as proposed solutions were the female voices behind those proposals. Many Americans—male and female—began to try out a new language in which "she" was as acceptable as "he" in the third person singular, in which "Miss" and "Mrs." conflated into "Ms." and in which "girls" had become "women." In some senses, the 1970s was the "women's studies decade," with a startling growth of feminist coursework in several U.S. academic institutions, the founding of women's committees in many disciplines, and the establishment of the National

Women's Studies Association. Then, because of huge strides toward equality at home, at work, and in the public consciousness, feminists and women in general became subject to a stunning backlash of negative and/or violent images of independent women conducted by the televangelists, the Catholic Church, the mass media, the Republican Party, and an increasing number of "New Right" organizations, such as the Eagle Forum spearheaded by Phyllis Schlafly.

In the early 1970s, four major sources of national momentum for feminists were the proposal for a national Equal Rights Amendment, congressional passage of Title IX of the Education Amendments of 1972, the Supreme Court decision in *Roe versus Wade*, and the aftershocks from the "Stonewall" police attack on a Greenwich Village gay bar. In establishing a woman's legal right to an abortion (within certain prescribed limits), the 1973 Supreme Court decision had the immediate impact of giving women more control over their bodies. It saved lives and changed lives. The ERA debate provided a platform for the discussion of the inequities experienced by women as workers and citizens. Congress sent the bill out to be ratified by the States in 1972, and a ten-year debate followed. Also in 1972, passage of Title IX supported the claim of U.S. women on education, and thus had resonance for the hiring of scholars in universities and the purchasing of equipment for junior high school girls' basketball teams. Stonewall was a point of no return for lesbians and gay men in the country. Six months before the beginning of the seventies, the raid on a Manhattan tavern ignited a gay and lesbian rights movement that manifested itself in public parades, self-help switchboards, legal aid centers, political lobbying, and caucuses among artists and scholars. Among the battles lesbians began to face was the confrontation of homophobia within the Women's Movement.

Although some antifeminists claim the second wave of feminism was a white, middle-class movement, in fact many of the early 1970s activists were women of color. In 1970, the North American Indian Association was founded by women from forty-three tribes. In 1971, six hundred Chicanas met at the first nationwide Chicana conference, where they passed a platform calling for legalized abortion and a resolution rebuking the Catholic Church. The Conference of Puerto Rican Women was founded in 1972. The next year the National Black Feminist Organization was founded (Hartmann, 70–71).

American courtrooms began to echo with women's voices in class action job discrimination suits and sexual harassment litigation. Meanwhile, the field of women's health was revolutionized by the publication of *Our Bodies, Ourselves* (1971), the exposure of forced sterilizations of women of color and poor women, broader distribution of contraceptives, and the establishment of women's health clinics. Karla Jay describes one of them in *Lavender Culture*:

> The health care workers explained to me in advance everything they were going to do and why. They also used simple language instead of the jargonese [that] straight, male physicians had used. And since the clinic took me seriously as a woman, they took my body seriously. The fee for this was $3 a few years ago when it opened. (61)

U.S. arts were changed with the opening of feminist and lesbian feminist galleries, theatre groups such as At The Foot of the Mountain in Minneapolis and the Westbeth Playwright's Feminist Collective in New York, and bookstores such as A Room of One's Own in Madison. The workplace was being redefined by pressure for better wages and working conditions (including maternity leave and day care). Indeed, the whole notion of paid work was being challenged by concepts such as comparable worth and salaried housework. Each of these changes resonated with others. One shift created another social disruption, and more territory was opened for question.

Books were among the most significant forces for social change, and the early 1970s revealed a revolution with the publication of Toni Cade Bambara's *The Black Women* (1970), Robin Morgan's *Sisterhood is Powerful* (1970), Eva Figes's *Patriarchal Attitudes* (1970), Shulamith Firestone's *The Dialectic of Sex* (1970), and Germaine Greer's *The Female Eunuch* (1971). The Feminist Press published its first book in 1971. Ms. Magazine was founded in 1972. Other channels of feminist communication included private conversation, consciousness-raising groups, rallies and demonstrations, feminist reporters gaining space in the mainstream media, and an increasingly aware female constituency on every level of the educational ladder.

With the passage of Title IX, it was safe to say women's studies was here to stay. In 1973, there were approximately 5,000 women's studies courses in the United States. By 1980, over 20,000 courses existed. By the end of the 1970s there were 350 women's studies programs around the country. Although these programs and ethnic studies programs were growing, women faculty and faculty of color still held fewer positions and positions of much lower rank than their white, male colleagues. It became clear that the project of reclaiming the academy had to take place on several fronts at once: hiring, promotion, and publication, as well as pedagogy. Women began to organize within disciplines to found committees and caucuses and to create interdisciplinary journals. The Modern Language Association's Women's Caucus first met in 1970. *Feminist Studies* was first published in 1972, and the first issue of *Signs* appeared in 1975. Feministas Unidas was founded in 1977. The National Women's Studies Association and *Sojourner: A Third World Women's Research Newsletter* were founded in 1977. In 1978, the Association of Black Women Historians was formed. Also emerging in the 1970s were women's research facilities and campus centers for outreach to community women.

The publication rate of articles on women and women's issues in journals of history, literature, education, and anthropology increased more than threefold between 1970 and 1980 (DuBois, 16). As the authors of *Feminist Scholarship: Kindling in the Groves of Academe* explain:

> The cumulative effect of the feminist critiques of the disciplines was to establish incontrovertibly the existence and varieties of male bias in traditional academic inquiry. This bias, however inadvertent, accepts and perpetuates the ideology of female inferiority. Whether the particular discipline has almost completely neglected women—as in history or philosophy—or treated them as incidental to central issues of research—as in literature or anthropology—or considered gender as an important factor for research—as in education—feminist scholars have shown that the assumption that male behavior and experience are the norm for the entire human race is common to all. So, too, do all the disciplines, whatever their other differences, provide a truncated and distorted picture of women, which reflects and justifies our society's oppressive stereotypes of what it is to be female. (36)

Academic feminist solidarity was not uncomplicated, and the feminist harmony was interrupted and stimulated by constituencies of women of color and lesbians who demanded a deeper commitment to inclusiveness. In 1974, less than one percent of the women's studies courses in the U.S. listed a focus on black women. As Gloria T. Hull and Barbara Smith write, in the introduction to the groundbreaking *All the Women Are White, All the Blacks Are Men, But Some of Us Are Brave: Black Women's Studies*:

> Clearly, then, if one looks for "hard data" concerning curriculum relating to Black women in the existing studies of academic institutions, we are seemingly nonexistent. And yet impressionistically and experientially it is obvious that more and more study is being done about Black women and, even more importantly, it is being done with an increasing consciousness of the impact of sexual-racial politics on Black women's lives. One thinks, for instance, of Alice Walker's groundbreaking course on Black women writers at Wellesley College in 1972, and how work of all sorts by and about Black women writers has since blossomed into a visible Black female literary "renaissance." (xxvi)

As progress was being made in the schools, the courts, the hospitals and the living rooms in the 1970s, right-wing men and women grew more and more nervous, and a powerful backlash ensued. Feminists emerged as enemies of the family and terrorists undermining the basic fabric of American life. In 1977, poor women's access to abortion was severely curtailed by the passage of the Hyde Amendment, legislation that only accelerated the antiabortion movement in the years to come. The Equal Rights Amendment was attacked as the harbinger of such disasters as homosexual marriage, women in combat, and unisex public toilets. Gradually, initial support for the legislation eroded as it was challenged by the Daughters of the American Revolution, the National Council of Catholic Women, fundamentalist

Protestant preachers, and lobbying organizations such as the Eagle Forum and smaller groups such as Utah's HOTDOGS (Humanitarians Opposed to the Degradation of Our Girls), which is affiliated with the John Birch Society (Hartmann, 135). Meanwhile, in municipalities around the country, lesbian and gay rights legislation was being defeated by homophobic activists. No doubt much of the antifeminism was fueled by the collective male ego wounded in our defeat in and withdrawal from Vietnam. In every phase of personal and public life, feminist gains were being eroded by what Susan I. Hartmann calls the "Countermobilization."

If the 1960s was a period during which women activists participated in and faced the contradictions of their unfair treatment in the New Left and Civil Rights movements, the 1970s was a decade when many women looked more closely at misogyny, and began to name and organize against numerous forms of violence against women. The FBI reported that every thirty seconds all American woman was raped and every eighteen seconds a woman was battered. Police observed that rape was increasingly accompanied by whippings, beatings or mutilation (Miner, 1981, 48). In 1970, New York Radical Feminists called a "Rape Speak Out." NOW started a Rape Task force in 1973. All over the country, as women were alerted to the dangers of rape, they tried to raise the consciousness of the courts, started self-defense courses and established rape crisis centers. By the end of the decade, forty states had new or revised rape statutes. Likewise, women made battery a public issue. The first feminist shelter was established in St. Paul, Minnesota in 1971, the product of a consciousness-raising group. As with rape, the public understanding of battery came about through feminist community organizing, educational panels, electoral lobbying, in-service training for police and hospital workers, and the establishment of sanctuaries for women who had been battered. By 1980, there were three hundred shelters nationally (Hartmann, 122–124).

By the late seventies, it had become apparent that the decade would bring both gains and losses, and that feminist strengths were threats to the orthodox of all stripes. Emblematic of this tension was the extravaganza of the National Women's Conference held in Houston in November, 1977. Two thousand delegates came from all over the country to discuss and vote on a national action platform. Issues affecting women of color and lesbians were well-represented. One of the most dramatic moments in the conference was when Betty Friedan, who had often been antagonistic to lesbians, spoke about the importance of homosexual rights. The delegates articulated strong support for child care, welfare reform, and abortion rights. Meanwhile, the streets outside the conference hall were a carnival of right-wing protest. Born-again Christians carried signs warning about eternal damnation. Phyllis Schlafly held a flag-draped press conference. And the national press had a field day.

At the end of the decade, the ground was laid for feminist advance and misogynist attack. In striking contrast to the large gains made with relative speed at the beginning of the 1970s by women inside and outside the academy, feminists now found increasing friction in every sphere. Women's rights activists began with the impetus and organizational tactics used successfully in the Civil Rights and Anti-War movements. Over the years, the New Right had learned to emulate some of these same strategies. Many feminists underestimated the deep and enduring nature of conservative resistance, and miscalculated the Right's material means to support that resistance. Perhaps some of us expected consciousness to be contagious. Perhaps a more philosophical aspect of the problem is related to the rhetorical limits of the discourse of equality. To a conservative, this abstract liberal ideal is vulnerable to all sorts of panic-ridden interpretations. Its generously unspecific nature invites abusive misrepresentation, such as the notion that affirmative action is "reverse discrimination" and that gay and lesbian civil rights ordinances are calling for "special rights." In the academy, once amused male colleagues were now responding more seriously and sourly to the growth of feminist books, articles, journals, and classes. Antifeminist harassment was being launched in the form of censorship, ridicule, job discrimination, and personal threat. Then, in 1980, U.S. voters elected Ronald Reagan, and fell into a long sleep.

* * *

The culture wars of the 1980s and 1990s include among their various targets feminism and feminists. U.S. culture is in the midst of an antifeminist rebound (unfortunately not the first time in U.S. history), directed against feminism as a theoretical approach and against feminists personally. The contemporary version has its own particular "New Right" face, even a grimace, that differs from those of the 1920s, or the 1940s but evokes older rallying forces such as laissez-faire economics and the glorification of family values, of femininity, and of motherhood within traditional nuclear models. However, feminism has an activist impulse. This enables constructive alliances with other oppressed groups, and brings feminism's goals in the 1980s and 1990s into conjunction with those of ethnic and multicultural studies. Hence, we witness that antifeminism in this period is accompanied often by antagonism to ethnic and multicultural studies. Negative reactions to feminism in academia, popular culture, and mass media today are camouflaged, even mystified, by wider attacks on women's studies, ethnic studies, and affirmative action policies. Further, such antiprogressive stances take refuge in the popular slogan of "political correctness," which is evoked in order to undercut modest progress in the educational and cultural life of the U.S.: the varied impacts of feminist thought inside and outside the academy, the establishment of women's studies and ethnic studies programs in academic institutions, and social welfare programs.

Antifeminism takes a variety of overt and subtle forms—intellectual devaluing and ridicule of feminist ideas, political baiting of feminists, and at times, physical threats. Antifeminist backlashes are targeted against feminism as a discipline and on feminists personally, often against the *perceived* power of feminists in contemporary times. Adherents of a traditional gender status quo portray a few well-established and visible feminist scholars as threatening. Such "threats" severely misrepresent the majority of women, who continue to endure vast gender inequities in this democratic nation. The attacks may be directed against women self-identified as feminists or those labelled with hostile intent as "feminists." A case in point is the man who gunned down fourteen women in a University of Montreal classroom because they were "all a bunch of fucking feminists."

It is important to recognize that these cultural wars are not simply academic matters. Part of a national debate, they seep into our daily lives through popular culture and mass-media rhetoric against poor people, gays and lesbians, immigrants,[5] and against safe abortions and other reproductive rights,[6] as well as, increasingly, in opposition to affirmative action. These negative messages against women and minorities enter both private and public spaces, broadcast into our living rooms via radio and television, discussed in our classrooms, reported in newspapers and magazines.

Susan Faludi provocatively discusses some of these issues in her book, *Backlash: The Undeclared War Against American Women*. Her introduction, ironically titled, "Blame It on Feminism" demystifies the many "grievances that contemporary American women have about their private and public lives" (ix). Popular media both celebrates and undercuts women's successes, often facetiously blaming feminism for women's unhappiness. "It must be all that equality that's causing all that pain," remarks Faludi, tongue in cheek. "Women are unhappy precisely because they are free."

In academia, Faludi cites how certain "experts" in legal studies, economics, sociology, and demography uphold that "equality doesn't mix with marriage and motherhood. And joining this bandwagon of attacks on feminism are some women who nonetheless consider themselves "feminist," and who are welcomed particularly by the mainstream publishing industry. What better than one of our own to condemn our goals, such as a successful career woman who bemoans the shortcomings of feminism (similar to nonwhite Dinesh D'Souza, who does the dirty work against minorities even better than a William Bennett or an Allan Bloom)? Let us call them gender insiders, these antifeminist feminists who are given increasing attention by a mainstream media that made Camille Paglia, "an embittered antifeminist academic ... [into] an overnight celebrity, landing [her] on the cover of *New York* and *Harper's* the same month, soon after launching a vitriolic attack on 'whining' feminists in her 1990 book *Sexual Personae: Art and Decadence from Nefertiti to Emily Dickinson*" (Faludi, 319).[7] The press merrily cashes in on Paglia's "antifeminist zingers," such as "If civilization had been left in female hands, we would still be living in grass huts." In her Preface to *Sexual Personae,* she notes, "My method is a form of sensationalism: I try to flesh out intellect with emotion.... Whenever sexual freedom is sought or achieved, sadomasochism will not be far behind.... Sex is a far darker power than feminism has admitted" (xiii, 3).

A few deriders of feminism such as Paglia receive much publicity, whereas among women in general, "75 to 95 percent credit the feminist campaign with improving their lives," states Faludi. "In public opinion surveys, women consistently rank their own inequality, at work and at home, among their most urgent concerns" (xv). Sadly, economic and social equality between men and women is hardly a reality when women constitute "two-thirds of all poor adults," and when "American women face the worst gender-based pay gap in the developed world" (Faludi, xiii). The fact that women still have to fight for an Equal Rights Amendment, for reproductive rights, maternity leave, affordable child care, and safe abortions' demonstrates that social, economic, and political equality for women is a long way off.

The 1980s backlash has a particular history, as do earlier ones in U.S. history. Each wave of antifeminism—1920s, 1940s, late 1970s—arises after certain gains in women's rights, and aims to erode such successes. Lois W. Banner remarks how the 1920s antifeminism, though "extensive... rarely denied women the right to live their lives as they saw fit. But the antifeminism of the postwar 1940s held women responsible for society's ills—either because they were failures as mothers or because they had left home for work" (212).[9] After the war, "'Rosie the Riveter' was replaced by the homemaker as the national feminine model." Women were bombarded by jingoistic psychologists who declared with dubious "scientific" evidence that women working outside the home were playing havoc with their children's mental states.

Contemporary antifeminism began in the late seventies among the religious Right. This fundamentalist thinking moved into the White House in the eighties with Reagan, and, by the mid-eighties, it had become socially acceptable to challenge women's struggles for equality. In her discussion of "Ironies of the 1980s," in *Born for Liberty,* Sara M. Evans notes that although "political feminism found hard times [during the Reagan era]... cultural transformations gave it advantages it had never had before.... [Reaganomics could not] significantly alter the gender shifts that had already taken place.... The real battle was over the meaning of those changes both for individuals and for society" (307).

The eighties saw substantial gains and losses for women. Support for ERA was very high in 1981, yet the amendment was struck down in 1982. Rather than the goal of equality being achieved, it was precisely the fear of women moving towards it that was perceived as a threat. Women's advancement in the workforce, however minimal in terms of actual numbers, was regarded with hostility—more than one woman (or minority) was often too many.[10]

Antifeminism of the 1980s and 1990s has operated in often insidious ways. Its uniqueness lies in its clever use of the very hard-earned *gains* of the feminist movement against women; women's successes are turned around as the very reasons for women's *losses.* The particularity of our current backlash lies in the increased power and capabilities of the media, including computerized information superhighways, electronic international mail networks, and other access into virtual realities that can ignore, negate, or render invisible the real conditions governing people's ordinary lives. Hollywood movies, popular psychology, conservative talk radio shows have found ways to turn on their head such goals as autonomy and independence that feminism struggled for, as if these gains in women's self-reliance are responsible now for all of women's ills, whether depression, unemployment, or teenage pregnancy. Publications, as different as the *New York Times, Vanity Fair, The Nation* have issued indictments against the women's movement with such headlines as "When Feminism Failed or The Awful Truth About Women's Lib"; "Professional women are suffering 'burnout' and succumbing to an 'infertility epidemic'"; "Single women are grieving from a 'man shortage'" (Faludi, ix). These myths, which ascribe women's woes to feminism, wish to do away with this "obsolete" feminist "thing." Other periodic outbursts of antifeminism are evident in increased incidents of violence against women (anti-abortionists, for instance, firebombing clinics, or threatening and killing doctors); culturally legitimized, even valorized violence in popular films; Rush Limbaugh's vastly popular radio shows with his humorous jibes at "femi-Nazi feminists."

One deleterious effect of contemporary antifeminism is that it has created a huge wedge between the very few celebrity women who have "made it," some of whom divorce themselves from the Women's Movement, and the vast numbers of working-class and working women who are still struggling for equal wages. Another tactic deployed by antifeminists is to pretend to be apolitical. On the contrary, attacks on feminism, whether in academia, popular culture, or mass media, are rooted in the conservative political climate of the eighties and nineties. These decades may well be remembered as a period of mean-spiritedness, of simplistic assertions of "individual rights and responsibilities" divorced from social and civic conscience. Attempts to dismantle affirmative action are veiled, often dishonestly, as "re-evaluations of an imperfect system." The loudest opponents of so-called reverse discrimination (beleaguered white men who feel that America for Americans—read "white"—is slipping away from their grip) have found new scapegoats in the nineties—immigrants, gays and lesbians (ballot initiatives in Oregon and Colorado), women and children (congressional debates about cutting off school lunches and aid to welfare mothers).

Contemporary antifeminist attacks are similarly launched by conservative upholders of ostensibly "value-free" scholarship and "pure" literary traditions. These adherents of a Western canonical tradition of humanistic learning are hostile not only to women's studies, but also to ethnic and multicultural studies. Their intellectual assaults are mounted often on the rhetoric of "political correctness" colloquially known as "PC." This anti–PC campaign undertakes overt and covert attacks on feminism as an ideology, with exaggerated claims of the power of feminists.

The difficulties of delineating the parameters of political correctness lie in the fluidity of the concept and its problematic appropriation by right-wing demagogues. Ironically, the loudest protestors who claim to be "silenced" by progressive aspects of feminism and multiculturalism invoke political correctness as a slogan to cut off debate and discussion. The most vociferous protectors of "free speech" see no contradiction in shutting up the voices of women and minorities.

Since antifeminist attacks are often couched in the rhetoric of accusations of political correctness, it is useful to examine two documents with opposing viewpoints—one by the conservative National Association of Scholars (NAS), and the other (formulated in response to NAS) by the liberal/ progressive Teachers for a Democratic Culture (TDC). Patricia Aufderheide's *Beyond PC: Towards a Politics of Understanding* presents a provocative selection of voices for and against this concept. Aufderheide's introduction attempts to define this slippery term:

> Is the issue, as *Newsweek* charged in the December 1990 cover story that triggered the media onslaught about PC, "totalitarian ways of teaching on American campuses?" Or, is it, as some in this anthology charge, largely a figment of the right-wing imagination, a strategy aimed at junking such programs as affirmative action? (1)

The National Association of Scholars has grown since 1987 to nearly 1,700 members with affiliates in twenty-five states. This Princeton, New Jersey-based group of traditionalists see themselves as "a disenfranchised minority within the academy." Many of their projects are funded by conservative foundations such as John Olin.[11] NAS puts forward its manifesto objecting to any kind of preferential provisions for women or minorities in recruitment, hiring, and retention. NAS believes that such "policies and practices involve either the application of a double standard or the repudiation of appropriate intellectual criteria.... Safeguarding intellectual freedom is of critical importance to the academy" (Aufderheide, 8). NAS objects to forms of "discriminatory harassment" that involve "punitive codes restricting 'insensitive' speech ... requirements that students take tendentious courses dealing with groups regarded as victimized" (8). The inclusion of race, gender, and class "relentlessly ... in preference to all other approaches to assessing the human condition" leads to increasing division on campus. NAS proposes that ethnic or gender studies courses should be allowed only if "they have genuine scholarly content and are not vehicles for political harangue or recruitment"

(10); it opposes "trendy methodologies" that include feminism. Its goals of fostering objective, humanistic knowledge are based on the claim that each individual be evaluated "on the basis of personal achievement and promise. A journal called *Heterodoxy: Articles and Animadversions on Political Correctness and Other Follies* also includes women's studies and feminists among its attacks. In a cover story, "Women's Studies Imperialists,' conservative anxieties are vented about "queer studies" and about women's studies' attempts to get "integrated" and to transform the curriculum rather than stay in their own "female" ghetto. Prominent feminist scholars like Johnnella Butler, Catharine Stimpson, Bettina Aptheker are ridiculed, whereas Camille Paglia, who derides women's studies as upholding "unchallenged groupthink," or Christina Hoff Sommers, who finds "quack scholarship" in the discipline, are applauded. The article also lambastes the Ford Foundation for supporting women's studies enterprises.[12]

In response to the concerted NAS campaign to malign the gains of diversity, feminism, and multiculturalism, and to present "an alarming picture of the state of contemporary education as a catastrophic collapse," a group called Teachers for a Democratic Culture (TDC) was formed.[13] TDC supports "curricular reforms influenced by multiculturalism and feminism," and asserts democratic principles of discussion and debate that are valued in U.S. education. TDC notes that, given the political changes of the last twenty years or so, women and minorities are present in increasing numbers in institutions of higher learning, and that their presence has inspired and often instigated curricular reforms. TDC contests the many "false claims" made by alarmists who believe that race and gender issues are taking precedence over the classics of Western civilization, "that teachers across the land are being silenced and politically intimidated; that the very concepts of reason, truth, and artistic standards are being subverted in favor of a crude ideological agenda." Rather, counters TDC, NAS and media supporters "are endangering education with a campaign of harassment and misrepresentation." A conservative trajectory similar to NAS's is evident in certain disturbing questions raised in Karen Lehrman's campus interviews with students: "Is women's studies failing women? Is feminist education limiting her potential?" (Lehrman, 45–51, 64–68).

Whereas TDC supports open discussion and debate "about the relations of culture, scholarship, and education to politics," NAS touts objectivity and humanistic knowledge, and insists that the "'truths' of 'Western civilization' should be the basis for our educational system." Manning Marable, in his column, "Along the Color Line: Why Conservatives Fear Multiculturalism," contests this claim to truth:

> As a professor of history, I know that there is no "truth" in anyone's history or textbooks. The history books in the past always reflected the interests and perspectives of people in power in America. That's why, until recently, Native Americans, Latinos, and African-Americans were excluded from all textbooks, and our achievements were ignored or stolen. When oppressed people successfully struggle for their democratic rights, the textbooks inevitably are changed.... Why are conservative intellectuals and foundations so frightened by multiculturalism? Behind their public rhetoric are several political realities.... By attacking multicultural education and affirmative action, they are deliberately manipulating racial and gender symbols to mobilize their supporters. (11)

The neoconservatives claim fallaciously that their educational goals of objectivity and truth as embodied in traditional humanistic teaching are devoid of political intent. As Catharine Stimpson remarks, "The attack on diversity is a rhetorical strategy by neoconservatives who have their own political agenda. Under the guise of defending objectivity and intellectual rigor, which is a lot of mishmash, they are trying to preserve the cultural and political supremacy of white heterosexual males" (quoted in Taylor, 32–40).

NAS grew out of a group who felt that they could not speak freely on issues such as affirmative action or feminism. They wanted the freedom to express racist or sexist views. John Taylor's essay, "Are You Politically Correct?" lumps together, in his own words, "the new fundamentalists" who include "an eclectic group" comprised of "multiculturalists, feminists, radical homosexuals, Marxists, New Historicists. What unites them ... is their conviction that Western culture and American society are thoroughly and hopelessly racist, sexist, oppressive" (34). Taylor cites several sensationalized examples, such as the incident at Harvard University when Professor Stephan Thernstrom was criticized for "racial insensitivity" in his course "Peopling in America." Faced with these "new fundamentalists," Thernstrom felt branded and accused, and he dropped the course. More recently, Rutgers University President, Francis Lawrence, was caught in a storm instigated by his comment that African-American students performed poorly on standardized tests because of their "genetic, hereditary background." Calls for Lawrence's resignation were averted not only because of his record as "a longtime civil rights advocate'" but by evoking political correctness: Did he "accidentally stumble into a controversial topic" asks Helaine Olen, "and is now falling victim to the vengeful winds of political correctness?" (A5).

In this climate of political conservatism, any criticism of racist or sexist views is regarded as silencing by a politically correct "thought police." Rather, as Stimpson points out, it is useful in our diverse society to develop greater sensitivity to language and to take "insulting language seriously." But such attempts are seen as trampling on freedom of expression, and on demanding "intellectual conformity enforced with harassment and intimidation." Taylor cites Camille Paglia, who likens this harassment to "fascism of the left," and Thernstrom, who characterizes it as "a new McCarthyism." In a similar victimology, Taylor translates the claims of the "gender feminists," who argue that "Western society is organized around a 'sex/gender system,' characterized by male dominance," very quickly and glibly into misanthropic attacks on males, the family, and heterosexuality. His discussion on date rape makes a mockery of the hard-won gains in defining the parameters of sexual assault. To give a legal name to social violence, whether it be "date rape," or "sexual harassment," named some thirty years ago, or what today we call antifeminist harassment, is threatening to the sexual status quo upheld by writers like Taylor.

The kinds of policing perpetrated blatantly by bodies such as NAS, however, are considered acceptable, the kinds that appear in NAS's journal, *Academic Questions,* which, as Jacob Weisberg notes, harps on "a few themes": "Academic feminism, in its various manifestations, is attacked in almost every issue. An article by Boston University sociologist Brigitte Berger equates the work of feminist Evelyn Fox Keller with Nazi physics. Peace studies, Critical Legal Studies" also come under attack (Weisberg, 83). Rather than desperately enforcing "a common culture" *(à la* Allan Bloom and E.D. Hirsch), Henry Giroux's suggestion from the opposite pole is worth considering—we need "a common ground for dialogue" within a truly democratic educational space. No master narratives with an *a priori* authority. Democracy, according to Giroux, "is expressed not in moral platitudes but in concrete struggles and practices that find expression in classroom social relations, everyday life, and memories of resistance and struggle" (8, 13). In its frenzied protection of a narrowly defined academic freedom and the sanctity of Western civilization, NAS has no compunction about attacking feminists. NAS's closed-mindedness would not even stop to consider that opening up the canon to the voices of women and minorities does not necessarily displace and silence canonic figures. As Stimpson explains, "To expand the canon is to enhance culture, not destroy it" (quoted in Weisberg, 86). Further, NAS's much-touted value of "objectivity" vanished when Lynne Cheney, head of the National Endowment for the Humanities, persuaded the Senate "to approve eight of her nominees, at least half of them members of the conservative National Association of Scholars" (Thompson & Tyagi, xv).

The extent to which neoconservative demagogues direct affairs, as university trustees or lawmakers, was demonstrated in a recent fracas when Angela Davis received a prestigious professorial award of $75,000 from the University of California, Santa Cruz to develop new ethnic studies courses at that institution over two and a half years. Republican lawmakers, uncomfortable with Davis's past (when she was wanted by the FBI, then tried and found *not* guilty of "murder and kidnapping [when] guns belonging to Davis were used in a shootout in Marin County" [Wallace, A27]), asked University of California President Jack W. Peltason to revoke the award. Senator Bill

Leonard commented, "At a time when we're trying to reconcile racial and gender differences, here's a person who's made a career of exacerbating those differences." He goes on to make a horrific analogy: honoring Davis is like celebrating a professor "who happened to have a side life as a grand dragon of the Ku Klux Klan. I see her as the leftist equivalent of that." Racist and sexist slurs, harassment of an intellectual, a feminist, are all part of "a concerted assault," as Davis herself put it, "against multicultural education." More specifically, neoconservatives also intend to attack the kind of research that this grant will support—Davis will use half the stipend "to create a Research Cluster on Women of Color in Collaboration and Conflict, which will develop curricula and host conferences" (Wallace, A3).

The conservative reaction to the increasing presence of women and minorities and to ethnic programs on campuses hardly recognizes facts and statistics, and dramatically exaggerates shifts in power. As Becky Thompson and Sangeeta Tyagi note: "Most college and university faculties in the United States still include less than 5 percent people of color. Only 13 percent of the full professors are women (of any race) compared to 10 percent in 1974, and 2.2 percent of full professors are African-American men or women" (xvi). These cultural wars over multiculturalism and political correctness are, as Troy Duster puts it, "about the shifting sands of racial privilege" (32). Ideologues such as Dinesh D'Souza propagate several myths about affirmative action and multiculturalism, namely that they create more divisiveness on campus, and that they dilute standards.[14] Countering these myths, Duster provides concrete historical reasons for affirmative action:

> It exists because over the past two hundred years, blacks and Latinos have had a difficult time entering higher education, and that legacy hasn't gone away.... The gap isn't closing; the economic barriers that restrict minority access to college aren't disappearing.
>
> But Americans' cultural memory lasts about five years, so the idea that affirmative action exists to redress past grievances doesn't resonate with today's students—of all colors. The notion that black people have a past of slavery and discrimination, that this is a fact of American history, is buried so deep in the consciousness of most students that it doesn't surface. The right wing says that if you bring that fact to the fore and teach it, that's called Oppression Studies, or "political correctness," and by telling people of color they should feel good about themselves, you're making white people feel bad about themselves. (32–33)

Dinesh D'Souza is a classic example of a race insider, a person of color aligned with a conservative, mainly white belief structure: like Linda Chavez, Clarence Thomas, and V.S. Naipaul, he has been lauded by mainstream media. D'Souza himself has a formidable right-wing record—as a former domestic policy analyst of the Reagan administration, managing editor of the neoconservative *Policy Review*, a founding editor of the *Dartmouth Review*, and a research fellow at the American Enterprise Institute.

D'Souza's essay "The Visigoths in Tweed" sets out the "dangers" that students face in a feminist liberal arts education: "brainwashing that deprecates Western learning and exalts a neo-Marxist ideology promoted in the name of multiculturalism" (12). D'Souza objects to the transformations in core curricula "in the name of diversity and multiculturalism," changes that are "Imposed by a university elite, not . . . voted upon or even discussed by the society at large." His rhetoric and others from NAS have portrayed the "dangers" of multicultural education as though studies of race and gender mark the end of Western civilization.

Conceding limited ground to the need for changing core curriculum—for no other reason than in response to changing student demographics—D'Souza advocates replacing Western by non-Western classics. Hence, the root concept of challenging domination, whether Western, or non-Western, completely escapes him. Further, he objects to various support services for minorities on college campuses, and presents an ahistoricized claim about the necessity of such services for disadvantaged groups. He complains as well about "other groups such as feminists and homosexuals" who "typically get into the game [by] claiming their own varieties of victim status."

Even as D'Souza is zealous in calling for scholarly facts and substantiation, he makes inaccurate claims—for instance, that "a contrived multiculturalism . . . frequently glamorizes Third World cultures. . . . In many of them feminism is virtually nonexistent, as indicated by such practices as dowries, widow-burning, and genital mutilation" (19). The fact that these oppressive practices exist does not discount the presence of feminist consciousness, and of numerous women's activist groups that exist all over the Third World. D'Souza would do well to gather scholarly data and facts on these life-and-death matters for women, though such feminist knowledge falls beyond the purview of his educational ideals. He also critiques certain prominent feminist scholars, quoting them simplistically and out of context: Alison Jaggar "denounces the traditional nuclear family as a 'cornerstone of women's oppression'", and Eve Sedgwick's work seeks to demonstrate "the homosexual bias in Western culture... through papers such as 'Jane Austen and the Masturbating Girl'" (21).

In this conservative climate, which threatens to roll back the hard-won gains of feminist and ethnic studies in the academy and in U.S. culture, it is still important for progressive people to be aware of the pitfalls and problems in the practical implementations of inclusive feminisms and multiculturalisms that respect difference even as they forge coalitions in working towards social change. In other words, given a powerful right-wing onslaught, progressive voices should not be silenced in engaging with troubling issues within well-meaning attempts at diversity in college curricula. So, even as we endorse tolerance, respect for, and knowledge of diverse cultures—some of the goals of a multicultural curriculum—we also recognize that multiculturalism has become a buzzword, and is used by different groups for their own ends. When multiculturalism is fashioned outside a progressive political context, it can be co-opted and appropriated under various "diversity" agendas. Exclusionary practices are common—for instance, white-woman bias in women's studies, or male bias in ethnic studies. As Thompson and Tyagi rightly argue, it is important to include "sophisticated analyses of the simultaneity of oppressions. These analyses absolutely depend upon accounting for multiple identities and sources of power" (xxv).

1994 has seen the ushering in of New Right politicians at the helm of the current Congress, who issue daily declarations of self-serving notions of "individual responsibility" that threaten to cut off assistance to the most vulnerable members of society—the poor, women, children. The Speaker of the House's (Ging)rich followers have no compunction about balancing the budget on the back of the Social Security Trust Fund; Congress can declare war quite blithely on affirmative action, under the subtle and dangerous rubric of "reevaluating a flawed system: Preferential treatment for minorities and women has outlived its time, they assert, citing success stories among women and minorities, "truly American creations" such as Clarence Thomas or Oprah Winfrey.

Even in these lean and mean times, women in this U.S. culture continue to make politicians, community leaders, and academics accountable; they insist on working towards socially responsible agendas where citizenship rights go along with duties and responsibilities, not only for the few and privileged but for the vast majority of working people. Feminists must still face the fact that some of the most basic tenets of feminist consciousness—that women define themselves, that they assert their rights as human beings—remain contested notions. Further, we must challenge the multiplicity of antifeminisms that face us in academia and in our daily lives.

Our historical overview of feminism and antifeminism has taken us from the 1960s civil rights struggle to the 1980s and 1990s culture wars. Today, on the brink of the next century, we recognize that antifeminist harassment is multidimensional, and takes overt or subtle forms. As we combat this current phenomenon, we recognize that feminists have to take on new battles, as attacks on feminism trade roles with hostility to ethnic studies, affirmative action, and multicultural education. The essays in this volume explore many of these issues: antifeminism becomes linked with due process and freedom of speech; with matters of academic advancement; with publishing and review; and with discriminations on the basis of age, race, and sexuality. We must make a concerted effort to name antifeminist harassment as such. This will combat the obfuscation of various discriminations under the problematic evocations of political correctness. Our tasks of naming, discussion, and analysis will bring us to possibilities of working towards a more just and humane society.

Notes

Special thanks to Shannon Olson, Rebecca Pierre, and Gretchen Scherer for their research and technical assistance, and to Jenny Putzi for historical research.

1. See Beal, 138–142. See also "A Black Feminist Statement," 13–22.
2. From a personal conversation between Moira Ferguson and Madonnah Thunder Hawk.
3. Katz, 139.
4. Linden-Ward, 8. By 1967, all fifty states had a similar status-of-women commission, which conducted research, held annual conventions, and sometimes published a newsletter.
5. Witness Proposition 187, a ballot initiative against immigrants that passed by a 59-to-41 margin in California. To the credit of the ACLU and the Mexican-American Legal Defense Fund, an injunction was filed late last year against Proposition 187. "Make no mistake," states the *Daily Bruin's* Thomas Overton. "Proposition 187 is unconstitutional. It represents a fundamental change in the nature of constitutional rights and benefits in that they are to be applied only to U.S. citizens. If you read through the Constitution, you will find no such disclaimer.... To call our respect for minority rights undemocratic is ridiculous." February 16, 1995: 19.
6. Sara M. Evans points out that by 1980, the National Right to Life Committee "had claimed 11 million members.... For right-to-life activists, abortion offended basic values about the meaning of womanhood, of sexuality, and of human life. They quickly became a significant political force because of their single-issue intensity." *Born for Liberty*, 305.
7. Faludi also cites other antifeminist voices that have joined the backlash. The text that could be "the most damaging to the feminist cause," notes Faludi, is Betty Friedan's *The Second Stage*. "The mother of the modern women's movement," who, in her 1963 classic, *The Feminine Mystique*, first expressed "the problem that has no name," Friedan now recants many of those radical feminist positions as "limited and wrong and distorted" (322–323).
8. Witness the recent onslaught on President Clinton's nominee for Surgeon General, Dr. Foster, whose nomination was in jeopardy because he had performed abortions. Although perfectly legal, abortions are portrayed as morally objectionable by right-wing propagandists and conservative politicians.
9. Banner's text also includes some wonderful photographs. See also Susan B. Anthony's *Out of the Kitchen, into the War* (New York: S. Daye, Inc., 1943); and Faludi, chap. III.
10. For instance, John Silber, President of Boston University charged that his English department had turned into a 'damn matriarchy'—when only six of its twenty faculty members were women" (Faludi, 64).
11. Marable quotes some staggering figures (reported in *The Chronicle of Higher Education*) of grants given by the Olin Foundation to conservative ideologues such as Dinesh D'Souza, who received $98,400; University of Chicago Professor Allan Bloom, $800,000; civil rights critic Linda Chavez, $25,000; and former Education Secretary William Bennett, $175,000. See also Diamond, 89–96.
12. Billingsley, "Women's Studies Imperialists," in *Heterodoxy* 1, 11–12. Other issues of *Heterodoxy* reflect this concerted campaign against feminist and multicultural studies, with racy titles like "Multicultural Mafia" (October 1992); "PC Riot" (June 1992); and "Transsexuals vs. Lesbians: The Last Battle in the Erogenous Zone" (October 1993).
13. "Statement of Principles," Teachers for a Democratic Culture. In *Beyond PC*, ed. Aufderheide, 67–70.
14. Particularly since the Republican takeover of Congress in November 1994, local newspapers and college campus dailies have been presenting debates on the necessity, or abolition, or reevaluation of affirmative action policies. Some recent examples worth reading include Cathleen Decker, "Affirmative Action Is Under Fire," *Los Angeles Times* (February 19, 1995): 1; J. Eugene Grigsby III, "California's Troubled Economy No Fault of Affirmative Action," *Los Angeles Times* (February 26, 1995): D2; and Clifford M. Tong, "Affirmative Action has Not Outlived Need," *Los Angeles Times* (February 27, 1995): B5.

Works Cited and Consulted

Aisenberg, Nadya and Mona Harrington. *Women of Academe: Outsiders in the Sacred Grove*. Amherst: University of Massachusetts Press, 1988.

Anzaldúa, Gloria, ed. *Making Face/Making Soul/Haciendo Caras: Creative and Critical Perspectives by Women of Color*. San Francisco: Aunt Lute Books, 1990.

Aptheker, Bettina. *Women's Legacy: Essays on Race, Sex, and Class in American History*. Amherst: University of Massachusetts Press, 1982.

Aufderheide, Patricia, ed. *Beyond PC: Toward a Politics of Understanding*. Saint Paul, MN: Graywolf Press, 1992.

Bambara, Toni Cade, ed. *The Black Women: An Anthology*. New York: New American Library, 1970.

Banner, Lois W. *Women in Modern America: A Brief History*. New York: Harcourt Brace, 1974.

Bannerji, Himani, et al. *Unsettling Relations: The University as a Site of Feminist Struggles*. Toronto: Women's Press, 1991.

Bataille, Gretchen and Kathleen M. Sands. *American Indian Women: Telling Their Lives*. Lincoln: University of Nebraska Press, 1984.

___. *American Indian Women: A Guide to Research.* New York: Garland Publishing, Inc., 1991.

Beal, Frances. "Double Jeopardy: To Be Black and Female." *Women and Womanhood in America,* ed. Ronald W. Hoagland. Lexington, MA: D.C. Heath, 1973.

Beers, David. "PC? B.S. Behind the Hysteria: How the Right Invented Victims of PC Police." *Mother Jones* 16:5 (September/October, 1991): 34–35, 64–65.

Bell, Roseann, Bettye J. Parker, and Beverly Guy-Shaftall, eds. *Sturdy Black Bridges: Visions of Black Women in Literature.* Garden City, NY: Anchor, 1979.

Billingsley, K.L. "Women's Studies Imperialists." *Heterodoxy: Articles and Animad versions on Political Correctness and Other Follies* 1:6 (November 1992).

Black Women's Liberation Group, Mount Vernon, New York. "Statement on Birth Control." *Sisterhood is Powerful,* ed. Robin Morgan. New York: Vintage, 1970.

Blea, Irene I. *La Chicana and the Intersection of Race, Class, and Gender.* New York: Praeger, 1992.

Bloom, Allan. *The Closing of the American Mind: How Higher Education Has Failed Democracy and Impoverished the Souls of Today's Students.* New York: Simon & Schuster, 1987.

Cantarow, Ellen. "Jessie Lopez de la Cruz," *Moving the Mountain: Women Working for Social Change,* ed. Ellen Cantarow. Old Westbury: The Feminist Press, 1980. 94–151.

Cochran, Jo Whitehorse et al., eds. *Changing Our Power: An Introduction to Women's Studies.* Dubuque: Kendall Hunt, 1988.

Cohen, Marcia. *The Sisterhood.* New York: Simon & Schuster, 1988.

Collins, Patricia Hill. *Black Feminist Thought: Knowledge, Consciousness, and the Politics of Empowerment.* Boston: Unwin Hyman, 1990. Reprint Routledge, 1991.

The Combahee River Collective. "A Black Feminist Statement." *All the Women Are White, All the Blacks Are Men, But Some of Us Are Brave: Black Women's Studies,* eds. Gloria T. Hull, Patricia Bell Scott, and Barbara Smith. Old Westbury, NY. The Feminist Press, 1982. 13–22.

Cotera, Martha P. *The Chicana Feminist.* Austin: Information Systems Development, 1977.

___. *Profile on the Mexican American Woman.* Austin: Statehome Publishing, 1976.

Crow Dog, Mary, with Richard Erdoes. *Lakota Women.* New York: Harper, 1990.

Cruikshank, Margaret. *Lesbian Studies, Present and Future.* New York: The Feminist Press, 1982.

D'Souza, Dinesh. *Illiberal Education: The Politics of Race and Sex on Campus.* New York: Vintage, 1991.

___. "The New Segregation on Campus," *The American Scholar* 60:1 (Winter, 1991): 17–30.

___. "The Visigoths in Tweed." *Beyond PC,* ed. Patricia Aufderheide.

Damon, Gene. "The Least of These: The Minority Where Screams Haven't Yet Been Heard." *Sisterhood is Powerful,* ed. Robin Morgan. New York. Vintage, 1970.

Davis, Angela. "Reflections on the Black Woman's Role in the Community of Slaves," *Black Scholar* 3 (December, 1971): 2–15.

___. *Angela Davis: An Autobiography.* New York: Random House, 1974.

___. *Culture and Politics.* New York: Random House, 1989.

___. *Race and Class.* New York.: Vintage, 1983.

Davis. Flora. *Moving the Mountain: The Women's Movement in America Since 1960.* New, York: Simon & Schuster, 1991.

Deckard, Barbara Sinclair. *The Women's Movement: Political, Socioeconomic, and Psychological Issues.* New York: Harper, 1979.

Diamond, Sara. "The Funding of the NAS." *Beyond PC,* ed. Patricia Aufderheide.

DuBois, Ellen Carol et al., eds. *Feminist Scholarship: Kindling in the Groves of Academe.* Urbana and Chicago: University of Illinois Press, 1987.

Duster, Troy. "They're Taking Over and Other Myths about Race on Campus." *Mother Jones* 16:5 (September/October 1991): 30–33, 63–64.

Echols, Alice. *Daring to be BAD: Radical Feminism in America 1967–1975.* Minneapolis: University of Minnesota Press, 1989.

Evans, Sara M. *Born for Liberty: A History of Women in America.* New York: The Free Press, 1989.

___. *Personal Politics: The Roots of Women's Liberation in the Civil Rights Movement and the New Left.* New York. Knopf, 1979.

___ and Harry C. Boyte. *Free Spaces: The Sources of Democratic Change in America.* New York: Harper and Row, 1986.

___. "Women in Twentieth Century America: An Overview." *The American Woman, 1987–88: A Report in Depth,* ed. Sara Rix (for The Women's Research and Education Institute of the Congressional Caucus for Women's Issues). New York & London: Norton, 1987.

Faludi, Susan. *Backlash: The Undeclared War on American Women.* New York: Crown Publishers, Inc., 1991.

___. "Blame It on Feminism." *Mother Jones* 16:5 (September/October, 1991): 24–29.

Figes, Eva. *Patriarchal Attitudes.* New York: Stein and Day, 1970.

Firestone, Shulamith. *The Dialectic of Sex: The Case for Feminist Revolution.* New York: William Morrow and Company, 1970.

Fitzgerald, Maureen, Connie Guberman, and Margie Wolfe, eds. *Still Ain't Satisfied! Canadian Feminism Today.* Toronto: The Women's Press, 1982.

Freeman, Jo, ed. *Woman: A Feminist Perspective*, 3rd ed. Palo Alto: Mayfield, 1984.

Friedan, Betty. *The Feminine Mystique*. New York: Dell, 1963.

Fritz, Leah. *Dreams and Dealers: An Intimate Appraisal of the Women's Movement*. Boston: Beacon Press, 1979.

Giddings, Paula. *When and Where I Enter: The Impact of Black Women on Race and Sex in America*. New York: William Morrow and Company, Inc., 1984.

Giroux, Henry A. *Living Dangerously: Multiculturalism and the Politics of Difference*. New York: Peter Lang, 1993.

Glickman, Rose. *Daughters of Feminists*. New York: St. Martin's, 1993.

Green, Rayna. *Native American Women: A Contexual Bibliography*. Bloomington: Indiana University Press, 1983.

Greer, Germaine. *The Female Eunuch*. New York: McGraw-Hill, 1971.

Harley, Sharon and Rosalyn Terborg-Penn, eds. *The Afro-American Women: Struggles and Images*. Port Washington, NY. and London: Kennikat Press, 1978.

Hartmann, Susan M. *From Margin to Mainstream: American Women and Politics Since 1960*. New York: Knopf, 1989.

Hirsch, E.D., Jr. *Cultural Literacy: What Every American Needs to Know*. Boston: Houghton Mifflin, 1987.

hooks, bell. *Ain't I a Woman: Black Women and Feminism*. Boston: South End Press, 1981.

Huff, Gloria T., Patricia Bell, and Barbara Smith. *All the Women Are White, All the Blacks Are Men, but Some of Us Are Brave: Black Women's Studies*. Old Westbury: The Feminist Press, 1982.

Jay, Karla and Allen Young, eds. *Lavender Culture*. New York: Jove, 1978.

____ and Joanne Glasgow, eds. *Lesbian Texts and Contexts: Radical Revisions*. New York: New York University Press, 1990.

Jones, Jacqueline. *Labor of Love, Labor of Sorrow: Black Women, Work and the Family, From Slavery to the Present*. New York: Vintage, 1985.

Joseph, Gloria I. and Jill Lewis. *Common Differences: Conflicts in Black and White Feminist Perspectives*. New York: Anchor, 1981.

Katz, Jane, ed. *I Am the Fire of Time: Voices of Native American Women*. New York: E. P. Dutton, 1977.

Kennedy, Flo. *Color Me Flo: My Hard Life and Good Times*. Englewood Cliffs, NJ: Prentice-Hall, 1976.

Lehrman, Karen. "Off Course: Is Women's Studies Failing Women?" *Mother Jones*. (September/October, 1993): 45–51, 64–68.

Lerner, Gerda. *Black Women in White America: A Documentary History*. New York: Vintage, 1972.

Linden-Ward, Blanche and Carol Hurd Green. *American Women in the 1960s: Changing the Future*. New York: T. Wayne, 1993.

Loeb, Catherine. "La Chicana: A Bibliographic Survey," *Frontiers* 5, 2 (Summer 1980): 59–74.

Longauex y Vasquez, Enriqueta. "The Mexican-American Woman." *Sisterhood is Powerful*, ed. Robin Morgan.

Lott, Juanita Tamayo, & Canta Pian. "Beyond Stereotypes and Statistics: Emergence of Asian and Pacific American Women." Washington D.C.: Organization of Pan Asian American Women and Women's Bureau/Dept. of Labor, 1979.

Marable, Manning. "Along the Color Line: Why Conservatives Fear Multiculturalism." *The Collegian* (University of Massachusetts, Amherst): November 10, 1993: 11.

Milkman, Ruth. *Women, Work and Protest: A Century of U.S. Women's Labor History*. London: Routledge & Kegan Paul, 1985.

Miner, Valerie. "Fantasies and Nightmares: The Red-Blooded Media," *Jump Cut: A Review of Contemporary Cinema* 26, Oakland, CA, December, 1981. 48–50.

____. *Rumors from the Cauldron: Selected Essays, Reviews and Reportage*. Ann Arbor: University of Michigan Press, 1992.

Mirandè, Alfredo and Evangelian Enriquez. *La Chicana: The Mexican-American Woman*. Chicago: University of Chicago Press, 1979.

____. *Mexican Women in the United States: Struggles Past and Present*. Los Angeles: University of California, Chicano Studies Research Center Publications, 1980.

Moraga, Cherríe and Gloria Anzaldúa, eds. *This Bridge Called My Back: Writings by Radical Women of Color*. Watertown, MA: Persophone Press, 1981. Reprint New York. Kitchen Table Press, 1983.

Morgan, Robin, ed. *Sisterhood Is Powerful, An Anthology of Writings From The Women's Liberation Movement*. New York: Vintage, 1970.

____, ed. Introduction. *Sisterhood Is Global: The International Women's Movement Anthology*. New York. Anchor, 1984.

Morrison, Toni, ed. *Race-ing, Justice, En-gendering Power. Essays on Anita Hill, Clarence Thomas, and the Construction of Social Reality*. New York: Pantheon, 1992.

Nieto, Sonia. *Affirming Diversity: The Sociopolitical Context of Multicultural Education*. New York. Longman, 1992.

Noble, Jeanne. *Beautiful Also Are the Souls of My Sisters: A History of Black Women in America*. Englewood Cliffs, NJ: Prentice-Hall, Inc., 1978.

Olen, Helaine. "Rutgers Remains Embroiled Over Power of a Few Words." *Los Angeles Times*, February 20, 1995: A5.

Paglia, Camille. *Sexual Personae: Art and Decadence from Nefertiti to Emily Dickinson*. New Haven and London: Yale University Press, 1990.

Rao, Aruna. *Gender Analysis in Development Planning. A Casebook*. West Hartford, CT: Kumarian Press, 1991.

_____, ed. *Women's Studies International: Nairobi and Beyond*. New York: The Feminist Press, 1991.

Rich, Adrienne. *Blood, Bread, and Poetry: Selected Prose 1979–1985*. New York: Norton, 1986.

Robinson, Lillian S. *Sex, Class and Culture*. Bloomington: Indiana University Press, 1978.

Rodney, Walter. *How Europe Underdeveloped Africa*. Washington, DC: Howard University Press, 1974.

Rodriguez, Richard. *Hunger of Memory: The Education of Richard Rodriguez*. New York: Godine, 1982.

Rukeyser, Muriel. *The Speed of Darkness*. New York. Vintage, 1971.

Schlesinger, Arthur. *The Disuniting of America*. New York: Norton, 1992.

Schultz, Debra L. "To Reclaim a Legacy of Diversity: Analyzing the 'Political Correctness' Debates in Higher Education." A report prepared by The National Council for Research on Women. 1993.

Shelley, Martha. "Notes of a Radical Lesbian." *Sisterhood is Powerful*, ed. Robin Morgan.

Sill, Geoffrey S., et al., eds. *Opening the American Mind: Race, Ethnicity, and Gender in Higher Education*. Newark: University of Delaware Press, 1993.

Simonson, Rick and Scott Walker, eds. *Multi-Cultural Literacy*. Saint Paul, MN: Graywolf Press, 1988.

Smith, Barbara, ed. *Home Girls: A Black Feminist Anthology*. New York: Kitchen Table Press, 1983.

Spender, Dale. *The Writing or the Sex? Or Why You Don't Have to Read Women's Writing to Know It's No Good*. New York: Pergamon Press, 1989.

Steinem, Gloria. *Moving Beyond Words*. New York: Simon & Schuster, 1994.

Swerdlow, Amy & Hanna Lessinger, eds. *Class, Race, and Sex: The Dynamics of Control*. Boston: G. K. Hall, 1983.

Takaki, Ronald. *A Different Mirror: A History of Multicultural America*. Boston: Little, Brown and Company, 1993.

Taylor, John. "Are You Politically Correct?" *New York Magazine*, January 21, 1991: 32–40.

Thompson, Becky and Sangeeta Tyagi, eds. *Beyond a Dream Deferred: Multicultural Education and the Politics of Excellence*. Minnesota and London: University of Minnesota Press, 1993.

Wallace, Amy. "Angela Davis Again at Center of UC Storm." *Los Angeles Times*, February 20, 1995: A3, 27.

Weisberg, Jacob, "NAS—Who Are These Guys, Anyway?" *Beyond PC*, ed. Patricia Aufderheide.

Williams, Patricia. *The Alchemy of Race and Rights*. Cambridge, MA: Harvard University Press, 1991.

Women's Studies Quarterly. Special Feature: Teaching the New Women's History. 15:1 and 2 (Spring/Summer, 1988).

Zinn, Howard. *S.N.C.C: The New Abolitionists*. Boston: Beacon Press, 1964.

CHAPTER 6

FEMINISM, POSTMODERNISM AND THEORETICAL DEVELOPMENTS

IMELDA WHELEHAN

Our language, intellectual history, and social forms are 'gendered'; there is no escape from this fact and from its consequences on our lives. Some of those consequences may be unintended, may even be fiercely resisted; our deepest desire may be to 'transcend gender dualities'; to not have our behaviour categorized as 'male' or 'female'. But, like it or not, in our present culture, our activities are coded as 'male' or 'female' and will function as such within the prevailing system of gender-power relations. The adoption of the 'professional' standards of academia is no more an activity devoid of gender politics than the current fashion in women's tailored suits and largely shouldered jackets is devoid of gender meaning. One cannot be 'gender neutral' in this culture.
(Bordo in Nicholson 1990:152)

I have already indicated that around the mid-'80s in academic circles a 'crisis' in feminism seemed to have been consensually acknowledged: the subject of feminism's differences of opinion was beginning to seem the most crucial in an era of critical retrospectives and summaries. Dominant 'strands' in feminist thought were marking their territory and consolidating their own methodological boundaries, and the impact of French psychoanalytic theory was changing the terms of feminist theoretical debate in the Anglo-American sphere. Radical feminism was increasingly vilified in British socialist feminist circles, and in the United States of America feminist radicalism had become associated with a narrower 'cultural feminist' position, which signalled a return to the celebration of the 'feminine', albeit from a woman-centred perspective. Socialist feminists were themselves more regularly defining their own political stance in terms of a departure from Marxist orthodoxy. Black and lesbian feminists were identifying themselves as organized groupings on the basis of race or sexual orientation, using much of their energies to signal the most grievous sins of white, bourgeois heterosexual feminists. Perhaps their combined critiques—more than any others—exposed the partial and exclusionary nature of the category of 'gender' as it had been used in other elements of feminist thought. Each grouping or 'strand', having been called upon to define its terms and its place within the matrix of feminism as a whole, seemed to settle into degrees of theoretical autonomy that eschewed any comprehensive attachment to male-oriented thought. However, by the latter half of the '80s, the question of male alliances—whether it be the entry of men into feminist thought as contributors and teachers, or the forging of liaisons with an increasingly sophisticated post-structuralist and postmodernist lobby—returned as perhaps the single most pressing debate of recent years.

Reprinted from *Modern Feminist Thought: From the Second Wave to 'Post-Feminism'*, by Imelda Whelehan, 1994. Copyright © 1994 Edinburgh University Press.

Feminism and Identity

Many theorists were at pains to demonstrate feminism's compatibility with postmodernist theory in signalling the end of modernity and its humanist account of individuality; they also offered a very significant critique of feminism—namely, its tenacious reliance upon gender difference as the single most important analytical category. This, it was suggested, demonstrated a reliance on totalizing and unifying categories—a revivification of the binarism that typified Western thought within modernity, and a consequently naive, or even regressive investment in notions of progress and continuity. While the radical potential of feminist contributions to postmodern thought were acknowledged because of their recognized contribution to reconceiving Western binarism, feminism was simultaneously regarded as one of 'the flawed grand narratives of modernity' (Featherstone, *Theory, Culture & Society*, Vol. 5, Nos 2–3, June 1988). Grand narratives were perceived from a postmodern perspective as potentially tyrannical and unhelpfully universalizing, and feminism's own meta-narrative of gender was regarded as having trapped feminists in ethno/heterocentric truth claims, which no longer had any currency in a postmodern world view. Nonetheless, it is significant that poststructuralism and postmodernism continue to be determined as something other than feminism, so that feminism remains contemporary theory's significant Other—a predictable and recurring relationship for feminism to academic thought. From the outset, it must therefore be emphasized that those figures acknowledged as having made a significant contribution to the development of postmodern perspectives in theory, art and literature are male. Feminists are perhaps justified in their suspicion that a dispersal of the meanings of gender in such a context fairly swiftly amounts to gender-blindness. In this light, a real danger lies in the possibility that in place of feminism's analysis of gender, originary meanings of gender difference are reinforced.

Within feminist ranks two points of conflict are currently receiving a significant degree of attention: (a) the escalation of 'identity politics' within the movement which threatens to turn feminist theory into a highly individualized, introverted and necessarily fragmented political stance; (b) a recognition that 'many feminist ideas become part of the common sense of our culture; yet those ideas may be expressed in forms we barely recognize as feminist' (Editorial, *Feminist Review*, No. 31, Spring 1989: 3). The two points intersect, of course; whether we recognize a particular stance as 'feminist' depends upon our sense of identity within a particular faction. Nonetheless, most feminists recognize and are antipathetic to a specific distortion of feminist ideas which is sustained within mainstream New Right ideology, identified as simultaneously pro-female and pro-family, and which offers itself primarily as a stance that recognizes and endorses women's current familial location as a position of strength:

> First, it promotes a 'pro-family' stance that views sexual politics, and particularly the politicization of personal relationships, as threatening to 'the family'. Second, it affirms gender differentiation and celebrates traditionally feminine qualities, particularly those associated with mothering. Finally, the new conservatives believe that struggle against male domination detracts from political agendas they consider more important. (Stacey in Mitchell and Oakley 1986: 222)

This view of feminism as detracting from the more important business of 'real' political enquiry is a familiar one for feminists: think of the reasons why many disaffected Left Wing women established feminist cadres in the late '60s and early '70s. Proponents of such a stance often allude to the dawnings of a 'post-feminist' age in which the worst excesses of second wave feminism can be discarded in favour of a political healing process in which the family can be once again made whole—freed from the indecent assaults of a sexual politics which has been held to deny the sanctity of personal privacy.

Perhaps the escalation of 'identity politics' was a contributing factor in feminists' general inability to produce a concerted response to such attacks, or at least to deny them any place in feminist thought. To deny them any currency would after all be to enact a tyrannous response to other 'pro-woman' forms of thought—to exacerbate both the problem of vying feminist identities and the question of who is 'allowed' to construct 'authentic' feminist responses to such challenges. Feminism's political roots are, after all, multifarious, and any such resistance might be seen to mark a precedent, where a feminist 'mainstream' could be construed as holding an unpalatable amount of authority over the utterances of more 'minority' groups. Identity politics, of course, need not be interpreted as a challenge against tyranny and exclusionism; they might be viewed as a positive sign that feminism remains a fluid site of healthy debate into the '90s. Nonetheless identity politics, taken to its logical extreme, facilitates a cacophony of warring feminist voices which can only announce their authority as speakers 'for' feminism by referring to the complex nature of their own subject positioning, of which being female is the lowest of common denominators. The result of such a tendency can be 'not to elucidate debate but to fix a woman somewhere along a predetermined hierarchy of oppressions in order to justify or contest a political opinion by reference to a speaker's identity' (Harriss, *Feminist Review*, No. 31, Spring 1989: 37).

There are clearly risks in deriving authority as a feminist speaker from one's own constellation of personal identities (as white, lesbian, working class, etc.), and a chief danger is to emphasize the boundaries between major strands of feminism as if they were fixed and immutable, rather than part of a debate which has as its shared goal the maintenance of a viable feminist contribution at both a localized and wider political context. Critiques offered by black and lesbian feminists have, for example, been salutory in changing and expanding the terms of reference of what was by default a white, heterosexual feminism; and the general thrust of this thesis has been to show how the acceptance of heterogeneity within the term 'feminism' can be beneficial to all women. It is possibly the case that identity politics has been construed as fragmentary by white feminists because it is their definitions of oppression that have been under attack.

Whether or not this is the case, identity politics were prefigured by the notion that 'the personal is political'. The primary effects of consciousness raising were arguably to suggest that achieving a feminist consciousness is largely a matter of finding a position which suits one's own public and personal context.

This may well give rise 'to a self-righteous assertion that if one inhabits a certain identity this gives one the legitimate and moral right to guilt trip others into particular ways of behaving' (Parmar, *Feminist Review*, No. 31, Spring 1989: 58). Of course consciousness raising was intended to be a preamble to collective action; but in the absence of a transformation of the social meanings of gender difference, the task of consciousness raising has to be repeated with every new generation, and in an era of proliferating academic discourses on feminism, consciousness raising of sorts can be a useful part of pedagogical practice. This can itself be rejuvenating for feminism, and might be practiced in order to forestall the truth claims of anti-feminists who would otherwise consign feminism unchallenged to the annals of recent history.

Feminism/Postmodernism: Theoretical Reflections

It is not only the phenomenon of the 'male feminist' that has caused feminists to rethink the dominant framework of their theories; since the mid-'80s feminist postmodern theorists such as Linda Nicholson have identified the continued existence of universalizing tendencies within feminist thought, observing that, 'it was the failure, common to many forms of academic scholarship, to recognize the embeddedness of its own assumptions within a specific historical context' (Nicholson 1990: 20). A particular trait in Western scholarship is the quest for objectivity, the notion that a critique can transcend the perspective of one individual or group, to carry truth claims that could be recognized as such by other individuals or groups. Although feminist groups among others have questioned the notion of neutrality and the means by which certain knowledges can be legitimated as truth, there do remain traces of dominant Western forms of thought within feminist methodology. Clearly the concept of patriarchy would be one example of a tendency towards ahistorical universalism, particularly when summoned by feminists in examining the 'cause' of women's oppression. Nonetheless I have previously outlined why an 'ahistorical' model of patriarchal power can be politically expedient in the face of totalizing exclusionary practices of existing historical ways of knowing. Postmodernist theorists locate the mode of objectivity as a symptom of modernity, a range of epistemic conditions which they would argue are waning. Postmodern relations of power therefore render claims of truth or falsehood illegitimate, and displace the unified category of 'woman' as subject—something perhaps that feminists are reluctant to part with on a political level. In addition postmodern positioning does not always help the feminist theorist negotiate a pathway through current materially and economically powerful political 'truth claims'.

The category of gender itself, and the way gender distinctions are culturally manifested, informs a feminist perspective on social realities which many would seem loath to relinquish. Fraser and Nicholson, however, suggest that interfaces between feminism and postmodernism would be mutually beneficial since, 'a postmodernist reflection on feminist theory reveals disabling vestiges of essentialism while a feminist reflection on postmodernism reveals androcentrism and political naivete' (Fraser and Nicholson in Nicholson 1990: 20). Here the relations between feminism and postmodernism are still seen to be tense; particularly, as the above quotation implies, because postmodernism emerges from a very male-identified reaction to modernity. Postmodernist critiques might be used by feminists to cleanse their own reflections of the worst kind of essentialism, but feminism's stake in modernity—or any perspective on male systems of power—can only be partial. Postmodernism has as one of its primary goals the aim of freeing itself from overarching philosophical givens, to ground social criticism within specific contexts and locales. Gone is the dependency upon notions of historical progression, the transcendence of reason and freedom—the meta-discourse (such as Marxism) is reduced to the status of just another discourse with no prior claim to particular privilege. Feminism, in the Lyotardian terms utilized by Fraser and Nicholson, would be just such another totalizing discourse, dependent as it is on the generalising categories of gender (or even race and class), which are regarded as too unitary and too homogenizing to be accommodated or utilized within a postmodern notion of subjectivity. However, there are grounds to suppose that even the displacement of the meta-narrative demands a social criticism that can embrace the local and contextual—and this would clearly be the case for a credible feminist response.

During the past decade many feminists have found previous accounts of female subjectivity to be too reductive—since at the very least they provide grounds for the exclusion of race, class and sexual orientation. But even the inclusion of such categories can be seen to totalize group identity in ways that preclude more cogent and 'localized' analyses of the constellation and mediation of power relationships. In any case, it could be argued that woman remains a totalizing theoretical category, within which other categories of 'otherness' are effaced. Politically, feminists have a strong investment in retaining the masculine/feminine binary in their discourse in order to uncover the multifarious means by which this binary still remains powerful; whereas utopian tendencies in postmodernist thought might envisage an end to the significance of such a binary. However, it might be advisable to consider Jameson's definition of postmodernism as 'not just another word for the description of a particular style', but:

> also, at least in my use, a periodizing concept whose function is to correlate the emergence of new formal features in culture with the emergence of a new type of social life and a new economic order—what is often euphemistically called modernization, postindustrial or consumer society, the society of the media or the spectacle, or multinational capitalism. (Kaplan 1988: 15)

Such a definition might prove useful to feminism since it offers the moment of postmodernism a historical location, whereby the material and ideological conditions that pertain within such a period can be investigated in relation to women in particular. Moreover, some feminists may be tempted to argue that a patriarchal ideology retains a rigid stronghold within a post-industrial capitalist society, just as it has been argued that the institutionalization of sexual difference can be perceived to predate capitalism,

Most feminists would accept, however, that the meanings and positioning of gender relations do change when there is a changing cluster of power networks, and the identification of a postmodern moment allows feminists to consider the condition of women as a distinct feature of postmodern social reality. If one of the significant aspects of the postmodern condition is the final dissolution of the myth of autonomous subjectivity, this may have a bearing on dominant feminist articulations of subjectivity, which often do depend upon notions of liberation which suggest a quest for a pre-existing putative autonomy available to masculine subjects. Jameson does not wish to suggest that the postmodern moment indicates a radical break with the period of modernity; rather it involves 'the restructuring of a certain number of elements already given: features that in an earlier period or system were subordinate now become dominant, and features that had been dominant again become secondary' (Kaplan 1988: 15). Jameson's assertion is made within the context of cultural productions; nonetheless in both the field of cultural production, and production in a wider sphere, feminism's chief problem is to ascertain whether one feature—the representation/positioning of women as subordinate/other—remains the same. In addition, despite the embeddedness of feminist discourse in identifying a 'reality' of gender difference which finds its intelligibility in essentialism or biology, the cultural logic of sexual difference has gained momentum from its historical longevity, resulting in the 'fact' of difference being entrenched in experience—not an easy category to theorize, or indeed to generalize about. Cynthia Cockburn looks back on the emergence of second wave politics and reflects upon the nebulous sense of difference which pervades feminism still:

> There was a material reason for the growth of difference-politics. It was a response to women's lived experience in the 1970s of struggling with men's response to feminism. We felt different. Not some essential or biological difference but an empowering difference born of our centuries-long experience as the subordinated half of the heterosexual couple. Our history had given us different values. (Chapman and Rutherford 1988: 326)

There may be much that a feminist can invest in the postmodern explosion of the binaries of classic Western thought. But might it not be the case that postmodernism itself derives impetus from a certain binarism in its demarcation of postmodernism and feminist postmodernism? Is it readily apparent that most postmodern reflections are any more gender conscious than other theoretical offerings by radical male academics have been? If dispensing with the binaries means that gender as category has no theoretical currency, then it would be difficult to interrogate postmodernism for instances of gender-blindness. Yet feminist interventions in postmodernism must do precisely that, and find that although large-scale power relationships can be rendered problematic in the delegitimation of the grand narrative, hierarchies of gendered power may exist in the spaces of postmodernist theory itself. Perhaps an analogy can be drawn here with Jonathan Rutherford's comments on the organization of political agendas: 'Men's power is not simply a sovereign, repressive force. It can be that, but it is a more complex phenomenon, and also operates through the ways in which politics and problems are defined, and in determining what are the real issues and priorities' (Chapman and Rutherford 1988: 43). Perhaps the priorities of postmodern theorists are by and large still too entrenched in announcing our epistemological and cultural break with modernity to wonder what women's place in modernity could possibly be defined as.

Modernism in art has often been described as a moment of high elitism and male exclusionary practices; the historical mode of process and objectivity yielded little insights from a feminist point of view. Women are necessarily embedded within these historical moments as material factors, but in terms of their relation to them as grand narratives, they have usually been quietly absent. Christine Di Stefano seems to be suspicious of the postmodern project itself as having an investment—if mainly in its sense of reaction and destabilizing of the models of modernist thought—in the basis of a gendered social organization which is still left intact by its neglect in mainstream postmodernism:

> The feminist case against postmodernism would seem to consist of several related claims. First, that postmodernism expresses the claims and needs of a constituency (white, privileged men of the industrialized West) that has already had an Enlightenment for itself and that is now ready and

willing to subject that legacy to critical scrutiny. Secondly, that objects of postmodernism's various critical and deconstructive efforts have been the creations of a similarly specific and partial constituency (beginning with Socrates, Plato, and Aristotle). Third, that mainstream postmodernist theory (Derrida, Lyotard, Rorty, Foucault) has been remarkably blind and insensitive to questions of gender in its own purportedly politicized rereadings of history, politics, and culture. Finally, that the postmodernist project if seriously adopted by feminists, would make any semblance of a feminist politics impossible. (Nicholson 1990: 75–6)

Stefano's concluding point—that postmodern theory renders feminist politics untenable—offers the bleakest outlook on feminism's engagement with postmodernism. The call to explode gender binaries, might well be perceived as an exhortation to 'gender neutrality', which all too easily slips us back into the bad old days of academic rigour and rationalism. Such a stance denies feminist academics the opportunity to analyse the impact of their own female identity in a social context, that in so many other ideological and material ways reminds us of our own femaleness as otherness. Susan Bordo perceives that this tendency displays further evidence of a backlash against second wave feminism—analogous to debates among some first wave American feminists, who called for an end to discussion focused on gender difference (Nicholson 1990: 152). Then as now, perspectives on the heterogeneity of female experience and aspirations led to an extension of the notion of human differences, a pull to accept differences of identity and their social impact as a fact of 'human' life.

It needs to be stated that other cultural 'outgroups' might also feel unprepared to dispense with their own totalizing and unitary categories, such as being black or gay or lesbian. Again these voices appear on the margins of postmodernism's mainstream, so that bell hooks' sense of being on 'the outside of the discourse looking in' (hooks 1991:24) might sum up how many non-white/non-male/non-heterosexuals feel; that they are a priori excluded, while at the same time being urged to dispense with their old-fashioned 'modern' ways of thinking. bell hooks points out that when race is discussed in a postmodern context, black women rarely merit a mention, and she convincingly identifies the aims of postmodern thought as themselves paradoxical:

> It is sadly ironic that the contemporary discourse which talks the most about heterogeneity, the decentred subject, declaring breakthroughs that allow recognition of Otherness, still directs its critical voice primarily to a specialized audience that shares a common language rooted in the very master narratives it claims to challenge. (hooks 1991: 25)

Nonetheless, she accepts that postmodern critiques of notions of identity and subjectivity are potentially effective tools for black people, who have after all collected politically under an identity—narrow and constrictive—foisted upon them by an imperialist ideology. For example, critiques of racism have not heretofore been concerned with the way that class mobility has fractured notions of collective identity; and it may well be in black theorists' interest to focus more upon the diverse and multiple experiences and meanings of racial difference. Yet hooks' exposure of the fact that postmodernist thought remains directed at the most privileged, appears to justify the caution with which feminists have in general received postmodern explorations into the sphere of gender, race and sexual identity.

In the face of the collapse of gender identity as a viable concept in a postmodernist worldview, a postmodernist feminist has to negotiate a pathway through the idea of a discourse which can be gender neutral. As Barrett and Phillips observe, 'feminists have become deeply suspicious of theoretical discourses that claim neutrality while speaking from a masculinist perspective, and have at times despaired of the possibility of "gender-neutral" thought' (Barrett and Phillips 1992: 1). This awareness that seeming gender neutrality has always connoted a patriarchal perspective in the past goes some way to explaining the degree of feminist skepticism around the postmodernist dispersal of explanatory categories of identity. Feminist concepts of identity and collectivity had gradually become more complex anyway; in particular because of increasing moves to theorize the triple oppressions of gender, race and class. They emphasize that 'we should certainly reject the simplistic teleology that later theory is therefore better theory, and that the best theory of all is the position from which we happen at the moment to be speaking' (Barrett and Phillips 1992: 7). There may well be concern about what happens to identity in the postmodern project since as Sylvia Walby points out, 'the fragmentation of macro-analytic concepts in the theorization of "race", gender and class is a typical part of the post-modernist project' (Barrett and Phillips 1992: 31). Walby further suggests that the postmodern project denouncing the categories of 'man' and 'woman' because there is no essentialist meaning to each category and that they therefore contain so many contradictory identities, may be a little precipitate. In common with other feminist critics who have explored postmodernist viewpoints she argues that,

> While gender relations could potentially take an infinite number of forms, in actuality there are some widely repeated features and considerable historical continuity. The signifiers of 'woman' and 'man' have sufficient and historical and cross-cultural continuity, despite some variations, to warrant such terms. (Barrett and Phillips 1992: 36)

There is no reason why feminists should not engage with developments in postmodern thought to the full; in fact one could reasonably argue that feminists and the progress of feminist discourse itself have been instrumental, if not essential, to post structuralist/postmodernist—developments. However, one has to retain an awareness that major movements in postmodern thought are seen as being located in 'male' theory; and the 'ownership' of high postmodern theory rests largely in male hands. This does not always allow sufficient space to scrutinize the relationship of discourse to materiality in this context, where discourse invests relations of power. Sylvia Walby suggests that 'rather than abandoning the modernist project of explaining the world, we should be developing the concepts and theories to explain gender, ethnicity and class' (Barrett and Phillips 1992: 48). Michele Barrett has identified how feminist and other oppositional groups can have a kneejerk negative response and 'who see what they call "discourse theory" as an ideologically suspect attempt to deny material reality' (Barrett and Phillips 1992: 209).

Playing with Difference: Essentialism, Gender and the Cyborg

The term 'essentialism' has often been used with negative connotations by many feminists; I have used it myself earlier in this work as shorthand description of a feminist stance which makes appeal to a discrete female 'nature'. Most feminists do of course see themselves as social constructionist, believing that gender is an effect of culture rather than a condition for its current configuration. Thus, essentialism and social constructionism take on the appearance of binary opposites; the former celebrating the fixity of female difference, and a revaluation of its social meanings; and the latter expressing a concrete denial of the innateness of sexual difference, arguing that difference is an effect of social and historical relations of power. Yet, as Diana Fuss has pointed out in *Essentially Speaking* (1989), the two terms are not mutually exclusive, and the use by social constructionists of the category 'gender' constitutes an appeal to a community of women as a group with a single identity, which inevitably assumes a broad shared essence. In other words, all political movements that focus on a particular identity (femaleness, gayness) as the basis for political action, effectively presuppose that particular properties define such groups, implying that there is an essence within identity which is fixed and can be unearthed through the discussion of an oppressed group's experiences of subjectivity.

All branches of feminist thought have valued experience, and the garnering of multifarious female experiences—in consciousness raising and in writing—has been a crucial feminist activity. As Diana Fuss has observed:

> The category of 'female experience' holds a particularly sacrosanct position on women's studies programs, programs which often draw on the very notion of hitherto repressed and devalued female experience to form the basis of a new feminist epistemology. (Fuss 1989: 113)

From the outset of the second wave, the explosion of experiential writing demonstrated that experiences are never unified or universal, but reflect differing relationships to class, race and sexual orientation—not to mention more localized variables. Yet the centrality of experience to feminist thought indicates a belief in the authenticity of experience, as if the woman who writes her own life as woman, reveals some previously suppressed truth about the state of being female. It is as if a woman can miraculously distance herself from the cultural and historical processes that make gender difference matter; yet as Fuss remarks, 'belief in the truth of Experience is as much an ideological production as belief in the experience of Truth' (Fuss 1989: 114). Narratives of experience do regularly yield common elements, which enhance feminist theoretical activities, and in this way the politics of identity is a useful tactic to initiate collective resistance to the patriarchal status quo. But it must be recognized that appeals to experience as authentic reconstructions of the nascent self risk reinstating difference as essence, and have resulted in the dissemination of identities within feminism that are often perceived as counter-productive.

There has been a tendency in feminist thought to recognize the constructedness of gendered identities, but at the same time see female appropriations of 'masculine' qualities in purely negative terms. Judith Butler prefaces her book *Gender Trouble* (1990) with the proposition that the binary framework which informs notions of gender only has real currency within a heterosexual world view, and asks, 'what happens to the subject and to the stability of gender categories when the epistemic regime of presumptive heterosexuality is unmasked as that which produces and reifies these ostensible categories of ontology?' (Butler 1990: viii). The meanings of gender, generally ascribed by feminists to the broad effect of patriarchal social organizations, is thus further recognized as being the product of a heteroreality, where heterosexuality has a clear investment in such delineations of difference. Gender, in Butler's view, is less stable than its 'official' meanings suggest, and she uses the example of female impersonator/film 'hero(ine)', Divine, to argue that his 'impersonation of women implicitly suggests that gender is a kind of persistent impersonation that passes as the real' (Butler 1990: viii). Drag, it is argued, can dramatize the fluidity of gender signifiers and can subvert and parody conventional meanings ascribed to gender difference in a pantomimic performance of their artificiality and arbitrariness. Butler, then, denies gender any originary credence, and considers how the parodic 'quoting' of gender binaries can decentre defining discourses within phallogocentrism for feminist purposes. This position develops the stance of Joan Nestle, who recognizes the resistance possibilities in the adoption of butch/femme roles, where meanings of gender are exposed as innately unstable and therefore ripe for reinterpretation. Other lesbian critics are, however, more sceptical; the most notable dissenter being Sheila Jeffreys:

> When a woman is being beaten by the brutal man she lives with is this because she has adopted the feminine gender in her appearance? Would it be a solution for her to adopt the masculine gender for the day and strut about in a work shirt or leather chaps? When gender is seen as an idea, or a form of appearance, then the oppression of women does disappear. (Jeffreys 1994:100)

Jeffreys' main concern is that any tendency to reduce the most effective meanings of gender differentiation to the level of play or parody depoliticizes the fact and effects of women's oppression. A common concern with poststructuralist/postmodern articulations of power is of course the fear that the political status of debates around the meanings and locations of gender are rendered ineffective; but Jeffreys' dogged essentialism around the issue of male sexuality being continually and ineluctably exploitative carries its own epistemological dangers.

The discussions throughout this book stand as testament to the fact that all feminists confront the problem that 'woman' as category cannot connote a common identity, and that it is debatable to what extent all women share a common form of oppression that outweighs other identities. If we accept that gender distinctions are an effect of culture, and that their meanings are constantly shifting within different historical and cultural formations, we necessarily accept that gender is always an ambiguous and contradictory category, which is independent of sex, 'with the consequence that man and masculine might just as easily signify a female body as a male one, and woman and feminine a male body as easily as a female one' (Butler 1990: 6). Within this context Butler argues that gay and lesbian citations of heterosexual conventions of gender organization (such as butch/femme) are not simply representations of heterosexual identities within a homosexual framework. Rather, such citation throws the constructedness of such categories into sharp relief, referring not to an original but a 'parody of the idea of the natural and original' (Butler 1990, 31).

Feminism's recourse to the representational category of 'woman' is also viewed by Butler as construct, in that feminism's appeal to the 'we' of womankind is always exclusionary. Butler asserts that gender's instability 'sets into question the foundational restrictions on feminist political theorizing and opens up other configurations, not only of genders and bodies, but of politics itself' (Butler 1990: 142). In other words, if politics did not appeal to categories of subjects deemed to own pre-existing originary identities, the binarism of gender relations as they are now understood might be exploded in favour of a polymorphous range of identities, that would facilitate a better understanding of how gender identity, and all entries into subjecthood are negotiated. Compelling as Butler's argument is, the notion of parody suggests an imitation of something that already exists; and even if, in the case of gender difference, this is the imitation of the idea of gender binarism, that idea itself, rather than any sense of its naturalness, has been and remains the focus of feminism's contestation of dominant patriarchal meanings of gender. The idea of appropriate gender socialization does have a material effect on the lives of women of whatever race or sexual orientation, although it is not the single determinant. Although the idea of parody as a tool in feminist politics is a seductive one, as I've suggested earlier on in this chapter, it is difficult to imagine a situation where denying the impact current meanings of gender difference have on women's lives would not result in a gender-neutral stance.

This is manifestly not the case in Butler's writing, and her thesis indicates the increasing tensions within lesbian feminism as to the range of sexual identities lesbians can or should have. These tensions have instigated new theoretical explorations into the appropriation and manipulation of gender difference—such as the meanings attributed to butch/femme roles. Susan Ardill and Sue O'Sullivan are concerned that in this we lose a feminist challenge to continued gender divisions and inequalities—particularly in the roles adopted by butch/femmes:

> Because lesbian experience is so untheorized and unsupported, even within radical or alternative cultures, any lesbian language of self-description and self-analysis has tended to remain underdeveloped. So these two words [butch/femme] have become dreadfully overburdened. (Ardill and O'Sullivan, *Feminist Review*, No. 34, Spring 1990: 80)

Butler would of course recognize in this a semantic richness, reflecting the continual dispersal of meaning around gender and the playful possibilities of ever-fluid butch/femme identification. Joan Nestle, in *A Restricted Country* (1987), demonstrates how important such identities were for lesbians in the 1950s in making lesbianism visible on the streets as a sexual style of its own, in enraging the heterosexual spectator, and in signalling the eroticism of lesbian differences, despite the threat of violence and censure:

> My understanding of why we angered straight spectators so is not that they saw us modeling ourselves after them, but just the opposite: we were a symbol of women's erotic autonomy, a sexual accomplishment that did not include them. The physical attacks were a direct attempt to break into this self-sufficient erotic partnership. (Nestle 1987: 102)

In an article on lesbian fashion in the 1990s, Inge Blackman and Kathryn Perry look at the increasing diversity of lesbian style signifiers that suggest and play with roles of butch/femme and S/M 'bottom' and 'top'. They add a cautionary note that, 'style may be subversive, but it can never become a substitute for direct political campaigning. If identity is a constantly shifting and changing phenomenon, it can no longer be a useful rallying cry for mobilizing people into action' (*Feminist Review*, No. 34, Spring 1990: 78). Whether lesbian role-play is subversive but not political continues to be debated, along with the question of whether the performance of difference necessarily reaffirms the power politics of heterosexual relationships.

Whether such a stance can be rendered politically useful in a broader feminist context remains to be seen; but such debates evidently enrich feminist discourse around the subject of compulsory heterosexuality and the politics of desire. Lesbian theorists remain the leaders in this field, since the political status of desire is as yet a much contested area, commonly avoided by straight feminists, and the notion of gender as parody of a non-existent 'natural' origin offers some challenging possibilities. Butler accurately identifies a paradox in feminism's location of gender as at once constructed and originary, and perhaps her situating parody as part of the politics of gay identity could be extended to heterosexual feminists' work on sexuality and subjectivity—to show the ways in which a sense of the parodic status of gender is already implicitly a part of the codification of heterosexual feminist discourse. Whether or not this extension of theories of otherness occurs, the value of such a position has clearly energized gay/lesbian theories, where the '90s has witnessed the modest beginnings of a new 'separatist' theoretical enterprise, with gay and lesbian theorists collaborating to produce such volumes as *Inside/Out* (1991); and new lesbian insights into feminist cultural criticism, such as *New Lesbian Criticism* (1992). In her introduction to *Inside/Out*, Diana Fuss asserts that 'what we need most urgently in gay and lesbian theory right now is a theory of marginality, subversion, dissidence, and othering' (Fuss 1991: 5). Perhaps this would also make an accurate assessment of feminism's current needs, which in its institutional embeddedness in the mainstream, loses its purchase on the fact of its marginality and otherness.

Perhaps one of the most sustained critiques of gendered binarism, and one of the most compelling images to emerge from feminism's cross fertilization with postmodernist thinking, is Donna Haraway's 'cyborg'. Neither organism nor machine, the cyborg marks a post-industrial, post-humanist fission between nature and culture, which transforms or deflects any originary meanings attributed to either term. The bio-technological contribution to social control remains, however, decidedly patriarchal, and 'the main trouble with cyborgs ... is that they are the illegitimate offspring of militarism and patriarchal capitalism, not to mention state socialism'; but, as she continues, 'illegitimate offspring are often exceedingly unfaithful to their origins' (Haraway in Weed 1989: 176). The cyborg, then, is not summoned by Haraway as a paradigm of the victim, caught up in the networks of what Foucault would term 'bio-power'; she is more interested in how cybernetics breaks down the humanist divisions between animal and human, mind and body, in a symbolic breach between nature and culture. For Haraway such an 'ironic' political stance as the one outlined in this essay, is an attempt to contribute to feminist debates around the politics of identity, by blocking the feminist tendency to retreat to pseudo-essentialist origins, extending the ground of 'new essentialist' discussions such as Butler's and Fuss's:

> Consciousness of exclusion through naming is acute. Identities seem contradictory, partial and strategic. With the hard-won recognition of their social and historical constitution, gender, race and class cannot provide the basis for belief in 'essential' unity. There is nothing about being 'female' that naturally binds women. There is not even such a state as 'being' female, itself a highly complex category constructed in contested sexual scientific discourses and other social entities. (Weed 1989: 179)

Haraway identifies consequent risks in contemporary feminists constantly summoning the quality of 'being' female (particularly through experiential narratives) in its tendency to mark feminism as a totalizing discourse. Her intention here is to make female identity itself ironic—something some lesbian theorists are also attempting to perform in their belief that gender parody such as butch/femme role-play disassembles dominant meanings of gender identity, rather than simply replicating relations of dominance and submission. Haraway is signalling a position that might also facilitate a renewed rhetoric of resistance and opposition which does not simply rely on an acceptance of the 'realities' of oppressive mechanisms. In a curious fashion her work carries resonances of that of Shulamith Firestone's *Dialectic of Sex*, although feminist critiques of this text have of course focused upon its underlying biologism. Haraway's account, however, denies biologism any privileged epistemological status; and in her portrayal of the cyborg she grounds biology and its possible connotations within shifting conditions of scientific discourse. Her ascription of the cyborgian subject does not deny the patriarchal rootedness of such a construction, but rather sees in the deflection of originary gender binarism, the possibilities of a new ironic form of resistance to existing relations of power.

Problems and Utopian Possibilities

No matter how enchanted one might be by the postmodernist redefinition of the categories masculine/feminine, and even male/female, feminists need to be able 'crudely' to assert that woman as category, encompassing the action and reaction of 'difference' in its many semantic layers, remains the subject and Subject of its political discourse. As Modleski avers, 'in the final analysis, it seems more important to struggle over what it means to be a woman than over whether or not to be one' (Modleski 1991: 20). The luxury of female anti-essentialism is still one only accorded to the privileged; non-white, non-heterosexual, non-bourgeois women are still finding political impetus in summoning up womanhood as identity, and femininity as a construct which excludes and punishes them most painfully of all—as bell hooks' summoning of Sojourner Truth's question, 'Ain't I a Woman?' as title for her 1982 text testifies.

One significant crisis in feminism is, I believe, the overwhelming consciousness that differing internal movements tend to create their own unwritten dos and don'ts; and women gaining access to feminist thought for the first time might be forgiven for feeling that they don't want to label themselves feminist because of the pejorative tone this term has culturally acquired. More importantly, they may feel that they cannot call themselves feminists, if they lack the 'qualifications' that certainly the more arcane branches of modern feminist thought seem to designate, a consideration strengthened by popular denunciations of feminism as prescriptive or even 'puritan'. Alison Light perceives the danger of a tone of piety creeping into feminism, perpetuating the complacency among (white) feminists that they are one of the 'chosen few', and she contests that 'Being a feminist, as I understand it, should not be like being in church: there are no blasphemies, no ritual incantations, no heretics and no saints' (Carr 1989: 28). I would agree with these sentiments, which perhaps deserve restating—despite their 'obviousness'—because recent debates among feminists give the lie to the notion that there are some fairly tenacious 'heresies' which need weeding out. Yet, paradoxically, we are in a position where there are some 'heretics' who use feminism to annihilate it, prompting a need for greater explicitness around the question of what feminism as discourse and action intends to achieve, and whether demarcated 'boundaries' are feasible. Whether or not such boundaries are desirable, they seem to be urgently needed.

Writing in 1971, Juliet Mitchell prophesied that the biggest single theoretical battle would be between radical and socialist feminists (Mitchell 1971: 91); here, Mitchell assumes that radical feminists will overcome their disaffection with the Left to combine their insights into women's experience and consciousness with a socialist feminist theory of women's oppression. Although the rift between these two positions has been demarcated many times since, in retrospect the major battle has been in the field of 'theory' itself and its possible disjunctions with a feminist political practice. Feminism has matured, and the potential sites for conflict—both within and outside feminist parameters—have multiplied. From largely eschewing political/theoretical coalitions with men during the '70s, in the '90s many feminists are forging new connections with men—at least at the level of postmodern critiques. The new battle for feminism, assuming that it survives the most recent crises of confidence/meaning outlined in this chapter, will be to find epistemological measures to defend its autonomy while enacting bridges between the politics of race, class, and sexual orientation. Many women who previously felt that their concerns were not addressed by the dominant forms of feminism might then recognize a newly strengthened location for their own resistance within a politics of heterogeneity. We live in an era which offers academic feminism some confusing messages. The shape and scope of women's studies in face of critical 'acceptance', has been transformed, yet the ideological pressures exerted by a patriarchal social reality still hold sway, and arguably are reinforced in a climate of recession and economic shrinkage.

Speaking of the interfaces between black male and female experiences of oppression and those experiences of white females, Kate Millett comments on how in the case of women and the perpetuation of the ideology of femininity, 'a certain handful of women are accorded higher status that they may perform a species of cultural policing over the rest' (Millett 1977: 57). It is tempting to see this tokenism filtering into increasing incidents of feminist interventions into 'high theory', particularly that of postmodernism. One of my chief concerns about the degree of acceptance, and even popularity, of feminist theoretical positions in academe is that such theorists are accorded by their male counterparts the 'honour' of being the cultural police force for feminism as a whole. Postmodern or poststructuralist feminism is viewed in this light as a sign of feminist thought at its most sophisticated, a methodology which renders other forms of feminist expression redundant. It suggests that feminists are being encouraged to forget the tribulations of their recent past, and throw in their hard-won resources with the anti-humanist men, whose investment in exploding humanist binarism might still represent a somewhat different agenda from that normally associated with feminism.

Feminism has always devoted time and energy to the anticipation of utopian possibilities of social transformation, as do all radical political positions to a greater or lesser extent. Perhaps the value of utopian preoccupations is undermined by postmodern critiques. When I attempt to identify the desirability or otherwise of the continuing production of feminist utopias as a viable political tactic, I recall Foucault's distinction between utopias and heterotopias in his Preface to *The Order of Things*:

> Utopias afford consolation: although they have no real locality there is nevertheless a fantastic, untroubled region in which they are able to unfold: they open up cities with vast avenues, superbly planted gardens, countries where life is easy, even though the road to them is chimerical. Heterotopias are disturbing, probably because they secretly undermine language, because they make it impossible to name this and that, because they shatter or tangle common names, because they destroy 'syntax' in advance, and not only the syntax with which we construct sentences but also that less apparent syntax which causes words and things . . . to 'hold together'. (Foucault 1970: xviii)

Foucault (citing Borges as an example of a writer of heterotopias) is here mocking conventional systems of coherence and classification, which comprise the formation of knowledges from which we seek access to the truth of being. Such ordering instances, it is asserted, provide the conditions of possibility of uttering 'truths', and of founding disciplines of empirical knowledge. Similarly, feminists have long been in the business of mocking, inverting or disrupting the existing 'order of things', particularly in observing that Western epistemology assumes orders which on closer scrutiny conform to and support the conditions of possibility of a distinctly masculine body of knowledge and truth claims. At the centre of this order is language which inscribes gendered and other identities in opposition to one another in the indefatigable tension of the 'either/or' logic of modern thought. In a sense feminists are out to destroy the syntax of phallogocentrism, to get to the cement that binds the logic of such thought together in such arbitrary terms, not in order to rebuild the structure of such syntax in a slightly different configuration, but in order to demonstrate that such a structure has no natural foundations whatever.

Utopias are the 'no-places' of a future where society has transformed into something other than our present realities. In order to construct utopias, writers of fiction or political theory have recourse to the dominant systems of the present to enact a critique of its inequities, or its mistakes. Feminist utopias also seek to enter that no-place where the meanings of gender and oppression are exploded as ever arbitrary relations of power with a chimerical link to the 'natural', which only proves to be an essence constructed from the meanings of social life in its ever changing social and cultural contexts. In offering such utopias feminists remind us of the 'no place' for women in current dominant ideological representations—and as they seek to gesture a future 'no place' for women as well as men, they might also be viewed as venturing a heterotopia of their own. Feminists do not, after all, envisage a future which is simply the obverse of the present; often the aim is to dispense with classic binarist thinking in favour of a multiplicity, which denies all essence, including what are thought of as biological imperatives, in order to think what is, in current discursive formations, radically 'unthinkable'. If we regard utopian texts such as Shulamith Firestone's *Dialectic of Sex* in this light, it is clearly inadequate simply to view her work as racked with essentialist truth claims about female biology. One might usefully review the intentions of Firestone's work, in common with other feminist writings, as an exhortation to women to think outside their current social reality, in order to articulate what has currently no 'language' of its own.

As Angelika Bammer suggests, utopian visions remain partial 'in both senses of the word: partisan and limited' (Bammer 1991: 155). As she indicates, this invites both negative and positive interpretations of the term: the negative side lies in the threat of exclusionism (particularly of the needs of less privileged groups of women), although the threat of the exclusion of men remains a powerful rhetorical challenge. Utopias are positive in the sense that feminists' multifarious and sometimes conflicting views of the desired shape of its utopias remind us that feminist thought is constantly reshaping and re-envisaging gender difference, and still has to focus upon reclaiming women's part in historical and cultural processes as a political necessity. The term heterotopia reminds us that not only are possible visions of the future multiple and ever changing, but that our critiques of the present draw upon multifarious perspectives on present social realities, specific to class, ethnic and sexual locations within patriarchy. Finally, the term heterotopia seems happily compatible with my exploration and affirmation of feminism's heterogeneity, where diversity and conflict might better ensure that our future is not a covert repetition of the shape of the past.

PART II

FEMINIST THEORETICAL AND RESEARCH PERSPECTIVES

A.

Theory and Research Methods

Chapter 7

Methods, Practice and Epistemology: The Debate about Feminism and Research

Mary Maynard

The question as to what constitutes feminist social research has been an issue for feminists for over a decade and there is now a considerable literature addressing the topic. It seems to be widely accepted by feminists themselves that there is a distinctively feminist mode of enquiry, although there is by no means agreement on what this might mean or involve. In fact, as Sandra Harding has pointed out, scrutiny of the arguments reveals some confusion in the terms that are central to the debate.[1] Harding usefully makes a distinction between discussions of method, of methodology and of epistemology. Whereas method refers to techniques for gathering research material, methodology provides both theory and analysis of the research process. Epistemology is concerned with providing a philosophical grounding for deciding what kinds of knowledge are possible and how we can ensure that they are both adequate and legitimate. Harding contends that the term 'method' is often used to refer to all three of these elements of research. This lack of clarity has impeded feminists in their quest convincingly to set out what is specifically 'feminist' about their work.

Despite the fact, however, that feminists have increasingly quoted and endorsed Harding's arguments, defining what feminism means in terms of doing research is still no easy matter. Different claims abound. Indeed, the task is made more difficult since there are disagreements both *within* each of the components which Harding has identified and *between* them. In this, of course, feminism is no different from the rest of the social sciences. One particular problem is reconciling the abstract analyses and recommendations made at the epistemological level, where there is burgeoning interest and writing, with the more concrete concerns of method and methodology faced by those carrying out empirical research. It is the concern of this chapter to disentangle and explore some of these issues. First, it will provide a critical overview of those arguments that have been central to feminist interest in method, research practice and epistemology. Secondly, it will consider some of the difficulties raised by this literature. Finally, the chapter will address selected key issues important to feminism if our work is to be taken seriously and be influential.

The Debate about Methods

The idea that feminism has a method of conducting social research which is specific to it has increasingly come under attack.[2] However, this was certainly a view put forward in the early stages of second wave feminist scholarship and it is one which continues to be espoused.[3] These arguments advocated and defended a qualitative approach to understanding women's lives as

---

Reprinted from *Researching Women's Lives from a Feminist Perspective*, edited by Mary Maynard and June Purvis, 1994. Copyright © 1994 Taylor and Francis.

against quantitative methods of enquiry. The arguments were rooted in a critique of what were perceived to be the dominant modes of doing research which were regarded as inhibiting a sociological understanding of women's experiences. Quantitative research (particularly surveys and questionnaires) was seen to represent a 'masculinist' form of knowing, where the emphasis was on the detachment of the researcher and the collection and measurement of 'objective' social facts through a (supposedly) value-free form of data collection. By contrast, the use of qualitative methods, which focus more on the subjective experiences and meanings of those being researched, was regarded as more appropriate to the kinds of knowledge that feminists wished to make available, as well as being more in keeping with the politics of doing research as a feminist. Semi-structured or unstructured interviewing has been the research technique most often associated with this stance, although this can, of course, produce both quantitative and qualitative data.

Initially, the feminist critique of quantification drew from the arguments of phenomenological sociologists, which were particularly influential in the early 1970s.[4] These sociologists claimed that the assumptions as to how actors structure their everyday worlds to be found within most questionnaire or interview schedules produce a falsely concrete body of data, which distort rather than reflect actors' meanings. Similarly, feminists have argued that the production of atomistic 'facts' and figures fractures people's lives.[5] Only one tiny part of experience is abstracted as the focus for attention and this is done in both a static and an atemporal fashion. Often the result of such an approach is a simple matrix of standardized variables which is unable to convey an indepth understanding of, or feeling for, the people under study. Further, research practices which utilize either pre-coded or pre-closed categories are often of limited use when trying to understand women's lives. This is because they are based on assumptions, often at an unrecognized and common-sense level, that the researcher is already sufficiently familiar with the phenomenon being investigated to be able to specify, in advance, the full range of experiences being studied and how these can be encapsulated, categorized and measured. Sociological research which is based upon such assumptions, it is argued, is neither exploratory nor investigatory. Rather, it assesses the extent, distribution or intensity of something which has been defined in advance of the research undertaken, by the researcher. Feminists have argued that there are aspects to women's lives which cannot be pre-known or pre-defined in such a way.

This position was particularly important at a time when feminist research was in its infancy and when women's lives and experiences were still largely invisible. What was most usefully required then was an approach to research which maximized the ability to explore experience, rather than impose externally defined structures on women's lives. Thus feminists emphasized the importance of listening to, recording and understanding women's own descriptions and accounts.[6] This strategy enabled researchers to extend knowledge of areas such as schooling and paid work, previously understood mainly from a male perspective. It also facilitated the development of new, woman-oriented fields of research, for example violence towards women, sexuality, childbirth and domesticity. At its heart was the tenet that feminist research must begin with an open-ended exploration of women's experiences, since only from that vantage point is it possible to see how their world is organized and the extent to which it differs from that of men.

With hindsight, however, it can be seen that this approach, which proved so beneficial to feminists in their early work, gradually developed into something of an unproblematized orthodoxy against which the political correctness, or otherwise, of *all* feminist research could be judged.[7] It began to be assumed that *only* qualitative methods, especially the indepth face-to-face interview, could really count in feminist terms and generate useful knowledge. Despite the fact that a number of feminist commentators *did* advocate the use of a range of research techniques and several deployed survey material and the statistical analysis of data to very effective critical ends,[8] the tendency to equate feminist work with a qualitative approach has persisted. One reason for this is the way in which quantification has been identified with the position of positivism, and positivism has become something of a *bête noire* in the quantitative versus qualitative debate.

Historically, what counts as positivism and its defining characteristics have been contested and have also changed.[9] The stereotypical view, however, and the one to which many feminists tend to subscribe, has focused on what counts as science. The emphasis here has been on deductivism. This involves the formulation of hypotheses about the world and the development of statements from them which are then tested to assess their validity. The existence of an independent and objective test (as is supposed to occur in laboratory experiments, for example), is crucial. It is this which ensures the facticity and reliability of the knowledge produced because it is uncontaminated by the subjective bias of the researcher. Science is thus characterized in terms of the objectivity of its method and the value-neutrality of the scientist. In textbook notions of positivism the resulting findings are fed back into and absorbed by the initial theory. This linear model of how research supposedly proceeds in the natural sciences is one which, some have argued, the social sciences need to pursue if they are to match the achievements of the other sciences.

The first point to be raised about this picture of positivism is, does it correspond to how science actually works? Developments in the sociology of knowledge and in the philosophy and sociology of science suggest otherwise and, although there are differing positions in the ensuing debate, plausible claims for the socially constructed nature of and investigator involvement in *all* research have been made.[10]

A second issue is to do with the implied relationship between the philosophical doctrine of positivism and empirical methods of research which involve measurement to provide numerical or statistically manipulatable data. In his very clear exposition of the nature of quantitative research Alan Bryman, for example, suggests that positivism and the use of quantitative methods are not necessarily the same thing, as is often assumed, and that there are 'aspects of the general approach of quantitative researchers which are not directly attributable to either positivism or the practices of the natural sciences'.[11] Bryman also questions the extent to which the terms qualitative and quantitative actually denote divergent assumptions about the nature and purpose of social research. He concludes that this is little more than an academic convention which took root in the 1960s and which 'has little to recommend it, either as a description of the research process or as a prescriptive view of how research should be done'.[12]

We also need to ask how far those doing quantitative research agree with the practices and assumptions which are attributed to them and used to criticize their work. Whilst it is no doubt the case that some *do* regard themselves as neutral researchers producing objective and value-free 'facts', others are more circumspect, acknowledging that providing figures involves as much of an act of social construction as any other kind of research. What is at issue, then, is whether positivism is *intrinsic* to quantitative research, and the answer appears to be that it is not. Catherine Marsh, for instance, has defended survey research against the charge of positivism, although she concedes that most of the textbook discussions do not allow a distinction between the two. Marsh suggests that there have been two kinds of attacks on surveys. One focuses on crude data collection and analysis and involves criticisms of poor research which most would agree with but which are not synonymous with surveys *per se*. The other focuses on the fact that the subjects of social research are conscious, language-speaking and meaning-creating. But, she argues, 'this is a problem for any social scientist, from the experimenter to the ethnographer, and is not confined to surveys'.[13] It is likely, then, that it is not so much quantification *per se* as naive quantification which is the problem.

A final point to be made is that in rejecting quantification, feminists have overlooked the contribution that research involving enumeration has made to our knowledge and understanding of women's experiences. Further, the *political* potential of such work must not be underestimated. The significance of violence in women's lives, for example, is underlined by studies showing the extent and severity of its incidence. Issues such as the feminization of poverty and women's lack of progress in achieving equality, on a number of dimensions, with men in paid work also benefit from work which demonstrates the problem numerically. This is not to argue that only work of this kind is useful or of interest. Such a position would be absurd. It is, however, to suggest that the time has come for some rethinking in terms of what are regarded as acceptable methods for feminists engaged in empirical research. This seems to encompass a recognition of the need for breadth as well as depth, as I have discovered in my own collaborative work on the Careers Service and on women's employment in the tourist industry, both of which used surveys in addition to other research techniques.[14]

Three things, in particular, are leading feminists to reconsider their position on method. First there is the need to acknowledge that the qualitative techniques they have tended to favour are not in and of themselves specific to feminism. Indeed, they are all an integral part of social science research and have their own histories of development and change outside and independent of feminism. Feminists may have appropriated these techniques, but they did not create them. They have also modified them, although they are not alone in doing so. In addition, a number of researchers have recently drawn attention to the ways in which the polarization of quantitative versus qualitative impoverishes research, and there have been calls for the use of multiple methods to be used in a complementary rather than a competitive way.[15] In their chapter for this book, for instance, Liz Kelly, Sheila Burton and Linda Regan clearly illustrate how this can be done to advantage in their work on child sexual abuse.[16] They argue that using questionnaires produced more reliable information than interviewing, because it allowed respondents anonymity in revealing distressing and sensitive experiences. This indicates that it is no longer tenable for the old orthodoxy to remain.

Feminism and Research Practice

If the arguments for the existence of a distinctive feminist method can be dismissed, what other grounds might there be for defining research as feminist? Another way in which feminists have answered this question is to turn to issues of methodology, which involves the theory and analysis of how research should proceed, how research questions might best be addressed and the criteria against which research findings might be evaluated. In doing so, feminists have tended to concentrate attention on two main areas of concern, the position from which distinctively feminist research questions might be asked and the political and ethical issues involved in the research process. Kelly has suggested the term 'feminist research practice' as helpful in this context, since it signals more clearly the wide-ranging nature of the points which feminists customarily address. Kelly argues that what distinguishes feminist research from other forms of research is 'the questions we have asked, the way we locate ourselves within our questions, and the purpose of our work'.[17] She thus draws attention to a range of issues which go beyond those relating specifically to method.

Many of those who have written about feminist research practice have indicated that a theoretical perspective, acknowledging the pervasive influence of gender divisions on social life, is one of its most important defining characteristics.[18] There are, however, differences over what this might mean. To begin with, there are different theoretical emphases. Perceiving the significance of gender in terms of division and inequality, for instance, implies a different theoretical perspective to that which emphasizes the importance of patriarchal power and control. Each approach is likely to lead to the posing of different sorts of questions and to the production of different kinds of knowledge and analysis. Further, it is not entirely clear what focusing on gender means in terms of the subjects of research. Some have argued that it entails a preeminent concern with women alone, and given their previous neglect this was especially important early on in feminist work.[19] Others have suggested that 'gender' implies women's relationship to men and that this also needs to be included, although examined from a woman's perspective, in any enquiry involved in understanding how women's experiences in a male world are structured.[20] Stanley and Wise have always maintained that a concern with gender necessarily means being prepared to focus on men and masculinity, with the intention of researching the powerful as well as the powerless.[21] Although this is still a relatively underdeveloped aspect of feminist research, it raises important questions about whether such work is solely about women's experiences, as has so often been claimed. A further issue here, and one which is currently a particularly important aspect of feminist debate, is the relationship of gender to other forms of oppression, for instance those of race, class and disability, and the need to include an awareness of this within the parameters of our research.

A second way in which an understanding of the feminist research process has developed, and a consequence of gender-conscious theory and politics, is in the modifications which have been made to existing techniques. It has already been pointed out that feminists have largely used interviewing in their work. But they have not, as is now well-known, adopted this strategy blindly. Feminists have been critical of the ways in which sociological research involves hierarchical power relationships.[22] Even non-scheduled interviewing and ethnographic methods can entail a deliberate separation of the researcher from the 'subject' of the researched. The researcher using qualitative methods may not be constrained by pre-coded questions, but is, nevertheless, exhorted by textbook guidelines to be emotionally detached, calculating and in control of the collection of data. Those researched are regarded, in this view of research, as the passive givers of information, with the researcher acting as a sponge soaking up the details provided. Feminists have rejected the inevitability of such a power hierarchy between researcher and researched. Instead, they have argued for the significance of a genuine, rather than an instrumental rapport between them. This, it has been claimed, encourages a non-exploitative relationship, where the person being studied is not treated simply as a source of data. Research becomes a means of sharing information and, rather than being seen as a source of bias, the personal involvement of the interviewer is an important element in establishing trust and thus obtaining good quality information.

The problem is that it is not entirely clear what the term 'good quality' might mean in this context. Does it refer to the authenticity of women's accounts, to reliable and valid information, or to material which has not been violated by researcher (re)interpretation? Who is to judge on these issues and using what kind of criteria? Further, it is not always so easy to reduce the power dynamics that are likely to be present in research and it is unlikely that they can ever be eradicated completely. As Janet Finch has indicated, if the researcher is educated and articulate it is very easy to encourage women to talk about aspects of their lives concerning which, on reflection, they might have preferred to remain silent.[23] It is easy too for feminists to deny that they have knowledge and skills in order to minimize differences between women, as Gelsthorpe has noted.[24] The problem of power dynamics may become particularly acute when men are the subjects of research. But here the difficulty is likely to be reversed, with the male respondent rather than the female researcher engaged in manipulation, as both Scott and Smart have described.[25]

A number of ways of dealing with these kinds of dilemma have been suggested. For example, feminist research is characterized by a concern to record the subjective experiences of doing research.[26] This concern with reflexivity, also to be found in some forms of ethnography, may be expressed in two rather differing ways. It can mean reflecting upon, critically examining and exploring analytically the nature of the research process in an attempt to demonstrate the assumptions about gender (and, increasingly, race, disability and other oppressive) relations which are built into a specific project.[27] It may also refer to understanding the 'intellectual autobiography' of researchers. This is important for Stanley and Wise who have been critical of the way in which social research dichotomizes objectivity versus subjectivity. They argue that the researcher is also a subject in her research and that her personal history is part of the process through which 'understanding' and 'conclusions' are reached.[28] In both cases gender is seen, not just as something to be studied, but as an integral dimension of the research process and therefore also to be examined. Such work on reflexivity means that feminists have been at the forefront of discussions about the need to be open and honest about the research process, although, clearly, there are no easy solutions to the issues which have been raised by them.

A final way in which feminist research practice might be said to be distinctive has been in its insistence on its political nature and potential to bring about change in women's lives. At one time this was summed up in the slogan that feminist research was 'on', 'by' and 'for' women and that it should be designed with the aim of producing knowledge which would transform patriarchy.[29] Such a claim is not, however, uncontentious, as Glucksmann's chapter in this volume indicates. It implies, for instance, that studies which cannot be directly linked to transformational politics are not feminist. It raises the question as to how far the researcher is in control of the extent and direction of any change which her research might bring about. In fact, different kinds of change are potentially involved. One is that associated with empowerment, literally helping to give people knowledge, energy and authority in order that they might act. Anne Opie has argued that there are at least three ways in which an individual may be personally empowered through participation in a research project.[30] These are through their contribution to making visible a social issue, the therapeutic effect of being able to reflect on and re-evaluate their experience as part of the process of being interviewed, and the generally subversive outcome that these first two consequences may generate. It is also possible, of course, that the researcher may be empowered in these ways as well.

Yet these are rather limited notions of the effects that research may have. To start with, it is by no means the case that all outcomes will be positive. It may be possible for participants in a study to have their consciousnesses raised without the corresponding channels for action being available. Feminists have raised questions about the ethics of research which, having generated all sorts of issues in respondents' minds, then abandons them to come to terms with these on their own. Kelly, for instance, has described the kind of support which she felt it necessary to provide for the women who talked to her about surviving sexual violence.[31] Writing about her research on women who have left violent partners, Kirkwood reveals that one of them declined to return for a second interview because she had found the first so traumatic.[32] Of course, it may be that a particular study has little or even no effect on participants. Still, it is important to be aware of the possible negative, as well as positive, outcomes that might arise.

Feminists have also written about the personal consequences on the researcher of undertaking particular kinds of research. Stanley and Wise, for example, argue that their consciousnesses as feminists were raised in such a profound way, as a result of their work on obscene telephone calls, that it affected their views of men, patriarchy and feminism.[33] Kirkwood found her research so emotionally stressful that she eventually sought counselling, although she argues that, retrospectively, she can see that these emotions played an important role in the quality of her analysis.[34]

Finally, it should be noted that even if research has little impact on the lives of those included in it, it may be important for the category of persons they are taken to represent. Thus, work on rape or women's housing problems may be too late to alleviate the suffering of those directly involved in it, but can contribute to legislation, policy or the behaviour of agencies in ways which later enhance the experiences of others.

This discussion of feminist research practice has drawn attention to a number of issues and debates in the field. Whilst it is clear that there is no one methodological approach or research practice specific to feminism, as some critics have erroneously claimed,[35] this should come as no surprise since feminism embraces a number of theoretical positions and perspectives. What *is* obvious, however, is the challenging and wide-ranging nature of the discussion which has developed; a discussion which has implications for the whole of social research and not just for the feminist variant of it. The next section addresses some of these implications further in an epistemological context.

Epistemology and the Nature of Feminist Knowledge

The feminist concern with epistemology has centred on the questions 'who knows what, about whom and how is this knowledge legitimized?'. An early feminist writer on this subject, Dorothy Smith, argued, for instance, that sociology was not just the study of men in society, it was also a 'male science of society' because its whole approach to the study of the social world was coloured by a masculinist bias.[36] Catharine MacKinnon has referred to this as the 'male epistemological stance' which she defines as men's power to create the world from their own point of view, which then becomes the truth to be described. For MacKinnon, although objectivity and science represent supposedly neutral positions, they are, in fact, gendered and partial.[37] Feminism not only challenges this partiality, it also critiques the purported generality, disinterestedness and universality of male accounts.

The main way in which this has been done is to confront the dichotomizing that is characteristic of Enlightenment thinking and the view of science which developed out of it. The Enlightenment pictured humanity as engaged in an effort to find universal moral and intellectual self-realization. Important here was the notion that reason. as employed philosophically and scientifically, could provide an objective, reliable and universal foundation for knowledge.[38] This, of course, is the origin of the pursuit of rationality and the positivistic position discussed previously. The knowledge generated would then be used to improve the quality of life and enable societies to develop and progress to higher forms of civilization. The legitimacy that such knowledge lay claim to was, however, rooted in a series of dualisms: reason and rationality versus emotion; mind versus body; subject versus object; objective truth versus ideology and the distortion of 'interests'. Feminists have pointed out not only that these polarizations mirror the dichotomy male/female, but that they are false in the way in which they imply opposite, unconnected extremes and consistently devalue the second component of these.[39]

One writer whose work in this area is well known is Sandra Harding. In Harding's view there are three stages in the development of feminist epistemology. The first of these, 'feminist empiricism', argues that it is possible to remove sexist and other biases from the processes of research, particularly when problems for study are initially being identified and defined, in the belief that, once these have been eliminated, value-neutral work will be produced.[40] Harding regards this as an attempt to reform 'bad' science, simply by 'adding' women into existing frameworks, rather than questioning the prejudiced assumptions that are constitutive of science *per se*. The second stage, and the one in which we are currently located, according to Harding, is that of the 'feminist standpoint'. Here the argument is that understanding women's lives from a committed feminist exploration of their experiences of oppression produces more complete and less distorted knowledge than that produced by men. Women lead lives that have significantly different contours and patterns to those of men, and their subjugated position provides the possibility of more complete and less perverse understandings. Thus, adopting a feminist standpoint can reveal the existence of forms of human relationships which may not be visible from the position of the 'ruling gender'.

In addition to 'feminist empiricism' and 'feminist standpoint' Harding suggests that there is a third epistemological position, that of feminist postmodernism. This, along with other variants of postmodernism, is critical of universalistic grand theories and rejects the existence of an authentic self. Its focus instead is on fragmentation, multiple subjectivities, pluralities and flux. Harding clearly does not regard these three stages of feminist epistemology as being absolutely distinct and she argues at one point, for instance, that the empiricism and standpoint positions are locked into dialogue with each other. Further, although she refers to the latter as 'transitional' she is also uneasy about any postmodern alternatives. While apparently agreeing with the postmodern critique of science as a doomed project, she also sees problems in adopting it wholeheartedly, because of the way in which it deconstructs and demeans gender as an issue. Thus, feminists cannot afford to give up the standpoint approach because it is 'central to transferring the power to change social relations from the "haves" to the "have-nots"'.[41] Postmodernism, in contrast, provides a vision of the future by deconstructing the possibilities as to what this might mean.

The idea of a 'feminist standpoint' has gained currency, although there are variations on precisely what this involves.[42] Harding herself identifies the standpoint position as a 'successor science'. She argues that objectivity should involve the critical scrutiny of *all* evidence marshalled as part of the research process. Conventional notions of objectivity are 'weak' because they include the researchers' hidden and unexplicated cultural agendas and assumptions.[43] 'Strong' objectivity, as represented by the feminist standpoint, includes the systematic examination of such background beliefs. It thus 'avoids damaging forms of relativism . . . and transforms the reflexivity of research from a problem into a scientific resource'.[44]

This idea of a successor science has been challenged by Stanley and Wise. They draw attention to 'silences' in Harding's work, particularly the lack of any real consideration of Black feminist and lesbian feminist points of view and argue that, rather than there being one standpoint, there are a range of different but equally valid ones.[45] Harding has recently attempted to overcome this problem and, in *Whose Science? Whose Knowledge?*, has included a section on 'others' (rather an unfortunate term suggesting deviation from some 'proper' norm). However, she does not deal with Stanley and Wise's central point; once the existence of several feminist stand*points* is admitted, then it becomes impossible to talk about 'strong' objectivity as a means of establishing superior or 'better' knowledge because there will, necessarily, be contested truth claims arising from the contextually grounded knowledge of the different standpoints. Stanley and Wise reject the idea of a successor science which, they say, still retains the implication that there is a social reality 'out there' that research can discover. Such 'foundationalism' is based on an insistence that 'truth' exists independently of the knower. They argue instead for a 'feminist fractured foundationalist epistemology'.[46] Whilst not disputing the existence of 'truth' and a material reality, judgments about them are always relative to the context within which such knowledge is produced.[47]

Those who defend the 'standpoint position', or one of its variants, deny that it signifies a collapse into total relativism, arguing, albeit sometimes for different reasons, that it occupies middle ground[48] in what is, conventionally and mistakenly, perceived as a foundationalism versus relativism dichotomy. There is still, however, the problem of the differing accounts which may emerge from different standpoints. While Stanley and Wise do not seem to regard this as an issue and write positively about such pluralism, others see difficulties.[49] Although it may be tempting to regard each standpoint as equally valid, this may be difficult when the power relations between women themselves differ. Things become particularly problematic, for example, when one standpoint contains elements or assumptions which are racist or heterosexist in nature.

Another issue relates to whether it is the standpoint of the individual or the group which is being referred to and what the relationship between them might be. Neither is it clear whether it is the standpoints of feminists or of women more generally which are to be the focus of attention. The terms 'feminist' and 'women's' are often used interchangeably in the literature and, although a feminist approach is almost definitionally one which starts out from women's experiences, most women are not feminists and would not necessarily agree with accounts of the social world generated from a feminist stance.[50]

The 'standpoint' debate is an important one for the ways in which it systematically sets out the specific characteristics of a feminist epistemology and shows how these have relevance for a number of issues (relativism and objectivity, for instance) which are continually debated within sociology more generally. As has been seen, however, there are still areas of contention so that the notion of standpoint is not as definitive as the term itself might imply. Other matters also pertinent to the debate will be addressed in the more general discussions which follow.

Methods, Research Practice and Epistemology: Linking the Terms of Debate

The above sections have considered some of the significant arguments and developments in the debate about the constitutive features of feminist research. The focus of this debate seems to have changed over the years. Initially concerned with the rather narrow issue of method, it then broadened out to include different aspects of research practice. Recently, interest has been more epistemological in nature. One reason for this has been feminists' involvement in discussions about postmodernism which involves questioning many conventional notions about the nature of science, the legitimacy of theory and the status of empirical research.[51]

Although there is no one particular model of what feminist research should be like, recurrent themes appear throughout the literature. There is the focus on women's experiences, for example, and the concern for ethical questions which guide research practices. Feminists are concerned with the role of the researcher in the research, and with countering the scientific philosophy and practice which is often associated with it. Although these themes, along with others, may not be specific to feminist work, the ways that they are treated (informed as they are by feminist theorizing about gender and feminist politics more generally), together with the manner in which they are combined, mean that it is possible to identify specific feminist research practices and epistemological positions.

There is a problem, however, in linking some of the arguments made at an epistemological level with what happens, or should happen, in terms of research practice and the use of particular research techniques. The discussion about feminist methods, for instance, which tends to have polarized qualitative versus quantitative approaches, is clearly at odds with the critique of the inhibiting effect of dualistic categorization that has been mounted by some feminists in the debate on epistemology. The methods literature has, thus, tended to reproduce the binary oppositions that have been criticized elsewhere, although there is now a move to advocate the importance of quantitative work, as indicated previously. Yet it is difficult to see how some of the issues currently at the forefront of epistemological concerns could really be empirically explored in anything other than qualitative work. The concern with the body and emotions as legitimate sources of knowledge, for example, with reflexivity and the critique of subject/object polarizations seem more appropriate to, and have more affinity with, research which employs relatively open-ended strategies. In many ways this should not surprise us. After all, as we have already seen, it was largely because of philosophical critiques of science and positivism that feminists developed their antipathy to quantification. But this now poses something of a problem because, despite feminists' disclaimers, the epistemological discussions still point to the overall legitimacy of qualitative studies, while researchers themselves are attempting to rehabilitate approaches that involve measurement and counting. This seems to indicate that arguments about what constitutes knowledge and discussions about methods of doing research are moving in opposite directions.

There is also divergence between the abstract analytical philosophizing which characterizes the literature on epistemology, particularly in its postmodernist form, and the more concrete language of that on methods and methodology. Can the former be translated into the practicalities of the latter? Whilst feminist postmodernism usefully directs attention to the fractured nature of womanhood, the possibilities of multiple identities and the dangers of totalizing theory, taken to their logical conclusions many of its precepts are inimical to the principles, never mind the practice, of undertaking empirical research. There are two main reasons for this. The first is that the social world is pictured as so fragmented, so individualistic, so totally in a state of flux that any attempt to present a more structured alternative, which, by its very nature, much social research does, is regarded as, a priori, mistaken. Not only is the task impossible, it is also seen as ill-conceived. A second reason is that the kind of research currently identified with the social sciences (be it surveys, interviews etc) is associated with precisely that, previously described, modernist Enlightenment tradition which postmodernism is trying to transcend. Whilst analyses of discourse and text are possible from within a postmodern perspective, anything which focuses on the materiality of human existence is virtually impossible, unless analyzed in terms of discourse and text. This does not mean, of course, that a postmodern approach has nothing to offer feminists. What it does mean is that because it contains radically different assumptions from those of other epistemological positions it has, potentially, different things to offer. Addressing this issue, Smart has described for example, how, in explaining rape, it is necessary to explore 'how women's bodies have become saturated with (hetero)sex, how codes of sexualized meanings are reproduced and sustained and to begin (or continue) the deconstruction of these meanings'.[52]

While this kind of work clearly makes a contribution to understanding the relationship between sexuality and sexual violence, it cannot be, and should not be regarded as, a substitute for other kinds of research. Two things are at issue here. The first relates to the problem of political intervention. If one major goal of feminist research is to challenge patriarchal structures and bring about some kind of social change. however conceived, then the postmodern approach, which eschews generalizations and emphasizes deconstruction, can only have a limited role in that endeavour. The second is the development of another kind of orthodoxy among feminists which advocates the postmodern approach as *the* way forward and appears dismissive of other kinds of work.[53] Not only does such a stance attempt to undermine other feminist positions, it also refutes the pragmatism which has been argued for in feminist research.[54] One element which is missing in most discussions of such work is the nature of the *external* constraints which are frequently faced. Not least of these are lack of time, money and other resources, in addition to the requirements imposed by funding bodies. That such facts intrude into and colour the research undertaken needs to be acknowledged. To the hard pressed researcher, being asked to reflect on intractable epistemological concerns can sometimes appear to be something of a dispensable luxury.

Critical Issues for Feminist Research

Currently, behind all the issues so far discussed in this chapter, there would seem to be three major and related concerns confronting feminists engaged in empirical social research. These are to do with the role of experience, the importance of 'race' and other forms of diversity, and the question of objectivity. One of the early driving forces of feminism was to challenge the passivity, subordination and silencing of women, by encouraging them to speak about their own condition and in so doing to confront the experts and dominant males with the limitations of their own knowledge and comprehension. Thus, the legitimacy of women's own understanding of their experiences is one of the hallmarks of feminism. An emphasis on experience is not, however, unproblematic. To begin with there is no such thing as 'raw' experience. Post-structuralist thinking clearly demonstrates that the very act of speaking about experience is to culturally and discursively constitute it.[55] People's accounts of their lives are culturally embedded. Their descriptions are, at the same time, a construction of the events that occurred, together with an interpretation of them.

The researcher is also, of course, involved in interpretation. There has been some discussion about this amongst feminists, with the suggestion that to do anything other than simply let women 'speak for themselves' constitutes violation. The problem with this is that it overlooks the fact that *all* feminist work is theoretically grounded; whatever perspective is adopted, feminism provides a theoretical framework concerned with gender divisions, women's oppression or patriarchal control which informs our understanding of the social world. It is disingenuous to imply otherwise. No feminist study can be politically neutral, completely inductive or solely based in grounded theory. This is a contradiction in terms.

Also at issue here is that, although women's experience may constitute a starting point for the production of feminist knowledge, it is not sufficient for understanding the processes and practices through which this is organized.[56] Dorothy Smith has written that

> A sociology for women must be able to disclose *for* women how their own social situation, their everyday world is organized and determined by social processes which are not knowable through the ordinary means through which we find our everyday world.[57]

To repeat and describe what women might have to say, while important, can lead to individuation and fragmentation, instead of analysis. Feminism has an obligation to go beyond citing experience in order to make connections which may not be visible from the purely experiential level alone. When researching women's lives we need to take their experience seriously, but we also, as Maureen Cain argues, need 'to take our own theory seriously' and 'use the theory to make sense of ... the experience'.[58] This is an interpretive and synthesizing process which *connects* experience to understanding.

One example, which draws particular attention to this issue, is the question of difference (as opposed to *differance*) in feminist literature[59] and the importance of diversity in women's experiences, based on social attributes such as class, sexuality, race, ethnicity and disability. To focus on such differences in terms of experience alone has several consequences. First, it encourages benign description which concentrates largely on distinctions in lifestyle, cultural practices etc. Second, it can exclude practices which oppress people with disabilities, an analysis of racism, classism, homophobia, heterosexism and detailed structural explorations of how specific forms of oppression are legitimated and maintained. Third, to imply that matters of class are significant to the experience of the working class alone, that 'race' is important for only some ethnic groups (for to be 'white' is also to have ethnicity), or that sexuality is relevant only to lesbians and gays is to miss the point. For these things structure *all* our lives, no matter how invisible they might be in experiential terms, and we are not excused from confronting them because we are not members of a particular oppressed group. The points made here are also relevant to the position of the standpoint epistemologies. It is not enough for each of the issues, so conveniently lumped together in the category 'difference', to be located in the experience of oppression of particular groups. If feminism is to fully confront racism and heterosexism, if it is to be able to analyze the interrelationships between class, race, gender and other forms of oppression, then it cannot let its focus of research remain with experience alone. One way of going beyond this is to use our theoretical knowledge to address some of the silences in our empirical work. It is not always necessary to include women who are white, black, working-class, lesbian or disabled in our research to be able to say something about racism, classism, heterosexism and disableism.

A final matter here concerns objectivity. Ramazanoglu has explained this in terms of how to produce scientific knowledge about meanings and social relationships, when people understand and experience these differently.[60] This is a problem that feminism shares with sociology more generally, although, as already discussed, some have advocated a feminist notion of 'strong' objectivity, while others have dismissed it as a problem altogether. But perhaps the issue is not so much about objectivity (with its positivistic connotations of facticity), nor of value-neutrality (and the supposed null effect of the researcher on her research), as about the soundness and reliability of feminist research. Feminist work needs to be rigorous if it is to be regarded as intellectually compelling, politically persuasive, policy-relevant and meaningful to anyone other than feminists themselves. At the moment, it appears that this is more easily dealt with on a practical level than on an epistemological one. At the very least this call for rigour involves being clear about one's theoretical assumptions, the nature of the research process, the criteria against which 'good' knowledge can be judged and the strategies used for interpretation and analysis. In feminist work the suggestion is that all of these things are made available for scrutiny, comment and (re)negotiation, as part of the process through which standards are evaluated and judged.

This chapter indicates that there is no one answer to the question 'what is feminist research?' and many contested issues of method, methodology and epistemology remain. It is clear, however, that, in contrast to more conventional discussions of research, which have a tendency to be somewhat arid, the debate within feminism is vibrant and dynamic. The issues that have been discussed here are important for feminism in several ways. Not only do they inform the research process, they also influence the empirical knowledge to be produced and the theoretical knowledge which will be constructed. The outcomes are, therefore, crucial for feminism taken as a whole.

Notes

The author is grateful to Bob Coles and Rosemary Deem for comments on an initial draft of this chapter.

1. Harding (1987). p. 2.
2. See, for example, Kelly *et al.* (1992a); Reinharz (1992); Stanley and Wise (1990).
3. See, for example, Bowles and Duelli Klein (1983); Reinharz (1983); Graham (1983).
4. For example, Cicourel (1974); Filmer *et al.* (1972).
5. Graham (1983, 1984).
6. Bowles and Duelli Klein (1983); Graham (1983, 1984); Stanley and Wise (1983).
7. Kelly *et al.* (1992a).
8. For the former see, for example, Stanley and Wise (1983); for the latter see, for example, Martin and Roberts (1984).
9. Maynard (1989). ch. 2.
10. The various positions are discussed in Harding (1986).
11. Bryman (1988). p. 42.
12. *Ibid.*, p. 125.

13. Marsh (1979).
14. Research on equal opportunities policies in the Careers Service, conducted with Bob Coles and Jo Riding, involved sending a questionnaire to all Principal Careers Officers in Great Britain to find out what kind of policies, with regard to gender, were in place, and what sorts of administrative procedures were being followed to ensure such policies were being pursued successfully, and to construct a catalogue of innovatory or good practices. A content analysis of policies and all relevant literature received was also undertaken. See Coles *et al.* (1988) and Coles and Maynard (1990). The research on women employed in the tourist sector was directed by Roy Carr-Hill and myself. In this, questionnaires delivered to the place of work were supplemented by interviews. See Carr-Hill and Maynard (1989).
15. Brannen (1992); McLaughlin (1991).
16. See also Kelly *et al.* (1992a).
17. Kelly (1988), p. 6.
18. Cook and Fonow (1986); Bowles and Duelli Klein (1983).
19. Duelli Klein (1983).
20. Cook and Fonow (1986); Gelsthorpe (1990).
21. Stanley and Wise (1993).
22. Oakley (1981).
23. Finch (1984).
24. Gelsthorpe (1992), p. 216.
25. Scott, S. (1984); Smart (1984).
26. Gelsthorpe (1990), p. 93.
27. Fonow and Cook (1991a).
28. Stanley and Wise (1993).
29. Duelli Klein (1983).
30. Opie (1992), p. 64.
31. Kelly (1988).
32. Kirkwood (1993).
33. Stanley and Wise (1991).
34. Kirkwood (1993).
35. Hammersley, M. (1992).
36. Smith (1988b).
37. MacKinnon (1982), pp. 23–4.
38. Flax (1987).
39. Harding (1986).
40. *Ibid.* It should be noted that Harding's critique is of empiri*cism*, which fetishizes facts as the only valid objects of knowledge, and not of empirical work *per se.*
41. *Ibid.*, p. 195.
42. Haraway (1988); Rose (1983); Stanley (1990a).
43. Harding (1991), p. 149.
44. *Ibid.*, p. 164.
45. Stanley and Wise (1990), p. 28.
46. Stanley and Wise (1993).
47. Stanley and Wise (1990). p. 41.
48. *Ibid.;* Harding (1991), p. 138.
49. Ramazanoglu (1989b).
50. *Ibid.*
51. Flax (1987); Nicholson (1990).
52. Smart (1990), p. 83.
53. For example, Hekman (1990).
54. Kelly *et al.* (1992a); Stanley and Wise (1990).
55. Foucault (1981, 1986).
56. Ramazanoglu (1989b).
57. Smith (1986), p. 6.
58. Cain (1986), p. 265.
59. Whereas 'difference' relates to diversity conceived in experiential terms, '*differance*' refers to competing constructions of meaning in a post-structuralist or postmodernist sense.
60. Ramazanoglu (1989b), p. 437.

CHAPTER 8

TWO FEMINISTS IN SEARCH OF AN INTERVIEW PRACTICE

LESLIE R. BLOOM

Are interviews a sort of neutered social encounter, divorced from issues relevant to other social situations, so that you accept behavior in interviews that you might expect to challenge elsewhere?
—Ribbens 1989, 579

Introduction

The first time I met Olivia was a chilly autumn night in 1990 when we were both attending a lecture given by Evelyn Fox Keller. A year later, when I began to seek participants for my study, she expressed an interest in being a respondent. Olivia was a second year professor at the university, and she identified herself as a feminist teacher.

At first I was worried about including her in the study because we knew so many of the same people in the university community, and I thought that this would jeopardize her anonymity. When I raised this concern, she told me that she knew that some people who read my work and knew her might figure out that she was the participant, but that this was something she could cope with. She also said that she really wanted to have both this opportunity for reflection on her life and the experience of being a research participant. Her desire to participate seemed to outweigh the risk of being identified. A second concern I raised was about my own discomfort with having a participant who was a professor, one who knew so many of the people I knew; I worried that this would make me feel very self-conscious. However, after some additional discussion about this concern and how we might deal with it, we agreed to work together. In the fall of 1991, Olivia (she chose the name because one of her favorite actresses is Olivia de Havilland!) and I began to work together.

In this chapter, I specifically focus on the interviewing process as central to research relationships in feminist methodology, particularly when the focus is on collecting personal narratives. Further, I examine the complexities of and then problematize the nature of power in research relationships. Toward these ends, I examine Olivia's and my discussions about and reflections on researcher and respondent roles in the interviews. My goals are to make sense of how feminist methodology was employed in practice and to reconceptualize it from the vantage point of hindsight.

Reprinted from *Under the Sign of Hope: Methodology and Narrative Interpretation*, by Leslie R. Bloom, 1998. Copyright © 1998 State University of New York Press.

Beginning Interviews

Olivia's and my first interview took place in her house. I entered the house with the usual anxieties of a first meeting and fears of a novice researcher. These anxieties and fears made voices screech in my mind: What am I going to say? What kind of respondent will she be? Because Olivia was a professor who was familiar with feminist methodology, I also had fears of being found incompetent in her eyes.

The living room we sat in was light, airy, and lovely, and I delighted in the hot-pink carnations in the vase on the coffee table. Like Olivia, I too enjoy keeping flowers in my house, and she told me about a great florist in town where I could, and subsequently did, buy flowers. Her cats joined us on the couch, and I admitted to her that cats make my eyes itchy and that they are my least favorite animals, in hopes that she would get them away from me! As she later joked, "My cats were very fond of you so I knew that you were okay. They are very good judges of character!" After we talked for a while about her house, gardening, flowers, and the merits of cats versus dogs, we began to discuss where our work together would lead.

Initially, Olivia and I talked about what I would do in terms of observing her teaching and what kinds of disclosures about my presence we would make to her graduate students. We discussed how we would keep the interviews unstructured, particularly that I would not be preparing interview questions for her. I also talked about how I was interested in using Olivia's narratives as a grounding from which theoretical decisions could be made. Indeed, we spent quite a lot of time talking through issues—how theory may be *a priori* or truly emerge from the "raw data" of narratives. We also talked about how I would be using feminist theory consistently and overtly as a lens through which to understand her life stories, while the other theoretical orientations that I would use would come later, depending on Olivia's narratives.

Our conversation was animated. We were both enthusiastic about being able to talk about books, theories, and methodological issues together, and we were eager to come to some mutual understanding about these in the context of feminism. I certainly felt more comfortable talking with her about methodology as this conversation progressed. Olivia then told me that one of the reasons she wanted to be in the study was out of a "sisterly desire to assist a feminist doctoral student," so it was no surprise that we were both excited about the prospect of exploring feminism and feminist methodology together.

Olivia too recalls the first part of this meeting as being enjoyable:

> I remember the first meeting. After our initial small talk, you took out the tape recorder and we began to talk about the project. This felt comfortable and it helped me to learn a little more about you; I had a chance to listen to you talk and learn a little about how you think. Perhaps more importantly, I was able to see how you interacted with me in a casual conversation. We spoke of our views on life history research and our thinking seemed quite compatible. I remember you said, "I don't know where this is going," in speaking about the project, which helped me to see that you really didn't have a plan all laid out. And I liked that.

Yet I did have a plan in my mind, albeit somewhat nebulous. What I did not have were interview questions! Although we did not discuss this plan at the first interview, Olivia and I had agreed that we shared the goal of embarking on a feminist methodological expedition. My plan might be described as an attempt to put into practice the following propositions that I had culled from various readings in feminist methodology and qualitative methodology more generally in preparing to do this research:

1. Feminist methodology should break down the one-way hierarchical framework of traditional interviewing techniques. Feminist interviews should be engaged, interactive, and open-ended. Feminist interviews should strive for intimacy from which long-lasting relationships may develop. Feminist interviews are dialogic in that both the researcher and respondent reveal themselves and reflect on these disclosures.

2. Feminist researchers give focused attention to and nonjudgmental validation of respondents' personal narratives.

3. Feminist researchers assume that what the respondents tell is true and that their participation is grounded in a sincere desire to explore their experiences.
4. In feminist methodology, the traditional "stranger-friend" continuum may be lengthened to be a "stranger-friend-surrogate family" continuum, which can allow the connection between women to be a source of both intellectual and personal knowledge.
5. Identification with respondents enhances researchers' interpretive abilities, rather than jeopardizes validity.
6. Through working closely with another woman, particularly a feminist, a sense of identification with her may emerge that can be a powerful source of insight.
7. Feminist researchers strive for egalitarian relationships with their respondents by making space for them to narrate their stories as they desire; by focusing on issues that are important to respondents; by returning transcripts to the respondents so they can participate in interpretation; and by respecting the editorial wishes of the respondents regarding the final product or text.

Further, I was beginning the interviews with Olivia with a strong interest in phenomenology. During that fall semester when I began interviewing Olivia, I was taking a course on the "Anthropology of the Body" with Professor Michael Jackson and reading his book, *Paths to a Clearing: Radical Empiricism and Ethnographic Inquiry* (1989). I was intrigued by the concept of radical empiricism and very interested in phenomenologically exploring the body (Bloom 1992). As Hammond, Howarth, and Keat explain, in phenomenology the focus is on the experiences of the individual and how an individual views herself as a subject-in-the-world (Hammond, Howarth, and Keat 1991). Therefore, in order to achieve this focus, feminist phenomenological interviewing "requires interviewer skills of restraint and listening as well as interviewees who are verbal and reflective. [An interviewer] asks almost no prepared questions" (Reinharz 1992, 21). Rather, questions emerge from the narratives of the interviewees. The major characteristic of feminist phenomenological interviews is that they are interviewee guided rather than researcher guided. Interviews tend to begin with one general question such as, "tell me about X" (Reinharz 1992, 21). While phenomenology is not inconsistent with feminist methodology, at that time I did not recognize the important contradiction between feminist methodology's call for conversational interviewing as a grounds for friendship building (Oakley 1981) and feminist phenomenology's call for researcher restraint.

To start the interview with Olivia, I suggested that she tell me about her early childhood, the situations or circumstances she remembered that, as I phrased the question, "might shed some light on who you are today as an *embodied* person." From my question emerged a number of stories about Olivia's childhood and family as she was growing up. Her first story, which focused on herself as a physically active and daring child (discussed in chapter 4), particularly reflects her concern with answering my question about embodiment. While Olivia's narratives of childhood seemed to me a smooth movement from discussing methodology to beginning the narration of her life history, for her the experience was quite different. She later recalled that

> when we stopped talking methodology and began the "formal" discussion about my life, our interaction seemed to change. Early in this discussion I sensed your reluctance to continue in a conversational mode. I felt like our conversation went from a comfortable dialogue to an unnatural monologue with the spotlight on me. You began asking some questions. And I told stories in response to those questions. I think we fell into a pattern of being the good listener and the good respondent.

Was I a "good listener"? What, for that matter, constitutes 'a "good listener" or "good researcher" in this situation? I recall that when I listened to the tapes later that day after this first interview, I criticized myself for talking too much. I would not have characterized myself as a "good listener"! And yet now, as I listen again to the tapes and read the transcripts of this first interview, I see that I did do quite a lot of listening that day, particularly during the earlier part of Olivia's narration.

Most of my contributions in the early part of the interview were questions to Olivia.

In her narratives, Olivia talked about playing sports as a child and the seriousness in the 1950s with which girls were socialized to femininity. My questions to her included: "Do you remember [your mother] telling you that you should act more 'lady-like'?"; "Did your father encourage you in your sports?"; "Do you remember a point where you started being more of what people would have thought of as feminine?"; "Do you remember how you felt about that?"; and "Do you find that this has carried over in your [adult] life?" These were the questions that I asked to encourage Olivia to talk more extensively about how she interpreted her experiences. Additional questions I asked were quite straightforward, and were used simply to clarify or elicit additional information. For example, I asked if her brother, about whom she was speaking, was older than she was. Early in the interview, I did not respond spontaneously to her stories with parallel stories, as one might with a friend in a "normal" conversation. However, toward the latter part of the interview, Olivia mentioned the apparent stereotypes of her parents' roles and relationship, and I joked, "Not in my family." My spontaneous response, perhaps particularly because it was spoken in a bantering tone, seemed to open the door for Olivia to ask me a direct question about my family, and for a short time we did talk more conversationally as I described my family in a parallel fashion to her descriptions. This part of the tape (noted in the transcripts) has a lot of laughter in it, which perhaps helped strengthen the connection between Olivia and me. Minister suggests, for example, that joking and laughter "reinforce communal bonds" (Minister 1991, 33).

Given my description of these interactions, would I be considered a "good listener" or "good researcher" in the context of feminist methodology? Feminist methodology, we recall, encourages interviews to be more like conversations between friends, and it encourages the researcher to give both focused attention to the respondents and non-judgmental validation of their experiences. Feminist phenomenological methodology asks researchers to be restrained and to listen carefully, constructing questions from what the respondents narrate. By describing me as a "good listener" Olivia acknowledged that I provided her with the focused attention and validation; however, I did not provide her with good conversation.

Being a "good listener" did not necessarily make me a "good researcher" for Olivia. To her, my responses seemed like "silences" in contrast to her longer narratives and more in-depth storytelling. This made her uncomfortable and self-conscious, as she later revealed:

> I do recall that whenever I ended a story you just remained silent, so I thought, well what else can I say? I was talking all of the time and all I could think about was how much I hated people who talked all the time. I also remember feeling compelled to reveal parts of my life that I had not shared with many of my closest friends. Why is that? Good girl syndrome? Like the good respondent, I felt obligated to keep talking, to say important things, and to do a mind and heart dump so that you would get the information you needed.

Being a "good respondent" is as problematic a role as being "good listener." To be a good respondent, it is necessary to be able to talk, to narrate experiences and feelings, and to reflect on these. From my perspective, Olivia *was* a "good respondent." She did respond to my obvious desire to "get the information" and to hear her narrate and then reflect on her life stories. Further, her initial narrative responded to the topic I had posed. And while my goal of eliciting her storytelling was not in conflict with her own desires to experience being a respondent, what Olivia felt in that first interview was that she had an obligation to "do a mind and heart dump" *for me*. From her perspective, being a "good respondent" was not a pleasurable experience.

When I left Olivia's house that day, I sensed her discomfort. She was agreeable about setting up another interview date, but there was a tension in the air. I wondered if I had offended her, particularly when I suggested to her that the hour was up. I was trying to keep to the time out of respect for her, but I worried that she felt that I had ended our time together abruptly, as if I had not been interested in what she had been telling me. I felt anxious and felt that I had disappointed her in some way.

When Olivia and I met again the following week, I began the session with the following question: "Would it be more natural or more comfortable if I talked more?" I hadn't planned to ask that; it just came to mind when we first sat down! Olivia responded that she too had wanted to talk about her feelings and reactions to the session, and she was curious about how I felt about it. What resulted was a rich conversation about our research goals and expectations.

One of the first things we talked through was whether or not it was useful to us to have me pose questions to her as a way to frame the interviews and amplify her stories. Olivia responded that my questions were helpful because they "keep the conversation going," but she also wanted me to "reflect on things or respond to things" more from my own experiences, because "it makes me think a little more about it. And it makes me feel less egocentric." She further revealed that what was most uncomfortable about the mostly one-sided storytelling was that it felt "more like a therapy kind of situation than it does an interchange or conversation. For me it's not that I can't do this, it's just that it probably isn't what I would picture as a true participatory exchange."

A few months later, reflecting again on the first interview, Olivia further revealed what the source of her discomfort had been:

> I have always been a private person. I have shared my life with a few special friends only. That first session felt intrusive. You knew so much about me and I knew nothing about you. My shell was broken open and the vulnerable meat of the clam was splayed to the sun, to the world. Yours remained tight and impenetrable.

From Olivia's description of me, I could visualize myself as the anthropologist in Paule Marshall's novel, cited at the opening of this book: For her, I was the "Juju" woman, the one who "could get a stone to tell you its life history . . . while you stay mum, your business to yourself." It was rather horrifying to hear her tell me that to her I seemed like the embodiment of the type of researcher I strove to challenge!

During the second interview I told her that I was uncomfortable with talking too much and felt that I was supposed to ask her questions and focus on her. I admitted to her that I was not comfortable self-disclosing too much during the interviews. Additionally, I told her that I worried about "speaking too much [because it] seems to me like I was taking control." I told her that I didn't want to take control because it wouldn't give her enough freedom to talk or to narrate her stories in an uninterrupted, open way. For Olivia, the freedom that I wanted to create for her through my restraint diminished the "naturalness" of the interaction:

> I think that questioning is a natural thing to do with each other. But what I found was happening was I kept cutting myself off from asking you questions that, if I were having a conversation with you, I would naturally ask. And so you have all these odd cuts in the conversation so that it ceases to be fluid and interactive.

Articulating what we each felt we were supposed to do and not supposed to do as respondent and researcher was central to our conversation. Olivia's sense that she was supposed to tell me lots of stories and not supposed to ask me questions about my life experiences, even though she wanted to, governed her interactions. Olivia was also governed by her concern that "we were going to get the things that you need to know." I was governed by a sense of responsibility to be an attentive listener who did not talk very much, especially about myself My ability to be an attentive listener and Olivia's ability to be a good storyteller were mutually nourishing; however, we agreed that we were not nourishing a relationship that either of us felt comfortable with. This conversation was extremely powerful for us, and it helped us to plan ways that we could better achieve feminist methodology. As Olivia later described it,

> This was probably one of the most powerful sessions we had together. It wasn't easy telling you that I wasn't comfortable because I didn't know how you would feel about that. I didn't want you to think I was being critical of you, but rather reflective about the process.

I did not feel criticized by Olivia when she revealed her thoughts to me, and I too found this session exciting in terms of our shared efforts to find a way that we could both feel comfortable with the research relationship.

Negotiating Research Relationships

At the end of this pivotal second conversation, Olivia and I talked about ways to shift the relationship to be more comfortable for each of us. We agreed that we would explore issues Olivia wanted to explore about her life and discussed whether these issues would be useful for my work. We made plans to get together in non-interview situations so that we could get to know each other on social and presumably more equal ground. And most importantly, we agreed to shift the agenda from interviewing about Olivia's life, to interweaving conversations about our life histories with conversations about methodology and the process that we were going through In Olivia's words, this was a time of "feeling kindredship and mutual struggle, neither of us knowing what the balance of conversation should be or exactly how to achieve it, but knowing that we wanted to explore the possibilities together."

One of the ways that Olivia and I tried to reframe or normalize our relationship was by meeting in a restaurant for lunch. I have always treasured lunchtime as a time to meet with women friends. Lunch with friends is an oasis in a busy day filled with dry meetings, paper grading, and superficial conversations with acquaintances unavoidable in the halls. I don't remember what we talked about that day, but what we talked about didn't matter to me as much as the fact that we did talk, and that we could meet over food rather than over a tape recorder.

During this phase of trying to get to know each other better, I went to one of her classes and participated in the activities she had planned. It was good for me to see her as a professor interacting with her students. On another day, instead of leaving the house before her husband came home as I usually did, I accepted the offered glass of wine and took the time to chat with them both. We also went to a Bonnie Raitt concert together, and had a wonderful time. All of these things helped me to get to know more about Olivia, "the meaningful actions that [she] engages in, the processes and activities that compose [her] life" (Reinharz 1983, 179). These shared activities gradually led to my gaining an understanding of Olivia as someone with whom I was able to talk more comfortably.

For Olivia, the first time she came to my house during the winter was special in terms of her getting to know me:

> I particularly remember the day you invited me to your home for one of our sessions. All traditional methods texts say that the interview should be held in a place where respondents are comfortable, like their homes. But ironically, seeing your home actually made me more comfortable with you. I felt I knew you better. You had beautiful spring flowers that you had "forced" from bulbs on the table, pictures of people you loved on book cases and the refrigerator—with a special place on your computer for a framed picture of your new nephew Zachary. You became a real person to me.
>
> Also, it was in your home where you were the most forthcoming about your own life. You told me about your family, your friend Patricia, and your confusions about relationships. We often don't think about the importance of the inquirer being comfortable if she is to engage in a truly interactive process. For the first time I began thinking of you as a friend and not simply as the person with whom I was working.

This time of trying to work things out to be more in accord with feminist methodology was good for both of us, and we both felt that we had achieved more rapport and a higher level of comfort. But had we found the feminist methodology we were searching for?

The Heteroglossia of Research Interviewing

Toward the end of our work together Olivia and I reflected on the time we had spent together, from our initial interview, through interpretations of her narratives, to the final writing of the research. While the focus of the interviews remained primarily on Olivia's life, she did come to feel that "we did a good job at [working toward establishing trust and intimacy] and it got easier and easier as we went further along in the process. And my discomfort with you which I had earlier completely went away later in the process." We agreed that although we had come a long way with creating a feminist framework for the research and had achieved a strong level of comfort with each other, we had not achieved the kind of conversational patterns that Oakley (1981) recommends. Nor, we agreed, did we form a friendship out of the research relationship, Olivia suggested that one reason we did not find new ways "to be" in the research relationship was that we were being pulled back to "old behaviors":

> I have all these expectations or notions built into my head about what my role is and what your role is and I think you do too. Even though we say we're going to do something different, I think it's hard to break out of that and we don't realize what some of the things are that are pulling us back to those old behaviors.

Olivia's analysis of the limitations on our attempts to create a feminist methodological context for our work together raises questions about how individuals do find ways to resist, subvert, and challenge normative roles and ways of thinking and believing and what prevents them from doing so. Bakhtin ([1935] 1981) also asks these questions about human agency in his theory of heteroglot discourses or heteroglossia. His theory is an enabling heuristic for making sense of successes and failures at "breaking out" of "old behaviors."

Bakhtin ([1935] 1981) explains that all individuals speak in heteroglot discourses that are governed by and emerge from the social, historical, and cultural contexts in which they are uttered. These socially situated heteroglot discourses are made up of a combination of authoritative and internally persuasive discourses that influence our thinking and behaviors. Internally persuasive discourses may be thought of as ways of thinking and being in the world in ways that engage us from within. They appeal to our hearts and minds. Internally persuasive discourses challenge the status quo, the authoritative discourses, and therefore, they function as interpretive lenses that allow us to see ourselves and the world in new and enabling ways. Bakhtin suggests that individuals who experience internally persuasive discourses discover awakened consciousness.

In contrast, authoritative discourses impose themselves from without. According to Bakhtin, an authoritative discourse has great power to "determine the very bases of our ideological interrelations with the world, the very basis of our behavior," because an authoritative discourse is

> located in a distanced zone, organically connected with a past that is felt to be hierarchically higher. It is, so to speak, the word of the fathers. Its authority was already *acknowledged* in the past. It is *a prior* discourse. It is therefore not a question of choosing it from among other possible discourses that are its equal. It is given (it sounds) in lofty spheres, not those of familiar contact. Its language is a special (as it were, hieratic) language. It can be profaned. It is akin to taboo, i.e., a name that must not be taken in vain. (original emphasis, Bakhtin [1935] 1981, 342)

Further, because "we encounter it with its authority already fused to it," an authoritative discourse "binds us, quite independent of any power it might have to persuade us internally" and profoundly influences our behaviors, relationships, and ways of thinking (Bakhtin [1935] 1981, 342).

Analyzing how qualitative research methodologies in general and feminist methodology in particular are constructed through these various authoritative and internally persuasive discourses, may shed light on why it was so difficult for Olivia and myself to locate ourselves comfortably within or achieve feminist methodology. Therefore, in the following section of this chapter, I would like to use Bakhtin's discourse framework for locating multiple, conflicting authoritative discourses and internally persuasive discourses. Further, I examine how these discourses functioned in the interviews specifically and the research relationship more generally. My hope is that this form of discourse analysis will help me begin to unravel some of the complexities of the interview process and research relationship. The three central discourses I will examine are the discourses of feminist methodology, the discourses of communication, and the discourses of the roles of power.

Discourses of Feminist Methodology

> One indicator of friendship is having someone to confide in and knowing that person will listen sympathetically to what you have to say. Another indication is reciprocity, in that confiding and listening are usually shared activities between close friends.... [But] close friends do not usually arrive with a taperecorder, listen carefully and sympathetically to what you have to say and then disappear.
> —Cotterill 1992, 599

One of the difficulties that Olivia and I experienced in our work together was coming to terms with what we each expected of ourselves and of each other as two women engaged in this feminist research project. The terrain for working out these expectations was the interview session, that specialized location where our roles were revealed, negotiated, and reframed. What I want to explore here are ways that Olivia and I were negotiating between competing internally persuasive discourses of models of feminist methodology, each with its own concept of the roles of "good researcher" and "good respondent" in the interview sessions.

Looking back at Olivia's articulations of her desires for the interview process, I see her use of words such as participatory, interactive, and conversational. As she explained at the end of the project, "I do like the more conversational approach where we would just talk and the stories would just come out ... even though it is a very inefficient way to do things." Thus, her conception of feminist methodology appears to be in accord with the model that Oakley (1981) and her followers describe. This model suggests that the interview becomes a site where women converse, reciprocate self-disclosure, and develop a relationship more akin to or resembling friendship or sisterhood than the conventional middle ground between stranger and friend.

For Olivia, therefore, we might say that Oakley's model of feminist methodology was internally persuasive and that she used this framework to evaluate herself and me. In this discourse, being a "good respondent" meant that she would have an interest in me as a person, encouraging me to talk about myself while I also encouraged her to talk about herself. Our success in doing this would be apparent in the equal amount of self-disclosure between us. Further, this discourse of feminist methodology attempts to diminish role differentiation, and her stress on the importance of conversation may also indicate an attempt to break down the differential roles of researcher and respondent. Her willingness to meet with me outside of the interview sessions, despite her busy schedule, also indicated that she was attempting to put into practice Oakley's suggestion that research respondents need to be committed and involved in the process. This conception of the research relationship seemed to be stable as an internally persuasive discourse to Olivia throughout the process and may offer one explanation of why being a "good respondent" (in the sense of her doing the majority of talking) was not achieving feminist methodology for Olivia.

But what was internally persuasive for me? What model was in my mind for being a "good researcher"? Going into the research, I recall being internally persuaded by Oakley's methodology as well as other descriptions of the empowering relationships between women articulated by feminist biographers and anthropologists. I believed that conversations between women would be a powerful alternative to the conventional interviewing and would therefore constitute a subversion of conventional qualitative methodology. I was intrigued by the idea that role differentiation could be diminished or eliminated.

However, I was also equally taken with the idea of interviews as respondent-guided—the kind of interviews where the respondents felt that they were given the opportunity for expressing themselves as they wished. This phenomenological model of feminist methodology, when put into practice, competes with the Oakley model. Engaged intellectually by two competing internally persuasive discourses, I see now that my practices leaned more toward the second model based on feminist phenomenology. Therefore, when striving to be a "good researcher," especially after Olivia articulated her discomfort with the first interview, I attempted to find a balance between the two models, not only to respond to Olivia's need not to be spotlighted, but also to fulfill my own interest in trying to "be" a feminist interviewer.

Upon reflection, I can see that what made this balancing difficult was that, in practice, the feminist phenomenological model was more internally persuasive (as my interview style attests) and more productive. In theory, however, the Oakley model was more internally persuasive because of its overt feminist challenge to conventional methods of interviewing and its privileging of the relational. Working with two discourses of feminist methodology simultaneously caused a tension for me, one that was not resolved during the research process.

Discourses of Communication, Or, Emily Post Does Discourse

> Olivia: I never did know what you were interested in or how much you wanted me to go into things. And that's because you were a good listener. You just took it in like you were willing to take what I gave you. You didn't want to probe or make me feel that I had to say something. I think that you were concerned with stepping in too far.... And I was concerned with telling you far more than you wanted to know or with boring you.

In his book on research interviewing, Charles Briggs (1986) suggests that in an interview situation, the rules of social science interviewing "preempt" the rules of normal, polite, social communication. He explains that "playing by the rules" of interviewing

> prompts the subordination of other components of the interaction to the mutual goal of the conscious transmission of interesting, accurate, and abundant information. When the system is working properly, the participants accept the roles assigned to them by the structure of the interview. Interviewers provide clear and interesting questions that enable respondents to exhibit their knowledge. These roles preempt the criteria that normally define these individuals' roles in society. (Briggs 1986, 56)

But what happens if interview rules and roles *compete with* rather than *preempt* the normal rules and roles of polite social communication, particularly between women? I want to suggest that in Olivia's and my interview sessions, we each struggled with multiple authoritative discourses and internally persuasive discourses of what constituted appropriate communication in our interview sessions. The two operative and influential authoritative discourses of communication were the discourses of *polite social communication* and *feminine communication*. Further, we were each working within a different model of interviewing depending on our internally persuasive feminist methodology. Finally, we each had a "normal" communication pattern that came into play in the interview sessions. When we look at communication with each of these concepts in mind, the palette from which we draw our understanding of communicative roles gets very messy in an intersubjective relationship.

Polite social communication, which I am framing as an authoritative discourse, might be characterized as turn-taking, listening and responding to the other, "making a long story short," and only asking questions appropriate to the relationship. Feminine modes of communication are similar to polite social communication. While feminine models may also be thought of as an authoritative discourse for women (even though they may also be personally internally persuasive), they emphasize empathetic listening and creating a relationship through personal disclosures (as opposed to only talking about things and events). As a communication event, the Oakleyan model of interviewing, which I am arguing Olivia was drawn to, is based on the feminine mode of communication as is typical of conversations found in friendships. The phenomenological model of interviewing that I was practicing, although it draws from the "feminine" skills of listening, might be thought of as a specialized speech event with specific roles for the participants that are not the same roles as those in "normal" polite social communication. With this set of interrelated ideas about communication in mind, how might we better understand the ways in which the discourses of methodology and communication influenced how Olivia and I communicated with each other?

Thinking about the relationship between my ways of communicating and my ways of interviewing has revealed to me, among other things, the powerful effects of my socialization as a child. When I was growing up, I was taught these rules of polite social communication, especially the rule about never asking people personal questions. I think that my mother thought it especially important that my brother and I be able to converse politely and properly with anyone in any social situation and we had a lot of practice doing so because we were always included at dinner parties when my parents had guests at the house. My parents quite frequently entertained their friends and graduate students from the university where my father worked. One event from when I was eleven or twelve stands out vividly for me. My parents had invited a couple to dinner: he was an Egyptian graduate student and she was from Boston and worked in Senator Ted Kennedy's office. I was fascinated with them and wanted to ask them lots of questions—him about Egypt and her about Senator Kennedy. I don't recall what I asked, but I clearly recall being told by my mother that it was not polite to ask whatever it was that I did ask. I remember feeling ashamed and embarrassed—demoted from dinner participant to child.

With this kind of disciplined socialization, it is no wonder that I felt both complimented and relieved when Olivia said that I was "very respectful not to probe beyond what I want to talk about": this is the good feeling that comes from fulfilling the demands of an authoritative discourse. Kathryn Anderson, reflecting on her interview style, also found herself adhering to the conventions of social communication, which made it difficult for her to ask probing questions:

> [M]y interview strategies were bound to some extent by the conventions of social discourse. The unwritten rules of conversation about appropriate questions and topics—especially the one that says "don't pry!"—kept me from encouraging women to make explicit the range of emotions surrounding events and experiences they related. (Anderson and Jack 1991, 13)

The authoritative discourse of polite social communication, especially as associated with women and feminine modes of communication, further mediated the kinds of responses I felt able to articulate when I was with Olivia. I felt that I was "forbidden" from voicing reactions to her narratives that might have been interpreted by her as confrontational. While there were times I may have thought to myself that "this can't be the whole story" or "that sounds like a romanticized memory," I never articulated these types of responses (even if more tactfully phrased) to her in the event that she would be offended by my doubt or disbelief.

If we think of feminist methodology as an internally persuasive discourse, however, we might have called it into practice to challenge these authoritative discourse/feminine requirements of politeness. But this only works if we think of feminist methodology as offering recommendations for interviews as different communication events than normal conversation. For example, feminist and feminist phenomenological methodologies encourage us or give us permission to ask probing questions as a means to help women explore their lives beyond the superficial. Further, feminist methodology may require us to voice disbelief and doubt, for as Reinharz explains, while feminist researchers may "begin a research project intending to believe the interviewee [they] *should* question the interviewee if she begins not to believe her" (emphasis added, Reinharz 1992, 29). A feminist phenomenological interview particularly may be seen to challenge polite social communication in that the respondent does not "make a long story short," but rather tells the long story in order to put her experiences into the words that she and the researcher can interpret.

I have also come to understand, with the help of my friend Patricia Sawin, that what might have been internally persuasive to me about feminist phenomenological interviewing is that it fit my customary communication style. In a discussion about this chapter, Patricia told me that after knowing me for two years, she felt that I had told her only a fraction about myself compared to what she had told me about herself. She also said that I have a discourse pattern that encourages the other person to talk more and that I typically do not share confidence for confidence. Therefore, when Olivia suggested that my "silences" about myself stemmed from how I was communicating as a researcher, she is right because, with hindsight, we can say that phenomenological interviewing was internally persuasive to me because of the type of person I am; but this is only part of the picture. It is equally true to say that this is how I communicate in a close friendship. But Olivia could not possibly have known this, because she and I were in an interview, not a friendship relationship.

Given the information she had about me, Olivia rightly concluded that the predominant way I communicated with her was not conducive to achieving her regulative ideal of feminist interviewing as a conversation. However, if Oakley's model allows for women to converse in "natural" ways, then my behavior might be judged equally successful, because I was doing what was natural *for me* in a friendship conversation. The problem, then, is having a rigid ideal of what a feminist, feminine, or woman-to-woman conversation should be as an internally persuasive discourse.

Feminist methodology may also be seen as supportive of and supported by the authoritative discourse of polite social communication and an equally authoritative discourse of feminine modes of communication. When the emphasis of feminist methodology is on conversation, turn-taking, and empathetic listening, women are asked to be polite not only in a conventional sense, but also in the feminine sense as well. Thus, internally persuasive and authoritative discourses work together to mediate the type of interactions that are possible and desirable. For Olivia, this may have been the case particularly in light of her articulations of feeling natural and unnatural. Being the focus of the interview made her feel that she was engaged in an "unnatural monologue" and that withholding questions from me was unnatural because "questioning is a natural thing to do" in social communication. It was not natural to tell a long story, and both feminist methodology and polite social communication contributed to her self-consciousness when she did so:

> One of the things I found in the interviews was that this autobiographical method of research was very inconsistent with how I typically talk about my life. I usually talk about my life through and with other people. If Jan [her best friend] and I were to sit and talk about my life, she would explore things, she would ask questions, and she would say, "well I remember a time" and then she would talk about herself. It would be a much more back and forth process.

If we return to the idea discussed above—that Olivia and I were working with competing internally persuasive discourses of feminist methodology—my will toward practicing feminist phenomenology created a conflict for her. That is, my interview style asked her to be a "good respondent" in the model that was internally persuasive to me, not her. Briggs describes this imposition of the researcher's communication style on the respondent as "communicative hegemony" (1986, 90). However, if the respondent is uncomfortable with the role, or if, as Briggs explains, respondents "are not accustomed to playing this [interview] game ... they are unlikely to accept this suppression of normal social criteria and ... may frame the 'interview' as another type of communicative event" (57). In a sense, making the communicative event into a conversation between women, rather than an interview, is what Olivia attempted when she "broke the frame" of phenomenological interviewing by asking me questions about myself.

Discourses of the Roles of Power

The final discourse that I want to explicate is the multiple roles of power in feminist methodology. I specifically want to examine how Olivia's multiple subject positions of respondent, professor, and feminist and my multiple subject positions of researcher, student, and feminist constituted a complex web of conflicting authoritative discourses and internally persuasive discourses about power in our research relationship.

In order to examine conflicting discourses of power in the research relationship, I want to mobilize one of the central claims of feminist theory—that individual, multiple subject positions are central to human relationships and that these multiple subject positions take on different meanings and levels of importance depending on particular situations and interpersonal relations. In the research relationship, the way that power functions depends greatly on the interrelationship between the multiple subject positions of the people involved in the research and the different discourses about those subject positions. What is crucial to unravel is the ways that conflicting discourses about the role of power in research emerge in research relationships as a result of the hierarchical structuring of particular subject positions. My hope is that by examining the conflicting discourses about the multiple subject positions in Olivia's and my research relationship, I may be able to discuss the complexities of the roles of power in feminist methodology and destabilize stagnant, authoritative discourses about how power functions in qualitative methodology more generally.

The Role of Power in Researcher-Respondent Subject Positions

> Little attention has been given to power relationships between women other than to assume that the researcher, by virtue of her education and status, is always more powerful than her respondents.
> —Cotterill 1992, 599

In qualitative methodology, it is a commonly accepted belief that the researcher has "The Power" in research relationships. As Laura Nader asserts, historically researchers have *consciously* placed themselves in positions of power because "the entirety of field work... depend[ed] upon a certain power relationship in favor of the anthropologist" (Nader 1969, 289). Recent critiques of how researchers' power is a form of colonization have raised awareness about the need to be reflective about how they exercise power over respondents. Similarly, Judith Stacey (1988) warned feminists about the ways that we may also participate in exploitative power relationships with our respondents.

The common thread in this genre of writing is that the respondent is envisioned in a social position "below" the researcher who, to use an often used (but rather offensive) term, "studies down" from a position of power over respondents. Researchers are understood to have power for many reasons. One central reason is that they often have economic and educational advantages over respondents, and in many cases, they also have white or male privilege. In feminist methodology, researchers are also said to be imbued with power because they are more free to leave the relationship than are the participants, which is a "significant power difference which remains constant" (Armstead 1995, 628; see also Stacey 1988). Even when feminist researchers themselves locate ways in which power is "shifting and, at times contradictory," they may still "accept that power ultimately lies with the researcher rather than the researched" because researchers, while they listen to what women want to say during interviews, "retain the power of redirection" and walk away with the interview data they wanted (Reay 1995, 211–213; see also Ribbens 1989). However, as Margaret LeCompte asserts, when researchers engaged in critical or emancipatory research define the respondents uniformly as "disempowered or oppressed, regardless of how the informants define themselves... the research is deeply constrained (Le Compte 1993, 13).

These totalizing conceptions of power consolidated in the researcher, while initially based on an understanding of the exploitative and colonizing practices of anthropology, have now become reified into an authoritative discourse. This discourse has constrained our research and therefore does not help us to understand power as complex, contextual, fluctuating, and, above all, relational (Friedman 1995). That is, while the *awareness* of researchers has been raised by the important critiques of colonization and exploitation, the discourses about the role of power are oversimplified. Further, the idea that the researcher has "The Power" over the participant is an authoritative, binary discourse that may function to disguise the ways that "the flow of power in multiple systems of domination is not always unidirectional" (Friedman 1995, 18). Power is situated and contextualized within particular intersubjective relationships. In accordance with Cotterill, I want to make a case that "issues of power and control which are fundamental to the research process shift and change, and within the interview situation the researcher as well as the researched is vulnerable. To deny that is to deny the subjective experience of the researcher as a woman" (1992, 605).

One effect of having power reified into an authoritative discourse is that we talk as if researchers *inherently* have more power in the research relationship. This problematic way of talking about the role of power stems from the dangerous and erroneous conflation of researcher power with researcher responsibility. This mode of discourse is further compounded by conflating researcher responsibility with researcher exploitation; it suggests that having the authority to collect data, interpret it, and produce a text is *inherently* an act of exploitation or even violence done by the researcher to the almost victimized respondent.

As a researcher, I began the process under the spell of this authoritative discourse of the role of power. I felt a great deal of anxiety about researcher power; consequently, I felt that putting into practice certain internally persuasive aspects of feminist methodology (such as those discussed above) would diminish my "power," and Olivia and I could have a more egalitarian relationship. Such is the lure of Oakley's model of feminist methodology! Therefore, I was particularly careful about giving the transcripts and tapes of the interviews to Olivia so that we would have shared ownership of them. We also used her transcripts to decide together on the path our subsequent interviews would take so that the research would answer questions she had about her own life (Harding 1987). I negotiated with Olivia the amount of input she wanted in the interpretation of her narratives; discussed with her the theoretical ways I would interpret her narratives; and worked with her on the final text so that she was comfortable having it go public. In accord with feminist methodology, I gave up what would conventionally be thought of as the researcher's interpretive or authorial "rights" in favor of shared rights, authorial responsibility, and diminished researcher power. Implementing these strategies into our research relationship did not mean that I was "giving up power" if power is taken to mean that I used her interviews for my work and my academic gains; however, implementing these strategies did mean that I was trying to be responsible to my work and my commitment to Olivia.

Further, because I gave Olivia the transcripts of the interviews and she was and is using them as the grounding for her own academic publishing, the stagnant notion that power is only situated in the researcher was challenged. Similarly, the idea that only the researcher gains from the research, making the research inherently exploitative, is also challenged. This example of how the unidirectional notion of power can be disrupted in practice emerges specifically from this type of relationship within an academic community; furthermore, it is connected with the context of "researching up" that is discussed next.

The Role of Power in Professor-Student Subject Positions

If power is contextual, complex, and unidirectional, this picture of the role of power in our research relationship is incomplete, for it negates the importance of Olivia's and my different subject positions as professor and student. This second hierarchical arrangement may be described as "researching up." Researching up is defined as conducting research in an elite setting with respondents who have more power and status than the researcher (Nader 1969). As Leslie Roman notes, researching up needs to be a feminist goal so that we can better understand "the cultural practices, social relations, and material conditions that structure the daily experiences and expectations of powerful groups" (1993, 307).

What seems curious to me now, is how conscious I was during the research process of diminishing conventional ways that researchers manifest power, while not consciously dealing with the ways that, as a student interviewing a professor, I was disempowered in this relationship. The unequal distribution of power that stemmed from "researching up" was probably more critical to our relationship than I understood at that time, and the authoritative discourse of the role of power in the professor-student relationship may well have functioned as a hidden episteme in the research relationship. This discourse becomes more apparent if we look at what was *not* said during the research process about power and if we reexamine the interviewing process in light of this discourse.

Like being a researcher, being a professor comes with an authoritative discourse of structural superiority in place. While feminist pedagogy offers a competing discourse, the structural realities of university life have managed to maintain the higher position of the professor in relation to the student. Therefore, while Olivia was not in a position to grade me—she was not "my" professor—her role as professor was no less powerful in my mind. Because we were in the same academic community, I felt worried about being judged by Olivia and feared offending her much of the time. I do not mean to suggest that I experienced incapacitating worries and fears; rather, it was an unspoken undercurrent that made me extra careful of how I interacted with her or interpreted her narratives. It was a vulnerability I experienced. While a desire to not hurt, offend or exploit each and every one of our respondents makes us hyperconscious of what we do and say, "researching up" adds an extra dimension to this concern: one that may contribute to the authoritative discourse of polite social communication—being the good polite, researcher and the "good listener."

Because she was the professor—that is, she was someone located structurally as my superior in an institutional setting we shared—she was positioned in such a way as to question my competence and knowledge based on her more advanced status in the academic community. For this reason, it may be understandable why I felt that I had failed in feminist methodology even though she did not say to me that I had: I knew I was not fulfilling her model of and desire for feminist methodology. This structural inequity may also, in part, account for Olivia's feelings of vulnerability as a respondent: it is not part of the usual professor-student relationship for the professor to disclose so much to a student.

The Role of Power in Feminist and Other Subject Positions

Olivia and I embarked on this project with the explicit naming of ourselves as feminists. Being feminists was not something either of us treated as insignificant: it was a consciously motivated component of our lives and subjectivity as well as a major commitment in our academic research and teaching. Feminism was a powerful, internally persuasive discourse to each of us. Reflecting on this shared commitment, I am left wondering how much this sense of identification with each other as being in a "sisterhood" contributed to the silence around issues of unequal power—as if our feminism had the magic to render impotent not only the power inequities discussed above, but a few additional ones as well.

Although Olivia and I intersected in some ways in terms of our subject positions and accesses to "power," we were more different than we ever discussed, and power was quite ambiguous and fluctuating in terms of our biographies. One similarity that gave us equal privilege was that we are both heterosexual. This made it easy for us to talk about gender differences and concerns about our heterosexual relationships as feminists. Our feminism also helped us to understand why we both highly valued our close friendships with our women friends. We did not, however, talk about our religious (ethnic) differences. While we often discussed racism in the public schools and our efforts in anti-racist pedagogy as white educators, my being Jewish complicates the notion of a shared whiteness, since whiteness is a modern social construction that not all Jews, including myself, share (Sacks 1994). Fluctuating axes of social class were also a grounding of our relationship. As a former corporate V.P. and then university professor, Olivia was middle-class when we worked together; however, she had been raised working-class and, as she told me, still felt a deeper connection with and concern for working-class women than middle-class women. Olivia's affiliations and history locate her simultaneously as working and middle-class.

I had been raised middle-class, although this positioning is not as simple as it sounds. At the time we were working together, I was not financially stable. I had just returned with very little from the Peace Corps and was living off student loans and graduate assistantships. As a result, I did not have a lot of financial security at that time, particularly given that graduate students often had to wait until just before the new academic year to find out if we were even being funded. Another disjuncture was that although Olivia and I were almost the same age, because we had grown up in such different regions of the country to such different families, we had less in common in terms of cultural experiences than we would have if we had been raised within the same class or if we had both grown up in the same type of geographic setting.

I highlight these differences, not because I think that they need to be interpreted exhaustively, but to provide some insight into the multiple grounding from which our fragile intersubjective research relationship emerged. Caught up in the research process and in our emerging relationship, I did not recall Mies's (1991) warning that identification, such as our identification as feminists, can cause blindness to differences, especially differences in power that exist among women.

Rethinking Feminist Methodology

> The alternative to relativism is partial, locatable, critical knowledges sustaining the possibility of webs of connections called solidarity in politics and shared conversations in epistemology.
> —Haraway 1991, 191

As a mode of examining women's lives, feminist methodology was and remains internally persuasive to me. I recognize the need to be able to talk about feminist methodology without resorting to either complete relativism or rule making (Reinharz 1992). Perhaps the only way to do this is to make sure that our discussions leave in the ambiguity and complexity of what it means to do feminist inquiry without denying that we can and sometimes do achieve feminist methodology; however, we still must acknowledge that each instance of feminist methodology differs because field relations are contextual and contingent, and intersubjective relationships are always in flux.

What I hope to add to the growing literature on feminist methodology through this chapter is my understanding of how important it is for us to have a more complex view of the concept of power and intersubjectivity in feminist methodology, one that emerges from an understanding of a complex relationship that is not permanently fixing the researcher in a position of power. Rather, we need to be more open and sensitive to how multiple desires and subject positions become enacted in various ways in our power dynamics. We need to reject conceptions of power in feminist methodology that do not attend to power's ambiguous ways of becoming manifest in interviews (see Newton and Stacey 1995). Power may fluctuate and vary depending not only on who is in the relationship, but on what is going on in both the researchers' and participants' lives and in the research process. Allowing for a more complex analysis of power dynamics through an understanding of intersubjectivity will help us to see how in some research relationships, power may alight on respondents and researchers with differing degrees of weight at different times and with different meanings in specific contexts.

We cannot eliminate power in research relationships, as much early feminist methodological literature hoped was possible. Nor, as Petra Munro maintains, is power "something feminists . . . have to be against," for power is not the same as domination (1995a, 110). Rather, the goal for feminists is to understand power's complexities and its influences on how we interact with each other. We must learn to notice power, analyze it, and name it when it manifests itself as it undoubtedly will.

I hope that my reflections on Olivia's and my research relationship contributes to the discussion about what a feminist interview can or might be as we rethink power and subjectivity in research. Questioning the idea that interviews are "unnatural" and that conversations are "natural" and therefore more desirable for feminist methodology is helpful for this discussion. If we understand both interviews and conversations as "natural" speech events, then striving for conversations in place of interviews may be less important in feminist relationships. What is more important is not whether one does an interview or a conversation, but that there is a resonance between the context of the relationship and the type of speech event that people have. If the relationship is a research relationship, perhaps it is less "natural" to have a conversation than to have an interview. What is at stake is the type of interview. Bakhtin's ([1952–3] 1986) later writings about "speech genres" are helpful here.

Bakhtin suggests that the form our utterances or speech acts take depends upon the genre in which we speak. He explains that "the genre in turn is determined by the subject matter, goal, and situation of the utterance" ([1952–3] 1986, 152–3). If the goal of the speech act is to collect narratives, then the genre is an interview: therefore, as Patricia Sawin argues, "perhaps it is a bit daft to say 'let's have a conversation' when what we want are narratives to interpret" (personal communication, 1997). Further, if the situation of the utterance or the goal of the speech act is friendship, then is it equally contradictory to say that we can conduct an interview? While I am not fully prepared to say that more conversational interviewing is not desirable, for I still think it is, I have come to understand that interviewing women is not a contradiction in terms. Rather, interviewing women *in exploitative ways* or in a dominating relationship is unethical and antithetical to feminist methodology. The participants of each relationship, then, will need to find a way of communicating in the project and will need to communicate about *how* they communicate. While this may mean that there is no way to say what feminist methodology is or is not in terms of methods in the field (and I think this is the point that Reinharz makes in her book, *Feminist Methods in Social Research*, that I had to experience to understand), it nonetheless must always have the political agenda of finding ways to better understand women's lives—our own, those of our participants, and the relationship between the two.

CHAPTER 9

DIS-STANCE AND OTHER STANCES: NEGOTIATIONS OF POWER INSIDE FEMINIST RESEARCH

MICHELLE FINE

> [F]eminist politics is not just a tolerable companion of feminist research but a necessary condition for generating less partial and perverse descriptions and explanations. In a socially stratified society, the objectivity of the results of research is increased by political activism by and on behalf of oppressed, exploited and dominated groups. Only through such struggles can we begin to see beneath the appearances created by an unjust social order to the reality of how this social order is in fact constructed and maintained.
> —Sandra Harding, *The science question in feminism*

Throughout the 1980s and into the 1990s, feminist researchers have been chatting busily in the kitchen of the social sciences, delighted by the vivid and disruptive possibilities of our scholarship on women's lives. Voyeurs, often, to the deep and radical transformations washing through the humanities and theoretical work in the social sciences. And dis-stanced witnesses to the breaths of feminist activism still alive. As we sit we worry, collectively and alone, about how best to unleash ourselves from our central contradiction—being researchers and being activist feminists (Crawford and Gentry 1989; Crawford and Marecek 1989b; Fine and Gordon 1989; Flax 1990; Hare-Mustin and Marecek 1990b; Kahn and Yoder 1990; Lykes and Stewart 1986; Morawski 1990; Parlee 1990; Payton 1984; Russo 1984; Smith and Stewart 1989; Unger 1990; Wittig 1985). We document at once the depths of violence and discrimination embedded in the lives of women (Amaro & Rousso 1987; Belle 1990; Blackman 1989; Brown 1987a; Gilkes, 1988; Lykes 1989; D. Smith 1987); and the complex maneuvers by which women deny such oppression (Crosby et al. 1989; Gilligan 1993; Majors 1994; Miller 1976; Taylor 1983). Harvesting substantial evidence of gender-, race/ethnic-, class-, disability-, and sexually-based oppression, we also know how meticulously women take care, make nice, and rarely, in our research, express outrage at the gendered politics of their lives (Brodbey and Fine 1988).

Many—not all—feminist social researchers report these stories, girdled in by now-stretched-out, but nonetheless intact, notions of neutrality and positivism, reliability, and truth. In narratives parallel to some of the women we study, some of us still smuggle our knowledge of social injustice into a discourse of science that fundamentally contains, and painfully undermines, the powerful politics of activist feminism. As is often the case with moments of social containment, feminists in the social sciences carry weighty evidence for a passionately disruptive transformation of our disciplines. And yet, as relatively new kids on the academic block, we also carry domesticating

---

Reprinted from *Power and Method: Political Activism and Educational Research*, edited by Andrew Gitlin, 1994. Copyright © 1994 Routledge (US).

responsibilities to keep this social science appearing dispassionately detached. And we manage these responsibilities differently. Valerie Walkerdine (1986) narrates this problem when she writes:

> I want, therefore, to demonstrate that women, positioned as teachers, mothers, carers and caring professionals... are held absolutely necessary for the moral order: they are responsible. This responsibility places women as at once safe, yet potentially dangerous (the bad mother). It places them as responsible for ensuring the possibility of democracy, and yet as deeply conservative.... My argument is that, quite simply, women of all classes have been placed as guardians of an order from which it is difficult to escape. (63)

Traditional social sciences have stubbornly refused to interrogate how we as researchers create our texts (see Becker 1986; Brodkey 1987; Reinharz 1988; Rosaldo 1989; Semin and Gergen 1990). Most particularly, this is the case for psychologists, where it is presumed that psychological theories and methods simply neutralize personal and political influences. When we write about "laws" of human behavior, our political stances may evaporate. That we are human inventors of some questions and repressors of others, shapers of the very contexts we study, coparticipants in our interviews, interpreters of others' stories and narrators of our own, is sometimes rendered irrelevant to the texts we publish. While feminists vary in how we manage this treacherous territory, we all manage it.

Donna Haraway (1988) caricatures the epistemological fetish with detachment as a "God trick... that mode of seeing that pretends to offer a vision that is from everywhere and nowhere, equally and fully" (584). Such narrative removal seeks to front universal truths while denying the privileges, interests, and politics of researchers. With Haraway and Sandra Harding (1986), feminist scholars have interrupted the membrane of objectivity across the academy and in their respective disciplines, refusing containment and asking how feminist politics can and do play, explicitly and subversively, in our intellectual lives.

Feminist researchers have clearly gained the most ground in the rethinking of our relationships with "subjects" and of the politics of power that loiter between us. British psychologist Sue Wilkinson (1986) characterizes feminist research in the following way:

> First, there is its reflexive and self reflective quality... an emphasis on the centrality of female experience directly implies its corollary: "ourselves as our own sources." Similarly, du Bois has emphasized the way in which the knower is part of the matrix of what is known; and Reinharz has required the researcher to ask her/himself how s/he has grown or changed in the process of research.
>
> Second, the relationship between the researcher and the researched will evidently be very different from that of the traditional "experimenter" and "subject." In feminist research, at the very least, both are to be regarded as having the same status: as participants or collaborators in the same enterprise....(13)

An early advocate of advocacy-based research, psychologist Carolyn Payton has long prodded the field about the bankruptcy of its "professional" social commitments. In the 1980s, she wrote:

> Please keep in mind that almost two decades ago the APA grappled with the question of the propriety of psychologists as a group advocating social change or taking part in political advocacy, and a process for dealing with such matters are suggested. Yet, here we are in 1983 still denying that we have any responsibility for or obligation to the society in which we live. We behave as if, along with study in this discipline, we inherit a dispensation from considering all matters concerning social consciousness barring those related to guild issues. (1984, 392)

Wilkinson (1986), Tiefer (1990), Payton (1984), and Patricia Hill-Collins, like feminist scholars across disciplines, situate themselves proudly atop a basic assumption that all research projects are (and should be) political; that researchers who represent themselves as detached only camouflage their deepest, most privileged interests (Rosaldo 1989). For instance, Hill-Collins articulates convincingly a political aesthetic that characterizes Black feminist consciousness.

But if feminist research is directed toward social transformations and if practices of "neutrality" primarily laminate deeply conservative interests of the social sciences, then feminist academic researchers face a central dilemma. That dilemma concerns the self-conscious role our politics can play as we pursue, passionately, our intellectual work. To this dilemma, Donna Haraway offers us passionate detachment through which she believes "men are bound to seek perspectives from those points of view which can never be known in advance, that promise something quite extraordinary, that is, knowledge potential for constructing worlds less organized by axes of domination (1988, 585)." Once full detachment has been revealed as illusory and the stuff of privilege, we can dip into the questions of "stances."

Reflecting on Stances

Studies which have as their focal point the alleged deviant attitudes and behaviors of Blacks are grounded within the racist assumptions and principals that only render Blacks open to further exploitation. The challenge to social scientists for a redefinition of the basic problem has been raised in terms of the "colonial analogy." It has been argued that the relationship between the researcher and his subjects, by definition, resembles that of the oppressor and the oppressed, because it is the oppressor who defines the problem, the nature of the research, and, to some extent, the quality of interaction between him and his subjects. This inability to understand and research the fundamental problem, neo-colonialism, prevents most social researchers from being able accurately to observe and analyze Black life and culture and the impact racism and oppression have upon Blacks. Their inability to understand the nature and effects of neo-colonialism in the same manner as Black people is rooted in the inherent bias of the social sciences. (Ladner 1971, iii)

Joyce Ladner wrote more than twenty years ago about the inherent racism, bred and obscured, that occurs when researchers elect to stand outside and reify the Self-Other hyphen of social research. Ladner knew then that researchers who sought to invent coherent Master Narratives needed, and created, "Others." The sharp edges of those works were best secured by the shadowed frays of the Other.

The articulate professional voices sounded legitimate against the noisy vernacular of the Other. The rationality of the researcher/writer calmed against the outrage of the Other. These texts sought to close contradictions, and by so doing they tranquilized the hyphen, ousting the Other, achieving dis-stance.

This essay here presumes that all researchers are agents, in the flesh (Caraway 1991) and in the collective, who choose, wittingly or not, from among a controversial and constraining set of political stances and epistemologies. Many deny these choices within veils of "neutrality," describing behaviors, attitudes, and preferences of Others, as if these descriptions were static and immutable, "out there," and unconnected to "Self" or political context. They represent these texts as if they were constructed without author(ity). Such texts refuse to ask why one research question or interpretation has prevailed over others, or why this researcher selected this set of questions over others. Such texts render oblique the ways in which we, as researchers, construct our analyses and narratives. Indeed, these texts are written as if researchers were simply vehicles for transmission, with no voice of their own. Such researchers position themselves in dis-stances, as ventriloquists.

Other researchers, in their texts, import to their work the voices of Discarded Others who offer daily or local meanings, which seemingly contrast with and interrupt hegemonic discourses and practices. With "voices" and "experiences" as the vehicles for social representation, these researchers typically claim little position for Self (Scott 1992).

Finally, some researchers fix themselves self-consciously as participatory activists. Their work seeks to unearth, disrupt, and transform existing ideological and/or institutional arrangements. Here, the researcher's stance frames the texts produced and carves out the space in which intellectual surprises surface. These writers position themselves as political and interrogating, fully explicit about their original positions and where their research took them.

I paint these three stances—ventriloquy, "voices," and activism—for feminist researchers to roll around, unpack, try on, discard. It seems crucial in the 1990s that social researchers who seek to be explicitly political (e.g., feminists, African Americans, poststructuralists, neo-

Marxists), as well as those who refuse to so acknowledge, should consider aloud, and together, the decisions we have made, through leakage and through pronouncements, in our research.

Ventriloquy

> Once upon a time, the introduction of writings of women and people of color were called politicizing the curriculum. Only *we* had politics (and its nasty little mate, ideology), whereas *they* had standards. (Robinson 1989)

Ventriloquy as a stance relies upon Haraway's God trick. The author tells Truth, has no gender, race, class, or stance. A condition of truth-telling is anonymity, and so it is with ventriloquy. Dramatizing ventriloquy as an academic stance, I offer a snip of institutional biography from an institution with which I've had some intimacy—The University of Pennsylvania.

In 1985, the University of Pennsylvania denied tenure to Dr. Rosalie Tung, then Associate Professor at the Wharton School. While Wharton justified the decision to not tenure Tung "on the grounds that the Wharton School is not interested in China related research," Tung maintained that her Department Chairman had sexually harassed her and that, after she insisted on a professional and not sexual relationship, he submitted a negative letter to the University's Personnel Committee, adversely influencing her tenure decision.

Tung brought the case to the Equal Employment Opportunity Commission (EEOC), which undertook an investigation, requesting documents from Penn. When the University refused to provide these documents, the Commission subpoenaed for Tung's tenure review file as well as those of the five male faculty members who had been tenured just prior to Tung. Penn argued the need to exclude all "confidential peer review information," and failed to provide (1) confidential letters written by Tung's evaluators, (2) the Department Chairman's letter of evaluation, (3) documents reflecting the internal deliberations of faculty committees considering applications for tenure, and (4) comparable portions of the tenure review of the five males. The Commission denied the University's application, for these exclusions.

The case made its way to the Supreme Court. Four years after denial of tenure, in a 9–0 vote, the Supreme Court found against Penn in a decision in which the justice wrote:

> We readily agree with the petitioner regarding that universities and colleges play significant roles in American society. Nor need we question, at this point, petitioner's assertion that confidentiality is important to the proper functioning of the peer review process under which many academic institutions operate. The costs that ensue from this disclosure, however, constitute only one side of the balance. As Congress has recognized, the costs associated with racial and sexual discrimination in institutions of higher learning are very substantial. Disclosure of peer review materials will be necessary in order for the Commission to determine whether illegal discrimination has taken place. Indeed, if there is a "smoking gun" to be found that demonstrates discrimination in tenure decisions, it is likely to be tucked away in peer review files. (*University of Pennsylvania v. EEOC* 58 USLW 4096, 1990)

Penn sought relief on the basis of that well-known precedential exemption for questions of confidentiality—*United States v. Nixon*, with Penn positioning itself with Nixon. Characterizing its First Amendment claim as one of "academic freedom," Penn argued that tenure-related evaluations have historically been written by scholars who have been provided with assurances of confidentiality. Such provisions of confidentiality, they argued, enable evaluators to be candid and institutions to make tenure decisions on the basis of "valid academic criteria." Disclosure of documents or names, Penn continued, would undermine the existing process of awarding tenure, and instigate a "chilling effect" on candid evaluations and discussions of candidates. They wrote:

> This will work to the detriment of universities, as less qualified persons achieve tenure causing the quality of instruction and scholarship to decline ... and also will result in divisiveness and tension, placing strain on faculty relations and impairing the free interchange of ideas that is a hallmark of academic freedom. (University of Pennsylvania, Petitioner v. EEOC, *U.S. Law Week* 1-9-90, #88-493)

To which the justices responded:

> Although it is possible that some evaluations may become less candid as the possibility of disclosure increases, others may simply ground their evaluations in special examples as illustrations in order to deflect potential claims of bias or unfairness. Not all academics will hesitate to stand up and be counted when they evaluate their peers.

Following the Supreme Court decision, Penn submitted to the EEOC a set of redacted documents from the Tung file in which all names and identifiers were removed from the texts. Penn maintained that if faculty were forced to commit their names to their judgments, that they would cower from "true" evaluations. The University took the terrifying position that only when authorship is obscured will truth prevail among academics.

Penn spoke for (but not with) its faculty. The position taken reminded many of Donna Haraway's God trick, in which researchers pronounce "truths" while whiting out their own authority so as to be unlocatable and irresponsible. Penn's position vis-à-vis the Supreme Court embodied institutionally researchers' refusal to acknowledge their personal involvements as they construct the very worlds they write about.

Ventriloquy is perhaps most bold when a university mandates the whiting out of authorship, but can be found in all research narratives in which researchers' privileges and interests are camouflaged. Ventriloquy means never having to say "I" in the text (Clark 1990); means treating subjects as objects while calling them subjects. And, ventriloquy requires the denial of all politics in the very political work of social research.

Voices

It's easy to be glib about the ventriloquism of researchers who seek asylum behind anonymous texts or texts in which they deny their authorial subjectivities. Somewhat closer to home, however, is a critical analysis of the ways in which scholars—critical ethnographers in particular—have used voices to accomplish a subtler form of ventriloquism. While such researchers appear to let the "Other" speak, just under the covers of those marginal, if now "liberated" voices, we hide. As Shulamitz Reinharz has written:

> By dealing in voices, we are affecting power relations. To listen to people is to empower them. But if you want to hear it, you have to go hear it, in their space, or in a safe space. Before you can expect to hear anything worth hearing, you have to examine the *power dynamics of the space and the social actors.*
>
> Second, you have to be the person someone else can talk to, and you have to be able to create a context where the person can speak and you can listen. That means we have to *study who we are and who we are in relation to those we study.*
>
> Third, you have to be willing to hear what someone is saying, even when it violates your expectations or threatens our interests. In other words, *if you want someone to tell it like it is, you have to hear it like it is.* (1988, 15–16) emphasis added

Voices offer a qualitative opportunity for scholars interested in generating critical, counter-hegemonic analyses of institutional arrangements. But they also offer a decoy. Through such work, many of us have been fortunate. We've collected rich and multi-situated voices from adolescents—dropouts in my case, teen parents for others (see Lesko 1988; McDade 1988; Sullivan 1990; Tolman 1990; Willis 1981). When I have spoken with adolescents, particularly low-income adolescents, it's consistently easy to gather up their stories of critique, dissent, contradictory consciousness, and quite vivid counter-hegemonic commentary, in order to tell a story. Low-income adolescents easily criticize their schools, challenge the relation of education credentials to labor-market participation, and name the hypocrisies that fuel societal terrors of sexualities (Fine and Zane 1989).

The ease with which such adolescents reflect (somewhat outrageous) versions of my own political stances, has grown more cumbersome, however, as my work has moved from gathering adolescent voices to soliciting those of adults. The stories of adults—be they teachers, parents, students, workers, etc.—constitute a much more dense mass of critical insights cast, typically, within "ruling-class" scripts (D. Smith 1987). A romantic reliance on these voices—as though they were rarified, innocent words of critique—represents a sophisticated form of ventriloquy, with lots of manipulation required. Unlike with teens, here I have struggled in the shadows of the voices of Others.

The complexities of relying upon adult voices are revealed in an evaluation research project involving low-income mothers of sixth-grade students living in Baltimore. Conducted collaboratively with Dr. Donnie Cook of the University of Maryland, this evaluation focuses on a Parent Empowerment Project developed by an advocacy organization for a randomly selected sample of 150 sixth-grade students and their parents or guardians.

The Baltimore women gave us (researchers and project staff) considerable pause about community organizing in the 1990s, but also gave us a chance to consider epistemological troubles with voices as a "raw form" of social science evidence.

Neither monolithic voices of critique nor single voices of institutional praise: These women were multiply situated and their perspectives were stuffed with social contradictions. The braiding of their commentary was rich, but not easily captured with the categories familiar to social analyses. Laced with perspectives of dominant classes, they wanted desperately to believe in public institutions, and at the same time they routinely witnessed the institutional inadequacies of the schools and felt absolutely responsible for the lives of children, who lived at levels of substantial economic disadvantage. These women set forth rich, complex, and hard-to-code voices (Condor 1986). Their experiences did not fit neatly the forms of theorizing available to me without my doing some "violence" to their raw narratives.

As Joan Scott has written on the topic of "experience," the presumption that we can take at face value the voices of experience as if they were the events per se, rather than stories about the events, is to dehistoricize and decontextualize the very experiences being reported. Scott argues that researchers who simply benignly transcribe social experiences fail to examine critically these constructions which seem so real to informants and are in such dire need of interpretation. Scott writes:

> The evidence of experience, whether conceived through a metaphor of visibility or in any other way that takes meaning as transparent, reproduces rather than contests given ideological systems—those that assume that the facts of history speak for themselves and, in the case of histories of gender, those that rest on notions of a natural or established opposition between sexual practices and social conventions, and between homosexuality and heterosexuality . . . the project of making experience visible precludes critical examination of the workings of the ideological system itself. (1992, 25)

Relying on "unadulterated voices" is fundamentally a decoy for an extended version of dis-stance and ventriloquy. Voices are, as Scott would contend, both "an interpretation and in need of an interpretation" (1992, 37). While researchers, particularly White feminists, need to worry about the imperialistic history of qualitative research that we have inherited and to contain the liberal impulse to "translate for" rather than "with" women across chasms of class, race, sexualities, politics, living arrangements, etc. (see Patai 1992), the refusal to theorize reflects either a form of theoretical condescension or hyper-protocol reserved only for Others with whom serious intellectual work and struggle are considered somehow inappropriate.

The interviews with the Baltimore women forced us to come clean; I had to reinsert consciously my interpretive self into my writings, with, but not through, the rendition of their voices. Researchers cannot write about/with/through adults' (or adolescents') voices as if the researchers had "said it all."

Social research cast through voices typically involves carving out pieces of narrative evidence that we select, edit, and deploy to border our arguments.

The problem is not that we tailor but that so few qualitative researchers reveal *that* we do this work, much less *how* we do this work.

A second dilemma arises when we rely on individual voices to produce social interpretations of group behavior. This often means repoliticizing perspectives narrated by people who have tried hard to represent themselves as nonpolitical. Our interpretations as researchers often betray the very concerted "individualism" and "apolitical nature" insisted on by narrators (Fox-Genovese 1991). This betrayal may well be essential analytically, but it nevertheless reflects the usually unacknowledged stances of researchers who navigate and camouflage theory through the richness of "native voices."

A third issue involves the popular romancing of the voices of women in poverty. Those of us who work to unearth personal stories tend to privilege contradiction, polyvocality, and subjugated voices. And then we often reproduce these voices as though they were relatively uncontaminated, free of power relations. Jill Morawski (1990), reminds feminists that, as we listen to the voices of Others, our work as psychologists is to critically interpret what we hear.

This critique of voices is by no means advanced to deny the legitimacy of rich interview material or other forms of qualitative data. On the contrary, it is meant for us to worry collectively that when voices—as isolated and innocent moments of experience—organize our research texts, there is often a subtle slide toward romantic, uncritical, and uneven handling, and a stable refusal, by researchers, to explicate our own stances and relations with these voices.

Before we leave voices, consider a most complicated instance of scholarly translation located at the hyphen of Othering—the brilliant work of Julie Blackman. A White social psychologist who works as an expert witness for White, Latina and African American battered women who have killed their abusers, Blackman enters courtrooms and retells the stories these women have told her—this time in standard English. She psychologizes and explains away the contradictions. She makes them acceptable. Blackman's project is to get these women a hearing from a jury of their peers. She has an impressive success rate for keeping these women out of jail (Blackman 1989).

Draped in white colonizing science, Julie and I and many Others have cut a deal. We invite the public to listen to the story because the teller is not the Other. Cut with the knives of racism and classism. Should we refuse? Do we merely reproduce power by playing to power? Do we regenerate the Other as we try to keep her from going to jail? Do we erase and silence as we trade on White/elite privilege?

As these scenes of scholarly translation vividly convey, feminist researchers are chronically and uncomfortably engaged in ethical decisions about how deeply to work with/for/despite those cast as Others and how seamlessly to represent the hyphen. I would differ with Judith Stacey when she writes:

> So, too, does the exploitative aspect of ethnographic process seem unavoidable. The lives, loves and tragedies that fieldwork informants share with a researcher are ultimately data-grist for the ethnographic mill, a mill that has a truly grinding power. More times than I would have liked, this study placed me in a ghoulish and structurally conflictual relationship to personal tragedy. (1991, 113)

To dis-stance is not to avoid the ethical complexities, or negotiations over power.

Activist Feminist Research

Activist research projects seek to unearth, interrupt, and open new frames for intellectual and political theory and practice (Fine and Vanderslice 1991). Researchers critique what seems "natural," recast "experience," connect the vocal to the structural and collective, spin images of what's possible. In such work, the researcher is clearly positioned (passionate) within the domain of a political question or stance, representing a space within which inquiry is pried open, inviting intellectual surprises to flourish (detachment) The text itself is conceived and authored with a critical eye toward "what is," attending seriously to local meanings, changes over time, dominant frames, and contextual contradictions. Within these texts, researchers carry a deep responsibility to assess critically and continually our own, as well as informants', changing positions. The strength of feminist activist research lies in its ability to open contradictions and conflicts within collaborative practices. Essential to an "activist" stance, then—be it feminist, African American, socialist-feminist, educational, or postmodern—is that researchers, activists, informants, and other audiences be engaged as critical participants in what Donna Haraway (1988) calls "power-sensitive conversations."

> Above all, rational knowledge does not pretend to disengagement: to be from everywhere and so nowhere, to be free from interpretation, from being represented, to be fully self-contained or fully formalizable. Rational knowledge is a process of ongoing critical interpretation among "fields" of

interpreters and decoders. *Rational knowledge is power-sensitive conversation.* Decoding and transcoding plus translation and criticism; all are necessary. (590)

Below, I try to capture some images of feminist activist scholarship, all of which share three distinctions. First, the author is explicit about the space in which she stands politically and theoretically—even as her stances are multiple, shifting, and mobile. Second, the text displays critical analyses of current social arrangements and their ideological frames. And third, the narrative reveals and invents disruptive images of "what could be" (Lather 1986).

Breaking the Silence

A move to activism occurs when research fractures the very ideologies that justify power inequities. In such work, researchers pry open social mythologies that others are committed to sealing. In the pieces of such scholarship cited below, we can hear the costs of breaking the silence for researchers at the margins.

In "Silence: Hispanic and Latina Women and AIDS," Ana Maria Alonso and Maria Teresa Koreck (1989) wedge open a political analysis of women and AIDS in the Latina community. They write about their contradictory loyalties to multiple intellectual, political, and cultural communities:

> The implications of denial are particularly deadly for Latina women.... Because of every way in which gender and sexuality are constructed, Latino men are not held accountable.... We almost did not write this paper. After much discussion, we decided that maintaining the silence is to cede terrain ... is to let dominant discourse define the politics of ethnicity, disease, sexuality and morality.... We can contest the power of the dominant discourses to define not only who we are and how we live, but also how we die. (57)

These women publicly resist in their narrative the cultures that both threaten and protect them. As border crossers themselves, holding membership in multiple communities (Rosaldo 1989) Alonso and Koreck refuse to collude in cultural or gendered betrayal. But as they remind us, while their project seeks to interrupt those silences which assault the lives of Latinas, the work of de-silencing is costly and dangerous to them.

Denaturalizing What Appears So Natural

Scholars interested in race, class, gender, sexuality, and disability know how quickly biological explanations seem to satisfy questions of perceived differences. These explanations float within an almost uninterruptible language of the "natural." If there is no other task that feminist activist researchers can accomplish, we can provoke a deep curiosity about (if not an intolerance for) that which is described as inevitable, immutable, and natural. Two examples may capture the work of splicing "what is" from "what must be."

Frigga Haug in a coauthored text *Female Sexualization*, writes with a German Marxist Feminist women's group committed to "collective memory work" on the sexualization of their bodies (1987). Sexualization, for the collective, involves the reduction and subjugation of women's bodies to a constant requirement to arouse male desire and, at the same time, to be normal. Haug and colleagues write the stories of their bodies with chapters focusing on hair, thighs, buttocks, cleavage, and parts that have grown to be sexually charged. These women track the sexual reconstruction of body parts once considered asexual. They spin histories of their social bodies and, by doing so, denaturalize that which appears to be so natural, so female, so in the body, and not the body politic. Their work forces a re-look at the social production of gender, sexuality, "nature," and, finally, desire.

Moving from bodies to classrooms, but still inside the unpacking of the natural, Patti Lather in *Getting Smart* (1991) invites researchers to look multiply at how we construct the stories we tell about others' data. She seeks to "explore what it means to write science differently" (xx) by framing and reframing interviews, reports, journal entries, and personal musings from her introductory women studies course. Interested in why women resist feminism, Lather refuses to tell the one natural story about these women. Instead, she spins four possible tales from her data:

> Each of the four tales I shall spin will be grounded in words generated via journals

and interviews from students across varied sections of this introductory women's studies class. Borrowing loosely from Van Maanen (1988), I call these a realist tale, a critical tale, a deconstructivist tale, and a reflexive tale. By "realist," I mean those stories which assume a found world, an empirical world knowable through adequate method and theory. By "critical", I mean those stories which assume underlying determining structures, for how power shapes the social world. Such structures are posited as largely invisible to common sense ways of making meaning but visible to those who probe below hegemonic meaning systems to produce counterhegemonic knowledge, knowledge intended to challenge dominant meaning systems. By "deconstructivist," I mean stories that foreground the unsaid in our saying, "the elisions, blind-spots, loci of the unsayable within texts" (Grosz 1989:184). Deconstruction moves against stories that appear to tell themselves. It creates stories that disclose their constructed nature. And, finally, by "reflexive," I mean those stories which bring the teller of the tale back into the narrative, embodied, desiring, invested in a variety of often contradictory privileges and struggles. (128–29)

By forcing readers to recognize the promiscuity of intellectual frames, within which we pour our data, Lather invites researchers and educators to "begin to understand how we are caught up in power situations of which we are, ourselves, the bearers [and to] foreground the limits of our lives and what we can do within those boundaries" (25). By text end, we can enjoy the freshness of Lather's questions: Who speaks? For what and to whom? Who listens? And we can recognize the partiality of any one interpretive frame, even if it is offered as the most natural or essential understanding.

Braiding Haug with Lather, whether the text is armpit hair or the story of women's resistance to feminism, both writers ask researchers/educators to engage critically in the process of interrogating how we have settled on the stories we tell; how else these stories could be told; how we can organize disruptively for "what could be."

Attaching What Is to What Could Be

Today there is a flurry of writing on "what could be," deepening social critiques of what "has been." By pressing readers to imagine what could be, a collection of writers has taken readers to the boundaries of current intellectual debates in order to conceive beyond, in order to provoke political possibilities. Such work is best exemplified by Lois Weis, in her text, *Working Class Without Work* (1990), and by Derrick Bell in his text, *And We Are Not Yet Saved* (1987). Work that disrupts ideological and theoretical "inevitables" must be recognized as deeply activist for social transformation.

In her text, *Working Class Without Work: High School Students in a De-industrializing America*, Weis describes an ethnography of White male and female students who attend a high school located in a recently deindustrialized working-class town. Weis analyzes working-class White male development as it is carved in opposition to young White women and adolescents of color, and she examines working-class White female development as an instance of incipient feminist awareness. She connects adolescent consciousness (male and female) to the erosion of labor markets and movements, and she anticipates theoretically that these young White working-class men could find comforting political respite within the New Right, while these young White working-class women could nestle comfortably within an emergent feminist politic. In so doing, Weis attaches her analyses of adolescent development to activist movements past and future. She achieves enormous theoretical advance by repoliticizing psychological development and by inviting readers to see how systematically schools depoliticize individuals from collective social movements that have shaped their lives.

As a talented critical ethnographer, Weis documents closely the ways in which schools not only reproduce but actually refuse to interrupt oppositional white male development. As a theorist of possibility, Weis advances these insights toward a rich melding of "what is" with a powerful sense of "what could be." She breaks silences and denaturalizes what is but, even further, she provokes readers to imagine multiple, postmodern possibilities of what could be, nurturing the social responsibilities among educators and readers to create that which is not yet.

Like Weis, Derrick Bell reframes what has been, and what could be, through a radical jolt of perspective. In *And We Are Not Yet Saved*, a series of legal chronicles, Bell writes through the voice and wisdom of fictitious Geneva Crenshaw. Each chronicle revisits a "racially based" judicial decision and shifts the historic discourse by forcing readers to tour U.S. history through a self-consciously African-American vantage point. The chronicles on desegregation, housing, and affirmative action force multiple readings of these decisions that were rendered ostensibly *for* people of color.

In the final chronicle, Bell describes the dystopia of the "Black Crime Cure." A group of young Black boys find some rocks that they eat, and in so doing they stop participating in criminal activities. Now, he notes, Whites can no longer reason that Blacks don't have housing, education, health care, or adequate living conditions because Blacks bring crime and poverty on themselves. With the Black Crime Cure, the White liberal explanation is removed. And he is relieved. These young boys pass the rocks onto their friends. All indulge, and pass them onto their children. Bell writes:

> Time does not permit a full recounting of how the Black Crime Cure was distributed across the country. While the stones seemed to give indigestion to whites who took them, they worked as they had in the cave for anyone with a substantial amount of African blood. Black people were overjoyed and looked forward to life without fear of attack in even the poorest neighborhoods. Whites also lost their fear of muggings, burglary and rape.
>
> But, now that blacks had forsaken crime and begun fighting it, the doors of opportunity, long closed to them because of their "criminal tendencies," were not opened more than a crack. All-white neighborhoods continued to resist the entry to blacks, save perhaps a few professionals. Employers did not hasten to make jobs available for those who once made their living preying on individuals and robbing stores. Nor did black schools, now models of disciplined decorum, much improve the quality of their teaching. Teachers who believed blacks too dangerous to teach continued their lackadaisical ways, rationalized now because blacks, they said, were too dumb to learn.
>
> Moreover, the Black Crime Cure drastically undermined the crime industry. Thousands of people lost jobs as police forces were reduced, court schedules were cut back and prisons closed. Manufacturers who provided weapons, uniforms and equipment of all forms to law enforcement agencies were brought to the brink of bankruptcy. Estimates of the dollar losses ran into the hundreds of millions.
>
> And most threatening of all, police—free of the constant menace of black crime and prodded by the citizenry—began to direct attention to the pervasive, long neglected problem of "white collar crime" and the noxious activities of politicians and their business supporters. Those in power, and the many more who always fear that any change will worsen their status, came to an unspoken but no less firm conclusion: fear of black crime has an important stabilizing effect on the nation (1987, 246–47)

Bell, throughout this text, assumes a disruptive narrative stance, unhooking the past, present, and future from the traditional, taken-for-granted notions. The text opens a series of social contradictions and unravels a powerful sense of activist possibility. Working backward (like Haug) and forward (like Weis and Austin), Bell explodes "common sense" (White?) notions of justice, entitlement, and progress and forces readers to reconsider explanations that have for so long suited, legitimized, and even perpetuated, racist hierarchies.

Both Weis and Bell position narratives inside intellectual spaces heretofore uncharted. They capture readers' imaginations with portrayals of adolescent identity and racial history cast in terms of what could be—impending with doom, and rich in possibilities.

Engaging in Participatory Activist Research

The fourth strategy for feminist research concerns participatory activist research. In the tradition of Kurt Lewin (1948) and Carolyn Payton (1984), this fourth strategy assumes that knowledge is best gathered in the midst of social change projects; that the partial perspectives of participants and observers can be collected by researchers in "power sensitive conversations" (Haraway 1988, 590), which need to be transformative—they cannot be just a pluralistic collection of voices but need to be a struggle. This word is, at once disruptive, transformative, and reflective; about understanding and about action; not about freezing the scene; but always about change (Gitlin, Siegel, and Boru 1989).

To illustrate: For over a decade, feminist psychologist Brinton Lykes (1989) has been engaged in political activism/research with Guatemalan Indian women in their struggles against political repression. Splicing activist politics with psychological research and a feminist commitment to collaboration, Lykes has woven a piece of work with these women in which

> we ... shared an interest in better understanding the conditions under which people come to understand themselves as actors constructing their future, as active participants in the social and political development of their people. We agreed that a project that documented the processes by which women, beginning with their immediate concerns, develop a political consciousness that is accompanied by action and gives social meaning to their activity, would contribute both to a better understanding of Guatemalan women's resistance efforts and, more generally, to our knowledge about the development of political self-consciousness among women. The project was conceived thus as a concrete resource for existing Guatemalan communities, as a vehicle for exploring a more theoretical problem of interest to theorists and to breaking the silence surrounding Guatemala's recent history. (171)

This group of women has collaborated with Lykes on the design for gathering, interpreting, and protecting the oral histories of women in refugee communities.

In her writings, Lykes is the exemplary poststructuralist narrator. Positioned multiply, and often contradictorily, she describes herself as an activist, collaborator, and researcher; as a native North American, a critical psychologist, and an overly "ethical" researcher (Lykes documents some telling negotiations over her construction of an "informed consent" form); a reflective interviewer and an anxious interviewee. Engaged over a decade with a set of activist refugees and psychologists, Lykes considers her project to be explicitly about liberatory struggle and its documentation. And she writes, beautifully and reflectively, about the consequences of such an agenda for psychological research practices.

One particularly compelling essay from this project concludes with a detailed analysis of the politics of collaborative research:

> The decision to engage in collaborative research does not *de facto* resolve competing interests. Nor does it minimize the importance of developing strategies for ensuring, for example, the anonymity of our informants, concerns that are even more critical in research with members of oppressed groups than in university-based work with college sophomores. Rather it affirms a commitment on the part of both researcher and participant to engage the research process as subjects, as constructors to our own reality (Lykes 1989, 179)

With Lykes, social research constructs a gendered archive of political resistance that would otherwise be buried within the deep history by the repression that characterizes these women's lives.

Reflecting Backward and Forward

I use this space to foreshadow a debate I am about to have with Daphne Patai, whose essay responds to my chapter and Patti Lather's. As you will see, Patai worries about the methodological and political implications of our chapters. I won't dispute her remarks except to explore an epistemological space in which we disagree profoundly; a space in need of conversation.

Patai writes for what she calls "intellectual independence." Deeply offended by researchers who nest, inside our scholarship, reflections on biography, position, and politics, she's right to conclude that we fundamentally part ways. *Dis-stance* was written explicitly to provoke conversations about the messy zones between and within politics and social research. I neither seek nor believe in "intellectual independence." I do yearn for any chance to talk, openly, with friends, colleagues, and activists about how to invent research for, with, and on social change.

Scholarship on school reform, racism, community life, violence against women, reproductive freedom ... sits at the messy nexus of theory, research and organizing. The *raison d'être*, for such research is to unsettle questions, texts, and collective struggles; to challenge what is, incite what could be, and help imagine a world that is not yet imagined.

Done critically and collectively with graduate students, community activists, educators, high-school students, and dropouts, this work trespasses borders of class, ethnicities, sexualities, genders, and politics. The collection of data, its interpretation, and our writings spin through a fragile, exhilarating, always tentative "we." "We" as Patai notes, is a utopian marker for a collective of differences in constant negotiation. "We" is not, as Patai suggests, an imperial net thrown over the bodies and minds of Others from my ivory tower. "We" is a political and intellectual stance; a wish worth aspiring toward; a fantasy never coherently achieved. "Our" work is a montage, and it is anything but intellectually independent.

I offer no apologies for the belief that intellectual questions are saturated in biography and politics and that they should be. I do want to be clear, however, about a point raised by Patai and by critics from the New Right. Researchers on the Left may begin with a set of intellectually and politically charged questions, but this does not mean that we force "ideological alignment." When we listen closely, to each other and our informants, we are surprised, and our intellectual work is transformed. We keep each other honest to forces of difference, divergence, and contradiction.

I set out, in *Dis-stance*, to begin a conversation with friends and colleagues about the messy borders of research self-consciously drenched in activism. Throwing a wide net around work I would consider activist, I tried to unroll some of the bumpier aspects of this work, reveal some of the more troubling questions, and slice open some of the more finely scarred tissues in this intellectual arena. I do this because my work, and many others', boils in a delicious but troubling stew of theory, politics, research, and activism, and because I believe intellectuals carry a responsibility to engage with struggles for democracy and justice.

As for "intellectual independence," I've never seen it, I don't believe in it, and I have no desire to share in the illusion. Collective democracies of difference, struggling over authority and validity at the hyphen between activism and research—now there's an illusion worth having.

References

Alonso, A., and Koreck, M. (1989). Silences: Hispanic and Latina women and AIDS. *Sexual Practices* 1 (1):101–124.

Amaro, H. (1989). *Women's reproductive rights in the age of AIDS: New threats to informed choice.* Article drafted from paper presented at the 97th Annual Convention of the American Psychological Association, August XX, New Orleans, LA.

Amaro, H., and Russo, N. F. (1987). Hispanic women and mental health: An overview of contemporary issues in research and practice. *Psychology of Women Quarterly* 11:393–408.

Austin, R. (1989). Sapphire Bound! *Wisconsin Law Review* 3; 539–578.

Becker, H. (1986). *Writing for social scientists: How to start and finish your thesis, book or article.* Chicago: Univ. of Chicago Press.

Bell, D. (1987). *And we are not yet saved: The elusive quest for racial justice.* New York: Basic Books.

Bell, D. (1990). Poverty and women's mental health. *American Psychologist* 45:385–89.

Blackman, J. (1989). *Intimate violence.* New York: Columbia Univ. Press.

Brodkey, L. (1987). *Academic writing as social practice.* Philadelphia: Temple Univ. Press.

Brodkey, L., and Fine, M. (1988). *Presence of body, absence of mind. Journal of Education* 170:84–99.

Brown, L. (1987a). Lesbians, weight, and eating: New analysis and perspectives. *Lesbian psychologies,* 294–309. Chicago: Univ. of Illinois Press.

Brown, L. (1987b). New voices, new visions: Toward a lesbian/gay paradigm for psychology. *Psychology of Women Quarterly* 13:445–58.

Caraway, N. (1991). *Segregated sisterhood.* Knoxville: Univ. of Tennessee Press.

Clark, M. (1990). The difficulty of saying "I": Identifying, analyzing and critiquing voices of self, difference, and discourse in college students' reading and writing about literature. Unpublished Ph.D. dissertation, Univ. of Pennsylvania, 1990.

Condor, A. (1986). Sex roles and "traditional" women: Feminist and intergroup perspectives. In S. Wilkinson (ed.), *Feminist social psychology: Developing theory and practice,* 97–118, Philadelphia: Open Univ. Press.

Crawford, M. (1989). Agreeing to differ: Feminist epistemologies and women's ways of knowing. In M. Crawford and M. Gentry (eds.), *Gender and thought: Psychological perspectives,* 128–45. New York: Springer-Verlag.

Crawford, M., and Gentry, M. (1989). *Gender and thought: Psychological perspectives.* New York: Springer-Verlag.

Crawford, M., and Marecek, J. (1989a). Psychology reconstructs the female, 1968–1988. *Psychology of Women Quarterly,* 13:147–66.

Crawford, M., and Marecek, J. (1989b). Feminist theory, feminist psychology: A bibliography of epistemology, critical analysis and applications. *Psychology of Women Quarterly* 13:477–92.

Crenshaw, K. Whose story is it, anyway? In T. Morrison (ed.), *Race-ing Justice, En-gendering Power,* 402–440. N.Y. Pantheon.

Crosby, F. (1984). The denial of personal discrimination. *American Behavioral Scientist* 27 (3):371–86.

Crosby, F., Pufall, A., Snyder, R.C., O'Connell, M., and Walen, P. (1989). Gender and thought: The role of the self-concept. In M. Crawford and M. Gentry (eds.), *Gender and thought: Psychological perspectives,* 100–127. New York: Springer-Verlag.

Fine, M., and Gordon, A. (1989). Feminist transformations of/ despite psychology. In M. Crawford and M. Gentry (eds.), *Gender and thought: Psychological perspectives,* 146–74. New York: Springer-Verlag.

Fine, M., and Vanderslice, V. (1991). Qualitative activist research: Reflections on politics and methods: In E. Posavac (ed.), *Methodological issues in applied social psychology.* New York: Plenum.

Fine, M., and Zane, N. (1989). On bein' wrapped tight: When low income females drop out of high school. In L. Weis (ed.), *Dropouts in schools: Issues, dilemmas and solutions,* 23–54. Albany, NY. State Univ. of New York Press.

Flax, J. (1990). *Thinking fragments: Psychoanalyses, feminism and post-modernism in the contemporary west.* Berkeley: Univ. of California Press.

Fox-Genovese, E. (1991). *Feminism without illusions.* Chapel Hill, NC: Univ. of North Carolina Press.

Gilkes, C. (1988). Building in many places: Multiple commitments and ideologies in Black women's community work. In A. Bookman and S. Morgan (eds.), *Women and the politics of empowerment,* 53–76. Philadelphia: Temple Univ. Press.

Gilligan C. (1993). Joining the resistance: Psychology, politics, girls and women. In L. Weis and M. Fine (eds.), *Beyond silenced voices,* 143–68. Albany, NY: State Univ. of New York Press.

Gitlin, A., Siegel, M., Boru, K. (1989). The politics of method: From leftist ethnography to educative research. *Qualitative Studies in Education* 2:237–53.

Grosz, E. (1988). The in(ter)vention of feminist knowledges. In Barbara Caine, E. Grosz, and M. deLepervanche (eds.), *Crossing boundaries: Feminisms and the critique of knowledges,* etc. 92–104. Sydney: Allen and Unwin.

Grosz, E. (1989). *Sexual subversions: Three French feminists.* Sydney, Aust.: Allen and Unwin.

Hare-Mustin, R., and Marecek, J. (1990a). Toward a feminist post-structural psychology: The modern self and the post-modern subject. Paper presented at the American Psychological Association, August 20. Boston, MA.

Hare-Mustin, R., and Marecek, J. (1990b). *Making a difference: Psychology and the construction of gender.* New Haven, CT: Yale Univ. Press.

Haraway, D. (1988). Situated knowledges: The Science question in feminism and the privilege of partial perspective. *Feminist Studies* 14(3):575–97.

Harding, S. (1986). *The science question in feminism.* Ithaca, NY: Cornell Univ. Press.

Haug, F. (1987). *Female sexualization: A collective work of memory.* London: Verso.

Hill-Collins, Patricia (19xx). *Black feminist thought.* New York: Routledge.

hooks, b. (1991a). *Yearning.* Boston: South End.

Kahn, A., and Yoder, J. (1990). Domination, subordination and the psychology of women: A theoretical framework. Paper presented at the American Psychological Association, August 20, Boston MA.

Ladner, J. (1971). *Tomorrow's tomorrow.* Garden City, NY: Doubleday.

Lather, P. (1986). Research as praxis. *Harvard Educational Review* 56(3):257–77.

Lather, P. (1990). Staying dumb? Student resistance to liberatory curriculum. Paper presented at annual conference of the American Educational Research Association, April, Boston, MA.

Lather, P. (1991). *Getting smart: Feminist research and pedagogy with/in the postmodern.* New York: Routledge.

Lesko, N. (1988). The curriculum of the body: Lessons from a Catholic high school. In B. Roman (ed.), *Becoming feminine: The politics of popular culture,* 123–42. New York: Falmer.

Lewin, K. (1948). *Resolving social conflicts: Selected papers on group dynamics.* New York: Harper.

Lykes, M. B. (1989). Dialogue with Guatemalan indian women: Critical perspectives on constructing collaborative research. In R. Unger (ed.), *Representations: Social constructions of gender,* 167–84. Amityville, NY: Baywood.

Lykes, B., and Stewart, A. (1986). Evaluating the feminist challenge to research in personality and social psychology, 1963–83. *Psychology of Women Quarterly* 10:393–412.

Majors, B. (1994). From social inequality to personal entitlement: The role of social comparisons, legitimacy appraisals and group membership. *Advances in Experimental Social Psychology* 26:293–355.

McDade, L. (1988). Ethnography and journalism: The critical difference. Paper presented at the Urban Ethnography Forum, February 19, University of Pennsylvania, Philadelphia, PA.

Miller, J. B. (1976). Toward a new psychology of women. Boston: Beacon.

Morawski, J. (1990). Toward the unimagined: Feminism and epistemology in psychology. In R. Hare-Mustin and J. Marecek (eds.), *Making a difference: Psychology and the construction of gender,* 159–83. New Haven, CT: Yale Univ. Press.

Patai, D. (1988). *Brazilian women speak: Contemporary life stories*. New Brunswick, NJ: Rutgers Univ. Press.

Patai, D. (1992). U.S. academics and third world women: Is ethical research possible? *In* S. Gluck and D. Patai (eds.), *Women's words*, 137–53. New York: Routledge.

Parlee, M. (1990). Psychology of menstruation and premenstrual syndrome. Unpublished manuscript, City University of New York, Graduate School and University Center, New York.

Payton, C. (1984). Who must do the hard things? *American Psychologist* 39(3):391–97.

Reinharz, S. (1988). The concept of voice. Paper presented at Human Diversity: Perspectives on People Context, June 8, University of Maryland, College Park, MD.

Robinson, L. (1989). What culture should mean. *The Nation* (September): 319–321.

Rosaldo, R. (1989). *Culture and truth: The remaking of social analysis*. Boston: Beacon.

Russo, N. (1984). *Women in the American psychological association*. Washington, DC: American Psychological Association.

Scott, J. (1992). *Experience*. In J. Butler and J. Scott (eds.), *Feminists theory; the political*, 22–39. New York: Routledge.

Semin, G., and Gergen, K. (1990). *Everyday understanding: Social and scientific implications*. London: Sage.

Smith, D. (1987). *The everyday world as problematic: A feminist sociology*. Boston: Northeastern Univ. Press.

Smith, J., and Stewart, A. (1989). Linking individual development with social changes. *American Psychologist* 44(1):30–42.

Stacey, J. (1991). Can there be a feminist ethnography? In S. Gluck and D. Palai (eds.), *Women's Words*, 111–120. New York: Routledge.

Sullivan, M. (1990). The male role in teenage pregnancy and parenting. New York Vara Institute of justice.

Taylor, S. (1983). Adjustment to threatening events. *American Psychology* 38:1161–73.

Tiefer, L., (1990). Gender and meaning in DSM-111 (and 111-R) sexual dysfunction. Paper presented at the American Psychological Association, August, Boston, MA.

Tolman, D. (1990). Discourses of adolescent girls' sexual desire in development psychology and feminist scholarship. Qualifying paper, Harvard University, Graduate School of Education.

Unger, R. (1990). Sources of variability: A feminist analysis. Paper presented at the American Psychological Association, August 24, Boston, MA.

Van Maanen, J. (1988). *Tales of the field: On writing ethnography*. Chicago: Univ. of Chicago Press.

Walkerdine, V. (1986). Post-stimulated theory and everyday social practices: The family and the school. In V. Wilkinson (ed.), *Feminist social psychology: Developing theory and practice*, 57–76, Philadelphia: Open Univ. Press.

Weis, L., (1990). *Working class without work: High school students in a de-industrializing economy*. New York: Routledge.

Wilkinson, S. (1986). *Feminist social psychology: Developing theory and practice*. Philadelphia: Open Univ. Press.

Willis, P. (1991). *Learning to labor: How working class kids get working class jobs*. Aldershot, England: Gower.

Wittig, M. A. (1985). Metatheoretical dilemmas in the psychology of gender. *American Psychologist* 40(7):800–811.

B.

Feminist Policy Studies

CHAPTER 10

POLICY ANALYSIS FOR POSTSECONDARY EDUCATION: FEMINIST AND CRITICAL PERSPECTIVES

ESTELA MARA BENSIMON AND CATHERINE MARSHALL

Rummaging through a long-forgotten manila folder labeled Feminism, Sexism, Women we came across headlines such as: 'Citing Sexism, Stanford Doctor Quits' (Leatherman, 1991), 'Walking Out on the Boys' (Leatherman, 1992), 'Rage in a Tenured Position', 'A Leading Feminist Literary Critic Quits Post at Columbia, Citing "Impossible" Atmosphere' (Heller, 1992), 'Woman who took on Harvard Law School over Tenure Denial sees "Vindication"' (Leatherman, 1993). These were stories about three female professors and their experiences in institutions and departments that are predominantly male in their faculty composition. The three professors are Frances Conley, the brain surgeon who quit her tenured professorship at Stanford Medical School after 25 years there because she wanted to protest what she described as a 'hostile environment' for women;[1] Carolyn Heilbrun, the holder of an endowed chair, past president of the Modern Language Association, a leading feminist literary critic, who unexpectedly submitted her resignation after 32 years in Columbia University's English department; and Clare Dalton who received a settlement of $260,000 after filing a complaint of sex discrimination when she was denied tenure by Harvard Law School (Heller, 1992; Leatherman, 1991; Leatherman, 1993).

The cases of Conley and Heilbrun, both of whom were tenured full professors with long academic careers, call attention to the particular ways in which universities can be unwelcoming to women, even after they have successfully completed the rites of the tenure passage. The experience of Dalton, whose work is in critical legal theories, calls attention to the difficulties women academics have in being accepted by mostly male peers as scholars, particularly when their work falls into a school of thought considered controversial. Dalton was denied tenure despite positive evaluations of her work by 12 external reviewers and only two negative reviews. Heilbrun's comments about her decision to leave Columbia University describe academic life in a masculinist culture. 'It's like a marriage ending, sad, exhausting—and infuriating because Columbia will continue to be run by male professors who behave like little boys saying "this is our secret treehouse club, no girls allowed"' (Leatherman, 1993). Heilbrun's comments were met with disbelief by her male colleagues, which is not surprising because the hostile environment she perceived is not a concrete thing or act but rather the cumulative effect of inequities which by themselves might appear insignificant but in combination can make women academics feel alien, exhausted and defeated. Among the inequities that Heilbrun experienced were denial of tenure to feminist scholars she supported and denial of admission to graduate applicants who specifically applied to study with

---

Reprinted from *Feminist Critical Policy Analysis II: A Perspective from Post-secondary Education*, Vol. 2, edited by C. Marshall, 1997. Copyright © 1997 Falmer Press.

Heilbrun. Several of Heilbrun's colleagues interviewed by a New York Times reporter were unsure of her first name, referring to her as Carol, Karla, and Caroline: several of her colleagues pointed out that she is married to a highly successful man and thus never needed to work, meaning that unlike theirs her career was a hobby: that she violated collegial norms by revealing confidential information about tenure committees; and the chair of the department, a much younger man, said of her. 'I truly respect Carolyn . . . I found her a very maternal figure . . .' (Matthews, 1992).

The premise of this book is that the theories and methods of conventional policy analysis are biased and therefore incapable of understanding the cases of the Heilbrun's, Conley's, and Dalton's and the other thousands of women professors, students and staff as resulting from structures, norms, practices, values and culture that are gendered. Conventional policy studies in postsecondary education assume that academic structures, processes and practices are gender blind. The lack of attention to gender, both as conceptual category and analytical lens, means that the differential experience of women and male academics is attributed to individual differences rather than to the consequences of a male ordered world (Scott, 1988).

From a conventional view, the stories of these three women would appear as unconnected individual cases, whereas from a feminist perspective they represent a pattern of institutionalized sexism. From a conventional policy view, the specific situations creating Heilbrun's, Conley's and Dalton's problems can be identified and corrected. In contrast, from a feminist perspective, policy solutions are sought from a focus on transforming the organizational context, not just remediating the individual case.

Women's Place in Postsecondary Education: An Invisible Majority

Even though women have constituted a majority of students in postsecondary education since 1979, earning more than half of all associate's, bachelor's, and master's degrees, and more than one-third of all doctorates (Touchton and Davis, 1991), higher education as a field of study has overlooked almost entirely women's roles as shapers and interpreters of the academy (Glazer, Bensimon and Townsend, 1993). Despite the strong presence of women in the student body, men outnumber women in positions of power, making the academy a world run by men. Nationally, about 88 per cent of presidents, provosts and chancellors are male, as are 87 per cent of full professors and 77 per cent of the trustees (Kolodny, 1993). Women who want to 'join the procession of educated men' (Woolf, 1966) continue to face a variety of obstacles related to their gender, yet, with the exception of the work of women scholars, in the great majority of research studies women are either invisible or they exist only in comparison to men. Despite a substantial policy-oriented literature on such topics as student retention, faculty productivity, leadership and administration of higher education, faculty careers, organizational change, resource allocation, teaching and learning and student outcomes, gender is not only rarely treated as a conceptual or analytical category, frequently it is completely overlooked.

When gender is acknowledged it is usually treated as a demographic characteristic, thus, when reference is made to women, it is in comparison to men. From such studies we have learned that female academics are less productive than male academics, that females move up the academic career ladder much more slowly than males, that women have heavier teaching loads than males, that women earn less than their male colleagues, etc. What is missing from postsecondary education is women-centered policy analysis. This chapter provides the theoretical and methodological tools to produce policy analysis that redresses this absence.

In order to provide a stage for the rest of the book, our purpose in this chapter is to answer two questions we anticipate will be in the minds of readers: 1) How do you read policy studies from a feminist perspective? And 2) How do you conduct feminist policy studies? The remainder of this chapter introduces the theoretical foundations underpinning feminist and critical theories, followed by a feminist critique of conventional policy analysis. Next we discuss selected studies whose conceptual design, analysis and interpretive methods exemplify feminist critical policy studies.[2]

What Makes a Theory Feminist and Critical?

Even though we often speak of feminist analysis or feminist theory in the singular the reality is that just as there is not a single theory of policy analysis there is also not a single theory of feminist analysis. To engage in critical feminist analysis it is necessary to have an understanding of the many feminisms, particularly the ideological positions that inform the questions they pose, the decisions made about research design, and most importantly the conclusions they derive and the recommendations they make for change. We wish to make clear that there is considerable variation among the various strands of feminism and we also want to make clear which of these strands represent our definition of feminist critical policy analysis.

Liberal feminism. Liberal feminism is a gentle, more politically/socially acceptable perspective, grounded in conceptions of individuals' civil rights, emphasizing women's equal access to domains where men dominate, chipping at the glass ceiling, relying on extant structures to make small changes to increase women's access to schools, professions, legislatures and presidencies (Hawksworth, 1994; Marshall, 1996).

The dominant ideology of liberal feminism is the attainment of equality. This perspective is commonly found in studies concerned with the status and achievement of women in positions and fields from which they have been traditionally excluded. The concern is more with equality in the sense of access and opportunity based on merit or credentials as opposed to equality of outcomes.

> Liberal feminists focus on public and professional life and want to assimilate women into all the levels of higher education and societal structures occupied by men. They seek the opportunity for women to compete for positions without being blocked by sex discrimination, and see higher education as the way for women to obtain the skills and credentials necessary for career success. The justification liberal feminists give for the education of women is based heavily on arguments of social utility (for example material productivity) and freedom of choice for individuals (Glazer, Bensimon and Townsend, 1993: 4).

Cultural feminism. Cultural feminist scholarship comprises works that posit women as *different* from men because from an early age they are socialized to take on roles associated with the female as mother, caretaker, nurturer, peacemaker, etc. This scholarship posits that women develop differently from men and therefore make judgments and decisions based on principles that give primacy to relationships and that are consistent with an ethic of caring (Belenky et al., 1986; Gilligan, 1982; Noddings, 1984).

Even though liberal and cultural feminisms have contributed to the development of feminist studies and have inspired institutional initiatives to improve the conditions of women in the academy, they also suffer shortcomings that limit the possibilities for social transformation. The liberal stance naively accepts token changes, expecting individual women to persevere in male domains (Marshall, 1996). Cultural feminism ignores that caring and nurturance have been relegated to the private sphere where they are rendered invisible because they are viewed as instinctual to women. In contrast, men's work has always been associated with the public sphere and, regardless of whether it was manual or mindwork, it has always been viewed as labor that is materially compensated. Thus even though cultural feminism has attempted to elevate 'women's ways' as valuable in the marketplace. (for example, women's ways of leading are touted as more consultative) it is still the case that in the context of a masculinist organizational culture the emphasis on women's ways legitimates stereotyping.

Power and politics feminisms.[3] Power and politics feminisms identify the range of structural, overt and subtle mechanisms through which men retain the power to define and control institutions, policy and women's activities, options and even their identity. The power of men to manage the social construction of identity, with man at the center, makes women *Other*; what and who women are can be molded to work in support, for example, of patriarchy in family life and capitalism in the gendered hierarchies of work and professions.

Control of legitimation processes determines what is viewed as valid and valuable in language, behavior, life and work goals, and the construction of knowledge. Accordingly, women's talk is marginalized, women's art is off-center, women's sports insignificant. Power and politics feminist scholars view men's power as pervasive and enduring because it is so solidly entrenched in the rules, activities and language of organized systems such as religion, education, health and law that we are not able to notice its workings. These scholars take Audre Lorde's sharp pronouncement, 'The Master's Tools will Never Dismantle the Master's House' (1984: 110) very seriously. For power and politics feminists the challenge is to construct alternative ways of problem-finding and policy analysis in order to transform organized systems to be responsive to differences. In contrast, for liberal feminists the challenge is to help women assimilate into the structures, values and norms of these systems.

The major difference between the liberal and power and politics feminist standpoint is that the former is a strategy of accommodation whereas the latter is a strategy of transformation. The authors in this volume write from a variety of perspectives, including standpoint theory (see Chapter 8 by Estela Mara Bensimon), poststructuralist theory (see Chapter 12 by Carmen Luke), black feminist theory (see Chapter 10 by bell hooks). However, despite having different preferences for conceptual frameworks the common thread across these works is that they share the intellectual and political agenda of power and politics feminism: to conduct rigorous research on women and the academy in order to transform it.

Postpositivist feminisms. Postpositivist feminisms, such as poststructuralism, post colonial, focus on the tremendous power men have derived by having always controlled language and the meaning system. Male dominance of language and meaning has enabled them to construct reality—history, knowledge and laws—from their vantage point and make it look as if theirs were the view from everywhere. Postpositivist feminists reject the concept of universals and posit instead a theory based on the analysis of differences, local context, specificity, for example, gender and race, and historicity (Barrett and Phillips, 1992).

Postpositivist feminists use theories of 'language, subjectivity, social processes and institutions to understand existing power relations and to identify areas and strategies for change' (Weedon, 1987: 40–1). The theories that make up postpositivism 'can analyze the workings of patriarchy in all its manifestations—ideological, institutional, organizational, subjective—accounting not only for continuities but also for change over time' (Scott, 1988: 33).

Critical theory. By illuminating the relationship between power and culture and the ideologies, knowledges and language, critical theorists have demonstrated how education, despite professing liberal values such as equal opportunity, nevertheless maintains systems, such as pedagogical approaches and curriculum content, that marginalize people, primarily on the basis of race and social class. (Ironically, critical theorists often ignore the intermix of class oppressions with sexism and racism.)[4]

Feminists have appropriated the analytical lenses of critical theory to understand how domination occurs in the intersection along lines of sex, race, sexual orientation and class. hooks notes 'sexism has always been a political stance' which 'informs the construction of masculinity for men of all races and classes' (1990: 59). As important, critical feminists reject Marxist determinism and explore how individuals resist oppression and negotiate their identities actively.

Combining Feminist, Critical and Policy Analysis

Power and politics as well as postpositivist feminist analyses *are* critical, but they add the focus on women. Accordingly, in feminist critical analysis there is a recognition of how patriarchy is manifest in the control of women's identities, including the identification of women with the private sphere, for example, portrayals of women academics as terrific teachers and unproductive researchers, and men with the public sphere. Feminist critical analysts view conventional policy studies methods as the products of disciplinary traditions that are androcentric and therefore reject them as the *master's tools*. Consistent with the feminist project of reconstructing the disciplines to include the missing voices of the Other(s), critical feminist analysts consciously incorporate into their studies gender as well as race, class, sexual orientation or other signifiers that are implicated in the construction of identities.

What, then, is feminist critical policy analysis? Borrowing from Patti Lather, we would say, 'very simply, to do feminist research is to put the social construction of gender at the center of one's inquiry . . . feminist researchers see gender as a basic organizing principle which profoundly shapes/mediates the conditions of our lives' (1991: 71). We see the project of feminist critical analysis as being twofold: 1) to critique or deconstruct conventional theories and explanations and reveal the gender biases (as well as racial, sexual, social class biases) inherent in commonly accepted theories, constructs, methodologies and concepts, and 2) to conduct analysis that is feminist both in its theoretical and methodological orientations. It involves reading policy studies with a critical awareness of how androcentrism is embedded in the disciplines, theories of knowledge and research designs that are foundational to conventional policy analysis and which ostensibly are neutral and neutered. Accordingly, feminist policy analysis involves the critique of knowledge gained from mainstream educational policy studies as well as the design of feminist educational policy studies.

In this chapter we discuss both aspects of feminist policy analysis—critique and design—and provide examples drawn from postsecondary education studies. In the next section we provide a critique of conventional policy analyses as androcentric.

What Makes Conventional Policy Analysis Androcentric?

Conventional policy studies represent the master's tool in that they are primarily a mechanism for powerholders to find cost effective ways to pursue their goals (Ball, 1990, Scheurich, 1994). To discern the master's tools we need to deconstruct the concepts, problems, subjects and interpretations that formulate policy studies. For even though gender may appear to be absent or irrelevant, ultimately the decisions that emerge from such studies do have gendered consequences. As has been pointed out, 'the notion of androcentrism suggests that assumptions, concepts, beliefs, arguments, theories, methods, laws, policies and institutions may all be "gendered"' (Hawkesworth, 1994: 105).

Posing the woman question is central to uncovering androcentric origins in theories and interpretations. To pose the woman question means determining to what extent conceptual frameworks, research designs, methodologies and the interpretation of findings fail 'to take into account the experiences and values that seem more typical of women than of men' (Bartlett, 1990: 837). The woman question pushes us to consider how the epistemological and ontological bases of conceptual frameworks may misrepresent the experiences of women thereby distorting our specific knowledge of phenomena—leadership, management, organization theory—as gender-encompassing (Bensimon, 1991). By posing the woman question, Bensimon documents the androcentric roots of organizational frames that are commonly used to understand how academic organizations function and suggests that the axioms of these frames (bureaucratic, collegial, political and symbolic) are more compatible with men's experience and understanding of leadership than women's. Typically androcentrism can be detected in the assumptions that undergird conventional policy analysis:

An implicit belief in a singular or universal concept of truth. Sandra Harding (1986) points out that the belief in a universal subject found in patriarchal theories has the effect of policing thought by assuming that the problems of some are in fact the problems of humankind. This assumption is commonplace in postsecondary education studies where the influence of 'academic man' is perpetuated by the use of he as the generic term for professor or in the reference to faculty as a class of people, undifferentiated, disembodied and sexless.

Ahistorical and decontextualized. It is not unusual for policy analysis to proceed as if subjects were without history and had the same relationship to their social environment. A major contribution of feminist scholarship has been its challenge of the conventional assumption that there is a correspondence between persons and their environments. By positing that women often live and work in social environments that oppose them (Westkott, 1985), feminist scholars put into question results of studies that attribute differences between women and men to individual characteristics. In postsecondary research there is ample documentation of the different rates of success between male and female academics; however, these studies rarely address the effects of a male dominant context on women's productivity. For example, the fact that women faculty give birth and raise children is not taken into account in studies of faculty productivity (Finkel and Olswang, 1996). Similarly, the six-year probationary period is a product of an era when men were free to pursue their academic careers while their wives took care of the home and children. Conventional policy studies rarely question the incompatibility between the biological and tenure clocks or recommend a more flexible probationary period (Finkel and Olswang, 1996).[5]

Assumption of objectivity and observer-neutrality. Conventional policy analysis assumes that everyone sees the same thing (Pateman and Gross, 1986). In contrast, feminist scholars insist that the observer's gender, race, social class and sexuality influence what research questions are asked, what is viewed as meriting analysis and how results are interpreted. For feminist scholars, knowledge that claims to be objective is really the ideology derived from the experiences and interests of privileged men (Harding, 1986: Hawkesworth, 1994).

Evaluating women on the basis of male norms. Even conventional policy analysis is androcentric when it includes women and their experiences as the focus but utilizes male norms to interpret them. Barbara Townsend (1993), after having reviewed 772 articles published in the three principal journals of postsecondary education during selected time periods in the 1960s through the 1990s, found only 30 studies that actually focused on women or addressed topics of concern to women. She also found that, even when documenting discrimination, most of the articles relied on male norms and values as the analytical and interpretive standard applied to women. Consequently, women often appeared as the source of the problem, and the solution was for them to become more like men. Townsend points out that these articles 'tend to project a world in which women must be better than men to succeed (compensatory scholarship) or one in which women's problems are emphasized, e.g., their experiences with sexual harassment, hiring and salary inequities (bifocal scholarship) (1993: 35).

Conventional, positivist, androcentric policy analysis do serve dominants, those who have positions allowing them to define the problems for public arena discourse and decide which problems to declare irrelevant or not on the agenda. However, the severe limitations of such studies are becoming more obvious as more women enter the academy and begin to question the status quo.

To sum it up, the combination of power and politics and postpositivist feminism with critical theory expands the policy arena and policy studies in areas that have been neglected. These perspectives enable us to notice details that we overlooked in our past readings of policy studies such as the micro-interactions at meetings and their meaning; the use of language; the negotiation for identity. These perspectives also help us see a policy community as an abstract entity when in fact it is a collection of professionals and advocates whose values and biases define who should be involved in the policy arena and whose interests should be taken into account in the formulation of policy.

Conducting Feminist Critical Policy Analysis

In addition to providing the tools of critique needed to dismantle the master's house feminist critical policy analysis is increasingly informing the design of studies. First, we offer a caveat: there is a misperception among those who are not knowledgeable of feminist theories that any work that focuses on women or issues that concern women is feminist (Townsend, 1993). An analysis of the demographic trends in graduate schools might highlight women's status but not be feminist. On the other hand, if the study's data were analyzed in connection to historically-embedded policy assumptions that structure universities around males, with a critique of the assumptions of current policies and programs, and presented an activist/advocacy stance for remaking institutional practices to be responsive to women, then it *would* be feminist critical analysis.

An example of the difference between policy studies about women versus feminist policy studies is provided in Chapter 6, 'Reframing research, informing policy analysis: Another view of women in the mathematics/science pipeline' where Frances Stage revisits one of her previous studies and re-envisions the findings and recommendations from a feminist critical perspective. In the original study, Stage and a colleague focused on the status of women aspiring to doctoral degrees in mathematics. In re-envisioning the original study from a feminist and critical perspective, Stage says, 'In retrospect, as I review our chapter I see that our recommendations focused primarily on the students themselves and were reactive in nature. Rather than suggesting change within a part of the higher education system that is not working, we limited our remarks to those [recommendations] that might be most acceptable in academe' (Chapter 6: 105).

For a study to be viewed as feminist critical policy analysis it is not sufficient to include women, it must include all aspects of each element discussed below:

It poses gender as a fundamental category. Harding notes that 'gender is a fundamental category within which meaning and value are assigned to everything in the world, a way of organizing human social relations' (1986: 57). Acker refers to gender as 'patterned, socially produced, distinctions between female and male, feminine and masculine' (1992: 250). When gender is viewed as a fundamental category, the researcher is more alert to the various ways in which gender structures experiences, relationships, processes, practices and outcomes. Thus feminist researchers have done extensive work to expose the *gendering* that goes on both in gender-explicit and gender-neutral practices, in organizational processes that advantage men and disadvantage women, and in practices that are patterned in terms of stereotypical male and female roles (Acker, 1992).

Feminist scholarship has been particularly helpful in pointing out that genderedness is not always overt and identifiable, such as sexist jokes as part of the culture of the workplace, but that in fact it is often 'deeply hidden in organizational processes and decisions that appear to have nothing to do with gender' (Acker, 1992: 251–2). For example, in 'Retrenchment in the 1980s: The politics of prestige and gender', Sheila Slaughter's (1993) research on retrenchment shows that retrenched fields were those with the greatest presence of women faculty and students. In 'Total quality management in the academy: A rebellious reading', Bensimon employs poststructuralist feminism to gender TQM, a popular corporate management approach that is now also the rage with academic administrators (1995).

It is concerned with the analysis of differences, local context, specificity (such as gender and race), and historicity (Barrett and Phillips, 1992). Feminist analysts assert that, in order for women to have a subject status that is equal to men's, women's difference must be recognized (Irigaray, 1993) rather than suppressed. This is in direct contradistinction with the assumption that gender blindness is a prerequisite for achieving equality between men and women. It declares false the widely held belief that gender blindness—the claim that the professor's sex is invisible —constitutes equal treatment for female and male academics. It declares that gender equity and a nonsexist academic workplace cannot be attained unless conscious attention is given to women's individuality as well as to relations between women and men. The eradication of overt and covert discrimination against women requires critical and gender-based appraisals of academic structures, practices and policies as well as the elimination of language and interactions that create overtly hostile, patronizing or indifferent workplaces for women (Tierney and Bensimon, 1996). Blindness to gender is, for example, what causes women faculty who are pregnant to feel aberrant. It is also what causes most institutions to lack maternity leave policies.

The data of feminist theory is the lived experience of women. 'One distinctive feature of feminist research is that it generates its problematic from the perspective of women's experience. It also uses these experiences as a significant indicator of the "reality" against which hypotheses are tested' (Harding, 1987: 7). The goal of the investigation is to answer questions and provide explanations about phenomena that women want and need rather than to answer the questions framed by men or by male controlled institutions. Further, the gender, race, class and cultural biases of the inquirer are assumed to be a part of the research and are subject to the same critical inquiry.

The goal is to transform institutions. Feminist analysis questions the purpose of the academy's structures, practices and values in order to do away with or reform those that disadvantage women and others. Conventional policy analysis approaches gender in relation to access and equity. The central question is why do women fare less well than men in their performance as professors, students, academic accomplishments, representation in positions of power, etc. Conceptually, the most grievous flaw of conventional policy analysis is that *discrimination* is posited as excluding women from participating in structures thought to be acceptable (Perreault, 1993). The goal of feminist policy analysis is to change institutions, not to add women. Whereas conventional policy analysis problematizes women (blame-the-victim approach), feminist policy analysis problematizes taken-for-granted practices such as the tenure system, making the probationary tenure period seven years, and the like (an investigate-and-fix-the-institution approach).

It is an interventionist strategy. The aim of feminist critical scholarship is to dismantle systems of power and replace them with more preferable ones (Pateman, 1986). Thus unlike conventional policy analysis where there is a pretension to neutrality and objectivity, feminist policy analysis is openly political and change-oriented.

> As a series of strategic interventions into patriarchal texts, feminist theory does not simply aim to reveal what is 'wrong' with, or false about, patriarchal theories—to replacing one 'truth' with another. It aims to render patriarchal systems and presumptions unable to function, unable to retain their dominance and power. It aims to make clear how such dominance has been possible; and to make it no longer viable (Gross, 1986: 197).

What Has Been Learned from Feminist Critical Policy Studies?

What makes feminist critical analysis compelling? Why should scholars of postsecondary education employ such analysis? Although the number of postsecondary education studies that adopt a feminist critical perspective is very small, they have been instructive in revealing what previously had gone unnoticed. From these studies we have a better understanding of:

- the academy as a patriarchal organization;
- the constrained assumptions in equity policy in the academy;
- the academic processes that reproduce gender inequities between men and women professors and students;
- the gendered consequences of neutral practices.

The Academy as a Patriarchal Organization

Feminist scholars of higher education depict the academy as a patriarchal organization in that male dominance is institutionalized throughout the system. They challenge the notion that women, when they enter the academy as students and professionals, are entering a 'sexually neutral world of "disinterested" and "universal perspectives"' (Rich, 1993: 123). The US university, according to Moore and Sagaria, in its origins and as it exists today, 'is deeply imbued with patriarchal ideology' (1993: 236). The ideology translates into political choices, skewing knowledge bases, curricula, policy and practices. The maintenance of this patriarchal ideology is made possible by coalitions of men in positions of power to determine 'who is chosen to study, who is chosen to teach and to do research, and what are the subjects most valued for research and instruction' (1993: 236). Citing classical works on the academy and the professoriate by prominent social scientists such as Blau, 1973; Bowen and Shuster, 1986; Jencks and Reisman, 1968; Wilson, 1979, they observe 'This male-defined culture and its ideology are so profound that most writers have been unaware of its existence or have not found it troubling' (1993: 233). This blindness or resistance is explained, first, in recognizing that facets of organizational cultures become constitutional—creating mind-sets and logics which frame and filter thinking, action, even feeling

(Sarason, 1982). It is explained, too, using Kuhn's notion of resistance to paradigm shifts (Kuhn, 1970).

Patriarchal ideology is also maintained through the control of scholarly journals, which are 'embedded with male bias in the selection of editors and in the matter and method of scholarship published in their volumes' (Moore and Sagaria, 1993: 236). Content analyses of journals dedicated to the scholarship of higher education reveal that they have very little to say about women in general and rarely present studies that are grounded in feminist theory. Two separate studies found a paucity of articles on women: the few articles with a focus on women could be classified into compensatory literature where women are presented as having to compensate for something they lack or into bifocal literature where male norms are employed to determine how men and women compare (Townsend, 1993, Twombly, 1993). The problem with this literature is that it depicts women as passive subjects, with no critique of the metanarrative of male-as-norm and women-as-other, and no sense of agency (women creating their own ways) or resistance to androcentric norms, political choices and institutional arrangements. Thus, they encourage and buttress policy solutions to help women overcome their deficits, leaving the patriarchal structures intact (for a fuller discussion of this problem see Chapter 6, by Stage).

To explain the underrepresentation of women in the professoriate, compensatory-oriented research focuses on women's not being socialized to be as career-oriented and ambitious as men as well as to their being responsible for child-rearing and other domestic duties which intrude into scholarly activities (Park, 1996). While feminist scholars do not dispute that these factors represent serious barriers to women academics, they maintain that 'focusing exclusively on such external factors may lead us to overlook the ways in which sexism is embedded in the structures, norms, and policies of the university itself' (Park, 1996: 47).

The Constrained Equity Policies in the Academy

Luce Irigaray maintains that 'In order to obtain subjective status equivalent to that of men, women must therefore gain recognition for their difference' (1993: 46). In the arena of policy analysis what this would mean is that unifying labels such as faculty, student, socialization, tenure, etc., would have to be redefined on the basis of particular subjectivities such as women faculty, black women administrators, Latina students, etc. Feminist policy analysis shows that the practice of universalizing concepts, as is customary in conventional policy analysis, defeats the intended purposes of affirmative action and equal access. Possibly one of the most important contributions of feminist policy analysis is that of showing that men are considerably more able to fit into the academic system as presently organized whereas for women fitting in depends on their ability and willingness to become more like men. Policy-makers, policies and programs in the academy embed that androcentric assumption uncritically; so do the women, often, as they unwittingly collude, trying to succeed in institutions built with men in mind.

Whether forceful policy is formulated affecting gender relations is a choice made *within a gender regime*. Recognizing the institutional and state patterns where power and policy and structures intertwine with gender is a crucial first step. As Apple says, 'Gender and its regulation is not just an afterthought in state policy . . . what concerns us most here—education—[is] to see the role of the state in gender politics even when it is not overtly discussed in official documents' (Apple, 1994: 356).

Studies of the policies formulated for gender equity (like Glazer's Chapter 4, this volume) reveal ineffective implementation and offer insights for constructing 'less domesticated and tamed' policies and programs (Marshall, 1996). Pay inequities persist but we understand how they are created and why there has been limited success in closing the gap (Hagedorn, 1996). Male dominance on trustee boards, non-enforcement of Title IX, the abandonment of affirmative action, and the failure to assign financial and other resources to support gender-equity initiatives provide evidence that gender-equity policy is often token, symbolic (Marshall, 1996; Sadker and Sadker, 1994; Stromquist's Chapter 3 in Volume I). From a conventional policy perspective inequities are viewed as gender-neutral and can be easily explained as the consequences of the academic market, i.e., 'you have to pay people according to market demands' or academic governance, i.e., 'change takes time' or the supply pool, 'there just aren't any women to hire/promote...' In contrast, feminist critical explanations emerge from gender/power analysis of the policy assumptions that impede change or legitimize inequities. (For example, universities paying professors of English literature, education, engineering and business by market demands systematically advantages males and disadvantages women.) Similarly, in the field of education women are disadvantaged by the practice of paying higher salaries to former school administrators who join the professoriate (without a research track record) than to women who have played by the rules of the game, i.e., engaged in research and publications.

Universities' policies on sexual harassment for the most part focus on students. In 'Betrayed by the academy' (1996) Dey, Korn and Sax refocus on women *faculty*, identifying incidence and effects of sexual harassment on women's careers, showing how a national survey, framed with questions grounded in women's experience, can elicit more than surface data. For example, exploring whether one's field and its gender balance influences incidence of harassment, they found, 'although female-dominated health-related fields have a low reported rate of harassment, education—which also has a tendency to be female-dominated—has a relatively high rate (18.3 per cent)' (1996: 161). Notwithstanding the authors' mistaken assumption that education is a female-dominated field (women predominate in the student body but not in the faculty, hence women are no more powerful) the incidence of sexual harassment they report is very alarming.

The Reproduction of Gender Inequities

Problem definition frames and drives the search for solutions. Policy studies and recommendations often frame 'the woman problem' as one of too few women; therefore the solution is to increase the number, thus improving the representation. Undeniably, adding more women particularly in positions of power should be a priority: however, we must also recognize that the mere presence of more women will not make much of a difference as long as most continue to go through college 'essentially uneducated about the dominant and dominating ideology and practice of patriarchy to which they have been subjected' (Moore and Sagaria, 1993: 236). Relatedly, Holland and Eisenhart in a study of the role of colleges in the reproductions of patriarchy concluded that 'despite the visibility of affirmative action programs and the women's movement, the conditions that promote women's acceptance of patriarchy have not been substantially altered' (1993: 306). These conditions include a peer-group culture that encourages and reinforces attractiveness and romantic relationships as primary sources of affirmation. Although the authors admit that the schools contribute to the creation of a patriarchal system they suggest that the influence of peer relations is much greater. In great part the invisibility of women in the curriculum contributes to women students' lack of consciousness about patriarchy and how they uphold traditional gender roles that are denigrating (Rich, 1993).

The Gendered Consequences of Neutral Practices

The project of feminist policy analysis in education is to disable patriarchy primarily through the research strategy of gendering everyday practices and traditions through which academic culture is created and recreated. Feminist policy analysts, rather than accepting such practices and traditions as inviolate elements of academic culture, have engaged in a systematic deconstruction. One of the primary contributions of feminist analysis has been in the area of academic socialization through studies of women graduate students and women professors which dispel the widely held belief that socialization is gender blind.

Typically socialization is understood as the initiation of prospective members to the culture of the institution, department and profession. Studies of graduate students in professional schools have documented the socialization processes involved in becoming a member of the medical or legal profession: studies of faculty have focused on the processes of moving from untenured assistant professor to a tenured senior professor. The literature on student and professorial socialization is voluminous and the great majority of it treats socialization as practices and rituals that newcomers must experience in order to become full-fledged members of a group. Becoming socialized or failing to do so is attributed to the individual. Consequently, in the literature on postsecondary education we will find explanations for college dropouts as the individual's failure to engage in activities that facilitate academic and social integration. Similarly, explanations for the denial of tenure focus on the individual's failure to engage in activities that facilitate research productivity.

Feminist policy analysis maintains that the relations between men and women at the department and institutional levels create different socialization experiences for women and men. Feminist studies of women faculty (Aisenberg and Harrington, 1988; Clark and Corcoran, 1986; Turner and Thompson, 1993) report that female graduate students and beginning faculty are frequently not part of professional and social circles where newcomers learn about the nonacademic aspects of being a professor such as how to negotiate salary, travel funds, release time and equipment. Similarly, studies report that when women enter the academy as tenure track faculty they often continue to remain outside the social and professional networks and are thus less likely to know the unstated criteria that senior faculty use in making decisions about tenure and promotion.

From a conventional perspective studies of the professoriate tend to look at why women are less successful than men in obtaining tenure and proceed to look for reasons in differences in productivity, effort, uses of time, work habits, etc. Feminist scholars approach the problem differently in that rather than asking why women fail to become socialized and integrated into the academic culture, they focus instead on documenting how seemingly neutral structures and policies contribute to the accumulation of advantage by males (usually white) and the accumulation of disadvantage by women. For example, in their study of women academics, Clark and Corcoran (1986) put gender at the center of their research by asking: 'What experiences have women had in the anticipatory socialization and the entry stages of a career that have gender salience?' 'How were sponsorship processes (advising, mentoring, collegiality) experienced by these women? What processes of accumulating advantages or disadvantages affected career progress and satisfaction for these women? Did these women perceive sex-based discrimination relative to educational preparation and employment processes, review procedures, assignments, rewards, and recognition?' (1986: 400). Acker and Feuerverger's Chapter 7 in this volume provides further insight into subtle aspects of reward systems.

In 'Administrative promotion: The structuring of opportunity within a university', Sagaria and Johnsrud, like Clark and Corcoran, document how supposedly neutral and gender blind practices produce different results in the promotion of men and women administrators. Their study reveals that building an administrative career requires continuous upward mobility and that men were more likely to be sponsored for administrative promotions for internal vacancies. They point out, 'individuals are sponsored or matched to a position through a process in which they are not systematically or openly evaluated for their merits for filling a position' (1992: 208). Based on their findings, they recommend that the practice of sponsorship of internal candidates be reshaped to promote affirmative action, for instance, by designating an internal candidate as 'under consideration only when such designation serves the goals of diversity' (1992: 209). They also point out that promotion practices which protect internal candidates from external competition disadvantages women and minorities because so few are in positions from which they can be promoted.

In 'Research, teaching, and service: Why shouldn't women's work count?' Shelley Park frames the problem of academic success for women as an institutional problem: rather than asking why women do less well, she asks how might the criteria for determining tenure contribute to differential patterns of success for men and women. She states:

> This article examines one way institutionalized sexism operates in the university setting by examining the gender roles and gender hierarchies implicit in (allegedly gender-neutral) university tenure and promotion policies. Current working assumptions regarding 1) what constitutes good research, teaching, and service and 2) the relative importance of each of these

endeavors reflect and perpetuate masculine values and practices, thus preventing the professional advancement of female faculty both individually and collectively (1996: 47).

Park's premise is that there is a gendered division of labor in the academy 'wherein research is implicitly deemed "men's work" and is explicitly valued, whereas teaching and service are characterized as "women's work" and explicitly devalued' (1996: 47). Citing the findings of studies that show women spend more time on teaching and service activities than men, Park argues that the rank ordering of research, teaching and service disproportionately disadvantages women. Specifically, in line with feminist analyses of the gendered symbolism that characterizes the public/private dichotomy, Park argues that research, the most valued indicator of academic performance, symbolizes mindwork which historically has been viewed as men's (paid/rewarded) work in a public place of employment whereas teaching and service symbolize nurturing activities which historically have been viewed as women's (unpaid/unrewarded) work in the privacy of the home.

In an article aptly titled 'Becoming gentlemen: Women's experiences at one ivy league school' Guinier, Fine and Balin (1994) focus on socialization as a process that disadvantages women in that success depends on their ability to behave more like men. Based on their study of women students at the University of Pennsylvania Law School, they report three findings: 1) Despite identical entry-level credentials, by the end of their first year in law school, men are three times more likely than women to be in the top 10 per cent of their law school class (p. 3); 2) even though first-year female law students exhibit more socially conscious attitudes than males by the third year, females' attitudes and aspirations are more like the men's: 3) a large number of women feel alienated by the way the Socratic method is used in large classroom instruction and have lower participation in classroom discussions than males.

From a conventional policy perspective these findings might inspire compensatory strategies to help women be better socialized to the norms and values of law school. For example, assertiveness training might be viewed as a solution to women's discomfort with the Socratic method. However, these authors interpret their results from a feminist perspective and focus on the structure of law school as the cause for the academic differences between women and men. They conclude that gender neutral practices in the law school are shown to have 'insidious effects of gender stratification in law school "socialization"' (Guinier et al., 1994: 98) and that it will not be sufficient to 'add women' but rather that there is dire need for a 'reinvention of law school, and a fundamental change in its teaching practices, institutional policies, and social organization' (1994: 100).

The studies we have discussed illuminate the elements of feminist policy analysis described earlier and demonstrate that expanding our definition of policy and our view of the policy arena with feminist and critical perspectives, along with the use of gendering as a policy analysis strategy, reveals biases in practices that otherwise would be invisible.

The Tools of Feminist Critical Policy Analysis[6]

Policy agendas have been constrained; gender questions and answers have been limited: higher educational journals with studies such as those in this volume are just now emerging. If reality is socially constructed and knowledge is culturally and historically determined, if politics and policy are enacted in micro-interaction as well as trustees' meetings and formal reports, if we critique the patriarchally constrained policy arrangements in higher education—then what methodologies and theories can be used? Feminist, critical, postmodern and poststructural theories and cultural views of policy arenas demand new agenda-framing.

Connecting postpositivist policy analysis with the feminist theories emphasizing analysis of power and politics *does* provide new ways of framing policy agendas for postsecondary education, and new policy analysis methodologies are emerging. Cost benefit analyses are less relevant than the microanalytic, sociolinguistic, ethnographic methodologies. Surveys are thrown away when it is clear that their questions, their Likert scales, etc., derive from theories that exclude women or that do not show an awareness of the genderedness inherent in social structures. Blue Ribbon Committee Reports and reform-minded documents go back to the drawing board when they make recommendations that benefit only an elite or that protect institutional stability and sacrifice programs that benefit marginalized groups, for example, restructuring strategies that result in the elimination of programs that have women as their primary beneficiaries. Thus, for every policy analysis and evaluation, the feminist critical analyst asks about every policy formulation: who benefits, who loses and how do females fare? Is the issue obviously about women (for example, should student medical insurance pay for abortions) or less obviously so (should the college raise the ceiling and the number of non-tenure track faculty?). Until now, with our defining feminist critical policy analysis, such demanding questions were not on the agenda.

Post-positivist policy analysis examines power brokers' biases, contests over conceptions of goals and decisions, with an array of interests, problem definitions and mechanisms for change (DeLeon, 1994; Kelly and Maynard-Mooney, 1993; Stone, 1988). Interpretive policy analysis identifies the normative stances, the assumptions and judgments about the political condition that do not meet a standard. The analyst clarifies the 'intentions and self-understandings of the agents involved' and reconstructs the 'practical reasoning' (Jennings, 1983). Narrative policy analysis uses stories to uncover 'the empirical, bureaucratic, legal, and political merits [that are] unknown or not agreed on' (Roe, 1989: 251) and identifies the better story. The analyst recognizes asymmetries and 'differential access to economic and political power of stakeholders (Roe, 1989: 266).

Ultimately, we need to construct a feminist theory of the state to explain the maintenance of gender regimes in the academy and other institutions. We need women-centered theories to develop strategies for change, theories that integrate gender issues with the realities of power and politics (Bowles and Klein, 1983; MacKinnon, 1982). The master's tools must be cast aside, in favor of discourse bringing into question all things that were common senses, structured and assumed, from male-female difference to male norms of leadership and power. A feminist theory of politics of education would assist in framing questions, policies and change strategies never seen before. All that is needed is the political choice to pursue these agendas.

Notes

1. Frances Conley withdrew her resignation after she was persuaded by the university and her colleagues that changes would be made to improve the environment for female medical students and professors.
2. See Chapter 1 of Volume I for a more complete discussion of these points.
3. We use this term to encompass the feminisms that focus on the deeply embedded cultural, political, economic and institutional power that maintains and reproduces patriarchy, including: Marxist, socialist, existentialist, poststructuralist, postmodern and radical (see Tong, 1989 and Weiler, 1988 for further nuances).
4. This is probably due to their grounding in Marxism and abstract theoretical discourse written by white males.
5. A tenured and prominent woman full professor, on being passed over for an endowed chair, said to one of us: 'I just know they think of me as not serious because I have a young child.' So the incompatibility probably affects more than just tenure processes.
6. For a more in-depth discussion of methodologies see Volume I, Chapter 1, called 'Dismantling and reconstructing policy analysis' by Catherine Marshall.

References

Acker, J. (1992) 'Gendering organizational theory', in Mills, A. and Tancred, P., *Gendering Organizational Analysis*, Newbury, CA, Sage Publications, pp. 248–60.

Aisenberg, N. and Harrington, M. (1988) *Women of Academe: Outsiders in the Sacred Grove*. Amherst, MA, The University of Massachusetts Press.

Apple, M. (1994) 'Texts and contexts: The state and gender in educational policy'. *Curriculum Inquiry*, 24(3), pp. 349–59.

Ball, S. (1990) *Politics and Policymaking in Education: Explorations in Policy Sociology*, London, Routledge.

Barrett, M. and Phillips, A. (Eds) (1992) *Destabilizing Theory: Contemporary Feminist Debates*, Stanford, CA, Stanford University Press.

Bartlett, K. T. (1990) 'Feminist legal methods', *Harvard Law Review*, 103(4), pp. 829–88.

Belenky, M. F., Clinchy, B., Goldberger, N. R. and Tarule, J. M. (1986) *Women's Ways of Knowing: The Development of Self*, Voice and Mind. New York. Basic Books.

Bensimon, E. M. (1991) 'A feminist reinterpretation of president's definitions of leadership', *Peabody Journal of Education*, pp. 143–56.

Bensimon, E. M. (1995) 'Total quality management in the academy: A rebellious reading', *Harvard Educational Review*, **65**(4), pp. 593–611.

Blau, P. (1973) *The Organization of Academic Work*, New York, John Wiley and Sons.

Bowen, H. R. and Shuster, J. H. (1986) *American Professors: A National Resource Imperiled*, Oxford, Oxford University Press.

Bowles, G. and Klein, R. D. (1983) 'Introduction: Theories of women's studies and the autonomy/integration debate', in Bowles, G. and Klein, R. D. (Eds) *Theories of Women's Studies*, London, Routledge and Kegan Paul, pp. 1–26.

Clark, S. M. and Corcoran, M. (1986) 'Perspectives in the professional socialization of women faculty: A case of accumulative disadvantage?', *Journal of Higher Education*, **57**(1), pp. 20–43.

Dey, E. L., Korn, J. S. and Sax, L. J. (1996) 'Betrayed by the academy: The sexual harassment of women college faculty', *Journal of Higher Education*, **67**(2), pp. 149–73.

Deleon, P. (1994) 'Reinventing the policy sciences: Three steps back to the future', *Policy Sciences*, **27**, pp. 77–94.

Finkel, S. K. and Olswang, S. G. (1996) 'Child rearing as a career impediment to women assistant professors', *The Review of Higher Education*, **19**(2), pp. 123–39.

Gilligan, C. (1982) *In a Different Voice: Psychological Theory and Women*, Cambridge, MA, Harvard University Press.

Glazer, J. S., Bensimon, E. M. and Townsend, B. K. (Eds) (1993) *Women in Higher Education: A Feminist Perspective*, Needham, MA, Ginn Press.

Gross, E. (1986) 'What is feminist theory?', in Pateman, C. and Gross, E. (Eds) *Feminist Challenges: Social and Political Theory*, Boston, MA, Northeastern University Press, pp. 190–204.

Guinier, L., Fine, M. and Balin, J. with Bartow, A. and Stachel, D. L. (1994) 'Becoming gentlemen: Women's experiences at one ivy league law school', *University of Pennsylvania Law Review*, **143**(1), pp. 1–110.

Hagedorn, L. S. (1996) 'Wage equity and female faculty job-satisfaction: The role of wage differentials in a job satisfaction causal model', *Research in Higher Education*, **37**(5), pp. 569–98.

Harding, S. (1986) *The Science Question in Feminism*, Ithaca, NY, Cornell University Press.

Harding, S. (Ed) (1987) *Feminism and Methodology*, Bloomington, IN, Indiana University Press.

Hawkesworth, M. (1994) 'Policy studies within a feminist frame', *Policy Sciences*, **27**, pp. 97–118.

Heller, S. (May 2, 1992) 'A leading feminist literary critic quits post at Columbia, citing "impossible" atmosphere', *The Chronicle of Higher Education*, A13–14.

Holland, D. C. and Eisenhart, M. A. (1993) 'Moments of discontent: University women and the gender status quo', in Glazer, J. S., Bensimon, E. M. and Townsend, B. K. (Eds) *Women in Higher Education: A Feminist Perspective*, Needham, MA, Ginn Press, pp. 293–310.

hooks, b. (1990) *Yearnings*, Boston, MA, South End Press.

Irigaray, L. (1993) *Je, Tu, Nous: Toward a Culture of Difference*, New York, Routledge.

Jencks, C. and Riesman, D. (1968) *The Academic Revolution*, Garden City, NY, Anchor Books.

Jennings, B. (1983) 'Interpretive social science and policy analysis', in Callahan, D. and Jennings, B. (Ed) *Ethics, the Social Sciences and Policy Analysis*, New York, Plenum Press.

Kelly, M. and Maynard-Moody, S. (1993) 'Policy analysis in the post-positivist era: Engaging stakeholders in evaluating the economic development districts program', *Public Administration Review*, **53**(2), pp. 135–42.

Kolodny, A. (1993) 'Raising standards while lowering anxieties: Rethinking the promotion and tenure process', unpublished paper, pp. 1–26.

Kuhn, T. S. (1970) *The Structure of Scientific Revolutions*, (2nd Ed) Chicago, IL, University of Chicago Press.

Lather, P. (1991) *Getting Smart: Feminist Research and Pedagogy With/In the Postmodern*, New York, Routledge.

Leatherman, C. (September 18, 1991) 'Stanford neurosurgeon decides to remain at university but sees continuing struggle against sex discrimination', *The Chronicle of Higher Education*, A19.

Leatherman, C. (October 6, 1993) 'Woman who took on Harvard Law School over tenure denial sees "Vindication"', *The Chronicle of Higher Education*, A19–20.

Lorde, A, (1984) 'The master's tools will never dismantle the master's house', in Lorde, A., *Sister Outsider*, Freedom, Crossing Press.

Mackinnon, C. (1982) 'Feminism. Marxism, method and the state', in Keohane, N., Rosaldo, M. Z. and Gelpi, B. C. (Eds) *Feminist Theory: A Critique of Ideology*, Chicago, IL, University of Chicago Press, pp. 1–30.

Marshall, C. (1996) 'Undomesticated gender policy', in Bank, B. J. and Hall, P. M. (Eds) *Gender, Equity and Schooling*, New York, Garland Publishing Co.

Matthews, A. (1992) 'Rage in a Tenured Position', *New York Times Magazine*.

Moore, K. M. and Sagaria, M. D. (1993) 'The situation of a women in research universities in the United States: Within the circles of power', in Glazer, J. S., Bensimon, E. M. and Townsend, B. K. (Eds), *Women in Higher Education: A Feminist Perspective*, Needham, MA, Ginn Press, pp. 227–40.

Noddings, N. (1984) *Caring: A Feminine Approach to Ethics and Moral Education*, New York, Teachers College Press.

Park, S. M. (1996) 'Research, teaching, and service: Why shouldn't women's work count?', *Journal of Higher Education*, **67**(1), pp. 46–84.

Pateman, C. (1986) 'The theoretical subversiveness of feminism', in Pateman, C. and Gross, E. (Eds) *Feminist Challenges: Social and Political Theory*, Boston, MA, Northeastern, pp. 1–10.

Pateman, C. and Gross, E. (Eds) (1986) *Feminist Challenges: Social and Political Theory*, Boston, Northeastern University Press.

Perreault, G. (1993) 'Contemporary feminist perspectives on women in higher education', in Glazer. J. S., Bensimon. E. M. and Townsend, B. K. (Eds) *Women in Higher Education: A Feminist Perspective*, 3–21, Needham, MA, Ginn Press, pp. 3–21.

Rich, A. (1993) 'Toward a woman-centered university', in Glazer, J. S., Bensimon, E. M. and Townsend. B. K. (Eds) *Women in Higher Education: A Feminist Perspective*, Needham, MA, Ginn Press, pp. 121–34.

Roe, E. M. (1989) 'Narrative analysis for the policy analyst: A case study of the 1980–1982 medfly controversy in California', *Journal of Policy Analysis and Management*, **8**(2), pp. 251–73.

Sadker, M. and Sadker, D. (1994) *Failing at Fairness: How America's Schools Cheat Girls*, New York, Charles Scribner's Sons.

Sagaria, M. D. and Johnsrud, L. K. (1992) 'Administrative promotion: The structuring of opportunity within a university', *The Review of Higher Education*, **51**(2), pp. 191–211.

Sarason, S. (1982) *The Culture of the School and the Problem of Change* (2nd Ed) Boston, MA, Allyn & Bacon.

Scheurich, J. J. (1994) 'Policy archeology: A new policy studies methodology', *Education Policy*, **9**(4), pp. 297–316.

Slaughter, S. (1993) 'Retrenchment in the 1980s: The politics of prestige and gender', *Journal of Higher Education*, **64**(3), pp. 250–82.

Scott, Joan W. (1988) 'Deconstruction equality-versus-difference: Or, the uses of poststructuralist theory for feminism', *Feminist Studies*, **14**(1)., pp. 33–50.

Stone, D. (1988) *Policy Paradox and Political Reason*, Glenview, IL, Scott, Foresman and Co.

Tierney, W. G. and Bensimon, E. M. (1996) *Promotion and Tenure: Community and Socialization in Academe*, New York, Suny Press.

Touchton, J. G. and Davis, L. (1991) *Fact Book on Women in Higher Education*, New York, American Council on Education and Macmillan Publishing.

Tong, R. (1989) *Feminist Thought: A Comprehensive Introduction*, Boulder, CO, Westview Press.

Townsend, B. K. (1993) 'Feminist scholarship in core higher education journals', *The Review of Higher Education*, **17**(1), pp. 21–41.

Twombly, S. (1993) 'What we know about women in community colleges: An examination of the literature using feminist phase theory', *Journal of Higher Education*, **64**(2), pp. 186–210.

Turner, C. S. and Thompson, J. R. (1993) 'Socializing women doctoral students: Minority and majority experiences', *The Review of Higher Education*, **16**(3), pp. 355–70.

Weedon, C. (1987) *Feminist Practice and Poststructuralist Theory*, Cambridge, MA, Blackwell.

Weiler, K. (1988) *Women Teaching for Change: Gender, Class, and Power*, South Hadley, MA, Bergin and Garvey Publishers, Inc.

Westkott, M. (1985) 'Feminist criticism of the social sciences', in Rich, S. L. and Phillips, A. (Eds) *Women's Experience and Education*, Harvard Educational Review, Reprint Series, No. 17, pp. 149–57.

Wilson, L. (1979) *American Academics: Then and Now*, New York, Oxford University Press.

Woolf, V. (1966) *Three Guineas*, New York, Harcourt Brace.

CHAPTER 11

ANALYZING BACKLASH: FEMINIST STANDPOINT THEORY AS ANALYTICAL TOOL

MARY HAWKESWORTH

Synopsis—Conceiving feminist standpoint theory as an analytical tool rather than as an epistemological doctrine, this article investigates the merits of this methodological approach for fostering an understanding of backlash politics and for identifying emancipatory political objectives in the late 20th century. The article examines competing theoretical accounts of affirmative action and welfare "reform" advanced by conservative women, liberal feminists, socialist feminists, black feminists, and postmodern feminists in order to make backlash more intelligible, to understand the forces that fuel it, and to devise strategies that empower women to resist oppression. By comparing these competing theoretical standpoints, the article also explores the contributions and limitations of standpoint theory as an analytical tool and as a method to engage pressing political issues. © 1999 Elsevier Science Ltd. All rights reserved.

From its origin in the work of Nancy Hartsock, feminist standpoint theory promised feminist scholarship a novel epistemology that could ground research in the truth embodied in women's experience. "Women's lives make available a particular and privileged vantage point on male supremacy, a vantage point which can ground a powerful critique of the phallocratic institutions and ideology which constitute capitalist patriarchy" (Hartsock, 1983, p. 284). According to Hartsock, the feminist standpoint offered a definitive account of "the real relations among human beings as inhuman, point[ing] beyond the present, and carrying a historically liberatory role" (Hartsock, 1983, p. 285). Thus, standpoint theory was to provide a bridge from knowledge to politics as cogent critiques would give rise to transformative praxis.

In its initial formulation, feminist standpoint theory followed classical Marxism in grounding ideology critique in a theory of objective truth and in drawing political prescriptions from a theory of the objective interests of women. Over the past decade, as feminist theorists have grappled with the Althusserian conception of ideology, postmodern conceptions of knowledge, and the powerful critiques advanced by black feminist and postcolonial feminist theorists, these objectivist moorings have slipped away. Feminist standpoint theorists have introduced conceptions of "situated knowledges" (Haraway, 1991, p. 188), "subjugated knowledges" (Collins, 1990, p. 233), and "strong objectivity" (Harding, 1991, p. 142; Harding, 1992, p. 584) in an effort to develop a conception of the feminist standpoint that can account for the multiplicity of women's perspectives and the diversity of women's experiences without succumbing to relativism. These efforts have not successfully resolved the problems of knowledge and agency that underlie standpoint theory, however. As an epistemological doctrine, feminist standpoint theory is seriously flawed. It entails a subjectivist approach to knowledge that privileges the experience of knowers as the source of knowledge without grappling with complex questions concerning the validity of particular knowledge claims. In relying upon experience as the ground of truth, feminist standpoint theory also fails to do justice to the fallibility of human knowers, the multiplicity and diversity of women's experiences, and the theoretical constitution of experience (Grant, 1993; Hawkesworth, 1989).

If standpoint theory fails as an account of knowledge and as a means to validate particular truth claims, are there other uses to which it might be put? In this article, I suggest that standpoint theory can be fruitfully adopted as an analytical tool. Imre Lakatos (1970) defined an analytical tool as a heuristic device that illuminates an area of inquiry, framing a set of questions for investigation, identifying puzzles or problems in need of exploration or clarification, and providing concepts and hypotheses to guide research (p. 132).

As an analytical tool, feminist standpoint theory has a number of advantages. It suggests a way of gathering data for analysis that presupposes multiplicity and complexity. The shift in feminist scholarship over the past decade from a notion of "the" feminist standpoint to a recognition of multiple feminist standpoints and multiple standpoints of women generates an analytical tool that accepts plurality as an inherent characteristic of the human condition. Rather than asserting the truth of any particular claim about experience, feminist standpoint theory as analytical tool requires the collection of competing claims advanced by women. In marked contrast to social science methodologies that claim value-neutrality, feminist standpoint theory as analytical tool acknowledges that claims about the world are theoretically mediated—constructed in relation to experience in light of a range of theoretical interests. Thus, feminist standpoint theory as analytical tool may offer a methodology markedly suited to the postpositivist recognition of the role that theoretical presuppositions play in cognition. By expanding the sphere of social science research to encompass the theoretical frameworks that support competing empirical claims, feminist standpoint theory as analytical tool may also identify new mechanisms to help resolve seemingly intractable political disputes. As an analytical tool, then, feminist standpoint theory may provide feminist scholars with new conceptual means to engage contemporary political issues.

To explore the potential uses of feminist standpoint theory as analytical tool, this article examines a range of competing explanations of antifeminist backlash, the "relentless whittling down process... to halt, or even reverse, women's quest for equality" (Faludi, 1991, p. xviii). Following standpoint theory's mandate to take up multiple perspectives, I compare accounts of two aspects of backlash—recent proposals to abolish affirmative action and "reform" welfare—advanced by conservative women, liberal feminists, socialist feminists, black feminists, and a postmodern feminist. By comparing the theoretical assumptions as well as the empirical claims within these conflicting accounts, I hope to illuminate the potential contributions and limitations of standpoint theory as an analytical tool and as a method to engage pressing political issues. I will also suggest that feminist standpoint theory as analytical tool is attuned to problems pertaining to objectivity masked by traditional social science methods. Feminist standpoint theory used as an analytical tool, then, may contribute to the construction of an objective account of political life, although not in the way that Nancy Hartsock originally suggested.

A Conservative Standpoint

Although the radical zeal of early, second-wave feminism sustained the illusion that certain "malestream" views were uniquely the products and perspectives of men (Daly, 1978; O'Brien, 1981), the increasing ranks of articulate antifeminist women destroys that naive vision. Phyllis Schlafly, Linda Chavez, Lynne Cheney, Beverly LeHaye, Anita Blair, Barbara Ledeen, and Laura Ingraham constitute a vocal conservative force who advance arguments concerning the evils of affirmative action and welfare that rival the views of Charles Murray, Lawrence Mead, and Paul Weyrich. Conservative women would deny that their views bear any relation to "backlash." On the contrary, their opposition to affirmative action and welfare stems from a deep conviction that life in the contemporary United States conforms to the fundamental promise of the doctrine of equal opportunity. The system operates as a meritocracy in which all have an equal opportunity to compete in a process designed to reward individual talent, initiative, and hard work.

Conservative women, like their male counterparts, deny that discrimination in hiring, wage scales, promotion, and admissions currently exists in the United States. While they acknowledge that African Americans as a group earn less than whites as a group, and that women as a group earn less than men as a group, and that both minorities and women constitute a smaller percentage of managerial and professional workers than of the general population, they deny that the explanation of these facts lies in deliberate discrimination. They suggest that a combination of personal choices made by individuals of their own free will and objective forces over which discrete individuals have no control, provide a more adequate explanation of these phenomena. Demonstrating a sophisticated grasp of issues in the philosophy of social science, conservative women cite a cardinal principle in statistical interpretation: correlation cannot prove causation. Thus, they point out that statistical data concerning the relative distribution of minorities and women in particular jobs are not sufficient to prove that intentional discrimination has occurred. Statistics cannot "prove" discrimination because proof of discrimination requires a demonstration of intentional exclusion of particular individuals by particular individuals. As a descriptive indicator that operates at the aggregate level, statistics can provide no information at all about individual intentions. Thus, any conclusion concerning the existence of discrimination in admissions, hiring or promotions, or pay drawn from statistical data, involves an unwarranted inference.

Conservative women suggest that the problem of underrepresentation does not reflect discrimination against qualified applicants, but rather reflects the fact that women and minorities lack the requisite qualifications for certain positions and therefore, either fail to apply or upon application are rightly rejected. The problem is primarily one of inadequate supply of qualified women and minority applicants, not one of demand hampered by willful discrimination. Lack of qualifications—not discrimination—impairs the employment potential of women and minorities. And the lack of qualifications among women and minorities relate to individual choices, for which ultimately individuals themselves are responsible. Women and minority individuals freely choose career patterns that differ from those of white males, and this crucial element of individual choice is routinely ignored in arguments that move from statistical underrepresentation to allegations of exclusion or discrimination. For this reason, affirmative action is clearly a misguided and inappropriate policy.

Affirmative action is designed as a social policy to end intentional discrimination in admission, employment, and promotion. Since any underrepresentation that currently exists is not related to any deliberate policies of discrimination, the disease and the cure are mismatched. The basic lack of correspondence between problem and solution stems from the failure to draw an important distinction between problems caused by deliberate individual actions, which are susceptible to solutions aimed at specific individuals, and problems caused by impersonal/objective social forces for which no individual can justly be held accountable.

Having diagnosed the cause of underrepresentation as an insufficient supply of qualified women and minority applicants, conservative women insist that affirmative action is synonymous with reverse discrimination: government policies necessitate the use of "quotas," the hiring of less qualified candidates, the obliteration of merit as a criterion of desert and consequently, the sacrifice of creative, hardworking individuals. Since qualified women and minority applicants are not available according to this analysis, it follows that school administrators and employers must engage in all these abuses in order to increase the number of women and blacks in their institutions as a demonstration to the government of their good faith." Giving less, qualified women and minority group members "preference" in admissions, hiring, and promotion can only result in new forms of discrimination that will entail the erosion of the principles of merit, scholarly quality, and integrity. Thus, affirmative action makes a mockery of the principle of desert, which itself provides the legitimation for denunciation of past discriminatory practices (Thernstrom & Thernstrom, 1997).

Affirmative action arbitrarily imposes responsibility for a collective problem upon specific individuals. It requires preferential treatment for "unqualified" women and minority group applicants and consequently, it discriminates in reverse against the "best qualified" candidates who just happen to be nonminority men. Such reverse discrimination is all the more intolerable because it undermines competition while allowing government bureaucrats to impose their subjective vision of the good upon the society at large. Bureaucratic intervention places universities and employers in the position of having to placate federal officials under penalty of loss of federal grants and contracts vital to their very survival. Thus, bureaucratic whim becomes a tyrannical task master that strips would-be federal contractors of their autonomy and their fidelity to standards of pure meritocratic excellence (Ladowsky, 1995).

In the absence of deliberate discriminatory policies in the contemporary United States, the only possible moral justification for the government's policies is compensatory justice for groups. Affirmative action must be understood as an effort to make reparation to blacks for a history of injustice. Yet this concept of compensatory injustices suffered by them as groups is completely incompatible with individual rights afforded by the U.S. Constitution. According to conservative women, affirmative action provides blanket preferential treatment for certain persons on the basis of race even if those persons did not personally suffer past injustices. Thus, preferential treatment for groups as a social policy is notoriously overinclusive. But it is simultaneously underinclusive for in providing compensation only for African Americans, it ignores the claims of other individuals who have personally suffered injustice yet who are not members of the groups targeted for compensation. Furthermore, reverse discrimination imposes the cost of compensation upon individuals who did not perpetrate the injustice and who cannot fairly be dubbed beneficiaries of the injustice since they neither sought the benefit nor had the opportunity to reject it. Put simply, reverse discrimination imposes the cost of compensation upon innocent parties. Thus, reverse discrimination can be faulted as both arbitrary in the distribution of benefits to the disadvantaged and in the assignment of the costs of compensation. Such rampant arbitrariness seriously impairs any moral justification for affirmative action.

Reverse discrimination substitutes concern with "abstract groups" and their purported rights for concern with living individuals. Focusing solely upon individuals who "make themselves," conservative women reject any notion of a legacy of group injury, just as they reject any notion of collective guilt on the part of the group who historically imposed the suffering. Therefore, conservative women construe affirmative action as an unconstitutional policy that subordinates individuals' rights to equal treatment to putative "group" rights to preferential treatment. According to conservative women, justice can require nothing more than the use of neutral principles, such as nondiscrimination, in admissions and employment. Since deliberate discrimination is not a contemporary problem, the use of neutral principles will promote meritocratic decisions while simultaneously according justice to individuals regardless of the group to which they happen to belong. For it will allow each individual to "make it" on his/her own.

Concern with the value of self-reliance and the development of social policies that hold individuals responsible for their own actions also fuels conservative women's attack on welfare. Accepting that the market economy affords employment opportunities to all who seek them, conservative women understand the causes of poverty in terms of the attitudes, the psychology, and the behavior of the poor. On this view, the problem to be addressed is a direct consequence of existing welfare policies that produce a class of people who adopt welfare as a way of life, who intentionally waste their skills and talents by willfully refusing to work.

Conservative women point to stories of individual upward mobility and success (e.g., Clarence Thomas) as proof that high rates of unemployment among disadvantaged groups cannot be explained by appeals to lack of jobs, discrimination, or other social conditions over which the disadvantaged have no control. The poor remain poor because they are unwilling to accept the jobs available to them. The underdevelopment of the work ethic is the fundamental problem of the poor and it is a problem attributable to welfare programs that provide benefits to recipients while expecting nothing in return. In direct contrast to the market that reinforces the work ethic in individuals by relating rewards to individuals' investments of effort and contributions to society, welfare undermines the value of such reciprocity by severing the connection between benefits and obligations. To rectify this problem, welfare programs should include a mandatory work requirement. Work must replace welfare in order to ensure the future prosperity of the currently disadvantaged members of society. Moreover, to facilitate recipients' integration into the mainstream of American life, an absolute lifetime limit (2–5 years) should be placed on receipt of welfare benefits (Kondrtas, 1995).

Once poverty is understood in terms of particular debilitating attitudes held by the poor, welfare-to-work programs emerge as an appropriate social policy designed specifically to alter individual attitudes toward work. Conservative women suggest that mandatory work requirements will generate a host of benefits for individual welfare recipients and for society. Requiring welfare recipients to work on a regular basis will help them to cultivate a work "habit," while simultaneously overcoming their fears of not being able to compete in a job market. On-the-job experience in public service projects will increase welfare recipients' feelings of self-worth and self-confidence as they realize they are contributing something of value to their communities. The dependency bred by reliance upon government hand-outs will be supplanted by a growing sense of self-sufficiency as participants gain a sense of mastery in their job assignments. The gradual accrual of job experience will enhance the marketable skills and hence the employability of welfare recipients. Over time, the regular exposure to the world of work, coupled with the newfound confidence and the acquisition of marketable skills, will facilitate the individual's transition from welfare to permanent paid employment in the private sector. Thus, the long-term consequence will be a reduction in state and federal expenditures for welfare as the total number of recipients is reduced due to job placements. State and federal governments will also realize immediate reductions in their welfare expenditures as those recipients who are unwilling to assume their work responsibilities are terminated from the welfare rolls. Work requirements also produce an additional residual benefit: reduction in the stigma associated with welfare. As the rolls are purged of welfare "cheats," welfare workers will encounter a new respect as the American public recognizes that the poor "have earned" the benefits that they receive.

Conservative proposals to return control of welfare programs to the states, ending the notion of an "entitlement" to public assistance, also call for significant reductions in expenditures for welfare. States are allowed to cut welfare allotments by 20% from the 1994 benefit levels and federal contributions through block grants will also be reduced over a 7-year period. Benefits to recipients will necessarily fall as a consequence. Reducing benefits while simultaneously requiring recipients to work off the benefits received will deter people from seeing welfare as an alternative to work. The image of welfare as a "pre-paid lifetime vacation plan," in the words of Ronald Reagan, would be permanently replaced by a conception of welfare as minimal subsistence support, administered with a sufficient degree of harshness and limitation in benefits that people who could work would be happy to get off and those who did work would stay off.

Like the "carrot and stick" of the market system (high wages as positive incentive, fear of unemployment as negative incentive), conservative women envision a revised welfare system that includes positive and negative incentives. As a positive incentive, work placement for welfare recipients affords the opportunity for the poor to develop work skills and habits, self-esteem, and confidence, as well as a basic "marketability." The assignment of individuals to menial jobs without pay as a condition for the receipt of minimal subsistence benefits and termination of benefits after a fixed number of years constitute the negative incentive. Both aspects of the "reform" proposals are central to their appeal; in combination they help restore the value of self-reliance, the discipline of capitalism, and the role of the market in the determination of merit.

A Liberal Feminist Standpoint

Taking conservative arguments at face value, liberal feminists have mobilized to present a different account of "equal opportunity" in the contemporary United States. Feminist scholars launched the Committee of One Hundred to join established groups such as the National

Organization for Women (NOW), the Feminist Majority, the Women's Equity Action League, and the American Association of University Women (AAUW) to present a compelling case that discrimination on the basis of race and gender persists in contemporary society and can be demonstrated. Rather than assuming that the United States represents a just and primarily nondiscriminatory society, liberal feminists suggest that empirical evidence documents widespread, albeit subtle, discrimination.

The Glass Ceiling Commission (1995) appointed by U.S. President George Bush, found, for example, that although white men constitute only 37% of the American population, they hold 95% of the top managerial jobs in Fortune 1000 corporations. If one looks beyond the realm of senior management in American corporations, 8.5% of working women hold jobs that are classified as executive/managerial, compared to 20% of working men. While 60% of American women who work full time outside the home are in clerical and service sector jobs, compared to 15% of working men. The situation for African Americans is even more bleak. There is only one black CEO in the Fortune 1000 corporations. Although African Americans constitute 12.9% of the American population, they hold 0.6% of the senior management positions and 3% of executive/managerial positions in the contemporary United States. In 1990, 3.2% of American physicians were African American (down from 4% in 1970); 3% of all lawyers were African American (up from 1.5% in 1970); and 4.5% of university professors were African American (no change since 1970) (Hacker, 1992).

Acknowledging that statistics cannot provide definitive indicators of discrimination, liberal feminists yet insist that the pervasiveness of statistical underrepresentation of women and minorities in higher education, in higher paying employment and in positions of prestige and power is sufficient to establish a prima facie case of discrimination. But liberal feminists do not rest their arguments concerning the persistence of discrimination upon a demonstration of underrepresentation alone, for, as conservatives have argued, any number of variables can be introduced to explain such underrepresentation. Instead, they emphasize "underutilization" in an effort to explode the myth that the principle cause of underrepresentation is the inadequate supply of qualified women and minority applicants. Underutilization is defined as having fewer women/minorities in a job category actually employed than would reasonably be expected from their availability in the labor pool. In universities, for example, the Ph.D. is a legitimate prerequisite for employment. In 1993, 45% of all the doctorates awarded to U.S. citizens went to women, but women constituted only 35% of the new hires in universities (American Council on Education, 1995). The phenomenon to be explained then, is not the dearth of minority or female professionals per se, but the dearth of such professionals given the availability of a certain percentage of qualified minority and female candidates. The pervasive underutilization of qualified women and minorities in the United States renders suspicious any explanation that emphasizes personal choice. For it seems unlikely that individuals who have invested great effort to become qualified to apply for certain careers should suddenly choose not to pursue those professions.

Moving beyond statistics of underrepresentation and underutilization, liberal feminists have also examined the evidence from controlled experiments to document persistent discrimination. A 1991 Urban Institute study, for example, demonstrated pervasive racial discrimination in hiring by conducting job "audits," which paired black job candidates with identically qualified white candidates in a range of job competitions. Although possessing equal grade-point averages and work experience, blacks were unable to advance as far in the hiring process as whites 20% of the time and were denied jobs offered to equally qualified whites 15% of the time. As the skill level of the job increased, so too did the tendency to discriminate (Turner, Fix, & Struyk, 1991).

Nearly 30 years of research in social psychology has documented a persistent pervasive gender and race bias in evaluation. Psychologists have documented that given identical qualifications or performances, there is a general tendency to give men more favorable evaluations than women and to give whites more favorable evaluations than minorities. Moreover, there is ample evidence to indicate that performance by women and minority group members is systematically downgraded by employers and school teachers and evaluated more positively when race or sex is unknown to the evaluator (Gutek & Stevens, 1979; Haefner, 1977; Nieva & Gutek, 1980; Rosen & Jerdee, 1974; Shaw, 1974). Thus, women and minorities experience a form of discrimination that exists over and above the problems of underrepresentation and pay differentials (Hughes, 1975 p. 26). They are treated as beings less worthy of respect than the average white male, not because of any individual weakness or failing but simply because they are members of a particular group.

The disrespect shown to women and minorities on the basis of their sex, race, or ethnicity highlights the fact that the competition for educational and economic opportunities is neither neutral nor fair, for women and minorities are judged by standards irrelevant to the competition. A tacit pro-white, pro-male bias in admissions, hiring, and evaluation procedures constitutes a form of discrimination that continues to harm women and minorities not because of their individual characteristics but because of their membership in particular groups.

On this view, one great benefit of affirmative action's insistence on good faith efforts to recruit women and minority candidates lies precisely in its ability to help "whites recognize that their own advantages are, in significant measure, group benefits, rather than individual achievements and that their own success has been, in part, a matter of their own superior group opportunities, purchased at the expense of opportunities for non-whites" (Livingston, 1979, p. 182). Recognition of the role played by race and gender privilege in decisions concerning admissions, hiring, and promotion procedures also suggests that neither the criteria employed in these decisions nor the individual employing them are "neutral" or "impersonal." It is not the market's "Invisible Hand" that determines applicants' merit and prospects for success, but the decisions of fallible administrators who serve as gatekeepers to the positions of power and privilege in contemporary society.

Given their diagnosis of the problem as ongoing discrimination in the form antiminority, antifemale bias, liberal feminists argue that affirmative action is a fair and appropriate remedy. As a mechanism for the cultivation of a recognition of the talent of all persons in society, affirmative action does not jeopardize principles of merit or standards of excellence. It simply prohibits situations in which the only ones allowed to demonstrate their merit are white males. Through the establishment of fair hiring practices and competition open to public inspection, affirmative action ensures that white men "compete fairly on the basis of merit, not fraternity, on demonstrated capability, not assumed superiority" (Pottinger, 1971, p. 29). By focusing attention on admitting, hiring, and promoting members of particular target groups, affirmative action draws attention to both the consequences of historic racism and sexism and to the extent, the gravity and the immediacy of the injuries still experienced by minorities and women in the United States.

Liberal feminists acknowledge that affirmative action causes white males to lose certain advantages, yet they deny that the loss constitutes a violation of individual rights. On the contrary, liberal feminists stress that white men currently occupying favored positions in existing organizations have themselves been the beneficiaries of some preferential treatment: "They are members of a group of persons who have been privileged in hiring and promotion in accordance with normal practices of long-standing, persons who have been offered better educational preparation than others of the same basic talents, persons whose egos have been strengthened more than members of other groups" (Held, 1975, p. 34). Because these white males did not deserve such preferential treatment, because they had no right to the advantages afforded by a racist and sexist society, no rights are being violated by the removal of those advantages. Policies to promote justice for the victims of injustice may require that white men lose their unwarranted privilege in society but they do not strip these individuals of legitimate rights.

In their efforts to engage the "war against poor women," liberal feminists have also launched a barrage of facts to counter persistent misrepresentations of the poor in conservative political rhetoric. Contrary to pernicious stereotypes, poor women do not see welfare as a desirable way of life. They do not "get pregnant" in order qualify for or increase welfare benefits. Indeed, Aid to Families with Dependent Children (AFDC) recipients have a lower fertility rate than other American women of childbearing age. The typical welfare recipient seeks assistance during a crisis caused by illness, unemployment, domestic violence, or divorce, relies upon public assistance for less than 2 years, and returns to the labor force at the earliest opportunity (Thomas, 1994).

Conservative stereotypes of the poor routinely invoke the "pathological theory of poverty," which attributes the cause of poverty to the characteristics or "defects" of the poor themselves (Handler, 1972, p. 3). Assuming that the market economy places success within the reach of any hardworking individual, conservatives assert that individual effort is all that stands between the rich and the poor. Thus, the poor are peculiarly responsible for their own fate. Those who choose to live in ignominious conditions by willfully refusing to take advantage of the opportunities that the free market affords are morally reprehensible. On this view, "laziness" or unwillingness to work is a form of moral defect for which the poor should be held strictly accountable.

Liberal feminists have pointed out that the pathological theory of poverty does not fit the facts of American poverty. An examination of the demographic characteristics of the poor suggests that the pathological theory is fundamentally flawed. "The poor" in the United States are a large and diverse group. Many of the "officially poor," that is, those who currently live below the "poverty line" set by the U.S. government, work full-time outside the home (Levitan & Shapiro, 1987; Spalter-Roth, Burr, Hartmann & Shaw, 1995). In 1995, a full-time employee working for minimum wages earned $2,000 a year less than the poverty line for a family of three (Chideya, 1995). Of the "officially poor," only 38 million Americans receive government assistance. Far more receive Supplemental Security Income (for the elderly, blind, and disabled) than received AFDC. More than two thirds of recipients of public assistance are unable to work because of age, disability, or caretaking responsibilities for preschool-aged children. Forty-eight percent of households with pretransfer incomes below the poverty line are headed by individuals aged 65 or older, another 12% are headed by disabled individuals, 7% are headed by women with children under the age of 6. Of the remaining households receiving public assistance, 7.5% are headed by persons who work full-time year-round but whose incomes are insufficient to meet family subsistence needs, 20.4% are headed by persons who are employed but not on a full-time basis, and 5% are headed by students (Danziger & Gottschalk, 1983, 1993; Edin & Lein, 1997).

Recent studies of AFDC recipients (the subset of the poor most frequently characterized in terms of the pathological theory of poverty) indicate that the belief that AFDC household heads do not work or will not work is simply mistaken. Although 63% of the 4 million women receiving AFDC benefits in 1995 had children under the age of 5 (Mink, 1996), 70% of AFDC households had at least one earner during the years on welfare. In 40% of these households, it is the head who earns the income, in the remainder, the earnings are those of older children within the household (Rein, 1982; Spalter-Roth et al. 1995). In direct contrast to popular stereotypes, black women receiving AFDC worked far more often than white women. There was also much greater movement between welfare and work than the pathological theory suggests. Only 2% of households receiving public benefits remain on welfare for 8 years or more (Thomas, 1994). The vast majority resorted to welfare to upgrade their total income because their earnings from work were inadequate or because their earning capacity had been temporarily undermined due to unemployment.

A number of studies of the attitudes of the poor toward work also challenge the pathological theory's accuracy. In answer to the question, "Do the poor want to work?," research on the work orientations of the poor has concluded that the poor do want to work. The work ethic is upheld strongly by AFDC recipients and work plays an important role in their life goals. Indeed, results from comprehensive studies of the attitudes of the poor toward work "unambiguously indicate that AFDC recipients, regardless of sex, age or race, identify their self-esteem with work as strongly as do the non-poor.... Despite their adverse position in society and their past failures in the labor force, these persons clearly upheld the work ethic and voiced strong commitments toward work" (Berkeley Planning Associates, Inc., 1980, p. 92; see also Edin & Lein, 1997; Goodale, 1973; Goodwin, 1972; Gueron & Pauly, 1991; Handier, 1995; Kaplan & Tausky, 1972; Schiller, 1973; Tienda & Stier, 1991).

From the liberal feminist standpoint, the pathological theory of poverty that underlies conservatives' demands for "welfare reform" rests upon a number of misconceptions. Contrary to the pathological view, the able-bodied poor share the American commitment to the work ethic and they do work. Their problem is not one of attitude but one of inadequate pay or inadequate employment opportunities (Edin & Lein, 1997; Handier, 1995). The market economy has not afforded these individuals the mythologized avenues of upward social mobility. Recent research suggests that even in an expanding economy, the market will not provide an escape from poverty for these individuals in the future. "The evidence from the recent past suggests that economic growth will not raise the earnings of the poor enough to enable many of them to escape poverty without government assistance. The major factor contributing to the reduction of poverty since 1996 seems to have been the growth in government transfers, which offset increases in poverty resulting from demographic changes and high unemployment rates. Economic growth *per se* seems to have had little effect" (Danziger & Gottschalk, 1983, p. 750).

The great majority of welfare recipients who have been involved with "workfare" and those who are now involved in welfare to work programs have been placed in low-level maintenance and clerical positions. Jobs such as cutting grass, picking up trash, washing dishes, mopping and waxing floors, driving senior citizen vans, moving furniture, childcare, and general office work have been typical (Burtless, 1995; Edin & Lein, 1997; Linden & Vincent, 1982). Evaluation studies note that program administrators have made no effort to offer participants jobs that utilize work skills that they already possess, nor have administrators made placements that enable participants to acquire marketable skills. Moreover, assignments tend to be in unskilled jobs, precisely the kind of jobs that are prone to elimination during periods of economic recession (Briggs, Rungeling, & Smith, 1980; Danziger & Gottschalk, 1993; DeParle, 1997; Friedman & Hausman, 1975; Rosen, 1980). Several evaluation studies suggest that placing welfare recipients in jobs that require few job skills actually lessens their chances of obtaining employment that affords sufficient income to escape poverty. A welfare recipient who succeeds in finding a job in the workforce equivalent to the welfare work assignment will earn too little to support a household (Bernstein & Goodwin, 1978; DeParle, 1997; Edin & Lein, 1997).

Liberal feminists situate backlash in the context of partisan politics. The increasingly vitriolic attack on poor women emerged in Reagan's 1970 gubernatorial campaign and has been a staple of Republican political rhetoric ever since, most recently reinvigorated in the 1994 Congressional elections in the form of the "Contract With America." California Governor Pete Wilson launched his attack on affirmative action as a tactic to advance his presidential aspirations; Senator Robert Dole introduced legislation to abolish all federal affirmative action programs for much the same reason. Trading on the Republican Party's "Southern strategy," Republican presidential aspirants hope that racism and sexism will help them secure the votes of the "social conservatives" (Melich, 1996).

To fight backlash then, liberal feminists are taking their arsenal of facts to the public forum. They have taken out full-page ads in, and submitted letters to the editors of the major national newspapers. They have formed a formidable lobby in Washington. They have staged vigils at the White House. They have conducted letter-writing campaigns, held press conferences, developed networks, and circulated information to groups across the country. They have organized sophisticated e-mail distribution mechanisms to orchestrate grassroots mobilization when critical votes are pending in Congress. They mobilized against Proposition 209, the California initiative to abolish affirmative action, organizing a house-to-house canvas by student volunteers during the summer of 1996. Under the banner, "A War Against Poor Women Is a War Against All Women," liberal feminists have sought to build solidarity among women in their fight to secure the minimal provisions of the American welfare state. Toward that end they launched a massive public education and voter registration campaign—"Freedom Summer '96"—to double the voter registration among those 18 to 24-year-olds and to encourage Americans to vote in order to save women's rights and civil rights (De Witt, 1996).

A Socialist Feminist Standpoint

Socialist feminists are profoundly ambivalent about affirmative action. As a policy developed within the bourgeois state to advance the interests of the privileged, affirmative action poses no threat to capitalism, to class hierarchy, or to the status quo. Indeed, affirmative action lends an air of credibility to capitalist patriarchy by erroneously suggesting that it can promote the interests and equality of women and people of color. It thereby situates discussions of racial and gender justice within the narrow and restrictive compass of "equal opportunity." By suggesting that discrimination is the primary problem that women and people of color face in contemporary society, affirmative action policies obscure and deny the structural and institutional framework of capitalist oppression. From a socialist feminist standpoint, policies that mask the complex dimensions of oppression are deeply problematic. "If one focuses on discrimination as the primary wrong groups suffer, then the more profound wrongs of exploitation, marginalization, powerlessness, cultural imperialism, and violence that we still suffer go undiscussed and unaddressed" (Young, 1990, pp. 196–197).

Long before affirmative action came under attack, socialist feminists offered a range of principled objections to this mode of liberal reformism. Affirmative action neither challenges nor transforms the hierarchical division of labor in the capitalist workplace. It merely seeks to change the race and gender composition of the elite. In eliminating racist and sexist hiring and admissions practices, affirmative action benefits the "most privileged" of the formerly disadvantaged, that is, the well-educated, middle-class women and people of color. As prominent "tokens" like Clarence Thomas, Linda Chavez, and Lynne Cheney make clear, there is no reason to believe that even a substantial increase in the representation of racial and gender groups in positions of power and prestige would benefit women and minorities in general. Indeed, the votes of Clarence Thomas on the Supreme Court in cases such as *Adarand v. Pena* make it painfully clear that the career advances of some "tokens" can have disastrous consequences for the oppressed. Thus the critical issue is not more women and minorities in power *per se*, but using power for progressive/socialist/feminist political ends. Neither race nor gender constitutes a guarantee of progressive political inclinations (Barrett, 1985, p. 242).

Socialist feminists have also pointed out that those who endorse affirmative action on the belief that women and people of color can work within the system to benefit the oppressed fail to recognize the power of institutional resistance to subversion from within and the likelihood of co-optation. On this view, feminist efforts to infiltrate hierarchies of power inevitably succumb to "careerism," to feminist accommodation to the status quo, or to the development of policies that heighten institutions' control over the oppressed (Barrett, 1985, p. 244).

Any socialist feminist effort to defend affirmative action illuminates this problematic. To defend affirmative action is to endorse a policy that reinforces a range of myths about the market's "just distribution" of jobs on the basis of "merit." Advocates of affirmative action promise that the elimination of race and gender bias will create the possibility for "true merit hiring." They trust that the notion of individual "qualifications" poses no insurmountable problems. They believe that it is "possible to measure, compare, and rank individual performance of job-related tasks using criteria that are normatively and culturally neutral" (Young, 1990, p. 193). Moreover, they accept the hierarchical organization of society, as well as the scarcity of positions of high income, power, and prestige, asking only that these positions be distributed on the basis of merit. The defense of affirmative action co-opts feminists into endorsing an inegalitarian competition in which the vast majority of competitors are destined to lose.

Socialist feminists have pointed out that "[e]ven if strong affirmative action programs existed in most institutions, they would have only a minor effect in altering the basic structure of group privilege and oppression in the United States. Since these programs require that racially or sexually preferred candidates be qualified, indeed highly qualified, they do nothing directly to increase opportunities for Blacks, Latinos, or women whose social environment and lack of resources make getting qualified nearly impossible for them" (Young, 1990, p. 199). To avoid being co-opted and to make significant contributions to the struggle for equality, feminists would be better off fighting the myth of a market-based meritocracy, challenging the justice of any hierarchical division of labor, and changing "the overall patterns of racial and gender stratification in our society [which] would require major changes in the structure of the economy, the process of job allocation, the character of the social division of labor and access to schooling and training" (Young, 1990, p. 199).

Although the logic of socialist feminist arguments concerning affirmative action is not changed by recent conservative attacks on affirmative action, the horizon of progressive political struggle has been constricted. Thus socialist feminists have joined coalitions to defend the small gains, made through such reformist strategies. They bring to these coalitions important concerns about the meaning of the conservative attack on liberal policies and the ideological functions of the "war" against women and people of color. From a socialist feminist standpoint, it is a mistake to construe these issues solely in terms of partisan electoral politics. The conservative vilification of women and the poor serves as a diversionary tactic that focuses attention on society's disadvantaged while masking structural transformations within capitalism. On this view, conservative arguments concerning the erosion of merit standards under affirmative action and conservative claims concerning the erosion of individual responsibility under welfare programs share crucial ideological affinities. Both reinforce individualist premises that structure policy debates in terms of individual success and failure, blinding the public to the possibility that social problems and economic crises can only be systematically addressed when treated structurally and collectively.

From a socialist feminist standpoint, the attack on poor women under the guise of "welfare reform" involves ideological distortions that cannot be grasped within a framework of partisan politics. Indeed, both the Democratic and the Republican parties made a commitment to "end welfare as we know it." Bill Clinton advanced the slogan during his 1992 bid for the presidency and the Republicans incorporated the idea into their "Contract with America" during the congressional elections in 1994. Both parties cooperated to pass legislation to replace AFDC entitlements with Temporary Assistance for Needy Families (TANF), which was signed into law by President Clinton in August 1996. According to socialist feminists relentless harangues against the poor in both parties' campaign rhetoric have produced systemic misperceptions in American politics: "A poll of 1994 voters found that one of five believed that welfare was *the largest* federal government expense, larger than the military budget. The reality is that AFDC spending since 1964 has amounted to less than 1.5 percent of federal outlays" (Sklar, 1995, p. 23).

While American voters are whipped into a frenzy of resentment against the "undeserving poor," the structural forces that threaten their fragile economic security go largely unnoticed. Changes in tax policy have produced the highest income inequality in the United States since 1929. During the past two decades, the share of the nation's income received by the top 5% of Americans increased nearly 25%, from 18.6 to 24.5%, while the share of income received by the poorest 20% fell by nearly 25%, from 5.7 to 4.3%. The richest quintile of Americans "earned" 46.9% of the nation's total income, while the middle 60% of the population earned 49.4%, and the poorest quintile earned 3.8% (Center on Hunger, Poverty, and Nutrition Policy, 1995). As corporate profits have soared since 1979, 43 million jobs, many of which were white-collar, high-paying positions, have been eliminated through "downsizing." Although there has been a net increase of 27 million jobs in the United States during this period, the newly created jobs are concentrated in the far less lucrative service sector. "The sting is in the nature of the replacement work. Whereas 25 years ago the vast majority of the people who were laid off found jobs that paid as well as their old ones, Labor Department numbers show that now only about 35% of laidoff workers end up in equally remunerative or better paid jobs" (Uchitelle & Kleinfield, 1996, pp. 1, 14). As the prospect of secure employment becomes increasingly rare, so too does the hope of earning a living wage. When adjusted for inflation, workforce-wide hourly wages fell 14% between 1973 and 1993. For those in the lowest ranks of the income pyramid, the loss in earning power has been much greater. "An unforgiving labor market, in recession and recovery alike, has hammered young, less-educated women.... Between 1979 and 1989, hourly wages plummeted for these women, falling most rapidly for African American women who didn't finish high school. This group's hourly wages, adjusted for inflation, fell 20% in that 10 year period" (Tilly & Albelda, 1994, p. 9). The unemployed have fared no better: the median AFDC payment has been slashed 47% since 1970, adjusting for inflation (Sklar, 1995, p. 22).

From a socialist feminist standpoint, "[i]mpoverished women don't create poverty any more than slaves created slavery. But they are primary scapegoats for illegitimate economics" (Sklar, 1995, p. 21). They provide a handy focal point for a vicious politics of resentment, while corporate greed escapes all public scrutiny. They provide the ideological camouflage for the

> ... fiscal doctrine of unlimited, unending deficit reduction [which] is not aimed at stable prices, full employment, and greater private investment. Rather, the motivations are to reduce the size of government, to disassemble the U.S. system of social insurance, and to maintain unyielding downward pressure on the price level. The implied economic policy is one of stagnation: a disproportionate weight is put on low inflation to the detriment of employment, investment, and general economic growth. The policy is also counter-redistributive: it favors wealth holders at the expense of wage-earners, the elderly, and the poor. If stated outright, these goals would be manifestly unpopular, so the sales pitch for extreme deficit reduction has to focus elsewhere—on creating and perpetuating misconceptions or downright superstitions about the federal budget and the public debt. (Sawicky, cited in Sklar, 1995, pp. 23-24)

For socialist feminists capitalism remains the underlying problem of the liberal democratic state. The politics of backlash manages to mask the increasing concentration of wealth by scapegoating African Americans, women, and the poor. As such, backlash must be understood as a brilliant strategic move in the new class war and it must be understood that backlash will be systematically addressed only when the underclasses mobilize effectively to expropriate their expropriators.

A Black Feminist Standpoint

The experiences of African Americans in the contemporary United States provide a markedly different framework within which to analyze antifeminist backlash. Both the attack on affirmative action and the war against poor women have been widely interpreted as a racist code, grounded in white supremacy, that reasserts racial stratification. Within this framework, race constitutes a "metalanguage" that reinscribes the master/slave relation in the policy discourses of the liberal welfare state (Higginbotham, 1992, p. 255). What appears so clearly to be "backlash" from a white feminist standpoint surfaces within this frame as perpetuation and consolidation of white privilege, a prophylactic against any systemic gains for African Americans.

From a black feminist standpoint, racially coded policy discourse operates at the boundaries of consciousness, mystifying the power dynamics of contemporary racial oppression and suggesting levels of black affluence and success and degrees of white victimization altogether inconsistent with any examination of prevailing social relations. (Able, 1993; Carby, 1987). Only with the framework of racial codes can one make sense of recent polls, such as that sponsored by the *Washington Post*, the Kaiser Family Foundation, and Harvard University, which found that a majority of whites believe that blacks are as well off or better off than whites: 46% of whites said that blacks on average held jobs of equal quality to those of whites, 6% said that blacks had jobs that were "a little better" than those held by whites, and another 6% said blacks had jobs that were "a lot better" than those held by whites. "The overwhelming majority of whites said that blacks have an equal chance to succeed, that whites bear no responsibility for the problems blacks face today, and that it's not the government's role to ensure that all races have equal jobs, pay, or housing" (Morin, 1995, p. A6). Only within the framework of racial codes can one comprehend how contrary to all empirical evidence, young white Americans have come to believe that they are more likely to be victims of reverse discrimination than African Americans or Hispanics are to suffer from racial bias (Chideya, 1995). By inverting prevailing power relations, racial codes insulate whites from the glaring evidence of racial inequality in our nation. They render Census Bureau statistics "unbelievable." Within racially coded discourse, Rush Limbaugh's wild imaginings have greater credibility than social science reports that document that the median income of white households was $32,960 in 1993, while the median income of black households was only $19,533; that 46.6% of black children under the age of 18 lived in poverty in 1992 compared with 16.9% of white children; that the unemployment rate for black adults was 9.2% in 1995, more than double the 4.3% for whites; that 31.7% of black teenagers actively seeking employment could not find work, while only 12.9% of white youth experienced the same problem (Rowan, 1995). Convinced by racially coded discourses that blacks are receiving "special" preferences, whites cannot comprehend that more black families were living in poverty in 1990 (37%) than in 1970 (34%) (Hacker, 1992).

From a black feminist standpoint, the myth of preferential treatment for blacks makes sense only within a framework that presupposes white superiority. Reinforced by the "scientific" racism of Richard Hernstein and Charles Murray's *The Bell Curve* (Hernstein & Murray, 1994) and Dinesh D'Souza's *The End of Racism* (D'Souza, 1995), many white Americans accept a vicious logic: blacks are intellectually inferior to whites, thus the only way they can attain positions of high pay, power, and prestige is through preferential treatment, which necessarily entails hiring "unqualified" blacks for positions that qualified whites "deserve." The language of reverse discrimination thus acts to consolidate the conviction of white superiority, while denigrating the talents of successful African Americans, sustaining the "stigma" associated with affirmative action that is so lamented by black conservatives. It also provides a soothing balm to the egos of thoroughly mediocre whites who can convince themselves that their failure to secure desired employment is the "fault" of blacks rather than the consequence of their own limited abilities.

Black feminists point out that racially coded policy discourse is thoroughly mystifying. Indeed, its commodification of otherness allows opposites to embrace (hooks, 1992). The very same whites who believe that blacks are *flourishing* during the era of corporate downsizing also believe that blacks *are* the pathological poor, who must be disciplined by the strictures of the market, forced from the welfare rolls (Bond, 1996). The rhetoric of "welfare reform" artfully reconfigures poverty as a "social/cultural/psychological pathology, corroborated by a public discourse of deficiency and remediation" (Polakow, 1993, p. 3). In projecting the image of "welfare cheats" as the fundamental problem of poverty policy, racially coded policy discourse constructs a poverty population of wanton, voraciously sexual, black adults, who pose a threat to American "family values." The distortions in this stereotype again eclipse the facts: that 10 million of the 14 million AFDC recipients are children under the age of 18 and that the majority of welfare recipients are white are facts that disappear in the tunnel vision of white supremacist "solipsism" (Spelman, 1988, p. 116; see also Edin & Lein, 1997).

Interrogating these ideological distortions, black feminists have situated the debate on "welfare reform" in the unrelenting history of racist practices of the American state. On this view, the war against poor women must be understood in relation to the long tradition of white hegemony that gave birth to slavery, the "separate but equal" doctrine, disenfranchising electoral practices, and the exclusion of domestics and agricultural laborers (black-dominant occupations) from social security provision. Within this tradition, the attack on welfare can be construed as a women first strategy in the Republican war against big government (Mink, 1996), a war that includes incursions against the economic gains made by African Americans who have found employment with the federal government. More than one third of all African American lawyers and 30% of all black scientists work for the federal government (Hacker, 1992). Employment in the federal bureaucracy, often in the "redistributive agencies" of the welfare state, has been the primary route to middle class existence for many African American women. "Great society programs in the 1960s heightened the importance of social welfare employment for all groups, particularly women. Between 1960 and 1980, human services accounted for 41% of the job gains for women compared with 21% for men. Among women, there were significant differences in the importance of human services employment for whites and blacks. For white women, the social welfare economy accounted for 39% of the job gain between 1960 and 1980; for black women, an even more dramatic 58%" (Erie, Rein, & Wiget, 1983, p. 103). "Downsizing" the government places the economic security, the precondition for autonomous citizenship, at risk for millions of African Americans.

Although welfare "reformers" construct themselves as the defenders of the American family, their racially coded diatribes against pregnant teens suggest that childbearing and childrearing are not rights secured to all citizens by the U.S. Constitution (Roberts, 1997). On the contrary, the recent welfare "reform" creates a class of women required by law to work outside the home, a move that denies the value of work involved in mothering, while infringing intolerably upon individual choices concerning childbearing and childrearing (Mink, 1996). Once again differential rights are accorded to Americans on the basis of race and economic duress. Patricia Hill Collins (1995) has suggested that the family must be understood as a discursive site of belonging that envelops issues of space, territory, and home. When blacks are constructed as a fundamental threat to American "family values," racism's code can be translated in a variety of vernaculars: there is no space of racial harmony; there is no room for racial integration; blacks have no home in white America; they are not welcome here.

Beverly Guy-Sheftall (1995) has noted that the idealized nuclear family, with the male breadwinner and the homemaker mother, is a bourgeois Eurocentric norm that bears little resemblance to family relations allowed slaves by their masters. When this norm is invoked by white Americans in the late 20th century, it must be understood as a hegemonic move designed to eradicate a perceived threat. In 1995, 60% of black children were raised in women-headed families. The love that black mothers afford their children, providing a sense of self-esteem that withstands the trials of racism and the onset of puberty, and the shared solidarity networks that foster collective responsibility among "other mothers" within the black community do indeed challenge the white bourgeois insistence that families must be heterosexual, nuclear, and male-dominant. Within this context, the castigation of welfare mothers and black teenage pregnancy when black teenagers constitute less than 12% of unmarried mothers (Usdansky, 1996) functions as a racist code that discursively constructs black families as a symbol of what must not be (Collins, 1990, 1995). When Norplant® implants for black teenagers in Baltimore high schools are added into the equation, the specter of Margaret Sanger's eugenic agenda seems far too close for comfort. Welfare "reform" becomes a guise for new social control mechanisms devised to ban poor black women from reproducing (Roberts, 1997). Incorporated into the policies of a racist state, "welfare reform" has a complex agenda: coercively enforcing white norms of feminine dependency, sexuality, morality and family; eliminating the economic security essential for equal citizenship; controlling the fertility of poor black women and thereby contributing to racial engineering; and reiterating the demand, unchanged since slavery, that black women be the "mules of the world" (Hurston, 1978, p. 29).

From a black feminist standpoint, racially coded policy discourses concerning affirmative action and "welfare reform" are symptoms of resurgent white supremacy. Although resistance must be mounted at these sites of contemporary oppression, these local struggles must be understood in the context of a larger campaign against racist hegemony. Success in securing a decent standard of living for poor women or in repulsing the conservative attack on affirmative action must be supplemented by systematic extirpation of the racism which is their root cause.

A Postmodern Feminist Perspective

The premises of postmodern feminism make the aggregation of the views of postmodern feminists problematic. Arguing that "women's experience is thoroughly constructed, historically and culturally varied, and interpreted without end" (Brown, 1995, p. 41), postmodern feminists caution that feminists must be wary of those who speak for women in terms that totalize and exclude. Calling instead for a politics of voice within a space of contestation, postmodern feminists insist that we must attend to "who speaks for whom as much as to what is said" (Yeatman, 1994, p. 15). In the words of Wendy Brown, "When the notion of a unified and coherent subject is abandoned, we ... cease to be able to speak of woman or for women in an unproblematic way ... dispensing with the unified subject does not mean ceasing to be able to speak about our experiences as women, only that our words cannot be legitimately deployed or construed as larger or longer than the moments of the lives they speak from" (pp. 40–41).

Recognizing such concerns for the particularity of individual perspective, this section will take up the view of just one postmodern feminist on backlash, one view that affords a vista markedly different from those considered to this point. In *States of Injury: Power and Freedom in Late Modernity*, Wendy Brown (1995) offers an interpretation of backlash in terms of the normalizing practices of the disciplinary state fueled by the psychological force of Nietzschean *ressentiment*. Seeking to illuminate a number of paradoxes of contemporary politics, Brown emphasizes that the Right's antigovernment discourse has masked a steady expansion of state powers and retrenchment of citizen rights over the past 20 years. While anti-statist rhetoric diverts attention from increasing state domination, it also incites liberal and leftist protectiveness toward the state:

> As the powers constituting late modern configurations of capitalism and the state have grown more complex, more pervasive, and simultaneously more difficult to track, both critical analyses of their power and a politics rooted in such a critique have tended to recede. Indeed Western leftists have largely forsaken analyses of the liberal state and capitalism as sites of domination and have focused instead on their implication in political and economic inequalities. At the same time, progressives have implicitly assumed the relatively unproblematic instrumental value of the state and capitalism in redressing such inequalities. (Brown, 1995, p. 10)

According to Brown (1995), this obliviousness to state domination locks progressive efforts that appeal to the state to remedy inequalities into a reactionary cycle that "reinstates rather than transforms the terms of domination that generated them" (p. 7). In appealing to the state for rights, African Americans, Hispanics, Jews, women, and gays and lesbians seek a legal protection that "discursively entrenches the injury-identity connection it denounces ... codify[ing] within the law the very powerlessness it seeks to redress ... discursively collud[ing] with the conversion of attribute into identity, of historical effect of power into presumed cause of victimization" (Brown, 1995, p. 21). Failing to recognize that politicized identity is itself a regulatory production of a disciplinary society, those who appeal to the liberal state for redress of injuries fail to comprehend that hard-won rights "imprison us within the subject positions they are secured to affirm and protect" (Brown, 1995, p. 120).

Brown argues that rather than contributing to an emancipatory project, rights privatize and depoliticize, mystifying and reifying "social powers (property and wealth, but also race, sexuality, and gender) as the natural possessions of private persons." (Brown, 1995, p. 123). In so doing, rights do not liberate us from relations of class, sexuality, gender, or race; on the contrary they obfuscate power relations, creating a fictive equality of sovereign subjects before the law. According to Brown (1995), it is precisely this conversion of social problems into matters of individualized, dehistoricized injury and entitlement that gives rise to claims of reverse discrimination.

Within the framework of Nietzschean *ressentiment*, a peculiar affinity emerges between the reverse discrimination claims of white men and the claims of racial and sexual discrimination advanced by women and people of color. Both are incited by "the moralizing revenge of the powerless, 'the triumph of the weak as weak'" (Brown, 1995, p. 67). According to Brown (1995),

> ... this incitement to *ressentiment* inheres in two related constitutive paradoxes of liberalism: that between individual liberty and social egalitarianism, a paradox which produces failure turned to recrimination by the subordinated, and guilt turned into resentment by the "successful"; and that between the individualism that legitimates liberalism and the cultural homogeneity required by its commitment to political universality, a paradox which stimulates the articulation

of politically significant differences on the one hand, and the suppression of them on the other. (p. 67)

From this Nietzschean perspective, the political tactics of both the proponents and opponents of affirmative action are fueled by the same desire to inscribe past and present injury in the law. As such, the tactics of both sides conform to the same impetus to avenge hurt and redistribute pain. In both instances, *ressentiment* "produces an affect (rage, righteousness) that overwhelms the hurt; and it produces a site of revenge to displace the hurt (a place to inflict hurt as the sufferer has been hurt). Together these operations both ameliorate (in Nietzsche's term *anaesthetize*) and externalize what is otherwise 'unendurable'" (Brown, 1995, p. 68).

The discursive construction of impoverished women as "dependents," an idiom that conveniently links images of addiction with images of childhood, can also be understood in terms of reactionary, victim-blaming politics of *ressentiment* and the disciplinary practices that produce dependent state subjects. But such an understanding problematizes solutions that appeal to the state for redress. Thus, Brown (1995) questions feminist tactics that would expand women's relationships to state institutions. Rather than empowering women, these "expanding relationships produce regulated, subordinated, and disciplined state subjects . . . reconfigur[ing] compulsory motherhood . . . intensifying the isolation of women in reproductive work, ghettoiz[ing] women in service work . . . exchanging dependence upon individual men for regulation by contemporary institutionalized processes of male domination" (p. 173).

Understanding backlash in terms of *ressentiment* and the disciplinary practices of the state makes the identification of progressive political tactics enormously complex. Brown (1995) notes that her critique of liberal rights discourses relevant to both the affirmative action debate and antipoverty policies "does not build toward policy recommendations or a specific political program" (p. 173). Nevertheless, she does suggest that to reconceptualize freedom in order to contest contemporary antidemocratic configurations of power, we must move beyond the political economy of perpetrator and victim that cedes political ground to moral and juridical ground thereby reducing politics to punishment (Brown, 1995, p. 27). To the extent that a politics fixed upon revenge is mired in the past injury that produced it, an emancipatory strategy must be oriented toward the future. Brown cautions that the centrality of "erased histories and historical invisibility" to the pain of "subjugated identities" mitigates against any embrace of "Nietzsche's counsel on the virtues of 'forgetting'" (Brown, 1995, p. 74). Instead, she suggests we begin a new political conversation in which the demand for revenge is supplanted by the demand for recognition. Within this radically democratic discourse, the ontological defensiveness of politicized identity would be replaced by contestation among "unwieldy and shifting pluralities adjudicating for themselves and their future on the basis of nothing more than their own habits and arguments" (Brown, 1995, p. 37). Within this mode of political speech, designed to "destabilize the formulation of identity as fixed position, entrenched history, mandated moral entailment," agonistic practices discursively forging an alternative future would banish the dispersion of blame for an unlivable present (Brown, 1995, pp. 75-76).

Standpoint Theory as Analytical Tool

As an analytical tool, feminist standpoint theory encourages researchers to consider competing accounts of the same phenomenon. But once multiple views have been collected, what is the analyst to do with them? Can incompatible claims be adjudicated? Are there criteria for determining the comparative merits of alternative accounts?

Judith Grant (1993) has suggested that feminist standpoint theory can be reinterpreted as a "self-consciously derived theoretical tool in service of a politics" (p. 119). On her view, conceiving feminist standpoints as an analytical tool shifts the focus from epistemological issues to feminist politics. As a heuristic device, the central concern is whether competing feminist standpoints can help us to make backlash intelligible, to understand the forces that fuel it, and to devise strategies that empower women to resist oppression. Within this context several questions require critical assessment: Does standpoint theory succeed in helping us comprehend the complexity of backlash? Does it help us chart an emancipatory feminist political course?

Each of the standpoints presented here was constructed largely from writings by and about women. Each tries to make sense of contemporary social relations. Each identifies issues of political concern and a direction for concerted political action. Examination of competing standpoints offers a systematic overview of the dimensions of backlash politics. And for those interested in fostering democratic politics, it could be argued, the competing standpoints on backlash identify the issues that must be taken up in public debate. Standpoint theory as analytical tool expands the terms of political discussion, airing claims too frequently silenced in the contemporary political fray. On this view, crucial differences among these views cannot be resolved at a theoretical level. They must be resolved through an open political struggle in which we as people decide what kind of a political community we wish to be.

While such an account of the utility of standpoint theory has much to commend it, in certain respects it seems too pat. It retreats too quickly from theoretical analysis to majority rule and in so doing replicates the subjectivist premises so characteristic of contemporary politics (MacIntyre, 1981). How are political participants to choose between the political prescriptions of conservative women, liberal feminists, socialist feminists, black feminists, and postmodern feminists? Is it all to be a matter of politics, interest accommodation, or the manipulative ploys of wiles and wills? If so, is there any hope for justice for disempowered groups?

Standpoint theory as epistemology insists that there are grounds for distinguishing between error and truth, for discriminating between a standpoint and ideology (Harding, 1991, 1992; Hirschmann, 1993; Rixecker, 1994). But in identifying the experiences of situated knowers as the ground for such distinctions, standpoint theory as epistemic doctrine leads us in an unhelpful direction, miring us in a mode of subjectivism that sustains both an unshakable conviction in the veracity of one's own experience and relativist resignation concerning the impossibility of adjudicating incompatible, experience-based claims (Hawkesworth, 1989). Competing appeals to "experience" acknowledge no criteria for choosing between incompatible accounts. In the absence of good reasons to sustain preference for one view over another, politics cannot help but become manipulative and rancorous (MacIntyre, 1981).

Perhaps there is another way to understand the utility of standpoint theory as analytical tool. Postpositivist conceptions of knowledge emphasize that theoretical presuppositions structure perception, the definition of an appropriate research question, the nature of acceptable evidence, data collection and analysis, and the interpretation of research findings. A methodology that requires investigation of multiple interpretations of the same phenomenon may help to illuminate the theoretical assumptions that frame and accredit the constitution of facticity within each explanatory account. By engaging competing theoretical frameworks, feminist standpoint theory as analytical tool can make visible dimensions of political analysis in need of critical assessment. Juxtaposing incompatible accounts forces the analyst to engage questions concerning the adequacy and internal consistency of the theoretical presuppositions, the standards of evidence and the models of explanation accredited by the competing accounts (Hawkesworth, 1988).

Consider, for example, the contradictory claims of conservative women and liberal feminists concerning the adequacy of the pathological theory of poverty. While these claims cannot be resolved by appealing to the experiences of the women who advance them, theoretical critiques of atomistic and methodological individualism in conjunction with aggregate economic data and survey research involving poor women can provide ample evidence of the flaws of the pathological account of poverty (Edin & Lein, 1997). Given the pervasive evidence against the pathological account, the question that must be investigated is why so many people find this erroneous account plausible. How can such "evidence blindness" be explained?

Standpoint theory as epistemology tends to appeal either to conceptions of ideology or to the sociology of knowledge to explain individual belief. But this also raises important theoretical issues. Many of the women who espouse conservative, liberal feminist, socialist feminist, black feminist, and postmodern feminist views come from remarkably similar class backgrounds and engage in similar kinds of intellectual labor. How then are we to explain their acceptance of such radically divergent views? Determinist and reductionist explanations simply cannot account for the diversity of political perspectives presented in this article.

All of the proponents of the varying views presented here claim to be dispelling distortions and mystifications. Conservative women argue that claims concerning racial and sexual discrimination distort the functioning of impersonal market forces. Liberal feminists, socialist feminists, and black feminists argue that conservative claims concerning reverse discrimination mystify relations of power and privilege in contemporary society. And postmodern feminist Wendy Brown (1995) argues that both gender-based and race-based discrimination claims and reverse discrimination claims mystify and mask the "slave morality" from which they emerge. No enumeration of the particular characteristics of individual knowers or the class background of academic women will explain these divergent beliefs. But a shift of focus from subjective knowers to analysis of the adequacy of divergent theoretical accounts of contemporary social life might help us to see how different theoretical frameworks structure perception, accredit evidence, and provide the rhetorical force for particular arguments, and in so doing, help us to assess the comparative merits of competing claims.

Consider, for example, the conviction of racial and sexual superiority that fuels conservative arguments that white men have a "right" to certain educational and employment opportunities that is violated when women and minorities are admitted or hired. Can this conviction persist once the premise of racial and sexual superiority is subjected to systematic critique? Can the assumption of a "right" to certain opportunities coexist with conservatives' acceptance of the market's premise that no one ever has a right to a job? What are the merits of the socialist feminist claim that a politics of resentment against the undeserving poor is being produced as strategic camouflage for the oppressive practices of late capitalism? What are the merits of Wendy Brown's claim that the victim-blaming politics of *ressentiment* is a product of the moralizing revenge of the powerless who wish to inscribe their injuries into law'? Can either or both these claims withstand scrutiny? Does an appeal to Nietzschean *ressentiment* place claims of reverse discrimination on the same plane as centuries of racial oppression'? Does the invocation of a "slave morality" create a false equivalence between the conjured injuries of privileged whites and the continuing harms experienced by people of color in the United States? Does the depiction of identity politics as "recrimination produced by failure" implicitly accredit the liberal meritocratic myths that the marginalized are "failures" and see themselves as such? Can socialist feminist critiques of capitalism adequately address the racial coding of contemporary backlash'? Can liberal feminist electoral strategies adequately engage the economic and racial dimensions of backlash politics?

To answer any of these questions, it is necessary to analyze and assess the theoretical presuppositions that structure contradictory observations and make divergent interpretations meaningful. This research agenda suggests that feminist standpoint theory as analytical tool has strengths that have been masked by exclusive examination of feminist standpoint claims on their epistemological merits. When feminist standpoint theory is understood as an analytical tool rather than an epistemic doctrine, it does a great service by illuminating problems that theoretical and empirical research must engage. Examining competing feminist standpoints reveals contentious theoretical assumptions and problematic prescriptions, as well as lacunae, that follow from them.

When trying to analyze backlash, all standpoints and perspectives are not equally insightful. Conservative women and liberal feminists operate within the same parameters of classical liberal theory. Within this theoretical framework, liberal feminists provide cogent arguments for rejecting the erroneous claims of conservatives. But precisely because they operate within the contours of the capitalist market, liberal feminists are markedly insensitive to the structural forces that undermine the promise of equal opportunity for a very large segment of the population. Socialist feminists raise important challenges to the moral legitimacy of a hierarchical division of labor and a mode of social organization that so viciously punishes the "losers" that it both produces and requires. But socialist feminists cannot account for the distortions that racism introduces to the normal operations of a capitalist market. Black feminists make visible the virulence and persistence of racism, but they fall back upon liberalism or socialism for economic analysis and tactics for political transformation. Postmodern feminist Wendy Brown (1995) reminds us that the state is not a neutral instrument and that normalizing practices threaten to ensnare emancipatory projects, but her call for a free space of contestation provides little direction for feminist praxis currently under threat from the forces of backlash and struggling to mobilize to counter those forces.

Theoretical analysis is no substitute for politics. Developing an adequate theoretical account of backlash will not determine the outcome of the next election. Nonetheless, theoretical analysis can help feminist activists become aware of the theoretical underpinnings and implications of our political arguments. It can help move feminist political debates beyond impasses created by *ad hominem* arguments, emotivist exchanges, and the devastating damage to coalition politics that flows from appeals to the authority of individual experience. If the adoption of standpoint theory as an analytical tool contributes to this end, then it makes good on Hartsock's (1983) promise to play a liberatory role, although not precisely in the way that Hartsock envisioned.

Feminist standpoint theory as analytical tool may also help us reconceptualize objectivity. The juxtaposition of competing theoretical accounts of backlash illuminates the role of social values in cognition, an illumination that has important implications for an adequate understanding of objectivity (Hawkesworth, 1992; Longino, 1990). Traditional methods in the social sciences are premised upon the assumption that the chief threat to objectivity is idiosyncrasy. Notions of replicability and intersubjective verification presume that the central obstacle to objectivity lies in the emotional and perceptual quirks of the subjective self that distort, confuse, and interfere with objective apprehension of the external world. Recognition of the theoretical constitution of facticity challenges the myth of radical idiosyncrasy and the optimistic assumption that intersubjective agreement can suffice to accredit knowledge once the bias of individual observers has been purged. If social values incorporated in a theoretical framework structure perceptions of the world, then intersubjective corroboration within that framework simply insulates those values from interrogation. Rather than function as the equivalent of objectivity, intersubjective consensus can shield shared values from critical reflection, truncate inquiry, and entrench error within intersubjectively "verified" theories. One virtue of standpoint theory as analytical tool is that it requires engagement of competing claims and competing theoretical frameworks. By examining the tacit presuppositions of alternative accounts, feminist standpoint theory as analytical tool helps make visible potential sources of error masked by mainstream social science methods. Attuned to the complex interaction between theoretical assumptions, social values, and discipline-specific methods in the constitution of facticity, feminist standpoint theory as analytical tool affords greater awareness of potential sources of error and a commitment to heightened interrogation of precisely that which is taken as unproblematic in competing accounts. As such, it may help us confront the contentious assumptions most deeply entrenched in our conceptual apparatus, fostering sustained critique of problematic assumptions that impair an objective grasp of the complex issues confronting contemporary political life.

References

Abel, Elizabeth. (1993). Black writing, white reading: Race and the politics of feminist interpretation. *Critical Inquiry, 19,* 470–498.

American Council on Education. (1995). *Making the case for affirmative action in higher education: A handbook for organizers.* Washington, DC: Author.

Barrett, Michele. (1985). *Women's oppression today: Problems in Marxist feminist analysis* (4th ed.). London: Verso.

Berkeley Planning Associates, Inc. (1980). *Evaluation design: Assessment of work-welfare projects.* Washington. DC: U.S. Department of Health and Human Services.

Bernstein, Blanche, & Goodwin, Leonard. (1978). Do work requirements accomplish anything? *Public Welfare, 32*(2), 36–45.

Bond, Julian. (1996), *Civil rights: Acting affirmatively*. Paper presented at the University of Louisville, KY, February.

Briggs, Vernon, Rungeling, Brian, & Smith, Lewis. (1980). Welfare reform and the plight of the poor in the rural south. *Monthly Labor Review, 103*(4), 28–30.

Brown, Wendy, (1995). *States of injury: Power and freedom in late modernity*. Princeton. NJ: Princeton University Press.

Burtless, Gary. (1995). Employment prospects of welfare recipients. In Demetra Smith Nightingale & Robert Haverman (Eds.), *The work alternative* (pp. 71–106). Washington, DC: The Urban Institute Press.

Carby, Hazel. (1987). *Reconstructing womanhood*. New York: Oxford University Press.

Center on Hunger, Poverty, and Nutrition Policy. (1995). *Statement on key welfare reform issues: The empirical evidence*. Medford, MA: Tufts University.

Chideya, Farai. (1995). *Don't believe the hype: Fighting cultural misinformation about African Americans*. New York: Plume/NAL-Dutton.

Collins, Patricia Hill. (1990). *Black feminist thought: Knowledge, consciousness and the politics of empowerment*. New York: Unwin Hyman.

Collins, Patricia Hill. (1995). *Through the lens of race/class/gender: Black family studies*. Paper presented at the University of Louisville, KY, November.

Daly, Mary. (1978). *GYN/ECOLOGY: The metaethics of radical feminism*. Boston: Beacon Press.

Danziger, Sheldon, & Gottschalk, Peter. (1983). The measurement of poverty: Implications for antipoverty policy. *American Behavioral Scientist, 26*, 739–756.

Danziger, Sheldon, & Gottschalk, Peter. (Eds.). (1993). *Uneven tides: Rising inequality in America*. New York: Russell Sage Foundation.

DeParle, Jason. (1997). Success and frustration as welfare rules change. *The New York Times*, December 30, pp. A1, A12–A13.

De Witt, Karen. (1996). New cause helps feminists appeal to younger women. *The New York Times*, February 5, p. A6.

D'Souza, Dinesh. (1995). *The end of racism: Principles for a multiracial society*. New York: Free Press.

Edin, Kathryn, & Lein, Laura. (1997). *Making ends meet: How single mothers survive welfare and low-wage work*. New York: Russell Sage Foundation.

Erie, Steven, Rein, Martin, & Wiget, Barbara. (1983). Women and the Reagan revolution: Thermidor for the social welfare economy. In Irene Diamond & Mary Shanley (Eds.), *Families, politics and public policy* (pp. 94–119). New York: Longman.

Faludi, Susan. (1991). *Backlash: The undeclared war against American women*. New York: Crown Publishers.

Friedman, Barry, & Hausman, Leonard. (1975). *Work and welfare patterns in low income families*. Waltham, MA: Brandeis University, Heller Graduate School For Advanced Studies in Welfare.

Glass Ceiling Commission. (1995). *Good for business: Making full use of the nation's human capital*. (Publication No. 029-016-00157-3). Washington, DC: U.S. Government Printing Office.

Goodale, James. (1973). Effects of personal background and training on work values of the hardcore unemployed. *Journal of Applied Psychology, 57*(1), 1–9.

Goodwin, Leonard. (1972). *Do the poor want to work? A socio-psychological study of work orientations*. Washington, DC: The Brookings Institute.

Grant, Judith. (1993). *Fundamental feminism: Contesting the core concepts of feminist theory*. New York: Routledge.

Gueron, Judith M., & Pauly, Edward. (1991). *From welfare to work*. New York: Russell Sage.

Gutek, Barbara, & Stevens, Denise. (1979). Differential responses of males and females to work situations that evoke sex-role stereotypes. *Journal of Vocational Behavior, 14*, 23–32.

Guy-Sheftall, Beverly. (1995). Words of fire: Black feminism since the 18th century. Paper presented at the University of Louisville, KY, March.

Hacker, Andrew. (1992). *Two nations: Black and white, separate, hostile, and unequal*. New York: Scribners.

Haefner, James. (1977). Race, age, sex, and competence in employee selection of the disadvantaged. *Journal of Applied Psychology, 62*, 199–202.

Handler, Joel. (1972). *Reforming the poor*. New York: Basic Books.

Handler, Joel. (1995). *The poverty of welfare reform*. New Haven: Yale University Press.

Haraway, Donna. (1991). *Simians, cyborgs and women: The reinvention of nature*. New York: Routledge.

Harding, Sandra. (1991). *Whose science? Whose knowledge? Thinking from women's lives*. Ithaca, NY: Cornell University Press.

Harding, Sandra. (1992). After the neutrality ideal: Science, politics, and strong objectivity. *Social Research, 59*, 567–587.

Hartsock, Nancy. (1983). The feminist standpoint: Developing the ground of a specifically feminist historical materialism. In Sandra Harding & Merrill Hintikka (Eds.), *Discovering reality: Feminist perspectives on epistemology, metaphysics, methodology, and philosophy of science* (pp. 283–310). Dordrecht, The Netherlands: D. Reidel.

Hawkesworth, Mary. (1988). *Theoretical issues in policy analysis*. Albany, NY: State University of New York Press.

Hawkesworth, Mary. (1989). Knowers, knowing, known: Feminist theory and claims of truth. *Signs, 14*, 533–557.

Hawkesworth, Mary. (1992). From objectivity to objectification: Feminist objections. *Annals of Scholarship, 8*, 451–477.

Held, Virginia. (1975). Reasonable progress and self-respect. In Tom Beauchamp (Ed), *Ethics and public policy* (pp. 31–43). Englewood Cliffs, NJ: Prentice Hall.

Hernstein, Richard J., & Murray, Charles. (1994). *The bell curve: Intelligence and class structure in American life*. New York: Free Press.

Higginbotham, Evelyn Brooks. (1992). African-American women's history and the metalanguage of race. *Signs, 17*, 251–274.

Hirschmann, Nancy J. (1993). *Rethinking obligation: A feminist method for political theory*. Ithaca, NY: Cornell University Press.

hooks, bell. (1992). *Black looks: Race and representation*. Boston: South End Press.

Hughes. Graham. (1975). Reparations for blacks. In Tom Beauchamp (Ed.), *Ethics and public policy* (pp. 20–30). Englewood Cliffs, NJ: Prentice Hall.

Hurston, Zora Neale. (1978). *Their eyes were watching God*. Urbana, IL: University of Illinois Press.

Kaplan, Roy, & Tausky, Curt. (1972). Work and the welfare Cadillac: The function of the commitment to work among the hard core unemployed. *Social Problems, 19*, 469–483.

Kondrtas, Anna. (1995). *News and views*. Washington, DC: The Independent Women's Forum.

Ladowsky, Ellen. (1995). That's no white male, that's my husband. *The Women's Quarterly, Spring*.

Lakatos, Imre. (1970). Falsification and the methodology of scientific research programmes. In Imre Lakatos & Alan Musgrave (Eds.), *Criticism and the growth of knowledge* (pp. 91–196). Cambridge, UK: Cambridge University Press.

Levitan, Sar A., & Shapiro, Issac. (1987). *Working but poor: America's contradiction*. Baltimore, MD: Johns Hopkins University Press.

Linden, Barbara, & Vincent, Deborah. (1982). *Workfare in theory and practice*. Washington, DC: National Social Science and Law Center.

Livingston, John. (1979). *Fair game: Inequality and affirmative action*. San Francisco: W.H. Freeman.

Longino, Helen. (1990). *Science as social knowledge: Values and objectivity in scientific inquiry*. Princeton, NJ: Princeton University Press.

MacIntyre, Alasdair. (1981). *After virtue*. Notre Dame, IN: University of Notre Dame Press.

Melich, Tanya. (1996). *The Republican war against women: An insider's report from behind the lines*. New York: Bantam Books.

Mink, Gwendolyn. (1996). *"Welfare reform": The attack on poor women*. Paper presented at the Annual Meeting of the Western Political Science Association, San Francisco, CA, March 15.

Morin. Richard. (1995). A nation divided. *The Courier Journal, October 8*, p. A6.

Nieva, Veronica, & Gutek, Barbara. (1980). Sex effects on evaluation. *Academy of Management Review, 5*, 267–276.

O'Brien, Mary. (1981). *The politics of reproduction*. London: Routledge and Kegan Paul.

Polakow, Valerie. (1993). *Lives on the edge: Single mothers and their children in the other America*. Chicago: University of Chicago Press.

Pottinger, J. Stanley. (1971). Come now, Professor Hook. *The New York Times, December 18*, p. A29.

Rein, Mildred. (1982). *Dilemmas of welfare policy*. New York: Praeger.

Rixecker, Stefanie. (1994). Expanding the discursive context of policy design: A matter of feminist standpoint epistemology. *Policy Sciences, 27* (2/3), 119–142.

Roberts, Dorothy. (1997). *Killing the black body: Race, reproduction, and the meaning of liberty*. New York: Pantheon.

Rosen, Benson, & Jerdee, Thomas. (1974). Influence of sex-role stereotypes on personnel decisions. *Journal of Applied Psychology, 59*(1), 9–14.

Rosen, Richard. (1980). Identifying states and areas prone to high and low unemployment. *Monthly Labor Review, 103*(3), 20–24.

Rowan, Carl. (1995). The "reverse discrimination" myth. *The Courier Journal, November 13*, p. A18.

Schiller, Bradley. (1973). Empirical studies of welfare stereotypes on employee selection. *Personnel Psychology, 25*, 333–338.

Sklar, Holly. (1995). Back to the raw deal. *Z Magazine, November*, pp. 19–24.

Spalter-Roth, Roberta, Burr, Beverly, Hartmann, Heidi, & Shaw, Louise. (1995). *Welfare that works: The working lives of AFDC recipients*. Washington, DC: Institute for Women's Policy Research.

Spelman, Elizabeth. (1988). *Inessential woman: Problems of exclusion in feminist thought*. Boston: Beacon Press.

Thernstrom, Abigail, & Thernstrom, Stephan. (1997) *America in black and white: One nation indivisible*. New York: Simon and Schuster.

Thomas, Susan, (1994). From the culture of poverty to the culture of single motherhood. *Women and Politics*. 14(2), 65–97.

Tienda, Marta, & Stier, Haya. 1991. Joblessness and shiftlessness: Labor force activity in Chicago's inner city. In

Amy, Chris, & Alberda, Randy, (1994), It's not working: Why many single mothers can't work their way out of poverty. *Dollars and Sense, November/December*, pp. 8–10.

Turner, Margery Austin, Fix, Michael, & Struyk, Raymond. (1991). *Opportunities denied, opportunities diminished: Discrimination in hiring.* Washington, DC: The Urban Institute.

Uchitelle, Louis, & Kleinfield, Nathan. (1996). On the battlefields of business, millions of casualties. *The New York Times,* March 3, pp. A1, A26–A29.

Usdansky. Margaret. (1996). While out-of-wedlock births soar, unwed moms don't fit stereotypes. *The Courier Journal,* February 25. p. H3.

Yeatman, Anna. (1994). *Postmodern revisionings of the political.* New York: Routledge.

Young, Iris. (1990). *Justice and the politics of difference.* Princeton, NJ: Princeton University Press.

Chapter 12

Affirmative Action and the Status of Women in the Academy

Judith S. Glazer

Affirmative action policies are under attack and while criticism of these policies is not new, the nature of the debate has shifted from implementation to termination.[1] The university has become a prime target for dismantling affirmative action as is evidenced by recent events at the University of California. The resolution approved by its Board of Regents on July 20, 1995, calling for the elimination by 1997 of race, religion, sex, color, ethnicity or national origin as criteria for admission, hiring and contracting on its nine campuses, provides a blueprint of the conflict that looms ahead.[2] The position of women, including women of color, will be directly affected by its outcome. In announcing the resolution, the governor proclaimed that: 'Merit, not the color of one's skin or gender, should be [public officials'] guiding principle'.[3] While the primary target of the debate has focused on preferential admissions policies for minorities within the nine-campus system, it is clear from the wording of the resolution that women will be affected. The University of Texas Law School has also been barred by a panel of federal judges from using race as a factor in admissions. This decision is now being appealed, and, as Hacker (1996: 21) points out, will give the Supreme Court the chance to revisit its 1978 Bakke decision, a 5–4 ruling that enabled the University of California at Davis Medical School to maintain a minority admissions policy.

This chapter is concerned with the extent to which affirmative action has benefited women in the academy in the past three decades. I begin with a brief discussion of feminist policy analysis and its application to affirmative action. In the next two sections, I discuss the response of American universities to affirmative action, focusing on the role and effectiveness of campus commissions on the status of women as one strategy for improving women's position in higher education. I conclude with some observations about the implications for women in the academy of efforts to dismantle affirmative action programs. This chapter is based on research I conducted in 1995 and early 1996. It was conducted in two phases: site visits to selected campuses with long commitments to improving women's status and the collection and analyses of recent commission documents and reports from a variety of sources. Throughout the chapter, I place women at the center of my inquiry, questioning assumptions about the role of the state and its institutions in eliminating sex discrimination and advancing women's position.

Feminist Theory and Feminist Policy Analysis

Theories of feminism and more recently models of feminist research advocate the importance of women's perspectives in assessing higher education and creating more inclusive systems. In 1991, I observed that the women's rights movement that had originated in tandem with the civil rights movement and was rooted in liberal values and belief systems had begun to take a more critical turn (Glazer, 1991). The advent of a conservative political agenda during the Reagan–Bush era of the 1980s combined with a growing skepticism in western intellectual thought influenced feminist scholars to look more critically at all ideologies, including their own, to reject the fragmentation that women experience in attempting to integrate their personal and professional lives, and to challenge the binary oppositions, 'in language, law, and other socially constituting systems, oppositions which privilege one presence—male, rationality, objectivity—and marginalize its opposite—female, irrationality, subjectivity' (Bartlett, 1993: 561). Five years after making these observations, the conservative discourse has become more insistent, moving rapidly from policy reform and modification to policy dismantling and termination. Postmodern feminists seek to deconstruct the policy process to reveal 'the hidden gender bias of a wide range of laws and assumptions' (1993: 561).

Policy scientists define termination as the adjustment of policies and programs that those in power determine have become redundant and unworkable and their replacement with another set of expectations and demands, triggering political contests that are different from those surrounding policy adoption and initiation (Bardach, 1976; Brewer, 1978).[4] Lasswell originated the concept of termination as one of seven 'power outcomes' in government decision-making (1956), but policymakers paid little attention to this idea during a period of rapid growth. By the mid-1970s, policy analysts were calling termination a series of fine tunings predicated on individual and organizational recognition of an imbalance between the political system and its relative domain in responding to new issues (deLeon, 1978) or a cyclical phase to eliminate dysfunctional or outmoded policies that had become part of the problem they were intended to solve (May and Wildavsky, 1978).

Feminist policy analysts reject the dominant view of male policy scientists that decisions regarding the continuation or termination of governmental policies should be based on such neutral evaluation criteria as resource management, cost effectiveness and organizational fit. They emphasize the importance of asking the woman question in conducting critical feminist policy analyses of government policies, a method designed 'to identify the gender implications of rules and practices that might otherwise seem neutral or objective...' (Bartlett, 1993: 551).

The work of Bartlett and other feminist legal scholars is particularly relevant in discussing affirmative action which is now being used as a wedge issue to divide white women and people of color. They reject the liberal feminist view that women can gain sex equality through their assimilation into alienating institutional structures. They adopt a more activist view of feminists as agents of transformational change. In asserting the need for redefining sex equality as the basis for a feminist jurisprudence, MacKinnon comments on the problems women encounter in a legal system based on sex inequality:

> Gender neutrality is the male standard. The special protection rule is the female standard. Masculinity or maleness is the referent for both. Approaching sex discrimination in this way, as if sex questions were difference questions and equality questions were sameness questions, merely provides two ways for the law to hold women to a male standard and to call that sex equality (MacKinnon, 1989: 221).

Williams comments on another aspect of sex discrimination law, which she terms *equality's riddle*, dealing with the impact of women's challenges to pregnancy rules under Title VII on their status and opportunity in the paid workforce. This issue is particularly important for women faculty, whose childbearing and tenure-track years often run simultaneously and for whom stop-the-clock policies are more often granted on a discretionary basis. She observes that the goal of the feminist legal movement has been twofold: 'to break down the legal barriers that restrict each sex to its predefined role and create a hierarchy based on gender' and 'to squeeze the male tilt out of a purportedly neutral legal structure and thus substitute genuine for merely formal gender neutrality' (Williams, 1993: 131). Becker problematizes the formal equality standard, viewing it as capable of effecting only limited change in an unresponsive legislative process and suggesting in her title that sexual equality awaits a Prince Charming who is unlikely to arrive, given the conservative mood of the Supreme Court and the fact that women have 'conflicting interests and visions of equality' (Becker, 1993: 234).

Radical feminists view universities as gendered hierarchies and question the basic premises of its policies and programs based on sex, age, color, class and other distinctions. They argue that 'feminist principles and liberal policies of equal opportunity are incompatible since liberalism is fundamentally patriarchal in theory and practice, despite the lip-service paid to women's rights and some of the benefits gained by women' (Coppock, Haydon and Richter, 1995: 48). Adherents of this perspective reject the reverse discrimination argument advanced by opponents of affirmative action as a patriarchal construct that seeks to perpetuate and reify historical male dominance in university organizations.

Drawing on the larger debate concerning the relationship between 'legal norms and gender hierarchies', Rhode (1991: 1736) links women's problems and those of other subordinated groups. She argues that institutions conceive sex disparities too narrowly, seldom focusing on 'the intersection of gender with other patterns of subordination such as class, race, ethnicity, age, and sexual orientation', reinforcing attitudes that deny their existence and fortifying 'the illusion that collective problems have been resolved' (1991: 1734). She urges feminists to expand their definition of what she calls the 'no-problem' problem in a society that views gender inequality as natural and to build support 'for the broader social initiatives that the problem in fact requires' (1991: 1736). Women in higher education are caught in a dilemma, largely excluded from full participation based on their perceived difference, and included with the expectation that they will adapt to existing institutional norms and accommodate their differences. The idea of female-friendly policies and programs is not taken into consideration either by laws or the policies they produce, and certainly not by the leadership in male-dominated institutions. Rhode argues persuasively that when institutions condone a 'self-perpetuating cycle of devaluation in which equality in formal rights masks inequality in daily experience', they support separate-but-equal world views of women's role and status (for example, that women are more likely to work part-time, take extended leaves, and place lower priority on advancement) without looking at the root causes of employment segregation and stratification, or alternatively, when they define equality in formal rather than substantive terms without demanding that equal access guarantees equal treatment and equal outcomes (1991: 1768). Eisenstein also rejects the liberal standard of equality for masking race and sex discrimination, marginalizing women and minorities, and reinforcing the 'standard of white heterosexual maleness'. In an essay on 'the myth of postracism', she explores how anti-government discourse was institutionalized by the late 1980s 'through a racialized discourse that piggy-backed women's issues along with it', substituting individual rights for equal opportunity and making the dismantling of affirmative action 'the centerpiece of this process' (1994: 40). She contends that gender hierarchies continue to thwart women's progress, and calls for a race-conscious feminist politics that critiques existing power relations. From a feminist perspective, attempts to achieve gender equity are governed by established power relations. Women, who are largely powerless within the university organization, must rely on male leadership to bring about substantive changes in their situation. It is the official discourse of that leadership, articulated by governing boards and presidents, that form the basis for state and institutional intervention in policies affecting women's role and status.

Affirmative Action in Historical Perspective

The development of affirmative action policy is a textbook case of policy incrementalism. It originated in the labor movement as a clause in the National Labor Relations Act of 1935, meaning that employers would be required to cease discriminatory practices against union members or organizers and take affirmative action on behalf of victims of discrimination (Skrentny, 1996). It was adopted as a civil rights initiative by President John Kennedy in 1961 in Executive Order 10925, calling on federal contractors to 'take affirmative action to ensure that the applicants are employed, and that employees are treated during employment, without regard to their race, creed, color, or national origin' (Skrentny, 1996: 7). It would take another decade and the threat of legal action by feminists for *sex* to be added to the list of protected classes that were covered by affirmative action statutes and executive orders. The symbiotic growth of the civil rights and women's movements between 1965 and 1970 brought new pressure on two presidents who were ideologically polar opposites—Lyndon Johnson and Richard Nixon—to include women as a protected class in federal affirmative action policies. Hacker speculates that Nixon's support of affirmative action was calculated to benefit African Americans at the same time as it inflamed blue collar workers, bringing them into the Republican camp and that 'Republicans are still betting that affirmative action will stir racial resentments in their favor' (1996: 21).

Four sets of statutes and executive orders were of particular interest to women: 1) the Equal Pay Act of 1963, the first sex discrimination legislation enacted, requiring equal pay for equal work regardless of sex; 2) Title IX of the Education Amendments of 1972, prohibiting sex discrimination in all federally assisted education programs in both public and private institutions receiving federal monies through grants, loans or contracts and also extending coverage to executive, administrative and professional employees; 3) Executive Order 11246, banning discrimination in employment by all employers with federal contracts, and requiring the development of affirmative action programs by all federal contractors and subcontractors with contracts more than $100,000 and with 100 or more employees; and 4) Title VII, as amended by the Equal Employment Opportunity Act of 1972, which forbade discrimination on the basis of race, color, national origin, religion or sex in any term, condition or privilege of employment, including sexual harassment.

This law was amended in March, 1972 to include all public and private educational institutions as well as state and local governments and it *applied to all employers, public or private, whether or not they received any federal funds* (Vetter, 1994: 3).

These statutes and executive orders gave sweeping powers to the federal government in monitoring the progress of all colleges and universities in achieving 'nondiscrimination on the basis of sex, race and ethnic origin' in all of its programs and activities. As a consequence, equal opportunity legislation became a means of categorizing professionals, not as individuals, but as members of a racial, ethnic or gender group (Stimpson, 1993). State and municipal regulations were modeled on the federal statutes, energizing women to form caucuses and organizations, pursue recourse in the courts, and monitor women's progress in the public sphere (Sandler, 1980: 2). Expectations were high that change would be immediate, pervasive and far-reaching.

The University Response

From the outset, 'passions, ideologies, strong opinions and established interests' permeated the advent of affirmative action on university campuses (Carnegie Council on Policy Studies, 1975). Two factors in particular mobilized universities into action. The Equal Employment Opportunity Act of 1972 necessitated copious reporting requirements based on workforce and utilization analyses of salary, benefits and advancement policies for all categories of employees and paving the way for legal action for noncompliance. The federal government filed more than 500 complaints against colleges and universities by 1973 (Stimpson, 1993: 8). Women's rights activists began their own campus-based investigations of admissions, employment and benefits policies and took collective legal action against discriminatory policies and practices in their institutions; by 1973, 1600 individual cases were filed with the EEOC, 45 per cent involving sex discrimination, 39 per cent race and ethnic discrimination, 12 per cent multiple allegations, and 4 percent religious discrimination (Stimpson, 1993: 8).

The educational establishment complained vigorously that federal regulations were costly, cumbersome, unreasonable and intrusive. At the same time, presidents responded by appointing affirmative action/equal opportunity officers to review existing policies, draft goals and timetables for admissions and employment, and ascertain that they were in compliance with the new regulations. Public posting of vacancies, affirmative action advertising, review of employment policies, initiation of recruitment and scholarship programs, and other strategies were implemented. Questions were raised about granting preferential treatment to women and minorities solely on the basis of their membership in a protected group, the conflict between faculty governance and federal regulatory policy, and the impact of goals and timetables and whether these were really quotas, and the charge that equality of individual opportunity was leading to 'a policy of group results' (Carnegie Council, 1975).

Proponents of affirmative action in higher education based their support on three arguments: compensating disadvantaged groups for prior discrimination; correcting current inequities by increasing the proportional representation of women and minorities; and enriching the institution through cultural and gender diversity (Francis, 1993; Tierney, 1996). Opponents, on the other hand, claimed that its primary use was political, a means of legitimizing reverse discrimination, mainly against white Anglo males, encouraging preferential treatment in admissions and hiring, and perpetuating the myth of female and minority inferiority.

At first, universities perceived affirmative action as a temporary, remedial measure that would be met through adherence to regulatory requirements and the implementation of nondiscriminatory policies and practices. However, it soon became apparent that salary, employment and tenure policies were construed by the federal government as grossly inadequate in meeting the test of equality and opportunity and that further steps would be needed to eliminate sex and race discrimination. Institutional sources of criticism related to the high cost of compliance due to onerous reporting and auditing requirements, allegations of reverse discrimination against white males, and the incompatibility between equal opportunity and merit in hiring, promotion and tenure (Gray and Schafer, 1981). Gray and Schafer (1981: 351) observed that decisions on faculty status were still subject to 'cronyism, the old-boy network, stereotyping, hiring men on potential and women on accomplishment' practices that did not end with the passage of anti-discrimination statutes and the issuance of executive orders. They speculated that written affirmative action plans had become pro forma exercises, unread and unacted upon by federal regulators and warned that unless reforms were instituted, the demise of equal opportunity was entirely possible. Four years later, the chair of Committee W asserted that 'academe has a long way to go to achieve the ideal of sex equity in faculty employment' (Gray. 1985: 40). She cited four related concerns: adverse judicial decisions on class certification, burden of proof, comparability of work and the use of statistics; continuing judicial deference to the educational establishment; the high psychic and financial costs of pursuing an individual or class action suit, making legal redress an empty dream for most faculty women; and the unlikelihood of legislative remedies or rigorous action from the EEOC. Women, she asserted, would be better served by reforming from within (Gray, 1985: 40).

The Campus Commission on the Status of Women

The campus commission on the status of women was one mechanism that research universities, in particular, adopted as a means of addressing women's demands and demonstrating their good faith efforts. I use the term *commission* generically to refer to task forces, committees and other entities sharing similar functions, i.e., to assess and recommend women's increased representation and improved status within a given institution. In seeking to determine the extent of women's progress in the past two decades, I have focused my attention on these commissions to measure their effectiveness in advancing women's interests. Undoubtedly, other mechanisms occur through human resources and equal opportunity offices, collective bargaining units, women's studies programs and university policies. Conceptualized within a liberal feminist framework, the women's commission had three related purposes: to demonstrate administrative support for the improvement of women's status, to give women a collective voice on campus, and to serve as a sounding board for women's concerns.

It originated in the 1960s as a response to the contemporary women's movement, the passage of equal employment statutes and executive orders, and the promise that sex and race discrimination would carry severe penalties. Their growth followed the establishment by Kennedy of a President's Commission on the Status of Women and of various state commissions throughout the 1960s. These politically inspired federal and state commissions gave women's rights activists unprecedented access to federal and state agencies and national and state platforms from which to publicize their agenda (Beuchler, 1990). They soon became advocacy organizations to break down barriers between the public and private sectors and to lobby for sex equity legislation and ratification of an Equal Rights Amendment.

By 1968, student and faculty activism played a significant role in the establishment of campus commissions to represent women's interests. Individual and class action lawsuits accelerated the change process and by 1970 colleges and universities responded by taking steps to increase the numbers of women on their campuses and to improve their professional standing. Equal opportunity and equal access became the twin mantras of the decade. The campus commission was a liberal feminist approach used by research universities, in particular, in addressing women's demands and demonstrating good faith efforts toward their advancement. At the University of Michigan, for example, the president appointed a Commission on Women in 1970 as a direct result of a class action complaint filed by women faculty and professional staff under Executive Order 11246. In this case, the federal government investigated and found the university guilty of 'blatant sex discrimination', withholding research funds until the administration acted to redress the gender imbalance. Similar actions occurred at other major universities, leading to the formation of commissions on women and workforce and utilization analyses.

By the mid-seventies, the ability of first-wave commissions to influence the university agenda for gender equity began to decline. Women interviewees, several of whom were now in leadership positions on their campuses offered several reasons: 1) the appointment of affirmative action/equal opportunity officers, reporting directly to the president, becoming his spokesperson, and, in many instances, acting in a legal capacity to adjudicate grievances and complaints; 2) the advent of women's studies programs as the focus of feminist intellectual activity, providing a new and alternate source of energy for academic women faculty and students; 3) the decline of campus activism paralleling the shrinking academic labor market, diminution of career advancement options, and the unionization of faculty and staff; and 4) the backlash against women in a time of diminishing resources and conflicting priorities as evidenced in reports of the chilly climate on campus for women students, women faculty and women administrators (Sandler and Hall, 1986) and the difficulties being encountered by women of color.

The Commission Strategy

The confluence of internal changes and external events motivated universities to reconstitute their commitment to women's concerns as the eighties came to a close. Women were then 53 per cent of all students but only 13 per cent of tenured full professors and 11 per cent of college presidents. While some problems had been resolved, several systemic issues resisted easy solutions: salary inequities, women's underrepresentation in scientific and professional fields, the resilience of the glass ceiling for women administrators, women's predominance on the lowest rungs of the ladder, and the differential treatment of women of color. In 1989, spurred on by the ACE Commission on Women in Higher Education (Shavlik, Touchton, and Pearson, 1989) as well as by growing recognition that the pipeline was not working, and pressures from minority students for a more visible commitment to campus diversity, presidents and governing boards formed committees, task forces and commissions to conduct needs analyses, collect data and set priorities for collective action. A major role of commissions in the nineties became the generation of statistical and anecdotal data on women's status and proposals for increasing their participation, correcting past inequities and addressing emerging issues.

Women's Commissions in the 1990s

More than two decades have now elapsed since the advent of affirmative action in higher education. Telephone, on-line, and in-person communications provided interesting insights into the current status of women's commissions and their prospects for the future. These interviews and conversations were supplemented with analyses of documents and reports of commission activities and demographic data. Three questions in particular provided the substance for my research. What is their current role? Have they made a difference? How do they view their future prospects in the current political climate?

Commissions have several practical functions: clarifying issues, setting priorities, collecting data, making recommendations, monitoring activities and serving as a sounding board and early warning system for the president. In institutions with well-established commissions, fiscal support and access to the highest levels of the administration, it is possible to influence the policy agenda. However, commissions are not risk-takers, priorities are set within a narrow band of acceptability and much of what is seen as progressive must be perceived as compatible with mainstream male values. For example, there is still a great deal of tokenism at the upper levels of university administration and therefore, women have limited access to the areas of finance, academic administration and other policy-making positions. Women's ability to attain full professorships, major grants, named chairs, presidencies and other forms of recognition and status is largely dependent on the indulgence of males in positions of power and influence.

The commission strategy illustrates the president's role as change agent and the impact of differences in leadership styles. Commissions gained their viability from presidents who are generally male and are unlikely to step outside the mainstream in conceptualizing commissions or in giving them space within the organization. On the other hand, they do demonstrate the limitations that the role of university governance plays in faculty hiring, promotion and tenure decisions. While the president can foster a more inclusive campus environment through his or her ability to generate resources and draw public attention to the issues, it is also true that deference must be paid to faculty and deans in making personnel decisions. Administrative appointments and promotions also tend to remain decentralized, making male dominance a self-fulfilling prophecy.

Commission staffs are small, some are *ad hoc* arrangements that self-destruct after conducting their study and presenting their recommendations, others are members of statewide consortia that report to a central office rather than the campus president. Some reports are analogous to master plans; they are issued and disseminated to a select group of trusted individuals within the university community, their recommendations are evaluated for cost effectiveness and consensus purposes, some discussion is held with the concerned parties, and depending on the compatibility of the recommendations with the goals of the administration, some proposals get implemented. Women's voices are rather muted and assertive women may find themselves being silenced by colleagues who recognize the risks in rocking the boat.

The anecdotal data I collected in my interviews underscore the resistance of universities to change and the subtle discriminatory practices that continue to thwart women's full participation. One workload issue, for example, concerns service demands on junior women faculty. A commission member observed that

> Junior women faculty are caught in a double bind. Although service is given very little weight in tenure and promotion decisions, women and minorities will not be given adequate consideration if search committees, promotion and tenure committees and executive committees consist exclusively of white men. Because the vast majority of our faculty are white men, to have a woman and a minority on every committee grossly overworks women, particularly at the assistant and associate professor levels.[5]

Access to institutional data varies considerably, however, and is largely dependent on the good will of the administration or on state policies governing release of this information, making it difficult to assess the extent of their effectiveness in removing gender-related pay inequities. Concern about reverse discrimination charges led one research university to engage in some rather interesting circumlocutions as they sought to rationalize gender-neutral equal opportunity policies and to equate gender equity and merit.

The 1993 National Study of Postsecondary Faculty (Zimbler, 1994) shows quite graphically that gender-neutral adjustments are ineffective routes to gender equity. For example, in fall 1992, the mean basic salary for female faculty in all program areas was 72.3 per cent of male faculty salaries. This disparity increased with rank and program status, for example, women full professors in professional programs (business, education and health sciences) earned 69.5 per cent of their male colleagues while women full professors in arts and sciences earned an average of 87.1 per cent of males. The disparity in mean total income for men and women faculty was more pronounced: 69.2 per cent in all program areas, from 61.8 per cent for full professors in professional programs to 81.7 per cent for 'other program areas' (agriculture, communications, home economics, library science, theology and interdisciplinary studies).

Despite their increased participation as faculty and administrators, barriers continue to deter women's full acceptance and, as commission data show, the numbers of tenured women faculty, academic administrators and university leaders continue to lag behind men at all levels and in all institutional categories. The data that preoccupy women's commissions reflect the national picture. By 1993–94, according to the National Center for Educational Statistics (Snyder and Hoffman, 1994), women students were 55.7 per cent of all undergraduates and 56.4 per cent of all graduate students including 40.2 per cent of all first-professional degree candidates. However, women accounted for only 31.5 per cent of a full-time instructional faculty compared to 68.5 per cent for men. The disproportionate number of male faculty is more pronounced at the full professor rank and in prestige fields. Even after two decades of affirmative action, women are still only 15.6 per cent of full professors compared to 84.4 per cent for men.

The situation in California is being mirrored in other states, and more than one commission director commented on legislative rumblings in their states for a ban on affirmative action. 'Each institution and each board of regents has its own priorities', one staff person told me. 'When our state system was established, we had a democratic governor. Now we have a republican governor and the regents, whom he has appointed, seem more concerned with restructuring and downsizing than with diversity. We have to wait and see how much weight will be given to the women's recommendations.'

In the final analysis, the institutional culture of most universities and colleges is not compatible with the needs and concerns of women in academia. Universities supporting commissions varied in size, prestige, mission and geographic location. However, the recurrent themes of the findings and recommendations issued by their women's commissions demonstrated strikingly similar concerns. More than two decades after affirmative action was enacted, women at prestigious universities cited the need for the administration to create a campus culture of support for women faculty, women mid-level administrators, women clerical staff and women graduate students. Some of the specific recommendations running through a number of reports related to salary equity (still an issue on many campuses), recruitment and tenure-track appointments in all-male departments, promotion and appointment of women into administrative leadership positions to counteract the ever-prevalent tokenism, and policies that facilitate women's combined family–work roles including mandatory stop-the-clock tenure policies and child care provisions.

When viewed from a feminist perspective, the underlying assumption of commission recommendations that new policies will solve old problems fails to recognize that basic attitudinal changes are needed to create female-friendly university systems. Rather than assert that women are more likely to work part-time than to earn tenure-track appointments, to teach more and publish less, to obtain their doctorates in the humanities rather than the hard sciences, to remain single or childless, to leave rather than remain at the university, to be assistant and associate administrators rather than in leadership positions, it would be appropriate to determine what it is about institutional structures that make them more compatible with men's lives.

When I asked one director to assess the effectiveness of her commission, she responded that a recent changing of the guard at the presidential level now meant she would report to a vice president instead. This change in leadership made it difficult for her to ascertain how much had been accomplished other than the easy things which she listed as family medical leave (now covered through federal legislation), flextime, campus child care, sexual harassment and campus security policies. She observed, 'The tough issues haven't been resolved. By this I mean promoting women into positions of authority, closing the salary gap, increasing the number of tenured women, recruiting and retaining women administrators, and doing more for junior faculty.' The slowness of changing the status quo is evident in the comments of another informant: 'There are explained differences between fields but unexplained differences due to gender.'

While commission members view their roles as 'advocacy, monitoring, vigilance, prodding, meeting periodically with the president and the provost, sometimes together, sometimes separately, publicizing data, making recommendations', they speculate that 'the extent to which clearly articulated institutional commitments fight with our political reality is an important question.' Site visits and in-person interviews document the persistence of problems in departments and professional schools that have been traditionally male-dominated, i.e., science, technology, business, law and medicine. They also substantiate the predominance of women faculty in assistant professor, part-time and non-tenure track positions, and in feminized low status fields. They reveal invisible barriers to women's full participation that are not evident in the national data but come to light from conversations about organizational culture and campus climate. Although the dearth of women faculty, including women of color, is often attributed to a nationwide shortage of qualified women in specialized fields, the anecdotal data raise questions about the accuracy of these beliefs. The low percentage of women faculty at the pinnacle of the profession should be an important warning signal that not enough has changed. Women continue to struggle for acceptance and success as they attempt to overcome inaccurate assumptions about their special needs. In a time of diminishing resources and conflicting priorities, gender equity remains an elusive goal.

Conclusions

The role of the commission has been largely symbolic, articulating a commitment to gender equity for women. The metaphorical significance of the millennium contributes added urgency to the message they disseminate within the university community regarding the need to affirm and respond to women's increasing participation as students and faculty by creating a transformative campus culture. However, as Tierney observes, the recent judicial ruling in the Hopwood case rejects the three premises on which affirmative action has been based: compensation, correction and diversification, arguing that 'specific, rather than general discrimination must be proved' (1996: 27). Gender becomes the 'no-problem' problem in this decision, not mentioned but implicit in the rejection by the court of race and ethnicity as valid criteria for admission to the University of Texas Law School. As Rhode argues, the intersection of gender with other patterns of subordination reinforces attitudes that denies their existence and strengthens the illusion that collective problems are resolved (1991: 1735). Although universities proclaim their continued commitment to affirmative action, if the Supreme Court upholds the Hopwood ruling, the rationale for commissions and other strategies to strengthen women's role and status in the university will be called into question. The retreat from goals, timetables and other accoutrements of affirmative action presents universities and commissions with potentially vexatious obstacles, making their work more difficult and their future role problematic.

Campus commissions provide a perspective on the university and its effectiveness in addressing women's concerns. In the first decade of affirmative action, pressure from the federal government triggered a flurry of activity on the part of universities and women became the main beneficiaries of these changes. However, major setbacks occurred in the 1980s as universities shifted their attention to retrenchment and restructuring and affirmative action mandates came under attack. Now in the 1990s, affirmative action is being perceived as dysfunctional, outmoded, and most recently, unconstitutional under the equal protection clause of the fourteenth amendment to the Constitution. Incremental change is rejected as an inadequate solution and dismantling and termination are proposed. Proponents of affirmative action acknowledge that even if affirmative action survives, 'it will be no more than a vestige of its former self' (Hacker, 1996: 28). Women, who are now the majority of students and whose numbers are increasing in the professoriate, need to make their voices heard in this debate and to assume a central role in the policy process, building on the lessons of commission activism as transformative agents of change.

Notes

1. An earlier version of this paper was presented at the annual meeting of the American Educational Research Association. New York City, April 12, 1996.
2. The resolution approved by the Board of Regents laid the groundwork to circulate petitions for the California Civil Rights Initiative, to be placed on the ballot in November 1996. CCRI asked voters to approve an extension of the ban on affirmative action to all state agencies and institutions and used similar language to federal equal opportunity statutes in affirming that: 'The state will not use race, sex, color, ethnicity, or national origin as it criterion for either discriminating against, or granting preferential treatment to, any individual or group in the operation of the state's system of public employment, education, or public contracting.'
3. Letter from Governor Wilson to Mr. Howard Leach, Chairman, University of California Board of Regents, June 1, 1995.
4. See J.S. Glazer (1984) for a case study of the termination of free tuition policy at the City University of New York in 1976.
5. This quotation and the quotations on pages 123 through 125 are excerpted from transcripts of personal interviews conducted with administrators and faculty in the course of site visits to research universities during 1995. By prior agreement, the identity of these informants remains confidential.

References

Bardach, E. (1976) 'Policy termination as a political process', *Policy Sciences*, 7, pp. 123–31.

Bartlett, K. T. (1993) 'Feminist legal methods', in WEISBERG, D. K. (Ed) *Feminist Legal Theory: Foundations*, Philadelphia, PA, Temple University Press, pp. 550–71.

Becker, M. E. (1993) 'Prince charming: Abstract equality', in WEISBERG, D. K. (Ed) *Feminist Legal Theory: Foundations*, Philadelphia, PA, Temple University Press, pp. 221–36.

Beuchler, S. M. (1990) *Women's Movements in the United States: Women's Suffrage, Equal Rights, and Beyond*, New Brunswick, NJ, Rutgers University Press.

Brewer, G. (1978) 'Termination: Hard choices—harder questions', *Public Administration Review.* **33**, pp. 338–51.

Carnegie Council on Policy Studies in Higher Education (1975) *Making Affirmative Action Work in Higher Education: An Analysis of Institutional and Federal Policies and Recommendations*, San Francisco, CA, Jossey-Bass.

Coppock, V., Haydon, D. and Richter, I. (1995) *The Illusions of 'Post-feminism': New Women, Old Myths*, London, Routledge.

deLeon, P. (1978) 'Public policy termination—An end and a beginning', *Policy Analysis*, 4, pp. 369–92.

Eisenstein, Z. R. (1994) 'United States politics and the myth of "post-racism"', *The Color of Gender: Reimaging Democracy*, Berkeley, CA, University of California Press, pp. 39–69.

Francis, L. L. (1993) 'In defense of affirmative action', in Cahn, S. M. (Ed) *Affirmative Action and the University: A Philosophical Inquiry*, Philadelphia, PA, Temple University Press, pp. 9–47.

Glazer, J. S. (1991) 'Feminism and professionalism in teaching and educational administration', *Educational Administration Quarterly*, **27**(3), pp. 321–42.

Glazer, J. S. (1984) 'Terminating entrenched policies in educational institutions: A case history of free tuition', *The Review of Higher Education*, 7(2), pp. 159–73.

Gray, M. W. (1985) 'Resisting sex discrimination against faculty women', *Academe*, 71, pp. 33–41.

Gray, M. W. and Schafer, A. T. (1981) 'Guidelines for equality: A proposal', *Academe*, 67, pp. 351–3.

Hacker, A. (1996) 'Goodbye to affirmative action?', *The New York Review of Books*, **XLIII**(12), July 11, pp. 21, 24–9.

Lasswell, H. D. (1956) *The Decision Process: Seven Categories of Functional Analysis*, College Park, MD, University of Maryland Press.

MacKinnon, C. (1989) *Toward a Feminist Theory of the State*, Cambridge, MA, Harvard University Press.

May, J. and Wildavsky, A. (1978) *The Policy Cycle*, Beverly Hills, CA, Sage.

Rhode, D. L. (1991) 'The "no-problem" problem: Feminist challenges and cultural change', *Yale Law Journal*, **100**, pp. 1731–93.

Sandler, B. R. (1980) 'Women on campus: A ten-year retrospect', *On Campus with Women*, **26**, Washington, DC, Association of American Colleges, pp. 2, 3.

Sandler, B. R. and Hall, R. (1986) 'The campus climate revisited: Chilly for women faculty, administrators, and students', in Glazer, J. ., Bensimon, E. M, and Townsend, H. K. (Eds) Needham Heights, MA, Ginn Press, pp. 175–204.

Shavlik, D. L., Touchton, J. F. and Pearson, C. R. (1989) *The New Agenda of Women in Higher Education: A Report of the ACE Commission on Women in Higher Education*, Washington, DC, American Council on Education.

Skrentny, J. D. (1996) *The Ironies of Affirmative Action; Politics, Culture, and Justice in America*, Chicago, IL, University of Chicago Press.

Snyder, T. D. and Hoffman, C. (1994) *Digest of Educational Statistics*, Washington, DC, Government Printing Office.

Stimpson, C. R. (1993) 'Has affirmative action gone astray?', *Thought and Action*, **VIII**, 2, pp. 5–26.

Tierney, W. G. (1996) *The Parameters of Affirmative Action: Equity and Excellence in the Academy*, Los Angeles, CA, Center for Higher Education Policy Analysis.

Vetter, B. (1994) *Professional Women and Minorities: A Total Resource Data Compendium*, Washington, DC, Commission on Professionals in Science and Technology.

Williams, W. W. (1993) 'Equality's riddle: Pregnancy and the equal treatment /special', treatment debate in Weisberg, D. K. (Ed) *Feminist Legal Theory: Foundations*, Philadelphia, PA, Temple University Press, pp. 128–55.

Zimbler, L. J. (1994) *Faculty and Instructional Staff: Who Are They and What Do They Do? 1993 National Study of Postsecondary Faculty*, Washington, DC, Office of Educational Research and Improvement.

CHAPTER 13

GENDER EQUITY IN COLLEGIATE SPORTS: THE ROLE OF ATHLETIC ASSOCIATIONS

LISA C. HUTCHENS AND BARBARA K. TOWNSEND

"No person in the United States shall, on the basis of sex, be excluded from participation in, be denied the benefits of, or be subjected to discrimination under any educational program or activity receiving federal financial assistance." (Education Amendments of 1972, Title IX)

Over twenty-five years have transpired since the passage of Title IX. During this quarter century there has been a tremendous growth of opportunities for women within collegiate sports, both as players and administrators. Along with these advancements have come increased spectator interest, increased media coverage, the training of women's teams for Olympic competition, and the development of women's professional leagues in basketball and softball (Riley 1997a).

Athletic associations—such as the American Association for Health, Physical Education, and Recreation (AAHPER), the Commission on Intercollegiate Athletics for Women (CIAW), and Association of Intercollegiate Athletics for Women (AIAW)—have been important players in the advancement of females within collegiate sports. Currently, however, women's athletic programs in four-year schools exist under the governance of two organizations, the National Collegiate Athletic Association (NCAA) and the National Association of Intercollegiate Athletics (NAIA), that also include men's athletic programs.

Some view this as a situation that potentially breeds gender inequity in intercollegiate athletic programs.

Statistics about the number of women in athletic programs and the dollars appropriated to them illustrate a lack of equity. According to a 1997 report from the Women's Sports Foundation, male athletes in NCAA Division I-A programs outnumbered females by almost a ratio of two to one, yet females made up approximately 55% of the student population (Sabo, 1997). The National Coalition for Women and Girls in Education reported that same year that for every new dollar spent on college sports for women, two new dollars were spent on men's sports. In addition, female college athletes received only 23% of athletic operating budgets, 38% of athletic scholarship dollars, and 27% of the money spent for recruiting new athletes (NCWGE, 1997). If gender equity is to become a reality, a commitment must be made by national athletic associations, colleges, universities, and the Office of Civil Rights (OCR) to seek rectification of existing gender discrimination. Then, and only then, will people see the necessary actions being taken to make women truly equal in the athletic arena (Parkhouse, 1990).

This article reviews the evolution of opportunities for females in college athletics at four-year institutions, including the impact of Title IX and subsequent court decisions. To fully understand the present dilemma of the gender equity movement in collegiate sports, the roles of various athletic associations, including the AIAW, the NAIA, and the NCAA, are analyzed. In addition, the Title IX initiatives implemented by the dominant athletic associations are examined.

Evolution of Women's Sports

The nineteenth century marked a period of tremendous cultural change as many women grew dissatisfied with their traditional roles in society and began to seek educational opportunities as a way to expand their roles in areas outside the home. Many physicians and educators, however, were convinced that the intellectual strain of receiving an education would damage the female reproductive system, especially if a female attended school during her time of puberty or adolescence (Gordon, 1989). It was believed that the brain and ovaries could not develop simultaneously. Ironically, it was this concern for upgrading a woman's maternal capacity that provided the impetus for the establishment of women's physical education, and eventually, athletic programs in this country (Rosenburg & Rosenburg, 1987).

As women exhibited the ability to endure the rigors of education, a transformation of concepts regarding the feminine idea occurred. A new image of independence and athletic vigor emerged, and with this new image came increased athletic opportunities. One such example was Wellesley College where calisthenics and sports were a required part of the curriculum and later became noted for training women college directors and physical education instructors (Park, 1987). Exercise for women began to gain credibility among the wealthy as outdoor activities such as horseback riding, archery, croquet, swimming, golf, and tennis allowed them to show off the latest styles in outdoor apparel at their exclusive clubs. In the 1870s these clubs began opening tournament play to women which resulted in the eventual formation of the National Archery Association, the U.S. National Lawn Tennis Association, and the U.S. Golf Association. These organizations sponsored the first national championships for women in archery (1879), tennis (1887), and golf (1895) (Cahn, 1994).

In 1892 Senda Berenson introduced the game of basketball to girls at Smith College, and by 1900 coeducational colleges, women's colleges, and normal schools were organizing women's teams across the United States (Smith, 1984). However, many female physical educators wanted to prevent the "win at all costs" mentality that was, they believed, so pervasive in men's athletics. Therefore, "sport for all" was the credo and intercollegiate competition was strongly opposed (Snyder & Spreitzer, 1978).

Formation of Women's Athletic Organizations

Collegiate sports for women developed in a relatively unified, controlled pattern across the United States as organizations governing women's athletics were formed and run by female physical educators with no external interference (Jensen, 1986). Three organizations concerned with establishing guidelines and policies for women's sports originated in the 1920s and continued to limit intercollegiate athletics until the 1960s (Acosta & Carpenter, 1985). These organizations were the Committee on Women's Athletics of the AAHPER, the Women's Division of the National Amateur Federation (WDNAF), and the National Association for Physical Education for College Women (NAPECW).

One of the popular means of providing sports participation without the formation of varsity athletics was the development of "play days" in which coeds from various colleges formed teams and competed in a number of sports (Snyder & Spreitzer, 1978). During the early 1930s, play days evolved into "sports days", which allowed for competition between schools but with rule modifications that reduced the competitive level (Cahn, 1994). By the mid-1930s, 80% of colleges participated in some variation of play day for women (Smith, 1984).

Play days and sport days continued to be the primary avenue for athletic competition through the 1940s as only 17% of colleges reported providing intercollegiate varsity sports for women. For those women without access to an intercollegiate athletic program yet wanting to pursue more serious competition, athletic opportunities had to be found where possible in municipal leagues, industrial recreation programs provided by local employers, the local YMCA, or the Amateur Athletic Association.

With the advent of contemporary feminism in the 1960s, significant changes began to occur. The number of females in the workforce increased significantly over the 1940s and 1950s, and women were appointed to highly visible political positions (The Feminist Majority 1995b). This groundswell of activity had an impact on athletics as well. Within the AAHPER, the Committee on Women's Athletics became the Division for Girls' and Women's Sports (DGWS) and developed into the most prominent organization in the governance of women's sports. In 1957, the DGWS, along with the WDNAF and the NAPECW, approved the inclusion of women's intercollegiate athletics in their areas of concern (Acosta & Carpenter, 1985). The three associations tried to jointly govern these athletic competitions, but confusion over the areas of control of each of the associations led to failure. By 1965 the DGWS, still under the umbrella of the AAHPER, had assumed solitary control in an attempt to place the direction of women's intercollegiate competition under one nationally visible structure (Jensen, 1986).

Under DGWS control, the highly skilled female athlete became the focus of attention, and intercollegiate championship competitions were initiated. As an increasing number of women became involved in high-level athletics, it became clear that the competence of women physical educators to handle the growing responsibilities in athletics was being tested. The time had come to establish a women's athletic organization separate from physical education (Jensen, 1986). In 1966 the CIAW was created to sponsor national championships and sanction women's intercollegiate athletic events. During the following six years, national championships were established for seven sports: golf in 1966; gymnastics and track and field in 1969; badminton, swimming, diving, and volleyball in 1970; and basketball in 1972 (Grant, 1989).

In 1971 the CIAW, with help from the DGWS, formed the AIAW, an organization that required institutional membership to pay annual dues (Grant, 1989). Created by women for women "who desired professional opportunities and athletic competition at the collegiate level" (Lopiano, 1986, p. 167), this organization had several priorities:

1. To use sport as a "means" to knowing oneself
2. To protect athletes from exploitation
3. To increase the level and type of sport options
4. To increase the skill of sport opportunity
5. To disprove myths about female athletes by showing strong, highly skilled competitors
6. To create capable female leaders
7. To improve career opportunities for women, and
8. To attack racial exploitation (Lopiano, 1986, p. 167).

Over 90% of its member institutions had women coaches (Thorngren & Eisenbarth, 1994) and athletic directors (VanderZwaag, 1988).

Development of Title IX

In 1972, "the single most important impetus for the explosion of girls' and women's participatory opportunities in sport" (Grant, 1989, p. 44) arrived with the passage of Title IX. However, the notion of increasing athletic opportunities for women was not the catalyst behind its passage. Rather, the catalyst was the denial in 1969 of a full-time faculty position to Bernice Sandler, who, with guidance from the Women's Equity Action League and the National Organization for Women, embarked on a national campaign to end sexual discrimination in education (Huggins, 1997). The issue of sex bias in education received added attention when Oregon Representative Edith Green introduced a higher education bill regarding gender equity and held what were the first ever hearings devoted to this topic. These hearings made sex discrimination in education a legitimate issue and were the first legislative step toward the enactment of Title IX (Riley, 1997b).

As the legislation was being sponsored through the Senate by Birch Bayh of Indiana, questions arose regarding the best methods for reaching gender equity. It took a House-Senate Conference Committee months to settle the differences between the two legislative bodies. The final legislation—the provision prohibiting sex discrimination in an education program or activity within an institution receiving federal funds—became Title IX of the Education Amendments of 1972 and was signed into law by President Richard Nixon on June 23, 1972. While developing the implementing regulations for Title IX, the then-U.S. Department of Health, Education and Welfare received more than 9700 comments and suggestions. The final Title IX regulations—34 C.F.R. Part 106—were signed on May 27, 1975 by President Gerald Ford (Riley, 1997b). Institutions were required to complete self-evaluations of their programs by July 21, 1976, but they had a three-year window, until July 21, 1978, to bring their programs into compliance (VanderZwaag, 1988).

Title IX Clarification

Title IX was passed with little controversy; however, soon after its passage, members of the NCAA complained that men's sports would suffer if women's sports had to be funded equally (The Feminist Majority, 1995a). In addition, confusion resulted from the broad language of Title IX as it contained the phrase "any education program or activity receiving Federal financial assistance." (Pieronek, 1994, p. 354) The question arose whether Title IX applied to an athletic program if the program or individual sports did not benefit directly from federal funds. Even the courts varied in their interpretations of the law as some excluded college athletics from the Title IX mandate when rendering judgments (Pieronek, 1994).

In response to criticism about the vagueness of the compliance requirements of the Title IX regulation, the OCR released its 1979 Intercollegiate Athletics Policy Interpretation, which included a more detailed method by which to measure equal athletic opportunity (Pieronek, 1994). Under this policy interpretation, the OCR applied a three-part test to help determine whether equal athletic opportunity was being provided. The three factors assessed were (1) whether the intercollegiate level participation opportunities for male and female students were provided in numbers proportionate to their respective enrollments; (2) whether the institution could show a history and continuing practice of program expansion for the underrepresented sex (typically female) which was responsive to their needs and interests; or (3) when no history of expansion was present, whether the institution could demonstrate that the interests and abilities of the underrepresented sex were being met by existing programs and opportunities. This interpretation provided colleges and universities with great flexibility since they were only required to meet one of the three criteria (Intercollegiate Athletics, 1996).

In addition to the three-part test, the OCR assessed other factors to determine equality of opportunity. The OCR required that (1) financial assistance based on athletic ability be allocated in proportion to the number of male and female students participating in intercollegiate athletics; (2) all other benefits, opportunities, and treatment afforded each sex be equivalent; and (3) the interests and abilities of students be accommodated to the extent necessary to provide equal athletic opportunities for both sexes (Achieving Gender Equity, 1995). Overall determination of compliance was to be based on the institution's program as a whole.

Initial Impact of Title IX on Women's Athletics

Initial institutional compliance with Title IX resulted in a tremendous growth in women's athletics from 1972 through 1982 (Grant, 1989). In 1973, the University of Miami, Florida, awarded the first athletic scholarships for women—a total of 15 in golf, swimming, diving, and tennis (Riley, 1997a). The average number of women's sports per school increased from 2.5 in 1973 to 6.48 in 1979 (Acosta & Carpenter, 1985), and in approximately the same time frame, women's athletic budgets grew 15% (Grant, 1989).

Athletic associations focusing on women's sports grew in size and scope. The MAW developed from its initial membership of 278 institutions in 1971–72 to 508 in 1973–74 to a peak of 973 in 1979–80, thus becoming the largest intercollegiate athletic governance organization in the nation at that time. In August 1980 a second athletics governing body, the NAIA, began to establish collegiate athletic programs for women, becoming the first national organization to offer competition for both women and men. That same year championships were held for women's teams in basketball, cross country, gymnastics, indoor and outdoor track and field, softball, tennis, and volleyball (NAIA Official Handbook, 1996). Post-season opportunities expanded from "open" championships in seven sports in 1972 to 41 national championships in 19 sports for three divisions that existed within the organization in 1982 (Grant, 1989). Division classification generally depended on the number of sports the college sponsored, with the largest number of athletic programs and facilities belonging to Division I, and those with smaller programs housed in Divisions II & III (Intercollegiate Athletics, 1996).

The 1975 AIAW Division I Basketball and Gymnastics Championships represented women's collegiate athletics' initial contact with major network television with $15,000 in revenue produced through NBC'S broadcasting of these events. By 1978, the figure had grown to almost $110,000 (Acosta & Carpenter, 1985). Further publicity was provided in 1979–80 when ESPN acquired the rights to televise selected Division II and III national championships (Grant, 1989).

Effects on Athletic Associations

The NCAA, an organization that at the time governed only men's athletic programs, participated in two major efforts to prevent, as stated by then NCAA Chief Executive Walter Byers, "the possible doom of intercollegiate athletics" (cited in Carpenter, 1985, p. 63). The NCAA lobbied on behalf of the "Tower Amendment," which sought to exclude revenue-producing sports, such as football and men's basketball, from the jurisdiction of Title IX (Carpenter, 1985). After this bill died in Congress, the NCAA went to court in 1980 and, in NCAA v. Califano, claimed that Title IX promoted a quota system which was in violation of the Fifth Amendment. Again, the NCAA's efforts were defeated (Acosta & Carpenter, 1985). After these two setbacks, the NCAA prepared to enter the realm of women's athletics by formulating a recommendation to offer championship competition for women. Not only was this a prerequisite for Title IX compliance, but increasing television revenues made the move much more palatable. In 1980 the NCAA Convention established 10 women's championships in two divisions and provided travel expenses to participating teams (Acosta & Carpenter, 1985).

This new posture by the NCAA was the beginning of the end for the AIAW, which found itself in competition with a financially superior association (Carpenter, 1985). The collapse of the AIAW occurred in 1982 due to the NCAA's initiation of Division I women's championships (Grant, 1989). The NCAA offered travel expenses to its sponsored championships, a benefit the AIAW could not match. Consequently, many schools moved their membership from the AIAW to the NCAA (Acosta & Carpenter, 1985).

The change in the majority of women's athletic programs to the male-dominated governance of the NCAA affected the gender composition of the coaching and administering of women's intercollegiate sports (Acosta & Carpenter, 1992). At institutions under NCAA control, the percentage of females coaching women's teams decreased from 90% in 1972 to 56% in 1985, and 90% of the Division I athletic programs for men and women were eventually merged and placed under male leadership (VanderZwaag, 1988).

The NAIA, which also established women's championships, experienced a similar fate in some regards. Its membership was composed primarily of small and often private institutions, where it was rare for a separation of men's and women's programs to occur. Authority over the women's programs was generally held by a male (D. Blackstock, personal communication, September 4, 1997), and on the national level, the majority of positions on standing committees and the Executive Committee were held by males, a trend that continues today (Grant, 1989).

Gender Equity in the 1980s

While women lost control, in most instances, of the governance of women's athletic programs, another major setback was experienced in 1984. In Grove City v. Bell, the Supreme Court ruled that only a program actually supported by federal funds was subject to the mandates of Title IX, and that any government grants paid directly to students did not meet the definition of federal funds because those monies were not directly funneled to the athletic programs or individual teams. Subsequently, the only laws that prevented sex discrimination in athletics were states' equal rights laws, which varied from state to state (Hendrickson, Lee, Loomis, & Olswang, 1996). Following Grove City v. Bell, a pessimistic mood prevailed among gender equity activists. Donna de Varona, a former Olympic gold medalist, stated at the time: "We're in the same position now that we were before the 1970s. It's true that there is more support for and acceptance of women's sports than ever before, but the mechanism that opened those doors (Title IX) is gone and we've already seen some erosion of women's opportunities in sports..." (cited in VanderZwaag, 1988, p. 237)

From 1984 to 1986, many allegations of female discrimination in intercollegiate athletics went uninvestigated as the OCR suspended or closed over 674 complaint investigations and 88 compliance review cases. In those few instances where allegations of discrimination were investigated, the OCR first had to establish whether a building was constructed with federal funds or whether a student was in a program funded by a federal agency. This information often had to be supplied by the colleges and universities themselves because reliable data on federal allocations were not available (Hendrickson et at., 1996). The OCR, due to a lack of funding as well as imprecise investigative procedures, became highly tolerant of disparities between the sexes (Thro & Snow, 1994). An institution was found to be in compliance if it voluntarily formed a committee to adopt a plan to correct possible violations (Durrant, 1992). Many colleges and universities quickly developed and adopted such plans without actually making an effort to put the plans into action (Grant, 1989).

A period of decline in regard to gender equity followed as indicated by the following statistics. In 1988 43% of the coaches of women's teams were female (Parkhouse, 1990), down from 54% in 1979 (Acosta and Carpenter, 1985). The number of women's teams per school stayed virtually the same as schools sponsored on average 7.15 in 1985 and 7.19 in 1989. While the number of sports offerings for females stayed somewhat constant, there was a trend toward replacing large roster teams with small roster teams, thus decreasing the number of participation opportunities for females (Acosta & Carpenter, 1992). Finally, in 1989, male athletes continued to represent the majority at both NCAA (67% male) and NAIA (60% male) institutions (Women's Sports Foundation, 1995).

Influence of Court Cases on Women's Athletics

It was mostly through court decisions that Title IX was redefined over the years. One case that set a precedent was Blair v. Washington State University in which female athletes and coaches at the university filed a discrimination lawsuit based on claims of inferior treatment in funding, fundraising efforts, publicity, scholarships, facilities, coaching, uniforms, and administrative support staff (Achieving Gender Equity, 1995). In 1987 the trial court ruled that the university discriminated against women and developed a funding formula based on the percentage of women in the undergraduate population. In devising the formula, however, football was excluded. The state's Supreme Court reversed on this single point claiming that no exception would be made for football. This ruling set a more stringent standard than previous Title IX interpretations for determining nondiscrimination based on accommodation of interests (Hendrickson et al., 1996).

The ruling in the Grove City College v. Bell case sent Congress back to work on reestablishing the intent of Title IX. On March 22, 1988, it passed the Civil Rights Restoration Act of 1987. This law superseded Grove City v. Bell by stating that "if any part of an institution receives federal financial assistance, the entire institution is required to be in compliance" (Crawford & Strope, 1996, p. 190). This interpretation covered the majority of U.S. colleges, including private schools, whose students received money from federal programs, for example, Pell Grants or Work-Study Loans; therefore, the majority of athletic programs were, once again, subjected to the mandates of Title IX (Thro & Snow, 1994).

A third step was taken toward greater Title IX adherence on February 26, 1992, when the U.S. Supreme Court handed down its decision in the Franklin v. Gwinnett County Public Schools case. For the first time plaintiffs successfully fought and received compensatory and punitive damages for intentional sex discrimination. This ruling served to empower victims of sex discrimination to proceed more vigorously with legal action (Achieving Gender Equity, 1995).

Together the Blair v. Washington State case, the Civil Rights Restoration Act, and Franklin v. Gwinnett County Public Schools case provided a clear indication that gender equity in athletic programs must be provided (Grant, 1989). Subsequently, the number of lawsuits filed on the basis of discrimination increased, many of which resulted in out-of-court settlements in favor of the plaintiffs (Final Report, 1993). Consequences for the colleges and universities involved monetary damages, attorneys' fees, court-mandated funding of women's programs, court control of athletic programs, and possible further litigation (Kramer & Marinelli, 1993).

Many institutions surmised that Title IX compliance would cost less than settling or defending lawsuits (Pieronek, 1994) because, unless challenged, an institution had the flexibility, granted by the OCR, to decide what initiatives to implement; however, if a court were asked to redress an alleged violation, the institution would have far less flexibility (Achieving Gender Equity, 1995). In addition, as long as an institution could show a history and continuing practice of program expansion which was responsive to the interests and abilities of the underrepresented sex, that institution would be considered in compliance (OCR, 1979). Gains were gradual because progress was made largely on a case-by-case basis, and the OCR's record of enforcing Title IX without court interference was inadequate (NCWGF, 1997).

Gender Equity in the NCAA

Eighteen years after the passage of Title IX, the NCAA finally, at the urging of its member colleges and universities, began to look at gender-equity as a serious issue and decided to undertake a gender-equity study covering all 847 NCAA member institutions across Divisions I, II, and III (Justus & Brake, 1995). Forms requesting information on each institution's expenditures for its athletic programs were mailed in June 1991. The results of the study were released in March 1992 and revealed that serious discrimination was prevalent among NCAA members (NCAA Gender-Equity Study, 1992). While the undergraduate enrollment was relatively even when divided by sex, 70% of the intercollegiate athletes were male with 83% of all recruiting dollars, 77% of the operating costs, and 70% of the scholarship dollars going to the men's programs (Final Report, 1993).

An NCAA Gender-Equity Task Force was formed that same year in response to the study (Acosta & Carpenter, 1992). Based on its recommendations, the NCAA made the following changes (Intercollegiate Athletics, 1996):

1. The principle of gender equity was incorporated into the NCAA's constitution, with the recognition that each college was responsible for adherence to Title IX.

2. An Athletics Certification Program was developed in 1993–94 in which Division I schools were required to evaluate their athletic programs and develop plans for improving them if Title IX compliance was not met. Schools failing to take corrective measures within an established time frame were to be ineligible for championship competition in all sports for up to one year. If after one year NCAA certification was still not met, the school was no longer to be an active member of the NCAA.

3. Nine emerging sports were identified to help schools achieve gender equity as well as to meet the interests and abilities of female athletes: archery, badminton, bowling, ice hockey, crew (rowing), squash, synchronized swimming, team handball, and water polo.

Publication of the NCAA Gender-Equity Report in 1992 was the first time information of this type had been made available; however, a limitation of the study was that the collected data were aggregated, thus it did not allow for the assessment of an individual institution's performance (Sabo, 1997). With the passage in 1994 of the Equity in Athletics Disclosure Act (EADA), all coeducational higher education institutions that participated in any federal financial program and sponsored intercollegiate athletics were required, beginning October 1, 1996, to annually disclose information regarding their athletic programs. This information was to include participation rates of both sexes, coaching salaries and expenses, student aid, and operating expenses (Intercollegiate Athletics, 1996).

In 1995, the NCAA conducted a follow-up study of its membership with the findings released in April 1997 (NCAA Gender-Equity Study, 1997). Small percentage gains for females were reported for both the average number of female athletes per institution and dollars available for operating expenses, recruiting, and scholarships. It was further noted that, 24 years after the passage of Title IX, only 70 of the 307 Division I schools (23%) had been certified by the Athletics Certification Program based on their efforts to satisfy the NCAA's gender equity principles. In addition, certification was not an indication of compliance, but rather, acknowledgment that the institution was making progress toward gender equity (Intercollegiate Athletics, 1996).

Gender Equity in the NAIA

While the NCAA slowly took steps to improve athletic offerings for women, the NAIA experienced its own unique problems as many of its member institutions, mostly the football-playing schools, exited. A decrease in its membership from 439 institutions in 1991–92 (Women's Sports Foundation, 1995) to 354 in 1997–98 resulted. Of these 354, seventy had dual membership with the NCAA, meaning that once their probationary period with the NCAA was over, they would leave the NAIA for full-time status with the NCAA. The initial movement of institutions to the NCAA paralleled what happened to the AIAW, as playoff-bound schools wanted total reimbursement for travel expenses. Since most of the NAIA sports and tournaments were not revenue-producing, costs for these smaller institutions proved expensive. Today, much of this continued movement stems from the NAIAs diminished image as its members, such as Transylvania, Cumberland, and Spring Hill, do not approach near the same level of national prominence as NCAA institutions such as Notre Dame, UCLA, Stanford, or the University of Michigan. Nor are NAIA regular season games and tournaments tied to lucrative TV contracts as are the NCAA's, in which its members receive a share of the revenues (D. Mosely, personal communication, October 23, 1997).

Within the remaining NAIA membership, competition often occurs among institutions that differ significantly in enrollment and athletic philosophy. For example, there are small schools such as Voorhees College in South Carolina with an enrollment of 860 and large schools such as Simon Fraser in Canada with almost 16,000 students. Philosophical differences are evident through comparison of the full slate of sports offerings of Western Washington University (eight men's, eight women's) to that of Bethany College, California (two men's, two women's), or by noting that some schools, such as Southwest Oklahoma State, play football, while others, such as Oklahoma Baptist, do not (Beazley, 1998). There are also contrasts in the number of scholarships awarded as Bethel College, Tennessee, awards a limited number of partial athletic grants-in-aid (S. Teel, personal communication, May 19, 1998); whereas, one of its common opponents, Union University, Tennessee, offers 54 full scholarships for one less sport (T. Sadler, personal communication, May 19, 1998).

Private liberal-art colleges, many of which have NAIA membership, have seen the percent of female undergraduate enrollments rise in recent years at larger rates than their larger state university counterparts (Gose, 1997). However, statistics reported by the Women's Sports Foundation (1995) for NAIA schools revealed that, as late as the 1992–93 academic year, male athletes still outnumbered their female counterparts.

The 1996 NAIA Official Handbook included gender equity as part of its printed statement of philosophy. Thus on paper the NAIA supported gender equity, but its actions to date do not reflect a proactive commitment. The NAIA National Office requires all member institutions to submit a year-end report outlining their scholarship programs. However, according to Lynn Adams, NAIA Vice President Championships: "Summaries or general information from these reports have not been made a part of our [NAIA] recording process;

therefore, that information is not presently available" (personal communication, September 27, 1996). A Gender-Equity Committee was appointed with the purpose of raising "the level of awareness about issues related to women in sport and to facilitate the advancement of women in sport and in the governance of all phases of the NAIA" (NAIA Official Handbook, 1996). However, its major activity thus far has been the implementation of workshops and national convention meetings on the subject of gender equity. To date, the NAIA has adopted no enforcement bylaws to expedite Title IX compliance by its member schools (D. Blackstock, May 20, 1998).

Conclusion and Implications

Women's Intercollegiate athletics have experienced unprecedented growth in the past twenty-six years since the passage of Title IX; however, many believe that the gender equity movement in athletics has stagnated. Much of the growth was realized in the 1980s, and progress is not synonymous with equality. According to Pedulla (1997), 80% or more of all colleges and universities were not in compliance with Title IX, yet the OCR has reduced the number of cases it investigated in subsequent years following 1995 (NCWGE, 1997).

Arguments abound on both sides of the gender equity issue as to what is fair and equitable while also being practical and manageable. Some athletic directors, such as Doug Dickey of the University of Tennessee, believe that the presence of football and its high participation level makes it virtually impossible to get the 50/50 split in participation rates that some Title IX advocates demand. However, it is football, that many athletic directors cite, as being the sport that funds the non-revenue sports on both sides of the gender line at their institutions (Climer, 1997). Pete Boone, Athletic Director at the University of Mississippi, stated that women's athletics for the 1996-1997 academic year accounted for 35-40% of the expenses at the school, but only produced about $15,000, a situation that had caused some schools to drop men's non-revenue sports unless football could provide adequate money (Hall, 1997).

Research by Dillon (1997a) seems to refute these claims. She reports that less than 40% of the 230 Division I colleges that played football in 1996-97 made money on the sport, and in the nearly 100 Division I schools without football programs, women still only constituted 44% of the athletic population. Additionally, Dillon (1997b) cites a Division I university with a football program that made a commitment to comply with Title IX. The University of Kansas, a member of one of the NCAAs elite football conferences—the Big 12, found donors who had an interest in women's sports and raised in excess of eight million dollars to help fund a new sports complex with facilities for both men and women, renovate the women's basketball locker room, and build a women's soccer field. The school is now raising $3 million annually for both men's and women's scholarships. As of 1995-96, women made up 49% of all students and 47% of the athletes.

Clearly, much needs to be done to increase colleges' and universities' commitment to provide gender equity in sports. Research conducted by the NCAA revealed the need for the association to take steps to raise the percentage of its members that adhere to the mandates of Title IX. Similar research focusing on its member institutions could indicate to the NAIA a similar need. Since tournament play, championship games, and bowl games provide member institutions with national recognition, and sometimes money, athletic associations have the ability and authority to exert some control in terms of requirements for institutional eligibility. Gender equity must be one of these requirements.

References

Achieving gender equity: A basic guide to Title IX for colleges and universities. (1995). Overland Park, KS: NCAA Gender-Equity Task Force.

Acosta, R.V., & Carpenter, L.J. (1985). Women in sport. In D. Chu, J. O. Segrave, & B. J. Becker (Eds.), *Sport and higher education* (pp. 314-317, 319). Champaign, IL: Human Kinetics Publishers Inc.

Acosta, R. V., & Carpenter, L. J. (1992). *Women in intercollegiate sport: A longitudinal study—fifteen year update, 1977-1992.* Brooklyn, NY: Brooklyn College. (ERIC Document Reproduction No. ED 352 337)

Beazley, C. (Ed.). (1996). *Blue book of college athletics for senior junior & community colleges.* Montgomery, AL: Athletic Publishing Company.

Blair v. Washington State University, 740 P.2d 1379 (Wash. 1987).

Cahn, S. K. (1994). *Coming on strong: Gender and sexuality in twentieth-century women's sport.* New York: The Free Press.

Carpenter, L. J. (1985). The impact of Title IX on women's intercollegiate sports. In A. T. Johnson, & J.H. Frey (Eds.), *Government and sport* (pp. 63–65). Totowa, NJ: Rowan & Allanheld.

Civil Rights Restoration Act of 1987, Pub. L. No. 100-259, 102 Stat. 28 (1988) (codified at 20 U.S.C. 1687).

Climer, D. (1997, May 25). Complying with Title IX not easy, but it's the law. *The Tennessean,* p. 16C.

Cohen v. Brown University, 991 F.2d 888 (1st Cir. 1993).

Cook v. Colgate University, 802 F. Supp. 737 (N.D.N.Y. 1992), vacated as moot, 992 F.2d 17 (2d Cir. 1993).

Crawford, J. D., & Strope, J. L. (1996). Gender equity in college athletics: How far have we really come in twenty years? *Education Law Reporter,* 5(1), 189–202.

Dillon, K. (1997a, October 9). *Money games inside the NCAA: NCAA certification program does little to improve gender equity.* Available: http://www.kcstar.com/cgi-bin/pubsys/page. . . .ncaa-article.pat?file=sports/30d99dfd.a08 [1997, October 18].

Dillon, K. (1997b, October 9). *Money games inside the NCAA: Schools make strides with eye toward equity.* Available: http://www.kcstar.com/cgi-bin/pubsys/page. . . .ncaa-article.pat?file=sports/30d99df9.a08 [1997, October 18].

Durrant, S. M. (1992, March). Title IX—its power and its limitations. *Journal of Physical Education, Recreation and Dance,* 63(3), 60–64.

Education Amendments of 1972, P.L.92-318, *Title IX-Prohibitions of Sex Discrimination,* July 1, 1972 (now codified as 20 U.S.C. $ 1681(a)).

Favia v. Indiana University of Pennsylvania, 812 F. Supp. 778 (WD. Pa. 1993).

Final report of the NCAA Gender-Equity Task Force. *(1993, July 26).* Overland Park, KS: NCAA.

Franklin v. Gwinnett County Public Schools, 112 S. Ct. 1028.

Gordon, L. D. (1989). Co-education on two campuses: Berkeley and Chicago, 1890–1912. In L. F. Goodchild, & H.S. Wechsler (Eds.), *ASHE reader on the history of higher education* (pp. 349–350). Needham Heights, MA: Ginn Press.

Gose, B. (1997, June 6). Liberal-arts colleges ask: Where have the men gone? *Chronicle of Higher Education,* 43(39), A35.

Grant, C. H. (1989). Recapturing the vision. *Journal of Physical Education, Recreation and Dance,* 60(3), 44–48.

Grove City College v. Bell, 465 U.S. 555 (1984).

Hall, B. (1997, October 1). Tigers, Rebs talk of money, and lack of it. *The Commercial Appeal,* p. D8.

Hendrickson, R. M., Lee, B. A., Loomis, F. D., & Olswang, S. G. (1996). The impact of the Civil Rights Restoration Act on higher education. *Education Law Reporter,* 100 (3), 671–690.

Huggins, S. (1997, July 21). Woman recalls how five words led to creation of Title IX. *The NCAA News,* p.5.

Intercollegiate athletics: Status of efforts to promote gender equity. *Report to the Honorable Cardiss Collins, House of Representatives (1996). (Report No. GAO/HEHS-97-10). Gaithersburg, MD: U.S. General Accounting Office* (ERIC Document Reproduction Service No. ED 402 300)

Jensen, J. (1986). Women's collegiate athletics: Incidents in the struggle for influence and control. In R. Lapchick (Ed.), *Fractured focus: Sport as a reflection of society* (pp. 151–158). Lexington, MA: Lexington Books.

Justus, J., & Brake, D. (1995). Title IX. *Journal of College and University Law,* 22(1), 48–62.

Kramer, W. D., & Marinelli, M. X. (1993, March 15). *Title IX in intercollegiate athletics; Litigation risks facing colleges and universities.* Washington, D.C.: American Council on Education.

Lopiano, D. A. (1986). A political analysis of the possibility of impact alternatives for the accomplishment of feminist objectives within American intercollegiate sport. In R. Lapchick (Ed.), *Fractured focus: Sport as a reflection of society* (p. 167). Lexington, MA: Lexington Books.

National Association of lntercollegiate Athletics official handbook *(1996, July).* Tulsa, OK: NAIA.

National Coalition for Women and Girls in Education. (1997, June 3). *Report card on Title IX at 25—athletics.* [WWW document]. Available: http://www.edc.org/WomensEquity/title9/athletics.html [1998, May 18].

NCAA gender-equity study: Summary of results. *(1992, March).* Overland Park, KS: NCAA. (ERIC Document Reproduction Service No. ED 345 593)

NCAA. Gender-equity study: Summary of results. *(1997, April).* Overland Park, KS: NCAA Gender Equity Task Force

Office for Civil Rights. *Title IX of the Education Amendments of 1972; Intercollegiate Athletics Policy Interpretation,* 44 Fed. Reg. 71413 et seq. (Dec. 11, 1979).

Park, R. J. (1987).*Sport, gender and society in a transatlantic Victorian perspective.* In J. Mangan & R. Park. (Eds.), *From 'fair sex' to feminism: Sport and the socialization of women in the industrial and post-industrial eras* (p. 77). London, England: Frank Cass & Co.

Parkhouse, B. L. (1990). A time to speak—you've come a long way, baby . . . dancing backwards and in heels. *Journal of Physical Education, Recreation and Dance,* 61(3), 72–75.

Pedulla, T. (1997, June 13). Women's sports leaders: Title IX makes headway. *USA Today*, p. 16C.

Pieronek, C. (1994). A clash of titans: College football v. Title IX. *Journal of College and University Law*, 20(3), 351–381.

Riley, R. W. (1997a, June). Achieving success under Title IX. Available:http://www.ed.gov/pubs/TitleIX/part5.html [1997, September 29].

Riley, R. W (1997b, June). Title IX: A sea change in gender equity in education. Available: http://www.ed.gov/pubs/Title IX/part3.html [1997, September 29].

Roberts v. Colorado State Bd. of Agriculture, 998 F.2d 824 (10th Cir. 1993), cert. denied, 114S. Ct. 580 (1993).

Rosenburg, C. S. & Rosenburg, C. R. (1987). The female animal: Medical and biological views of women and their role in nineteenth-century America. In J. Mangum & R. Park (eds.), *From fair sex' to feminism: Sport and the socialization of women in the industrial and post-industrial eras* (pp. 13–22). London, England: Frank Cass & Co.

Sabo, D. (1997, June 23). *The Women's Sports Foundation gender equity report card: A survey of athletic opportunity in American higher education*. East Meadow, NY: Women's Sports Foundation.

Smith, R. A. (1984). The rise of basketball for women in colleges. In S.A. Reiss (Ed.), *The American sporting experience: A historical anthology of sport in America* (pp. 243–245). Champaign, IL: Leisure Press.

Stanley v. University of Southern California, 13 F.3d 1313 (9th Cir. 1994).

Snyder, E. E., & Spreitzer, E. (1978). *Social aspects of sports*. Englewood Cliffs, NJ: Prentice-Hall, Inc.

The Feminist Majority Foundation. (1995a). *Empowering women in sports*. Available: http://www.feminist.org/research/sports2html#intro [1998, May 18].

The Feminist Majority Foundation. (1995b). *The Feminist Chronicles*. Available: http://www.feminist.org/research/chronicles/part2.html [1998, May 19].

Thorngren, C. M., & Eisenbarth, B. S. (1994, June). Games yet to be played: Equity in sport leadership. *Women's Educational Equity Act Digest*, p. 2–3.

Thro, W. E., & Snow, B. A. (1994). Cohen v. Brown University and the future of intercollegiate and interscholastic athletics. West's Education Law, 3(1), 11–28.

VanderZwaag, H. J. (1988). *Policy development in sport.* Indianapolis: Benchmark Press, Inc.

Women's Sports Foundation. (1995, October). *Participation statistics packet*. East Meadow, NY: Author.

Lisa C. Hutchens is Assistant Professor of Physical Education, Wellness, and Sport at Union University and co-head coach of the school's NAIA women's basketball team. She has served as an instructor and assistant coach for the past seven years. **Barbara K Townsend** is Professor of Higher Education in the Department of Leadership at the University of Memphis. She has served as chair of the department and as Associate Dean of the School of Education at Loyola University Chicago.

CHAPTER 14

CRUEL ENVIRONMENTS: SEXUAL ABUSE AND HARASSMENT IN THE ACADEMY

LINDA SERRA HAGEDORN

If any human society—large or small, simple or complex, based on the most rudimentary hunting and fishing or on the whole intricate interchange of manufactured product—is to survive, it must have a pattern of social life that comes to terms with the differences between the sexes. (Margaret Mead, 1996, p. 163)

Chapter Purpose

The truth is out. For many former and present college students, faculty, staff, and administrators the college campus represents a cruel environment. The tragedy of this statement stands vivid against the campus stereotype as an environment of comfort, nurture, and deep intellectual involvement which creates an overtly positive experience leading to wonderful memories and loyal alumni. Sadly, judging from the continually growing number of sexual abuse and harassment complaints and lawsuits, the problem is not diminishing. Rather, this pervasive, complex, and sensitive problem continues to swell despite recent policies instituted at virtually all postsecondary institutions. It appears that a fresh look or different perspective is warranted. This chapter has a threefold purpose. First, it will present a broad review of sexual harassment and abuse. Second, it will seek to explain why the college campus is the frequent location for sexual abuse and harassment. Finally, the chapter will recommend steps to thwart the increasing incidence of all forms of sexual abuse in the academy.

Due to the nature, extent, and pervasiveness of sexual harassment and abuse, the pertinent studies and literature reside in many disciplines. Accordingly, my research extended to the literature bases of anthropology, sociology, psychology, criminal justice, law, medicine, and understandably higher education. With this broad sweep of the literature, I will present sexual abuse and harassment in the academy through a slightly different lens. Sexual harassment will be presented as an act of gender abuse on a continuum with sexual assault and rape. Using the literature specific to gender abuse and rape, I will demonstrate how the college environment is especially conducive to all acts of gender abuse. Finally, in light of this perspective, I will focus on present campus policies as well as to suggest methods and policies to produce college campus environments that are less cruel. In short, this chapter will serve as a digest of the literature effectively evolving into a theoretical framework for future policy formulation.

Reprinted from *Higher Education: Handbook of Theory and Research*, Vol. XIV, by Linda Serra Hagedorn, 1999. Copyright © 1999 Agathon Press.

Background

The sexual harassment of women on college campuses most likely began when women first entered higher education. A poem published in the University of California's student publication, The Pelican, in 1914 provides a succinct glimpse into the college environment faced by the female students of the early 20th century:

> When Dolly used to go to Class to make an eight o'clock,
> The blasé seniors, sweater clad, her passageway would block:
> And smokers on old North Hall steps would never move their feet,
> But crowd the sidewalk to the curb, so Dolly took the street.
> For co-eds in the good old days walked by with modest mien:
>
> They never were obtrusive, they were neither heard nor seen.
> They dressed in khaki, greys and drabs: and powder? Not a grain.
> They went in for that high brow stuff. (They made themselves quite plain.)
>
> But now when Dolly goes, she's class! Her motor class at noon.
> She barely makes a one o'clock and thinks that quite too soon.
> A Senior with her cigarettes, a Junior with her books.
> With men the same, what is the change? Why, only Dolly's looks.
>
> Now carmine lips and low done hair and costume from Lucille
> Whose clinging chiffons hide her liens and likewise half reveal.
> The streets are crowded to the walk; our Dolly knows the trick:
> She goes in for that eye brow stuff, for Dolly is some chic.
> (as cited in Gordon, 1990, p. 86)

In the late 20th century, the infamous Clarence Thomas–Anita Hill national hearings brought the topic of sexual harassment to the news' forefront, which resulted in a spate of published literature and research, much of it specifically targeting institutions of education. Recent studies and inquiries paint bleak pictures indicating sexual harassment is rampant and pervasive in school and college environments. For instance, according to a survey by the American Association of University Women (1993) approximately 4 out of 5 female students (81%) have experienced some form of sexual harassment incident related to their education. When confined to college experiences, other researchers report approximately 25% to 75% of all female students have been the victim of some form of sexual harassment (AAUW, 1993; Adams, Kotke, and Padgitt, 1983; Brown and Maestro-Scherer, 1986; Gruber, 1990; Paludi, 1990). When confined to harassment specifically from college instructors, Dziech and Weiner (1984) reported 30% of the women in their survey reported victimization.

Due to a dearth of research, the extent of sexual harassment to college staff, faculty, and administrators remains ambiguous. For female faculty, studies have shown the rates of sexual harassment may be between 20% and 49% (Chronicle of Higher Education, 11/2/93; Fitzgerald et al. 1988). For nonacademic staff, the rate is probably similar to that found in other public and private institutions; approximately 50% of employed females (Brown and Maestro-Scherer, 1986; Fitzgerald et al, 1988). The wide disparity and range in incidence rates reflects the lack of concrete definitions of sexual harassment and the continued reliance on individual interpretations of incidents, conversations, and occurrences. Dey, Korn, and Sax (1994) found that reported incidence rates were significantly lower when survey respondents were directly asked if they had experienced incidents of sexual harassment as compared with reported rates when respondents were asked if they had experienced specific types of behavior commonly included under the sexual harassment definition. Regardless of the study, the definition, or the circumstances, most researchers agree that the proportion of postsecondary students, faculty, staff, and administrators who have experienced sexual harassment in some form is very high (AAUW, 1993; Brown and Maestro-Scherer, 1986; Fitzgerald et al., 1988; Sandroff, 1992; Sandler and Shoop, 1997a). Moreover, the true extent of the problem may lie hidden as the National Council for Research on Women (1992) estimates that only about 10% of sexual harassment incidents are actually reported.

Table 1. Definition Matrix of Key Sexual Harassment Terms		
Term	Definition	College/University Examples
Sexual Harassment	A general usage term referring to "verbal or physical conduct of a sexual nature, imposed on the basis of sex, by an employee or agent of a recipient that denies, limits, provides different, or conditions the provision of aid, benefits, services or treatment protected by Title IX" (Office for Civil Rights, 1981; p. 2). Incidents of sexual harassment can be classified as either *quid pro quo* or hostile environment.	a. Administrator refers to the female faculty in his department as tokens b. Male college professor asks for sexual favors from his female students in return for passing grades in the class
Quid Pro Quo	The most obvious, yet least common form of sexual harassment. Literally, "Something given in exchange for something else" (Sandler and Shoop, 1997b) Involves the direct request of sexual favors	a. An administrator promises a favorable evaluation to a faculty member if she will spend the weekend with him b. A college professor promises authorship on a research project if the graduate student provides sexual favors
Hostile Environment	A pattern of unwelcome sexually oriented conduct, atmosphere, or environment that a reasonable woman would find intimidating or offensive (Shoop, 1997)	a. A math professor regularly implies that women cannot excel in mathematics b. A group of fraternity members regularly whistle and taunt women on their way to class
Peer Harassment	A form of hostile environment harassment that is perpetrated between people having no power differential, such as student on student	a. A male student regularly ogles and stares at female students who are trying to study in the university library b. Male physics professors refuse the department's sole female professor's request to co-author a research project telling her that a woman could not possibly perform research of the same caliber as the male researchers
Verbal Sexual Harassment	Written or spoken comments of a sexual nature about someone's clothing, body, or activities. Includes sexual jokes, inappropriate questions regarding sexuality, whistling, or other verbal comments.	a. Lewd jokes b. Sexual epithets chanted during sporting events
Physical Sexual Harassment	Unwelcome physical contact based on sex	a. Instructor makes a habit of stroking the backs of female students b. A male student purposely bumping into a female student in the hallway
Visual Sexual Harassment	The use of or display of items that are sexual in nature	a. Displays of pornographic material in residence halls b. A professor mixes a slide of a nude model among slides consistent with lecture material.

Table 1. Definition Matrix of Key Sexual Harassment Terms (Continued)		
Contrapower Harassment	Harassment by a subordinate to a superior (Benson, 1984) Contrapower harassment occurs despite an inverse in the power relationship between the actors	a. A student attempts to seduce her professor in order to gain an assistantship
Gender Harassment or Misogyny	Actions depicting a general hostility towards women	a. Pornographic displays in the residence halls b. The use of sexual epithets or slurs demeaning to women chanted during athletic events
Gay Bashing	Harassment based on sexual orientation	a. Gay students become the victim of taunting, teasing, and joking b. A lesbian assistant professor is denied tenure because her research area is gay students
Consensual Relationships	A "romantic" relationship between two individuals with a direct power differential, such as a professor and his student	a. A department head is dating a professor in her department b. A professor is romantically involved with his teaching assistant
Sexual Discrimination	Any treatment or consequences stemming solely from one's gender or sexual orientation	a. A professor is not granted travel funds because she is pregnant b. An applicant is denied a job interview because of his homosexuality
Sexual Assault or Sexual Abuse	Unwanted sexual contact that is achieved by force or violence	a. Date rape b. A professor is forced to perfom a sexual act by a perpetrator armed with a knife
Sexual Touching	Uninvited physical contact with sexual overtones	a. Pinching b. Grabbing c. Slapping
Sexual Materials	"Pornographic materials or objects which sexually debase women or womanhood" (Gruber, 1992, p. 452)	a. Pornographic movies b. Displays from sex magazines c. A fraternity house decorated with bras
Title VII	A component of the Civil Rights Act of 1964 which provides the right to work in an environment free from discrimination, intimidation, derision, or offensive insults	Provides workers at colleges and universities with legal protection against all forms of sexual discrimination
Title IX	A component of the Education Amendments of 1972 which defined the school as the student's workplace	Title IX provides Title VII coverage to college and university students
Relational Advances	Repeated requests for a social relationship with repetition to the extent of harassment	Repeated requests for dates despite firm negative responses
Micro Inequalities	Outwardly small, unimportant events that collectively create "stress"	a. Sexist jokes in a classroom b. Inappropriate comments

Definitions

In this chapter I chose to focus on the sexual harassment and abuse of women by men. Most scholars agree that the distribution of power, misogynous forces within society, contemporary gender expectations, and current sex roles make the harassment and abuse of women far more likely than that of men (Brandenburg, 1982, 1997; Hotelling and Zuber 1997; Sandler and Shoop, 1997; Superson, 1993). As an example I offer a study of sexual harassment performed at Cornell University which found that 90% of reported incidents were men harassing women while only 1% were women harassing men and 9% consisted of harassment by a person of the same sex (Parrot, 1991; as reported in Brandenburg, 1997). Moreover, the harassment of men by women or the harassment of same sex individuals may have totally different dynamics that should be addressed separately and extensively. However, this emphasis and focus should in no way be interpreted that the harassment of men, same sex individuals, or harassment based on sexual orientation is less heinous, less offensive, or of less importance.

Since the nomenclature associated with sexual harassment is relatively new, associated definitions are in the process of being formed and redefined through the judicial system. Table 1 presents a definition matrix of some of the more important sexual harassment and abuse terms used in this chapter. The table also includes simple examples of the terms as placed in the higher education context.

The Sexual Abuse Continuum

Although sexual abuse has traditionally been defined in terms of physical violence and injury, contemporary definitions now include psychological abuses such as harassment. Although psychological abuse is harder to define or quantify than physical violations, its emotional and physical effects may be equally devastating. Furthermore, Hart and Brassard (1991) argued that any separation of physical and psychological abuse "overly simplifies the topic and denies reality" (p. 63). As such, I present the forms of sexual abuse (including harassment) on a sexual abuse continuum with physical acts of abuse including rape (see Figure 1 for a graphic representation of the continuum). The sexual abuse continuum is supported by scholars in criminal justice, women's studies, sociology, and education. Till (1980) proposed a popular report on sexual harassment that utilized a similar continuum of five categories from generalized sexist remarks or behaviors to sexual crimes (including but not limited to rape). More recently, Quina (1996) explored the sexual exploitation continuum in greater detail and boldly stated:

> All forms of sexual harassment share important commonalties with rape. While harassment is usually less physically intrusive and less violent or life-threatening, it is not substantially different structurally or socially from rape. This conceptual framework defines rape and harassment as sexual assaults lying on a continuum of sexual exploitation, varying in degree of physical intrusion and potential physical injury to the victim. At the pole of the least physically violent, this continuum begins with verbal assaults, including sexually offensive jokes or degrading comments, also called "gender harassment" (e.g., Fitzgerald and Ormerod, 1991). At the pole of the most violent are rape, murder, and femicide. On such a scale, sexual harassment and rape are relatively close together. In fact, many assaults now called "harassment"—those involving sexual contact"—are legally the equivalent of rape. (page 183–184)

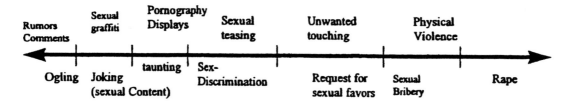

Figure 1. The Sexual Abuse Continuum

Although the depiction of the sexual abuse continuum implies degrees of severity in a general sense, it is not to be strictly interpreted or applicable for every case or for every individual. For example, although the continuum presents ogling as a slightly lesser offense than teasing, these terms are open to individual interpretation and context. It is very likely that consistent and repeated ogling will have a more serious psychological effect than a single isolated incident of sexual teasing despite the placement on the continuum.

It is also imperative that I clearly state the inclusion of "lesser forms" of sexual harassment on the same continuum as rape is not to be interpreted as belittling the atrocity of rape. Rape is a heinous and cruel crime that can emotionally and physically devastate a victim. For the sake of comparison, I offer an analogy of a theft continuum. Whereas shoplifting small items might be on one end of a theft continuum the other extremity might include multi-million dollar embezzlement. Certainly the two crimes are not equal, but they share similarities in definition and origin despite vast differences in degree and effect.

Implications of Sexual Harassment on Campus

Colleges and universities are both ethically and legally responsible to curtail all forms of sexual harassment and abuse and to promote an environment free of discrimination for its staff, faculty, and students. Certainly offensive or unprofessional behavior undermines the academic environment that is promised by college catalogs and included in mission statements. Offensive conduct may also violate state and federal laws thus putting both the institution and the offender in jeopardy of legal actions and punitive damages.

Ethical

The college or university's responsibility to its students, staff, faculty, and administration extends beyond that of most employers or many other types of institutions. Educational institutions (i.e., preschools, elementary schools, high schools, colleges, etc.) have additional ethical responsibilities related to their "in loco parentis"[1] status. In other words, educational institutions must ethically include the psychological, physical, and scholarly needs of students in their care. Of course, acts of physical abuse are against the law and can produce serious long-lasting effects. But, the well-documented and serious aftermath of sexual harassment also cannot be ignored. Studies have shown that sexual harassment may reduce self-esteem, jeopardize emotional stability, interfere or curtail career plans, corrupt interpersonal relationships, and generally create personal havoc (Brandenburg, 1997; AAUW, 1993; Paludi and Barickman, 1991; Shoop and Hayhow, 1994). Physical problems have also been recorded as effects of sexual harassment. Victims have complained of insomnia, headaches, and gastrointestinal disturbances (MacKinnon, 1979). And, of course, sexual harassment can "reduce the quality of education, diminish academic achievement, and ultimately may lower earning power" (Hotelling, 1991, p. 500) thus creating an environment that is totally counter to the purpose of educational institutions (Benson and Thomson, 1982). In 1989 the American Council on Education (ACE) urged all member institutions to adopt policies to inhibit sexual harassment. Since that time, most postsecondary institutions have recognized their responsibility, have followed ACE's advice, and have created policies and procedures to eliminate sexual harassment on campus. In addition, most institutions have adopted clear procedures for filing and resolving complaints related to harassment. In many institutions, these policies are reviewed on a regular basis and are published in the college newspaper or other campus-wide publications. Many institutions have chosen to disseminate the information via pamphlets, notices, flyers, posters or on the Internet.

Legal

Of course colleges and universities have more than just an ethical responsibility to eliminate sexual harassment. They are required by law to monitor and prevent sexual discrimination and harassment; provide a suitable, non-hostile environment; as well as provide appropriate procedures for the reporting and subsequent aftermath if sexual harassment should occur. To appropriately frame sexual harassment within the college environment, a short summary of the pertinent laws and cases will be presented.

Title VII. Strictly speaking, Title VII of the Civil Rights Act of 1964 protects employees (not students) of postsecondary institutions from all aspects of discrimination on the basis of gender, race, color, religion or national origin including conflicts involving hiring, firing, promotion, wages, disability, leaves, and retirement (Shoop, 1997). However, the Equal Employment Opportunity Commission (EEOC) issued its Sexual Harassment Guidelines in 1980, which more broadly defined sexual harassment as a violation of Title VII. Both the quid pro quo and hostile environment forms of sexual harassment are proscribed under Title VII.

Quid pro quo is the least common but most clearly recognized type of sexual harassment. It occurs when "submission to or rejection of unwelcome sexual conduct is used by a person with authority in the organization as the basis for making employment decisions affecting a subordinate employee" (Gillio and Bell, 1997, p. 189). Quid pro quo is clear and unmistakable taking the form of exchange of sexual favors for employment related returns. By its definition, the quid pro quo form of sexual harassment can only be committed by an individual with authority and power. Unlike other forms of harassment, quid pro quo accusations may be based on only a single incident (Conte, 1997). Regardless of circumstances, institutions have generally been found liable for quid pro quo forms of harassment.

The more common form of sexual harassment is labeled hostile environment. This form of harassment can occur "even if it leads to no tangible or economic job consequences" (EEOC, 1990, p. 2) and unlike the quid pro quo form, can occur between people of equal status (employee-on-employee or student-on-student). Hostile environment is broadly defined and may consist of any number of situations interpreted to cause extreme discomfort, embarrassment, or consistent irritation based on sex. Courts have interpreted hostile environments to include repeated requests for sexual favors, frequent use of vulgar language, displays of sexually offensive or explicit materials, and other situations that may demean and/or intimidate an individual to such an extent that it affects her ability to perform job tasks (Conte, 1997). To legally prove hostile environment the victim must prove that the conduct was 1) sexual in nature, 2) unwelcome, and 3) sufficiently severe or persistent to "alter the terms or conditions of employment" (Gillio and Bell, 1997, p. 190). In addition, the employer must have been aware, or should have been aware, that these disturbances were occurring. To clarify the hostile environment definition, courts have applied the "reasonable person" or "reasonable woman" standard (Brandenburg, 1997). The interpretation is, a hostile environment is one in which a typical or reasonable woman would feel discomfort, or embarrassment. Liability in hostile environment cases is usually decided through negligence standards; the employer is liable if the situation was known or should have been known and prompt remedial action was not taken (Gillio and Bell, 1997).

Title IX. Sexual harassment of students was not recognized under Title VII until 1981 when the Office of Civil Rights of the U.S. Department of Education included sexual harassment incidents as violations of the protections of Title IX of the Education Amendments of 1972. Thus, Title IX extended Title VII protection against sexual harassment to students thus broadly defining the definition of workplace to include schools and colleges (Baker, 1997; Shoop, 1997). Literally, Title IX prohibits any sex-based situation or decision that limits the "enjoyment of any rights, privilege, advantage or opportunity" related to federally funded educational programs (34 C.F.R. § 106.31 (b)(7). The dual interpretation of Title VII and Title IX provides students with protection from quid pro quo forms of harassment by teachers and professors and extends hostile environment definitions to student-on-student transgressions.

The Civil Rights Act of 1991. The Civil Rights Act of 1991 recast the federal court's view of sexual harassment providing compensatory and punitive damages, expert witness fees, and jury trials (Conte, 1997; Sandler and Shoop, 1997). Although compensatory damages may be granted from private employers as well as from local, state, or federal government agencies; punitive damages[2] can only be awarded from the private sector. Under compensatory damages, the Civil Rights Act allows for the recovery of expenses for medical or psychiatric treatment, pain and suffering, inconvenience, and other nonpecuniary losses (Conte,

1997). Punitive damages can only be claimed by proving "malice or reckless indifference to federally protected rights" (Conte, 1997, p. 65).

Significant court cases. As with most complex and circumstance-dependent situations, many of the legal aspects of sexual harassment have been decided through litigation in courts of law. There are numerous cases regarding students, faculty, and staff of schools and colleges on which legal precedence has been established and on which new cases are based. Table 2 presents some of the more significant court cases and outcomes that are pertinent to this chapter.

Sexual harassment is a relatively new term in the process of evolving in both its definition and in the determination of specific liability and damages. The more than 10,000 cases of sexual harassment filed with the Equal Employment Opportunity Commission (EEOC) each year (Gutek, 1997) attests to the permeation of sexual harassment in U.S. society. Despite the numerous complaints, some would agree with Superson (1993) that victims still lack sufficient and clear legal recourse.

Consensual Relations

Although neither Title VII nor Title IX expressly prohibit consensual relationships between professors and students,[3] the potential for exploitation and/or abuse is clear. The ability of students to freely consent to sexual relationships with individuals possessing power over their academic futures is extremely ambiguous. So despite the fact that consensual relationships are not illegal per se, liability under the anti-sex bias provisions of Title IX does apply. Since federal courts can award

Table 2. Significant Sexual Harassment Court Cases Impacting Education		
Case	*Cite*	*Outcome*
Alexander v. Yale	459 F. Supp. 1 (D. Conn. 1977)	*Quid pro quo* sexual harassment is sexual discrimination under Title IX.
Cannon v. University of Chicago	441 U.S. 677 (1979)	Title IX could be used for a private lawsuit claim of sex discrimination in educational institutions.
Korf v. Ball State University	726 G.2d 1222 (7th cir. 1984)	University professors have an ethical obligation that should be considered when assessing if sexual harassment has occurred.
Moire v. Temple University School	613 F. Supp. 1360 (E.D. Pa. 1985)	Action on hostile environment peer harassment can proceed under Title IX.
Meritor Savings Bank, FSB, v. Vinson	477 U.S. 57 (1986)	Sexual harassment is actionable under Title VII.
Franklin v. Gwinnett County Public Schools	112 S.Ct. 1028 (1992)	Student may seek monetary damages under Title IX for sexual harassment.
Harris v. Forklift Systems, Inc.	114 S.Ct. 367 (1993)	Defined the hostile work environment as one in which a reasonable person would find abusive.
Doe v. Petaluma City School District	830 F. Supp. 1560 (N.D. Cal. 1993)	Individuals may not be held liable for discrimination under Title IX.
Patricia H. v. Berkeley Unified School District	830 F. Supp. (N.D. Cal. 1993)	Student may file a hostile environment claim under Title IX.
Karibian v. Columbia University	No. 93-7188 (2nd Cir. 1994)	Employers are liable if supervisors create a hostile work environment.

monetary settlements to students[4] ruled victims of Title IX discrimination, numerous institutions have developed policies and regulations to govern consensual alliances between professors and students. An article in the Chronicle of Higher Education (Wagner, 1993) went so far as to advocate immediate dismissal for all faculty members who breach appropriate professional boundaries and establish or maintain a sexual relationship with students. Other organizations have adopted policies dealing with consensual relations when dealing with similar circumstances. For instance, the American Psychological Association prohibits psychology faculty from entering sexual relationships with students (Stamler, Pace, and Stone, 1997). Individual opinions on consensual relationships run the gamut from viewing them as private matters beyond the purview of the institution to definite grounds for dismissal, but there is general agreement that relationships between professors and students are generally problematic (Paludi, 1997; Sandler and Shoop, 1997).

Issues of Intent

The legal and definitional aspects of sexual harassment are further clouded by questions of the intent of the perpetrator. Numerous campus incidents perceived by the perpetrator as joking or teasing, pure fun, or nothing more than playful mischief can be interpreted quite differently by the target. I offer the following personal incident as an example. As an undergraduate I clearly remember entering a male professor's office to discuss my progress and immediately noticed he displayed a popular poster of scantily clad female models. Each model was wearing a football helmet depicting the college's football team emblem and one of the women was posed with a football. The poster's printed message "Let's play ball" had a clear sexual overtone. The male professor may have felt that the poster was an amusing and novel way to show his support of the college team. However, the fact that the incident remains vivid despite the passage of more than 25 years is a testament to the discomfort and unease that the poster instilled.

Legally and morally, sexual harassment is defined by the impact of the action, not the perpetrator's intent. Part of the problem with "issues of intent" lies with perceptual differences between men and women. Studies have shown that propositions and conversations perceived as sexually offensive by women may be the results of intended flattering by men (Riger, 1991). Other studies regarding gender differences in perceptions found that while men may discern certain female behaviors as sexual in nature, women are more likely to perceive the same actions as just friendly (Abbey, 1982; Gutek and Morasch, 1982; Saal, Johnson, and Weber, 1989; Shotland and Craig, 1988). For instance whereas a woman who initiates a conversation, accepts a date, or telephones a man may be acting without sexual intent, men are more likely to interpret these actions as sexually inviting.

Sexual Harassment Theories

As established in this chapter, despite negative consequences and illegality, sexual harassment is widespread. This section will examine some of the "whys". Why is sexual harassment so prevalent on college campuses? Why do so many male professors, administrators, and students commit these offenses? Although no single theory can explain the full spectrum of sexual harassment on campus, Tangri and Hayes (1997) offer an analogy helpful in understanding the "whys". They liken the behaviors leading to sexual harassment to the layers of skin on an onion.

> ... The "deep structure" or innermost layers represent species wide evolutionary behavioral adaptations and other biological processes; the next layers represent sociocultural norms, values, and institutions; the next layers represent organizational structures and arrangements; and the outermost layer represents idiosyncratic individual and dyadic characteristics, the most outwardly visible variables. (p. 113)

The theories explaining sexual harassment are a result of the research and subsequent theories which attempt to explain rape and other sexually abusive acts. Based on my interpretation of Tangri and Hayes (1997) as well as other related research and theories, I include Figure 2 as a visual representation of a macro theory portraying the interrelationships between each of the sexual harassment theories herein defined.

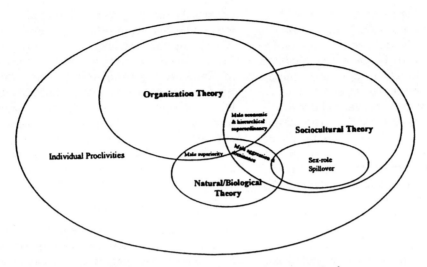

Figure 2. Sexual Harassment Theories in a Macro Design

The Natural/Biological Theory

The biological theory corresponds to a "deep structure" or theory explaining sexual harassment. Blaming the sexual harassing behaviors of men on naturally endowed stronger sex drives, this theory attributes sexual harassing behaviors on raging male hormones rather than discriminatory intent. Despite the many versions of the natural/biological theory in the related literature; in simple language all of them are remakes of the old "boys will be boys" justification. Since the college campus typically has an abundance of young males at the peak of their sexual drives plus an equal number of young women the natural/biological theory has been used to explain the large number of sexual abuse and harassment incidents. However most researchers find little evidence that this theory can explain or excuse the sexually harassing behaviors of men. Despite the lack of evidence that males share a proclivity toward sexually abusive behaviors (Tangri and Hayes, 1997), statistics from the Bureau of Justice undoubtedly indicate that males far outnumber females as the perpetrators of aggressive and sexually oriented crimes (U.S. Department of Justice, August, 1995).

The Organization Theory

Organization theory rationalizes sexual harassment through aspects of workplace environments that may provide opportunities for stratification by gender, attenuate gender differentiation, or sanction or approve harassment (Tangri, Burt, and Johnson, 1982). As such, the organization theory of sexual harassment investigates the structures inherent in organizations or institutions that allows the abuse or promotion of organizational power using gender as a backdrop. The culture of the typical workplace or educational institution empowers individuals by virtue of position such that coercion or intimidation of others in lesser positions is possible (and sometimes even promoted). In colleges and universities, similar to other organizations, it is more likely to find males in positions of power and females delegated to the more subordinate roles. In general, stratification creates vulnerable subordinates.

The National Center for Education Statistics (1996) illustrates the gender imbalance of organizational power in higher education. While 67% of faculty are male, more than half of undergraduates (54%) and master level students (52%) are female. For doctoral level students, 37.8% are female (Hussar and Gerald, 1996). However, college administration remains predominantly male. Of the 2,906 college presidents only 16% (453) are female; the vast majority presiding over women's colleges and community colleges (Office of Women in Higher Education, April, 1995).

Another aspect of the organization theory is that sexual harassment is more prevalent in organizations that encourage or promote a sexualized atmosphere (Gutek, 1985; Haavio-

Mannila, Kauppinen-Toropainen, and Kandolin, 1988; Tangri, Burt, and Johnson, 1982). In other words, organizations with the nonprofessional atmosphere of frequent ribald talking, joking, and/or seductive dress, may unintentionally be promoting sexual miscommunication. This theory may be very applicable to institutions of higher education who despite their strong mission statements characterizing them as bastions of intellectual pursuit may exude a sexualized atmosphere. The sexualized environment of colleges and universities will be expanded later in the chapter.

The Sociocultural Theory

According to the sociocultural model, sexual harassment functions as a tool to maintain male-female sex norms such that males retain occupational dominance and females remain subordinate (Tangri, Burt, and Johnson, 1982). This theory may also be viewed as the maintenance of a patriarchal social system legitimized by acculturated social beliefs (MacKinnon, 1979). The deep roots of this theory include society's rewards for aggressive and domineering behaviors in males and for submissive, passive, and acquiescent behaviors in females (Tangri, Burt, and Johnson, 1982). According to this theory, rape and the fear of rape function as an instrument of control to keep women in their appropriate social positions (Baron and Straus, 1989).

A variation or subset of the sociocultural theory is what Gutek and Morasch (1982) termed "sex-role spillover." Sex-role spillover occurs when learned gender-based expectations are inappropriately injected into the workplace (or educational institution) promoting the salience of gender identity over that of work identity. For example, female faculty are perceived and expected to be nurturing, compassionate, and more placid than their male counterparts despite identical job titles and requirements. This prominence of sex-role spillover is due to gender identity which tends to be much more powerful than either work identity or social identity (Hotelling and Zuber, 1997). It is important to note that sex-based expectations are held by both men and women. In other words, while a man may perceive a female student as a "sex object" the student may likewise perceive herself and find personal value in that role (Gutek and Morasch, 1982). Our society promotes the evaluation of women by their physical appearance, accordingly women self-evaluate by appearance.

In short, the sociocultural theory explains why sexual harassment and abuse are prevalent in college—campuses reflect the same cultural mores as society. Males are expected to be macho, strong, powerful, and leaders while females are expected to be sweet, demure, attractive, and in need of male leadership.

Individual Proclivities

Perhaps intuitive, but independent of the three models of harassment the likelihood of someone becoming an harasser or a victim is also dependent on individual proclivities. The three major models herein described, whether considered individually or as a collective whole, are inadequate in the face of the complex nature of sexual harassment and human behavior in the late 20th century. The need to consider individual proclivities becomes obvious with a simplistic and singular look at each of the three theories. For instance, through the lens of the natural/biological model all men on campus would be harassers save for individual differences. In the organizational model, all students and staff at a specific university would act similarly due to their common surroundings and organizational norms. And, from the viewpoint of the sociocultural model, all Americans would share similar perceptions of appropriate campus behaviors based on our membership in the same culture. Therefore, Figure 2 depicts the three sexual harassment theories as subject to individual proclivities.[5] Note also that the three theories are not discrete, but rather overlap in both definition and application. For instance, both the natural/biological theory and the sociocultural theory include the role of male aggression and dominance. The difference, however, is that where the sociocultural model attributes these differences to learned behaviors the natural/biological model attributes these behaviors solely to biology. An example of the overlap between the organizational theory and the sociocultural theory is the economic and hierarchical superordinancy of males in the academy as a result of their superordinancy in society in general. Overlap between the natural/biological and the organizational theories is evident in the male superiority myth. Of course the three models present different perspectives with respect to potential policy and subsequent societal and organizational change. Whereas the natural/biological model provides no hope that males will ever overcome their aggressive and dominant biological programming, the organizational and sociocultural models provide optimism. These theories predict and promote change as a result of societal and organizational behaviors. In the short run, policy to annihilate sexual harassment in postsecondary institutions must be viewed through the organizational theory; that is policies focused on behaviors on campus. However, in the long run, if sexual harassment is to be effectively curtailed or even eliminated societal changes under the sociocultural theory are required.

Sexual Harassment and the Sexual Abuse Continuum

I will now describe the origin of the sexual abuse continuum that was introduced earlier in the chapter (Figure 1) as well as expand on and explain the relationship between sexual harassment and rape. The purpose of this section is to present a better understanding of 1) the relationship between harassment and rape; 2) present the components of an environment conducive to acts of sexual abuse such as rape; and 3) to compare the environment of the typical college or university campus to the features and situations found to be related to sexual abuse.

Sexual Harassment and Rape

The relationship of sexual harassment with other forms of sexual abuse including rape has been firmly established in previous literature (Bell et al., 1992; Gutek and Morasch, 1982; Till, 1980; MacKinnon, 1979; Quina, 1996). In fact, the sexual harassment theories presented earlier are direct outgrowths of rape theories. The fundamental differences between rape and harassment cannot be denied, but because they share the themes of exploitation of power, beliefs in male entitlement, and the lack of personal or cultural conscience preventing or hindering such actions, harassment theories were naturally patterned after rape theories. One major difference between the two acts is the type of power exploited. Whereas the exploitation of physical power is fundamental to rape; the exploited power of sexual harassment may be more economic, social, or cultural in nature. While it is evident that a college dean possesses a direct economic power over the non-tenured professor, the professor possesses an equally potent, yet fundamentally different, power over the student. At first glance it may appear that the power differential is absent in cases of peer and contrapower harassment. But theorists have pointed out that there is always a power differential between men and women regardless of workplace position or vested authority (Brandenburg, 1997). It may be that power needs a looser definition such as that provided by Huston (1983) as "the ability to achieve ends through influence" (p. 170). Or, it may be that cultural expectations exert a social power equally strong as economic. Women nurtured in a patriarchal society that espouses myths of male superiority may succumb to peer or contrapower harassment because they believe that females should be passive, believe the male superiority myth, fear appearing prudish, have been conditioned to interpret all male attention as flattery, or feel that significant values lie only in the physical body rather than in any other realm. Indeed, sexual harassment like rape declares the power of the perpetrator over that of the victim while reinforcing the power of males over that of females despite the workplace or academic position of the actors.

Another major difference between rape or other violent sexual assault and the actions typically classified as sexual harassment is the type and severity of abuse. Whereas rape and sexual assault contain physical, psychological, and emotional abuse, the abuse of sexual harassment is usually limited to the psychological. It is interesting to note that when Follingstad and colleagues analyzed abuse and the factors that moderate physical and psychological symptoms of battered women, they included verbal harassment, threats, and isolation from social support networks in the psychological abuse categories (Follingstad et al, 1990; 1991). Others have pointed out that the physical and the non-physical abuse types may appear distinct in theory, but in reality, this separation is less apparent (Hart and Brassard, 1991). Physically violent acts almost always leave psychological scars and psychologically abusive acts often create physical problems. The intertwine of physical, emotional, and psychological abuse supports the use of the continuum.

The typical abuser. Through the study of men most likely to rape, much can be learned about the men most likely to sexually harass and abuse on campus. In the criminal justice and sociology literature, a connection was established by several researchers who found substantive links between men with rape supportive belief systems and men who were accepting of sexually harassing behaviors (Murrell and Dietz-Huler, 1993; Pryor, 1987; Reilly et al, 1991). It must be said that the direct study of the harasser is difficult because it is hindered by a natural reluctance to admit to harassing behaviors. Furthermore, many harassers feel that they are the true victims of society and that their only crime was being misunderstood by those seeking vindictive actions on males (Brewer, 1982; Pryor, 1987; USMSPB, 1981). Although the study of rapists is also fraught with similar difficulties, there have been several studies of convicted rapists. However, since the rapists who have been caught and subsequently convicted represent only a small portion of the men who actually rape[6], the generalizability of these studies has also been questioned. The four rapist types consistently identified in earlier literature (see Cohen, Seghorn, and Calmas, 1969; Cohen et al., 1971) as well as sexually abusive or harassing counterparts are presented in Table 3.

Despite motive or other particulars, most sexual abusers are "habitual" and repeat their various kinds of assaults (Freeman-Longo and Wall, 1986; Rosenfeld, 1985). Also, the criminal justice literature supports that most sexual offenders see assault as a form of seduction (Crowell and Burgess, 1996; Quina, 1996). The "rape myth" has been consistently identified as a precursor to a mindset capable of sexual assault (and hence also harassment). Believers in this myth see most accusations of rape based on the lies and deceit of women. In short, these men feel that women "lead men on" with their actions, mode of dress, or conversations; enjoy physical force despite their claims to the contrary; require a firm hand to be "kept in their place"; and that "no" must be taken in context and frequently means "yes." Stated simply, the rape myth embodies a belief system that women want to be raped and sexual relationships are naturally adversarial. In concert with the findings of Wolfe and Baker (1980), most rapists believe their actions did not constitute a rape or that rape was totally justified. The rape myth is compatible with the natural/biological theory that depicts men as the slaves of their sex drives who can easily be driven to frenzy by female temptresses. The general discussion of rapists is pertinent to higher education because studies have estimated that between 25 to 35% of college men accept some variety of the rape myth (Giacopassi and Dull, 1986; Gilmartin-Zena, 1987). A study by Holcomb and colleagues (1991) found that one-third of college men reported that women are often responsible for rape, and 14% of the college

Table 3. Taxonomy of Rapists and Sexual Harassment Counterparts*

Rapist type	Why does he rape?	What motivates him to rape?	What is the sexually harassing counterpart?
Displaced Aggression	In response to feelings of anger and unworthiness	To humiliate and degrade women	Harassers who act in response to displaced anger
Compensatory	In response to environmental stimuli	To exhibit sexual potency and power	Harassers who act when the appropriate opportunity arises
Sexual Aggressive	To obtain excitement	To bring pain to the victim and to obtain dominance and control	Harassers who act to openly deride and purposely hurt or degrade women

*Adapted from Bartol and Bartol, 1986

men felt men were incapable of controlling their aggressive behavior when attracted to a woman.

A classic study by Malamuth (1981) provided evidence that many "normal" men may have rape proclivities. Among a sample of male college students, Malamuth found 35% admitted to being capable of rape if they were assured that no ill effects would occur to them. Using Malamuth's techniques Pryor (1987) also utilized the proclivities of the typical rapist to validate the proclivities of those who are likely to sexually harass. Like Malamuth, Pryor presented male college students with ten scenarios that contained situations with inherent power differentials such that males were cast in the dominant role. Respondents were instructed to choose a course of action assuming no negative consequences could result. Each set of responses included one alternative that was sexually exploitive. Through these tests Pryor found that likely harassers hold similar attitudes and beliefs as those who are likely to sexually abuse and victimize. Specifically, he found that men likely to harass are more likely to be authoritarian, act in sexually exploitive ways, describe themselves in super-macho type terms, and blame or excuse their actions on situational variables. More recently, Quina (1996) explored the similarities between men likely to harass and those likely to rape. She argued that although rape myths are believed and practiced by both rapists and harassers, the extent and intensity of actions separates the two kinds of abusers.

In the case of compensatory and impulsive rapists (see Table 3), circumstances or situational variables will make rape more likely. Numerous studies have linked the use of alcohol or drugs with subsequent sexually abusive acts (Bachman, 1994; Kantor and Straus, 1987; Muehlenhard and Linton, 1987; Koss et al, 1988). In virtually all categories of crime, perpetrators are more likely to be under the influence. Bachman (1994) reported that approximately 50% of rape victims described their offender as under the influence of drugs and/or alcohol at the time of the crime. Many reasons for the connection between alcohol, drugs, and sexual abuse have been offered. For instance, the use of alcohol or drugs by men may interfere with cognition processes such that women's actions intended as neutral may be misinterpreted as sexual (Crowell and Burgess, 1996). Another indirect explanation may be that alcohol or drug use may place women in locations where abuse is more likely to occur or that women indulging in alcohol and/or drugs may be perceived as more sexually available (Crowd and Burgess, 1996). In the words of Sanday (1990) "a drunken woman is not defined as being in need of protection and help, but as 'asking for it'" (p. 11).

Figure 3 presents a graphical display of the typical harasser and the role played by belief in rape myths. Note that the figure also includes extenuating circumstances that may encourage harassment. These circumstances are especially important when dealing with compensatory types whose actions grow out of environmen-

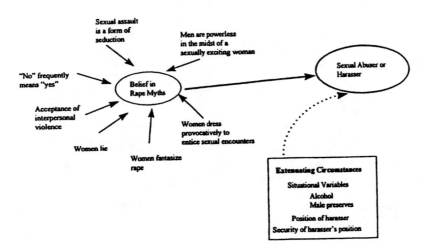

Figure 3. The Typical Abuser

tal stimuli. The dotted connection indicates that although extenuating circumstances may make harassment more likely, the mere presence of these circumstances can not create an harasser.

The typical sexual abuse victim. Similar to the situation of abusers, by studying the characteristics of those most likely to be victims of rape, much can be learned about the women on campus most likely to be sexually harassed. Although learning to cope with the threat of sexual victimization should be a necessary developmental task for all women, characteristics of the more likely victim have been identified. Predictably, the single and best predictor of victimization is gender. But, just being female does not put all women at equal risk (U.S. Department of Justice, August, 1995). Age and marital status have been identified as powerful predictors because women are most likely to be victimized if they are single and between the ages of 20 and 24 (Bachman, 1994). Since most incidents are between individuals of the same race, race may also have some predictive ability (Bachman, 1994). Personality characteristics may place some women at greater risk than others. Bait and O'Brien (1985) identified the "feminine" characteristics; quiet or passive, nurturing, kind, and/or helpful as risk increasers. After a thorough review of the literature, Crowell and Burgess (1996) listed the predictors of rape victimization as 1) having a background of childhood sexual abuse, 2) liberal or loose sexual attitudes, 3) extensive use of alcohol or drugs, and 4) a history of many sexual partners. Lastly, there are situational variables that place women in settings that increase the chances of an encounter with an offender. For instance, women who live, work, or socialize 1) in high crime areas, 2) late at night, 3) in establishments associated with high crime rates (such as some bars), 4) are frequently alone and 4) in "sexually oriented" environments may be more vulnerable to sexual assault and rape (Crowell and Burgess, 1996).

The sexual abuse continuum supports the same factors that place women at increased risk of rape, also places them as more likely victims of other forms of sexual abuse including harassment. Separate from the rape literature, several authors have made lists of the characteristics that may make women more vulnerable to sexual harassment on college and university campuses (for example Fitzgerald, Hulin, and Drasgow, 1995; Sandler and Shoop, 1997; Paludi, 1997). Those characteristics listed and tested in the literature include:

- Women (students and faculty) in male-dominated fields or disciplines
- Graduate students working closely with faculty (especially when student and faculty are close in age)

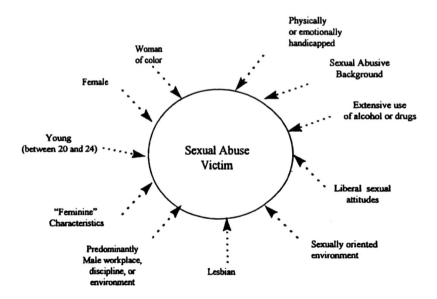

Figure 4. Extenuating Circumstances to Sexual Abuse Victimization

- Women of color or minority status
- Lesbians
- Those in small colleges or departments
- The economically disadvantaged or occupationally dependent
- The physically or emotionally disabled
- Women with a history of sexual abuse
- The unassertive, quiet, or socially isolated

Figure 4 presents the extenuating circumstances (or contributing factors) that may make a woman a more likely victim of sexual harassment. By no means does the figure imply that these characteristics cause a woman to be a victim or that the blame for the harassment should be placed on the victim. However, the factors do appear to have a cumulative effect on sexual harassment victimization.

Being a victim of any kind of sexual abuse, including harassment, takes its toll on the individual. The more severe forms of abuse and/or the length of its duration may determine the severity of the aftereffects. The aftermath of rape, the most severe form of sexual abuse, has been identified and labeled rape trauma syndrome.

Rape trauma syndrome. Rape and other sexually abusive acts leave scars. Rape trauma syndrome, the psychological aftermath of rape, was first identified in 1974 by Burgess and Holmstrom. Basically, rape trauma syndrome is the resulting physical, psychological, and behavioral reactions that follow an act of rape. Like other life-threatening events, the symptoms of rape trauma syndrome remain long after the event. Specific reactions depend on many factors, but may include changes in sleep, guilt, grief, recurring thoughts, lower self-esteem, body image distortion, fear, phobias, acute stress, and problems making or maintaining intimate relationships (Burgess and Hazelwood, 1995; Goodman et al., 1993).

Sexual harassment syndrome. Another commonality that rape shares with sexual harassment is the victim's aftermath. Many researchers have reported the existence of a sexual harassment syndrome that is much like its counterpart for rape (for example; Meek and Lynch, 1983; Quina, 1996; Rabinowitz, 1990; Schneider, 1987). The sexual harassment syndrome can cause many symptoms including fears, flashbacks, anxiety, depression, as well as causing the victim to alter her lifestyle to avoid or otherwise cope with the harasser (Alliance Against Sexual Coercion, 1981; Meek and Lynch; 1983; Quina, 1990). Unfortunately, the victim who is personally coping with sexual harassment syndrome, may find little comfort or understanding from others. Donnerstein and Linz (1994) argued that the media's display of violence against women bears a portion of the blame for society's unsympathetic treatment of many harassment victims. A callousness has evolved and the American public is not easily shocked or surprised by inappropriate treatment.

Furthermore, like in cases of rape, the victim is frequently blamed. Until recently, rape was the only crime in which the victim had to prove that she resisted the attack (Crowell and Burgess, 1996). Although courts no longer require signs of resistance and corroboration of witnesses in cases of rape, the burden of proof still falls on the victim. Likewise, sexual harassment victims bear the burden of proof. They are confronted with questions like "what did you say to bring that on?"; "what were you wearing?"; "why didn't you just quit or leave?"; and "why didn't you report this earlier"? Each of these questions ignores the fact that the perpetrator (not the victim) was in control and responsible for the situation. Furthermore, these responses ignore the fact that consequences, many of which are severe, occur with reporting. Fear of losing one's job, failing the course, or being labeled a "troublemaker" may deter women from reacting in a timely manner and reporting incidents. And, many women are unaware of how or to whom harassment cases should be reported.

The continuum. Rape and sexual harassment share many commonalties. They are both rooted in power dynamics, deal with gender roles, share similar offender characteristics, portray cultural stereotypes that may not be representative, leave severe emotional (and sometimes physical) scars, and leave their survivors transformed (Quina, 1996). Both sexual harassment and rape are serious offenses that are predominantly characterized by male on female, the powerful on the powerless, and the perpetrator on the victim. Society has historically not been sympathetic to victims of either rape or harassment. Despite the powerless status of the victim, she must explain why it happened, how it happened, and what she did to make it stop.

The College Environment

This section of the chapter will illustrate how factors common to many college campuses may be conducive to acts of sexual harassment and other forms of sexual abuse. I will illustrate how the factors and situations that have been shown to be conducive to rape, the predictors of sexual abusers, as well as the factors that make a woman a more likely victim may be present on the typical college campus. This perspective may reveal why acts of sexual abuse are so prevalent on campus and why the number of cases continues to escalate. More importantly, this perspective may clarify the areas needful of new and additional scrutiny as well as serve as a springboard for policies to curtail sexually abusive acts on campus.

Male Preserves

Rape and harassment are more likely to occur in an environment depicted as a "male preserve" (Fain and Anderton, 1987). Historically, whereas college campuses have been bastions for males, females were relegated to subordinate roles. The strong influence of fraternities and the promotion of "football as king" exists on many campuses. Although sororities and female athletics have also been established at many institutions, the strength and popularity of these activities pale when compared to their male counterparts.

Gender ratios have been found to contribute to the likelihood of harassment (Gutek, 1985; Hotelling and Zuber, 1997; Ryan and Kenig, 1991). The predominant male population in disciplines such as math, architecture, and the hard sciences create male preserves that may put females in these disciplines at additional risk of harassment. Disciplines such as education, nursing, social work, and library science that traditionally attract more females are sometimes treated as second tier—not receiving the same level of funding, faculty salaries, or status as the disciplines occupied with a preponderance of men. The high administrative posts of most colleges remain predominantly male (American Council on Education, 1996) thus creating the situation where men are more frequently in positions of power over women.

The Issue of Power

Aside from the issue of gender, the college campus has a hierarchical structure consisting of multiple layers of true power relationships. Administrators have power over professors and staff; professors over graduate assistants and other students; and graduate assistants over undergraduates. Adding to the hierarchy, the superordinate in each of these dyads is generally older and more experienced than the subordinate. The inherent hierarchical structure of colleges and universities provide an environment in which those who are inclined to take advantage of power have the opportunity to do so.

A Sexualized Atmosphere

I argue that the college campus offers a sexualized atmosphere similar to that found to promote all forms of sexual abuse. First of all, the traditional undergraduate is at or near the age range of maximum risk of sexual abuse (20–24 years of age) (Bachman, 1994). Pornographic movies, magazines, and books can often be found on campus, especially in fraternity houses (Sanday, 1990). Secondly, since college is the first opportunity for the majority of traditionally aged students to liberate themselves from parents or other authority figures, many students adopt new liberal attitudes and experiment with sex. A survey by the American Social Health Association (1995) found 85% of female college students reported being sexually active, one-fourth of the college women reported at least one coerced sexual act, approximately half reported having sexual relations with four or more men, and 7% reported more than 20 partners. Similarly, a survey of 100 students at a New Jersey college found the majority of students engaging in high risk sexual activity on a regular basis (Gainey, 1993). Although postsecondary institutions do not overtly promote sex, coed dormitories, male athlete worship, frequent use of profane language, little sister practices at fraternities, parties involving alcohol, and other related activities common to the college campus create an environment with multiple sexual overtones. The sexually charged atmosphere created by these multiple factors creates an environment conducive to all forms of sexual abuse.

Alcohol

Chen and Kandel (1995) found the traditional college age (18 to 21 years of age) to be the time for the heaviest use of alcohol among U.S. drinkers. Approximately 88% of college students report alcohol use (Shalala, 1995) and 40% report binge drinking (Johnston, O'Malley, and Bachman, 1996). Certainly this behavior is troublesome for numerous reasons, but research has indicated that alcohol use by men is related to greater sexual aggression, sexual harassment, and other sexually abusive acts (Benson, Charleton, and Goodhart, 1992; Berkowitz, 1992; Kantor and Straus, 1987; Koss et al, 1988; Koss and Gaines, 1993; Matthews, 1993; Muehlenhard and Linton, 1987). A study of reported sexual offenses at one university found that the majority of male perpetrators and about half of the female victims were using alcohol at the time of the incident (Frintner and Rubinson, 1993). Other studies of college campus environments found correlations between the frequency of binge drinking and the number of reported sexual assaults (Wechsler et al., 1994; Wechsler et al., 1995).

The relationship between alcohol and various types of sexual abuse may take multiple forms. For instance, men under the influence of alcohol are more likely to interpret the neutral actions of women as sexual interest, are less likely to honor a woman's refusal of a sexual advance, and may misinterpret a woman's consumption of alcohol as a sign of sexual availability (Abbey, Ross, and McDuffie, 1995; Crowd and Burgess, 1996).

Alcohol misuse is not an innocent rite of passage for college students. For some, alcohol leads to sexual abuse and harassment and is one of several of the contributing factors that targets college and university campuses as an unsafe environment. The relationship between alcohol and harassment may be heightened by other conditions on campus—for instance, the Greek system.

Greek Life

Fraternities and sororities can provide positive social interaction, campus involvement, foster lifelong relationships, encourage community service, and instill college loyalty. The Greek system is not inherently evil or wrong, but when misused may create a higher likelihood of sexual harassment and abuse.

Several studies have found fraternity brothers to consume more alcohol (Marlatt, Baer, and Larimer, 1995; Wechsler, Dowdall, Davenport, and Castillo, 1995), to be less responsible drinkers (Klein, 1992; Tampke, 1990), to engage in more unsafe sexual practices, and to be involved in more abusive dating experiences (Worth, Matthews, and Coleman, 1990). Furthermore, while Bryan (1987) indicated that 70% of reported gang rapes occurred during fraternity parties, Ehrhart and Sandler (1992) reported that the majority of campus gang rapes involved fraternity members. In a comprehensive study of fraternity gang rape, Sanday (1990) related the actions and thought processes of some fraternity members. She recorded incidents of fraternity members plying women with drugs and alcohol in order to more easily conquer them and thus obtain sexual relations, the practice of "working out a yes" (p. 11), "pulling train" (a fraternity term for gang rape) (p. 4), and rationalizing these activities by describing the victim as "wanting it" (p. 13). Membership in the fraternity provides a young man with greater feelings of power because he now has his fraternity brothers as allies. On an individual level the brother may feel that his masculine identity is being formed and strengthened. However, for some individuality may actually be threatened by the group think mentality that intertwines brotherhood, misogyny, and phallocentrism.

Similarly, there is evidence linking sorority membership with incidents of sexual abuse. The results of a study of 140 sorority women found that almost half reported being victims of some form of sexual coercion, almost one-fourth reported at least one rape attempt and 17% reported being actual victims of rape (Copenhaven and Grauerholz, 1991). More than half of the sorority women claiming to be victims of rape reported that the rape occurred in a fraternity house or that a fraternity member was the perpetrator.

Other aspects of Greek life may also directly or indirectly encourage sexual harassment and abuse through social contexts that tolerate or even encourage sexual exploitation. For instance, Kalof and Cargill (1991) found fraternity members to hold more traditionally male attitudes as well as to be more dominant while finding sorority members to be more submissive than independent students. Each of these traits was shown earlier to be related to sexual abuse and harassment. A study of sorority women (Atlas and Morier, 1994) found them more likely to use alcohol in excess, to express a desire for exhibitionism, and to attend numerous parties than independent women.

Finally, Rhoads (1995) observed fraternity life at a major research university, and reported numerous incidents where brothers viewed and treated women as less than human beings and as general targets for sexual manipulation. In his words, "Consistent throughout most of the reported fraternity assaults is a pattern whereby fraternity members view women in subordinate terms such as sexual objects; women are seen to be unworthy of human dignity and undeserving of normal human rights" (Rhoads, 1995, p. 308).

Collectively, although Greek life does not directly cause harassment, the fraternity/sorority actions, parties, and promoted belief system may be another contributing factor to cruel environments on some college campuses.

Athletics

Like fraternities and sororities, athletics play an active role in campus life and can yield many positive outcomes for participants. It cannot be denied that athletics promote social development for spectators and athletes, produces school pride, and can generate needed funds for the institution. But athletics also has a dark side. The connection between athletics and lower-than-expected academic gains for student participants is a frequent topic of discussion both in the media and in the research literature. Much of the anecdotal and research literature supports a connection with competitive campus athletics and violence in general. Male college athletes are overrepresented in reports of sexual assault and harassment (Corset, Benedict, and McDonald, 1995; Crosset, Ptacek, McDonald, and Benedict, 1996) A study at a western university found that male athletes scored lower on a moral development test (Baldizan and Frey, 1995). A study of 477 male undergraduates at a large southeastern university found athletes had a higher proclivity to rape (Boeringer, 1996). And a large study by Koss and Gaines (1993) found a significant proportion of variance of sexual aggression was explained by athletic participation. The evidence linking student athletes with sexual violence and harassment is clear. The reasons for the link may be equally clear. Too often the aggression, power, and dominance that are appropriate in sports may be transferred to personal interactions, thus allowing the special power and social status assigned to athletes to be misused. Of course, athletics do not cause sexual abuse. But the evidence that athletes are over-represented in incidents of sexual abuse and harassment is undeniable.

Sex-Role Spillover

All of the aspects described in this section contribute to the inflated rate of sexual incidents on college campuses. Collectively, these conditions can be linked with the phenomenon of sex-role spillover that was earlier introduced. Other less obvious examples of sex-role spillover include female students steered toward or self-selecting only "gender appropriate" fields; erotically appealing cheerleading outfits; the assumptions that women may enter fields in the social sciences while men are suited for the hard sciences. All of these situations serve as suitable examples of gender-expected activity in college. In accordance with the sociocultural theory, an environment differentiated and stratified by gender sets the stage for subsequent restraint and harassment. Furthermore, the sex-role spillover atmosphere on college campuses may perpetuate sexual abuse and harassment through contagion. The role of contagion is based on a laboratory study by Pryor, LaVite, and Stoller (1993) who found that college men with harassing proclivities would emulate the behavior of a harassing role model. Thus exposure to an environment where harassment takes place, may encourage some men to perpetuate the cruel cycle.

Throughout this section I have presented my arguments describing the college campus as a cruel environment for many women as well as conducive to acts of sexual abuse and harassment. Although I have pointed to the Greek system, athletics, the use of alcohol and other factors as contributors to a cruel environment, causation was never implied. In other words, if the factors discussed herein were completely eliminated from campus life sexual abuse would not become extinct. It may be that factors such as fraternities, sororities, athletics, and alcohol contribute to sexual abuse not because of the mindset they promote, but rather through the attraction of individuals with proclivities to be abusive or abused. The reader is directed to Figure 5 where the factors relating sexual abuse in the collegiate environment are pictorially displayed. Note that the extenuating circumstances presented in Figures 3 and 4 are now expanded to show a relationship to the sexual abuser and victim.

Restructuring the College Environment

There are no simple or easy answers to a complex situation like sexual abuse on campus. The sheer number of books, articles, and pamphlets dedicated to annihilating the phenomenon serve only as a testament to the inefficiency of past efforts. The last section of this chapter will examine what colleges and universities have done to curtail sexual harassment and abuse. This section will also provide a framework for the restructure of the college environment to produce campuses that are less inviting to sexual abuse and harassment.

Sexual harassment and abuse policy statements. After reading more than 50 college or university policy statements regarding sexual harassment and/or abuse I conclude that virtually all of them could be subtitled "thou shalt not or else." Consistently the statements provided the following three components; (1) presentation of definitions of harassing or abusive behaviors on campus, (2) a statement clearly stating that sexual abuse will not be tolerated, and (3) encouragement to promptly report all incidents. While many statements included listings of the sanctions the institution planned for perpetrators or protections to be accorded to victims, others included instructions on how or to whom incidents should be reported. Many institutions ignored the topic of consensual relationships, some provided a short prohibition against relationships between institutional persons with direct professional power differentials, while a few institutions had long complicated separate documentation regarding the topic. Despite great variation in length, institutional policy statements were found to be quite similar overall. Of course published policy statements may not reflect a college or university's total plan to eliminate sexual incidents, but according to the available documentation, the majority of steps to suppress unwanted behaviors such as sexual harassment and abuse is the use of threats, reprimands, and penalties for offenses *after* they take place. This type of tactic has been shown to be ineffective in the long run, does not eliminate the tendency to behave in inappropriate ways, and may result in escape or avoidance behaviors (Skinner, 1971). In other words, although a clear policy that delineates punitive actions once harassment is determined may be sufficient to deter some would-be offenders, it is insufficient as the sole deterrent. As an exam-

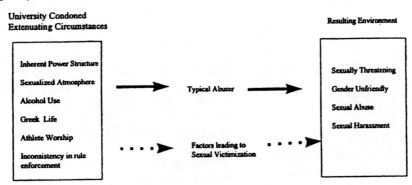

Figure 5. Factors Contributing to a Cruel Environment

ple, I offer the problem of driving over the posted speed limit. Despite the use of fines and even the possible loss of driving privileges, a ride on any expressway in the U.S. quickly reveals the ineffectiveness of relying solely on punitive actions in an attempt to curb speeding. Taking this example even further, some drivers purposely break speeding laws and openly use a radar detector to avoid punitive actions. Similarly, although many campus harassers may be aware of their institution's disapproval of and punitive actions resulting from sexual abuse and harassment, some will take evasive measures to make detection of the incident less likely. It is very improbable that a campus harasser will adopt the mindset "now that I know the university doesn't want me to sexually harass, I will just stop." It may be argued that personnel and students need to be better educated and informed of the exact consequences and subsequent punitive actions of inappropriate behaviors, but the ineffectiveness of the sole use of punitive actions will prevail.

Framework for a Less Cruel Environment

The Seven "A's

The campus is a microcosm of society. Like society, actions are promoted and supported through a mechanism I have labeled the seven "A's": (1) attention, (2) approval, (3) affection, (4) appreciation (5) awards (6) autonomy and (7) affirmation. Returning to the factors contributing to sexual abuse and harassments on campus I will now investigate past practices of placement of the seven A's.

Male preserves. Even a cursory look at many university newspapers reveals where the lion's share of *attention* is placed: male athletics. Campus *approval* is great when the teams win and the *affection* of the entire campus community is evident. The importance and eminence of the male athletics programs are *affirmed* through the funds allotted to them. Institutions *affirm* the superiority of athletics over academics through the numerous programs and techniques to keep athletes from being disqualified due to poor academic performance. As earlier stated, athletics are not wrong in and of themselves, but the level of *attention* and *awards* provided to male athletics merits reexamination and realignment in accordance with the college mission statement's emphasis of an academic and intellectual community.

Greek life. The campus environment provides many reinforcements to Greek life. *Approval* is provided to live off-campus under less supervision and less rules. Typically fraternity and sorority members are *awarded* privileged residential status in classic homes with much larger living quarters than in any dormitory, with more control over food and drink and extensively more *autonomy*. Moreover, Greek organizations receive much *attention* and *affection* through parties and other gatherings. Not only is group *acceptance* and camaraderie fostered but each person is awarded lifetime membership in the sisterhood or brotherhood. *Approval* is even evident in the campus store where T-shirts, stickers, and other memorabilia with fraternity and sorority symbols are sold. All in all, the campus provides many encouragements to Greek life.

Alcohol. Even though the use of alcohol (and drugs) is not directly promoted by colleges and universities, it does appear that *approval* is indirectly provided. The serving of alcohol at fraternities and sororities is a practice that only the most fundamentally religious institutions would dare to deny. *Acknowledging* alcohol use and doing little to control it, indirectly equals campus *approval*.

Inconsistencies. Despite the reliance on a policy of punitive actions after the deed has been committed, colleges and universities do not always react with consistency. For instance, Williams and Brake (1997) recently reported an incident involving two college football players accused of raping a first-year college student. Although one man was found guilty by university officials and suspended for two semesters, the suspension is scheduled to take effect *after* the perpetrator graduates. Although this scenario is not typical, the university involved indirectly (but clearly) granted *approval* of rape, declared great *affection* and *appreciation* for student athletes, and *affirmed* the importance of sports over the safety and well-being of female students.

Misuse of informal complaints. A growing phenomenon is the use of campus disciplinary hearings even in situations involving serious and violent crimes. Of course it is to the college's distinct advantage to handle cases internally, thus avoiding the expenses and risks of having incidents tried in courts of law as well as to avoid negative media coverage. In the case of sexual harassment and abuse the use of this tactic is fraught with problems. For instance, the decision may rest in the hands of professors, administrators, and sometimes even students who have neither the authority nor the training to act in this regard. Furthermore, the results of the hearing are protected from disclosure by the Family Educational Rights and Privacy Act (Wagner, 1996). According to Eileen Wagner, an attorney specializing in education and woman's rights law, colleges often do not report even the most serious crimes to the police (1996). Although, the informal complaint mode may be appropriate for some situations, inappropriate use of "in house" settlements may also lay the groundwork for a more cruel environment.

As an example I offer an incident related in the book *Fraternity Gang Rape* (Sanday, 1990). At an undisclosed university a professor of law was the appointed hearing officer in an incident of an alleged gang rape that occurred in a fraternity house. The hearing officer ordered the fraternity suspended for six months while not taking action against any of the accused individuals. As a settlement, the alleged victim was paid a "substantial sum of money by the university to stave off a civil suit" (p. xvii). The "substantial sum of money" was tax-exempt university funds that the university donors most likely never intended to be spent for this purpose. Using an on-campus hearing minimized negative publicity for the institution. However, this procedure obscured the true dangers on campus. Using the seven A's framework, the institution *affirmed* the right of fraternity members to treat women as objects. By paying the alleged victim for her silence, the institution *awarded* a scheme in which the campus would continue to shine in a positive light despite a possibly cruel and dangerous environment. Lastly, by avoiding litigation and not pursuing criminal prosecution of the individual perpetrators, the university unmistakably sided with the perpetrators thus showing a misaligned *approval* of the action.

The BAD

Institutions must reassess how, when, and where they have applied the seven A's. This framework provides a proactive approach to creating an environment where sexual abuse and harassment are less likely to occur rather than only adopting a reactive stance that deals with problems after they occur. A proactive approach, however, must be placed in tandem with a policy package that leaves no doubt that sexually harassing and abusive actions will not be tolerated while at the same time **B**ans, **A**bolishes, and **D**iscourages (acronym BAD) those factors leading to a cruel environment. The framework of the "seven A's," the courage to file criminal charges when warranted, the application of the acronym "BAD," as well as the need for a strong enforced sexual harassment policy is presented as Figure 6. Note that the "BAD" includes activities such as amorous relationships within professional power differentials, campus-related alcohol consumption, excessive athletic hero worship, negative fraternity/sorority activities, gender-related power structures, visual harassment, and inconsistencies in rule enforcement.

The prohibited actions or as I have labeled it, the "BAD" are generally listed in the college or university's sexual harassment policy statement. A strong policy statement that clearly states the university's position is extremely important in averting sexually oriented incidents. In general, the policy must contain clear prohibitions of specific inappropriate behaviors, the aftermath if activities perceived to be sexually abusive or harassing are performed, encouragement to promptly report incidents, and clear statement of the rights of those who feel they have been abused. Of course, even the best of policies is totally ineffective when the target individuals are not informed of the policy content. Therefore every policy must have a comprehensive dissemination procedure that reaches all members of the campus community. Just because students, staff, and faculty have been informed of the policies it should not be assumed that it is universally understood and committed to long-term memory. For this reason, a dissemination policy should be scheduled at regular intervals, published in the school newspaper or other campus publica-

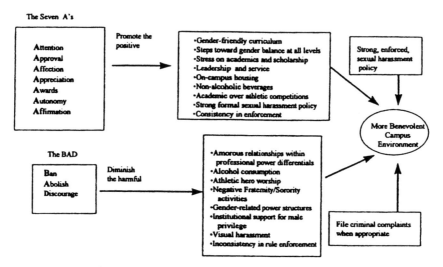

Figure 6. Framework for a Less Cruel Environment

tions, prominently displayed on the Internet, and definitely not obscurely buried.

Grievance and reporting procedures should take in account the psychological issues inherent in sexual harassment and abuse as well as eliminate, to the greatest possible extent, retaliation by the alleged harasser. Since victims of sexual harassment may already feel powerless, alone, and out of favor with university personnel, further victimization must be avoided. In other words, the grievance process should not place the complainant in the position of defending her actions (or lack of actions), but rather allow her to function as a reporter of the facts.

Suggestions—Positive Practices for Improving the College Environment

Administrator Practices

Any changes in the environment will most likely be initiated or at the very least must be approved by administration. For this reason it is imperative that administrators be aware of the extent and seriousness of sexual harassment, be informed of the consequences of the status quo, be wary of situations that may exacerbate or even encourage negative outcomes, and most importantly, be courageous to take steps to initiate change. Although educating administrators, faculty, staff, and students about sexual harassment and abuse is important, the initiative cannot merely start and end there. A suggestion is to incorporate a proactive posture by providing approval to activities conducive to a gender-friendly environment rather than only employing the typical "damage control" after-the-fact actions. Consistent follow-up of the "BAD" as well as the application of the "seven A's" earlier suggested (i.e., attention, approval, affection, appreciation, awards, autonomy, and affirmation) when behavior is deserving of praise may promote changes in the environment and subsequent changes in behavior. Administrators who knowingly allow and condone the contexts in which sexual harassment and abuse breed, have a share of the responsibility for the consequences.

Administrators should also examine the appropriateness of adjudication of sexual abuse and harassment cases on campus. It is virtually impossible for administrators and faculty, who are employees of the institution, to be unbiased with respect to the college (Wagner, 1996). Members of the law enforcement community are professionally trained in the investigation and prosecution of sexually abusive situations and can offer assistance to victims of sexual violence. College employees and students have neither the training nor experience to work in this delicate area.

Instruction, curriculum, and the faculty. A powerful means of changing the college environment may be the use of more gender friendly curriculum and educational strategies.

A classroom environment where women are treated as equals, are given equal attention, are not the frequent subject of jokes, not treated as sex objects and are equally valued will spillover into other environmental arenas. The college curriculum may contribute to a positive environment through the inclusion and acknowledgment of the contributions of women. Finally, the environment will be more gender appropriate when faculty, administrative, and staff ranks are gender balanced to demonstrate that capability, talent, and competence are not defined by gender. Although outwardly a difficult task, colleges and universities can increase female participation in predominantly male disciplines through a more gender friendly environment. Female students are entering male-dominated fields like engineering in increasing numbers, but the retention rate within the major remains poor (Hagedorn, Nora, and Pascarella, 1996). Policies to retain students after they have enrolled are as necessary as the policies aimed at recruitment. To attract and retain qualified female faculty, salary schedules should be monitored for signs of gender or other bias. And, when inconsistencies are found steps to correct any bias must be promptly taken.

Student services. Student service professionals can be pivotal in the change. Although the appropriate actions are dependent on the size, type, and location of the institution. Positive actions may include:

- Sponsoring more academically focused seminars, dialogues, speakers, and concerts.
- Rather than the typical Greek style life, establish housing based on student academic majors (i.e., an engineering house, a social work house, a nursing house, etc). Entrance requirements to these houses can be based on GPA and department recommendations.
- Consider in-dorm fraternities and sororities. By dedicating a floor of a college dormitory to a Greek chapter, students can enjoy the camaraderie of Greek life while residential life professionals can maintain control and provide adequate guardianship services.

- Enforce rules that permit only non-alcoholic refreshments to be served at campus-related events.
- Encourage and reward students to participate in academic competitions.
- Require positive service projects from student organizations. An example might be for a student organization to conduct a program to safely escort students who may feel threatened to the Women's Center or other safe location.
- Conduct regular seminars and/or workshops for students, staff, and faculty which include the definitions, prohibitions, and procedures to report sexual abuse and harassment.
- Keep praise for athletic triumph in context. Colleges are not the NFL, athletics are only peripheral to the institution's mission.
- Maintain a zero tolerance for visual harassment. Displays or graffiti of a sexual nature should be promptly removed.
- Although a grievance procedure must be sufficiently robust to provide protection against false claims, various channels for the reporting of sexual harassment incidents should be made available so that reluctance or embarrassment is minimized.
- If a crime is committed—promptly report it.
- Consistent with the literature, a strong formal policy must be adopted and publicized.
- Create an office of sexual harassment prevention and policy or have a trained sexual harassment adviser on staff.
- In all situations, practice consistency, consistency, consistency!

Conclusions

There are no easy answers. For those women who have experienced sexual harassment or abuse on college campuses the descriptor "cruel environment" is apt. The procedures, rules, admonitions, and policies of the past are obviously impotent to counter the rising numbers of incidents. A problem this pervasive requires a serious look at the environment that appears to support the incidents. Are practices common to the campus inadvertently promoting gender inequality and as such encouraging harassment? This chapter points out several areas in which this appears to be the case.

Naturally, the blame does not rest solely on the institution because it plays only a cross-sectional role in the experiences of students and employees. Taking those first positive steps to create a more-gender friendly environment, to promote academic over hostile endeavors, and to adhere to the true mission of the institution may establish institutions with a more benevolent environment for all.

Notes

1. Locus parentis exists in institutions of education such that the institution is responsible for the care and control of students in the absence of supervision by parents and guardians (Black, 1991).
2. Punitive damages are capped at $50,000 for employers with 100 or less employees; $100,000 for employers with 101 to 200 employees; $200,000 for employers with 201 to 500 employees and $300,000 for employers with more than 500 employees (Conte, 1997).
3. Although this section specifically targets relationships between professors and students, the dynamics are the same between staff and students or administration and students. The issue is one of power and not specifically of job title.
4. Decided from the federal court case Franklin v. Gwinnet County Public Schools 830 F. Supp. (N.D. Cal. 1993)
5. Proclivities is loosely interpreted and can include previous environmental factors (childhood experiences, family structure, etc.) as well as genetic inheritance. In other words, individual proclivities refers to the emotional structure the student, staff, faculty, or administrator brings to the institution.
6. Over 500,000 rapes are reported annually. However, it is estimated that the true number of committed rapes may be 3 times this number (U.S. Department of Justice, 1995).
7. Although this statement specifically pertains to large four-year universities, it must be stated that smaller universities and even liberal arts colleges are placing increased importance on competitive athletics.

References

Abbey, A. (1982). Sex differences in attributions for friendly behavior: Do males misperceive females' friendliness? *Journal of Personality and Social Psychology* 42: 830–838.

Abbey, A., Ross, L. T., and McDuffie, D. *(1995).* Alcohol's role in sexual assault. In R. R. Watson, (ed.), *Drug and Alcohol Abuse Reviews, VoL T: Addictive Behaviors in Women.* Totowa NJ: Humana Press.

Adams, J. W., Kotke, J. L., and Padgitt, J. S. (1983). Sexual harassment of university students. *Journal of College Student Personnel* 24: 484–490.

Alliance Against Sexual Coercion. (1981). *Fighting Sexual Harassment: An Advocacy Handbook.* Boston: Alyson.

American Association of University Women (AAUW) (1993). *Hostile Hallways: The AAUW Survey on Sexual Harassment in America's Schools.* Washington, DC: Author

American Council on Education (1992). *Sexual Harassment on Campus: A Policy and Program of Deterrence.* American Council on Education, Washington DC.

American Council on Education (1996). *Higher Education Facts in Brief.* Author: Washington DC

American Social Health Association (1995*).* Internet site: http://sunsite.unc.edu/ASHA/press/college032395.html

Atlas, G., and Morier, D. (1994). The sorority rush process: Self-selection, acceptance criteria, and the effect of rejection. *Journal of College Student Development* 35(5): 346–353.

Bachman, R. (January, 1994). Violence against women: A national crime victimization survey report. NCJ-145325 U.S. Department of Justice: Office of Justice Programs, Bureau of Justice Statistics.

Baker, C. N. (1997) Proposed Title IX guidelines on sex-based harassment of students. In E. K. Cole (ed.). *Sexual Harassment on Campus: A Legal Compendium* (Third Edition), Washington DC: National Association of College and University Attorneys.

Baldizan, L., and Frey, J. H. (1995). Athletics and moral development: Regulatory and ethical issues. *College Student Affairs Journal* 15(1): 3343.

Baron, L, and Straus, M. A. (1989). *Four Theories of Rape in American Society: A State-level Analysis.* New Haven, CT: Yale University Press.

Bart, P., and O'Brien, P. H. (1985). *Stopping Rape: Successful Survival Strategies.* Elmsford, NY: Pergamon.

Bartol, C. R. and Bartol, A. M. (1986). *Criminal Behavior.* Englewood Cliffs, NJ: Prentice Hall.

Bell, S. T., Kuriloff, P. J., Lottes, I., Nathanson, J., Judge, T., and Fogelson-Turer, K. (1992). Rape callousness in college freshman: An investigation of the sociocultural model of aggression towards women. *Journal of College Student Development* 33:454–461.

Benson, D., Charlton, C., and Goodhart, F. (1992). Acquaintance rape on campus: a literature review. *Journal of American College Health* 40:157–165.

Benson, D. J., and Thomson, G. E. (1982). Sexual harassment on a university campus: The confluence of authority relations, sexual interest and gender stratification. *Social Problems* 29: 236–251.

Berkowitz, A. (1992). College men as perpetrators of acquaintance rape and sexual assault: A review of recent research. *Journal of American College Health* 40:175–181.

Black, H. C. (1991). *Black's Law Dictionary*. West Publishing Co.: St. Paul, MN.

Boeringer, S. B. (1996). Influences of fraternity membership, athletics, and male living arrangements on sexual aggression. *Violence Against Women* 2(2): 134–147.

Brandenburg, J. B. (1982). Sexual harassment in the university: Guidelines for establishing a grievance procedure. *Signs: Journal of Women in Culture and Society* 8:320–336.

Brandenburg, J. B. (1997). *Confronting Sexual Harassment: What Schools and Colleges Can Do*. New York: Teachers College Press.

Brewer, M. (1982). Further beyond nine to five: An integration and future directions. *Journal of Social Issues* 38: 149–158.

Brown, W. A., and Maestro-Scherer, J. (1986). Assessing sexual harassment and public safety: A survey of Cornell women. Unpublished report, Cornell Office of Equal Opportunity.

Bryan, W. A. (1987). Contemporary fraternity and sorority issues. In R.B. Winston Jr. and W. R. Nettles III (eds.), *Fraternities and Sororities on the Contemporary College Campus*. San Francisco: Jossey-Bass.

Burgess, A. W., and Hazelwood, R. R. (1995). The victim's perspective. In R. R. Hazelwood and A. W. Burgess (eds.), *Practical Aspects of Rape Investigation: A Multidisciplinary Approach*. Boca Raton, FL: CRC Press.

Burgess, A. W., and Holmstrom, L. S. (1974). Rape trauma syndrome. *American Journal of Psychiatry* 131: 413–418.

Chen, K., and Kandel, D. B. (1995). The natural history of drug use from adolescence to the midthirties in a general population sample. *American Journal of Public Health* 85(1): 41–47.

Cohen, M. L., Garafalo, R., Boucher, R., and Seghorn, T. (1971). The psychology of rapists. *Seminars in Psychiatry* 3: 307–327.

Cohen, M. L., Seghorn, T., and Calznas, W. (1969). Sociometric study of the sex offender. *Journal of Abnormal Psychology* 74:249–255.

Conte, A. (1997). Legal theories of sexual harassment. In W. O'Donohue (ed.), *Sexual Harassment Theory Research and Treatment*. Boston: Allyn and Bacon.

Copenhaver, S., and Grauerholz, E. (1991). Sexual victimization among sorority women: Exploring the link between sexual violence and institutional practices. *Sex Roles: A Journal of Research* 24(1–2): 31–41.

Crosset, T. W, Benedict, J. R., and McDonald, M. A. (1995). Male student-athletes reported for sexual assault: A survey of campus police departments and judicial affairs offices. *Journal of Sport and Social Issues* 19(2): 126–140).

Crosset, T. W., Ptacek, J., McDonald, M. A., and Benedict, J. R. (1996). Male student-athletes and violence against women: A survey of campus judicial affairs offices. *Violence Against Women* 2(2): 163–179.

Crowell, N. A., and Burgess, A. W. (eds.) (1996). *Understanding Violence Against Women*. Washington, DC: National Academy Press.

Dey, E. L., Korn, J. S., and Sax, L. J. (1996). Betrayed by the academy: The sexual harassment of women college faculty. *Journal of Higher Education* 67(2): 149–173.

Donnerstein, E., and Linz, D. (1994). Sexual violence in the mass media. In M. Costanzo and S. Oskamp (eds.), *Violence and the Law*. Newbury Park, CA: Sage.

Dziech, B. W., and Wiener, L. (1984). *The Lecherous Professor: Sexual Harassment on Campus*. Boston: Beacon Press.

Ehrhart, J. K., and Sandler, B. R. (1992). *Campus Gang Rape: Party Games?* Washington DC: Center for Women Policy Studies.

Equal Employment Opportunity Commission (1990, March). Policy guidance on current issues of sexual harassment. (Notice N-915-050). City, State: Author.

Fain, T. C., and Anderton, D. L. (1987). Sexual harassment: Organizational context and diffuse status. *Sex Roles* 5/6:291–311.

Female faculty members and students at Harvard report sexual harassment (1993, Nov. 2). *Chronicle of Higher Education* 27(10).

Fitzgerald, L. F., Hulin, C. L., and Drasgow, F. (1995). The antecedents and consequences of sexual harassment in organizations: An integrated model. In G. P. Keita and J. J. Hurrell. Jr. (eds.). *Job Stress in a Changing Workforce: Investigating Gender Diversity, and Family Issues*. Washington, DC: American Psychological Association.

Fitzgerald, L. F., and Ormerod, A. J. (1991). Perceptions of sexual harassment: The influence of gender and context. *Psychology of Women Quarterly* 15: 281–294.

Fitzgerald, L. F., Shullman, S. L., Bailey, N., Richards, M., Swecher, J., Gold, Y., Ormerod, M., and Weitzman, L. (1988). The incidence and dimensions of sexual harassment in academia and the workplace. *Journal of Vocational Behavior* 32: 152–175.

Follingstad, D. R., Rutledge, L. L., Berg, B. J., Hause, E. S., and Polek, D. S. (1990). The role of emotional abuse in physically abusive relationships. *Journal of Family Violence* 5(2): 107–120.

Follingstad. D. R., Brennan, A. F., Hause, E. S., Polek, D. S., and Rutledge, L. L. (1991). Factors motivating physical and psychological symptoms of battered women. *Journal of Family Violence* 6: 81–95.

Freeman-Longo, R. E., and Wall, R. V. (1986). Changing a lifetime of sexual crime. *Psychology Today* March: 58–64.

Frintner, M. R, and Rubinson, L. (1993). Acquaintance rape: The influence of alcohol, fraternity membership, and sports team membership. *Journal of Sex Education and Therapy* 19(4): 272–284.

Gainey, R. (1993). *A Study of Undergraduate College Students' Alcohol Consumption Related to High-risk Sexual Activity*. East Lansing, MI: (ERIC Document Reproduction Services No. ED361 636).

Giacopassi, D. J., and Dull, R. T. (1986). Gender and racial differences in the acceptance of rape myths within a college population. *Sex Roles* 15: 63–75.

Gillio, V. A., and Bell, G. V. (1997). Sexual harassment: New problems and new solutions. In E. K. Cole (ed.), *Sexual Harassment on Campus: A Legal Compendium* (3rd Edition). Washington, DC: National Association of College and University Attorneys.

Gilmartin-Zena, P. (1987). Attitudes toward rape: Student characteristics as predictors. *Free Inquiry in Creative Sociology*: 15: 175–182.

Goodman, L. A., Koss, M. P., Fitzgerald, L. F., Russo, N. F. and Keita, G. (1993). Male violence against women: Current research and future directions. *American Psychologist* 48(10): 1054–1058.

Gordon, L. D. (1990). *Gender and Higher Education in the Progressive Era*. New Haven, CT: Yale University Press.

Gruber, J. E. (1990). Methodological problems and policy implications in sexual harassment research. *Population Research and Policy Review* 9: 235–254.

Gutek, B. A. (1985). *Sex and the Workplace: Impact of Sexual Behavior and Harassment on Women, Men and Organizations*. San Francisco: Jossey-Bass.

Gutek, B. A. (1997). Sexual harassment policy initiatives. In W. O'Donohue (ed), *Sexual Harassment Theory Research, and Treatment*. Boston: Allyn and Bacon.

Gutek, B. A., and Morasch, B. (1982). Sex-ratios, sex-role spillover, and sexual harassment of women at work. *Journal of Social Issues* 38: 55–74.

Haavio-Mannila, E., Kauppinen-Toropainen, K., and Kandolin, I. (1988). The effect of sex composition of the workplace on friendship, romance, and sex at work. In B. A. Gutek, A. Stromberg, and L. Larwood (eds.), *Women and Work: An Annual Review* (vol 3). Beverly Hills, CA: Sage.

Hagedorn, L. S., Nora A., and Pascarella, E. T. (1996). Pre-occupational segregation among first-year college students: An application of the Duncan dissimilarity index. *Journal of College Student Development* 37(4): 425–437.

Hart, S. N. and Brassard, M. R. (1991). The prevalence of personality disorder among wife assaulters. *Journal of Personality Disorders* 7(4): 328–340.

Holcomb, D. R., Holcomb, L. C., Sondag, K. A., and Williams, N. (1991). Attitudes about date rape: Gender differences among college students. *College Student Journal* 25(4): 434–439.

Hotelling, K. (1991). Sexual harassment: A problem shielded by silence. *Journal of Counseling and Development* 69(6): 497–500.

Hotelling, K., and Zuber, B. A. (1997). Feminist issues in sexual harassment. In W. O'Donohue (ed.), *Sexual Harassment Theory Research and Treatment*. Boston: Allyn and Bacon.

Huston, T. (1983). Power. In H. Kelly, E. Berscheid, A. Christensen, J. H. Harvey, T. L. Huston, G. Levinger, E. McClintock, L. A. Pepla, and D. R. Peterson (eds.), *Close Relationships*. New York: Freeman.

Hussar, W. J., Gerald, D. E. (1996). *Projections of Education Statistics to 2006*, 25th ed. (NCES 96-661) Washington, DC: National Center for Education Statistics, Office of Educational Research and Improvement, U.S. Dept. of Education.

Johnston, L. D., O'Malley, P. M., and Bachman, J. G. (1996) *National Survey Results on Drug Use from the Monitoring the Future Study 1975–1994: College Students and Young Adults*. Rockville, MD: National Institute on Drug Abuse.

Kalof, L, and Cargill, T. (1991). Fraternity and sorority membership and gender dominance attitudes. *Sex Roles: A Journal of Research* 25(7): 417–423.

Kantor, G. K., and Straus, M. A. (1987). The drunken bum theory of wife beating. *Social Problems* 34(3): 213–230.

Klein, H. (1992). College students' attitudes toward the use of alcoholic beverages. *Journal of Alcohol and Drug Education* 37(3): 35–52.

Koss, M. P., Dinero, T. E., Seibel, C. A., and Cox, S. L. (1988). Stranger and acquaintance rape. *Psychology of Women Quarterly* 12:1–24.

Koss, M. P. and Gaines, J. A. (1993). The prediction of sexual aggression by alcohol use, athletic participation, and fraternity affiliation. *Journal of Interpersonal Violence* 8(1): 94–108.

MacKinnon, C. (1979). *Sexual Harassment of Working Women.* New Haven, CT: Yale University Press.

Malamuth, N. (1981). Rape proclivity among males. *Journal of Social Issues* 37: 138–157.

Marlatt, G. A., Baer, J. S., and Larimer, M. (1995). Preventing alcohol abuse in college students: A harm-reduction approach. In G.M. Boyd, J. Howard, and R.A. Zucker (eds.) *Alcohol Problems Among Adolescents: Current Directions in Prevention Research.* Hillsdale, NJ: Erlbaum.

Matthews, A. (1993, March 7). The campus crime wave. *New York Times Magazine:* 47:38–42.

Mead, M. (1996). *Male and Female: The Classic Study of the Sexes.* New York: Quill.

Meek, P., and Lynch, A. (1983). Establishing an informal grievance procedure for cases of sexual harassment of students. *Journal of NAWDAC* (Winter): 30–33.

Muehlenhard, C. L., and Linton, M. A. (1987). Date rape and sexual aggression in dating situations: Incidence and risk factors. *Journal of Counseling Psychology* 34:186–196.

Murrell, A. J., and Dietz-Huler, B. L. (1993). Gender identity and adversarial sexual beliefs as predictors of attitudes toward sexual harassment. *Psychology of Women Quarterly* 17: 169–175.

National Center for Educational Statistics. (1996). The Digest of Education Statistics, Table 221.—Full-time instructional faculty in institutions of higher education by race/ethnicity, academic rank, and sex: Fall, 1993. [Online]. Available: http:/nces01.ed/gov/NCES/search/digest.idq ?TextRestriction=facultyandmode=titl andCiMaxRecordsPerPage=10andCiScope=%2FNCES%2Fpubs%2Fd96%2FandTemplateName=digestandCiTemplate=%2FNCES%2Fsearch%2Fd igest. htxandCiort=rank%5Bd%5DandHTMLQueryForm=%2FNCES%2Fpubs%2Fd96%2Findex.html [1997, August 7].

National Council for Research on Women (1992) *Sexual harassment: Research and resources.* New York: Author.

Office of Women in Higher Education (April 15, 1995). *Women Chief Executive Officers of US. Colleges and Universities.* Washington, DC: American Council of Education.

Paludi, M. A. (ed.). (1990). *Ivory Power: Sexual Harassment on Campus.* Albany: State University of New York Press.

Paludi, M. A. (1997). Sexual harassment in schools. In W. O'Donohue (ed.), *Sexual Harassment Theory Research, and Treatment.* Boston: Allyn and Bacon.

Paludi, M. A., and Barickman, R. B. (eds.). (1991). *Academic and Workplace Sexual Harassment: A Resource Manual.* Albany: State University of New York Press.

Parrot, A. (1991, October 7). Improving the quality of life at Cornell: A presentation on sexism, sexual harassment, and acquaintance rape. Panel discussion conducted at the President's Council of Cornell Women, New York.

Pryor, J. B. (1987). Sexual harassment proclivities in men. *Sex Roles* 17(5–6): 269–290.

Pryor, J. B., LaVite, C., and Stoller, L. (1993). A social psychological analysis of sexual harassment: The person/situation interaction. *Journal of Vocational Behavior* (Special issue) 42: 68–83.

Quinn, K. (1990). The victimizations of women. In M.A. Paludi (ed.), *Ivory Power: Sexual Harassment on Campus.* Albany, NY: SUNY Press.

Quina, K. (1996). Sexual harassment and rape: A continuum of exploitation. In M. A. Paludi (ed.), *Sexual Harassment on College Campuses: Abusing the Ivory Tower.* Albany: State University of New York Press.

Rabinowitz, V. C. (1990). Coping with sexual harassment. In M. A. Paludi (ed.), *Ivory Power: Sexual Harassment on Campus.* Albany, NY: SUNY Press.

Reilly, M. E., Lott, B., Caldwell, D., and DeLuca, L. (1991). Tolerance for sexual harassment related to self-reported sexual victimization. *Gender and Society* 6(1).

Rhoads, R. A. (1995). Whales tales, dog piles, and beer goggles: An ethnographic case study of fraternity life. *Anthropology and Education Quarterly* 26(3): 306–323

Riger, S. (1991). Gender dilemmas in sexual harassment policies and procedures. *American Psychologist* 46(5): 497–505.

Rosenfeld, A. H. (1985). Discovering and dealing with deviant sex [Report on work of Abel, Becker, and Mittleman]. *Psychology Today* (April): 8–10.

Ryan, J., and Kenig, S. (1991). Risk and ideology in sexual harassment. *Sociological Inquiry* 61:231–241.

Saal, F. E., Johnson, C. B., and Weber, N. (1989). Friendly or sexy? It depends on whom you ask. *Psychology of Women Quarterly* 13: 263–276.

Sunday, P. R. (1990). *Fraternity Gang Rape.* New York: New York University Press.

Sandler, B. R., and Shoop, R. J. (1997b) What is sexual harassment? In B. R. Sandler and RJ. Shoop (eds.), *Sexual Harassment on Campus: A Guide for Administrators, Faculty, and Students.* Boston: Allyn and Bacon.

Sandroff, R. (1992) Sexual harassment: The inside story. *Working Woman* 17(6): 47, 49–51, 78.

Schneider, B. E. (1987). Graduate women, sexual harassment, and university policy. *Journal of Higher Education* 58(1): 46–63.

Shalala, D. E. (1995, June). Message from Secretary of Health and Human Services Donna E. Shalala. National Institute on Alcohol Abuse and Alcoholism, Alcohol Alert–No. 29 PH 357.

Shoop, R. J. (1997) The legal context of sexual harassment on campus. In B. R. Sandler and R.J. Shoop (eds.), *Sexual Harassment on Campus: A Guide For Administrators, Faculty and Students.* Boston: Allyn and Bacon.

Shoop, R. J., and Hayhow, J. W. (1994). *Sexual Harassment in Our Schools*. Needham Heights, MA: Allyn and Bacon.

Shotland, L., and Craig, J. (1988). Can men and women differentiate between friendly and sexually interested behavior? *Social Psychology Quarterly* 34: 990–999.

Skinner, B. F. (1971). *Beyond Freedom and Dignity*. New York. Alfred A. Knopf.

Stamler, V. L, Pace, D., and Stone, G. L. (1997). Sexual intimacy between university faculty and students: Educational issues and interventions. *NASPA Journal* 34(3): 217–228.

Superson, A. M. (1993). A feminist definition of sexual harassment *Journal of Social Philosophy*: 24, 46–64.

Tampke, D. R. (1990). Alcohol behavior, risk perception, and fraternity and sorority membership. *NASPA Journal* 28(1): 71–77.

Tangri, S. S., Burt, M. R., and Johnson, L. B. (1982). Sexual harassment at work: Three explanatory models. In E. Wall (ed.), *Sexual Harassment: Confrontations and Decisions* (pp. 89–109). (Reprinted from *The Journal of Social Issues*, (1982) 38(4), pp. 33–54.)

Till, F. J. (1980). Sexual harassment: A report on the sexual harassment of students. Report of the National Advisory Council on Women's Educational Program.

United States Department of Justice (1995, August). *Violence Against Women: Estimates from the Redesigned Survey*. (Report No. NCJ-154348). Washington. D.C.: Bureau of Justice Statistics Special Report

United States Merit Systems Protection Board. (1981). *Sexual Harassment in the Federal Workplace. Is It a Problem?* Washington, DC: U.S. Government Printing Office.

Wagner, E. N. (1993). Fantasies of true love in academe. *The Chronicle of Higher Education* (May 26): B1–B3.

Wagner, E. N. (1996). The secret on-campus adjudication of sexual assault [Online], Available: http://www.woconline.org/ONLINE/wagner.html [1997, August, 27].

Wechsler, H., Davenport. A., Dowdall, G., Moeykens, B., and Castillo, S. (1994). Health and behavioral consequences of binge drinking in college: A national survey of students at 140 campuses. *Journal of the American Medical Association* 272(21): 1672–1677.

Wechsler, H., Dowdall, G. W., Davenport, A., and Castillo, S. (1995). Correlates of college student binge drinking. *American Journal of Public Health* 85(7): 921–926.

Wechsler, H., Moeykens, B., Davenport, A., Castillo, S., and Hansen, J. (1995). The adverse impact of heavy episodic drinkers on other college students. *Journal of Studies on Alcohol* 56 (6): 628–634.

Williams, V., and Brake, D. L. (1997). Sexual harassment: Let the punishment fit the crime. *Chronicle of Higher Education* (April 18): 43(32), A56.

Wolfe, J. and Baker, V. (1980). Characteristics of imprisoned rapists and circumstances of the rape. In E. G. Warner (ed.), *Rape and Sexual Assault*. Germantown, MD: Aspen Systems Co.

Worth, D. M., Matthews, P. A., and Coleman, W. R. (1990). Sex role, group affiliation, family background, and courtship violence in college students. *Journal of College Student Development* 31(3): 250–254.

Chapter 15

Texts and Repression: Hazards for Feminists in the Academy

Dorothy Smith

Introduction

This chapter explores discourses and the intertextuality of discursive texts, not as literary or philosophical events, but as local practices organizing a sequential social act. Two texts will be examined. They make up a sequence, a kind of 'conversation,' though not by any means a friendly one. The sequence of texts is analysed for how it shapes public debate, articulating particular institutional sites, in this case, a university in Western Canada, into widening circles of debate and controversy. The texts to be explored concern issues of sexism raised in relation to a department of political science at a Canadian university. The controversy or debate that they generated reverberated through Canadian academic institutions, the networks of the women's movement in Canada, and to some extent the mass media, connecting with the larger politics of that counter-movement Sidney Blumenthal (1986) calls the 'counter-establishment' and Susan Faludi (1992), 'backlash.'

This investigation is preoccupied with discourse as it happens in sequences of social action, inseparable from such sequences and as constitutive and coordinating them. Here I am interested in repression as a textual practice and specifically in how an objectifying discourse can subdue the expression of divergent perspectives and experiences generated in the everyday actualities of social organization, supplanting them with an objectified form of 'consciousness.' In general, I want to learn more about how texts coordinate subjectivities or consciousnesses, the latter conceived as 'active' and inseparable from people in their activities, and, in this context, how texts that universalize or objectify, create forms of consciousness that override the 'naturally' occurring diversity of perspectives and experiences. Here, I think, is where the power that Michel Foucault (1980) attributes to knowledge comes into operation. Such universalizing or objectifying discourses operate to coordinate people's diversities of experience, perspective, and interest into a unified frame at the institutional level. They may indeed be constitutive of what we mean by 'institutions'.

The story begins before we have a text to work on in the experiences of women students (graduate and undergraduate) and junior faculty in a department of political science. A committee led by one of the junior faculty made a report (hereafter, the Report) to the department describing, in the familiar itemizing form, the chilly climate that women experience in the department. That is the first text. It was presented and discussed at a faculty meeting in the spring of 1993. The second is a letter (hereafter, the Letter) responding to the Report, written by the tenured men in the depart-

---

Reprinted from *Writing the Social: Critique, Theory, and Investigations*, by Dorothy Smith, 1998. Copyright © 1998 University of Toronto Press.

ment and addressed to the junior member of faculty who chaired the committee. It is copied to the vice-president academic, the president of the faculty association, and all regular faculty (of the department). In the Letter, the tenured male faculty members of the department call on the junior faculty member to withdraw the Report on the grounds that it makes unjustified accusations of gross misconduct against them. Later, as the controversy widens, involving feminists elsewhere in Canada, academic and political networks among political scientists (many of them on the left politically), and the media, the Letter can be seen, I suggest, as a critical intervention at *the institutional level* that redefines the terms in which the issue will be debated, establishing the hegemony of a juridical discourse, with its language of allegations, evidence, due process, and so forth. The 'application' of the juridical discourse, I suggest, reproduces *at the institutional level* the forms of exclusion that the notion of 'chilly climate' assembles for women at the pre-predicative level of the gender organization of the university. One of the features of this controversy, of which I too was and am a part (and, of course, this paper as well), is the effectiveness of the juridical discourse of the Letter in redefining the intentions and competence of the Report. In effect, I and others I have talked to were captured by the text of the Letter and came to evaluate the original critique in its terms. Though we might sympathize with the women who wrote the Report, we were also critical of its methodological failings. Writing this in a hotel room in Fredericton, New Brunswick, I've just come from a conversation in which I discussed with friends who live there our experiences of that capture. We talked about how, though the Report spoke of what we'd at various times experienced ourselves, we had also been critical of its failure to measure up to the standards of evidence called for by the male faculty's Letter.

When women in the academy raise issues of sexism and racism or simply when we talk about it, the notion of a 'chilly climate' comes to hand. For us, it fishes up out of our experience an open-ended collection of instances. I've talked to women critical of the 'climate' committee's Report who yet say, 'I know what they're talking about.' And when I talk about these issues in a public setting, women in the audience are nodding their heads, smiling (maybe grimacing), turning to one another to make whispered comments. I can see that this notion and the kinds of instances it collects calls up experiences of their own that they can recognize as instances belonging in the collection. Sometimes they add to my collection by coming forward at the end of a talk to tell me of them.

This knowing-what-we-are-talking-about does not translate readily into terms that can be recognized and attended to at the institutional level of organization. Somehow what has appeared obvious gets dissolved into a collection of items each one of which by itself can be resolved into 'subjectivity,' or 'Well, it doesn't only happen to women,' or 'So he was bit rude/insensitive,' or 'where's your evidence?' The notion of 'chilly climate' and its ability to collect experiences fails when it comes to raising the issue at the level of the universalizing discourses in which the order of the academy is formulated. I want to understand how it happens that what may be obvious to feminists is not only invisible to the majority of their male colleagues or teachers, but can be so readily suppressed at the level of the institutional order. In analyzing the dialogue in texts that initiated a major controversy I hope to map the social organization of institutional repression in a way that will help us to see how it comes about.

I begin by formulating the kind of social organization of gender in which the experiences recognized by feminist discourse arise. I want to show how it generates different sites of experience for women and men. This is followed by a description and analysis of the 'chilly climate' Report and, very briefly, what happened when it was presented to the faculty meeting of the political science department. Then I describe the Letter written by the eight male tenured faculty and analyze its retroactive reading of the Report.

From the first text to the second text there is (a) a shift in venue from the department to the institutional level of the university; and (b) a repositioning of the issue from the feminist discourse in which the report was framed to a juridical discourse. The latter extends the umbrella of a regulatory order over how the issue is subsequently defined and discussed. The language of allegations, charges, evidence, and due process displaces feminist discourse and the experiences it has enabled women to recognize. It is a language that seems to be incapable of recognizing the kinds of experiences recognized by feminist discourse, depreciating and degrading what we have to report in forcing it into the framework of accusations, charges, allegations, and so forth. Its objectifying practices, vital in defending the freedoms of individuals against the state, come into play in this context to suppress and subordinate. Issues of due process, entitling the accused to identify their accusers and to respond to the specifics of their accusations, take on an oppressive cast where the accused stand in a relation of authority and superior power over those who are their 'accusers.'

Though subsequently withdrawn, the Letter provided the framework for public discussions within and beyond the university. The juridical discourse organizes how issues are represented and how they are addressed, *on both sides*. Its version of what happened also became a resource in the building of a 'backlash' discourse seeking to protect the academic freedoms of university faculty against the threat of 'inclusiveness' (Richer and Weir 1995). In this process, the problems of making changes in the local practices of sexism and racism that are part of the daily working life of universities disappear from view *at the institutional level*.

I am not arguing that this sequence of two texts represents a turning point (though it may have been); rather, it epitomizes an increasingly general deployment of a juridical discourse as a means of defending the *status quo ante* in universities against both feminist and anti-racist critiques. By the time a similar 'affair' had emerged at another Western Canadian university, the regulatory jurisdiction of the juridical discourse had already been established and came to hand in discrediting a critique of both sexism and racism launched by graduate students in that university's department of political science (Marchak 1996; Smith 1997).

A Brief Excursus on Method

Briefly, something about the method of analysis here. I have tried to avoid becoming technical. But I want to mark a difference in a method of reading that I discovered when I was working earlier on two versions of an event that took place in 1968 in Berkeley, California (Smith 1990d). We, I writing and you reading, are people whose work is deeply implicated in reading and writing, pages of print or computer screens. We take for granted the texts before us—that we can move back and forth in them, that we can read them in relation to one another much as those did who investigated and reported on the Berkeley matter (going back and forth to try to arrive at a 'balanced' view of the matter). In my analysis of the two versions of the Berkeley event, I at first compared one account with the other, looking for differences, for where they converged, and so on. But then I came upon what I have since made into a methodological instruction for myself: investigate/analyse texts as they (might) 'occur' in actuality, namely, in some sequence of action in relation to each other. In the case of the alternate versions of the event in Berkeley, one account was superseded by the other; the second account was, in fact, designed to subsume and displace the first.

In my experience of these texts as a sequential course of reading, I found that the second provided a set of instructions for rereading the first. The retroactive reading was of a particular and interesting kind. It did not contradict the first. Rather, it subsumed it, so that the first person accounts in the first text could be read as partial observations of what was *really* going on. The second text rewrote the events, supplying a level of organization that reinterpreted the observed events as expressions of an institutional order. The distinctive competence of its 'administrative' language was to subsume the descriptive language of the first. When the two texts I am examining in this chapter are viewed in this manner, analogous processes can be seen to be at work. The Letter reconstructs the feminist critique of the department made in the 'climate' committee's report. It is that reconstruction which is the focus here.

In a sense, the analysis also discovers my own practices of reading. Like others who had taken the part of the 'chilly climate' committee, I had nonetheless adopted the framework supplied by the Letter in looking at the Report as imperfectly researched and lacking the kind of evidence needed to sustain the 'allegations' the Letter instructed us to see it as making. The kinds of criticisms of the methodology of the Report, voiced or unvoiced, that I described above are organized, I think, by taking on the Letter's framework in a retroactive reading. It took the analysis reported in this chapter for me to be able to see how I had been implicated and how the Letter had been active in organizing my consciousness.

Intersections of Gender with the Regimes of University and Discourse

Gender organization is in large part historically sedimented and transmitted through local practices passed on hand-to-hand, so to speak, over generations. For the centuries of their history in Europe, universities have been exclusively for men. For centuries, knowledge and learning were among men, and men spoke to and wrote for other men. Back in 1964, Jessie Bernard (1964) discovered what she called the 'stag' effect: when men were asked to name those they held to be significant in their field, they named only men, even when there were women who had done work considered to be important. Here was a residue sedimented by an exclusively masculine history. I imagine that men took the maleness of their university and discursive colleagues for granted. Excluding women was built into their daily lives. Men's achievements were oriented to work done by other men, aiming for other men's esteem and recognition. Their everyday working lives were lived in a world in which women were never colleagues. If there at all, women were secretaries, research assistants, sessional instructors, cleaners, food servers or students —but never equals and co-participants. At home, there were wives and daughters, irrelevant to their work. I imagine how they talked only to other men about things that mattered, and that the things that mattered were what men talked about. Their camaraderie included men's jokes and comments on the physical attractiveness or otherwise of the women they encountered. They did not think of women students as those who might become colleagues; they sometimes looked at them from within the circle of male collectivity as sexual objects; they were sometimes useful; they were often irrelevant. Occasionally, a male faculty member married a student; there was occasional sex, an occasional affair.

I imagine an ethnography of a contemporary university department that would display the gender organization sedimented in the everyday work processes regulated by the university as a regime. It is this everyday level of social organization that remains largely out of sight. To help us envisage this level of organization, I am helped here by reading Alison Lee's (1996) account of the gender organization of a high-school classroom in which a course in geography was being taught:

> [T]he most lasting impression I have of this classroom is of boys' voices... of male voices physically swamping girls'... [the boys'] voices were often loud, the physiological difference combining with the classroom spatial arrangements and their apparent sense of freedom to produce their voices in ways which asserted their presence fairly effectively... there was a marked absence of girls' voices, despite their physical presence in the room. (Lee 1996: 72–3)

How familiar this is to those of us who have been reading the feminist studies of female-male interaction and have come to be able to observe what goes on around us! Lee continues:

> Boys swamped girls in visible ways as well, through their numbers, the massing of their bodies in clusters around the room, their occupation of most of the space. Indeed, there was a strong sense of centre and periphery in the distribution of bodies in space. Girls sat together in the front left-hand corner and seldom left this space. Individual boys and groups of boys, on the other hand, moved regularly around the classroom space, visiting each other. (Lee 1996: 73)

Allowing for differences in going from the local to the institutional level, we can surely find an analogous gender organization in those university departments still bearing the sediments of their masculinist history.

In the past of the university, women, if present at all in an academic role— as students, research assistants, researchers, instructors, and occasionally as faculty—were not members of the university on the same footing with men; their work did not count; they were not people who had things of significance to say. If a woman were doing valuable work, it could be appropriated without scruple or acknowledgment. Only men could be the subjects of scientific sentences since, in the virtual world of scientific discourse, only men were constituted 'author.' Were a woman to occupy a position of authority, the contradiction between that position's authority and her subjectlessness as a woman would create uneasiness. A male colleague wrote of a woman university administrator of some years past that 'she received an elaborate courtesy that was not born of respect but rather, of unease ... she was not perceived as another academic administrator to be judged on the basis of her competence, but as a different kind of creature' (quoted in Backhouse, Harris, Michell, and Wylie 1995: 100). In university classrooms, men oriented (and orient) to men as those who were or would be legitimate participants in the same academic world. A collectivity of men could (and can) be activated across the faculty-student status boundary by telling jokes about women, denigrating women's competence, and being sarcastic at women's expense (particularly, of course, when women are present). A woman physics major at Duke University in the 1990s tells this story:

> On a physics test, her professor included the following example: Starting with the lungs and using Bernoulli's equation, describe in full physical detail the production of the sound 'Ohhh' by our lone sophomoric female physics major. An anatomical sketch would be helpful. (Quoted in Sandler, Silverberg, and Hall 1996:33)

Women's local relationship to the universalized male subject was built into and reproduced by gendered speech genres in which women were excised as subjects, in which they were sexual objects and served as sexualized metaphors for objects, in which the standpoint of (white) men was exclusive vis-à-vis those it constituted as other—women and non-white peoples among them.

I imagine the absolute normality of the regime of masculinity in the university; I imagine it being just the way people lived and worked; I imagine the everyday ordinary language of hallway, cafeteria, bar, and classroom as building in the exclusion of women as subjects/speakers. The everyday working life of a university department is also organized by the discourse or discourses of the discipline the department represents. Here, too, are worlds still largely male-dominated whose authorized speakers (Smith 1987) are mainly male. It is an intellectual tradition largely written from the point of view of the men who made it. It is also an intellectual world that has been assembled from within an exclusively European tradition, which therefore organizes the work of classroom, the resources of library, and the language, objects, and conventions of discourse as a centre defining others who are not represented as subjects or authorized speakers (Said 1979). The experiences, interests, and associations of men of a certain class and race bled into the paradigms of the humanities and social sciences, and even into the natural sciences (Spanier 1995: 149). In going to work in the library, listening to lectures, taking notes, working on papers, or taking tests, a woman student would not find a discourse in which, as a woman, she could appear as subject. Women or students from histories or cultures that were and are discursively excluded as subjects, and who may today be finding themselves as subjects and speakers in specialized programs (Women's Studies, Native Studies, and so on), are still absent or marginalized in mainstream discourse.

Projected into the present, this past has never been disavowed. The relations of discourse authorize and affirm the historically sedimented local organization of race and gender in the everyday worklife of faculty and student. Still today the majority of faculty are white men. In the local regime of a particular university, they are the authorized speakers and teachers of the discourses of their discipline. They are the authorized regulators of classrooms and assigned readings and those authorized to judge students' products. In the classroom, and the graduate classroom in particular, women and men are taught by men who can enter the discourses they teach without an experience of denial of presence, voice, and subject position. A self-insulating, self-reproducing system created in the past is decanted into the everyday ordinariness of the present.

The Feminist Critique

For women students and faculty in the university, a feminist discourse named what we had experienced but had not known how to speak. To women who know enough of feminist discourse to know how to name and see what is going on around them in the university, the taken-for-granted everyday practices of a male-dominated society display an ordinary, and pervasive, sexism. This is the reason the phrase 'a chilly climate for women' resonates. It originated in a report written in 1982 by Roberta Hall and Bernice Sandler (1982), where it was used to describe 'the myriad small inequities that by themselves seem unimportant, but taken together create a chilling environment' (Sandler, Silverberg, and Hall 1996: 1). An unsystematically assembled list drawn from my own experience, from interviews with women faculty in departments of political science in Canada, and from reading yields the following:

- Visitors to the department meeting you in the hallway ask for information or directions (are you a secretary?).
- You feel strangled in faculty meetings.
- You practise speaking complete sentences and paragraphs, rather than handing the completion of your meaning over to another by devices such as 'you know.'
- Your colleague in the next door office stops by on his way to lunch with 'the boys' (your colleagues) and doesn't ask you to come along.
- You are junior faculty, untenured, working at night in your office, and the chair of the department drops by for a chat which has no purpose or point—is he going to make a pass?
- When an assistant dean comes to address the sociology faculty to emphasize the importance of toughening up grading, his language is inclusive only of men—'you young men,' he says, 'get hot under the collar . . .'
- When you try to raise issues of gender equity in hiring in a departmental search committee meeting, the chair shouts at you.
- When you have protested first to your chair, then to the dean, about being harassed by male students in an introductory sociology course in which you have made women a topic, nothing is done and you know you have only succeeded in exhibiting yourself as someone who cannot manage her classroom.
- When a distinguished woman scholar in your field is invited to give a lecture, none of the men in the department come—'But I don't do feminist theory,' they say when asked why.
- In seminars and meetings, the men interrupt or ignore you; when you raise an issue, it's hard to get it discussed by them; and so on.

These are instances from the faculty side. A similar list could be written based on the experience of women students; and, from either side, of the experience of racism or homophobia.

The notion of climate does not define specific acts or kinds of behaviour; it locates the generalized character of a regime that is vested in the routine and everyday and in the ordinary as well as the technical languages which regenerate the local orderliness of the everyday work of a university. It is all around us and nowhere in particular, like the weather. Analogously the exclusions of non-white people, organized *variously* through state and economic organization, are articulated as the taken-for-granted local practices of universities.

When women students and a junior member of the faculty of the University of Victoria (Canada), constituted as the Committee to Make the Department More Supportive of Women (set up a year earlier), the 'climate' committee for short, made a critique of sexism in the Department of Political Science, they appealed implicitly to principles of rational discourse fundamental to the university. They sought to correct barriers, which feminist discourse has enabled us to recognize, to their full and equal participation in the academic discourses that the university sustains.

The historically sedimented masculine university creates major gender asymmetries. A symmetry of presence of women and men as subjects for each other has been lacking in the discourses it houses. Among other practices deforming the symmetry of presence in academic contexts is men's orienting to women in an exclusively sexual mode: 'Call me fussy,' said one woman student, 'I just object to someone staring at my bust all the time' (President's Advisory Committee on the Status of Women, University of Saskatchewan 1995: 186). Attending to a woman as a sexual object *in a professional context* displaces her as subject in a professional mode. Within the discourses of the sciences and humanities, men have been subjects for women, but women have not been subjects for men; and, until this women's movement, perhaps not even for each other or themselves.

Feminist discourse has developed categories that name, specify, and collect what it is about men's taken-for-granted and everyday working practices and modes of relating in the university that undermines women's participation as full equals in the discourses of the sciences and humanities. The concept of a 'chilly climate' is one. It expresses the pervasiveness of the problem, rather than specific acts.

Beginning in people's experience presupposes divergent perspectives and different interpretations. People bring to any moment of activity the deposits of their idiosyncratic biographies. But differences are also structured in the social organization of their everyday activities with others, and these, though modified by what individuals bring to the situation, are not idiosyncratic. Women can join in funding and recognizing experiences we have in common.

Men are situated differently in these historically sedimented gender relations and, for the most part, do not participate in a discourse that enables recognition of what it is that feminists are pointing to when we say: 'This is sexist.' 'One of the hardest things about working in my Faculty is that they don't know they have a problem. The majority of my Faculty would say they don't discriminate. Yet they make such obvious sexist comments' (woman faculty member, quoted in Backhouse, Harris, Michael, and Wylie 1995: 120). While feminists have no difficulty in recognizing in the Report written by the 'climate' committee of the University of Victoria's Political Science Department the lineaments of barriers we have experienced, men generally seem not to do so. Feminists who read the Report may say, as I did when I first read it, 'Well, it may not be put together as effectively as it might, but I know just what they're talking about.' We are reading as knowledgeable practitioners of the discourse within which the Report is written. It is familiar ground. It is clear that it has not been at all obvious to the male faculty who respond to it.

Men, however, are for the most part not competent readers, if readers at all, of feminist discourse. Nor are they sensitized by experiencing the uneasiness, dismay, anxiety, sometimes anger, which women may experience and which feminist discourse recognizes. The feminist critique does not raise issues for them at the level of academic discourse, where criticism is a familiar hazard, but at the level of their taken-for-granted and largely unreflective ways of doing things and of the very normality of the ways in which they relate to one another and to women.

The Report of the 'Climate' Committee

The report of the 'climate' committee was presented to the Department of Political Science in the spring of 1993. The members of the committee identified in the final paragraph of the Report were two graduate and three undergraduate students, and its chair, a junior faculty member (untenured). The Report is not in highly formalized form. It is not on letterhead paper; it is typed, but not expertly formatted (the format of sub-headings displaces levels); it is not paginated. The date appears to have been added in a different typeface (I suspect it was typewritten onto an original computer-generated text). This does not create a problem of authenticity since there is no question about when it was delivered. It is identified in the first paragraph as the work of a committee that the Department of Political Science set up the previous year in response to concerns 'regarding the discouraging and unsupportive environment experienced by... women students' that surfaced during the report of the department's Graduate Review Committee (Department of Political Science, minutes, 11 May 1992). The Report is thus clearly located as departmental business, authorized by the department.

The Report is, it says, 'preliminary.' There is no extended account of its method of production. In the introductory paragraph, it is said that the Report 'emerg[ed] from discussions with . . . women students.' The final paragraph refers to the committee's method of proceeding. '[It] has consulted widely with the student body and the Political Science Women's Caucus of the Course Union, and through a variety of meetings, forums and exchanges.'

The introductory section of the Report places the responsibility for change with the department as a whole, noting that it has already recognized its responsibilities in this respect by recent hirings aimed at rectifying its gender imbalance. However, concerns are expressed that the Report may meet with 'hostility, indifference, and the calling into question of women's credibility and right to participate in and make representation to the department on issues of equity.' These concerns had arisen because, earlier in the year, the Women's Caucus of the Political Science Course Union had made representations with respect to the hiring process then under way in the department and had been sharply rebuffed.

The general format of the Report is as follows: there are five major headings, under each of which instances of departmental 'practices' are described, followed by recommendations for change; the headings are 'Teaching,' 'Class Content,' 'Funding,' 'Sexual Harassment and Everyday Hostility,' and 'Hiring.' The Report concludes with a section titled 'Further Recommendations,' which is followed by the paragraph referred to above.

The sections display a regular structure. Each opens with a general statement about 'barriers' faced by women in the area designated by the heading. This is followed by several descriptive items that provide specific illustrations of the general statement. The descriptive items are mixed in character. Some refer to particular incidents, for example, under the heading 'Teaching': 'faculty comments such as "feminism is just Marxism in a skirt" and "feminism is just political puff."' Others generalize across a range of incidents, clearly relying on the feminist discourse on the academy for the concepts that assemble them: 'professors do not interrupt men who are dominating seminars or class participation, and do not encourage and support women speaking.' Still others make use of such categories of feminist discourse as 'sexist' without further specification: 'professors often refuse to allow women students to respond to extremely sexist and anti-feminist comments made in class by male students.' All sections conclude with recommendations for measures the department should take to remedy the situations they describe. These add up to a comprehensive program of change. In a sense, the Report is a hybrid, formulating its issues in an objectifying style, avoiding the identification of particular individuals, and attributing the problems to the department as a whole rather than to the individuals who were originally involved in the incidents described. At the same time, it has relied throughout, in generating its examples, on what feminist discourse recognizes in women's experience.

The Male Faculty Response

The Letter from the eight male tenured faculty is the second text. Addressed to the junior member of faculty who chaired the 'climate' committee, it was written some days after a departmental meeting at which the Report was discussed. Written on letterhead paper and 'professionally' formatted (though there are a number of minor typographical errors), it was accompanied with a memorandum informing the junior faculty member that copies of the Letter had been sent to the dean, the academic vice-president, and to the president of the faculty association, as well as to all regular faculty members (presumably of the department). Using departmental letterhead appropriates for the Letter the authority of the institutional site. Copying the Letter to officers in the administrative hierarchy repositions the issues, at least as the Letter formulates, taking them from the departmental level to the level of the university at large, and thereby opting out of the collegial process in the department.

The Letter denies that the Report 'reflect[s] the reality' of the department. It asserts that the Report makes 'two utterly false statements [*sic*],' and that these are so damaging to the reputations of male faculty in the department that discussion cannot be pursued until they are withdrawn." The Letter then quotes from the section of the Report headed 'Sexual Harassment and Everyday Hostility' as follows:

'Female staff and students experience harassment and hostility. The range of behaviours that women experience include the following: sexist and racist treatment of students in the class and during consulations [sic] ... sexual advances at social gatherings by male faculty members to students' (quoted in Bilson and Berger 1994: 12–13). These statements indicate, they claim, 'a pattern of corrupt and repugnant behaviours' and are 'so obviously damaging' to their reputations that they must be retracted. The formulation of statements as generalities implies that 'there have been many instances' of sexism and that 'more than one faculty member has made sexual advances to more than one student on more than one occasion.' It is their belief they state, that 'there are no incidents whatsoever of the behaviours described; the events described in the Report have never happened. The Letter then challenges Professor Brodribb to provide evidence supporting the statements made in the Report 'to the proper university authorities,' using the university's procedures for investigating sexual harassment, and to agree to abide by the results of the investigation. If, however, she cannot 'provide credible evidence to substantiate the assertions,' then they 'demand an unqualified apology and retraction' (Bilson and Berger 1994: 40) by a date six days from the date of the Letter. Collegial discussion, the Letter indicated, cannot be resumed until the matter is resolved. If credible evidence is not produced and no apology and retraction made, 'then it will be necessary . . . to take further steps to protect our reputations. This clause has been widely interpreted, including by the external reviewers (Bilson and Berger 1994: 41), as a threat to take legal action.

Reconstructing the 'Climate' Report

Michel Foucault's theory of discourse (Foucault 1972; 1981) proposes that the categories, concepts, theories, epistemologies, and methods of positing the objects and relations of discourse are constituted in its rules and conventions. The discourse on which the Letter relies is juridical. It is a discourse with the power to reorganize and subordinate other discourses. It is a particular practice of this power that is examined here in an analysis of how the Letter interprets and retroactively redefines the Report.

Central to the Letter is the construction of its discursive objects—assertions 'alleging sexist and racist behavior [sic]' and 'suggesting gross sexual misconduct,' indicating 'a pattern of corrupt and repugnant behaviours [sic].' The imposition of a juridical template over the Report generates these objects. It is useful to follow Stanley Fish's (1967) recommendation to analyse a text as a course of reading in which its meaning is built sequentially. I have taken his advice in analysing the Letter's 'conversation' with the Report as a sequence of steps, or perhaps devices, each next one of which relies on previous steps.

Step 1

The juridically relevant segments of the Report, namely its references to sexual harassment, sexism, and racism, are brought into focus; the remainder is discarded. The effect is to displace the Report as an account of a generalized 'climate' in the Department of Political Science. The section 'Sexual Harassment and Everyday Hostility,' which contains these references, is reproduced below in its entirety (the numbering is for purposes of referencing and does not appear in the original):

1. SEXUAL HARASSMENT AND EVERYDAY HOSTILITY
2. Subtle (and not so subtle) forms of sexual harassment are a
3. significant barrier to women's full and equal participation in the department.
4. Female staff and students experience harassment and hostility. The range of
5. behaviours that women experience include the following:
6. —comments about the 'feminist imperialists'
7. —comments like 'I'm not going to be evaluated by the feminist police'
8. —sexist and racist treatment of students in the class and during consultations
9. —sexual advances at social gatherings by male faculty members to students

10. —pitting women against each other during class (eg. calling upon a devout
11. —anti-feminist woman to argue it out with a feminist)
12. —interruption or blocking of conversations and exchanges between women,
13. —especially when these seminar discussions focus on feminism
14. —the general silencing of women in seminar classes
15. —disparaging scholarship on women, or ridiculing material that deals with
16. —women's perceptions or [sic] in class and informally (eg. derogatory
17. —comments about 'the feminists' and 'feminism'
18. —sexist humour as a classroom device
19. *We recommend that this behaviour stop.
20. *We also recommend that faculty, staff and students who are addressing
21. issues of sexual harassment receive departmental support.
22. *We recommend that the Department take leadership in formulating a serious
23. and unequivocal policy against sexual harassment. This policy may serve as
24. an example to other sections of the University community.
25. *We recommend that an effective and serious approach to women's safety
26. become part. of the mandate of Traffic & Security.

Step 2

The objectionable 'assertions' are extracted from the surrounding text of the original for quotation in the Letter. Two passages are selected (lines 4–5 and 8–9) and reassembled to make up the following passage:

> Female staff and students experience harassment and hostility. The range of behaviours that women experience include the following: sexist and racist treatment of students in the class and during consulations [sic]... sexual advances at social gatherings by male faculty members to students. (Quoted in Bilson and Berger 1994: 12–13)

Stripping away the context and adjusting the continuity produces a passage representing the Report that is fitted to the Letter's account of the offending assertions, as follows:

(a) The first sentence (lines 2–3 above) of the section is omitted. It defines the significance of sexual harassment as a barrier to women's 'full and equal participation in the department.' Omitting it removes any indication of the Report's claimed intention to treat the behaviours described as attributes of the department rather than to focus on the behaviour of individual members of the department. Omitting any reference to the Report's recommendations regarding the department's role in making change (lines 19–26) has a similar effect.

(b) The first two items (lines 6–7) in the list of the 'range of behaviours' are omitted. This omission is not noted in the letter. The remainder of the items (lines 10–18) illustrating the theme are also omitted. Thus, any passages incompatible with the Letter's reading of the Report as making 'allegations' of 'corrupt and repugnant behaviours' have been eliminated.

In reading the Report, I found the use of the concept of 'sexual harassment' equivocal. I think this is because it locates an intersection of discourses. As formalized procedures for dealing with complaints of sexual harassment have been established in universities, sexual harassment has come to be juridically defined and to be restricted increasingly to specifically sexual forms of harassment. The 'Report of the Review Committee into the Political Science Department,' written by Beth Bilson and Thomas R. Berger, cites a judicial decision formulating just such a restricted definition (Bilson and Berger 1994: 22). There is, however, a feminist usage that defines it more broadly to include behaviour that expresses hostility towards women or denigrates them as women. This usage is still current in the feminist literature and tends to survive institutionally where universities have harassment procedures which also take up racial harassment.

As I start to read this section of the Report, its introductory paragraph (lines 2–5) tells me to discard the first of these interpretations (i.e., the juridical). The 'range' of the examples (lines 6–18) confirm the second, broader interpretation. In omitting all but two of the items, the Letter restricts interpretation of 'sexual harassment' to the juridical, ruling out the broader feminist interpretation.

Step 3

Tracing a course of reading through the Letter, the reconstructed segment attributed to the Report can be seen as the object referred to in the Letter's next move—the construction of the 'assertions' as 'obviously damaging to our reputations.' 'Obviously' instructs the reader to register the reputational damage as what anyone could see. We have seen in step 2 how the groundwork for this has been laid. The next move is to articulate the 'objects' within the framework and juridical language of the Letter. The items illustrating 'sexual harassment and everyday hostility' can now be read as 'unfounded assertions' 'alleging sexist and racist behavior' and 'suggesting gross sexual misconduct,' together 'indicat[ing] a pattern of corrupt and repugnant behaviours.'

Step 4

The course of reading that the Letter sets up for the reader upgrades the rhetorical value of references to 'sexist behavior':

(a) The original wording of the Report is reconstructed in a juridical language: 'sexual advances at social gatherings' (the Report.) becomes gross sexual misconduct' (the Letter). An intertextual tie is set up between the 'assertions' and grounds for dismissal of faculty that may be written into disciplinary clauses of faculty–university contracts and/or into the formalized sexual harassment procedures of the university. There are implications, therefore, that more than reputation could be at stake.

(b) Stripping away all other items except the reference to sexist and racist treatment of students has had the general rhetorical effect of enhancing the offensive value of the assertions. I found the jump from 'sexual advances at social gatherings' to 'gross sexual misconduct' rather startling. It is a rhetorical shift in the offensive value of the item as it appeared in the Report; but accomplished, as it is, in step-by-step fashion, the reader does not necessarily recognize how steep the shift has been.

In later texts, further along in the widening controversy, there are further upgradings. These are also filtered through the ordinary process through which one text refers back to another, which refers back to another, and so on. Readers, however, don't generally lay the texts side by side to compare them. Being accused of making sexual advances to students at parties would hardly warrant the formality of the Letter's indictment. Upgrading the offence brings it to a level commensurate with the outrage the Letter expresses. Here is the groundwork for further upgradings, first in an informally distributed paper written by one of the signatories to the Letter (who refers to 'allegations' of 'truly corrupt and violent behaviour') (Magnusson 1993: 5); and, later; John Fekete performs a further upgrading—'sexual advances' by faculty to students at social affairs become 'sex-crimes' (Fekete 1994: 294).

Step 5

Juridical discourse is objectifying. It preempts diversities of consciousness and experience. Its procedures subdue such differences to methods of dispelling ambiguity, of the determination of what constitutes good evidence, and so forth. Categories must have a determinate reference to events, states of affairs, and so on, independent of the statements that use them. The wording of the Report must be reshaped into formulations of definite acts performed by actual and identifiable individuals. Once denied as charges or accusations, they must meet criteria of proper evidence. Determination of truth and falsity is a project integral to the practice of objectivity and to arriving at an account capable of overriding what you think, what I think, what she thinks. In the first two paragraphs of the Letter, a falsehood/reality contrast is introduced: the Report 'provides a portrait of our department which, in our view, does not reflect reality'; and 'there are two utterly false statements [sic] in the report...The sequence I have analyzed as a course of construction follows. Only then can the junior faculty member chairing the 'chilly climate' committee be challenged to produce 'credible evidence' for 'the proper university authorities.' The insistence on a retraction if credible evidence is lacking relies on a whole course of construction that has transformed the Report's delineation of a 'climate' into allegations of determinate and improper acts committed by definite people on definite occasions for which evidence must be brought to if their truth or falsity is to be assessed.

To my count, the Report lists twenty illustrative items; the Letter focuses on only two. Some of these items describe students in class being treated, either by the instructor or by other students, in ways that should surely be considered as less than the best professional practice, regardless of whether women or men are involved. Instructors are described as treating women students and what they put forward with contempt; as allowing, even encouraging, 'harassing' behaviour from male students in class that is continued outside class; as allowing male students to dominate classroom discussions; as making 'patronizing and demeaning comments on work submitted'; and so on. These are not made an issue in the Letter. Nor are the questions the Report raises about the lack of feminist content in mandatory political science courses and of feminist and Native instructors. In stripping down the Report to fit the juridical frame, the Letter disables the Report's attempt to make visible a taken-for-granted gender order that deformed the conditions of women's full and equal participation in the discourse of political science.

At what point does criticism become accusation? At what point does the detailing of critique become 'charges' and 'allegations'? The theory of symbolic interaction and its echoes in ethnomethodology tell us that it is the response to the act that gives the latter its determinate character. Here we see an act, the Report, given definition in the terms, syntax and methods of juridical discourse. The institutional character of the Letter elevates the Report to its own status. It was publicized in an article in the *Globe and Mail* (Wilson 1993), which appeared shortly after the date of the Letter. Its interpretation comes to dominate the debates that followed, including the issues focused on by the external review (Bilson and Berger 1994). In a sense, the Letter *produces the accusations of which it complains*. The external reviewers observed: 'It is all very well to say that the purpose of the report of the Chilly Climate Committee was not to indict individuals. Yet that is its effect' (Bilson and Berger 1994: 55). It is an effect that the Letter itself creates in its retroactive reconstitution of the Report as a formalized and public or semi-public document, reinterpreted in a juridical mode.

Juridical Discourse and Institutional Debate

The social organization of the everyday in which the women's experiences originated were worked up into the text of the Report in meetings and discussions among them. The Report is entered into a departmental sequence of action: it originated when the committee was set up by a decision of a departmental meeting in the previous year; it is delivered at a departmental meeting; is discussed; further work on it is called for. Faculty at the meeting did not welcome the Report, and, at the male faculty's request, it was forwarded to the equity office of the university. No move had been taken by that office by the date of the Letter, which lodged the 'accusations' at the institutional level by 'copying' the letter to the dean, the vice-president (academic), and the president of the faculty association. The projected, but incomplete, departmental sequence of producing, reading, and responding to a text that attempts to describe typical aspects of women's experiences in the department is abruptly preempted by the men's Letter. The latter launches the issue into institutional space not only of the university but also, implied in the threat to take 'further steps to protect our reputations,' of law and state. It establishes the discourse that will regulate debate, providing schemata, terms, discursive objects, an epistemology (positivist), and methodological conventions for determining the truth-value of propositions. The external review written by Beth Bilson and Thomas Berger, despite its generally sympathetic treatment of the issues raised by the 'chilly climate' Report, clearly adopts its problematic from the Letter.

To read is to expose oneself to capture. It is to risk being entered by an organization of language and making it ours. The power of a text bearing the marks of authority when it is launched into public space is considerable. As readers are captured, it comes to provide the terms of discussion with others similarly caught. I have referred to my own experience of such capture earlier. In setting the terms and schemata of debate, the Letter establishes a shift in focus from the issues about women's situation in the department to the damage to the male faculty's reputations and issues of due process. As debate engages, the terms and schemata that will organize it have already been put in place, a powerful and ordinary feature of the regulation of public discourse.

Thus the juridical interpretation and the texts it organizes are foundational to the debate that follows. Reviewed from the standpoint established by the Letter, the Report is evaluated in terms of evidential requirements which an internal critique of the department would not have called for. As an internal document, the Report could be taken to be *pointing out* what could be observed by any member of the department; indeed, some of my interview data suggests that what the committee intended was to make concrete and explicit issues which had been left vague and ambiguous in a previous report to the department on this and related topics. The Letter, however, relocates the Report at the institutional level as well as subduing it to juridical discourse.

Juridical discourse organizes subsequent criticisms of the Report. The Report is treated as if it had been intended originally as a public text launched at the institutional level. The 'Report of the Review Committee into the Political Science Department' (Bilson and Berger 1994), the last and most authoritative of a series of reviews of the events, is fully in the juridical mode. Though generally favourable to the Report, it criticizes its methodology, drawing on a critique by a distinguished feminist sociologist who had been consulted by members of the 'chilly climate' committee (Bilson and Berger 1994: 17–19); it deplores the Report's ambiguous use of terms such as 'sexism' and 'harassment' (ibid.: 24), supplying its own authoritative and undimensional definitions, based on a judicial decision; criticizes the Report's reliance on women's experience; and is particularly critical of the violations of due process in the 'accusations' it makes against the men. Once it is launched into public space, the Report is examined for methodological standards of objectivity which are not normally required of internal departmental documents, particularly those that are preliminaries to departmental discussion. It is called to this level of accountability in the process of being redefined and recast through the steps taken by the senior male faculty of the department.

The Letter's reading of the Report establishes a template that can be distilled from later stories, reviews, and so on: *women make serious accusations of sexism or sexual harassment against men, damaging their reputations and putting them at risk of serious penalties. It turns out, however, either that there are no objective grounds for their accusations or that the behaviour they describe is trivial.* This template structures how this or similar controversies are reported in the public media: male faculty at universities are unjustly accused, and false or misleading allegations are made; professors are accused of serious, even criminal, misconduct that, upon investigation, is seen to be trivial and/or unsubstantiated; universities fail to observe due process and proceed to 'punish' the professors before allegations have been substantiated. The stories are produced out of a sequence of actions mandated by a juridical discourse. The analysis above has displayed the substructure of one such story. We can see how an internal criticism of a department once read juridically and transposed into a public arena can be read as an 'accusation of 'wrongdoing. Once 'normal rules of justice and due process are applied, the issue becomes the wrong done the professors rather than the women's critique.

John Fekete's (1994) critique of what he calls 'a new authoritarianism' (1994) in universities describes 'professors on trial.' Among them are those whose Letter is under examination here. His account of the Report of the 'climate' committee relies on the Letter's productive work as well as on a later contribution (Magnusson 1993) to the bitterness of the debate. He tells us that the Report 'suggests... a pattern of corrupt and violent behaviour (289) and that 'sex-crime charges' were made (294). The *Alberta Report* (1995) describes the 'climate' committee's Report as making 'baseless accusations' 'of fostering academic bigotry and sexually harassing female undergrads' against 'unnamed male professors'(38). The introductory paragraph of a frontpage article in the *Globe and Mail* (Saunders 1995) presents a critique of what is described as the use of sexual harassment codes to discipline professors 'for ironic comments, passing glances and lectures that students or fellow faculty find upsetting' (A1). The article argues that' . . . for professors accused of wrongdoing, the normal rules of justice and due process frequently do not apply' (A1). Citing the case examined here as an example, the article suggests that some universities have allowed 'individual professors—or even entire departments, through so-called "chilly climate" investigations—to be disciplined for a wide range of actions that stop short of genuine sexual harassment . . '(A3). At another university, a move by the administration to suspend graduate admissions to a department of which criticisms of racism and sexism had been made, becomes, when it is interpreted by the juridical discourse's mandated course of action (Smith 1990d), punishment dealt out without due process. Interpreted otherwise, say, in terms of a university administration's responsibilities to its students, the administration's edict would have read, not as punishment improperly applied, but as an appropriate administrative intervention in a department that it had judged to have rather serious problems with its graduate program.

The 'wide range of actions' that constitute the body of the Report's critique become, when this template is imposed, only a resource for demonstrating the frivolous nature of the accusations that the women have made. Instances drawn from the feminist critique, particularly those that go back to the issues of 'climate,' are represented as groundless or trivial—the *Globe and Mail* article has the subhead 'Ruffled Feathers on Campus' (Saunders 1995: A3). In a later and analogous episode at another Western Canadian university, the Civil Liberties Association reviewing a report on the situation prepared by a lawyer, commented 'that in the thirty-two pages of repetitive allegations, the preponderance were "minor in nature" and did "not obviously provide a basis for a claim of racism or sexism"' (Marchak 1996: 114). The same structure generates the stories travelling the gossip channels among academics involved in a movement identifying itself with 'academic freedom' and opposing those who raise issues of gender or racial inequities in universities. I heard some of these stories at the 1997 conference 'Academic Freedom and the Inclusive University' at the University of British Columbia. For example: a story of women who went on a packaged tour and brought a case under the Human Rights Code for sexual discrimination against the tour operator because he arranged for them to be served croissants for breakfast; the story of one of the professors involved in the case I have discussed here as having been accused of sexual harassment by one of the student members of the 'chilly climate' committee *when,* the teller of the tale reported with some pleasure, *they had never even met.* Michèle Le Doeuff, quoted in the introduction to the Report, writes that as a philosopher, on the one hand, she faces 'fierce opposition' and, on the other hand, is told that 'you are making a lot of fuss about nothing'(Le Doeuff in Climate Committee 1993).

Discussion

I have wanted to write this not as a micro-sociology that addresses only the local setting in which it arises, but to make a sociological investigation of a particular local sequence of action as it participates in a general institutional level of organization. Generalized and generalizing discourses participate in the organization of local sequences of text-mediated action and hence in the ongoing reproducing of the university as a regime coordinating local resources of funding, personnel, real estate, teaching responsibilities, and so on, with discourses organized extra-locally and hooking up with other universities and other institutions.

Reproduced at the level of the public text-mediated relations of discourse, the juridical offers devices that can be used to pre-empt the recognition of experientially based criticisms of sexism or racism in institutional settings. The analysis shows a passage from women's experience into an objectifying discourse as a locally organized sequence of action that is from the outset coordinated with extra-locally organized discourses. In a sense, the sequence of two texts is a sequence of discourses in which the juridical is successful in suspending the efficacy, at least for this sequence, of a feminist discourse specifically aimed at giving expression to experience, even providing generalized forms in which it can be objectified (made independent of particular subjectivities). The method of analysis explores texts as they are entered into and are integral to the organization of sequences of action. The organizing or regulating operation of texts allows us to see how the unfolding and open-ended character of actual people's activities achieves what can be described as 'organization' or 'institution.' Printed and published, texts supply a *standardized, replicable form of words,* detachable from the particular local setting in which the original sequence of action occurred. Texts can be thought of as supplying one part in a conversation, but a part that can be standardized across multiple conversations in different local settings and at different times. Analysis, therefore, of texts as constituents of particular local sequences of action discovers the extra-local organization of discourse and, in a sense, how it can be described as discourse and hence as something existing independently of particular sites of reading and talk. What Michel Foucault (1981) calls 'the order of discourse' organizes, even *regulates,* particular text-reader conversations and particular sequences of action.

In the sequence I have described and analysed here, the order of juridical discourse can be seen also as having the 'capacity' to supersede or subsume other discourses. It relies on an epistemological 'theory,' built into the notion of 'evidence,' that there is a reality knowable in the same way by anyone, against which statements about it can be tested. Its procedures are objectifying, displacing particular perspectives and experiences. A single version of events or deeds has to be produced that is independent of its experiential, and hence necessarily partial, ground. It constructs a determinate event or act for which evidence can be produced and hence relies on what is describable and knowable independently of particular viewpoints. It operates with something like an 'override' device which subdues diverging perspectives. It does not know how to handle different experiences of *one event* other than by discarding one or even both, in favour of an 'objective' version—what really happened.

The issues raised by feminist 'chilly climate' discourse are not readily fitted to such a discourse. Gender organization at the level of the everyday is necessarily reciprocal. It is not the same for women as for men. Alison Lee's description of the interactions of boys and girls in a high-school geography class illuminates these reciprocities. Experiences arising in these relations will diverge *systematically*. Hence it *may be difficult to align stories told by women and stories told by men of the 'same' situation.* The problems that the 'chilly climate' discourse enables women to recognize do not readily resolve into specific acts, let alone acts describable as 'corrupt and repugnant' (the Letter). Imagine the girls in Lee's geography class making their feminist critique. It would be full of those 'myriad small inequities that by themselves seem unimportant' (Sandler, Silverberg, and Hall 1996: 1). Feminists writing on the topic commonly refer to problems of specifying just where the problems they encounter lie and how to describe them. Susan Prentice writes:

> ... climate is pervasive and systemic, the result of compounded effects, it becomes difficult to pinpoint exactly what initiatives would 'warm' or remedy the climate... Paula Caplan has pointed out that women faculty and students experience the climate as a 'ton of feathers.' (Prentice 1996: 3)

For the juridical order of discourse, the everyday social organization of gender relations presents problems: it is not easy to produce systematic descriptions of acts or categories of acts that can be identified and recognized again; the acts themselves are embedded in and part of a social organization that generates systematic differences and reciprocities of experience for women and men.

Objectifying discourses have a special status in institutions. They may, indeed, provide for what we mean by 'institution.' Patricia Marchak (1996) sees the critiques of racism and sexism as a threat to the universality and objectivity that are foundational to the university and the authority of its faculty to teach and judge. In speaking from women's experience, women are speaking from one side of an historically normalized organization of social relations in which men, and not women, have represented and derived their authority from the objectified order. Public challenge to the gender order of domination threaded into the texture of faculty–faculty and faculty–student relationships threatens what Joan Landes describes as 'the masquerade through which the (male) particular was able to posture behind the veil of the universal' (Landes 1995: 98). 'Chilly climate' discourse exposes the masquerade and puts in question the authority that relies on the objectified order.

The 'chilly climate' Report, aimed at changing a department's practices, was brought to the 'governing' body of the department as a step in initiating change. It performed an act of judgment, evaluating the department, criticizing its gender order and, either directly or by implication, the men occupying the institutionally defined positions of power and authority within it. An act of judgment constitutes the authority of those who judge. Here are women judging men, students and junior faculty judging senior faculty. For the men to respond by accepting the validity of the critique would imply acceptance of the authority of those who judge in this matter, reversing the institutional standing of the male tenured faculty vis-à-vis junior faculty and students and, in making visible 'the male particular behind the veil of the universal,' putting their authority as faculty in question. The Report claims implicitly, under principles of symmetry and reciprocity, the right to judge the judges. The Letter redresses the balance of authority to judge in the direction of the established gender regime. *It restores the coincidence of gender and formal institutional hierarchies that is challenged by the Report.* The eight male faculty, signatories to the Letter, are constituted as subjects within juridical discourse; they appropriate its authority in challenging the feminist critique.

At the surface constituted by the texts, the local settings of the course of action of which they were originally part do not appear. In the ensuing controversy, it is the texts that define the issues. They are all that ascend from the particular local setting into the strata of discourse. They do not travel with the debris of actuality. The social organization supplied by the texts themselves admit only the categories written into them. In the Letter the parties to the sequence appear as equals (notice that the Letter is addressed to the junior faculty member alone and does not include the students as addressees; nor does it identify the differences in status). The signatories have been 'accused'; due process requires that they should have all opportunity of confronting their accuser and the particulars of the accusation so that they can defend themselves. The local setting has disappeared, including the gendered character of the university's regime and the relative positions of participants in it. That these are senior male faculty with tenure, including the chair of the department, confronting women students and a junior faculty member undergoing tenure review, is not admissible to the discourse it contains. Invisible also at the surface of these texts is the fact that these are men who have played their part in the university at large, been present on its senate, participated in its faculty association, served on committees, been present on formal occasions, and met less formally in a variety of settings with other members of faculty. Some had direct connections with the provincial government then in power, and all or most, have extensive connections with political scientists in other parts of Canada. In short, they are men who are widely respected and known; men of substance and standing within the institutional order. In writing the Letter and circulating other documents in support of their position, they had taken for granted, as the writers of the Report had not, that they could command university resources, such as the worktime and skills of departmental support staff, as well as departmental technologies of producing and reproducing documents; they had taken for granted that their Letter could be properly produced on official departmental stationery, be distributed by departmental staff, and later, when they feared that the Report had been distributed widely throughout the country, that they could mail the texts of their rebuttals to faculty members in universities across the country. Though the students active on the committee were not directly addressed by the Letter and the Report carries no names, they had been present at the departmental meeting at which the Report was discussed and were known to male faculty. All members of the committee were potentially exposed to direct or indirect penalties by those with various forms of power over them, including command over resources of the university to use against them. These aspects of what was happening as the sequence of texts originally unfolded are missing from the textual surfaces and *become inadmissible* to the text-reader conversations to which they articulate elsewhere or elsewhen. The connection of the sequence of texts to the everyday gender order of the university is disrupted. *The validity of the critique rather than its substance becomes the issue to be debated.*

Jürgen Habermas's (1970) formulation of the ideal speech situation as foundational to an ethic of rational discourse offers, I suggest, principles by which universities could take up critiques of sexism and racism as legitimate issues. He holds that rationality, truth, and justice rely on the principles of the ideal speech situation in which speakers seek to be understood, to tell the truth, in terms of their own feelings as well as what they know of the world beyond their own subjectivity, and justice rely on the principles of the ideal speech situation on which speakers seek to be understood, to tell the truth, in terms of their own feelings as well as what they know of the world beyond their own subjectivity, and to be accepted by the other as speaking in terms of norms and values they share. The relationship is reciprocal. Each party is both speaker and hearer and recognizes the other as such; there is full mutual recognition of each participant as a subject and a symmetry of the presence of subjects for each other; no one participant is privileged in the performance of dialogic roles, with the implication that though one may teach, the other too is recognized as a subject who may argue and question. Theorizing an ideal speech situation as foundational to rational discourse enables identification of sources that 'deform' its realization. Deformations may arise from 'the social structure on the basis of asymmetries in the performance of dialogue roles' (Habermas 1970: 144). Rationality, for Habermas, is a form of life free from the deformations of arbitrary domination.

The concept of the ideal speech situation offers a foundation for rationality other than Landes' 'masquerade of objectivity' that is uncovered when other subject positions are granted admission. It extrapolates from the very existence of speech and from the intention to understand and be understood built into it. In its ideality, it entails symmetry and reciprocity among subjects in the relationship. It offers not a description but a measure against which the actual can be evaluated. It is specifically attentive to deformations of its ideality arising from the 'social structure' in which the speech situation is set, particularly those that are not fully conscious.

Gender and race are deformations of the ideal speech situation that have been taken for granted in the work life of universities. To criticize these is not to undermine the very fabric of the university by undermining the claim to objectivity and objective judgment on which the authority of its faculty is based, as Marchak (1996) suggests. On the contrary, it is to discover deformations that injure the university's commitment to rationality and truth and its claims to universality. Furthermore, a dialogue conducted under 'rules' of symmetry and reciprocity in the 'ideal speech situation' would proceed very differently from that which ensued from the 'chilly climate' Report. The problem of the gender organization of the everyday—that what women experience is not what men experience and vice versa—would be recognized from the outset. Both parties would have been committed to listening to each other. Both parties would be committed to the possibility of being changed in the course of dialogue. The women might say, 'Listen, here are some of the things that we have experienced in classrooms as students or in meetings and hallways and offices as faculty: we have been silenced, ridiculed, ignored, depreciated. And the men would say: 'We don't know what you're talking about. And the women say: 'Just listen, just be prepared to believe that this is what we experience in our relationships with you.' White feminists have entered into just such dialogues with women of colour in which we (white feminists) have learned something of what it is that we (white people) may be doing that silences, marginalizes, and depreciates women of colour. To take such critiques seriously means examining them, not as accusations, but rather as a realization of the university's commitment to rationality and truth that calls for a reappraisal of its taken-for-granted everyday practices.

Far from threatening the foundations of the university, critiques of racism and sexism are better understood as committed to removing deformations that have been historically sedimented in the everyday working life and the intellectual practices of universities in North America. Those who make the critique can be seen as measuring a university against an implicit ideal of fully reciprocal and symmetrical dialogue as foundational to universities' claims to universality and commitment to rational discourse.

PART III

Women as Academic Leaders, Faculty and Students

A.

Women Leaders

CHAPTER 16

THE LEADERSHIP CHALLENGE FOR WOMEN COLLEGE PRESIDENTS

MARGARET JABLONSKI

Considerable research on leadership in general, and on higher education in particular, outlines traditional leadership theory (Stodgill, 1974; Bass, 1985; Bennis and Nanus, 1985; Schon, 1984; Chaffee & Tierney, 1988; Neumann & Bensimon, 1990; Birnbaum, 1989). There is a conspicuous lack of research, however, on women leaders in colleges and universities (Shakeshaft, 1987,1989). It is time for us to listen to the women leading our institutions and to learn from their experience.

In this article, I examine the leadership styles of seven women college presidents by summarizing their perceptions of their leadership styles. Profiles of women leaders in academia emerge, including their ideas on what it means to be a female executive. I also examine the perceptions of some of the faculty who interact with the presidents. If there are differences between the leaders' perceptions of their styles and what others believe or experience, what may be contributing to this discrepancy? Answers to these questions have implications for women as leaders in academia.

Four factors influenced the framework for this study: the practical experiences of women as academic leaders described in the literature and discussed at conferences, the traditional literature on leadership, emerging alternative models for leadership and human development, and my interest in women's issues in academia. A review of leadership literature yielded more than 350 definitions of leadership as of the early 1990s. Instead of focusing on power or influence theories or organizational models, I examined leadership and gender, approaching this study as a feminist researcher exploring how women view the world and their place in it. I expected to find that women college presidents successfully employed alternative, participatory leadership styles, such as those described in some gender studies (Desjardins, 1989; Shakeshaft, 1987; Haring-Hidore et al., 1990, Aisenberg & Harrington, 1988). In the analysis of the interviews, it became clear that these presidents *believed they utilized participatory and empowering forms of leadership, but their faculties' perceptions often differed.*

Leadership Theory

The literature on leadership can be organized into categories such as trait approaches, power or influence theories, behavioral models, contingency factors, and organizational constructions (Stodgill, 1974; Bass, 1981; Bensimon, Neumann, & Birnbaum, 1989). The traditional trait research lists desirable or necessary traits such as assertiveness, originality, sociability, humor, risk-taking, rational decision-making, and self-confidence as common to successful leaders (Stodgill, 1974; Bass, 1981; Bennis & Nanus, 1985). Although trait theory research no longer continues as a major

---

Reprinted from *Initiatives*, Vol. 57, Issue 4, 1996. Copyright © 1996 National Association for Women in Education.

focus of study, many previous studies in academia describe successful presidents in terms of characteristics such as superior judgment, decisiveness, confidence, rational thought, and charisma (Fisher, 1984). Trait research related to gender examines the concept of gender in relation to masculine and feminine traits (Korabik, 1982; Leary, 1985; Marshall, 1985; Bem, 1984, 1987; Deaux & Kite, 1987, others). Some research concludes that gender is the primary cognitive identification because our culture values it as such (Bem, 1984; 1987). Feminine qualities include caring, nurturing, maintaining, supporting, healing, reflection, and evaluating (Leary,1985).

Another major category of research focuses upon how leaders influence followers and the reciprocal relationship between leaders and followers. Societal changes in the United States such as movement to a global economy, changes in organizational design, and a transition from a mechanistic world view to a contextual, complex, and relational paradigm (Rogers, 1988) forces the rethinking of conventional leadership theories to include transforming expectations. Transformational leaders use such strategies as articulating a vision, providing meaning through communication, and developing trust among group members (Bennis & Nanus, 1985). Coaching is commonly used in academia instead of controlling or coercing followers, and personal power is used more often than organizational power (Krausz, 1984).

Gender studies with women subjects appear to point to the use of one style: participatory. Women are more likely to empower subordinates by using participatory management (DiBrito & DiBrito, 1986; Shakeshaft, 1987). Women in both business and education are found to have an open, people-oriented philosophy of leadership that includes communication, motivation, goal direction, fairness, teamwork, delegation, and participatory decision-making (Burstyn, 1980; Funk, 1988; Morgan, 1986).

Much research on gender and sex role orientation points to an incongruity between women's sex role and status and their occupational role and status (Kantor, 1977; Lafontaine & McKenzie, 1985; Deaux & Kite, 1987; Dachler, 1988). Women are evaluated on being feminine and managerial at the same time.

When women act in a manner that emphasizes the feminine, they risk losing their authority. When they act "managerial," they are sanctioned by both men and women (Nivea & Gutek, 1981).

A consideration of environment, leader-follower relations, and roles in contingency leadership theory is missing from most of the research on women and leadership. A contingent approach is developed in the feminist research model where multiple perspectives are explored. In this paradigm, the context of a situation determines the meaning for each participant (Marshall, 1985).

Gender-based research on women in academic administration does not fall precisely into traditional organizational models. For example, Maslow's hierarchy of needs is based on the world of work according to males: the highest level being self-actualization in the economic realm (Schein, 1980). Feminist research suggests different priorities for women, including maintaining relationships and fostering community (Gilligan, 1982; Miller, 1986; Shakeshaft, 1987).

Qualitative Research Methods

The use of qualitative methods has improved the study of leadership by introducing a wider range of contextual variables into the analysis of leadership styles (Bryman, Bresnen, Beardsworth, & Keil, 1988). Some of the most highly regarded studies in the past decade on leadership used interviewing as one or the only approach (Peters & Waterman, 1982, Bennis & Nanus, 1985). Interviewing appears to be a particularly relevant approach to studying women (Oakley, 1981; Belenky et al., 1986; Hegelsen, 1990). Qualitative research assumes that the perspective of another can be made explicit using methods such as observation and interviewing (Patton, 1980; Miles & Huberman, 1984).

In order to gain detailed descriptive information of how each of the presidents viewed themselves as leaders, this study used the qualitative method of interviewing. To determine congruence between the leader's perspective and that of her faculty, I explored similar topics with five faculty members on each campus, using an interview guide for all subjects. However, the interview was open to change in direction based on the individual.

The seven presidents in this project were drawn from the northeast, where approximately 12 percent of the colleges are led by women. All but one were presidents of smaller institutions, ranging in size from 1,000 to 3,000 undergraduate students. Their tenure as CEOs ranged from under two years to 10 years or more. Three had made a conscious choice to seek the presidency and sought out career opportunities, such as an academic vice presidency, to develop leadership skills. Six of the seven presidents hold a doctoral degree and the majority had been accomplished faculty before assuming the presidency.

The majority of women were married (5 of 7) and four have children (1.4 average); one was divorced and one single. All were in their late forties or early fifties. The presidents represented nondenominational campuses: two private liberal arts schools, two women's colleges, two state institutions, and one technical college; five of the institutions were private and two public. The number of full-time faculty on their campuses ranged from 25 to over 300. Five of the institutions had never before had a woman as president.

Perceptions of Presidents

The presidents described themselves, for the most part, as different from many of their male predecessors. They believed they used participatory techniques, empowered others, and led their campuses by collaboration, participation, and open communication. The generative leadership model developed by Sagaria and Johnsrud (1988) describes a process that encourages participation, creativity, empowerment, and open communication. The generative model provides a framework for organizing the material derived from the interviews with the presidents. The following themes related to the generative leadership model were derived from the data: empowerment, collaboration, communication, and decision-making. The fifth theme of feminism emerged from this study and is added to the model. Generative leaders create a work culture that values people. Such leadership engenders trust, collaboration, shared decision-making, connections between people, and valuing of differences. Although generative leadership was not defined as "female," Sagaria and Johnsrud (1988) indicated that women used generative leadership.

Empowerment

These presidents sought to build a community on campus by giving power and ownership to others. "The more people feel empowered the more comfortable they are at including other people in decision-making," said one president.

Four presidents described how it was important to "empower people" or "enable" others. One president discussed methods of including people on committees and giving them "the room they need" to grow and develop. This ability to empower others was central to the majority of the president's generative styles.

> My goal ... is to be empowering to people. So that I really bring out the best of the people around me. I believe it is very important in a job like this to be able to rely on the strength of others. The most important decisions you make are decisions about your key colleagues.

Another president described what she would not do: she would not manipulate others.

> Finally I would say in all this that any sense of condescension, paternalism, is just dead wrong. So you don't do this because you think these people are on a chess board to be manipulated. This is not manipulation.

Several presidents made the distinction between involving people in the process, asking for their feedback, and building a consensus. They recognized that there would be times when consensus was not possible, such as around budget reductions and personnel decisions. In these cases, providing a sense of direction is required. These presidents acknowledged that even though they may want to empower others, the situation may call for a different approach.

Collaboration

Realizing that collaboration requires people to work together to solve problems, these presidents said they were not as "respectful" of hierarchy and they sought to decentralize decision-making. One president described her leadership style this way:

> Finding the right people, empowering them, and having them work together, even without me, so their patterns of collaboration hold up well. Somewhat blurring the lines of hierarchy for getting things done, but not blurring them for making sure that people feel responsible for certain kinds of things. This place is extremely participatory and process oriented.

Participation by all members of a group in decision-making can take significant amounts of time. The processes of collaboration require more time than does the effort of one person. The presidents usually thought it was time well invested, even when their agenda took longer to move along. They also believed in having people participate in the implementation of the agenda.

Communication

The majority considered it important to listen to others, especially faculty. These women were not reluctant to share ideas early on, ask for feedback, and change their minds. They also acknowledged that once the expectation of a more participatory form of communication had been established, people sometimes got confused when it appeared a decision was made unilaterally or against the recommendations of the group. This was evident on several campuses in connection with budget and personnel decisions, which the presidents generally made alone after seeking advice.

Two of the presidents discussed a link between communication and gender, one that takes into consideration the parties involved in the communication process. This relates to the desire for women to maintain and foster connections with others (Miller, 1986; Gilligan, 1982).

> I would really prefer to find ways of communicating and of solving problems so that we don't diminish anybody. And I've noticed that this is not a priority in the world at large. I find that generally a female, rather than a male tends to do this. Men are much more willing than I am to have a head-on confrontation.

Decision-making

In generative leadership, the leader values shared decision-making both as a process and as a means of enhancing outcomes (Sagaria & Johnsrud, 1988). A preference for involving others in decision-making was seen in this study. The presidents gathered information from a variety of sources and asked for advice before making decisions.

> I think there have been times when people wanted me to just make a decision—period, to get it out of the way, where I wasn't willing to do that without listening to more people. It is frustrating to people sometimes.

> We had a very long and arduous and thorough study of what the master plan for the college should be. There were many people involved: faculty, students, trustees and various possibilities and overall conceptual plans. In the end a master plan was adopted that I think most people understood, and it is working out.

The presidents I interviewed seemed much more concerned about the process of decision-making than their male counterparts in the literature (Schein, 1980; Hershey & Blanchard, 1982). In some areas, they were willing to have the community make the decision for them. For example, one college community demanded divestment of company stocks with business in South Africa and persuaded the president to take action.

The presidents reserved the right to make final decisions in two areas: budget and personnel. The budget process at these colleges followed the traditional models of bureaucratic management. In the personnel area, however, the presidents appeared reluctant to terminate staff, acknowledging this as a concern or "failure" for them. They gave examples of critical personnel decisions when they waited longer than they should have to act. In each case, the conflict was around the concept of interdependence and cooperation between team members to carry out the vision of the president.

> I believe it is very important in a job like this to be able to rely on the strength of others. The most important decisions you make are decisions about your key colleagues. If you get the right people doing the right things, then the whole place goes

swimmingly. If you don't then you spend all of your time trying to repair your errors.

The literature on women's identity development supports this concept of maintaining relationships, sometimes at a cost to oneself or to the institution (Miller, 1984; Surrey, 1985).

> I was not sufficiently sensitive to personnel decisions at the beginning. I didn't realize how important they could be. It wasn't like a problem in political science where you analyze the pros and cons, and decide whether someone goes or stays. You have to think about this person is like an organ in a body, and they mesh through veins and arteries and bones with lots of other people. And if you lift the person out, it isn't as though everything else is fine. You have to think about the connections, and everything else is going to bleed. Who is going to feel threatened, or unsupported, or unhappy.

This feeling mirrors that reported on by Miller (1986) in her analysis of women as subordinates, serving the needs of others and developing in the context of connections with others. If affiliations are central to a woman's life, then breaking such a connection becomes a threatening or difficult thing to do, even for these powerful women.

> I wish I had responded to personnel problems more quickly. I thought if it involved people then I should take my time. I kept the finance person longer than I should have, and the academic dean longer than I should have. I have a problem letting people go. Whose responsibility is it when people fail?

Making the tough decisions, including saying no when necessary and appropriate was described as a difficult part of the position. Women have traditionally been the ones to smooth things over and to make sure everyone feels positive with the outcome of a situation.

> If I take a position on something, do something that makes a lot of people unhappy, one of my jobs is to make it possible for those people to handle that unhappiness in a way that is better than worse... Yes, there is a great amount of diplomacy, but I started with a situation which an action had to be taken. It is not just mediating, I'm talking about where it starts with the issue of principle, but that is not enough to make tough decisions and make them right. That is only the beginning.

One president was a clear exception in this area. She was directive, forceful, and decisive. She made very difficult personnel decisions about three of her vice presidents within the first year of her tenure. She terminated one of them and fought with the board of trustees over her power and authority to do so. This president said "I was willing to go to the wall to fight over who was going to run the place. I was not willing to just sit in the chair. I had to win".

Finally, several of the presidents indicated that in certain instances, they would like to be more decisive but felt constrained by the process-oriented environment. They struggled with the question of when it is important to retain authority for decision-making and when the outcome is more important than the process.

> This place is extremely participatory and process-oriented, and sometimes I do get frustrated with that. Because I think we have too many committees and too many people who need to be consulted. So that if I had my druthers, I suppose I would be more presumptive than I can be. At another kind of an institution I might make more decisions more quickly without waiting for the process to unfold.

This president recognized that the more empowered the community is, the greater the debate and the longer the process may be.

Faculty Perceptions of Women Presidents

I interviewed thirty-five faculty on seven campuses about the leadership style of their female president. Only two of the seven presidents were described by their faculty as generative leaders. The majority of the faculty on five campuses in this study used the language of traditional male leadership theory in describing their presidents.

Three leadership styles were attributed to the majority of presidents in this study: hierarchical, entrepreneurial, and task oriented (Astin & Scherei, 1980). The hierarchical president acts as a focal point, taking in information and making most of the decisions. The entrepreneurial president takes risks, is competitive and aggressive. The task-oriented president operates as a functionalist, exhibiting competence and effectiveness. Some faculty saw their presidents as controlling the academic environment, directing others instead of empowering them, and using an inner circle of confidants to manage the campus. At least one president agreed, saying, "I think that there has been a major move away from an attempt to create more collaborative and consensual approaches to a more hierarchical."

Faculty descriptions of the leadership of women presidents were usually indistinguishable from those that might have been made of male presidents. All were described as very strong, competent individuals. The faculty expressed concerns about the hierarchical, bureaucratic approach and the need for power and control they perceived in their presidents. They thought their presidents were directive and purposeful in coordinating the management of the campuses, adopting a rational, analytical approach to problem-solving. The faculty perceived their presidents as often frustrated by faculty governance which demanded committee participation.

> I think it is an aggressive style of knowing what she wants and going after it. I think the committee has input and she listens. I am not sure that will change her mind . . . I think it is an instant gut sort of reaction.

The faculty feared that their presidents could not lead their colleges through difficult financial times. The presidents were forced to spend much of their time on budget issues, fundraising, personnel issues, and dealing with external constituencies, while faculty wanted an academic leader who would influence the curriculum and the campus community.

> I think she gave up too quickly on her vision of what was needed for the college because it was hard for her. She talked about wanting to create a collaborative community environment where the quality of life was important and the community would do a lot of shared decision-making. I think she underestimated how hard it was, and rather than go back and keep trying at it, she threw up her hands.

The Issue of Gender

Five of the presidents wove women's issues, the concept of feminism, achieving equality, and appreciating the uniqueness and differences of women into their conversations. A few spoke of the impact of the women's movement on their lives, the importance of women's networks and associations to them, the scholarship they have engaged in around the topic of feminism. The two women's college presidents spoke about the importance of leading an institution for women by celebrating contributions of women and providing a role model for others. Some talked of hiring women to affect the culture of the college. The presidents structured opportunities where mentoring could develop. One president described a clear connection between gender and leadership.

> It seems to me there are ways in which women, in our culture, in this time in history, I qualify on those grounds, tend to use very different styles than men. Not always, and not by every individual. We are not talking about absolute gender differences . . . It seems to me that women are more likely to be process oriented, more likely to be attentive to the nuances of individual people's differences and needs, less likely to think hierarchically and bureaucratically, and less likely to be comfortable with authoritarian modes of behavior.

Although these presidents considered work to be central to their lives, they wove relationships and family into their depictions of themselves. They integrated their professional and personal selves, valuing caring and nurturing aspects, as well as independence and autonomy. All of them mentioned family as a source of support and as a distraction from their work.

Faculty were ambiguous or negative about the link between gender and presidential leadership style. At three colleges, no consensus existed among the faculty on the effect gender may have on leadership style. In general, the faculty resisted equating stereotypical notions of "feminine" behavior with their presidents, instead describing them in traditional male terms: analytical, aggressive, tough, and strong-willed. These three presidents were found to be gender neutral or acting in a stereotypical male approach.

Some other faculty use stereotypically negative metaphors to describe their president: the heroine, the mother, the matriarch, the nun. Another described the president as a feminine, soft woman who "does nice things with her hair and is proud of her figure. She's very much a woman." Others indicated that their president had adopted traditional male patterns of communication such as being direct, looking one in the eye, speaking in a deep tone of voice.

Although both male and female faculty members discussed their desire to have their presidents adopt alternative leadership styles, the voices of the female faculty were more passionate. "She refuses to get drawn into conversations that set up a sort of polemic about women and gender... If I make statements that women do science differently than men, she is all over me." In some cases, the female faculty clearly expected a more participatory leadership style from the female president than they had demanded from previous male presidents. The majority of the faculty were clearly conflicted about the issue of gender relating to the leadership style of their president.

Conclusions and Speculations

This study led to many questions: Why did the women here describe themselves as generative leaders? What accounts for the discrepancies between the presidents and their faculties' perspectives? Is the traditional model of leadership a necessary one in some conditions?

The presidents, in general, believed they used a participatory style that empowered others as "the right thing to do." Many of them cited leadership development programs or the emerging literature in the field when describing their style. Another factor influencing their conversations about leadership was their participation in other leadership studies (5 of 7), which had provided them with feedback on their styles and terminology to frame their experiences. In their interviews, they may have presented their sense of what they wanted to be, or are trying to be, instead of how they really are. They may have unintentionally omitted "negative" perceptions they had received about themselves, or they may have wanted to portray a more positive image for this study.

My observation of the presidents and the faculty members in this study is that they developed expectations about leadership and gender over their lifetimes. Cultural, social, environmental, and organizational influences on the individual development of each president appeared to be primarily traditional. They had male role models, male boards of trustees to report to, and many male faculty leaders to deal with. In theory, the presidents espoused generative leadership, but their colleges' governance structures, committees, and boards of trustees could not support such a model. Organizations need to be structured differently to accommodate alternative leadership styles.

Both male and female faculty appeared to be in conflict over their hope to see a more participatory style from their presidents and a desire for strong, aggressive leaders. This discrepancy would also follow if they accepted the stereotypical caretaker role for women and projected it onto their female president. In this case, faculty, and women faculty in particular, could not help but be disappointed when their presidents were not as nurturing and caring as they expected. If the organizational constraints are the same for male and female presidents, then women CEOs are clearly at a disadvantage when being evaluated as leaders. Our expectations for leadership by women need to be congruent with expectations of leadership by men.

Several important questions arose from this study which need further exploration: What factors contribute to the gap between theory and practice in leadership? Should a female president change her style to address faculty concerns or the needs of the college? Do faculty, especially female faculty, expect too much from their female president? Is the academic environment conducive to generative leadership?

This study of seven women college presidents provided an opportunity for the women to describe their leadership styles, and for some faculty to discuss their perceptions of presidential leadership. The findings discussed here may help presidents and faculty develop a deeper understanding of the complex nature of academic leadership. We need to reexamine our expectations of women as presidents in light of the realities of their positions and organizations. Women presidents and other senior-level women in academia would benefit from continuing discussion of the discrepancies found here.

References

Aisenberg, N., & Harrington, M. (1988). *Women of academe.* Amherst: University of Massachusetts Press.

Astin, A., & Scheirei, R. (1980). *Maximizing leadership effectiveness.* San Francisco: Jossey Bass Publishers.

Bass, B. (1981). *Stodgill's handbook of leadership.* New York: Free Press.

Bass, B. (1985). *Leadership and performance beyond expectation.* New York: Free Press.

Belenky, M.F., Clinchy, B.M., Goldberger, N.R., & Tarule, J.M. (1986). *Women's ways of knowing.* New York: Basic Books.

Bem, S.L. (1984). *Androgyny and gender schema theory: A conceptual and empirical integration.* Paper presented at the Nebraska Symposium on Motivation.

Bem, S.L. (1987) Is androgyny a solution? In M. Walsh, (Ed.) *The psychology of women* (pp. 206–225). New Haven: Yale University Press.

Bennis, W., & Nanus, B. (1985). *Leaders: The strategies for taking charge.* New York: Harper & Row.

Bensimon, E., Neumann, A., & Birnbaum, R. (1989). *Making sense of administrative leadership: The "L" word in higher education.* ASHE-ERIC Higher Education Report No. 1. Washington, DC: The George Washington University, School of Education and Human Development

Birnbaum, R. (1989). The implicit leadership theories of college and university presidents. *Review of Higher Education* 60(2), 123-135.

Bryman, A., Bresnen, M., Beardsworth, A., & Keil, T. (1988). Qualitative research and the study of leadership. *Human Relations* 41(1), 13–30.

Burstyn, J. (1980). Historical perspectives on women in educational leadership. In S.K. Biklen & M. Brannigan (Eds.), *Women and educational leadership* (pp. 65–75). Lexington, MA: D.C. Heath & Company.

Chaffee, E., & Tierney, W. (1988). *Collegiate culture and leadership strategies.* New York: American Council on Education/Macmillan.

Dachler, P. (1988). Constraints on the emergence of new vistas in leadership and management research: An epistemological overview. In J. Hunt, R. Baliga, B. Rajarman, P. Cachlere, & C. Schriesheim (Eds.), *Emerging leadership vistas.* Lexington, MA: D.C. Heath & Company.

Deaux, K. & Kite, M. (1987). Thinking about gender. In B. Hess & M. Ferre (Eds.), *Analyzing gender.* Beverly Hills, CA: Sage Publications.

Desjardins, C. (1989). Gender issues and community college leadership. *AAWCIC Journal,* 5–10.

DiBrito, C., Carpenter, S. & DiBrito, W. (1986). Women in leadership and management: Review of the literature 1985 update. *NASPA Journal* 23(3), 22–31.

Fisher, J. (1984). *The power of the presidency.* New York: MacMillan Publishers.

Funk, C. (1988, May). *Career paths and working patterns of women in mid-management roles in business and education.* Paper presented at Women and Work Conference, May 1988.

Gilligan, C. (1982). *In a different voice.* Cambridge: Harvard University Press.

Haring-Hidore, M., Freeman, S., Phelps, S., Spann, N., & Wooten, R. (1990). Women administrators' ways of knowing. *Education and Urban Society* 22(2), 170–181.

Helgesen, S. (1990). *The female advantage: Women's ways of leadership.* New York: Doubleday.

Hersey, P., & Blanchard, K. (1982). *Management of organizational behavior.* Englewood Cliffs: Prentice Hall.

Kanter, R.M. (1977) *Men and women of the corporation.* New York: Basic Books.

Korabik, A. (1982). Sex role orientation and leadership style. *International Journal of Women's Studies* 5, 329–337.

Krausz, R. (1985). Power and leadership in organizations. *Transactional Analysis Journal* 16, 85–94.

Lafontaine, E., & McKenzie, B.J. (1985). Being out on the inside of higher education administration: Women's role and status incongruity. In P. Farrant (Ed.), *Strategies and attitudes: Women in educational administration* (pp. 145–151). Washington, DC: National Association for Women Deans, Administrators, and Counselors.

Leary, M. (1985). Men and women—What are the differences and does it matter? *Management Education and Development* 16,140–154.

Marshall, J. (1985). Paths of personal and professional development for women managers. *Management Education and Development* 16,169–179.

Miles., M., & Huberman, AM. (1984). *Qualitative data analysis.* Beverly Hills, CA: Sage Publications.

Miller, J. (1986) *Toward a new psychology of women.* Boston: Beacon Press.

Morgan L. (1986). *Leadership and managerial styles of top-level women administrators in four-year institutions of higher education.* (Doctoral Dissertation, University of Pittsburgh, 1986).

Neumann, A., & Bensimon, E. (1990). Constructing the presidency: College presidents' images of their leadership roles— A comparative study. *Journal of Higher Education* 61(6), 678–701.

Nivea, V., & Gutek, B. (1981). *Women and work: A psychological perspective.* New York: Praeger Publishers.

Oakley, A. (1981). Interviewing women: A contradiction in terms. In H. Roberts (Ed.), *Doing feminist research* (pp. 31–49). London: Routledge & Kegan Paul Co.

Patton, M. (1980). *Qualitative evaluation methods*. Beverly Hills, CA: Sage Publications.

Peters, T.J., & Waterman, R.H. (1982). *In search of excellence: Lessons from America's best-run companies.* New York: Harper & Row.

Rogers, J. (1988). New paradigm leadership: Integrating the female ethos. *Initiatives* 51(4), 1–8.

Sagaria, M.D., & Johnsrud, L.K. (1988). Generative leadership. In Sagaria, M. D. (Ed.), *Empowering Women: Leadership Development Strategies on Campus.* New Directions for Student Services, 13–26. San Francisco: Jossey Bass Publishers.

Schein, E.(1980). *Organizational psychology,* 3rd ed. Englewood Cliffs: Prentice-Hall, Inc.

Schon, D. (1984). Leadership as reflection-in-action. In T.J. Sergiovanni & J.E. Corbally (Eds.), *Leadership and organizational culture: New perspectives on administrative theory and practice* (Urbana, IL: University of Illinois Press. pp. 36-63).

Shakeshaft, C. (1987). *Women in educational administration.* Newbury Park, CA: Sage Publications.

Shakeshaft, C. (1989). The gender gap in research in educational administration. *Educational Administration Quarterly* 25(4), 324–337.

Stodgill, R. (1974). *Stodgill's handbook of leadership: A survey of theory.* New York: Free Press.

Surrey, J. (1985). *Self-in relation: A theory of women's sense of self.* Wellesley MA: Stone Center Papers.

Margaret Jablonski is Associate Dean, Residence and Campus Activities, at the Massachusetts Institute of Technology.

CHAPTER 17

WOMEN AND THE COMMUNITY COLLEGE PRESIDENCY: CHALLENGES AND POSSIBILITIES

DEBORAH M. DICROCE

This chapter analyzes the impact of women on the community college presidency and their potential to make a unique contribution by connecting the characteristic strengths of their gender to the power of their office.

"Few things that can happen to a nation are more important than the invention of a new form of verse." So declared twentieth-century English poet T. S. Eliot (1927, p. xii). As part of my presidential inaugural address in September 1989, I used this quote to illustrate the dramatic effect the community college has had on American higher education. Now, almost six years later, I return to Eliot's words to establish the thesis of this chapter. This time, however, the new verse form is women community college presidents. Quite pointedly, my thesis is this: by connecting the characteristic strengths of their gender to the power of their office, women who are community college presidents have a golden opportunity to make a unique contribution to their institutions and society as a whole. They are what is happening to today's community college. They are indeed its new verse form, and their success in realizing the possibilities and meeting the challenges of their office has ramifications for society at large. This chapter explores the multiple connections among the multiple realities of this thesis by portraying the current status of women in the presidency, defining the leadership characteristics of women presidents, connecting these characteristics to a clarion call for new executive leadership, relating this call to the community college presidency, and proposing a framework for women presidents to effect meaningful institutional change and impact the larger public policy issues of academe and society at large.

Status of Women in the Presidency

Without question, women have made significant progress in attaining presidencies in American two-year and four-year institutions. According to the American Council on Education's most recent published analysis of women chief executive officers ("More Women Leading Higher Education Institutions," 1992, p. 1), 348, or 12 percent of the 3,000-plus chief executive officers (CEOs) employed in academe are women. This figure represents a 135 percent increase in the number of women CEOs heading American collegiate institutions between 1975 and 1992. An informal analysis of a March 19, 1993, ACE roster of women CEOs suggests that the trend, although slowing down, is continuing. As of that date, 379, or 12.6 percent of the CEOs were women.

Although increases are found in all types of institutions, they are especially significant in the two-year public sector. Of the 348 women CEOs in 1992, 136, or 39 percent headed two-year institutions and, of these, 77.9 percent were in the public sector. The 1993 roster puts the figure at 153, or 40.4 percent, with 81.7 percent in the public sector.

The point is that two-year colleges appear to be at the forefront in placing women in their presidencies. The question is why. On the one hand, one might expect the community college to be the pacesetter in hiring women presidents. Since its founding, it has been hailed as the "people's college," "democracy's college," and "opportunity's college." With women over half its student body, it demonstrates a strong commitment to the values of open access, diversity, and inclusiveness. On the other hand, the steadily rising number of women presidents in the community college may simply be a result of the institution's lower hierarchical status in academe. Put less diplomatically, the community college is at the bottom of the power rung anyway; why not leave the messy business of women CEOs to it?

Interestingly, women CEOs at the senior institutional level inadvertently give some credence to the latter explanation. In a 1991 news story in the *Chronicle of Higher Education*, several women CEOs were interviewed on the status of women presidents (Leatherman, 1991). They agreed that women have made considerable strides in the presidential arena; however, they also agreed that women have had less opportunity for the "plum leadership jobs" and are often left in the position of "tak[ing] on the presidency at a troubled institution, or be[ing] offered none at all" (Leatherman, 1991, p. A19). Said Paula Brownlee, the former president of Hollins College, "There's no conspiracy about it. I think it is a matter of what are the alternative options for the women versus the alternative options for the men. I suspect for women the range is not as great" (Leatherman, 1991, p. A19). What are the implications for the community college presidency? At the time of the news article, 41 percent of the 360 women CEOs were at two-year colleges (Leatherman, 1991, p. A20), yet no community college president was interviewed for the piece. One cannot help but speculate why.

Regardless of reason, the connection between gender and power is difficult to miss. However, the community college offers the ideal setting for women presidents to provide the leadership to redefine the connection and, in so doing, to have a positive impact on their institutions, the larger higher education community, and society as a whole.

Leadership Characteristics of Women Presidents

"If we had a keen vision and feeling of all ordinary human life, it would be like hearing the grass grow and the squirrel's heart beat, and we should die of that roar which lies on the other side of silence" (G. Eliot, 1872, p. 189). Most versed in women's studies recognize these words as an oft-quoted excerpt from George Eliot's *Middlemarch* (1872). For purposes here, they are a powerful context for an analysis of the leadership characteristics of women presidents. Indeed these characteristics are rooted deeply in Eliot's "other side of silence."

Carol Gilligan's *In a Different Voice* (1982) does an excellent job of penetrating this "other side." Gilligan traces the development of women's morality to notions of responsibility and care. She contends there is a difference between men's and women's decision-making and judgment calls. For women, she argues, there is less likely to be a sense of "blind justice" that relies on abstract laws and absolute impartiality. Instead, women tend to have a context of moral choice which acknowledges both that the needs of individuals cannot always be deduced from general rules and principles and that moral choice must be determined inductively from the particular experiences each participant brings to the situation. In contrast to the male vision of a hierarchy of power, women view the world as a web of relationships.

Others have amplified on Gilligan's work. Belenky, Clinchy, Goldberger, and Tarule (1986) take Gilligan's idea of moral choice for women and identify what they call "women's ways of knowing." They claim that women come to know through silence, through listening to the voices of others, through the quest for self, through the voice of reason, and through connecting all of the above. Josselson (1987) takes Gilligan's sense of self and suggests it affects women's individual approaches to forming relationships, making decisions about family and children, pursuing careers, developing religious beliefs and worldviews, and more. And, in her rather provocative book, *The Female World,* Bernard (1981) provides a comprehensive study of the female ethos, concluding the female world is based on an ethos of love and duty whereas the male world is based on an ethos of power and competition. For all, the notion of interconnectedness holds a paramount place in women's reasoning structures.

Finding the roar to this "other side of silence" has led to a plethora of research which strongly supports the notion that women's leadership styles differ from men's. Rosener (1990) studied men and women executives with similar backgrounds and concluded that the way they managed was different. Rosener found men to lead through a series of what she calls "transactions," rewarding employees for a job well done and punishing them for a job poorly done. She found women leaders more interested in transforming people's self-interest into organizational goals, with the women being quick to encourage participation, share power and information, enhance other people's self-worth, and get others excited about their work.

"The Web" Versus "The Pyramid." Helgesen's work (1990a) paints a similar picture. Helgesen conducted an in-depth study of four women executives and found them to be successful precisely because they did not follow what some might call the more traditional (male) model of management. For example, they freely exhibited and used such stereotypically female strengths as supporting, encouraging and teaching, soliciting input, and, in general, creating a positive, collegial work environment. As Helgesen puts it, women leaders like being "in the center of things, rather than at the top, which they perceived as a lonely and disconnected position" (Helgesen, 1990a, p. 44). Consequently, they often avoid traditional hierarchies in favor of "circular management," metaphorically being a part of "the web" rather than "the pyramid" (Helgesen, 1990b, p. F13).

"Women's Leadership." Numerous other studies done over the past several years have led to similar conclusions. However, the surest sign that the differences in women's and men's leadership styles have become institutionalized is the special billing they receive in Aburdene and Naisbitt's *Megatrends for Women* (1992).

Aburdene and Naisbitt coined the term "women's leadership" to describe what they consider to be a leadership personality that reflects "women's values" and subsequently translates them into "leadership behavior" (p. 89).

Specifically, they identify 25 leadership behaviors and cluster them into six central traits as follows:

> *Empower.* Women "reward" rather than "punish," "invite speaking out" rather than "demand respect," are "motivators" rather than "drill sergeants," "value creativity" rather than "impose discipline," are interested in "vision" rather than the "bottom line."
>
> *Restructure.* Women seek to "change" rather than "control," "connect" rather than "rank," establish a "network" rather than a "hierarchy." They are "holistic" and "systemic" rather than "mechanistic" and "compartmental." They are "flexible" rather than "rigid."
>
> *Teaching.* Women "facilitate" rather than "give orders." They prefer the "teaching archetype" to the "military archetype."
>
> *Role Model.* Women "act as role models"; they do not "issue orders."
>
> *Openness.* Women cultivate a "nourishing environment for growth." They "reach out" rather than up or down. They advocate "information availability" rather than "information control."
>
> *Questioner.* Women "ask the right questions" rather than "know all the answers."
> [Aburdene and Naisbitt, 1992, p. 91]

So how well does this research depict the leadership characteristics of women who are community college presidents? According to the work of Gillett-Karam (1994), it reflects them quite well. Gillett-Karam attempted to see to what extent (if any) five cluster dimensions of transformational leadership—namely, vision, people orientation, motivation orientation, empowerment, and values orientation—were gender based. Although she found the general clusters as a whole were not gender based, four "separate behaviors" within the clusters were significantly higher for women and two were significantly higher for men. The "feminine" behaviors were as follows: "(1) risk taking or taking appropriate risks to bring about change, a *vision* behavior; (2) demonstrates caring and respect for individual differences, a *people* behavior; (3) acts collaboratively, an *influence* behavior; and (4) builds openness and trust, a *values* behavior" (Gillett-Karam, 1994, p. 103).

The "masculine" behaviors were as follows: "(1) rewards others contingent on their effort and performance, a *people* behavior; and (2) is characterized by a bias for action, an *influence* behavior" (Gillett-Karam, 1994, p. 103).

In short, Gillett-Karam's findings corroborate the more general research conducted on women executives. They also characterize a recent group of impressive dissertation studies on women community college presidents (Adams, 1993; Guill, 1991; Mennuti, 1987; Miles, 1986; Sanders, 1990; Schmidt, 1990), which collectively lends further credence to Aburdene and Naisbitt's (1992) model of women's leadership. Suffice it to say that George Eliot's "other side of silence" is silent no more. Clearly women are beginning to redefine the power structure by redefining what constitutes effective leadership.

Clarion Call for New Executive Leadership

The New Paradigm. In virtually all fields of knowledge, researchers have begun to define a shift in the way the world operates. They refer to it as the "new paradigm." This new paradigm is characterized by a "world ordered by heterarchy" not hierarchy, with information and authority flowing across channels and input from all members of a defined entity considered valid and important (Lincoln, 1985, p. 34). It is "holographic" and "perspectival" rather than "mechanical" and "objective" (Kuh, Whitt, and Shedd, 1987, pp. 14, 23). It defines the world less in terms of "linear causality" where there is a direct connection between an action and its outcomes and more in terms of "mutual causality . . . where A and B cannot be separated into simple cause-effect relationships" (Schwartz and Ogilvy, 1979, p. 14). With this new paradigm has come a clarion call for new executive leadership. The call is resounding in both the business world and academe. It is being answered with a new leadership that manifests many of the leadership characteristics distinctly labeled as "feminine."

Framing the New Leadership. Of particular use in defining the new leadership is the recent work of Bolman and Deal (1991) on reframing organizations. Bolman and Deal developed a model for "integrated leadership" within the context of four situational frames. The frames are *structural*, where the leader analyzes and designs as the "social architect"; *human resource*, where the leader supports and empowers as the "catalyst or servant"; *political*, where the leader advocates and builds coalitions as the "advocate"; and *symbolic*, where the leader inspires and frames the experience as "prophet or poet" (Bolman and Deal, 1991, pp. 423–445). Bolman and Deal contend that the effective leader is comfortable moving in and out of the frames as the situation demands.

Interestingly the four frames resonate the roar of women from the "other side of silence." For example, they adopt (inadvertently, no doubt) Gilligan's (1982) notion of responsibility and care, giving decision making a context of moral choice. They also place the effective leader in Helgesen's (1990) web, in the center of things organizationally rather than on top of the hierarchical pyramid.

Corporate Quest for New Leadership. Adaptations of women's leadership are especially evident in the corporate world's call for new executive leadership. From its many perspectives (Guest, 1986; Kanter, 1989; Zaleznik, 1989), this new executive leadership also resonates "the other side of silence." It reflects Bernard's (1981) ethos of love and duty as well as Aburdene and Naisbitt's (1992) emphasis on empowerment, restructuring, teaching, role modeling, openness, and questioning. It also has the transformational elements of Gillett-Karam's (1994) "feminine" behaviors—namely, caring and respect, risk taking, collaboration, and openness and trust. Suffice it to say that what was once called a woman's leadership style in the twentieth century has now become the new leadership for the twenty-first century.

The New Executive Leadership and the Community College Presidency

What then are the implications of this new leadership for those who lead community colleges? In his landmark study of the community college presidency, Vaughan (1986) notes that the role of the community college president has undergone a dramatic metamorphosis over the last thirty years as community colleges themselves have changed. The ideal profile of the community college president today embraces the Leadership characteristics defined earlier in this chapter as belonging to the new leadership for the twenty-first century Indeed, recent studies of community college CEOs draw from a common lexicon to describe the effective executive Leader. The lexicon includes descriptors like "facilitator," "social convener," "interdependence," "inclusiveness," "collaboration," "visionary," "high energy" "risk taking," "openness," "human relation interactional skills," "trustworthy," "motivator," and "flexibility," (Duncan and Harlacher, 1991; Vaughan, Mellander, and Blois, 1994). One professional journal ("More Women Leading Higher Education Institutions," 1991) even featured the elegant photograph of a symphony conductor on its cover to illustrate the "leadership for the new millennium" (p. 1). Given the edge that women who are community college presidents have on this new leadership, they are well positioned to make unique contributions to their institutions and society as a whole.

Framework for Action

And what exactly are these contributions? Exactly how should these women presidents proceed? I propose the following actions as a blueprint for those who are women community college presidents to effect meaningful change at their institutions and impact larger public policy issues of academe and society at large. Of course, although the elaborations of each action are focused specifically on women presidents, the general actions are useful ones for men presidents also.

Initially break down institutional gender stereotypes. For obvious reasons, most women who enter the community college presidency do so making history for their respective institutions. In other words, as they assume the presidency they forever break the gender barrier at their institutions, creating a new "first" for the institution and often for the larger community the college serves. Above all else, women presidents must embrace the powerful symbol of the moment. And they must recognize the reality that not everyone inside and outside the institution is bursting with joy over their presidential appointment; in fact, there is most likely a bet or two riding on how long the new first will last. Nonetheless, carpe diem! Through the symbolic power of their office, women presidents can break down institutional gender stereotypes to the benefit of all faculty, staff, and students.

Penetrate institution's power structure and redefine its sense of power. Women can also use the power of their office to affect their institutions' power structures and, in so doing, to create institutional climates conducive to a collective redefining of power. Most institutions have at least some form of a "good old boy" network. They also have a collection of self-identified people who qualify only for membership in the institution's disenfranchised club. Neither the network nor the disenfranchised group hail exclusively from one gender, one ethnic background, one anything. Yet the former tends to exhibit predominantly "masculine" behavior and the latter predominantly "feminine" behavior. The opportunity (and challenge) that women presidents have is to redefine the institutional structure which gives life to both entities.

Although the best strategy for doing so is clearly individual to the institution and its culture, some obvious places to look include the institution's overall governance structure, its process for appointments to important committees, its promotion and tenure policy and practices, its recruitment and hiring policy and practices, and its salary structure. Women presidents are also well positioned to model a power structure built less on hierarchy and more on relationship, with a free exchange of information and an openness for collegial debate and discussion. They can be mentors for women faculty and staff and role models for women students. In short, through the strengths of their gender and the power of their office, women presidents can "find the voice of their reluctant followers" (Couto, 1993, p. 1) and make it the voice of a redefined sense of institutional power.

Use power of office to alter gender-related institutional policy. No community college is an island. In the most fundamental sense, community colleges are a microcosm of society at large and, as such, mirror the good and bad of that society. Sexual misconduct is a very real societal bad; yet it is often given only lip service at the people's colleges. Women community college presidents are uniquely positioned to ensure that their institutions adopt and enforce strong policies on sexual assault and sexual harassment. They can use the power of their office to "heighten [the] awareness of the need and create opportunities for [the full college community] to develop a stronger global perspective... [and] to foster a deeper understanding of violence in all its forms" (American Council on Education, 1994, p. 7). In short, they can use it to build community for the brave new world of a new century and its community colleges.

Raise collegial consciousness and initiate collegial dialogue on gender and related issues. The roar of George Eliot's "other side of silence" is alive and well on today's community college campuses. It is filled with the deafening silence of often painful collegial memories and manifests itself in isolated events of gender and related matters long ago swept under the rug institutionally. It yearns to be heard but has, for too long, thought it really had no voice. It has many reluctant followers—some men, some women; some people of color, some white; some homosexual, some heterosexual. It spans the breadth and depth of the institution's being, covering such topical areas as campus civility, multicultural diversity, collegial power, equal opportunity and conflict resolution. Simply put, women community college presidents can use the power of their office and the strengths of their gender to give this "silence" an institutional voice.

Become an active player for public policy development and debate beyond the college level. At the 1990 ACE Women Presidents' Summit, Johnetta Cole, president of Spelman College, evoked the words of the abolitionist and suffragist Sojourner Truth: "Now if one woman in one garden was said to turn the world upside down, surely all of these womenfolk here can turn it right side up again" (Blum, 1990, p. A15). Here, in large measure, lies the ultimate challenge and opportunity for women community college presidents—to somehow turn the world "right side up again." In other words, women community college presidents can contribute to society's larger agendas by becoming active players for public policy development and debate in the regional, state, and national arenas.

In 1994 ACE'S Office of Women in Higher Education published *A Blueprint for Leadership: How Women College and University Presidents Can Shape the Future.* An outgrowth of the 1993 ACE Women Presidents' Summit, this document articulated the vision for the involvement of the higher education woman executive in matters beyond her campus. As such, it has a particular relevance for women presidents in the community college. The document outlines three broad areas in which women CEOs should become involved, namely, redefinitions of war and peace, the economy and environment, and the intersection of public and private life. However, the defined areas of involvement and specific ways to be involved are of far less importance than the rallying call for involvement. As the new leadership for democracy's colleges, women community college presidents must answer this call.

Conclusion: A Call to Action

T. S. Eliot is really quite correct: "Few things that can happen to a nation are more important than the invention of a new form of verse" (1927, p. xii). For the community college, that new verse form is women community college presidents. To be sure, the challenges facing this new invention are immense but the opportunities are equally so. May those who lead answer the call to action. Society at large shall indeed be the ultimate beneficiary

References

Aburdene, P., and Naisbitt, J. *Megatrends for Women.* New York: Villard Books, 1992.

Adams, C. "Leadership Characteristics of Four Community College Women Presidents: A Case Study." Unpublished doctoral dissertation, Colorado State University, 1993.

American Council on Education. *A Blueprint for Leadership: How Women College and University Presidents Can Shape the Future.* Washington, D.C.: American Council on Education, 1994.

Belenky, M., Clinchy, B., Goldberger, N., and Tarule, J. *Women's Ways of Knowing.* New York: Basic Books, 1986.

Bernard, J. *The Female World.* New York: Free Press, 1981.

Blum, D. "165 Female College Presidents 'Honor Progress, Connect with Each Other,' and Commiserate." *Chronicle of Higher Education*, Dec. 19, 1990, pp. A13, A14.

Bolman, L., and Deal, I. *Reframing Organizations*. San Francisco: Jossey-Bass, 1991.

Couto, R. "Leadership in the 21st Century: Finding the Voice of Reluctant Followers." Paper presented at the annual meeting of the Virginia Social Science Association, Lexington, Mar. 26, 1993.

Duncan, A., and Harlacher, E. "The Twenty-First Century Executive Leader." *Community College Review*, 1991, 18 (4), 39–47.

Eliot, G. *Middlemarch*. London: Penguin Books, 1872.

Eliot, T. S. *Shakespeare and the Stoicism of Seneca*. London: Oxford University Press, 1927.

Gillett-Karam, R. "Women and Leadership." In G. Baker (ed.), *A Handbook on the Community College in America*. Westport, Conn.: Greenwood Press, 1994.

Gilligan, C. *In a Different Voice*. Cambridge, Mass.: Harvard University Press, 1982.

Guest, R. "Management Imperatives for the Year 2000." *California Management Review*, 1986, 28 (4), 62–70.

Guill, J. "Conflict Management Style Preferences of Community College Presidents." Unpublished doctoral dissertation, University of Virginia, 1991.

Helgesen, S. *The Female Advantage: Women's Ways of Leadership*. New York: Doubleday Currency, 1990a.

Helgesen, S. "The Pyramid and the Web." *New York Times Forum*, May 27, 1990b, p. F13.

Josselson, R. *Finding Herself: Pathways to Identity Development in Women*. San Francisco: Jossey-Bass, 1987.

Kanter, R. "The New Managerial Work." *Harvard Business Review*, 1989, 67, 85–92.

Kuh, G., Whitt, E., and Shedd, J. *Student Affairs Work 2001: A Paradigmatic Odyssey*. Alexandria, Va.: American College Personnel Association, 1987.

Leatherman, C. "Colleges Hire More Female Presidents, But Questions Linger About Their Clout." *Chronicle of Higher Education*, Nov. 6, 1991, pp. A19–A21.

Lincoln, Y. *Organizational Theory and Inquiry*. Newbury Park, Calif.: Sage, 1985.

Mennuti, R. "An Exploration of Moral Orientation, Gender and the Nature of the Dilemma in Moral Reasoning of Community College Presidents." Unpublished doctoral dissertation, Virginia Polytechnic Institute and State University, 1987.

Miles, K. "A Naturalistic Inquiry into the Administrative Behavior of a Top-Level Woman Executive in a Two-Year College." Unpublished doctoral dissertation, University of Colorado, Boulder, 1986.

"More Women Leading Higher Education Institutions." *Higher Education & National Affairs*, June 8, 1992, pp. 1, 3.

Rosener, J. "Ways Women Lead." *Harvard Business Review*, 1990, 68, 119–125.

Sanders, S. "A Profile of Experienced Women Chief Executive Officers of Two-Year Colleges." Unpublished doctoral dissertation, University of Arkansas, 1989.

Schmidt, M. "Gender Balance and Leadership: A Study of Community College Presidents' Leadership Described in Gender Related Terms." Unpublished doctoral dissertation, Seattle University, 1990.

Schwartz, P., and Ogilvy, J. *The Emergent Paradigm*. Analytical Report no. 7, Values and Lifestyles Program. Menlo Park, Calif.: SRI International, 1979.

Vaughan, G., Mellander, G., and Blois, B. *The Community College Presidency*. New York: Macmillan, 1986.

Vaughan, G., Mellander, G., and Blois, B. *The Community College Presidency: Current Status and Future Outlook*. Washington, D.C.: American Association of Community Colleges, 1994.

Zaleznik, A. *The Managerial Mystique: Restoring Leadership in Business*. New York: Harper-Collins, 1989.

Deborah M. DiCroce is president of Piedmont Virginia Community College in Charlottesville.

CHAPTER 18

ASIAN WOMEN LEADERS OF HIGHER EDUCATION

LORI M. IDETA AND JOANNE E. COOPER

Stereotypes of Asian Americans abound. If not being noted for their docileness and passivity (Nakanishi, 1993), they are touted as the model minority (Chun, 1995; Escueta & O'Brien, 1995). This latter generalization has evolved partially because students of certain ethnicities within the category of "Asian American" pursue higher education in substantial numbers (Escueta & O'Brien, 1995). When one examines Asian representation in roles other than that of student, however, the numbers decrease dramatically (Carter & Wilson, 1995; OWHE/ACE, 1995).

Nakanishi (1993) asserts that the representation and administrative experiences of Asian Pacific Americans in higher education's faculty and administrative ranks have not received "sufficient policy or programmatic attention," (p. 57). Suzuki (1994) calls for more qualitative studies conducted on smaller sample groups and using techniques such as in-depth interviews to understand the nature of the "glass ceiling" that Asian Americans "apparently encounter as they try to move upward to the higher levels of administration" in postsecondary education (pp. 278–281). For Asian American women, encounters with this glass ceiling are frequent. Research on women in higher education (Aisenberg & Harrington, 1986) and on women leaders (Astin & Leland, 1991) has urged us to move beyond mere facts and figures and has emphasized the need for the study of the lives of individual women "as a means of understanding the antecedents of activism and passion—the driving forces in leadership behavior" (Astin & Leland, 1991, p. 160). Asian American women stand at the crossroads of our understanding of women and leadership. Through their perspectives at the boundaries of culture and organization, they bring new understandings of leadership and of individual transformation.

Little is known about the experiences of Asian women in higher education either as students or as they begin to move into the ranks of faculty and administrative positions. What pressures do they encounter and how do they respond to these stresses?

In response to the concern over the low representation of Asian American leaders and in an effort to understand the lives of diverse women in higher education, to uncover the driving forces behind their work as leaders, we examined the lives of four Asian American women administrators. Research on these minority leaders furthers the past work on women in the academy discussed above, by breaking silences and giving voice to the tensions that these women experience in their work settings. This process, according to Aisenberg & Harrington (1988), is the key to creating a countersystem of social order in the academy that "opposes excessive hierarchy and exclusivity in holding of authority . . . that incorporates diversity, spreads authority through processes of cooperation, resists centrality . . . and protects individuality," (p. 136).

This study examined the lives of Asian (Chinese, Filipino, and Japanese) American women who were all senior-level leaders of post-secondary education. They were from varying states,

---

Reprinted from *Everyday Knowledge and Uncommon Truths: Life Writings of Women's Experience In and Outside of the Academy*, edited by L. K. Christian-Smith and K. S. Kellor 1997. Copyright © 1997 Westview Press (Perseus Books).

varying institutions, and varying institutional types. Personal experience methods (Clandinin & Connelly, 1994) were used to elicit these women's stories and through them, the narrative understanding of their professional practices. The narratives in this chapter were collaboratively constructed with the study's participants. Each narrative was co-authored by the researcher and the individual whose story was being written. Through a feminist-cultural lens, we offer the critical events in these women's lives which have led to their ability to survive and to work in their institutions of higher education. The results of this study refute the commonly held misconceptions of Asians as a "model minority" which will become the focus of this chapter.

Misconceptions of the Asian "Model Minority"

Asians have long been touted as the "model minority," (Chun, 1995; Suzuki, 1995; Sue & Okazaki, 1995). As such, Asian Americans are considered successes in all that they pursue, especially in the realm of academia. Nakanishi (1993) explores three basic misconceptions which arise out of society's stereotypical view of Asian Pacific Americans.

The first misconception is closely tied to the assumption that Asian Pacific Americans are "especially successful and talented in academics," (p. 52). The reality, however, is vastly different. Nakanishi (1993) asserts that Asian Pacific Americans, like other minority groups and women in general, decline substantially in numbers as one moves up the academic ladder from high school graduation through college, graduate school and into the ranks of faculty and administrators.

The second misconception is that Asian Pacific Americans do not face discrimination or unfair employment practices in higher education institutions. Nakanishi claims that this view combines two widely accepted but false notions. The first is the claim that Asian Pacific Americans have been fully accepted into American life and no longer encounter either overt or covert racial discrimination in their social and professional interactions. The second notion is that colleges and universities are unique places of employment which are "somehow more tolerant, more enlightened, more objective, and more open to new ideas" and are "free of bias and subjectivity," (pp. 53–54). Nakanishi asserts that one manner in which this biased treatment emerges is in the negative reactions to and evaluations of multicultural work conducted by ethnic minorities.

The third misconception is that Asian Pacific Americans who encounter problems in their employment or promotion are more inclined than any other minority group to walk away and not contest unfair denial of tenure or promotion. This misconception is fueled by the stereotype that Asian Pacific Americans are "passive, docile, and are expected to quietly fade away" when conflict arises (p. 55).

The results of our study generated evidence to refute the second misconception, and provided support to refute the third stereotype, held of Asian Americans by society. In contrast to Nakanishi's (1993) focus on Asian Pacific Americans, this study focused on Asian women of Chinese, Filipino, and Japanese ethnicities. Through the methodology of narrative these women revealed stories of both the adversity and support they have faced and continue to encounter as professional women in a field dominated by White males.

The Power of Narrative

Scholars of narrative inquiry such as Clandinin & Connelly (1992), Elbaz (1991), and Grossman, (1987) assert that story is an important component of understanding teacher's conceptions of their professional and personal lives. However, few narrative studies have focused on administrators at any educational level.

One of the main rationales for using narrative in examining the lives of women higher education leaders is that narrative is viewed as an "especially appropriate form of women's knowing and expression" (Belenky, Clinchy, Goldberger, & Tarule, 1986; Carter, 1993; Helle, 1991). Carter (1993) asserts that we must "dignify the stories of women's work so that we will not degrade what they do" (p. 11).

Heilbrun (1988) states, "Few studies of the last twenty years, and, of course, even fewer in earlier years, have concerned themselves with women's biographies or autobiographies" (p. 29). To Heilbrun, women's access to narratives is more than a matter of having the right to tell one's story. Rather, she views the ability and the right of women to talk about their lives, as central to issues of power and control.

In order for women to gain control of their stories and of their own lives, they must recognize the fact that they have the right to tell their own stories. This means breaking away from the long-accepted standard of men narrating both men's and women's stories. Weiland (1994) states, "In (Heilbrun's) view, the stories of women needed to be freed of their dependence on the forms of male narrative, biography being then an epistemological project formed primarily by gender, and, hence, promoting redefinition of what is worth knowing about lives" (p. 104). In the case of Asian women, their stories have been doubly silenced, both as females and as Asians.

Lessons from the Third Wave of Feminism

Collins (1991) asserts that people of color, especially women of color, have always been expected to put their concerns into the language and structure of the dominant group. This, she states, changes the meaning of what she and others have to say. In the Third Wave of feminism, Collins, and other Black feminist writers, such as Audre Lorde (1995), are finding their own approaches to writing and their own voices in telling their stories.

There have been three "waves" of feminism used to illustrate the evolution of feminist theory and contribute critical information to our understanding of society's views of women and women's views of themselves. The First Wave began in the 1700s and ended when women secured the right to vote in 1920. The Second Wave emerged on the heels of World War II and flourished during the 1960s. Although these two waves of feminism enhanced our thinking and improved the lives of women, the Third Wave of feminism has attacked previous feminist thought and writings as being too White, too middle-class (Nicholson, 1990), and too universalizing of all women's experiences (Kelly, Burton, & Regan, 1994). In addition, the philosophies and writings of the movements have also silenced women of color who have been left out of the arena of mainstream feminism since its inception (Collins, 1991). Current feminist scholars are calling for research that attends to participants' ethnicity, class, color, etc., in addition to issues of gender (Frankenberg, 1993; Lorde, 1995; Collins, 1991). Where the prime targets of feminist critiques were once male-dominated narratives emerging within male-dominated disciplines, now feminist criticism has turned on its own narratives.

Collins (1991) further asserts that we need to reconceptualize people who have multiple identities. She urges us to stop conceptualizing, for example, gender first, then adding race, then adding, religion, etc. Rather, Collins states that she sees all facets of identity as interlocking and interactive. The three constructions of race, class, and gender are, for women of color, an umbrella of dominance (hooks, 1989; Smith, 1987). One construction cannot exist without the other. The theory that all characteristics are interlocking rather than additive is reaffirmed in the findings of this study and moves us away from defining people through separate and fractured identities.

The narratives that follow reveal interlocking and interactive identities that serve to refute the current misconceptions of Asian American women.

Snap-Shots of the Women's Narratives

The most dominant theme which emerged from this study was the participants' ability to become stronger when confronted by discriminating situations. Rather than responding with passivity, these women used their experiences as springboards for more determined action and as sources of strength, growth, and deeper understanding. Their experiences help correct two of the misconceptions explored by Nakanishi (1993): that Asian Pacific Americans do not face discrimination or unfair employment practices in higher education, and that when they encounter discrimination, they are more likely to respond passively, to "quietly fade away" in the face of conflict.

The four Asian women whose narratives follow recalled incidents in which they faced racism or sexism in their places of employment. These women's written narratives give us insight into the discrimination they have endured and their struggles to respond in ways that address the conflicting demands placed on them by their own sense of identity their workplace, and their family expectations.

The narratives of Jane and Ayla shed light on the misconception that Asians do not face discrimination. In fact, as Asian women, even in senior-level positions, these administrators continue to encounter both racist and sexist situations in the world of higher education. The larger question is how to respond to these situations. Here the narratives of Sally and Audrey address the additional misconception that Asians (and perhaps most especially Asian women) confront these situations with passivity and without contesting unfair treatment.

Discrimination in Institutions of Higher Education

Jane. Jane's experiences as a Chinese immigrant in a predominantly White state underscore the ignorance and insensitivity Asian Americans have encountered. Although much of the discrimination she faces is subtle rather than blatant, it is nevertheless pervasive and debilitating. Unfortunately, it comes from both the White community and from other minorities who erroneously assume that Asians are not "real minorities" and have therefore experienced few barriers to their success. Jane's response has been to make the work of equal opportunity her life's work.

Jane is the sixth daughter and eighth of ten children of Chinese immigrants. Jane and her siblings were born and raised in a predominantly White state and in conditions which would be described today as urban poverty. Jane was discouraged by her family to pursue a college degree as girls of her generation were expected to marry and bear many sons. Despite the lack of support she received, Jane went on to a local college where she was the only student of color. On her first night in the dormitories, Jane was overwhelmed with visitors who "came down to my dorm room to look at 'the Chinaman' because they had never seen one before."

Jane went on to secure a teaching position at the college level while working on her doctoral studies. She reflects on the unreasonable work load expectations she was handed by her superiors in her days as a fledgling faculty member. She also recalls the denial of her request for an extension to complete her dissertation which was posed as an ultimatum for her to retain her job. Jane later learned that such extensions had been granted to her White, male colleagues and, although with less frequency, to her White, female colleagues.

Jane asserts that both positive and negative interactions with family and community as well as the larger society have strengthened her ability to withstand the many forms of criticisms and judgmental reactions that seem to be part and parcel of working in the areas of civil rights, EEO and diversity. Today, Jane serves as the Director of the Center for Multicultural Affairs of a large, public research university. While she feels she is able to handle the "invisible" or "colorblind" treatment; the neglectful, often insensitive and patronizing behaviors; and the frequent "drill" questions (Where did you come from? No, where did you *really* come from? Where/How/When did you learn to speak English so well?); she does not deny the emotions that arise when these situations occur. Perhaps the most difficult to address and ultimately the most damaging to one's sense of self is that of being denied opportunities for personal and professional growth and development because of one's race, ethnicity, or gender, because of assumptions about one's worthiness, or whether "someone like her" could succeed.

Jane finds being a female Asian American has its own specific challenges. While she has not been subjected very often to overt discrimination, nor have there been many refusals to interact or work with her, it is not always possible to ignore subtle signals which indicate that while one may not be openly excluded, neither are there the indicators that one is included. This seems to be an especially universal perception among people of color. Moreover, Asian Americans in positions like hers may also be questioned by people representing other racial/ethnic groups since there is the assumption that as "model minorities," Asian American are not "real" minorities.

Jane has amassed her encounters with discrimination and used them as the driving force behind her life's work. Of her dedication to issues of equity Jane says "There are days when I wonder, 'What am I doing? Are we doing the right thing? Are we headed toward our goals? Are we using the right map or blueprint? Are we using the right tools and methods?' Well, there *are* no maps. [There are] no blueprints."

The lack of a guide or how-to handbook for creating the desired university community does not deter Jane. She persists in working in an unpopular area that is fraught with resistance referred by some as "Just another P.C. bandwagon." Jane knows there are no easy answers, but perhaps that is the challenge that motivates her. She shares, "I humorously use phrases like 'Chinese water torture' as a description of my persistence—I keep at it until what needs to happen, happens."

Ayla. As an immigrant to the United States, Ayla categorizes the discrimination she has faced in two ways. First, there are those who see her as downtrodden and want to champion her causes in order to help out the poor minority woman. Second, are those who have real questions about her ability because she is Filipino and wonder subtly if she is able do the job. Ayla faces both these challenges with a determination to be heard and to be respected for her abilities.

The second daughter, and youngest child of an English father and a Malay-Chinese mother, Ayla was born and raised in the Philippines. Ayla's immersion into the all-girls' schools she attended as a child was critical in empowering her as a young woman. Ayla went on to receive her college degrees in the United States. Currently, Ayla serves as the faculty developer for a public research institution.

Ayla has found that her ethnicity, rather than her status as a woman administrator, seems to cloud the judgment of some of those with whom she works. Ayla believes that those members of the dominant ethnic class are often unaware that they approach her and other ethnic minority administrators in these disturbing and disrespectful ways. She says, "(There are those that say), 'I want to be the one to help this minority rise to glory,' and there are those who look at you and (think) maybe you can't handle the job." She admits that these actions are very subtle, "but it comes through in the oddest ways."

Although mainly confronted by ethnic bias, Ayla does not deny that gender has certainly been an issue for many women in the academy. She feels fortunate to be in the field of education, where women are better represented than in other professions. She admits that if she is experiencing discrimination in a field populated by a large number of females, she shudders to imagine the experiences of women in fields largely dominated by men. Her negative experiences are common to many women. She tells a tale of being ignored at meetings only to witness that when a male reiterated her already stated idea or question, he received affirmation or credit for his contribution. To deal with these events, this leader has learned to speak up and repeatedly say, "I think I said that ten minutes ago." Over the course of her career she has learned this and other strategies for gaining voice and "establishing equity" in those meetings and in her life. These approaches have earned Ayla the reputation of being "tough." Despite the struggles, Ayla continues to champion for equity issues for women and ethnic minorities, particularly those of Filipino ancestry.

Contemplating retirement, Ayla is only now able to say that she is "comfortable" with who she is as a woman and as an administrator. When questioned about this process of self discovery and acceptance she revealed, "You get better at it. You get better at it with everyday experience."

Not Going Quietly

Next the narratives of Sally and Audrey illuminate the ways in which Asian women have responded to discrimination when they have encountered it. These responses are a complex blend of strategies arising out of their status as women, their cultural heritage as Asians, the particular workplace pressures they face in their institutional settings and their own individual leadership styles. In general, these responses begin to undermine the myth that Asians do not challenge the status quo when they encounter racism. As Asian women, they describe the layered oppressions of racism and sexism, often responding with renewed determination to stand up, speak out, and fight for the right to their own identity in the academy. For Sally, this response includes careful reflection on who she is as a woman and how this might affect her future career plans. For

Audrey it is a fighting stance, one in which she fiercely defends her staff, whom she describes as "family."

Sally. Sally has encountered prejudice from the minority as well as the White community. As a woman of mixed Asian race, Sally spans the boundaries between White and Asian communities as well as between Filipino and Japanese communities. In addition, her work takes her into the interstices between public K–12 education and higher education, a space where she encounters additional pressures to meet the expectations of each institution's organizational culture. For Sally, at this particular juncture in her life, these expectations have centered more on her role as a woman than on her ethnicity. Her response has been to reflect carefully on her own identity and her subsequent professional goals. Surviving as a woman in a "man's game" and whether this requires more conformity than she is willing to give have been constant questions for Sally.

Currently, Sally serves as Director of Articulated Curricula for a community college. Sally realizes that although she views herself as a competent *person,* others see her as a *woman.* Perhaps still competent, but nevertheless, a woman. Her male colleagues to whom she relates so well, do not include her when they venture out to the golf course or local bars to conduct business. She has come to endure the reality that her acceptance of diversity is not always a two way street. Her gender and her mix of ethnicities are often boundaries she faces within her institution. The culture of the community college in which Sally works is one dominated by White males. Despite the large number of ethnic minorities in her community, Sally believes that the institution is prejudiced against people of color. Being born and raised in the community, and being of Filipino/Japanese ancestry, Sally realizes that she has many strikes against her.

Recently, Sally has spent a great deal of time reflecting on her path as articulation coordinator. She always aspired to rise up the bureaucratic ladder and be a top level administrator. Now, she is questioning this long held dream. Sally is questioning if upward mobility is still really what she desires. Her identity has always rested on the title of her position. Now, she realizes that her identity is centered around her family—her husband, son, grandmother, mother, father, and siblings. She finds herself enjoying her role as nurturer to her family and co-workers. Perhaps, she says, expanding herself horizontally in her position is actually more appealing. She elaborates " though I don't have everything sorted out, I'm getting to like who I am. I'm getting to see that indeed Sally is a woman, that has definite woman needs and issues that have to be addressed in this lifetime as a woman. And never mind playing this man's role or this man's game, because you're always going to lose because you're not yourself."

Sally is now at a crossroads. She wonders if her long-held need for security means she will conform to the norms of the institution or if she has the energy to continue being unique. She feels the tension between climbing the career ladder and being nurturing in the workplace. She wonders how she can successfully explore herself as a woman and still survive the male game of higher education. Sally shares, "It is truly a man's game . . . and what I'm learning is how to survive as a woman by playing a game that's more aligned with my identity as a woman and being appreciated and still survive . . ."

Audrey. Early in her career Audrey faced triple layered discrimination due to her young age, her gender, and her ethnicity. Her response was not one of passivity, as described by the myth Nakanishi (1993) discusses, but one of fierce and determined resistance. She continues to be true to her values in the face of administrative requests to "drop the matter," submitting rebuttals, and going to bat for employees as well as standing up for herself as she encounters racist or sexist attitudes. These actions certainly belie the misconception that Asians will not contest unfair treatment, but instead are likely to "quietly fade away."

The personification of the Asian American stereotype, Audrey is not. While school teachers expected Audrey to have high test scores to be placed in the honors program, she did not. While society expected Audrey to excel in mathematics and be able to attend UCLA, she did not. And while higher administration expected Audrey to be quiet, complacent, and submissive, Audrey is not.

Audrey was born into a highly conservative Republican family in California. She was raised in a Black ghetto in which she witnessed tremendous racial discrimination of her neighbors and friends while, as an Asian child, she was viewed as a member of the "model minority" and expected to succeed in the academic realm. Audrey has battled the stereotypes of racism her entire life. Her experiences as a higher education administrator have not been any different. She shares, "People have found it easy to dump on me—easy to jump to conclusions—to blame before fact-finding. Is it because I was a comparatively young Asian woman?"

Audrey currently serves as the Dean of Student Development at a public community college where she actively works to promote equity issues. When Audrey's institution recently undertook a new evaluation system, Audrey's composure was tested to its limits. Audrey described the results of her evaluation as a "scathing attack." Some of the comments received read, "She is racially biased against Whites, she only hires minorities." "She comes to our office and only greets Blacks and Asian Americans." "She is intolerant." "She is pushy." "She has embarrassed me." These painful comments were amidst other comments which read, "She's a role model." "She's a visible leader." "She's a student advocate." The president of the faculty senate also wrote, "I don't know much about her, but rumor has it that she doesn't get along with her staff." He submitted this statement despite the fact that he had met with one of Audrey's staff members and she reportedly told him, "No, (Audrey) gets along well with all of us, that's not a problem." The same faculty senate president also wrote, "(Audrey) tends to appear at various functions." Audrey explains that she often organizes numerous functions on campus and thus, "shows up" to direct, emcee or oversee them.

In response to her evaluation, Audrey submitted a five page rebuttal requesting further clarification on several points. She shares that the administration refused to respond. She says, "The chancellor came up and told me, 'You know you're wonderful. You know we think you're doing a great job. Drop the issue. Don't push this any further.'" The administration then sent Audrey a three line memo stating that her comments were received and were on file. She immediately wrote back stating," . . . you're finished with it, I am too. Now, please give me a letter of recommendation. I need to move on." Audrey reports she has yet to receive a response from the administration.

Audrey reflects:

> One of the biggest lessons I learned from this is that when you avail yourself to staff, the more out there you are, the more vulnerable you are . . . The more you put yourself out there, the more you become like family . . . you're still in a leadership role and so they expect you're going to be that close to everybody. So I walk a very dangerous tight rope because of that, you know?

Audrey is currently working at maintaining harmony amongst her staff. Although she would like to be personally connected to each one, it is difficult as her staff has grown from ten employees to seventy.

Despite the difficulties, Audrey still holds to her values of equity and equal opportunity for all. She continues to work fiercely for diversity issues and to speak for those who do not have a voice in the bureaucracy of education. Audrey believes this dedication comes from a lifetime of what she calls a "second class nature" which she has had to combat her entire life.

Audrey perseveres despite her internal war. She attempts to mentor her staff by facilitating their networking and appointing them to committees in her place. Audrey considers mentoring those to come after her as critical. She asserts, "I have to do that because if I don't replace myself, then I didn't create anything." She explains that she has witnessed too many social movements and programs fall to pieces when great leaders do not take the time to nurture others to take their places. She states, "If you don't take the time to grow your own, then it won't happen."

Discussion

Collectively, these women represent various ethnicities within the broad category of *Asian American*. Through the revelation of critical incidents in their lives, we have learned that their experiences with racism have differed and have been painful. Instead of displaying the stereotypical characteristics others expected of Asian women (i.e., docileness, passivity, silence), especially during challenging times, these women became stronger and more determined to prove those who held those misperceptions of them wrong.

Most of these women were able to single out a series of incidents over their lifetimes in which they were confronted by racial or gender discrimination. Rather than becoming disempowered by these experiences, the women grew more determined in their goals for success. For some of the women, their choice to work in the field of education or to work for equity issues, was the direct result of the critical encounters they had with racism. In many ways, the racism these women faced early in their lives became one of the most compelling findings of the study because of its impact on the participants' identity formation.

The participants of this study faced sexism in one form or another. The individual details of how the women responded to these incidents vary as greatly as the occurrences themselves. However, the common thread which ties them all together is that all the women took the anger, shame, resentment, or bitterness which resulted from these run-ins and became strengthened to counter any wrong impressions of them. Instead of losing faith in other women when they experienced greater discrimination from females than males, they assumed a larger role in fostering young women.

Given the stories of racism and sexism encountered by the participants of this study, there is evidence to refute the second misconception of Asian Americans as reported by Nakanishi (1993) that Asian Pacific Americans do not face discrimination in American higher education institutions. These narratives support Nakanishi's assertion that Asian Pacific Americans have not been fully accepted into American life and that they continue to encounter discrimination. The fact that numerous incidents of discrimination occurred within these women's work environments refutes the stereotype that colleges and universities are more tolerant and more enlightened than other institutions (Nakanishi, 1993, p. 54). Audrey's experiences of facing greater discrimination because she assertively works for equity issues, further supports Nakanishi's assertion that ethnic minorities and women who pursue scholarship concerning multicultural issues, often receive hostile reactions to and evaluations of their work (p. 54).

The women's anti-stereotypical response of transforming the negativity of discriminating situations into catalysts of strength can be traced, for some women, to their families' responses to their complaints. When some of the women attempted to speak with their families about their encounters with discrimination, they received responses stating that these encounters were "no big deal," or that they should simply ignore them. For these women, the internalization of grief and the response of determination may have been the only possible response because nothing less was expected of them. They were expected to be strong. Not all of the women in this study reported this type of message from their families, yet they all reported more determination in response to discriminating situations. This determination provides evidence to refute the third commonly held misconception as reported by Nakanishi (1993), that Asian Pacific Americans who encounter problems in their employment are more inclined to walk away from the situation in a passive manner (p. 55).

Asian women leaders seem to live within the confines of powerful paradoxes. As Asian females they struggle in organizations which define leaders as primarily male and White. In addition, organizations simultaneously reward leaders for behaviors such as fortitude, courage, and heroism (Morgan, 1986), while punishing women for displaying these behaviors because they are considered to be gender inappropriate. Asian women face compounding cultural demands that increase this tension between their roles as women and their roles as leaders. The participants of this study were both rewarded and admonished in their organizations for the same behaviors. Behaviors which are typical of leaders (displays of power, authority, and fortitude) are considered atypical for women and doubly atypical for Asian women. As Bloom and Munro (1995) assert "Our very understandings of terms like power and authority are located in and dependent on gendered understandings in which male behavior is constituted in opposition to female behavior (Butler, 1990). To be female is to not have authority. Thus, to be a female administrator is necessarily a contradiction in terms" (p. 104).

For Asian women, this becomes a double contradiction, given the standard of cultural expectations that Asian women are to be more compliant or subservient in their behavior. These contradictory expectations manifest themselves both at home and at work, creating a kind of schizophrenic existence in which some women reported being subservient at home and assertive in the workplace. Yet, even when the women display power and authority in their workplaces, they work against the contradictory cultural stereotypes of what it means to be a woman, and what it means to be an Asian woman in our society.

Compounding these dilemmas are cultural expectations that Asian women should succeed outside the home in order to bring honor to the family. Here, family expectations presume these women to display courage and fortitude when they face discrimination in their professional lives. Thus, they are confronted with multiple paradoxical demands in the workplace as women leaders and as Asian women. To be an Asian woman demands that one be, if anything, less assertive than one's White counterparts. To be Asian also demands that one display courage in the face of adversity, so as not to bring shame to the family name. These conflicting and contradictory demands create what Bloom & Munro (1995) define as "nonunitary" or fractured selves (p. 107).

Summary

Through the mutual construction of written narratives, four senior-level Asian women leaders gave voice to their experiences as ethnic minorities and as females in the predominantly White male arena of postsecondary education. They were also given the space to reflect on how their gender and ethnicity have become lenses through which they perceive the world. Evidence emerged from this process to refute common misconceptions of Asian Americans. The women of this study faced sexism and racism in their careers as higher education leaders. The painful and often subtle stories they shared are powerful evidence to refute the myth that Asian Americans do not face discrimination in institutions of post-secondary education (Nakanishi, 1993). The manner in which these women were able to transform these sexist and racist encounters into catalysts for greater strength, determination, and advocacy stands as evidence to contradict the misconception that Asian Americans would be more apt to passively walk away from such problems (Nakanishi, 1993).

The time is right for the stereotypical perceptions of Asians to change. As we enter a new century, society is faced with a diversification previously unknown to the world. Third Wave conceptions speak a truth that can no longer be ignored. Women are already the majority gender on campuses of higher education. By the turn of the century, it is estimated that the Asian American population will be ten million strong (Hsia, 1988). It is logical to then assume that Asian American women will soon become a significant presence on campuses in roles other than that of student. Although our study was conducted on a small sample, it is our hope that it creates a deeper and greater understanding of the struggles and strengths of Asian women. For the discrimination that this population encounters in the world of higher education is tremendous, but so are the contributions they have to offer.

End Note Reflections

The coming together of two women authors from diverse backgrounds served to strengthen this study. Joanne is an established professor of higher education with expertise in the area of narrative inquiry. She was raised in a White, middle-class environment in Oregon. Lori is a recent Ed.D. graduate and is a new professional in the area of student affairs administration. She is the fourth-generation of her Japanese-American family to call Hawaii home. With an innate understanding of Asian culture, Lori was able to gain deeper insights into what the project participants were relaying through their interviews and narratives. She was also able to feel the tensions the women experienced between family and work and understood the very natural tendency to create family in the workplace. In addition, Lori's own family background, where her mother was the breadwinner and her father the househusband, has led her to an interest in women and leadership. She first saw women take a leadership role in her own life at a very young age. Her mother has served as a model of what strong women can do when they are determined to do what they must. For her, the words of Eleanor Roosevelt ring true, "You must do the thing you think you cannot do." Thus, in studying Asian American women leaders of higher education, Lori was able to bring to the study all that she was and all that she represented. Standpoint epistemology informs us that a person occupying the same space in society as her participants is a definite strength. Joanne's abilities, because of her location outside of the culture and background of the participants of the study, were equally valuable. While delineating themes from the interviews and narratives, Joanne was quick to discover ones which were so second-nature to Lori that they were not visible. For example, in analyzing the women's narratives, Joanne immediately recognized the importance of the women's philosophy of bringing the concept of family into their work environments. Joanne had unearthed a concept deserving of attention and exploration which was so commonplace for Lori that she was unable to recognize it as a theme in the study.

As a young professional in an area nearly void of senior-level Asian women administrators, Lori quickly became an admirer of the project participants. Joanne helped to temper Lori's tendency to revere the women in the study, which arose naturally from her strong Asian cultural value to respect one's elders. Together they successfully negotiated the balance between celebrating the successes of the participants and presenting a clear picture of their lives and struggles.

Writing together has helped both Lori and Joanne to "work the hyphens" of othering, as described by Michelle Fine (1994). As an Asian American, Lori brought knowledge of her culture to this work. As a Caucasian American with eighteen years of experience in institutions of higher education, Joanne contributed knowledge of mainstream culture, as well as knowledge of academic cultures. Both women function simultaneously as insiders and outsiders to the cultures and issues addressed in this study. While functioning as insider/outsider to Asian cultural values and the culture of higher education, both women function as insiders to the understandings of what it is to be female. Thus, they simultaneously worked the hyphens of their mutual existences, forming at times a balanced equation, at other times highlighting the knowledge and strengths of one particular author. Through this work we seek to uncover ourselves and our own investments, rather than "burying the contradictions that percolate at the Self-Other hyphen" (Fine, 1994, p. 70). With Fine, we believe our work breathes "a renewed sense of possibility" into the work of Asian/Caucasian, advisor/student, administrator/faculty, local/mainland, female/female, bonds, dichotomies and contradictions that percolate at our own personal hyphen.

References

Aisenberg, N., & Harrington, M. (1986). *Women of academe: Outsiders in the sacred grove.* Amherst: University of Massachusetts Press.

Astin, H. S., & Leland, C. (1991). *Women of influence, women of vision: A cross generational study of leaders and social change.* San Francisco: Jossey-Bass, Inc. Publishers.

Belenky, M. J., Clinchy, B. M., Goldberger, N. R., & Tarule, J. M. (1986). *Women's ways of knowing.* New York: Basic Books.

Bloom, L., & Munro, P. (1995). Conflicts of selves: Nonunitary subjectivity in women administrators' life history narratives. In J. A. Hatch & R. Wisniewski (Eds.), *Life history and narrative* (pp. 99–112).

Bordo, S. (1990). Feminism, postmodernism, and gender-skepticism. In L. J. Nicholson (Ed.), *Feminism/Postmodernism* (pp. 133–56). New York: Routledge.

Carter, D. J., & Wilson, R. (1995). *Thirteenth Annual Status Report on Minorities in Higher Education.* Washington, DC, American Council on Education.

Carter, K. (1993, Jan.–Feb.). The place of story in the study of teaching and teacher education. *Educational Researcher,* 5–12.

Chun, K. T. (1995). The myth of Asian American success and its educational ramifications. In D. T. Nakanishi & T. Y. Nishida (Eds.), *The Asian American educational experience* (pp. 95–112). New York: Routledge.

Clandinin, D. J. & Connelly, F. M. (1992). Teacher as curriculum maker. In P. Jackson (Ed.), *Handbook of research on curriculum* (pp. 363–401). New York: Macmillan.

Clandinin, D. J. & Connelly, F. M. (1994). In N. K. Denzin & Y. S. Lincoln (Eds.), *Personal experience methods. Handbook of qualitative research* (pp. 413–427). Thousand Oaks: Sage Publications, Inc.

Collins, P. H. (1991). *Black feminist thought: Knowledge, consciousness, and the politics of empowerment.* New York: Routledge.

Cooper, J. E. & Heck, R. H. (1993). Using narrative in the study of school administration. *International Journal of Qualitative Studies in Education.*

Elbaz, F. (1991). Research on teacher's knowledge: The evolution of a discourse. *Journal of Curriculum Studies, 23,* 1–19.

Escueta, E. & O'Brien, E. (1995). Asian Americans in higher education: Trends and issues. In D. T. Nakanishi & T. Y. Nishida (Eds.), *The Asian American educational experience* (pp. 259–272). New York: Routledge.

Fine, M. (1994). Working the hyphens: Reinventing self and other in qualitative research. In N. K. Denzin & Y. S. Lincoln (Eds.), *Handbook of qualitative research.* (pp. 70–82). Thousand Oaks: Sage Publications.

Frankenberg, R. (1993). *The social construction of whiteness: White women, race matters.* Minneapolis: University of Minnesota Press.

Grossman, P. (1987). *A tale of two teachers: The role of subject matter orientation in teaching.* Paper presented at the Annual Meeting of the American Educational Research Association, Washington, DC.

Heilbrun, C. G. (1988). *Writing a woman's life.* New York: W. W. Norton.

Helle, A. P (1991). Reading women's autobiographies: A map of reconstructed knowing. In C. Witherell & N. Noddings (Eds.), *Stories lives tell: Narrative and dialogue in education* (pp. 48–66). New York: Teachers College Press.

hooks, b. (1989). *Talking back: Thinking feminist, thinking black.* Boston: South End Press.

Hsia, J. (1988). *Asian Americans in higher education and at work.* New Jersey: Lawrence Erlbaum Assoc.

Kelly, L., Burton, S. & Regan, L. (1994). Researching women's lives or studying women's oppression? Reflections on what constitutes feminist research. In M. Maynard & I. Purvis (Eds.), *Researching women's lives from a feminist perspective* (pp. 27–48). Bristol: Taylor & Francis.

Lorde, A. (1995). Age, race, class, and sex: Women redefining difference. In M. L. Andersen & P. H. Collins (Eds.), *Race, class, and gender: An anthology second edition* (pp. 532–540). Belmont, CA: Wadsworth.

Miles, M. B. & Huberman, A. M. (1984). *Qualitative data analysis: A sourcebook of new methods.* Beverly Hills: Sage Publications.

Morgan, G. (1986). *Images of Organization.* Newbury Park, Sage Publications.

Nakanishi, D. T. (1993, Spring). Asian Pacific Americans in higher education: Faculty and administrative representation and tenure. *New directions for teaching and learning, 53,* 51–59. San Francisco: Jossey-Bass Publishers.

Nicholson, L. J. (Ed.). (1990). *Feminism/Postmodernism.* New York: Routledge.

Office of Women in Higher Education. American Council on Education. (1995). *Women presidents in U.S. colleges and universities.* Washington, DC: OWHE.

Smith, D. E. (1987). *The everyday world as problematic: A feminist sociology.* Boston: Northeastern University Press.

Sue, S. & Okazaki, S. (1995). Asian American educational achievements: A phenomenon in search of an explanation. In D. T. Nakanishi & T. Y. Nishida (Eds.), *The Asian American educational experience* (pp. 133–145). New York: Routledge.

Suzuki, B. H. (1994). Higher education issues in the Asian American community. In M. J. Justiz, R. Wilson & L. G. Bjork (Eds.), *Minorities in higher education* (pp. 258–285). American Council on Education. Oryx Press.

Suzuki, B. H. (1995). Education and the socialization of Asian Americans: A revolutionist analysis of the "model minority" thesis. In D. I. Nakanishi and T. Y. Nishida (Eds.), *The Asian American educational experience* (pp. 113–132). New York: Routledge.

Tripp, D. (1994). Teachers' lives, critical incidents, and professional practice. *Qualitative Studies in Education, 7*(1), 65–76.

Weiland, S. (1994, Summer). Writing the academic life: Faculty careers in narrative perspective. *The Review of Higher Education, 17*(4), 395–422.

CHAPTER 19

HOW DEANS OF WOMEN BECAME MEN

ROBERT A. SCHWARTZ

Introduction

In 1870, women accounted for only 21% of the undergraduate population. By 1890, the numbers had climbed to 35%. By 1920, women represented 47% of the undergraduate students enrolled in American colleges and universities (Graham, 1978, pp. 759–793). As the enrollment of women increased, many college presidents appointed female faculty members to advise, assist, and counsel female students. These women were given the title "dean of women" to reflect their new dual roles.

Deans of women were asked to serve a dual role on the college campuses from the 1890s till the 1930s. In that transitional period, the deans were to oversee the new "minority" population on campus—women. In this capacity, they would insulate the historically male campuses from the women and, in turn, protect and guide the women, a distinct social and cultural minority despite the rapid increase in their enrollment. On the other hand, most deans were first and foremost faculty. They were academics who had trained for the scholarly life and were eager for the opportunity to teach, write, and conduct research. They were concerned about the intellectual and scholarly development of women, especially in competition with men. Then as now, women had to be better to be equal.

Coeducation and Regionalism

Prior to the turn of the century, few opportunities existed in which women could experience higher education in a coeducational setting, either as students or faculty. Although Oberlin College in Ohio had admitted four women as early as 1837, relatively few coeducational experiences existed prior to the Civil War (Rudolph, 1990). Even at Oberlin, women took a different, lesser curriculum than men and were assigned different college duties. While the men studied Greek, Latin, and rhetoric, women studied in a Female Department. While men prepared for the ministry, women cooked, washed, and cleaned (Solomon, 1985, pp. 21–22).

After the Civil War, the rationales both for and against the admission of women were as widespread as the institutions. Geography played a role; many colleges in the East and South steadfastly refused to admit women while, in the Middle West and West, new state colleges in Iowa, Indiana, Michigan, and California opened their doors as coeducational institutions (Rudolph, 1990, pp. 307–328). Economics and the prohibitive cost of operating two separate campuses, one for men and another for women, was an avoidable expense if coeducation was adopted at the outset. The need for more teachers in the "common schools" which had spread to the Midwest also encouraged the higher education of women, more and more often in state institutions such as teachers colleges and normal schools.

Yet college presidents and senior faculty on many campuses were unsettled by the presence of women. Even such ardent proponents of coeducation as President James Burrill Angell of Michigan, had been educated in a generation when students and faculty were exclusively male. Women in college raised concerns about propriety, delicate matters of health, and female "problems" as well as the institutional responsibility to families to protect the safety, sexual virtue, and reputations of daughters far from home.[1] The deans of women were the perfect solution to the dilemma. They could not only attend to any "female" concerns but also could maintain an appropriate "woman's sphere" of domestic responsibility and tranquillity, the image of which dominated respectable society in Victorian America. As president of Wellesley (1881–1887), Alice Freeman Palmer created the "cottage system," a collection of small houses for group living, as a safe *domus* for Wellesley students.[2]

The First Deans of Women

Alice Freeman Palmer became the nation's first dean of women in 1892. A graduate of the University of Michigan, Palmer had been a very popular president of Wellesley College until she resigned upon marrying Harvard philosopher George Herbert Palmer in 1887 (Solomon, 1980). Lobbied incessantly by William Rainey Harper, Palmer agreed to be dean of women and professor of history at the University of Chicago in 1892 only on condition that she serve part time. Palmer was reluctant to leave the sophistication of the Boston area and her husband of five years for more than a few months at a time. He refused an offered position that would have allowed him to accompany her. (Palmer, 1909). To share the work of her new office, Alice Palmer persuaded Harper to hire her good friend and protegee, Marion Talbot, as Dean of Women for the University College and assistant professor of domestic sciences. When Palmer resigned three years later, Harper promoted Talbot to the deanship (Talbot, 1925).

The appointment of other deans of women followed quickly, paralleling the increases in the enrollment of women. In 1903, Marion Talbot of Chicago called the first meeting of deans of women for which a record survives.[3] Seventeen deans of women, representing the Universities of Chicago, Illinois, Wisconsin, Colorado, Kansas, Iowa, Ohio State, and Michigan, Indiana University, and Northwestern, Ripon, Carleton, Lawrence, Barnard, Oberlin, Beloit, and Illinois College attended (NADW, 1927). The deans' agenda included the housing of women students, training in etiquette and social skills, women's self-government, leadership opportunities for women students, and women's intercollegiate athletics.

Later in the same decade, organizations representing state colleges, private colleges, and teachers colleges formed representative organizations. In 1915, Lois Kimball Mathews, dean of women and associate professor of history at the University of Wisconsin, published the first book on *The Dean of Women*. Many deans of women were eager to pursue graduate degrees to advance their skills and credibility. In response, Teachers College of Columbia University established a graduate program in 1916 specifically to train deans of women. In 1917, the National Association of Deans of Women (NADW), was established as a branch of the National Education Association (NADW, 1927).

In the five decades from the 1890s through World War II, the deans of women established the foundations of professional practice for student affairs and higher education administration, including graduate study, the development of professional associations, research on students, college environments, and student guidance and counseling. They developed a body of professional literature which included journals, research reports, and books.

These deans worked hard to "professionalize" the position of dean and to legitimize their roles on the still predominantly male college campus. As women, they saw their role, profession, and gender as inextricably tied together (Cott, 1987; Chafe, 1972). The deans of women were early champions of the scientific methods of guidance for students. They often challenged each other and their campuses to "do the right thing" by women. At their first meeting in Chicago in 1903, they passed a resolution condemning "gender segregation" in higher education (NADW, 1927).

However, many of their significant accomplishments have been lost or ignored in compilations of the modern history of higher education. What remains is an unfortunate caricature of deans of women as "snooping battle axes" (Rhatighan, 1978)—prudish spinsters who bedeviled the harmless funseeking of their students.

In large part, in my opinion, this inaccurate view results from the male voice's domination of written and oral histories of American colleges and universities. Even to the present, the accomplishments of deans of women have rarely received honest evaluation, validation, or appreciation. Rather, they have been discounted, discredited, or ignored. In reality, the deans of women were consummate professionals who anchored much of their work to the academic principles of rigorous research and scholarly dissemination of their findings. Many of the significant and well-established practices of student affairs work and higher education administrations that exist today were first put in place through the work of the deans of women. This paper presents a closer examination of these deans, revealing a much different story than the stereotype which has survived.

Professional Development

As early as 1904, the deans of women began to organize professional associations. While the scope of many of the early associations was limited, it gave the deans an opportunity for professional contact and connections. These associations were organized by institutional type: Deans of Women in State Universities, Deans of Women in Private Colleges, and so on. The NADW's History Committee reported that attendance at these early meetings often numbered only 12 or 14 women (NADW, 1927, pp. 214–217), but these meetings were still significant in that they represented a determined effort to share ideas and information and to support each other professionally and, in large measure, personally.

The deans of women diligently and rigorously built their profession on the bedrock of academic discipline, research, and publication. Many of the deans appointed in the late decades of the 19th century and early decades of the 20th already held advanced degrees in their own fields. Most held faculty rank and continued to teach despite the added responsibility of the deanship. As Lois Kimball Mathews (1915) noted in *The Dean of Women*, a dean "must win her spurs in the classroom.... There is no more effective place for inculcating respect for women's powers and equipment than on the teaching side of a desk in the college classroom" (pp. 32–33). In 1928, Jane Jones, a graduate student at Teachers College, published her research on 263 deans of women titled *A Personnel Study of Women Deans in Colleges and Universities*. In her sample, 91% (n = 238) of these women had earned at least a bachelor's degree, 57% (151) had also earned a master's degree, and 15% (40) had earned the doctorate. In response to the question "Do you hold academic rank?" 74.9% (197) did. Of those deans who held faculty positions, the breakdown of rank was: lecturer 0.9% (1); instructor 8.8% (23); assistant professor 12.9% (34); associate professor 12.9% (34); and professor 39.9% (105) (pp. 12–14).

They reported teaching in 36 academic areas; but most were grouped in traditional arts and sciences: English (57), history (21), hygiene (17), French (16), education (15), and home economics (10). Some, like Marion Talbot, were in pioneering disciplines like household sanitation and the domestic sciences that gave rise to ecological sciences later in the century (Rossiter, 1982). In short, the deans of women were not academic lightweights.

Research and Publications

The diligent Ruth Strang, professor of education at Teachers College at Columbia, headed the Research Committee of the National Association of Deans of Women through the 1930s. Strang and her colleagues at Teachers College, Sarah Sturtevant and later Esther Lloyd-Jones, oversaw many graduate research projects and regularly published their own work. In the preface to the report of the NADW Research Committee in 1934, Strang noted:

The position of dean of women has both artistic and scientific aspects. The artistic side is represented in the inspirational and philosophical articles; the scientific aspect in the description survey and experimental study of plans and procedures of work with individuals. It has been the self-imposed task of the Research Committee to summarize the investigations relating to the work of dean of women, and to make available annually the more or less scientific body of professional subject-matter published during the year. (NADW, 1934, p. 56)

Responding to her own rhetorical question, "What lines and types of research are needed?" Strang editorialized:

Articles on guidance in educational magazines during the past five years have predominantly been descriptions of guidance programs and practices. Only 140 of the 461 articles analyzed involved some systematic investigation. Professors and directors of guidance emphasize the need for measures of the effects of guidance services and opportunities. Well-planned programs of guidance should be set up, groups of students followed through these programs, complete records kept at each step and the results carefully measured. (NADW, 1934, p. 129)

Under Strang's leadership, the Research Committee identified 115 articles in their bibliography for 1934 alone. Through Strang's influence, comparable reports and bibliographies were prepared by the Research Committees and published in the *Yearbooks* of the National Association of Deans of Women in 1935, 1936, and 1937.

In addition to the research effort, more books joined *The Education of Women* by Marion Talbot (1910) and *The Dean of Women* by Lois Kimball Mathews. Anna E. Pierce, dean of women at the New York State College for Teachers produced *Deans and Advisers of Women and Girls* in 1928. Jane Jones's research (1928) was published in Contributions to Education, a series sponsored by the Teachers College. Another graduate study, *The Effective Dean of Women: A Study of the Personal and Professional Characteristics of a Selected Group of Deans of Women*, appeared in 1932, written by another dean, Eunice Mae Acheson. Teachers College faculty members Sarah Sturtevant and Ruth Strang contributed their own research, *A Personnel Study of Deans of Women in Teachers College and Normal Schools*, in 1928, followed by *A Personnel Study of Deans of Girls in High School* in 1929. Their much larger 1940 study, *A Personnel Study of Deans of Women in Colleges, Universities, and Normal Schools* updated the earlier works.

By the mid-1930s, 40 years after the first deans of women were appointed and a mere 17 years after the national association was formed, deans of women had firmly established themselves in higher education administration. The first deans were well-respected academic women who had committed themselves to their disciplines. While they were determined to provide counsel and support to young women, they also focused on the prerequisites of scholarship as the road to respect in academe. Accordingly, the early deans wrote books, conducted research, published articles, and established professional associations. In turn, the associations developed journals and held annual conferences for the further dissemination of knowledge and the advancement of the profession.

The deans of women also oversaw the establishment of graduate study and degrees for the training of new deans of women as well as the expansion of research related to the field. The faculty teaching in graduate programs, especially at Teachers College, represented some of the strongest researchers and practitioners in guidance and counseling which had emerged from the "personnel" movement initiated by Walter Dill Scott, a psychologist and later president of Northwestern University. When Esther Lloyd-Jones joined the faculty at Teachers College in New York, for example, she brought with her first-hand experience as a dean as well as strong research skills developed during her time at Northwestern under Scott's tutelage.

The Personnel Movement

Walter Dill Scott developed the concept of "personnel psychology" as a young psychology professor at Northwestern. Through a battery of tests, extensive interviews, and meticulous record-keeping, each individual in an organization was chronicled and categorized by family background, personnel interests, aptitude, and vocational and career aspirations. In the college setting, records on individual students allowed the trained observer to assess the student's developmental progress, not only toward a college degree but also a successful occupation and, ideally, a fulfilling life. The underlying hypothesis of this movement was that, rather than leaving vocation, personal satisfaction, and social efficiency to whimsy and chance, proper personnel and guidance techniques enabled personnel directors to direct and support student's energies towards constructive and useful ends.

Initially designed to complement the "efficiency movement" in industry, Scott's ideas were applied, first, to draftees in World War I and later to students at Northwestern. The concept spread to other institutions through Scott's protégés such as L. B. Hopkins who became president of Wabash College. Hopkins wrote his own version of Scott's personnel philosophy for higher education, *Personnel Procedure in Education*, published in 1926 by the American Council on Education (ACE).[4] When Esther Lloyd-Jones moved to Teachers College after graduate work and a faculty position at Northwestern, she used "personnel" concepts with graduate students and deans of women. Her own book, *Student Personnel Work at Northwestern University*, was published in 1929.

During the 1930s, "student personnel" programs became widespread and popular; using psychology and vocational guidance would become the dominant theme of the late 1940s and 1950s. Having embraced the concept in the early 1930s, the deans of women were far ahead of their time. Not only were the graduate faculty at Teachers College and other institutions promoting the very latest in psychological sciences for work with college students, but the deans of women through their national association also spread the word to their members on college campuses across the country.

When a new coordinating body, the Council of Guidance and Personnel Associations (CPGA), was initiated in 1934, members of the National Association of Deans of Women were immediately involved as officers. Through the leadership of women such as Thrysa Amos, Sarah Sturtevant, and Esther Lloyd-Jones, this council encouraged the further involvement of deans of women and women in other positions, such as appointment secretaries, in national associations promoting the personnel movement. By 1936, the CPGA represented the common interests of 12 member organizations. Other organizations in the new CPGA included the American College Personnel Association, the Personnel Research Federation, and the Teachers College Personnel Association, to name only three. This coordinated effort consolidated the increasing interest in the personnel movement nationwide.[5]

As early as 1931, a report on land-grant colleges by the U.S. Commissioner of Education had noted:

> The term "personnel service" has been carried over into the colleges from industry, where it came into prominence just after the [first] World War. . . . Industry uses personnel work in selecting, teaching, lessening turnover, conserving health, and providing recreation for its workers. . . . When colleges took over this type of work . . . the fundamental aim . . . [was] service to the student as an individual. [However,] the colleges have for years been obtaining and filing away vast numbers of records, a source for limitless research, that, rightly used, might throw much light on many of their unsolved problems. (pp. 420–424)

In 1937, the ACE published a monograph reporting the work of a 17-member Subcommittee on Student Welfare which enthusiastically promoted the concept of "student personnel." It urged college and university presidents and faculty to guide students through courses, vocations, and even the extracurriculum with the aid of student personnel procedures. This subcommittee included Esther Lloyd-Jones and Thrysa Amos, both active in many of the activities of deans of women (ACE, 1937).

Over time, the student personnel concept won many supporters. The deans of women saw the new philosophy as sound theory put into practice and as a benefit to women students. By emphasizing social efficiency and tying vocation to skills and ability, not just physical attributes, the personnel concept was friendlier to women than other existing methods of selection and training.

What the deans could not know was that the personnel movement carried within it the seeds of destruction for their own profession as deans of women. At Northwestern, Walter Scott had encouraged the coordination of personnel offices and workers under a single director of personnel for greater efficiency. When records were kept in several offices or duplicated by several workers, much effort was wasted. While the logic of efficiency was irresistible, the social fact of American administrative hierarchy in the 1930s was also inescapable: Whether in the army, a factory, or a college, the administrative head of any large operation was almost certainly going to be a man.

Deans of Men

After the appointment of the deans of women at the University of Chicago, most colleges and universities in the United States slowly began adding the office of dean of men during the 1910s and 1920s.[6] After performing numerous tasks of a dean for several years, Thomas Arkle Clark, a professor of rhetoric and English at the University of Illinois, received the official title of dean of men in 1909. Clark's appointment was followed by others at Purdue, Iowa, and Wisconsin to name only a few other state coeducational institutions. While the admission of women created change on campus, demanding administrative response, male students were more often left to fend for themselves as they had traditionally been.

Given the concentration of deans of men in the Midwest, it is not surprising that the first recorded meeting of deans of men took place at a Big Ten institution. Scott Goodnight, dean of men at the University of Wisconsin, takes credit for arranging a meeting in Madison in 1919 "for a discussion of our problems" (NADM, 1934, p. 28). Goodnight, with some urging from Robert Rienow, dean of men at Iowa, called the meeting because of his concern for student disciplinary matters between the schools. He recalled:

> Without authorization from anybody, I wired Minnesota, Iowa, Illinois, Indiana and Michigan to come on over. The idea of founding a permanent organization or creating a professional association was the farthest thing from my mind when I invited the boys to come in for a weekend so that we might discuss our common tribulations more intimately. It was after the first meeting had proved so pleasant and stimulating that the proposal was made to repeat it. (NADM, 1934, p. 32)

The session was a great success. Another meeting followed in 1920. In 1921, the gathering formally organized under the name of the National Association of Deans of Men and authorized the publication of the meeting's minutes.

The meetings were social and club-like in contrast to the professionalism of the national conferences of the deans of women. The deans of men enjoyed the opportunity to converse, to enjoy local hospitalities and activities, and to regale each other with tales from their campuses. Over time, issues of professionalism, graduate study, and the role of the dean of men were topics of discussion, but they were addressed in a more affable, informal manner with less emphasis on scholarship and research than the deans of women demonstrated in their sessions.

For example, Stanley Coulter, dean of men at Purdue University, captured the informal and jovial tone of these early meetings:

> What is a Dean of Men? I have tried to define him. When the Board of Trustees elected me Dean of Men, I wrote to them very respectfully and asked them to give me the duties of the Dean of Men. They wrote back that they did not know what they were but when I found out to let them know. I worked all the rest of the year trying to find out. I discovered that every unpleasant task that the president or the faculty did not want to do was my task. I was convinced that the Dean of Men's office was intended as the dumping ground of all unpleasant things. (NADM, 1928, p. 37).

Part of the deans of men's organizational task was to search for a campus persona with which they were comfortable. They were concerned that they not be perceived only as "disciplinarians" whose primary role was to punish young men who ran afoul of college or university rules and regulations.[7] As a group, they practiced a benevolent, pipe-smoking, older brother type of *in loco parentis*.

Change on Campus and the Deans

During the Roaring 1920s, college students became the first collective student population large enough to rewrite the rules, and they demanded life on their own terms. In the *Ohio State Lantern* in 1922, one coed declared:

> Are we as bad as we are painted? We are. We do all the things that our mothers, fathers, aunts and uncles do not sanction, and we do them knowingly. We are not young innocents—... We are ... smoking, dancing like Voodoo devotees, dressing décolleté, "petting" and drinking. We do these things because we honestly enjoy the attendant physical sensations.... The college girl—particularly the girl in the coeducational institution—is a plucky, coolheaded individual who thinks naturally.... The girl does not stand aloof—she and the man meet on common ground.... (Qtd. in Fass, 1976, p. 307)

Fass (1976) has noted the importance of this shift in women's traditional roles:

> The American woman had been the special stabilizer of nineteenth-century society. [Instead of the] stable mother secure in her morality and her home [was the] "giddy flapper, rouged and clipped, careening in a drunken stupor to the lewd strains of a jazz quartet" (pp. 23–25).

Some deans of women reacted with outrage and moral indignation. For example, Anna Pierce, dean at a state college in upstate New York, used her book, *Deans and Advisers to Women and Girls* (1928) to lament the abandonment of the moral codes which defined women's roles throughout the nineteenth century and to urge the familiar themes of separate spheres for men and women.

However, most deans appear to have taken many of these social changes in stride. Minutes from the national meetings of deans of women do not record a significant reaction or undue concern about the new "youth generation," a term employed by *Life* magazine to describe the campus scene. William J. Alderman, dean of men at Beloit College, wittily characterized the college campuses of the 1920s as a:

> heterogony of monstrosities—bobbed haired daughters of Satan in their early nicotines; tardy sons of Hoyle who have an aversion for the hardy sons of toil; emulous coeds who indulge in such fatuous anachronisms as breaking the endurance record for the tango;... The daughters of culture have married the sons of prosperity and are sending their offspring to universities and colleges because it is fashionable, convenient and prudential. (NADM,1928, p. 43).

Nonetheless, the deans of men more typically reacted to change on campus, in contrast to the participatory stance of the deans of women, who typically used their professional associations and their own research to guide their responses. The deans of men, like Thomas Clark and others, stood for a paternalistic, *in loco parentis* approach to these concerns. They often appealed to the "good" nature of their men and used discipline as a tool for social development.

Further, the disciplinary records for the period indicate that women students were less likely to engage in behavior which resulted in disciplinary action. A 1932 survey of 31 land-grant colleges shows that 2,914 women (7% of all women enrolled) were disciplined, while men in 40 institutions who were disciplined during the same period numbered 11,683 (12.5% of those enrolled) (*Report of the U.S. Commissioner of Education, 1932*). Far more students, male and female alike, were put on probation or suspended for "poor grades" than for "drinking," "sex," or "automobiles." Thus, deans of men were indeed busier than the deans of women when it came to campus discipline, but their primary source of concern was academic performance, not moral behavior. Robert Rienow, dean of men at the University of Iowa, admitted at the 1928 NADM meeting: "For thirteen years I kidded myself that I was not a disciplinarian. But in the last few years I have learned that I was [always] pulling the chestnuts out of the fire for someone" (NADM, 1928, p. 41).

Training for Deans of Men

Beyond discipline and approaches to student conduct, the most obvious disparity between deans of men and deans of women was the ongoing debate over professional training and graduate study. F. F. Bradshaw, dean of men at the University of North Carolina argued in 1931:

> The deanship stands to some extent at a fork in the road... whether we are to be solely campus disciplinarians or whether we are to be administrative coordinators of the institution's work from the point of view of the whole individual student and the point of view of group life of students. (NADM, 1931, p. 108)

However, he was apparently a minority voice against a majority position of jocular but determined amateurism holding that graduate study was of little use to anyone seeking to be a dean. Speaking in the same 1931 conference of deans of men, Joseph Bursley, dean of men at the University of Michigan, countered Bradshaw's argument, not with evidence, but with the cheerful assertion: "I am afraid that I am not in sympathy with the idea of any course of training for the position of Dean of Men.... The best and most successful Deans of Men are born and not made" (p. 103). Bursley did offer a slight concession, although whether it can be taken seriously is another matter:

> There is one place where I believe that preparedness is absolutely essential to the success of a dean of men—that is in the selection of a wife. The very best preparation he [the dean] can have for his work is to marry the right woman. If she is the right kind, a dean's wife does just as much to earn his salary as he does, and if she is not, he might as well quit before he starts. (NADM, 1931, p. 104)

Five years later, Frederick R. Turner, successor to Thomas Arkle Clark as Dean of Men at the University of Illinois, repeated an identical assertion to the annual conference of the National Association of Deans of Women:

> I am... chairman of a special committee [of the National Association of Deans of Men] to study and report on... the preparation [of the] dean of men... The general opinion of those who have served long and successfully, and those who have observed successful deans of men, is that there is no satisfactory training [to be a dean], at least from the academic standpoint, for the simple reason that the best deans are born that way and not trained that way. (NADW, 1936, p. 104)

Part of his address was reporting the work of a committee he had chaired on "preparation for work as a dean of men" that had surveyed respondents. In response to a question about what practical training would be helpful, the top responses were "apprenticeship to a Dean of Men (n = 68);" "work with activities (43)," "administrative duties (30)," "counseling and interviewing (27)," "dormitory proctor (18)," and "business experience (16)." Other suggestions ranged from "Y.M.C.A. work" to "grade tests" to "speaking in public" (NADW, 1936, pp. 104–106).

There is no record of the reaction of the highly professionalized deans of women to this survey. However, in 1937, William H. Cowley got the attention of the deans of men with an address on "The Disappearing Dean of Men." Cowley, director of education research at Ohio State, spelled out the future for the assembled deans in a simple and straightforward thesis: As the need for student personnel services expanded within higher education, the office of the dean of men would cease to exist. While "deans for student relations" and "instructional" or academic deans had "grown out of the same tree"—Charles W. Eliot's administration at Harvard—both had changed significantly over time.

Cowley saw the existing distribution of student personnel functions as an obstacle to efficiency. For example, the student's application form is "replete with information of high value to the members of the personnel staff other than the admissions officer" (NADM, 1937, p. 94); however, probably no one else ever saw it and other campus offices collected the same information all over again, wasting their time and the students'. In essence, Cowley claimed:

> All student personnel services are but different types of the same sort of activity.... A basic unity runs throughout them all. If the assumption is sound, then it follows, it seems to me, that somehow they should all be made to work together in unison, that they should all move forward in step, that, in brief, they should all be coordinated. (p. 94).

Cowley sketched "three roads" to such coordination. In the first possibility, the dean of men would become this needed personnel coordinator. The second "road" made the dean subordinate to a coordinator of personnel services. The third option eliminated the positions of both dean of men and women, as Earlham, William and Mary, Iowa State, and Northwestern had already done. He found possible but improbable the idea that matters would remain much as they were.

The turn towards student personnel services in higher education, Cowley told the deans, was irreversible and universal. While "sitting deans" might be named coordinator or director of personnel in the revamped organization, much would depend on the incumbent. Each dean would have to be evaluated on his own merits. A successful transition would depend on the dean of men's "training, his temperament, his intellectual range, his ability as an executive, and . . . his spirit" (p. 99).

Two of the many questions to which Cowley responded after the presentation of his paper was a particularly telling one: Would a dean of women also be "subordinate"? Would it be possible for a woman to be promoted to the top spot? Cowley responded, "It seems to me there isn't any reason deans of women shouldn't go up if they are equal to it. I think we can say that the deans of women are in exactly the same position as deans of men" (p. 99).

Cowley was a member of the Student Welfare Committee of the American Council on Education, which had just published *The Student Personnel Point of View* (ACE, 1937). He was simply reporting on the committee's work. But Cowley commanded a good bit of respect and his presentation forced the deans of men to reexamine their position on campus.

Still, nothing really changed for ten or fifteen years—not until deans of men and other male administrators accepted the inevitability of the "personnel movement" in the late 1940s and early 1950s.[8] As campuses adopted the "student personnel" philosophy as envisioned by the American Council on Education in 1937, it was the position of dean of women which systematically disappeared from most college and university campuses. As men swarmed to college campuses after World War II in response to the Serviceman's Readjustment Act (GI Bill), opportunities for women were diminished. Eventually, the dominance of men on college campuses defeated the need to recognize and maintain a role for women on campus.

Post-World War II Developments

The position of dean of women was threatened after World War II both in numbers and as a symbol. Although women's representation on campuses had climbed steadily from 1870 through the 1920s, their inclusion on campus had never been easy. The Great Depression in the 1930s and national attention on World War II in the 1940s further redirected social energies away from education. When the country returned to domestic issues following World War II, the press for "normalcy" and rush to reward men for the "war effort" ignored the role women had played in achieving success. In many cases, this reaction galvanized attitudes which can best be described as "anti-women;" including the slow but steady erosion of women's presence on college campuses (Chafe, 1972).

Barbara Solomon (1980) and Patricia Graham (1978) cite enrollment statistics from 1870 to 1950 that describe a slow but steady decline in the enrollment of women from 1930 through the 1950s. From representing 47% of undergraduates in 1920, women's enrollment dropped to only 21% of undergraduates by the mid-1950s (Graham, 1978), even though the raw numbers of women in higher education continued to rise. At first glance, this decline may not appear to be much of a problem since women who desired an education obviously had no trouble gaining admittance by the thousands. However, the culture of the campus became increasingly indifferent and even hostile towards women. The patronizing tone is captured by the universally prevalent joke that women were just in college to earn their "MRS" degree. Chafe (1972) and others have documented the determined effort to keep women in the home and out of the workplace in the post-war era. In simple terms, there was a social reconstruction of the 19th century concept of "separate spheres," with women's place being located exclusively in the home. As evidence, we need look no further than the baby boom generation born in the late 1940s and 1950s.

The position of dean of women was an inevitable victim of the pervasive hostility that greeted women in general on campus, while the position of dean of men assumed new administrative importance. In 1951, the National Association of Deans of Men changed its name to the more contemporary National Association of Student Personnel Administrators. On individual campuses, the office of dean of men expanded to become dean for student personnel, dean of students, and vice-presidents for student personnel services during the 1950s. Meanwhile, deans of women were given lesser positions, dismissed, or allowed to retire quietly. In 1952, Louise Spenser reported that the number of deans of women reporting to a "coordinated" office or to a dean of students had risen to 12% as compared to 2% in 1936. Many of the deans of women who responded to Spenser's survey, based on responses from 472 colleges and universities, gave anecdotal evidence that they could sense problems in the future. Spenser herself, analyzing her data, queried, "Shall the needs, and problems, and interests of women students be represented by a man who is generally far removed from the problems . . . ?" (p. 107). This status problem was not unique to deans of women. William Chafe (1972) documents that "women fell from 25% of all auto workers in 1944 to 7.5% in April 1946. Overall, females comprised 60% of all workers released from employment in the early months after the war [World War II] and were laid off at a rate 75% higher than men" (p. 180). Among deans of women, the trend would persist across the next several decades till the office was virtually extinct. The NADW, the professional association, became the National Association of Women Deans, Administrators, and Counselors (NAWDAC) in the 1960s, trying to reverse its declining membership with broader appeal.

Summary and Conclusion

Many explanations can be offered, but the simplest are probably the most accurate. In brief, women were not welcome on college campuses during the period, a trend which reached its zenith in the 1950s. As a lightning rod for women's involvement on campus, the dean of women was no longer a positive force for change but a pariah. The caricature of spinsterly, "snooping battle axes" (Rhatigan, 1978) gained credence in the 1950s, allowing the final denigration of a proud, respected, and pioneering professional—the dean of women. Instead of the recognition and respect which many of the deans of women deserved for the establishment of graduate study, research, professional associations, and a significant body of professional literature, the deans of women saw their roles and offices erode and eventually disappear.

The new personnel directors suggested by Cowley and the *Student Personnel Point of View* in 1937 were finally appointed in the late 1940s and during the 1950s. While many of the deans of men were realigned into such positions as dean for student personnel, dean of students, and vice presidents for student personnel services, deans of women were given lesser positions, dismissed, or allowed to retire quietly. To insure their new roles, in 1951, the National Association of Deans of Men changed its name to the more contemporary National Association of Student Personnel Administrators. The deans of men finally got the message. The ideas, theories, concepts, research, and goals of the deans of women went forward, but the deans of women did not. The deans of women became men.

From the 1950s to the 1990s, men assumed the primary roles as deans, vice presidents, leading authors, and national spokespersons for higher education and student affairs issues, research, and policy. In truth, they were simply advancing the ideology of the women who had preceded them in earlier decades. Ironically, higher education administration and student affairs continue to attract more women than men to graduate preparation programs. And following the pattern described above, most of the top administrative positions still go to men.

Footnotes

1. One of the most pronounced diatribes against higher education for women came in a 1873 book, *Sex in Education; Or a Fair Chance for Girls*, by Edward H. Clarke, a Boston physician specializing in diseases of the eye and nerves. Clarke argued that women were incapable of both serious intellectual work and child-rearing. Too much study would atrophy

the womb. His book went into 17 printings before 1885.
2. Palmer herself moved from the president's house to a cottage. During the 1890s at the University of Chicago, Palmer and Marian Talbot attempted, through the Beatrice Hotel and later a women's residence hall on campus, to recreate the "cottage system" for women students (Talbot, 1925).
3. Marion Talbot was following the example of her mother, who in 1888 had organized the charter session of the Association of Collegiate Alumnae, a meeting attended by both Marion Talbot and Alice Freeman. There is a mention of an earlier meeting in 1902 but no minutes have survived. This association did some of the earliest research on women in American colleges, a function that the National Association of Deans of Women picked up with enthusiasm and carried out with impressive professionalism.
4. George Zook, U.S. Commissioner of Education and later president of ACE, became an early and zealous convert to the concepts of the personnel movement. Zook, Hopkins, and Lloyd-Jones all served on an ACE committee in 1937 credited with drawing greater attention to the new philosophy of student personnel in higher education through publishing the *Student Personnel Point of View* (SPPV), a monograph still published and studied today.
5. The CPGA was later renamed the American Guidance and Personnel Association (APGA).
6. Le Baron Russell Briggs, an English professor at Harvard, was appointed "dean for students" in 1890 by Charles William Eliot, who was attempting to delegate some of his administrative tasks. Briggs thus preceded Alice Palmer and Marion Talbot at Chicago. Eliot simultaneously appointed another faculty member as academic dean (Eliot, 1908; Brown, 1936).
7. Among Thomas Clark's publications is a collection of tales dealing with miscreant students, aptly titled, *Discipline and the Derelict: Being a Series of Essays on Some of Those Who Tread the Green Carpet* (1921).
8. This same "personnel movement" was the subject of Lloyd-Jones's book in 1929 and had been embraced by the leadership of the National Association of Deans of Women in the 1930s. In this aspect, they were at least a decade in advance of their male counterparts.

References

American Council on Education. (1937). *The student personnel point of view*. Washington, DC: Author.

Acheson, E. M. (1932).*The effective dean of women: A study of the personal and professional characteristics of a selected group of deans of women*. Chicago: University of Illinois.

Brown, R. W. (1928). *Dean Briggs*. New York: Harper.

Chafe, W. H. (1972). *The American woman: Her changing social, economic and political roles, 1920–1970*. New York: Oxford University Press.

Chafe, W. H. (1977). *Women and equality*. New York: Oxford University Press.

Clark, T. A. (1921). *Discipline and the derelict: Being a series of essays on some of those who tread the green carpet*. New York: Macmillan, 1921.

Cott, N. R (1987). *The grounding of modern feminism*. New Haven, CT: Yale University Press.

Eliot, C. W. (1908). *University administration*. New York: Houghton Mifflin.

Fass, P (1977). *The damned and the beautiful: American youth in the 1920's*. New York: Oxford University Press.

Graham, P. A. (1978). Expansion and exclusion: A history of women in American higher education. *Signs: Journal of Women in Culture and Society, 3*, 759–773.

Hopkins, L. B. (1926). *Personnel procedure in education*. Washington, DC: American Council on Education.

Lloyd-Jones, E. (1929). *Student personnel work at Northwestern University*. New York: Harper & Brothers.

Jones, J. (1928). *A personnel study of women deans in colleges and universities*. Contributions to Education, No. 319. New York: Teachers College, Columbia University.

Mathews, L. K. (1915). *The dean of women*. Cambridge, MA: Riverside Press.

NADM. National Association of Deans of Men. (Annual.) *Secretarial Notes of the Annual Conferences of the National Association of Deans of Men*. Title also *Secretarial Proceedings of the National Association of Deans and Advisers to Men*. Lawrence, KS: Republican Publishing Company. I cite the following issues by year in the text: 10th conference in 1928, 11th conference in 1929, 13th conference in 1931, 14th conference in 1932, 15th conference in 1933, 16th conference in 1934, 18th conference in 1936, 26th conference in 1944. Library, Indiana University.

NADW. National Association of Deans of Women. *Yearbook of the National Association of the Deans of Women*. I cite the following issues in the text: 1927, 1928, 1934, 1936. Library, Indiana University.

Palmer, G. H. (1909). *The Life of Alice Freeman Palmer*. Boston: Houghton Mifflin.

Pierce, A. M. (1928). *Deans and advisers to women and girls*. New York: Professional and Technical Press.

Rhatigan, J. J. (1978). A corrective look back. In J. Appleton, C. Briggs, & J. J. Rhatigan (Eds.), *Pieces of eight: The rites, roles and styles of the dean by eight who have been there* (pp. 9–41). Portland, OR: NASPA Institute of Research and Development.

Rudolph, E. (1990). *The American college and university: A history*. Athens: University of Georgia Press.

Rossiter, M. W. (1982). *Women scientists in America: Struggles and strategies to 1940*. Baltimore, MD: Johns Hopkins Press.

Solomon, B. M. (1980). *In the company of educated women: A history of women and higher education in America*. New Haven, CT: Yale University Press.

Spenser, L. W. (1952). *Eleven years of change in the role of the dean of women in colleges, universities, and teachers colleges*. Unpublished doctoral dissertation, Teachers College, Columbia University, New York.

Sturtevant, S., & Strang, R. (1928). *A personnel study of deans of women in teachers college and normal schools*. Contributions to Education, No. 319. New York: Teachers College Press.

Sturtevant, S., & Strang, R. (1929). *A personnel study of deans of girls in high school*. Contributions to Education, No. 393. New York: Teachers College Press.

Sturtevant, S., Strang, R., & McKim, M. (1940). *A personnel study of deans of women in colleges, universities, and normal schools*. Contributions to Education, No. 787. New York: Teachers College Press.

Talbot, M. (1910). *The education of women*. Chicago: University of Chicago Press.

Talbot, M. (1925). *More than lore: Reminiscences of Marion Talbot*. Chicago: University of Chicago Press.

Zook, G. (1937, May). Presidential report for the American Council on Education, 1937, *Educational Record, 14*.

Robert A. Schwartz is currently an Assistant Professor in the College of Education at the University of South Carolina in Columbia. His research interests include the history of higher education, women, and student services. He has recently completed research on women in higher education and also African American women in graduate study.

B.

WOMEN FACULTY

CHAPTER 20

RESEARCH, TEACHING, AND SERVICE
Why Shouldn't Women's Work Count?

SHELLEY M. PARK

Introduction

Despite myths concerning the efficacy of affirmative action programs, there are still relatively few women in academia. Moreover, the female professors one does encounter in the academy are apt to be found in lower-paying, less prestigious, and less secure positions [6, 12, 18, 71, 83]. Educational cutbacks combined with fewer tenure-track positions and more restrictive criteria for tenure and promotion have given rise to a "revolving door" phenomenon, wherein adjunct and junior faculty are rotated through entry level positions without serious consideration for tenure [42, 44]. This has created a new class of "gypsy scholars" [14], an intellectual "proletariat" [87] who—in order to eke out a living—move from one low-paying, dead-end teaching post to another. This proletariat is disproportionately female.

There are several explanations for this. Some people claim that women are simply not socialized to be as career-oriented or ambitious as men. Others point to the fact that women still are largely responsible for child-rearing and housekeeping, thus giving them less time and energy to forge successful career paths. Though there undoubtedly is some truth to such explanations, focusing exclusively on such external factors may lead us to overlook the ways in which sexism is embedded in the structures, norms, and policies of the university itself.

Organizational theorists have recently begun to grapple with the ways in which allegedly sex-neutral corporations and bureaucracies are dominated by masculine principles and structures which lead to advantages for male employees and disadvantages for female employees [1, 16, 45, 46]. Central to this analysis has been the uncovering of a gendered division of labor in corporations, which arises through the institutionalization of organizational roles that "carry characteristic images of the kinds of people that should occupy them" [46, p. 250]. Thus, certain tasks, such as managing money, may be gender-typed as masculine, whereas other tasks, such as dealing with clients, may be gender-typed as feminine, replicating the gender stereotypes that exist outside the corporation. Such gender-typing of (abstract) jobs subsequently leads to filling these occupational positions with specific persons who are biologically male or female [1]. This further reinforces the initial assumption that certain work is "men's work," whereas other work is "women's work" [45]. "Men's work" is, moreover, typically depicted as involving greater complexity and difficulty than "women's work" and thus enjoys greater status and rewards than "women's work" [1]. Hence, the gender-role segregation results in a gender-role hierarchy in which the jobs identified as (culturally) feminine and allocated to (biological) women are undervalued and underpaid.

This article examines one way institutionalized sexism operates in the university setting by examining the gender roles and gender hierarchies implicit in (allegedly gender-neutral) university tenure and promotion policies. Current working assumptions regarding (1) what constitutes good research, teaching, and service and (2) the relative importance of each of these endeavors reflect and perpetuate masculine values and practices, thus preventing the professional advancement of female faculty both individually and collectively. A gendered division of labor exists within (as outside) the contemporary academy wherein research is implicitly deemed "men's work" and is explicitly valued, whereas teaching and service are characterized as "women's work" and explicitly devalued.

The Prevailing Criteria for Tenure and Promotion

There are three criteria by which candidates for tenure and promotion are judged: research, teaching, and service; however, these criteria are not equally weighted. Though all faculty are expected to do some service, few (if any) faculty members have ever been denied tenure on the basis of insufficient service [47]. And though all faculty are expected to do some teaching, outstanding teaching will not by itself guarantee someone tenure. The decisive factor in tenure and promotion (and salary) decisions is research [14, 15, 18, 25, 26, 34, 47, 54, 84].

Research is decisive in two ways. First, research is necessary for successful promotion: if a candidate's research is deemed inadequate, no amount of teaching or service will compensate for this. Lewis cites the following example of evaluative reasoning regarding a candidate for full professor: "Her performance as a teacher and as someone who has rendered university service has been outstanding. Regrettably, her scholarship although of high quality when it has appeared has been quite limited. I sincerely believe that her record viewed without respect to such questions as affirmative action, etc. would not lead to the conclusion that she be promoted" [54, pp. 98–99]. Second, research may be sufficient for successful promotion: excellent research will counterbalance almost all other deficiencies in a faculty member's record, except complete "dereliction of duty" [47]. In the words of one untenured faculty member: "To achieve tenure ... one need not have any service, and need only demonstrate minimal competence as a teacher; ... research is the *only* consideration for *tenure* that actually seems to count" [25, p. 137]. Only when a faculty member's research is borderline (adequate, but not outstanding), will her or his teaching or service record become a central focus of the review proceedings. According to both statistical analyses and personal interviews, this emphasis on research in tenure and promotion reviews holds across all disciplines and all types of institutions, except two-year colleges [15, 18, 34].

The relative importance attributed to research, teaching, and service is reflected also in the ranking of activities within each of these categories of evaluation. For example, within the category of research, publishing is deemed a more noteworthy activity than presenting papers at conferences (akin to lecturing) or editing or reviewing for a journal (akin to grading). And within the category of publishing, publishing articles in scholarly journals (for other researchers) is considered more important than publishing textbooks (for students), and both of these activities carry far more weight than publishing essays in the popular media (for the general populace)—an activity typically deemed utterly insignificant for the purposes of tenure and promotion review. Finally, within the category of publishing scholarly works, publishing purely theoretical articles often ranks above publishing articles which "merely" apply theory to a problem and, typically, both of these rank above publishing educationally oriented articles [17]. Thus, one finds the pattern of prioritizing research over teaching and service replicated within the relative rankings of subspecies of research itself. The more "pure" the scholarship is (in form, content, and intended audience), the more value that research is accorded. To the degree that scholarship is "tainted" by its affiliation with teaching or service-related activities, it is devalued [6].

Similar considerations pertain to the rankings of subspecies of teaching and service activities, respectively. The more closely a teaching activity is related to research the more highly it will be valued, and the more closely a teaching activity is related to service the less likely it will be valued. Thus, for example, teaching graduate courses carries more status than teaching undergraduate courses; and both of these are ranked above administering an academic program or advising and counseling students.

Likewise, although service, in general, carries little weight in faculty evaluations, certain types of service—such as being an officer or chair of a national professional organization (an organization that sponsors a research journal and/or academic conferences)—may be noteworthy. Certainly, such professional service is typically deemed more noteworthy than university service, which, in turn, is deemed more noteworthy than community service. Service to one's campus, though expected, is considered relatively unimportant in the review process. The only exception to this may be holding an administrative post—especially if such a post is related to issues of teaching (for example, the dean of graduate studies) or, better yet, research (for example, the vice-president in charge of research). Such administrative activities will carry far more weight than membership on university committees, which, in turn, will be accorded greater significance than, for example, advising student organizations. Finally, service to one's civic community, while morally admirable, is unlikely to be considered a professional virtue when the time for promotion comes. This is so even when such public service is intimately related to one's professional expertise. In summary form the rank ordering of criteria for faculty evaluation is roughly as displayed in Table 1.

The emphasis on research publication in the contemporary academy is a primary cause of stress for faculty—especially for female faculty [84]. Yet, the general consensus within and across universities concerning the rank ordering of the faculty activities listed above implies that current institutional policies regarding tenure and promotion policies are fair and easily justified. But this is simply not the case.

Table 1. Criteria for Tenure and Promotion

Research	Teaching	Service

Publishing
  professional journals
  professional books
    theoretical
    applied
    pedagogical		

Publishing
  textbooks
  instructional materials		

Conference presentations	Classroom performance
	  graduate
	  undergraduate
	    upper division
	    lower division	

Editing/reviewing for a journal		Professional service

		University service
		  administration
		  committees
		  student clubs

	Advising/ counseling students	
Magazine/newspaper articles		Public service

Below, various rationales for the reigning faculty evaluation and reward system are examined. Unless propped up by a set of unexamined presuppositions regarding the justification of a gender-role hierarchy, each of these putative justifications fails.

Research Separates the Men from the Boys . . . and the Women

Why should research be the primary criterion for tenure and promotion? One line of argument, which focuses on research as an indicator of faculty merit, goes something like this: "Research separates the men from the boys (or the women from the girls). Teaching and service won't serve this function because everyone teaches and does committee work."[1] A variation on this theme argues that "Teaching and service won't serve this function because there is no satisfactory way of evaluating teaching and service." According to the first line of reasoning, research performance is the only factor that *differentiates* faculty presumed to be equal in other respects. According to the second line of reasoning, research performance is the only factor by which faculty members can be *objectively* evaluated, even if they are unequal in other respects.

"Everyone Teaches and Serves"

Is research the only factor that will demonstrate faculty merit? Though it is true that everyone teaches and serves on committees, this line of reasoning overlooks the following facts. First, not everyone teaches the same number of courses. Course loads vary among universities, departments and even within departments. Those engaged in research are often given course reductions and/or sabbatical leaves. Secondly, not everyone teaches the same number of students. Even where course loads are similar, class sizes may be vastly different. Those who teach core courses will service many more students than those who teach specialty courses; and those who teach undergraduates will have much larger classes than those who teach graduate students. Finally, professors vary in the amount of effort they expend per course and per student. Some faculty members frequently develop new courses and assignments or redesign old ones, while others teach from the same notes year in and year out. Some faculty members assign essays, while others evaluate students by computer-graded multiple choice examinations. Some faculty members have grading assistants, others do not. Some spend hours writing detailed comments on each student essay, while others just skim and grade. Some faculty members spend hours advising and mentoring students, while others are unapproachable or unavailable even during their scheduled office hours.

Similarly, though it is true that everyone is given committee assignments, not everyone serves on the same number of committees and not everyone spends the same number of hours on committee work. Some committees meet weekly, and others meet once or twice a year. Some committee members prepare for meetings and spend time outside the meeting doing homework, seriously examining the issues, lobbying for proposals and so forth, while other committee members rarely show up for scheduled meetings.

Simply to say that "everyone teaches" obscures crucial differences among courses and among teachers. Likewise, to say that "everyone serves" obscures important differences among committees and among their respective members. In doing so, the argument for prioritizing research both exploits and obscures the gender bias in university tenure and promotion policy.

In treating teaching and service as undifferentiated activities, the argument for prioritizing research utilizes a technique commonly used to devalue women's work and, thus, rationalize the unpaid or underpaid status of that work. It assumes that there is no difference between good and bad teaching (and service) or, that if there is, this difference is unaccounted for by levels of skill, because these are activities that are *instinctual* or *natural* for those who perform them. Consider, for example, Stigler's claim that "there are, nationally, many more good teachers of undergraduates than there are good researchers" [77, p. 74]. This makes little sense if teaching is a learned skill in light of the fact that graduate students receive little or no pedagogical training but a considerable amount of research training [11]. The notion that anyone can teach well, like the notion that anyone can parent (or more specifically mother) well, *assumes* that these activities are uncreative, unchallenging, and unskilled. Similarly, the notion that anyone can perform service activities well, like the notion that anyone can be a good housekeeper or waitress, *assumes* that such activities are unskilled and require little thought or effort. As Smith argues, this is an assumption that could only arise from a specific perspective, namely the (masculine) perspective of those who do not routinely or seriously engage in such labor [76].

Teaching duties have fallen and continue to fall disproportionately to women [6, 8, 18, 19, 42, 60, 71, 83, 90]. In 1980, 53 percent of male faculty at four-year institutions, but only 35 percent of female faculty, taught eight or fewer hours per week. Conversely, 28 percent of female faculty, but only 15 percent of male faculty taught thirteen or more hours per week [42]. Eleven percent of female faculty, compared to 7.5 percent of male faculty, spent seventeen or more hours per week teaching [8]. In the late 1980s, the gender gap had narrowed slightly, but female faculty were still significantly more likely than male faculty to spend the bulk of their time on teaching and teaching-related activities. In 1988 faculty women were spending, on average, 61 percent of their time teaching, whereas faculty men spent only 54 percent of their time teaching [83, p. 152]. In 1989–90, 43 percent of all male faculty, but only 36 percent of female faculty, taught eight or fewer hours per week. Conversely, 27 percent of female faculty, compared to 20 percent of male faculty, taught thirteen or more hours per week. Eleven percent of female faculty, compared to 8 percent of male faculty, spent seventeen or more hours per week in the classroom [6].

In addition to spending more hours per week in the classroom, women spend more time preparing for their classes and more time advising students than do their male colleagues [6]. This may be related to the fact that women are more likely to be assigned undergraduate and remedial classes. In 1989, 58 percent of women, but only 48 percent of men, were teaching undergraduates exclusively [19]. Twenty percent of women, but only 13 percent of men, taught remedial skills classes [6]. Yet, even among those faculty teaching undergraduates exclusively, women spend more time preparing for teaching than do their male colleagues [19].

Such disparity in teaching responsibilities is not surprising given that female faculty members are largely concentrated in ranks, disciplines, and institutions that have higher than average teaching expectations. In 1989, women comprised 45 percent of instructors, 38 percent of assistant professors, 26 percent of associate professors and 13.7 percent of all full professors.[2] Almost half of female faculty were concentrated in health-related fields, education, English, and the social sciences.[3] Finally, women accounted for 38 percent of all full-time community college faculty, 28 percent of private four-year college faculty, 21 percent of public research university faculty, 27 percent of other public university faculty and only 19 percent of private research university faculty [1, p. 33; see also 6, 18, 62, 83]. Within the twenty most prestigious research universities, women held only 17 percent of full-time faculty positions in 1986, with a descending proportion of higher-ranked positions: 32 percent of assistant professorships, 22 percent of associate professorships, and 8 percent of full professorships [62, p. 232]. Thus, women—including both white and minority women—are apt to find themselves in places and stations with fewer resources and heavier teaching loads than their male counterparts [3, 6, 90].

Moreover, one might speculate that due to disciplinary specializations combined with low rank, female faculty will carry disproportionately heavy grading and advising loads for each of the classes they teach. For example, instructors and assistant professors in English may be assigned lower-division composition courses which necessitate the frequent grading of essays and consultations with each individual student. And junior faculty in nursing, social work, or education may spend numerous hours organizing and supervising student internships. In all disciplines, faculty occupying lower ranks are apt to find themselves teaching sections of introductory or general education courses with large numbers of students, many of whom are young and in need of personal as well as intellectual guidance.

In light of the above considerations, it is not surprising to find out that tenure and promotion processes are a primary source of stress for female faculty. In its 1989 National Survey of Faculty, the Carnegie Foundation discovered that 74 percent of female faculty believed, contrary to the prevailing paradigm, that "teaching effectiveness should be the primary criterion for promotion of faculty" [18, p. 64].

Like teaching activities, service activities differ along gender lines. In addition to spending more time advising students, female faculty members engage in significantly more, and different types of, service activities than their male counterparts [3]. In 1988, the U.S. Department of Education found that female faculty, across all types of institutions, devoted a greater percentage of their time to institutional service activities than did male faculty [83, p. 153]. In 1990 the Carnegie Foundation concurred that female faculty were the most active participants in the daily campus governance process, "even though they devoted more time to the teaching function than did men, they were significantly more active in the work of the faculty senate, administrative advisory committees, and other campus-wide bodies" [19, p. 42]. Faculty women are also more likely than men to volunteer time and expertise to extra-institutional projects [83, p. 151].

There are several reasons for these differences. First, female and minority faculty members—and especially minority female faculty—may have more "opportunities" for serving student groups and community organizations, as well as individual students, because they are sought out by other women or minority members as positive role models or because of their areas of research interest [60, 71]. Second, faculty women (unlike men of color) are more likely to be approached by students with personal, as well as academic, concerns on the expectation that women will be more caring and sensitive than men [75]. Third, women, as well as men of color, are given more "opportunities" for university service than white men. For example, they may be asked to serve on various committees in order to guarantee representation of their group or simply to symbolize their institution's commitment to affirmative action and diversity goals [35, 43, 60, 63, 71]. Finally, women (unlike men of color) are thought "to enjoy and to excel in the 'pattern maintenance' chores that governance involves" [60, p. 131, see also 75, 82]. Yet, neither this belief nor tokenism extend to the more prestigious, more powerful, and better paying administrative positions.

Women still have limited opportunities to formulate university policies as presidents, vice-presidents, academic deans, and department chairs. Tenured female faculty, especially faculty women of color, are often overlooked for high-visibility and high-status administrative posts, while frequently steered toward "dead-end special" positions, such as director of minority affairs or affirmative action officer—"positions that usually have no advancement track in the academic structure" [71, p. 192; see also 5, 28]. For the most part, as Sandler contends, "women administrators remain concentrated in a small number of low-status areas that are traditionally viewed as women's fields (such as nursing and home-economics) or in care-taking roles (such as in student affairs and affirmative action) or in other academic support roles (such as admissions officer, registrar, or bookstore manager)" [71, p. 176].

In sum, though all university faculty are expected to teach and to serve, as well as to research, male and female faculty exhibit significantly different patterns of research, teaching, and service. Men, as a group, devote a higher portion of their time to research activities, whereas women, as a group, devote a much higher percentage of their time to teaching and service activities than do men. The result is that men publish more extensively than do women [3, 6, 7, 12, 18, 19, 83]. In 1979, Cole reported that, over their career, men averaged 12.6 publications compared to 7.6 for women [23]. A decade later, as more and more institutions moved into the "publish or perish" mode, the gender gap in publishing rates remained significant. Men published almost twice as many articles and books as women from 1986–88 [83, p. 156]. In 1989, 35 percent of men, but only 13 percent of women, had published eleven or more articles in professional journals; and 49 percent of men, but only 36 percent of women had ever published or edited a book [15, A-19, A-20].

These differences in "research productivity" can be explained by women's structural position in the university: women, as a group, carry heavier teaching loads, bear greater responsibility for undergraduate education, and have more service commitments. Women also have less access to graduate teaching assistants, travel funds, research monies, laboratory equipment, and release time for research [6, 19, 30, 90]. The net result is that utilizing research as the primary criterion for tenure and promotion, while devaluing teaching and service, will not separate the men from the boys (or the women from the girls) so much as it will separate the men from the women. As Harding claims, women are, in large part, assigned responsibility for domestic and emotional labor in their workplaces as well as in their homes, whereas men are assigned the "head" work. And, as in the home, these two functions are causally related. It is because faculty (and other) women manage daily domestic affairs and perform caregiving work that faculty men are free to "immerse themselves in the world of abstract concepts" [38, p. 55]. Yet, the distinctly social (as opposed to natural) character of women's work is invisible from the male vantage point [55, 76]. Hence, inside the university, as outside it, we find a gendered division of labor wherein women assume primary responsibility for nurturing the young and serving men, but receive little credit for doing so.

"Just Say No"

A standard response to such concerns is to advise female faculty—especially those who are untenured—to "just say no" to such extra assignments. "Don't do so much course preparation. Don't serve on so many committees. Don't spend so much time on things other than research" [see, for example 2, p. 395]. There are two difficulties with this response.

First, the response is naive. It assumes that junior, female faculty can refuse teaching and service appointments with few, if any, negative repercussions. This is a dubious assumption, which demonstrates little thoughtfulness about relations of power inside the academy.[4] Junior faculty often have little control over their teaching loads, class sizes, or course assignments. The much touted "academic freedom" does not extend to the freedom to refuse teaching assignments—especially not for untenured faculty who need to prove to their colleagues that they are "team players." Nor is it easy for junior faculty to "say no" to service assignments "offered" them by their superiors (their chair, their dean, their university president—in short, those people who can effectively deny their tenure). Though they may receive little credit for accepting these tasks, untenured faculty will fear reprisal for rejecting them. This double-bind is exacerbated for female faculty whose participation on university committees raises a dilemma unique to women and minorities: "Either they must accept more committee assignments than their male colleagues or face the charge of being uncooperative in satisfying a demand [for representation] that they themselves created" [82, p. 230; see also 71, 75].

In addition to being naive, the advice to refuse teaching and service obligations begs the question. Even if a young, untenured faculty person *could* refuse certain teaching and service obligations without repercussions, the notion that she *should* say "no" *assumes* that this work is unimportant or, at any rate, less important than research. But this assumption is precisely what is at issue.

Women may feel that the time they devote to teaching and advising *is* important for several reasons. First, women, like minority men, are apt to place a greater emphasis on curricular and pedagogical issues than white males insofar as they are more likely to perceive, and work to correct, biases in traditional curricula. As Rich notes, traditional disciplinary canons have repeatedly obscured and devalued the history and experiences of women: "Outside of women's studies... we live with textbooks, research studies, scholarly sources and lectures that treat women as a subspecies, mentioned only as peripheral to the history of man" [68, p. 123]. That women have noted this and are working to correct it is evidenced by the fact that faculty women are more likely than faculty men to develop new courses that incorporate gender as well as broader cultural concerns. Faculty women are six times more likely than their male colleagues to teach a women's studies course and more than twice as likely to incorporate readings on women or gender issues into all of their undergraduate courses. Women are also significantly more likely than men to teach ethnic studies courses, incorporate readings on racial or ethnic issues into their courses, and attend workshops dealing with issues of gender, race, and culture [6].

The style, as well as the content, of traditional pedagogy may serve to exclude and alienate women. As Belenky et al. have argued, women's ways of knowing may be stifled by the traditional lecture format, wherein the professor appears as the omnipotent authority, takes few risks, and permits the students to see only the product and not the process of his thinking [10]. This format silences women by treating them as merely the passive receptacles for someone else's truth. This silencing is further exacerbated by traditional evaluation techniques which emphasize grades based on the product, rather than the process of student learning. More conducive to women's intellectual, emotional, and personal development is a pedagogy that emphasizes "connection over separation, understanding and acceptance over assessment, and collaboration over debate"; a pedagogy that "accord[s] respect to and allow[s] time for the knowledge that emerges from firsthand experience" and, instead of imposing the instructor's own expectations and requirements, "encourage[s] students to evolve their own patterns of work based on the problems they are pursuing" [10, p. 229].

That women are also (at least implicitly) aware of this and working to improve pedagogical techniques is evidenced by the fact that faculty women are significantly less likely than their male colleagues to use extensive lecturing as their primary instructional method. Conversely, women are significantly more likely to use class discussion, cooperative learning, experiential learning, field work, group (as well as independent) projects, and student-developed activities as methods of instruction. Faculty women also utilize a greater variety of evaluation techniques than faculty men. While women do utilize standard assessment techniques, such as mid-term and final examinations and multiple choice quizzes, women are significantly more likely than men to assign weekly essays and student presentations and to involve students in evaluating one another's work. Women faculty are also significantly less likely to grade on a curve [6].

In addition to spending more time on their teaching, women, like minority men, may place a greater priority on advising students because they are more likely to perceive themselves as having a special responsibility to student members of their own demographic constituency. They may be more aware of the social, personal, and academic difficulties faced by young women or young men of color on a campus marked by explicit or implicit sexual and racial politics, more knowledgeable about (institutional and extra-institutional) sources of support, and better able to provide pragmatic advice. Yet, because of the small numbers of female and minority faculty at research institutions, such a sense of responsibility may leave such faculty members feeling torn by conflicting expectations. The advice to resolve such role conflicts by simply prioritizing research is problematic insofar as it ignores the very real needs of students. In the words of one faculty member: "I prefer research... [but] it's not so easy—there is standard advice both to new faculty and to women—'You don't have to spend so much time with students.' But in my case, often because they're foreign students, *they really do need time*.... I've spent a lot of time and... am trying to regain a balance" [75, p. 60, emphasis mine].

Finally, women (unlike men of color) may feel that the time they devote to their teaching is important because of their gendered ethical perspective. The advice to spend less time with students in order to devote more time to one's personal research projects encourages faculty to reason in terms of what Gilligan names a (masculine) "ethics of justice" rather than a (feminine) "ethics of care" [37]. According to Gilligan, men are trained to make moral decisions by establishing a rational hierarchy of (abstract) rights and duties, whereas women are socialized to define morality in terms of responsibilities that stem from compassion for and (concrete) connection with others. These different ethical perspectives are exemplified in male and female faculty's attitudes towards teaching. Not only do women spend more time on teaching and teaching-related activities, they also teach differently than men. As noted above, women are significantly more likely than men to utilize collaborative learning techniques. These differences in pedagogical style appear related to differences in pedagogical goals. While almost all (male and female) faculty emphasize the importance of developing undergraduates' ability to *think* clearly, female faculty are significantly more likely than male faculty to cite the *personal, professional, moral, emotional, and social* development of their students as essential goals of their teaching. In 1989–90, 77 percent of women, compared to 64 percent of men, claimed that enhancing their students' self-understanding was an essential educational goal. Seventy-one percent of women, compared to 58 percent of men, aimed to prepare students for employment. Seventy-one percent of women, compared to 60 percent of men, wanted to help students develop personal values, and 62 percent of women, compared to 54 percent of men, hoped to develop their students' moral character. Fifty percent of women, but only 36 percent of men, attempted to provide for the emotional development of their students. Women were also significantly more likely than men to cite "enhancing students' out-of-class experience" and "preparing students for family living" as essential educational goals [6, pp. 63, 83]. These differences in pedagogical goals suggest that female faculty are less likely than their male colleagues to view their students (dispassionately) as merely the abstract holders of intellectual rights and more apt to connect with them (compassionately) as concrete, embodied human beings with diverse, complex needs. To the extent that this is true, women may find the advice to stop spending time with students morally problematic and difficult to heed.

For similar reasons to those given above, women (and minorities) may view their service work as important and have difficulty abandoning it. Women (and minority) faculty are more likely to devote time to service activities insofar as they are more likely than white men to perceive the need for change in the policies, procedures, and institutional structure of the university. Women (and minority) faculty are also more likely to perceive themselves as having a special responsibility to other female (and minority) faculty and, indeed, to other women (and minorities) outside of the academy. For both these reasons women may accept—or even seek out—positions on various university committees. They may also freely devote time to mentoring their more junior colleagues, give free public talks, and volunteering for community projects.

Allen notes that gender and ethnicity affect faculty workloads and research productivity and suggests that the lower research productivity of white women, African American women, and African American men is attributable, in part, to different values and priorities: "Faculty members from different demographic groups... have different attitudes about and expectations for academic work. [There is] a possible mismatch between institutional demands and the perspectives of women and minority faculty members" [3, p. 34]. This mismatch is exemplified by women's attitudes toward service, as well as their attitudes toward teaching. Women are less likely than men to emphasize research and significantly more likely than men to emphasize being a good colleague, providing services to the community, and participating in committee and administrative work as important professional goals. This indicates that women's professional priorities are less likely than men's to be aligned with the research priority of the contemporary academy. In 1989–90, for example, 86 percent of women cited collegiality as professionally important, whereas only 52 percent viewed engaging in research as important. And women viewed community service as equal in importance to research [6, pp. 62, 82].

The notion that female faculty should cut back on their teaching and service work in order to devote more time to their research makes sense only if one prioritizes women's *individual* efforts to advance within the system over women's *collective* efforts to transform prevailing norms and practices. It thus ignores the fact that faculty women may feel a responsibility to, and compassion for, both their female colleagues and their female students, in addition to women outside the academy [9, 56, 68]. Teaching and service activities are crucial for the personal, intellectual, and professional advancement of academic women as a group. Insofar as tenured faculty women see mentoring untenured faculty as an imposition, it will be difficult to retain female faculty. Insofar as female faculty view teaching and advising female students burdensome, it will be difficult to bring more women into faculty posts. As Rich notes, fragmentation among academic women "is merely a replication of the fragmentation from each other that we undergo in the society outside." If academic women accept the premise that their professional advancement, job security, and opportunities for scholarship "lie in propitiating and identifying with men who have some power" (for example, tenured male researchers, chairs, deans, journal editors), they will continue to find themselves "in competition with each other and blinded to [their] common struggles" [68, p. 124].

One of the primary barriers to success for female faculty is the "lack of a supportive, even hospitable, climate" [90, p. 176; see also 71]. Faculty women often cite intellectual and social isolation as a primary source of job dissatisfaction [5, 6, 90]. This isolation is perpetuated by a masculine ethic of competition and individualism. As one administrative woman says, "I find it difficult to get ahead personally if it involves competition.... I [do] strive to better myself... but always within the context of cooperating with other people; ... some people [try] to make a name for themselves ... at the expense of other people.... It has been a real problem for me.... I often wonder if I'm going to be successful in this kind of position.... I don't like competition that requires that in order for one person to win another has to lose" [2, p. 396]. Intellectual and social isolation is also perpetuated by an exclusive focus on research productivity. As one black faculty woman states: "I want to live my life. I do not want to sit in cloistered halls... writing academic papers for the rest of my life. That isn't a life" [5, p. 192].

In addition to being a source of personal dissatisfaction, intellectual and social isolation—often experienced most severely by minority academic women—prevents women's professional advancement. Despite the prevailing notion that academic success results solely from individual talent and hard work, "moving through the system of rewards and status requires knowing colleagues who can provide the guidance, support and astute insight into the political processes of the institution" [90, p. 177].

These considerations suggest that advising women to abandon teaching and service responsibilities for the sake of enhancing their research productivity is misguided. It is important for women to engage in teaching and service activities both for their own growth as individuals, and for their advancement as a group. Classroom and advising activities, while time-consuming for faculty women, may also provide a source of human relationship for women that makes their work more meaningful. And committee and community work may likewise fend off feelings of social isolation, in addition to providing important intellectual and professional contacts—especially for nontenured women. As the Carnegie Foundation's survey results suggest, faculty who are located at teaching institutions (liberal arts and community colleges), and those who actively participate in university governance, are more likely to perceive a "sense of community" on their campus and are less likely to leave their institution [18, 19].

In sum, the notion that women should improve their research productivity by refusing anything more than minimal teaching and service responsibilities arises from a masculine perspective that mirrors sexist attitudes that exist outside the academy. In privileging research, it values the abstract theoretical labor of men, while it simultaneously exploits and devalues the concrete emotional and domestic labor of women (wives, secretaries, research assistants, adjunct teachers, and "regular" female faculty) that makes theoretical activity possible [38, 68, 76]. In inviting "exceptional" women to join the ranks of researchers, it encourages women to likewise exploit and devalue (unpaid or underpaid) "women's work"—thus ensuring that those chosen few will remain tokens.

"But, There's No Way to Evaluate Teaching and Service"

Some individuals acknowledge difficulties with valuing research more highly than teaching and service, but argue nonetheless for retaining the present faculty evaluation system on pragmatic grounds. "While the present system of measuring faculty merit may not be perfect," the argument goes, "it is too difficult to objectively measure the quality of faculty teaching and service" [see, for example, 75, p. 52]. This response denotes a lack of imagination and highlights the double standard used to evaluate research, on the one hand, and teaching and service, on the other.

It is certainly not impossible—although it may be time-consuming—to assess the quality of a faculty member's teaching and service. Though it is true that current methods of evaluating teaching are fraught with difficulties, these methods could be refined, developed, and expanded to achieve more accurate and objective results. Currently, student responses to multiple-choice questionnaires are the primary tool used in evaluating classroom performance, but the objectivity of these student evaluations of faculty has been the subject of much debate [34]. For example, there is evidence that high student evaluations of faculty correlate positively with high faculty evaluations of students and small class sizes [67, 89]. Thus, those who resist grade inflation and teach large classes may be unfairly penalized. There is also evidence that women faculty are rated more negatively by students than male faculty [71, 75].

Yet, with a little imagination (and a little research), one can easily find ways to overcome or at least compensate for these difficulties. First, the student evaluation tool could itself be refined to de-emphasize the "grading" of faculty and instead emphasize students' reasons for valuing or devaluing a course or instructor.[5] Second, student evaluations could be examined alongside records of grade distribution and class size. Finally, student evaluations could be supplemented by peer evaluations, a chair evaluation, a dean evaluation, the evaluation of external referees, and a self-evaluation. The evaluations of faculty by their peers and superiors could be based on classroom visits, interviews with a representative sampling of current and former students, evidence of scholarship (including, but not limited to publication) relating to the faculty member's teaching methods or course content, evidence of new courses developed or revisions to existing courses, and samples of teaching materials, such as syllabi, reading lists, handouts, assignment sheets, tests, and copies of graded work and completed student theses and dissertations [57, 73, 86, 89]. Utilizing a diverse array of evaluators and evaluative tools should help counteract potential bias and render reasonably accurate results.

Although there has been sparse scholarship concerning evaluations of faculty service, here too one can imagine reasonably objective methods of making such evaluations. As in evaluating teaching, evaluating service should rely on a spectrum of evidence. Such evidence might include the testimony of colleagues in professional organizations, university and college co-committee members and committee chairs, departmental colleagues and chairs, members of community groups or businesses a faculty member has served, and members of student organizations a faculty member has advised. In addition to such testimonial evidence, evaluators might also examine written documents from committee and other archives, active policies and programs that have resulted from service commitments, scholarship related to a faculty member's service, and self-evaluations of service.

In addition to looking at the *quality* of a professor's teaching and service, a tenure and promotion committee should also consider the *quantity* of her teaching and service. Pertinent information here includes the number of courses taught per year (including overload teaching at branch campuses), total student contact hours (courses taught x the number of students in each course), the number of different course preparations, the number of new courses developed, the number of students assigned for advisement and placement, and the number of student theses, dissertations, practicums, and independent studies supervised. With regard to service, relevant information would include the number of professional or administrative offices held and the length of time served in those posts, the number of university committees served on (along with a rough approximation of the number and length of times those committees meet per year), the number of community presentations given, the number of student organizations advised and the length of time served as an advisor, and the amount of consulting work done.

Though one might argue that the quantity of one's teaching and service should be less important than its quality, both need to be taken into account, because women do a disproportionate amount of teaching and service and one might expect there to be an inverse relationship between the two factors. Simply put, the larger the number of students one is responsible for teaching, the less "quality time" one will be able to spend with each individual student. Likewise, the more service assignments one accepts, the less time one may have to devote to each assignment.

One might also hypothesize an inverse relationship between the quantity and quality of research. While proponents of the present criteria for tenure and promotion overemphasize the importance and difficulties of assessing teaching and service quality, they deemphasize the importance and difficulties of assessing research quality. Indeed, most evidence suggests that research is assessed merely according to quantity, rather than quality, of publication.

Over twenty years ago, the Commission on Academic Tenure in Higher Education bemoaned the results of this assessment process: "Review committees are impressed by the number of publications rather than by their significance. Extrinsic signs such as the general reputation of journals or publishers are often substituted for a positive assessment of the work itself. Nontenured members of faculties, believing that largely quantitative tests of publication prevail, lose confidence in the evaluation process and are often prompted to undertake quick projects that will expand their bibliographies, rather than to work on more difficult or more long-term projects" [cited in 86, p. 34]. Yet, in 1989, the Carnegie Foundation reported a continued institutional emphasis on quantity of publication. Fifty-seven percent of the faculty surveyed believed that the number of publications was important in tenure decisions, and 38 percent reported that at their institution publications were merely counted, not qualitatively assessed. Among faculty at four-year institutions, these numbers jumped to 80 percent and 47 percent, respectively [18, pp. 49, 50].

This quantity over quality approach to assessing research publication encourages conservative research that can be completed within a short time. It also encourages the submission of articles for publication without the refinement of ideas that might otherwise take place. In both these ways, emphasis on "research productivity" may lead faculty to compromise their personal and intellectual values. Assistant and associate professors surveyed by Verrier reveal that they are "taking on short-term, conservative research projects, often not central to their current research interests nor tapping into their more creative energies. Research activity is directed to tasks that they believe will be rewarded—for example, attaining grants, writing a book, publishing a steady output of 'least publishable units'" [84, p. 116].

There is, thus, a double standard that pertains to the assessment of research, on the one hand, and teaching and service, on the other. Although measuring the quality of research, teaching, and service is not impossible, it is clearly more difficult and more time-consuming than simply counting the number of articles published, courses taught, and committees served on. The import of this difficulty is different, however, for teaching and service than it is for research. The difficulty of assessing teaching and service quality results in a devaluation of these activities, while the difficulty of assessing research quality results in the adoption of a quantitative approach to measurement.

Women, as a group, are negatively affected by this double standard. The emphasis on teaching quality over quantity ensures that female faculty are not rewarded for carrying higher than average teaching loads. And the emphasis on research quantity over quality ensures that female faculty will be penalized for having shorter than average publication lists. Feminists (and other innovators) will be particularly hard hit by prevailing methods of assessment. Feminist scholarship is, by definition, not conservative. It seeks to radically redefine concepts, issues, research paradigms, and pedagogical methods. This scholarship represents one of the most significant research developments in the latter twentieth century, but it is time-consuming scholarship [54]. Thus, institutional norms that emphasize quantity over quality of research will inevitably devalue the research contribution of the feminist scholar.

Research Has Instrumental Value

The arguments for prioritizing research over teaching and service examined above focus on the necessity of utilizing the research criterion in evaluating the relative *merit* of faculty members. These arguments fail insofar as "research productivity" is, at best, only one of several indicators of faculty merit. There is, however, another set of arguments for emphasizing research in tenure and promotion reviews—arguments that focus instead on the *usefulness* of research and, hence, researchers. These arguments, to be examined below, are as follows: (1) research advances and disseminates knowledge, (2) research aids teaching, and (3) research enhances personal and institutional reputation.

"Research Produces and Disseminates Knowledge"

It is often argued that research is integral to the mission of the university in that it advances and disseminates knowledge. Producing and disseminating knowledge is (and should be) a central part of a university's mission. But whether or not it is plausible to view research as the primary or, indeed, only avenue to pursuing this goal depends on how we interpret "research." It also depends on questions surrounding what sort of knowledge is produced and whom it is intended to reach. Although research, understood as an activity leading to scholarly publication, is an important method of producing and disseminating certain types of knowledge to particular groups of people, research in this narrow sense is neither sufficient nor necessary for carrying out the university's more general scholarly mission.

Publishing the results of one's experimental or theoretical investigations is not sufficient for the dissemination of knowledge. Publication depends on the prior conception, development, and completion of a successful, or at least minimally interesting, research project—a project that may have involved several acknowledged and unacknowledged persons and institutions besides those who have written up the results. One can publish, and thus disseminate knowledge, without doing the research that actually produces the knowledge. As Schiebinger notes, the history of science as a history of man-made discoveries has overlooked the fact that women "have served science well in their positions as invisible assistants" [72, p. 264]. The wives, daughters, and sisters of male scientists, barred from the public world of science and refused access to necessary resources—yet nonetheless devoted to science—often became the private (and unacknowledged) assistants to their male relatives in the nineteenth century. In the twentieth century, it is not uncommon for graduate students or junior faculty members in the natural and social sciences to perform laboratory experiments, take polls, or compile statistics—much as wives, daughters, and sisters previously did—the results of which are summarized and published by their advisors or mentors. Within the academy, as outside of it, a division of labor may exist such that the person or persons who are responsible for beginning a project may not be the same person or persons who finalize that work or distribute (and receive credit for) the resulting product. To equate research and publication obscures this (often gendered and always class-based) division of labor.

Moreover, publishing in scholarly journals is not the only, or even the best, method of disseminating knowledge. Given the typically small number of people who read most academic journals and treatises, publishing in the popular media may be a more effective method of disseminating knowledge. Yet, as already noted, current tenure and promotion criteria trivialize this activity, as the following comments from a social scientist further indicate: "My research on women and obesity had been published in the public media (where it had apparently been contaminated). The provost asked me for examples of my work and I gave him some of the press releases as an indication that the larger community was interested in it. Instead of asking me for copies of the papers on which these press releases were based, he [said] my material was not substantively academic" [78, p. 50].

"All too often," as hooks notes, "educators, especially university professors, fear their work will not be valued by other academics if it is presented in a way that makes it accessible to a wider audience" [41, p. 111]. This fear is no mere paranoia. Current tenure and promotion guidelines devalue—indeed may negatively value—research topics and styles that are interesting and accessible to a general audience, encouraging instead a form of scholarship that is both elitist and exclusionary [68]. This suggests that arguments for prioritizing faculty research based on the university's mission to disseminate knowledge may be disingenuous. If university administrators are genuinely concerned to provide intellectual ideas and discoveries to as many people as possible, they should encourage, rather than dismiss, those faculty who are interested and skilled in reaching mass audiences.

Teaching, conference presentations, and community talks are also effective, yet devalued, methods of disseminating knowledge. Like publishing in the popular media, these methods of spreading knowledge undoubtedly reach a greater number and more diverse groups of people (including more women) than are reached by publishing in academic journals. Unlike publishing in any print media, however, these oral methods of spreading knowledge have the advantage of reaching people who cannot read or write. Until everyone in this country is literate, intellectual ideas must still be spread by word of mouth. In addition to reaching a wider and more diverse audience, oral methods of communication also have the advantage of permitting the audience to "ask questions, clarify issues, give feedback" [41, p. 110]. Thus these alternative methods of reaching people might help to extend and transform, as well as disseminate, knowledge.

"Better Researchers Are Better Teachers"

Because it seems *prima facie* reasonable, at least to taxpayers, parents of students, and students themselves, to see a professor's primary responsibility as that of teaching, many university administrators have begun to emphasize the connections between research and teaching. We are told that "professors actively involved in research will be better teachers." Is this true? Not necessarily. Whether or not research involvement enhances our teaching depends, once again, on how we define research. It also depends on whom and how we teach.

The expectation that doing research will improve a faculty member's teaching is based largely on the assumption that "scholarship makes a professor more knowledgeable and that a more knowledgeable professor makes a better teacher" [31, p. 145].[6] But this is simply not true if we equate scholarship with research, measured in terms of number of publications. Indeed, Friedrich and Michalek discovered that "more active researchers are seen as being less knowledgeable. This result is consistent with the argument that research may increase a teacher's knowledge in a specific area at the expense of more general knowledge.... Immersion in research apparently can breed a narrowness that detracts from the broad-based knowledgeability that students perceive as being an important element of good teaching" [31, pp. 153, 160].

Research, as defined for the purposes of tenure and promotion reviews, is an activity that results in a finished *product*—a journal article, book, or other creative work.[7] Scholarship that contributes to faculty knowledgeability and hence to good teaching, however, is best understood as professional development—doing library work, reading, making inquiries, attending workshops, using computers, improving one's communication skills, and so forth. Faculty women spend more time than faculty men on these sorts of professional development activities [6, 83]. This aspect of women's scholarship may not result in a concrete product and is best understood as an ongoing *process* [13, 14].

In sum, although there is a plausible connection between *professional development* and good teaching, the connection between *publishing* and teaching is more dubious. An effective teacher must be knowledgeable about her subject matter, including recent developments in her field, but it is not necessary for an effective teacher to have a long list of publications or the notoriety that may come with such publication [11]. Attending conferences, workshops, reading relevant materials, and honing certain skills may be sufficient. Indeed, doing more than this may, and in many instances does, detract from the quality of one's teaching.

There is an overwhelming amount of evidence which suggests that, in general, faculty make forced choices between teaching and research. Over half of the faculty surveyed at research and doctorate universities claim that at their institution "the pressure to publish reduces the quality of teaching" [18, p. 51]. And although some empirical studies suggest that the pursuit of research enhances teaching effectiveness [30], most studies of the relationship between research and teaching suggest either that they vary independently, or that they are negatively correlated [3, 11, 14, 15, 27, 31, 52, 60, 61]. The most recent studies typically suggest that teaching and research may have been complementary in the past, but now stand in an inverse relationship with more research coming at the expense of teaching time. Allen explains this as follows: "A generation ago, faculty members resolved conflicts between teaching and research by expanding their workweeks. But the eight-hour growth to a fifty-three-hour workweek makes future increases unrealistic, and faculty members invest hours at the margin to rewarded and recognized activities" [3, p. 30]. As Keohane suggests, while discovering and sharing knowledge are related, "at the pragmatic level of the disposition of professorial time and the deployment of resources, research and teaching often do conflict. Time spent in the laboratory or library grappling with a research problem competes with time spent elsewhere, including the classroom. Time spent preparing to convey knowledge to undergraduates in terms that will be sensible to them is time not spent describing the results of one's research to informed colleagues. Following up on a graduate seminar over coffee in the common room takes time that might have been spent at the computer writing the next grant proposal" [51, p. 105; see also 22].

These considerations suggest that the present argument is also disingenuous [61]. Surely university administrators recognize—certainly they should recognize—the time allocation problems that current faculty face. Moreover, if a primary value of research is its perceived benefits for teaching, then one might wonder why teaching activities are less respected and rewarded than research activities.

Nonetheless, the assumption that teaching and research are complementary rather than competing activities may make sense if one teaches specialized, senior, or graduate level courses [42, 52]. Although, in general, time spent on research will take time away from teaching and vice versa, "it is also conceivable that particular types of teaching may have complementary effects on research activity, thus enhancing an individual's research record and likelihood of promotion.... For instance, graduate level teaching might increase access to high quality advisees or graduate research assistants. Also, teaching courses in one's specialty might complement an individual's research activities" [52, p. 152].

Boyer likewise suggests that scholarly investigation and classroom instruction will often mesh in the context of a graduate seminar, noting, "At that level, faculty and student cultures intersect and, further, graduate faculty often have a very light teaching load to accommodate their research." "But," he continues, "at the undergraduate level, and most especially in general education courses, research work often competes with classroom obligations, both in time and content. Faculty assigned to teach such courses frequently must take shortcuts in their research or rely heavily on teaching assistants—an arrangement that is often less than satisfactory for both student and professor" [15, p. 55].

Once again, this suggests that current tenure and promotion guidelines are a source of job stress for faculty. Junior female faculty will suffer a distinct disadvantage, because they not only carry heavier teaching loads but are significantly less likely to be assigned graduate courses [52, 60]. Whereas faculty teaching graduate courses (predominantly male) need to know a lot about a little, faculty teaching lower-division, general education, undergraduate courses (disproportionately female) need to know a little about a lot. The former more specialized knowledge will, but the latter more general knowledge will not, easily translate into publication.

"Research Enhances Reputation"

Despite all this, if one desires to enhance one's academic reputation or advance one's academic status, one must publish—often and in the right places. One's name must regularly appear in print in relevant journals, periodicals, conference proceedings, and citation indexes in order to achieve professional recognition within one's field. In the contemporary academy, it is professional recognition in this sense that counts, but once again we should ask whether or not this is what *should* count, or at any rate whether or not this is *all* that should count. Why should research, in the sense of publication, be "the currency of the realm" [81, p. 462]?

One final—although not very persuasive—rationale for rewarding publishing researchers more highly than effective teachers or servers concerns the prestige that research brings to an institution. In a nutshell, the argument is that hiring, retaining, promoting, and otherwise rewarding those who do research will enhance a university's—and a university administrator's—reputation. As Cole notes, the current emphasis on faculty research productivity stems from competition among universities "to be 'the best' and to be *perceived* as among the best." Such perceptions, he contends, "will not result from hiring and promoting those who have extraordinary track records as teachers," but will instead come from hiring faculty "whose research publications are envied by others; . . . institutional legitimacy is obtained predominantly through research achievements. That is what academic leaders have coveted; . . . research excellence is a measure of an academic leader's performance in office . . . [and] legitimates the university's claim to greatness" [22, p. 24; see also 61].

This response is useful in highlighting the fact that a university does not operate in isolation, but instead operates as part of a (relatively homogenous) higher education system [15]. Thus, the value placed on research *within* a particular institution reflects (and is reflected by) the value placed on research *among* universities. Yet, the response fails to be persuasive because—like other arguments considered above—it largely begs the question. We still want to know *why* research should be so highly prized, envied, and coveted.

The arguments for ranking universities on the basis of their research output parallel those offered in support of promoting faculty on the basis of their research productivity, and they suffer the same flaws. One argument suggests that because all universities and colleges provide classes and serve their constituencies, research is the only means of *differentiating* academic institutions. This argument, like the argument for treating research as the sole indicator of faculty merit, treats teaching and service as homogenous activities. But this overlooks the unquestionable differences in the quantity, quality, types, and sizes of classes, and the wide variety in students' campus experiences, from one institution to another [14]. Likewise, it ignores differences in the quantity, quality, and types of services offered among institutions and the alternative constituencies served by different institutions.

A second argument admits these forms of diversity among universities, but maintains that research excellence is, nonetheless, the only way to *objectively* evaluate (and rank) academic institutions. In the words of one administrator, there is no "trustworthy interinstitutional metric" for judging the quality of an institution's teaching or service comparable to the one available for judging an institution's research excellence [51, p. 106]. This argument, like the pragmatic argument for using research productivity as the primary indicator of faculty merit, suggests a lack of imagination. One suspects that the absence of an "interinstitutional metric" for evaluating teaching, advising, and service is the result, rather than the cause, of a devaluation of these activities.

Tuchman, Gapinski, and Hagemann suggest that greater recognition accrues to research than to teaching and service because "the output of researchers is more visible, consisting of articles, books, and other published pieces which often attract a national audience. . . . [Teaching and service] activities are more inclined to receive local rather than national recognition" [80, p. 93]. This raises two further questions: Why is national recognition more important than local recognition? And why (and to whom) is research more nationally visible?

To be nationally rather than locally recognized, in the present context, is not tantamount to being visible to more people. Nor does it entail being visible to a more diverse range of people. Teaching and service-oriented faculty are visible to large numbers and to a diverse group of people—students, department and university colleagues, members of community, public and business organizations, and so forth. Research-oriented faculty, on the other hand, may be visible to a relatively small number and to a homogenous group of people—other academics at other universities whose (typically narrow) areas of research interest match their own.

Thus, although publishing may be both necessary and sufficient for enhancing a narrow academic reputation *within* small (albeit national) academic circles, it is not necessarily the most effective method of building good will that goes *beyond* those circles. Teaching and community service are integral to building a personal and institutional reputation among one's students and members of one's local community for honesty, integrity, fairness, caring, and compassion. Building such an institutional reputation is unlikely, however, if the faculty within a university are only rewarded—indeed, only retained—for single-minded efforts to produce lengthy, jargon-filled treatises on topics of interest only to fellow specialists.

Redefining Scholarship and Women's Roles as Scholars

It is only by virtue of the ambiguity of the term "research" that arguments for prioritizing research as a criterion for tenure and promotion appear plausible. Research, conceived as a search for truth, is an important factor in expanding the boundaries of knowledge. But research, measured in terms of quantitative output, mitigates against the development of novel ideas and approaches. Research, understood as professional development, is an important factor in pedagogical effectiveness. But research, in the sense of scholarly publication, favors disseminating specialized knowledge to an elite circle over providing general knowledge and useful skills to a diverse public. Yet, it is only research narrowly understood as publication and measured quantitatively that counts substantially toward individual and institutional advancement. When it is said that research is integral to the mission of the university, therefore, we must be careful to scrutinize what, precisely, is meant by research. We must also initiate a serious dialogue concerning what, exactly, the mission of the university is.

The Mission of the University in Historical Perspective

For the past several decades, the prevailing assumption has been that the mission of the university is "to advance, disseminate and apply knowledge" in that order [6, 51, 65, 66]. "Basic" or "pure" research has been prioritized with teaching and public service tacked on as ancillary goals. The mission of the university has not always been conceived this way, however. The contemporary American research university is "a hybrid" of several earlier traditions [51, p. 103].

In the seventeenth and eighteenth centuries, the mission of the academy was largely a *moral* and *spiritual* one: "the colonial college ... focused on the student—on building character and preparing new generations for civic and religious leadership" [15, p. 3]. American colleges, such as Harvard, were built on the British undergraduate teaching model, where students were the central focus of academic life, and faculty were hired to serve as "educational mentors" within and outside of the classroom [p. 4]. This conception of the mission of the academy, which respected teaching as a vocation, continued into the nineteenth century at institutions such as Harvard, but was slowly transformed by an alternative conception advanced by the nation's first technical schools.

From the early nineteenth to the early twentieth century, the mission of the academy came to be viewed as largely a *practical* and *economic* one: higher education's focus shifted "from the shaping of young lives to the building of a nation" [15, p. 4]. Early technical schools emphasized the goal of training young people to build railroads, bridges, and other parts of the American infrastructure. Colleges such as Harvard, while still emphasizing classroom instruction, began to link teaching to the institution's role "in the service of business and economic prosperity" [p. 4]. In the latter half of the nineteenth century, the new land-grant universities focused on providing knowledge that would improve agriculture and manufacturing. Thus, "American education, once devoted primarily to the intellectual and moral development of students, added service as a mission." Although Stanford's president may have overstated the case, declaring in 1903, "The entire university movement in the twentieth century is toward reality and practicality," most agreed that higher education was justified in terms of its usefulness [15, p. 5].

Only recently has the mission of the academy come to be viewed as largely a *theoretical* and (allegedly) *objective* one. While research began to emerge as a central part of the university's mission in the mid-nineteenth century, the university's research agenda was, at that time, practically indistinguishable from its teaching and service goals. "Professors were hired to teach the science that was already known" so that students could apply this knowledge in their work and communities— "to add to that knowledge was not expected" [88, pp. 5, 51]. By the latter part of the nineteenth century, however, the universities of Pennsylvania, Harvard, Columbia, Princeton, and the newly founded University of Chicago began to emphasize graduate education modeled on the Ph.D. programs of the German research university—a model that required original research culminating in the doctoral dissertation. By the turn of the century, evaluations of faculty at several institutions were also beginning to stress the importance of research productivity. At these institutions, research became sharply distinguished from teaching and service. Though undergraduate education remained a function of the university, "for many professors, class and lecture work became almost incidental." Service likewise became devalued: "Some even considered it a violation of the integrity of the university, since the prevailing Germanic model demanded that the professor view the everyday world from a distance" [15, p. 9].

With the exception of the German-inspired research universities, however, most universities and colleges continued to define their mission in terms of undergraduate education and service until the mid-twentieth century. Until World War II, "academic concerns were primarily practical and local, not theoretical and national" [65, p. 199]. During World War II, however, service took on a more national perspective and scientific research gained public recognition as integral to the security of the nation. Federal funding for research increased dramatically over the next four decades, and the research priority which had previously characterized only a few institutions became widely shared [65]. Today, undergraduate education and community service goals have been overshadowed by an emphasis on graduate education and research at almost all academic institutions. With the exception of two-year colleges, post-secondary institutions have shifted their focus "from the student to the professoriate, from general to specialized education, and from loyalty to the campus [and local community] to loyalty to the profession" [15, p. 13].

In the post-cold war period, however, the public has become increasingly skeptical concerning the justification of research institutions' "claims on the public purse," and federal research monies have been drastically reduced [65]. More generally, the public has questioned the accountability of the academy and academics, as faculty retreat from the classroom to esoteric research projects that seem ingly disconnected from both national cerns and local community needs. federal funds for research and declining public support for higher education has left academic institutions competing for increasingly scarce resources at the same time that research costs are escalating and student enrollments are burgeoning [61]. Yet, the research emphasis among and within universities has remained largely unquestioned. One result has been, as suggested above, "the emotional and economic exploitation of women" for the sake of "the 'work' of a few men" [68, p. 124]. Less external research monies, combined with an increased internal emphasis on the importance of research has made current tenure and promotion criteria increasingly difficult to meet. This has been especially true for women who may have little time (and in some cases little inclination) for grant-writing and article-publishing given their extensive teaching and service responsibilities and their tendency to take these responsibilities seriously.

An Alternative Model for Evaluating Faculty: Rereading Boyer through Feminist Lenses

Women—and those who care about women's place in the academy—can respond to this situation in two ways: by problematizing women or by problematizing the criteria by which women (and others) are evaluated. The favored response, thus far, has been the former. Even "progressive academics" whose scholarship emphasizes "the importance of critiquing and resisting racist and/or sexist discourse... rarely problematize the elitist practices and division of labour which produce 'superior thinkers' and 'proper scholarly practices of conceptualizing' in their own workplaces" [59, p. 120]. Women have been mentored (when they have been mentored at all) to cut back on the time they devote to teaching and service in order to concentrate on their research. The assumption underlying this advice—usually given by well-intentioned liberals, including liberal feminists—is that individual women can improve their situation if they choose to. This assumption portrays the successes and failures of women as the consequence of freely made personal choices, thus ignoring the fact that the university's current organizational culture depends upon a gendered division of labor.

Additionally, as noted above, advising women to refuse anything more than minimal teaching and service responsibilities in order to pursue their research arises from a masculine perspective that mirrors sexist attitudes outside the academy. Such advice assumes that child-rearing (teaching, advising, mentoring, and nurturing students), homemaking (departmental and institutional service), and volunteer work (community service) are unimportant, uncreative, and unchallenging tasks. No satisfactory argument is given as to why such tasks are unimportant—or at least less important than individual research. Instead this is simply assumed from the outset.

Yet, clearly, this assumption is problematic. After all, the survival of an academic institution depends on the willingness and ability of *some group of people* to teach classes, advise students, manage day-to-day operations, and build and maintain community relationships. Developing good teacher-student and university-community relations is especially important within the current social context wherein higher education is rapidly losing public support. Yet, as long as these tasks remain depicted and devalued as "women's work," few male faculty will choose these roles. As we have seen, the group of people who currently fill teaching and service roles are women. Some of these women are also successful researchers—what Astin and Davis term "superacademic women" [6], but the majority are increasingly drawn from a surplus labor pool of (so-called) part-time faculty who are underpaid, receive few benefits, and have no access to the resources necessary to transform their position to that of a "regular" (that is, tenured) faculty member. This suggests that feminists need to urge a reevaluation of the reigning faculty evaluation system.

One way to transform the university into a place that truly values women and fairly evaluates women's contributions is suggested by recent (re)definitions of scholarship [15, 26]. Boyer, for example, urges university faculty and administrators to overcome the myopic definition of research as the production of scholarly articles and books and to focus instead on scholarship, (re)defined broadly as encompassing the scholarship of discovery, integration, application, and teaching [15, p. 16]. Although Boyer does not argue for this expanded definition of scholarship on explicitly feminist grounds, both his thinking and his conclusions are conducive to feminism and suggest a set of criteria for tenure and promotion that would be more woman (and feminist)-friendly than those currently in place.

The scholarship of discovery "comes closest to what is meant when academics speak of 'research'" [15, p. 17]. It includes research publication that contributes to "the stock of human knowledge," but emphasizes "not just the outcome, but the process, and especially the passion [that] give meaning to the effort" and contributes to the intellectual atmosphere of a campus. This is consistent with feminist disavowals of the passion/reason dichotomy, as well as contemporary feminist revisionings of knowledge as an ongoing process [24, 36, 38, 39, 74, 79]. Moreover, in moving away from an exclusive focus on the product of research, the scholarship of discovery avoids the commodification of knowledge and the related devaluation of the producer (the laborer) vis-à-vis the marketer (the publisher). Finally, the scholarship of discovery, as reconceptualized here, is viewed as meritorious by virtue of its local (campus), and not merely its national (professional), contribution.

The scholarship of integration is closely related to the scholarship of discovery but emphasizes "the connectedness of things." It involves "doing research at the boundaries where fields converge" and thus emphasizes the importance of interdisciplinary research, such as that undertaken by many women's studies faculty. The scholarship of integration further emphasizes the need to interpret (both old and new) discoveries by "illuminating data in a revealing way" and "fitting one's own research—or the research of others—into larger intellectual patterns" in order to overcome the "pedantry" that can result from overspecialization [15, pp. 18, 19]. Feminist theory is integrative in just this way—it seeks to synthesize the results of investigation and detect patterns [33].

As suggested above, however, theory should not be disengaged from practice. While feminist scholarship requires a commitment to connecting disciplines, drawing together ideas, and reinterpreting evidence, it also requires connecting research to teaching and service, drawing together people and reinterpreting the role of the academic (and the academy) in the larger community. These latter activities would be encouraged by tenure and promotion criteria that emphasize the scholarship of application and teaching alongside the scholarship of discovery and integration.

The scholarship of application ties research to service by encouraging the scholar to ask "How can knowledge be responsibly applied to consequential problems? How can it be helpful to individuals as well as institutions? And further, can social problems *themselves* define an agenda for scholarly investigation?" [15, p. 21]. Thus, the scholarship of application encourages the scholar to passionately engage with, rather than dispassionately study, the world. It also requires scholars to be responsible for both the direction and the consequences of their research. In both these ways, it supports the feminist contention that researchers must give up the flawed distinction between objectivity and subjectivity [21, 24, 36, 38, 39, 48, 56, 79]. The scholarship of application recognizes a dynamic relationship between the intellectual and the personal, between theory and practice. Personal experiences and social and political concerns may give rise to intellectual analyses which are tested by further experience and experiment. Theorizing suggests new ways of designing environmental policies, treating illnesses, engineering buildings, solving economic problems, and serving local communities; the practical application of ideas, in turn, tests theories and gives rise to new intellectual understandings. Thus, rather than devaluing service as trivial, nonintellectual, or even anti-intellectual (because personal commitments compromise objectivity), an institution that acknowledged the scholarship of service would value service as "serious, demanding work," which produces as well as applies knowledge [15, p. 22].

Finally, the scholarship of teaching ties research to teaching, by emphasizing that "good teaching means that faculty, as scholars, are also learners" [15, p. 24]. Good teaching is not something that anyone can do; it requires knowledge of one's subject matter and the ability to organize, synthesize, and communicate knowledge in meaningful ways to a non-specialist audience [11, 61]. More importantly, it requires the ability to "stimulate active, not passive, learning" and provide students with the capacity to go on learning after their college days are over." Thus, effective teaching requires a willingness to interact with students, to engage them in discussion, encourage them to think critically and creatively, listen to their comments and questions, and to "be pushed in new creative directions" oneself [15, p. 24]. This portrayal of good teaching is consistent with feminist and multicultural models of pedagogy, which view teaching as a collaborative endeavor most likely to succeed where classes are transformed into learning communities [9, 10, 55, 59, 74]. Moreover, the model of teaching suggested here deemphasizes the mere "dissemination" of knowledge and reemphasizes both the importance and the difficulty of reproducing (and empowering) knowers. Thus, an institution that acknowledged the scholarship of teaching could no longer trivialize this facet of academic "women's work."

The university, as we currently encounter it, is—as Rich suggests—"above all a hierarchy" [68, p. 124]. Moreover, it is a hierarchy built on the exploitation of women: the contemporary research university replicates the patriarchal family wherein fathers are breadwinners, mothers are domestic laborers, and prodigious daughters are encouraged to identify with their fathers and brothers more strongly than their mothers or sisters [68, pp. 125, 129]. If we are to transform the university into a more woman-centered institution, then we must begin by deconstructing this gendered hierarchy. A primary focus of this effort must be the prevailing criteria for promotion and tenure.

Following Boyer, revised criteria for faculty evaluation might be depicted, nonhierarchically, as in Figure 1. As this figure indicates, these various academic functions are interrelated: application of existing knowledge may result in discoveries that can be integrated into the curriculum, and which may, in turn, prompt new interpretations of evidence, and so on. Yet, analyzing these faculty functions serves to highlight the diversity of faculty talents and contributions that deserve recognition in the tenure and promotion process. In order to assess fairly each faculty member's contributions and skills, we will need to develop an equally diverse set of evaluative tools. As suggested above, this is not impossible. Yet, it is complex and time-consuming. Hence, succeeding at this task will require considerable and diverse resources, and participation in this effort should itself be rewarded.

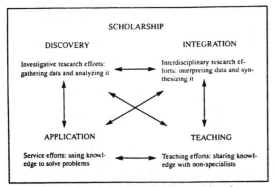

Figure 1. Scholarshp Reconceptualized Following Boyer [15]

Notes

1. Here and below, the arguments offered in favor of the prevailing tenure and promotion paradigm are gleaned from conversations with colleagues and administrators in formal and informal settings. Explicit arguments for prioritizing research productivity in evaluations of faculty are rarely found in the published literature, demonstrating that this paradigm is the current "null hypothesis" [22]. The burden of proof is assumed to fall to those who would contest this paradigm.

2. Minority women, as women in general, were concentrated in lower ranks, comprising 7 percent of instructors, 5 percent of assistant professors, 3 percent of associate professors, and 1.4 percent of full professors. Minority men while comprising a relatively small proportion of faculty (like minority women) were fairly evenly distributed across ranks, indicating they have been more successful than minority women in gaining promotion, but less successful than white men.

3. Here again both white and minority women follow similar patterns of concentration, while minority men are more evenly dispersed across disciplines than women, but less evenly dispersed across disciplines than white men.

4. As Frye notes, "Differences in power are always manifested in asymmetrical access" [32, p. 103]. Superiors can refuse access to subordinates, but those who are subordinate (in this case, junior faculty) cannot easily refuse access to their bosses (in this case, chairs, deans, and upper administrators).

5. This would also have the welcome effect of better enabling faculty to improve their courses.

6. It might also be argued that active involvement in research makes a teacher more lively, enthusiastic, interesting, challenging, and organized. The only variable linking research to effective teaching, however, is organization. And it is plausible to suggest that good organizational skills are a source, rather than an effect, of good research [31].

7. This article emphasizes the importance of scholarly publication to successful tenure and promotion outcomes. This emphasis, like the university's emphasis, is problematic for those faculty who work in the visual or performing arts. The contributions of painters, photographers, sculptors, actors, and musicians—like the contributions of women—would be better recognized by the revised criteria for tenure and promotion suggested at the end of this article.

References

1. Acker, J. "Hierarchies, Jobs, and Bodies: A Theory of Gendered Organizations." In *Women in Higher Education: A Feminist Perspective*, edited by J. S. Glazer, E. M. Bensimon, and B. K. Townsend, pp. 81–95. Needham Heights, Mass.: Ginn Press, 1993.
2. Aisenberg, N., and M. Harrington. "Rules of the Game." In *Women in Higher Education: A Feminist Perspective*, edited by J. S. Glazer, E. M. Bensimon, and B. K. Townsend, pp. 387–98. Needham Heights, Mass.: Ginn Press, 1993.
3. Allen, H. L. "Workload and Productivity in an Accountability Era." *NEA 1994 Almanac of Higher Education* (1994), 25–38.
4. Altbach, P. G., and L. S. Lewis. "Reforming Higher Education: A Modest Proposal." *Thought and Action*, 9 (1994), 31–40.
5. Andrews, A. R. "Balancing the Personal and Professional." In *Spirit, Space and Survival: African American Women in (White) Academe*, edited by J. James and R. Farmer, pp. 179–95. New York: Routledge, 1993.
6. Astin, A. W., W. S. Korn, and E. L. Lewis. *The American College Teacher: National Norms for the 1989–90 HERI Faculty Survey*. Los Angeles, Calif.: Higher Education Research Institute, Graduate School of Education, UCLA, 1991.
7. Astin, H. S., and D. E. Davis. "Research Productivity across the Life and Career Cycles: Facilitators and Barriers for Women." In *Women in Higher Education: A Feminist Perspective*, edited by J. S. Glazer, E. M. Bensimon, and B. K. Townsend, pp. 415–23. Needham Heights, Mass.: Ginn Press, 1993.
8. Astin H. S., and M. B. Snyder. "A Decade of Response." *Change*, 14 (1982), 26–31, 59.

9. Bannerji, H., et al. *Unsettling Relations: The University as a Site of Feminist Struggles.* Boston, Mass.: Southend Press, 1992.
10. Belenky, M. F., B. M. Clinchy, N. R. Goldberger, and J. M. Tarule. *Women's Ways of Knowing: The Development of Self, Voice, and Mind.* New York: Basic Books, 1986.
11. Bess, J. L. "College Teachers: Miscast Professionals." *Change* 22, (May/June 1990), 19–22.
12. Billard, L. "Twenty Years Later: Is There Parity for Academic Women?" *Thought and Action*, 10 (1994), 115–44.
13. Blackburn, R. T., J. P. Bieber, J. H. Lawrence, and L. Trautvetter. "Faculty at Work: Focus on Research, Scholarship and Service." *Research in Higher Education*, 32 (1991), 385–413.
14. Boyer, E. L. *College: The Undergraduate Experience in America.* New York: Oxford University Press, 1986.
15. _____. *Scholarship Re-Considered: Priorities of the Professoriate.* Princeton, N.J.: Carnegie Foundation for the Advancement of Teaching, 1990.
16. Calas, M. B., and L. Smircich. "Re-Writing Gender into Organizational Theorizing." In *Women in Higher Education: A Feminist Perspective*, edited by J. S. Glazer, E. M. Bensimon, and B. K. Townsend, pp. 97–117. Needham Heights, Mass.: Ginn Press, 1993.
17. Campbell, D. K., J. Gaertner, and R. P. Vecchio. "Perceptions of Promotion and Tenure Criteria: A Survey of Accounting Educators." *Journal of Accounting Education*, 1 (1983), 83–92.
18. Carnegie Foundation. *The Condition of the Professoriate: Attitudes and Trends 1989.* Princeton, N.J.: Carnegie Foundation for the Advancement of Teaching, 1989.
19. _____. "Women Faculty Excel as Campus Citizens." *Change*, 22 (Sept/Oct 1990), 39–43.
20. Clark, S. M., and M. Corcoran. "Perspectives on the Professional Socialization of Women Faculty: A Case of Accumulative Disadvantage?" *Journal of Higher Education*, 57 (January/February 1986), 20–43.
21. Code, L. *Epistemic Responsibility.* Hanover, N.H.: Brown University Press, 1987.
22. Cole, J. R. "Balancing Acts: Dilemmas of Choice Facing Research Universities." *Daedelus*, 122 (1993), 1–35.
23. _____. *Fair Science: Women in the Scientific Community.* New York: Free Press, 1979.
24. Collins, P. H. "Toward an Afrocentric Feminist Epistemology." *Black Feminist Thought, Consciousness, Knowledge, and the Politics of Empowerment.* Boston, Mass.: Unwin Hyman, (1990), 201–20.
25. ly, F., and B. K. Townsend. "The Chair's in Tenure Acquisition." *Thought and Action* 9 (1994), 125–46.
26. W. T. "Teaching and Scholarship: Adapting American Higher Education to Hard [Times]." *Journal of Higher Education*, 65 (January/February 1994), 45–57.
27. Fairweather, J. S. "The Value of Teaching, Research, and Service." *1994 NEA Almanac of Higher Education*, (1994) 39–58.
28. Farmer, R. "Place but not Importance: The Race for Inclusion in Academe." In *Spirit, Space and Survival: African American Women in (White) Academe*, edited by J. James and R. Farmer, pp. 196–217. New York: Routledge, 1993.
29. Finnegan, D. E. "Segmentation in the Academic Labor Market." *Journal of Higher Education*, 64 (November/December 1994), 23–24.
30. Finkelstein, J. J. *The American Academic Profession.* Columbus: Ohio State University Press, 1984.
31. Friedrich, R. J., and S. J. Michalak, Jr. "Why Doesn't Research Improve Teaching?" *Journal of Higher Education*, 54 (March/April 1983), 145–63.
32. Frye, M. *The Politics of Reality: Essays in Feminist Theory.* Trumansburg, N. Y.: The Crossing Press, 1983.
33. Frye, M. "The Possibility of Feminist Theory." In *Theoretical Perspectives on Sex Difference*, edited by D. L. Rhode, pp. 174–84. New Haven, Conn.: Yale University Press, 1990.
34. Gabbin, A. L., S. N. Cairns, and R. L. Benke (eds.). *Faculty Performance Indicators.* Harrisonberg, Va.: Center for Research in Accounting Information, James Madison University, 1990.
35. Garcia, R. L. "Affirmative Action Hiring." *Journal of Higher Education*, 45 (April 1974), 268–76.
36. Garry, A., and M. Pearsall (eds.). *Women, Knowledge, and Reality: Explorations in Feminist Philosophy.* Boston, Mass.: Unwin Hyman, 1989.
37. Gilligan, C. *In a Different Voice: Psychological Theory and Women's Development.* Cambridge and London: Harvard University Press, 1982.
38. Harding, S. "Rethinking Standpoint Epistemology: What is 'Strong Objectivity'?" In *Feminist Epistemologies*, edited by L. Alcoff and E. Potter, pp. 49–82. New York and London: Routledge, 1993.
39. Harding, S., and M. B. Hintikka (eds.). *Discovering Reality: Feminist Perspectives on Epistemology, Metaphysics, Methodology, and Philosophy of Science.* Dordrecht and Boston: D. Reidel, 1983.
40. Heald, S. "Pianos to Pedagogy: Pursuing the Educational Subject." In *Unsettling Relations: The University as a Site of Feminist Struggles*, edited by H. Bannerji, L. Carty, K. Dehli, S. Heald, and K. McKenna, pp. 129–49. Boston, Mass: Southend Press, 1992.
41. hooks, b. *Feminist Theory: From Margin to Center.* Boston, Mass.: Southend Press, 1984.
42. Hornig, L. S. "Untenured and Tenuous: The Status of Women Faculty." *Annals of the American Academy of Political and Social Science*, 448 (1980), 115–25.

43. Howe, R. "Retrenchment Policies and Practices: A Summary." *Journal of the College and University Personnel Association*, 31 (1980), 136–47.
44. Jacobs, J. A. *Revolving Doors: Sex Segregation and Women's Careers*. Stanford, Calif.: Stanford University Press, 1989.
45. Johnsrud, L. K., and R. H. Heck. "Administrative Promotion within a University: The Cumulative Impact of Gender." *Journal of Higher Education*, 65 (January/February 1994), 25–44.
46. Kanter, R. M. *Men and Women of the Corporation*. New York: Basic Books, 1977.
47. Kasten, K. L. "Tenure and Merit Pay as Rewards for Research, Teaching, and Service at a Research University." *Journal of Higher Education*, 55 (July/August 1984), 500–514.
48. Keller, E. F. *Reflections on Gender and Science*. New Haven, Conn.: Yale University Press, 1985.
49. Kember, D., and L. Gow. "Orientations to Teaching and their Effect on the Quality of Student Learning." *Journal of Higher Education*, 65 (January/February 1994), 58–74.
50. Kemp, A. A. *Women's Work: Degraded and Devalued*. Englewood Cliffs, N.J.: Prentice-Hall, 1994.
51. Keohane, N. O. "The Mission of the Research University." *Daedalus*, 122 (1993), 101–25.
52. Kingsbury Jones, L., S. A. Hoenack, and M. Hammida. "Career Development of Tenure-Track Assistant Professors." *Thought and Action*, 9 (1994), 147–72.
53. Lie, S. S., L. Malik, and D. Harris (eds.) *The Gender Gap in Higher Education*. London: Kogan Page, 1994.
54. Lewis, L. S. "Academic Tenure: Its Recipients and Effects." *Annals of the American Academy of Political and Social Science*, 448 (1980), 86–101.
55. Maher, F. A. "Toward a Richer Theory of Feminist Pedagogy: A Comparison of 'Liberation' and 'Gender' Models for Teaching and Learning." *Journal of Education*, 169 (1987), 91–100.
56. Mairs, N. *Voice Lessons: On Becoming a Woman Writer*. Boston, Mass.: Beacon Press, 1994.
57. Marsh, H. W. "Validity of Students' Evaluation of College Teaching: A Multitrait-Multimethod Analysis." *Journal of Educational Psychology*, 74 (1982), 264–79.
58. McElrath, K. "Gender, Career Disruption, and Academic Rewards." *Journal of Higher Education*, 63 (May/June 1992), 269–81.
59. McKenna, K. "Subjects of Discourse: Learning the Language that Counts." In *Unsettling Relations: The University as a Site of Feminist Struggles*, edited by H. Bannerji, L. Carty, K. Dehli, S. Heald, and K. McKenna, pp. 109–28. Boston, Mass.: Southend Press, 1992.
60. Menges, R. J., and W. H. Exum. "Barriers to the Progress of Women and Minority Faculty." *Journal of Higher Education*, 54 (March/April 1983), 123–43.
61. Miller, L. H. "Hubris in the Academy: Can Teaching Survive an Overweening Quest for Excellence?" *Change*, 22 (Sept/Oct 1990), 9–11, 53.
62. Moore, K. M., and M. D. Sagaria. "The Situation of Women in Research Universities in the United States." In *Women in Higher Education: A Feminist Perspective*, edited by J. S. Glazer, E. M. Bensimon, and B. K. Townsend, pp. 227–40. Needham Heights, Mass.: Ginn Press, 1993.
63. Moore, W., and L. Wagstaff. *Black Faculty in White Colleges*. San Francisco: Jossey-Bass, 1974.
64. Neumann, Y., and E. Finaly-Neumann. "The Support-Stress Paradigm and Faculty Research Publication." *Journal of Higher Education*, 61 (September/October 1990), 565–80.
65. Nichols, R. W. "Federal Science Policy and Universities: Consequences of Success." *Daedalus*, 122 (1993), 197–223.
66. Perkin, H. "The Historical Perspective." In *Perspectives on Higher Education: Eight Disciplinary and Comparative Views*, edited by B. R. Clark, 23–39. Berkeley, Calif.: University of California Press, 1984.
67. Powell, R. W. "Grades, Learning, and Student Evaluation of Instruction." *Research in Higher Education*, 7 (1977), 193–205.
68. Rich, A. "Toward a Woman-Centered University." In *Women in Higher Education: A Feminist Perspective*, edited by J. S. Glazer, E. M. Bensimon, and B. K. Townsend, pp. 121–34. Needham Heights, Mass.: Ginn Press, 1993.
69. Root, L. S. "Faculty Evaluation: Reliability of Peer Assessments of Research, Teaching, and Service." *Research in Higher Education*, 26 (1987), 71–84.
70. Sampson, E. E. "Scientific Paradigms and Social Values: Wanted—a Scientific Revolution." *Journal of Personality and Social Psychology*, 36 (1978), 1332–43.
71. Sandler, B. R. "The Campus Climate Revisited: Chilly for Women Faculty, Administrators, and Graduate Students." In *Women in Higher Education: A Feminist Perspective*, edited by J. S. Glazer, E. M. Bensimon, and B. K. Townsend, pp. 175–203. Needham Heights, Mass.: Ginn Press, 1993.
72. Schiebinger, L. *The Mind Has No Sex? Women in the Origins of Modern Science*. Cambridge, Mass.: Harvard University Press, 1989.
73. Seldin, P. "Faculty Evaluations: Surveying Policy and Practices." *Change*, 16 (1984), 29–33.
74. Sleeter, C. E. (ed.) *Empowerment through Multicultural Education*. Albany, N.Y.: SUNY Press, 1991.
75. Simeone, A. *Academic Women: Working toward Equality*. South Hadley, Mass.: Bergin and Garvey, 1987.

76. Smith, D. E. "Women's Perspective as a Radical Critique of Sociology." In *Feminism and Methodology*, edited by S. Harding, pp. 84–96. Bloomington: Indiana University Press, 1987.
77. Stigler, S. M. "Competition and the Research Universities." *Daedalus*, 122 (1993), 157–77.
78. Theodore, A. *The Campus Troublemakers: Academic Women in Protest*. Houston, Tex.: Cap and Gown Press, 1986.
79. Tuana, N. (ed.). *Feminism and Science*. Bloomington and Indianapolis: Indiana University Press, 1989.
80. Tuckman, H. P., J. H. Gapinski, and R. P. Hagemann. "Faculty Skills and the Salary Structure in Academe: A Market Perspective." *The American Economic Review*, 67 (1977), 692–702.
81. Tuckman, H. P., and R. P. Hagemann. "An Analysis of the Reward Structure in Two Disciplines." *Journal of Higher Education*, 47 (July/August 1976), 447–64.
82. Turk, T. G. "Women Faculty in Higher Education: Academic Administration and Governance in a State University System, 1966–1977." *Pacific Sociological Review*, 24 (1981), 212–36.
83. U. S. Department of Education. *Profiles of Faculty in Higher Education Institutions, 1988*. Washington, D.C.: National Center for Education Statistics, 1991.
84. Verrier, D. A. "Perceptions of Life on the Tenure Track." *Thought and Action*, 9 (1994), 95–124.
85. Wanner, R., L. S. Lewis, and D. I. Gregario. "Research Productivity in Academia: A Comparative Study of the Sciences, Social Sciences, and Humanities." *Sociology of Education*, 54 (1981), 238–53.
86. Whitman, N., and E. Weiss. *Faculty Evaluation: The Use of Explicit Criteria for Promotion, Retention, and Tenure*. Washington, D.C.: American Association for Higher Education, 1982.
87. Winkler, K. J. "Women Historians Have Greater Access to Some Jobs but Remain Concentrated in Underpaid Ranks." *Chronicle of Higher Education*, 12 January 1981, p. 8.
88. Wolfle, D. *The Home of Science: The Role of the University*. New York: Columbia University Press, 1968.
89. Wright, P., R. Wittington, and G. E. Whittenburg. "Student Ratings of Teaching Effectiveness: What the Research Reveals." *Journal of Accounting Education*, 2 (1984), 5–30.
90. Wunsch, M. A., and L. K. Johnsrud. "Breaking Barriers: Mentoring Junior Faculty Women for Professional Development and Retention." *To Improve the Academy*, 11 (1992), 175–87.

I wish to thank the participants in the 1994 Women in Higher Education Conference, especially Kathryn Seidel, and also the anonymous reviewers for the Journal of Higher Education for their encouragement, suggestions, and constructive criticism of earlier drafts of this article.

Shelley M. Park is an assistant professor of philosophy at the University of Central Florida, Orlando.

CHAPTER 21

(EN)GENDER(ING) SOCIALIZATION

WILLIAM G. TIERNEY AND ESTELA MARA BENSIMON

"I had two offers. At the first place, when I went for the interview I met the chair, and the man who will be the next chair, and the man who is the dean, and the man who's been in the department the longest time, and the man who teaches religion, and it was like a little club of men. I just met with the senior men in the department. I didn't meet any junior faculty. I didn't meet any women. I know there were women in the department, but they didn't schedule me to meet any of them. They didn't take me out to dinner the night before. They didn't give me breakfast. I assumed that there was an internal candidate and they were just going through the motions. But they ended up offering me the job.

"Two days later, I came for the interview here, and it was like sunshine after rain. It was the most thoughtful of all of the five campus interviews. They did things like giving me twenty minutes to myself between meetings with people. At the other place, I had forty-five minute meetings with people starting at eight thirty in the morning and going through until seven at night without a break. Here people escorted me from one place to another, so that I got to meet people without feeling as if they were interviewing me. In my schedule they had the names of the persons that would take me to each meeting and the name of the person who would pick me up. At the other place, I actually wrote the schedule down myself while the chair read it to me."

This woman was more fortunate than the man we introduced in the previous chapter. Having received only one offer, he was obliged to accept a position in an institution that made him uneasy. She received job offers from both institutions, giving her a choice. As might have been expected, she accepted the position in the latter institution and told the chair at the former one that she was declining their offer because "I can't imagine what it would be like to walk into that department every day."

In view of the inconsiderate treatment this applicant received at the former institution, her decision did not come as a surprise. What surprised us, however, was that she rejected it even though she was offered $7,000 more than the salary she is receiving at her present institution.

It is commonly assumed that faculty search committees know how to conduct a campus visit so that the candidate leaves with the impression that their institution would be a good place to begin or continue one's academic career. When the interview involves a woman or a minority group member and the search committee is all male and/or all white, what is said and done is viewed through the lenses of gender and race. A department conveys significant messages about its culture and the climate for women when a sexist remark made by a member of the search committee is greeted with chuckles, or the candidate is told by a senior professor that he will have to skip the interview luncheon because he has a tennis date, or very few of the senior faculty show up for the candidate's job talk, or the all-male faculty spends more time arguing with one another than talking with the candidate.

Reprinted from *Promotion and Tenure: Community and Socialization in Academe*, by William G. Tierney and Estela Mara Bensimon, 1996. Copyright © 1996 State University of New York Press.

Our interviews with administrative leaders and department chairs suggest that senior faculty, the great majority of whom is white males, are unaware of the gendered and racial connotations of their conduct, language, mode of interaction, gestures, etc. Often senior faculty and administrators mistakenly assume that being blind to gender or race assures women and minority applicants that they will be given equal consideration and judged solely on the basis of merit and credentials. Indeed, the interview excerpts with which we opened the previous chapter and this one support this view: Men and women can be subjected to equally bad interview situations. However, the cumulative effect of patronizing, sexist, or tactless behavior on the part of an all-male search committee has unique implications for women in that it compels them to function in a climate that is neither supportive nor affirming.

In the previous chapter, we discussed the tenure and promotion years; in this one we shall focus on the particular experiences of women.[1] We contend that gender equity and nonsexist academic workplaces cannot be attained unless conscious attention is given to relations between men and women. We wish to dispel the widely held belief that gender blindness—the claim that the professor's sex is invisible—constitutes equal treatment for female and male academics. To the contrary, we maintain that the eradication of overt and covert discrimination against women requires critical and gender-based appraisals of academic structures, practices, and policies as well as the elimination of language and interactions that create overtly hostile, patronizing, or indifferent workplaces for women. Our premise is that the relations between men and women at the departmental and institutional levels create different socialization experiences. In this chapter we use gender as the lens to analyze the impact on women of socialization practices and experiences discussed in chapter 3. Ninety-nine junior faculty women were interviewed for this project. We are cognizant of the importance of differentiating among women on the basis of race, social class, and sexual orientation, and shall specify racial or ethnic identities when doing so does not violate our pledge of confidentiality. Further, this chapter is based largely on interviews with white women for several reasons: (1) the number of nonwhite U.S. women interviewed is very small and (2) gender and race or gender and ethnicity are not inseparable, so in those cases when these women spoke from the standpoint of their racial or ethnic identities we included them in the next chapter, which is on racial and ethnic faculty in predominantly white institutions.

Socialization as a Gendered Practice

Typically, socialization is understood as the initiation of prospective members into a culture of the institution, department, and profession. It is represented as a rite of passage that begins with probationary membership in the department and concludes, if one is successful, with the granting of lifetime tenure or, if unsuccessful, with immediate termination.

Women's Initiation

Preparing for a candidate's campus visit is not simply a matter of scheduling a series of meetings, announcing the candidate's "job talk," and arranging a real-estate tour. Just as the institution is looking the candidate over, the candidate is also forming impressions that will influence what offer she will accept, as well as her attitude toward prospective colleagues.

A feminist scholar being interviewed for a gender-studies position in a predominantly male department in one of the traditional disciplines described her interview as follows:

> We were having dinner and this one guy, he just kind of laughed and said 'Well, I think it is some kind of a joke . . . I don't know why we are doing this [looking to hire a feminist scholar].' All through the evening he expressed amusement by the efforts of marginalized people to try to position themselves within organizations and institutions where they don't really have the right to be.

Eventually the chair of the department apologized to the candidate and made it clear that they were truly interested in her. She was able to get over her anger and continue with the interview. When the position was offered, she accepted it. However, the treatment she received might have been a preview of the obstacles that could arise during her review for tenure and promotion. As a safeguard, she accepted the position with the condition that a faculty member from Women's Studies would be included in the department's review committee.

This white woman accepted the offer because she had no other job possibilities at the time; but had she received an offer from a department more hospitable to women and feminist scholarship in an equally prestigious institution, she probably would have taken it.

Off-putting interviews were uncommon; for the most part women spoke positively about their interviews. Still, most of the institutions we visited did not have guidelines that dealt specifically with the concerns of female candidates. To reiterate a point made in the previous chapter, the purpose of these vignettes is to portray specific problems that different individuals discussed. A thoughtful response ought not to be relief that such instances have not happened on one's own campus, but rather, proactive planning to ensure that they do not occur in the future. Our point is not that one institution is good and another bad, but that gendered relations are a fact of life. If we are to deal with such differences successfully, we must face them more forthrightly than we have done in the past.

Only one academic administrator had promulgated recruitment practices that spoke directly to the concerns of women and minorities. Starting from the premise that "the relationship the department develops with this person begins at the interview process and it has to start positively," this administrator established recruitment approaches centered on gender and race such as the following:

- Using language and graphics in job announcements that stressed the value of interdisciplinary scholarship and working and living in a multicultural community;
- Placing position announcements in specialized publications such as the *Women's Review of Books*;
- Ending the custom of interviewing candidates in hotel bedrooms at the site of disciplinary conferences (e.g., MLA, ASA);
- Organizing at least one lunch or one dinner for the candidate with people like themselves in order to get a frank assessment of the community. If it was a woman, then it was an all-women's lunch or dinner. If it was a minority person, it was a lunch or dinner with people from their ethnic, racial, or cultural background.

The institutions in our study were conscious of affirmative action and targeting recruitment efforts toward women and minorities. However, beyond recruiting women and minority applicants, there was not much evidence that practices had been modified to avert gender- or race-based inequities at the point of hiring. For example, the custom of individual salary negotiations has been shown to place women at a disadvantage, particularly those who had not been mentored as graduate students and instructed on negotiation rituals and courtship customs that are common in hiring practices in the academy. Women often receive starting salaries that are lower than those of their male peers because they don't know what to ask for or how to negotiate. A white woman at a research university told us, "I didn't think about negotiating. I felt lucky that I was getting a tenure-track job. I wanted to say to the chair, 'I am really happy to come and I want the job, and you have really been nice', and bring it to a closure."

As luck would have it, this woman ended up with a very good salary as well as other benefits she did not think to ask for: a travel budget for her research, a computer, and reimbursement for moving expenses. Had she gone to another institution or even to a different department in the same university, she probably would not have done as well. She was fortunate in having been appointed to an academic unit led by an administrator who had a policy of providing all new faculty members with substantially the same salaries, research budgets, and travel allowances. Speaking about the policy, the administrator who initiated it said,

> I told the department heads that women cannot bargain as aggressively as men. I told them, "I don't care whether they bargain or not." Just because a man says he needs a computer and the woman doesn't,

that doesn't mean he gets the computer and she doesn't. If he gets a computer, she gets a computer. If she gets a research budget, he gets a research budget.

The woman who ended up with more than she asked for was a beneficiary of the new equity policy. She was hired at the same time as a Latino and received a salary and benefits package that was practically the same as the one he had bargained for himself. Had this policy not been in place she probably would have started at a lower salary than that of her male colleague.

The problem with this practice, as well-intentioned as it is, is that it is still disadvantageous for women: "Women can't play as well as men, so we have to help them," rather than "The process is unfair so we have to eliminate bargaining." We should stress the latter.

Arriving on Campus: Women's First Impressions

The location, size, and furnishings of office space usually reflects one's status. More established faculty members get spacious, cheerful offices, and probationary faculty get the small, somber cubicles. Different messages about power relations are conveyed by such decisions as who gets an office with a window, who has to make do with a used computer, who gets a new executive chair, and who gets wall-to-wall carpeting. A woman who walks into an office stocked with supplies, personalized cards, a working computer, and a functioning telephone gets a different message about the culture of the department than the one who learns on her first day that it will be six months before she is assigned an office.

The following are brief descriptions of the arrival experiences of five assistant professors, all of whom are newcomers in a very small institution.

White Male
Newcomer #1: I have been made to feel very welcome. When I ask for money, I get it. A few days after I arrived, the president called me to set up a meeting so we could get acquainted.

White Woman
Newcomer #2: I arrived to an empty department. No one was here. I was responsible for setting up my office. I had to figure out how to get my computer set up and in working order.

White Woman
Newcomer #3: It was totally chaotic. I did not get an office for months. I think it is inconceivable that they would have expected a man to function without an office.

White Woman
Newcomer #4: Well, I didn't get my computer until I'd been here for five weeks, so I missed all of the events that were only announced on e-mail.

African-American Woman
Newcomer #5: I had to get my own keys, computer, telephone, stationery. I didn't know there was a mailroom, and I just only got the key for it [more than a month after she arrived].

What impressions might one form based on the experiences of these new faculty members? A superficial interpretation is that the women's bad experiences compared to the man's good one suggest that structure accords privileges to men and places women at a disadvantage. However, the opening vignette in the previous chapter shows a white man whose initial campus experiences were as unwelcoming as those of the four women, suggesting that anyone, regardless of sex or race, may have a negative initial campus experience.

Our purpose is not to portray this institution as a bad place for women (in fact, the general consensus among the women interviewed was that it was a good place), or to document a systematic pattern of gender and race bias. Rather, by juxtaposing the experiences of these five professors, we want to show that the problem is not one of overt sexism or discrimination but rather that unwelcoming climates are created by unconscious actions that take on gendered meanings. From a gender perspective, the five vignettes could be interpreted as reflecting sex role stereotypes, e.g., "Men need to be cared for" and "Women know how to make do on their own."

Clearly, no one planned to treat the women differently from the man, it just worked out that way. The women's less-than-warm receptions were accidents of circumstance; nevertheless, it is important for members of an institution or department to reflect on the cumulative effect of such incidents on the climate for women. Unfortunately, we tend to dismiss such incidents as one-time occurrences or degender them with rational explanations: for example "The man was a star in his field," and that is why he was treated differently; "Woman #2's chair took time off for a vacation and forgot to order her computer"; "Woman #3 had the misfortune of being a casualty in an interdepartmental feud over office space"; "Woman #4 wanted a highly specialized computer that was delayed at the manufacturer"; and "Woman #5's department chair had a reputation for not being very thoughtful."

We do not contend that the pattern of gender discrimination suggested by the five vignettes is the result of overt sexist practices or from intentional acts of hostility. Without a doubt, lack of administrative acumen is certainly a major cause for the poorly planned receptions of new faculty. Furthermore, we believe that patterns of organization that place women at a disadvantage or reinforce their status as the "other" are produced by the absence of gender consciousness in the minds of decision-makers and its invisibility in the cultures of departments and institutions, as well as in the structures of tenure and promotion. Blindness to gender and gender relations in the construction of meaning prevents academic leaders, men and women, from discerning the multiple "readings" of institutional life. The challenge, then, is to consider how a female assistant professor in an all-male department might be inclined to "read" lack of planning for her arrival as a form of sexism. That is, individuals who have the power and authority to influence institutional functioning have to be adept at using gender as the lens through which they discern their institution's structures, practices, and culture.

Only Woman #3 raised the possibility of gender bias: "It is inconceivable that they would have expected a man to function without an office." The other women did not suspect discrimination based on sex. Yes, they complained about the lack of forethought and preparation for their arrival, and they were generally annoyed, but they did not view themselves as victims of discrimination stemming from a masculinist culture. Rather, they felt very positive about the institution and attributed the lack of preparation for their arrival to external circumstances: lack of space, lack of clerical assistance, overworked administrators, etc. The minority woman, however, pointed out, "If this had been my first job, I would probably have taken things like the office and the computer as personal—you know, that they didn't think I was very important." A white woman with previous experience said that if this had been her first job she would have felt "vulnerable" and "lost."

In another institution sex stereotyping became obvious in the assigning of advisees. A white woman professor in the sciences who was the only one in her program said, "It's almost like they are on automatic pilot. If it's a woman, they assign her to me, or the women come to me, because they've been assigned to somebody else, and they say: 'I don't know what he's talking about, so could I have you for an advisor?'" When we asked this woman what the chair would do if she asked him to reduce her advisement load, she responded: "I think he would be quite willing to do that for me, if I asked . . . but I would feel like I am abandoning them [women students]."

Joining the Professoriate

Virginia Woolf's essay, *Three Guineas*, moves us to ask, "On what terms shall women join the professoriate?" What must women do to be accepted by the tenured faculty? The comments that follow reveal the pressures imposed on women who join male-dominated cultures:

> They are kind of patronizing, but I don't think they will try to hurt us [the junior faculty]. I am not worried about that, but I just feel that it is a kind of burden to get along with them all of the time. The main thing is just getting along with the guy colleagues . . . sometimes I feel uncomfortable, personally, with them. (Asian-American woman)

I smile. I am nice. I try to always feel like I am in a good humor and that I am not challenging anyone, but especially I smile, and it drives me nuts sometimes. If I did not smile or had the personality of some of my [male] colleagues I would be out on my ear. The men can get away with being nerds, but there is no way I could get away with that, even if I wasn't doing feminist things. (White woman)

These passages are taken from interviews with two women, one an Asian American and the other white. Both are assistant professors at the same institution but in different departments. Although they are in different disciplines and in buildings at opposite ends of a sprawling campus, they have developed similar strategies to fit in. They engage in what we call "smile work" tactics to get along in departments dominated by senior male colleagues.

Doing "Smile Work"

"Smile work" takes many different forms, but basically it is a culturally imposed strategy women use to fit into departments with a tradition of male dominance. Sometimes these are departments in which the faculty have not internalized the need to be more diverse and have hired women and/or minorities because of external pressures to comply with affirmative action goals. Typically, they tend to think of equal opportunity as "adding women" without reconsidering socialization practices in order to be more welcoming. Male-dominated cultures encourage feminine stereotypical behaviors that make women appear "unobjectionable," congenial, and cheerful rather than strident and unpredictable.

At a small college, a senior male professor reminisced about the "patriarchal" ways of the past, lamenting that "the faculty club is no longer a place where the wives and children come on Friday nights." A white woman administrator at the same college said, "There is a substantial number of faculty who remember the time when they were masters of the universe . . . and they are still living in that culture." A white man in a research university said of his department, "There is still a definite gender bias, especially among the senior people. I think you're probably a couple of steps ahead if you are a white male around here, but that's probably just stating what people already know or stating the obvious." In institutions such as these, where the imprint of a patriarchal past is still quite discernible, women employ the behavioral and symbolic practices of "smile work" in conscious ways.

Smile work entails the symbolic management of behavior to present oneself as being pleasing and agreeable. An assistant professor in a different working relationship with a very powerful senior professor said,

I accommodate him by backing out, by joking with him, by pretending that we get along and that I don't mind hearing about his sex life.

On the surface, she behaves like a good-natured colleague, a "team player," one of the guys. The act of accommodation inherent in smile work can be costly, a fact she admitted the very moment we entered her office. Before getting started with the interview, she said, "I am so glad you are here . . . I have no one to talk with about these things." She then told us of her decision to move to another institution:

As long as I remain here, I feel I will never be able to establish my own identity. He [senior colleague] makes me feel like a glorified graduate student, and it is very hard on my self-esteem . . . but I cannot afford to have him as my enemy at tenure time. I have to live with this situation.

What this individual has to do in order to survive and succeed involves identity, not "only" adaptation. A man has to learn the code, but that doesn't necessarily mean that he has to conceal who he is, whereas a woman in this situation may be obliged to falsify herself to a greater extent. The point is not to say that men have it easier, but that the same "problem" must be interpreted in a variety of ways.

Women who felt pressured into being accommodating spoke about feelings of powerlessness, loss of self, and lack of self-confidence. A feminist scholar complained that a senior professor treated her as if she were "his personal property." "He wanted to boss me, introduce me around as if I were his protégé," she said. She resented the subordinating gestures of her colleague and would have liked to bring them to his attention. However, she received a negative mid-tenure review, and "rather than making a big thing out of it," she said, "I was advised to try to win over one of the professors who voted against me... so I am trying to win this person over, using regular, you know, normal ways." Then she added the caveat: "I want to have positive evaluations, but I am not going to lose my dignity."

In a hierarchical and status-conscious structure, the dualism of "senior" versus "junior" underscores differences in power, knowledge, and prestige that characterize relationships between experts and novices. Indeed, at one institution we visited, the participants had replaced the term "junior faculty" with one they felt was less objectionable and power-laden—"probationary faculty." The status of novice is full of contradictions, uncertainties, and anxieties about one's worth. For women in predominantly male departments, the difficulties are intensified by the combined politics of tenure and promotion and gender relations. A Latina told us, "I have to demonstrate I am humble and malleable" in order to succeed. An Asian woman described a faculty meeting with new graduate students that was "dominated by one of the senior men.... when my turn to speak came, I mentioned that I do traditional things and that I also teach courses on feminist topics. I made it known that I have several interests. Immediately after I said that, he warned the graduate students to be focused in one area. I felt he was undermining me because I did not just do traditional stuff."

One cannot know for sure whether the senior professor's remarks were triggered by her comments, and if they were whether their intended meaning was as she interpreted it. However, in an environment where outstanding graduate students can enhance professors' status and prestige, the professor's admonition "to focus" took on a derogatory meaning. The comment emphasized the woman's junior status, which she feared would make her appear as inexperienced and, therefore, not necessarily a prime choice to serve as dissertation advisor for doctoral students.

Doing "Mom Work"

Another form of accommodation that women engaged in was "mom work," a term used by an assistant professor to describe the imposition of nurturing and caretaking roles on women. Just as some department cultures fostered "smile work," others promulgated the stereotype of the nurturing woman. The pressure to perform "mom work" was greatest in small private colleges. These are colleges with a greater-than-usual dependency on tuition revenues and where there is an unstated expectation for faculty to be popular with students and their parents.

According to one white woman, the pressure to be popular with students was "amplified for female professors." "It's a personality issue. You have to, you know, be extroverted and be willing to disclose personal issues, personal information; they [students] definitely look for some personal information." A gay white man said, "I team-taught a class with a woman, and some of the comments in the evaluations were surprising... they said she giggled like an adolescent, and I didn't perceive her like that at all... she joked the way male professors often do, and the students shot her down because she is a woman." He also remarked that students "tend to cling to women professors, and when they are not allowed to cling, when the female professor tries to make her own time, she's considered selfish, whereas with the male professor, it's like he has more important things to do." In the same vein, a white woman made this observation:

> We are expected to be more nurturing, more forgiving, more disclosing. Being forgiving is very important. Forgiving students for not meeting a deadline, for not being able to find a printer or typewriter, or because athletics or jobs interfere with coming to class. There is a whole lot of forgiving to do.

In response to a reprimand provoked by a student's complaint, a white woman said:

> I got a letter from the faculty personnel committee saying that "we hope that you make yourself available to students." So I had to respond. I showed them that I had set aside six hours a week for office hours and that I gave students my home phone number as well as my office number.

Another white woman observed:

> We are expected to be good teachers, and when a man does a good job teaching, he gets complimented. When a man in the department is a nurturing father, he is seen

as caring, and when a woman runs around taking care of her kids, it's seen as that she's simply doing her role, or worse, as interfering with her work.

A woman faculty member attributed her difficulties with male students to the college's "informal culture," in which males felt free to be more aggressive. She said:

> I had males, typically sitting at the back of the room, who seemed to make it a point of challenging me, getting me on an issue to the point where, for some reason, it appeared to be a way of testing me, or playing out some power struggle.

However, a colleague of hers disagreed:

> I think there are other factors that contribute to it, too, besides the informality. I think the student population at this college is less diverse in terms of economic and cultural background than you would find in other schools, for example at a community college. The students feel a camaraderie that lets them exhibit "machismo"; they have permission from each other to do that. A lot of times it comes from the male athletes, and I am not sure our P.E. faculty is doing enough to tell the male athletes that that's not acceptable.

One white woman said, "I would not go to senior faculty members with this problem because I don't know how they would react." Instead, she says, "I start questioning them [the male students], I move over, I'm standing, they're sitting, you know, I make a real blatant power move on these guys. I stand right next to them, and I start calling on them, by name, and asking them questions, and if they're not prepared, which frequently happens to be the case, that pretty much takes care of the situation."

Not all women, however, know how to use confrontation to affirm their authority, nor should they have to. This is not an isolated teaching problem experienced by some female faculty. Rather, it is a problem that arises from an institution's culture, and as such, it needs to be addressed at the institutional level. As one of these women pointed out "... this is a gender issue, and I think the men's sports coaches can say we've had enough of this, we want a different culture ... but they are not saying that. They say, 'Oh well, that's just the jocks, and jocks will be jocks.'... You know, it's a variation of 'boys will be boys.'"

Pressure to do "mom work" was also obvious from how frequently female faculty members were enlisted into doing more than a fair share of a department's domestic-type work. A white woman spoke about agreeing to teach a required freshman seminar for the third consecutive year even though the department had a policy that no one should have to teach it for more than two years. She said,

> They have to twist arms to get people to teach the required freshman seminar. The chair was in a bind, and when he said, "Could you think about doing it another year?" I said, "Sure" because it is fun to teach.

The catch was that the professor who teaches the seminar also becomes the advisor of that year's freshman cohort. After three years, this professor's advisement load had grown to approximately 60 students, about 10 times the advising loads of the tenured faculty.

Studies of women in academe (Aisenberg and Harrington 1988; Turner and Thompson 1993; Clark and Corcoran, 1986) report that female graduate students and beginning faculty are frequently not part of professional and social circles in which newcomers learn about the nonacademic aspects of being a professor, such as how to negotiate one's salary, travel funds, release time, and equipment. Similarly, studies report that when women enter the academy as tenure-track faculty, they often remain outside the social and professional networks and, therefore, they are less likely to know the unstated criteria that senior faculty use in making decisions about tenure and promotion. Faculty who lack the strategic knowledge necessary for making informed choices end up like the professor above, accepting extra "domestic" work only to realize later (and sometimes too late) that it has very little value as a criterion for promotion and tenure. The professor who volunteered to teach the freshman seminar for the third consecutive year now regretted having done so:

> I really shouldn't have been teaching the first year seminar. I thought at the time it would be a wonderful course to teach, and it will be a big plus in the service department. Well, service you can just about write

off, if you do anything in the way of service, it will be ok. I should have just protected my time, and said: "I haven't got time to do this and still do a lot of scholarly stuff. Find somebody else." But the department chair was desperate for somebody to do it, and when I said, "Sure," I wasn't thinking that it would be more negative than positive.

This professor blames herself for not having been more assertive. But what about the department chair? Shouldn't he have known better? How fair was it for the chair, given his position of authority, to make her choose between helping him out or appearing uncooperative? Clearly, the chair did not intend to overburden the professor. Nevertheless, he overburdened her because he failed to recognize the appearance of there being a choice. The professor could have said yes, or she could have said no. In a power relationship this is not a choice that can be freely exercised.

Similarly, we do not agree with the position taken by a provost at a research university who told us, "One thing that I tell them [women and minority faculty] is that saying 'no' in itself may be a good thing. If the department head says 'How would you like to teach the 100-level introductory course?' and they say, 'No,' then that sends a message to the department head that this person is really committed to working with graduate students and doing research." While this is certainly good advice on how to survive and succeed in a research-oriented culture, it places the onus for being socialized on the untenured woman. Also, it is possible that a white man's refusal to teach introductory-level undergraduate courses may be more acceptable than the same response from a woman. His refusal conforms to the stereotypical male script, i.e., teaching interferes with his research, but her refusal departs from the stereotypical female script, i.e., she is not acquiescent.

Ideally, junior faculty should be able to rely on their chairs for support, advice, and mentoring, and it is therefore unfair and thoughtless to make requests that junior faculty may feel they cannot refuse. A woman faced with this very predicament said,

> I tried very hard to not succumb to what felt like a lot of pressure to participate [in committees] from my chair. I'm trying to establish myself as a part of the community here, and if I, you know, back up and say, "Wait a minute! The rules say you can't make me do this," what kind of image am I painting of myself? And, you know, it is important to be accepted by my colleagues, and that's quite a bit of pressure.

The culture of the department structures the behaviors, choices, and self-presentation of junior faculty. A woman with more than three years on the tenure track told us that she would advise a newly appointed assistant professor "to play the academic strategy game: Take time away from teaching and don't be available for committee work." Ironically, she admitted that she had not followed her own advice: "I haven't done that because I get a lot of my human needs met by teaching and servicing." The point is that in a departmental culture structured according to the preferences of the male faculty, women may view service activities that take them away from research and writing as opportunities to establish relationships outside their departments. Department chairs who may be in favor of more diverse hiring do not realize that faculty members who are one-of-a-kind often have difficulty in dealing with alienating departmental cultures. Spending time with students, devoting themselves to teaching, and volunteering for service rather than representing what women are naturally predisposed to do well may be nothing more than opportunities for connecting with others and forming relationships. Department chairs who understand this can take measures to help female faculty members to establish social and professional networks.

Women and Collegiality

Being included as a colleague was a persistent concern for many women. One white woman said,

> I have zero collegiality in my department. They don't know what I do. I feel alienated, not on an equal footing with the men. Sometimes I have lunch in the faculty club and see the guys from my department eating together. In the three years I have been here, no one has asked me to have lunch.

In contrast, another white woman in the same department (different sub-specialty) said the opposite about her colleagues:

> It is a very congenial group. Most of us have lunch together almost every day. We know where to look for each other. Even though I am the only woman, I always feel I can go over.

Needless to say, there could be any number of reasons for one woman feeling left out of the collegial circle and another feeling included. Perhaps one is more extroverted than the other; perhaps the first woman's colleagues have not realized that the socialization of newcomers is their responsibility. We noted in the previous chapter that one woman thought men did not "invite" others for lunch, so she behaved just like the men, whereas another woman commented that she had never been asked to lunch. The woman who saw herself as being part of the inside group felt that her colleagues were familiar with her work. In contrast, the woman who felt excluded from the men's circle declared, "They don't know what I do."

Collegiality is far more likely to occur when there is a shared orientation to the discipline. For example, the woman who felt included by her male colleagues mentioned that a Marxist or a feminist would probably disrupt the group's harmony. Additionally, the unspoken rules of collegiality meant that she had to put up with "backlash" humor. She said,

> There is a professor who jokes about white men not being able to get jobs . . . he says it jokingly, but you can tell he has serious feelings about it. . . . I think he accepts me now, but he was one of the senior faculty who did not want me here. . . . No one says anything to him . . . they shrug it off; they say, "That is just the way he is."

In contrast, a white woman with a distinctively different approach to her discipline and teaching found herself

> getting slammed [by colleagues] for being ideological and political in the classroom. They said my teaching could be supplemented by more authority-centered criticism, meaning that instead of allowing student voices, I should lecture. It rankled me. I was angry. I thought they would respect my work.

Senior women, particularly if they were the only female full professor, were not necessarily any more responsive to junior females than were the senior men. For example, a white junior woman said of a senior colleague, "I have asked her to have lunch, but she is very overworked and has not responded."

Women in the Sciences and Engineering

Women in mathematics and the sciences who were often the "only woman" spoke about their loneliness. Asked what it is like to be a female professor, a white woman said, "In the math department, it's a very lonely experience. . . . Math is a very male subject . . . the expectation of how a mathematician thinks, or how a mathematician operates are very masculine expectations. A lot of mathematicians tend to be very aggressive people, very argumentative . . . and that is not my personality at all. . . . part of it is just me, but I think in general female mathematicians tend to be not nearly so argumentative as the males . . . so I find it very difficult to operate in that sort of environment, it is very hard to handle."

Women in male-identified fields often sensed a lack of respect or interest from their colleagues and felt marginalized. This mathematician said,

> It makes me question how valuable I am, because I always have this sense that I should be different from how I am. And I find it very oppressive, I have a feeling that I am always kind of struggling to justify myself. I always feel that I somehow am not . . . I have to work to gain their respect . . . and, I don't want to have to think that much about it, I want to just be able to go about my activities, to do my teaching, to learn, you know, new kinds of scholarly stuff, and instead I have to worry about all those other issues, and it takes a lot of energy.

A colleague in the sciences, also a white woman, agreed: "I also find it very lonely, even though two out of the five faculty in my department are women." She described the difference between the sciences and liberal arts as follows: "I have a sense that there is a much tighter and more supportive group of women who are in the humanities and social sciences departments. They're all in the same building, it's easier to run into people, it's easier to make connections with people."

Both the mathematician and the scientist were assigned service responsibilities that fit the category of "mom work." As one put it, she was asked to do "things that are kind of peripheral to both teaching and scholarship." One was the editor of the department's newsletter and the other was the advisor for all pre-med students, which entailed "a lot of administrative work related to providing support for students applying to medical schools." She said, "I do a lot of public relations, I meet with the parents, and I go and talk to groups of new students.

Structured Absences: The Sexless Professorial Body

"I am a little self-conscious about being the professor with a child," said a white woman. An Asian-American recalled, "I felt uncomfortable mentioning that I had a child or that I had a relatively newborn baby at the time of the interview. I had gone on another job interview at the time I was eight months pregnant, and when the faculty saw I was expecting, they looked shocked... them seeing me as a pregnant woman was an immediate negative reaction. Once they found out I was pregnant, their attitudes toward me changed." A third woman admitted, "I felt that if my child was sick, I'd be too embarrassed to miss class... no one else has a family, so I felt some tension about having kids."

At another institution, individuals commented that when a man had a child, "it was a moment for celebration, but when a woman had a child she heard comments such as, 'I hope this doesn't jeopardize tenure.'" One woman who had a child when she arrived in her department recalled that everyone was understanding; "but when I had my second child, it was clear that I'd made a mistake. 'Don't you know about birth control?' someone actually said." Another person in the institution remarked that when this individual brought her infant to the college, the male faculty disapproved of how the department had become a "daycare center." In contrast, at a small college, a woman said, "I have two young kids who manage to get sick at the beginning of every semester I've taught, and I don't get any grief when I teach my class and run right home... I assume that it's not specific to me, it's just a flexible kind of place that acknowledges that people have lives outside of the institution." And she added, "It made *all* of me feel welcome, not just the part that the institution was going to get a benefit out of."

Before affirmative action and women's entry into the academy the professorial image was that of the "academic man"; when we spoke about a college professor, the image conjured up was masculine and we always used "he" when speaking about an unspecified professor. Nowadays we talk about faculty as if they are an undifferentiated class of people, disembodied and sexless. This generalized image of faculty makes some women professors with children feel aberrant. "Structuring absence" is the term used by a male professor to describe the academy's "muteness about personal lives." He said,

> It is symptomatic of a structuring absence... just as other things are there because they're structured, this one is deliberately unspoken. Things are formed around that, people don't talk about the difficulties of their home life because they're not supposed to. It's not gallant, it's not jock enough, it's not steroid enough.

The "structured absence" of the personal sphere creates disadvantages for women with children that most institutions are not addressing adequately. Institutionally sponsored day care services are rare. Even though some institutions made provisions for stopping the tenure clock for women who gave birth, none had paid maternity leaves that were longer than a few weeks. The lack of paid maternity leave policies left it to the discretion of department chairs and their willingness to circumvent regulations in order to grant semester-long leaves to female faculty members with a newborn child. One professor said "the chair was supportive once he found out a precedent had been set, but he did not initiate anything." A Latina in a commuting marriage said, "In this university, everything seems to happen at the department level, and your chair can make your life miserable." Fortunately, her department chair was unusually understanding and sensitive about the personal lives of faculty. He told us, "Smart people tend to marry smart people," and went on to say:

> I have one woman whose husband is a foreign service officer stationed in another country, so they commute. I have another whose husband is involved in a job that takes him all over the world without much notice. These are strains that did not exist to the same degree 10 or 15 years ago, and we have not figured out how to accommodate them in the process of promotion and tenure.

He also observed,

> We have a pregnancy leave policy, and if a faculty member is adversely affected by a pregnancy they could stop the tenure clock for one year. It made great sense. Guess who took advantage of it the most—male faculty members even though their productivity may not be as adversely affected as that of their wives.

Sometimes long-term leaves could be managed only if other members of the faculty were willing to cover for the absent professor. This arrangement was neither fair to the colleagues who assumed the extra work nor to the women who became dependent on and indebted to the kindness of others. For example, the male professor who said, "My colleague, she managed to get pregnant so she would deliver in the middle of the school year," was obviously annoyed. Clearly, it is unrealistic to expect women faculty to schedule the time of conception so that childbirth coincides with the slow season in academia. It is also unrealistic for institutions not to have provisions that protect professors who also happen to be women and mothers.

None of the women were bitter or angry about the impact this "structuring absence" had on them. Quite the contrary, they were grateful for the kindness and understanding of their department chairs. One woman said, "He went to bat for me and got me a medical leave so I got paid anyway." Another woman said, "The chair of my department has been real supportive of me. When I had my baby, he *allowed* me to not teach for a semester. I had six months off, and I was able to stay home with my son. It is not a university policy, it is just something he did to try and help me."

A minority woman who was herself directly affected was moved to work on the institutionalization of paid maternity leaves. She said, "Right now it is very individualized, and some departments have been very hostile to pregnant women who approach the chair and ask not even for a leave but just a lighter teaching load."

While all the institutions in the study have made progress in terms of hiring women faculty and bridging the gender gap, the culture of the institutions and departments in some critical ways still operates according to norms from a time when the prototypical professor was a white male whose wife stayed home and took care of their children. Indeed, the lack of paid maternity leave policies accentuates women's difference from the norm. Lack of paid maternity leave policies disempowers women because it forces them to be dependent on and be indebted to the goodwill of individuals whose support they need to succeed as academics.

Characteristics of Women-Affirming Cultures

Up to this point, we have concentrated on the cultural barriers women must overcome to establish themselves and be accepted in male-identified academic milieus. The academic cultures we have described seem more indifferent to women than openly contemptuous of them, more likely to exhibit institutionalized rather than overt sexism. Feminist scholars have called attention to the "invisible paradigms" (Shuster & VanDyne, 1984), the "communal unconscious" (Aiken et al., 1987) that structures departmental and institutional cultures that pose barriers to the integration of women faculty. As we have already mentioned, we heard few reports of egregious sex discrimination or sex harassment. Women expressed discomfort, annoyance, and frustration with male dominance that permeated their departments and institutions, but none described her situation as so horribly oppressive as to be intolerable. None of the women said they planned to give up their plans for an academic career; none expressed regrets about having chosen the professoriate as their vocation.

By the same token, few of the women described their departments or institutions as being totally affirming for women, and a relatively small number described department or institutional characteristics that made them good for women. Among the factors that women identified as contributing to a positive climate were chairs who were sensitive to the personal lives of women, an equity-oriented institutional ethos, and a critical mass of women.

One said:

> In this department being a woman is great. We have a lot of them. Of the five junior faculty, three are women. My colleagues treat me as though they think I am smart and that I am worthy of consideration when we are debating.

Agreeing with her colleague, the second woman said:

> They have done a very nice job of recruiting women, so I would say, for the most part, there aren't a lot of gender issues. I have not ever been treated in a condescending manner. I have no sense that women are treated as second-class citizens and that our work is not taken seriously.... We are not shoved off to marginal or minor committees.... The year I came in, they hired five faculty; three of those were filled with women.

These two women have been appointed to a newly created multidisciplinary department in which junior faculty outnumber senior faculty. The youthfulness of the department along with its multidisciplinary mission create an ethos that values diversity.

However, it also helped that the ideological orientation of these two women was congruent with mainstream theories and research methods. For example, one professor, although interested in issues of social inequality, was nevertheless a mainstream quantitative researcher. She said,

> If I would have been more radical, more of an activist, I suspect that it would have been more difficult. This department is mainstream enough that I would have really had to be on my toes to rise above the kinds of critiques that everybody was going to come ready to launch at me.

The other woman observed, "If I was a deconstructionist feminist, it wouldn't play very well at all, but I can't imagine them hiring anyone quite that radical. I would say that if it's relatively mainstream feminist types of issues, it would not be problematic."

Finally, the department chair was pivotal in creating the climate that made these women feel recognized and respected as professionals. The Latina said,

> He always encourages me to show him my work. He is very complimentary... when my teaching evaluations come back and they are positive, he comes in and he tells me. He is not guarded in his praise. He is very complimentary of my performance.

She also praised him for his sensitivity to unique personal circumstances. She said,

> My husband and I commute, and the chair has been very understanding when I have had to leave on a Friday to go spend a long weekend with my husband. He treats me like a professional... as long as I do my work he lets the reins loose.... He lets me arrange things however it accommodates me best.

At a different institution, a woman from the Middle East described her chair as thoughtful, sensitive, and "wonderful." She said, "We talk all the time. Not only was my office completely set up when I arrived, but he knew that my husband needs to finish his dissertation, so he gave me an extra key to my office and put another big table in there for him so he could work there, too."

Along with leadership, institutional mission can be a powerful influence on the culture of an institution. A woman who left a large research-oriented university for a small teaching-oriented college with a strong commitment to a multicultural mission said that the difference between the two places was "startling" and that she "couldn't have looked for an institution that would have been the complete opposite [of research university] any more closely than this college." She said,

> When I arrived, the woman who runs the computer center offered me anything that I needed. The dean has always said, "Please stop by and talk to me," as has the president of the college, and it's genuine. You can tell they would welcome you to stop

and chat with them, and tell them how things are going.

She also commented on being

> quite surprised at the number of females that are in administrative positions with power, and not just figurehead sorts of positions. I haven't noticed any blatant sexism.... I feel I have been respected by everybody that I have come in contact with.

She concluded by saying, "I feel like I'm waiting for the other shoe to drop. You know, that this can't be reality."

A critical mass of women also contributes to the creation of affirming climates for women. A white woman who had done her graduate work at a prestigious northeast university and started her career in a small college said, "Having been in a university environment that was incredibly hostile to women, coming here seems like heaven. There are a lot of women senior faculty. In the university, there was only one in the department, and she was very token." A white professor of economics in a department where three of the six faculty members are women said, "It is very unusual; in other colleges I would have been the token female. Here they weren't looking for a woman because they didn't need to fill any gender gap." Being among other women meant not having the feeling "constantly that you have to join a men's club." A European Latina said, "It makes a difference. In the university I came from, women were marginalized ... here whenever we want to bring a speaker, we bring a feminist.... All the senior women in the department are in the key university committees where important decisions get made."

Even though department chairs, deans, and vice presidents spoke about affirmative action and efforts to recruit women, almost none of these academic leaders stated that the dismantling of institutionalized forms of sexism was one of their priorities. The reason was not that they did not care, rather the state of "communal unconscious" that develops from the internalization of the "invisible paradigms" that structure the culture of the academy and the disciplines prevents senior faculty and administrators from seeing how their very practices might create and reproduce institutionalized forms of sexism. In other words, it is possible for academic leaders to target recruitment efforts toward women and minorities without giving much thought to transforming male-identified departmental cultures. The meritocratic discourse of promotion and tenure is effective camouflage for the gendered aspects of seemingly neutral practices. As a consequence, individuals in positions of authority, power, and influence construe affirmative action as a matter of "adding women" to a presumably gender-neutral structure. Just as feminist scholars have pointed out that making the curriculum more inclusive is not simply a matter of adding women to syllabi but rather demands the "deconstruction and reconstruction" of the disciplines in order to be truly transformative, the same can be said about the integration of women into the professoriate.

The one exception to the "add women" approach was a dean and feminist scholar who was willing to discard recruitment, hiring, and evaluation practices that undermine the achievement of integrating the academy. She said,

> When I walked in the door there were three lawsuits in process: two by minority women and one by an Anglo [sic] woman in different departments charging the institution with discrimination not only in the promotion and tenure process, but in the ways that they had been treated during their time here. I also found that we had a very poor record of hiring and retaining women in most of the departments and that the most serious problems were at the senior levels where there were simply no women in most departments.

Thus she changed position announcements to appeal more directly to women and minority applicants:

> We changed our advertisements ... the way in which we physically presented ourselves in advertisements, we talked about what it is to be a multicultural community. I then had all the faculty who were going to be on interview committees meet with the affirmative action officer. We put our advertisements in places that they have never been before, like the *Women's Review of Books*.

Furthermore, faculty search procedures were structured to increase the likelihood of women and minority candidates:

> The first year, I said to the committees that all the searches would be affirmative action. I told them "You are going to have two piles. One pile is white males and the other pile is minorities and women. Only if you cannot find a viable candidate in the pile of minorities and women can you go to the white male pile."

Additionally, women and minorities were well represented in faculty research committees but were also protected from being overburdened:

> I said, "From hence forward all search committees will be gender balanced with an equal number of males and females and one-third minority representation." Needless to say, we did not have enough minorities or women in each department to make up committees, so we borrowed them from department to department. But that mean some women and some minority faculty were being tediously borrowed. So, I said to department heads, "Any faculty member who is being borrowed has got to have course relief." I gave this faculty one course relief and used them to develop the search committees.

Search committees were less likely to dismiss candidates whose work did not conform to normative concepts of scientific research because "they were so differently composed that the applications were read differently."

These gender and race motivated interventions produced tangible results:

> We got a very different cohort than we have gotten before. During my first years our hires were 70% women and about 30% were minorities. It doesn't mean I did not hire any white males. I did hire some white males.

To increase women's chances for success and retention, this dean invented a mentoring system that avoids placing the senior professors (most of whom are men) in the role of superior and the junior female faculty member in the role of subordinate. Instead of creating mentoring pairs, each newcomer was assigned three mentors: one male and one female, neither of whom are from the same department as the junior faculty member, and the third person is another junior faculty member. Newcomers are paired up with faculty mentors on the basis of non-academic interests, mainly to encourage professors to establish some common ground through shared interests (e.g., hobbies, sports, children, etc.). The hoped-for outcome is that personal knowledge will break down ideological and generational barriers between senior and junior faculty. A woman who took part in this program said:

> I was assigned three mentors. Two are full professors and the other one is an assistant professor. The dean mandates that one of the mentors be an assistant professor so that mentoring is not based on power relations. One of the mentors is a really wonderful super professor from another department who is interested in post-colonial stuff and that was good for me. The dean provides free lunches for the mentoring group twice a semester.

Women faculty praised the dean for her initiatives against what they perceived as gender-based inequities. One woman said, "She has done some extremely important work here as a feminist dean.... Her presence has made a big difference in the achievement of things like unofficial leaves for women who give birth and that we are now able to request a stoppage of the tenure clock when we give birth. This did not exist before her." However, she encountered considerable resistance from long-time faculty. One professor said, "She is a very strong feminist, and the faculty don't agree with her tactics."

Women-Centered Structures

Feminist administrators with the power to challenge institutionalized forms of sexism are rare in most colleges and universities. Women-centered academic structures, however, which are now more common, were mentioned repeatedly as places that alleviate the loneliness and alienation felt by female faculty members. Among the twelve institutions included in the study, all but one had a women's studies program.

For some women faculty, these academic programs were far more important in providing collegial support than their home departments. A feminist scholar in a very conservative, male-dominated department said, "If I get weirded out about what's going on here, I can call one of the faculty in women's studies and say I just need to talk about what's going on." Another said, "Once I got here, I found out that there is a really strong women's studies program with a wonderful director, and I found a lot of colleagues with whom I could exchange ideas." She added, "That makes a big difference in making the university seem attractive and deciding to remain here."

In a small liberal arts college, a female faculty member in a science department told us that she had just come from "the Feminist Seminar":

> We are a group of faculty who gets together once a month to discuss feminist scholarship.... I wouldn't make myself read Tony Morrison's new edited volume [*Race-ing Justice, En-gendering Power*] if there wasn't some motivation for doing so.

In addition to providing a place for intellectual development, the seminar provided her with personal support:

> It's a way for me to connect with women senior faculty who are in some sense role models for me, as a new faculty person here.

A man who was doing research on "the celebration of the gladiator as the ultimate jock" said, "My male colleagues are cordial but they never ask about my work" and pointed out that he has found more support in a feminist faculty seminar.

We asked faculty members if their participation in a feminist seminar counted as scholarship or professional service. One professor said, "This is an extra.... We are doing important work ... this year we are focusing on readings related to racism, and it is critical that faculty be involved in such discussions, but that's not acknowledged as a legitimate contribution to the academic atmosphere."

Women's academic groups are also responsible for much of the formal and informal mentoring that women receive. A woman mentioned, "A group of us started the women's faculty group when we were new here. We've had several programs on tenure and how to prepare for it, and on career plans and how to direct your writing and to organize your life so you can teach and write and be a person at the same time." After having attended a roundtable discussion organized by the women's faculty group, an assistant professor told us, "Women who have served on the tenure committee came to speak to us, and it was there that I learned that an edited volume doesn't count the same way as submitting my work to a specialized journal would. People would hear me give talks at conferences and would say, 'I'd like you to submit that to the book I'm editing.' If I had known earlier, I probably would have turned down some requests and done different kinds of writing on my own."

In presenting these stories, it is not our intent to concoct a composite profile of "the woman's experience in the tenure track." Rather, we have used them to illustrate the multiplicity of women's experiences and also to show that these experiences are shaped by the intersections of gender, race, ethnicity, and culture (institutional and departmental).

The stories provide understandings of how some female faculty members, most of whom are white, enact their academic roles and how they respond to the cultures of their departments and institutions. The stories have a familiar ring in that they reiterate circumstances that have contributed to women leaving the academy before the tenure decision (Bronstein, Rothblum and Solomon 1993), publishing less than men (Astin and Davis 1985), taking longer than men to achieve tenure and promotions to associate or full professor (Bentley and Blackburn 1992), lacking characteristics associated with exemplary newcomers (Boice 1992), and to gravitate toward "intentional intellectual communities" (Gumport 1990) in search of academic and social support. In looking at these stories through the lenses of critical and feminist postmodernism, we extend previous analyses of the status of women academics from the individual level (e.g., behaviors, personality, attitudes) to the institutional level, thereby revealing cultural norms that pose a barrier to the socialization of women (Bronstein, Rothblum and Solomon 1993; Fox 1985). This suggests that the particular experience of a female junior professor is shaped not only by her individual behaviors but also, and perhaps more significantly, by gender and power relations that typify the culture of a department or institution. What this means is that from a critical and feminist postmodernist standpoint, we interpret "smile work" and "mom work" as behavioral patterns produced by male-identified academic cultures. That is to say, the problem is not that women suffer from work overload only because they have not figured out how to protect their time or because they do not know how to say "no" to the requests of others. Neither is the problem one of women doing more service work or more teaching because such work fulfills "women's needs" to feel useful, needed, and competent. Nor can we attribute it to being symptomatic of the "feminine version of the academic career pattern" (Dwyer, Flynn and Inman 1993). Rather, a critical and feminist postmodernist standpoint frames "mom work" as a cultural norm in settings that are predominantly male yet are not conscious of how this maleness structures the lives of female and male faculty members according to traditional gender roles. Additionaly, the gender and power relations in academic settings can be so alienating that doing service might make women feel less invisible, less isolated, less lonely. A woman's sense of invisibility or isolation or loneliness is not simply a matter of developing a more outgoing personality. Institutional cultures also need to change seemingly innocent and natural practices that have the effect of placing women at a disadvantage and silencing them.

The experiences of professors in more women-affirming academic departments suggest that academic leaders can create organizational cultures that are responsive to gender differences. For example, department chairs who recognized the interdependence between the private and public lives of faculty and made accommodations for women's responsibilities in the private sphere created environments in which gender difference did not translate into an impairment or negative condition. The positive as well as the negative experiences reported by these women suggest that there are a variety of ways in which academic leaders can transform the cultures of their departments, schools, or institutions. For example, women spoke highly of department chairs who provided them with feedback about their work, were cognizant of their accomplishments, and acknowledged them. Seemingly innocuous comments from a department chair, such as "Your course evaluations came in and they are just great," or "Your presentation in the graduate seminar has sparked a lot of interest," or "I plan to use your article on . . . as one of the required readings for my class" are symbolic gestures of recognition, respect, and acceptance.

Note

1. None of the women we interviewed identified themselves as lesbian; thus we are not able to discuss the particular experience of lesbian junior faculty. However, lesbian existences in the tenure track have been provided in other works (e.g., Bensimon 1992; Bronstein, Rothblum and Solomon 1993).

CHAPTER 22

FEMINISTS AT WORK: COLLABORATIVE RELATIONSHIPS AMONG WOMEN FACULTY

CYNTHIA SULLIVAN DICKENS AND MARY ANN D. SAGARIA

Since the first women's studies program was formally approved at San Diego State University in 1970 (Musil, 1992), women's studies programs have rapidly developed and become a part of higher education institutions, particularly at research universities. Women associated with these programs are developing successful careers and conducting significant research. Building meaningful careers in research institutions often means that faculty members must successfully manage conflicts that develop between their commitments and the prevailing norms of their discipline or professional field. Because of women's minority status, however, the professional relationships and friendships that a woman faculty member forms with other academic women on her campus or elsewhere may be of particular importance in helping her to construct an identity as a legitimate scholar, develop effective research strategies, and overcome feelings of isolation (Jensen, 1982; Kaufman, 1978). Moreover, these relationships may provide the instrumental and emotional support that many women either need or desire to pursue their particular scholarly interests in competitive research institutions.

To work in collaboration with other scholars with whom they share a gender consciousness as well as research interests arguably offers a variety of professional and personal advantages to women who share feminist values and political commitments. Collaborative scholarship, however, is not universally valued in the academy. As a feminist sociologist and frequent collaborator, Mary Frank Fox (1985) noted:

> Freedom and independence are certainly strong precepts in science and scholarship . . . and scholarship tends to attract the "solitary mind." Yet the solitary dispositions and independent norms of science and scholarship are contravened by the communalism of the work. . . . The communalism and exchange of research engenders cooperation and interdependence. . . . We need to know much more about the way in which collegiality operates. (p. 271)

Nor is collaboration well explicated in the scholarly literature. Studies of faculty collaboration, particularly studies employing qualitative methods, are rare (Austin & Baldwin, 1991) and little is known about the social relationships that develop among women faculty who work collaboratively in the competitive and individualistic culture of American research universities. The purpose of this study was to describe collaborative relationships among women faculty members as they reflect the interrelationships among feminism, collaboration, and scholarship—specifically, the relationships that develop among feminist women who collaborate in their scholarship.

Women, The Academy, and Collaboration

Academic Women's Status

Although women have held faculty positions in American colleges and universities since the nineteenth century, they were rarely the focus of social science research until the mid-sixties when Jessie Bernard (1964) presented an argument for bringing more women into higher education to address the shortage of qualified instructional faculty. By the late 1960s, however, faculty women in the social sciences were focusing attention on doctoral-trained women and were comparing their academic careers with those of men along such dimensions as field, marital status, children, productivity, income, and other professional and personal characteristics. Simon, Clark, and Galway (1967, p. 236) found that the differences between men and women's academic careers were both relatively small and decreasing but that women faculty felt they had failed to gain full acceptance in the academic "club."

Other studies of faculty women documented the under-representation of women in specific institutions and fields and began to explore career pattern variations (Bayer & Astin, 1975; Graham, 1970, 1978; Lewin & Duchan, 1971; Tidball, 1976). Particularly after the passage of affirmative action legislation, scholars of higher education carefully scrutinized the careers, status, and productivity of women faculty members and tried to explain the continuing evidence of discrimination against women despite their gains on a number of traditional productivity measures (Astin, 1978). Kaufman (1978), looking at structural, rather than psychological barriers, explored collegial-friend relationships and concluded that women's exclusion from male networks isolated them from important informal contacts, leaving them at a professional disadvantage.

Subsequent research on academic women acknowledged women's disadvantage (Clark & Corcoran, 1986; Fox, 1984) and frequent isolation in an institutional culture long dominated by men. Menges and Exum (1983) argued that women and minority faculty progressed more slowly through the academic ranks because of the distinctive problems that they faced in negotiating peer review processes that favor the scholarship and career patterns associated with white males. Langland and Gove (1981) observed that women's studies programs had begun to alter faculty scholarship but had yet to substantially influence the traditional curriculum; they noted that women's studies remained the voice of the outsider in academe.

Without minimizing the obstacles that academic women continued to face in their struggles to succeed as "women-of-knowledge;" Simeone (1987) contended that the situation for women had improved, citing as evidence

> the growing prominence of women's studies and feminist scholarship, the expansion of women's scholarly and professional networks for communication and support, the increasing numbers of women faculty at research institutions, the implementation of anti-discrimination laws, and the increasing publication rates for women. (p. 75)

Although many scholars agreed with Simeone's argument, research in the 1990s has continued to provide insights into women's isolation and exclusion from informal male networks and positions of power (Moore & Sagaria, 1991), while others have theorized that connected and caring relationships characterize women in general (Ashton-Jones & Thomas, 1991; Belenky, Clinchy, Goldberger, & Tarule, 1986; Noddings, 1986). For example, after Moore and Sagaria (1991) documented the under-representation of academic women in positions of power in leading research universities and editorial boards, they then argued the need to rethink graduate education and junior faculty experiences, reshaping them from periods of individualistic challenge and competition to times of mutual investment in talent development, generativity, and collaboration. They urged an examination of feminist scholars' working relationships to garner possible evidence about whether the practices of feminist scholars reflect feminist theory and advocacy.

Women's Friendships, Values, and Culture

The values and relationships that have long been associated with women in Western culture—nurturance, reciprocity, intimacy, mutuality, and care and concern for others—appear repeatedly both implicitly and explicitly in the literature on collaboration. Appley and Winder (1977) developed a theory of collaboration that evoked themes of caring, commitment, and consciousness (or reflexivity) that tend to be characteristics of feminist inquiry. They conceptualized collaboration as a relational value system that provides an alternative to competition and hierarchy and identified three characteristics:

> (1) individuals in a group share mutual aspirations and a common conceptual framework; (2) the interactions among individuals are characterized by "justice as fairness"; (3) these aspirations and conceptualizations are characterized by each individual's consciousness of her or his motives toward the other; by caring or concern for the other; and by commitment to work with the other over time provided that this commitment is a matter of choice. (p. 281)

Historical inquiry into the lives of 18th- and 19th-century American women—particularly white, middle-class women—supports this contemporary construct of women's collaboration, documenting and providing further insights into the ties between feminism and collaboration. Drawing upon diaries, letters, and personal records, feminist historians have demonstrated the importance and significance of women's associations with other women. Writing before Appley and Winder, Smith-Rosenberg (1975) described American society as characterized by a rigid gender-role differentiation that led to the development of supportive networks of women within a "women's sphere." These networks in the family and in the larger society grew out of women's mutual affection and shared experience and provided an important sense of continuity within a rapidly changing society. Cott (1977) asserted that women's friendships were particularly attractive because they represented peer relationships: "Female friendships assumed a new value in women's lives in this era because relations between equals—'peer relationships'—were superseding hierarchical relationships as the desired norms of human interaction" (p. 187). She further suggested that women's reliance on each other "embodied a new kind of group consciousness, one which could develop into a political consciousness" (p. 194).

Freedman (1979) identified linkages between the 19th-century culture of white, native-born, middle-class women and feminist politics. She argued that the rise of women's societies and organizations, or "female institution building," although not necessarily representing a political strategy, nevertheless provided those women with resources integral to the emergence of feminist politics. Freedman further suggested that the integrationist strategies which replaced separatism after the success of the suffrage movement may explain the erosion of the women's culture and the decline of feminism after 1920. Applying her theses to women in universities, she observed:

> The success of the first generation of female academics did not survive past the 1920s, not only because of men's resistance, but, as Rosalind Rosenberg [1979] has explained, "Success isolated women from their culture and placed them in an alien and often hostile community." Many academics who cut off their ties to other women lost the old feminine supports but had no other supports to replace them. (p. 522)

Freedman concluded from the history of women's institution building—with contemporary women's studies departments serving as just one notable example—that women must draw on the cultural resources that emanate from a separate and distinct women's culture while continuing to examine that culture critically.

Rosenberg's (1979) research into the feminization of the curriculum at the University of Chicago at the turn of the century revealed the extent of women's gains and losses as a result of their integration into male-dominated universities. "The triumph of higher education in America had a major impact on feminism," she asserted.

> The ideological change fostered by work in the social sciences freed women from the restrictions imposed by old prejudices about female inferiority, but at the same time undermined the sense of support women had enjoyed as members of a distinctive and self-consciously separate community. Having won a place within higher education, women suffered the strain of no

longer feeling secure in the old, separate world of womanhood and maternal nurture, without being fully accepted or feeling comfortable within the new world of professionalism and science. (p. 338)

Irish scholar O'Connor's (1992) critical review of the research into women's friendships extended the work of Cott, Freedman, Rosenberg, and Smith-Rosenberg. O'Connor concluded that women's friendships have been overlooked and frequently trivialized as an area of research. Further, she argued that friendship is a culturally constructed form of relationship. It varies according to historical and cultural influences, affects the individual's identity and well-being, and plays an important part in reflecting and reinforcing class position and marital status.

Collaboration and Coauthorship in Academic Scholarship

Research on collaboration has focused primarily on coauthorship. Male scientists who dominated "big science" provided scholarly interest in coauthorship and teamwork that appeared in the social science literature in the decades after World War II (Eaton, 1951; Hagstrom, 1964, 1965). By the 1970s and 1980s, however, such studies included women as subjects; their authorship and public acknowledgment of their contributions increased. Chubin (1974) and Mackie (1976) found that women as well as men published a significant amount of collaborative research, although women who published collaboratively tended to receive first-author recognition less often than men. Wilkie and Allen (1975) found that two women were much more likely to collaborate equally than two men or a man and a woman. Fox and Faver's (1984) research on the advantages and disadvantages of collaboration among social scientists indicated that, while collaborative scholars benefit from opportunities to join resources and alleviate academic isolation, possible disadvantages include time required for negotiation, financial costs, and personal investments necessary to maintain the relationship.

When studying styles of collaborative scholarship among male academic chemists, Bayer and Smart (1991) found that, over time, the proportion of single-authored and dual-authored papers declined and the proportion of published team research papers increased. By mid-career, more than half of a typical scholar's published papers were multi-authored. Analyzing authorship patterns in sociology journals, Ward and Grant (1991) found coauthorship more common than single authorship for both women and men, although women coauthored more frequently than men. They also found that both women and men scholars writing on gender coauthored more frequently than scholars writing on other topics; rates of coauthorship were lower in national mainstream journals than in other sources; and women were less likely to occupy the dominant-author position in mainstream journal articles than elsewhere.

In a 1992 interpretive study, Baldwin and Austin analyzed the language that participants used to describe long-term collaborative partnerships. Finding that faculty members in the field of higher education used a variety of metaphors to describe their collaborative relationships, they concluded that "[a] good collaborative relationship has many of the qualities of a good marriage, a successful creative alliance, or a winning sports team" (p. 8). Taken together, the scholarship on faculty women's status, feminist perspectives on women's friendships and culture, and academic collaboration suggests that collaboration among feminist scholars may have an impact on both their work and their identity.

Methodology

To examine the social relationships that develop among feminist women who collaborate in their research, we chose an interpretive research design with interviews. The approach was well suited to retrieve the meanings that individual and groups of scholars construct from their experiences as collaborators while maintaining a feminist grounding in the lived experiences of women (Fonow & Cook, 1991). Thus, this study differs from the majority of social science studies of collaboration that typically have used bibliometric or survey methods and have often focused on citation counts and name-ordering patterns. (For examples, see

Hagstom, 1965; Smart & Bayer, 1986; Ward & Grant, 1991.)

We developed, piloted, and refined an interview protocol containing 35 open-ended questions. It was organized into four categories covering (a) the culture of the research university, (b) collaboration, (c) the evolving scholar, and (d) feminism. This study is derived from parts of three categories—collaboration, the evolving scholar, and feminism. The other category, the research community's culture, lay beyond the focus of paper. The pilot study consisted of individual and group interviews at a public research university in the Midwest with faculty women who identified themselves as feminists.

In the actual data collection and analysis phase, we audio tape-recorded, transcribed, and analyzed the interviews, which varied in length from 45 minutes to over two hours. We also collected curricula vitae and other written documents, including published journal articles, conference papers, and manuscripts in progress, later using them for limited triangulation purposes.

We coded and thematically analyzed data based on Strauss and Corbin's (1990) open coding process, developing categories based on both inductive and deductive processes. For example, in considering the occurrence of collaborative research, we considered antecedent conditions, specific properties, context, intervening conditions, and strategies that scholars used to manage and respond to collaboration in relationship to the context and consequences. By organizing the coded bits of data around each specific collaborative event, we were able to see new themes. The identification of these themes led to the refinement of the research questions which then became the basis for a higher level coding scheme. Rereading and recoding each transcript with the major themes clearly in mind resulted in making visible linkages that had been too embedded in the narratives to be noticed earlier. The quotations we have chosen to include in this article are those that best illustrate a particular finding.

We used a purposeful, criterion-based sampling technique (Patton, 1990) to identify participants for the study, selecting women who met the following criteria: (a) They were employed as a full-time tenured or tenure-accruing faculty member at one of two Carnegie classification Research I universities; (b) They held a core, joint, or adjunct appointment[1] in a department of women's studies; and (c) they had collaborated with another woman on a research project, a scholarly paper or article, or a creative arts project.

Early in the spring of 1993, we contacted women's studies departments at two Research I universities. From a list of faculty names, we then contacted women by mail. Twenty-nine women returned response letters indicating that they had collaborated with another woman and were interested in participating in the study. The 26 women in the final sample represented 18 different academic departments and fields in the social sciences, humanities, and professional schools. Thus, they are similar in disciplinary or professional field to women's studies faculty in most research institutions (Rosser, 1986). Six participants were assistant professors, eleven were associate professors and nine were full professors. There are fewer assistant professors represented in the sample than in the national distribution of women faculty in research universities. This finding might seem surprising, but faculty participants repeatedly reported that they were advised not to collaborate as junior faculty. An additional explanation is that women may delay their affiliation with women's studies programs until after receiving tenure if the women's studies unit is not their tenure-accruing unit.

Three of the participants were women of color and 23 were white, although two of the white participants identified themselves as having other ethnic backgrounds or national heritages. Fourteen of the women described themselves as currently having life partners; 12 were married, eight said they were currently single or divorced, and three identified themselves as lesbians. The women had a total of 14 children and/or stepchildren. Participants ranged in age from their mid-thirties to their late sixties and had earned their highest degree between 1955 and 1990.

Findings

Collaborative scholarship was an ongoing process for most feminist faculty. At the time of the study, the majority of feminist scholars both had been and were collaborating in their scholarship with a variety of individuals, including friends and colleagues, students and advisors, and partners or spouses. Some majority women had designed studies and coauthored publications only with other white American women; others had worked closely with women of color and women of other nationalities and ethnicities and with men as well as women. Similarly, some women of color had collaborated only with other women of color while others had collaborated with minority and majority men and women. Some participants had worked almost entirely in collaborative research relationships; others had formally collaborated only once on a publication or paper. Also, the rank of the participant appeared to have little bearing on when an individual collaborated or on the nature of the collaboration. The one exception was that fewer assistant professors than associate and full professors collaborated. Again, the reason was that most participants perceived collaboration as a liability to establishing their reputations as scholars.

Among the various collaborative practices, four distinctive collaborative relationships emerged in the study: pedagogical, instrumental, professional, and intimate. "Pedagogical" collaborations exhibited a concern for professional nurturance and growth by a more experienced individual who worked with a less experienced individual. "Instrumental" relationships were formed for a specific work output. "Professional" collaborations were characterized by a shared research agenda, multiple collaborative projects, and a longer term collegial relationship. "Intimate" collaborations were characterized by an emotional and intellectual closeness, shared understandings, and an ease of communication.

Although we present these relationships as four separate types, in practice they are both fluid and discrete. Some collaborative relationships can be easily categorized. As other collaborative relationships evolve, they may subtly change from one type of relationship to another. Still other relationships do not easily lend themselves to being described as any particular type. Moreover, participants who frequently collaborated may have been involved in one relationship that was pedagogical, another that was more instrumental, and a third that was intimate. Although no one pattern predominated, the pedagogical pattern involving a senior and junior colleague in a teaching-learning relationship was the most common of the four patterns and was the most likely to evolve into a different type of relationship over time.

Pedagogical Collaboration: Nurturance

For faculty in this study, nurturing the development of others was an important aspect of their feminism and of their perception of the scholarly role. A majority of the participants agreed that working closely with another scholar on a shared intellectual project was an important way to foster growth and learning. Thus, collaboration as a form of teaching or mentoring was described often and by a majority of the participants. Faculty who collaborated with students and senior faculty who collaborated with their junior and usually younger, less-experienced colleagues practiced this form of collaboration.

Collaboration in Associate Professor Phyllis Brown's[2] social sciences department is a value the departmental faculty share and represents the most commonly found collaboration in mainstream academia. She observed much student/faculty collaboration of that kind. "A lot of it centers around busy faculty with lots of ideas. Students are interested in some of these same things." Including students in research that leads to jointly authored papers was viewed as a way "of getting research out in a place with not very many resources—a better way than paying students just to collect data." Brown hinted, however, at some ambivalence about collaborating with students and admitted that she chose her collaborators carefully. "I collaborate mostly with female students.... I view collaboration with students as a mutual thing." She added: "Part of my feminism was trying to get into the system, so that, for example, I can choose what doctoral students' committees I'll be on—and they tend to be heavily women, or men who[m] I valued.... I'll put my energy into helping minority students who are weak and some women who are weak. I can't help all of the weak students."

Being part of a student/faculty research group not only added to Dr. Lisa Gamble's feelings of professional competence but helped her develop close friendships with other women scholars. An associate professor in a professional field, she explained: "You still feel a real close bond with those people—socially and emotionally as well as professionally—knowing that those are your colleagues who[m] you can go to when you need help." As a faculty member, however, she had serious concerns about the possible exploitation of students. Like most of the other participants in the study, Gamble did not agree that faculty should coauthor a student's research "unless the faculty member really writes or contributes something significant." She admitted that her opinion was not the dominant one in her department and described it as "an ethical issue without a right answer."

Dr. Marian Thomas's experience as a new assistant professor working with a graduate student demonstrated that faculty, too, can be vulnerable in student/faculty research. Thomas recounted an unhappy experience with a graduate assistant who became interested in data she was collecting for Marian's research. Unaware of the ethics of the situation, the student took Thomas's data and worked on the topic with another faculty member. Despite the experience, Marian welcomed the opportunity to work with students who are interested in her area. Having lacked female mentors and collaborative opportunities as a student, she was aware of just how important and advantageous they could be. She credited her collaborative research experience with a senior colleague for her growth as a feminist and as a scholar.

Dr. Jill Hastings, a social sciences assistant professor, described her feminism as motivating her to help other women recognize their choices and "not get locked into certain ideas of how you're supposed to do things." She described herself as committed to empowering her students and recalled the importance of her own collaboration with a competent female scholar whom she could emulate. "Collaborating with her allowed me to feel more valued," she explained, and she wanted to function in that same capacity with students. "Even though I've done a lot of research, I still think of myself primarily as a teacher," and teaching is one way she expressed her feminism.

Professor Nancy Connor, a full professor in a professional field who was beginning to talk about retirement, had few opportunities to direct doctoral dissertations and to write with students because of her particular research specialty. Nevertheless, she was committed to helping women and young scholars. She observed:

> If you can pair some experience with inexperience, it really helps to serve in a mentoring way to that person coming along. I'd like to see a lot more of that—particularly young scholars now. The tenure mill is tough—they're scrambling for six years. If they can get some help, it's useful to them. On the other side of that, sometimes young scholars are a real shot in the arm for somebody like me.

Sharing Connor's commitment to younger scholars, Dr. Edith Ross, also a professor in a professional field, described her own feminist stance toward collaboration:

> Collaboration is working in a fashion where everybody has input, that everybody's empowered to have equal input. . . . If I'm a senior now, a senior person in my field, and I'm working with more junior women . . . we're listed equally. I may have contributed more because of my experience, but I don't want to get into that issue. Others mentored me. Now I will mentor others.

Instrumental Collaboration: Pragmatism

Instrumental collaboration encompasses relationships that were formed to accomplish a specific objective or to work on a single project. Scholars came together in instrumental collaborations for primarily practical reasons, such as needing someone with a particular skill or resource to complement their own research expertise. Another reason for engaging in an instrumental collaboration was desiring the experience of working on a particular project, investigating a topic of special interest, or working with a particular person. Some collaborations with students and new faculty were more pragmatic than pedagogical even though learning was a benefit. As Professor Betty Line in a professional school recalled:

> Politically it was very important to collaborate when I was young, because I needed the strength of the senior people. They

needed my abilities, but they had years and status. So there are times early in my career where I was the worker and they were the name and we used each other mutually.

An associate professor in a professional field, Patricia Carter described her reason for collaborating on a survey with a colleague at another institution as their mutual need to publish. "She had the expertise in the area and we were friends—she was in the same kind of situation I was—in terms of publications." Pat described how they "carved it in half" after completing the survey with each approaching the data from a different point of view. They published two coauthored articles.

A social scientist, Dr. Ellen Frank commented that she had "coauthors all over the place" and suggested that instrumental relationships can be motivated by a need to generate research. Frank, an associate professor, admitted that few people worked together in her field 15 years ago but that it has become increasingly common as the field becomes more like the natural sciences. She described herself as having been drawn increasingly into collaborative work over time. "It's very nice. You can keep a lot of balls in the air at one time." She admitted, however, that collaboration requires compromise and a willingness to give up some control: "Sometimes the paper doesn't look exactly like the way you would have written it."

Joining with other researchers to generate articles—to increase one's efficiency and productivity—was more frequently seen in the social sciences than in other fields represented in this study. However, women in the humanities also collaborated for pragmatic reasons, often joining forces to coedit a journal or anthology or to take on a larger project than one could do alone. Much like Frank's description of collaboration as a division of labor, collaborators in the humanities also divided up the work in ways that were perceived as efficient, reflecting their particular strengths and interests. For example, Dr. Marjorie Baker, a professor in the humanities, described how she and her collaborating partner prepared a commemorative volume. "I worked mostly with the publisher... and when there were problems with contributors, it was [her] turn to get on their case. She oversaw the final preparation of the copy editing." They both wrote essays for the volume and collaborated on the introduction. Assistant Professor Suzanne Smith described her collaboration similarly:

> It appeared that we had the perfect combination of all the resources to get the project going.... It was something that needed to be done, and we thought we could do it.... Together we had enough need, enough resources, enough opportunity to think the project into existence.

Professional Partnership Collaboration: Shared Agendas

Less common than other types of collaborative relationships, professional partnerships were characterized by shared research agendas and long-term relationships that often lasted several years and through many research and writing projects. The relationships that developed between professional collaborators were cordial and friendly, but they lacked the intensity that characterized intimate collaborations. Dr. Nina Caruso, an assistant professor in a social science discipline, was currently involved in a large, sponsored, multi-year project that was, or had the potential to become, a professional collaboration. She typically had several research projects and collaborative relationships going at one time, some pedagogical and others intimate. However, Caruso's relationships occasionally had characteristics of the long-term professional relationships that lead to multiple publications over several years. Caruso described herself as a "private" person who separated her personal life from her professional life. Discussing her relationships with her colleagues, she explained:

> Most of my collaborators are friends of mine.... Basically [the relationships] evolved as friendships after the research part. And we socialize. But we usually socialize [in a way] that is removed from the actual work that we're doing. There is a distinction between what's social and what's work.

Dr. Taylor Woodrow, whose activities best illustrate professional partnership collaboration, had several long-term relationships over the course of her scholarly career. A social sciences professor, she portrayed her relationships as friendly "but never to the point that it [being friendly] dominates." Describing her current research partnership, she explained:

> I'd say we're good collegial friends.... We go to professional meetings together, room together to save money ... and the families are friendly.... There is a difference between a good collegial friend and a good friend. There is always a little reserve with a collegial friend that you're not going to have with a personal friend.

Her current professional collaboration was "a long-term successful one with grants, papers, a book, and presentations." The relationship had begun more than six years before the study:

> We sort of plunged in—we sort of knew each other a little bit socially, both women, both in the department, both at about the same career stage. We had very similar methodological interests and complementary substantive interests. That turned out to be a very good basis for collaboration. But I didn't really know her. We sort of ignored that.

Woodrow's involvement in long-term research relationships provided a view of collaboration that was missing in the stories of many of the participants. She talked about how her experiences as a doctoral student helped her in "laying the foundation for the first major collaborative relationship that I did have as a professional" and how she learned to put differences aside and maintain a positive relationship:

> You have to be a little bit easy-going in these relationships ... or they'll dissolve.... It's not exactly like a marriage, but everybody has to give more than 50%.... You do have to understand the ebb and flow. If you're terribly picky or you're terribly demanding in your collaborative relationship, they will not work.

Intimate Collaboration: Intellectual and Emotional Closeness

Special personal and professional relationships were formed by women in this study who shared their ideas and their scholarly lives with very close friends, life partners, and other family members. Also included in this category are close collaborative relationships that developed between women scholars who shared the same racial or ethnic identity, other than that of the dominant Anglo group, and expressed that shared identity in their work. Associate Professor Maggie Grant's current relationship with her friend, colleague, and collaborator is unlike any professional relationship Maggie had ever had. A solitary person who was happy to be at home alone with a book, she laughed at how her collaborator kept her connected—"forever dragging me around." A real plus in their collaboration, she believes, is their ease in communication: "We've got this code. We can say two or three words and she'll know what I'm talking about. We agree on most things."

Others involved in intimate collaborations also reported the importance of shared understandings. Professor Lori Boothe struggled to explain the process of writing with her life partner and laughed, "It's really funny. It seems like this utterly natural division of labor.... We don't even have to talk about it." For Dr. Karen Bell, an associate professor in the humanities, and Nina Caruso, those easy relationships came in their collaborations with other women of color. Caruso also laughed when explaining, "I think some of the things that you'd have to explain to an Anglo woman you don't necessarily have to explain. But also I think how we view the world and how we view certain things. It's also shaped by that." Bell wondered, "I don't know whether it's because [she] is my friend and we have the same aspirations, the same rhythms—we were like Frick and Frack. We laugh about that so much now." More seriously, she continued, "We are two people who are dedicated to teaching.... We are highly politicized, very conscious of our racial and gender positioning in mainstream academia at this point in the century."

Associate Professor Sally Miller agreed that communication with her collaborator, a female sibling, was easy, describing how they understand each other's looks and moods. Collaboration with a close relative, however, meant that they occasionally have to deal with feelings of jealousy, competition, and resentment. Miller described a relationship that was both permanent and changing:

> We always used to have each other read our papers that we'd done singly and critique each other. And there was a time when she stopped giving hers to me. And

then I stopped too. But now she's started up again, and I don't know what prompted that or what prompted the stopping. I think there was an awareness of something going on and some kind of resentment. I don't know.

"Sharing" is a key word in the stories that feminist women told about their "intimate" collaborations. Jill Hastings pointed out that the perception of collegiality was a reason many of them were attracted to the academy in the first place. As Maggie Grant, Nina Caruso, and Karen Bell illustrate, they often shared a way of talking, a network of friends, membership in a particular culture, and other aspects of their personal and professional lives. Occasionally, they shared homes and families. Sally Miller collaborated with students, former students, and most frequently with her sister. Lori Boothe and Phyllis Brown collaborated with their life partners. Collaborating with a loved one added another dimension to an already complex and emotionally intimate relationship. Lori explained, "We're partners as well as collaborators, so this is a small part of the whole piece of our relationship.... I suppose in a way it makes us even closer."

The Interaction of Feminism, Collaboration, and Scholarship

Faculty women who are committed to feminism, scholarship, and collaboration reveal in their words that their commitments intersect in diverse and powerful ways. A dominant theme flowing through the feminist faculty narratives is the importance of personal values. Participants repeatedly expressed the desire to integrate such feminist values as nurturance, mutuality, cooperation, and reciprocity into their scholarship and to select topics and methods that reflect their commitments to other women, their communities, and to equality and social justice. Although women in this study rarely used the word *values* in their stories, they repeatedly used value-laden words such as *equal, empowering, democratic, sharing,* and *trusting,* to describe both their relationships and the culture they desire to create. Lori Boothe, a full professor in the humanities, observed that collaboration seems like a very feminist mode of work. Edith Ross, a full professor in a professional field, described working with a jealous and controlling faculty member as "the opposite of collaboration. It's a very hierarchical notion."

Many women in the study believed that collaboration, like their relationships, can and should model feminist values. They strove for relationships that empowered women and other groups that had been excluded or undervalued. They worked to establish an atmosphere of mutual respect, trust, and support. Equality and democracy are central values in feminist relationships and were concepts that recurred in the participants' stories. Myra Kramer, an associate professor of color in the social sciences saw collaboration as reflecting both feminist and Afrocentric values. Karen Bell, an associate professor of color in the humanities, firmly believed that collaboration was a way "for women to do differently in the academy ... to really make our voices heard." Sally Miller, a white associate professor in the social sciences concurred:

> I think working together in a collaborative, cooperative, non-competitive way is one way in which feminism can be modeled to the world.... It seems to me that kind of a commitment is very different than what we see in normal departments and normal scholarship where the mode is very much "attack another position in order to make your position look good." This whole collaboration notion suggests there is another way.

Agreeing with Sally Miller, Pat Carter, a white associate professor in a professional school, views the dominant academic culture as pushing people "not only to go against their values but to exploit others." She describes the connection between her values and collaboration, "The values I usually end up advocating have to do with teamwork, cooperation, understanding, mutual respect—so collaboration fits right in [with] all that." In short, working closely with a feminist collaborator can give a scholar the courage to proclaim her own feminism in an environment that is hostile to feminist politics, scholarship, and pedagogy.

Discussion

This study indicates that collaboration is a common practice among feminist scholars. The participants in this study typically sought membership in a supportive community. They experienced a lack of close relationships with other women as a professional and sometimes personal disadvantage. Thus, they chose to counter that disadvantage in their work with professionally productive relationships with women. This study documents four patterns of collaborative relationships. Three of the patterns—pedagogical, instrumental, and professional—manifested forms and features somewhat similar to those observed by other researchers. For example, Wilkie and Allen (1975) identified three forms of academic teams as complementary, supplementary, and coequal. Later, Smart and Bayer (1986) modified Hagstrom's (1964) traditional partnership types into complementary, supplementary, and master-apprentice. Although the participants in this study also collaborated in ways that could be labeled with some of these same terms, most of them recognized and rejected the power and authority structure implied in these forms, especially master-apprentice and supplementary. Therefore, we chose to give them names that described the purpose or essence of the collaborative relationship rather than its authority structure.

This study, furthermore, differs from antecedent scholarship on academic teams, coauthorship, and collaboration by identifying intimate collaboration as a fourth relationship pattern, one which heretofore has been invisible and or undocumented in published work. Intimate collaboration is characterized by an intellectual and emotional closeness between partners. Not surprisingly, the affective qualities enmeshed in academic research relationships have not been captured by traditional quantitative research methods. Moreover, the majority of studies of collaboration and coauthorship in university scholarship have been conducted by and focused exclusively on academic men (see, for example, Bayer & Smart, 1991). In explicating collaboration and coauthorship about men there has been no mention of intimacy as a quality of those relationships. In contrast, as feminist scholars have written about qualitative aspects of women's research relationships, they have suggested that some women derive great satisfaction from social relationships and that they approach research as a communal endeavor (Ward & Grant, 1991).

Also, because feminist methodology considers reflexivity a valued source of knowledge (Cook & Fonow, 1986), intimate collaboration could further enhance self-reflection.

In the present research, some feminist scholars' stories about close personal scholarly relationships with women describe intellectual intimacy as an integrated construct that defies extricating one dimension from the other. Consequently, the interview data do not lead to the conclusion that women's academic careers are less important than their personal relationships, a patriarchal stereotype with which professional women in all fields have been burdened. In fact, findings from this study regarding the friendships that women faculty form with their collaborators in professional, pedagogical, and instrumental relationships suggested diversity. Some women preferred to maintain a professional distance from their academic colleagues, even those with whom they socialized. They described their professional lives as separate from their personal lives. Others preferred to combine work and close friendships. It is significant to note that no participant, however, felt that she compromised her work to maintain a friendship. At the same time, several feminists indicated that they chose not to collaborate with other women if they felt that professional involvement would harm their personal relationship.

It is not surprising that disciplinary norms determined likely forms of collaborative scholarship. Women in the humanities were likely to coauthor or coedit books while women in professional fields were more likely to collaborate on research projects and journal publications. However, even within a particular discipline or field, colleagues valued collaboration differently. For example, in an area of the humanities one feminist faculty member's coauthored book was well received and rewarded while in another area of the humanities a feminist faculty member's coauthored book was dismissed by her colleagues. In all fields, participants consistently described their desire to function as democratic, equal partners rather than as hierarchical team leaders, thus lending support to Wilkie and Allen's (1975) finding that women prefer to collaborate with other women as equals. Even in pedagogical teams consisting of junior and senior faculty or students and professors, women in this study resisted the implications of hierarchy and authority implicit in the masculine "master/apprentice" relationship. Instrumental teams consisting of specialists who might be viewed as "supplementary" collaborators were also described as operating according to a democratic model. Sensitive to relationships of power and exploitation, women faculty in this study attempted to establish relationships based on mutual respect, trust, and support.

As feminist women who were building careers in research universities where the vast majority of tenured faculty are white men, the enactment of their commitments to feminism and scholarship demanded both emotional and intellectual resources. Despite the fact that some women faculty either lacked the opportunity or chose not to collaborate formally until later in their careers, the participants in this study found that collaboration with other women was a powerful way to create and to share their ideas and their intra-institutional and extra-institutional resources. Far from viewing their collaborations with other women as disadvantageous, most women in this study preferred them and considered them advantageous, thus further corroborating academic feminists' valuing and seeking membership in a supportive community (Reinharz, 1984). In reality, the faculty in this study experience a lack of close relationships with other women scholars as a professional disadvantage, and they are committed to countering that disadvantage in their work with other women.

Implications

This study contributes to knowledge about the relationships and friendships that help to support and define academic careers and contribute to productive scholarly lives. At the same time, it focuses only on women's studies faculty in research universities. Although we made efforts to maximize diversity in rank, discipline, race and ethnicity, sexual orientation, and other demographic characteristics, the study does not purport to describe all faculty women or all women's studies faculty. Further studies are needed to consider (a) women who work in other types of colleges and universities where research opportunities and expectations are limited; (b) women in the natural sciences or professional schools, such as engineering and medicine, where collaborative research is the norm; (c) women faculty who are not affiliated with women's studies programs; (d) women who work in administrative positions; and (e) collaborating faculty women whose careers have been unfulfilling or unsuccessful and who have left the research university environment. Also, the small number of women of color, lesbian scholars who chose to discuss their sexual orientation, and the absence of individuals with physical disabilities in this study precluded the possibility of explicating how "characteristics" associated with isolation influence collaboration. An understanding of feminism, scholarship, and collaboration would be enhanced by hearing the stories of women faculty in these important groups.

We interviewed participants individually and privately rather than as collaborating pairs or teams. Discussing collaboration with groups of women might provide a view of relationships and socially constructed identities that is missing in this study.

The quality of a publication is an important factor in evaluating faculty scholarship, whether it is produced individually or collaboratively. The design of this study precluded considering the quality of scholarship. Thoughtful inquiry into the relationship between individually and collaboratively generated scholarship and quality is necessary.

Conversations with women who collaborate successfully suggest that in-depth studies are also needed to explore other common types of collaboration, with student/faculty research partnerships being a particularly rich area for study. Similarly, other collaborations that display power and status differences, such as those involving women and men, junior and senior faculty, and African American and white faculty, deserve scholarly attention. These collaborative relationships raise questions about how the partners manage their differences and how these perceived differences both advance and inhibit meaningful scholarship and satisfying relationships.

This study is an attempt to describe and understand some of the intersections of scholarship, feminism, and collaboration in the lives of a selected group of women faculty. Clearly, there is need for additional investigation if these relationships are to be well understood and generalizations are to be made. The caveats in this study should not, however, obfuscate the finding that feminist scholars' cultural knowledge and values are woven together with their feminism, scholarship, and collaboration. To seek to understand feminist scholars' friendships and other social relationships and to capture the meanings those women make of their lives is to acknowledge their struggles and achievements and to further illuminate the dynamics of integrating one's life and one's scholarship as a model for others.

Footnotes

1 This criterion was used to identify feminist faculty members. Research universities selected as sites of the study had a formal process of reviewing a scholar's research and course content for coherence with the feminist ideology and goals of the women's studies program.

2 All participants' names used in this paper are pseudonyms. References to their specific institutions, schools, departments, and fields, other than women's studies, have been omitted to protect the identities of the individual participants.

References

Appley, D. G., & Winder, A. E. (1977). Values, attitudes, and skills. *Journal of Applied Behavioral Sciences, 13*(3), 279–291.

Ashton-Jones, E., & Thomas, D. K. (1991). Composition, collaboration, and women's ways of knowing: A conversation with Mary Belenky. In G. Olson & I. Gale (Eds.), *(Inter)views: Cross-disciplinary perspectives on rhetoric and literacy* (pp. 27–44). Carbondale: Southern Illinois University.

Astin, H. S. (1978). Factors affecting women's scholarly productivity. In A. S. Astin & W. Z. Hirsch (Eds.), *The higher education of women* (pp. 133–157). New York: Praeger.

Austin, A. E., & Baldwin, R. G. (1991). *Faculty collaboration: Enhancing the quality of scholarship and teaching.* ASHE-ERIC Higher Education Report, No. 7. Washington, DC: George Washington, School of Education and Human Development.

Baldwin, R. G., & Austin, A. E. (1992, October). *Toward greater understanding of faculty collaboration: Metaphors, emerging theory, and collaborators' advice.* Paper presented at the Annual Meeting of the Association for the Study of Higher Education. Minneapolis, MN.

Bayer, A. E., & Astin, H. S. (1975). Sex differentials in the academic reward system. *Science, 188*, 796–802.

Bayer, A. E., & Smart, J. C. (1991). Career publication patterns and collaborative "styles" in American academic science. *Journal of Higher Education, 62*, 613–636.

Belenky, M. F., Clinchy, B. M., Goldberger, N. R., & Tarule, J. M. (1986). *Women's ways of knowing: The development of self, voice, and mind.* New York: Basic Books.

Bernard, J. (1964). *Academic women.* University Park, PA: University Press.

Chubin, D. (1974). Sociological manpower and womanpower: Sex differences in career patterns of two cohorts of American doctorate sociologists. *American Sociologists, 9,* 83–92.

Clark, S. M., & Corcoran, M. (1986). Perspectives on the professional socialization of women faculty: A case of accumulative disadvantage? *Journal of Higher Education, 57,* 20–43.

Cook, J. A., & Fonow, M. M. (1986). Knowledge and women's interests: Issues of epistemology and methodology in feminist sociological research. *Sociological Inquiry, 56,* 2–27.

Cott, N. F. (1977). *The Bonds of Womanhood: "Woman's Sphere" in New England, 1780–1835.* New Haven, CT: Yale University Press.

Eaton, J. W. (1951). Social processes of professional teamwork. *American Sociological Review, 16,* 707–713.

Fonow, M. M., & Cook, J. A. (1991). Back to the future: A look at the second wave of feminist epistemology and methodology. In M. M. Fonow & J. A. Cook (Eds.), *Beyond methodology: Feminist scholarship as lived research* (pp. 1–15). Bloomington: Indiana University.

Fox, M. F. (1984). Women and higher education: Sex differentials in the status of students and scholars. In J. Freeman (Ed.), *Women: A feminist perspective* (3rd ed., pp. 238–255). Palo Alto, CA: Mayfield.

Fox, M. F. (1985). Publication, performance, and reward in science and scholarship. In J. C. Smart (Ed.), *Higher education: Handbook of theory and research* (Vol. 1, pp. 255–282). New York: Agathon.

Fox, M. F. & Faver, C. (1984). Independence and cooperation in research: The motivations and costs of collaboration. *Journal of Higher Education, 55,* 347–359.

Freedman, E. (1979, Fall). Separatism as strategy: Female institution building and American feminism, 1870–1930. *Feminist Studies, 5*(3), 512–529.

Graham, P. A. (1970). Women in academe. *Science, 169,* 1284–1290.

Graham, P. A. (1978). Expansion and exclusion: A history of women in American higher education. *Signs: Journal of Women in Culture and Society, 3*(4), 759–773.

Hagstrom, W. O. (1964). Traditional and modern forms of scientific teamwork. *Administrative Science Quarterly, 9*, 241–263.

Hagstrom, W. O. (1965). *The scientific community*. New York: Basic Books.

Jensen, K. (1982). Women's work and academic culture: Adaptations and confrontations. *Higher Education, 11*, 67–83.

Kaufman, D. R. (1978). Associational ties in academe: Some male and female differences. *Sex Roles, 4*(1), 9–21.

Langland, E., & Gove, W. (Eds.) (1981). *A feminist perspective in the academy: The difference it makes*. Chicago: University of Chicago.

Lewin, A. Y., & Duchan, L. (1971). Women in academia. *Science, 173*, 892–895.

Mackie, M. (1976). Professional women's collegial relations and productivity: Female sociologists' journal publications, 1967 and 1973. *Sociology and Social Research, 61*, 277–293.

Menges, R. J., & Exum, W. H. (1983). Barriers to the progress of women and minority faculty. *Journal of Higher Education, 54*(2), 123–144.

Moore, K. M., & Sagaria, M. A. D. (1991). The situation of women in research universities in the United States: Within the inner circles of academic power. In G. P. Kelly & S. Slaughter (Eds.), *Women's higher education in comparative perspective* (pp. 185–200). Dordrect, The Netherlands: Kluwer.

Musil, C. T. (1992). *The courage to question: Women's studies and student learning. Executive summary*. Washington, DC: Association of American Colleges.

Noddings, N. (1986). Fidelity in teaching, teacher education, and research for teaching. *Harvard Educational Review, 56*(4), 496–511.

O'Connor, P. (1992). *Friendships Between Women*. New York: Guilford.

Patton, M. Q. (1990). *Qualitative evaluation and research methods*. Newbury Park, CA: Sage.

Reinharz, S. (1984). *On becoming a social scientist*. New Brunswick, N. J.: Transaction Books.

Rosenberg, R. (1979). The academic prism: The new view of American women. In R. Berkin & M. B. Norton (Eds.), *Women of America: A history* (pp. 318–341). Boston: Houghton Mifflin.

Rosser, S. V. (1986). The relationship between women's studies and women in science. In R. Bleier (Ed.), *Feminist approaches to science* (pp. 165–180). New York: Pergamon.

Simeone, A. (1987). *Academic women: Working toward equality*. South Hadley, MA: Bergin & Garvey.

Simon, R. J., Clark, S. M., & Galway, K. (1967). The woman Ph.D.: A recent profile. *Social Problems, 15*(2), 221–236.

Smart, J. C., & Bayer, A. E. (1986). Author collaboration and impact: A note on citation rates of single and multiple authored articles. *Scientometrics, 10*, 297–305.

Smith-Rosenberg, C. (1975). The female world of love and ritual: Relations between women in nineteenth-century America. *Signs: Journal of Women in Culture and Society, 1*(1), 1–29.

Strauss, A., & Corbin, J. (1990). *Basics of qualitative research: Grounded theory procedures and techniques*. Newbury Park, CA: Sage.

Tidball, E. (1976). Of men and research. *Journal of Higher Education, 47*(4), 373–389.

Ward, K. B., & Grant, L. (1991). Co-authorship, gender, and publication among sociologists. In M. M. Fonow & J. Cook (Eds.), *Feminist strategies in the study of gender* (pp. 248–264). Bloomington: Indiana University.

Wilkie, J. R., & Allen, I. L. (1975). Women sociologists and co-authorship with men. *American Sociologist, 10*, 19–24.

Appendix
Interview Guide Questions

1. Collaboration

- Have you been encouraged by your colleagues to work collaboratively? How?
- How do you define collaboration? (What does the word "collaboration" mean to you?) Is this the way it is defined in your discipline? Do you agree with that definition?
- How does your department/college encourage or discourage collaborative scholarly work?
- Have you ever been told not to collaborate or coauthor a paper?
- Have you ever been told not to collaborate with other women? With other feminists?
- Have there been times in your career when collaboration seemed more attractive than other times?
- Were you given opportunities to collaborate when you were a student?
- Do you ever collaborate with your students now?
- Have you had a collaborative research partnership which has been particularly meaningful in your development as a scholar? Would you tell me about it?
- How did you happen to become collaborating partner(s)?

- How do (did) you make decisions regarding who does what?
- Did problems come up during your collaboration? How were they resolved?
- Did you publish the results of the study? Was the paper coauthored and collaboratively written?
- How did you handle issues of authorship?
- Have you ever experienced any feelings of competition when you are involved in a collaborative project? How did you manage those impulses?
- What words would you use to describe your involvement in a collaborative project? (Fun?)
- What are the benefits of collaborative scholarship from your experience? The disadvantages? Trade-offs?
- Will you continue to do collaborative research and writing? (Why or why not?)

2. The Evolving Scholar

- Have you changed as a result of your collaboration? Describe that change. (Probes: Do you feel more competent? More self-confident?)
- Has the type of research and writing you do changed as a result of your collaboration?
- Has your relationship with your partner(s) changed during the course of this research project?
- Describe how the relationship has developed.
- Have your relationships with other women faculty been strengthened by working together collaboratively? In what ways?

3. Feminism

- What does being a feminist mean to you? Has this meaning changed for you over the years?
- In what ways do you see your scholarship as having a political motive or purpose?
- How does your scholarship relate to your feminism?
- How does collaboration relate to your feminism?

Cynthia Sullivan Dickens, who died in January 1997 of cancer, was an Assistant Professor of Educational Leadership at Mississippi State University at Starkville where she taught courses in higher education and student affairs. She earlier served in a variety of administrative leadership positions, including Vice President for Students Affairs at Northern Kentucky University. She began research on women's scholarly collaboration while earning a Ph.D. in higher education at The Ohio State University.
Mary Ann Danowitz Sagaria is an Associate Professor in the School of Educational Policy and Leadership and a faculty associate in the Department of Women's Studies at The Ohio State University. Much of her published scholarship has been collaborative and is in the areas of leadership, administrative careers, and diversity and inclusivity in higher education.

CHAPTER 23

FOR COLORED GIRLS WHO HAVE CONSIDERED SUICIDE WHEN THE ACADEMY'S NOT ENOUGH: REFLECTIONS OF AN AFRICAN AMERICAN WOMAN SCHOLAR

GLORIA LADSON-BILLINGS

[We] deal intimately with the White power structure and cultural apparatus, and the inner realities of the Black world at one and the same time. —Harold Cruse, *The Crisis of the Negro Intellectual*

And ain't I a woman?
—Sojourner Truth

I begin this chapter with apologies to Ntozake Shange.[1] However, the power and urgency of her language best speak to me when I think about my position as an African American woman in the predominantly white, male world of the academy. Certainly, I have not seriously considered suicide because of professional challenges and difficulties. My working-class, African American family background assures me that no "job" is worth dying for. And it is just this attitude of blurring the distinction between "job" and "career" that has sustained me in the rigors of academic life. I attempt to write this chapter somewhere within the nexus of my life as an African American woman and an African American woman scholar. I deliberately write this narrative within and outside of my personal life because I believe that my personal life (or who I am as a person) informs and shapes who I am as a scholar. I resist notions of myself as an "objective" researcher when what I research is so intricately linked to the life I have lived and continue to live.

In this chapter, the reader has the opportunity to hear whispers of my "inner voice" that are self-reflective about the cultural and educational world that has shaped me. Without these "voices from within" the story is woefully incomplete. Even with my selective sharing of the narrative that is my life, the story still is partial. The reader is privy only to that which I choose to share, but that I would share it at all represents a break with much of traditional academic writing.

Going to School

"Now remember, when we go downtown people will be staring at us," said Mrs. Gray, the accelerated reading teacher. "They'll be staring at us because they're not used to seeing groups of Negro children walking in and out of the best downtown stores." I had been in downtown stores many

---

Reprinted from *Learning from Our Lives: Women, Research, and Autobiography in Education,* edited by A. Neumann and P. L. Peterson, 1997. Copyright © 1997 Teachers College, Columbia University.

times but this was a special Christmas visit for a group of "special" readers. At my segregated elementary school, it never occurred to me that African American students weren't as smart as other children. We were told so often and in many ways. But, this special visit to watch the dancing fountain in John Wanamaker's Department Store Christmas Show was a public declaration that we were special—we were smart.

Except for a brief period in junior high school, I remember enjoying school. I reveled in the life of the mind. Books and the world of words brought me great comfort (most of the time). But the luxury of spending one's life reading and thinking seemed far beyond my grasp. I had to "make a living" and making a living meant having a secure and stable *job*!

Life in the academy was not one I selected for myself, consciously. I entered college without any idea about what I wanted to do. I knew I enjoyed history and writing. In my secret life I was a writer, but just thinking about saying that aloud made me laugh. I could see it all clearly. After earning a bachelor's degree I would return to the solitude of my room (in my parents' home) to think and write. Never mind that most of my family's resources had gone to secure my education. Never mind that there was an expectation that I would both take care of myself (financially) and contribute to the family.[2] I merely would announce that I had returned home a "writer" and each morning while other family members marched off to work, I would retreat to my "study" and "write." The entire imagined scene was ludicrous.

What was more imaginable was the "sensible" (and understandable) profession of teaching. Everyone knew that teaching was a "good job" (almost as secure as working at the post office). I would have job security, good benefits, summers "off," and a "short" work day. Best of all, I could continue living in the world of intellectual activity.

Although I enjoyed teaching and supervising for ten years in a large urban school district, there was less intellectual activity and more work involved than I imagined. I taught middle grades (7–8) and intermediate (4–6) students for eight of those ten years. For two years I served as a social studies/science collaborator (or consultant) for one of the city's eight geographic area districts. My area consisted of forty-four schools with approximately four thousand teachers. My job was to respond to the teachers' curriculum and instructional needs as requested. In actuality I spent too much time observing struggling teachers for principals who wanted documentation they could use to fire them. By 1978 I could not resist the lure of graduate school. Still I lacked a clear notion of what I would "do" as a result of graduate study. I just knew that graduate school would be a place to once again read and study.

However, the difference between the "me" who attended undergraduate school and the "me" who attended graduate school was dramatic. One month after I entered undergraduate school (in mid year), Malcom X was assassinated and my hope for strong, militant, black leadership filled with righteous indignation was dashed. Throughout my collegiate years the Vietnam War raged on while many of the male students at my historically black college campus struggled to maintain a high enough grade point average to keep them from being drafted. Too many of them lost that battle and found themselves in Southeast Asia fighting a war they did not understand.

By the time I graduated in 1968, Martin Luther King, Jr. had been assassinated and once again a void in black leadership was apparent. Robert Kennedy would be slain before I turned in my first professional employment application. It was a time of death and dying, protests and riots. My own coming of age was inextricably linked to the larger changing consciousness of African Americans who were challenging the existing social order in new ways. Rather than a cry of "let us in," which had seemed to shape the discourse of the early civil rights struggle for school desegregation and public accommodation, there were increasing calls for self-definition and self-determination among African Americans and other people of color. This confluence of social change, my interests in intellectual and political activity, and my reawakened sense of myself as an African American woman, all pointed me toward finding ways to make a closer fit between my "work life" and my "real life."

You Can't Get There From Here

It is the summer of 1993 and I am meeting with a group of African American and Latino undergraduate students who are a part of a special program aimed at mentoring them into graduate school. During the course of the meeting one student asks, "How did you make it through graduate school, all the way to a Ph.D.? What should we be doing?" I remember laughing aloud and saying to the student, "Do you realize how much farther ahead you are than I was as an undergraduate? I didn't even know there was any such thing as graduate school!" I was not lying to them.

In my family, the term "doctor" was reserved for someone who could write you a prescription or preach fire and brimstone. After I received my doctorate my father would explain to friends and family that I wasn't a "healing doctor, just a *writing* doctor." While there was no overt opposition to my returning to school, there was no real support. I was a parent with responsibilities. Why would I give up my job—my good job—to go back to school? I could not expect my family to support what they did not understand. I especially could not expect them to support what I, myself, could not explain.

My first weeks in graduate school had me rethinking why I had given up my secure teaching job. The whole experience seemed surreal. People were speaking an alien language and arguing over seemingly meaningless problems at the same time *real* people were struggling with *real* problems. I was reminded that for many children, school is not a *real* place. My solace in those first weeks of graduate school came as a result of a decision I had made to not take advantage of campus housing. I felt the need to live in a "familiar" community. Thus I found housing in a nearby African American community.

While my days were spent in the "unreal" world of graduate school, my nights and evenings were spent in the real world of a struggling, largely African American and Latino school district geographically located near a prestigious university and alongside a predominantly white school system that was reputedly among the best in the state. The parents of the African American and Latino school system's "town-gown" issues were not the typical ones of zoning permits and fraternity raucousness. Sitting in the shadow of a "great" university, they wondered why the fact that their children were failing at unprecedented rates seemed not to be an issue for scholarly inquiry. Their questions were my questions and became the principal way for me to merge my personal interests and community politics with my professional goals. Their struggles helped me articulate the meaning that education and educational research could have in the lives of African American people.

That commitment—to make what I got from graduate school meaningful—was more of a challenge than I anticipated. My graduate school had one African American faculty member (not in my area) who was preparing to leave. Other African American graduate students who expressed an interest in the African American community were either discouraged or struggling with little faculty mentorship or support. The general pattern of successful graduate study meant attaching oneself to a faculty member via a research project or teaching assistantship. But there were no research projects focused on African American education.

My years of teaching and supervision in a large urban school district meant that I was qualified for a teaching assistantship in the school of education's relatively small (thirty to forty students) teacher education program.

> My job as a supervisor would be a snap. I was required to supervise eight social studies interns. After all, I had recently had the responsibility of "supervising" 4,000 teachers in 44 separate school sites—44,000 students, and that was just my geographic region. Sometimes I had to respond to supervisory requests system-wide—280 schools, 13,000 teachers, more than a quarter of a million students. I didn't kid myself about what I did. I was a firefighter. I did damage control. Working with eight eager beaver student teachers was something I could do in my sleep.

Even though I regarded my work as relatively easy, I was not prepared for the sense of alienation I would feel as an African American woman.

> "Aren't there any other black supervisors in the teacher education program?" I asked.

"You mean there is one?" came the reply from a third-year African American doctoral student. "Yeah, I'm supervising," I said. "How'd you pull that off?" she asked.

In many ways graduate school was a pleasant divergence from the cares of the world. I found the work enjoyable, if not inspiring. The first years of course work seemed a lot like having a day at an amusement park. There were so many different rides and attractions from which to sample, and yet you knew you could never do it all.

Graduate school did not get "hard" for me until I had to declare a research interest. The closer I got to having to make that declaration, the more arduous just getting up and going to campus became.

> My course work is winding down. I am supervising four students and teaching the methods course for my advisor while he is on sabbatical. I have a part-time job at a local middle school. At home, I am parenting a pre-teen son and serve as chairperson of his school's advisory committee. I wake up each morning with a headache. It plagues me throughout the day and accompanies me to bed every night. Not prone to headaches, I go to an optometrist to have my eyes examined. Two prescriptions and two pairs of eyeglasses later I am still suffering with a nonstop headache. I drag myself to the campus health center. The doctor can find nothing wrong with me. "No, you don't have a brain tumor." "No, your sinuses look fine." "Do you have a history of migraines?" The quarter is ending and we are returning home for Christmas. As the plane touches down at Philadelphia International Airport, I notice that my headache has disappeared. For the next three weeks I am headache free. Ten minutes after we return to San Francisco, I feel like my head is going to explode.

Members of my graduate school cohort are busy "collecting data." They want to know how to "improve students' memory," or how to "determine young children's understanding of chronology," or do "analyses of social problems in elementary social studies textbooks." I did not even have a question and could not imagine being interested in the things they were busy researching.

Someone who was a dissertator during my first year told me that this phase of graduate school was akin to the "loneliness of the long-distance runner." And, while the sports metaphor made sense to me, my perception of what I was experiencing seemed more like the solitary and isolated picture of a James Meredith walking swiftly to and from classes at "Ole Miss" or the little girl marching up the steps of a school accompanied by two National Guardsmen.

Now, lest I be misunderstood, I must make clear that my graduate school experience was never one of overt racism or discrimination. I think I was relatively well liked and had little or no trouble getting along with classmates and professors. My loneliness resulted from "intellectual segregation," not social segregation. I had no mentors who were interested in the issues of race and racism in the same way I was. I found some intellectual stimulation in my minor department—anthropology. Culture was a real thing in the anthro department. My challenge was to transpose the notions of "exotic" culture to investigations of a marginalized culture like my own.

My "salvation" came in the form of the Afro-American Studies Program.[3] After attending a lecture given by the chair of the program, I talked my way into her undergraduate course, entitled "The Afro-American in Fact and Fiction." As I surveyed the syllabus and required readings, I smiled to myself. I had read almost every book listed, Ellison's *The Invisible Man*, Chinua Achebe's *Things Fall Apart*, Camara Laye's *The Dark Child*, Harriet Beecher Stowe's *Uncle Tom's Cabin*, Frederick Douglass's narrative. This would be a snap. Here I was a "mature" student sitting in a class with younger African American students with a reading list filled with texts I already knew. I was just happy to know that for a little over an hour, three times a week, I would be in an all-black intellectual space. It was a comforting feeling.

To my surprise, this class on texts that I "knew" was one of the most difficult and challenging I had encountered at this prestigious institution. It was an Afro-Am course, but the professor, an Afro-Caribbean female (a black woman!) was talking to us about Foucault and Bourdieu—"regimes of truth" and "prescriptive modes of rationality." We would do "multiple readings" of texts. We would "interrogate meaning." We would wrestle with the "imaginary social significations" of race, class, and gender. A few students dropped out after the first two weeks. Many seemed lost throughout the quarter. I was as excited and invigorated as I had ever been in school. I was spending "way too much time" reading for my "undergraduate" class. Although there were obvious differences in the curriculum and the teaching styles, this course reminded me of my sophomore humanities course. For me, the common denominator was a strong black woman academician, confident in her persona, well-grounded in her subject area—a rarity in my college career:

> "Don't take Dr. Jones's humanities section, she's too hard!" That was sound advice from juniors and seniors who had learned the hard way. I didn't need a course that was too hard. I was already taking nineteen units in an attempt to graduate early. I couldn't be sabotaged by a required humanities course. I had to stay on the dean's list to keep my scholarship. My eyes were tearing as I kept turning the pages of the timetable trying to find a humanities section that would fit my schedule. As it stood, the only one that fit was Dr. Jones's and I didn't need that kind of grief. Unsuccessful in my quest for the most desirable schedule, I find myself sitting in Dr. Jones's classroom. She walks in dressed in black from head to toe, wearing makeup that looked as if it had been applied by an undertaker. She could be a slightly darker version of the Addams Family mother, Morticia. She begins right away rattling off information about Dante, Greek and Roman myths, Chaucer, Milton. I am terrified and at the same time intrigued. She is both mesmerizing and brilliant. Throughout the semester I never miss a class. I read and study constantly and emerge with the grade of A. More importantly, I understand that the arena of the academy is *not* off limits to black women.

My time in the undergraduate Afro-Am course was less a respite from the all-encompassing "whiteness" of the ed school than it was an opportunity to rethink and reenvision the relationships between and among race, culture, and education. If I could read Ellison and Douglass in a new way, perhaps I could read education and anthropology in new ways. In what ways were these disciplines "socially constructed" and how did these social constructions intersect with race and gender? What were the implications of these constructions for the educational lives of African American children?

In my circuitous route from the ed school to the anthropology department, to Afro-Am, I was beginning to formulate a question—a question I do not think I would have gotten to in the narrow confines of the School of Education. Taking the long way around may have saved my (intellectual) life.

Living the Life of a "Public Intellectual"[4]

Space constraints do not allow me to tell the entire story of my graduate school career. Suffice it to say I "found" a question, researched it, wrote a dissertation, and defended it. But in this section I attempt to discuss the integration of personal, public (sociocultural/civic), and intellectual interests.

Like most academics I gave serious thought to the rigors of the academy—teaching, service, and above all else, scholarship. But I believe I was less interested in the proliferation of my work than whether or not the work had meaning for those whom I intended to serve. Thus in this section of the chapter I move away from my personal narrative toward a theory of African American female intellectual life. I feel compelled to make this switch because African American and other scholars of color rarely have the luxury of considering only their personal sojourns. Rather, our position in the academy is typically the result of collective struggle and support. Thus our understanding of our roles includes an intertwining of the personal and the public—the intellectual and the emotional—the scholarly and the political.

I approach this theory of African American female intellectual life as theory-in-the-making—unfinished and open-ended. I begin contemplation of this theory with a historical glance back to those who have previously pondered and theorized the dilemmas of African American intellectual life.

W. E. B. DuBois declared it at the turn of the century. Carter G. Woodson refined it in the 1930s. Harold Cruse named it in the 1960s. Jacqueline Mitchell restated it in the 1980s, and Cornel West reframed it in the 1990s. The "it" is what Cruse termed "the crisis of the Negro intellectual."

In *Keeping Faith*, West asserts that "[T]he choice of becoming a black intellectual is an act of self-imposed marginality" (p. 67) and in charting options for African American intellectuals, he suggests four possible models: the bourgeois, the Marxist, the Foucaultian, and the insurgency. Below I attempt to summarize each of these models.

The bourgeois model is characterized by its quest for legitimation. In West's terms, this model "sets intellectual limits, in that one is prone to adopt uncritically prevailing paradigms predominant in the bourgeois academy" (p. 76). An African American scholar who adopts this model might ask, "What are the rules of the academy? What must I do to achieve and be rewarded by the existing structure? Rather than commitment to scholarship or community, this model reflects commitment to self in a personal, self-aggrandizing manner that never questions the legitimacy of the academy. Indeed, in an attempt to curry favor the bourgeois black intellectual seeks conformity within the institution and conducts "safe" scholarship or seeks "safe" positions within a scholarly discourse.[5] The second model, West argues, is the Marxist model, a model that allows access to the "least xenophobic white intellectual subculture available to black intellectuals" (p. 78). However, its early liberatory benefits are lessened because it "tends to stifle the further development of black critical consciousness and attitudes" (p. 79). Thus, an African American scholar who adheres to this model may enjoy the opportunity to engage in intellectual pursuits that challenge the dominant paradigms, but those challenges will rarely, if ever, be linked to the everyday circumstances of people outside of the academy.

The Foucaultian model constitutes the black intellectual as a postmodern skeptic. By interrogating the "regimes of truth" that are constructed by discursive practices and institutional power, black intellectuals in this model participate in a reconception of what it means to be an intellectual. Rather than struggle, in West's terms, "on behalf" (p. 81) of the truth, African American intellectuals in this tradition struggle over the status of the truth. Thus the work of the black intellectual as postmodern skeptic becomes that of uncovering myths of representation and challenging so-called universals.[6] However, its shortcoming lies in its provision of "ideological and social distance from insurgent black movements for liberation" (p. 81). In African American parlance it allows the intellectual to "talk the talk without walking the walk." Finally, the insurgency model calls for a melding of the positive aspects of the preceding models. From the bourgeois model it lifts the determination and will but reshapes it for collective rather than individual benefit. From the Marxist model it acknowledges the structural constraints without becoming enmeshed in an economic determinism. From the Foucaultian model it maintains a worldly skepticism about power relations but speaks directly to the specificity of African American life, history, and culture.

However, for all of the theoretical rigor and intellectual seductiveness of West's formulations, his model fails to acknowledge a salient feature of my intellectual life—gender. Thus, while white women can and have written persuasively about the challenges of women in the academy[7] and African American men have done likewise around issues of race, it is only the African American female who can speak to the specificity of coping with this "dual otherness."[8]

In *Theorizing Black Feminisms*, Stanlie James says that, "[A]lthough Black women are often characterized as victims, theorizing is a form of agency that provides them with opportunities to 'learn, think, imagine, judge, listen, speak, write, and act'—which transforms not only the individual (from victim to activist, for example) but the community, and the society as well" (p. 2). This act of theorizing from an African American woman's perspective, although marginalized in the literature, is not new. As far back as the late 1800s, Anna Julia Cooper, in *A Voice from the South by a Black Woman of the South*, conceived the black woman's intellectual and political position thusly: "She is confronted by a woman question and a race problem, and is as yet an unknown or unacknowledged factor in both" (p. 27).

Rose Brewer argues that "Black feminist theorizing places African American women at the center of the analyses" (p. 15). For too long critiques of academic life have been one-dimensional along either race or gender lines.

However, in 1982, three black women scholars, Gloria Hull, Patricia Bell-Scott, and B. Smith, initiated scholarly work in "Black Women's Studies" in which they summarized the shortcomings of both black studies and women's studies:

> Women's studies courses... focused almost exclusively upon the lives of White women. Black studies, which was much too often male-dominated, also ignored Black women.... Because of White women's racism and Black men's sexism, there was no room in either area for serious consideration of the lives of Black women. And even when they have considered Black women, White women usually have not had the capacity to analyze racial politics and Black culture, and Black men have remained blind or resistant to the implications of sexual politics in Black women's lives. (pp. xx–xxi)

So entrenched are the notions of either black studies or women's studies that even on one historically black women's college campus there was debate about the legitimacy of a black women's studies program.[9] However, black women's epistemology revolves around notions of "the simultaneity of oppression."[10] Therefore, no study of black women is complete without an understanding of the intersections and interactions of race, class, and gender. These intersections/interactions apply both within and outside of the academy.

Making Sense and Scholarship on My Own Terms

As an African American female, public intellectual, I struggle to do intellectual work that is politically significant and culturally grounded. I struggle to do this work as a way to acknowledge and revere those who have gone before me and as a way to pave the path for those who must come after. This struggle is grounded both in what I choose to study and how I choose to study it. Study of African American life and culture has been legitimated even when situated in a deficit model.[11] Problems faced by African Americans in schooling are almost legendary. From school desegregation to resegregation, scholars of various races and ethnicities have attempted to unravel the knotty complexities of African Americans' failed schooling experiences. Thus my research interest is not perceived as "alien" in the academy.

However, my academic struggle primarily has been one of methodology and theoretical grounding. Indeed, while the academy may be more tolerant of what scholars choose to study, it can sometimes be rigidly dogmatic about how research is to be conducted. Thus theoretical frameworks must be precisely explicated to support the work—particularly that work done in unconventional ways.

Patricia Hill Collins's work on black feminist epistemology provides a theoretical and conceptual platform on which to rest my methodology. Collins's notion of a black feminist epistemology is based on the propositions of (1) concrete experience as a criterion of meaning, (2) the use of dialogue in assessing knowledge claims, (3) the ethic of caring, and (4) the ethic of personal accountability.

Concrete Experiences as a Criterion of Meaning

This dimension suggests that only black women can truly know what it is to be a black woman. As straightforward as this sounds, its import should not be minimized. It underscores the significance of what Patricia Hill Collins refers to as "two types of knowing—knowledge and wisdom" (p. 209). Thus "individuals who have lived through the experiences about which they claim to be experts are more believable and credible than those who have merely read or thought about such experience" (p. 209). This particular stance means the life of an academic often is treated with skepticism unless it can be supplemented with real life experiences.

In my own work, I have attempted to work with people in settings with which I have had some familiarity. Thus my work with successful teachers of African American children was conducted in a community with schools very similar to ones where I have worked and lived. My experiences, although unique to my life, lend credibility to my work. I, too, have struggled to be a successful teacher of African American students. I have confronted some of the same bureaucratic, institutional, and structural challenges that the teachers in my research do. Our shared experience as teachers with analogous situations made entree into this setting, with these participants, easier and faster.

The Use of Dialogue in Assessing Knowledge Claims

In this dimension, Collins points to the importance of creating equal status relationships via dialogue. "Dialogue implies talk between two subjects, not the speech of subject and object. It is a humanizing speech, one that challenges and resists domination" (p. 212).[12] By "talking with" rather than "talking to" other black women, African American women have the opportunity to deconstruct the specificity of their own experiences and make connections between and among those that are more representative of collective experiences of black women. This give and take of dialogue makes struggling together to make meaning a powerful experience of self-definition and self-discovery (recovery).[13] Dialogue was the hallmark of my investigation with successful teachers of African American students. Initially, my conversations with parents to locate the teachers meant I had to talk "with" the parents to get their candid impressions of which teachers were most successful with African American students. Subsequently, I entered into dialogue with each teacher as a part of the ethnographic interviews,[14] and later in our conversations about her teaching, and finally as we met together to view videotaped examples of each teacher's teaching. In our full group meetings—the research collective—we participated in lively discussions and dialogue that reflected African American linguistic style. Our talk was filled with overlapping speech, interruptions, Black English Vernacular (BEV) expressions and syntax. Unlike a recitation where the teacher (or leader) "lobs" a question and the student fires back an answer—something like a tennis match—we participated in a more diffuse, collective questioning and answering. Perhaps the best metaphor would be, more like a volleyball game. Someone might "serve" up a question and it got "batted around" several times before another question emerged. Question asking and answering were a shared responsibility. The researcher was not privileged to pose and determine the questions while the "researched" answered.

The Ethic of Caring

Although some white feminists have identified the ethic of caring[15] as an aspect of women's scholarship, Collins reiterates its centrality to black women's lives (and scholarship): "[T]he ethic of caring suggests that personal expressiveness, emotions, and empathy are central to the knowledge validation process" (p. 215). Collins further points out that these convergent notions of white and black women about caring do not negate its importance in developing and understanding an Afrocentric feminist epistemology.

In my research with successful teachers of African American students, I needed to demonstrate a level of caring for and about the teachers. I was asking them for unlimited access to their classrooms as well as posing hard questions about their practice. Because their community often had been under the scholarly gaze of the research community, I had to demonstrate genuine caring to guarantee their continued participation. Several ways that I attempted to demonstrate an ethic of caring were by listening to the teachers throughout the process, sharing every aspect of the process and documentation, and religiously guarding their identities and their privacy.

The Ethic of Personal Accountability

The final dimension of Patricia Hill Collins's theoretical position suggests that knowledge claims must be grounded in individual character, values, and ethics. While the dispassionate, "objective," white, masculinist discourse allows people with radically differing public positions to socialize and mingle in private, a black feminist epistemology argues that private qualities have bearing on public standpoints. Thus not only what was said but who said it gives meaning and interpretation to knowledge claims.

How then do I, an African American female scholar, meld the disparate pieces of my own schooling experiences with the persistent crises of black intellectuals and the particular dilemmas of black women scholars? For the most part, my work has been an attempt to explain myself. Despite the wide acceptance (or at least recognition) of the cultural ecological model[16] which posits an explanation of African American school failure, my own life is testimony to alternative explanations for African American school achievement. Thus my work has been an attempt to reorient the thinking about African American school performance away from failure and deficit to a proactive pragmatism grounded in the successful practices of exemplary teachers of African American students.[17] I am compelled to engage in this work for personal as well as public reasons. As a parent who has had to help her children negotiate the uneven and precarious terrain of public schooling, I am dismayed to see how regularly African American children are assumed to lack the "appropriate tools" (read intelligence).

> "Oh, don't tell me you've got Kevin in your class," remarked a teacher in the teachers' lounge. "What's wrong with him, is he a problem?" "Oh, no, he's actually a very nice kid, but that mother!" My information comes from a friend who was listening in on that conversation. Yes, I am that mother, a title I wear with distinction because it tells people not to "mess over" my children. Unfortunately, I cannot be that mother for every child and the specialized treatment I am able to broker for my own children never impacts the children of those parents who are too tired, too intimidated, or too unfamiliar with school procedures to challenge the negative perceptions held by too many teachers.

I need to do the kind of research that will help make the system more equitable and just. Thus one of the earliest questions the decision to conduct this kind of research evoked was, "How do you capture 'pedagogical excellence'?"[18] A meta-question within a black women's epistemology was, "How do you capture it in ways that are consistent with the cultural values and ethos of a particular community?" As a member of the African American community[19] I felt comfortable about the nature of my research, but I treaded carefully regarding the way I conducted it.[20]

Initially I began talking with African American parents about who they thought were excellent teachers for their children. I chose African American churches as the places where I might find numbers of African American parents who might be willing to talk with me. While the parents were used to and comfortable with the idea of talking about teachers, several seemed surprised that their suggestions were to be taken seriously. However, my recollections about parents, in general, and African American parents, in particular, were that they had keen insights about teachers and teaching. Even when parents were unaware of pedagogical and curriculum innovations, their ability to talk about the interpersonal and subtle aspects of school–home relations helped them make evaluations that served their purposes.

The parents took their role as assessors of teacher "goodness" very seriously. They offered examples of teacher behaviors and interactions, comparative data (for example, comparing siblings' and other relatives' experiences), and levels of improved student achievement as evidence for the kinds of recommendations they made. Some common threads among the teachers they recommended were teachers who "respected them" and believed that they knew something about what was best for their children. They reported that when their children were in these "good" teachers' classrooms, they demonstrated an enthusiasm for school and what the parents termed a "good attitude" toward school and learning.

By the time I was able to meet with and talk to the identified teachers, I had rethought the way I was to conduct this research several times.[21] How could I learn about teachers' expertise without the teachers' participating in the project beyond the data collection and into the analysis and interpretation? I realized that I could not. Now, instead of a project where I interviewed, observed, and videotaped teachers and, subsequently, retreated to the solitude of my office where I would reconstruct the teachers' experiences and say for them what they were doing and why, I was now considering a different tack.

At the analysis stage of the project, I convened the teachers to create a "research collaborative." Instead of my telling teachers what they were doing (and, perhaps, why they were doing it), I employed a modified version of the group conversation[22] method" designed, in Joyce King and Carolyn Mitchell's words, to "reduce social tension . . . and help participants identify shared experiences and to facilitate the discussion of highly personal or deeply felt emotional issues" (p. 3).

Over the next two years I listened and learned from expert teachers whose practice I had observed, videotaped, and discussed with them on an individual basis. But here in this intimate group setting, teachers talked, agreed, disagreed, laughed, and almost cried. Even though they were not all African American teachers (five of the eight participants were African American, three were white), the African American teachers took a leadership role in the discussion. The form, pace, and style of their conversations were similar to African American informal speech. Throughout the conversations participants talked in an overlapping style—interrupting, completing each other's sentences. Their conversational pattern reminded me of a novice white teacher who had worked in their district and indicated that she could not organize her students into cooperative groups because "they just talk too much." She went on to say, "I guess it's cultural, because the black teachers talk all the time too!" Despite her pejorative way of expressing it, this white teacher had observed that oral expression was valued in this community. Their "talking all the time" was, for me, a research heaven.

As I listened, both during their conversations and during transcription, I marveled at the ways they melded their lives as teachers and as vital members of their communities. I was reminded of my own teachers who seemed also to work in ways that were consistent with the lives they led. Their ability to "make sense" of the two worlds in which they lived reminded me of disjunctures in my own life. I wanted to do academic work and be a committed advocate for my community. Would that advocacy compromise my research? Would my biases mean that I would not have the capacity to recognize the problems as well as the strengths of my community? Would my work gain acceptance in the academy if I pursued my work in this way? Why was I even asking myself these questions?

The academy is shaped by many social forces. More women of color are defining and redefining their roles within it. New ways of thinking about teaching and research have provided spaces for women scholars to challenge old assumptions about what it means to be in the academy.[23] While both the women's movement and the black studies movement have helped increase the parameters of academic work, new paradigms emerging from black women's scholarship provide me with a liberatory lens through which to view and construct my scholarly life. The academy and my scholarly life need not be in conflict with the community and cultural work I do (and intend to do).

In some ways my coming to terms with my scholarly life and my personal/cultural life is not unlike coming to terms with the dual identity of African American-ness. Growing up in the segregated 1950s and early 1960s, one could not escape the derogation and denigration of Africa (and blackness). That was not an identity many embraced with ease. Even though my fifth-grade teacher had worked to correct the prevalent images, still I was assaulted by images of Africa as a "dark" continent and its inhabitants as "primitive" and "uncivilized." It was not unto the pride-filled civil rights era that I, like many others, began to understand the ways Africa's reality had been systematically denied and distorted. To affirm our newfound heritage we wore our hair in huge natural crowns and adorned our bodies with African fabrics. We declared that black was beautiful and made peace with the history and heritage that had been stolen by others and hidden by our own. We were Africans, but were we Americans?

Coming to terms with my American-ness was another matter. How could one feel a civic (or even personal) commitment to a nation that rejected you? You were not wanted in its schools, could not sit at its dime-store lunch counters, and could not try on a hat in its department stores. How could you "pledge allegiance" when you had seen the men in your life serve in the armed services, only to be subjected to various and sundry humiliations at the hands of local police officers? How could you think "my country, 'tis of thee" when there were no representations of you (particularly of you as a black female) in any aspect of public life? But to think that I led a miserable life, horribly scarred by racism, would be a mistake. My life was perhaps more safe, secure, and nurturing than my own children's. My sense of belonging within my community was apparent. I did not lament not being accepted by America. I imagine the feeling was mutual.

However, with time and maturity I began to understand that without the profound impact of Africans (and African Americans) on this nation, there may not have been an America as we know it. My claim to this country is as legitimate as anyone's. But we are in an era when contestation over what it means to be an American is at the center of our public debate. I have come to understand that my African-ness does not diminish my American-ness and vice versa. My identity is not an either/or proposition. Rather, it is both/and. In the same way my scholarship and my personal/cultural life are not either/or propositions. I do scholarly work that both challenges and enhances my personal/cultural life. I live a personal/cultural life that challenges and enhances my scholarly work. I am a "colored girl" who has attempted to make life in the academy satisfying and meaningful "enuf."

Notes

1. Ntozake Shange's "choreopoem," *For colored girls who have considered suicide when the rainbow's not enuf*, brought the African American woman's experiences and perspectives to life for the theater-going public.
2. The notion of "mutuality"—a reciprocal relationship in a network of social obligation—is discussed by Joyce Elaine King and Carolyn Ann Mitchell in *Black Mothers to Sons: Juxtaposing African American Literature With Social Practice* as a key feature of African American cultural values and by Patricia Hill Collins in *Black Feminist Thought: Knowledge, Consciousness, and the Politics of Empowerment*.
3. The currently accepted term *African American* was not in use during my graduate school years. The term *Afro-American*, or *Afro-Am*, was commonly used on many campuses.
4. I borrow the term *public intellectual*, its use and meaning, from my colleague and friend, Joyce E. King.
5. Ishmael Reed, in his novel *Japanese by Spring*, has a black character, Professor Puttbutt, who exemplifies this bourgeois model.
6. For a discussion of the current debate about African American scholars and postmodernism, see *The Black Scholar* (October-November 1993), which contains a special section on the "multicultural debate."
7. See, for example, Code, 1991; Arnot, 1982; and Martin, 1982.
8. For a discussion of "dual otherness," see Dubois, [1903] 1989.
9. Guy-Sheftall, 1993.
10. Brewer, 1993.
11. See, for example, Bettleheim, 1968; Bloom, Davis, and Hess, 1965; and Ornstein, 1971.
12. hooks, cited in Collins, 1990.
13. hooks, 1993.
14. Spradley, 1979.
15. Noddings, 1984.
16. Ogbu, 1978, 1987.
17. Ladson-Billings, 1994.
18. Ladson-Billings, 1990.
19. I do not want to suggest that there is one monolithic African American community. By identifying myself as a "member" I am suggesting that I see African Americans as my primary cultural group and believe there are a number of values, beliefs, attitudes, linguistic styles, expressive styles, etc., that we hold in common.
20. This concern over methodology emanated from my awareness that many African American communities have participated in research (both willingly and unwittingly) that has ill-served them. Thus research that is designed allegedly to help African Americans has been constructed to maintain stereotypes and distortions about the nature of the community. I was decidedly conscious of the need to be respectful and in a "learner mode" throughout the research process.
21. After talking with the parents, I also talked with school principals. Teachers whose names appeared on both the parents' and principals' lists were invited to participate in the study.
22. DuBois and Li, 1971.
23. Examples include Weiler, 1988, and Lather, 1986.

Bibliography

Achebe, Chinua. 1958. *Things Fall Apart*. London: Heinemann.

Arnot, Madeleine. 1982. "Male Hegemony, Social Class, and Women's Education." *Journal of Education* 164: 64–89.

Bettleheim, Bruno. 1968. "Teaching the Disadvantaged." *National Educational Association Journal* 54: 8–12.

Bloom, Benjamin, Allison Davis, and Robert Hess. 1965. *Compensatory Education for Cultural Deprivation*. New York: Holt, Rinehart and Winston.

Brewer, Rose. 1993. "Theorizing Race, Class, and Gender: The New Scholarship of Black Feminist Intellectuals and Black Women's Labor." In *Theorizing Black Feminisms*, Stanlie M. James and Abena P. A. Busia, eds. New York: Routledge, 13–30.

Code, Lorraine 1991. *What Can She Know? Feminist Theory and the Construction of Knowledge*. Ithaca, NY: Cornell University Press.

Collins, Patricia Hill. 1991. *Black Feminist Thought: Knowledge, Consciousness, and the Politics of Empowerment*. New York: Routledge.

Cooper, Anna Julia. 1892. *A Voice from the South by a Black Woman of the South*. Ohio: Aldine.

Cruse, Harold. 1967. *The Crisis of the Negro Intellectual: From Its Origins to the Present*. New York: William Morrow.

Douglass, Frederick. [1845] 1973. *Narrative of the Life of Frederick Douglass, an American Slave*. New York: Anchor.

DuBois, Rachel Davis, and Mew-soong Li. 1971. *Reducing Social Tension and Conflict: The Group Conversation Method*. New York: Association.

DuBois, W. E. B. [1903] 1989. *The Souls of Black Folks*. New York: Penguin.

Ellison, Ralph. 1952. *The Invisible Man*. New York: Modern Library.

Fauset, Arthur. 1938. *Sojourner Truth, God's Faithful Pilgrim*. Chapel Hill: University of North Carolina Press.

Guy-Sheftall, Beverly. 1993. "A Black Feminist Perspective on Transforming the Academy: The Case of Spelman College." In *Theorizing Black Feminisms*, Stanlie M. James and Abena P. A. Busia, eds. New York: Routledge, 77–89.

hooks, bell. 1989. *Talking Back: Thinking Feminist, Thinking Black*. Boston: South End.

hooks, bell. 1993. *Sisters of the Yam: Black Women and Self-Recovery*. Boston: South End.

Hull, Gloria T., Patricia Bell-Scott, and Barbara Smith, eds. 1982. *All the Women Are White, All the Blacks Are Men, but Some of Us Are Brave*. Old Westbury, NY: Feminist Press.

James, Stanlie M. 1993. Introduction to *Theorizing Black Feminisms: The Visionary Pragmatism of Black Women*, Stanlie M. James and Abena P. A. Busia, eds. New York: Routledge.

King, Joyce Elaine, and Carolyn Ann Mitchell. 1990. *Black Mothers to Sons: Juxtaposing African American Literature With Social Practice*. New York: Peter Lang.

Ladson-Billings, Gloria. 1990. "Like Lightning in a Bottle: Attempting to Capture the Pedagogical Excellence of Successful Teachers of Black Students." *International Journal of Qualitative Studies in Education* 3: 335–344.

Ladson-Billings, Gloria. 1994. *The Dreamkeepers: Successful Teachers for African American Students*. San Francisco: Jossey-Bass.

Lather, Patti. 1986. "Research as Praxis." *Harvard Educational Review* 56: 257–277.

Laye, Camara. 1954. *The Dark Child*, trans. James Kirkup, Ernest Jones, and Elaine Gottlieb. New York: Noonday.

Martin, Jane Roland. 1982. "Excluding Women From the Educational Realm." *Harvard Educational Review* 52: 133–148.

Mitchell, Jacqueline. 1982. "Reflections of a Black Social Scientist: Some Struggles, Some Doubts, Some Hopes." *Harvard Educational Review* 52: 27–44.

"The Multicultural Debate." 1993. *The Black Scholar* 23 (3–4): 48–80.

Noddings, Nel. 1984. *Caring: A Feminine Approach to Ethics and Moral Education*. Berkeley: University of California Press.

Ogbu, John. 1978. *Minority Education and Caste: The American System in Cross-Cultural Perspective*. New York: Academic Press.

Ogbu, John. 1987. "Variability in Minority School Performance: A Problem in Search of an Explanation." *Anthropology and Educational Quarterly* 18: 312–334.

Ornstein, Alan. 1971. "The Need for Research on Teaching the Disadvantaged." *The Journal of Negro Education* 40: 133–139.

Reed, Ishmael. 1993. *Japanese by Spring*. New York: Atheneum.

Shange, Ntozake. *For colored girls who have considered suicide when the rainbow's not enuf: A Choreopoem*. New York: Macmillan, 1977.

Spradley, James P. 1979. *The Ethnographic Interview*. New York: Holt, Rinehart and Winston.

Stowe, Harriet Beecher. 1938. *Uncle Tom's Cabin: Or, Life Among the Lowly*. Garden City, NY: Nelson Doubleday.

Weller, Kathleen. 1988. *Women Teaching for Change*. New York: Bergin and Garvey.

West, Cornel. 1993. *Keeping Faith*. New York: Routledge.

Woodson, Carter G. 1993. *The Miseducation of the Negro*. Washington, DC: Association.

Learning from Our Lives: Women, Research, and Autobiography in Education, Copyright © 1997 by Teachers College, Columbia University. All rights reserved. ISBN 0-8077-3593-0 (pbk), ISBN 0-8077-3594-9 (cloth). Prior to photocopying items for classroom use, please contact the Copyright Clearance Center, Customer Service, 222 Rosewood Dr., Danvers, MA 01923, USA, tel. (508) 750-8400.

CHAPTER 24

WHO IS YOUR MOTHER?
Red Roots of White Feminism

PAULA GUNN ALLEN

At Laguna Pueblo in New Mexico, "Who is your mother?" is an important question. At Laguna, one of several of the ancient Keres gynocratic societies of the region, your mother's identity is the key to your own identity. Among the Keres, every individual has a place within the universe—human and nonhuman—and that place is defined by clan membership. In turn, clan membership is dependent on matrilineal descent. Of course, your mother is not only that woman whose womb formed and released you—the term refers in every individual case to an entire generation of women whose psychic, and consequently physical, "shape" made the psychic existence of the following generation possible. But naming your own mother (or her equivalent) enables people to place you precisely within the universal web of your life, in each of its dimensions: cultural, spiritual, personal, and historical.

Among the Keres, "context" and "matrix" are equivalent terms, and both refer to approximately the same thing as knowing your derivation and place. Failure to know your mother, that is, your position and its attendant traditions, history, and place in the scheme of things, is failure to remember your significance, your reality, your right relationship to earth and society. It is the same thing as being lost—isolated, abandoned, self-estranged, and alienated from your own life. This importance of tradition in the life of every member of the community is not confined to Keres Indians; all American Indian Nations place great value on traditionalism.

The Native American sense of the importance of continuity with one's cultural origins runs counter to contemporary American ideas: in many instances, the immigrants to America have been eager to cast off cultural ties, often seeing their antecedents as backward, restrictive, even shameful. Rejection of tradition constitutes one of the major features of American life, an attitude that reaches far back into American colonial history and that now is validated by virtually every cultural institution in the country. Feminist practice, at least in the cultural artifacts the community values most, follows this cultural trend as well.

The American idea that the best and the brightest should willingly reject and repudiate their origins leads to an allied idea—that history, like everything in the past, is of little value and should be forgotten as quickly as possible. This all too often causes us to reinvent the wheel continually. We find ourselves discovering our collective pasts over and over, having to retake ground already covered by women in the preceding decades and centuries. The Native American view, which highly values maintenance of traditional customs, values, and perspectives, might result in slower societal change and in quite a bit less social upheaval, but it has the advantage of providing a solid sense of identity and lowered levels of psychological and interpersonal conflict.

Reprinted from *The Graywolf Annual Five: Multicultural Literacy,* edited by R. Simonson & S. Walker, 1988. Copyright © 1988 Graywolf Press.

Contemporary Indian communities value individual members who are deeply connected to the traditional ways of their people, even after centuries of concerted and brutal effort on the part of the American government, the churches, and the corporate system to break the connections between individuals and their tribal world. In fact, in the view of the traditionals, rejection of one's culture—one's traditions, language, people—is the result of colonial oppression and is hardly to be applauded. They believe that the roots of oppression are to be found in the loss of tradition and memory because that loss is always accompanied by a loss of a positive sense of self. In short, Indians think it is important to remember, while Americans believe it is important to forget.

The traditional Indians' view can have a significant impact if it is expanded to mean that the sources of social, political, and philosophical thought in the Americas not only should be recognized and honored by Native Americans but should be embraced by American society. If American society judiciously modeled the traditions of the various Native Nations, the place of women in society would become central, the distribution of goods and power would be egalitarian, the elderly would be respected, honored, and protected as a primary social and cultural resource, the ideals of physical beauty would be considerably enlarged (to include "fat," strong-featured women, gray-haired, and wrinkled individuals, and others who in contemporary American culture are viewed as "ugly"). Additionally, the destruction of the biota, the life sphere, and the natural resources of the planet would be curtailed, and the spiritual nature of human and nonhuman life would become a primary organizing principle of human society. And if the traditional tribal systems that are emulated included pacifist ones, war would cease to be a major method of human problem solving.

Re-membering Connections and Histories

The belief that rejection of tradition and of history is a useful reponse to life is reflected in America's amazing loss of memory concerning its origins in the matrix and context of Native America. America does not seem to remember that it derived its wealth, its values, its food, much of its medicine, and a large part of its "dream" from Native America. It is ignorant of the genesis of its culture in this Native American land, and that ignorance helps to perpetuate the long-standing European and Middle Eastern monotheistic, hierarchical, patriarchal cultures' oppression of women, gays, and lesbians, people of color, working class, unemployed people, and the elderly. Hardly anyone in America speculates that the constitutional system of government might be as much a product of American Indian ideas and practices as of colonial American and Anglo-European revolutionary fervor.

Even though Indians are officially and informally ignored as intellectual movers and shapers in the United States, Britain, and Europe, they are peoples with ancient tenure on this soil. During the ages when tribal societies existed in the Americas largely untouched by patriarchal oppression, they developed elaborate systems of thought that included science, philosophy, and government based on a belief in the central importance of female energies, autonomy of individuals, cooperation, human dignity, human freedom, and egalitarian distribution of status, goods, and services. Respect for others, reverence for life, and, as a by-product, pacifism as a way of life; importance of kinship ties in the customary ordering of social interaction; a sense of the sacredness and mystery of existence; balance and harmony in relationships both sacred and secular were all features of life among the tribal confederacies and nations. And in those that lived by the largest number of these principles, gynarchy was the norm rather than the exception. Those systems are as yet unmatched in any contemporary industrial, agrarian, or postindustrial society on earth.

There are many female gods recognized and honored by the tribes and Nations. Femaleness was highly valued, both respected and feared, and all social institutions reflected this attitude. Even modern sayings, such as the Cheyenne statement that a people is not conquered until the hearts of the women are on the ground, express the Indians' understanding that without the power of woman the people will not live, but with it, they will endure and prosper.

Indians did not confine this belief in the central importance of female energy to matters of worship. Among many of the tribes (perhaps as many as 70 percent of them in North America alone), this belief was reflected in all of their social institutions. The Iroquois Constitution or White Roots of Peace, also called the Great Law of the Iroquois, codified the Matrons' decision-making and economic power:

> The lineal descent of the people of the Five Fires [the Iroquois Nations] shall run in the female line. Women shall be considered the progenitors of the Nation. They shall own the land and the soil. Men and women shall follow the status of their mothers. (Article 44)
>
> The women heirs of the chieftainship titles of the League shall be called Oiner or Otinner [Noble] for all time to come. (Article 45)
>
> If a disobedient chief persists in his disobedience after three warnings [by his female relatives, by his male relatives, and by one of his fellow council members, in that order], the matter shall go to the council of War Chiefs. The Chiefs shall then take away the title of the erring chief *by order of the women in whom the title is vested.* When the chief is deposed, the women shall notify the chiefs of the League ... and the chiefs of the League shall sanction the act. The women will then select another of their sons as a candidate and the chiefs shall elect him. (Article 19) (Emphasis mine)[1]

The Matrons held so much policy-making power traditionally that once, when their position was threatened they demanded its return, and consequently the power of women was fundamental in shaping the Iroquois Confederation sometime in the sixteenth or early seventeenth century. It was women

> who fought what may have been the first successful feminist rebellion in the New World. The year was 1600, or thereabouts, when these tribal feminists decided that they had had enough of unregulated warfare by their men. Lysistratas among the Indian women proclaimed a boycott on lovemaking and childbearing. Until the men conceded to them the power to decide upon war and peace, there would be no more warriors. Since the men believed that the women alone knew the secret of childbirth, the rebellion was instantly successful.

In the Constitution of Deganawidah the founder of the Iroquois Confederation of Nations had said: "He caused the body of our mother, the woman, to be of great worth and honor. He purposed that she shall be endowed and entrusted with the birth and upbringing of men, and that she shall have the care of all that is planted by which life is sustained and supported and the power to breathe is fortified: *and moreover that the warriors shall be her assistants.*"

The footnote of history was curiously supplied when Susan B. Anthony began her "Votes for Women" movement two and a half centuries later. Unknowingly the feminists chose to hold their founding convention of latter-day suffragettes in the town of Seneca [Falls], New York. The site was just a stone's throw from the old council house where the Iroquois women had plotted their feminist rebellion. (Emphasis mine)[2]

Beliefs, attitudes, and laws such as these became part of the vision of American feminists and of other human liberation movements around the world. Yet feminists too often believe that no one has ever experienced the kind of society that empowered women and made that empowerment the basis of its rules of civilization. The price the feminist community must pay because it is not aware of the recent presence of gynarchical societies on this continent is unnecessary confusion, division, and much lost time.

The Root of Oppression is Loss of Memory

An odd thing occurs in the minds of Americans when Indian civilization is mentioned: little or nothing. As I write this, I am aware of how far removed my version of the roots of American feminism must seem to those steeped in either mainstream or radical versions of feminism's history. I am keenly aware of the lack of image Americans have about our continent's recent past. I am intensely conscious of popular notions of Indian women as beasts of burden, squaws, traitors, or, at best, vanished denizens of a long-lost wilderness. How odd, then, must my contention seem that the gynocratic tribes of the American continent provided the basis for all the dreams of liberation that characterize the modern world.

We as feminists must be aware of our history on this continent. We need to recognize that the same forces that devastated the gynarchies of Britain and the Continent also devastated the ancient African civilizations, and we must know that those same materialistic, antispiritual forces are presently engaged in wiping out the same gynarchical values, along with the peoples who adhere to them, in Latin America. I am convinced that those wars were and continue to be about the imposition of patriarchal civilization over the holistic, pacifist, and spirit-based gynarchies they supplant. To that end the wars of imperial conquest have not been solely or even mostly waged over the land and its resources, but they have been fought within the bodies, minds, and hearts of the people of the earth for dominion over them. I think this is the reason traditionals say we must remember our origins, our cultures, our histories, our mothers and grandmothers, for without that memory, which implies continuance rather than nostalgia, we are doomed to engulfment by a paradigm that is fundamentally inimical to the vitality, autonomy, and self-empowerment essential for satisfying, high-quality life.

The vision that impels feminists to action was the vision of the Grandmothers' society, the society that was captured in the words of the sixteenth-century explorer Peter Martyr nearly five hundred years ago. It is the same vision repeated over and over by radical thinkers of Europe and America, from François Villon to John Locke, from William Shakespeare to Thomas Jefferson, from Karl Marx to Friedrich Engels, from Benito Juarez to Martin Luther King, from Elizabeth Cady Stanton to Judy Grahn, from Harriet Tubman to Audre Lorde, from Emma Goldman to Bella Abzug, from Malinalli to Cherrie Moraga, and from Iyatiku to me. That vision as Martyr told it is of a country where there are "no soldiers, no gendarmes or police, no nobles, kings, regents, prefects, or judges, no prisons, no lawsuits . . . All are equal and free," or so Friedrich Engels recounts Martyr's words.[3]

Columbus wrote:

> Nor have I been able to learn whether they [the inhabitants of the islands he visited on his first journey to the New World] held personal property, for it seemed to me that whatever one had, they all took shares of . . . They are so ingenuous and free with all they have, that no one would believe it who has not seen it; of anything that they possess, if it be asked of them, they never say no; on the contrary, they invite you to share it and show as much love as if their hearts went with it.[4]

At least that's how the Native Caribbean people acted when the whites first came among them; American Indians are the despair of social workers, bosses, and missionaries even now because of their deeply ingrained tendency to spend all they have, mostly on others. In any case, as the historian William Brandon notes,

> the Indian *seemed* free, to European eyes, gloriously free, to the European soul shaped by centuries of toil and tyranny, and this impression operated profoundly on the process of history and the development of America. Something in the peculiar character of the Indian world gave an impression of classlessness, of propertylessness, and that in turn led to an impression, as H. H. Bancroft put it, of "humanity unrestrained . . . in the exercise of liberty absolute."[5]

A Feminist Heroine

Early in the women's suffrage movement, Eva Emery Dye, an Oregon suffragette, went looking for a heroine to embody her vision of feminism. She wanted a historical figure whose life would symbolize the strengthened power of women. She found Sacagawea (or Sacajawea) buried in the journals of Lewis and Clark. The Shoshoni teenager had traveled with the Lewis and Clark expedition, carrying her infant son, and on a small number of occasions acted as translator.[6]

Dye declared that Sacagawea, whose name is thought to mean Bird Woman, had been the guide to the historic expedition, and through Dye's work Sacagawea became enshrined in American memory as a moving force and friend of the whites, leading them in the settlement of western North America.[7]

But Native American roots of white feminism reach back beyond Sacagawea. The earliest white women on this continent were well acquainted with tribal women. They were neighbors to a number of tribes and often shared food, information, child care, and health care. Of course little is made of these encounters in official histories of colonial America, the period from the Revolution to the Civil War, or on the evermoving frontier. Nor, to my knowledge, has either the significance or incidence of intermarriage between Indian and white or between Indian and Black been explored. By and large, the study of Indian-white relations has been focused on government and treaty relations, warfare, missionization, and education. It has been almost entirely documented in terms of formal white Christian patriarchal impacts and assaults on Native Americans, though they are not often characterized as assaults but as "civilizing the savages." Particularly in organs of popular culture and miseducation, the focus has been on what whites imagine to be degradation of Indian women ("squaws"), their equally imagined love of white government and white conquest ("princesses"), and the horrifyingly misleading, fanciful tales of "bloodthirsty, backward primitives" assaulting white Christian settlers who were looking for life, liberty, and happiness in their chosen land.

But, regardless of official versions of relations between Indians and whites or other segments of the American population, the fact remains that great numbers of apparently "white" or "Black" Americans carry notable degrees of Indian blood. With that blood has come the culture of the Indians, informing the lifestyles, attitudes, and values of their descendants. Somewhere along the line—and often quite recently—an Indian woman was giving birth to and raising the children of a family both officially and informally designated as white or Black—not Indian. In view of this, it should be evident that one of the major enterprises of Indian women in America has been the transfer of Indian values and culture to as large and influential a segment of American immigrant populations as possible. Their success in this endeavor is amply demonstrated in the Indian values and social styles that increasingly characterize American life. Among these must be included "permissive" childrearing practices, for imprisoning, torturing, caning, strapping, starving, or verbally abusing children was considered outrageous behavior. Native Americans did not believe that physical or psychological abuse of children would result in their edification. They did not believe that children are born in sin, are congenitally predisposed to evil, or that a good parent who wishes the child to gain salvation, achieve success, or earn the respect of her or his fellows can be helped to those ends by physical or emotional torture.

The early Americans saw the strongly protective attitude of the Indian people as a mark of their "savagery"—as they saw the Indian's habit of bathing frequently, their sexual openness, their liking for scant clothing, their raucous laughter at most things, their suspicion and derision of authoritarian structures, their quick pride, their genuine courtesy, their willingness to share what they had with others less fortunate than they, their egalitarianism, their ability to act as if various lifestyles were a normal part of living, and their granting that women were of equal or, in individual cases, of greater value than men.

Yet the very qualities that marked Indian life in the sixteenth century have, over the centuries since contact between the two worlds occurred, come to mark much of contemporary American life. And those qualities, which I believe have passed into white culture from Indian culture, are the very ones that fundamentalists, immigrants from Europe, the Middle East, and Asia often find the most reprehensible. Third- and fourth-generation Americans indulge in growing nudity, informality in social relations, egalitarianism, and the rearing of women who value autonomy, strength, freedom, and personal dignity—and who are often derided by European, Asian, and Middle Eastern men for those qualities. Contemporary Americans value leisure almost as much as tribal people do. They find themselves increasingly unable to accept child abuse as a reasonable way to nurture. They bathe more than any other industrial people on earth—much to the scorn of their white cousins across the Atlantic, and they sometimes enjoy a good laugh even at their own expense (though they still have a less developed sense of the ridiculous than one might wish).

Contemporary Americans find themselves more and more likely to adopt a "live and let live" attitude in matters of personal sexual and social styles. Two-thirds of their diet and a large share of their medications and medical treatments mirror or are directly derived from Native American sources. Indianization is not a simple concept, to be sure, and it is one that Americans often find themselves resisting; but it is a process that has taken place, regardless of American resistance to recognizing the source of many if not most of American's vaunted freedoms in our personal, family, social, and political arenas.

This is not to say that Americans have become Indian in every attitude, value, or social institution. Unfortunately, Americans have a way to go in learning how to live in the world in ways that improve the quality of life for each individual while doing minimal damage to the biota, but they have adapted certain basic qualities of perception and certain attitudes that are moving them in that direction.

An Indian-Focused Version of American History

American colonial ideas of self-government came as much from the colonists' observations of tribal governments as from their Protestant or Greco-Roman heritage. Neither Greece nor Rome had the kind of pluralistic democracy as that concept has been understood in the United States since Andrew Jackson, but the tribes, particularly the gynarchical tribal confederacies, did. It is true that the *oligarchic* form of government that colonial Americans established was originally based on Greco-Roman systems in a number of important ways, such as its restriction of citizenship to propertied white males over twenty-one years of age, but it was never a form that Americans as a whole have been entirely comfortable with. Politics and government in the United States during the Federalist period also reflected the English common-law system as it had evolved under patriarchal feudalism and monarchy—hence the United States' retention of slavery and restriction of citizenship to propertied white males.

The Federalists did make one notable change in the feudal system from which their political system derived on its Anglo side. They rejected blooded aristocracy and monarchy. This idea came from the Protestant Revolt to be sure, but it was at least reinforced by colonial America's proximity to American Indian nonfeudal confederacies and their concourse with those confederacies over the two hundred years of the colonial era. It was this proximity and concourse that enabled the revolutionary theorists to "dream up" a system in which all local polities would contribute to and be protected by a central governing body responsible for implementing policies that bore on the common interest of all. It should also be noted that the Reformation followed Columbus's contact with the Americas and that his and Martyr's reports concerning Native Americans' free and easy egalitarianism were in circulation by the time the Reformation took hold.

The Iroquois federal system, like that of several in the vicinity of the American colonies, is remarkably similar to the organization of the federal system of the United States. It was made up of local, "state," and federal bodies composed of executive, legislative, and judicial branches. The Council of Matrons was the executive: it instituted and determined general policy. The village, tribal (several villages), and Confederate councils determined and implemented policies when they did not conflict with the broader Council's decisions or with theological precepts that ultimately determined policy at all levels. The judicial was composed of the men's councils and the Matron's council, who sat together to make decisions. Because the matrons were the ceremonial center of the system, they were also the prime policymakers.

Obviously, there are major differences between the structure of the contemporary American government and that of the Iroquois. Two of those differences were and are crucial to the process of just government. The Iroquois system is spirit-based, while that of the United States is secular, and the Iroquois Clan Matrons formed the executive. The female executive function was directly tied to the ritual nature of the Iroquois politic, for the executive was lodged in the hands of the Matrons of particular clans across village, tribe, and national lines. The executive office was hereditary, and only sons of eligible clans could serve, at the behest of the Matrons of their clans, on the councils at the three levels. Certain daughters inherited the office of Clan Matron through their clan affiliations. No one could impeach or disempower a Matron, though her violation of certain laws could result in her ineligibility for the Matron's council. For example, a woman who married *and took her husband's name* could not hold the title Matron.

American ideals of social justice came into sharp focus through the commentaries of Iroquois observers who traveled in France in the colonial period. These observers expressed horror at the great gap between the lifestyles of the wealthy and the poor, remarking to the French philosopher Montaigne, who would heavily influence the radical communities of Europe, England, and America, that "they had noticed that in Europe there seemed to be two moities, consisting of the rich 'full gorged' with wealth, and the poor, starving 'and bare with need and povertie.' The Indian tourists not only marveled at the division, but marveled that the poor endured 'such an injustice, and that they took not the others by the throte, or set fire on their house.'"[8] It must be noted that the urban poor eventually did just that in the French Revolution. The writings of Montaigne and of those he influenced provided the theoretical framework and the vision that propelled the struggle for liberty, justice, and equality on the Continent and later throughout the British empire.

The feminist idea of power as it ideally accrues to women stems from tribal sources. The central importance of the clan Matrons in the formulation and determination of domestic and foreign policy as well as in their primary role in the ritual and ceremonial life of their respective Nations was the single most important attribute of the Iroquois, as of the Cherokee and Muskogee, who traditionally inhabited the southern Atlantic region. The latter peoples were removed to what is now Oklahoma during the Jackson administration, but prior to the American Revolution they had regular and frequent communication with and impact on both the British colonizers and later the American people, including the African peoples brought here as slaves.

Ethnographer Lewis Henry Morgan wrote an account of Iroquoian matriarchal culture, published in 1877,[9] that heavily influenced Marx and the development of communism, particularly lending it the idea of the liberation of women from patriarchal dominance. The early socialists in Europe, especially in Russia, saw women's liberation as a central aspect of the socialist revolution. Indeed, the basic ideas of socialism, the egalitarian distribution of goods and power, the peaceful ordering of society, and the right of every member of society to participate in the work and benefits of that society, are ideas that pervade American Indian political thought and action. And it is through various channels—the informal but deeply effective Indianization of Europeans, and christianizing Africans, the social and political theory of the confederacies feuding and then intertwining with European dreams of liberty and justice, and, more recently, the work of Morgan and the writings of Marx and Engels—that the age-old gynarchical systems of egalitarian government found their way into contemporary feminist theory.

When Eva Emery Dye discovered Sacagawea and honored her as the guiding spirit of American womanhood, she may have been wrong in bare historical fact, but she was quite accurate in terms of deeper truth. The statues that have been erected depicting Sacagawea as a Matron in her prime signify an understanding in the American mind, however unconscious, that the source of just government, of right ordering of social relationships, the dream of "liberty and justice for all" can be gained only by following the Indian Matrons' guidance. For, as Dr. Anna Howard Shaw said of Sacagawea at the National American Woman's Suffrage Association in 1905:

> Forerunner of civilization, great leader of men, patient and motherly woman, we bow our hearts to do you honor! ... May we the daughters of an alien race ... learn the lessons of calm endurance, of patient persistence and unfaltering courage exemplified in your life, in our efforts to lead men through the Pass of justice, which goes over the mountains of prejudice and conservatism to the broad land of the perfect freedom of a true republic; one in which men and women together shall in perfect equality solve the problems of a nation that knows no caste, no race, no sex in opportunity, in responsibility or in justice! May 'the eternal womanly' ever lead us on![10]

CHAPTER 25

A WOMAN OUT OF CONTROL:
DECONSTRUCTING SEXISM AND RACISM IN THE UNIVERSITY[1]

ROXANA NG

At the conclusion of a course I taught on minority groups and race relations, a male student brought a complaint against me, charging that I used the class as a platform for feminism. He claimed that as a "white male" he felt completely marginalized. This incident is not unique. In the first year I taught, a male student circulated a petition complaining to the administration that half the materials in my course on "cross-cultural education" contained references to women and gender relations. I was pleased that I had unwittingly achieved a balanced curriculum, but the student and the administration disagreed that this was desirable, and I was asked to change the contents for the remainder of the course (Ng 1991). On at least two other occasions, complaining (male) students have physically threatened me. Indeed, complaints of this kind about my courses' contents and my pedagogical methods have recurred during my ten years' teaching in the university.

The advice administrators and colleagues have given me concerning these incidents generally revolves around contents and styles: perhaps I can tone down my lectures somewhat; change to less controversial materials; acquire more teaching techniques; prepare better. (With reference to the course on "cross-cultural education," the administration suggested I use videos and let the students draw their own conclusions.) As I continued to analyze how gender, race, and class relations operate dynamically in interactional settings, however, I realized that what I experienced has less to do with my competence as a teacher than with who I am.

I am a feminist and a member of a racial minority. My scholarly work focuses on integrating analyses of gender with those of race and vice versa. My insistence on teaching ethnic and race relations with a feminist perspective, and on challenging Eurocentric assumptions in feminist theorizing, has consistently got me into trouble throughout my university teaching career.

Using a critical incident that occurred in one of the courses I teach, I want to draw attention, in this chapter, to how sexism and racism as *power dynamics* operate in everyday life to disempower feminist and other minority teachers. These dynamics, as we are discovering, affect how our formal authority is perceived and received by students, and, by extension, the degree to which we can be effective teachers, especially if our teaching challenges existing norms and forms of thinking and behavior in the classroom, in the university, and in society. (See, for example, in chronological order: Nielsen 1979; Heald 1989; Ng 1991; Hoodfar, this volume.)

Reprinted from *Radical In<Ter>ventions: Identity, Politics, and Difference/s in Educational Praxis*, edited by S. DeCastell & M. Bryson, 1997. Copyright © 1997 State University of New York Press.

In their introduction to a special issue of the *Canadian Journal of Education* on feminist pedagogy, Briskin and Coulter (1992) identified three power axes in the classroom: between teacher and students; between students and teacher, especially women and teachers who are women of color; and among students (257). Here I examine an additional power axis: between the minority teacher and her/his colleague(s) in relation to the handling of student complaints. I show how gender and race relations interact to undermine the authority and credibility of minority[2] faculty members, and I deconstruct the complexity of sexism and racism as interlocking relations operating in a specific situation to maintain the subordination and marginalization of minority teachers. The complex and multifaceted character of the critical incident on which I base my analysis illustrates the pervasiveness of sexism and racism and raises questions about the assumption of neutrality and fairness when university administrators and other staff members are asked to adjudicate complaints.

Although my discussion focuses on the teacher's experience, I suggest that other minority staff and students encounter similar situations, in which their experiences are frequently exacerbated because of their relative powerlessness in the university hierarchy. My discussion therefore raises issues about existing equity measures and about how to make the university more inclusive when people enter and participate in it as *unequal* subjects. In the conclusion, I propose an antisexist, antiracist approach to educational matters.

The Incident

Although I use one incident instead of a variety of examples, I am not treating it as typical or generalizable of similar types of situations. Following Dorothy Smith's (1987) method of problematizing the everyday world, my purpose here is to explicate the social organization that produced and reinforced my position as a gendered and racialized subject in the university. Here is how Smith puts it:

> If you've located an individual experience in the social relations which determine it, then although that individual experience might be idiosyncratic, the social relations are not idiosyncratic. [All experiences] are generated out of, and are aspects of the social relations of our time, of corporate capitalism. These social relations are discernible, although not fully present or explicable in the experiences of people whose lives, by reason of their membership in a capitalist society, are organized by capitalism. (quoted in Campbell n.d.)

The dynamics that partly shaped the interactions described in the incident involve relations of gender, race, and class. These relations, which I call "sexism" and "racism," are not peculiar to this incident but are rather relations that have developed over time in North America and elsewhere as groups of people have interacted. They have become systemic; that is, they are taken for granted and not ordinarily open to interrogation. In examining the incident, my intention is not to attribute blame or to identify victims, but to explicate the systemic character of sexism and racism as they are manifested in institutionalized interactional settings. I maintain that in so doing, we move away from treating these incidents as idiosyncratic, isolated "wrongdoing" perpetrated by a few individuals with attitudinal problems. Instead, we aim at a fundamental re-examination of the structures and relations of universities, which have marginalized and excluded certain groups of people historically and continue to do so despite equity measures implemented in the last ten years or so.

In this particular incident, a student (who identified himself as a "white,"[3] immigrant male) brought a complaint against me regarding a course I taught on minority groups and race relations, one of my primary teaching subjects in various universities since 1982.[4] In this kind of course, I always include discussions of women as a minority group and of race and gender dynamics. As I develop and refine these courses, I incorporate meditative and physical exercises, in addition to small group discussions, as a way to rupture standard modes of scholarly inquiry, which artificially separate body and soul from mind (Currie 1992). These courses are both stimulating and contentious, and although most students seem to enjoy them, I receive complaints every time I teach them. What I report here, then, is not unusual. It signals and pinpoints how approaches that deviate from the perceived norm of teaching can be threatening to and are resisted by students.

Interestingly, the student complainant attended classes for the first four or five weeks, then was absent until the third-last class. During that class, he became very agitated when, in our discussion on antiracist education, we included women's experiences of discrimination. At one point he became extremely angry, interrupted the discussion, and insisted on talking about something else. I interceded and brought the discussion back on track. I also pointed out that this kind of interruption and the ways male and female students reacted to it illustrated the gender dynamics we had been discussing for the past couple of weeks.[5]

The student did not come to the last two classes and complained to the administration about my teaching[6]—at a meeting I attended. During the meeting, he charged that the meditative and physical exercises I conducted (the reasons for which I had explained clearly) were completely inappropriate in a graduate class and that my course outline did not specify my feminist perspective. He further complained that the reading materials, which he had to pay for, were exclusively on feminism and not on race relations, which was untrue. I refused to enter into a debate about the reading materials and suggested that whether they were exclusively feminist was a matter open to examination. He then charged that I was using the course to advance a particular political agenda. He felt that in intercepting his disruption of the last class he had attended, I had marginalized him as a "white male."

Three times in the meeting he told the administrator I was "a woman out of control." When I pointed out that my perspective was very clearly disclosed during the first two classes (indeed, I encouraged students who did not like my approach to withdraw from the course), he turned to the administrator and said, "But I thought it was a phase she was going through. I didn't think that she would keep on like this when I returned after a five-week absence." He finally threatened to take me and the department to court for "false advertising." He told us that his girlfriend, a lawyer, was waiting outside.

During the entire meeting, the administrator maintained a neutral stance. At the end of the student's complaint, he asked the student what would have constituted an acceptable approach, given that we obviously had different perceptions about the course and how it was handled. The student replied that at a minimum he would have expected me to state my perspective explicitly in the course outline. I interjected at this point that if I was to make my perspective explicit, I would expect all my colleagues to do the same. The student replied, "But I don't have problems with other courses! I only have problems with yours." He added that he would ask "a gay" to make his perspective explicit also.[7]

After the student left, the administrator expressed sympathy but suggested I seriously consider the student's request. Apparently the issue of legality (students are getting more militant about the products we claim to deliver and the products we actually do deliver) had been raised at the senior level of the university administration. I declined consideration of the student's request about my course outline and suggested the matter should be raised formally in a faculty meeting.

Sexism and Racism as Systemic

Much work combating sexism and racism in the education system has emphasized attitudinal and curricular changes (for instance, prejudice awareness/reduction workshops; measures against sexual and racial harassment; introducing other cultures into the curriculum, especially under the rubric of multicultural education). These changes, important and necessary though they are, are based on what Mohanty (1990) has identified as a "liberal pluralist" conception of diversity. Mohanty points out that "the race industry" and prejudice-reduction workshops in universities reduce historical and institutional inequality to an individualist and psychological level:

> In focusing on "the healing of past wounds" this approach also equates the positions of dominant and subordinate groups, erasing all power inequities and hierarchies.... [T]he location of the source of "oppression" and "change" in individuals suggests an elision between ideological and structural understandings of power and domination and individual, psycho-

logical understandings of power. (Mohanty 1990, 198)

Whereas the institution of women's studies has brought about a radical rethinking of gender relations in society, especially in Western societies, this cannot be said of curricular reform on race. Frequently, attempts in this area take an additive approach, adding an article (or two) to existing materials. There has been insufficient reconceptualization of how race matters in the structuring of social experiences inside and outside the academy. Even more insidious and stifling is the frequency with which, as Mohanty has pointed out, members of minority groups (both faculty and students) are tokenized when racism is treated as an individualistic and attitudinal property. That means that

> specific "differences" (of personality, posture, behavior, etc.) of one woman of color stand in for the difference of the whole collective, and a collective voice is assumed in place of an individual voice.... [T]his results in the reduction or averaging of Third World peoples [for example] in terms of individual personality characteristics. (Mohanty 1990, 194)

This approach overlooks the fact that power dynamics, based on one's race, gender, ability, and other characteristics, operate in mundane, taken-for-granted, and "commonsense" ways. Thus, although attitudinal changes and multicultural education (for example) are necessary points of departure for creating an inclusive university, they do not address the embeddedness of sexism and racism as routine operation in the university.

I want to go beyond treating sexism and racism as if they reside only in certain individuals, to examine their *systemic* properties. I begin with the premise that sexism and racism are two systems of oppression and inequality based on the ideology of the superiority of one race and/or gender over others. Thus, "white" European men, especially those of British and sometimes French descent, will typically see themselves as superior to women and to people with other ethnic and racial origins. Systems of ideas and practices have been developed to justify and support this notion of superiority. In Canada these ideas and practices originate in colonization by the British and the French.[8] Over time, ideas about the superiority and inferiority of different groups become accepted ways of thinking and being. Certain behaviors and modes of operation are eventually taken for granted; they become ways of excluding those who do not belong to the dominant group(s).

This understanding is derived from Gramsci's analysis of ideology and of how certain ideas become hegemonic and "commonsensical" over time. Commonsense thinking is uncritical, episodic, and disjointed, but it is also powerful because it is taken for granted (Gramsci 1971, 321–43). Once an idea becomes common sense, it is no longer questioned. In applying Gramsci's historical discussion to racism in contemporary British society, Stuart Hall observes: "[Ideologies] work most effectively when we are not aware that how we formulate and construct a statement about the world is underpinned by ideological premises; when our formulations seem to be simply descriptive statements about how things are (i.e. must be), or of what we can 'take-for-granted' (Hall, quoted in Lawrence 1982, 46).

Collin Leys[9] suggests that when an ideology becomes completely normalized, it is embedded in language. Some examples of commonsense statements are: "Blacks are good at sports but not at academic subjects"; "Women are nurturing"; "Unemployed people are lazy." Although these ideas may originally have been developed by the dominant group, they have become ways cohorts of individuals are "normally" thought of; they are popularly held beliefs.

These normalized ways of thinking (frequently referred to as "stereotyping") have real and profound consequences for people's lives. In her ethnographic research on how high school students are streamed into vocational programs, Jackson found that Chinese boys were advised to go into vocational-stream accounting courses which effectively curtailed their entrance into university. This advice was based on guidance counselors' perception that these boys were good at math but not so good with language. Similarly, Chinese girls were routinely streamed into secretarial programs (Jackson 1987).

Let me give another example from my own research as illustration. My analysis (Ng 1992) of immigration policy reveals that when a household applies to Canada for landed immigrant status, usually only one member of the household is granted "independent" status; the other members are granted "family class" status. This classification system usually accords the man/husband, seen to be the household head, independent status, and designates the woman/wife and children family class immigrants. This system is based on the Western notion of the "nuclear family" with the man/husband being the head of the household; it ignores the facts that other societies have different family structures and that the wife and adult children make essential contributions to the household economy. Furthermore, since family class immigrants are seen as dependents, they are not eligible for state assistance (such as training subsidies) available to the household head. In an immigrant household, then, often the husband can receive such assistance, while the wife is ineligible by virtue of her classification, rendering her dependent on and subordinate to her husband. This is an instance of how sexism operates objectively and routinely in Canadian institutions and illustrates what I mean by "systemic" sexism.

Sexism and racism are systemic in that, routinized in institutions, they have become ways of thinking about and treating groups of people unequally as if these ideas and treatments are "normal"; they are "common sense" and thus not open to interrogation. These ways of doing things keep certain individuals and groups in dominant and subordinate positions, producing the structural inequality we see both in the education system and in the workplace.

Institutionalized sexism and racism are enacted in "everyday" interactions (Smith 1987). In the example of immigration policy above, when an immigration officer classifies people according to the law, she is implicated in the reinforcement of sexism in relation to the immigrant woman regardless of her "personal" attitude toward the person so classified. The way counselors stream Chinese boys and girls into "terminal" vocational programs is another case in point. Acts of sexism and racism, then, go beyond personal intentions and attitudes precisely because they are embedded in institutions and because individuals have different (and at times multiple and contradictory) locations within institutions. Sexism and racism are *power relations* that have crystallized in organizational actions in which we are implicated by virtue of our membership in institutions. We are not and cannot be exempted from them. To see sexism and racism as systemic, then, is to understand that power dynamics (including forms of inclusion and exclusion) permeate the settings in which we live and work. Knowing how these dynamics work can thus be a first step in eradicating sexism and racism.

In analyzing the specific incident introduced at the outset of this chapter, I want to draw attention to the more general interactional dimension of power relations operating as forms of exclusion and marginalization by recognizing that, in addition to our structural positions as students, faculty, and staff in the academy, we are, at the same time, gendered and racialized subjects. Our race and gender, as well as other socially and ideologically constructed characteristics, shape how we see ourselves and how we are seen. They affect, enable, and disable how we negotiate our ways through the university system.

I use "socially and ideologically constructed" to refer to the identification of biological, sexual, and other characteristics as absolute differences. The term "races," for example, is used to denote the supposed differences, based on skin color, brain size, and physical features, and so on, of conventionally differentiated groups of people. These differences, treated as "natural" and therefore immutable, are then used to justify the domination of one group over another. In fact, the construction of different groups as "races" varies historically and across societies (see Miles 1989; Ng 1989; 1993).

To see members of the university community as gendered and racialized subjects is to understand and to acknowledge that we are not created equal. The social structure of inequality on the basis of class, gender, race, ability, and so on, which leaks into and becomes integral to everyday life in the academy, means that we do not participate in the academy as equals.

Deconstructing the Incident

The incident cited above raises four central issues. First, it raises the issue of neutrality, objectivity, and fairness in adjudicating complaints about teaching that challenges societal norms. When dealing with these and other complaints, university administrators and staff frequently take a "neutral" and "objective" stance in the interest of "fairness." To be neutral is to adopt a disinterested position, to presume that people are equal or the same, and to overlook the inequalities that people embody as a result of their unique biographies and their social locations. This neutral stance is the cornerstone of the Western intellectual tradition, established by men to engender and safeguard their privilege and institutionalized in the academy, it is important to keep in mind, at a time when the university was the exclusive domain of certain classes of men.

Feminist scholarship has challenged the notion of objectivity and demonstrated that so-called objective universal knowledge is constructed by men for men (see Smith 1974; Spender 1980). Adrienne Rich (1976) contends that the "detachment" and "disinterest" that constitute objectivity in scientific inquiry are the terms men apply to their own subjectivity.[10] Mary O'Brien (1981) calls this "malestream" thought. Susan Bordo (1987) reminds us that the exclusive preoccupation with reason in scholarly pursuit is a product of Cartesian thinking, which creates an artificial dualism, separating the mind/intellect and the body/emotion. This idea that "truth" exists independent of the social and physical location of the knower is carried over to the adjudication of disputes in the university. But Martin and Mohanty (1986) point out, "The claim to a lack of identity or positionality is itself based on privilege, on a refusal to accept responsibility for one's implication in actual historical or social relations, on a denial that positionalities exist or that they matter, the denial of one's own personal history and the claim to a total separation from it" (208).

It is interesting and revealing that, in spite of (or because of?) our unequal structural positions, the administrator in the incident I recounted attempted to treat the student's complaint on "equal footing" with my course design and pedagogical methods and that he did not see anything out of the ordinary about a student calling a faculty member "a woman out of control." (If he did think this was peculiar, he chose to ignore it, since he did not mention it either during or after the meeting.) This *pretense* of fairness was immensely disempowering to me as a minority teacher, especially since the student deliberately adopted a tone that denigrated me. As Patricia Williams says, "If faculty do not treat women as colleagues, then students will not treat women as members of the faculty" (1991, 63). This example shows precisely how sexism is normalized in men's, and frequently women's, collective consciousness. The attempt at fairness in this instance reveals how men collude with each other, intentionally or unwittingly, to restore the status quo of male dominance (see also Burstyn 1985).[11]

The second issue the incident raises is that of student resistance. This is a complex issue because students resist for different and contradictory reasons: they resist curriculum that challenges the status quo, especially if they identify with the status quo; they resist because certain materials make them realize and reflect on their own oppression; they resist because both the contents and the teacher represent authority in power structures that marginalize them (consider, for instance, the youths in Willis' [1977] and McClaren's [1989] studies); they resist for other social and psychological reasons (see Lewis 1990) too numerous to list here. Here I draw attention to the challenges we encounter in the classroom because of *who we are* as gendered and racialized subjects. Challenges to male teachers, as a colleague observed when I discussed the above incident in a faculty meeting, are frequently directed at course materials, and disagreements are played out as intellectual debates. In the case of a minority faculty member, both course materials and the teacher become targets. As a member of a racial minority and a woman, I have no authority despite my formal position. But it is not only my authority that is at stake here. The knowledge I embody and transmit is also suspect—I *am* a woman out of control. The sexism and racism in this case are based not only on the student's attitude toward minorities in general; they are also based on his attitude toward minorities in positions of authority whose knowledge and expertise are dubious. In reflecting on her own teaching about women in the third world, Homa Hoodfar (this volume) reports on similar experiences. In one course, for example, Hoodfar reports that her knowledge was finally accepted by the students only when it was corroborated by her white female colleague, who gave a guest lecture on the position of women in Uganda.

Third, this incident raises the issue of language. In his outbursts both in the class and in the meeting with the administrator, the student asserted that I was marginalizing him as a "white male." His language use is instructive: as marginalized groups are included and incorporated into the academy, the mainstream is appropriating and subverting feminist and other liberatory discourses for use against the very groups who developed these discourses in the first place. Statements such as "I don't feel safe [or comfortable]" and "I feel silenced [or marginalized]" are now widely used to describe individuals' experiences. This is another instance of the individualization and trivialization of collective experiences;[12] it erases the inequality among people due to race, gender, class, sexual preference, ability, and so on, and reduces systemic inequality to personal feelings. Liberatory language is thus normalized, so that the "white" male student, feeling threatened because his taken-for-granted way of thinking and acting is challenged, can assert that he is "silenced" or "marginalized."

Finally, as universities are increasingly geared toward a consumer and corporate model (Newson and Buchbinder 1988), they have become marketplaces rather than places for people to interrogate existing knowledges and to create new ones. Although I believe that there must be accountability in teaching, and I recognize that students can be and have been shortchanged, I also know, having taught in universities for the last ten years, that student complaints are launched and threats of legal action are evoked in very specific situations: usually when a student is threatened by knowledges that rupture her commonsense understanding of the world. Threats of legality are intended to restore the status quo.[13] In the specific incident discussed above, the legal threat was a tactically clever move on the part of the student, and it bared his class position and his recognition that what was at issue here was power, which he knew he had as a white male and which he intended to use. Raising the possible legal consequences of my pedagogy captured the administrator's attention and summoned[14] him in his role as an administrator rather than as my colleague. That the student threatened legal action and that he received a neutral, if not sympathetic, hearing resulted from his subject position as a "white," articulate male who could invoke the law on his side.

Against the Grain: Combating Sexism and Racism in the University

To conclude, I want to explore how we may begin to combat sexism and racism in the university in light of my preceding conceptualization and analysis. I recommend that we try to think and act "against the grain"[15] in handling various kinds of pedagogical situations. To act against the grain requires one first to recognize that—and how—routinized courses of action and interactions within the university are imbued with unequal power distributions which produce and reinforce various forms of marginalization and exclusion. Thus, a commitment to redress these power relations involves interventions and actions that may appear "counter-intuitive."[16] We need to rupture ways university business and interactions are "normally" conducted.

In introducing the notion of working against the grain, obviously I am speaking not to those interested in preserving the status quo, but to the increasing numbers of groups and individuals who wish to make the university more inclusive of previously marginalized and disadvantaged groups (recognizing that they by no means represent a monolithic interest or position).

To work against the grain is to recognize that education is not neutral; it is contested. Mohanty (1990) points out that "education represents both a struggle for meaning and a struggle over power relations. [It is] a central terrain where power and politics operate out of the lived culture of individuals and groups situated in asymmetrical social and political positions" (184). We must develop a critical awareness of the power dynamics operating in institutional relations and of the fact that people participate in institutions as unequal subjects. To this end we must take an antisexist and antiracist approach to understanding and acting upon institutional relations, rather than overlooking the embeddedness of gender, race, class, and other forms of inequality that shape our interactions.

In her exploration of feminist pedagogy, Linda Briskin makes a clear distinction between nonsexist and antisexist education, a distinction which is critical to our understanding here. She asserts that nonsexism is an approach which attempts to neutralize sexual inequality by pretending that gender can be made irrelevant in the classroom (Briskin 1990a; 1990b). Thus, for instance, neither asserting that male and female students should have equal time to speak nor giving them equal time adequately rectifies the endemic problem of sexism in the classroom. One of Briskin's students reported that in her political science tutorials, when a male student spoke, everyone paid attention, but when a female student spoke, the class acted as if no one was speaking (Briskin 1990a, 13). Neutrality conceals the unequal distribution of power.

An antisexist and antiracist approach would acknowledge explicitly that we are all gendered, racialized, and differently constructed subjects who do not interact as equals. This goes beyond formulating sexism and racism in individualist terms and treating them as ("flawed") personal attitudes. Terry Wolverton (1983) discovered the difference between nonracism and antiracism in her consciousness-raising attempt: "I had confused the act of trying to appear not to be racist with actively working to eliminate racism. Trying to appear not racist had made me deny my racism, and therefore exclude the possibility of change" (191). Being antisexist and antiracist means seeing sexism and racism as systemic and interpersonal (rather than individual) and combating sexism and racism collectively, not just personally (as if somehow a person could cleanse himself of sexism and racism).

The first thing we must do, regardless of whether we belong to minority groups, is to break the conspiracy of silence that has ensured the perpetuation of sexism, racism, and other forms of marginalization and exclusion in the university. Patricia Williams' closing remark in her article "Blockbusting the Canon" (1991) is worth quoting at length here:

> It's great to turn the other cheek in the face of fighting words; it's probably even wise to run. But it's not a great way to maintain authority in the classroom.... "[J]ust ignoring" verbal challenges from my law students is a good way to deliver myself into the category of the utterly powerless. If, moreover, my white or male colleagues pursue the same path (student insult, embarrassed pause, the teacher keeps on teaching as though nothing had happened), we have collectively created that peculiar institutional silence that is known as a moral vacuum. (63)

Taking an antisexist and antiracist approach means we cannot be complacent as individual teachers or as members of the different collectivities to which we belong (for instance, on committees and in faculty associations). We must speak out against normalized courses of action that maintain existing inequality, although this may alienate us from those in power as well as those close to us. We must actively support our minority colleagues in their teaching, administrative, and other responsibilities and consciously open up spaces for previously silenced or marginalized voices to be heard. We must create spaces for students to interrogate existing paradigms and to explore alternative ones and support them in other endeavors. We must also constantly interrogate our own taken-for-granted ways of acting, thinking, and being in the world.

To explore what these principles may mean in concrete action, I return to the critical incident. I am not suggesting that administrators and staff handling and adjudicating disputes should categorically take the side of "the minority teacher/student." However, I am suggesting that the assessment of any situation should take account of people's varying subject positions within and outside the university. In this case, although the student's complaint was legitimate in that he felt uncomfortable with the materials and my instructions, his behaviour in class and in the meeting was not. It was explicitly sexist and implicitly racist; it was aimed at undermining my authority and expertise.

Administratively, to resolve such a dispute, the student could be advised to withdraw from courses with which he has problems rather than waiting until the end of the term. An appropriate administrative response could be to arrange for the student to withdraw from the course, even though the official deadline had passed (which was actually what this student wanted and proceeded to do).

Pedagogically, the student's complaint, with its sexist, racist, and homophobic subtext, presents an excellent opportunity for challenging the assumptions in his thinking and for educating him about academic freedom. This kind of situation is a valuable pedagogical moment that can be used to engage students in what we teach in a formal classroom setting. To work against the grain as an educator is to close the perceived gap between the formal and the "hidden" curriculum and to use any opportunity we can to challenge normalized and normalizing forms of behavior and thinking.[17]

The concept of academic freedom could be deployed in this instance to educate the student about the nature of university education and about his consumer-oriented mentality toward university education; university education is intended to expose students to a range of perspectives and experiences, not to confirm and/or reinforce their limited views of the world. Taking Fernando's and his colleagues' (Fernando, Hartley, Nowak, and Swinehart 1990) definition of the role of an intellectual and an academic to be that of a social critic trained to challenge dogma and to express critical views (6), it can be argued that a fundamental aspect of our freedom and responsibility as academics is to expose the political and contested nature of education.[18]

Finally, I want briefly to take up the issue of safety and comfort, because these words have become currency in debates around discourses and practices that challenge existing modes of thinking and working. Understanding oppression and doing antiracist work is by definition unsafe and uncomfortable, because both involve a serious (and frequently threatening) effort to interrogate our privilege as well as our powerlessness.[19] To speak of safety and comfort is to speak from a position of privilege, relative though it may be. For those who have existed too long on the margins, life has never been safe or comfortable. Understanding and eliminating oppression and inequality oblige us to examine our relative privilege, to move out of our internalized positions as victims, to take control over our lives, and to take responsibility for change. Such an undertaking is by definition risky and therefore requires commitment to a different vision of society than that which we now take for granted.

Teaching and learning against the grain is not easy, comfortable, or safe. It is protracted, difficult, uncomfortable, painful, and risky. It involves struggles with our colleagues and our students, as well as within ourselves. It is, in short, a challenge, but it is one we ought no longer to have to take up alone, unsupported by the institutions within which we conduct our professional lives.

Notes

1. This article is based on my presentation on a panel entitled Racism, Sexism and Homophobia: Some Threats to Inclusivity and Academic Freedom in the University, at the OCUFA (Ontario Confederation of University Faculty Associations) Status of Women's Conference on Developing Strategies for the Inclusive University, 5–6 February 1993, in Toronto. The other panel members were Johann St. Lewis and David Rayside. Thanks are due Suzanne de Castell, David Bray, Linda Briskin, Roger Simon, and Rebecca Coulter for comments on earlier drafts of this article. Special thanks to Linda Briskin for the title.
2. I use the term *minority* in the standard sociological sense to refer to people who are relatively powerless in a society. Thus, even though women are numerically the majority, they are a "minority" in terms of power and influence. Similarly, ethnic and racial minorities, especially nonwhites, constitute a minority in this society. To avoid repetition, I use the term *minority* to refer both to women and to ethnic/racial minorities.
3. I use the term "white" in quotation marks to emphasize that "white," similar to "colored," is a socially and ideologically constructed term. Its designation changes historically according to the dominant-subordinate relations in a given society. I use "white" to refer to groups who have taken part in Canada's colonization and who are perceived to be or who perceive themselves to be part of the dominant groups. In this case, the student referred to himself as a "white male"; his original language, however, was not English. He also told the class he was an immigrant and had been discriminated against in relation to his legal status; but in the course he did not draw parallels between his own marginality as an immigrant and the experiences of other marginalized groups.
4. I am deliberately vague about details of the course to protect the identity of individuals involved. I want to emphasize that my intent is not to personalize the story, but to highlight

the embeddedness of gender and racial dynamics in our experiences.
5. It was clear that this student had upset everyone in the class. Some students became angry. Some, especially the younger female students, immediately took on a nurturing role (see Lewis 1990), attempting to protect him from other students' anger and to painstakingly explain to him the parallels between women's subordination and the subordination of ethnic and racial minorities. When the only other male student in the class spoke up and confronted him about his sexism, he at last took notice, and, in my view, took on the male student as an equal (as opposed to a bunch of hysterical women trying to overwhelm him). By this time the discussion had become a tennis match between the two men, so, using materials we read in the course, I pointed out the gender dynamics occurring in our midst.
6. In highlighting the focus of this article, I have to omit details that detract from the main theme(s). What brought this student's complaint to the administration was actually more complicated. Briefly, in addition to resenting what had occurred in the last class he had attended, the student was upset that I had asked him to make up, by means of written work, the work the class had done in his absence (e.g., small group discussions, debates, and writing exercises). He felt I was being unjust because his absence was due to medical reasons (which I accepted), but I insisted on his making up the work because of the length of his absence. He felt I was discriminating against him because I asked him to do "extra" work not mentioned in the course outline (which specifically stated that attendance, though ungraded, was required). This was unacceptable to him, hence his request for mediation. In the meeting, however, he completely bypassed the original issue and instead criticized the course.
7. This comment, made spontaneously, illustrates both the normalization of heterosexism and the overlapping character of forms of subordination.
8. This is a cursory and simplistic presentation of the complex history of Canada's colonial past. Space and time prevent a fuller exploration and explication of this topic, except to say that although I recognize the subordination of French-speaking peoples, I want to note the two key colonizers of Canada.
9. Special lecture by Collin Leys organized by Tuula Lindholm for a Gramsci study group on March 21, 1993.
10. For an excellent discussion of objective versus subjective knowledge and the constitution of objectivity, see Currie (1992).
11. The myth of objectivity of school knowledge has also been challenged by those writing about the hidden curriculum. For a useful summary, see Giroux (1981).
12. See also Mohanty (1990, 193–96) who raises an important critique of the use of the term *experience* in liberatory discourses which becomes individualized in the university.
13. I base this claim on my own experience and on informal conversations with minority faculty over the past ten years of my university teaching career. Given the corporatization and rise of politically correct movements in universities, I think this area is worthy of further investigation.
14. I borrow this term from Susan Heald's analysis of state formation (Heald 1990, 149). To summon is to call forth or to command a particular aspect of our multidimensional and contradictory identity.
15. Various writers have used this term—see Cochran-Smith (1991), Ng (1991), and Simon (1992). Although these authors attach slightly different significance and meaning to the term, it generally denotes educational practices aimed at instilling critical perspectives and consciousness in students in the classroom. I suggest it should be extended to our work in other settings.
16. The term *counter-intuitive* is borrowed from Linda Briskin, who used it in a workshop, Negotiating Power in the Inclusive Classroom, we co-facilitated for the Toronto Board of Education on January 21, 1993. Similar to being "against the grain," being counter-intuitive is to interrogate what we take for granted as the "natural" ways of doing things.
17. Realistically, of course, we cannot and do not seize *every* moment presented to us; however, critical pedagogical moments arise more often than we "normally" think of in our work, and they can be deployed as consciousness-raising opportunities for ourselves and others.
18. The meaning of academic freedom, like the role of education itself, is a topic of heated debates. I will not elaborate on this subject here except to say that the discussion in Fernando and others (1990), together with the literature on critical pedagogy, can be used to reconceptualize the academic freedom debate and related notions of "objectivity" and "fairness."
19. I thank the students in my advanced seminar Sexism, Racism, and Colonialism: Pedagogical Implications (spring 1993) for helping me clarify my own thinking on this subject.

References

Bordo, S. (1987). *The flight to objectivity: Essays on cartesianism and culture*. Albany: State University of New York Press.

Briskin, L. (1990a). *Feminist pedagogy: Teaching and learning liberation* (Feminist Perspectives, No. 19). Ottawa: Canadian Research Institute for the Advancement of Women.

_____. (1990b). Gender in the classroom. *CORE [Newsletter of the Centre for Support of Teaching, York University], 1*(1), 2–3.

Briskin, L., and Coulter, R. P. (1992). Feminist pedagogy: Challenging the normative. *Canadian Journal of Education, 17,* 247–263.

Burstyn, V. (1985). Masculine dominance and the state. In V. Burstyn & D. E. Smith, *Women, class, family and the state* (pp. 45–89). Toronto: Garamond Press.

Campbell, M. (n. d.). *An experimental research practicum based on the Wollstonecraft Research Group.* Unpublished manuscript, Ontario Institute for Studies in Education, Department of Sociology, Toronto.

Cochran-Smith, M. (1991). Learning to teach against the grain. *Harvard Educational Review, 61,* 279–310.

Currie, D. H. (1992). Subject-ivity in the classroom: Feminism meets academe. *Canadian Journal of Education, 17,* 341–364.

Fernando, L., Hartley, N., Nowak, M., and Swinehart, T. (1990). *Academic freedom 1990: A human rights report.* London: Zed Books, with World University Service, Geneva.

Giroux, H. (1981). Schooling and the myth of objectivity: Stalking the politics of the hidden curriculum. *McGill Journal of Education, 16,* 282–304.

Gramsci, A. (1971). *Selections from the prison notebooks* (Q. Hoare & G. Nowell Smith, Eds. and Trans.). New York: International Publishers.

Heald, S. (1989). The madwoman out of the attic: Feminist teaching in the margin. *Resources for Feminist Research, 18*(4), 22–26.

_____. (1990). "Making democracy practical": Voluntarism and hob creation. In R. Ng, G. Walker, & J. Muller (Eds.), *Community organization and the Canadian state* (pp. 147–164). Toronto: Garamond Press.

Jackson, N. (1987). Ethnicity and vocational choice. In J. Young (Ed.), *Breaking the mosaic: Ethnic identities in Canadian schooling* (pp. 165–182). Toronto: Garamond Press.

Lawrence, E. (1982). Just plain common sense: The "roots" of racism. In *The Empire strikes back: Race and racism in 70s Britain* (pp. 42–94). Birmingham: University of Birmingham, Centre for Contemporary Cultural Studies.

Lewis, M. (1990). Interrupting patriarchy: Politics, resistance, and transformation in the feminist classroom. *Harvard Educational Review, 60,* 467–488.

Martin, B., and Mohanty, C. T. (1986). Feminist politics: What's home got to do with it? In T. de Lauretis (Ed.), *Feminist studies/critical studies* (pp. 191–212). Bloomington: Indiana University Press.

McLaren, P (1989). *Life in schools.* Toronto: Irwin Publishing.

Miles, R. (1989). *Racism.* London: Routledge.

Mohanty, C. T. (1990). On race and voice: Challenges for liberal education in the 1990s. *Cultural Critique, 14,* 179–208.

Newson, J., and Buchbinder, H. (1988). *The university means business: Universities, corporations and academic work.* Toronto: Garamond Press.

Nielsen, L. L. (1979). Sexism and self-healing in the university. *Harvard Educational Review, 49,* 467–476.

Ng, R. (1989). Sexism, racism, and Canadian nationalism. In J. Vorst et al. (Eds.), *Race, class, gender: Bonds and barriers* (pp. 10–25). Toronto: Between the Lines Press, with the Society for Socialist Studies.

_____. (1991). Teaching against the grain: Contradictions for the minority teacher. In J. S. Gaskell & A. T. McLaren (Eds.), *Women and education* (2nd ed.) (pp. 99–115). Calgary: Detselig Enterprises.

_____. (1992). Managing female immigration: A case of institutional sexism and racism. *Canadian Woman Studies, 12,* 20–23.

_____. (1993). Racism, sexism, and nation building in Canada. In C. McCarthy & W. Crichlow (Eds.), *Race, identity, and representation in education* (pp. 50–59). New York: Routledge.

O'Brien, M. (1981). *The politics of reproduction.* London: Routledge and Kegan Paul.

Rich, A. (1976). Women's studies: Renaissance or revolution? *Women's Studies, 3*(2), 35–47.

Simon, R. L. (1992). *Teaching against the grain: Texts for a pedagogy of possibility.* Toronto: Ontario Institute for Studies in Education.

Smith, D. E. (1974). Women's perspective as a radical critique of sociology. *Sociological Inquiry, 44,* 7–13.

_____. (1987). *The everyday world as problematic: A feminist sociology.* Toronto: University of Toronto Press.

Spender, D. (1980). *Man made language* (2nd ed.). London: Routledge & Kegan Paul.

Williams, P. J. (1991, September/October). Blockbusting the canon. *Ms., 11*(2), 59–63.

Willis, P. (1977). *Learning to labour: How working class kids get working class jobs.* New York: Columbia University Press.

Wolverton, T. (1983). Unlearning complicity, remembering resistance: White women's anti-racism education. In C. Bunch & S. Pollack (Eds.), *Learning our way: Essays in feminist education* (pp. 187–199). Trumansburg, NY: The Crossing Press.

C.

Women Students

Chapter 26

Of Gentlemen and Role Models

Lani Guinier

In 1984 I returned to Yale Law School to participate on a panel of mainly black alumni reminiscing about the thirty years since *Brown v. Board of Education*. It was a symposium sponsored by the current black students, who were eager to hear the voices of those who came before them. Each of us spoke for ten minutes in a room adorned by the traditional portraits of larger-than-life white men. It was the same classroom in which, ten years earlier, I had sat for Business Units (corporations) with a white male professor who addressed all of us, male and female, as *gentlemen*. Every morning, at ten minutes after the hour, he would enter the classroom and greet the upturned faces: "Good morning, *gentlemen*." He explained this ritual the first day. He had been teaching for many years; he was a creature of habit. He readily acknowledged the presence of the few "ladies" by then in attendance, but admonished those of us born into that other gender not to feel excluded by his greeting. We, too, in his mind, were simply *gentlemen*.

In his view, *gentlemen* was an asexual term, one reserved for reference to those who shared a certain civilized view of the world and who exhibited a similarly civilized demeanor. If we were not already, law school would certainly teach us how to be *gentlemen*. *Gentlemen* of the bar maintain distance from their clients, are capable of arguing both sides of any issue, and, while situated in a white male perspective, are ignorant of differences of culture, gender, and race.[1] That lesson was at the heart of becoming a professional. By his lights, the greeting was a form of honorific. It evoked the traditional values of legal education to train detached, neutral problem solvers. It anticipated the perception, if not the reality, of all of us becoming *gentlemen*.

It took many intervening years for me to gain the confidence to question directly this term that symbolically stripped me of my race, my gender, and my voice.[2] Now, seated at the podium in the familiar classroom preparing to address a race- and gender-mixed audience, I felt the weight of the presence of those stern, larger-than-life *gentlemen* portraits. For me, this was still not a safe place.[3]

Yet all the men on the panel reminded us how they felt to return "home," with fondly revealed stories about their three years in law school. The three black men may not have felt safe either, but they each introduced their talks with brief yet loving recollections of their law school experiences.

It was my turn. No empowering memories stirred my voice. I had no personal anecdotes for the profound senses of alienation and isolation caught in my throat every time I opened my mouth. Nothing resonated there in that room for a black woman, even after my ten years as an impassioned civil rights attorney. Instead I promptly began my formal remarks, trying as hard as I could to find my voice in a room in which those portraits spoke louder than I ever could. I spoke slowly and carefully, never once admitting, except by my presence on the podium, that I had ever been a student at that school or in that room before. I summoned as much authority as I could to be heard over the sounds of silence erupting from those giant images of *gentlemen* hanging on the wall, and

---

Reprinted from *Critical Race Feminism: A Reader*, edited by Adrien Katherine Wing, 1997. Copyright © 1997 New York University Press.

from my own ever-present memory of slowly *disappearing* each morning and becoming a *gentleman* of Business Units I.

Immediately after my presentation, the other black woman on the panel rose to speak. She too did not introduce herself with personal experiences or warm reminiscences about her past association with the law school, but, like me, remained upright and dignified. Afterwards, she and I huddled together to talk about how different the law school we had experienced was from the one recollected by our male colleagues.

We were the *disappeareds*, she and I. The alienation stirred by our return to the place where we first became *gentlemen* was too profound and silencing to share except between ourselves. Continuously scrutinized by those larger-than-life portraits, our humanity, culture, frames of reference, and identity as women of color were dislocated by those memories of our law school experience.[4] We were the minority within a minority whose existence, even physical presence, had been swallowed up within "neutral" terms and other marginalizing traditions associated with educating *gentlemen*. Except at private intersections of blackness and womanhood, our voices had been silenced.[5]

Four years later, at the first Women of Color and the Law Conference, I again returned to Yale Law School. I was invited to speak at a panel entitled "Roots in Our Communities: What Roles for Lawyers and Professionals?" This time I was invited by young female students of color who asked me to speak explicitly about the personal choices and conflicts I had experienced in my career as a black female civil rights attorney. At the conference, I tried to overcome my training as a surrogate *gentleman* who distances her personal self from her professional self. I also tried to overcome the self-protective silence that earlier helped me survive as a *gentleman* in Business Units I. This time I found my voice.

I revealed myself in context, talking about my family, my colleagues, my adversaries, and my clients. In all my professional roles, I experienced what Mari Matsuda calls "multiple consciousness," meaning the bifurcated thinking that allows one to shift back and forth between one's personal consciousness and the white male perspective that dominates the legal profession.[6] Multiple consciousness allows us to operate within mainstream discourse and "within the details of our own special knowledge,"[7] producing both madness and genius.

Multiple consciousness provides intellectual camouflage and emotional support for the outsider who always feels the threeness[8] of race, gender, and marginality. It engenders the spirit of W. E. B. Du Bois's idea of double-consciousness, two warring selves within one black body, living within the "veil" yet gifted with "second-sight."[9] Even while performing insider roles, many of us still function as outsiders. As a black woman civil rights attorney with insider privileges and outsider consciousness, I moved along the perimeter of cultural norms (roots, community, race, and gender) and cultivated status (mainstream professional role) as an explorer and translator of these different identities.

For outsiders, who do not experience the world through color blindness or gender neutrality, multiple consciousness is a cultural norm. Those with outsider consciousness live with the peculiar sensation of always looking at one's self through the eyes of others. We are self-conscious precisely because of, not in spite of, our race and gender. In our insider roles, we are still outsiders. As a result, we experience color blindness, gender neutrality, and individual perspective as unfamiliar, mainstream, existential luxuries. "Neutrality" feels very different from the perspective of an outsider.[10] A race-neutral, gender-neutered perspective is apparently enjoyed, to the extent it exists at all, by *gentlemen*: those with a white male perspective, those in the majority, and those *gentlemen* surrogates to whom the majority grants insider privileges. For self-conscious, second-sighted outsiders, multiple consciousness centers marginality and names reality.[11]

I recounted to the students at the conference how multiple consciousness often became a burden in my professional relationships with male lawyers and colleagues. I was never certain when to situate myself outside a white male perspective or with whom to disengage from value-neutral problem solving. Even my mother complained that sometimes I "cross-examined" her.

As a law professor, I now take the podium daily under the watchful eyes of those ever-dominant portraits of *gentlemen* that still guard the periphery. I am at the podium; but for women and people of color like myself, this is not yet a safe place. Legal education still teaches value-neutral detachment. As legal educators we still distance our personal selves from our professional selves. Our race and our gender and those of the litigants in our casebooks are still, for the most part, an unspoken subtext.

Nevertheless, recent events remind me that my presence in legal education offers some students refuge. Renewed calls have been made for more black women law professors to be "role models" for black female students.[12] In the conventional sense of the term, I function not only as a teacher but as a symbol for certain student voices and aspirations.[13]

Repercussions from these public calls for more black women role models prompt me to explore further the uneasiness I have with the role model rationale for hiring black women law professors. I do not object to being a role model—even if I had a choice about the matter, which I probably do not. Indeed, I do feel special responsibilities as a black woman law professor. But in my eyes I am a mentor more than a role model. As such, I rely on a *communicative* discourse,[14] actively and constructively listening to empower my students' own voices. As a teacher I act as a mentor who takes from the margin[15] to facilitate student reflection, insight, and professional responsibility.

I prefer the term "mentor" to "role model" in part because I worry about the way the role model argument is often used to diminish the role outsiders play, a role that benefits insiders as well as other outsiders. I question the way the role model argument measures successful outsiders by an insider yardstick. In addition, I take issue with the representational justification currently in vogue. Role models may grant a passport to power or status to people who then take no account of how they arrived at their destination.

The first problem with the role model argument is that it trivializes the important contribution that outsiders make in diversifying a faculty. Presenting black women law professors primarily as role models ignores their roles as scholars and intellectual leaders whose presence on a faculty might alter the institution's character, introducing a different prism and perspective.[16] Black women legal scholars may challenge their white male colleagues to perform their own roles better.

Using her outsider perspective, a black woman law professor may take "information from the margin to transform how we think about the whole."[17] She contributes to legal education not merely through her physical presence but by pulling from the richness and rootedness of her experience, by continuously reaching for the transformative possibilities of her role.[18]

But the term "role model" is often used insidiously to refer only to a faculty "mascot" who counsels and keeps students in line, a pacifier of the status quo who won't bite the hand that uplifted her.[19] As prototypes of achievement, role models illustrate, through example, the possibility of success for their constituency. In fact, black role models may become powerful symbolic reference points serving as camouflage for the continued legacy of past discrimination.[20] Institutionally acceptable role models may simply convey the message "we have overcome" in language calculated to exact admiration from, but not necessarily to inspire, those not yet overcoming.

Black women role models are also defended as group spokespersons or "spokesmodels."[21] For example, some blacks claim that as teachers they have "a clear, racial representational function," meaning that they both "comprehend" and "represent" the needs and interests of all black students. Thus, some argue that black women role models *represent* aspiring young black women's needs and affirm the status of black women as law school citizens who can participate in the process of making policy decisions that affect their lives in law school and beyond.

The representational view posits an inspirational figure based disproportionately on mere physical attributes, potentially institutionalizing acceptable or assimilated "*gentlemen* of color" to serve as group representatives to the outside world. By their presence, such role models presumably articulate black interests and act as living symbols of the equal opportunity process.

But these aspects of the role model as spokesperson overemphasize the representational value of passive, individual success unconnected to a dynamic, rooted concept of socially responsible, emotionally engaged leadership. Without an introspective or reflective understanding of their own experience, and an open ear listening and responding to the voices of group and nongroup members, the role model as respectable insider simply presents success as an illusion of privilege. The possibilities for social change become the possibilities for individual advancement.

To realize their value as catalysts for meaningful group "upward mobility" (meaning mobility beyond their own individual advantage), role models need ties to their community: heeding their own accounts of their experience and internalizing reference points of what is or should be responsible and responsive behavior. For me, role models should be more than mere *"gentlemen* of color"—detached, neutral, wooden images for emulation or admiration.

Role models have responsibilities, not just privileges. To be effective group representatives rather than institutionally acceptable achievers, role models must reflect the values of the group whose aspirations they symbolize. Role models should be people with whom members of the out-group identify and should be held accountable to other outsider aspirants. Especially to the extent they are seen as agents for others, role models need to nurture their roots, not just model their roles.

This rootedness needs to be incorporated more directly into the definition of the term "role model." As a self-referential term, "role model" fits only to the extent that my own polar experiences—as a marginalized student and as an empowered and empowering civil rights attorney—root me in the sturdy soil and rocky terrain of multiple consciousness. Rooted in community, a law professor can be "an organic intellectual with affiliations not restricted to the walls of the academic institution."[22] She can produce legal scholarship and engage in educational instruction, not in isolation, but in solidarity with other like-minded scholars. Authenticity and faithfulness to her own voice connect her to "the richness of [her] own experience" and empower her to overcome silencing even by well-intentioned white male colleagues.[23] Her stories help construct a shared reality as a means of "psychic self-preservation" and of "lessening [her] own subordination."[24]

Students—those to whom a teacher should be accountable—often find her stories empowering. In this sense, an effective teacher is less a role model than a mentor, an educator who empowers through feedback, guidance, and sharing rather than one who commands through example, visibility, or physical stature. I find meaning in this alternative, mentoring view of the so-called role model relationship.

Mentors see learning as an active process that builds on students' emotional engagement and emphasizes the mutuality of their role in the educational conversation. Second-sighted within the "veil," a mentor may draw on the outsider consciousness of a minority group advocate and member. From this vantage point, she may see that women and students of color, already silenced by their status and their low numbers, respond less enthusiastically to learning by intimidation than to teaching techniques that foster security and respect for multiple viewpoints.

I do not aspire to be a cultural icon in the conventional or group representative sense. I value my role as a translator and facilitator, a beneficiary of and contributor to a transformed and transformative educational conversation with black women, people of color, and minority viewpoints of all colors. But I play this role not just for black women, or even for people of color. Despite special concerns and responsibilities to engage particular students, I take information from the margin to transform the educational dialogue for *all* my students. I play the role of teacher, mentor, counselor, and educational facilitator for white male students too.[25] As if peeling an onion, I unlayer these preliminary, still tentative thoughts on our continuing negotiation over shared cultural space. I puzzle over demystifying the traditional image of legal educators and lawyers as detached, problem-solving, neutral *gentlemen*. The nature of my own education and of the schools with which I have associated makes it difficult either to reject the opportunities afforded passive symbols of achievement or to transcend traditional, established ways of viewing the world.

Nevertheless, through the process of careful listening and mutual discovery, I join other black women in telling our stories. Collective action engages our personal selves with our professional roles, asserts the value of our lived experiences, takes account of the way others perceive our contribution, and attempts to empower and build community. A rooted, communicative discourse emboldens us to explore the unclaimed territory of our experience on the margins of legal education.

Many more law professors of color, including black women, should be hired, but not simply to "unbecome" *gentlemen* or to become role models instead. Indeed, to the extent that we are role models, it is not because we become *gentlemen* with race and gender added. To be a role model is not just a privilege, but a responsibility to those who come after us and to those whom we follow.

Thus, I write this essay to collaborate with other black women law professors, to find our voices, and to help other people find theirs. And if we find in our voices a race, a gender, and an outsider perspective with roots deep in the rocky terrain and sturdy soil of multiple consciousness, we also may finally dislodge from our throats the alienation and isolation begotten by *gentlemen* orthodoxies, including those everpresent *gentlemen* portraits that still guard the citadel.[26]

Notes

1. For the purpose of this essay, the term "*gentlemen*" describes the lawyers' role as that of being neutral, dispassionate, unemotional but courteous advocates for a client's interest. While "gentlemen" primarily refers to males, and in particular to those of good breeding, it assumes men who possess neither a race nor a gender. Compare Peggy McIntosh, *White Privilege and Male Privilege: A Personal/Account (Coming to See Correspondences through Work in Women's Studies* (1990) (Working Paper no. 189, Wellesley College Center for Research on Women) (for white men, their race and gender are an "invisible package of unearned assets").
2. In law school I resisted through silence. Only later did I learn to question out loud how much of a gentleman I ever was, or even how much of a lady I ever could be.
3. In some ways, the gigantic male portraits symbolized my alienation as a student from class, race, and gender privilege. Yet, because I had attended an Ivy League college, perhaps it is surprising that I continued to find the *gentlemen's* portraits so alienating. My intuition is that law school, as a professional school, was simply more homogeneous, with even more explicitly homogenizing institutional norms (such as value-neutral detachment), than I had either expected or previously experienced.
4. See Suzanne Homer & Lois Schwartz, *Admitted but Not Accepted: Outsiders Take an Inside Look at Law School*, 5 Berkeley Women's L.J. 1, 37–38, 43–44 (1989–90) ("marginalized persons" develop a counter-code of silence in response to an interrogation technique and an educational atmosphere that are perceived as assaulting their privacy and dignity; "women and persons of color experience frustration instead of growth" when forced to develop an identity within an academic institution dominated by a white male perspective).
5. Indeed, our sense of disassociation appears consistent with the contemporary school experience of other black women and black girls. *See* Suzanne Daley, *Little Girls Lost Their Self-Esteem on Way to Adolescence, Study Finds*, N.Y. Times, Jan. 9, 1991, at B9 (survey of three thousand adolescents concluded that black girls in high school draw apparent self-confidence "from their families and communities rather than the school system"; in order to maintain their self-esteem, black girls must disassociate themselves from school experience). Although admittedly neither as intense or painful, my invisibility also revived memories of my father's experience a generation earlier as the only black student entering Harvard College in 1929. *See* C. Gerald Fraser, *Ewart Guinier, 79, Who Headed Afro-American Studies at Harvard*, N.Y. Times, Feb. 7, 1990, at B7 ("Because of his color, Mr. Guinier said, he was barred from the dormitories, was denied financial aid because he had failed to send his picture with his application, and was spoken to inside and outside of class by only one person").
6. Mari J. Matsuda, *When the First Quail Calls: Multiple Consciousness as Jurisprudential Method*, 11 Women's Rts. L. Rep. 1 (1989).
7. Id.
8. *See* W. E. B. Du Bois, *The Souls of Black Folk* 16–17 (A. C. McClurg, 1903).
9. Id.
10. Richard Delgado, *Storytelling for Oppositionists and Others; A Plea for Narrative*, 87 Mich. L. Rev. 2411, 2425 (1989). As a black woman who has experienced minority status and stigma associated with my race and/or gender, I am self-conscious about both race and gender.
11. *See* Kimberlé Williams Crenshaw, *Race, Reform, and Retrenchment: Transformation and Legitimation in Antidiscrimination Law*, 101 Harv. L. Rev. 1331, 1336 (1988) (describing blacks' greatest political resource as the ability to speak and share a collective identity based on experiences of racism and to "name [their] political reality").
12. Indeed, my decision to join this anthology of self-reflective essays was precipitated by the

role model characterizations that abounded during Derrick Bell's protest in the spring of 1990. Claiming he could not function as a "role model" for women students, Bell refused to accept his Harvard Law School salary until a woman of color was hired as a professor. See Fox Butterfield, *Harvard Law School Torn by Race Issue*, N.Y. Times, Apr. 26, 1990, at A20 ("As a male," Bell said, he "could not serve as a role model for female black students").

13. A role model may be nurturing mentor, symbol of achievement, or template for how this particular role might be performed. See the chapter by Anita L. Allen, *On Being a Role Model*, in this volume (the conspicuous presence of role models as symbolic achievers may rebut assumptions of group inferiority that undermine student confidence and performance).

14. Iris M. Young, Justice, Democracy and Group Difference 9–15 (Sept. 1, 1990) (unpublished paper prepared for presentation to the American Political Science Association, on file with the *Berkeley Women's Law Journal*) (describing a communicative model of democracy that rejects a disciplined, unemotional style of expression, which often operates to exclude, silence, and disadvantage members of some groups; communicative style does not require emotional detachment or rigid argumentation but employs a broader conception of permissible forms of discourse, including personal narrative).

15. Harlon L. Dalton, *The Clouded Prism*, 22 Harv. C.R.-C.L. L. Rev. 435, 444 (1987) (quoting bell hooks: "With creativity and an open mind, 'we can use information from the margin to transform how we think about the whole.'").

16. Delgado, *supra* note 10, at 2421.

17. See Dalton, *supra* note 15, at 444.

18. Richard Delgado, *When A Story Is Just a Story: Does Voice Really Matter?*, 76 Va. L. Rev. 95, 99 (1990) (describing outsiders' accessibility to and stake in disseminating information that persons without their experiences may not have).

19. Delgado, *supra* note 10, at 2423–27 (describing conventional faculty concern that black professor who causes trouble by stirring up students "wouldn't be a good role model even for the minorities," at 2426 n. 45).

20. Regina Austin, *Sapphire Bound!*, 1989 Wis. L. Rev. 539, 575 (also chapter 35 in this volume) (role models who offer "pride" and "positive identities" are not substitutes for effective, committed teachers and leaders).

21. See Lani Guinier, *The Triumph of Tokenism: The Voting Rights Act and the Theory of Black Electoral Success*, 89 Mich. L. Rev. (1991) (spokesmodels are attractive group spokespersons with no accountability to group goals; the term "spokesmodel" derives from the television program Star Search, in which young women are scouted for their poise, looks, and articulation).

22. Kendall Thomas, Remarks at the AALS Annual Meeting, Law and Interpretation Section, Washington, D.C. (Jan. 4, 1991).

23. *See* Dalton, *supra* note 15, at 441.

24. Delgado, supra note 10, at 2436.

25. Although the law school admits a class of almost one-half women, and for the first time in 1990, one-third nonwhite persons, my upper-level courses have always consisted primarily of white men. This is not surprising, considering the small absolute number of African American, Asian American, and Latin American students, and the relatively small percentage of these students admitted prior to 1990.

26. And we may eventually help the *gentlemen* change the pictures. In 1990, a student group organized by women and people of color at the University of Pennsylvania raised enough money, with the active support of the dean, to commission the first "official" portrait of a black woman law school graduate, Sadie T. M. Alexander. In the course of writing this essay I learned to my great surprise that at Yale Law School a seminar room display of graduates practicing public interest law now also includes the photograph of at least one black woman—me.

CHAPTER 27

DETOUR FROM NOWHERE: THE REMARKABLE JOURNEY OF A RE-ENTRY COMMUNITY COLLEGE WOMAN

SANDRIA RODRIGUEZ

In *Our Town*, a deceptively simple play about small town life in turn-of-the century New Hampshire, Thornton Wilder depicts two housewives who "cooked three meals a day—one of 'em for twenty years, the other for forty—and no summer vacation. They brought up two children apiece, washed, cleaned the house, and *never a nervous breakdown*." Wilder's speaker muses about the hard lot of women in early twentieth-century America: "It's like what one of those Middle West poets said: You've got to love life to have life, and you've got to have life to love life.... It's what they call a vicious circle" (1938, p. 47).

In spite of technological advances, many of today's women find themselves caught up in the vicious circle experienced by Wilder's fictional women nearly a hundred years ago. Instead of becoming easier, the challenge of living a full, responsible, enjoyable life for women seems to have become increasingly difficult. Nowhere is this more evident than among poor women who seek to better their lives by pursuing higher education while juggling jobs outside the home as well as familial responsibilities. That some can do so without suffering nervous breakdowns or worse is testament to the power of the will and the resiliency of the human spirit.

Many of the recent publications on re-entry women in postsecondary education illuminate these expanding ranks of women as being among the heroes of the modern age. Rice and Meyer (1989) point out that the number of re-entry women in higher education has more than doubled over the past 20 years and that the most frequent reason for their re-entry is economic need. Ironically, while these women tend to enroll in male-dominated job-related areas such as business and health-related fields, unlike their male counterparts many still wind up in traditionally female occupations which pay far less. Re-entry women experience other problems that are different from those encountered by males or younger women: they generally have primary responsibility for child rearing and other family matters; they suffer a disproportionate amount of stress, guilt, and anxiety over their myriad responsibilities; their success is often dependent on behavioral and emotional support from spouses and other family members; and, at some postsecondary institutions, there is a lack of support services to help re-entry women overcome the barriers to furthering their education. In light of the battles faced by re-entry women, including the hardship of financing a college education while making financial ends meet at home, it is not surprising that 95 percent of re-entry women are part-time rather than full-time students and that, at least in the community college setting, they stop out more often and take longer to earn their degrees than do most of their

---

Reprinted from *Initiatives*, Vol. 58, No. 1, 1997. Copyright © 1997 National Association for Women in Education.

male counterparts (Dillon, 1990). Indeed, the literature indicates that re-entry women at community colleges, in particular, confront their own set of challenges.

In her study of Italian-American re-entry community college women, for instance, DeGregoria (1987) found that the women she studied were daunted by a lack of family support, sex role stereotyping, and negative images of Italian Americans. Similarly, LaPaglia (1994) discovered that beyond the demeaning connotations associated with community colleges, reentry women experienced feelings of marginalization and frustration, the latter resulting from juggling multiple roles and responsibilities, especially with inadequate financial resources. Osterkamp and Hullett (1983) found that community college policies often discriminate against re-entry women, who tend to be part-time students, by making degree completion, the acquiring of financial aid, job placement, and access to child care on campus extremely difficult if not impossible for any student who is not full time. Freeman (1989) discovered that colleges discriminate against women by simply failing to act on their behalf. Freeman's description of college as a "null educational environment" (p. 223) for women echoes the re-entry community college woman's portrayal in much of the literature.

In this article, my intent is to illuminate the particular challenges and triumphs experienced by many re-entry women in the community college setting. In particular, I profile one re-entry woman at a community college in northeastern Illinois. Marnie's story offers an instructive blueprint for understanding how a nontraditional-aged woman can beat the odds. Moreover, it offers insights into how a college can facilitate the success of re-entry women. After telling Marnie's story, I offer several suggestions aimed at improving the educational experiences of re-entry community college women.

The idea to use the in-depth interview as the data collection method for this article grew out of my work experience. As an associate dean in a suburban community college where 52 percent of the students are women and the average age of the students is 31, I often meet re-entry women who are furiously battling the odds in order to further their education. One day at my campus, I encountered a seven-months pregnant mother of six who had traveled ten miles by bus to take an asthmatic child to a hospital emergency room before taking a bus from the hospital to the campus. She spoke with me about obstacles she faced in trying to attend college, and I was able to help her in creating a schedule that would meet her needs. Afterward, ashamed to smile because she was missing several front teeth, the mother shielded her mouth with her hand as delight at receiving simple kindnesses brought a huge grin to her face. She was deeply moved upon discovering that, by making a few phone calls and using the fax machine to expedite her registration process, I had saved her money and miles of additional travel by bus. She expressed extreme surprise that compassionate consideration would be given to her financial needs, her degree of readiness for academic endeavor, and her child-care requirements. The portrait of life which she exemplified in rich detail, juxtaposed against her murmured aspirations for herself and her children, fueled my recognition that the re-entry woman's community college experience, in all its difficult and glorious permutations, should be understood by community college personnel. I decided to study one re-entry woman's story in depth as a first step to understanding in full relief who re-entry women are, what their educational needs are, and how community colleges can help to best meet their needs.

In order to select a subject for my study, I began to talk with colleagues at my own institution and at neighboring colleges about re-entry women they knew who had overcome many of the common barriers to a college education and had achieved their educational goals at the community college level. Using this snowball sampling method, I interviewed a number of potential subjects, finally settling on a woman whom I will call "Marnie Davis." Marnie and I engaged in many hours of dialogue, during which I asked her questions about her family background, her motivations to go to college, her community college experiences, and those events, experiences, attitudes, or people that promoted or prevented her educational success. I took copious notes throughout. Rather than analyzing and presenting my interview material in terms of recurrent themes, as is often the case in qualitative research (Schatzman & Strauss, 1973; Yin, 1984), I chose instead to reconstruct what I had learned from Marnie in a more holistic, flowing narrative. After I had a rough draft, I shared this narrative with Marnie and asked her to correct any errors of fact (Lincoln & Guba, 1985). It is my hope that the vivid images in Marnie's story will make community college personnel and other educators more aware of the obstacles faced by many re-entry women and that their awareness will lead to their responsible activism on re-entry women's behalf. The story that follows has Marnie's seal of approval.

Marnie's Story

My name is Marnie Davis. They call me a "re-entry woman" and that's funny because when I first came to college, I wasn't re-entering anything. I'd barely gotten out of elementary school. I had only made it to my first year of high school when I quit. Me and Catholic school didn't mix. I just couldn't get school work, especially math. I was kept back so many times they started passing me because I was getting old. I'd get straight F's and they'd pass me. In eighth grade, my teacher decided she was going to teach me math; I was gonna get it. So she went way down to my level. She showed me exactly how to do decimals, and I got it. I learned decimals in the eighth grade while the other kids were learning algebra. I learned decimals perfect and I got an A+; my report card said A+. In ninth grade, they put me in fast algebra. I said, "Wait a minute. I'm an idiot. I can't do math. I just learned decimals. At least let me go in regular math." And they said, "Nope. It says A+ right here. You're in fast algebra."

And I remember when my mother got out "Snow White" and I read the first page. When I finished, I didn't know anything that I'd read. They didn't have help for learning-disabled kids in Catholic school, and I quit when I turned 16, just after I got in ninth grade. I was angry and frustrated, and I took everything out on my parents. They kicked me out of the house. That's when the Outlaws, a biker gang, started raising me.

They taught me don't lie, don't rip on anybody, or you will get hurt. And they taught me to read, my first husband did. It was a book about John Wayne Gacy. He told me just take my time reading it over and over. I would read a page about four times. And I really got into it, it was so interesting. The first few books I read, I read like that, reading everything over about four times. And then I found myself not having to read everything over to understand it.

The Outlaws taught me honor. You don't hurt the gang. When one guy raped a girl, some of the gang took a gallon of gasoline and they took him out to this clearing where there was a stump. They nailed his privates to that stump, they gave him a sharp hatchet, and then they doused the stump with the gasoline and set it afire. He used the hatchet to get loose and bled to death before he got to the highway.

The Outlaws taught me a woman's place. You don't get married; you just say, "That's my old lady. That's my old man." And the motorcycle is more important than the woman. It goes in the bedroom, too, and the woman could be traded for a new fender for the motorcycle if one were needed. A woman has to be valuable. She has to prostitute or she has to deal. I didn't have to prostitute; I dealt. But I took a lot of beatings from my first husband and my second husband so, after my son was born, I went home and my parents took me in. I was 20 years old.

I started college because my parents worked and I needed to help my little brother with his homework. He needed to understand computers, and I didn't know anything about them. My mother found a continuing education computer course at the community college and enrolled me in it. Almost everybody in class was a policeman and I knew them all. It was like old home week. The teacher showed us how to do things; then she walked around and helped everyone who needed help. I found out that I could do what people showed me how to do. I did great in that class. It wasn't like school. It even met at night. So I took two other computer classes. My family was helping to take care of my son, and I started working and hitting the bars at night. I wound up back out there with the Outlaws. When my second son was four, the law took him away from me, awarding custody to his abusive father. At that time, I was working in a factory taking care of my children, and I should not have lost my baby. When I allow myself to look inward to the edges of my memory and face the pain that I have felt, nothing touches it. Nothing comes close to the sorrow of losing my child. I went deep into cocaine. I almost died, and I wanted to die.

My third husband beat me all the time. I had broken bones, a broken nose, teeth knocked out, black eyes, bruises, and I had to go to work like that. I have been in the hospital many times from beatings.

I didn't get back to college until 1990, six years after losing my youngest boy. I re-entered to get my GED. I had been interviewed but not chosen for a job because I didn't have an associate degree, and I had to train the guy they hired! I needed a GED to get into college credit classes. I was ashamed of my ignorance, and I would hide my GED book under my coat so no one in the halls would know what an idiot I was. My husband kept telling me how stupid and ugly I was, but I got A's in my class. I got my GED and began taking college credit courses toward my associate degree. I didn't go to counseling for help because my teachers were so willing to work with me. But not my math teacher. For help in math, I went to a foreigner, a computer lab specialist who taught me algebra in plain English and began teaching me computers.

My husband would rip up my books, put them in the toilet, keep me up all night fighting so I would be too tired to concentrate in class the next day. I would get off the bus and he would beat me all through the house. My grades plummeted to C's. I remember it was December 20, the last day of school, and I was eager for my grades to come in the mail. My husband claimed I was messing around with somebody. He picked up my son and threw him into a wall. I intervened, and then I took a really bad beating. I was barely able to walk, but I got to a 7-Eleven and called the police. They took me back to my house, but my husband had left.

He came back on New Year's eve, said he was sorry, that he would never hit me again. The next morning he woke up and kicked the living crap out of me. He ground my wrists and ankles under his sharp boot heels, and he said he was going to kill me. It took the police one year to pick him up for that crime, but he has just now gotten out of jail for it. He served two and a half years. He has called my family and said that he has learned to be an undertaker and that he will be the last person to see me alive. The cops say they can't do anything to him because he hasn't done anything yet.

I've certainly done something. It's 1996 and, since 1990, I have earned almost two associate degrees. I have a degree in business administration with a computer information systems emphasis. I have only a couple of courses to go to complete my data processing degree. I am a certified network administrator in 3.12 and 4.1 systems from Novell, and I am working on becoming a certified network engineer from Novell. I love learning. I never want to leave college. I've had husbands telling me I'm stupid and ugly. But I've had all these people in this college telling me I'm really smart. They gave me two student-worker jobs—one in personnel and one in a computer lab. Most of my teachers would ask how I'm doing and would encourage me. I still can't spell, but I'm a computer whiz. I sometimes teach computers to college employees and, as a computer specialist for the college, I supervise computer functions in an entire division. College did it for me. College made the difference in my life. I went to counseling the other day to find out what I need to get my bachelor's degree. The counselor said I'm almost there. I only need 36 hours to get my bachelor's. That's only 12 courses.

People tell me all the time that I teach computers really well. I break it down so everyone can understand. I want to become a college teacher. I know I can do it because I already am somebody, and when you're somebody, you can do anything you set your heart and mind on doing.

Lessons From Marnie's Story

After you listen to Marnie Davis, some of the barriers to her educational success seem apparent. As a child, she had not fit into the range of normality that would allow her Catholic schooling to meet her educational needs. Even though Marnie's mother had gone to college and was a registered nurse, neither she nor Marnie's father seemed capable of reconciling this frustrated and rebellious child with the strict religious tenets of their very Catholic household. Marnie was one of eight children whose parents seemed to love them equally. Yet, her inability to fit into the society of the classroom heralded her increasing inability to fit into mainstream society or into the society of her family. The pedagogical and epistemological practices in the elementary and high schools that Marnie attended were generally inappropriate for a child of her needs.

While the spirit of rebellion against a nonsupportive spouse (Rice, 1982) may have figured peripherally in Marnie's ability to persist in college, her physical resilience and desire to better the life chances for herself and her child were greatly significant, as was the support and encouragement of her parents and siblings. But Marnie believes that one of the most important contributors to her ability to persist and to succeed was the quality of attention that she received at the community college. Her first course in computers was taught by a woman who became a role model. There were some "excellent women faculty" in data processing, one of her major areas of study. Faculty seemed genuinely interested in discovering how they could accommodate the different learning styles of their students. The financial aid office was very responsive to Marnie, and through her status as a student worker, her financial situation actually improved when she became a full-time student. She began receiving public assistance and was able to move from her rat and roach infested apartment under a bar. While being on welfare was embarrassing to Marnie, the days of not being able to feed her son (or of feeding him but not eating herself) were gone.

Although Marnie was still suffering physical and mental abuse at home, her college experience was empowering. In English classes, Marnie learned to use her imagination. She was taught (by a male English teacher) that what she thinks is actually important and that her reasoned ideas enhanced the quality of class discussions. When she was revising one of her first papers for this English class, Marnie's husband told her that it was stupid for her to waste time on the paper, that she had not done well because she is a dummy, that he could dash off in a minute a better paper than she could write. Her husband actually wrote a paper to show Marnie how superior his skills were to her own. While she did not share her opinion with him, she thought his paper was "crud." He was very upset that, after revision, Marnie earned an A on her paper. With that English paper, the college had proved effective in tipping the balance of Marnie's self-esteem in an upward position. "For most of my life I had believed that I was ugly and dumb," said Marnie, a beautiful, hazel-eyed, tastefully dressed, 30-something slip of a woman with an infectious laugh and a mane of curly blond hair. "But when you've got a whole lot of educated people helping you to prove that you are somebody, you stop believing the jerk that you live with."

In the community college milieu, Marnie's case is not as unusual as one might think. Many women who are poorly educated, financially bereft, and in abusive, life-threatening relationships have been able to reconstruct their lives within the context of the community college. Building on Marnie's experience and drawing from the research and writings on re-entry women in community colleges, I offer the following recommendations to enhance the educational experience for re-entry women at community colleges.

- Actively recruit re-entry women. They add a rich dimension to the classroom and often serve as models of maturity for traditional-aged students (LaPaglia, 1995).
- Provide inexpensive child care, transportation, and tutorial help for those who need it (Cardenas & Warren, 1991).
- Make sure that admissions and financial aid policies do not discriminate against re-entry women. If scholarships and awards are based exclusively on class rank or ACT and SAT scores, many deserving older women may be excluded from receiving them because their school experience predates or did not include the criteria (Betz, 1994).
- Provide student employment opportunities for re-entry women that will help them to sharpen their academic, social, and career-related skills (Osterkamp & Hullett, 1983).
- Provide in-service training for faculty that will heighten their sensibility to the special needs of re-entry women, since these needs may have an impact on re-entry women's academic performance (Cardenas & Warren, 1991).

- Ensure flexible class scheduling by providing evening and weekend college opportunities. Initiatives of this sort will allow re-entry women to more easily adjust their schedules to accommodate their course loads (Vriend, 1975).
- Establish outreach programs with area adult education agencies to recruit women and to facilitate their smooth transition to college (Rice & Meyer, 1989).
- Hire women faculty to teach in traditionally male-dominated disciplines such as computer science, mathematics, and engineering. Mentors for women in these areas remain remarkably scarce (Gutek & Nieva, 1995; Betz, 1994).
- Initiate the formation of on-campus support/study groups for re-entry women (Rice & Meyer, 1989).
- Work to ensure that each college employee is well versed in and committed to the principles and practices of excellent customer service. While the entire college community should be treated with compassion and respect, vulnerable students often are clinging to persistence by a fragile thread which could be easily severed by callous, disrespectful treatment from college employees (Rotkis & McDaniel, 1993).
- Demystify the college-going process. Outreach efforts must genuinely extend to poor, older, academically underprepared, working class, and non-aspiring potential re-entry women. Institutionally based strategies for such outreach should be augmented by college employees' individual, one-on-one endeavors to reach, recruit, and retain nontraditional-aged women (Sidel, 1994).
- Provide professional growth opportunities for all faculty in the development of "women's leadership" behaviors (Aburdene & Naisbitt, 1992). Focusing on feminine behaviors such as empowering, restructuring, facilitating, modeling, and questioning in teaching rather than on masculine or control-oriented epistemological models encourages re-entry women to participate in dialogical, collaborative, and democratic ways of teaching and learning (DiCroce, 1995; Belenky, Clinchy, Goldberger, & Tarule, 1986).

The need for educational reform to empower re-entry community college women becomes more urgent as greater numbers of nontraditional-aged women join the ranks of college students. Issues of educational opportunity for re-entry women must be seriously considered with viable and timely solutions as required outcomes. Central to these solutions must be the discovery and implementation of ways to ease the transition to college for re-entry women as well as ways to enhance their ability to persist. Similarly, we need to influence re-entry women to select and follow the career paths that will best help them to realize their potential as productive, happy citizens instead of automatically locking themselves into "feminine" occupations. All areas of student life, including those academic disciplines which have traditionally been seen as non-welcoming to women, must encourage and support their ongoing inclusion. Finally, re-entry women should be fully included in the definitions of and solutions to student-based issues surrounding the community college experience.

As we begin to take these basic steps toward developing the prodigious talents of re-entry women such as Marnie Davis, we will commensurately promote society's advancement. After all, equality of educational opportunity for re-entry community college women empowers society even as it empowers the women themselves to actualize their potential and to achieve their goals. Lack of such empowerment denies the development of our most precious natural resource, our people. Women, like minds, are terrible things to waste.

I thank Jennifer Grant Haworth and an anonymous reviewer for their constructive comments on an earlier draft of this article. I thank "Marnie Davis" for sharing her story.

References

Aburdene, P., & Naisbitt, J. (1992). *Megatrends for women*. New York: Villard Books.

Belenky, M. F., Clinchy, B. M., Goldberger, N. R., & Tarule, J. M. (1986). *Women's Ways of knowing: Development of self, voice, and mind*. New York: Basic Books.

Betz, N. E. (1994). Basic issues and concepts in career counseling for women. In W. B. Walsh & S. H. Osipow (Eds.), *Career counseling for women* (pp. 1–41). Hillsdale, New Jersey: Lawrence Erlbaum Associates.

Betz, N. E. (1994). Career counseling for women in the sciences and engineering. In W. B. Walsh & S. H. Osipow (Eds.) *Career counseling for women* (pp. 237–261). Hillsdale, New Jersey: Lawrence Erlbaum Associates.

Cardenas, R., & Warren, E. (1991). Community college access: Barriers and bridges. In D. Angel & A. Barrera (Eds.), *Rekindling minority enrollment* (p. 1522). San Francisco: Jossey-Bass.

DeGregoria, B. (1987). Counseling the nontraditional Italian-American student. *Community Review*, 8 (1), 38–41.

DiCroce, D. M. (1995). Women and the community college presidency: Challenges and possibilities. In B. K. Townsend (Ed.), *Gender and power in the community college* (pp. 79–88). San Francisco: Jossey-Bass.

Dillon, P. H. (1990). The myth of the two-year college: Length and variation in the time students take to complete associate degree requirements. Research Report. Los Angeles Community College District. Office of Research, Planning, and Development, 1–21.

Feingold, S. N. (1975). Career barriers—are they falling down? In E. House & M. E. Katzell (Eds.), *Facilitating career development for girls and women* (pp. 15–28). Washington, D.C.: National Vocational Guidance Association.

Freeman, J. (1989). How to discriminate against women without really trying. In J. Freeman (Ed.), *Women: A feminist perspective* (pp. 217–232). Palo Alto: Mayfield.

Gilligan, C. (1982). Woman's place in man's life cycle. In C. Gilligan, *In a different voice: Psychological theory and women*. Cambridge, MA: Harvard University Press.

Gutek, B. A., & Nieva, V. F. (1979). Determinants of career choice in women. In B. A. Gutek (Ed.), *Enhancing women's career development* (pp. 7–20). San Francisco: Jossey-Bass.

LaPaglia, N. (1994). Storytellers: The image of the two-year college in American fiction and in women's journals. Position paper. DeKalb, IL: LEPS Press.

LaPaglia, N. (1995). The interplay of gender and social class in the community college. In B. K. Townsend (Ed.), *Gender and power in the community college* (pp. 47–55). San Francisco: Jossey-Bass.

Lincoln, Y. S., & Guba, E. G. (1985). *Naturalistic inquiry*. Beverly Hills, CA: Sage.

Osterkamp, D., & Hullett, P. (1983). Re-entry women and part-time students: An overview with relevant statistics. Position Paper. Bakersfield College, CA. EDRS.

Patterson, C. D., & Blank, T. D. (1985, March). Doubt, struggle and growth: a profile of the mature woman in the student role. Paper presented at the annual meeting of the Eastern Psychological Association, Boston, MA.

Rice, J. K., & Meyer, S. (1989). Continuing education for women. In J. K. Rice, *Handbook of adult and continuing education*. San Francisco: Jossey-Bass.

Rice, J. K. (1982, September). Spouse support: Couples in educational transition. *Lifelong Learning: The Adult Years*, 4–6.

Rotkis, J., & McDaniel, N. (1993). Creating a special place in the community college for unique students. *Community College Journal of Research and Practice* 17, 315–32.

Schatzman, L., & Strauss, A. L. (1973). *Field research strategies for a natural sociology*. Englewood Cliffs, N.J.: Prentice-Hall.

Sidel, R. (1994). *Battling bias: The struggle for identity and community on college campuses*. New York: Viking.

Vriend, T. J. (1975). The community college in career development of women. In E. House, & M. E. Katzell (Eds.), *Facilitating career development for girls and women* (pp. 67–70). Washington, D.C.: National Vocational Guidance Association.

Wilder, T. (1938). *Our Town*. New York: Harper & Row.

Yin, R. K. (1984). *Case study research: Design and methods*. Beverly Hills, CA: Sage.

Sandria Rodriguez is Associate Dean of Communication Arts, Humanities, and Fine Arts at the College of Lake County in Grayslake, Illinois. She has taught English at the junior high, high school, and community college levels. She is completing her Ph.D. at Loyola University Chicago. Her dissertation is on first-generation college graduates.

CHAPTER 28

BLACK AND FEMALE:
REFLECTIONS ON GRADUATE SCHOOL

bell hooks

Searching for material to read in a class about women and race, I found an essay in *Heresies: Racism is the Issue* that fascinated me. I realized that it was one of the first written discussions of the struggles black English majors (and particularly black women) face when we study at predominantly white universities. The essay, "On Becoming A Feminist Writer," is by Carole Gregory. She begins by explaining that she has been raised in racially-segregated neighborhoods but that no one had ever really explained "white racism or white male sexism." Psychically, she was not prepared to confront head-on these aspects of social reality, yet they were made visible as soon as she registered for classes.

> Chewing on a brown pipe, a white professor said, "English departments do not hire Negroes or women." Like a guillotine, his voice sought to take my head off. Racism in my hometown was an economic code of etiquette which stifled Negroes and women.
>
> "If you are supposed to explain these courses, that's all I want," I answered. Yet I wanted to kill this man. Only my conditioning as a female kept me from striking his volcanic red face. My murderous impulses were raging.

Her essay chronicles her struggles to pursue a discipline which interests her without allowing racism or sexism to defeat and destroy her intellectual curiosity, her desire to teach. The words of this white male American Literature professor echo in her mind years later when she finds employment difficult, when she confronts the reality that black university teachers of English are rare. Although she is writing in 1982, she concludes her essay with the comment:

> Many years ago, an American literature professor had cursed the destiny of "Negroes and women." There was truth in his ugly words. Have you ever had a Black woman for an English teacher in the North? Few of us are able to earn a living. For the past few years, I have worked as an adjunct in English. Teaching brings me great satisfaction; starving does not. . . . I still remember the red color of the face which said, "English departments do not hire Negroes or women." Can women change this indictment? These are the fragments I add to my journal.

Reading Carole Gregory's essay, I recalled that in all my years of studying in English department classes, I had never been taught by a black woman. In my years of teaching, I have encountered students both in English classes and other disciplines who have never been taught by black women. Raised in segregated schools until my sophomore year of high school, I had wonderful black women teachers as role models. It never occurred to me that I would not find them in university classrooms. Yet I studied at four universities—Stanford, University of Wisconsin, University of

---

Reprinted from *Talking Back: Thinking Feminist, Thinking Black*, by bell hooks, 1989. Copyright © 1989 South End Press.

Southern California, and the University of California, Santa Cruz—and I did not once have the opportunity to study with a black woman English professor. They were never members of the faculty. I considered myself lucky to study with one black male professor at Stanford who was visiting and another at the University of Southern California even though both were reluctant to support and encourage black female students. Despite their sexism and internalized racism, I appreciated them as teachers and felt they affirmed that black scholars could teach literature, could work in English departments. They offered a degree of support and affirmation, however relative, that countered the intense racism and sexism of many white professors.

Changing hiring practices have meant that there are increasingly more black professors in predominately white universities, but their presence only mediates in a minor way the racism and sexism of white professors, especially white males. I had not developed this dread as an undergraduate because there it was simply assumed that black students, and particularly black female students, were not bright enough to make it in graduate school. While these racist and sexist opinions were rarely directly stated, the message was conveyed through various humiliations that were aimed at shaming students, at breaking our spirit. We were terrorized. As an undergraduate, I carefully avoided those professors who made it clear that the presence of any black students in their classes was not desired. Unlike Carole Gregory's first encounter, they did not make direct racist statements. Instead, they communicated their message in subtle ways—forgetting to call your name when reading the roll, avoiding looking at you, pretending they do not hear you when you speak, and at times ignoring you altogether.

The first time this happened to me I was puzzled and frightened. It was clear to me and all the other white students that the professor, a white male, was directing aggressive mistreatment solely at me. These other students shared with me that it was not likely that I would pass the class no matter how good my work, that the professor would find something wrong with it. They never suggested that this treatment was informed by racism and sexism; it was just that the professor had for whatever "unapparent" reasons decided to dislike me. Of course, there were rare occasions when taking a course meant so much to me that I tried to confront racism, to talk with the professor, and there were required courses. Whenever I tried to talk with professors about racism, they always denied any culpability. Often I was told, "I don't even notice that you are black."

In graduate school, it was especially hard to choose courses that would not be taught by professors who were quite racist. Even though one could resist by naming the problem and confronting the person, it was rarely possible to find anyone who could take such accusations seriously. Individual white professors were supported by white-supremacist institutions, by racist colleagues, by hierarchies that placed the word of the professor above that of the student. When I would tell the more supportive professors about racism comments that were said behind closed doors, during office hours, there would always be an expression of disbelief, surprise, and suspicion about the accuracy of what I was reporting. Mostly they listened because they felt it was their liberal duty to do so. Their disbelief, their refusal to take responsibility for white racism made it impossible for them to show authentic concern or help. One professor of 18th century literature by white writers invited me to his office to tell me that he would personally see to it that I would never receive a graduate degree. I, like many other students in the class, had written a paper in a style that he disapproved of, yet only I was given this response. It was often in the very areas of British and American literature where racism abounds in the texts studied that I would encounter racist individuals.

Gradually, I began to shift my interest in early American literature to more modern and contemporary works. This shift was influenced greatly by an encounter with a white male professor of American literature whose racism and sexism was unchecked. In his classes, I, as well as other students, was subjected to racist and sexist jokes. Any of us that he considered should not be in graduate school were the objects of particular scorn and ridicule. When we gave oral presentations, we were told our work was stupid, pathetic, and were not allowed to finish. If we resisted in any way, the situation worsened. When I went to speak with him about his attitude, I was told that I was not really graduate school material, that I should drop out. My anger surfaced and I began to shout, to cry. I remember yelling wildly, "Do you love me? And if you don't love me then how can you have any insight about my concerns and abilities? And who are you to make such suggestions on the basis of one class." He of course was not making a suggestion. His was a course one had to pass to graduate. He was telling me that I could avoid the systematic abuse by simply dropping out. I would not drop out. I continued to work even though it was clear that I would not succeed, even as the persecution became more intense. And even though I constantly resisted.

In time, my spirits were more and more depressed. I began to dream of entering the professor's office with a loaded gun. There I would demand that he listen, that he experience the fear, the humiliation. In my dreams I could hear his pleading voice begging me not to shoot, to remain calm. As soon as I put the gun down he would become his old self again. Ultimately in the dream the only answer was to shoot, to shoot to kill. When this dream became so consistently a part of my waking fantasies, I knew that it was time for me to take a break from graduate school. Even so I felt as though his terrorism had succeeded, that he had indeed broken my spirit. It was this feeling that led me to return to graduate school, to his classes, because I felt I had given him too much power over me and I needed to regain that sense of self and personal integrity that I allowed him to diminish. Through much of my graduate school career, I was told that "I did not have the proper demeanor of a graduate student." In one graduate program, the black woman before me, who was also subjected to racist and sexist aggression, would tell me that they would say she was not as smart as me but she knew her place. I did not know my place. Young white radicals began to use the phrase "student as nigger" precisely to call attention to the way in which hierarchies within universities encouraged domination of the powerless by the powerful. At many universities the proper demeanor of a graduate student is exemplary when that student is obedient, when he or she does not challenge or resist authority.

During graduate school, white students would tell me that it was important not to question, challenge, or resist. Their tolerance level seemed much higher than my own or that of other black students. Critically reflecting on the differences between us, it was apparent that many of the white students were from privileged class backgrounds. Tolerating the humiliations and degradations we were subjected to in graduate school did not radically call into question their integrity, their sense of self-worth. Those of us who were coming from underprivileged class backgrounds, who were black, often were able to attend college only because we had consistently defied those who had attempted to make us believe we were smart but not "smart enough"; guidance counselors who refused to tell us about certain colleges because they already knew we would not be accepted; parents who were not necessarily supportive of graduate work, etc. White students were not living daily in a world outside campus life where they also had to resist degradation, humiliation. To them, tolerating forms of exploitation and domination in graduate school did not evoke images of a lifetime spent tolerating abuse. They would endure certain forms of domination and abuse, accepting it as an initiation process that would conclude when they became the person in power. In some ways they regarded graduate school and its many humiliations as a game, and they submitted to playing the role of subordinate. I and many other students, especially non-white students from non-privileged backgrounds, were unable to accept and play this "game." Often we were ambivalent about the rewards promised. Many of us were not seeking to be in a position of power over others. Though we wished to teach, we did not want to exert coercive authoritarian rule over others. Clearly those students who played the game best were usually white males and they did not face discrimination, exploitation, and abuse in many other areas of their lives.

Many black graduate students I knew were concerned about whether we were striving to participate in structures of domination and were uncertain about whether we could assume positions of authority. We could not envision assuming oppressive roles. For some of us, failure, failing, being failed began to look like a positive alternative, a way out, a solution. This was especially true for those students who felt they were suffering mentally, who felt that they would never be able to recover a sense of wholeness or well-being. In recent years, campus awareness of the absence of support for international students who have many conflicts and dilemmas in an environment that does not acknowledge their cultural codes has led to the development of support networks. Yet there has been little recognition that there are black students and other non-white students who suffer similar problems, who come from backgrounds where we learned different cultural codes. For example, we may learn that it is important not to accept coercive authoritarian rule from someone who is not a family elder—hence we may have difficulties accepting strangers assuming such a role.

Not long ago, I was at a small party with faculty from a major liberal California university, which until recently had no black professors in the English department who were permanent staff, though there were sometimes visiting scholars. One non-white faculty member and myself began to talk about the problems facing black graduate students studying in English departments. We joked about the racism within English departments, commenting that other disciplines were slightly more willing to accept study of the lives and works of non-white people yet such work is rarely affirmed in English departments where the study of literature usually consists of many works by white men and a few by white women. We talked about how some departments were struggling to change. Speaking about his department, he commented that they have only a few black male graduate students, sometimes none, that at one time two black students, one male and one female, had been accepted and both had serious mental health problems. At departmental meetings, white faculty suggested that this indicated that black students just did not have the wherewithal to succeed in this graduate program. For a time, no black students were admitted. His story revealed that part of the burden these students may have felt, which many of us have felt, is that our performance will have future implications for all black students and this knowledge heightens one's performance anxiety from the very beginning. Unfortunately, racist biases often lead departments to see the behavior of one black student as an indication of the way all black students will perform academically. Certainly, if individual white students have difficulty adjusting or succeeding within a graduate program, it is not seen as an indication that all other white students will fail.

The combined forces of racism and sexism often make the black female graduate experience differ in kind from that of the black male experience. While he may be subjected to racial biases, his maleness may serve to mediate the extent to which he will be attacked, dominated, etc. Often it is assumed that black males are better able to succeed at graduate school in English than black females. While many white scholars may be aware of a black male intellectual tradition, they rarely know about black female intellectuals. African-American intellectual traditions, like those of white people, have been male-dominated. People who know the names of W.E.B. DuBois or Martin Delaney may have never heard of Mary Church Terrell or Anna Cooper. The small numbers of black women in permanent positions in academic institutions do not constitute a significant presence, one strong enough to challenge racist and sexist biases. Often the only black woman white professors have encountered is a domestic worker in their home. Yet there are no sociological studies that I know of which examine whether a group who has been seen as not having intellectual capability will automatically be accorded respect and recognition if they enter positions that suggest they are representative scholars. Often black women are such an "invisible presence" on campuses that many students may not be aware that any black women teach at the universities they attend.

Given the reality of racism and sexism, being awarded advanced degrees does not mean that black women will achieve equity with black men or other groups in the profession. Full-time, non-white women comprise less than 3 percent of the total faculty on most campuses. Racism and sexism, particularly on the graduate level, shape and influence both the academic performance and employment of black female academics. During my years of graduate work in English, I was often faced with the hostility of white students who felt that because I was black and female I would have no trouble finding a job. This was usually the response from professors as well if I expressed fear of not finding employment. Ironically, no one ever acknowledged that we were never taught by any of these black women who were taking all the jobs. No one wanted to see that perhaps racism and sexism militate against the hiring of black women even though we are seen as a group that will be given priority, preferential status. Such assumptions, which are usually rooted in the logic of affirmative action hiring, do not include recognition of the ways most universities do not strive to attain diversity of faculty and that often diversity means hiring one non-white person, one black person. When I and other black women graduate students surveyed English departments in the United States, we did not see masses of black women and rightly felt concerned about our futures.

Moving around often, I attended several graduate schools but finally finished my work at the University of California, Santa Cruz where I found support despite the prevalence of racism and sexism. Since I had much past experience, I was able to talk with white faculty members before entering the program about whether they would be receptive and supportive of my desire to focus on African-American writers. I was given positive reassurance that proved accurate. More and more, there are university settings where black female graduate students and black graduate students can study in supportive atmospheres. Racism and sexism are always present yet they do not necessarily shape all areas of graduate students working in English departments, I hear that many of the problems have not changed, that they experience the same intense isolation and loneliness that characterized my experience. This is why I think it is important that black women in higher education write and talk about our experiences, about survival strategies. When I was having a very difficult time, I read *Working It Out*. Despite the fact that the academics who described the way in which sexism had shaped their academic experience in graduate school were white women, I was encouraged by their resistance, by their perseverance, by their success. Reading their stories helped me feel less alone. I wrote this essay because of the many conversations I have had with black female graduate students who despair, who are frustrated, who are fearful that the experiences they are having are unique. I want them to know that they are not alone, that the problems that arise, the obstacles created by racism and sexism are real—that they do exist—they do hurt but they are not insurmountable. Perhaps these words will give solace, will intensify their courage, and renew their spirit.

CHAPTER 29

DIS/CONNECTING LITERACY AND SEXUALITY: SPEAKING THE UNSPEAKABLE IN THE CLASSROOM

KATHLEEN ROCKHILL

I view the telling of our personal stories of subordination as an essential political act because without our stories recovered the past haunts the present and hopelessly claims the future.

(McMahon, 1991, p. 33)

"Dis/connecting literacy and sexuality"—when I write these words, I think of how literacy[1] and sexuality[2] are profoundly connected, especially through their opposition, in women's lives, but, absolutely disconnected in educational discourse and practice. Who speaks of literacy and sexuality in the same space? While this disconnection reflects the erasure of women's experience from the social production of knowledge, it is sedimented by practices of institutionalized heterosexism which regulate sexuality as private, unspeakable, and, for women, in opposition to intellectual performance. It is indicative of these separations that educators who advocate literacy for "empowerment" do not ask, "What does it mean to speak of power for a woman whose subordination is accomplished through sexual objectification?" This question is especially pertinent for critical literacy, for "woman's" sexual subordination hinges upon her not threatening male authority, an authority which is threatened by her attaining higher levels of literacy.

Foucault's (1982) argument that power operates through consensus rather than coercion, in the form of discursive practices that shape the subject's thoughts and regulate conduct, does not appear to have affected the ways in which literacy, even critical literacy, is approached. If power is not "out there" in the form of some external identifiable enemy, but internalized through processes of social inscription that shape the way we think—that is, the landscapes of our subjectivities—then how is it possible to approach the acquisition of literacy as a process of critical learning? Traditional literacy practices have been radically challenged by the work of Paulo Freire and other progressive educators who have recognized that acquisition of "the word" is not a neutral process and that "education for critical consciousness" is important to counter the colonizing effects of literacy acquisition. Still, models of popular education assume that learners are a homogenous group, innocent, free in some way of conflict, and that there is consensus, within and among group participants, who are united in their opposition to "power," which is named as "out there," "external," "coercive" (capitalists, the military, and so on) (Rockhill, 1988). Ironically, in assuming the learner to be a kind of blank slate, traditional conceptions of the learner as lacking in critical knowledge about (his) world and of the teacher as the knower, the one with the unproblematically correct approach to political analysis and action, are reinforced. Although lip service is paid to the subject's ideological inscription, it is

---

Reprinted from *Critical Literacy: Politics, Praxis, and the Postmodern*, edited by C. Lankshear & P. McLaren, 1993. Copyright © 1993 State University of New York Press.

assumed that the teacher, somehow, has attained a level of critical consciousness that students have not.

As a feminist concerned about education for radical change, I have been struggling for several years to develop an educational approach that can take up questions of social inscription as integral to processes of critical consciousness through (dis)identifications—experience seen as refracted through prisms of power relations lived as the normalized practices of daily life. How do these processes, relations, and practices differ according to one's social location; that is, how do the class, race, ethnicity, age, physical ability, gender, and sexuality of the learner enter into the challenges posed for literacy work? Although critical approaches to literacy have been important in the development of learner-centered approaches to teaching (Gaber-Katz and Watson, 1991), it is time to recognize that the learner is not a neutral person, but different persons who are gendered, raced, classed, and so on, and located, in all probability, at the margins of mainstream society. Moreover, that person's subjectivity has been formed in such a way that he or she is apt to have "internalized" social prescriptions about what is seen to be desirable behavior; hence racism, sexism, classism, and so on are experienced as inadequacy and self-loathing in relation to white, male-defined standards. Many women, for example, hate themselves for not measuring up to idealized images of feminine beauty at the same time as they desire to be, to match, as closely as possible, those images.

Feminism has scarcely touched the field of adult education; the area of literacy is no exception. This is beginning to shift, but the struggle is a formidable one. In my own faculty the battles have been brutal, fought largely around hirings, with feminist candidates consistently dismissed as "narrow, dogmatic, ideological," their work defined as having nothing to do with adult education, a profound threat to the humanitarian values of "the field." I am struck by the ways in which the current dismissal of feminism strongly replicates the delegitimation of working-class education as a base for practice that took place in the 1930s, when the field of workers' education was captured and defined by professional educators. In a historical study of the era (Rockhill, 1985), I describe how the professional field of adult education was institutionalized through a series of discursive practices that delegitimized class-based education as ideological, separatist, undemocratic, and biased, the very antithesis of liberal egalitarian educational values. Instead of considering a separate, class-based education that might serve to provide a base from which workers collectively could define, study, and critique their class location, educators felt that their responsibility was to provide a place wherein individual adults could be given a second chance to acquire the skills necessary to succeed in the system. These forms continue to define legitimate practice; equality of opportunity through functional literacy is the overarching goal, not literacy for critical consciousness and political action. Separate education for women in which a feminist agenda is the announced goal of the course is virtually unthinkable.

What does all of this have to do with the question of literacy and sexuality? If literacy is about "empowerment" through acquisition and critical awareness of "the word," and if women are subjugated through our sexualization—that is, the manipulation of our desire to be "feminine subjects" who are, by definition, not independent, intelligent, and educated—and if the boundaries of education are set so that literacy and sexuality shall never meet, then what does literacy as empowerment for women mean? Which women? What does it mean if feminism, the analysis and practice of addressing women's subordination through sexual objectification, is deemed to be "irrelevant" and/or a "threat" to the true values of adult education and literacy?

Literacy, sexuality, and power

> In order to perpetuate itself, every oppression must corrupt or distort those various sources of power within the culture of the oppressed that can provide energy for change. For women this has meant a suppression of the erotic as a considered source of power and information in our lives.
> (Lorde, 1984)

The separation of literacy from sexuality is deeply sedimented in the construction of educational work, as well as in the semiotic codes of "woman." To be an educated woman is to be without sex; to be "sexy" is to be desirable, to be vulnerable. To walk into a classroom mandates that we hide our sexual beings (bodies) in the closet. As long as education carries the symbolic meaning of power, it runs against the grain of women's "allowed" (however dangerous and contradictory) domain of "power," her sexual desirability to men.

Catherine MacKinnon (1989) argues that, for women, dominance is eroticized; "woman" does not exist as a "being" independent of the male gaze, which shapes her desire. The meaning of her existence is in her service of and accessibility to men. Sexuality, in this schema, is not limited to narrowly defined sexual acts, but is conceived much more broadly as "a pervasive dimension of social life, one that permeates the whole, a dimension along which gender occurs and through which gender is socially constituted" (p. 130).

> Sexuality... is a form of power. Gender, as socially constructed, embodies it, not the reverse. Women and men are divided by gender, made into the sexes as we know them, by the social requirements of its dominant form, heterosexuality, which institutionalizes male sexual dominance and female sexual submission. If this is true, sexuality is the linchpin of gender inequality... sexuality is gendered as gender is sexualized. Male and female are created through the eroticization of dominance and submission." (p. 113)

In their work, F. Haug *et al.* (1987) demonstrate how female socialization is primarily a process of female sexualization. As girls learn how to become women, they learn how to acquire competence as sexualized feminine subjects. Through their collective project in memory work, the authors vividly reveal how "sexuality is represented through a whole set of rules which do not just relate to the genitalia but govern the body as a whole, the way it is treated or clothed, bodily hygiene and so on." They go on to point out that sexuality is regulated through *hetero*sexuality, "which constitutes both the envisaged goal and the framework within which we already move" (p. 212).

To see sexuality broadly, as a full range of beliefs, assumptions, representations, and social practices that regulate women through our (hetero) sexualization, is a controversial move among feminists. In describing the "institution of heterosexuality," Teresa deLauretis (1990) provides a key to understanding why it is everywhere and nowhere at the same time:

> The tenacious mental habit of associating sexuality (as sexual *acts* between people) with the private sphere or individual privacy, even as one is constantly surrounded by representations of sexuality... tends to deny the obvious—the very public nature of the discourses on sexuality and what Foucault has called "the technology of sex," the social mechanisms (from the educational system to jurisprudence, from medicine to the media, and so forth) that regulate sexuality and effectively enforce it—*and* that regulate and enforce it as *heterosexuality*. (p. 129)

In education, by and large, sexuality is regulated by its absence, by the severance of the body from the mind, by the relegation of sexuality to the "private" sphere, the sphere of the unspeakable. Even more significantly, I argue that in "our" society women are regulated through the direct opposition of intellectuality to sexuality; to be "woman" is to be sexual, not intellectual. What I am saying is nothing new. Girls learn at a young age not to be too smart if we want to be popular, not to be too sexy if we want to be accepted intellectually. As Michelle Fine (1988) argues, where sexuality does enter educational discourse in high schools, it does so in terms set to regulate girls to be heterosexual, celibate until marriage, and monogamous; sexuality, as a "desire of her own," does not exist in education.[3] For a teenage girl, "achievement" is accomplished through the acquisition of a steady boyfriend of the highest possible status, not school performance. As Angela McRobbie (1991) notes, "One of their [schools'] central functions is to reproduce the sexual division of labour, so that girls come willingly to accept their subordinate status in society" (p. 44). That it is common knowledge that intellectuality and sexuality are opposed for girls and women, and yet never present in discourses about education and literacy, is illustrative of the regulation of sexuality through its absence, and, even further, its unspeakableness, especially if spoken in terms of personal experience in classrooms. This may be especially true of adult education classrooms, which is particularly ironic given that "the field" prides itself on being "experience based" and "learner centered." Whose experience? Which learners?

Intellectuality and sexuality are in opposition for women because education potentially provides an alternative source of power. There is the possibility of independence from men, both materially—in terms of time, space, money, and work—and in thought. That they are opposed partly affirms MacKinnon's argument: what man wants an uppity woman? I think of my own experience, of how men used to phrase my desirability to them in terms of my difference from other academic women, my accessibility, my vulnerability, my tentativeness, my sexiness. In order to counter my intellectuality I learned to deny my mind, to claim "my power" through appearing to be sexually desirable to men. And yet this posed a bind for me in the university, where to appear sexual was to become a target of ridicule, charged with inappropriate behavior and appearance.

To name sex as a power relationship between men and women through which women are subordinated is a threat to deeply sedimented social practices and forms that go far beyond individual male-female relationships, and yet—this is the contradiction—the "power" of this relationship is precisely that it is experienced individually, as one's intimately lived connection to others, to socially sanctioned sources of hope, happiness, and love. Why is there so much resistance to naming heterosexuality as a formative social institution which organizes relations between men and women in "our" society? Does the naming of heterosexism have to mean the erasure of race and class, and/or the invalidation of the possibility of "egalitarian" male-female partnerships? Can the traps of universalism and essentialism be addressed by considering how heterosexism is simultaneously organized according to race and class? How can we shift the ground of the analysis from "innate characteristics" that fix all men as violent and all women as victims to look at the social relations and discursive formations that position men in a dominant relationship to women as mediated by race and class? How is "Woman" framed as "heterosexual" in various societies, and how is that image also codified along the lines of class, race, age, beauty, and so forth?

It is true that theories of women's sexual oppression have not taken into account power differences among women, especially with respect to race and class. This is an important critique. White Western feminist academics—and I am one—cannot claim to speak for all women; we truly do not know, and are not positioned to know, how sexism, racism, and classism work across various social locations. I have no doubt that I am most conscious of my subordination as a woman through my sexual subordination because this is the primary site through which I have lived oppression; the shape of that oppression was influenced by class and to some degree by race.[4] Still, I am uneasy about critiques that would dismiss sexuality as a site of women's oppression because it does not speak to race and class. Instead of throwing out the possibility that women are oppressed through sexuality, I would like to open up the question of *how* the sexual subjugation of women may work, and how it may work very differently according to one's social location. As Mohanty (1988) observes, "Male violence (if indeed that is the appropriate label) must be theorized and interpreted *within* specific societies, both in order to understand it better, as well as in order to effectively organize to change it" (p. 67).

Part of the difficulty with understanding *how*, in Foucault's terms, the "deployment of sexuality" actually works is in its reduction to discourse and, with it, the erasure of the lived bodies of historically located subjects who are lodged in relationships of power (deLauretis, 1987). As MacKinnon (1989) observes, although it has become common to speak of sexuality as socially constructed, "seldom specified is what, socially, it is constructed of, far less who does the constructing or how, when, or where... Power is everywhere therefore nowhere, diffuse rather than pervasively hegemonic" (p. 131). And I would add, who receives the constructing, how meaning may be made differently by women in different locations, with different investments in white male-defined mandates of female sexuality. Just as Haug *et al.* begin to open up the "rules" young girls learn to live by, and how they are learned, we need investigations that can begin to explicate how external ordering (social inscription) is lodged in concrete ongoing social relations reproduced differently across social domains over the life span.

Focusing on the social relations that produce women's subordination differently according to race leads Aída Hurtado (1989) to theorize that differences in women's relational position to white male privilege account for differing, contradictory dynamics through which women are subordinated: whereas white women are seduced into "femininity," women of color are rejected.

> White men need white women in a way that they do not need women of color because women of color cannot fulfill white men's need for racially pure offspring. This fact creates differences in the *relational position* of the groups—distance from and access to the source of privilege, white men. Thus, white women, as a group, are subordinated through seduction, women of color, as a group, through rejection. Class position, of course, affects the probability of obtaining the rewards of seduction and the sanctions of rejection. (p. 844)

Although I wonder whether, even for white women, regulation through seduction doesn't depend upon the surety of "rejection" if one cannot live up to or does not follow the norms and rules of white feminine performance, Hurtado makes the crucial point that these dynamics will work very differently depending upon the possibility of access to white male privilege. And, as Mohanty (1988) argues, the category *women of color* has a homogenizing effect that conceals class, cultural, and racial specificities. Cherríe Moraga, writing from within the specificity of Chicano culture, shows how the violation by white males of the Mexicana (Chicana) is taken up among her people in such a way that the Chicana who does not couple with the Chicano male is slandered as a betrayer of her race. Moraga raises the question of the relationship of "women of color" to "men of color," and how that is defined by women's relationship to white male power. As Moraga (1983) argues, the loyalty of the Chicana to her race is defined by her loyalty to the Chicano male, a loyalty that can turn woman against woman:

> What looks like betrayal between women on the basis of race originates, I believe, in sexism/heterosexism. Chicanas begin to turn our backs on each other to gain male approval or to avoid being sexually stigmatized by them under the name of puta, vendita, jota. (p. 98)

The sexual legacy passed down to the Mexicana/Chicana is the legacy of betrayal, pivoting around the historical/mythical female figure of Malintzin Tenepal. As translator and strategic advisor and mistress to the Spanish conqueror of Mexico, Hernan Cortez, Malintzin is considered the mother of the mestizo people. But unlike La Virgin de Guadalupe, she is not revered as the Virgin Mother, but rather slandered as La Chingada, meaning "fucked one," or La Vendida, sell-out to the white race. (p. 99)

So little has been documented as to the actual suffering Chicanas have experienced resisting or succumbing to the sexual demands of white men. The ways we have internalized the sexual hatred and exploitation they have displayed against us are probably too numerous and too ingrained to even identify. If the Chicana, like her brother, suspects other women of betrayal, then she must, in the most profound sense, suspect herself. How deep her suspicions run will measure how ardently she defends her commitment, above all, to the Chicano male. As obedient sister/daughter/lover she is the committed heterosexual, the socially acceptable Chicana. Even if she's politically radical, sex remains the bottom line on which she proves her commitment to her race. (p. 105)

Literacy as threat/desire

> In writing close to the other of the other, I can only choose to maintain a self-reflexively critical relationship toward the material, a relationship that defines both the subject written and the writing subject, undoing the I while asking "what do I want wanting to *know* you or me?"
> (Minh-ha, 1989)

Some years ago I worked on a research project about the experiences of Spanish-speaking immigrants to West Los Angeles in learning English. Several years later, I published my interpretation of the experiences of the women interviewed, theorizing that the acquisition of English language literacy was highly contradictory for them, a strong desire that also posed a threat to their lives as constructed (Rockhill, 1987b, 1987c). Although my interpretation is necessarily limited by my not being of the same culture and class as the women who told their stories, and I struggle with the racism implicit in that process, still it was in this work that the profound educational bind faced by women came powerfully home to me. Here I first linked what had been separated in my mind—stories of sexual violence—with stories of educational (non)participation. This was ironic in a way, because I knew from my own history the profound threat that the education of women posed to the men with whom they were in a relationship; the violence it provoked written in my bones. Still, they remained separated from me. Setting out to study literacy practices, I did not inquire about intimate relationships, but did ask for stories about the experience of immigration, as well as detailed specificities of language situations where English was encountered, which provided concrete settings for understanding the ways in which language learning was interconnected with the structure of daily life.

Because of the gendered structure of the world in which they were lodged, the women interviewed were more dependent than men upon classroom instruction in order to learn English; yet the women were often hampered from participation because of either subtle or overt opposition in the home, their structural location as women. The intricate texture of how heterosexuality is lived as sexual oppression was outlined in bold relief by the extent of the women's isolation and their dependence upon men in the home. The women we interviewed did not drive, did not have access to a car, were not permitted to go out of their homes, and/or were terrified to do so because of crime (woman as target) and not knowing enough English to defend themselves. Unlike men, they could not learn English informally because of the structure of women's work, which is bifurcated between dead-end factory, domestic, and field jobs requiring no talk and highly literacy dependent jobs in clerical, secretarial, and women's caring professions. To advance, literacy in English is crucial, and, since women have less access to learning the language informally, they are extremely dependent upon classes but denied continuing access because of time pressure and/or the threat that their participation can pose to the family; the fear is that the woman will become more educated than her husband, more independent, and be influenced by Western "gringa" feminism. At that same time, the man is more vulnerable than ever, typically with a deplorable short-term heavy manual labor job with a high incidence of disability and unemployment, and at a deficit in not knowing how to work the system. All of these factors are compounded enormously if one's presence in the country is uncertain, either as an illegal immigrant or as a refugee. Literacy is about language and education as well as the specific skills of reading and writing; its meaning is integral to the social relations in which it is embedded. When attending literacy classes represents "becoming educated," for a woman to step out of the house and attend a class can upset the power relations of the traditional family. To "empower" her may be to put her "safety" at risk. In the case of ESL, for the women interviewed, English language literacy was a compelling desire, *and*, as a symbol of educational attainment in a different (dominant) cultural formation, it posed a threat to the stasis of their lives and loves.

In reporting this research, I struggled with my fears that my interpretation was racist and/or would feed into the racist stereotyping of "the other." Although I was absolutely certain that violence is not limited to the population under study, I recognized that it has a particular coloration because of the dynamics of immigration, language, culture, and racism—and that this has to be taken into account in doing educational programming. Since then, other studies have begun to show the dis/connections between education and sexuality for different populations of women. Even today, as I pick up the daily newspaper, there is an account of violence toward Filipino women (Reid, 1991). While pointing out that no community is free of violence against women, one of the workers interviewed for the story goes on to report how, "because of language and cultural barriers, some women remain trapped, not knowing where to turn." Almost as an aside, another of the workers comments, "Being intelligent and vocal is considered masculine in our culture." To be "Woman" is not to be "outspoken." In a study that I am currently engaged in with Patricia Tomic, the community workers interviewed confirm the extreme isolation of Spanish-speaking immigrant and refugee women, the violence some experience in their homes, their terror of going out of the house, calling for help, or participating in educational programs. Often it is not until they separate from their male partners that they act upon their desire to learn English systematically and pursue their educations.

Where not knowing the dominant language is involved, the dis/connections between education and sexuality can lead to extreme social isolation, even greater dependency upon the male, shame, and self-degradation. What does it mean for a woman suddenly to be rendered "illiterate," to be drastically displaced, without knowledge of "the word" or of the social system to which it refers? And when access to "the word" carries with it access to gringo culture, the image of the educated Western woman with her more "independent" ways, does literacy then pose the possibility of "another way of being woman"?

How do race and class work differently and together in conjunction with sexuality to colonize women? Even where English is the first language, the drama of literacy is about the desire for movement from one class location to another. To what extent are literacy classes, and the life skill training that often accompanies them, really about learning the appearances of white middle-class performance for women (Morton, 1985)? How do these changes, whether real or anticipated, affect the relationships of women to friends, family, and lovers? Is there an underside to the fairytale of Pygmalian, to the romance of literacy as the passport to a life of comfort and success?

It is crucial to emphasize that male violence toward some women who participate in literacy and educational programs is not limited to non-English-speaking families. Presenting initial documentation from a study conducted under the auspices of the Canadian Congress for Learning Opportunities for Women (CCLOW), researcher Betty-Ann Lloyd notes that "many, many women face violence from men if they dare to go back to school." As one participant in the study puts it, "When a woman becomes involved in a literacy program, when she's becoming more independent, the man is losing his grip and he's becoming more violent and more aggressive and attempting more control." Another notes, "Low education does help keep you where you are. That's why men become so threatened when you start to finish your program and you might look at some kind of training. You may not be so dependent" (Lloyd, 1991, p. 33). Significantly, each connects violence to the perceived greater independence of the woman, a "threat" more likely as further educational possibilities develop.

I also wonder at the implication of childhood sexual abuse, as well as of ongoing sexualization/violence in the way many women are treated, for educational performance. "Low self-esteem" has so repeatedly been named as the central problem women must overcome to participate in education that it has the status of commonplace knowledge. What's behind it?

"Stupid! Illiterate! Whore!" How often I heard that refrain in my Los Angeles studies. To be sexualized is to be rendered stupid, the "dumb blonde" in dominant culture, always accessible: without a thought—or desire—of one's own. Day-in and day-out abuse: what are its effects? As one literacy worker puts it,

> Violence in the home... causes a lack of self-worth, a lack of self-esteem, a lack of confidence. If you're being told you're stupid or worthless for so many years you start to believe it... I think every time they're abused it's "How can I go back to school? I'm stupid. How can I make that effort to get out there, that first step to get out there?" (Lloyd, 1991, p. 33)

The privatization of sexuality, its mas(c)ualization as "pleasure," the systemic silencing of women's lived experiences of sex, and the splitting of education from "the personal" keep us from exploring the linkages between sexuality and educational performance. We don't know because we don't ask, don't want to probe, don't want to violate, don't want to know.

Like me, Belenky *et al.* (1986) did not originally think to ask about sexual abuse in their study of "women's ways of knowing." It was midway through their study, after many women had mentioned that sexual trauma had significantly affected their learning, before the researchers began systematically to ask about it. The evidence they have suggests that there may be a strong connection between sexual abuse, lacking a sense of voice, and unquestioned trust in authorities. I know from my own work on incest that it had profound effects upon my sense of self, a deep fear of being seen, of taking up space. This is corroborated by the work of Anne-Louise Brookes (1988). I know only enough to know that the relationship between intellectuality and sexuality must be a complex one for girls who are abused. I "survived" by escaping into my head; I do not know what happens if the head is not experienced as a "safe" place, if one has been controlled by being systematically told that one is stupid, dumb, if one has been asked, "Just who the hell do you think you are to think . . . ?" Consider the erosion of self-esteem, to be told you are a dumb, stupid slut . . .

The argument for culturally specific approaches to literacy is reinforced by Jenny Horsman's sensitive study of literacy in the lives of women in rural Nova Scotia, *Something in My Mind Besides the Everyday* (1990). Detailing a range of violence in women's lives, from sexual abuse to psychological abuse to childhood pregnancy to isolation and poverty, the heartbreaking piece of the story for me is how women take on social judgments and believe that they are to blame for the failures of their lives. Still, Horsman captures the fighting spirit of the women she interviews, their determination to find a place in the world for themselves and their children:

> I think it's probably pretty strange to anyone that doesn't realize the kind of a life that a battered woman lives . . . I made it my little mini war trying to win battle after battle to get my own little place, my own little piece of myself . . . I want to work . . . to work at something that I can enjoy getting up in the morning where I think I'm accomplishing something, where I get paid a reasonable amount to live on . . . I'm asking for the moon and the stars and everything else. (Alice, quoted on back cover)

Horsman observes that the lives of the women she studied are

> organized in relation to the needs of others. This organization is essentially *dis*organization, women living their lives around the demands of their male partners, and children, and sometimes also extended family members . . . Dependence—on men, on inadequately paid work and on social service assistance—is threaded through the lives. (p. 85)

Dependence leads to violence: "The violence of these women's lives is frequently obscured by the illusion that illiteracy creates women's problems—that it is illiteracy that "disables" women or "chains" them in prison. In that way our attention is focussed not on the disorganizations of women's lives but on women's failure to become literate" (p. 86).

Thus so the "dream" of literacy:—the desire that we as educators, policymakers, and employers co-create that women take on as their own—"become literate, become educated, and your life will change. If you don't, you alone are at fault."

In "Literacy as Threat/Desire" (1987b), I put forth a similar argument. It is not so much a question of whether literacy "in fact" makes any difference in women's (in)dependence as it is the symbolic vision of education as transforming one's life, transporting one into the "safety" of the middle-class home, white picket fence and all. And education may be, "in reality," women's only ticket out of poverty—and it may not make a difference.

Toward a feminist agenda in literacy

> Moving from silence into speech is . . . a gesture of defiance that heals, that makes a new life and new growth possible. It is that act of speech, of "talking back," that is no mere gesture of empty words, that is the expression of our movement from object to subject—the liberated voice.
> (hooks, 1989, p. 9)

Education is turned to by women in search of a way out of the cycles of dependency in which their lives are enmeshed. This is all we have to offer, really: either that or institutionalization. I recall watching a film by Brenda Longfellow (1981) in which a woman who had been battered finally made her way into a training program. I recall feeling quite sick and angry at the view that this was the "happy ending" of the film, theoretically the romance of the "career" taking the place of romantic love. Although I don't want to deny that education, as a move toward possible economic independence, *is* essential, I also want to ask whether a course or a job is enough to end the cycle of violence in which battered women are caught.

Having spent my life trying to overcome the effects of sexual abuse in my childhood, situations played out over and over as an adult through my (re)positioning as "woman," as sexual object, as one who has and had no worth other than as a body, I want to scream out "No!—Literacy alone is not enough." We need to learn how to resist and refuse our social inscription as "woman," especially since our primary sites of rebellion are also sexually inscribed—as the Whore—the rampantly heterosexual. [5]

So what does "critical literacy" look like for women? If you make it to "our" classes, what do we do? What might explicitly feminist approaches look like? If critical literacy is about "emancipation," "empowerment," how can the various ways in which power works to subordinate women be taken into account? Insofar as power works through our bodies, through our sexual objectification as "feminine," through the formation of our subjectivities, of our consciousnesses, what does this suggest as possibilities for educational approaches to critical consciousness? And what are the implications for women if education is highly charged, posing a threat to our socially designated source of power, "our" (hetero)sexuality?

To address, seriously, the question of women's power, it is essential to open up the ways in which we are implicated in institutionalized heterosexism: the ways in which we live heterosexism, not only in our intimate relationships, but also in public settings, where we are also positioned as the sexualized female, and the ways in which our very identity—our sense of self, our subjectivity—has been shaped by heterosexism, as defined through the prisms of class, race, and culture. Because they are so close to the bone, because they touch our deepest places of emotional investment and wounding, opening up these questions in the classroom can be charged with emotion and conflict, the "danger" of sliding into the slippery domain of therapy ever present. And yet, I know from my teaching that these are critical questions, questions that link what is experienced as personal inadequacy to social positioning and political practices, and that they can be explored in the classroom if personal experiences, disagreements, and confrontations are respected as places from which to begin to talk.

Insofar as we understand power as the ordering of our conduct through the formation of our subjectivities, our identities, as Teresa deLauretis (1990) points out, a key question becomes, how can we *(dis)identify*? If power works through discursive formations of seduction/rejection to manipulate desire, the very construction of "self," of identity, and if the identities formed are in relation to dominant ideologies and deeply sedimented in ongoing social relations, how can we find a standpoint from which to "see through" and resist social inscriptions? And if *"we"* are all so formed, how are we formed differently, according to our social location and positioning relative to white male privilege? I emphasize "we" because teachers do not stand apart from their students, free of social inscription. If anything, teachers may more closely approximate dominant images of power, be more blinded by the possibility of being "seduced," than their students. How do we learn to (dis)identify from hegemonic conceptions of "woman" *as well as* recognize that not all women identify in the same ways? How do we learn to take into account the simultaneity of oppressions through gender, race, class, and sexuality, come to understand and respect their collusion in the constitution of differences through sameness and sameness through difference? Don't differing and complex social locations suggest differing processes of (dis)identifying, as well as multiple and changing (dis)identifications? Doesn't difference in location also suggest differences in the ways and content of knowings, situated knowledges that may differ from dominant conceptions (Luttrell, 1989; Collins, 1989)? Isn't part of the whirl that education poses for those whose experiences have not been fully co-opted by dominant descriptions of their realities immense discomfort, distance, and chaos? [6]

One of the most troubling questions posed by poststructural theory is the question of agency, and the possibility of taking a critical stance, of seeing from a vantage outside of or alongside our inscription. I want to argue that inscription is totalizing but not total. The "social" is not a monolith, not uniform, often contradictory, and our experience of "it" depends in part upon our locations. This affects both what we know and how we know. As deLauretis (1990) argues, there is a place outside of consciousness, perhaps the "unconscious," that resists total inscription. And, as Haug *et al.* point out, discursive formations work through social relations. Using the image of a huge fishing net as what establishes the order of the social whole, the reader is asked to consider *how* the net is woven and *cast*. Herein lies a key for critical approaches to education; social relations are multiple, sometimes contradictory, and, like a net, full of w/holes.

In my work I have used the image of invisible concrete walls that regulate us as in a maze. As I see it, the goal of critical education is to learn how to (re)cognize the walls of the maze and how they are held in place. The bleak vision is seeing that I have been trained like a rat to run through and perform effectively in the maze. As long as I can negotiate the treacherous channels of the maze, I carry in me the illusion of safety, comfort, order, and competence. This is the "negative" theoretical moment, when I must "deconstruct," giving up old safeties. The hopeful vision—the positive moment—is in learning how to see the trap of the maze, to recognize the taken-for-granted rules and assumptions that govern my behavior, to see how they are reproduced and ingrained in everyday practices and relationships, and to see how they are relived in my bodily and emotional responses. The painful reality is that I learn to recognize the boundary of the maze only when I run into its invisible concrete walls head on; as my belief in the course of action prescribed by the walls crumbles, I fall into chaos, disorder, the void of not knowing how to be, how to perform, who I am. In time resistance shifts to more conscious forms of rebellion, of (re)cognition. I know my (re)production when I feel my breath stop, the pressure rise in my head, and the knot form in my gut, when I refuse to be trampled on any longer, saying "NO," finding "support" to resist, to affirm that "I'm not crazy," that what I "know" is valid, . . . and rebuilding . . . rebuilding . . . rebuilding. . . .

Questions about "experience" and the validity of knowledge from experience have plagued me for some time. Although I do not agree with the liberal humanist assumption that experience is in some way "pure," "innocent," or "true," I do recognize a knowing from my experience. I believe that consciousness is ideologically formed, that we have to struggle to understand how our experience is shaped and reproduced through dominant cultural/structural forms. Yet I have worked too long and hard not to recognize that there is a place where I also "know," where my experience has not been totally colonized by ideology, where I have not absolutely "forgotten" in order to survive, to feel "safe," by shaping my experience to fit dominant cultural norms. Perhaps deLauretis is right: it is that part of my "unconscious" that is "eccentric"; it is lodged in my social location as a woman, and it is in that location of difference that the possibility of resistance—of a lesbian stance—rests.

A domain of experience for women that poses an extremely controversial place from which to speak is sexuality, especially if what is spoken challenges dominant constructions that either silence or regulate sexuality as heterosexuality. Although I do not want to argue that "a lesbian stance" is the only place from which inscriptions of heterosexuality can be challenged, I think that the greater a woman's investment in heterosexuality, the more threatening and emotionally laden are its challenges. Still, women who identify as heterosexual can and do challenge their inscription, often from within the frame of heterosexuality, and sometimes in ways that counter it (Williams, 1991).

This brings me back to the question of differences in location and how those differences may speak to less totalizing forms of social inscription, while at the same time the costs of refusing to play according to the rules of the dominant society may be greater. In what kind of a "crazy-making" position would this place one? Is it possible that the processes and possibilities of critical consciousness may play out very differently according to our investment in *not* seeing? Perhaps the greater our privilege is along particular dimensions, the more we have to gain by not seeing, or only seeing so far, or in ways that do not undermine our "loyalties." Yet if sites of rebellion are also socially inscribed (Willis, 1977; McRobbie, 1991), perhaps the picture is more complex. I think that this may be especially true for women where differences in class and race location may pose diametrically opposed possibilities for how one lives the "social outlaw" and/or whether one can choose to trade in sexuality or intellectuality.

Whatever, chances are high that our students know more than their teachers about concrete aspects of their lives that are missing from or (mis)represented in dominant forms of discourse. Unless they can bring their experiences into the classrooms and we can truly learn to listen—to hear their stories—to learn what they know, that they know, and *how* they have come to know what they know, I don't see how we can talk of critical literacy (Razack, 1990). And, through the validation of their experience as knowledge, perhaps they will come to value that they too "know"—and just perhaps "low self-esteem" will be less of a problem. How do we deal with differences in experiential knowings, knowings that are not innocent of ideological inscription, that may be contradictory, that may even violate the knowings of others in the group?

In my work I have found that the implications of truly listening, of encouraging students to speak their exceptionality, to speak their difference, their anger, their pain, has had a revolutionary impact upon my teaching. Like bell hooks (1989) and Audre Lorde (1984), I have come to understand my approach to teaching to be confrontational, and I am learning the importance of listening to the "defiant speech" (hooks, 1989; Ellsworth, 1989) of those who disagree with me, the texts in use, or the generalizing "we" that develops as differences are eclipsed. Painfully, I am coming to know that I do not know. As Ellsworth (1989) learned, all knowledge, even the teacher's, is partial; it is framed through one's social location, one's life experience and history. But this is not easy. To truly allow a space where defiance can be spoken means that classes are conflictual and confrontational. Like most women, I have been sexualized to care for others, not to confront; I am terrified of anger; I struggle to welcome it as a moment of truth.

These moments of speaking exceptionality, of defiant speech, are experienced as emotionally charged interruptions in the classroom. It is not uncommon for a person who has been silent[7] suddenly to erupt, with angry words at last, rupturing silences imposed by seeing one's experience violated or erased by classroom discourse. I recall vividly the moment when I first publicly spoke from my knowledge and location as a sexually abused woman and child, in an emotional torrent unleashing years of tears and rage, and I recall the frenzy that this placed me in because I felt that, as a teacher, I had no right to so ab/use my power, "imposing" my emotions on the women participating in the class. All I had wanted to do was to critique feminist theories of motherhood that explained female socialization in terms of "connection" to the mother, while erasing violence, especially the raped violence of the father that I had experienced. I knew painfully of what I spoke and could no longer tolerate the gaping disjuncture between what had been emblazoned in my bones and the abstract theoretical discourse of feminism. As I spoke, years of silenced emotions erupted. In breaking these rules of silence, I've come to see how sexuality, as lived, and emotional outbursts, on the part of the students *and* teacher, are beyond the boundaries of proper classroom conduct. I still struggle with emotional expression and questions of power, and find no easy answer. Although I do not want to impose my emotion, I cannot expect students to enter into the vulnerable place of expressing their feelings if I stay safely masked, hiding behind the role of teacher.

Uma Narayan (1988) argues that the oppressed have "epistemic privilege," "insider knowledge" about the nature of their oppression. She makes a useful distinction between (1) knowledge gained through causal and structural analysis of oppression, and (2) immediate knowledge of everyday life under oppression: "They know first-hand the detailed and concrete ways in which oppression defines the spaces in which they live and how it affects their lives" (p. 36). Moreover, the insider (the oppressed) knows these in an emotionally embodied way, as a "truth" which the outsider may seek to understand but can never fully know in the same way. Although Narayan's description does not take into account differences in consciousness of the oppressed, or multiple social locations among the oppressed that mean that knowledge is always partial, shifting, and changing, her distinction is still useful in thinking about education for critical consciousness. I don't want to risk separating theory from experience, but it seems to me that education for critical consciousness is about the integration of both kinds of knowledge identified by Narayan. It means that experiences as emotionally embodied must be linked to post-structural analyses of one's experience as socially mediated and constructed. The post-structural turn, which argues that subjectivities are ideologically formed, means that we must hold in question even what we think we know through experience. So to Narayan's two distinctions I would add critical self-reflexivity, or developing the capacity to see *how* one's subjectivity, one's interpretation of experience, one's knowledge, is lodged in social relations and shaped by discursive formations.

That the emotions are central to critical consciousness I've come to understand in two ways: one is the emotional tenacity of our attachment to how we have learned to become. As Haug *et al.* point out, in the process of learning *how* to become a sexualized female, one acquires a competence, a sense of safety and pleasure in that competence; to let go is to feel incompetent, to lose one's sense of self, to fall into an abyss. And our emotions are deeply etched in our bodies; to "understand" what is happening does not mean we can change it. We are deeply invested in the "safety" of the ways we have learned to be, the "safety" of the known, the familiar of the (hetero)sexualized feminine. It is quite terrifying to upset this, especially since those ways of being are not individual to us, but socially prescribed, mandated. Our fear of change, our sense of impending threat, is justified. Minnie Bruce Pratt (1984) writes of the exclusions, the denials, that this sense of safety, of home, depends upon, a safety that does not get called into question until old ways of being become untenable. Pratt describes how, when she became a lesbian, she stepped "outside the circle of protection" she had taken for granted. She writes that "we experience change as loss" "because it is: the old lies and ways of living, habitual, familiar, comfortable, fitting us like our skin, were *ours*. Our fear of losses can keep us from changing. What is it, exactly, that we are afraid to lose?" (p. 39). Fears of loss are not limited to our psychic lives. Every time we interrupt, speak defiantly, and/or name our differences, we risk the loss of our community, home, and friends. So too in the classroom, difference is spoken at great risk—but what is this "safety" which depends upon silence, politeness, and "comfortable" speech?

Berenice Fisher (1987) notes that emotions are integral to the process of consciousness raising and of feminist pedagogy, but we know very little about how to work with them; we assume that in some way, once we understand the social roots of our emotions, our "true" emotions will emerge. Fisher draws upon the work of Audre Lorde, on the power of the erotic and of anger as liberatory, to ask how we can learn to use the emotions in approaches to feminist teaching, and describes her use of theatrical forms to encourage classroom participants to "embody" the standpoints of others and to talk about their feelings about doing so.

I have also struggled for many years now to bring a full range of emotions into the classroom. I have wanted to provide a space where participants can embody our learning, speak from and challenge our experiences as women, find the courage to name our exceptionality from the normalizing "we" of the classroom even with respect to feminism. I know of no model for this kind of education. I refuse to run from pain, conflict, and anger in the classroom; I refuse to set up safeties that are predicated upon false assumptions of trust, of an inclusive "we." I want to bring our bodies, our sexualities, the full "strength of the erotic" (Lorde, 1984), into our classroom. The more I push, the more I've come to see the deep chasm that's developed between the mind and the body, education and therapy. The extent to which the sexual, the body, and the emotional are seen as the domain of therapy and not of education becomes clearer as these boundaries are pushed.

These divisions are reflected in some of the reactions I've had to my written work. When I read the "Chaos" (1987a) piece, in which I write emotionally about my experience and the erasure of incest and sexual abuse from educational and scholarly work, I am urged to go into therapy, to work through pain and anger. When I speak about literacy as threat/desire, I am told, "But we cannot possibly take up that kind of work in the classroom." To address that doubleness of threat and desire, to take seriously the possibility that educational participation can be a site of violence for women, cannot be done within the framework of education; that is the domain of therapy.

Consciousness raising is a painful process. It upsets our world as we know it. If literacy poses a threat to women, how much greater will that threat be if it is also tied to a critical analysis of our situations? The power we confront is not some alien enemy but ourselves, the ways we have learned to be as feminized objects, our life as we have understood it, including the hope for safety and salvation through romance, the home, and the family.

These longings for safety are reproduced in the classroom. As educators, we do all we can to stave off conflict, to avoid unpleasant emotional experiences, to make everyone feel comfortable, liked. We shun disruption—and yet, it is only through disruption, I believe, that critical learning can take place. As Magda Lewis (1990) observes,

> We cannot expect that students will readily appropriate a political stance that is truly counter-hegemonic, unless we also acknowledge the ways in which our feminist practice/politics *creates*, rather than ameliorates, feelings of threat: the threat of abandonment, the threat of having to struggle with unequal power relations, the threat of psychological/social/sexual, as well as economic and political marginality; the threat of retributive violence—threats lived in concrete embodied ways. (p. 485)

Does this feel too hot to touch? Perhaps. Over the years I have found researchers and educators arguing that questions of violence toward women cannot be taken up, for we are unprepared to deal with the consequences of what might be opened. Although I see this as a legitimate concern, I am also appalled by the arrogance of the assumption that silence is safer for the woman who is being abused. Although I don't want to deny the need for more resources, more training, who exactly are we protecting when we ignore the bruises on the woman before us? Imagine what it is like to live in the isolation of violence sealed tightly behind the "safety" of four walls—to have absolutely no corner in which to hide.

Women's stories are coming into literacy classrooms (Doiron, 1987; Gaber-Katz and Horsman, 1988; Green, 1990). Whether this is due to "learner-centered" curricular approaches that encourage students to write their stories, to increasing numbers of feminist teachers who create safer spaces for these stories to be told, and/or to the sharp rise in public discourse about sexual abuse, the boundaries of the speakable have been shifting in education. When women do speak out, especially when they talk together in women's groups, issues of violence are frequently raised; but, as Garber, Horsman, and Westall (1991) point out, generally teachers feel ill-equipped to deal with these situations, want to be able to rescue the women and/or are fearful of the pain that talking may evoke. As literacy workers, they stress the necessity of finding ways to collaborate with those who work in the area of violence against women, and of paying more attention to teachers' stories, for they too are often in struggle. I think that this is a crucial point, not only to see the teacher's standpoint and to provide bases for support, but also to undo the idea of the "illiterate other," as though in some way the teacher—bound to be a woman—is exempt from, above, or beyond the violence of her own social inscriptions.

This raises the question posed by Uma Narayan of power and the epistemic privilege of the oppressed. The reality is that the classroom is not the same as a CR group. Participants do not freely choose each other, safety and trust cannot be assumed, and there are power differences—between teacher and student, but also among students. Especially troublesome in my teaching has been learning how to allow for power differences in knowledge, whether due to the "epistemic privilege" of social location, to assumptions of the greater "political correctness" of one position over another, or to differences in access to the privileged discourse operating in any particular classroom. To disagree, or to speak with authority, is difficult for women and can be very painful. In her thesis, Marian McMahon (1987) vividly describes the conflict she has experienced between caring for others and speaking with authority. I see this as another way in which the opposition between sexuality and intellectuality is played out: a key aspect of our sexual inscription as women is caring for others, including taking responsibility for the nurturing, flattering, and nonthreatening support of their egos, whereas intellectuality implies authority, the possibility of disagreeing, seeing things differently. This can be quite terrifying for women, since to disagree, to challenge, runs counter to our desire to be nice, to take care of others, to make things run smoothly, to feel comfortable for all.

In order to form an identity in opposition, or as deLauretis puts it, to (dis)identify, I believe it is necessary to have separate spaces in which to work collectively to see how what is taken for granted as natural and normal, as the way one must be, is socially inscribed and can be resisted—and, most important, is not a function of individual disorder, but of social ordering. Although not "safe," separate spaces are at least "safer," and it is in these spaces that women begin to talk without feeling they must take care of men and/or be silenced by male prescriptions of the talkable. Although classrooms are deeply inscribed by patriarchal relations whether or not men are present, at least the nonphysical presence of males makes it possible to take up female sexualization in a way that their presence hinders. Significantly "women-only" programs are typically viewed as an "impossibility," for "what about the men?" (Lloyd, 1991). Still, some question how the work of literacy can be done successfully unless the emotional and situational issues and violences faced by women are addressed (Garber, Horsman, and Westall, 1991). In the research it has supported, CCLOW recommends "woman-positive" programming in literacy, with local programs deciding on the approach. Clearly "woman positive" is an important beginning, but we need also to learn how to maintain vigilance in asking "which women?"

How do we approach this work in ways that do not repeat the mistake of assuming universal woman—that all women are the same? How do we teach in ways that encourage rather than conceal differences, and how do we relate these to differences in power among women? What is the relevance of more work that takes on feminist analyses of privilege with respect to race and class for women whose lives are lived as anything but privilege? Are there other approaches that can open up questions of difference and show how these are lodged in relations of power? Ellsworth (1989) suggests the formation of affinity groups to address dynamics of oppression as they are reenacted in the classsroom. Also stressing the necessity of using classroom dynamics as a place from which to work, Lewis (1990) articulates the irony that the "feminist critique of social relations reproduces exactly the practices we are critiquing" (p. 486). I agree with Ellsworth and Lewis, and would add that I have found it crucial that I become sensitive to my power as a teacher, my words take on the power of teacher, no matter how hard I work to divest myself of that power.

I have found memory work or storytelling to be the process that works best for me. In this work, I also participate in the writings, revealing my inner struggles with inscription. I use the term *memory work* rather than *autobiography* because I want to stress the possibility of this work as having a social and political dimension. Garber, Horsman, and Westall (1991) question endless autobiography and storytelling, asking where it gets us. In a disturbing but important review of the stories of incest survivors, Louise Armstrong (1990) goes so far as to argue that "the personal is apolitical." I rebel against this, especially coming at a time when women are just beginning to speak our stories. When our stories are left to the domain of therapy, they are depoliticized. As educators, I think the crucial question is, how can we politicize the personal? Collective memory work may hold a key.

In this, I've found the work of Haug et al. (1987) to be especially suggestive. In their approach, participants write individual and then collective stories based upon childhood experiences of various parts of the body—for example, legs, hair, "the body." In my teaching, I've found that photographs are especially evocative as we study each other's progressive accomplishment in acquiring "the look"—how it is that we learn how we must be, what photographs we have, why they were taken and chosen, and what lies outside the frame, the story behind the pictures chosen.

In talking about our memories, I work with participants to situate stories in time and place, to recall specific details, physical appearances, people present or absent, their probable stories, the beliefs and activities that frame the remembered event, its perceived significance, and so on. In this way, we work at historically and socially locating our stories, uncovering commonalities and differences, looking for the ways in which processes of regulation work through "taken-for-granted-as-normal" beliefs and practices that continue to shape our lives.

I've also used "memory work" to push through impasses and conflicts in the classroom. Here I ask whether participants would like to write something brief to express what the situation evokes for them; then, the next time we meet, we read our words one after another, without interruption or discussion, until all voices have filled the room like a cacophony of sound. First we hear, really try to hear, from where each person speaks, and then we talk, searching for dis/connections between our experience of the current situation and past events, and among our collective experiences. These moments are powerful ones emotionally as well as intellectually, as we begin to see beyond the personal of our private stories to trace the ways in which we have been socially and politically shaped. So memory serves as a lever to see how our subjectivities have been and continue to be constructed, even in classroom practices, how we struggle with resistance, and the risks of refusal.

Endings

I don't know what relevance my experience of teaching at the graduate level has for literacy teaching. In this writing I feel frustrated by my lack of experience in teaching literacy, and yet I cannot separate my research and thinking on the topic from my teaching. Perhaps the final challenge of the postmodern critique is to the ways in which expertise and knowledge get constructed. How is it that I am the one invited to write on critical literacy, and why do I agree? The latter question is especially troubling to me. I feel passionately about the contradictions of which I write, about the challenge that sexuality as power poses for literacy and the education of women, about the importance of emotional embodiment, of the erotic, to learning. I refuse to let go of the violence that women face, and I want to learn how to see locational differences in how that violence is lived, but whether I am an "authority" on literacy is another question.

I end because I cannot go on any longer; I have no conclusion. To tie all of the foregoing together would be to bring closure where there can be none. To quote Nancy Simms (1991), "I see literacy as political. And advocacy role is very much a part of it. The issues aren't coming together. We have to talk about how literacy connects with racism, homophobia, classism, sexism" (p. 28)

In my work, I continue to use autobiography and memory work. To some extent, this paper is one form of that approach. As Arlene Schenke (1991) contends, "A genealogy of memory-work should offer strategies of commitment that are relational, provisional, deliberately ambivalent and continuously in process (p. 13). It should be an opening, ideally, to continuing reflection and critique, a story that "never stops beginning or ending. It appears headless and bottomless for it is built on differences. Its (in)finitude subverts every notion of completeness and its frame remains a non-totalizable one" (Minh-ha, 1989, p. 2).

Notes

* So many conversations and confrontations have shaped my thinking over the years. My deepest debt is to the Latina and Chicana women who participated in the Los Angeles research. Since then, students in my classes, members of CCLOW's Literacy Advisory Board, participants in my "memory work" groups, friends within and without these groups, have been crucial to my work. A special thanks to Becky, who labored through several drafts of this paper with me.
1. I use the term *literacy* broadly, to mean discrete sets of reading and writing practices, as well as symbolically, as in "to be literate," "to be educated." Hence, *literacy* and *education* are sometimes used interchangeably when the reference is to the symbolic, that is, the intellectual- and/or class-associated dimensions of literacy. Furthermore, I think of literacy as a "process of acquiring more education" for women which signals a change in a woman's relationship to education in her life.
2. I also use the term *sexuality* broadly as the full range of institutionalized social practices, beliefs, and assumptions that define woman as woman—as the object of desire and/or caretaker of men. This is developed more fully in the text. Although I do not want to argue that all men are violators and all women are victims, I do see, in the social construction of "woman," that she has been "essentialized" as an object of male desire. In this paper, I speak of sexuality primarily in terms of violence because, as constructed in opposition to education and women's increased independence from men, that is how it is lived. This does not mean that sexuality cannot also be experienced as pleasure, even in forms that some consider to be violent. What would "a desire of her own" look like for women?
3. Fine's work raises the question of the relationship of desire to violence in the representation of sexuality in schooling. She argues that girls are presented with an image of heterosexual relations in which men are depicted as violent and women as victims. In contrast to Fine's research, the life skills curricula with which I am familiar do not take up the question of sexuality as violence at all; the underlying framework appears to be

lodged in libertarian approaches to sexuality as pleasure. Hence, even when sexual learnings from parents are presented, they are given in terms of parental openness about bodies, touch, and so on; the possibility of violence, or of sex as a power relation, is not suggested. See, for example, Zaph et al. (1983). My appreciation to Becky Anweiler for bringing this work to my attention.

4. How do we bring race, class, and sexuality together in our analysis? In my work, I have found that the closer I am to dominant standards, or "privilege," the harder it is to see how the "isms" work. I see class as deeply tied to the sexual drama I lived as a child: my parents' determination to move into the middle class, the importance of my mother's education as the daughter of working-class Italian immigrants to that movement, and the very conflictual position in which this placed my father, who was from a dirt-poor farming background and who worked as a laborer, taking out his sense of male inadequacy, his rage, through violence against his children. Threatened by the developing class difference between him and my mother, her intellectual development, did he turn to me?

5. My thesis is that, in Western societies, the dominant way available to girls and women to live out their "rebellion" against straight middle-class norms is through being "wild," a wildness defined through sexual power—the sexier, the more available, the greater a woman's sense of power. How this varies according to social location, especially with respect to class and race, is an important question. The work of Angela McRobbie on working-class girls in England suggests the relevance of looking at girls' sexual desires in terms of perceived possibilities for educational pursuit.

6. I think of my own experiences of sexual abuse, the educational mandate that I leave my body, sexuality, and experience out of the classroom, and the deep pain and chaos that I felt in having systematically to separate what I knew in my history from what I was allowed to present and produce in the classroom. Finally, one day I was able to find the clarity to name, to stand by the "integrity" of, my experience, to take exception without turning the blame inward as my shame and inadequacy, and to at last find the courage to speak my difference publicly.

7. In emphasizing the importance of defiant speech, I do not want to lose sight of the communicative presence and power of silence. See Arlene Schenke's work for a critique of "voice" in critical pedagogy. Also highly suggestive is her use of Foucault's genealogy as a method from which to approach critical teaching through memory work in ESL classes.

References

Armstrong, L. (1990). "The personal is apolitical." *Women's Review of Books*, March 1991, 7(6), 1–4.

Belenky, M. F., et al. (1986). *Women's Ways of Knowing: The Development of Self, Voice and Mind*. New York: Basic Books.

Brookes, A.L. (1988). *Feminist Pedagogy: A Subject In/formation*. Unpublished doctoral dissertation, University of Toronto.

Collins, P. H. (1989). "The Social Construction of Black Feminist Thought." *Signs*, 14(4), 745–773.

deLauretis, T. (1987). *Technologies of Gender: Essays in Theory, Film and Fiction*. Bloomington: Indiana University Press.

———. (1990). "Eccentric Subjects: Feminist Theory and Historical Consciousness." *Feminist Studies*, 16(1), 115–150.

Doiron, R. (1987). *My Name is Rose*. Toronto: East End Literacy.

Ellsworth, E. (1989). "Why Doesn't This Feel Empowering? Working Through the Repressive Myths of Critical Pedagogy." *Harvard Educational Review*, 59(3), 297–324.

Fine, M. (1988). "Sexuality, Schooling and Adolescent Females: The Missing Discourse of Desire." *Harvard Educational Review*, 58(1), 29–53.

Fisher, B. (1987). "The Heart Has Its Reasons: Feelings, Thinking and Community-Building in Feminist Education." *Women's Studies Quarterly*, 15(3–4), Fall/Winter, 47–58.

Foucault, M. (1982). "The Subject and Power." In H.L. Dreyfus and Paul Rabinow (eds.), *Beyond Structuralism and Hermeneutics*. Chicago: University of Chicago Press, pp. 208–226.

Gaber-Katz, E., and Horsman, J. (1988). "Is It Her Voice If She Speaks Their Words?" *Canadian Woman Studies: Woman and Literacy*, 9(3–4), 117–120.

Gaber-Katz, E., and Watson, G.M. (1991). *The Land That We Dream of . . . A Participatory Study of Community-Based Literacy*. Toronto: OISE Press.

Garber, N., Horsman, J., and Westall, T. (1991). "Feminism and Literacy." In N. Breen (ed.,) *Women, Literacy and Action: A Handbook*. Toronto: Ontario Literacy Coalition, pp. 6–21.

Green, A. R. (1990). *Coming Out of My Shell*. St. John's Newfoundland: Rabittown Literacy Program.

Haug, F., et al. (1987). *Female Sexualization: A Collective Work of Memory*. London: Verso.

hooks, b. (1989). *Talking Back: Thinking Feminist. Thinking Black*. Boston: South End Press.

Horsman, J. (1990). *Something in My Mind besides the Everyday: Women and Literacy*. Toronto: Women's Press.

Hurtado, A. (1989). "Relating to Privilege: Seduction and Rejection in the Subordination of White Women and Women of Color." *Signs*, 14(4), 833–855.

Lewis, M. (1990). "Interrupting Patriarchy: Politics Resistance and Transformation in the Feminist Classroom." *Harvard Educational Review*, 60(4), 467–488.

Lloyd, B.-A. (1991). *Discovering the Strength of Our Voices: Women and Literacy Programs*. Toronto: Canadian Congress for Learning Opportunities for Women.

Longfellow, B. (1981). *Breaking Out*. 27 min./16 mm. Toronto: Development Education Center.

Lorde, A. (1984). *Sister/Outsider*. New York: The Crossing Press.

Luttrell, W. (1989). "Working-Class Women's Ways of Knowing: Effects of Gender, Race and Class." *Sociology of Education*, 62 (Jan.), 33–46.

MacKinnon, C. A. (1989). *Towards a Feminist Theory of the State*. Cambridge: Harvard University Press.

McMahon, M. (1987). *Telling Tales out of School: The ABC's of Repression in Education*. Unpublished master's thesis, University of Toronto.

_____. (1991). "Nursing Histories: Reviving Life in Abandoned Selves." *Feminist Review*, 35, 23–37.

McRobbie, A. (1991). *Feminism and Youth Culture: From 'Jackie' to 'Just Seventeen.'* Boston: Unwin Hyman.

Minh-ha, T. (1989). *Woman, Native, Other*. Bloomington: Indiana University Press.

Mohanty, C. (1988). "Under Western Eyes: Feminist Scholarship and Colonial Discourses." *Feminist Review*, 30, 62–88.

Moraga, C. (1983). *Loving in the War Years*. Boston: South End Press.

Morton, J. (1985). *Assessing Vocational Readiness in Low Income Women: An Exploration into the Construction and Use of Ideology*. Published master's thesis, University of Toronto.

Narayan, U. (1988). "Working Together Across Difference: Some Considerations on Emotions and Political Practice." *Hypatia*, 3(2), 31–47.

Pratt, M. B. (1984). "Identity: Skin Blood Heart." In E. Bulkin, M.B. Pratt, B. Smith, *Yours in struggle*. New York: Long Haul Press, pp. 9–63.

Razack, S. (1990). Storytelling for social change. Unpublished draft manuscript.

Reid, S. (1991). "Filipino Women Battle Abuse: Victims Urged to End Silence Imposed by Cultural and Language Barriers." *Toronto Star* (March 14, 1991) p. A23.

Rockhill, K. (1985). "Ideological Solidification and Liberalism in University Adult Education: Confrontation Over Workers' Education in the USA." In R. Taylor, K. Rockhill and R. Fieldhouse *University Adult Education in England and the USA*. London: Croom Helm, pp. 175–220.

_____. (1987a). "The Chaos of Subjectivity in the Ordered Halls of Academe." *Canadian Woman Studies*, 8(4), 12–17.

_____. (1987b). "Literacy as Threat/Desire: Longing to be SOMEBODY." In J. Gaskell and A. McLaren (eds.), *Women and Education: A Canadian Perspective*. Calgary: Detselig Enterprises, pp. 315–331.

_____. (1987c). "Gender, Language and the Politics of Literacy." *British Journal of Sociology of Education*, 8(2), 153–167.

_____. (1988). "e-MAN-ci-patory Literacy." *Canadian Woman Studies*, 9(3–4), 113–115.

Schenke, A. (1991). *Speaking the Autobiographical "I" in Poststructuralist Practice: A Pedagogy of Voice and Memory-Work*. Unpublished master's thesis, University of Toronto.

Simms, N. (1991). "Looking at 'Ism's': Visible Minority Women and Literacy." Interview by M. Breen (ed.), *Women Literacy and Action: A Handbook*. Toronto: Ontario Literacy Coalition, pp. 22–30.

Williams, B. J. (1991). *Notes Passed between Hostages: Feminist Writing and the Politics of Self-Representation*. Unpublished doctoral thesis, University of Toronto.

Willis, P. (1977). *Learning to Labor: How Working Class Kids Get Working Class Jobs*. New York: Columbia University Press.

Zaph, M. B., et al. (1983). *Discovering Life Skills*. Vol. 3. Toronto: YWCA.

CHAPTER 30

LESSONS FROM A YOUNG FEMINIST COLLECTIVE

TIYA MILES

for the women of the Rag with love and good wishes

The room overflowed with women. They stretched out across the floor, leaned against chair backs and chair legs, their faces open with excitement. I found a space among them and listened to the six who had called the meeting explain their plan to create the only feminist journal on the Harvard-Radcliffe campus. They stressed that although they had been the catalyst for the formation of the group, they did not expect or want to be the leaders. They proposed a method of consensus for decision making and suggested that the positions of facilitator, time keeper and vibes watcher (whose job it was to monitor the tension in the room and notice if people were being silenced) should rotate on a voluntary basis.

Our initial act of consensus was to decide on a title for the magazine. The final choice, after what seemed like hours of debate, was *The Rag: A Feminist Journal of Politics and Culture*. Soon the name outgrew the journal itself and came to refer to the group of women who constituted the collective. In those early weeks, we became fond of saying with a smirk, "I'm on the Rag."

Our first planned event was a discussion forum to generate ideas for the topic of our premiere issue. In the fall of 1991, we gathered in the Lyman Common Room to talk about the theme of "control." We sat in a wide circle and munched on snacks while we voiced personal experiences and observations. The conversation branched in several directions. We discussed issues ranging from the injustice of being perpetually vulnerable to sexual attack on the streets to oppressive societal beauty ideals. I felt invigorated by the energy, challenged by the ideas and supported by the words that echoed my own thoughts. It was in this forum that I was first able to voice and begin to transform my negative self-concept, which was rooted in my long-held belief that as a black woman, my hair and features were ugly.

The weekly Rag meetings forged an incredible bond among the twenty or so of us who attended regularly. Most of us were writing essays, and we would spend the time editing pieces, discussing current events on and off campus and sharing personal feelings.

At the end of fall semester, when it was time to distribute copies of our first issue, we met at Dunster House with charged expectation. Thrilled by the sight of our newly published journals, we picked them up, ran our hands over the covers and flipped through the pages rereading our words. We had caused a ripple of interest and criticism among our fellow students, some of whom flung the terms "lesbian" and "angry" as intended slurs. And now, as we prepared to tell them where we stood and where they could go, we felt formidable. We laughed and yelled as we dropped off stacks of journals at first-year dorms, upper-class "houses" and libraries. Our thoughts in print

---

Reprinted from *Listen Up: Voices From the Next Feminist Generation*, edited by B. Findlen, 1995. Copyright © 1995 Seal Press.

(particularly personal accounts of rape and a description of giving "Uncle Sam" a blow job) caused a messy splash in the Harvard sea.

Two semesters and two journals later, fifteen of us sat in a small room with angry mouths stretched across our faces and tears pressing out of our eyes. The energy we felt had a different character now—heavy, tense, rife with blame and defensiveness. The Rag was tearing from the pull of problems that had been so small at first, we hadn't noticed them. Resentment about cliques and an inner circle bubbled under the surface. Racial and class conflicts had crept up like weeds. During several meetings and informal discussions in the spring of 1992, we tried to talk out our difficulties and ended up drawing battle lines.

Our organizational problems seemed to have taken root at that very first meeting, while we were reveling in the creation of a supportive forum for our opinions. Although the journal's creators had attempted to disseminate power and control, their central role remained.

The journal creators and a few others handled the collective's business responsibilities outside of regular meetings. Discontent arose among other members of the collective who felt left out of such an important Rag function. The group discussed this problem at several meetings, but all attempts at change failed. When the business group incorporated its work into weekly meetings, our already drawn-out Thursday night sessions became hours long. And because the business group knew more about the subject than other Rag members, finance discussions often turned into reports. When the business crew scheduled open brunch meetings, no one attended. At the same time that some Rag members continued to feel excluded, those who handled business resented being blamed for doing more than their share of the work.

Somehow, a small group of Rag members had kept what seemed to be a disproportionate amount of responsibility and power. And although we all felt the problem, we did not know how to excise it. As more people joined the collective, the situation worsened. The journal creators and those who had attended the founding meeting were perceived to have (and perhaps took on) a possessive attitude, as if we owned the journal and were the only legitimate members of the group.

In the middle of the Rag's second year, racial strife developed out of what was intended to be an innocuous proposal. Another Rag woman and I were also members of the Association of Black Radcliffe Women. During a meeting of that group, ABRW members expressed anger at the title of an upcoming Black Students Association dance—"The Boody Slam Jam." The ABRW women felt that the slogan reinforced negative portrayals of black women's bodies. The women argued that these portrayals, common in popular music videos and songs such as "Baby Got Back" and "Poison" (which includes the lines: "That girl is poison. You can't trust a big butt and a smile"), caricatured black women's behinds and emphasized them as sexual objects. Although this concern led to a discussion of ABRW members' wider interest in feminist issues, many of the women were opposed to joining the Rag and writing about their thoughts. They felt an aversion to the term "feminist," which they thought described a white, even racist movement, and they saw the Rag as a quintessential "feminist" group.

The other joint ABRW/Rag member and I related this discussion at a Rag meeting. We suggested that *The Rag* change its subtitle to a "Womanist" or "Feminist and Womanist Journal of Politics and Culture" as a signal to other black women that the collective was an open, welcoming space. The debate over this suggestion revealed Rag members' unspoken racial tensions and opened the floodgates of the group's internal conflicts.

When we introduced the idea of the subtitle change, a rash of impassioned reactions followed in the group of four black women (two of them biracial), two Asian women, and several white women. Some felt that womanism, as first defined by Alice Walker, was an admirable ideology, but others felt that it wasn't radical enough because it included a commitment to the liberation of oppressed men. Some white women rejected the idea that there could be legitimate reasons for not wanting to call oneself a feminist; one woman termed such people "wishy-washy" and implied that changing the subtitle would be an act of weakness.

The two of us who had suggested the change pointed out the self-oriented perspective of some white feminists which blocked them from seeing the necessity of black women's and men's struggling together for survival in a racist society. We also argued that requiring women to identify themselves as feminists excluded like-minded, politically active black women and categorized them as weak. One biracial black woman, who called herself a feminist and explained how long it had taken her to gather the strength to do so, felt that we were excluding her by holding up a narrow black feminist authenticity that defined mainstream feminism as antiblack.

Class conflicts piggybacked racial discord. In other meetings that semester, a black woman who had taken a year off to work in order to fund the rest of her college education expressed resentment at what she viewed as the insensitivity of wealthy white women. A few Rag parents had donated hundreds of dollars to the magazine, and one Rag member had offered her family's summer house as a retreat site. The black woman, who had no such funds or house to offer the group, felt that her worth and strength as a group member were diminished by those women's obvious economic power. Other women pointed out that it would be impossible for us to publish without those funds. A white woman revealed her family's extensive wealth and said she felt both angry and hurt at being blamed for who she was and things she had no control over.

We never recovered from the accusations, resentment and tension that doused us. The spring of my senior year, *The Rag* was not published. The year after I graduated, remaining Rag members published the pieces that had been written the year before, and then the group dissolved. We had lasted only two years.

During those final meetings, I often tried to understand what had happened to us. Now, as I look back with the hindsight afforded by time, reading and many conversations, I can pinpoint a constellation of problems that have weakened many young feminist groups. Many of the women on the Rag had awakened to feminist consciousness only recently and were unfamiliar with feminist history and contemporary feminist theory. We were not aware of the need for individual self-analysis or for recognition of our own role in oppressing and silencing others. We were so focused on our individual development and liberation that we failed to reach out to women with different experiences and to plan group activism.

Perhaps the main problem was our ignorance of feminist history. We should have read the warnings, reflections and advice of the many older women who had already struggled with the dilemmas we faced. In fact, the importance of knowing history in the struggle against oppression is an issue in many of these women's writings. Audre Lorde writes in *Sister Outsider*, "By ignoring the past we are encouraged to repeat its mistakes.... [H]istorical amnesia... keeps us working to invent the wheel every time we have to go to the store for bread."[1]

In *Daring To Be Bad*, Alice Echols traces the development of radical feminist groups in the late sixties and seventies. Over twenty years ago, the women Echols discusses fought and split over issues of leadership, hierarchy, race, class, sexual orientation and feminist authenticity—many of the problems that disintegrated the Rag. Like the women in those early groups, we strove toward an ideal of collective decision making and equal power but ended up with a certain degree of centralized power and internal strife. A group discussion of this historical account (as well as others) might have prepared Rag members for the difficulties we would face in the realm of organization and decision making.

An early awareness of the potential for these pitfalls would have forced us to rethink our organizational procedures (or lack thereof), rather than glossing over them with vague notions of sharing and inclusivity. We might have decided to collectively choose a small group that would handle business for the duration of a semester. In this way, important matters would be handled efficiently, but concentration of responsibility and power would not be arbitrary or static. Similarly, we might have chosen a structured means of incorporating new members into the group to lessen feelings of possessiveness on the part of old members and exclusion on the part of new members.

Our lack of historical knowledge also contributed to the racial tensions and misunderstandings between us. As Patricia Hill Collins points out in *Black Feminist Thought*, black women have a longstanding feminist intellectual tradition, which has often been suppressed in feminist contexts as well as mainstream culture. Many black women are unaware that we have deep roots in feminist consciousness and that our foremothers have always been involved in feminist struggle. Our misinformation about feminist history—the false idea that feminist thought and activism in the United States have been exclusive to white women—led some of us in ABRW to reject feminism immediately and refuse to work with white women who claimed the label. White women's lack of knowledge about black feminist history led some of them to automatically deny black women's critiques of white feminist racism and to categorize womanism as a watered-down version of "real" feminism.

Black feminist theorists Patricia Hill Collins, bell hooks and Audre Lorde point to the necessity for all feminists to critically assess themselves to determine the ways in which they participate in systems of oppression. In *Feminist Theory: From Margin to Center*, hooks discusses black women's feelings of self-alienation, a result of living in a climate in which they are devalued: "Women of color must confront our absorption of white supremacist beliefs, 'internalized racism,' which may lead us to feel self-hate, to vent anger and rage at injustice at one another rather than at oppressive forces."[2] hooks encourages black women to affirm blackness and "decolonize" our minds to free ourselves from the restraints of oppressive ideologies.[3] Perhaps the black woman on the Rag who had taken a year off to work felt devalued not only because of the white women's actions, but also because she had accepted the cultural correlation between wealth and worth.

Middle- and upper-class white feminists must also examine their acceptance of racist and classist assumptions as well as their privilege in order for a group to flourish. Some white Rag members became defensive and resistant to dialogue when issues of race emerged and were insensitive to the ways in which their privilege and cross-cultural ignorance hurt women of color. The white women's offhand rejection of womanism as a viable theory and equation of their experiences with the oppression of black women might have been avoided if they had critically considered their own positions and assumptions. If the women whose parents funded the magazine had reflected upon how that deed might affect less privileged women, perhaps they would have thought about other options, such as having their parents donate anonymously.

At times black Rag members duplicated some of these mistakes as a result of not considering our individual positions in relation to other black women and other women of color. Some of us fell into the myth of the existence of what hooks calls "monolithic [racial] experiences"[4] and assumed that most black women shared our feminist perspective. We vehemently advanced the consensus of a few black women to the degree that a biracial black woman felt that she was excluded and that her experience was being defined as inauthentic. In addition to this, we contributed to other women's invisibility by making only a marginal effort to widen our discussion to embrace women of color who were not black. Audre Lorde's piercing words are applicable to all members of feminist groups: "The true focus of revolutionary change is never merely the oppressive situations which we seek to escape, but that piece of the oppressor which is planted deep within each of us."[5]

When the Rag women gathered at that first meeting, we all harbored burning issues that warmed or scalded us from within. The opportunity to voice and share these feelings motivated us to produce the journal and bonded us as a group. But this foundation of individual desire and need crumbled as time went on. Once we had expressed the thoughts that we had bottled up inside, our task seemed less urgent and our energy level waned. This static focus on our individual experiences and problems deterred us from seeking out and listening to other women's experiences. If we had stretched beyond the boundaries of our group, perhaps we would have invited older women in our community to join discussions and gained the opportunity to learn from their wisdom. Perhaps we would have attracted a variety of women to participate in the earliest stages of Rag development and combined all of our insights and energy to create a more dynamic collective.

If we had reached out to other women, we might have opened space for discussion of our differences before we were consumed by them.

We might have learned about each other's specific life experiences and dismantled our assumptions about other groups. Early exploration of our differences and individual definitions of feminism might have forestalled our retreat into defensiveness and closed-mindedness when conflicts arose. As Audre Lorde envisioned, we might have been able to "recognize differences among women who are our equals, neither inferior nor superior, and devise ways to use each others' difference to enrich our visions and our joint struggles."[6]

bell hooks also emphasizes the danger of group members becoming so entrenched in the exploration of personal feelings and experiences that they do not move from consciousness to action. Although the Rag did produce four journals, we never published beyond that, and only once did we move into the realm of activism. If funneled into action, the consciousness that was developing in the Rag might have had a tremendous impact on our campus and beyond. As a group we might have participated in demonstrations for minority faculty hiring, lesbian and gay rights and divestiture. We might have planned clever actions against the all-male, elite Harvard clubs that offended many Rag members. We also might have participated in any of the many social service activities organized by other students on campus. For example, one Rag member who also did public service work gave a copy of *The Rag* to a mother who lived in the housing development where she volunteered. After reading an essay about popular animated films (such as *The Little Mermaid*) having a negative impact on the self-esteem of girls of color, the mother responded that she had never considered the subject and that she had not been aware that feminism was concerned with girls of color. Perhaps the Rag could have followed up on her interest and offered to work with mothers in that community to create greater awareness of the issue and to collect books and films that contained positive and inclusive portrayals of girls.

My experience in the Rag leads me to imagine the following picture of a vital, growing young feminist group. A commitment to encourage and a responsibility to challenge form the roots. The study of feminist histories, intergenerational communication, self-analysis, dialogue, activism and respect for diversity shape the branches. And the women—in their myriad textures and colors, in their possibilities for flying in the face of the wind—are the seeds, pods and blossoms.

Notes

1. Audre Lorde, *Sister Outsider* (Trumansburg, New York: Crossing Press, 1984), p. 117.
2. bell hooks, *Feminist Theory: From Margin to Center* (Boston: South End Press, 1984), p. 55.
3. bell hooks, *Black Looks* (Boston: South End Press, 1992), p. 10.
4. hooks, *Feminist Theory: From Margin to Center*, p. 57.
5. Lorde, p. 123.
6. Lorde, p. 122.

Part IV

Comparative and International Perspectives

Chapter 31

Multicultural and Global Feminism

Rosemarie Putnam Tong

Multicultural and global feminists share with postmodern feminists a view of the self as fragmented. However, for multicultural and global feminists, the roots of this fragmentation are primarily cultural, racial, and ethnic rather than sexual, psychological, and literary. There are many similarities between multicultural and global feminism. Both challenge "female essentialism," the view that the idea of "woman" exists as some sort of Platonic form each and every flesh-and-blood woman somehow fits; and both disavow "female chauvinism," the tendency of some women, privileged on account of their race or class, for example, to presume to speak on behalf of all women.

Despite the important similarities that link multicultural and global feminists, there are nonetheless some major differences that distinguish them. Multicultural feminism is based on the insight that even in one nation—the United States of America, for instance—all women are not created or constructed equal. Depending on her race and class but also on her sexual preference, age, religion, education attainment, occupation, marital status, health condition, and so on, each and every woman in the United States will experience her oppression as an American woman differently. Adding to the insights of multicultural feminists, global feminists further stress that depending on whether a woman is a citizen of a First World or a Third World nation, an advanced industrial or a developing nation, a nation that is colonialist or colonized, she will experience oppression differently.

Multicultural Feminism: An Overview

Because my experiences are those of an American woman, in this chapter I write about multicultural feminism in the United States. Moreover, I stress issues of race and class not because I think race and class are always of more concern to American women than sexual preference and age, for example, but because issues of race and class have a particularly long history in the United States. Furthermore, many multicultural feminists have themselves focused on these issues. In a similar vein I focus on the differences between black and white women for largely pragmatic reasons. It is not that I am totally unaware of or disinterested in the issues confronting Asian American women, Native American women, Hispanic women, lesbian women, old women, women from religious traditions other than Christianity, or disabled women. It is simply that I am unable effectively to communicate the thoughts of the large number of different kinds of women who have themselves written about their unique experiences of oppression. I apologize to those women whose voices are not explicitly heard in these pages and ask them, as well as those whose voices are heard here, to

---

Reprinted from *Contemporary Feminist Thought*, Second Edition, by Rosemarie Putnam Tong, 1998. Copyright © 1998 Westview Press (Perseus Books).

read my reflections on multicultural feminism simply as the attempt of one woman to understand how she both is and is not like other women.

The Roots of Multicultural Feminism in the United States

In some ways multicultural *feminist* thought is related to multicultural thought, an ideology that supports diversity and is currently highly popular in the United States. However, Americans have not always celebrated diversity. Unity was the goal of earlier generations, who maintained that the United States represented the idea of *e pluribus unum*, "out of many, one." According to historian Arthur M. Schlesinger Jr., early immigrants to the United States wanted to become a new people. He specifically noted the eighteenth-century French immigrant J. Hector St. John de Crèvecoeur, who spoke eloquently about trading in his old identity for a new one:

> Crèvecoeur's conception was of a brand new nationality created by individuals who, in repudiating their homelands and joining to make new lives, melted away ancient ethnic differences. Most of those intrepid Europeans who had torn up their roots to brave the wild Atlantic and attain America wanted to forget a horrid past and to embrace a hopeful future. They *expected* to become Americans. Their goals were escape, deliverance, assimilation. They saw America as a transforming nation, banishing old loyalties and forging a new national identity based on common political ideals.[1]

During the nineteenth century and for the first half of the twentieth century, the trend toward "escape, deliverance, assimilation" continued. Indeed, until the end of World War II, the majority of immigrants to the United States willingly jumped into America's so-called melting pot, first described by Israel Zangwill in a 1909 play:

> There she lies, the great melting pot—listen! Can't you hear the roaring and the bubbling? There gapes her mouth—The harbor where a thousand feeders come from the ends of the world to pour in their human freight. Ah, what a stirring and a seething! Celt and Latin, Slav and Teuton, Greek and Syrian,—black and yellow—... East and West, North and South, the palm and the pine, the pole and the equator, the crescent and the cross—how the Great Alchemist melts and fuses them with his purging flame! Here shall they all unite to build the Republic of man and the Kingdom of God.... Peace, peace, to all you unborn millions, fated to fill this giant continent.[2]

For a variety of reasons, most of them having to do with how "the Great Alchemist" seemed to be cooking a homogeneous, white cream soup rather than a heterogeneous gumbo or minestrone, the old many-united-into-one gospel gave way to a new one-divided-into-many gospel by the second half of the twentieth century. Schlesinger noted this new gospel condemned Crèvecoeur's "vision of individuals of all nations melted into a new race in favor of an opposite vision: a nation of groups, differentiated in their ancestries, invisible in their diverse identities."[3] Assimilation gave way to ethnicity, and integration deferred to separatism as the "salad bowl" or "quilt" metaphor for the United States displaced the old melting-pot metaphor.[4] Multiculturalism had been born.

Usually defined as a "social-intellectual movement that promotes the value of diversity as a core principle and insists that all cultural groups be treated with respect and as equals,"[5] multiculturalism met with much criticism during the late 1980s and throughout the 1990s. Of all the arguments raised against multiculturalism, those focusing on its tendency to undermine social solidarity were the strongest. For example, Joseph Raz, himself a supporter of multiculturalism, conceded to his critics: "Without a deep feeling of solidarity, a political society will disintegrate into quarreling factions. Solidarity is required if people are to feel concerned about each other's fortunes and to be willing to make sacrifices for other people. Without such willingness the possibility of a peaceful political society disappears."[6] Critics of multiculturalism insisted labels such as *African American*, *Asian American*, *Hispanic American*, and *Native American* were perniciously divisive. These critics longed for a homogeneous America and "American Americans."

In support of multiculturalism, its defenders noted that all too often "mainstream" Americans presume the "all-American kid" is a baseball-playing, apple-pie-eating, blue-eyed, blond-haired, very white kid. In reaction to this sketch of the typical American, Americans who do not look "all-American" but who nonetheless regard themselves as true Americans emphasize or celebrate their native roots as essential to their *unique* way of looking "American." They assert, "We should learn to think of our [society] as consisting not of a majority and minorities but of a plurality of cultural groups."[7] We do not all have to look, act, speak, and think alike to be American. What we need instead is to cultivate mutual toleration, respect, and knowledge of each other's cultures and to make sure we *all* possess the skills and rights necessary to compete in the economic market and the political arena.[8]

Multicultural feminists applaud multicultural thinkers' celebration of difference, lamenting that traditional feminist theorists often failed to distinguish between the condition of white, middle-class, heterosexual, Christian women in advanced and affluent Western industrialized countries and the very different conditions of other women with varying backgrounds. In *Inessential Woman: Problems of Exclusion in Feminist Thought*, Elizabeth Spelman sought to explain the reasons for this puzzling failure. In her estimation, traditional feminist theorists went wrong because they thought they could overcome women's oppression simply by maintaining not only women's *sameness* to men but also women's *sameness* to each other. They reasoned, said Spelman, that if all people are the same, then all people are equal. No one is anyone else's "superior" or "inferior." Unfortunately, continued Spelman, traditional feminist theorists did not realize that it is possible to oppress people by denying human difference as well as by denying human sameness.[9] Referring to women's oppression in particular, she explained her point about difference and sameness as follows:

> The assertion of differences among women can operate oppressively if one marks the differences and then suggests that one of the groups so differentiated is more important or more human or in some sense better than the other. But on the other hand, to stress the unity of women is no guarantee against hierarchical ranking, if what one says is true or characteristic of some as a class is only true or characteristic of some women: for then women who cannot be so characterized are in effect not counted as women. When Stanton said that women should get the vote before Africans, Chinese, Germans, and Irish, she obviously was relying on a concept of "woman" that blinded her to the "womanness" of many women.[10]

Spelman urged contemporary feminist theorists to resist the impulse to gloss over women's differences, as if there exists some sort of "woman" into whom all of women's autobiographical differences flow and dissolve. In particular, she pleaded with them not to make the mistake historian Kenneth Stampp made when he asserted "that innately Negroes are, after all, only white men with black skins, nothing more, nothing else."[11] Why, asked Spelman, is it that *Negroes* are only white men with black skins, nothing more, nothing else? Why is it not instead that *Caucasians* are only black men with white skins, nothing more, nothing else? If a white man can imagine himself protesting his reduction to a black man with white skin, why does he have trouble imagining a black man protesting his reduction to a white man with black skin? Could it be that whites still think "white" is definitely the best way to be, that is, that white people are somehow the gold standard for all people? Noting there are many well-intentioned "Stampps" within the ranks of traditional feminist theorists, Spelman observed: "If, like Stampp, I believe that the woman in every woman is a woman just like me, and if I also assume that there is no difference between being white and being a woman, then seeing another woman 'as a woman' will involve seeing her as fundamentally like the woman I am. In other words, the womanness underneath the Black woman's skin is a white woman's, and deep down inside the Latino woman is an Anglo woman waiting to burst through a cultural shroud."[12] No wonder, said Spelman, that so many women of color reject traditional feminist thought. A valid feminist theory must take the differences among women seriously; it cannot claim all women are "just like me."

Black Women and Feminism: The Interlocking Systems of Gender, Race, and Class

Although a wide variety of feminists in the United States expressed dissatisfaction with "white" feminism, black feminists were among the first to voice their grievances systematically and extensively. To be sure, the concerns that black feminists, including African American feminists, raised about "white" feminism were not *identical* to those raised by Hispanic American, Asian American, and Native American feminists, for example. Nevertheless, they resonated well enough with the concerns of these and other U.S. minority women (for example, lesbians and disabled women) to constitute a major challenge to "white" feminism. Black feminists told white feminists that women of color and other minority women see the world differently than do white women and other privileged women and that unless "white" feminism stopped being "white," its message would be meaningless to women of color and other minority women.

Among the central claims of black feminists is the inseparability of the structures and systems of gender, race, and culture. Most black feminists deny it is possible for women to focus exclusively on their oppression *as women*. On the contrary, each woman, or each relatively distinct group of women, needs to understand how everything about her—the color of her skin, the amount of money in her purse, the condition of her body, the sex of the person(s) with whom she is intimate, the date on her birth certificate—provides part of the explanation for her subordinate status. As Spelman commented: "It is not as if there is a goddess somewhere who made lots of little identical 'woman' units and then, in order to spruce up the world a bit for herself, decided to put some of the units in black bodies, some in white bodies, some in the bodies of kitchen maids in seventeenth-century France some in the bodies of English, Israeli, and Indian prime ministers."[13] On the contrary, implied Spelman. The "goddess" made *millions* of women—a far more demanding and creative process.

When black feminists tell white feminists they need to understand more fully the intersection of racism, sexism, classism in the lives of black women, not all white feminists respond appropriately to U.S. black women's "multiple jeopardy."[14] Some white feminists react in the nineteenth-century style of Elizabeth Cady Stanton, who, we will recall, insisted that the fight against sexism must take priority over the fight against all other isms, including the very ugly racism and classism. These white feminists accuse black feminists of too easily forgiving the sexist sins of black men, of feeling sorry for their most immediate and intimate oppressors. Other white feminists react in an overly apologetic way, vowing to fight against racism (and to a lesser degree classism) before mounting an attack on sexism. They beg black women to forgive them for their racist (and classist) sins.

Distressed and dismayed by the apparent inability of many white feminists to *understand* what black feminists actually mean by expressions such as "multiple jeopardy" and "interlocking systems of oppression," bell hooks claimed in no uncertain terms that racism, sexism, and classism are not separable in fact, even if they are separable in theory. No one of these forms of oppression can be eliminated prior to the elimination of any other.[15] Oppression is a many-headed beast capable of regenerating any one of the heads temporarily severed from its bloated body. The *whole body* of the beast is the appropriate target for those who wish to end its reign of terror. In an equally direct manner, Audre Lorde noted that "as a forty-nine-year-old Black lesbian feminist socialist, mother of two, including one boy, and a member of an interracial couple," she understood the concept of multiple jeopardy all too well, since she usually found herself a member of some group "defined as other, deviant, inferior[16] or just plain wrong." The way to overcome this kind of marginality, said Lorde, is not "to pluck out some one aspect of [oneself] and present this as [a] meaningful whole,"[17] as if one could solve all of one's problems simply by fighting racism *or* sexism *or* classism *or* homophobia *or* ableism (Lorde experienced even more alienation subsequent to a mastectomy).[18] Rather, the way to overcome one's otherness is to "integrate all the parts of who I am, openly, allowing power from particular sources of my living to flow back and forth freely through all my different selves, without the restrictions of externally imposed definition."[19] Lorde asserted she fights indiscriminately against the forces of oppression, including "that piece of the oppressor"[20] within herself. Her one and only priority is to create a society in which everyone is truly equal and where "different" does not mean "inferior" but instead "unique."

Furthering the analyses of hooks and Lorde, Patricia Hill Collins argued that in the United States black women's oppression is systematized and structured along three interdependent dimensions. First, the *economic* dimension of black women's oppression relegates black women to "ghettoization in service occupations."[21] Second, the *political* dimension of black women's oppression denies black women the rights and privileges routinely extended to all white men and many white women, including the very important right to an equal education.[22] Third, the *ideological* dimension of black women's oppression imposes a freedom-restricting set of "controlling images" on black women, serving to justify as well as explain white men's and (to a lesser extent) white women's treatment of black women. Commented Collins: "From the mammies, Jezebels, and breeder women of slavery to the smiling Aunt Jemimas on pancake mix boxes, ubiquitous Black prostitutes, and ever-present welfare mothers of contemporary popular culture, the nexus of negative stereotypical images applied to African-American women has been fundamental to Black women's oppression."[23] Collins theorized the ideological dimension was more powerful in maintaining black women's oppression than either the economic or political dimension. She stated that "race, class, and gender oppression could not continue without powerful ideological justification for their existence"[24] and stressed that black feminists must work to free African American women from the "mammy," "matriarch," welfare recipient, and "hot momma" stereotypes. Until blacks as well as whites stop thinking in stereotypical terms about black women, black women will not be free to be themselves.

Although black feminists often focus on economic and political issues, contrary to some misconceptions they also address many sexual issues. To be sure, black feminists have been loathe to make a "public issue" of sexism in the black community for fear of feeding some whites' misperception that black men are more sexually voracious and violent than white men or, the related view, that black women, like their "menfolk," have enormous sexual appetites.[25] Nevertheless, many black feminists have decided to risk such misperceptions. Among the most eloquent of them has been hooks.

Noting the extent to which black men have used disturbing gendered metaphors to describe the nature of blacks' struggle for freedom, hooks explained:

> The discourse of black resistance almost always equated freedom with manhood, the economic and material domination of black men with castration, emasculation. Accepting these sexual metaphors forged a bond between oppressed black men and their male oppressors. They shared the patriarchal belief that revolutionary struggle was really about the erect phallus, the ability of men to establish political dominance that could correspond to sexual dominance. . . . Many of us have never forgotten that moment in *Soul on Ice* when Eldridge Cleaver, writing about the need to "redeem my conquered manhood," described raping black women as practice for the eventual rape of white women. Remember that readers were not shocked or horrified by this glamorization of rape as a weapon of terrorism men might use to express rage about other forms of domination, about their struggle for power with other men. Given the sexist context of the culture, it made sense.[26]

But, continued hooks, that black men have suffered does not negate that black women have also suffered, not only at the hands of their white oppressors but also at the hands of black men. This latter suffering, no less than the former, must be addressed, in hooks's estimation. In other words, the black community must confront its own sexism, and black women must challenge black as well as white pornographers, sexual harassers, and rapists, for example, by holding them accountable for their role in oppressing women, particularly black women.

Although white and black feminists define pornography differently, they agree it is degrading when it represents depersonalized sexual exchanges devoid or nearly devoid of mutual respect, that is, when it describes or depicts sexual exchanges in which the desires and experiences of at least one participant are not regarded by the other participant(s) as having a validity and importance equal to his/her/their own. Although some black feminists dismiss the radical-cultural feminist antipornography campaign as an instance of misplaced "white" outrage—a spewing of venom that only white, middle-class, "spoiled" women who have adequate food, shelter, clothing, education, and jobs can afford—other black feminists regard pornography as a relevant and significant issue. For example, Tracey Gardner expressed the view that more black women would take pornography seriously if they realized just how bad it is.[27] She claimed that many black women, like many white women, *think* they know what pornography is. They may have seen copies of *Playboy* or *Jiveboy*; they may have attended an X-rated movie; they may have heard about urban "combat zones" or even visited them. But it is unlikely that these same women have also seen violent porn (in which women are tortured) or have spent time cruising New York City's Forty-Second Street or its equivalent. Pornography is not so much about cute *Playboy* bunnies as it is about depicting women as raw meat or a cluster of dismembered body parts.

Over and beyond sexist pornography, there exists a whole genre of racist pornography. Unlike those feminists who assume pornography primarily affects white women, Collins argued that "the treatment of Black women's bodies in nineteenth-century Europe and the United States may be the foundation upon which contemporary pornography as the representation of women's objectification, domination, and control is based."[28] She noted that in antebellum America, at least in the South, men did not need pornographic representations because they "could become voyeurs of black women on the auction block."[29] Collins described the objectification of the black female body in the person of Sarah Bartmann, the so-called Hottentot Venus. Bartmann, an African woman, was often displayed at fashionable Parisian parties as a sexual curiosity. Wealthy Europeans gladly paid royal sums to view her genitalia and buttocks, which remain on display in Paris to this day. In other words, stressed Collins, many white men (and also white women) paid to see a live pornographic show in which the sexuality of Bartmann was represented as *the* sexuality of all African women (and men): a physical, animal-like sexuality, supposedly different from the sexuality of white men and women. No wonder, then, when black women appear in pornographic magazines targeted for white men, they are frequently portrayed as animals (usually cats such as tigers, leopards, and cheetahs) being chained or caged by the "great white hunter."

Even worse than the kind of racist pornography white men use, said writer Alice Walker, is the kind of racist pornography black men use. Sometimes black men's racist pornography shows a black man getting a white woman to perform a sexual act no white man would dare ask her to perform. Here the racist message is that when black men get power, they intend to have "their way" with white women. At other times black men's racist pornography depicts even more hurtful scenes: for example, one showing a black man defecating or urinating on a black woman. Here the racist message is that black men do not take pride in anything or anyone black. In her moving essay "Coming Apart," Walker described a black man's feelings as he finally comes to terms with his use of racist pornography:

> What he has refused to see . . . is that where white women are depicted in pornography as "objects," black women are depicted as animals. Where white women are at least depicted as human bodies if not beings, black women are depicted as shit. He begins to feel sick. For he realizes that he has bought some if not all the advertisements about women, black and white. And further, inevitably, he has bought the advertisements about himself. In pornography the black man is portrayed as being capable of fucking anything . . . even a piece of shit. He is defined solely by the size, readiness and unselectivity of his cock.[30]

In degrading women, but particularly his own women, the black man degrades himself. He also helps set the stage for black women's sexual harassment.

Like white women, black women are not strangers to sexual harassment, defined as unwanted sexual attention of a nondiscriminatory or discriminatory sort. Nondiscriminatory sexual harassment occurs when the harasser has no official control over the women he harasses. Discriminatory sexual harassment occurs when the harasser is in a position of authority or power allowing him to make better or worse the educational or occupational situation of the women he harasses.

When it comes to discriminatory sexual harassment, the focus of this analysis, black women are leaders in the efforts to stop its incursions into the workplace and into academia. As in pornography, power plays directed against black women are likely to have racist as well as sexist overtones. Black women, especially poor black women, are particularly vulnerable to sexual harassment because of their pressing need for education and employment. When white men harass black women, they use sex not only to control black women as *women* but also to demean them as *black* women (racism + sexism) or as *poor* black women (classism + racism + sexism). Sexual harassers tend to take advantage of those whom they perceive as most vulnerable; and whether "white" America cares to face it or not, black women epitomize as well as enflesh the vulnerability of their people's slave past.[31]

Black men, too, sexually harass women.[32] However, the sexual harassment of a black woman by a black man is qualitatively different from the sexual harassment of a black woman by a white man; it is also qualitatively different from the sexual harassment of a white woman by a black man.[33] When a white woman is sexually harassed by a black supervisor or employer, "being white" will probably work to her advantage in the same way "being white" works to a white woman's advantage when she is raped by a black man. The "system" will be more inclined to believe her story; "white" society assumes black men *want* white women as "trophies." In contrast, when a black woman is sexually harassed by a powerful white man, "being black" will probably not work to her advantage, although it should, given that in the past white slave owners usually got their "way" with their black female slaves. The rewards for pleasing the master and the punishments for displeasing the master were such that black female slaves quickly learned to say yes to their masters' sexual advances. Nevertheless, even though the legacy of slavery continues to distort sexual relations between blacks and whites, so powerful is the stereotype of the black "hot mamma" that judges and juries are inclined to believe that the guilty party is the black female employee, not her white male employer. She is the supposed temptress who threw her black body at him to give him a taste of what his uptight, lily-white wife could never give him. Similarly, when black female employees charge black male employers with sexually inappropriate behavior, courts are far more likely to see an instance of sexual attraction gone sour than an instance of genuine sexual harassment. In this connection, the Anita Hill–Clarence Thomas case is most instructive.

In 1991 Anita Hill, a young black lawyer with an impeccable personal and professional record, alleged Clarence Thomas sexually harassed her when she was under his supervision. At the time Hill made these allegations, Thomas was a candidate for a seat on the Supreme Court. Indeed, one of the reasons Hill gave for the time lag between Thomas's alleged harassment and her coming forward with her complaints was precisely that she could no longer keep silent about her abuse. In her estimation a sexual harasser had no business serving on the U.S. Supreme Court. However reluctant she had previously been to air her story in public because of possible risks to her career, she felt she could not continue to hold her tongue.

Criticism of Hill's decision to go public was particularly strong among blacks. They considered her disloyal to the black community and held her in disdain for jeopardizing the confirmation of the *only* black candidate President George Bush would nominate to the Supreme Court.[34] Moreover, Thomas himself linked Hill's allegations against him with the lynching of black men in the "old days." At his Senate confirmation hearings, he declared, "I will not provide the rope for my own lynching."[35] After hearing Hill's and Thomas's divergent accounts of their relationship, the fourteen white men on the Senate committee in charge of Thomas's confirmation hearings unanimously endorsed his candidacy to the Supreme Court. In the process of doing so, several members of the committee attacked Hill's character. One went so far as to suggest she had fabricated the whole story as part of a *liberal* plot to ruin *conservative* Thomas's chances for Senate confirmation. Reflecting on these attacks, journalist Jack E. Hill commented:

> Black women's complaints about sexist behavior are taken even less seriously than white women's. Held down by racism and the sexism of both black and white males, black females are one of society's most oppressed groups. Yet their attempts to call attention to their plight routinely provoke storms of energetic denial of the legitimacy of their complaints. An example: the denunciations that were heaped on Alice Walker for her novel *The Color Purple* and the film that was based on it. Some critics falsely charged that Walker was a lesbian who hated black men because she created a heroine who was savagely mistreated by nearly every black male she encountered.[36]

To make matters even worse for Hill, polls revealed that although *feminists* supported her, 49 percent of American women, black and white, either sided with Thomas or proclaimed the Hill–Thomas "showdown" a draw.[37] In particular, less-advantaged women felt that despite her humble roots, the highly educated and very successful Hill was not really one of them. Anne Rungold, media director for the Democratic Party, stated: "Both working-class women and highly educated women put up with sexual harassment every day.... But the perception among working-class women is that a Yale degree just gives you the right to make a federal case out of it. Besides, if you can't get a good-paying job somewhere else, what good is that degree anyway?"[38] In some ways the Hill–Thomas case played out as it did because these two blacks were perceived as "white" and "rich" and therefore as not *really* black.

Like pornography and sexual harassment, rape assumes different forms in black and white women's lives. In her book *Women, Race and Class*, Angela Davis claimed white feminists ranging from Susan Brownmiller to Jean MacKellar to Diana Russell helped resuscitate the "old racist myth of the Black rapist" who yearns to abuse white women sexually.[39] MacKellar, for example, noted that 90 percent of all reported rapes in the United States are committed by black men, even though the FBI's corresponding figure is 47 percent.[40] Similarly, of the twenty-two rape cases Diana Russell described, more than 50 percent involved women who had been raped by men of color, even though only 26 percent of the original ninety-five cases she studied involved men of color.[41] By presenting their statistics in such ways, Davis observed, MacKellar and Russell obscured the real social causes of rape. Since only a small fraction of rapes are ever reported, it could be women are more inclined to report poor or black rapists than rich or white rapists. Although this is conjecture, it is not idle speculation. The law prefers not to catch rich, respected, or powerful men in its snares. Therefore, a woman who is raped by a pillar of the community, especially a white pillar, is likely to leave bad enough alone by not reporting her rapist to the authorities. As a result, there is no way of estimating how many women are raped by "nice" white doctors, lawyers, professors, and businessmen.

Davis was most distressed by what she perceived as the contributions of Brownmiller, MacKellar, and Russell to white society's irrational fears about the "violent black man." She took particular exception to some passages in Brownmiller's influential book on rape, *Against Our Will: Men, Women, and Rape*. She claimed that Brownmiller implied, for example, that the average black man agrees with Eldridge Cleaver's statement that rape is an "insurrectionary act" against "white society." Commented Davis: "It seems as if she [Susan Brownmiller] wants to intentionally conjure up in her readers' imaginations armies of Black men, their penises erect, charging full speed ahead toward the most conveniently placed white woman."[42] Such a view of black men, stressed Davis, is one that feeds the flames of the racist fires continuing to warm the passions of bigoted people.

In the nineteenth century, wrote Davis, thousands of black men were lynched by white men. For several years, these lynchings were justified as necessary to prevent "Negro conspiracies, Negro insurrections, Negro schemes to murder all the white people, Negro plots to burn the town and to commit violence generally."[43] When it became obvious that no such conspiracies, insurrections, schemes, or plots were brewing, another reason was offered to justify white society's lynching of black men: to save white women from black men's sexual assaults. These sexual assaults were often "trumped up," if not by white women then by white men. Nevertheless, the lynchings continued despite the concerted efforts of black anti-lynching crusaders such as Ida B. Wells, Mary Church Terrell, and Mary Talbert, all of whom did their best through the 1890s and early 1900s to expose these "justified lynchings" for what they really were—unjustified murders of innocent black men. Not until 1930, when white women, under the leadership of Jessie Daniel Ames, established the Association of Southern Women for the Prevention of Lynching, did the tide of lynching reverse itself and abate. These white women refused to "allow those bent upon personal revenge and savagery to mount acts of violence and lawlessness in the name of women."[44] Commending these white women for their convictions and courage, Davis nonetheless expressed regret it took white women so long to respond to the repeated pleas of their black sisters.

Currently, many black women are not certain whether they should press for more stringent rape laws. On the one hand, they are well aware that black men who rape white women (or who are accused of raping white women) are often treated more harshly than white men who rape black women (or white women). Since 1930, of the 455 men who were legally executed in the United States for a rape conviction, 89 percent were black. In a majority of these cases, the rape victim was a white woman. In Florida alone, between 1940 and 1964, six white men who raped white women were executed; in comparison, eighty-four blacks were prosecuted for raping white women and forty-five were executed. And no rapist, white or black, who violated a black woman received the death penalty.[45] In view of such statistics, black women want white feminists to work with them to make certain that new rape laws will be enforced fairly, irrespective of skin color.

On the other hand, black women are also well aware that most rapes are intraracial, not interracial, and that however hard it is for a white woman to "prove" she has been raped by a white man, it is even harder for a black woman to "prove" she has been raped by a black man. Not only is the white community likely to trivialize her complaints, dismissing her rape as just "one of those things *those* people do to each other," but the black community is likely to condemn her as a "traitor," urging her to set her priorities straight.

Focusing on black women's confusion about what to do about rape, Barbara Omolade analyzed the heavily publicized Central Park jogger case. On April 19, 1989, a young white female jogger was brutally assaulted and raped by a group of young black men in New York's Central Park. Both the black and white community were appalled by the attack. Indeed, said Omolade, Mayor Koch spoke of "a whole city filled with distress and pain at the plight of this young girl."[46] Because this was a black-on-white rape, the media predictably turned a "polarized racial lens on the crime,"[47] describing the alleged assailants as "animals" and "their actions in the park a form of wilding."[48] As it turned out, the alleged assailants were seemingly "good" black boys who came from hardworking, churchgoing families and whose guilt was far from certain.

Although black feminists expressed concern that the alleged rapists of the Central Park jogger were being "railroaded," they were still eager to consider the *sexist* as well as *racist* implications of the case, said Omolade. Acknowledging that the law is often unfair to black men, Omolade nonetheless stressed that black men are *victimizers* as well as *victims* and that no one knows this better than black women. She commented:

> The . . . case occurred during a social science blitz about "endangered" Black males being poor, jailed, uneducated, and despised. The Black man then became a heroic and besieged "victim" of white racism whose "endangered status" is used to rationalize and justify his violence. The pain of Black women and children who are "endangered" by these same Black men is ignored.
>
> Although the young Black men of the [Central Park jogger] case are from a community with little economic, political, or social power, and have been found guilty of raping a woman from a *race* and community with all such power, they are also from a *gender* which can rape and abuse women of their race with the same impunity white men use in murdering or judging Black men. What construct other than sexism can be offered to explain Black resistance to condemning all forms of rape irrespective of the victim's color? What other than rejec-

tion of the value of the Black female body can explain the Black community's protests and furor about the guilt or innocence of the ... boys who allegedly raped a white woman, and its lack of concern about the boys who harass and rape Black women every day![49]

Omolade emphasized that sexism within the black community has to be confronted. There comes a time when black women's concerns should be moved from the back burner to the front burner. However serious the concerns of black men are, the concerns of black women are equally serious.

Global Feminism: An Overview

Global feminism differs from multicultural feminism because it focuses on the oppressive results of colonial and nationalist policies and practices, how Big Government and Big Business divide the world into the so-called First World (the realm of the haves) and the so-called Third World (the realm of the have-nots). Agreeing with multicultural feminists that the definition of feminism must be broadened to include all the things that oppress women, whether based on race or class or resulting from imperialism or colonialism, global feminists stress "the oppression of women in one part of the world is often affected by what happens in another, and that no woman is free until the conditions of oppression of women are eliminated everywhere."[50] Committed to the task of dispelling misunderstandings and creating alliances between Third World women and First World women, global feminists aim to widen the scope of feminist thought.

Believing that First World women are interested only in sexual issues or in making the case that gender discrimination is the worst form of oppression a woman can experience, many Third World women emphasize they are far more concerned about political and economic issues than sexual issues. They also stress that in their experience their oppression as women is not nearly so bad as their oppression as Third World people. Thus, many Third World women reject the label *feminist*. In its stead, they embrace Alice Walker's term *womanist*. Walker defined a "womanist" as "a Black feminist or woman of color" committed to the "survival and wholeness of entire people, male and female."[51]

In reaction to Third World women's critique of feminism, some First World feminists object that "womanists" do women a disservice by minimizing gender discrimination. However, most First World feminists are highly receptive to Third World women's reservations about feminism. They admit the time has come for feminists to redefine "feminism." In fact, some First World feminists are so eager to make up for their past neglect of Third World women's issues that they insist *only* Third World women's issues are important. First World women should, they claim, simply count their blessings and beg Third World women's forgiveness for their contribution to Third World women's and men's oppression. Not only are First World men guilty of exploiting Third World people, so, too, are First World women.[52]

Other First World feminists believe that it is not necessary for First World women to deny the legitimacy of their own concerns in order to acknowledge their role in oppressing Third World people. They stress that global feminism is not about privileging the concerns of Third World women over those of First World women. Rather, global feminism is about women, from all over the world, coming together as true equals to discuss their commonalities and differences as honestly as possible in a mutual effort to secure what Charlotte Bunch identified as the two long-term goals of global feminism:

1. ... the right of women to freedom of choice, and the power to control our own lives within and outside of the home. Having control over our lives and our bodies is essential to ensure a sense of dignity and autonomy for every woman.

2. ... the removal of all forms of inequity and oppression through the creation of a more just social and economic order, nationally and internationally. This means the involvement of women in national liberation struggles, in plans for national development, and in local and global struggles for change.[53]

For global feminists, the personal and the political are one. What goes on in the privacy of one's home, including one's bedroom, affects the ways in which men and women relate in the larger social order. Sexual and reproductive freedom should be of no more or less importance to women than economic and political justice. Socialist feminist Emily Woo Yamaski made this point most forcefully when she stated: "I cannot be an Asian American on Monday, a woman on Tuesday, a lesbian on Wednesday, a worker/student on Thursday, and a political radical on Friday. I am all these things every day."[54]

Over and beyond emphasizing the interconnections among the various kinds of oppression each woman faces in her own life, global feminists stress the links among the various kinds of oppression women in all parts of the world experience. For global feminists, the local is global and the global is local. What an individual woman does in the United States affects the lives of women all over the world; and, correlatively, what women all over the world do affects the life of the woman in the United States. Bunch explained:

> To make global feminist consciousness a powerful force in the world demands that we make the local, global and the global, local. Such a movement is not based on international travel and conferences, although these may be useful, but must be centered on a sense of connectedness among women active at the grass roots in various regions. For women in industrialized countries, this connectedness must be based in the authenticity of our struggles at home, in our need to learn from others, and in our efforts to understand the global implications of our actions, not in liberal guilt, condescending charity, or the false imposition of our models on others. Thus, for example, when we fight to have a birth control device banned in the United States because it is unsafe, we must simultaneously demand that it be destroyed rather than dumped on women in the Third World.[55]

Feminist *practice* is a theme global feminists repeatedly announce.

Diversity and Commonality

Although global feminists insist women are interconnected, they caution women that in order to understand what binds them together, women must first understand what separates them. Women cannot work together *as true equals* to resolve issues concerning them unless women first recognize the depths of their differences. According to Audre Lorde, when a feminist walks into a room filled with women from all over the world, she probably does not want to confront her differences from all of them. It is simply too threatening to her notions about "sisterhood" to focus on women's "manyness," so she strains to focus on women's "oneness." Lorde stressed that it is precisely this type of behavior that explains feminists' inability to forge the kind of alliances necessary to create a better world. She stated:

> Advocating the mere tolerance of difference between women is the grossest reformism. It is a total denial of the creative function of difference in our lives. Difference must not be merely tolerated, but seen as a fund of necessary polarities between which our creativity can spark like a dialectic. Only then does the necessity for interdependency become unthreatening. Only within that interdependency of different strengths, acknowledged and equal, can the power to seek new ways of being in the world generate, as well as the courage and sustenance to act where there are no charters.[56]

Just because a feminist wants to work with women very different from her—who may, for example, have suffered oppressions far more harmful to body, mind, and spirit than the ones she has suffered—does not mean she should deny who she is. Nor does it mean she should keep her counsel for fear of offending others. On the contrary, to refuse to reveal one's self to others is to assume that others are not capable of coming to terms with one. "Although I think I have what it takes to understand others, I doubt that they share this ability": To think in such a fashion is the height of arrogance in global feminists' view.

"Women's Issues" Versus "Political Issues"

Among the differences global feminists address is the tendency of some women to stress sexual and reproductive issues and other women to stress economic and political issues. In 1975 the United Nations declared the years 1975–1985 the Decade of Women, instructing all its members to give women the same opportunities for advancement in the economic, cultural, religious, political, and judicial fields that men have. Three international women's conferences punctuated the Decade of Women: a beginning conference held in Mexico City (1975); a midpoint conference held in Copenhagen (1980); and a final, twelve-day conference held in Nairobi, Kenya (1985). More than 2,000 delegates from 140 countries attended the final meeting. In addition, some 13,000 delegates participated in Forum 85, a loosely confederated group of 157 nongovernmental organizations. Although global feminists generally looked forward to each of these conferences, many of them worried that a women's conference sponsored by a "patriarchal" organization like the United Nations was subject to problems. It was bound to serve, as Robin Morgan claimed, not women's interests but Big Brother's interests.[57]

As it turned out, problems between First World women and Third World women did emerge at each of the international women's conferences held between 1975 and 1985. In the estimation of several First World women who attended these meetings, so-called political issues often took center stage, as so-called women's issues were shunted aside. They claimed, for example, that at the Mexico City conference the delegates of communist, Asian, Latin American, and African states were instructed by their respective governments to engage solely in "politics" and to eschew issues related to women's human rights; that at the Copenhagen conference "more heat was generated about 'Zionism,' 'racism,' and 'Western imperialism' than about the basic rights of women and their legally deprived status in over 75 of the 118 countries attending";[58] and that at the Nairobi conference, as well as at Forum 85, "once again, political cliches and ideological harangues, associated with East–West and North–South disputes in the General Assembly of the U.N., dominated proceedings."[59] Referring in particular to the Nairobi conference and Forum 85, critic Eschel Rhoodie observed:

> Even the subject of the right of women to choose when and how many children to have did not make the grade. Yet this issue is one of the most important ones to be addressed by women's organizations and governments in the Third World. It failed to become a central rallying point in Kenya, the venue of the conference, the capital of a country where men's blind and irresponsible resistance to birth control has produced the highest birthrate in the world, creating catastrophic social and economic problems and condemning women to remain in a centuries-old stereotype.[60]

The leader of the U.S. delegation, Maureen Reagan, reportedly summed up the Nairobi conference as "an orgy of [political and ideological] hypocrisy."[61]

Global feminists urge First World women critical of the UN international women's conferences to reconsider their objections to them. Conceding that Big Brother indeed used some women at these meetings to support political causes that weaken rather than strengthen women's status, global feminists nonetheless remain convinced that so-called political issues and so-called women's issues are not necessarily opposed. They also remain convinced that it is a mistake to think that feminists must always privilege women's issues over political issues; sometimes sexual and reproductive issues must, as many Third World women presently believe, defer to economic and political issues.

Third World women's priorities help explain why some of them view First World women as arrogant know-it-alls, who are totally ignorant about real oppression. Nawal el Saadawi, an Egyptian writer, was particularly critical of First World women's supposed powers of perception. She noted: "Western women often go to countries such as Sudan and 'see' only clitoridectomy, but never notice the role of multinational corporations and their exploited labor."[62] In other words, First World women frequently fail to appreciate the extent to which *they* are the economic and political oppressors of women (and men) in the Third World. The same U.S. woman who is willing to attend protests against clitoridectomy might not be willing to attend protests against the multinational corporation that pays her or her husband a substantial salary.

Global feminists stress that the distinction between so-called political issues and so-called women's issues is false. There is, they say, no boundary between these two kinds of issues. On the contrary, they co-constitute each other.[63] In this connection, global feminist Angela Gillian quoted a Cape Verdean woman, who, together with several other women, had invited her to address their daughters about the importance of higher education:

> I want my daughter to take part in what is taking place in this country. If she gets married now, she will never participate in the change. I don't want her to be like me. I am married to a good man. As you know about 40 percent of Cape Verdian men are labourers in Europe, and my husband is in Holland. That house over there that we are building brick by brick right next to this little cabin is being made with the money he sends home. Every two years he gets one month's vacation, and comes home to meet the baby he made the last time, and to make a new one. I don't want that for my daughter. I've heard that it is possible to prevent pregnancy by knowing the calendar. Please teach our girls how to count the days so that they can control their pregnancies.[64]

Gillian commented that for this woman the issue was not *men's* oppression of women but how an inequitable international labor system causes both men and women to construct their family relations in deleterious ways. No wonder, said Gillian, that many Third World women are convinced that "the separation of sexism from the political, economic, *and* racial is a strategy of elites. As such it becomes a tool to confuse the real issues around which most of world's women struggle."[65]

Stressing that *everything* is a women's issue, many global feminists went to each of the three UN international women's conferences wanting very much to erase the arbitrary line between so-called women's issues and so-called political issues and to bridge the gap between the perspectives of First World and Third World women. For example, as Charlotte Bunch prepared for the Nairobi conference, she hoped to set a broad agenda not limited to sexual and reproduction issues. She said: "Racism is a woman's issue, just as is anti-Semitism, Palestinian homelessness, rural development, ecology, the persecution of lesbians, and the exploitive practices of global corporations. Domination on the basis of race, class, religion, sexual preference, economics, or nationality cannot be seen as a mere additive to the oppression of women by gender. Rather, all these factors help to shape the very forms of that oppression."[66]

Nowhere is the complex interplay between multiple forms of oppression more clear than with respect to the old reproduction-controlling technologies (contraception, sterilization, and abortion) and the new reproduction-aiding technologies (intrauterine donor insemination and in vitro fertilization). Whether such technologies and the social arrangements associated with some of them (e.g., surrogate motherhood) are women-liberating or women-oppressing depends largely on a woman's class, race, sexual preference, religion, and nationality. For example, although virtually all U.S. women express concerns about the safety, efficacy, convenience, and availability of contraception, sterilization, and abortion, most white, middle-class heterosexual women believe they would be far less free and well-off without these reproduction-controlling technologies.

But the largely positive view that white, middle-class, heterosexual women hold regarding reproduction-controlling technologies is *not* the view *all* U.S. women share. All too often, some racist and classist (as well as sexist) American healthcare practitioners and politicians have used (or sought to use) the reproduction-controlling technologies for eugenic or cost-saving purposes. For example, in the 1960s the so-called rule of 120, which precluded sterilization of a woman unless her age times the number of her living children equaled 120 or more,[67] was widely followed by obstetricians and gynecologists when it came to healthy, white, middle-class, married women—a fact that angered these advantaged women. They wanted physicians to adopt more permissive sterilization policies. What these advantaged women failed to realize, at least initially, was that the same obstetricians and gynecologists who were reluctant to sterilize them were often only too happy to sterilize women of color, especially indigent ones.

Indeed, in some southern states, sterilizations of indigent black women were so common that they were irreverently referred to as "Mississippi appendectomies."[68] More recently, but in the same manner, some legislators have drafted policies and laws linking fertile women's welfare eligibility to their willingness to use the contraceptive Norplant. In the estimation of these lawmakers, unless a woman agrees to use this long-term contraceptive implant, she and any children she might already have should be denied Aid to Families with Dependent Children.[69]

The kind of policies and laws described above caused many U.S. women of color, particularly those whose incomes are very low, to suspect "white" America has eugenic designs on "black" America. Some of these women claim that "white" America is so eager to limit the growth of the black population that it forces the abortion "choice" as well as the contraception "choice" and sterilization "choice" on black women and other women of color. In support of their claim, they note that some of the most fervent right-to-lifers also advocate limiting or cutting benefits to welfare mothers—even though such limits and cuts might cause more than a few welfare mothers to terminate their pregnancies. Realizing the extent to which a woman's race and class affects the scope of her reproductive freedom, Alison Jaggar commented: "A real choice about abortion requires that a woman should be able to opt to have her child, as well as to abort it. This means that the full right to life of the child must be guaranteed, either by community aid to the mother who wishes to raise it herself, or by the provision of alternative arrangements that do not put the child who is not raised by its own mother at any significant disadvantage."[70]

If the situation with respect to women's use of reproduction-controlling and reproduction-assisting technologies is unclear in the United States, it is even more unclear worldwide. In the former Soviet Union, women have the right to abort. However, most of them are forced to exercise this right routinely (on average twelve to fourteen times during their lifetimes) because contraceptives, although legal, are extremely difficult to obtain.[71]

Even more worrisome than the former Soviet Union's policies are those of China, where a one-child-per-family policy remains on the books, enforced more strenuously in some regions of the country than in others. In the early 1980s Chinese government officials decided to monitor the fertility of approximately 340 million Chinese women, going so far as to track their menstrual cycles. They also decided to punish couples who had more than one child and to reward those who complied with the one-child policy. A variety of economic penalties were levied against the former; in contrast, the latter were given pay raises of up to 40 percent, extended maternity leaves, and better housing.[72] In 1995 a new generation of Chinese government officials stepped up the effort to decrease the size of China's population. They posted signs warning women to report every three months to a local clinic for a pregnancy test or else face a large fine. In addition, officials urged women with one child either to be sterilized or to accept an intrauterine device. Failure to comply with such urgings proved to be no small matter in some rural outposts. After blasting into rubble the home of a family with three children, government dynamiters in the village of Xiaoxi warned its shocked inhabitants, "Those who do not obey the family planning policies will be those who lose their fortunes."[73]

Equally if not even more threatening to women's reproductive freedom are India's amniocentesis policies. First developed to discover genetic abnormalities in the fetus, amniocentesis is now routinely used in India as a sex determination test with the purpose of eliminating female fetuses. The test is inexpensive and women supposedly "want" it, particularly if they already have one or more daughters, each of whom will eventually require a costly wedding dowry.

When Indian feminists campaigned for a ban on sex determination, their protest was heard, but in a way that backfired on them. GAMET-NICS, a U.S. company with clinics in many Third World countries, devised a preconception sex-selection technology. Using this method, technicians separate Y chromosomes, which are the male sex determinants, from X chromosomes. At present they are able to select sperm containing 80 percent of Y chromosomes, which are then injected into the woman. Although this method is more costly than amniocentesis followed by abortion and although it, like its predecessor method, promises to make Indian women an "endangered species," it struck many Indians as more "humane" than amniocentesis and abortion. Reflecting on this new technology, Maria Mies, who is both an ecofeminist and a global feminist, commented: "This example shows clearly that the sexist and racist ideology is closely interwoven with capitalist profit motives, that the logic of selection and elimination has a definite economic base. Patriarchy and racism are not only ethically rejectable ideologies, they mean *business* indeed."[74]

No less a woman's issue than reproduction is production. As Robin Morgan noted, "Women are the world's proletariat."[75] Even though housework constitutes 60 to 80 percent of most nations' economics, housework continues to suffer from "gross national product invisibility." To deny that women work, stressed Morgan, is absurd. Women constitute almost the totality of the world's food producers and are responsible for most of the world's hand portage of water and fuel. In most nations handicrafts are largely or solely the products of female labor, and in most nations women compose a large portion of tourist industry workers, particularly the sex tourism industry in Asia (catering to businessmen who pay for the sexual services of women in the countries they visit).[76] In addition multinational corporations use women as a cheap source of labor, failing to provide them with the training they provide men and firing them whenever it proves profitable to do so. Women are migrant and seasonal workers in agrarian countries and part-time laborers in industrialized countries.

Worldwide, women work a so-called double day, doing eight or more hours of "invisible" work at home (housework, childcare, eldercare, sick care) and eight or more hours of "visible" work outside the home. When governments and businesses respond to women's complaints about having to work too hard, they typically do so in ways that do not improve women's situations. They tell overworked women to work part time or to get on a mommy track, strategies that often render women virtually ineligible for substantial promotions and pay increases. Or, worse, governments and businesses pass laws and develop policies that "protect" women from supposedly "harmful" high-paying jobs. As if this is not bad enough, governments and businesses often fail to understand women's complaints about their "double day" of work, recommending ridiculous or insulting solutions. For example, Cuba's Fidel Castro once proposed that "hairdressers remain open during the evening to ease the burden of the woman who is employed during the day but needs to be attractive in her house wifing role at night."[77]

Reflecting on how hard women work and how little government and business has done to ameliorate women's lot, Morgan concluded this state of affairs obtains because Big Brother's interests are not served by providing women the same kind of work and economic security it provides men. Whether Big Brother lives in the First World or Third World, "a marginal female labor force is a highly convenient asset: cheap, always available, easily and callously disposed of."[78] In Morgan's estimation, women's oppression as producers is clearly equal to if not greater than their oppression as reproducers.

Although First World women are disadvantaged workers relative to First World men, Morgan conceded that they are advantaged workers relative to Third World people, including Third World men. She also acknowledged that First World proposals to solve the Third World's economic problems—in particular so-called development economics strategies—often work to the detriment of Third World people, especially Third World women. (However, Morgan did not discuss the specific ways in which development economics strategies help consolidate the First World's power in the Third World.)

Detailing how the First World's "you-can-catch-up-to-us" policies serve the interests of the First World far more than the interests of the Third World, Maria Mies claimed that First World economists make promises to Third World people they have no hope of keeping. They tell Third World people that they can attain the same standard of living First World people enjoy. But down deep, First World economists doubt the truth of their stories about endless progress and limitless growth.[79] For example, observing that the world's population will swell to 11 billion after the year 2050, Mies stated: "If of these eleven billion people the per capita energy consumption was similar to that of Americans in the mid-1970s, conventional oil resources would be exhausted in 34–74 years."⁸⁰

Because the First World already finds it difficult to maintain its high standard of living, Mies speculated that whatever the First World gives the Third World in the way of benefits, it extracts in the way of costs. Specifically, the First World passes on to its Third World "partners" the economic, social, and ecological costs it cannot afford to pay without dropping from First World status to something more akin to Third World status. Commented Mies:

> The relationship between colonized and colonizer is based not on any measure of partnership but rather on the latter's coercion and violence in its dealings with the former. This relationship is in fact the secret of unlimited growth in the centers of accumulation. If externalization of all the costs of industrial production were not possible, if they had to be borne by the industrialized countries themselves, that is if they were internalized, an immediate end to unlimited growth would be inevitable.⁸¹

In sum, stressed Mies, "catching-up development" is not feasible, and this for two reasons: (1) There are only so many resources to divide among humankind, and they are currently inequitably distributed and consumed; and (2) the existing "colonial world order" needs to maintain the economic gap it promises to eliminate in order to maintain its present power.

What is more, not only is "catching-up development" not feasible, it is not *desirable* in Mies's estimation. She claimed the First World's "good life" is actually a very *bad* life insofar as human relationships are concerned. First World people are too busy making money to spend time with each other. They are so strained and stressed they gradually lose any sense of selfhood or ultimate meaning. First World people run the rat race, day after day, until the day they die. Their children inherit their considerable material goods, and the meaningless cycle of running and dying continues.

Mies also stressed that "catching-up development" has a role within the First World as well. First World women are offered the opportunity to catch up to First World men. However, to keep this promise, like the similar one to Third World people, is, once again, neither feasible nor desirable. First, whether promises of freedom, equality, and self-determination are kept depends on who controls the money and who has the power in a society; and in the First World *men* still control most of the money and most of the power. In order for First World women to "catch up" to First World men, First World men would have to be willing to share all of society's resources *equally* with First World women. At present such willingness on the part of First World men is not apparent.

Second, even in the affluent First World the "system" can afford only so many women to get the kind of money and power they need to be as free, equal, and self-determining as men are. Since First World men are not currently willing to share their money and power equally with First World women, First World women's best chance for "liberation" would then seem to depend to a greater or lesser extent on Third World people's, especially Third World women's, oppression. Mies explained: "Only while women in Asia, Africa or Latin America can be forced to work for much lower wages than those in affluent societies—and this is made possible through the debt trap—can enough capital be accumulated in the rich countries so that even unemployed women are guaranteed a minimum income; but all unemployed women in the world cannot expect this. Within a world system based on exploitation 'some are more equal than others.'"⁸²

Third, because money and power are limited goods for which self-interested human beings will inevitably compete, there is no ethical basis for solidarity among human beings in general or women in particular. Mies offered the following example:

> It may be in the interest of Third World women working in the garment industry for export, to get higher wages, or even wages equivalent to those paid in the industrialized countries; but if they actually received these wages then the working-class woman in the North could hardly afford to buy those garments, or buy as many of them as she does now. In her interest the price of these garments must remain low. Hence the interests of these two sets of women who are linked through the world market are antagonistic.⁸³

As long as the possession of material goods and power is equated with human happiness, there will be the kind of competition and antagonism that inevitably leads to conflict and even war. Women will be set against women multiculturally and globally and against their own men nationally.

From the perspective of global feminists, stressed Mies, the First World must abandon its view of the "good life" and substitute for it a view predicated not on the *quantity* of one's possessions and power but on the *quality* of one's relationships. In addition the First World must confront the material world's limits and vow to live within these limits. Only then will it be possible to create a new world order, in which divisions such as First World–Third World are incomprehensible. Finally, from the perspective of global feminists, women should take the lead in devising and implementing the systems, structures, policies, and programs needed to effect this transformation. In their estimation, it is women, particularly Third World women, who seem to know better than men, including Third World men, that the truly good life is not the rich, powerful life. In this connection, Mies described the experiences of her collaborator, Vandana Shiva, during a conference about the "green movement" in South Africa:

> While the main leaders and speakers seemed to expect South Africa's economic and ecological problems to be solved through full integration into the growth-oriented world economy, the women, who had so far borne the burden of modernization and development, were much more sceptical. One 60-year-old woman said that, 'The (government's) betterment scheme has been the best strategy to push us into the depth of poverty. It accelerated the migratory system.'
>
> The men were forced to migrate to the cities in search of jobs, whereas the women, together with the old and the children, had to try to survive in the rural areas. Meanwhile, the white government destroyed all assets and possessions by which the women tried to maintain their subsistence. 'We were dispossessed of our goats, donkeys and other animals. They were taken away by force and we got only 20 cents as compensation per head.'
>
> This woman had experienced the contradictory impact of 'betterment' or development as the government understood it. She knew that some must always pay the price for this development and that usually its victims are the women. Therefore she was not enthusiastic about further integration of the new non-racist democratic South Africa into the world market. Rather she demanded land and the security of independent subsistence.[84]

Production, no less than reproduction, is clearly a woman's issue.

The One and the Many: Ethical Absolutism Versus Ethical Relativism

That women are different and that they have different priorities is a tenet of global feminism. So, too, is the view that depending on where, when, how, and with whom she lives a woman will experience forms of oppression unique to those who share her circumstances. All this suggests that in order to be a global feminist, one must first be a multicultural feminist. According to Mies and Shiva, the East–West confrontations that preoccupied us from World War I onward and the North–South tensions that currently confront us effectively ended not only "all socialist dreams and utopias" but also "all universal" ideologies based on the conception of a common human nature.[85] Belief in oneness, as many postmodern feminists insist, is Eurocentric, egocentric, and phallogocentric. We must deconstruct the "one" so people can be *themselves*—not the other. Moreover, as many environmentalists claim, because natural and cultural diversity is a precondition for the maintenance of life on the planet, we must oppose the "homogenization of culture on the U.S. coca-cola and fast-food model" and the destruction of life forms "according to the demands of profit-oriented industries."[86]

Attracted to the view that the "many" needs to replace the "one," global feminists theorize that by parity of reasoning ethical relativism, the theory that ethical judgments are applicable only to the time and place in which they arise, needs to replace ethical absolutism, the theory that ethical judgments are applicable to all times and all places. But this is easier said than done. Ethical relativism poses a serious threat to feminism. For example, Mies and Shiva noted the total espousal of ethical relativism implies the global feminists "must accept even violence, and such patriarchal and exploitative institutions and customs as dowry, female genital mutilation, India's caste system.... Taken to extremes the emphasis on 'difference' could lead to losing sight of all commonalities, making even communication impossible."[87] In other words, if the idea of difference makes it impossible for women in one culture to communicate with women in another culture, global feminists might as well forget their plans to build a new world order. Such an order is neither viable nor welcome if people are so different they cannot even make sense of each other's words.

To get even clearer on why ethical relativism is a stumbling block for global feminists in particular, it is useful to focus on female circumcision/genital mutilation, a practice that has prompted some heated disputes between First World and Third World women. In her book *No Longer Patient*, feminist bioethicist Susan Sherwin noted it is indeed true that most feminists, not just global feminists, tend toward ethical relativism. Feminists supposedly regard ethical relativism as less oppressive than ethical absolutism. Yet according to Sherwin, feminists who rightly flee from the oppressiveness of an ethical absolutism that refuses to recognize difference may also wrongly flee from the universality of an ethical absolutism that permits them to say that oppression is always wrong. Feminists, she said, need to be able to say something is *wrong* before they try to make it *right*. A relativist critic is an oxymoron. If your decisions are as good as mine, then how can I possibly criticize you, or you me? asked Sherwin. We two are perfect; there is simply no need for either one or both of us to change our minds or course of action. Socially speaking, ethical relativism would seem to cost all feminists, including global feminists, the possibility of moral progress—of a better tomorrow, of a new world order.

In an attempt to elucidate just how difficult it is for a feminist to steer a course between the Scylla of ethical absolutism and the Charybdis of ethical relativism, Sherwin focused on the widespread practice of female circumcision/ genital mutilation in many African and Middle Eastern countries. She noted more than 84 million women now living have undergone this painful, frequently unsanitary, often harmful surgical procedure. Among the justifications for female circumcision/genital mutilation are "custom, religion, family honor, cleanliness, aesthetics, initiation, assurance of virginity, promotion of social and political cohesion, enhancement of fertility, improvement of male sexual pleasure, and prevention of female promiscuity."[88] Although large numbers of women as well as men within these countries endorse this practice, Sherwin still judged it wrong. In proclaiming the wrongness of female circumcision/genital mutilation, however, Sherwin realized she was walking down a perilous path. All too often "moral absolutism" has been used to support cultural dominance. Oppressors make the leap from "There is a truth" to "*I know* that truth, but you do not." Nevertheless, Sherwin claimed that in their desire to show proper respect for cultural diversity and to eschew the role of oppressor, feminists must be careful not to pull the moral carpet out from under themselves. Surely, some actions are so egregiously wrong—for example, rape—that feminists must simply say, "Rape is *wrong*," even if some culture or another happens to endorse rape. In taking this step, however, feminists must explain why they decided to violate their general rule of respect for cultural difference.[89]

Sherwin conceded it is easier to be a traditional ethical relativist than a feminist ethical relativist. Whereas the traditional ethical relativist is willing to live with his or her inability to condemn a practice such as female circumcision/genital mutilation (or, I suppose, even rape) if the majority of a population accepts it, the feminist ethical relativist is not. Sherwin agreed with traditional ethical relativists "that we do not have access to anything more foundational than community standards in ethics,"[90] but she claimed some communities are morally worse than other communities. A community that structures its relations in terms of patterns of domination and subordination, she said, is not worthy of moral trust; and unless a community is morally trustworthy, feminist relativists are not obligated to tolerate, let alone respect, its standards.

Before feminists decide to trust a community's standards, they must, emphasized Sherwin, make some baseline judgments about its moral methodology. If the community's standards are the result of a truly democratic conversation, then those standards, however disconcerting, ought to be tolerated, indeed respected, by feminist relativists. So, for example, if it turns out all segments of a society practicing female circumcision/genital mutilation truly endorse it—that no affected group has been forced to support this practice as the result of "coercion, exploitation, ignorance, deception, or even indifference"[91]—then it is a nonoppressive practice. However, in Sherwin's estimation, it is doubtful that *all* the segments of the societies practicing female circumcision/genital mutilation truly support it. Indeed, there is increasing evidence that support for female circumcision/genital mutilation is waning even in those nations that currently practice it. For example, over a decade ago, Kenyan president Daniel Moi condemned female circumcision/genital mutilation. Like many other people in his government, he believed the practice harms women and children physically and psychologically. Urging his people to put aside one of their long-standing traditions, Moi stressed that no nation, especially a developing one like Kenya, can afford to harm its own human resources. Kenya's future depends on each of its citizens being as healthy and happy as possible.[92]

Conceding it is not simple to determine whether a community is oppressive or nonoppressive—or just *how* oppressive a community must be before feminist ethical relativists mistrust its moral judgments—Sherwin sought additional guidance for feminists from David Wong, a nontraditional (but still nonfeminist) moral philosopher. Wong claimed that two equally justified, equally true, opposed moral positions can exist side by side. The individuals who espouse these two separate positions, however, should not interfere with each other's ends unless such interference would be "acceptable to them were they fully rational and informed of all relevant circumstances."[93] In order to clarify his meaning, Wong gave the example of abortion. As he saw it, people fight endlessly over abortion, but neither the antiabortion nor the pro-choice camps can rationally convert the other side. Both positions are grounded in reflective, well-established moral systems. Both positions, therefore, are probably morally justified. Referring to his own "justification principle," Wong again stressed that since no fully rational and informed person is willing to accept active interference with his or her ends, both the conservatives and the liberals should confine themselves to verbal volleying.[94] Each side should simply respect the moral convictions of the other and make it impossible, or nearly impossible, for the other side to follow its own ethical lights.

What is wrong with Wong's otherwise helpful position on ethical relativism, said Sherwin, is its acceptance of the conservatives' and liberals' respective moral systems as equally well established. In her estimation, Wong failed to ask certain crucial questions: namely, How did the systems come to be? Whose interests do they foster? And whose interests do they impede?[95] These questions are the kind of questions feminist ethical relativists should ask. The answers will probably reveal not only that the conservative position favors fetuses' and men's interests over women's interests but also that the conservative goal of stopping abortion limits liberals in ways that the liberal goal of safe, affordable, and accessible abortion does not limit conservatives.

The conservatives would block liberals from doing something they believe is right—having an abortion because one is not ready, willing, or able to be a parent; yet the liberals would not stop the conservatives from doing something they believe is right—not having an abortion because of their beliefs about the personhood of fetuses. The bumper sticker that reads "Don't like abortion? Don't have one!" comes close to making Sherwin's distinction succinctly. To the degree conservative abortion policies block liberals in a way liberal abortion policies do not block conservatives, feminists may actively interfere with conservatives on the grounds that conservative abortion policies are less "democratic" than liberal abortion policies.

> A feminist moral relativism demands that we consider who controls moral decision-making within a community and what effect that control has on the least privileged members of that community. Both at home and abroad, it gives us grounds to criticize the practices that a majority believes acceptable if those practices are a result of oppressive power differentials. It will not, however, always tell us precisely what is the morally right thing to do, because there is no single set of moral

truths we can decipher. Feminist moral relativism remains absolutist on the question of the moral wrong of oppression but is relativist on other moral matters; in this way, it is better able to incorporate feminist moral sensibilities.[96]

Apparently, not all differences are created equal.

However promising the future of feminist relativism may be, at present it cannot escape all of its absolutist tendencies. Feminist moral relativists want to respect difference, but they reserve the right to judge *which* differences among individuals or groups should be respected. They imply that "consent" plays the crucial role in determining whether oppression does or does not exist and therefore whether a culture's practice should or should not be respected. But is "consent" really the only factor or even the most important factor in determining whether a practice is absolutely wrong? Or is there another equally important or even more important factor that makes certain states of affairs absolutely right or absolutely wrong? Are there, for example, certain things to which all people have a moral claim, no matter when, where, or how they live?

According to Mies and Shiva, there is a basis for claiming that at its most basic level morality is indeed absolute and universal. Its fundamental function is to meet the physical and psychological needs *all* people have in common, for unless these needs are met, a human being cannot give meaningful "consent." An absolutism or universalism built on meeting fundamental human needs is, in Mies and Shiva's estimation, very different from an absolutism or universalism based on recognizing human rights. They explained:

> This universalism does not deal in abstract universal human "rights" but rather in common human needs which can be satisfied only if the life-sustaining networks and processes are kept intact and alive. These symbioses, or "living interconnectednesses," both in nature and in human society are the only guarantee that life in its fullest sense can continue on this planet. These fundamental needs: for food, shelter, clothing; for affection, care and love; for dignity and identity, for knowledge and freedom, leisure and joy, are common to all people, irrespective of culture, ideology, race, political and economic system and class.[97]

Thus, global feminists must ask themselves if female circumcision/genital mutilation serves a fundamental human need before they make any proclamation about its rightness or wrongness. More important, they must assume that if women in one culture are capable of recognizing fundamental human needs, so, too, are women in every other culture. If I think I can know that female circumcision/genital mutilation, as practiced, does not serve any fundamental human need, then I must assume women in other cultures can come to the same conclusion.

Conclusion

Multicultural and global feminism present a great challenge to feminism: how to unite women in, through, and despite their differences. In general, multicultural and global feminists have offered women two ways to achieve unity in diversity. The first consists in working toward sisterhood or friendship. For example, in the introduction to *Sisterhood Is Global*, Robin Morgan stressed that when all is said and done, women are not really so very different. Provided women ask each other "*sincere* questions about difference," said Morgan, they will see each other as searching for the same thing: namely, a *self* ("self-identity," "an articulation of self-hood," "self-realization," "self-image," "the right to be oneself").[98]

Furthering Morgan's point, Elizabeth Spelman itemized the kind of "sincere" questions multicultural and global feminists must ask. Among these questions are the following: "What do I and can I know about women from whom I differ in terms of race, culture, class, ethnicity?"[99] "What happens when oppressors want to undo racism or other oppression; how do they go about acquiring knowledge about others, knowledge whose absence is now regretted?"[100] Among the many ways to find answers to these questions, said Spelman, is to "read books, take classes, open your eyes and ears or whatever instruments of awareness you might be blessed with, go to conferences planned and produced by the people about whom you wish to learn and manage not to be intrusive."[101] Other ways are to try to imagine what other women's lives are like and to be tolerant of difference no matter how much it threatens one. Of course, said Spelman, imagining how it is with others and tolerating others is far different from perceiving others and welcoming others. She explained the difference between imagining and perceiving as follows:

> When I am perceiving someone, I must be prepared to receive new information all the time, to adapt my actions accordingly, and to have my feelings develop in response to what the person is doing, whether I like what she is doing or not. When simply imagining her, I can escape from the demands her reality puts on me and instead construct her in my mind in such a way that I can possess her, make her into someone or something who never talks back, who poses no difficulties for me, who conforms to my desires much more than the real person does.[102]

Later Spelman elucidated the important distinction between tolerating someone's opinion and welcoming someone's opinion. She claimed that merely to tolerate a viewpoint is to fail "actively" to seek it out as a *serious* critique of one's own viewpoint. If I am just tolerating you, I am not open to really changing myself. I am not prepared to be your friend; instead, I am simply willing not to be your enemy.

In a dialogical essay she coauthored with Maria Lugones, Spelman stressed that in order to develop an adequate (multicultural and global) feminist theory, a wide variety of women have to formulate it together. But in her sections of the essay, Lugones asked Spelman what motive the women who were previously left out of theory-making would have for doing this. Perhaps they want to be left alone to do theory themselves, in their own voices. Furthermore, Lugones wondered, what motive would the women who were previously the ones in charge of theory-making have for doing this? Why would they want to join women who told them they could come and listen to their discussions, provided they were, as they had once been, "unobtrusive, unimportant, patient to the point of tears," yet willing to learn new lessons from women who might view them "as of no consequence except as an object of mistrust?"[103] Would the motive of the former theory-makers be self-interest, either in the sense of getting to know the other so as to better dominate her or in the sense of "self-growth or self-expansion," feeding off the rich "difference" of the other? If so, stressed Lugones, white women and First World women need to know they will not be *tolerated*, let alone *welcomed* by women of color and Third World women.

Moreover, continued Lugones, white women and First World women need to know that if they wish to do theory with women of color and Third World women out of a sense of duty, understood as an act of noblesse oblige or as an anemic substitute for love, then they should be prepared for rejection. There will be no opportunity for sisterhood, for entering the world of the other. Lugones stressed that First World women and white women who use the language of duty do little more than agree *not* to use their "education" to "overwhelm," "research," and keep on the defensive Third World women and women of color.[104]

If the feminists who have been at the center of theory want to do theory with the feminists who have been at the margins of theory, their motive must be nothing short of friendship, according to Lugones. Unless one woman wants to be another woman's friend, she will be unable to summon the psychic energy to travel to that woman's world in order to see her living her life there as a self rather than the other. According to Morgan, Spelman, and Lugones, the chief task of multicultural and global feminists is, therefore, to inspire women to want to be each other's friends.

Disagreeing with Morgan's, Spelman's, and Lugones's views on the essential goal of multicultural and global feminism are a variety of thinkers, including bell hooks, Audre Lorde, and Iris Young. Although hooks and Lorde sometimes employed the language of sisterhood in their writings, for them sisterhood is a *political* rather than a *personal* concept. Women can be sisters in the sense of being political comrades, but only if they are willing to truly confront their differences. "Imagining," "perceiving," "tolerating," and "welcoming" are fine, insofar as they go; but confronting differences requires far more painful activities, like being enraged and being shamed. There is a difference, hooks emphasized, between "bourgeois-women's-liberation" sisterhood and multicultural-and-global-feminist sisterhood. The former focuses on women's "supporting" each other, where support serves "as a prop or a foundation for a weak structure" and where women, emphasizing their "shared victimization," give each other "unqualified approval."[105] The latter rejects this sentimental brand of sisterhood and offers in its stead a type of sisterhood that begins with women's confronting and combating each other's differences and ends with their using these very same differences to "accelerate their positive advance" toward the goals they share in common. As hooks explained: "Women do not need to eradicate difference to feel solidarity. We do not need to share common oppression to fight equally to end oppression.... We can be sisters united by shared interests and beliefs, united in our appreciation for diversity, united in our struggle to end sexist oppression, united in political solidarity."[106] Lorde also stressed the importance of maintaining women's differences rather than trying to transcend them. She claimed, for example, that feminists don't have to love each other in order to work with each other.[107] In the same vein, Iris Young observed that although women should not be enemies, they should not expect to be friends. They should simply be content to be "strangers."[108]

Rejecting the homogenizing, conformist tendencies of the language of community and family, Young argued that feminists should not try to be "sisters" and "friends" with women whose worlds are radically different than their own. As Nancie Caraway noted, for Young "insistence on the ideal of shared subjectivity... leads to undesirable political implications."[109] Young repeatedly urged feminists, among other political theorists and activists, to distrust the desire "for reciprocal recognition and identification with others... because it denies differences in the concrete sense of making it difficult for people to respect those with whom they do not identify."[110] She claimed, said Caraway, that multicultural and global feminists should not want to be sisters or friends because such desires "thwart our principled calls for heterogeneity in feminism."[111]

The choice between the sisterhood of friendship and the sisterhood of political solidarity is an important one. Multicultural and global feminists might need to make this choice once and for all in the future, but for now the overall consensus seems to be a both-and approach in which political alliances become opportunities for women to form personal friendships. In this connection it might be the case that none other than Aristotle had some good advice for feminists. There are, according to Aristotle, three kinds of friendship: the kind of friendship people who are of *use* to each other have (for example, professional colleagues); the kind of friendship people who enjoy the same sorts of pleasures have (for example, "drinking buddies" and dance partners); and the kind of friendship people who share meaningful goals and tasks in common have (for example, famine relief workers and women against oppression). To be this last kind of friend, said Aristotle, is to be a "partner in virtue and a friend in action."[112] Perhaps this is precisely the kind of friends multicultural and global feminists should want to be.

Notes

1. Arthur M. Schlesinger Jr., *The Disuniting of America* (Knoxville, Tenn.: Whittle Books, 1991), p. 2.
2. Jung Young Lee, *Marginality: The Key to Multicultural Theology* (Minneapolis: Fortress Press, 1995), p. 35. Lee is citing Israel Zangwill, *The Melting Pot: a Drama in Four Acts*.
3. Schlesinger, *The Disuniting of America*, p. 2.
4. See, for example, Angela Y. Davis, "Gender, Class, and Multiculturalism, Avery R. Gordon and Christopher Newfield, eds. (Minneapolis: University of Minnesota Press, 1996) pp. 40-48.
5. Blaine J. Fowers and Frank C. Richardson, "Why is Multiculturalism Good?" *American Psychologist* 51, no. 6 (June 1996): 609.
6. Joseph Raz, "Multiculturalism: A Liberal Perspective," *Dissent* (Winter 1994): 74.
7. Ibid., p. 78.
8. Ibid., p. 77.
9. Elizabeth V. Spelman, *Inessential Woman: Problems of Exclusion in Feminist Thought*, (Boston: Beacon Press, 1988) p. 11.
10. Ibid , pp. 11-12.
11. Ibid., p12.
12. Ibid., p13.
13. Spelman, *Inessential Woman: Problems of Exclusion in Feminist Thought*, p. 158
14. Deborah King, "Multiple Jeopardy: The Context of a Black Feminist Ideology", in *Feminist Frameworks*, 3rd edition, Alison M. Jaggar and Paula S. Rothenberg, eds. (New York: McGraw-Hill, 1993) p. 220.
15. bell hooks, *Yearning: Race, Gender, and Cultural Politics* (Boston: South End Press, 1990) p. 59

16. Audre Lorde, "Age, Race, Class, and Sex: Women Redefining Difference," in *Race, Class, and Gender*, 2d edition, Margaret L. Andersen and Patricia Hill Collins, eds. (Belmont, Calif.: Wadsworth,1995) p. 532.
17. Ibid., p. 539.
18. Lorde, *The Cancer Journals*, (San Francisco: Spinster/Aunt Lute, 1980).
19. Lorde "Age, Race, Class, and Sex: Women Redefining Difference," p. 539.
20. Ibid.
21. Patricia Hill Collins, *Black Feminist Thought: Knowledge, Conciousness, and the Politics of Empowerment* (Boston: Unwin Hyman, 1990) p. 6.
22. Ibid.
23. Ibid., p. 7.
24. Ibid., p. 67.
25. Jill Lewis, "Sexual Division of Power: Motivations of the Women's Liberation Movement," in Gloria I. Joseph and Jill Lewis *Common Differences: Conflicts in Black and White Feminist Perspectives*, (Garden City, N.Y.: Anchor/Doubleday,1981) pp. 44-45
26. hooks, *Yearning: Race, Gender, and Cultural Politics*, pp.58-59.
27. Tracey Gardner, "Racism in Pornography and the Womeln's Movement," in *Take Back The Night*, Laura Lederer, ed. (New York: William Morrow, 1986) p. 112.
28. Collins, *Black Feminist Thought: Knowledge, Conciousness, and the Politics of Empowerment*, p. 168.
29. Ibid.
30. Alice Walker, "Coming Apart" in *Take Back The Night*, Laura Lederer, ed., p. 103.
31. Raymond M. Lane, "A Man's World: An Update on Sexual Harassment," *Village Voice*, December 16-22, 1981, pp. 1, 15, 16.
32. Karen Lindsey, "Sexual Harassment on the Job," *Ms.*, November, 1977, p. 48.
33. Catharine A. MacKinnon, *Sexual Harassment of Working Women*, (New Haven, Conn.: Yale University Press, 1979) p. 31.
34. Jack E Hill, "The Stereotypes of Race," *Time*, October 21, 1991, p. 66.
35. Ibid.
36. Ibid.
37. Priscilla Painton, "Woman Power," *Time*, October 28, 1991, p. 24.
38. Ibid.
39. Angela Y. Davis, *Women, Race and Class*, (New York: Random House, 1981) p. 196.
40. Jean MacKellar, *Rape, the Bait and the Trap* (New York: Crown Publishers, 1975) p. 72.
41. Diana Russell, *The Politics of Rape: The Victim's Perspective*, (New York: Stein & Day, 1975) p. 163.
42. Davis, *Women, Race and Class*, p. 197.
43. Frederick Douglass, "The Lesson of the Hour," Pamphlet published in 1894; reprinted under the title "Why is the Negro Lynched?" in Philip S. Foner, *The Life and Writings of Frederick Douglass* (New York: International Publishers, 1950) vol. 4, p. 501.
44. Jesse Daniel Ames, *The Changing Character of lynching 1931-41*, (New York: AMS Press, 1973).
45. Marvin E. Wolfgang and Marc Riedel "Rape, Race, and the Death Penalty in Georgia," *American Journal of Orthopsychiatry*, 45 (July 1975): 658-669.
46. Elizabeth V. Spelman, *Inessential Woman: Problems of Exclusion in Feminist Thought*, (Boston: Beacon Press, 1988) p. 11.
47. Ibid., p. 184.
48. Ibid.
49. Ibid., p. 189.
50. Carlotte Bunch, "Prospects for Global Feminism," in *Feminist Frameworks*, Jagger and Rothenberg, eds. p. 249.
51. Alice Walker, *In Search of Our Mothers' Gardens*, (New York: Harcourt Brace Jovanovich, 1983) p. xi.
52. Ann Russo, "'We Cannot Live Without Our lives': White Women, Anti-Racism, and Feminism," in *Third World Women and the Politics of Feminism*, Chandra Talpads Mohanty, Ann Russo, and Lourde Torres, eds. (Bloomington: Indiana University Press, 1991) pp. 304-305.
53. Bunch, "Prospects for Global Feminism," p. 250.
54. Quoted in Nellie Wong, "Socialist Feminism: Our Bridge to Freedom," in *Third World Women and the Politics of Feminism*, Mohanty, Russo, and Torres, eds. p. 293.
55. Bunch, "Prospects for Global Feminism," p. 251.
56. Audre Lorde, *Sister Outsider*, (Trumansburg, N.Y.: Crossing Press, 1984) p. 111.
57. Robin Morgan, *Sisterhood is Global*, (Garden City, N.Y.: Anchor, 1984) p. 35.
58. Eschel M. Rhoodie, *Discrimination Against Women: A Global Surbey of the Economic, Educational, Social and Political Status of Women*, (London: McDarland, 1989) p. 19.
59. Ibid.
60. Ibid. p. 20.
61. Angela Gillian, "Women's Equality and National Liberation," in *Third World Women and the Politics of Feminism*, Mohanty, Russo, and Torres, eds. p. 218.
62. Ibid. p. 224.
63. Ibid. p. 229.
64. Ibid.
65. Ibid.
66. Carlotte Bunch, "U.N. World Conference in Nairobi," *Ms.*, June, 1985, p. 82.
67. Adele Clark, "Subtle Forms of Sterilization Abuse: A Reproductive Rights Analysis," in *Test-tube Women: What Future for Motherhood?*, Rita Arditti, Renate Duelli Klein, and Shelley Minden, eds. (London: Pandora Press, 1985) p. 198.
68. Helen Rodriguez-Treas, "Sterilization Abuse" in *Biological Woman: The Convenient Myth*,

Ruth Hubbard, Mary Sue Henifin, and Barbara Fried, eds. (Cambridge, Mass.: Schenkman, 1982) p. 150.
69. "Contraceptive Raises Ethical Concerns," *Medical Ethics Advisor* 9, no. 2 (February 1991): 17
70. Alison Jaggar, "Abortion and a Woman's Right to Decide," in *Woman and Philosophy: Toward a Theory of Liberation*, Carol C. Gould and Max W. Wartofsky, eds. (New York: Putnam's, 1976) p. 357.
71. Morgan, *Sisterhood is Global*.
72. Nicholas D. Kristof, "China's Birth Rate on the Rise Again as Official Sanctions Are Ignored," *New York Times*, April 21 1987, p. 1.
73. Patrick E. Tyler, "Population Control in China Falls to Coercion and Evasion," *New York Times*, June 25, 1995 pp. 1, 6.
74. Maria Mies, "New Reproductive Technologies: Sexist and Racist Implications," in Maria Mies and Vandana Shiva, *Ecofeminism*, p. 305.
75. Angela Gillian, "Women's Equality and National Liberation," in *Third World Women and the Politics of Feminism*, Mohanty, Russo, and Torres, eds. p. 218.
76. Ibid. p. 765.
77. Ibid. p. 16.
78. Ibid.
79. Maria Mies, "The Myths of Catching-up Development," in Mies and Shiva, *Ecofeminism*, p. 58.
80. Ibid. p. 60.
81. Ibid. p. 59.
82. Ibid. p. 66.
83. Ibid. p. 67.
84. Maria Mies, "The Need for a New Vision," in Mies and Shiva, *Ecofeminism*, p. 305.
85. Mies and Shiva, "Introduction: Why We Wrote This Book Together," in Mies and Shiva, *Ecofeminism*, pp. 10-11.
86. Ibid. p. 11.
87. Ibid. pp. 11-12.
88. Susan Sherwin, *No Longer Patient: Feminist Ethics and Health Care* (Philadelphia: Temple University Press, 1992), p. 62.
89. Ibid. p. 65.
90. Ibid. p. 67.
91. Ibid. p. 69.
92. Leonard J. Kouba and Judith Muasher, "Female Circumcision in Africa: An Overview," *African Studies Review*, 28, no. 1 (March 1988): 105-109.
93. Sherwin, *No Longer Patient: Feminist Ethics and Health Care*, p.71.
94. Ibid.
95. Ibid.
96. Ibid. p. 75.
97. Mies and Shiva, "Introduction: Why We Wrote This Book Together," in Mies and Shiva, *Ecofeminism*, p. 13.
98. Morgan *Sisterhood is Global*, p. 36
99. Spellman, *Inessential Woman: Problems of Exclusion in Feminist Thought*, p. 178.
100. Ibid.
101. Ibid. pp. 178-179.
102. Ibid. p. 181.
103. Maria Lugones and Elizabeth Spelman, "Have We Got a Theory for You! Feminist Theory, Cultural Inperialism, and the Demand for 'the Woman's Voice,'" in *Feminist Philosophies*, Janet A. Kourany, James P. Sterba, and Rosemarie Tong, eds. (Englewood Cliffs, N.J.: Prentice-Hall, 1992) p. 388.
104. Ibid. p. 389.
105. bell hooks, Feminist Theory: From Margin to Center (Boston: South End Press, 1984) p. 404.
106. Ibid
107. Lorde *Sister Outsider*, p. 113.
108. Iris Marion Young, "The Ideal of Community and the Politics of Difference," *Feminism/Postmodernism*, Linda J. Nicholson, ed. (New York: Routledge, 1990) p. 308.
109. Nancy Caraway, *Segregated Sisterhood: Racism and the Politics of American Feminism*, p. 206.
110. Young, "The Ideal of Community and the Politics of Difference," p. 311.
111. Caraway, *Segregated Sisterhood: Racism and the Politics of American Feminism*, p. 206.
112. Aristotle, *Nichomachean Ethics*, in *The Works of Aristotle Translated into English*, W.D. Ross, ed. (London: Oxford University Press, 1963).

CHAPTER 32

INTERNATIONALIZING THE CORE CURRICULUM

PATRICE MCDERMOTT

This is the first of three essays linked by the theme "Borders, Boundaries, and Feminist Pedagogy: Internationalizing the Women's Studies Core Curriculum at the University of Maryland." The essays and the courses they describe were inspired by the Ford Foundation's Summer Institute on Women and Gender in an Era of Global Change, a faculty development seminar offered at the University of Maryland, College Park in 1995.

General Issues in Internationalizing the Core Curriculum

As the authors of this cluster of essays, we write as feminist scholars committed to creating women's studies curricula that take account of, and respond to, the global forces profoundly shaping women's lives in the late twentieth century. We are convinced that women's studies core curricula that remain exclusively oriented to U.S. content and Western feminist perspectives no longer meet the standards of scholarly rigor and political relevance that define our field. We also argue that, given the wide variety of women's studies courses offered within any particular institution, efforts to truly centralize international perspectives in the core curriculum are best served by focusing on introductory women's studies courses and upper-level feminist theory courses. These are the two courses in the curriculum most often required for women's studies students, and these above all others are designed to introduce students to the central concerns, key terms, core concepts, and basic theoretical perspectives that help define the field.

We came to this project after participating together in the Ford Foundation's Summer Institute on Women and Gender in an Era of Global Change, under the direction of Deborah Rosenfelt at the University of Maryland, College Park campus. However, we teach on different campuses, within different program structures, addressing different audiences within the University of Maryland system. Carole McCann and I teach at the University of Maryland, Baltimore County campus (UMBC), a midsized research institution with a particular emphasis on fields related to science and technology. UMBC has a student population of 10,600, most of whom are in-state residents, and is the most ethnically diverse of the campuses. UMBC has an interdisciplinary women's studies program that relies primarily on full-time affiliate and part-time adjunct faculty to teach its courses. UMBC offers a women's studies minor through the program and a major through the interdisciplinary studies program. Carole McCann's Theories of Feminism course is the required capstone course for all women's studies minors and majors at UMBC. Cindy Gissendanner teaches at Towson University, a regional comprehensive university that, for over a century, was the teachers' college in the UM system. Towson serves approximately 14,000 students, 12 percent of whom describe themselves as students of color. Women's studies at Towson is an interdisciplinary program of study that was first offered to students in the early 1970s. Towson's introductory women's studies

Reprinted from *Women's Studies Quarterly*, 3 & 4, 1998. Copyright © 1998 Women's Studies Quarterly.

course, Women in Perspective, is counted in the institution's general education requirements; thus, women's studies generally offers approximately 15 sections of the course each semester. Since the vast majority of full-time tenured and tenure-track women's studies faculty hold its appointments outside of the women's studies department, sections of Women in Perspective have been taught predominantly, though not exclusively, by part-time adjunct faculty.[1] Seung-kyung Kim teaches at the University of Maryland, College Park campus (UMCP), which, with a combined graduate and undergraduate enrollment of more than 34,000, is the largest campus in the UM system. UMCP is home to one of the largest and most diverse women's studies departments in the country, offering both undergraduate and graduate degrees. Theories of Feminism at UMCP is required for all women's studies majors and can also be used by the general student population to fulfill general university requirements. UMCP is host to the Ford Foundation's National Curriculum Transformation Project, the academic journal *Feminist Studies,* and the National Women's Studies Association.

Given our different institutional contexts, program structures, and class compositions, we were not surprised that each of us encountered unique problems in the process of curriculum transformation. However, despite such institutional variations, we discovered that all of us grappled with at least five general issues in our attempt to internationalize the content of our core women's studies courses.

The first general issue has to do with a question of *balance.* How does one add new material to an already overloaded syllabus without resorting to an "add and stir" formula that simply tacks on new material in a marginalized, extraneous manner?[2] Similarly, how does one successfully introduce new material designed to fundamentally reorient the core curriculum when the women's studies curriculum itself is already underresourced and overburdened? Many introductory women's studies courses in U.S. universities already attempt to encompass the diversity of female experience within the Western Hemisphere; can such a course be stretched even further to cover the entire globe? What can reasonably be accomplished in a feminist theory course when an institution only supports one upper-level offering and the expansion of the field already requires an introductory feminist theory course, an advanced feminist theory course, a history of feminism course, a postmodern feminist theory course, and now a global feminist theory course?

The second issue concerns the use of *theoretical and experiential* perspectives of non-U.S. women in U.S. classrooms. How does one incorporate ideas that have been developed by emergent and postcolonial feminists in a way that centralizes their theoretical perspectives in U.S. classrooms, rather than just using their experiences to illustrate predefined Western feminist theories? This raises a third, related point; international voices brought into U.S.-based curricula must be fully *contextualized* according to each author's unique social location. Moving the analysis beyond exclusively Western interpretive frames requires a careful situating of each author's voice according to *indigenously* defined intersections of race, class, ethnicity, sexuality, religion, language, and nation. A fourth issue concerns how one might frame such a wide variety of globe-hopping texts and experiences for undergraduate students. Is it even possible to accurately historicize and effectively anchor so many disparate accounts of gender experience in one semester? If not, then what are the most useful ways to self-consciously mark and learn from the course's inclusions and exclusions?

Fifth, we considered the challenge in selecting materials for a course that will illuminate but not reproduce colonial relationships in the classroom. How does one ensure that comparative international materials consistently present women as active and authoritative agents in the world? Recent criticisms of U.S. feminism have cautioned against turning non-Western subjects into "exoticized others"[3] or, in Ella Shohat's words, Western feminism's ultimate poster children.[4] If done well, the use of truly international perspectives in women's studies courses should fundamentally reframe the classroom. Indeed, the implications of even the most basic geopolitical categories, like First World/Third World, developed/undeveloped, Western/Eastern, global north/global south, international/transnational, and global/universal, may be explicitly revealed for the first time in U.S. classrooms.

And finally, each of these general issues continuously interacts with those more idiosyncratic features that always operate in any classroom. What is the institutional context of the course? What are the composition and needs of the institution's student body? How does the instructor's social location, pedagogical style, and intellectual predilections determine the efficacy of international course content? In the following essays, Cindy Gissendanner, Seung-kyung Kim, and Carole McCann will address these general issues from the vantage point of their particular experiences in bringing comparative international material on women into what had been predominantly U.S-based and Western-influenced core courses. First, I would like to set the background as I see it.

Politics of the Core Curriculum in Women's Studies

For nearly thirty years feminist scholars in the United States have dedicated themselves to producing a body of knowledge designed to illuminate women's lives and simultaneously to improve the conditions under which they live. These activists/scholars successfully established women's studies as feminist territory within North American universities and continue to use it as a basis for more widespread social change. Feminists were not interested in simply creating a self-contained discipline reserved for the study of women; nor did they merely want to forge analytical frameworks across the disciplines that would integrate new content on women into traditional fields. While these marked steps along the way, feminist scholars aimed for nothing less than a transformation of the theoretical foundations of the entire curriculum—"a feminist revolution in knowledge."[5] Recent studies of the impact of curriculum transformation projects across the disciplines have documented the far-reaching influence of feminist research.[6] But, as a scholar of the intellectual and institutional history of feminist research, I am convinced that an equally valuable legacy of the feminist revolution in knowledge must be understood in terms of the structures that feminist work has made available within the modern university.

The university is an authoritative institution in the United States that is one of the sites for primary producing, legitimating, and disseminating specialized knowledge to the larger society. By engaging in a complex set of relationships with the university, feminists have earned a tenuous interpretive authority in discussions of gender in larger arenas of public debate. But, despite its success within North American universities, women's studies has remained less fully institutionalized than traditional disciplines.[7] Women's studies differs from most fields because it is more likely to be organized into programs that award certificates and minors, offer cross-listed courses, and rely on adjunct faculty appointments. It is less likely to achieve the status of autonomous departments that offer undergraduate and graduate degrees, retain full administrative authority over its curriculum, and possess a conventional complement of tenured and tenure-track faculty to call its own. And, when it comes to new curricular proposals, women's studies, unlike traditional disciplines, is continually forced to defend its intellectual merit and rearticulate the ways it does, or does not, differ from the academic norm. Given the budgetary constraints of the modern university and the larger political climate in which feminists operate, it is unlikely that the institutional pressures that have marginalized women's studies will ease in the near future. Consequently, most women's studies faculty and supporters will need to make even more effective use of, if not simply defend their control over, the institutional mechanisms currently available to women's studies programs.

Many of those working to transform knowledge within the university have found that the core curriculum, that is, the few courses students are *required* to take in order to receive a women's studies certificate or degree, remains one of the few institutional devices over which feminist scholars exert considerable control. The core curriculum, in effect, embodies the fundamental, shared intellectual and political tenets that define the field and are considered required knowledge for all women's studies students. Women's studies, however, is a field made up of many feminisms and interpretive communities. Consequently, the core curriculum has been dynamic and contested terrain during the field's thirty-year history. No single set of ideas or politics can fully explain the multiple ways in which gender intersects with race, sexuality, ethnicity, class, and religion in women's lives. And yet course offerings and faculty lines are finite entities within the modern university. Articulating the core curriculum, then, becomes more than just a struggle over intellectual constructs. It becomes a complicated political practice with real material consequences. The core curriculum not only anchors a field of study; it also helps determine who gets published, who gets read, how resources are distributed, and how power relations are reproduced or challenged within the university and the larger society.

Globalization

During the same thirty years in which women's studies gained an institutional presence on U.S. university campuses, larger global forces, which collectively have come to be known as "globalization," have altered the conditions of women's lives. Danish analysts Hans-Henrik Holm and George Sorenson define globalization as the processes associated with economic, political, and social interaction across national boundaries that have been intensifying in breadth and depth on a global scale since the early 1970s. The proliferation of multinational corporations, the creation of transnational economies, and their combined effect on local communities, markets, and labor, have become the most visible features of globalization. Under such conditions, capital is no longer contained within geographical allegiances or sovereign boundaries. A few hundred multinational corporations and a handful of transnational organizations, including the World Bank and the International Monetary Fund (IMF), now exert enormous influence on national and local economic conditions through structural adjustment policies. Changes in communication technologies have given capital the capacity to flow around the world at lightning speed through a few privately owned, centralized information operations. This free-floating capital, in turn, has helped create "megacities" that are centers of international communication, such as Tokyo, London, Mexico City, Sao Paulo, Bangkok, and New York, which too often place the needs of transnational industry above those of local populations. Similarly, depletion of natural resources and protection of the environment have become globally interdependent processes. In yet another related change, national sovereignty is waning at the same moment that nationalisms built on ethnic, religious, racial, regional, and tribal divisions are increasing. The resulting economic upheaval and political unrest have helped create an unprecedented number of mass-migrating populations on a global scale, increasing the number of refugees from 3 million in 1970 to 27 million in 1994.[8]

The unprecedented acceleration of transnational integration has created intersecting economic, technological, and political "global webs," which entangle and transform the lives of women across great geographical distances.[9] The multinationals' search for cheap pools of offshore labor has combined with the Third World debt crisis to drive an unprecedented number of women into formal and informal market activity, while simultaneously increasing their household responsibilities.[10] Real wages are falling for women in industrialized nations, at the same time that social programs designed to function as safety nets for those living in the most impoverished conditions have been drastically reduced. World Bank and IMF structural adjustment policies often result not only in increased unemployment but in a concomitant reduction in public expenditures on social services, including health care and education, that are central to stabilizing women's lives. Environmental degradation, including reductions in fresh water supplies and the depletion of soil fertility, affects women's lives in particular, since, especially in rural areas, women are responsible for collecting natural resources for family use. Additionally, women and children now make up 80 percent of the refugees displaced by war and political conflict worldwide.[11] Struggles over nationalism often recast women into more traditional, confining roles or ask women to place the needs of the emerging nation before their gender-based interests. And all the while, Western images of female sexuality are broadcast across the globe through the ever-expanding use of technology for free market activity. Clearly, understanding and confronting these powerful gendered structures of modern globalization must be a central task of women's studies as an interdisciplinary field and feminism as a transnational force.

Transnational Social Movements

Activists learned quickly that the many social and political problems associated with globalization could no longer be countered effectively from within national boundaries. Many of those committed to human rights, environmental issues, fair labor practices, and refugee aid began their work as citizen-activists unaffiliated with their governments. They created transnational social movements that may prove, more than any other social or political entity, to be the fullest embodiment of resistant forms of globalization in the twenty-first century. This "globalization from below," made up of local and transnational movements spinning their own global webs, has been described by Richard Falk as the only hope we have of attaining justice in a capital-driven new world order.[12]

The 1970s feminist transnational boycott of Nestle products brought together nearly 100 private organizations and local entities in 65 countries. The boycott ultimately forced Nestle to abandon its Third World marketing practices and led to the passage of the 1981 World Health Organization Code of Conduct, which governs the marketing and sale of infant formula. The Nestle boycott was one of the first transnational feminist campaigns. Today, indigenous, emergent, and postcolonial feminisms and activists are shaping the future of global women's movements. Their ideas are reverberating throughout the United States and abroad, if fitfully.[13]

Paralleling the increase of transnational feminist activism from the mid-1980s to the present, global interrogations of Western feminist thought have complicated women's studies in the United States.[14] This work has challenged the conceptual framework of the field and redefined the geopolitical boundaries of courses in ways that make it increasingly clear that the local and the global are inextricably bound together in understanding women's lives. Feminist theorist Chandra Mohanty was one of the first to argue that Western feminist domination of women's studies distorted the complexity and challenge of Third World women's voices. Mohanty now argues that the inescapable effects of globalization mean that feminist scholars must frame new questions about feminist scholarship in the twenty-first century. If a certain political logic has historically motivated various cultural constructions of race and gender within national borders, says Mohanty, that logic is now crossing those borders in ways that never before seemed possible. The challenge to feminist scholars now, according to Mohanty, is to create a curriculum that illuminates the multiple levels of colonization at work in globalization and tracks the power of its political logic as it crosses international boundaries.[15]

Notes

1. The Towson program received a three-year curriculum transformation grant from the U.S. Department of Education's Fund for the Improvement of Postsecondary Education (FIPSE) in the early 1980s to conduct faculty workshops in various sectors of the university that were designed to help faculty infuse women's studies scholarship into introductory survey courses. The grant was aimed at mainstreaming women's studies into courses that served as the basis of the Towson's general education core, which ensured that students took courses in a wide array of disciplines. The general education requirements have been significantly restructured beginning in the 1996–97 academic year. How this restructuring, which groups Women in Perspective with courses in a category called "Cultural Pluralism," will affect enrollment in the introductory women's studies course remains to be seen.

2. Concerns about further marginalizing nondominant experiences through course structure have been raised by a number of curriculum analysts, including: Judy Nolte Lensink, "Strategies for Integrating International Material in the Introductory Women's Studies Course," *Women's Studies International Forum* 14, no. 4 (1991): 227–283; Susan Hardy Aiken et al., *Changing Our Minds: Feminist Transformation of Knowledge* (Albany: State University of New York Press, 1988); Janice Monk et al., "Reaching for Global Feminism in the Curriculum," *Women's Studies International Forum* 14, no. 4 (1991): 239–247.

3. Aihwa Ong, "Colonialism and Modernity: Feminist Representations of Women in Non-Western Societies," *Inscriptions* (1988): 79–93; Cheryl Johnson-Odim, "Common Themes,

Different Contexts: Third World Women and Feminism" and Chandra Talpade Mohanty, "Under Western Eyes: Feminist Scholarship and Colonial Discourses," in Mohanty et al., eds., *Third World Women and the Politics of Feminism* (Bloomington, IN: Indiana University Press, 1992); and Ella Shohat, "Notes on the 'Post-colonial,'" *Social Text* 31/32 (1993): 99–113.

4. Ella Shohat, "Unthinking Eurocentrism: Gender and Global Media,"(Globalization, Gender, and Culture Lecture Series, University of Maryland, College Park, February 27, 1995).

5. Judith Stacey, "Disloyal to the Disciplines: A Feminist Trajectory in the Borderlands," in *Feminisms in the Academy*, Donna Stanton and Abigail J. Stewart, eds. (Ann Arbor: University of Michigan Press, 1995), 311.

6. Works that trace the influence of feminist scholarship in the academy include: Stanton and Stewart, eds., *Feminisms in the Academy*; Elizabeth Minnich, *Transforming Knowledge* (Philadelphia: Temple University Press, 1990), Elizabeth Minnich et al., eds., *Reconstructing the Academy: Women's Education and Women's Studies* (Chicago: University of Chicago Press, 1988); Aiken et al., *Changing Our Minds*; and Marilyn Schuster and Susan Van Dyne, *Women's Place in the Academy: Transforming the Liberal Arts Curriculum* (Lanham, MD: Rowman and Littlefield, 1985).

7. Throughout its existence, proponents of women's studies in the United States have never settled the question of whether it is more desirable to affect curriculum transformation fully from within existing institutional structures of the modern university or, since women's studies is a form of oppositional studies, to deconstruct the theoretical assumptions of traditional knowledge from a more marginalized, but less compromised, institutional location. See Marilyn Boxer, "For and About Women: The Theory and Practice of Women's Studies in the U.S.," *Signs: A Journal of Women in Culture and Society* 7 (1982): 661–95; Vivian P. Makovsky and Michele A. Paludi, "Feminism and Women's Studies in the Academy," in *Foundations for a Feminist Restructuring of the Academic Disciplines*, Michele Paludi and Gertrude A. Steuernagel, eds. (New York: Haworth Press, 1990), 1–37; and Elizabeth Langland and Walter Gove, *A Feminist Perspective in the Academy: The Difference It Makes* (Chicago: University of Chicago Press, 1981).

8. *The UN and the Advancement of Women 1945–1995* (New York: United Nations, Department of Public Information, 1996), 34. Cf. *Beyond Beijing: After the Promise of the UN Conference on Women* (New York: The National Council for Research on Women, 1997).

9. The concept of "global webs" and the ways in which such global integration creates social and political disintegration are explained by Richard Barnet and John Cavanagh in *Global Dreams: Imperial Corporations and the New World Order* (New York: Simon and Schuster, 1994).

10. Shelly Feldman, "Crises, Poverty and Gender Inequality: Current Themes and Issues," in *Unequal Burden: Economic Crises, Persistent Poverty, and Women's Work*, Lourdes Beneria and Shelly Feldman, eds. (Oxford: Westview Press, 1992), 22.

11. Jodi Jacobson, "Women's Health: The Price of Poverty" in *The Health of Women: A Global Perspective*, Marge Koblinsky et al., eds. (Oxford: Westview Press, 1993).

12. Richard Falk, "The Making of Global Citizenship" In *Global Visions: Beyond the New World Order*, Jeremy Brecher et al., eds. (Boston: South End Press, 1993), 39–50.

13. The growth of indigenous women's organizations is reflected in the fact that only 300 nongovernmental organizations (NGOs) attended the United Nations Third World Conference on Women in 1985 and 2,000 NGOs attended the Fourth World Conference in 1995. Cited in Florence Howe, "Editorial," *Women's Studies Quarterly* (spring/summer 1996): 6.

14. Most of the scholarly journals in the field of women's studies have devoted special issues or article clusters to bringing international perspectives to feminist research and teaching, including: *Feminist Studies* "Global Feminism after Beijing," 22, no. 2 (fall 1996); *Signs* "Postcolonial, Emergent, and Indigenous Feminisms," 20, no. 4 (summer 1995); *NWSA Journal* "Global Perspectives," 8, no. 1 (spring 1996); *Women's Studies International Forum* "Western Women and Imperialism" 13, no. 4 (1990) and "Reaching for Global Feminism in the Curriculum," 14, no. 4 (1991); and *Women's Studies Quarterly* "Teaching Women's Studies from an International Perspective" (spring/summer 1990) and "Beijing and Beyond: Toward the Twenty-first Century of Women" (spring/summer 1996). Recent anthologies devoted to centering non-Western perspectives in feminist scholarship include: Chandra Mohanty et al., eds., *Third World Women and the Politics of Feminism* (Bloomington: Indiana University Press, 1991); Nupur Chaudri and Margaret Strobel, eds., *Western Women and Imperialism: Complicity and Resistance* (Bloomington: Indiana University Press, 1992); Najma Chowdhury and Barbara Nelson, eds., *Women and Politics Worldwide* (New Haven: Yale University Press, 1994); Amrita Basu and C. Elizabeth McGrory, eds., *The Challenge of Local Feminisms: Women's Movements in Global Perspective* (Boulder, Colo.: Westview Press, 1995); and Angela Miles, *Integrative Feminisms: Building Global Visions 1960s–1990s* (New York: Routledge, 1995).

15. Chandra Mohanty, "Inclusive Scholarship Across the Disciplines: Epistemological Earthquakes and Psychic Shocks" (paper presented at the New Jersey Project Tenth-Anniversary Conference: "Transforming the Curriculum Ten Years Later," Clifton, N.J., November 1, 1996).

Patrice McDermott is associate professor of American Studies and associate dean of the College of Arts and Sciences at the University of Maryland, Baltimore County campus. Her book, *Politics and Scholarship: Feminist Academic Journals and the Production of Knowledge* (University of Illinois Press, 1994) received the NWSA/Illinois Press Book Awaard. Her articles on Feminist Studies and NWSA Journal. McDermott is currently working on a study of oppositional knowledges and cultural authority in contemporary U.S. public discourse.

CHAPTER 33

TRENDS IN THE GENDER GAP IN HIGHER EDUCATION

SUZANNE STIVER LIE AND LYNDA MALIK[1]

Women's early struggle as intellectuals

During its early history, the university was a forbidden world for women; those who attempted to enter experienced a wide variety of discriminatory practices. Graphic examples are Nawojka of Poland (Chapter 13) who had to disguise herself as a man when attending Cracow University in the fourteenth century and Anna Maria van Schurman from The Netherlands (Chapter 10) who was made to conceal herself behind a curtain in order to follow university lectures at the University of Leiden in the seventeenth century. Evidence from the seventeenth and eighteenth centuries suggests that, although not in the mainstream of scientific and intellectual activity, women (particularly from the aristocracy and the artisan classes) were interested in the sciences—in princely courts, informal salons, the artisan workshop and king's academies. However, as scientific endeavours began to be concentrated in established academies and universities and science itself became a legitimate profession, women were increasingly excluded from scientific activity (Schiebinger, 1989).

In the late nineteenth or even in the twentieth century, women as a group began to pressure for admission to higher education in many countries around the world. The industrial revolution enabled those from the upper and middle classes to have more leisure time and a surplus of single women from the middle classes led to pressure on the universities to provide an education which would prepare them to earn a livelihood. Arguments used to exclude women from universities were reminiscent of Aristotelian and Confucian views of women's intelligence, and at this time emphasized the adverse effects of education on women's health.

In 1833, Oberlin College in the United States was the first university to officially admit women to higher education. Subsequently in many countries university barriers came tumbling down (Table 4, Statistical Appendix).

The gender gap: current trends

Unequal distribution of wealth, rank and power are found currently in all higher education systems. Although the *doxa* theoretically requires that the distribution be based on achieved criteria (such as theoretical innovation or contribution to knowledge), ascribed characteristics everywhere

---

Reprinted from *The Gender Gap in Higher Education: World Yearbook of Education*, by Suzanne Stiver Lie and Lynda Malik, 1994. Copyright © 1994 Kogan Page Publishers.

play a critical role. Among the ascribed characteristics which are related to an individual's position on the hierarchy, none is more important than gender.

In this volume the gender gap in higher education among students, faculty and administration in 17 countries has been documented and analysed. In each country women have been found to be under-represented in positions of prestige and power. However, when the gender gap is considered in terms of size, history, current trends and ideological and contextual underpinnings, it is far from uniform. In certain countries, including Poland, Bulgaria, France, the United States and Turkey, the relative position of university women has improved dramatically in this century. However, in many others opportunities appear to be narrowing as a consequence of political and cultural developments.

Even in those countries where the position of university women has improved, it would be a mistake to conclude that this improvement has been linear; rather it has generally been, as described by Margaret Sutherland (Chapter 16 in this volume), one step backwards for each two steps forward. In the United States there has been a marked rise in the number of women receiving master's degrees and doctorates; however, in the immediate post-World War II period these figures dipped sharply, and only in 1972 did they regain the rate prevalent in the 1930s. In China the rate of women's relative enrolment in higher education has remained stable during the past 20 years after a substantial spurt 40 years ago. In Russia at Moscow State University the percentage of female students fell from 54 in 1985 to 45 in 1991.

The same trends may be observed among the faculty in many countries, where after relatively good years in the late 1960s and 70s the percentage of women in top faculty positions is now decreasing. The poor economic environment has led to a university restructuring in the Netherlands, United Kingdom and Norway, among others. These restructuring plans emphasize a cost-benefit approach and fiscal efficiency which often directly conflict with the positive action programmes introduced earlier. In the United Kingdom women now fill fewer senior university posts than they did a decade ago and the current trend is to increase the number of short-term appointments. In Norway and the Netherlands this restructuring of academic ranks led to increased competition for fewer positions. In many countries, therefore, it can be seen that women are running fast to stay put.

Vertical gender stratification

It might be expected that as the pool of women who are enrolled in higher education increases, the proportion who receive first level and higher degrees would correspondingly increase, and that this growth would be reflected in the percentages of women in various ranks in the university hierarchy. The female proportions of students enrolled in higher education has increased in most countries under consideration, and in the majority is approaching or has exceeded 50 per cent (Table 5, Statistical Appendix). These impressive figures are related, in some countries, to even greater proportions of the total number of (first degree) university graduates who are female.

However, in most countries the female proportions of those who receive higher degrees drops sharply. Outstanding exceptions to this trend are Australia, Poland and Turkey. Other countries which have relatively uniform percentages of female student enrolment and degree attainment are France, the United Kingdom and the United States. Since advanced degrees are necessary for a career in higher education, it is clear that the low proportions of women on university faculties is determined, to a large extent, by the low proportions of female advanced-degree recipients.

In this regard, a number of questions need to be addressed. These include an examination of the conditions which lead high proportions of women students in some countries, but not others, to pursue advanced study. In countries where women constitute a large proportion of those receiving advanced degrees, are they also a significant proportion of the faculty? What is the distribution of ranks in countries where women do constitute a significant portion of academic personnel?

Of the 17 countries included in this volume, only in Australia, Poland and Turkey were the female proportions of those who took higher degrees approximately the same as the female proportion of first-degree recipients. At first glance few countries would seem to be more disparate than Australia, Poland and Turkey. Although the latter two have approximately the same per capita GNP, the religious traditions of all three countries differ, as do their political and cultural history in this century. The infant mortality rate per 1,000 live births of Australia is 7.2 (one of the world's lowest), while Poland's is double that (16.3) and Turkey's (59.5) is more than three times as high as the one in Poland (Table 1 in the Statistical Appendix).

In Turkey higher education was restricted to a small élite. Women from this group were encouraged to pursue advanced studies, both as a source of prestige and as a means of achieving financial security—the golden bracelet. Upon completion of advanced studies, their social class position provided them with an advantage in the competition for university positions. In Poland two circumstances combined to encourage women to attain advanced degrees and secure university positions: the great demand for faculty to fill vacant academic positions (as a result of the death, during World War II, of two-thirds of the academic staff), and the stress placed on employment as a means of achieving equality for women. In Australia the stable proportion of undergraduates, bachelors and higher-degree recipients appears to be related to the change from an élite to a mass system of tertiary education in which Colleges of Advanced Education (traditionally popular among women) were combined with universities in a unified system.

Proportions of women on the faculties in the countries we studied range from a high of 37.1 (for Poland) to a low of 11.0 (in Iran). Stability in student enrolment and degree attainment is generally positively related to female share of faculty positions (although this is not true in all countries, particularly Bulgaria and Australia).

The proportion of female faculty in most countries is also positively related to the proportion of women having high rank. Those countries with the highest percentages of women on the faculty are also, in general, those in which a woman is most likely to have achieved the rank of full professor. For example, in Poland and Bulgaria, which have the highest proportions of women faculty (31.7

Table 19.1 *Relative position of women in higher education*

	% of Faculty who are Female	% of Full Professors who are Female
Poland	31.7	16.9
Bulgaria	30.8	12.0
France	27.1	11.4
USA	26.0	14.0
Turkey	25.0	20.0
Russia	24.3	11.3
Norway	24.2	9.3
China	23.8	11.0
Greece	20.5	6.3
UK	20.5	4.9
Australia	18.6	7.4
E Germany	18.6	4.9
W Germany	16.6	5.2
Botswana	13.9	—
Netherlands	13.2	2.3
Pakistan	11.8	4.2
Iran	11.0	5.9

Source: Based on figures in Table 6 in the Statistical Appendix.

and 30.75, respectively), women are most likely to have achieved the rank of full professor. In Iran and Pakistan, where women do not constitute a high proportion of the faculty, they are also among the least likely to be full professors.

Female proportions of total higher education faculty and full professors can be considered indicators of the extent of gender stratification. Table 19.1 makes it clear that this is not exclusively determined by any single factor. Countries with small academic gender gaps are found in the East and the West, in societies which have experienced structural upheavals and in those which have not.

Horizontal gender stratification: subjects 'fit for women'

Regarding the horizontal aspects of gender stratification, culturally derived notions of appropriate male and female behaviour strongly affect choices of fields of study and careers. The overall tendency in most countries is for women to predominate both as students and faculty in social science, humanities and education. However, history shows that subjects 'fit for women' have changed over the decades. In Norway, mathematics and natural sciences were the choices of the women pioneers in universities in the late 1800s. Classical Greek and Latin were the disciplines with most prestige and were regarded as beyond the abilities of women. In Turkey, in the decade following their entry into academe, women were more strongly represented in the faculties of natural sciences (44 per cent) than in the humanities (22 per cent). At this time the Turkish alphabet was Latinized and the government was attempting to modernize the country. The fields of law, economics and business, where the men were concentrated, were considered more critical to Turkey's development than the natural sciences. The natural sciences, including chemistry, physiology, zoology and microbiology, which were then regarded as unusual choices by many women, were typical in Iran, Turkey and Pakistan, as they prepared women to serve the women of their countries as physicians.

In the former Soviet Union and Eastern Europe after World War II, acute shortages of skilled labour facilitated many women's entry into non-traditional studies and careers. The percentages of women in traditional 'male' disciplines (engineering, economics, medicine, mathematics and the natural sciences) are high. For example, in Poland, 60 per cent of mathematics and natural science students were women in 1991-2 and in the former German Democratic Republic (in 1987) 46 per cent.

Although in many Western countries there has been a significant shift away from conventional 'women's' fields, the presence of women in natural science and technical disciplines is still considerably lower than in Eastern Europe. For example, in Greece 26 per cent of the students in the natural sciences in 1970 were women; in 1990 this figure reached 36.3 per cent. In the United States a similar shift has been noted, which although it is small on a percentage basis, is impressive numerically: in 1989, women constituted 29.7 per cent of undergraduate students in the physical sciences; in 1979-80 this was 23.7 per cent (Chamberlain, 1988).

Women administrators: room at the top?

There are two types of policy-making structures in most universities: the professional and the bureaucratic. The professional structure consists of university presidents (rectors), department heads, deans and collegiate bodies such as faculty councils and committees. The bureaucratic-managerial structure controls the operational and support aspects of the institution. The autonomy of these structures is limited to a greater or lesser degree by the state. For example, in Chapter 4 Nicolina Sretenova outlines the limited autonomy which had prevailed under the Communists in Bulgaria, the government's conception of 'political correctness' having become a major consideration in the selection of students and faculty. In Norway national priorities regarding gender equality have had considerable impact at the administrative level, but continue to meet considerable resistance among the (mostly male) faculty.

There has been little systematic study of either the professional or the bureaucratic structure of universities (Moore, 1987). In this volume, only three countries—France, Turkey and Norway—examined both of these and they all found similar trends: most of the bureaucratic staff are women and their presence is inversely related to rank. In Norway, however, women have made dramatic gains in their share of administrative leadership positions in the last three decades (from 21 to 58 per cent).

Women's leadership positions on the professional level are generally even lower than that at the bureaucratic level. For instance, in Botswana women are completely absent from the university council and among the deans, and only 15 per cent of the department heads are women. In Turkey the percentage of women among presidents and deans is 9.8. In the United States the proportion of heads of colleges and universities has risen from 5 per cent, during the 1970s, to 10 per cent currently.

If a woman does achieve a top position, she appears as a 'miraculous exception'. Moi (1992) argues that members of minority groups who do succeed in a system are at least as likely to identify with it as to turn against its unjust distribution of symbolic capital. Women also seldom figure on powerful selection committees which decide faculty appointments. For instance, in Norway almost 90 per cent of these committees were male-only in 1984.

Summary

History and culture set the stage for contemporary developments. In societies with backgrounds of relative gender equality (such as that prevailing among the peasants of Bulgaria and the fishermen/farmers of Norway), the groundwork was laid for egalitarian ideology and practice. In those in which gender roles have been highly differentiated and stratified, acceptance of egalitarian codes is more problematical.

The tenacity of traditional values is apparent in many countries, including Turkey and China. In Turkey the Kemalist reforms were superimposed on a conservative and highly stratified society. The new norms were coopted by the upper classes, including particularly those who supported the regime, but encountered resistance from others in the population, especially from those in rural areas. The effect of this duality was that within the university, class became more salient than gender in the processes of recruitment and promotion. Thus, a society which has remained traditional in many ways has developed a university system with one of the smallest gender gaps in the world. In China, in spite of the revolution and institutionalization of egalitarian gender codes, entrenched views remain influential. Within the university, as elsewhere in society, formal and informal mechanisms operate to keep most women out of positions of power.

Although traditions importantly influence modern life, they do not entirely determine the course of events. Norms and values change as a consequence of altered circumstances and diffusion. Interesting examples of normative change are provided by France and the United States, where the development of egalitarian programmes has led to (relatively) small academic gender gaps.

The case of Germany is particularly instructive in this context, in light of the contrasting developments in the eastern and western sectors during the post-World War II period. In the East the commitment to equality brought about a change in the composition of the student body (which began to include large numbers of students from working-class families) and in the female proportion of those who were awarded the two highest degrees. It is interesting to note, however, that, as in Norway, the ideological and political changes were not strongly reflected in the academic ranking; the proportion of female academics in East Germany in the top two grades remained lower than the corresponding proportions in West Germany.

The interaction of structural, cultural (ideological) and economic factors may be observed in Poland and Iran. In Iran, when the Western-looking regime of the Shah was replaced by the inward-focused government of Ayatollah Khomeini, a fundamental structural upheaval occurred. Traditional elites were replaced by a coalition of clerics who articulated the grievances of the urban shopkeepers and others who felt shut out and alienated from the wave of prosperity which the Shah's regime had brought to the upper classes. This structural realignment was accompanied by a dramatic cultural shift which centred around the revival of traditional norms and values. However, the limitations which the latter imposed on the participation of women in public life, and in the university in particular, were mitigated by the need to fill positions left vacant in the wake of Iran's war with Iraq.

In Poland the circumstances were analogous. The fall of Communism brought about massive structural change which was accompanied by a sharp cultural shift in the direction of capitalism, Catholicism and other traditional patterns. As in Iran, the negative impact of these changes on academic women is mitigated by economic factors.

If structural factors are defined as characteristics of a society's state and class structure (Skocpol, 1979), it is clear that dramatic structural changes have less effect on the gender gap than do cultural patterns. In some of the most egalitarian societies, revolutions have not occurred, whereas in many societies where the state and class structure have undergone basic transformation, the gender gap remains pervasive.

One generally assumes that as egalitarian norms become widely accepted, the position of disadvantaged groups (including women) improves. However, we have found that while generally true, this is not always the case. In Turkey the Kemalist de-emphasis on Islam was related to a decline in the relevance of gender as a criterion of social differentiation. As less importance was placed on gender, increased attention was focused on class. The relatively large proportion of university women selected on this basis were able to maximize their opportunities because of the availability of domestic help. Thus, sharp differentiation between classes helps to explain the small size of the higher education gender gap in Turkey. In egalitarian societies where household servants have disappeared, academic (and other professional) women argue that their household responsibilities impede their careers.

Nevertheless, in general, an egalitarian normative system does seem to reduce the gender gap in higher education. In fact this effect is so powerful that it appears in some countries to override the adverse effects of poor economic conditions. Significant exceptions to this trend are Norway and the Netherlands where formal commitments to equality co-exist with high levels of economic development, and yet the higher education gender gaps are still relatively great.

It is also important to note that gender stratification is not monolithic. Factors related to the ranking of students, faculty and administration appear to differ. While the proportion of women students in higher education is nearing or has achieved parity in many countries, this is not true of faculty (particularly at the upper ranks) or of administration. Although it has been argued that as the pool of qualified academic women grows their proportions in the academic and administrative hierarchies will automatically increase, so far this has not occurred. A key question in this regard concerns the choices made by individual women. Having internalized potentially conflicting sets of norms regarding family and career, in most countries female university students decide not to obtain advanced degrees. This choice is related primarily to conceptions of the 'proper' role of women in society, and economic factors. Thus, the stage is set for the under-representation of women at high levels of the university. Throughout her career the university woman is confronted by this conflicting set of goals, and this uneasy situation occurs within a social/cultural context which impedes her access to high positions.

Lie (1978) has argued that the value system and work structure of science is an exaggeration of so-called 'masculine' characteristics. Some feminist scholars have challenged the scientific canon, showing women have been excluded from the priorities of science and questioning the central values of the scientific ethos and methods. There has been a proliferation of women's research over the past two decades which Professor Emeritus Jessie Bernard (1989) has provocatively labelled the 'feminist enlightenment'.

Through their own networks and alliances, women have developed Women's Studies courses and programmes and research centres both within and outside of the university system. Although these incentives have met with considerable resistance from the (male) establishment (see Chapter 11 in this volume), Margaret Sutherland (Chapter 16 of this volume) rightly points out that the development of Women's Studies has been one of the most remarkable innovations in the curriculum of higher education in our time. We might add it is also one of the greatest successes of the women's movement. Although the relationship between the existence of a higher education gender gap and a women's movement is equivocal, Women's Studies document gender inequalities and question traditional patriarchal assumptions. From their beginning in the United States in the late 1960s, they have spread like a chain reaction throughout the academic world. Table 7 in the Statistical Appendix shows that all the countries in this volume, with the exception of Uzbekistan and Bulgaria, have started either Women's Studies courses, programmes or research centres within the context of their university structures.

Concluding thoughts

In each country most indicators show an improvement in the life of women during this century. Everywhere we find an increase in life expectancy and literacy rates. Institutionalized discrimination against women appears to be on the wane and this is symbolized by the ubiquity of female suffrage.

Nevertheless, nowhere do women and men share power and privilege equally, and this is illustrated very clearly in the academic world. Considering students, faculty and administrators separately, it is clear that the greatest gains (numerically) have been made among the students. However, although the proportions of male and female university students are approximately equal in many countries, women tend to specialize in fields which do not prepare them for future positions of prestige and power.

Women faculty are concentrated in the lower academic ranks; most investigators report that this is due to lower research and publication rates which are the main avenues of academic advancement. Although some studies have not found marital status to be a good predictor of publication rates, when age and number of children are taken into account, the relationship between gender and publication rates is clarified. Academic women report, and the data confirm, that the presence of young children hinders publication (see Chapters 11 and 17).

High-level administrators in most countries are unlikely to be women, although in a few countries great strides have been made with the implementation of affirmative action programmes.

Although in most countries in this volume gender-based discrimination has been legally abolished, substantial numbers of university women report instances where they have been victimized by latent or informal forms of discrimination.

The smallest academic gender gaps have been found in countries where egalitarian traditions are combined with economic opportunities. In the face of adverse economic circumstances, even a powerful feminist movement and a strong governmental emphasis on equality do not appear to appreciably reduce the size of the gender gap. This means that there is no universal solution to the question of the gender gap in higher education. Each country operates within its own historical and cultural context and must work out its own unique solutions.

Note

1. No order of seniority is implied.

CHAPTER 34

WOMEN ACADEMIC LEADERS IN A LATIN AMERICAN UNIVERSITY: RECONCILING THE PARADOXES OF PROFESSIONAL LIVES*

SUSAN B. TWOMBLY

Abstract. This study used interviews with 18 women in positions of academic leadership at the University of Costa Rica to explore such questions as (1) why do women seem to have success attaining positions? (2) how did these women get to their current positions? (3) what obstacles did they meet along the way and what facilitated their journey? (4) what is the relationship of machismo and institutional culture to women's professional choices and lives? A secondary purpose of the study was to provide insight into the lives of professional Latin American women, about which little is known. Traditional Western theories used to explain women's careers lead to the conclusion that Costa Rican women are oppressed and discriminated against in their quest for academic careers. An interpretivist framework focusing on the meaning women give to their lives suggests a different conclusion. Comparing themselves to women in the larger society, academic women described themselves as leading privileged lives in which rules are gender blind and women can achieve through hard work and dedication.

Introduction

In most Western countries teaching is a female profession, especially at the elementary level. University teaching and administration, however, are usually male domains (Ruijs 1993, p. 535). Feminist critics of U.S. universities have described universities as male defined cultures (Moore and Sagaria 1993). In my own U.S. university there are few women in prominent positions of power and responsibility; and although women are increasingly gaining department chair positions, the first female dean of education was appointed in 1994 as only the third woman dean in the university. (The other two were in nursing and social welfare.) More recently, a woman was named dean of the College of Liberal Arts and Sciences, the largest, most powerful academic unit on campus, and a woman was appointed Associate Provost. My university is hardly unique. Women students outnumber men in North American colleges and universities, and yet women's struggle to gain faculty and administrative positions, and thus access to sites of influence, in these culturally powerful institutions has been less than totally successful (see for example, Aisenberg and Harrington 1988; Finkel and Olswang 1996; Moore and Sagaria 1991; Tack and Patitu 1992).

These patterns are replicated in Europe as well (Eliou 1991; Ruijs 1993). Ruijs (1993, pp. 532–535) reported that women represented between 13 and 32 percent of university teaching staffs in 8 European countries and Turkey. Only between 1% and 20% became professors, and women were rarely found in administrative positions. Worldwide, control of educational institutions at all levels, and especially of culturally powerful universities, is typically in the hands of men. Eliou (1991) notes the emergence of universal patterns of disadvantage for academic women such as underrepresentation, gender differentials in rank and otherwise constrained careers. Ironically, Ruijs (1993) found higher percentages of women in educational management positions in Portugal, Greece, Spain and Ireland, countries not known for equal opportunities for women. She did not provide an explanation of this curious phenomenon, which is replicated in the case of Costa Rica: the percentage of women faculty and administrators is relatively higher than in countries thought to be more "enlightened" with respect to gender equality.

In 1993 approximately 25 women held positions of authority in the University of Costa Rica (UCR), one of the premier Central American public universities. Many of these women were directors of their respective *escuelas* or departments, four were deans, and three occupied positions in the highest ranks of the university. That four deanships should be held by women—including the deanship of the School of Engineering—was surprising. Women had narrowly lost recent elections for rector and two women contended for this position in the most recent election. Although these 25 women constituted a relatively small percentage (about 15%) of the total number of administrators at UCR, finding any women in such important positions is noteworthy. In several cases these were not the first women to have held these administrative positions. The School of Education has had a long history of distinguished women deans. Moreover, 25 is more administrators than one would have expected to find at a comparable U.S. university in 1992.

The relative prominence of women in positions of authority in UCR makes it an important site in which to explore answers the following questions: (1) why do women seem to have success attaining positions? (2) how did these women get to their current positions? (3) what obstacles did they meet along the way and what facilitated their journey? (4) what is the relationship of machismo and institutional culture to women's professional choices and lives? Although scholars have attempted to explain the lack of women in positions of influence in Western universities, we know little about university women in Latin America. In fact, we know less about the potentially powerful class of Latin American professional women—including university professors and administrators—than we do about poor, rural and working class women in these countries.

Peter Winn (1992) notes that Western ideas about Latin American women are shaped by myths and contradictory stereotypes that die hard. These stereotypes include the long-suffering and all-forgiving madonna; the exotic sexpot; the predatory and threatening Eva Perón; the powerless wife; the unskilled worker, poor and illiterate (313–314). Western scholars have also succumbed to perpetuating stereotypes of Latin American women as more oppressed than Western women (Behar 1993). Thus, an important secondary purpose of this study was to shed light on the professional lives of a group of Latin American women with the purpose of counteracting the traditional stereotypes.

Conceptual framework

In the absence of appropriate theoretical frameworks grounded in a Latin American experience a very general socio-structural framework was used as a point of departure to guide this study. Within this framework two major perspectives have been used to explain women's success or lack thereof in North American universities. The first of these is the individual perspective (Kanter 1977, p. 261; Epstein 1988, pp. 46–98; Shakeshaft 1987, p. 82). This perspective attributes the lack of women in administrative positions to biological, cognitive or socialization differences between men and women. Common arguments are that women lack sufficient experience or educational degrees, women fear failure, women can't make decisions or women are socialized to be caring instead of competitive. This approach tends to blame the individual for some of the inequities faced by women and to advocate individual remediation as the solution to these inequities (Kanter 1977, p. 261). Sex role socialization is frequently offered as the explanation for the differences between men and women. As Epstein (1988) defines it, "socialization into sex roles focuses on the process by which the sexes assume different personality characteristics, skills, and preferences" (137). Socialization can lead to sex segregation in organizations because, according to the theory, men and women have different abilities and preferences leading them to select occupations that value sex-appropriate skills, while ignoring other types of occupations.

The second perspective looks to structural sources to explain women's lack of success (Epstein 1988, pp. 136–164).[1] This perspective holds that institutional patterns shape the choices individuals make and are, in turn, maintained and reinforced by those choices. Kanter (1977, p. 262) argued that the structure of opportunity within organizations, power, and numbers actually shaped women's aspirations and motivation to climb the organizational ladder and their lack of ability to do so. This perspective focuses on both formal and informal structures of organizations that affect career opportunities either positively or negatively and includes normative prescriptions and practices as well as actual organizational structure. Entrance requirements, well-defined career ladders, tradition, colleague groups, and mentors are all examples of formal or informal structural aspects of organizations having the potential to restrict or enhance women's roles in organizations. Behavior of women, according to this school of thought, is conditioned by these structures, and is not the product of female deficiencies.

In addition, Aisenberg and Harrington's (1988) discussion of the effects of the marriage plot and the adventure plot on academic women was useful. The marriage plot represents the norm that women's proper role is to marry and to support her husband and children. Even single women are affected by the marriage plot because of society's expectation that all women should marry and raise children. The adventure or quest plot represents a setting forth to search for or provide service to society in a more public way than raising children (Aisenberg and Harrington, pp. 6–19). Aisenberg and Harrington argue that the conflict between the old, private (marriage plot) versus the new, public (adventure plot) is a primary point of tension for professional women as they prepare for and negotiate the rules that govern academic careers and attempt to find a voice in the academy.

Using these perspectives as a starting point, I interviewed 18 of the 25 women who held elected positions of authority in April, 1993. The interview protocol was developed with the assistance of Costa Rican colleagues in the gender studies program. Interviews were conducted in Spanish, often amidst a great deal of street noise and frequent interruptions, and lasted between 45 minutes and 2 hours. Interviews were taped, and the parts of the interviews relevant for this paper were transcribed. The focus of the interviews was on the trajectory of professional life beginning with the decision to attend university, factors that helped or hindered professional advancement in the university, how gender affected success as defined by the women themselves, and the role of women in Costa Rican society. Additional questions dealt with administrative work, power, definitions of and attitudes toward feminism, and their responsibility to provide examples for other women. The reader is reminded that in most cases, although these women did not all come from elite families, they were speaking from the relatively elite positions of professional women who had succeeded according to their definitions of success.

This study is limited by lack of comparative data from a group of male administrators in the same university; space considerations prevent a comparison with existing data on North American and other women administrators. Unfortunately there are few published studies of Latin American women administrators or professors. Much of that which is publically accessible consists of descriptive statistics (e.g., López Núñez 1997; Méndez, Davis and Delgadillo 1989) or is not directly relevant to the focus of this particular study (e.g., Stromquist 1992b). A final limitation is that the author's native language is not Spanish. This may have limited the ability to probe deeply and the interviewee's willingness to answer honestly. However, the author had worked alongside the interviewed women for almost a year planning an international women's congress, and the study had the blessing of the director of that congress. Most respondents seemed to prefer discussing certain aspects of their lives (the personal/private) more than others (the professional). They were cautious about attributing their experiences to discrimination. In at least one case this could have had something to do with not wanting to be critical to an outsider or it may have had more to do with different definitions of discrimination. Generally speaking, interviewees did not seem to be evasive. Because of the paucity of qualitative analyses and lack of theoretical frameworks based on a Latin American experience, the interview protocol was kept simple in an attempt to generate relevant responses without predetermining those responses or forcing the responses into a North American framework.

In the pages that follow, I first describe the women administrators at the University of Costa Rica: who they are and how they achieved their current status in 1993. In the second section I explore factors that the women participants in this study identified as having facilitated or hindered their professional development, including the electoral process. In the third section I argue that while the traditional approaches applied to Western women's careers would lead us to conclude that women in positions of power at UCR are oppressed and discriminated against in their quest for university positions, an interpretivist framework focusing on the meaning these women gave to their experiences leads to a different conclusion. In so doing, I will challenge the common stereotype that Latin American women are helpless victims of an oppressive patriarchal society.

Background

Women in Costa Rica: A brief overview

Girls and women fare relatively well in this small, rural Central American country in which the extremes of wealth and poverty so characteristic of much of Latin America are unfamiliar. In 1991, women comprised 49.5% of the total population of approximately 3,100,000 persons (Market Data 1991–1992). Two of the factors that work in favor of women are a low birthrate (4.3 children per family) and a relatively high level of education (García and Gomáriz 1989). Between 1960 and 1988 the percentage of women in the workforce increased from 17% to 29.9% (excluding domestic labor) (Valdes, Gomáriz and García 1993).

It is the area of education that distinguishes Costa Rica most from its neighbors. Only 7.4% of the female population was classified as illiterate in 1984 (Valdes, Gomáriz and García 1993). In 1990, Costa Rica had the second lowest (behind Argentina) overall female illiteracy rate (under 20%) in Latin America (Stromquist 1992a, p. 26). Furthermore, women constituted 50% or more of the students at every level of education except that of higher education, in which their participation lagged behind that of men only slightly (Blanco, Delgadillo and Méndez 1989; Valdes, Gomáriz and García 1993). In 1990, 37% of the University of Costa Rica faculty were women (Universidad de Costa Rica 1992) compared to approximately 10% of Peruvian academics (Stromquist 1992) and between 5% and 22% in U.S. research universities (Moore and Sagaria 1993). In Central America, public universities in Panama and Nicaragua had slightly higher percentages of women faculty during this same time period, a fact Méndez Davis and Delgadillo (1989) attribute to war and political unrest in those countries. UCR has an active gender studies program. A virtual alphabet soup of governmental and non-governmental activist women's organizations exists in the country, leading Leitinger (1997) to conclude that Costa Rica is at the vanguard of the women's movement in Latin America.

Some caution is warranted however. Educational equality does not necessarily mean social equality, and Costa Rican women face many obstacles (Bonder 1992; Mendiola 1992). In fact, despite this picture of relative equality, the women interviewed described the society in which they live as very traditional and they noted that women face a number of serious problems, especially violence.

Gender relations in Costa Rica, as in most of Latin America, are guided by the ideology of machismo and its corollary, marianismo. With it roots in Spanish colonial ideas and teachings of the Catholic church, machismo is a "system of gender relations which exaggerates the differences between men and women according to their so-called 'natural' qualities and determines what is acceptable behavior from each" (Fisher 1993, p. 3). Machismo asserts the superiority of men over women and valorizes strong, aggressive and virile behavior in men and encourages women to be dependent, self-sacrificing, submissive and emotional (Fisher, 4). Conversely marianismo glorifies motherhood and teaches women to be self-sacrificing guardians of the family and fosters a gender division of labor in which men perform public, productive functions and women the reproductive, private ones (Tiano 1997). Although the aspects of marianismo that exalt women's moral superiority may have been abandoned, other aspects, such as beliefs about appropriate work roles for women still exist (Winn 1992, p. 315). Latin American women have a history of using these cultural stereotypes and ideals to achieve social goals. Many well known Latin American resistance movements, such as the Mothers of the Plaza de Mayo, have been successful precisely because women exploited their roles as mothers, which governments and their armies have been unwilling to challenge (Fisher 1992; Winn 1992).

University organizational structure

Formal and informal structures are two of the keys to understanding women's success or failure in obtaining high level positions in higher education. The University of Costa Rica is an impressive university located on a large, attractively landscaped campus in San Pedro, a suburb of San José. It was founded in 1940 and enrolls approximately 30,000 students in five faculties. In 1988, UCR employed over 2,500 persons in faculty roles; 1,482 were tenured faculty (Oficina de Planificación 1988, p. 20). The University is governed by the University Assembly (consisting of all tenured faculty); the University Council, a representative group elected to make policy; the Rector (president) and five appointed vice rectors: academic affairs, research, community outreach, administrative affairs, and student affairs. The institution is divided into *facultades* (colleges), *escuelas* (departments), sections, agricultural stations, research centers and institutes, and has four regional centers located throughout the country. After the rector, the Director of the University Council is the most powerful position in the university.

Each school is headed by an elected dean and a college assembly, each department by an elected director. Terms for all elected positions are four years with the possibility of reelection for one additional term. In schools divided into departments, directors or department chairpersons hold more direct power than deans. See Table 1 for a listing of areas, schools and departments.

Academic careers in UCR are constrained by the electoral process and more generally by the boundaries of the University. The electoral process makes planning a career in administration difficult for both men and women. Only tenured professors holding the rank of associate or full-professor (*catedrático*) can stand for election. For university-wide positions, such as rector, all members of the University Assembly have the right to vote. This includes students who have representation equal to 33% of the faculty. This voting pattern is replicated at the *facultad* (school) and *escuela* (departmental) levels. In contrast to some countries, such as Ecuador, secretaries, janitors and other non-faculty staff exert much influence on university affairs through the union but have little say in electing officials. As we shall see, voting plays an interesting role for women: it helps them in local (school and departmental) elections and hurts them in university-wide elections.

The academic labor market at the major Costa Rican universities is very much an institutionally bounded one. Generally speaking little mobility occurs between universities. In most cases individuals hold faculty positions in the institutions from which they received their first degree. This is viewed as quite normal and acceptable. (In the newer, private universities this may not be the case as most faculty will have degrees from one of the major universities.)

As in the United States, the key entry point to academic administration is a faculty position. The typical career path is to begin teaching as an *interino* (part-time) and then to compete for a position in *propiedad* (with tenure) when one becomes available. A brief description of the ranks, promotion process and a statistical view of women faculty is given below.

Women in the University of Costa Rica: A statistical picture

The updated official list of university administrators issued in January, 1992, included the following women: Vice-president of Academic Affairs, Vice-president of Community Outreach, Director of the University Council (a full-time, elected position), a member of the University Council, the Dean of Engineering, Dean of Education, Dean of Fine Arts and Dean of Letters, and five vice-deans including the graduate division. Thus, women held five deanships out of 13. Ten women held positions as directors of schools (departments) out of 41 departments while 11 served as subdirectors. Two women directed interdisciplinary careers (majors) and women directed the law and education research institutes (2 out of 10 total). Assistant directors of three of these were women. Out of 17 research centers, 4 were headed by women *(La Gaceta* 1992).

The data reported in Table 1 indicate that women faculty were more highly represented in some areas and departments than in others, namely in the areas of Arts and Letters, Social Sciences and Health. Because each area represents a wide range of academic schools and departments, women's participation must be analyzed carefully. From a comparative perspective, the most interesting figures are those in the sciences. Even within the area of Engineering and Architecture, where the percentage of women was low, 21% of the faculty in Industrial Engineering, 27% in Architecture, and 38% in Computer Science were women. Women were also well-represented in the schools of pharmacy and microbiology and the Department of Nursing.

Obtaining a faculty position is one thing, but promotion to the highest academic ranks is quite another. An individual who is hired for a position in *propiedad* (with tenure) moves through a series of ranks beginning with instructor, adjunct, and associate, to the highest rank of *catedrático*. At the time of this study there was no time limit for moving from one rank to another. Criteria for promotion from

Table 1. Women faculty by academic unit, July 1990

Academic unit	Percent	Number	Academic unit	Percent	Number
Total	36.5	854	Faculty of Education	61.3	98
General studies	45.5	45	Administration	27.3	6
Area of arts and letters	48.4	104	Teacher Education	67.2	41
Faculty of Fine Arts	32.6	30	Counseling and Spec. Ed.	80.0	32
Theater	33.3	4	Physical Education	41.7	10
Music	34.0	17	Library Science	75.0	9
Art	31.0	9	Faculty of Law	14.1	11
Faculty of Letters	60.2	74	Area of engineering and architecture	14.5	42
Philology/Linguistics	60.7	17			
Philosophy	33.3	8	Faculty of Agriculture	13.0	10
Modern Languages	68.6	48	Ag. Economics	14.3	2
Area of basic sciences	24.1	49	Fitotechnology	9.1	3
Faculty of Sciences	24.1	49	Animal Science	14.3	4
Biology	50.0	14	Food Technology		
Physics	16.3	8	Faculty of Engineering	15.1	32
Geology	10.0	2	Agricultural Engineering	18.2	2
Mathematics	22.1	17	Civil Engineering		
Chemistry	28.6	8	Electrical		
Area of social sciences	43.2	260	Industrial	20.7	6
Faculty of Economics	26.1	42	Mechanical	9.5	2
Business Administration	18.5	12	Chemical	15.8	3
Public Administration	44.0	11	Architecture	26.7	4
Economics	20.5	9	Topography	9.55	2
Statistics	37.0	10	Computer Science	38.2	13
Faculty of Social Sciences	52.6	120	Area of health	33.3	154
Anthropology & Sociology	49.2	29	Faculty of Pharmacy	52.4	11
Communication	39.3	11	Faculty of Medicine	32.8	107
Political Science	40.0	4	Nursing	96.2	50
History and Geography	42.4	25	Medicine	17.4	39
Psychology	63.3	31	Faculty of Microbiology	44.0	22
Social Work	87.0	20	Faculty of Dentistry	21.2	14

Source: Pertil del Funcionario Docente. UCR, Oficina de Planificación Universitaria, 1992.

one rank to the next highest include publications, teaching experience, degrees attained, and mastery of foreign languages. The review system involves accumulating points and is overseen by a central university committee.

The only available data revealed that women were more highly represented in the lower ranks (Blanco, Delgadillo and Méndez 1989). In 1987, 47% of women faculty were at the rank of instructor compared to 40% of the men. At the other end of the spectrum, 26% of the men held the rank of associate and 21% that of *catedrático* compared to 24.3% and 11.9% (up from 6.2% in 1982) of the women, respectively. However, 11.9% is approximately double the percentage of women holding full professorships in major U.S. research universities in the same time period (Moore and Sagaria 1993, p. 232) and much higher than the percentages reported for various European countries (Ruijs 1993). The percentage of women in the upper ranks at UCR is important because one must hold at least the rank of associate to stand for election to positions of authority. Thus women were not as well represented in the ranks that have the most influence within the University (González 1993, personal communication). Because there has been no study of the promotion process at UCR, the reasons for this gap are not known.

Background charactistics

The research on academic women's careers suggests that several important background variables are useful in explaining women's success or failure in achieving professional status.

Social class

Elite studies look to background characteristics, such as social class, to explain membership in elite groups (Epstein 1988). The women interviewed for this study ranged in age from late 20s to mid-50s. The majority were in their 40s. As they explained, they had benefited from an open society in which social mobility was common. In contrast to the perhaps two dimensional stereotype of women in developing countries as being either rich and educated or poor and uneducated, these women came from varied social backgrounds. Some of them clearly came from wealthy and/or socially prestigious families. "I come from a family with a long academic tradition," said the Dean of Letters. "My grandfather, my uncle, and my father were academics who participated in the political reform of [19]48, with the writing of the Constitution of [19]49 and later with the University reform of the [19]50s and beyond." The Vice Rector of Academic Affairs completed all of her post secondary education in the U.S., suggesting that she came from a family with substantial resources.

There were, however, women who came from poor homes. The Director of the University Council described hers as "a very poor family." Her father left home when she was young. As a consequence she had to work while attending public schools. The Dean of the Faculty of Education did not describe her family as being financially poor but rather as lacking education: "My parents had a very low level of education.... My father gave up his business activity and continued as a *campesino* with a small coffee farm." "The cultural environment was not very rich," she added, "but the socioeconomic situation of the family was adequate—not abundant—but adequate. I never had to look for work when I was a child." The majority described themselves as middle class, as do most Costa Ricans.

Regardless of class backgrounds, many of these women described challenging family situations, such as death of a father, that forced them to alter plans, take on additional responsibilities and to find jobs to pay the bills. One woman spoke for the rest when she said that these challenges forced her "to work and to fight hard to complete my studies and maintain my family's properties. It was a fight for the well-being of a family."

Socialization and education

In Costa Rica, as in most Latin American countries, the *licenciatura* (one year of study beyond the bachelor's degree) is the minimal degree required for obtaining most faculty positions. Therefore a university education (but not a master's or doctoral degree) is a necessary first step to attaining a faculty position.

The motivation to attend (or not to attend) college for these women came from two primary sources: the family and the self. For most of these women the motivation and support to attend university arose in the family and for most was a normal part of family life. Frequently, one or the other parent was credited with providing special support. For example, "The idea of being a professor was born in the home," said a director of a scientific research center. She credited her mother with the fact that she and her brothers and sisters were encouraged to get an education:

> Mother ... did not study, but thought that all her children should become professionals. Perhaps because of her own frustration at not being able to work she always cultivated in all of us the idea of becoming professionals. Not all of us did, but she gave us all, within limitations of the family, the same possibilities.

The recently elected member of the University Council observed that her family believed that a university education was the key to achieving economic status to match the social status they already possessed.

For some, attending university was not a conscious decision. "From the time I was a child, it wasn't my decision. It was a family decision" said one woman. Yet another said, "There was never any discussion that I was going to study in the university. My father could not finish his education. Later, when we were grown, he entered university in the United States and completed a master's degree. We were four girls and one boy. It was assumed that everyone studied. It was the tradition.... My mother was a professor of mathematics." The Dean of Letters added, "I lived from the time I was a child in an environment of university reform ... for me it [attending university] was not an aspiration. It was a fact of life."

Their families encouraged them to study even though they were girls. The director of the Department of Sociology and Anthropology noted that "There was not any exclusion. Because the perspective of our parents was to study and to keep studying." The Dean of Letters talked about the relationship of gender and studying in her academic family: "My family was very traditional in its view of gender with respect to the roles of men and women in society.... I also had an advantage: an open-minded father who told me that the important thing was to do what I wanted to do. He opened doors for me and supported me."

The Dean of Education stressed that her parents' lack of education did not negatively affect her family's support for education: "Within this more or less culturally limited environment, my parents gave me the facilities—the stimulus to be an adequate student. Performing well in elementary school motivated my parents because they had their plans that all of us were going to study and all of us are professionals." She confirmed what more than one said, "We all studied and found that education was the mechanism to mobility and this stimulated us further."

The Director of the Department of Nutrition was one of the few who encountered opposition in her home. She was the seventh of nine children.

> My mother was machista, but my father was not. Mother had the conception that the woman was born to marry and have children. This was her role. She shouldn't even think about studying. My older brothers were all given the opportunity to study, however, they left school at the end of high school.... It was his [father's] help that enabled me to continue school. I earned good grades and it was clear to me that I wanted to study. My mother strongly opposed me during my first year in high school. After the first year, when she realized that I could do well, she gave me more support. When she realized I was serious, the pressure diminished.

However, she ran into the opposition of her mother again when it came time to actually attend university. She won a scholarship to study nutrition in Guatemala, but her mother did not want her to leave the country. After some convincing, her father gave his permission.

Obtaining a university education was not so easy for several women and these were the women who found the motivation to pursue higher education within themselves. The Director of the University Council had the support of a grandmother and an aunt to study, but she located the motivation to seek a university education within herself: "In that era, children of poor families did not have access to education. My case is exceptional. Why? Because I always wanted to have a university degree. I am a very tenacious woman." The director of one of the research institutes also located the motivation within herself. She noted that after having to take care of her family and losing much of her childhood, "I decided to improve myself professionally."

The Director of Counseling and Special Education, in her late 50s, led a rather traditional life until her children went to college:

> I went to the high school of the highest class in Costa Rica, where they educate the wives of presidents—a nun's school.... I married at 18 thinking that it was bad to work, that it was bad to get divorced—never. I should have all the children I could, do all the official work associated with the house and be a model super woman.... I didn't recognize my own needs. My husband was sexist, encouraged by me.... He wanted to have lots of children. During the first 10 years of marriage I didn't work. I had 5 children and adopted one more. In these ten years I felt a tremendous need for some sort of community life. I worked in social work. I started a project with poor people—sort of a cooperative. It was a wonderful experience, but it resulted in lots of problems with my husband. When my children entered the University, I did as well. I completed general studies at the same time they did. I wanted to study social work.

Perhaps one of the reasons that most of these women did not face more opposition is that families believed that women needed an education in order to manage a house, as described by one department director: "How I was socialized in the home was very influential. I was not socialized to assume only the household chores, but I learned to administer the house as well as do the domestic chores."

Academic career

I was concerned with three stages in these women's university careers: pursuit of advanced degrees, entry into a career in the University of Costa Rica, and path to current position, including barriers and facilitating factors.

Advanced degrees

One of the questions posed in research on academic women's careers is whether they have the requisite degrees to compete for jobs; and if not, what are the barriers that prevent them from earning these degrees. The *licenciatura* is the minimal degree required to obtain a faculty position and higher degrees are not absolutely necessary to ascend faculty ranks, which creates a level playing field that may prove to be an advantage for women. Available data for 1987 showed that, overall, women faculty at UCR (56.2%) were more likely than men (49.6%) to hold the *licenciatura* as the highest degree (Perfil 1988, p. 12). Conversely, 18.4% of the men held master's degrees compared to 15% of the women (Perfil 1988, p. 12). Relatively few of the total faculty held doctorates (12%). Of those who did, men (15%) were twice as likely as women (7%) to hold this degree (Perfil 1988, p. 12). It is clear that men were more likely than women faculty members to have earned master's and even doctoral degrees.

Based on the women interviewed for this study, it would appear that holding advanced degrees was an advantage for attaining elected administrative positions. Compared to the total population of faculty, the women administrators in this study comprised a relatively elite group. Six of the 18 (33%) women held doctorates, all from foreign universities; and 11 or 61% held master's degrees, some from foreign universities and others from UCR. The *licenciatura* was the highest degree for only one woman. The percentages of women administrators holding advanced degrees were significantly higher than overall percentages of men holding these degrees; however, statistics on the percentage of male administrators holding advanced degrees were not available. In some ways it is not surprising that individuals with advanced degrees assume such leadership roles. Funding organizations, such as Fulbright, often support candidates who are leaders or who have demonstrated leadership potential.

Earning advanced degrees is, however, no easy proposition for either men or women. In most cases, it is necessary to leave the country to earn advanced degrees. Most of the women interviewed had studied in the U.S., but others earned degrees in Canada, Belgium and other

Latin American countries. Leaving the country for doctoral and many master's degrees is an obstacle for men and women alike, but it is particularly difficult for women. One of the prerequisites to study abroad is money. Most of the women interviewed for this study relied on some form of scholarship support from UCR itself or from other organizations. During its early years, UCR adopted an aggressive policy of sending faculty abroad to earn advanced degrees.

Availability of scholarships and the scholarship selection process play a critical role in determining who will earn advanced degrees. According to the women interviewed, the scholarship application process was gender blind; however, there was a catch: convincing husbands to take leaves from jobs to accompany them. The result was a self-selection process in which women were less likely than men to even apply for scholarships. While several of the younger women reported very supportive spouses who had taken a year or two from their own jobs to accompany their wives, this was not common especially among the older women. The Dean of Letters described some of the difficulties women faced:

> Embassies and universities occasionally throw roadblocks in the way of women. They [embassies] ask personal questions about the family. 'Are you married? How may children do you have? Are you going with your husband?' One knows that the scholarships really do not include the family. This is very important. If I am single, it is very easy.

UCR was also criticized for not providing sufficient economic support for divorced women with children.

Only one or two women reported feeling any sort of discrimination or obstacles blocking their paths to success in foreign universities. The Director of the University Council had been told by her thesis director in Belgium she was not capable of earning the Ph.D. "He disqualified me from the very beginning and he was very arrogant. He challenged my identity as a woman." She won the highest prize given in Belgium for doctoral study.

First university position

Several patterns emerged from the 18 career histories. Only the Dean of Letters, the Director of the University Council, and one other woman spoke of wanting to be academics from the time they were children and of intentionally seeking academic jobs. Many started out in other careers and were then "called" to the University. For example, the Dean of Engineering, the Director of the Nursing Department and several women in the Faculty of Education had begun careers in positions outside of the University. This was possible, in part, because of tremendous growth of the University of Costa Rica as a result of university reform of the 1950s and 1970s. The Dean of Engineering noted how lucky she was: "I began to study engineering and then along came the Reform of 1957. The University grew, creating opportunities for employment. I was lucky to choose a career in demand." The Dean of Fine Arts had just returned to UCR with a master's degree in photography when the Department of Photography was opened, creating opportunities for her to join the faculty. The Dean of Education said, "I was surprised in 1972 when they called me from the Faculty and told me that they wanted me to come and help with a teaching practicum." The Director of the Department of Anthropology and Sociology described the role of recent university reform further: "The Third Congress (1970s) created the social conception of the University. Because of this Congress much attention was then devoted to social work. Many of the social science positions were created then. Women as well as men benefited." She went on to say that this boom had ended, "Many entered in *propiedad* before me. I was one of the last who could do so."

For two others the struggle to enter the University was somewhat more difficult for largely idiosyncratic reasons. In the case of the director of a research institute, she had earned her doctorate in the United States and returned to integrate herself in the University to find that if she wanted a job in the University, it could only be working on a specific project. The Director of Counseling and Special Education was denied her first request for a job by the Dean of Education (her aunt) who believed a married woman should stay at home with children.

Current position

The third aspect of these women's careers involved getting the position that they held when interviewed. All of the positions held by these women, save one, were elected positions. Conversations with a woman who had narrowly lost the election for rector in the early 1980s and observations of a rather nasty election for seats on the University Council led me to approach the interviews with the tentative hypothesis that the election process would be a major barrier to women seeking administrative posts because of its highly public nature. Surprisingly, the election process was reported to be somewhat problematic for some women but not as much of an obstacle as anticipated. Of course, the women interviewed for this study were winners, not losers, of elections. In fact, the electoral process may have helped women in female dominated areas.

Although most of the women did not report experiencing the nasty campaign politics of the woman who had narrowly lost the recent election for rector, they did report being subjected to a double standard. "Women have to be purer than men," observed one woman. The recently elected member of the University Council explained how the election process worked against her:

> All of the other candidates from my area were men, men who had followed traditional university careers. I had [only] been coordinator of the master's program in the School of Education. The men had held ministry positions. There were very subtle things. In one round table discussion they wanted me to speak first. I declined because it is a disadvantage to go first, and we drew straws. There is a tendency to attack one's personal life. There is more interest in elections for high positions and more weapons are used. In the case of the married woman, they invent a lover. If one has one, it becomes public. If one doesn't have a lover, they invent one. It isn't the same for a man. In my case they attacked me on a professional issue.

A number of women reinforced the fact that a double standard operates with respect to personal life. In two cases, the candidates' husbands were also a member of the same unit. These women reportedly had to convince their colleagues that they were not mere puppets for their husbands who actually would run things. As one woman said, "No one has ever asked any of the previous directors about the influence their spouses had over them." Perhaps because most women held positions in areas where women constituted the majority, they did not generally feel that the election process worked against them. The stakes were higher for positions of higher rank and elections potentially more volatile.

Most denied actively seeking the position they held at the time this study was conducted and characterized their election as "accidental". The Dean of Engineering had recently returned to UCR. For a period she only worked part-time and then some colleagues suggested that she run for dean. "And that's how it began," she said. The Dean of Fine Arts also said that she did not seek the position, but friends suggested she run. This particular woman had had no previous formal administrative responsibilities, but had coordinated the graphic arts program, the largest in the Faculty. The Vice Rector had more than 20 years of working within the University with several periods outside but in the field of education:

> I was in the Government four years as a consultant to the Minister of Education, also a woman, during the years 1978–82. Now I am in this administrative position. They called me and here I am. This was unexpected. Tomorrow something else may happen or not.

In the nutrition department, the faculty in *propiedad* took turns being director. Another dean did not speak directly of how she got to her present position but made it clear she was doing it to repay a debt to the University: ". . . after receiving a scholarship like the one I received from the University I have paid it back and fulfilled my administrative debts by occupying this high position for four years. No more," she said laughing. Several women were motivated by a sense of obligation to society. Many of these women were somewhat surprised that they were actually good at administration.

Several women actively sought their administrative positions. The director of the University Council had held numerous positions within the public workers union at the university, country and international levels.

She had been an unsuccessful candidate for the position of rector. The recently elected member of the University Council had not held other elected positions before running for the Council, but had come to realize that, while she liked teaching and research, she could not change the system as a professor. In order to do that she had to enter politics. She defeated numerous strong male candidates to win the right to represent the social science area. This woman was one of two female (losing) candidates for rector in 1995. One department director had recently returned from earning a second master's degree in the U.S. when the election for director of her department occurred. She found her department to be lacking in some things which she believed she could provide, many of which were women's issues: "I decided that only I could provide these things and launched my campaign for the position." This was her first administrative position.

Location in the university

One of the arguments made by sociologists and scholars who have studied women in educational organizations is that women are ghettoized and marginalized in certain female professions or certain areas within professions, usually areas with low status and little power. Such segregation is often explained as a function of sex role socialization in which women are socialized to choose careers that value sex-appropriate skills. With several notable exceptions, the women in positions of power in the University of Costa Rica were in departments or schools in which women constituted the majority or near majority of students and faculty. This was true in fact as well as in perception. "In the University the majority of women are in positions identified especially for women. There are a few exceptions and in these cases women have achieved the positions with a base of support," explained the Director of the University Council. She went on to say:

> Although in UCR there are many women in positions of power, there are certain careers which are considered women's fields.... Engineering and medicine are masculine. The culture of the country is masculine. If we talk of women in positions of power in this University, we are talking about women who are *luchadoras*, very strong women with a very strong trajectory of struggle, and they are outstanding from an academic point of view.

Confirming the sex role socialization notion, the Vice Rector for Academic Affairs explained: "The educational system is discriminatory at the level of training of students.... When students select majors self-discriminating factors enter, perhaps cultural and universal factors. Women tend to choose certain types of careers."

Sex role socialization and societal norms may explain how most women end up in certain fields, but it does not explain how they are able to rise to positions of leadership. Four reasons emerged from the interviews. First, women were successful for the most part in areas in which women predominated as faculty and students. The university system facilitated women's access to positions of authority in fields in which there are more women to vote. A department director explained: "The assembly in the School of Medicine is 80% men. Men are going to win any election for this reason." At the time the interviews were conducted, the School of Education was dominated by women with only the Department of Educational Administration headed by a man. The only other male in the Assembly was the student representative. However, it did not always follow, said some, that women would win elections just because there were more women in a school or department. For example, the School of Education had had male deans. The system of electing administrators did seem to facilitate women's chances of attaining positions in certain areas as most women in this study, with a few important exceptions, were in units dominated numerically by women.

Power differentials among positions was a second explanation for women's success in attaining in attaining deanships. The Dean of Education explained:

> We are women deans in schools divided in departments. Why? Because the power in these schools is held by the departments. The dean is more or less a coordinator. Some would say a figurehead, but I don't agree with that. Deanships in schools not divided in departments, such as law and pharmacy do not have women deans." [A woman had recently held the deanship of the School of Law.] Who are the deans

then? "X" in Letters—school divided in departments, "Y" in Engineering—also divided in departments. She is very important. There should not be a woman dean in Engineering . . .

With few exceptions, women had more success obtaining deanships in faculties divided into departments where deans reportedly had less power than department directors. Even in those faculties, the deans, and the position itself were viewed as symbolically important; and in fact, many deanships in departments divided into schools were held by men.

Thirdly, teaching, the primary emphasis of the Latin American university, is considered legitimate female work as the Dean of Letters described:

> We have always said that Letters is one of the most matriarchal of the schools in the entire university. Traditionally, teaching has been viewed as women's work. Here, primary, and later secondary education, has always been in hands of women. It was assumed that women were mothers and therefore good teachers. Above all, primary education was seen as an extension of the home, and education was directed by women. The School of Letters was a school that primarily trained for teaching. However, this has changed some recently. There has been greater specialization and now we have postgraduate studies and emphasis on research has increased. But fortunately this happened when women already had the territory clearly controlled.

Finally, some positions were believed to be designated for women. Several of the women noted that the position of vice rector for academic affairs was a position for women. "The vice rectorship of academic affairs is always in women's hands, because of its relationship to teaching. This is also a stereotype, but there have been extraordinary women in this position," said one woman. Another woman suggested that this was only compensation for the rector always being a man.

These findings support the arguments that structure determines women's opportunity. Women obtained top level positions in areas dominated by women almost by default and not necessarily due to gender loyalty. In fact, several women noted that men support other men but that women do not yet support other women out of solidarity. Women expressed ambivalent attitudes toward gender segmentation in the university. They expressed concern about ghettos of powerlessness and agreed that women should be able to pursue any field of study, but many also spoke very positively about why they were in a "woman's field." One dean even spoke defiantly about women having her area under control.

There are several ways to think about women being segregated in women's fields. On the one hand, women working in traditional women's fields such as nutrition, education, and health have an opportunity to affect services essential to the well-being of women and of a developing society. From a comparative perspective, although women have historically dominated some fields such as home economics and nursing in U.S. universities, women have not dominated high level faculty or administrative positions in such traditional "women's fields" as education or social welfare. Moreover, some social science fields that were considered appropriate for women at UCR, such as sociology and psychology, are not necessarily dominated by women in the U.S. So, even though women attained powerful positions in women's fields, at least they gained positions of power in these fields. The downside is that fields traditionally associated with women do not have as much political influence as medicine and law where there were fewer women professors.

Obstacles and facilitating factors

Each of the interviewees was asked to discuss factors which had facilitated and inhibited their careers. In order to put their comments in context, it is important to understand that success for these women was defined very broadly to include recognition as a good teacher and as an expert in one's field. Election to positions of authority was only one indication of this recognition. (U.S. benchmarks of earning tenure and promotion were not applicable here.)

Obstacles facing women in UCR, as described by those who held positions of power, can be grouped into two major categories: application of a double standard to women and sex stereotyping. Related to both of these issues, and often intermingled in discussions, was that of the family. Interestingly, although family responsibilities were described as a limitation on women's time to engage in research and scholarship, overall family was not labeled an obstacle.

With few exceptions, these women believed that it was more difficult for them than their male colleagues to achieve success. "I can't speak of equality," said the Director of the University Council. "We have to be two times better to succeed in the University. If one is equal in qualifications, the man has more opportunities; but if a woman stands out and excels, she can achieve success more easily than a man.... For the Council, one has to be an outstanding woman in order to win. Men get points just for being men."

In commenting on success in the university, the Dean of Letters laughed as she said:

> Success? Officially or unofficially? Officially by ability, curriculum vitae and academic area. Unofficially, to be male carries more weight.... In practice one observes very subtle obstacles. For example, stereotypes function as rationality for men.... Recognition of scientific publications is very easy. However, recognition of literary works is much more complicated, and art is even more difficult. One has to demonstrate doubly that literary work and art have value because traditionally women are associated with emotion and men with science.

"Stereotypes still put women in subordinate positions. We aren't good administrators. We are good secretaries," said one woman. Moreover, "It costs women more to hold an administrative position." This was largely due to family responsibilities. All but four of the women interviewed were married or had been divorced. Only these four and two of the younger, recently married women, did not have children. The three women in the highest positions were single, as predicted by one of the department directors. These women were viewed as being able to take on top positions because they did not have husbands and children. However, because they clearly violated accepted norms for women, they probably faced other obstacles.

Studies of U.S. women faculty show that women believe they have heavier workloads than their male colleagues and that this differential disadvantages them. Women in UCR also reported differences between them and their male colleagues involving time but it was not a workload differential within the university. In fact, as the major source of financial support for the family, low university salaries forced men to hold second jobs outside UCR. This reportedly reduced their dedication to their university careers. Women, on the other hand, could dedicate 100% to the university because they were not expected to support a family.

Many of the women interviewed drew a distinction between those factors that affected their roles as women and the university system. Most agreed with the dean who said: "The university system does not disadvantage women. It is the real time available that limits one." She asked, "does the woman have time to write? time for professional development? time to learn another language? Can she make the decision to go to another country to study if her husband is not an academic? These are the limitations." "Success doesn't have anything to do with sex," added one department director. "It is a matter of will, intention, ability, and free time."

One director's description of her efforts to produce scholarship shows how her time was limited. "In spite of a good family situation, it is hard to do research. One has to achieve a balance between family and work. One can't dedicate much more time to one area or the other. I am a housewife, nurse, wife, mother. This affects my ability and time to commit myself to reset, thinking and conceptualizing." For those who had children it was clear that their primary responsibility was to the children, especially while the children were young. These findings correspond to those described by Korean academic women (Johnsrud 1995). Korean women did not describe workload differentials as negatively affecting them, but they did identify differential expectations for performance and differences in available time due to family obligations (30).

One of the structural factors that facilitated women's careers was that UCR was quite flexible in allowing women with full-time appointments to work part-time when necessary, there were no time limits for promotions, and one could teach in *interino* (instructor) status for as long as one wished. However, these advantages could also work against women. One recently married department director explained that she had entered her faculty career at the same time as several friends. Due to family obligations, the friends had not been promoted. She went on to say that this weighed on all of the women in her department who had children.

Some of these women had full-time housekeepers to care for the children; however, full-time help was too expensive for some. The Dean of Education remarked that even though she did have help in her home, she still bore the majority of the responsibility for transporting the children, helping them with their homework, and managing the home. She described her day:

> Yesterday I worked here (at the University) until 2 in the afternoon. I went home (about 15 miles from the University). I worked at home with the children a little. I left them at school and returned to a meeting of the Council of the School of Education. In the meantime I ran to buy some things for the children. On the way home I went to buy some groceries and returned to my house at 7:30. Then, for the next two hours I helped the children.... We have something that most North American families don't have: domestic help. However, the maid is more likely to attend to the man of the house. I can arrive very late and very tired, but she never asks me if I would like a cup of tea or if she can help me with anything. She shines my husband's shoes, puts out his clothes, asks him if he wants tea, etc. This is the structure I would change.

The Director of Physical Education spoke more favorably about the crucial role played by domestic employees in her professional life. More than one woman in this study complained about the lack of quality day care centers.

When asked specifically about the role of the family, the women generally agreed that societal expectations of women were the single most important limitation for women in general. One woman who worked in a highly technical, typically masculine, field in which men were suspicious of her competence made the following comment:

> Independent of whether there is open discrimination or not, of whether there are children or "empleadas", the woman has to do the housework. It is an unequal situation, very bothersome. One supposes also that if the woman accepts work outside of the home, she is a bad mother. People are going to ask why you aren't attending to your children. All my life I have been called a bad mother, even by some of my colleagues. The former director of my department used to ask me what I was doing at the University, why wasn't I home with the children? It is a catch-22. There is no way to come out well because if you are a mother, you can't be a good worker.

The fact that women described families as the most significant limiting factor in their careers and yet, when asked directly, did not label family responsibilities as an obstacle or problem is not easily explained. Perhaps the best explanation is that limitations were attributed to the larger society rather than to the university itself.

Obtaining postgraduate degrees and knowledge of foreign languages were mentioned as important criteria for moving through the ranks (although not necessarily to obtain positions) and could be an obstacle for women as discussed earlier. The difficulty in going abroad to study was summarized by one woman: "The opportunities are greater for men to leave to get a graduate degree than for women because of their commitment as mothers." This woman also offered the opinion that people still believed that education for a man was a better investment than for a woman. In general, these women believed that they lived in a place and time in which, in the words of one, "Men can rise in the ranks more easily because it is easier for them to travel outside of the country."

Not all agreed the university presented greater obstacles for women than for men. Several women echoed the sentiments of one research center director: "The obstacles are not very great." "They are surmountable.... It costs to assimilate.... It depends in part on personality. There are men who have been affected because their personality is weak. It almost does not matter whether one is male or female, but rather the personality counts more and what one wants in life." Another woman noted that she had:

personally not experienced any difficulty. It is a cultural problem, the limitations that one faces. It is also a problem of defining priorities.... For me, at a certain time my first priority was to be a mother, second was a professor, and third was to be a researcher. The limitation that one has is to define priorities. Obstacles one defines oneself.

"I have not faced any obstacles," said the Vice Rector "At the level of society, that is where women face obstacles...."

While societal and cultural factors were identified as inhibitors, the women in this study largely credited themselves for their success and some overcame significant personal obstacles to obtain an education. Also, these women became professionals at a time when competent women could get ahead. For example, The Director of the University Council reported, "If one has equal professional qualifications to a man, the man has more opportunities. If a woman stands out and excels she can achieve success more easily than a man...."

A director of a scientific research institute attributed her success to her character: "I have never been one to stay behind." One department director became pregnant out of wedlock before having finished her education. She made the very difficult decision not to marry the father:

> If I had married, I would not have worked, would not have earned my master's degree.... I would have run into a wall. The father of the child had told me that I could not work, but because I had my undergraduate degree and an established job I could not become the housewife he wanted me to be.

"To be the only woman in a major had certain advantages," reported the Director of Computer Sciences; "While I felt alone, it gave me pleasure to belong to this elite." "It's all personal attitude," said the Dean of Engineering: "I speak the language without losing my femininity. They respect me and I have always played within the men's rules even though they represent a handicap for me."

Others cited additional factors that helped them. The Director of Counseling and Special Education complained about the lack of support from her husband. He had been against her working until recently. This woman, who had raised five children before entering the University herself, told the story of how she finally gained confidence in herself by making the decision to donate a kidney to a student. This marked an important point in her life. Up to this point, she had not made significant decisions without approval of her husband. After this decision, "I lost the fear of making decisions."

It was clear that on a personal level, all of the interviewed women had worked hard to succeed, by their own accounts at least twice as hard as their male colleagues, and their ability to do so was a result of personal characteristics and having survived many battles.

However, the University was also described as being a good place for women to work—better than private industry. Two aspects of the university were particularly helpful to women: its flexibility and its growth during the 70s and 80s when most of these women began their careers. In the words of one director:

> The advantages of UCR facilitate the entrance of women.... In one sense machismo favors this. Because women are married it is not their responsibility to guarantee work stability. I can be *interino* and if they need me, fine; and if they do not, I do not have the same pressure that men have. Above all, the university woman does not have to maintain the family economically. The University also permits us to work part time when we have to. In a private company one can not work part time.

As discussed earlier, these particular women also benefited from seeking university careers during a period in which the university was growing rapidly and needed faculty. However, as one department director noted, the boom had ended. The effect this will have on the number and percentage of women in the University is not known. Other important factors facilitated university careers for women: term limits on the length and number of times one could hold a position provided opportunity within the university, teaching at even the university level was viewed as appropriate for women, and the system of academic ranks was perceived to be "cold" and objective.

Although several of the younger women credited their very helpful husbands for making their ability to hold administrative positions possible, any reference to mentors was missing. Although one or two women noted the importance of role models to their professional development, such as former deans, ministers of education and a woman who had run for rector recently, mentors, reportedly essential to success of academic women in North America, were apparently not a factor for Costa Rican women academic leaders. Even when I described the specific meaning of the term, which is the same in Spanish, they did not identify influential mentors. Johnsrud (1995) arrived at similar conclusions in her study of Korean women. Mentors may be a culturally embedded aid for women that is not universal.

In sum, women in positions of authority in UCR had conflicting views about the situation for women in the university. Generally speaking, although there were obstacles, these women downplayed these obstacles and viewed the university as a good place for them.

Discussion

From a Western perspective, it is possible to argue that, despite their personal success, the women in this study, and all women at UCR, faced a situation unequal to that of their male colleagues. They described a very traditional society in which women were clearly expected to fulfill certain roles as mothers and family caregivers. They identified few barriers to professional advancement that did not have something to do with family and/or stereotypes about women. Although the university was described as a good place for women to work, and in fact, did appear to have some structural features that facilitated women's academic careers, all was not well. Even though most agreed that policies and practices were gender blind, there was also some agreement that to be male carried more weight, a double standard was applied to women, and most noticeably, opportunities for women were greater in certain less powerful, "women's fields" than in other more influential ones. Strong personalities, supportive families and a flexible university enabled these women administrators to succeed and rise to the top of their professions.

These women's own constructions of their lives revealed many paradoxes: policies were described as being cold and objective, and yet women had to work twice as hard and be twice as good as men; women were "segregated" in "women's fields," and yet the university was not discriminatory; women were subjected to societal stereotypes about appropriate roles for women, and yet the university was a good place to work; and most curiously, role expectations for mothers restricted women's time to produce the necessary scholarship to ascend in the ranks and ability to go abroad to earn advanced degrees, and yet families were not described as specific obstacles. The traditional individual and structural approaches to interpreting women's careers do not enable us to satisfactorily reconcile these seemingly contradictory portrayals of women's lives within the University of Costa Rica.

Acker and Feuerverger (1997) offer reference group theory as a useful framework for resolving some of women's contradictory assessments of their own situation. Reference group theory proposes that one's judgment about one's own situation is relative depending on the comparison group. In Canada and the U.S., women academics compare themselves to their male colleagues, which results in a generally negative view about their lives. The women in this study, however, located themselves as a subculture of the larger machista society; and compared to women in general, they clearly viewed themselves as privileged. If they faced discrimination, it was imposed by that larger society and its views about women, not by the university. This parallels the larger women's movement in Costa Rica. Rather than an intellectual movement driven by theoreticians, the movement is very much directed toward solving "real" problems, such as poverty, hunger, and violence. By comparison to these problems, the concerns of academic women have received little attention.

With all of its faults, the women in positions of authority generally perceived UCR to be an oasis in an otherwise machista society; and the university itself, they believed, did not limit their participation. Time and time again women said that the university was a good place to work. Laws and university policy, they believed, established a more or less equal situation for men and women, while societal expectations and stereotypes inhibited women's ability to achieve by restricting the time they had to devote to activities such as publishing, their ability to study abroad, and the way women were viewed. Although some women talked specifically about discrimination, about having to work twice as hard and be twice as competent as men, the old boys network, and other ways in which they were disadvantaged, they largely described the rules as gender blind. In this respect, the university was a subculture that countered values of the larger society at least for women in positions of power.

Various structural explanations for UCR's seeming receptivity to women were given, such as the coincidence of UCR's growth with the availability of women to assume positions, flexibility, relatively low professorial salaries (although a university professorship is considered to be a relatively high status position), the university's emphasis during its own critical formative years on preparing secondary teachers, the fact that Latin American universities are primarily teaching institutions, and the belief that teaching, regardless of level, was an acceptable role for women.

However, these successful academic women attributed their success first and foremost to their own personal characteristics. Even the four women who specifically discussed discrimination against women talked about women being able to succeed through excellence, tenacity and political savvy as they themselves had. In short, although they compared themselves to their male colleagues with respect to being subjected to a double standard, these women who were successful felt proud to have succeeded in this environment. This is consistent with belief in individual efficacy based on a strong sense of individualism and self-worth Leitinger (1997) attributes to Costa Rican women and with the Korean women studied by Johnsrud (1995).

The confusion arises in perceived role of family in careers of these academic women. Although society was "blamed" for creating restrictive expectations for women and family obligations were often cited as imposing limitations on academic women, family, itself, was not labeled an obstacle to achievement. Rather, children limited the time one had to devote to academic tasks necessary to succeed in the university. However, none of the 18 women discussed family in a negative way. All 18 women (even the single women) believed that a woman's first priority was to her children and that priorities shifted as the children grew. They did not use negative terms, such as burden or obstacle to describe family. The idea that one might have to choose between family and career did not even enter the conversation. Here we find a more positive construction of the relationship between family and work than is typical of North American academic women (For example, Aisenberg and Harrington 1988; Finkel and Olswang 1996). One might argue that Latin American middle and upper class women have the luxury of domestic help and extended families to counteract the career drag of family; however, the women in this study did not talk much about either.

Interpreting the lives of Costa Rican academic women seems to call for a more complex, or at least different, view of the relationship between the personal and professional lives of women than typically found in research on Western academic women. As Guzmán Stein (1997) argues, liberal and Marxist theorists tend to see women as victims of oppressive structures whereas there is increasing evidence to show the existence and nature of women's resistance and management of subordination. There are many examples of this in Latin America: the Mothers and Grandmothers of the Plaza de Mayo to name two examples. Women neither define discrimination nor can they or do they always resort to means of resistance considered conventional by Western scholars (Guzmán Stein 1997; Phillips 1991).

The works of Patricia Hill Collins (1990) and Mary Catherine Bateson (1990) provide alternative views that are useful, particularly for understanding the role of family in professional lives. Hill Collins argues that the traditional approaches to understanding families based on a middle class North American and European norm is problematic for African American women, and I would suggest it is problematic for Latin American women as well. This was not a study of families *per se* and does not permit us to formulate a conception of the Costa Rican family. However, the simple division of the world into public (paid labor) and private (family) spheres with all of its negative consequences for women may not apply to the case of professional women in Costa Rica. These academic women seemed to draw great strength from their families and in some cases talked about having great power in the family unit. Many reported making all of the important family decisions, especially those having to do with the children. Although we might see the academic women subject participants in this study as oppressed by family responsibilities, importantly they made the distinction between being affected by family responsibilities and oppressed by them. Rather they saw themselves as strong-willed, capable women who were able to overcome the obstacles they had encountered.

Bateson (1990) portrays lives as a series of negotiations and attempts to reconcile contradictions. These academic administrators, in fact, viewed themselves as privileged to be working in an organization that was favorable toward women. They all were subjected to societal expectations to marry and yet had also bought into the idea that women could assume public professional lives. Their lives were a series of situations in which they negotiated and renegotiated the public and private aspects of their lives depending on the age of children and professional roles. By leaving the country to pursue advanced degrees and assuming professional positions, they sought to break the pattern of women being primarily wives and mothers. Even though they were hesitant to call themselves feminists, models or leaders, the women administrators at UCR, in their individual attempts to reconcile the pushes and pulls of societal demands and professional desires, were creating alternatives in which forced choices of work or family were rejected in favor of more complex lives. The strength of their story lies in their very constructions of self as strong, active agents who were making a contribution to society, rather than as passive victims of a machista society. Herein lies the lesson these women offer to others. In many ways, their experience confirms the "universal patterns" noted by Eliou (1991); however, in other ways, Costa Rican women, like the Korean women studied by Johnsrud (1995), provide support for alternative conceptions of successful academic lives and the factors that influence those lives.

*An earlier version of this chapter was presented at the Annual Meeting of the American Educational Research Association, New Orleans, LA, April 8, 1994.

CHAPTER 35

ACADEMIC FEMINISM: LIVING THE CONTRADICTIONS

SUE MIDDLETON

Academic feminists are multiply marginal. As women, we are a minority among male academics; as women academics, we are anomalous among women and are seen as elitist by some grassroots feminist activists. As feminists, we are "other" to some women academics. As feminist academics teaching women's studies, we are associated with a vulnerable field of marginal status. The multiple positionings of academic feminists have been usefully framed by Nancy Fraser (1989):

> In relation to our academic disciplines, we function as the academic wing of an expert public. In relation to extra-academic social movements . . . we function as the expert wing of an oppositional public. In addition, many of us relate to still other publics. As teachers, we try to foster an emergent pedagogical counterculture. As faculty advisors, we try to provide guidance and lend legitimacy to radical student groups on our campuses. Finally, as critical public intellectuals, we try to inject our perspectives into whatever cultural or political public spheres we have access to. (p. xii)

This chapter explores the everyday working lives of feminist university teachers—the ways in which, in the various dimensions of our lives, "oppositional discourses and expert discourses intersect" (Fraser, 1989, p. xii). I use my own experiences as a teacher of "Women and Education" courses within a university as a case study of the politics of feminist knowledge in an educational institution.

Like many feminist courses, my "Women and Education" course is positioned in two undergraduate university programs: education and women's studies. This dual location brings women's studies students into a course that would otherwise contain only education students. As a teacher of and contributor to courses in both programs, I take my educational knowledge into classes in women's studies and bring my feminism into those in the education department. My feminism and my educational theories inform my public and private life outside the university, and my feminist community activities influence my curricula.

> Blurred boundaries; intersections; fluidities—ebbs and flows in time and space; harsh interruptions . . . these will not "write themselves" in tidy arguments. They will not follow linear paths, or submit to the ordered hierarchies of headings. The sociological voice is interrupted by "internal talk" (Noddings, 1991, p. 164). The logic of argument is disturbed by anger, laughter, pain. Across the screens of my reasoning drift the faces of students, the words of colleagues, reflections of the greening trees by the lake I pass on my walk from kitchen to classroom. . . . My typing fingers follow the driftings of consciousness, transfix in print scores of their tunes and cacophonies. Refusing to remain

---

Reprinted from *Educating Feminists: Life Histories and Pedagogies*, by Sue Middleton, 1993. Copyright © 1993 Teachers College Press.

in the "sensible emptiness" (Pagano, 1991, p. 193) of theory, they compose narratives, "tell stories" about my experience of "being a feminist academic."

"Telling stories" becomes a basis for educational theorizing. Life histories, biographies, autobiographies now form the basis for a growing literature in educational theory (Casey, 1988; Goodson, 1988: Goodson, 1992; Schaafsma, 1990; Witherell & Noddings, 1991).

I am composing a polyphonic score; a counterpoint of many voices. I speak as a teacher, a feminist activist, a sociologist, a politician, a "public intellectual," a citizen. You will hear "the ghosts of students past"[1] and the loud arias of sociologists. Sometimes the voices are solos; sometimes they sing in harmonies; sometimes they shout—a rebellious rabble. While some sing the scores of previous composers, others indulge in free improvisations.

An Encounter

It is a still morning—the birds are strangely silent. I try to think abstractly of the structuring of educational knowledge but find myself thinking of Joe—a student past, who will not stay out of sight in the shelved pages of my doctoral thesis. He takes over my thoughts. As Janet Miller (1990) has argued, "curriculum is centred within students' and teachers' biographies, histories, and social relationships" (p. 2).

Joe was Maori, of about my age, of working-class rural origins, and a primary school teacher. He was taking my multicultural course, a course I convened in the mid-1980s. The course was called "Teaching in Multicultural Settings." As a Pakeha, I felt competent to teach about the ethnocentrism and colonial power relations in which school knowledges are inscribed. However, I refused to teach about the experiences and perspectives of Maori and other cultural minorities. Consequently, I relied heavily on visiting Maori and other ethnic minority speakers. When I organized the course, I focused it on issues of racism and class oppression. I believed that as Pakeha and middle class, I was positioned within the oppressor class rather than the oppressed class in New Zealand society.

As a feminist, I was particularly concerned that Maori women's voices be heard among the visiting speakers and in the set readings, for Maori academic scholarship, like its Pakeha counterpart, has been seen as male dominated (Irwin, 1992b; Te Awekotuku, 1984). Within the Waikato region where I work, there were at that time many prominent Maori women educators. My educational and feminist networks gave me access to such women. Accordingly, my course included more women than men speakers. One student wrote in her end-of-course evaluation that "the high proportion of women speakers was unnecessary."

Apart from that, I was unaware that my feminism was showing in this course to any significant degree. However, no doubt, some students would have seen me as having a reputation as a feminist on campus. For example, for part of 1983, I was acting convenor of the women's studies program.

> Jo Anne Pagano says (1991), "I think we all have a tendency to fictionalize ourselves when we write about ourselves. Force is added to the impulse when autobiographical work will function in some judgmental scheme" (p. 194). These narratives, the stories I construct about my feminist university work, are brought into being by and within the academic power relations that are their object of inquiry. As "an academic book," this will be positioned in various "judgmental schemes." I choose carefully which feelings, thoughts, and information are to enter such public domains. My accounts are positioned and partial.

After several weeks of absence from class, Joe came to see me in my office. He had stayed away, he said, because my feminism had put him off at first. He had found it incomprehensible that I, as a Pakeha academic, could consider myself oppressed.[2]

> I wasn't talking about women in general. I mean I'm not uncomfortable with Maori women, and if they are more eloquent and more forceful and higher ranking in terms of society, that doesn't worry me at all. But what it was, what I was trying to tell you was, that being Pakeha as you were, and being in charge of the place, and the rangatira [leader] of the course.... What it did was remind me of certain things I learned in school. And the fact was that then, you know, there were girls who were white, pretty from the Pakeha point of view, dressed nicely, they ate nice lunches, and

they were successful in school. And the thing that I always remembered was that they would giggle at my, and my relations', and my friends' clumsiness in using the English language. And they would laugh at us when we were strapped because we didn't do our spelling or our maths or we didn't get enough right. We were walloped in front of them. This kind of an attitude, this kind of a feeling within me towards women, white women especially, has always been there. And when I hear feminists going on about how tough their lives are and being oppressed by men, I understand that, I agree. But they've got bloody higher chances than I had, and I'm a Maori man. Now, relate that to Maori culture, where a man is pretty well assured of a place or a dominant position, you know. And a woman too, but there are different criteria for measuring it.... I find it difficult to side with the radical elements. You know, it was sort of hard. I was thinking, "Goddamn it, here she is, she's running this thing and she is saying that women are being oppressed." And I'm thinking, "Goddamn it, she ought to have lived some of my life and see what it's like." That's what I was sort of trying to get at. I think, a bit of resentment on my part. Then I thought, "How stupid. I've just got to get along—why the hell—I've just got to get along there and learn what there is to learn." And so that's what I did. It was getting to the stage when I was having dreams about those days, and I knew it was coming from this course ... you know, school days, getting the strap ... and those girls giggling and laughing. And us boys ganging together and beating up some other poor person, or going and playing football and pumping the hell out of anyone we could get hold of. But you know, in that way I'm also very pleased to have confronted that problem and come to terms with it.

Without realizing it, I had taken my feminism into an education course. While I had tried to bring to the foreground issues of class and race, Joe had read me as a radical feminist who prioritized my own oppression as a woman. My presence as a Pakeha woman in a position of power in education had surfaced in his consciousness the taunts and pains inflicted in his school days by middle-class Pakeha girls.

As Patti Lather (1991) has argued, "rather than dismiss student resistance to our classroom practice as false consciousness," we should "explore what these resistances have to teach us about our own impositional tendencies" (p. 76). From Joe, I learned about some of the ways my teaching and my personality could be read. I had not wanted my Pakeha academic feminism to overshadow the horrors of racism. I decided that I would in the future position myself much more overtly with respect to issues of race and class at the beginning of all my courses so that students could deconstruct my teaching if they needed to. The autobiographical account—the archaeology of my pedagogy outlined in chapter 1 of this book—had its origins in such encounters.

The Politics of Academic Women's Studies

Pedagogies are created in institutions: preschools, schools, universities, and colleges. The institutional structures within which they come to form are influenced by the historical and political events, the material conditions, and the cultural contexts of their time and place. Pedagogies are rendered desirable and conceived of as possible within the political configurations of an institutional culture. Much of our work as academics involves analyzing and participating in the power relations of the institutions within which we write and teach. To explore this, I shall move beyond the personal by positioning myself within the disembodied conversations—the discourses—of curriculum theory. I speak for a while with my sociological voice.

To understand the positioning of women's studies within university structures, the work of the British sociologist Basil Bernstein is useful. Bernstein saw the organization of educational knowledge as patterned on two major "knowledge codes": "collection codes" and "integrated codes." He used the term "collection code" to refer to patterns of curriculum organization in which the contents of various academic subjects are insulated from one another through such organizational devices as compartmentalized timetabling, hierarchical subject-based departments, and subject specialization among teachers. Conversely, the term "integrated code" refers to curricula in which boundaries between contents or disciplines are blurred. The teaching is often done by staff from a number of different departments. Many university women's studies programs share the characteristics of an integrated code.

According to Bernstein (1971), the dominant knowledge code in modern secondary schools and universities is the collection code, in which "knowledge... is private property with its own power structure and market situation" (p. 56). Collection codes structure collegial relationships—within and between disciplines and departments—in hierarchical, encapsulated, and competitive ways.

> Where knowledge is regulated through a collection code, the knowledge is organised and distributed through a series of well-insulated subject hierarchies. Such a structure points to oligarchic control of the institution, through formal and informal meetings of heads of department with the head or principal of the institution. Thus, senior staff will have strong horizontal work relationships (that is, with their peers in other subject hierarchies) and strong vertical work relationships within their own department. However, junior staff are likely to have only vertical (within the subject hierarchy) allegiances and work relationships. (p. 61)

Sociologists and historians of the curriculum have argued that the existing collection code classification of educational knowledge into subjects in universities reflects the power struggles of groups of male academics as much as any epistemological categorization of academic knowledge (Arnot, 1982; Bernstein, 1971; Coyner, 1983; Goodson, 1988; Spender, 1981; Spender, 1982a). Due to historical circumstances, some fields of study have constructed a power base and, because they are represented at the higher levels of decision making, can arrest the development of new subjects that might compete with them for scarce resources.

In contrast, integrated code subjects such as women's studies are administered by "a committee system of staff... which will perform monitoring functions" (Bernstein, 1971, p. 65). In contrast to subjects structured according to the hierarchies of a collection-coded discipline, integrated code subjects such as women's studies are often not represented directly at the most senior levels of decision making. As Bernstein described it, the administrative anomaly of an integrated code within an institution structured according to a collection code creates "a type of organizational system that encourages gossip, intrigue, and a conspiracy theory about the workings of the organization, as both the administration and the acts of teaching are invisible to the majority of the staff" (p. 61). I shall use this model as a framework for a brief discussion of the changing institutional structures and political dynamics in which my teaching of "Women and Education" takes place.

The women's studies program to which my course contributes began as one course in 1974 (Ritchie, 1982; Seymour, 1976). By 1981, the year I began to contribute to the program, it had grown to a total of six undergraduate courses. Four of these, including "Women and Education" were subject based and taught from their host departments. Two were interdisciplinary and team-taught by women from several departments. Cross-listing meant that students could take departmental courses such as "Women and Education" as part of their women's studies package (at that time not a major, but only a minor for a social science degree).

Women's studies was administered and coordinated by a voluntary committee on women's studies, which included students and other interested members of the university feminist community, as well as those who taught the various courses. The majority of the teachers were untenured, and during one financial crisis in the institution, 46% of the women academics, including the majority of the feminists on the faculty, were threatened with termination of their contracts.[3] With no departmental structure or staffing of its own, the program was continually at risk. It was not formally represented at the higher levels of decision making and survived largely through the lobbying of senior staff by junior staff. At this time, the information networks among the program's feminist staff and students were riddled with the gossip, intrigue, and conspiracy theories identified by Bernstein as characteristic of the politics of integrated codes within hierarchical collection-coded institutions.

These institutional fragmentations were superimposed on a feminist movement whose boundaries were not confined within the academy. Like its counterparts elsewhere,

Waikato's women's studies program was organic to various feminist communities outside the university gates. Although individuals were positioned unequally within the university as teachers and students, outside the university in various feminist organizations, networks, and activities, we were positioned differently in relation to one another—as coworkers, as activists, and as friends.

In Hamilton, New Zealand, as in many university cities elsewhere, academic women's studies was cultivated in the soils of wider feminist movements and debates. For example, the evolution of our program took place in an environment of local and international debates about the place of feminist knowledge in the academy. Many liberal feminists supported the development of university programs in women's studies as a way of encouraging women into academic scholarship and of combating sexism within other disciplines (Bernard, 1973; Tobias, 1978.) Some radical feminists, however, criticized the institutionalization of women's studies courses in an academic context, arguing that the setting up of an elite hierarchy of feminist "experts" defeated one of the objects of feminism, which was to challenge the hierarchical structuring of academic knowledge (Rich, 1976). As Dale Spender (1982a) argued:

> ... feminists ... seek an end to hierarchies and standards, as they have been constructed, on the grounds that they are *not* an inherent part of learning, but of a stratified society ... in the current context where a body of knowledge is rapidly becoming available, and where the possibility of "transmission" exists—with all its concomitant attributes of hierarchies and competition—it may be very important for feminism to focus on past achievements and to keep the cooperative model in mind, for it could begin to get "lost" as feminism enters institutions. (p. 169)

The 1970s and early 1980s saw heated debates among feminists on this question. While liberal feminists pressured women to succeed in terms of the institution, separatists accused those who did so of becoming coopted agents of the male power elite. Academic feminists were accused of exploiting the movement to gain privileges.

As feminist university teachers, we were positioned inside the feminist educational theories and debates that were the objects of our curriculum. It became impossible to separate content from form. The traditional divisions identified in curriculum theory—the binary oppositions between the overt and covert and between intentional and hidden dimensions of curricula—collapsed.

Feminists in a Classroom

When I started "Women and Education" in 1981, it was the only university course of its type in the country. As I explained in chapter 2, to gain credibility for the course and to have it accepted as a part of the degree requirements, I structured it as a conventional academic discipline. The first half of the course consisted of an introduction to the typologies of feminist educational theories and was taught as a guided reading program. Classes took the form of prepared discussions of the set material and corresponding exercises in the study guide. The guided reading section of the course was assessed by an essay and an open book test. Although much of the content of this part of the course was radical, the format was in the liberal mode of initiation into a body of theory and did not in itself challenge the dominant style of university teaching (Hirst, 1975; Peters, 1966). Students were required to read and critique examples of writings that exemplified conservative (e.g., biologically determinist) perspectives, liberal perspectives, Marxist, radical feminist, Maori, and socialist-feminist perspectives on women's education.

This approach, I believed, would allow students of all backgrounds and persuasions to work on developing, stating, refining, and critiquing their own theoretical positions. The majority were education students—either teachers in training or experienced teachers. These students had a knowledge of schools, some familiarity with educational theory, and maybe little knowledge of or interest in feminism. Some were suspicious of or opposed to feminist ideas. Conversely, some of the women's studies students who were coming in from other disciplines may have previously given little thought to educational theory or processes but had some prior knowledge of feminist history and ideas and had become very interested in women's issues. Several of the women's studies students had strong radical feminist theoretical beliefs and political agendas. Within the class, conflicts developed between the nonfeminist/liberal students and those who were passionately converted to radical and separatist feminism. Such students became impatient with what they saw as retracing their steps by being required to work through liberal and Marxist concepts, which they had long ago rejected.

The second part of the "Women and Education" course was designed to encourage students to state their own theoretical positions and to use these to analyze an aspect of women's education that was of particular relevance to them: their own or their children's educational experiences, a political project with which they were involved, and an aspect of education policy. Radical students who were members of feminist collectives could then include theoretical analyses and documentation of their own political activities on and off campus. Several feminist students used this opportunity to challenge the course and my teaching of it as hierarchical and antifeminist.

I quote from the essay of one such student—I shall call her Diane:

> The very act of writing this essay involves me, as a radical feminist, in a series of contradictions. Firstly, I am required to present a critique of my university education by presenting a piece of work in what I see as a patriarchal academic mode—that is, an essay which requires that I legitimize my own experience by providing "adequate referencing." I am obliged to validate my experience by quoting the writing of those who have "succeeded" in the very institutions that I am attacking, and therefore have enough academic "clout" to earn credibility and the privilege of access to publishing resources. Furthermore, I had a limited choice of topic for presentation and the end product is subject to assessment by a person placed above me in a hierarchical system, who will "grade" it and rank me on a success/failure scale using "standards" which I had no hand in setting. Paradoxically, in order to challenge the structure, value systems, and operation of the university, I am forced to use those very forms which I find distasteful and alien—result: academic schizophrenia.

As a student and an intellectual, Diane was positioned inside the academy. As a radical feminist, she positioned herself outside it. Because I was a power figure—the designer, selector, and assessor of her knowledge—Diane positioned herself in relation to me as an antagonist.

Within the class that year, debates took place between the liberal and radical feminist students. These are exemplified in the following excerpt from a tape-recorded class evaluation at the end of the course:

CATHERINE: Assessment implies that there is a standard, that you either fail or you win.
TANYA: I agree, but the university just won't allow a course without assessment.
JOANNE: Well, then, it's not a feminist course, and women's studies is just part of the status quo and women's studies is no challenge to the establishment.
BETTY: Are you saying that the course is mere tokenism then?
JOANNE: I'm saying that it's maintaining the status quo.
BETTY: What do you suggest?
JOANNE: What do I suggest? Well I don't think that real feminist women's studies can happen in the university.
BETTY: Where do you think it could happen?
JOANNE: I think it happens "out there" in consciousness-raising groups, in informal groups.
AMY: Can I come in? Even though I largely agree with you that things can be done better, and differently, and more feminist-oriented outside the university, don't you think it's also good that there's something here within the institution?
SANDRA: There's a lot of people here that probably wouldn't have been exposed to it otherwise.
MARY: I think that the course is important and I think that it should be within the university. What goes on outside, and this comes down again to the thing about what we mean by being educated ... I hope that it doesn't stop here, that it's something that goes on all the time. All Sue is doing is passing on what she has learned, what she has gathered, to us, and we can go further.

But for me Sue has got the know-how, because she's been in contact with more of the research, etcetera, etcetera, that's been done than you and I have. I know that we could go to the library and we could look up "feminism" and we could look up the various subsections and we could read them, but I think that with a course, we're all different I know, but with a course we're forced to look at certain readings which we mightn't do otherwise on our own. I'm only pointing out why I think it's important that we have a leader.

JOANNE: That you have a leader.

BETTY: Yes, that I need a leader.

Like the feminist students who were criticizing academic women's studies, I was positioned both inside and outside the dominant discourses of my discipline. At the time, I, too, was struggling for legitimacy in order to survive in the academy. The legitimacy, status, and continuation of the "Women and Education" course was by no means assured. These were the years in which I was drawing my map of feminist educational theories—struggling to make a discipline that would be sufficiently acceptable to gain legitimacy within the degree structure. I was also designing a feminist doctoral thesis under two male supervisors. I was a very recent recruit to university teaching—a person who, in younger days, would never have dreamed that an academic career was possible. Like many women academics, I felt shaky, insecure in my role as an expert, disbelieving in my right to teach and my authority (Aisenberg & Harrington, 1988). I was working in a small city; I needed the personal and professional support of local feminist networks.

The conflict I have described was a minor incident. But there were many other much more painful conflicts among campus feminists. Feminist writings and feminist folklore record numerous examples of the ways in which, in the early 1980s, feminists who were teaching and studying in universities were torn apart during institutional conflicts. Women were pulled by divided loyalties and found themselves positioned on opposite sides during struggles over assessment (Fletcher, 1991), appointments and tenure, and sexual harassment. We had believed in the solidarity of sisterhood (Jones & Guy, 1992). Sisterhood shattered into jagged splinters.

Feminism and Pedagogy

I was then, as I do now, designing my curriculum with two pedagogical principles in mind: the importance of teaching about existing feminist educational theories and research and the importance of students' personal knowledge and experiences as a grounding for their own educational theories and strategies. I wanted my students to have available to them some theoretical tools with which to craft their understandings of experiences—to focus also, as Maxine Greene (1988) has expressed it, "on the range of human intelligences, the multiple layers of language and symbol systems available for ordering experience and making sense of the lived world" (p. 125).

As discussed previously, many feminist writers, especially those of radical feminist persuasions, have argued that a feminist pedagogy is a student-centered pedagogy that emphasizes the educational worthwhileness of using students' personal experiences as a basis for learning. As received knowledge, theories—even feminist theories—can become "conceptual imperialism" (Stanley & Wise, 1983). Some have argued that certain formal teaching techniques, such as imparting knowledge through top-down methods such as formal lecturing, is inherently unfeminist. Previous discussions of such questions can be usefully grouped into three major sets of arguments: political, empirical, and psychological.

Political rationales are derived from various versions of the consciousness-raising model, which developed in the early phases of the second wave of feminism. Consciousness raising originated in grassroots settings and has been adapted for more academic situations. It was a technique of finding words for what Betty Friedan (1963) described as "problems with no names," as women met in informal groups to share their "sense of something wrong" (Mitchell, 1973) with their experiences as women in particular (usually middle-class, white, Western, and urban) settings. It was a way of making knowledge where no prior written records remained (Spender, 1978, 1981).

Ann Foreman (1977) described consciousness raising as a process in which women learn

> to look at themselves through their own eyes rather than through those of men ... it is the ... often painful process of breaking through the experience of femininity. By discussing and comparing their individual experiences, women develop an understanding of the emotional structures of their dependency (p. 151).

Critics argued that within this framework, experience was conceptualized as unproblematic: It was assumed that pure experience could be described and was in and of itself valid knowledge. A politics grounded in consciousness raising rested on women's experiences to provide a basis for all oppositional women's knowledge and feminist culture. Such assumptions, said socialist feminists, rendered invisible the material conditions and power relations of the wider capitalist/patriarchal society that structured such experiences. For example, Sheila Rowbotham (1973) wrote that "the problem created by simply rejecting everything that is, and inverting male values to make a female culture out of everything not male is that the distortions of oppression are perpetuated" (p. ix). Juliet Mitchell (1973) commented that "the rise of the oppressed should not be a glorification of oppressed characteristics" (p. 178). What was needed, they argued, were historical and materialist analyses that would contextualize women's experiences within the wider power dynamics in which they had come to form. The teaching of theory within this perspective was an aid to liberation.

Although some have grounded feminists' preferences for student-centered pedagogies in political imperatives, others have seen these primarily as a historical fact. Empirical research supports the claim that women teachers—to a greater degree than men teachers—prefer the pedagogies that are based on students' personal knowledge. For example, in a study of academic women in Massachusetts, Nadya Aisenberg and Mona Harrington (1988) noted a tendency for women's scholarship in their various disciplines to focus "on the relation of actual daily experience to larger social or moral patterns" (p. 94). Similarly, all of the feminist school teachers in Kathleen Weiler's (1988) study "mentioned the value of nurturance and caring in themselves and their work-values that are emphasized as positive aspects of women's experience...." (p. 78). The Catholic religious and Jewish women in Kathleen Casey's thesis on feminist teachers spoke of "a genuine care of children" as their major motivation for becoming teachers; a "kind of attachment," argues Casey, that "has enormous potential for progressive action" (1988, p. 225). The New Zealand feminist teachers in my own study (see chapter 4) expressed similar concerns.

Marxists, sociologists, and socialist feminists have sought explanations in the historical and material conditions of women's work (Bernstein, 1975; May, 1992a). Women teachers have worked disproportionately with infants and younger children, but men have worked disproportionately with adolescents closer to the public world of work. Various forms of progressivism in which students make choices and express themselves freely have taken root more readily in the lower-status feminine world of early childhood education than they have in the higher-status masculine domain of formal secondary and higher education levels.

A third set of writers have drawn on psychological theories, such as object relations (Chodorow, 1978; Gilligan, 1982), to argue that student-centered pedagogies are grounded in an inherently feminine epistemology (Grumet, 1988). Such writers have argued that in Western cultures, from infancy, masculine identities are defined through separation from the mother and that adult men are often threatened by intimacy and have difficulty with personal relationships. In contrast, from infancy, female gender identity is defined through attachment (identification with the mother); many adult women feel threatened by separation and have problems with individuation. According to Carol Gilligan (1982), these distinctive developmental patterns, which result from the fact that it is women who are the primary care givers of infants, predispose men toward abstraction ("a morality of rights or fairness") and women toward connectedness ("an ethic of responsibility based on equity, the recognition of differences in need" [p. 164]).

Drawing on such object relations theories, radical feminist curriculum theorists such as Madeleine Grumet see feminists' espousal of student-centered pedagogies as expressions of women's essential femininity. As teachers, women draw their "experiences of reproduction and nurturance into the epistemological systems and curricular forms that constitute the discourse and practice of public education" (Grumet, 1988, p. 3). Concerns with what Nel Noddings (1991) calls "caring and interpersonal reasoning" structure such feminist, or women-centered, curricula.

If we leave aside some major criticisms that have been made of the essentialism of these positions (Grosz, 1990; Sayers, 1986), these positions do lend support to the previous arguments that, for a variety of reasons, many women teachers place great emphasis in their classes on students' personal experiences and knowledge. This preference for student-centered pedagogies has been made prescriptive in much feminist educational writing (Bowles & Klein, 1983; Culley & Portuges, 1985). Such approaches are in contradiction to the dominant and accepted teaching styles in a university, and as many feminist writers have observed, feminists' emphasis on the personal in teaching and research has brought about accusations of unscholarliness (see chapters 1 and 2). My own pedagogy, as outlined in this book, has been an attempt to weave together the personal, the theoretical, and the political.

The various student-centered pedagogies in which personal experiences can be shared are difficult in introductory courses, which may contain hundreds of students. Furthermore, continuity and intimacy between teachers and students are particularly difficult in a team-teaching situation. Many introductory women's studies courses take the form of a formal lecture with a succession of different lecturers followed by small tutorial discussion groups. Somewhat ironically, such a structure is imposed by the collective/cooperative/cross-departmental structures that are characteristic of an integrated knowledge code. As Bernstein has explained (1971):

> Integrated codes will, at the level of the teachers, probably create homogeneity in teaching practice ... integrated codes will reduce the discretion of the teacher in direct relation to the strength of the integrated code (number of teachers coordinated by the code). (p. 60)

Two Lectures

My "Women and Education" course (department based within the dominant collection knowledge code) permits me great autonomy as a teacher. However, my occasional contributions to the large, core women's studies courses (interdepartmental within the subordinate integrated knowledge code) take the form of formal lectures. On the podium, facing the serried rows of students, I am positioned as an expert.

> When I was a student in the 1960s, lecturing seemed such a tidy activity. Lecturers read books, summarized their contents, wrote neat notes, and read them to the students. . . . Feminist knowledge resists such tidiness. It will not stay encapsulated between the covers of books, it will not follow the neat meanderings of rationally argued lecture notes. The waters of "women's everyday lives" leak onto the pages. "Writing a women's studies lecture" is to confluence the streams in our experience that are diverted and dammed by conventional academic practices.

On August 7, 1987, I was to give a lecture on "Marxism and feminism" to the first-year-level introductory feminist theory class taught within the Centre for Women's Studies. I was invited to give this lecture because of my background in Marxist theory and my espoused socialist feminist perspective.

The night before this lecture, I had been distracted from its preparation by an item on the television. Some months previously, feminist women had published an article in an upmarket Auckland magazine in which they had argued that at a major Auckland public hospital, women diagnosed as having carcinoma in situ had been given unconventional treatments as part of their doctors' medical research (Coney & Bunkle, 1987). The women had not been told that they were in research or that their treatments were unconventional or controversial. Several of the women had developed full-blown uterine cancers and subsequently died. The television report that night concerned the outcomes of an official inquiry into the matter.

> On the night of August 6, 1987—the night of the television report, and the night before my lecture on Marxism and feminism—I

dreamed I was standing at an inquiry desk in a large, busy hospital. I had been running and was out of breath. I was struggling to hold onto a huge pile of "dangerous information," which kept growing larger and larger. I felt anxious that it not get into the wrong hands—it was dangerous to women and must only be given to those who recognised this and who were sufficiently concerned about it to try and stop it. As I stood there, pleading with the chaotically indifferent people behind the desk, the pile kept growing, engulfing me—bits began blowing away in a sudden crescendoing wind.... Then I found myself in a university lecture theatre about to give the lecture on Marxism and feminism. On the overhead projector I placed a transparency. But it was not the one I had prepared, with its typed quotations from *Capital* and *The German Ideology*. Instead, it was a line drawing—an outline—of the body of a naked woman. Where her breasts should have been was a gaping hole, emerging from which was a giant parrot's beak. I woke suddenly—fearful, anxious....

Like any account of a remembered dream, this one is open to multiple readings. At the time, I analyzed it as follows.[4] I saw it as signifying my experiencing of deep contradictions: a blurring of conventional boundaries between sexuality and intellectuality, between good and bad images of female sexuality, and between feminist sexual politics and the fundamental liberal freedom of access to knowledge and information. I had gone to sleep thinking about and feeling several things: anxiety about my unprepared lecture and joy and grief at the outcome of the inquiry into the unfortunate experiment at National Women's Hospital. Like my dream, this inquiry had concerned issues of sexuality, power, and knowledge. The inquiry had shown that women had died as a result of being denied information about their own bodies; knowledge about their disease (carcinoma in situ) had been alienated from them, appropriated by doctors as *their* intellectual property as data for experimental purposes.

A few days before having this dream, I had returned from what was my second sitting of the Indecent Publications Tribunal in Wellington. In preparation, I had read 4 books and 117 pornographic magazines. In the dream, pornographic images had intruded into my intellectual discourse—in this instance, Marxist theory. The woman's body on the screen was mutilated—as in pornography, women's bodies are symbolically mutilated and distorted.

As a member of the Indecent Publications Tribunal, I act as what Nancy Fraser (1989) described as a "critical public intellectual" (p. xii). My expertise—my professional knowledge as an educator who had specialized in women's issues—was a reason for my nomination by my local member of Parliament and my subsequent selection by the minister of justice during the now-displaced Labour government's administration.

The Indecent Publications Tribunal consists of four members of the public plus a barrister of at least 7 years' standing as chair. We work within the Ministry of Justice. Our statutory role is to categorize sexually explicit and/or violent printed materials according to legal criteria as specified in the Indecent Publications Act of 1963. Indecent, as defined in the act (section 2), "includes describing, depicting, expressing, or otherwise dealing with matters of sex, horror, crime, cruelty, or violence in a manner that is injurious to the public good."

Printed materials that come within the terms of the act are regulated and monitored through banning or classifying in ways designed to limit their availability to certain classes of persons—for example, persons aged 18 and over. The tribunal, then, is an ideological state apparatus backed by the coercive powers of the justice system (Althusser, 1971). Like a court, it often makes decisions on grounds of precedent—former decisions often reached by former tribunal members.

Having official, public responsibility for deciding what constitutes injury to the public good has been work that has embodied profound contradictions in both the professional and the personal dimensions of my life. It has affected me intellectually and emotionally at both conscious and unconscious levels. The problems it poses—intellectual, emotional, and political—have seeped into the content of my teaching.

Shortly after I was appointed,[5] I was invited to give a lecture to a second-year education course: "Education and the Individual." The students had been studying Freud under the guidance of two of my male colleagues—one a philosopher, the other a psychologist.

The topic they had invited me in to speak about was "Psychoanalysis, Sexuality, and Feminism." My reading in this field had been stimulated by my struggle with issues pertaining to pornography. I thought that psychoanalytic theories would be a useful aid to understanding this because the object of psychoanalysis as a mode of inquiry is the understanding of human sexuality and the ways its repression generates dreams, fantasies, wishes and desires—as well as neuroses and more severe mental disorders. Feminist readings of psychoanalytic materials—such as Juliet Mitchell's (1974) reading—offered ways of understanding male sexual fantasies as they have been constituted within patriarchal/capitalist cultures. Pornography depicts selected male sexual fantasies.

In my lecture, I discussed Lacan's view that Freud had intended the phenomena of penis envy and castration anxiety—central to the Oedipal drama—to be read in symbolic rather than literally biological terms (Grosz, 1989; Mitchell & Rose, 1982; Sayers, 1986). For Lacanians, the phallus is the privileged signifier of patriarchal cultures. To illustrate the phallic symbol, I screened slides made from photographs in so-called soft-porn magazines—magazines that I had supported some weeks previously in gaining R18 classifications and that could as a result be purchased at news stands throughout the country. In the clinical sterility of a university lecture theater, what had appeared to me in the context of hundreds of other pornographic images as relatively harmless now appeared as symbolic rape.

> Two of the slides were taken from a series of colour photos—a striptease sequence, which was a common format in some of the magazines. The model is called "Ruth." She is a scientist, in her laboratory, wearing a white coat. Beside her, on the bench, is a microscope and a flask. Frame by frame, she removes her clothes, until she is lying naked on the hard wooden bench. In one shot, the cold steel shaft of the microscope points parallel to her vagina—a symbolic erection. In the final shot, she lies prostrate, clasping over her belly a round glass flask full of liquid.
>
> There in the lecture room, the image was horrific. As a scientist, "Ruth" was a power-figure, clad in the white coat of authority. An intellectual. The striptease reduces her to "just another fuck." A receptacle for sperm. A toilet.
>
> The phallic symbol of the microscope and the uterine symbol of the filled flask remind me of Marion Cotton—a New Zealand woman who was raped with broken bottles until she died.

But certain male colleagues would tell me this is "all in my head." What's wrong with showing a scientist as sexy? At one tribunal hearing, a feminist member of the tribunal questioned a witness about a striptease sequence photographed in a rubbish tip—"the garbage man's daughter." Did this not imply that women were rubbish? He argued that the photographs did not imply this to him. Rather, they embodied a contradiction: how could anything so beautiful be found in a place like this?

The Rational Individual: Living the Contradictions

Within the feminist classroom—even in the context of a formal lecture—the public domains of theory collide with the personal worlds of experience. Such collisions also occur in other spaces in the institution: in institutional relations outside the classroom setting. I have found myself and my censoring activities becoming objects of prurient interest for some male colleagues and associates. There's a covert sniggering from some of the men. I get lots of "Can I help you read the books?" nudge, wink. On one such occasion, I answered that I would very much appreciate the man's assistance in advising me how to categorize a huge pile of gay men's magazines and then proceeded to describe the penises in these pictures. He did not pursue the matter. There is a feeling of being contaminated, polluted, or unclean as a result of being on this tribunal. Some people have commented to me that I should not have accepted this job. It's not a nice thing to do. Nice girls don't. The materials become a secret—I become furtive, anxious about violations of my private spaces. I have had to develop strategies for dealing with such invasions.

The magazines arrive in the early mornings by courier—flung onto the front porch with a loud thud around 6.00 AM, which is one of my favorite times of the day. I am usually reading or writing. The arrival of the material at this hour violates my privacy, my intellectual morning calm. I groan when I hear the pack arrive. Twenty volumes devoted, for example, to rubber or vinyl fetish, sodomy, "big tits," or spanking hold the promise only of monotony, subterfuge, and the suspension of intellectual engagement in the act of reading.

When and where to read the magazines became a problem. My daughter has been told that the courier packs contain pornography, why I read it, and what I feel about it. I have told her that it mainly presents images of women as objects, not as people. I used to but no longer read at work in my office behind locked doors. It would be awkward to be caught in the act by students and some of my more conservative colleagues. Once opened, the packs become a problem. It's as if they emit a foul gas. I hide the opened packs. I don't want children coming across them. Nor do I want my office at work or my study at home—my spaces—becoming arenas of prurient interest. I feel unclean after reading some of this material. I need to bathe.

As an intellectual, I am expected to make rational judgments about pornography. But it is a genre designed to cater to the irrational—the sexual fantasies, desires, and fetishes that lie deep in the mysteries of the unconscious. As such, they affect the intellectual reader as well as the prurient consumer for whom they are designed.

As a feminist and a censor, I straddle the contradictions within Western constructions of the individual: between the rational and the sexual dimensions of experience. Such contradictions have been usefully explored by some postmodernist feminists (Fraser, 1989; Lather, 1991; Nicholson, 1990a; Weedon, 1987). Drawing on Derrida and other deconstructionists, these writers have argued that the theoretical apparatuses available to Western scholars bifurcate consciousness (D. Smith, 1987) and create splits between reason and passion, logic and emotion, the intellectual and the sensual/sexual dimensions of human existence. Such binary oppositions, they argue, are hierarchical: The first term in the dualisms I have listed here is privileged over the second. Within modern conceptualizations of the individual, reason must rule over emotion. From my positioning as a censor—from within the apparatus of ruling—I must make rational judgments about the permissibility of certain forms of erotic discourse.

Generations of feminist philosophers have studied the Western liberal ideal of the rationally autonomous individual as a male construction (Eisenstein, 1981; Fraser, 1989; Martin, 1987; Vetterling-Braggin et al., 1977). For example, in 1792, Mary Wollstonecraft (1792/1978) criticized the male Enlightenment social philosophers of her time—in particular, Rousseau—for having a model of reason that was socially constructed by them as unattainable by women. Women, these philosophies argued, were intellectually inferior by nature and could therefore justifiably be denied full citizenship. They were creatures of passion whose education must teach them purity and ways of making themselves pleasing to men. But, like the male liberals of their day, first-wave liberal feminists believed that civilization rested on the rule of reason over passion. Women, they argued, lacked equal reasoning power only because they had been denied adequate education. Only this would enable them to play an equal part with men in public life (Mill, 1869/1983).

Liberal, including liberal feminist, theories have had difficulty accommodating human sexuality. As Engels (1891/1971) argued in the 19th century, under capitalism, men could live by a double standard. Their wives, through monogamous fidelity, would ensure the reproduction of the family and the rightful inheritance of property. A sexual underclass of women—hidden from public recognition—could service their sexual pleasures. Women were thereby divided into classes of good women and bad women—a bifurcation that structures women's lives today. Intellectual (rational) women were faced with several options: to deny their sexuality (an asexual spinsterhood), to become respectable wives and mothers (abandoning careers or subordinating these to the demands and desires of family members), or to become bohemian (unrespectable) members of an intellectual/artistic demimonde.

Contemporary liberal discourses such as those of the New Right (see chapters 1 and 6) constitute the individual—the citizen in modern states—as primarily rational, competitive, and engaged in the pursuit of self-interest. Like previous liberal theories, these cannot accommodate female sexuality. Bad sex is to be controlled through censorship (the imposition of rational criteria). However, even good sex for women—reproductive heterosexuality within a stable relationship—falls outside modern liberal constructions of the individual (Martin, 1982, 1987).

In 1987—when I was writing the lectures discussed earlier—I was, like many of my academic colleagues, reading the vast number of government and departmental reports that were being produced with alarming rapidity as part of the restructuring of education. As critical public intellectuals, we wrote academic critiques, submissions to select committees, and letters to ministers and officials. As part of a collaborative project, I undertook a feminist reading of the New Zealand Treasury's briefing papers on education (Lauder, Middleton, Boston, & Wylie, 1988). In the Treasury's (1987) 400-page report—a New Right analysis of education as a private commodity—I found the following statement:

> The question of equitable access to childcare for working mothers is essentially one of public policy—whether affirmative action is required to assist the life-chances of women. The assumption is not just that the benefits of child-rearing do not compensate for the disadvantages from what would be (without the compensation) the result of *an irrational desire to have children*. Or, in the case of unplanned children, that the public should compensate parents for the unexpected net loss. The validity of these assumptions will not be self-evident to all, and depends largely on conclusions reached about the degree of community responsibility for having children. (p. 57) (Emphasis mine)

Within this and other market-liberal (New Right economic) texts, motherhood—legitimate female reproductive heterosexuality—is construed as contradictory to the idea of the citizen—the rationally autonomous individual. According to the Treasury papers, the rational individual competes in the marketplace, and having children is an irrational decision because it prevents this. At the same time, women's unpaid work in the family is viewed as an essential part of their children's education. Women who wish to work outside the home are seen as endangering their children's well-being. As individuals competing in self-interest, mothers and children are locked in conflict (Middleton, 1990a). As in pornography, women are considered in opposition to the masculine ideal of individualized, competitive, and autonomous rationality. Only men—and asexual women—can be the rationally autonomous subjects that such versions of liberalism demand.

Conclusion

As a woman, as a public intellectual, as a university teacher/researcher/writer, and as a feminist, I am positioned inside the contradictions in liberal constructions of the individual. In my teaching about women and education, I seek to deconstruct the androcentrism of major educational theories, including those that have informed recent educational restructuring policy. I also aim to show students how we are positioned inside what we are studying. The positionings of my students within the various nonfeminist and feminist discourses of women's education will be addressed in the following chapters.

Notes

1. With apologies to Charles Dickens, *A Christmas Carol*.
2. After this conversation, I asked Joe if he would be willing to be interviewed as part of my ongoing research into feminist and antiracist teaching. He agreed and came to my office on another occasion to make the tape from which this quotation has been extracted.
3. Details of this event, and of a fuller sociological analysis of the Waikato University women's studies program, are in Middleton (1987a). The original analysis of untenured staff was done in collaboration with Logan Moss and other members of the untenured staff support group.
4. This analysis was brought into being by a request from Allanah Ryan of Massey University. As editor of *Sites*, an interdisciplinary journal, she asked me to write about my experiences on the Indecent Publications Tribunal for a special issue on the role of critical intellectuals in New Zealand society. The paper appeared in the summer 1988 issue of *Sites* (Middleton, 1988a).
5. My appointment is for 5 years; at the time of writing, I have completed 4 years of service. I am now the longest-serving member on the tribunal. I have seen changes not only in personnel but also in the criteria on which decisions are made. I have therefore played a part in changing the precedents for legal decision-making. This will be a topic for a future analysis.

Part V

Feminist Pedagogy and Curriculum Transformation

CHAPTER 36

CHALLENGING THE TRADITIONAL CURRICULUM

MARILYN JACOBY BOXER

Questioning The Content Of Higher Education

Florence Howe has characterized the women's studies movement as the third stage in a long encounter of American women with higher education. In the eighteenth century no institution for higher learning in the United States admitted women to its student body. In the early national period, following what the historian Linda Kerber labels "the great debate over the capacities of women's minds," women sought to gain admittance to seminaries and colleges where they were likely to be offered a separate course of study for "ladies." In the late nineteenth century, they demanded access to the "men's curriculum," a claim that was posed with special intensity at newly founded women's colleges and was followed by an extended period of putative "co-education" in the many institutions that increasingly accepted students of both sexes. Several generations of women both took and taught the men's curriculum, believing all the while in what Howe terms the "myths of coeducation." Quoting the late historian Joan Kelly, Howe notes the phenomenon of a "new double vision" (with one eye seeing men, and the other seeing women) that in the late 1960s and 1970s led a more radical generation to challenge the content of what they now discerned to be "men's studies." In this third period, they demanded fundamental change in the courses and curricula that reinforced stereotypes about, and supported continuing discrimination against, women by perpetuating misinformation about and ignorance of women's history, lives, and perspectives. To remedy the flaws and fill the gaps, they created women's studies.[1]

In retrospect, the initial strategy of demanding terminology, topics, and even whole courses inclusive of women seems more modest than militant. As Annette Kolodny points out with reference to literary criticism, feminists were simply seeking "an honored berth on that ongoing intellectual journey." However, as the new converts peered into car after car, they found what they saw disturbing. Confirming Kelly's findings, they observed that sometimes women were missing altogether, sometimes women appeared only in images that reflected men's perspectives, and sometimes women's activities and everything considered feminine were devalued. But soon, traveling beyond rediscovered foremothers and asking what women had done in the male-defined world, they began to formulate new questions. As Elisabeth Young-Bruehl points out, they "made a revolution by adding to the query, What do women want? the question, How and by whom have women's wants been determined? It is one thing, for example, when a psychological study is con-

---

Reprinted from *When Women Ask the Questions: Creating Women's Studies in America*, by Marilyn Jacoby Boxer, 1998. Copyright © 1998 Johns Hopkins University Press.

ducted to try to assess differences between women and men, and quite another when the assumptions—the perceptual and conceptual biases—that shape such a study are themselves the object of study." In essence, the new women thinkers asked, Who's driving this train, where is it going, and why? Almost half a century after Virginia Woolf's famous query about the destination of the "procession of educated men," scholars in women's studies began to question whether they wanted only to join the parade or also to change its route and objective.[2] They questioned virtually everything about higher education.

The development of women's studies demonstrates the truth in the observation that "questions are instruments of perception." The process of challenging the "men's curriculum" began with new questions, which led to a search for new sources, new methods, new definitions, and new interpretations. In discipline after discipline, feminist scholars, mostly but not exclusively women, have applied the tools provided by the "masters" who trained them to examine the contents and structure of "the master's house." While Audre Lorde argued that "the master's tools will never dismantle the master's house," feminist scholars have wielded the instruments with sufficient skill to make a major impact on the academy. Though hardly a dismantling, refurnishing if not remodeling is well under way. Thousands of articles have been published in both disciplinary and interdisciplinary journals and in anthologies issued by numerous university and trade publishers. Large numbers of books have appeared, and virtually every scholarly press now promotes a women's (and gender) studies list. The sheer volume of publications suggests the impressive dimensions of the academic feminist enterprise and, to quote the subtitle of one volume, "the difference it makes."[3]

In that volume's lead essay on that "difference," Patricia Meyer Spacks discusses how Jane Austen was portrayed and the way in which Austen's work was assessed before and after the emergence of feminist criticism. She begins with a 1961 essay, "Jane Austen: A Depreciation," whose author observed Austen's neglect of the great events of history and pronounced her ideals to be "irredeemably humdrum" and her "ethical standards . . . monotonously subdued," presumably to match her "so narrowly and so contentedly confined" experience. Not quite two decades later, critics were pointing to Austen's "revolutionary" contribution, citing the "less obvious, nastier, more resilient and energetic female characters who enact her rebellious dissent from her culture." Spacks comments that it would be "difficult for men writing about that woman ever to sound quite the same again. . . . Feminist criticism, in other words, has provoked new debates: arguably the most important contribution any critical mode can make." "Never before in history," she observes, "have so many people declared so loudly that women *matter*." With that new consciousness, Spacks describes how she herself has begun to read Austen differently, now noticing—and not taking for granted—the "tiny stories of sexual betrayal embedded" in her work.[4]

This re-visioning process, through which Spacks, now a professor of English at the University of Virginia, became a feminist critic, is exemplary. A decade later, twenty well-published literary scholars, most of whom held tenured faculty positions at major research universities, described similar experiences in an anthology appropriately entitled *Changing Subjects*. From the interaction of their changing personal and professional lives emerged new subjects, new subjectivities, and a new field of academic endeavor. These scholars came of age with the rebirth of feminism, which, they reflected, "transformed our lives and our scholarship. We saw it as a growing point that enabled us to connect our deepest passions and energies with our work, to think more deeply and originally." These feminist scholars have renewed the meaning of the term *intellectuel engagé*, refusing what Yeats called the choice between "perfection of the life, or of the work" and fashioning in the intersection a new and distinctive field of literary criticism.[5]

By 1980 the immense scope of the women's studies project and the possibilities it provided were becoming clear. Nannerl O. Keohane—then a professor of political science at Stanford, later the president of Wellesley College, and now the president of Duke University—commented, in an essay on the difference that women's studies might make in her field, that it was likely that "more would be learned about women and politics in the 1970s than in all previous decades of the history of the discipline combined." After identifying aspects of political science (such as the dominance of men in the public sphere that constituted its primary subject matter) that had contributed to the field's silence about women, she wondered why so little attention had been paid to the exceptions (why there was no *"eminence rose"* to parallel the *eminence grise*) or to the variety of ways in which basic categories such as authority might be exercised and experienced. The inclusion of women would serve to broaden the field to include material dealing with the participation of women in political life, the treatment of women by political theorists, the legal and moral issues related to women's concerns, the importance of language related to sex differences, and the structures of social and institutional power. There was plenty of "work cut out for us," she told her readers.[6]

The disciplines subject to feminist criticism are probably co-extensive with the intellectual concerns of the contemporary professoriate. Surveying just a few recent volumes on the impact of feminist research, one finds articles on anthropology, archaeology, art, biology, classics, economics, education, English, French, Spanish, ethnic studies, history, literary criticism, philosophy, political science, psychiatry, religious studies, sociology, theater, and more—especially if one includes subdisciplines and interdisciplinary fields. At least two publishers, Oxford University Press and Twayne Publishers, have established series devoted to the impact of feminism on disciplines in the arts and sciences. Twayne plans to publish

> volumes on anthropology, art history bioethics, biology, classics, education, economics, film, history, law, literature, music, philosophy, political science, psychology, religion, sociology, and theater.... [The press] anticipate[s] that each one will combine the virtues of accessibility with original interpretations of central issues of gender, genre, methodology, and historical perspective. These are the questions that feminism has explicitly and implicitly unsettled in every field of knowledge, forcing us all to reconsider how we learn, how we choose what we learn, and how we change what and how we learn.[7]

Across the disciplines, scholars in women's studies have adopted strategies that can for the most part be categorized under a few rubrics that are often used to frame the inquiry. One typical anthology uses as section headings "The Articulation of Gender as an Analytical Category"; "Methodological Moves from Margin to Center"; "The Sticking Power of Stereotypes"; and "Paradigmatic Implications." Women's studies, often itself accused of bias, uses these means to assert a "lack of objectivity in science that has permitted an all-too-ready acceptance of what are essentially unproved explanations of unproved gender differences." Another collection of essays begins its table of contents with "Outsiders Within: Challenging the Disciplines," followed by "The Difference That Gender Makes" and "Feminism and the Politics of Intellectual Inquiry"; in the last section, "Dialogues: Feminist Scholarship and/in the Disciplines," the first section's challenge has turned to dialogue. From a mid-1990s perspective, the editors of this volume identify anthropology, literature, and history as fields "deeply transformed" by feminist scholarship; economics, political science, psychology, and sociology as less so; and, within language studies, French more than Italian or Spanish. They call attention as well to a "paradigm shift" within women's studies itself, due to recognition of the "particularity" of the "'woman' in women's studies." The profundity of the impact on the disciplines varies, they suggest, according to the degree to which the field itself is self-reflective. This may be one reason that women's studies has moved more slowly in the natural sciences. By the 1990s, however, Sue V. Rosser felt that feminism had stimulated new approaches to biological research and had "begun to play a substantial role in policies, funding, and technological development and application in areas of women's health, reproductive technologies, and the environment."[8]

The range of fields influenced by women's studies is likely to increase further as a result of efforts such as a new three-year project on "women and scientific literacy," sponsored by the Association of American Colleges and Universities with funding from the National Science Foundation. Its purpose is to "make science more attractive to women by integrating it into women's-studies courses and incorporating new scholarship on gender studies into the teaching of science and mathematics." Ten institutions, all with "strong" women's studies programs, were selected from among seventy-six applicants to participate.⁹

Women's studies has become increasingly visible in academic journals. In addition to examining feminist critiques of methodologies, interpretations, and "invisible paradigms," one multidisciplinary group assessed the impact of women's studies scholarship by analyzing patterns of publication of articles on women between 1966 and 1980 by the major journals in anthropology, education, history, literature, and philosophy. Their study of ten publications in each discipline provides suggestive data on feminist influence. Granting problems of definition, especially in anthropology, education, and literature, where dominant traditions encompassed the study of topics that might be assumed to have included woman-oriented analyses (e.g., kinship studies and mythology) but in fact most often did not, they counted publication rates by discipline as well as change at five-year intervals over the fifteen-year period. In the aggregate, the publication of articles on women increased dramatically. Between 1966–70 and 1971–75, the number almost doubled (from 32.6 articles per year to 63.2), rising to 84.6 by 1976–80 (constituting, however, just 5.31% at the highest). Among the five fields, the most pronounced change occurred in history, where the percentage of articles on women grew from 1.1 percent of all research published to 6.45 percent; and expanded in presence from four to all ten journals. In philosophy, the increase in number was much smaller—but began from a base of zero.¹⁰ In view of the exponential growth of women's studies, a replication of this study today might well show dramatic change. Chapter 9 presents data on the increasing prevalence of Ph.D. dissertations (from which many publications ensue) in women's studies.

Academic feminism's encounters with the disciplines reflected its ambiguous stance and the often ambivalent position of its practitioners—located both within and in opposition to the traditional fields. For some the goal was simply to conduct research, to add knowledge about women to the canon, and to "mainstream" feminist scholarship, in order to gain legitimacy for women's studies. For others the new approach spanned disciplinary borders and engaged the foundations of all fields of knowledge. Using feminist criticism as the vehicle through which to assert radical attacks on the epistemological presuppositions, bodies of knowledge, and methodologies of the fields in which they were trained, some feminist scholars, influenced by European thinkers, participated in criticism of what they considered "master narratives" or "totalizing theories" that they associated with the Enlightenment. Others sought to recuperate the Enlightenment for feminism, pointing out the ways in which feminism itself depended on concepts and values derived from that intellectual source (see chapter 6).

Critics of the academy have attributed great influence to women studies because of its challenge to the curriculum. The late Page Smith, a traditional if idiosyncratic historian concerned with the dangers of "presentism," specialization, relativism, and the decline of spiritual and universalistic values in the academy, saw women's studies as both symptom and cause. Commenting on the argument that female scholars should not study women because they lacked objectivity, Smith said, "What was laughable [in the traditional academicians' resistance to feminist criticism] was that it never occurred to white males to question *their* objectivity." Despite grave misgivings about its rapid growth and "imperialistic form" on his campus, Smith perceived women's studies as advancing his agenda: "It is difficult to overestimate the importance of women in undermining the academy's notion of 'objectivity.' . . . By accelerating the process of fragmentation, already far along, Women's Studies may force a re-evaluation of the whole of higher education." Smith also grudgingly credited academic feminists with being "the last utopians." For Claire Goldberg Moses, women's historian and long-time editor of *Feminist Studies*, and for the postmodernist literary scholar Leslie Wahl Rabine, academic feminism had major responsibility for what they term the "contemporary crisis of the disciplines, abetted and in large measure instigated by women's studies."¹¹

Page Smith hoped that by "breaking the disciplines," women's studies would hasten the end of a century of increasing specialization. Using that provocative term as her title, Florence Howe has drawn an interesting parallel between the "transformation of the curriculum" by the newly emerging sciences in the late nineteenth century and the transformation sought by feminist scholars today. Only after the late-nineteenth-century battle did the disciplines now deemed "traditional" emerge to supplant an earlier, holistic, religious, and morally focused "discipline" that constituted higher learning (for an elite intended for leadership in the ministry, law, and society). The new "galaxy" of specialized disciplines, rapidly organized into departments, became today's powerful mainstream with which feminist scholars contend.[12]

Whether challenging or defending the traditional academic disciplines, partisans on both sides of the curricular debates tend to forget that "school subjects are constructions too." Jane Roland Martin, a philosopher of education, has examined what she terms "the dogma of god-given subjects," pointing out that people tend to recognize as a subject suitable for study "only those things which in the past have been considered suitable candidates for a general and a liberal education. There is a much greater range to choose from than we realize."

> Neither Chairs, Hamburgers nor Humphrey Bogart has the ring of a bona fide subject to most of us. Yet if we shed our narrow frame of reference we realize not only that these can be subjects, but that they undoubtedly are—Chairs a subject in a curriculum for furniture makers, Hamburgers a subject in a curriculum for McDonald trainees, Humphrey Bogart a subject in a curriculum for film enthusiasts. Even a brief glance at the wide variety of curricula there are should convince us that anything can be a subject; that French, Mathematics and Physics can give way to Identity, Community and the Reality of Material Objects or to the Rights of Animals, Mary Queen of Scots and Dying.
>
> Anything can be a subject because subjects are made, not found. They are not "out there" waiting for us, but are human constructions.

Martin goes on to discuss the judgments of "importance" that determine what "subject-entities" become subjects of study, and the ways in which teaching goals determine their usage. In another essay she traces the process through which a double standard may be applied in decisions concerning which subject-entities are chosen and which are seen to constitute a worthy "field of knowledge."[13]

Comparing politics and education, for example, Martin argues that while both exist as important social activities and institutions, only the former, taught as political science or government, has become accepted as a basic field of knowledge suitable for general or liberal education.

> Why have curriculum makers favored politics as a subject-entity over education? Politics' advantage is that, considering it one of society's "productive" processes, North American culture has situated it in the public world and placed it in men's care. Education's problem is that even though school has moved it out of the private home and into the public world, it is seen as a "reproductive" societal process whose "natural" practitioners are still assumed to be women.

In Martin's view, the exclusion or trivialization of women-dominated activities as subjects of study constitutes a kind of "hidden curriculum in the validation of one gender, its associated tasks, traits, and functions, and the denigration of the other." She would revise the definition of subjects of study and fields of knowledge to include not only women's studies but the "3 C's of caring, concern, and connection." "Compassion 101a need no more be listed in a school's course offerings than Objectivity 101a is now." But the definition of an educated person would be expanded, in the spirit of John Dewey, turning education into what Martin would call "a journey of integration, not alienation," which, in her opinion, it now is.[14]

Institutional Transformation Projects and Phase Theory

The use of radical rhetoric such as "breaking the disciplines" and the suggestion of fanciful ideas such as "Compassion 101a" are consistent with the far-reaching aspirations of women's studies' initial call for transformation not just of courses and curricula but also of institutions and societies. Women's studies advocates made Charlotte Bunch's comment that it was not enough to "add women and stir" into a feminist cliché.[15] They elaborated on it by repeating the geographer Janice

Monk's observation that one could not "integrat[e] the concept of a round earth into a course that assumes a flat earth."[16] Adding the new scholarship on women to existing stores of knowledge would necessarily require fundamental change in the assumptions, interpretations, and structures that shape intellectual domains. New questions would have to be asked; new sources identified; new categories of analysis and methods of conducting research and interpreting evidence devised. No simple additive process would do. As early as 1976, when Princeton University faculty conducted a study of several hundred course outlines from 172 departments in several institutions and found minimal curricular impact by the new scholarship on women, it was clear that change would not come quickly or easily.[17]

An immense effort toward that end soon began. Described variously as mainstreaming, integrating, transforming, or gender-balancing the curriculum, it was underwritten by government agencies and private foundations as well as universities. In 1981, the Southwest Institute for Research on Women (SIROW) at the University of Arizona, with funding from the National Endowment for the Humanities (NEH) and the Rockefeller Family Fund, organized an invitational workshop entitled "Integrating Women's Studies into the Curriculum." That same year, the Ford, Lilly, and Johnson Foundations provided support for a second invitational conference for this purpose. Soon, across the country, other conferences were convened, institutes held, reports issued, and proceedings published, all testifying to the vitality of the "transformation" movement. Increasing responsiveness to the diversity among women (as discussed in chapter 5) and collaboration between ethnic studies and women's studies programs encouraged inclusion of a rapidly growing body of research on women of color. Projects at Memphis State University and at Spelman College, in association with other institutions of higher education in Atlanta, provided exemplary models for transforming curricula, both within women's studies and across the broader reaches of academia.[18] Drawing on several published reports in the early to mid-1980s, Mariam Chamberlain, director of a three-year study of the status and prospects of women in higher education that was sponsored jointly by the Ford, Carnegie, and Russell Sage Foundations, could report that "feminist scholarship has indeed begun to alter the state of knowledge of the disciplines." "But," she declared, "women's studies has yet to have any substantial influence on the traditional curriculum." From a longer perspective, in 1991 Ellen Messer-Davidow concluded more optimistically that feminist inquiry, while it had "not transformed" the disciplines, had "altered" them. For Messer-Davidow, more fundamental change would require greater "know-how" about the ways in which human agents can affect social systems.[19] The intellectual tools for further change are now readily available.

By 1992 almost two hundred curriculum transformation projects had been reported. In 1993, a National Center for Curriculum Transformation Resources on Women (NCCTRW), partially supported by the Ford Foundation and the Department of Education's Fund for the Improvement of Postsecondary Education, was established at Towson State University, in Maryland, to provide continuing leadership. A recent NCCTRW catalog includes a list of curriculum consultants in many disciplines, representing major research universities and leading liberal arts colleges across the country; bibliographic resources; Internet resources; suggestions for obtaining funds for transformation projects; designs for evaluating curricula; "discipline analysis" essays in sixteen fields; panels of experts in seven areas; and essays on diverse interdisciplinary and international perspectives. While research that explores the results of such efforts remains relatively scarce, several "before and after" studies of course syllabi suggest that faculty participation in transformation projects does make a difference. According to one recent review, "It is rare that a faculty member participates in one of these projects without making changes: Some add one or more new texts or concepts; some integrate material throughout the course; some completely change the structure and topics of the course to make the study of gender and cultural diversity central."[20]

Among the national leaders in transformation efforts whose names appear on the NCCTRW's list of consultants and are frequently cited in the literature are Elizabeth Kamarck Minnich and Peggy McIntosh. The philosopher Minnich (once a graduate assistant to Hannah Arendt) has published a book explaining that she set as her task thinking through the *"root problem underlying the dominant meaning system that informs our curricula."* It was Minnich who in 1979 had grasped the revolutionary potential of replacing an androcentric, or male-centered, perspective with a woman-centered view of the world. In a memorable phrase, she compared the epistemological impact of replacing androcentric with gynocentric scholarship to "Copernicus shattering our geo-centricity, Darwin shattering our species-centricity. We are shattering andro-centricity, and the change is as fundamental, as dangerous, as exciting." Now her search produced "really only a few basic realizations." Stubbornly and pervasively embedded in common knowledge, the root problem, she argued,

> reappears in different guises in all fields and throughout the dominant tradition. It is, simply, that while the majority of humankind was excluded from education and the making of what has been called knowledge, *the dominant few not only defined themselves as the inclusive kind of human but also as the norm and the ideal.*
>
> *Faulty generalization,* even universalization, is compounded by ... privileging central *singular* terms, notably "man" and "mankind," which lead directly to such singular abstract notions—and ideals—as "the citizen," "the philosopher," "the poet." Such singularity makes thinking of plurality, let alone diversity, very difficult indeed.... Whole systems of knowledge built around such concepts come to appear to have neither contexts nor consequences that should be considered central (rather than peripheral) to their truths and meaning. The result is *partial knowledge* masquerading as general, even universal.

Given these systemic errors, only fundamental reconception of "false universals" could open the dominant curriculum to the new scholarship. It would then be necessary to revisit basic questions about human existence.[21]

While Minnich justified the necessity of transformation, analysis of the process of change was provided by the historian Peggy McIntosh, director of a faculty development program at the Wellesley College Center for Research on Women. Under McIntosh's leadership, for several years the center offered fellowship awards for residence at Wellesley to scholars working to integrate materials on women into the traditional curriculum. It gave faculty resident in New England stipends for attendance at regional seminars on the implications of the new scholarship and gave matching funds to institutions around the country that invited consultants on integration to work with their faculties. Drawing on the field of history for her model, McIntosh built on the pioneering work of Gerda Lerner, who called in 1969 for a new conceptual framework in women's history, to lay out a progressive transformation process. Lerner projected five phases for the transition: recognizing that women have a history (which differs by class); then seeking women's contributions to "male-defined society"; conceptualizing women as a group "defined in their own terms"; posing new questions about history based on knowledge of women, including rethinking traditional periodization from women's perspective; and reconceptualizing the discipline to create a total human history. McIntosh outlined the five phases as:

Phase 1: Womanless History
Phase 2: Women in History
Phase 3: Women as a Problem, Anomaly, or Absence in History
Phase 4: Women as History
Phase 5: History Reconstructed, Redefined, and Transformed to Include Us All[22]

Writing in the foreword to a guidebook, published by Betty Schmitz in 1985, that includes designs for overall project management, examples of campus projects, and resources for revision, McIntosh characterizes the transformation process as a dynamic faculty development project to enhance the teaching and learning of a new curriculum. "Phase theory" may also be used for content analysis of an existing program, to assess the extent of "gendered knowledge" present in a given course or curriculum. McIntosh's five phases, expanded slightly, generalized, and interwoven with the developmental schemes of several other analysts, reappear in the six "stages of curriculum change" developed by Marilyn R. Schuster and Susan R. Van Dyne, professors, and former deans, at Smith College, which appeared in both the *Harvard Educational Review* and an anthology of essays on transformation that they edited and published with support from McIntosh and the Wellesley Col-

Table 1. Stages of Change in the Curriculum and the Classroom

Stages	Questions	Incentives	Means	Outcomes	Classroom Practice
1. Invisibility	Who are the truly great thinkers/actors in history?	Maintaining standards of excellence	Back to basics	Pre-1960s, exclusionary core curriculum; fixed products, universal values	Students as passive vessels
2. Search for missing women, absent "minorities"	Who are the great women? Where is the female Shakespeare?	Affirmative action/compensatory	Add data within existing paradigms	"Exceptional" women added to the curriculum; role models sought for women and "minority" students	Notice the presence of female and minority students
3. Minorities understood as oppressed; women as subordinate in male-dominated society	Why has history of "minorities" been ignored? Why is women's work considered marginal?	Anger/social justice Intellectual	Protest existing paradigms, but within perspective of dominant group	"Images of women" courses, African-American studies begins	Student engages more in debate; may resist identification with gender or ethnic group
4. Women studied on own terms, oppressed experience; cultures studied from insider's perspective	What was/is women's experience? What are differences among women? (attention to race, class, sexuality, cultural differences, different meanings of gender)		Outside existing paradigms; develop competing paradigms	Links among ethnic studies, cross-cultural studies, and women's studies; interdisciplinary courses	Student values own experience, gathers data from more familiar sources

Table 1. Stages of Change in the Curriculum and the Classroom (Continued)

Stages	Questions	Incentives	Means	Outcomes	Classroom Practice
5. New scholarship challenges the disciplines	Question adequacy of current definitions of historical periods, norms for behavior? How must questions change to account for gender, ethnicity, class and sexuality in context? Shift from stable subject to shifting subject positions.	Epistemology	Testing the paradigms; gender, race, class and sexuality as categories of analysis	Beginnings of transformation; theory courses	Teacher as coach, student as collaborator
6. Visibility; transformed curriculum	How are gender, race, class, sexuality, imbricated? How can we account more fully for diversity of human experience?	Inclusive vision founded on attention to differences and diversity rather than sameness and generalization	Transform the paradigms	Reconceptualized, inclusive core; dynamic process, transformed introductory courses	Empowered student, knowledge defined as much by skills, abilities, as by content

Source: Elaine Hedges, *Getting Started: Planning Curriculum Transformation* (Towson, Md.: National Center for Curriculum Transformation Resources on Women, 1997), 92. Prepared by Susan R. Van Dyne and Marilyn R. Schuster, Smith College, Northampton, Mass., 1983; updated 1996. Reprinted by permission of Susan R. Van Dyne and Marilyn R. Schuster, and the National Center for Curriculum Transformation Resources on Women.

lege Center for Research on Women (see table 1). The contributors to this volume included leaders of transformation projects spanning the country, at public and private, large and small institutions, major research universities along with liberal arts colleges. This work also highlights the first partnership project to link black studies and women's studies in transformation efforts.[23]

Reviewing more than fifty projects, Schuster and Van Dyne found three predominant models for institution-wide change: "top-down," "piggy-back," and "bottom-up," each with varying strengths and risks. They recognized the importance of respecting local conditions but warned against "mere assimilation of what's most affordable or readily acceptable," and they emphasized the necessity of offering an "inclusive vision ... not merely white women's studies ... [and including also] our own often-silenced minorities such as lesbians."[24]

The results of the many curriculum transformation projects remain uncertain, and like many other educational processes, these projects may bear fruit only after years of maturation. What is all too clear is that these efforts may encounter serious resistance. Reporting on one of the largest curriculum integration projects, a four-year effort at the University of Arizona, begun in 1981 with sponsorship by the NEH, a multidisciplinary team called attention to the many ways in which their efforts had proved frustrating. Involving forty-five participants from thirteen departments, who were mostly typical of tenured men at universities everywhere, the project provided the volunteer participants either stipends or released time, and required that they attend seminars and revise at least one course to include materials about women.

While the project evaluators reported that many did make "measurable alterations in the perspective and content of their courses," they also felt as directors that they had "seriously underestimated the magnitude and intractability of the resistance [they] would confront." They found reading and hearing on the part of many participants to be "cursory" and "selective," their agreement "polite" but "limited," and the changes induced superficial and minimal. The cross-disciplinary team was accused of "territorial invasion"; their work was contested as "ideologically motivated," while their critics left the "ideological grounding of their own epistemologies unexplored." The team, comprising younger female experts facing senior male colleagues, experienced in their leadership roles an "inverted gender dynamics" in which they were perceived either as a "police force" or as a "group of schoolteachers." They concluded that "the tools of rationality alone are inadequate to the task of intellectual change when the investments in ideas regarding gender are deep-seated and self-interested for all parties." The fundamental proposition guiding women's studies, the social construction of gender, was contested with sociobiological interpretations, leading the team to introduce the following year readings on biology and to recommend that biological issues should be highlighted early in curriculum integration projects. The "authority of the *texts*" was not enough to change men's minds. The Arizona team, tempered by its trial, provided a wealth of suggestions for future efforts.[25]

Transformation projects may also run aground for other reasons. As noted in chapter 2, the absence of tenure lines that permit faculty to concentrate all of their academic work in women's studies may mean that curriculum transformation becomes "something they [do] on the side." If left to others who are less knowledgeable, it may lose its critical edge and be diluted. At one rural research university, "diversity" came to equal "variety," and a major effort at changing the curriculum to encompass the new scholarship on both race and gender failed. Evaluations of that attempt suggest that ignorance is at least as great an obstacle as hostility. Success requires education in the fundamental perspectives of women's studies, especially its epistemological claims about the positionality of knowledge.[26]

The most extensive of all transformation endeavors is the New Jersey Project on Inclusive Scholarship, Curriculum, and Teaching, funded by the state of New Jersey and William Paterson College. Established in 1986 with a line item of $100,000 in the state's higher education budget, an additional $25,000 to $50,000 from the state department of education's New Jersey Humanities Grant program, and various in-kind contributions from the college, the project survived the elimination of the New Jersey Department of Education as well as attacks from the National Association of Scholars and others. More than a decade later it was still publishing *Transformations*, a semiannual, nationally distributed journal, and sponsoring numerous conferences, networks, exhibits, and special events. Journal issues generally include experiential studies of curriculum revision in various disciplines, suggestions for integrating material on nondominant groups of women (and men), discussions of pedagogy, model course outlines, bibliographies, and reviews of books and other instructional media. Beyond answering "why" and advising "how-to," the project (especially through its journal) also "protects change-minded professors from isolation on their campuses," according to one women's studies coordinator for whom it seems to have made "all the difference."[27]

The challenge to tradition from women's studies elicited criticism from former NEH director Lynne Cheney, who objected to a comment in *Transformations* that "a truly transformed curriculum wouldn't contain a Western Civilization course" (ignoring the movement within the field of history itself to replace Western Civilization with World History as a foundational course). Cheney also mocked the use of Minnich's audacious comparison of the impact of re-visioning in women's studies—the replacement of androcentricity with women-centered learning—with the Copernican revolution by citing an erroneous statement about the astronomer's discovery as indicative of "low levels of scientific literacy in women's studies departments." Cheney reserved her strongest criticism for the work of "the ubiquitous Peggy McIntosh" and the taxpayer-supported New Jersey project, which she sees, along with numerous other contemporary intellectual projects, as putting "scholarship and teaching into the service of politics" (see chapter 8).[28]

Curriculum change projects have encountered criticism on other grounds as well. Margaret Andersen spoke for many who found the terminology problematic: "mainstreaming" implies the existence of one stream when there are many; "balancing" suggests that all claims to truth are equal; "integrating" suggests the possible loss of feminist goals through assimilation. Furthermore, transformation requires personal change, not just new knowledge.[29] Sandra Coyner expressed the fears of others for whom externally funded transformation projects threatened the movement toward the establishment of women's studies programs, potentially diverting resources and weakening the rationale for developing the "discipline" itself. If material on women were diffused throughout the curriculum, would a need for separate courses and autonomous centers of feminist scholarship still be perceived? Was women's studies' goal to accomplish a finite mission, reach a final stage in the transformation of knowledge, and then make a graceful exit? Coyner thought not. Some of these questions reappear in contemporary debates on naming (*women's studies* versus *gender studies*) as well.

Speaking at a 1989 panel discussion entitled "Transforming the Knowledge Base," Coyner expressed the opinion that the authors of "stage theories" had confused a "developmental stage" and a "historical stage." They had likely experienced the various types of change successively as they participated in the creation of women's studies knowledge; for them it was useful to think in terms of stages. But what of the new generation? Would women's studies preserve its feminist thrust if transformed into "the highest form of knowledge?" Coyner wrote, "I came to women's studies through the women's movement and such ideas as 'the personal is political,' there is sexism, there is patriarchy, and there is women's solidarity. Now I meet students coming to women's studies through deconstruction. They start in a very different world." It was crucial, felt Coyner, to maintain a separate "space" for women's studies. This was a reiteration of her call, initially put forward at the first annual meeting of the National Women's Studies Association in 1979, for the establishment of women's studies as a separate discipline.[30]

Women's Studies as a New Discipline

Coyner spoke initially at a time when "mainstreaming" across the disciplines was promoted as women's studies' ultimate strategy, but, in her view, this approach encountered more resistance than receptivity. Appearing everywhere, women's studies had a home nowhere. Survival for the long haul, she argued, required that "Women's Studies should abandon our fierce adherence to 'interdisciplinarity' and become more like an academic discipline." "Interdisciplinarity" was a fact of life in women's studies, indicative perhaps more of its multiple locations and marginality than of any intellectual coherence or collaborative joining of work by people trained in different fields. Most research continued to emerge from the disciplines; traditional departments held the keys to faculty status and survival. Coyner focused also on the disadvantages to faculty of split assignments and dual loyalties.[31]

Despite such problems as what Catharine Stimpson, in her capacity as founding editor of the interdisciplinary journal *Signs*, termed the "fallacy of misplaced originality" (the discovery, by a scholar trained in one field, of something that is familiar in another), there were also intellectual arguments favoring Coyner's resolution that women's studies should be declared a discipline. Drawing on intellectual history and philosophical debates over the structure of knowledge, she anticipated a number of rebuttals, including the allegation that women's studies, unlike other fields, was not "objective" or "apolitical." Coyner found her most convincing argument by borrowing Thomas Kuhn's theory of scientific revolutions. Point by point she elucidated parallels between the stages of development of women's studies and the processes that, in Kuhn's scheme, led to the establishment and then replacement of "normative science." In Kuhnian terms, women's studies was at a "pre-paradigm" stage and feminist scholars were ready for "disciplining ourselves." Coyner saw women's studies as challenging established paradigms, identifying useful methods and concepts, creating new professional structures, and generally fomenting an intellectual revolution that would, ultimately, lead to a new normative science. It was time to abandon other disciplinary identities and "to think like a women's studies person." Women's studies required a separate location as a department, where practitioners could control their own curriculum, schedule their own classes, and hire their own faculty, who would be evaluated specifically for their teaching and research on women. Eventually, with the development of the Ph.D. degree in women's studies, graduates trained in several traditional disciplines would be prepared to bring true interdisciplinarity to the new field. Meanwhile, women's studies practitioners "could now pay more attention to each other and correspondingly less to our colleagues in the traditional disciplines." The community of scholars, professional associations, and "shared language" that served other sciences already existed in women's studies. Typically, the shared concepts that were emerging did not fit established paradigms; the Kuhnian period of anomaly and crisis leading to a scientific revolution was well under way in women's studies. New paradigms were emerging in and across the disciplines.[32]

The application of a Kuhnian model outside the natural sciences has been faulted on various grounds. Reflecting on the decades of feminist scholarship and her experience of curriculum transformation at the University of Arizona, Myra Dinnerstein questioned the usefulness of the "paradigm shift" concept. She drew on the work of the anthropologist Marilyn Strathern to suggest that the Kuhnian analysis may be inappropriate for disciplines with multiple perspectives, where competing points of view frequently coexist. Furthermore, she noted, women's studies must reinterpret the meaning of calls for curriculum transformation in the light of the post-modernist challenge to truth claims (further discussed in chapter 6).[33]

Apart from considerations of disciplinary definitions, the appeal of departmentalization has continued. In Coyner's 1979 vision, women's studies would, after the revolution, become an autonomous discipline for which, she noted, the appropriate structure was a department. Evelyn Torton Beck, then chair of women's studies at the University of Maryland, College Park, cited Coyner as she reiterated this position a decade later. Declaring that proponents of women's studies should not "acquiesce in our own marginality," she argued that it was "time to insist that women's studies be recognized as a newly established discipline which can be properly taught only within an autonomous department by faculty whose 'tenure home' is women's studies." For women's studies, with its ambition to cross academic borders and transform entire domains of knowledge, the implications of structure loom larger than perhaps they do in other fields. As women's studies develops, its multidisciplinarity will stimulate thought across intellectual and institutional boundaries. But to overcome the potential problem of partial knowledge and incomplete perspective, it must develop new models to facilitate the labor-intensive and costly work essential to good interdisciplinary research and teaching. Bonnie Zimmerman, former chair of the women's studies department at San Diego State University, anticipates that women's studies will create "complex learning communities" to push the cutting edge in intellectual work.[34]

By maintaining a stance that recognizes the need to institutionalize women's studies as if it were a discipline as well as to transform the curriculum of many other disciplines, women's studies can perhaps help to create a new model for a larger academic world increasingly expanding beyond long-established forms. The debate over structure is complicated by the existence of an extensive discussion about the uniqueness of "women's ways of knowing" and our ways of doing scholarly work. If women's studies is a "discipline," what are its defining characteristics? Is there a specifically feminist methodology?

The search for particular feminist approaches to method and methodology grows out of the recognition that traditional ways of creating knowledge have led to false views of women. The philosophers of science Sandra Harding and Evelyn Fox Keller are two leading voices among the many who have raised the question of feminist method. Asking, "Is there a feminist method?" Harding responds by distinguishing between "methods of inquiry," or ways of collecting information and documenting experience, and "methodology," which she defines as theory plus analysis; she answers yes on method and no on methodology. In her view, what is new in feminist work is its grounding in women's experiences, its purpose of seeking research intended to serve women, and its placing of researcher and subject in "the same critical plane." Keller argues, against conventional understanding and scientists' claims, that "method and theory may constitute a natural continuum." Referring to the work of Barbara McClintock, she links paradigm with methodological style.[35]

The feminist challenge is more profound than the simple question of a unique feminist method. Feminist analysts often answer such inquiry by broadening the context. Women's studies they see as part of the larger post-positivist movement that goes back a hundred years and more, to a much older tradition that denies the existence of absolute knowledge. Joyce McCarl Nielsen, for example, associates the feminist approach to research with other philosophical perspectives that challenge positivistic scientific method: namely, hermeneutics and critical theory. With the former it shares a belief in the importance attached to social interaction and the meanings attached to human behavior by the subjects themselves. Like the latter, it rejects the claim that any position can be neutral or disinterested, and it adopts a commitment to liberating people from constricting ideologies. In these schools of thought, as in feminism, knowledge is seen as socially constructed and interpreted.

Nielsen also points to two events within the natural sciences in the twentieth century which advanced the "demythologizing" of science as "pure truth in an ultimate sense": the development of quantum physics and Thomas Kuhn's reinterpretation of scientific progress as a historical process of paradigm transitions. Following the path sketched by Sandra Coyner in 1979, Nielsen notes the ways in which Kuhn's work can serve to explain the emergence of women's—feminist—studies. First she points to the "presence and awareness of anomalies.... What is important is not only that they exist... but that scientists take note of them and define them as counterinstances that challenge the truth or accuracy of the dominant paradigm, rather than defining them as irrelevant, bothersome, and unimportant minor deviations." This describes closely, in feminist perspective, the treatment of women in the construction of knowledge. Kuhn's second necessary condition for a paradigm shift, or scientific revolution, is "the presence of an alternative paradigm"—and what else is women's studies? In Nielsen's words, "to consciously adopt a women's perspective means to see things one did not see before and also to see the familiar rather differently." As examples of feminist inquiry that brought anomalies to the fore and led to alternative explanations, Nielsen offers two famous instances: Joan Kelly's 1977 essay "Did Women Have a Renaissance?" and Carol Gilligan's 1982 book *In a Different Voice*. These studies led, respectively, to questioning the grounds of periodization in history and to alternative views of human moral development. In other disciplines, similar cases abound.[36]

The revision, if not revolution, in perspective that was provoked by feminist criticism has created a new framework within which reforms and new, revised, and more nuanced interpretations will continue to emerge. Throughout the humanities, women's studies and other antipositivistic schools of thought have stimulated increased self-reflexivity and methodological self-consciousness. For all the talk of "feminist methods," no one approach is unique to women's studies. On the contrary, feminist researchers employ many methods. Coyner, for one, finds nothing wrong with using any or all of "the master's tools." Associating herself with Sandra Harding's views, she takes a pragmatic approach: "We should look at methodologies that have worked for us, find out what characterizes them, and call that feminist methodology instead of letting the prescriptive writings of people who say 'this is what you have to do for your work to be feminist' define what is feminist." Harding also warns against making a fetish of method. Method, she explains, arose with the institutionalization of science, as a way of enforcing "norms of inquiry" that operated as a sort of "invisible administrator" to enforce rules. Seen as emancipatory in an earlier age that was breaking away from the authority of church and state, "rule by method" no longer serves that purpose. In particular, principles calling for value-free, uninvolved approaches to research should be replaced with "conscious partiality" and active participation.[37]

However, feminist scholars assert that feminist researchers should share guiding principles. The sociologists Judith A. Cook and Mary Margaret Fonow suggest the following five: (1) "attending to the significance of gender and gender asymmetry"; (2) recognizing the "centrality of consciousness-raising" as a key to interpretation; (3) "challeng[ing] the norm of objectivity that assumes that the subject and object of research can be separated"; (4) considering the "ethical implications" of treating persons as research objects; and (5) employing research means toward the "empowerment of women and transformation of patriarchal social institutions." Cook and Fonow also turn from prescription to description and identify four common themes in much contemporary feminist scholarship: "the role of reflexivity"; "an action orientation"; "attention to the component of the research act"; and "use of the situation at hand."[38]

The way in which adopting such principles affects scholarship is captured in the sociologist Judith Stacey's "trajectory in the borderlands," her account of an "accidental ethnology" of white families who lived and worked in the Silicon Valley of northern California. Originally intended as a comparative study of "working-class gender relationships under postindustrial conditions" among white and Latino families, Stacey's "formal research design ... unraveled rapidly." She describes how her initial two interviews challenged her preconceptions by revealing a putative feminist to be a convert to evangelical Christianity and a long-abused wife to be a feminist. Lured by the unexpected into an ethnology reported in a "reflexive, first-person, and occasionally dialogic narrative style," Stacey offers her work as an example of "undisciplined" research. Both postmodernist and humanist, it is feminist as well. Not only does Stacey transgress what she considers "arbitrary and increasingly atavistic disciplinary divisions of knowledge" but she declares that she has now "adopted that surprising new feminist fashion here of studying men."[39]

If women's studies does not have any singular method, it does have a pervasive attitude. Implicit when not explicit in its affinity with hermeneutics, critical theory, and various standpoint perspectives is a firm rejection of the positivist stance toward objectivity which has served to define many social science disciplines as well as scientific method. Often seen as a core value of the academy, fundamental to the search for truth, the notion of objectivity is rejected by many feminists, who see it instead as a mask for bias. Critics of women's studies frequently use the concept of objectivity as a handy tool for attack. But feminist scholars who challenge the dominant tradition and its creators for their slanted views of women build on a long heritage. In the early fifteenth century, Christine de Pizan lamented that the ills men attributed to women existed in their own minds, not in female nature; "the books that so sayeth, women made them not."[40]

Half a millennium later, feminist critics reiterate this point. According to the historian Christie Farnham, "It is the lack of objectivity in science," which "has permitted an all-too-ready acceptance of what are essentially unproven explanations of unproven gender differences," that has spurred feminist research. The literary critic Leslie W. Rabine notes that "men used a rhetoric of objectivity as a kind of armored vehicle for projecting masculine subjectivity." The sociologist Margaret Andersen declares that "women's labor makes the male mode of operation—detached and rational—possible."[41]

Male objectivity/female subjectivity appears in the feminist lexicon as one more false and uneven dichotomy. Carol P. Christ, writing from the perspective of religious studies, calls on feminist scholars to "deconstruct and disavow the *ethos of objectivity*." However, she also warns of the difficulty of that task, which is due not only to an "androcentric veil" that shields judgments of value and power structures in the university but also to the dualism that posits irrationality and chaos as objectivity's opposite. For the defenders of objectivity, Christ argues, "ways of thinking not firmly rooted in so-called rational principles lead directly back to the chaos monster, to Nazi Germany." For objectivity's feminist critics, it merely hides the perspective from which a speaker speaks, offering disembodied speech and a god's-eye "view from nowhere." It may also disregard the influence of language differences that affect perception. Norma Alarcón has criticized native English-speaking Americans for inventing theory that ignores the "linguistic status" of subjects, failing to acknowledge that "we are culturally constituted in and through language in complex ways and not just engendered in a homogeneous situation."[42]

The importance of the debate over objectivity in the feminist challenge to the traditional curriculum justifies taking a closer look at the uses of objectivity in the academy. The ideal of objectivity did not achieve its place on the university heights without struggle. In recent studies that buttress the feminist argument, intellectual historians have traced its role in the professionalization of the social sciences in the United States. Peter Novick, a historian of science, portrays objectivity as the "noble dream" of founders of the American historical profession. In "Objectivity Enthroned," the first part of his 1988 book, Novick demonstrates objectivity's importance and utility, amid a crisis of authority in American intellectual life, in separating amateurs from professional keepers of the past. By redefining their audiences, standardizing their technique, privileging academic over activist goals, and separating fact from value, historians created a myth of the reality of the past. They portrayed historical truth as correspondence to that reality, to be uncovered progressively by the application of a Baconian scientific method and reported in monographic literature in which, following the style of Flaubert, the "direct appearance of the author was anathema." Presented objectively, interpreted impartially, this recovered fact constituted the ideal to which the professional historians aspired, and on which they built their "discipline."[43]

In a subsequent section of the book entitled "Objectivity Besieged," Novick follows the collapse of consensus in the 1920s and 1930s. War guilt, revisionist challenges to dominant interpretations of the Civil War and Reconstruction, and postwar developments in physics, music, painting, linguistics, psychology, anthropology, and law all challenged the founding myth. Objectivity was reinterpreted following World War II, Novick asserts, and a Whiggish Western civilization dominated general education until collapse began again in the mid-1960s, this time instigated by leftist historians and abetted a bit later by minority groups and women. Today, Novick found, objectivity was "in crisis"; this finding was developed in a chapter entitled "Every Group Its Own Historian"—a title borrowed from the presidential address of Carl Becker to the American Historical Association in 1931. There would have been, of course, few female, or feminist, historians in Becker's audience to applaud.

In this historical perspective, contemporary feminist (and postmodernist) challenges to objectivity seem less radical than they are sometimes said to be. Objectivity historicized is objectivity dethroned. For feminists, explains the anthropologist Donna Haraway, a frequent participant in the "objectivity debates," "objectivity means quite simply *situated knowledges*." This is not, she explains, an invitation to relativism—a bogey often employed in objectivity's defense. Instead it offers an alternative: "partial, locatable, critical knowledges sustaining the possibility of webs of connections called solidarity in politics and shared conversations in epistemology."[44]

It may not be easy to distinguish Haraway's position from the classic *ad hominem* argument that dismisses a point of view because of its origin. If truth exists, it should be possible to state it—but who can do so, and in what language? In an article in which he sets out to explain what is at stake in contemporary curriculum debates, the philosopher John Searle acknowledges that "objectivity only functions relative to a shared 'background' of cognitive capacities and hence is, in a sense, a form of intersubjectivity." Searle asserts that "a public language presupposes a public world." Some feminist scholars would say that this is exactly so: knowledge is produced through conversation. The question is, who gets to participate and who defines the terms? Often unspoken in the debate is the distribution of power to decide outcomes. Who gets the last word—the right to name what will be known as reality? Who tells the truth(s) about women?[45]

Critics such as Searle complain of the "Nietzscheanized Left" (borrowing Allan Bloom's term) and chastise women's studies for departing from the norms of what Searle calls the "Western Rationalistic Tradition" in their efforts to destabilize concepts and rename accepted versions of reality. As women lead the search to find and tell new truths about women, and feminist scholarship grows apace, they join a long line of critics of objectivity. Nevertheless, they are often singled out as a force especially destructive of traditional wisdom and values. As Joyce Appleby, Margaret Jacob, and Lynn Hunt point out in *Telling the Truth about History*, "a great transformation has recently occurred in Western Thinking about knowledge.... As the twentieth century closes, it becomes obvious that new definitions of truth and objectivity are needed in every field of knowledge.... The chief cause of the present crisis of knowledge is the collapse on all fronts of intellectual and political absolutism." As befits intellectual leaders in a democratic society, the authors conclude their work with the statement "Telling the truth takes a collective effort."[46]

Transformation projects in women's studies represent academic feminists' collective effort to add women's voices to the conversations through which knowledge is created and transmitted. Often that has meant attacking the disciplines. After hundreds of organized projects and thousands of individual efforts in women's studies, and challenges by many other interdisciplinary programs as well, the disciplines nevertheless retain their structure, their courses, and their curriculum largely intact. Sometimes women are added and not stirred. Despite the success of academic feminists in gaining legitimacy for their work, tenure and many excellent positions for themselves, and institutional acceptance for their courses, curricula, and programs, women's studies often remains marginalized, which fuels continuing debates about its structure, future, and especially in the last decade, even its name. Grounded in and shaped by the disciplines, where most of its research continues to take place, women's studies thrives both as an interdisciplinary community and, probably even more, as a vital presence within communities based on discipline. Existing both inside and outside traditional academic structures, feminist scholars now ponder "how to be or not to be marginal at one and the same time." Ellen Messer-Davidow, in a thoughtful article assessing the impact of women's studies' success in institutionalizing academic feminism, finds that the "disciplinary grid ... disempowers women."[47]

Messer-Davidow's concern is primarily with the loss of impetus toward the use of academic change to leverage social change. Exploring the extent to which women's studies programs teach courses that are explicitly about social change, Messer-Davidow surveyed the curricula of two dozen "large, radical, community-oriented and/or prestigious programs" and found that only four emphasized change or taught practice. One of the questions initially raised in the debates over "mainstreaming women's studies" and "transforming the curriculum" was whether success would kill women's studies. Many of the founders transferred their energies from the women's liberation movement to the women's studies movement and have not, Messer-Davidow points out, engaged in community-based social action since the early 1970s. However, beyond suggesting that investigators become involved with their subjects in social science research and adding curricular coursework and internships in "social change" (which, interestingly, resonates with a national movement toward institutionalizing "service learning"), Messer-Davidow has little to offer about the "how" side of her article's title, "Know-How."[48]

The relationship between women's studies and the (other) disciplines invokes questions of institutional structure as well as intellectual boundaries, and the controversy over "autonomy versus integration" of the early 1980s reappears in another guise in the 1990s, as a debate over naming. Not only the structural separation of women's studies but also the use of the term *women* to define and label the field was seen by some as perpetuating a dichotomy in which woman is subordinate to man, and as reinforcing ahistorical, essentialist views of sexual differences. *Gender-balancing* and *gender studies*, advocated sometimes as less threatening terms for the academic feminist project because they include men, can also be construed as the more radical approach, for they imply dissolving concepts, categories, and institutions that maintain a dichotomous inequality. For those who recognize gender as a social system that pervades all institutions (family, sexuality, economy, politics, law, marriage, and education) and permeates the intellectual foundations of knowledge, *gender feminism*—a term used pejoratively by the critic Christina Hoff Sommers—is the way to achieve transformation in the university as well as in society (see chapter 6).[49]

For others, however, fundamental change through women's studies requires not only revision of organizational structures in the academy and changes in curricula but also alternative ways of delivering instruction. Many hold the view that how to teach is as important as what to teach. Classroom organization and environment matter as much as the syllabus. Transformation necessitates not only revising course content, sources, and interpretations and "breaking the disciplines" by blurring the genres and also the genders, but also bridging the separation between cognitive and affective modes of learning. In this view it is essential to connect the content of courses with the character of students' lives. Effective instruction—teaching that would "take"—must link inquiry with experience in the lives of both faculty and students. Much of this could be lost in projects focused primarily on transforming the curriculum. Like the authors of the 1969 book *Teaching as a Subversive Activity*,[50] some feminist educators believe that in education as well as in media, "the medium is the message," and they seek to alter virtually every aspect of the teaching-learning experience.

Experiments in creating totally alternative educational environments have been relatively few, largely in the form of summer "institutes" or "communities" where feminists struggled over problems of content, structure, and funding. While they provided spaces in which women could think and be together "free of the constrictions of male-dominated institutions," these efforts never served as a viable alternative to women's studies in mainstream higher education in the United States.[51] Instead, efforts to open the academy to feminist education meant adding to the challenge to the curriculum efforts to change the learning environment through what came to be called "feminist pedagogy."

Notes

1. Florence Howe, "Feminism and the Education of Women (1975)," in *Myths of Coeducation: Selected Essays, 1964-1983* (Bloomington: Indiana University Press, 1984), 175-205; and idem, "Myths of Coeducation (1978)," in ibid., 206-20; Linda Kerber, "'Why Should Girls Be Learn'd and Wise?': Two Centuries of Higher Education of Women as Seen through the Unfinished Work of Alice Mary Baldwin," in Faragher and Howe, eds., *Women and Higher Education in American History*, 18-42, quotation on 20. On the history of black women's education in the United States, see Linda M. Perkins, "The Education of Black Women in the Nineteenth Century," in Ibid., 64-86; and Jeanne Noble, "The Higher Education of Black Women in the Twentieth Century," in ibid., 87-106. See also Barbara Miller Solomon, *In the Company of Educated Women: A History of Women and Higher Education in America* (New Haven: Yale University Press, 1985)

2. Annette Kolodny, "Dancing through the Minefield: Some Observations on the Theory and Practice of a Feminist Literary Criticism," *Feminist Studies* 6, no. I (spring 1980): 1-25, quotation on 6; Elisabeth Young-Bruehl, "The Education of Women as Philosophers," in Minnich, O'Barr, and Rosenfeld, eds., *Reconstructing the Academy*, 9-23, quotation on 11; originally published in *Signs* 12, no. 2 (winter 1987): 207-21.

3. On questions and perception, see Neil Postman and Charles Weingartner, *Teaching as a Subversive Activity* (New York: Delta, 1969), 121; Audre Lorde, "The Master's Tools Will Never Dismantle the Master's House," in *Sister Outsider: Essays and Speeches* (Freedom, Calif.: Crossing Press, 1984), 110-13.

4. Patricia Meyer Spacks, "The Difference it Makes," in Langland and Gove, eds., *Feminist Perspective in the Academy*, 7-24, quotation on 7-9, 17; originally published in *Soundings: An*

Interdisciplinary Journal 64, no. 4 (winter 1981): 343-60.
5. Gayle Greene and Coppélia Kahn, "Introduction," in Greene and Kahn, eds., *Changing Subjects*, 1; William Butler Yeats, "The Choice," in *Selected Poems and Three Plays*, 3d ed. (New York: Macmillan, 1962), 138.
6. Nannerl O. Keohane, "Speaking From Silence: Women and the Science of Politics," in Langland and Gove, eds., *Feminist Perspective in the Academy*, 86-100, quotations on 86,89,98.
7. Claire Sprague, editor of the Twayne series, in foreword to Judith P. Zinsser, *History and Feminism: A Glass Half Full* (New York: Twayne, 1993), vii; see also Sue V. Rosser, *Biology and Feminism: A Dynamic Interaction* (New York: Twayne, 1992).
8. For a typical anthology, see Farnham, ed., *Impact of Feminist Research*, vii, viii; on lack of objectivity in science, see Christie Farnham, "Introduction: The Same or Different?," in ibid., 1-8, quotations on 2. For collection of essays, see Stanton and Stewart, eds., *Feminisms in the Academy*, v, vi; on fields trasnsformed and paradigm shift, Domna C. Stanton and Abigail J. Stewart, "Introduction: Remodeling Relations: Women's Studies and the Disciplines," in ibid., 1-16, quotations on 5, 7; Rosser, *Biology and Feminism*, 133. On the resistance of science to women's studies, see Helen E. Longino and Evelynn Hammonds, "Conflicts and Tensions in the Feminist study of Gender and Science," in Hirsch and Keller, eds., *Conflicts in Feminism*, 164-83.
9. "'In' Box," *Chronicle of Higher Education*, Feb. 14, 1997, A10.
10. Ellen Carol DuBois et al., *Feminist Scholarship: Kindling in the Groves of Academe* (Urbana: University of Illinois Press, 1987), 157-94, data on 165-70. On anthropology, see also di Leonardo, ed., *Gender at the Crossroads of Knowledge*. More recently, Susan Christopher reports working with her thesis advisor, Patricia Gumport, at Stanford's School of Education to collect content analysis data from two "gatekeeping" journals each in history, philosophy, and sociology for the period 1960-90; this study remains incomplete. Susan Christopher, personal communication, Nov. 18 1996.
11. Claire Goldberg Moses and Leslie Wahl Rabine, *Feminism, Socialism, and French Romanticism* (Bloomington: Indiana University Press, 1993), 2; Page Smith, *Killing the Spirit: Higher Education in America* (New York: Viking, 1990), 19, 289-92.
12. Florence Howe, "Breaking the Disciplines: In the Nineteenth Century and Today (1978)," in *Myths of Coeducation*, 221-30.
13. Jane Roland Martin, *Changing the Educational Landscape: Philosophy, Women, and Curriculum* (New York: Routledge, 1994), 188-91.
14. Ibid., 208-9, 21, 229-31.
15. Bunch explains her meaning as follows: "Another view of feminism that has limited us is what Mary Hunt and I labeled the 'add women and stir' approach to change. I do believe in adding women and stirring, in many situations, but the women added have to be willing to stir up the mix so that it no longer looks the same, so that we are reorienting whatever we've been stirred into. Feminism must be more than adding women into structures as they are; it must also be about transforming those institutions, making them more humane." Bunch, *Passionate Politics: Feminist Theory in Action* (New York: St. Martin's Press, 1987), 140; the volume contains her collected essays, 1968-1986.
16. In her original statement, Janice Monk, addressing an audience of geographers on the necessity of curriculum transformation, said, "as an analogy, consider integrating the concept of a round earth into a course that assumes a flat earth." Monk, "Integrating Women into the Geography Curriculum," *Journal of Geography* 82, no. 6 (1983): 271-73, quotation on 271.
17. On the early study of the impact of women's studies, see Chamberlain, ed., *Women in Academe*, 156.
18. Betty Shmitz et al., "Women's Studies and Curriculum Transformation," in Banks and Bank, eds., *Handbook of Research on Multicultural Education*, 708-28. See also Friedman et al., eds, *Creating an Inclusive College Curriculum*.
19. Chamberlain, ed., Women in Academe, 158; Ellen Messer-Davidow, "Know-How," in Hartman and Messer-Davidow, eds., *(En)Gendering Knowledge*, 281-309, quotation on 281.
20. Schmitz et al., "Women's Studies and Curriculum Transformation," 720.
21. Elizabeth Kamarck Minnich, *Transforming Knowledge* (Philadelphia: Temple University Press, 1990), 2, 37-38, 177, 178, 181; for Copernicus and Darwin, see idem, "Friends and Critics: The Feminist Academy," in Beth Reed, ed., *Toward a Feminist Transformation of the Academy: Proceedings of the Fifth Annual GLCA [Great Lakes Colleges Association] Women's Studies Conference, Nov. 2-4, 1979* (Ann Arbor, Mich.: Great Lakes College Association Women's Studies Program, 1980), I-II, quotation on 7.
22. For McIntosh, see Betty Schmitz, *Integrating Women's Studies into the Curriculum: A Guide and Bibliography* (Old Westbury, N.Y.: Feminist Press, 1985), esp. 26. See also Mary Kay Thompson Tetreault, "Feminist Phase Theory," *Journal of Higher Education* 56 (July-Aug. 1985): 363-84. Tetrault also identified five phases, which she termed "male scholarship, compensatory scholarship, bifocal scholarship, feminist scholarship, and multifocal or relational scholarship"(367). Several of the schemes are reviewed and discussen in relation to liberal arts and sciences disciplines by Margaret L. Andersen, "Changing the Curriculum in Higher Education," *Signs* 12, no. 2 (winter 1987): 222-54. For Lerner, see Gerda Lerner, "New Approaches to the Study of Women in American History," *Journal of So-*

cial History 3 no. I (fall 1969): 53-62; and idem, Placing Women in History : Definitions and Challenges." *Feminist Studies* 3, no.1-2 (fall 1975): 5-14, both also in her *The Majority Finds its Past: Placing Women in History* (New York: Oxford University Press, 1979). For the use of phase theory in a study of incorporating gender into a required core curriculum, see Susan Christopher, "Gendered Knowledge in the Core Curriculum" (Paper presented at National Women's Studies Association annual meeting, Skidmore College, New York, 1996); the paper is based on idem, "Required Knowledge: Incorporating Gender into a Core Curriculum" (Ph.D. diss., Stanford University, 1995).

23. See also Marilyn R. Schuster and Susan R. Van Dyne, "Stages of Curriculum Transformation," in Schuster and Van Dyne, eds., *Women's Place in the Academy*, 13-29, chart on 16. In 1996, Schuster and Van Dyne updated their chart on curriculum transformation, which now appears as "Stages of Change in the Curriculum and the Classroom," reprinted here as table I, from Elaine Hedges, *Getting Started: Planning Curriculum Transformation* (Towson, Md.: National Center for Curriculum Transformation Resources on Women, 1997), 92.

24. Marilyn R. Schuster and Susan R. Van Dyne, "Changeing the Institution," in Schuster and Van Dyne, eds., *Women's Place in the Academy*, 91-97, quotation on 97.

25. Susan Hardy Aiken et al., "Trying Transformations: Curriculum Integration and the Problem of Resistance," Signs 12, no. 2 (winter 1987): 255-75, quotations on 258, 261-64, 273.

26. See Lynne Goodstein, "The Failure of Curriculum Transformation at a Major Public University: When 'Diversity' Equals 'Variety'" NWSA Journal 6 no. I (spring 1994): 82-102; and "Lynne Goodstein Responds," ibid., 6, no. 2 (summer1994): 308-13, quotation on 311; and the forum on that project in ibid., 6, no. 2 (summer 1994): 291-313, especially Paula Rothenberg, "Rural U.: a Cautionary Tale," ibid., 6, no.2 (summer 1994): 291-98.

27. Ellen G. Friedman of Trenton State College, quoted in Joye Mercer, "Curricular Project in New Jersey Faces an Uncertain Future," Chronicle of Higher Education, Nov. 23, 1994, A26.

28. Lynne V. Cheney, *Telling the Truth: Why Our Culture and Our Country Have Stopped Making Sense—and What We Can Do about It* (New York: Simon and Schuster, 1995), 97,101,106. Cheney refers to Anne Fausto-Sterling, "Race, Gender, and Science," *Transformations* 2, no. 2 (fall 1992): 5-6.

29. Andersen, "Changing the Curriculum," 228-30; see also the discussion of terminology in Schmitz, *Integrating Women's Studies*, 7-8.

30. Sandra Coyner, *Transforming the Knowledge Base: A Panel Discussion at the National Network of Women's Caucuses, First Biennial Meeting, 1989* (New York: National Council forResearch on Women, 1990), 6-7.

31. Sandra Coyner, "Women's Studies as an Academic Discipline: Why and How to Do It," in Bowles and Klein, eds., *Theories of Women's Studies*, 46-71, quotation on 46; idem, "The Ideas of Mainstreaming: and the Disciplines," *Frontiers VIII*, no. 3 (1986): 87-95. For other views on the question of autonomy, see Deborah Rosenfelt, "What Women's Studies Professors Do That Mainstreaming Can't," *Women's Studies International Forum* 7 no. 3 (1984): 167-75; Peggy McIntosh and Elizabeth Kamarck Minnich, "Varieties of Women's Studies," ibid.,7, no. 3 (1984): 139-48. These issues have been articulated more recently by Domna Stanton and Abigail Stewart in "Remodeling Relations: Women's Studies and the Disciplines," in Stanton and Stewart, eds., *Feminisms in the Academy*, 1-16, esp. 10.

32. Coyner, "Women's Studies as an Academic Discipline," 59, 64, quotation from Stimpson on 57.

33. Myra Dinnerstein, "Questions for the Nineties," *Women's Review of Books* 6, no. 5 (Feb. 1989), 13. See also Marilyn Strathern, "An Awkward Relationship: The Case of Feminismm and Anthropology," *Signs* 12, no. 2 (winter 1987): 276-92.

34. Evelyn Torton Beck, "Asking for the Future," *Women's Review of Books* 6, no. 5 (Feb. 1989): 22; Bonnie Zimmerman, presentation on "Curricular Issues for the Twenty-first Century," at "The Next Twenty-five Years," women's studies program admintrators' conference, Arizona State University, Tempe, Feb. 13-15, 1997.

35. Sandra Harding, "Introduction: Is There a Feminist Method?," in Harding, ed., *Feminism and Methodology*, 1-14. See also idem, *The Science Question in Feminism* (Ithaca: Cornell University Press, 1986); and idem, *Whose Science? Whose Knowledge? Thinking from Women's Lives* (Ithaca: Cornell University Prss, 1991). For Evelyn Fox Keller, see her "Feminism and Science," in Keller and Longino, eds., *Feminism and Science*, 28-40, quotation on 38.

36. Joyce McCarl Nielsen, "Introduction," in Nielsen, ed., *Feminist Research Methods*, 1-37, quotations on 12-13, 20. See also Keller and Longino, eds., *Feminism and Science*.

37. Coyner, *Transforming the Knowledge Base*, 16; Harding, *Science Question in Feminism*, 228-29. For "conscious partiality," see Maria Mies, "Toward a Methodology for Feminist Research," in Bowles and Klein, eds., *Theories of Women's Studies*, 117-39, quotation on 122.

38. Judith A. Cook and Mary Margaret Fonow, "Knowledge and Women's Interests: Issues of Epistemology and Methodology in Feminist Sociological Research," in Nielsen, ed., *Feminist Research Methods*, 69-93, quotations on 72-73; idem, "Back to the Future: A Look at the Second Wave of Feminist Epistemology and

Methodology," in Fonow and Cook, eds., *Beyond Methodology*, 1-15.
39. Judith Stacey, "Disloyal to the Disciplines: A Feminist Trajectory in the Borderlands," in Stanton and Stewart, eds., *Feminisms in the Academy*, 311-29, quotations on 316-18, 320, 324-25.
40. Christine de Pizan, quoted in Boxer and Quataert, eds., *Connecting Spheres*, 9.
41. Farnham, "Introduction," 1-8, quotation on 2; Leslie W. Rabine, "Stormy Weather: A Memoir of the Second Wave," in Greene and Kahn, eds., *Changing Subjects*, 216; Margaret L. Andersen, *Thinking About Women: Sociological and Feminist Perspectives* (New York: Macmillan, 1983), 232.
42. Carol P. Christ, "Toward a Paradigm Shift in the Academy and in Religious Studies," in Farnham, ed., *Impact of Feminist Research*, 53-76, quotations on 54, 55-56; Norma Alarcón, "The Theoretical Subject(s) of *This Bridge Called My Back* and Anglo-American Feminism," in Anzaldúa, ed., *Making Face, Making Soul*, 363-64.
43. Peter Novick, *That Noble Dream: The "Objectivity Question" and the American Historical Profession* (New York: Cambridge University Press, 1988), quotation on 40. See also Mark C. Smith, Social Science in the Crucible: The American Debate over Objectivity and Purpose, 1918-1941 (Durham, N.C.: Duke University Press, 1994).
44. Donna Haraway, "Situated Knowledges: The Science Question in Feminism and the Privilege of Partial Perspective," *Feminist Studies*,14, no. 3 (1988): 575-99, quotations on 581, 584.
45. John R. Searle, "Rationality and Realism, What is at Stake?," in Cole, Barber, and Graubard, eds., *Research University in a Time of Discontent*, 55-83, quotations on 68-81. For a good example of feminist redefinitiion, challenging the "Western Rationalistic Tradition" (Searle's capitals), see Toril Moi, "Representation of Patriarchy: Sexuality and Epistemology in Freud's Dora," *Feminist Review* 9 (Oct. 1981):60-74. For new ways to conceptualize objectivity, see Sandra Harding, "Rethinking Standpoint Epistemology: What is 'Strong Objectivity'?," in Alcoff and Potter, eds., *Feminist Epistemologies*, 49-82.
46. Searle, "Rationality and Realism"71; Joyce Appleby, Lynn Hunt, and Margaret Jacob, *Telling the Truth about History* (New York: W.W. Norton, 1994), quotations on 276, 309.
47. Messer-Davidow, "Know-How," 289. On marginality, see Stanton and Stewart, "Remodeling Relations," 3.
48. Messer-Davidow, "Know-How," 307 n. 53.
49. The team charged with curriculum transformation at Lewis and Clark College in Oregon defined their task as "gender-balancing" for reasons of strategy as well as theory, explaining, "We needed an unthreatening term to designate our comprehensive concerns." Susan Kirschner, Jane Monnig Atkinson, and Elizabeth Arch, "Reassessing Coeducation," in Schuster and Van Dyne, eds., *Women's Place in the Academy*, 36.
50. Postman and Weingartner, *Teaching as a Subversive Activity*, 16-24.
51. For reports on the 1975 Sagaris Institute in Vermont, the Califia Communities of 1976-83, and the Feminist Studies Workshop in Los Angeles in 1973 which led to the L.A. Women's Building and several other alternative structures, see "Alternative Structures for Feminist Education," pt. 2 of Bunch and Pollack, eds., *Learning Our Way*, 113-245; Ruth Iskin, "Feminist Education at the Feminist Studio Workshop," in ibid., 169-86, quotation on 169. For a women's studies movement that developed largely outside of institutions of higher education, see Ann Taylor Allen, "Women's Studies as Cultural Movement and Academic Discipline in the United States and West Germany: the Early Phase," *Women in Germany Yearbook* 9 (1993):1-25; and idem, "The March Through the Institutions: Women's Studies in the United States and West and East Germany, 1980-1995," *Signs* 22no. I (autumn 1996): 152-80.

CHAPTER 37

WRITING EVERYBODY IN

MYRNA GOLDENBERG AND BARBARA STOUT

When Montgomery College and four other Maryland community colleges engaged in projects to bring recent scholarship on women and minorities into the curriculum, they were participating in the continuous pattern of change that has characterized American higher education for over three centuries. These projects are significant to community college teaching, especially the teaching of English, for three reasons: Their subject matter coincides with the community college student body; their principles acknowledge the community college teaching situation; and their results include expanded uses of writing and attention to language in many disciplines. Participating faculty were reminded of the power of language to shape thinking.

Since the early eighteenth century, college curriculum has been through constant change—though usually slowly and often contentiously—to accommodate new knowledge, new ways of conceiving and transmitting knowledge, and new student populations. The expansion of the curriculum has always paralleled and continues to parallel the democratization of both the student population and the system of higher education. The fundamental movement is well known: from the early clerical/classical schools with their small, selected numbers of young, male, nearly all white students to today's plenitude of all kinds and sizes of institutions, serving men and women in all adult age groups from the multiple cultures that comprise the nation.

Changes in curriculum eventually followed the expansion of the student population and the expansion of knowledge itself. In the late nineteenth century, the founding of women's colleges and the limited enrollment of women into major colleges and universities led to the development of new fields, such as home economics and social work. In the late 1940s, the phenomenon of mass education, largely attributed to the introduction of the G.I. Bill and the establishment of a national network of community colleges, markedly expanded the student population not only by numbers but, more importantly, by social demographics. Working-class and minority veterans, encouraged by the G.I. Bill, enrolled in colleges and universities and changed the curriculum through their experiences and insights. Their interests were honed by the war as well as by their often unprivileged backgrounds. They demanded a serious, practical course of study that prepared them for advanced study or good careers. Many were married men. Reluctant or unable to become typical undergraduates, they were probably the original nontraditional students. And many of them went to their local community colleges. Then, in the 1960s and 1970s, desegregation and gender equity regulations led to minority studies and women's studies programs. Most recently, the assertion that knowledge is socially constructed has expanded the curriculum by challenging the status quo and by questioning the claim of objectivity. This pattern of growth continues, with the interaction

---

Reprinted from *Women's Studies Quarterly*, 3&4, 1996. copyright© 1996 *Women's Studies Quarterly*.

of scholarship, student populations, and curriculum reform ongoing—at times quietly, at times controversially.

About 85 colleges and universities have participated in serious efforts to transform higher education curriculum so that it reflects the experiences and contributions of women and minorities. Given the strong links between this effort and community college demographics, it seems that increasing numbers of community colleges will get involved. So far, these projects have included community colleges in California, colleges in the Rocky Mountain/Western States projects, colleges in New Jersey as part of that state's Transformation Project, and the Maryland colleges that are the focus of this essay. Montgomery College is fortunate to have had enough interest, support, and leadership from faculty and administrators for involvement in two projects—one of its own and then the larger collaborative effort between Maryland colleges and Towson State University.

The first curriculum transformation project at Montgomery College was the Balancing the Curriculum Institute, a six-week summer project in 1987 and again in 1988 during which twelve self-selected faculty agreed to study a set of readings gathered by the institute director, to revise a unit of a course, to critique one another's revisions, and to again revise the unit. Faculty from art history, biology, chemistry, computer science, English, history, psychology, and sociology were funded by the college, receiving a stipend and a book allowance. This project was repeated the following summer, attracting another twelve faculty.

The second project, called the Towson State University/Maryland Community Colleges Project, involved six institutions and took place over four semesters and one summer, therefore demanding a large amount of coordination and planning. (See "Faculty Development: A Consortial Model," by Myrna Goldenberg and Shirley Parry, in this volume.)

While each of the five community colleges that participated in this project represents a distinct population, together they depict the character of the community college student body nationwide. One campus is primarily urban and African American, and women make up 72 percent of its enrollment; three campuses are suburban, with white, international, immigrant, and African-American students all visibly present; the fifth campus is less racially diverse but serves rural students as well as urban and suburban residents. In total, these colleges enroll 60 percent women and significant numbers of older students, especially adults returning— often as single parents (usually mothers)—for training or retraining. Montgomery College, the flagship college of the larger collaborative project by virtue of its previous curriculum reform project, enrolls 15 percent of all the African-American students in Maryland community colleges, 53 percent of the Hispanic students, 50 percent of the Asian students, 25 percent of the physically challenged students, and leads the state in the number of students taking English for Speakers of Other Languages.

Principles

These two projects were based on seven principles that are important to any substantial curriculum transformation project in a community college. First, review of relevant scholarship and research is the essential starting point. Community college students have as much right to academic currency as university students, but because the community college teaching load does not provide incentive for research, faculty often need and welcome the opportunity to update themselves and to provide solid, newly conceived information to the students.[1]

Second, a focus on pedagogy is vital. Community colleges are teaching institutions, so good community college faculty are concerned about effective teaching. Because of the nature of these projects, feminist pedagogy has to be defined, discussed, and practiced. Feminist pedagogy creates active learning, uses as much collaboration as possible, respects every student as a learner, and expects students to assume responsibility for learning—ideas common to the writing-across-the-curriculum movement as well as to the community college mission. It is, in a word, a pedagogy of empowerment. The projects modeled this kind of pedagogy: Workshops were participatory, faculty actually changed courses rather than simply listening to presentations, they shared their work, and they were required to keep and submit journals tracing their work and thinking as they reformed their course or courses.

Third, changes must be appropriate to introductory courses and, simultaneously, introductory courses must be inclusive, accurate, and up-to-date. Introductory surveys establish the boundaries and key points by which students come to see the nature and scope of a subject. The language of a subject, the significance of its content, the influence of the subject on other subjects both current and past, the relevance of the subject in today's world, its major and minor issues—all are packaged in the introductory course, the staple of community college teaching. Today, students need to have the full view of a subject provided by the multiple vision that comes from scholarship which does not ignore gender, race, class, sexual preference, and ethnicity.

Fourth, both faculty and colleges must make substantial commitments. In these projects, faculty were compensated and were also accountable. They had to attend and participate; they had to submit revised courses; they had to keep and turn in journals, which showed their engagement and also evaluated all aspects of the project. Tight budgets make it difficult for colleges to find resources, but significant curriculum reform cannot occur without institutional support and funding.

Fifth, multiple views must be respected. The act of incorporating new paradigms reminds us that knowledge is constructed by people, that people are shaped by the knowledge that they study, that knowledge is usually expressed in language that cannot be fully accurate, and that the reformulation of knowledge is constant and continual.

Sixth, projects are only beginnings. Curriculum reform is a continuing process. Follow-up sessions for reports on how course revisions have worked and dissemination of revisions to other faculty need to be arranged. Participating faculty need opportunities to take revisions to the next stage.

Seventh, significant curriculum reform usually occurs in stages. Because these projects concentrated on scholarship on white women and minorities of both sexes, they followed a variation of the stage theories developed by Lerner, McIntosh, Schuster and Van Dyne, Tetreault, and others, all of which provide useful tools for evaluating the level of reformulation of a course.

Stage Theory

These projects defined the stages they went through as integration, transformation, and reconceptualization. Further, a course was understood as circumscribed by its content, language, and pedagogy, which are the components of all courses. At each of the three stages, the instructor considers content, pedagogy, and language, asking the same set of questions: Where are the women and minority men? Why are they missing? What are the effects of exclusion? How would this course change if it reflected the scholarship on women and minority men? How can the language be more accurate? How can I teach more effectively? Each question takes on a different texture and emphasis at stages two and three as the instructor gains perspective and information from each preceding stage.

The objective of the first stage, integration, is to begin consciously to use gender and race as categories of analysis and as subject matters worthy of study. The instructor will add material on women and minority men; add assignments that send students to multicultural and feminist sources; add awareness to the classroom through announcements of new books, lectures, or films; and eliminate sexist and racist language, metaphors, stereotypes, and norms. The instructor also moves toward feminist pedagogy, emphasizing collaborative learning. At the end of this stage, the course has been changed because material on and by women and minority men has been added, but the broad outlines and boundaries of the course remain the same.

In the second stage, transformation, the students and instructor develop bibliographies that include works by and about women and minority men. Here the course is changed by what is added *and* deleted. Instructors use new works and women and minority men as exemplars. They reperiodize and reorganize the course, fully incorporating the experiences of women and minority men, They ask, were the Dark Ages dark for all women? How did manifest destiny apply to American minorities? They include nontraditional genres like letters and diaries, and, in that process, validate forms that have been excluded. They change the course topics to reflect the fullness of the subject. In literature, for example, instructors include letters and orally transmitted folk tales; Linda Brent might replace Frederick Douglass in a crowded course outline. At this stage, the course is essentially transformed in that the key elements have been changed: Criteria of what is good are redefined; Lady Byron, Caroline Herschell, Aphra Behn are included as major contributors, not merely added as supplemental curiosities.

In the third and final stage, reconceptualization, the instructor gives the course new shape and vision, and challenges all assumptions: language, content, organization of knowledge, the politics and power structures of the discipline. Because of the breadth of this stage, project participants did not reach it during the span of the project, but they were at least able to grasp its concept.

Content

Dealing with new scholarship means, first of all, changes in the content of courses and attention to the methods by which content is established. Some of the content changes from these projects are no longer startling because of the accepted position these ideas have taken in some disciplines in the few years since these projects began. Textbooks by major publishers now incorporate scholarship on women and minority men at least in literature, history, and sociology.

However, the changes made in course content, whether obvious or surprising, indicate how great the need was to balance the curriculum to provide instruction that validates the experiences of the majority of community college students. Courses in ten disciplines were changed in the following ways:

Arts:

- examining effects of the privileging of forms such as oil painting, symphonies, and operas—which often require expensive media, training, and civic support—as major, and classifying forms such as work songs, blues, ceremonial music of nonwestern cultures, ceramics, textiles, and jewelry as minor;
- exploring images of women and minority men in art, drama, film;
- determining the implications of valuing form, style, and technique over subject matter; abstraction vs. human concern;
- rediscovering female and minority male composers, painters, sculptors, photographers, patrons;
- including nonwestern scales, rhythms, and forms;
- seeing connections between values and progress;
- asking, who are the tastemakers? whence their criteria?

Biology:

- examining the contributions of women scientists, such as Rosalind Franklin, Barbara McClintock, Martha Chase, Rachel Carson, Rosalyn Yalow, Helen Taussig, and Candace Pert as integral parts of the course rather than as add ons;
- determining the evaluative point of view about research findings, methods, and applications: The aspirin/heart attack study using over 22,000 male physicians—why were women not included? Are the results applicable to females? Are conclusions which are based on small sample populations or relatively homogeneous groups, such as patients at veterans hospitals, valid generalizations to the whole population?
- acknowledging that science is not truly objective—that biases, personal animosities, rhetorical and metaphorical language, and contradictory views exist in science as well as in all other communities.

Business:

- adding specific material about women managers;
- increasing use of Labor Department statistics and other current documents about men/women/minorities salary and job categories;
- discussing working and family issues;

- discussing gender, race, and ethnic issues in advertising;
- discussing comparable worth.

Composition:

- considering textbooks for positive images of all groups, multicultural perspectives;
- increasing the use of peer editing;
- including journals and other informal writing both in the composition class and for use in other classes;
- sharing one's own writing;
- assigning topics dealing with race and gender;
- two concerns about teaching argument: lack of emphasis in textbooks on reaching consensus; students' unwillingness to challenge or take a stand.

Criminal Justice:

- analyzing depictions of judges, police officers, criminals, attorneys, and victims in pictures, drawings, and cartoons;
- considering women as offenders and professionals;
- reclassifying rape as a violent—not sexual—crime and the impact of such reclassification on offenders, victims, and the judicial system.

History:

- understanding how one group has been accepted as universal and normative, automatically marginalizing the others;
- using race, class, and gender as core themes, rather than including them as problems;
- questioning periodization and labels: asking how women, slaves, and workers experienced the golden era of fifth-century Greece or the stimulation of the Renaissance;
- looking at many human experiences in historical eras: for example, in the pre-Civil War South, looking at the master and the mistress of plantations, female and male slaves, men and women as yeoman farmers;
- examining the role of women in economic systems from the gathering/hunting societies to modern socialism, communism, and capitalism:
- increasing the use of primary sources and nontraditional sources, such as letters, diaries, advertisements: For example, a course unit on the Lowell Mill girls, using slides of photographs of the mills, a typical day's schedule, selections from the *Lowell Offering*, a magazine produced by and for the girls which both glossed over and revealed the realities of their lives.

Literature (American):

- including Native American, Hispanic-American, and Asian-American texts;
- paying more attention to slave narratives and seeing differences between female and male slave experiences;
- adding Zora Neale Hurston and other women writers to a course in African-American literature that has been dominated by male writers.

Literature (World):

- examining the myths of Eve and Pandora as models for images/life patterns in the western world;
- providing gender analysis of the Iliad, the Odyssey, and the Aeneid;
- discovering insights into positions of women in the classical world through the dramas;
- pursuing a shift from exclusively European and North American texts to inclusion of African and Latin American texts;
- providing organization by themes: nature, love, family life, work, war/violence, with emphasis on multiplicity of views.

Nursing:

- adding cultural history of women as related to the development of nursing;
- considering the importance of gender in nursing;
- providing images of nurses in the media, arts, and literature;
- exploring the relationships between war and nursing;
- discussing the economic and political questions of equal pay and comparable worth;
- discovering the voice (or silence) of nurses in politics and policy.

Psychology:

- determining gender differences in mental illness;
- examining gender roles and mental disorders, such as depression, agoraphobia, eating disorders, alcoholism,
- considering the bias in scientific research—methodological bias in subject selection for psychological studies;
- exploring the implications of the use of male norms for evaluating women;
- discussing the cultural attitudes toward menstruation and menopause and the impact on women's self-esteem (contrast with attitudes toward male puberty and middle age);
- exploring the social dilemmas associated with prostitution and pornography.

Sociology:

- making race, class, gender, ethnicity more visible as tools of analysis;
- providing more critical evaluation of theories;
- comparing shopping malls that cater to different groups, noting differences in shops and services and racial assumptions about consumers;
- exploring gender stereotyping in children's stories and fairy tales;
- exploring considerations of domestic violence;
- examining novels about social problems.

Pedagogy/Active Learning

The Montgomery College Project and the Towson University/Maryland Community Colleges Project encouraged faculty to establish a participatory classroom atmosphere, one in which students collaborate with one another and with the instructor to enhance their learning. The primary goal is to move from "received" to "connected" and finally to "constructed" knowledge and passionate knowing.[2] Another goal is to construct courses that help students "integrate the skills of critical thinking with respect for and ability to work with others."[3]

Faculty included in their courses small-group work and student presentations, which build confidence as well as increase knowledge of course content. Instructors usually counted such activities in grading students. Faculty members also developed assignments, like journals and interviews, to increase personal involvement and to show students how their experiences and their worlds are the starting points for research into larger questions.

When they share classroom power through more student involvement, faculty do not abdicate their responsibility, nor do they make their jobs easier. Instructors still must transmit knowledge that defines their discipline; they must choose books and other materials; give lectures, tests, and grades; lead discussions; and carefully plan, monitor, guide, and evaluate student participation. Sensitivity, a great deal of flexibility, good humor, and much planning are essential when adopting inclusive teaching methods, but those methods are judged by both instructors and students as to whether they are worth the efforts. Transformation projects and writing-across-the-curriculum projects share this commitment to active, engaged learning.

Pedagogy/Teaching through Writing

Naturally, English faculty gave much attention to writing assignments as they revised their courses. Composition as well as literature courses were changed, so English faculty had special opportunities to apply composition research and to see its connections with feminist pedagogy. But faculty in other disciplines used writing in redesigned courses to a surprising extent. The required journals had shown clearly how informal writing can connect a learner with course material. In addition, many project faculty had participated in writing-across-the-curriculum efforts because they are the kind of faculty who are always interested in improving their teaching effectiveness.

In their revised courses, many faculty included writing in traditional modes, like research papers, case studies, summaries, essay exams, book/article/film/performance/exhibit reviews, and field trip reports. Increased time for drafting and revising was often scheduled, and more assignments were given. One sociology instructor who wanted students to see writing both as a dialogue with him and as an instrument of learning stated this policy, which rewarded promptness and revision, in his course syllabus:

> All assignments turned in on time can be revised until you are satisfied with the results and your understanding of the material. Late papers will be accepted for two weeks, but they will not receive comments and cannot be revised. . . .

Faculty also used informal writing: journals, response papers, "thinking" papers, reports of small-group discussion, one-minute writings, written questions about material or for use in examinations, and computer conferencing.

Two criminal justice faculty said that they increasingly find journals to be "our most useful tool." They ask for some entries to be done at home and some written in class, and count journal writing in the course grade. Some of their prompts include:

- Describe yourself and your relationship to this course, including your course goals.
- Describe the effects of race, gender, age, social class, and physical appearance on your own experiences with the criminal justice system and with crime.
- React to visual and print media coverage of crime issues (with which we are constantly bombarded). Write about the portrayal of victims, of offenders, of authority and power, of the victim-offender relationship.

These instructors said, "Almost all students have improved their writing ability, perhaps more in terms of thoughtful expression than in style and form."

An instructor in hotel/motel management used what she called a reactive journal. She asked her students to write informally to such assignments as those listed below, and remarked recently that now she can't teach without this personal writing:

- In your work in the hospitality industry, have you ever experienced racism or sexism—either as a victim or an observer? Describe what you saw and felt.
- Analyze the climate of the organization in which you are working in terms of the presence or absence of sexist or racist attitudes.
- Write a work autobiography telling of jobs you have had in the hospitality industry, how you acquired them, and what you learned from them.
- Analyze your managerial strengths and weaknesses. How would your management style differ from those of managers you have worked for in the hospitality industry?
- Do you think a person's management style has anything to do with his/her gender?

Two English faculty members, one in composition and one in literature, asked students to use journals as seedbeds for formal papers. The composition instructor joined her students in the process by developing one of her own journal entries into an article that she planned to submit for publication.

Pedagogy/Textbooks

Curriculum reform requires attention to textbooks and, in these projects, to analysis of the presence and treatment of women and minority men. Recently published books generally avoid overtly sexist language like the universal "he" and the misleading "man," but vestiges still remain. Nursing faculty worry about the continuing representation of nurses as "she's" and doctors as "he's." Philosophy faculty noted that the use of "man" and "men," especially in model syllogisms, can exclude women: All men are mortal. Mary is therefore a man...? Social science faculty noticed that women and minority men are too often ghettoized into chapters as "problems" or questions. Art faculty observed an improvement in a widely used text: In the book's 1963 edition, there were no plates of works by women or minority men; in a 1986 printing, among 1,079 plates, eighteen were by women and one was by a man of color. English composition and literature anthologies have become noticeably more inclusive in the last few years, in response to new scholarship and faculty insistence on its use.

Language

The language of a course defines its subject matter and values. Language is both the substance and the means of conveying substance. Obviously, such a complex issue is central to curriculum transformation. But just as project faculty could only be awakened to the issue in three semesters, language can only be touched on here. Focusing on language, project faculty looked for conscious and unconscious metaphors that establish attitudes: the taming of the wilderness, virgin land, settling of the West, Columbus's "discovery" of the hemisphere already populated by millions of people, labels of "progress" and "development," calling a community of female seals a "harem." All disciplines employ locutions that may not represent a concept accurately and that may, at the same time, perpetuate gender and cultural stereotypes.

The conceptual effect of common dualisms was also addressed. Polarities like masculine/feminine, black/white, active/passive make it difficult to conceive of the complex and more accurate patterns of reality. Faculty discussed the implications of using common metaphors and dualisms, and developed a heightened sensitivity to the power of language to either stifle or stimulate reader/student response.

Conclusion

The student body will continue to grow in number and diversity, and the curriculum will need reform, just as it always has. For the near future, it seems important for community college faculty and students to have the opportunity to update in the areas on which this essay has focused. The special mission of the community college, which is to empower its students by moving them from passive to active learning, verifies the need for more transformation projects. Finally, in their awareness of the constructing power of language, English faculty will continue to do research, to stay current in the growing body of research in composition and literature, to try to help students and colleagues understand how writing and learning are connected, to prepare students for writing in other courses, and finally to help students become independent, critical learners, as well as thoughtful members of their own communities and of that larger but increasingly fragile community, the world.

Notes

1. Goldenberg, M., and Kievitt, F. D. "The Community College Scholar/Teacher Revisited." *Community College Humanities Review,* 9 (1988): 108–115.
2. Belenky, M. R., et al. *Women's Ways of Knowing.* New York: Basic Books, 1986.
3. Shrewsbury, C. M. "What Is Feminist Pedagogy?" *Women's Studies Quarterly,* 15 (1987): 6–11.

The recipient of the ACCT 1996 William H. Meardy Faculty Member Award, **Myrna Goldenberg** teaches English and women's studies at Montgomery College in Maryland. She is codirector of several local, state, and national curriculum transformation projects, including the Ford Foundation Curriculum Mainstreaming Teaching Initiative and the FIPSE Towson State/Maryland Community Colleges Project.

She has published *numerous articles* on curriculum transformation, American Jewish women, and Holocaust studies, and she lectures frequently, both nationally and internationally, on women in the Holocaust.

Barbara Stout, professor of English at Montgomery College, participated in Montgomery College's Balancing the Curriculum Institute and the Towson State/Maryland Community Colleges Project. She is secretary of the Conference on College Composition and Communication.

A slightly different version of this essay appears in *Two-Year College English: Essays for a New Century*, edited by Mark Reynolds (Urbana, IL: NCTE, 1994). Copyright © 1994

CHAPTER 38

LESBIAN INSTRUCTOR COMES OUT
The Personal Is Pedagogy

JANET WRIGHT

I have been coming out as a lesbian in my social work and women's studies classes now for 6 years. Since I use personal narratives in my teachings and I expect my students to honestly examine themselves, their histories and cultures, and their values as they become social workers, I feel strongly that my ability to talk honestly and openly about myself and my family is a necessity. However, I am more aware now than I was when I originally wrote this article of the emotional toll that coming out in the classroom takes on me. In this article I emphasize the positive effects of coming out both on myself and on my students—who so clearly benefit from authenticity. I remain convinced that the benefits outweigh the costs for me, as well. However, I am struck and challenged by the fact that it hasn't gotten any easier for me over the years and that the initial experience of coming out still leaves me feeling raw and too vulnerable. My thinking now is focused on how to renegotiate and transform this experience of fear and vulnerability for myself.

In the fall of 1990, when I had been a full-time instructor at the University of Wisconsin-Whitewater for one year, I decided to come out as a lesbian during the section on sexual orientation in my Human Behavior and the Social Environment class. I had been nervous for over a week before this class was to take place. But as I looked out at the 25 faces that had grown familiar in 6 weeks of classes, my fear became nauseatingly cold. Why is coming out always so hard, I later wondered. Perhaps because I fear that the other(s) will cease perceiving me as an individual and instead lock me into a category they label perverse or sick or immoral.

During my first year of teaching, I had brought in gay and lesbian friends to be the "dyke/gay for a day." This was the protocol I learned as a teaching assistant in women's studies elsewhere. The technique aimed at "normalizing" gay/lesbian life without risking tainting the women's studies department with a confirmation of the rumors—that we were all lesbians anyway, so there was no need to take our words seriously. The professor had suggested that if I wanted to come out, I do it when *I* was the instructor of the course, not as a teaching assistant.

I was accepting the challenge. I was tired of the evasions. I felt dirty during class discussions of sexual orientation, as if I were eavesdropping on conversations not meant for me. In order to teach in the way that I was most comfortable—using dialogue and narrative—I had to be able to model self-disclosure. There was no longer a choice. It was a risk I had decided to take.

I began that class by illuminating my fears, and then explaining why I decided to come out. The students were silent. I discussed the myths about gay men and lesbians, especially the myths I find most offensive—that lesbians hate men and that homosexuals molest and recruit children. The students were silent. I told them my own story of coming out as a lesbian. The students were silent. I dismissed class early, with instructions to bring any question they had about gays or lesbians, written with no name, to the next class (see Appendix A). They filed out silently.

I sat dejectedly in my chair in the classroom, trying to breathe, trying to calm my jumbled thoughts and feelings. Interrupting my thoughts, one of the students walked back in. I braced myself. She said, "I just wanted to tell you that I am a lesbian, although I've never really said that before, and I have never felt so validated in all of my life. Thank you for your courage."

That comment was the first of a stream of feedback from students that has almost without exception validated and confirmed my decision to come out in that and in subsequent classes.

"I don't understand why you had to come out in class," a student commented once in a discussion on sexual orientation. "That seems like something too private to talk about in classes."

Self-doubt flooded up within me as I attempted to answer the question. The familiar scornful comment, "I don't mind if people are homosexuals. I just wish they wouldn't *flaunt* it," was repeated in my mind. I had decided to come out in classes because it felt right, but clearly the time had come for a more logical, critical analysis with which to expand on my empathic understanding. Why did I feel it was a good strategy to come out in my classes—and a *strategy* for exactly what?

There are at least three possible targets or receivers of the act of coming out in classes: the instructor herself or himself, the students, and the university community. What are the ramifications of coming out for these different receivers?

The Impacts on the Instructor

Secrecy, the closet, is a shell often worn by gay men and lesbians to protect us from violence and from biased judgments and unfair treatment. Secrecy can be used to enhance and protect life and is an indispensable tool in protecting and maintaining identity (Bok, 1983). But secrecy can also damage those who are attempting to "pass." "Passing" prevents building a liberation movement. It prevents us from fighting back, from attacking the myths and superstitions. As Kantrowitz (1984) said about passing as a Jew, "Anyone who has heard, as I have, Jew-hating remarks said to her face because the speaker thought she didn't look Jewish knows both the survival value and the knife twist of passing."

Empowerment comes from acting on one's own behalf. "If I am not for myself, who will be?" (Kantrowitz, 1984). If I cannot stand up for myself and articulate my own concerns, then how can I help others to understand and care about them? Coming out is one step on the road to acceptance and liberation.

The argument that one's sexual preference is something private and intimate ("I don't talk about *my* sexuality!") does not apply to coming out. Coming out is not a discussion of intimate sexual details, it is a discussion of identity. This is what keeps it from being a narcissistic attention-seeking ploy. The Personal Is Political was a powerful political slogan because "it insisted on the primacy of the personal, not in a narcissistic way, but in its implied meaning of the self as a site for politicization, which was in this society a very radical challenge to notions of self and identity" (hooks, 1989). Naming and giving voice to one's experience is the first step in learning about domination and how it functions. The key for the instructor is to link discussions of personal identity to knowledge of how to work towards changing and transforming the oppressive parts of society. Coming out, then, becomes part of the struggle against dominant/subordinate thinking.

Secrets also isolate and distance us from others, leading to inauthenticity in relationships. Both radical educators (Freire, 1989) and feminist pedagogists (Noddings, 1991; Belenky et al., 1986) emphasize the importance of the relationship between the teacher and the student. Solas (1990) found that social work students perceived that the most important component of overall teaching effectiveness was the relationship between the educator and themselves. The best teachers, they felt, were willing to help students and were approachable. Both Gordon (1974) and Rogers (1969) emphasize the teacher–student relationship. Rogers identifies three qualities that facilitate learning:

1. Realness in the facilitator of learning.
2. Prizing, acceptance, and trust—prizing the learner.
3. Empathic understanding.

Gordon argues that there are five traits in a good teacher–student relationship:

1. Openness or transparency, so that each is able to risk directness and honesty with the other.
2. Caring, so that each knows that she/he is valued by the other.
3. Interdependence of one on the other.
4. Separateness, to allow each to grow and to develop her/his uniqueness, creativity, and individuality.
5. Mutual needs meeting, so that neither's needs are met at the expense of the other's needs.

Effective teachers, then, are authentic and willing to self-disclose as a means of reducing hierarchy and of sparking dialogue.

Freire (1989) refutes what he calls the "banking concept of education," in which "knowledge is a gift bestowed by those who consider themselves knowledgeable upon those whom they consider to know nothing" (p. 58). This type of education simply perpetuates a system of domination and subordination. Instead, Freire calls teachers to teach through dialogue, practicing "co-intentional" education that minimizes hierarchy between teacher and student and emphasizes partnership in the pursuit of knowledge.

An authentic relationship between the instructor and the students benefits the instructor by decreasing the distance between them. The instructor is able to teach using her/his own life experiences as examples and as case histories. There is less need to guard oneself, and the instructor can more easily build a sense of shared humanity. Heterosexuals, who don't have to guard this core part of themselves (who, for example, speak candidly about partners and celebrations and holidays) may have difficulty understanding the guardedness and sacrifice of spontaneity that accompanies the closet. Being oneself, being real, makes the art of teaching more comfortable and more relaxed. As Uribe and Harbeck (1992) write, "A major aspect of hiding is the ever present need to self-monitor" (p. 15). We can concentrate our energies on the lessons at hand, unencumbered by the fear of discovery, if we are out to students. This authentic relationship not only benefits the instructor but also benefits the students.

The Impacts on the Students

The relationship between the student and the instructor creates the climate in which learning takes place. Creating an atmosphere of acceptance and mutual caring may predicate the ability to think critically, especially for women students. Nofz (1990) writes, "The inevitable result of criticism without positive affirmation is a great reluctance to share ideas that one holds worthy of examination."

When a teacher can be open and honest about her/his own life, even the difficult parts, students feel safer, more respected, and trusted. This relationship is the fertile ground where learning can take root. As Greene (1991) puts it, "It may be that education can only take place when we can be the friends of one another's minds." When the teacher offers the students stories of her/his own struggles with identity, with overcoming oppression, the students can discover connections with themselves—and "penetrate barriers to understanding" (Witherell, 1991). Stories, Witherell continues, enable us to imagine "the experience and the feeling of the other" (p. 94).

In some classes over the past 2 years, I have distributed an additional evaluation form along with the anonymous end-of-semester evaluation (see Appendix C). This form explores the effects of my coming out in the classroom. The first question asks, "In this class, as part of the section on sexual orientation, the instructor 'came out' as a lesbian. What effect did this have on you?" Students choose to check one of the following categories:

- No effect
- Positive effect; I learned something from it
- Negative effect; it wasn't helpful
- Should have kept it to herself

Out of 56 questionnaires, no students have checked the last two responses. Forty-nine students have checked that it had a positive effect on them and seven said that it had no effect. Of those seven who checked the "no effect" line, several went on to explain that they had already had considerable exposure to gay/lesbian issues.

On the second question, "Did this enhance your learning and your ability to understand the issues involved in sexual orientation and homophobia?", 53 students checked "yes." All of the three students who checked "no" cited that they already understood the issues. Some of the student comments are illuminating on the value of coming out in establishing an open classroom atmosphere.

> I think it took a lot for the instructor to come forth and tell us she's a homosexual. I have a lot of respect for her because she's not pretending to be someone she's not.

> I have plenty of friends that are homosexuals/gay. But I do feel that it helped a lot of other students and *made the atmosphere a more sharing one* [my emphasis].

> I realized that the stereotypes are so inaccurate that you hear. It was good for the class to hear a personal story which is very normal and not odd.

> I got a greater understanding of the myths and stereotypes surrounding homophobia in our society and had more factual, personal experience material to absorb—I got to *feel* [my emphasis] what gays and lesbians have to endure and as a result am much more tolerant.

Although positive affirmation and encouragement are important in a classroom, they are not sufficient to create a comfortable dialogue. If we expect students to share life experiences, to examine them critically in light of new knowledge, then we are encouraging them to take risks. If, as Nofz (1990) says, we as professors refuse to take similar risks, we set a powerful example of disassociating one's life from one's education.

We need to share more of our own struggles with inquiry, not just the end results of what we have learned. Each time we allow our students to see that we, too, sometimes face uncertainty, or have a nagging personal experience that cannot be fitted neatly into the disciplinary wisdom, we invite our students to join in that struggle.

MacDermid et al. (1992) concur:

> Separation (between learners and educators) is emphasized when learners are asked to use their personal experience as bases for building knowledge but the educator does not do the same; the learners are being asked to take risks (by revealing personal information) that the educator does not take. Personal stories revealed by educators allow learners to see them from a human perspective, enhancing the felt connectedness between them and minimizing the gap between the personal and the political.

Feminist educators (Noddings, 1984; Witherell, 1991; Belenky et al., 1986) emphasize that most women (and perhaps most men, too) learn best through a pedagogy that emphasizes connectedness between learner and educator, among learners, and between learners and experience. Dialogue, which necessitates a genuine interest in the other, is an important key to learning (Grumet, 1981). Self-disclosure opens the possibility for true connected, respectful, critical dialogue.

Another way that an instructor's coming out can be beneficial to students is that it provides a model. Providing models of gay/lesbian teachers is important for both gay/lesbian students and for heterosexual students. It helps to break the sense of isolation, hopelessness, and fear experienced by gay and lesbian students. Gay and lesbian students, like any other oppressed group, need their elders as models and guides. But gay and lesbian teachers feel especially constrained. Coming out may cost us our jobs. We could be accused or suspected of molesting or recruiting young impressionable students. A major component of every oppression is isolation, but it is overwhelmingly potent in the oppression of gays and lesbians because we can't always even identify each other.

Recent estimates by the Department of Health and Human Services suggest that of the more than 5,000 suicides annually of young men and women between the ages of 15 and 24, more than 30% of them may be directly related to emotional turmoil over sexual preference issues and societal prejudices surrounding same-sex relationships (Harbeck, 1992). Uribe and Harbeck (1992) believe that gay, lesbian, and bisexual adolescents may be at higher risk of dysfunction, partially because of a lack of positive role modeling influences and experiences and their dependence on parents, peer groups, and educators who may be unwilling or unable to provide emotional support. In their study of homosexual adolescents, Uribe and Harbeck found that: "One of the most significant facts was their feelings that they existed in a box, with no adults to talk to, no traditional support structures to lean on for help in sorting out their problems, and no young people like themselves with whom to socialize" (p. 15). Recognizing that some gay/lesbian people have genuine and terrible constraints on coming out at work, those of us who can, must. The lives of young lesbians and gay men are depending on our strength.

For heterosexual students, the presence of an openly gay or lesbian teacher can provide them with an important model, too. Many heterosexual students may believe that they have never known a gay man or lesbian. This invisibility allows the stereotypes and myths to persist. One student commented on her/his class evaluation:

> I guess I was extremely prejudiced toward homosexuals before I took this class. I have never had contact with a homosexual before, at least not as far as I'd known. I realized that I have to accept people for their individual characteristics and attributes, rather than for their sexual preference. I'm no longer homophobic at all. I think Janet did a great job. She was very open and honest.

Harbeck (1992) notes that several psychological studies have demonstrated that if a heterosexual individual knows a homosexual, then acceptance increases as stereotypical responses decrease.

Bias is not only an intellectually learned process, it is also emotional. Therefore, unlearning bias must have an emotional component. When a teacher comes out as lesbian or gay, the student must confront bias and oppression on a personal level. The out lesbian/gay teacher who can dialogue with students about the oppression she/he experiences will help students personalize the issues—oppression can take on a new, more personal meaning. Students may be freed to more critically examine oppression in their own lives. For example, one student spoke about her experience with being hospitalized for phobias in high school, the stereotypes people held about mental illness, and the effects of this on her life. Students have, after the teacher's disclosure, examined experiences with eating disorders, being a Jew in a Christian society, rape and sexual abuse, child abuse and woman abuse, alcoholism, and so on. The students' abilities to critically examine these experiences in an accepting classroom atmosphere have been empowering and, in some instances, healing. Secrets tend to foster feelings of shame. Openness can dissipate these feelings.

Student comments on my class evaluation forms support the idea that they learned about oppression from the instructor's coming out:

> I am glad you came out in class. I feel some of those same fears. I am anorexic/bulimic. People have a lot of misconceptions on this.

> I want to thank you for your respect for us. My dad is gay and he never hides it. He is proud.

> I had no clue nor ever thought of the sexual orientation of the instructor. It made me realize that anyone can be gay/lesbian and it doesn't make them any less of a person.

> I had a negative attitude toward gays and lesbians, probably because I never knew any. But now I realize that they are just people too.

> I used to be very against homosexuals because I didn't understand them. The information given helped me understand what these people are about.

> I—not to my knowledge—have never met a homosexual person. I guess I was a little

homophobic—but I have an open mind. I'm glad I know.

It's better to see people who represent the stereotypes in our society in order to disprove them. I think it is easy for people to hold bias until they are confronted by a person who presents an image of fact.

You once said in class that we are all prejudiced because we are raised to be, and that sometimes we are too "liberal" to admit our prejudice and at first I wanted to be defensive. But yet, when I went with my friends, some of whom are gay, to various bars and felt uncomfortable, I was angry with myself for feeling uncomfortable. I realized that my feelings had no basis and that you were right.

Modeling as a visible gay or lesbian teacher takes on other meanings, too. By being out, we model honesty. We validate difference. We show that individuals have choices—choices to be the men and women that they are, regardless of societal prescription. At a time in their lives when traditional students are just beginning to listen to their own voices over their peer group, over parents—we model the values of being oneself, authentically and without reserve. And this is one of the most important lessons of life.

Impact on the University

When instructors and other staff are openly gay and lesbian, the university and their respective departments will no longer be as free to operate under the assumption of heterosexuality. A struggle between conflicting values on lesbian/gay issues at Oberlin College illustrates this. On the one hand, the institution was among the first to adopt nondiscrimination clauses for sexual orientation. On the other hand, there is a strong emphasis and focus on heterosexual orthodoxy—that traditional heterosexual roles for men and women are the only truly acceptable ones. Gay men and lesbian women, for example, are not supported in political activities. However, if administrators are aware of gay and lesbian faculty and staff, they may realize that the topic is "on the table" and their actions and policies can be and will be challenged.

Identified gay and lesbian faculty and staff will also be used by the university and the department as consultants. Although there is danger of tokenism ("Let's make sure there's a lesbian on the committee"), even tokenism can be progress. On the one hand, it is insulting to think that one person can even attempt to speak for as heterogeneous a group as gay men and lesbians. On the other hand, at least the topic is addressed. And, the modeling takes place on a collegial level as well—administrators and colleagues are forced to see and acknowledge a gay man or lesbian woman. Stereotyping becomes less viable.

Suggestions for Departments

The fear of backlash is well-founded, of course. It occurs as any oppressed group advocates for its own equal rights, and homophobia consists of a unique blend of hatred, fear, and moral indignation. There will be violence, both physical and emotional, against gay men and lesbians, their supporters, and those wrongly suspected of being gay or lesbian. However, some academic departments will choose to contribute to an atmosphere of acceptance rather than ignore the struggle. It is not necessary to wait for a faculty member to come out or to recruit a gay or lesbian faculty member in order to begin this process. Following are some suggestions for departments and faculty.

1. Adopt a resolution on sexual orientation (see Appendix B). A resolution makes very clear the attitudes and intentions of the department around sexual orientation. This resolution can be included in the student handbook, distributed and discussed in classes, and pointed out to every potential faculty and staff member. This is a crucial step in structuring a safe environment for gay men and lesbians.

2. Posters, decorations, pamphlets, and handouts in and from the department can project a positive image of gays and lesbians and an accepting departmental attitude.

3. Examples of gay and lesbian couples and families as well as counseling issues such as coming out should be common

in role plays and practice classes. Policy and research classes can incorporate gay and lesbian issues. Most important, faculty can use inclusive language, such as *partners* instead of *husband and wife*. Lesbian and gay reality is thereby integrated into and validated by the curriculum.

4. Departments must recognize and discuss the possible ramifications of a colleague coming out to students. Heterosexual students may seek information and understanding from heterosexual faculty on gay/lesbian issues. Are faculty sufficiently prepared and comfortable with their own views? How will the department handle extremely homophobic students? Is there an attempt to screen such students out of the profession? How? What if students refuse to have the lesbian/gay instructor as an advisor? How will the department respond to a sudden drop in student evaluations? When faculty grapple with these issues, they acknowledge the unique oppression they are confronting.

Department chairs need to be aware of the dangers and opportunities that open to an out faculty member in the university. An identified gay/lesbian faculty member may be seized on by university administration, leading to the dangers of tokenism and overextension.

On the other hand, an out faculty member can enrich the perceptions of and discussions on oppression for departments as well as for university administrations.

5. Heterosexual faculty members can come out as strong supporters of gay/lesbian rights by discussing their own participation in a gay rights march, by relating their own experiences with gay brothers, sons, and lesbian daughters, and sisters, gay/lesbian friends. Faculty members might attend and later discuss a meeting of P-FLAG (Parents and Friends of Lesbians and Gays)—or better yet, plan a field trip and take the students along.

Faculty members could try wearing pink triangle buttons for a day and discussing their own personal reactions and fears, as well as the reactions from others.

Faculty members can write letters to the school paper, protesting homophobic statements or events or supporting gay/lesbians rights.

Perhaps most important, faculty members could discuss in classes their own processes in shedding their homophobia. Students desperately need heterosexual models who can honestly discuss their homophobia and their methods for combatting it.

Conclusion

Coming out in the classroom is not the only strategy for fighting homophobia and heterosexism. It is not appropriate for all classes or for all lesbian/gay faculty members to come out to students. "Each teacher has her or his individual methods of teaching, of reaching the students, of creating a rapport that permits some learning to occur" (Khayatt, 1992, p. 173). The labels can be uncomfortable—*straight* or *queer; heterosexual* or *homosexual*—because they once again reinforce dualistic and simplistic thinking. Sexuality, gender roles, and identity are complex concepts that cannot be adequately or comfortably pigeonholed into rigid labels. An instructor who teaches a graduate level course on sexuality, for example, might consciously reject the notion of identifying her/his present place on the continuums. Coming out may not make sense for instructors of certain large lecture classes or certain topics. Context is always an important factor in decision making.

However, there is an important function for those educators who are willing and able to self-identify as lesbian or gay. Societal hatred, fear, and misunderstanding are focused on the stereotyped images of gay and lesbian. One way of diffusing the potency of those labels is by redefining them, reframing them, so that they lose their negative power. Coming out in the classroom opens the dialogue on sexual orientation and on oppression on the personal level. This can be empowering for the faculty person as well as the lesbian and gay students. But it can also model an authenticity and acceptance that challenges, empowers, and honors all the classroom participants who, regardless of sexual orientation or preference, are unique and diverse individuals.

References

Allen, Katherine R., & Crosie-Burnet, Margaret. (1992). Innovative ways and controversial issues in teaching about families: A special collection on family pedagogy. *Family Relations, 41*, 9–11.

Belenky, Mary Field, Clinchy, Blythe, Goldberger, Nancy Rule, & Tarule, Jill. (1986). *Women's ways of knowing*. New York: Basic Books.

Bok, Sissela. (1983). *Secrets: On the ethics of concealment and revelation*. New York: Vintage Books.

Freire, Paulo. (1989). *Pedagogy of the oppressed*. New York: Continuum.

Gordon, Thomas. (1974). *TET: Teacher effectiveness training*. New York: Peter H. Wyden.

Greene, Maxine. (1991). Foreword. In Witherell, Carol, and Noddings, Nel (Eds.), *Stories lives tell: Narrative and dialogue in education* (pp. 83–95). New York: Teachers College Press.

Grumet, Madeleine R. (1981). Conception, Contradiction and Curriculum. *Journal of Curriculum Theorizing, 3*, 292.

Harbeck, Karen M. (Ed.). (1992). *Coming out of the classroom closet*. New York: Haworth Press.

Hegel, Georg Wilhelm Friedrich. (1967). *The phenomenology of mind*. New York: Harper and Row.

hooks, bell. (1989). *Talking back: Thinking feminist, thinking black*. Boston: South End Press.

Kantrowitz, Melanie. (1984). *Anti-Semitism, racism, and coalitions*. Speech given in Minneapolis, MN.

Khayatt, Madiha Didi. (1992). *Lesbian teachers: An invisible presence*. New York: State University of New York Press.

MacDermid, Shelley M., Jurich, Joan, Myers-Walls, Judith A., & Pelo, Ann. (1992). Feminist teaching: Effective education. *Family Relations, 41*, 31–38.

Noddings, Nel. (1991). *Caring: A feminine approach to ethics and moral education*. Berkeley: University of California Press.

Nofz, Michael. (1990). The classroom and the "real world"—are they worlds apart? *Teaching Forum, 12* (pp. 1–3). Undergraduate Teaching Improvement Council, University of Wisconsin System.

Pharr, Suzanne. (1988). *Homophobia: A weapon of sexism*. Little Rock: Chardon Press.

Postman, Neil, & Weingartner, Charles. (1969). *Teaching as a subversive activity*. New York: Dell.

Rich, Adrienne. (1980). Foreword. In J. P. Stanley & S. Wolfe (Eds.), *The coming out stories* (pp. xi–xiii). Watertown, MA: Persephone Press.

Rogers, Carl R. (1969). *Freedom to learn*. Columbus, OH: Charles E. Merrill.

Solas, John. (1990). Effective teaching as construed by social work students. *Journal of Social Work Education, 26*, 145–154.

Uribe, Virginia, & Harbeck, Karen M. (1992). Addressing the needs of lesbian, gay, and bisexual youth: The origins of PROJECT 10 and school-based intervention. In Harbeck, Karen M. (Ed.), *Coming Out of the Classroom Closet* (pp. 9–28). New York: Haworth Press.

Witherell, Carol. (1991). The self in narrative: A journey into paradox. In Witherell, Carol, & Noddings, Nel (Eds.), *Stories lives tell: Narrative and dialogue in education* (pp. 83–95). New York: Teachers College Press.

Witherell, Carol, & Noddings, Nel (Eds.). (1991). *Stories lives tell: Narrative and dialogue in education*. New York: Teachers College Press.

Appendix A

Questions from Students

What follows is a sampling of anonymous, written questions that students have given me in Human Behavior and the Social Environment classes. This format of asking students to hand in anonymous questions that the instructor takes home to consider and answers in the next class period has been very successful.

What brought about your change in behavior, or what made you realize your true feelings?

When did you know? Who did you tell?

Did you know when you were married?

How does one know that one is gay/lesbian?

A homosexual student wrote an article on how homosexuals need more effort on coming out of the closet, standing up for their rights, etc.—then signed it "anonymously"—why would they do this and totally contradict themselves?

Family

How did your family handle your homosexuality—first your parents and then your children—after you were previously in a heterosexual relationship?

How do your parents feel? Brothers, sisters?

How did you explain to your family (children and parents) about your sexual preference?

How does having and/or growing up in a household with a homosexual parent(s) affect children?

Do your kids get teased or beat-up, are they afraid to bring friends home, or embarrassed to be seen in public with you?

What were your children's first reactions?

Dating/Relationships

Where do lesbians and gay men go to meet other homosexuals, other than gay bars? Do you have a partner at this time?

Is it the same kind of love if you were "in love" with a man?

What is it that you like about your partner? Are you currently involved with someone? Are you and your partner sexually involved? How do you introduce your partner?

Do you go places (bars, etc.) where you interact with other lesbians?

How did you approach your first lesbian relationship? Was it awkward? Did you make a date like everyone else?

Friends

How do men treat you when they find out you are a lesbian?

How did the other professors react?

Are your previous boyfriends offended?

Are other women afraid of you, or afraid to touch you normally, because of your sexual preference?

Marriage/Husband

Are your biological children from your ex-husband?

The book says that most people know their sexual preference before age 20. If that is true, why do many homosexual people enter into heterosexual marriages?

What does your husband think and what happened in your marriage?

Did your ex-husband know?

Sex

What do lesbians do for sexual arousal or stimulation with each other? Do you still have heterosexual desires? Has anyone expected that you were into every other kind of thing (like group sex, or whatever)?

Causes

Do you think homosexuality could be genetically linked?

Do you think people are born gay?

What was the reason for you becoming a lesbian?

Legal Issues

Is it legal for lesbians and gay men to marry in Wisconsin? In any state?

On what grounds would child custody be granted or not to the gay/lesbian parent?

Have you ever been discriminated against because you are a lesbian?

Religion

What are your religious beliefs and how does it affect your sexual orientation?

Miscellaneous

Do lesbians still feel "feminine"?

Comments

I think it took a lot of courage for you to tell our class about this—I think it's cool that you're not ashamed of who you are and if anything, I think it makes one a better person admitting to oneself and others about who you are and what you believe. I don't see you any differently than from the first day of class.

I applaud your openness. Many students never knew a gay or lesbian and just heard stories. You are giving them an excellent example.

Appendix B

Resolution Regarding Sexual Orientation

Whereas discrimination against gay men and lesbians is still legal in most states and is widely practiced and accepted throughout the United States;

Whereas there is no known cause of homosexuality and it appears to be a naturally occurring human diversity which is present in at least 10% of the human population;

Whereas gay men and lesbians are as psychologically and emotionally adjusted as the rest of the population;

Whereas no harm comes to other peoples as a result of a homosexual orientation;

Whereas the social work profession has historically committed itself to the goal of social equality and the elimination of oppressions; and

Whereas the National Association of Social Workers Code of Ethics prohibits discrimination on the basis of one's sexual orientation;

We, the faculty and staff of the Department of Social Work, University of Wisconsin, Whitewater, are resolved:

To educate and raise awareness in social work students about the oppressions of homophobia and heterosexism and their harmful effects on society as a whole;

To work against the discrimination of gay men and lesbians wherever it exists in the University community;

To improve the University climate for the gay men and lesbians who are faculty/staff, classified staff, and students, and

To work for the acceptance of gay men and lesbians as full-fledged members of society, entitled to the same rights, responsibilities, and respect as any other citizen.[1]

Appendix C
Evaluation Form

In this class, as part of the section on sexual orientation, the instructor "came out" as a lesbian. What effect did this have on you?

- No effect
- Positive effect; I learned something from it
- Negative effect; it wasn't helpful
- Should have kept it to herself

Did this enhance your learning and your ability to understand issues involved in sexual orientation and homophobia?

Why or why not?

How do you think the instructor could have improved your learning experience on the issue of sexual orientation?

Note

1. This Resolution was adopted by the University of Wisconsin–Whitewater, Department of Social Work Faculty, January 1991.

Janet Wright has a PhD in Social Welfare from the University of Wisconsin–Madison and is presently the Chair of the Social Work Department at the University of Wisconsin–Whitewater. Her book on lesbian step families is expected to be published by the Haworth Press in 1998.

CHAPTER 39

KNOWLEDGE AS BAIT: FEMINISM, VOICE, AND THE PEDAGOGICAL UNCONSCIOUS

LAURIE FINKE

To what extent should we accept Paulo Freire's assertion that education is never a neutral process, but either facilitates "the integration of the younger generation into the logic of the present system," thereby encouraging them to internalize its values, or becomes a "practice of freedom" and a means of enabling students to participate in the transformation of that system (15; see also Davis, "Manifesto")? For the last two decades, feminist teachers committed to creating education that would also be a "practice of freedom" for students, especially for women, have attempted to promote more egalitarian classrooms responsive to differences not only of gender, but also of class, race, sexual preference, ethnicity, and age. Crucial to this goal of developing new pedagogies that are participatory, experiential, and non-hierarchical—a goal shared with those practicing "liberatory," "oppositional," or "radical" pedagogies—have been concepts like "empowerment," "student voice," "dialogue," and "critical thinking," concepts that entail a new understanding of the nature and roles of "knowledge" in teaching and learning.

Under these various labels, however, efforts by both feminist and radical teachers to promote nonauthoritarian classroom environments have often ended up mystifying the very forms of authority they sought to exorcise, authority that is both institutionally and psychically embedded in the social relations of education. They have done so because these relations cannot so easily be reduced to a simple dichotomy between conformity and resistance. Indeed, that dialectic continually founders on the rocks of such anxiety-producing paradoxes as the feminist teacher who attempts to subvert the institution of education while participating in its unequal system of rewards and punishments, or the feminist student who tries to bring down the patriarchal system while maintaining a high enough GPA to get into graduate school, or even the nonfeminist student negotiating a graduation requirement. The social relations of education can be comprehended only within a complex network of intersecting tensions that include not only conformity and resistance, but also identification and rebellion, love and power. They must account for not only the vertical relations between teacher and student, but also the horizontal relations among students.

Unable to articulate a pedagogical politics that is not simply oppositional, some feminists write about pedagogy as if they believe that the classroom is a universal and a historical space, rather than a local and particular space embedded within a specific institutional culture that serves a range of disciplinary and institutional objectives. To be sure, both feminists and other radical educators have already begun to examine the political shortcomings of pedagogies that strip both students and teachers of their specific political investments in the name of "rational" analysis and "critical thinking" (Ellsworth; Tetreault and Maher, "Doing Feminist Ethnography," "Breaking

Through Illusion"; Graff; Penley; and Treichler). While I do not wish to ignore the significance of these critiques, I want to explore the psychic investments that come into play in feminist classrooms but that may be mystified by an unexamined commitment to egalitarian ideas about learning. In particular, I shall examine the ways in which all pedagogy—including feminist pedagogy—is driven by a psychic interplay of desire and power among teachers and students. While I recognize that this analysis is not unique to feminist teaching and that many of its particulars are shared by other radical teachers, my interest is specifically in what *feminist* teachers say about their teaching and in the ways in which psychoanalytic thinking might enable feminist teachers to come to terms with the roles of power and authority. I assume feminist pedagogy does not exist in a vacuum. It interacts with, influences, and is influenced by other approaches to teaching. This essay is one instance of an attempt to bring feminist teaching into dialogue with other radical pedagogical practices—in particular with the practices of psychoanalysis. This is what I mean by the "pedagogical unconscious" of my title, a term Gregory Jay has used to describe student resistance and ignorance not as a passive state—as an absence of information—but as an "active dynamic of negation" which effective teaching must engage (789). Tied to a feminist political analysis of the social relations of gender, this concept should enable a more complex vision than feminist pedagogy has allowed of classroom dynamics, which are inevitably as conflicted as nurturing, as competitive as collaborative, and as contradictory as complementary.

Ordinarily we consider teaching as a public practice that operates consciously and rationally; psychoanalysis, in contrast, is a private practice that engages the unconscious and the irrational. For this reason, the two might seem antithetical (Penley 131; Millot; Emerson 255–57). Feminist pedagogy seems a particularly hostile ground for psychoanalytic thinking because the former shares with the liberatory pedagogy of Paulo Freire the belief that oppression, once it is rationally exposed through a critical analysis that springs from the dialogue between student and teacher, can be effectively resisted. Feminist pedagogies have their origins in the consciousness-raising movement of the sixties and so would subscribe to Freire's formulation of human beings as "conscious beings, and consciousness as consciousness intent upon the world" (66; see also Treichler 68–69). Such a formulation would seem to have little political use for a concept of the unconscious, for that which is unknowable to consciousness.

But this appeal to consciousness-raising cannot tell us why the student who can intelligently critique patriarchal institutions in a brilliant seminar paper can still suffer from date rape, domestic violence, an eating disorder, or a crisis of sexual identity. Feminist teachers, however total their commitment to theoretical analysis, can neither banish entirely nor fully illuminate the psychic lives of their students because the classroom itself is part of the cultural matrix within which its participants' psyches have been produced. Both teachers and students are, at least in part, constituted by the dominant discourses and practices they oppose and seek to demystify. Feminist pedagogy, then, must avoid reproducing a simplistic inside/outside dichotomy which locates oppression, anxiety, and resistance either exclusively within the individual, the result of psychic forces of which the individual is not consciously aware, or exclusively outside of the individual in the cultural and historical forces that act on her. The one approach privileges neurosis—hysteria in particular—and the other victimization (Rose). The former calls for a psychoanalytic pedagogy; the latter, a political one. The task of a feminist pedagogy seems to demand some integration of both approaches.

By writing an essay on psychoanalysis and pedagogy, I do not wish to suggest that feminist pedagogy can or ought to be explained only in psychoanalytic terms or to set psychoanalysis up as a "master" narrative for pedagogy. Nor do I wish to engage in any *apologia* for bringing these two practices to dialogue with each other. Although I am aware of the potentially productive feminist resistance to psychoanalysis—one that is always political—there is already a large body of literature on this resistance (Bernheimer and Kahane, Feldstein and Roof, Garner et al.). The process of thinking through the relationship between psychoanalysis and feminist pedagogy is undoubtedly an anxious one. Having no previous commitments to psychoanalytic feminism, I feel caught between the often keen insights of psychoanalytic feminist critics, on the one hand,

and the distrust and often open hostility of other feminist scholars (my own divided self included), on the other. The dilemma created by such competing approaches potentially reduces all feminists to either naïve and unsophisticated "empiricists" or dutiful daughters mimicking the master discourse. It seems to me that feminism cannot be content with either an apolitical theory or an untheorized politics. The question that then poses itself concerning the relations between psychoanalysis and feminist pedagogy is not only how psychoanalysis might reveal the unconscious of feminist pedagogy, but, equally important, how a feminist pedagogy might repoliticize psychoanalysis.

For this reason, I want to begin my investigation of the dialogue between psychoanalysis and feminist pedagogy by exploring a literal scene of teaching—women's teaching in the shadow of patriarchy—that appears in a very political play, Shakespeare's *Henry V*. This scene, which describes a particular kind of pedagogy, is marginal to the main plot of the play, perhaps included to create "comic relief." It follows immediately on Henry's victory against the French at Harfleur. In it, Katherine, the French princess who will later be married to Henry to cement a dynastic merger between the English and French, learns some English from Alice, her lady-in-waiting. The "language lesson" is composed entirely in French:

> *Kath:* Alice, tu as été en Angleterre, et tu bien parles le langage.
> *Alice:* Un peu, madame.
> *Kath:* Je te prie, m'enseigner; il faut que j'apprenne à parler. Comment appelez-vous la main en Anglois? (3.4.1–6)

The conscious, or rational, goal of this pedagogical exchange is to teach Katherine the language of her soon-to-be adopted country. This simple cognitive act posits a one-to-one correspondence between words and things in which signifiers can be exchanged between different languages while the signifieds remain unaffected by the exchange. "La main" can become "de hand" with no violence to the actual appendage.

The enunciation of this "language lesson," however, proves a more complex affair than the cognitive exchange of signifiers between teacher and student suggests. Ronald Schleifer defines enunciation as the "act of utterance, the performance of discourse," as opposed to the utterance or statement itself (802). The exchange between Katherine and her lady-in-waiting is driven by conflicting articulations of power, desire, status, and resistance—not only those of the two characters in the scene but also those of many others who are absent from it. "Teach it to me," Katherine says to her lady-in-waiting, "I *want* to learn it." But Katherine's desire reflects her acceptance of the realities of power and dynastic politics in the war between her father and her future husband. Katherine functions in the play as a token of exchange between the warring French and English monarchies; her offspring presumably will unite the two realms and end their warfare (Henry the Sixth, "in infant bands crowned King/of France and England"). As the language lesson proceeds, we notice that the words Katherine asks to have translated are all parts of her body: hands, fingers, nails, arm, elbow, neck, chin, and foot. But what Katherine "learns" is far more than such English equivalents of French words: she also learns how the female body is constructed and deployed in the aristocratic and militaristic culture of "chivalry." She learns this not through the agency of the lady-in-waiting, the ostensible "teacher" in this transaction, but through the desires of those men who, while not actually present in the scene, establish the conditions of its enacting, its "enunciation." In effect, the lesson has a subconscious; both Katherine and her lady-in-waiting have internalized the desires of others. Katherine is "schooled"—by another woman and her social subordinate—to define herself as a body, an object of sexual exchange in feudo-dynastic politics.

At the same time, Katherine resists both the conscious and the unconscious "lessons"—resists, that is, the desires both of those present and those absent—by punning on French-English homonyms. In saying "resists," I am not speaking of conscious and effective political resistance that I might urge feminists to adopt so as to effect change. What I mean is that Katherine plays the "student," adopting a position of ignorance that both Felman and Jay attribute to the pedagogical unconscious (Felman 28–31; Jay 786–87). Engaging this resistance, they argue, is crucial to any true pedagogical practice informed by psychoanalytic insight. Katherine mistakes the English "elbow" for the French "bilbow," or sword, and the English "nail" for the French "mail," mimicking the militaristic language that dominates the play but that is especially prominent in the preceding scene depicting Henry's siege of Harfleur (3.4.29, 45). She also mistakes the English "foot" and "gown" for the French "foutre" and "con," setting up an obscene pun which even late twentieth-century editions of Shakespeare refuse to gloss:

> Le foot et le count! O Seigneur Dieu! ils sont les mots de son mauvais, corruptible, gros, et impudique, et non pour les dames de honneur d'user. Je ne voudrais prononcer ces mots devant les seigneurs de France pour tout le monde. Foh! le foot et le count! (3.4.52–56)

These obscene puns, which she would refuse to speak in public before "les seigneurs," suggest her perhaps unconscious resistance to being reduced to a "good fuck" or a "cunt." This scene, then, subtly defines and limits Katherine's role within the play's politics, while it offers a mode of resistance—the slippage in and between languages—to its cultural and political imperialism. Although the play contains Katherine's "resistance" and the final courting scene covers over the slippages between the French and English languages, this scene provides a moment through which we might tease out a potential feminist politics of psychoanalysis.

Katherine's unconscious desires, manifested in lapses of speech and in wordplay (see Freud, *Jokes*), are shaped by and in resistance to the political and social concerns of the Renaissance aristocracy within which individuals are gendered. In *Henry V*, the individual psyche and the social world are never seen in isolation from each other; the play discourages the separation of the individual and the social so central to the philosophy of liberal individualism. What complicates both feminist and psychoanalytic critiques of pedagogy is the liberal enlightenment concept of the individual embedded within the philosophies of education, psychoanalysis, and liberal feminism. All tend to conceive of the "individual" in opposition to the "social" so that consciousness or the "psyche" is constructed as individual, whereas ideology, conceived of as false consciousness, operates in the realm of the social, particularly the political. The operations of the psyche and politics end up opposing one another, rather than emerging in dialogic relation. The feminist critique of psychoanalysis asserts that psychoanalytic discourse explains ideology and history only in terms of universalized and static psychic formations (Smith 84–85). Implicit in Lacan's rereading of Freud, however, is some recognition of the complex interrelationships between the individual and the social, the psychic and the political. If, as Lacan has argued, the psyche is organized as a language, then, like a language, it must be a social process explained in terms of ideology, conceived not simply as false consciousness, but in Althusserian terms as those lived practices, meanings, and values that effectively ensure the maintenance and reproduction of social power. In an effectively politicized feminist psychoanalysis, the individual woman's psyche must be construed as a social and ideological process, constituted by and within language and culture and not some kind of private interiority. "Raising" her consciousness is not simply a matter of translating isolated private and prelinguistic experiences into discourse, but of negotiating the ways in which she, like Katherine, is culturally and ideologically embedded in history. Both consciousness and the unconscious are processes, the ongoing productions of an internalized ideology in Western society of "individuality," which is itself an ideologically delimited and unstable sign.

Despite what it has to tell us about the relationships between the individual and her social environment, however, the "language lesson" in *Henry V* stands as a model against which a feminist pedagogy would want to define itself. Katherine merely parrots the list of words and sounds she has been "given"; her resistance to its conscious and unconscious agendas can be registered only through the subversion of mimicry. As I suggested above, it hardly constitutes an effective political resistance. Most feminist teachers, when they talk about teaching, speak of a desire to "empower" the learner to tell her own stories rather than parroting those of the dominant culture. Even more specifically, they seek to give "voice" to those who have been silenced and alienated by traditional pedagogical practices that privilege hierarchy, authority, "rigor," and exclusivity, and that value abstract and objective knowledge over subjective and experiential knowledge.

The authors of *Women's Ways of Knowing* testify to the persistence of "voice" among the female students they interviewed as a powerful metaphor to describe learning experiences that contrasts with the metaphors of vision traditional pedagogies employ to describe cognition:

> What we had not anticipated was that "voice" was more than an academic shorthand for a person's point of view. Well after we were into our interviews with women, we became aware that it is a metaphor that can apply to many aspects of women's experience and development. In describing their lives women commonly talked about voice and silence: "speaking up," "speaking out," "being silenced," "not being heard," "really listening," "really talking, " "words as weapons," "feeling deaf and dumb," "having no words," "saying what you mean," "listening to be heard," and so on in an endless variety of connotations all having to do with sense of mind, self-worth, and feelings of isolation from or connection to others. We found that women repeatedly used the metaphor of voice to depict their intellectual and ethical development; and that the development of a sense of voice, mind, and self were intricately intertwined. (18)

Despite the prominence of the metaphor of "voice" within feminist pedagogy (see also Tetreaut and Maher, "Doing Feminist Ethnography"), it still remains an elusive concept. We assume we know what we mean when we say we want our students to discover their own "voice," and the term itself becomes a kind of mantra we chant. But, as an unexamined assumption, the metaphor of voice repeats Katherine's language lesson in *Henry V*, tying feminist pedagogy to an essentially female body. Yet even a moment's reflection on the voice as a physical attribute might serve to undermine the self-evident nature of the metaphor. When we hear our voices mechanically reproduced on a tape recorder, the experience is alienating; we might even deny altogether that they are ours. Furthermore, that "voice," which was once located in a body, is now detached from it and infinitely reproducible, a simulacrum or copy without an original bodily presence to authorize it. The interrogation of such boundaries may enable us to explore the peculiar forms of resistance feminist pedagogies have marginalized or missed altogether.

The metaphor of voice grounds feminist pedagogy in the (female) body and in an essentialist notion of a core "self' who produces language or "voice" manufactured out of "experiences." This "self" is assumed to precede social life so that the detrimental effects of a patriarchal society on the individual are correctable once adjustments have been made to release the "voice" which will speak for the "self." Yet all of these terms—self, voice, experience—have been placed under erasure by poststructuralist semiotics and by Lacanian psychoanalysis, which define these concepts in terms of their radical discursivity. The "self" who can have a voice is not independent and preexistent; it is fashioned out of the discursive and semiotic practices of patriarchy within and against which the gendered self fashions its "identity" (de Lauretis 18). In this respect, the process feminist pedagogy seeks to describe is not the student's *discovering* a voice that is already there, but her *fashioning* one from the discursive environment through and in which the feminist subject emerges. The difference may seem subtle, but it is crucial to a theoretical understanding of a feminist pedagogy of voice. Pedagogy attempts to intervene in the ongoing processes by which the subject is fashioned and to affect that fashioning in a particular direction. Feminist pedagogy as a "practice of freedom" attempts to fashion a female subject who is "empowered" to participate in the transformation of her world. But before we can consider what that might mean in pedagogic practice, we must consider what we mean by the "subject."

Poststructuralist analysis, particularly that dependent upon the works of Lacan, replaces terms like "self" or "individual"—with their connotations of autonomy and unity—with the term "subject," which more fully captures the sense of subjection, of the self's fashioning by its insertion into an already articulated symbolic economy. What prevents this concept from becoming totalitarian (the subject is completely subjected to forces outside of her control) or quietistic (the subject can never do anything to alter or refashion herself) is that the subject is never fully complete; it is always in the process of being fashioned, always a shifting and heterogeneous field of meaning. As a result, this subject-in-process is always simultaneously a product *and* producer of the symbolic economy.

If poststructuralist semiotics is right in describing the formation of the subject as a discursive process, and if Lacanian psychoanalysis is correct in describing that subject as fundamentally heterogeneous, split, and not fully present or known to itself, then we need to rethink the very notion that what is significant about teaching is available for conscious and rational analysis. Pedagogy must also be characterized by some form of intervention in the "unconscious," by a dynamic interchange between the unconscious of both teacher and learner. It is crucial, though, to avoid mystifying or reifying the psychoanalytic "unconscious." The unconscious after Lacan can no longer be seen as a "moral occult" (Brooks 202), nor is it a "reification of the human being" (Lacan 64). It is not a preexistent entity any more than the "self" is. Like the conscious self, it is an effect of discourse, of enunciation. Lacan does away with the reified Freudian topography of ego, id, and superego and returns to Freud's earlier division between conscious and unconscious, attempting to describe a dynamic process by which the "self" comes into being—enters semiosis—through its interactions with the world: "psychoanalysis can locate the unconscious, as Lacan does, not behind or below consciousness as an agent of impulses we do not recognize (but which is always susceptible to cognition), but rather inhabiting enunciation itself, a *function,* not a *cause,* of discourse" (Schleifer 804). Since education is also a "function of discourse," such a view of the unconscious makes more plausible its appropriation as a critical term in a discussion of pedagogy.

What forms the unconscious—if we can talk about its having form at all—is the countless and innumerable pragmatic, semiotic, and linguistic "events" and cues that we have encountered, internalized, and then forgotten, but that form part of our production of language and meaning from infancy on. The process begins in infancy, in the infant's experience of her body in the pre-mirror stage, which Lacan describes as laying down "letters" (Ragland-Sullivan 20). These "letters" operate as "local signifiers" that create and inform the unconscious. The process continues throughout the subject's lifetime and is crucial to understanding Lacan's notion of subjectivity as a culturally and linguistically mediated process. Lacan does not separate the conscious and the unconscious as rigorously as Freud does, although he recognizes them as distinct orders. Instead, he introduces two new terms—the *moi* and the *je*—which mediate between the conscious and unconscious and prevent them from becoming reified concepts. "Subjects reconstitute themselves for each other . . . by exchanging ego *(moi)* through language *(je)* as symbols" (Ragland-Sullivan 43). The subject, then, is at once dual and contradictory; it is at the same time fixed and continually in play (calling upon both senses of that term). The unconscious simultaneously attributes "permanence, identity, and substantiality" to the subject and its objects *and* reveals the illusory nature of that unity in its "gaps, ambiguities, and scars" (Ragland-Sullivan 43).

The psychological growth and development of the individual is always thoroughly implicated in the social and, thus, in the ideological. "The process described as being 'assimilated' into culture . . . covers over a multiplicity of complex processes of reaction, resistance, subversion, acquiescence and acceptance" (Hodge and Kress 240). Outside of the family, the educational system is the primary "state apparatus" or "disciplinary mechanism" through which such assimilation takes place. In a chapter of *Social Semiotics* entitled "Entering Semiosis: Training Subjects for Culture," Hodge and Kress attempt to describe a very small portion of this "assimilation"—both cognitive and affective—which contributes to the formation of an unconscious in teaching of all kinds: in the informal exchanges between a mother and a toddler, in a nursery school "discussion," and in an elementary school "report." Teaching, then, I would argue, not only engages the unconscious, but is implicated in the very formation of the unconscious itself. The unconscious constitutes what Felman has called "a kind of *unmeant knowledge* which escapes intentionality and meaning, a knowledge which is spoken by the language of the subject (spoken, for instance, by his slips or by his dreams), but which the subject cannot recognize, assume as *his* [sic]" and thus appropriate (28). To agree with this statement is not to privilege the unconscious as some realm of freedom from authority. On the contrary, it is to engage with that authority precisely where it is the most effective because the least calculated.

This unmeant knowledge, spoken but unrecognized, suggests that knowledge, like the subject, is also fundamentally split and heterogeneous. Feminist pedagogies have recognized intuitively that traditional pedagogical strategies cannot "get at" this "unmeant knowledge," but they have been unable to theorize the consequences, to engage and use it as a "practice of freedom" by interrogating the realm of their own authority. In practical terms they have been unable to develop strategies to teach to such a conception of "unmeant knowledge." Traditional pedagogy speaks of an exchange of information between conscious and rational egos. The teacher who has mastered a particular "field" of knowledge transmits that knowledge to students. This is the kind of teaching Freire describes with his metaphor of "banking," an educational practice in which teachers make deposits of knowledge in students. This transmission implies certain practices—the lecture, the Socratic dialogue, the exam, even the research paper—all of which function to manage the flow of knowledge (defined as finite information) as a bank manages the flow of currency, and all of which, despite our protests to the contrary, are practices found in most colleges and universities. In an institution in which knowledge is conceived of as finite, the method of transmission will be linear, temporal, continuous, and progressive (numbered sequences of courses, distribution requirements, and "capstone" courses are just a few of the practices that instantiate this concept of knowledge). Both students and teachers are universalized; the method is the same whatever the historical moment, location, institution, discipline, or the gender, race, or class of the participants. But such practices quite often fail students (in both senses of the term) not simply because they are oppressive but because they deny what Felman calls the "irreducibility of knowledge." "Human knowledge," she writes, "is, by definition, that which is untotalizing, that which rules out any possibility of totalizing what it knows or of eradicating its own ignorance" (29). Such a conception of knowledge as always unmasterable requires a mode of teaching, a practice which, much like the analytic situation, proceeds not progressively through time, but through resistance and "through breakthroughs, leaps, discontinuities, regressions, and deferred action" (27).

The practical consequence of this discontinuous view of learning is to return us to the question of voice from a new direction. We may ask ourselves, as feminist teachers, what we mean when we ask our students to "discover" their own voices. In my experience, we often do not mean the same thing that our students assume we mean. Surely we do not want them to spout whatever comes into their heads. So when they take us at our word, we are often frustrated by their failure to meet our (often unstated) expectations, and they are angry at our refusal to validate their "experiences" and to respect their "voices." At some time we have all been puzzled and hurt by such resistance. To understand it, we need to be honest enough to realize that, as feminists, we want our students to fashion a particular kind of voice that corresponds to our own desires as teachers, desires which have been authorized by the discursive practices of our disciplines and fields: English, anthropology, history, and more specifically, feminism. To be sure, we might suggest something like "freewriting" as a heuristic strategy. Just as the free associations of the analysand provide the interpretive material for the analyst's hermeneutic method, so the student's first thoughts on a subject will subsequently be shaped by the interactions between teacher and student into a standard disciplinary "narrative." We certainly do not want our students merely to parrot us, to "bank" and mimic our words mindlessly. However, in feminist classrooms, we tend to privilege certain kinds of "personal" or "experiential" disclosures over others, and we are not satisfied simply to allow students to recount their experiences without theorizing how they are woven into the fabric of patriarchal social relations, without understanding the ways in which their experiences fit into a critique of patriarchy.

To understand more fully the ways in which we, as feminist teachers, desire our students to discover "voice," we must assess the relationship between teacher and student. While recognizing that the classroom creates a complex network of both hierarchical and horizontal relationships, both between teacher and students and among students, I have chosen to focus in what follows primarily on the teacher–student dyad because it seems most amenable to a psychoanalytic method. One stratagem by which feminist teachers have attempted to create more egalitarian classrooms is by relinquishing the teacher's traditional position of "mastery." Thus, Janet Robyns writes:

> [Feminist teachers] were not set up as knowers among a group of nonknowers. They were more like part-time assistants. They helped as much as they could by giving information about their experiences. . . . The "teacher" did not remain the same person. In sharing our knowledge, our thoughts and experiences, the "teacher" rotated among us. Each functioned as teacher at times because each had something to offer. There was no knower/nonknower, judge/judged hierarchy. (Robyns 53; cited in Treichler 66)

The problem, as Treichler and Penley have pointed out, is that such attempts to eliminate authority serve only to mystify "the hierarchical distribution of power embodied by the university's institutional structure" (Treichler 71; Penley 138). The strategy may have been more or less successful during a time when feminist teachers were themselves in precarious and vulnerable positions within the academy, when many were untenured or adjunct faculty. But as feminist teachers have achieved tenure and full-professor status, the fiction of the teacher-less classroom becomes harder to maintain. Students enter the classroom believing that the teacher knows the "right" answer; her refusal to reveal that answer—and feminist teachers quite often claim that they have no "right" answers—can and often does cause more distress than empowerment. Regardless of our attempts to de-center our authority as teachers, we must evaluate our students and must do so from the position of a "subject supposed to know."

The students' positing of mastery and knowledge in an "other" creates the effect psychoanalysts call transference: "As soon as there is somewhere a subject presumed to know, there is transference" (Lacan, cited in Felman 35). Many scholars have recognized the role of transference in pedagogy. As Robert Con Davis has argued, this transference has consequences for and indeed defines the relationship between teacher and student:

> The teacher subject to this transference can still legitimately teach but does so as an imaginary projection, presenting knowledge as a kind of bait (promising everything) that lures the student into the recognition of the unconscious discourse they both articulate so that, ideally, as the instruction succeeds, the student will find a place from which to produce (rather than merely repeat) language. The student in this Freudian model marks the site of the continual possibility of speech, of discourse—initially a suppressed articulation in someone else's language but eventually a site of language with its own relation to the unconscious. ("Pedagogy" 752)

It strikes me that Davis's description may provide a starting point from which feminist teachers may begin to articulate more fully what we mean by "voice." An analysis of transference may enable us to unpack the workings of classroom authority—both real and imagined—by focusing our attention away from the content of teaching—the exchange of signifieds—and toward the dramas of identification and resistance that accompany the exchange of signifiers. That is, away from enunciated content and toward voice.

In the case study in which he first introduced the term, Freud maintained that he failed to complete Dora's analysis because he "did not succeed in mastering the transference in good time" (*Dora* 140). She remained silenced, a hysteric all her life, unable to produce rather than merely repeat language (one of the symptoms from which Dora suffered was aphonia—an occasional loss of voice). I would like to suggest that what feminists mean when we invoke the concept of "voice" might more accurately be described as the successful mastering of a transference. My choice of the term "mastering," no doubt distasteful to many feminists, enables me to call attention to the necessary inequity of transference relationships. Lacan writes that "transference *is* love . . .; it is love directed toward, addressed to, knowledge" (cited in Felman 35). But that love—which Freud argued is originally the love for the parent which is successively transferred to other objects, to teachers or the analyst, for instance—is possible only within a highly unequal relationship; it inevitably involves power, inevitably creates a relationship of imagined mastery and simultaneous identification with and resistance toward that mastery. The relationship between teacher and student, then, can be no more equal than the relationship between mother and child so valued by many feminists. An analysis of transference will necessarily be an analysis of the power relationships involved in teaching. Inequality sets off a process of discovery leading to "a place from which [the student can] produce (rather than merely repeat) language," or to what Belenky et al. refer to as "voice" (Davis, "Pedagogy" 752). This inequality—the student's position of ignorance and resistance, the teacher's of supposed knowledge and mastery—is the "bait."

At the same time, I wonder, is it really only the teacher—to whom the student certainly attributes mastery—who masters the transference? Or is the teacher's role as "subject supposed to know" at least in part imaginary and, therefore, as Davis suggests, also a "bait" that "lures" the student into "a recognition of the unconscious discourse they both share"? Lacan's rereading of transference encourages just this sort of ambiguity: "What, therefore, is meant by interpreting the transference?" he writes. "Nothing other than a ruse to fill in the emptiness of [a] deadlock. But while it may be deceptive, this ruse serves a purpose by setting off the whole process again" (71). The slippage between Freud's "mastering" and Lacan's "interpreting" suggests something of the nature of Lacan's revision of Freud. The power relation involved is rendered more ambiguous—a "ruse"—directing attention away from the content of the relationship (mastery) to its discursive strategies (interpretation). The "end" of interpretation is less final than that of mastery. The analyst's (or teacher's) acts of interpretation are not the end of the lesson; they are its pretext. Like Katherine's language lesson in *Henry V*, this "ruse" or "bait" reminds us that teaching and the acquisition of knowledge cannot be comprehended merely as the straightforward exchange of information. That exchange is the bait which enables the student's ignorance and resistance to come into play as dynamic forces in the constitution of knowledge in the classroom.

The advantage of thinking of knowledge as "bait" is that it grants the student some agency in the acquisition of knowledge or in the discovery of a "site of language with its own relation to the unconscious" (Davis, "Pedagogy" 752). It is the power of the student's resistance that provides the opportunity for this discovery, which, as Felman suggests, calls into question the opposition between knowledge and ignorance and opens up the possibility for a more profound conception of learning. Resistance takes many forms in the classroom, some of which are encouraged, whereas others are not. For instance, feminist teachers encourage and reward students' resistance to gender inequalities of all kinds, and at least expect and cope more or less well with students' resistance to their authority as feminists and to feminism's knowledge and insights. Because these forms of resistance in feminist classrooms are enacted primarily at the level of content, I will not deal with them in detail. Rather, I would like to examine a less often recognized form of a resistance, a form working not through content but through voice. In this case, the student resists being freed *from* the teacher's authority; her resistance takes the form of extreme identification, which results in anger and frustration when that identification is resisted by the subject supposed to know. By analyzing resistance through such discursive strategies, I can redirect talk about student "voice" to show how, through transference, a student may find a (provisional) place from which to produce, rather than merely repeat, language.

In my undergraduate feminist theory class, I have begun requiring students to keep a diary on their term projects as they research and write them. The purpose is to focus their attention as much on the process of theorizing as on its products—the theories themselves. This provides them with a space in which to monitor their own relation to the often alienating discourses of theory, which means, quite often, their relationship to the teacher, the "subject supposed to know" theory. Usually I have a hard time convincing students (especially outside of composition classes) of the utility of writing that has no direct relation to the writing on which they will be evaluated. Mostly they tolerate it as busy work, and sometimes it is. But occasionally such writing functions as a kind of "bait," serving less to illuminate for them the conscious and rational process of writing than to create spaces in which they might glimpse some of the unconscious processes that accompany learning. These diaries have on occasion yielded some insights into the processes of transference I have been describing. For this reason, I would like to look at the diary of one student in a feminist theory class.

E. L. began feminist theory as a last term senior, a student with a 3.77 GPA (she relates this in her diary), looking forward to graduate school, fully confident of her own sense of "self" and confident that she had found her own "voice." This confidence that she knows what is expected of her is reflected in her first entry, 14 April:

> Ever since the first week of classes, when I discovered that I would be required to write a major term paper for each class, I have been searching for topics. I always have plenty of ideas and interests. My problem usually comes when I have to start narrowing the topics down so they will be doable in a few week's time. I walk 5 miles a day by myself. This is usually when I kick around ideas in my head. Once I have an idea, I try to talk to someone about it. For me, it helps to extrovert my ideas and get feedback. I almost always learn as I speak.

Yet that confidence was much more fragile than either she or I suspected, and it quickly shattered. The experience of writing a term paper for feminist theory created enormous psychic distress, frustration, anger, and resistance. Given her academic history, her difficulties took me by surprise. We struggled together throughout the term to see why she could not complete this paper as easily as others she had written. Her diary provides a record of that struggle. I do not claim that her situation is unique either to this class or to feminist classes. Most teachers will recognize in E. L. students of both sexes whom they have encountered (although in my experience this student is typically female). As I suggested earlier, students' resistance to being freed *from* authority may at times be as intense as their resistance to authority. I am interested in the particular forms E. L.'s resistance took, and in the discursive strategies she used to express it. Her difficulties seemed to be triggered by the supposedly nonauthoritarian context of my feminist classroom, in which I had relinquished certain forms of authority and mastery I ordinarily do not relinquish in other kinds of classes.

In her opening entry E. L. reveals the first stage of Lacan's stages or "patterns" of psychoanalytic transference by identifying with the "teacher," suggesting, at this early stage, as Ragland-Sullivan notes, that "the emphasis is on likeness and the analyst [in this case the teacher] is perceived as a counterpart" (37). She assumes that her "ideas and interests," her desires, correspond to those of her teachers and that this correspondence gives her a kind of control or mastery over the process of writing.

E. L.'s reaction five days later to her own first exploratory efforts at producing feminist theory reveals the fragility of her own hard-won sense of identity, of control and mastery:

> I think [the assignment to write an exploratory essay on the topic chosen for the term project] distracted me from my original idea. That is fine, I guess—but I don't like being confused. I like knowing what I am trying to say when I write. I don't think I knew what I was trying to say in that essay.

This was to become a persistent theme in E. L.'s diary. The harder she pressed me to reveal "what kind of paper I wanted," the more unwilling or unable I was to tell her what she wanted to hear. I say this without complacency because it was both frustrating and embarrassing to realize that perhaps I did not know myself what I wanted. In the psychoanalytic situation, as the ideal "subject supposed to know" is revealed as an illusion, an "imaginary projection," there is a parallel "disintegration of the analysand's supposition of knowing." Ragland-Sullivan describes this process in the analysand as a disintegration of the self. Because the unified *moi* (the ideal ego) gives the subject a sense of "self cohesion," "any unraveling of the strands that went into weaving that identity as a conviction of 'being' causes a debeing of being: a sense of fragmenting" (37).

That sense of unraveling, of fragmentation, occurs in the student too as she begins to discover a threat to her own very fragile sense of being and reacts to restore it. This position, which feels like a loss of identity, is distressing, as E. L. begins to reveal in the same entry:

> I don't understand what kind of a paper the final draft is to be. Are we writing humanities type papers, or social science

papers, reviewing the literature, or making up our own theories?

Her growing sense of fragmentation reveals itself in her sense of the fragmentation of knowledge into "disciplines" lacking cohesiveness and connection: somehow the skills required for writing a social science paper are useless if one is supposed to be writing a "humanities type paper" or "making up our own theories." It is as if each of these different "types" of writing requires a different voice and thus a different projection of her "self."

E. L.'s distress reaches a peak with the evaluation of her rough draft, which is hardly surprising; this is the point in the term at which students see the teacher not simply as a "part-time assistant," as Robyns suggests (53), or one who "nurtures" the students' ideas. She has to evaluate, to judge their work as well. At this moment students most keenly feel the teacher's power. For students who have eagerly accepted as empowering the ideology of feminist egalitarianism this discovery can be painfully disillusioning. As the entries for 19 May and 1 June suggest, E. L.'s frustrations were largely directed at me; I was both failing to validate her usual "voice" and failing to make available a knowledge she could consume:

> 19 May: Well, I got my rough draft back. I don't know what kind of reaction I expected—but I was certainly surprised by your comments. Too smooth—read like a final exam. Hmm. Secretly that is quite a compliment. But I have spent a lot of time trying to figure you out and realize that that is not a compliment coming from you. A compliment is what you said about my exploratory essay: provocative. That is what I will aim for in my final draft.
>
> 1 June: Today I talked w/ you in your office. I was in a stupor from staying up all night writing a rough draft of [another] term paper. I must say, it was much simpler than this project—but I did not learn even a fraction of what I am learning doing this.... I realize over and over how I totally write for other people. I know what [Professor C.] wants to hear and how he wants to hear it—so I do it. I have been trying to figure you out—but you are so different from other profs I've had.... You suggested that I start at the end where I thought it was falling apart and you thought it was just getting interesting. How funny.

These two entries begin to uncover the resistance being enacted in this relationship. I commented that her rough draft read like a final exam to suggest that this student repeats language but is anxious about producing it. This student, who thought she already had a "voice," but finds herself suddenly struggling, measures success by her ability to align herself in identification with the teacher. Her inability to fix me with a secure identity threatens her identity, resulting in her sense that things are "falling apart." To her credit, she does at least recognize that she is encountering a qualitatively different kind of learning from that she has experienced in other classes. It is more painful because it exposes the fragility of her sense of self, but it is also more productive because it becomes the means by which she interrogates her own relationship to learning.

Ragland-Sullivan could be describing this student's experiences when she describes psychoanalytic transference:

> When the other (analyst) reflects an ideal unity—supports one's *moi* identifications—the narcissistic slope of the *moi* is gratified. When the ideal is shattered, the avatar of aggressiveness arises and shows itself in projected blame, disenchantment, intimations of fragmentation, and so forth. The goal of aggressiveness here is to protect the *moi* from perceiving the tenuous fragility of its own formation.... The insistence of the *moi* on retaining its (fictional) unity of individual perception constitutes what psychoanalysts call resistance. From another perspective, however, one might call this stubbornness a survival insistence. (38)

E. L. could feel confident of her identity and "voice" as long as she could stay within the boundaries of her previous experiences with teachers, as long as she is asked only to reproduce those forms of enunciation she has already mastered. I use the term "enunciation" rather than, say, "knowledge" because it seems to me that what is at stake in this case is not knowledge itself, its signifieds. E. L. had no difficulty understanding the material she was reading; she was not resistant to feminist analysis. Her problem lay in what to *do* with that knowledge, in how to employ its signifiers beyond merely repeating them, a difficulty of enunciation. When she was asked to explore rhetorical situations that she had not mastered, when her ideal of learning was shaken, she produced what, for lack of a better term, we might call symptoms which included "blame, disenchantment, intimations of fragmentation." E. L.'s thinking of her difficulties in this assignment in relation to her assignments in another, more traditional class in which her usual repertoire of behaviors is adequate supports my belief that her difficulties lie in the enunciatory, or performative, dimension of learning. At stake here, as Schleifer has argued in another context, is "not the transference of pre-existing *feelings* from one object to another . . . but the transference of *discursive strategies* from one situation to another" (805; emphasis mine).

In many students, such psychic fragmentation and distress frequently bring on what I would call rhetorical symptoms. This is not entirely surprising since the unconscious is "acted out on the surface of discourse" (Schleifer 804). In Freudian psychology, hysterics quite often produced symptoms that manifested themselves in linguistic disorders. In the most celebrated case, that of Anna O., the German feminist Bertha Pappenheim who was analyzed by Freud's early collaborator Josef Breuer, Breuer describes the "deep-going functional disorganization of her speech":

> She lost her command of grammar and syntax; she no longer conjugated verbs, and eventually she used only the infinitive, for the most part incorrectly formed from the weak past participle, and she omitted both the definite and indefinite article. In the process of time she became almost completely deprived of words. (Gay 64)

Because the signifiers of knowledge in the academy are primarily written, it seems reasonable that its symptoms of distress, of ego fragmentation, working on the "surface of discourse" would primarily be manifested in the rhetorical dimension of language, occurring on both the macro level of written discourse—in organizational difficulties—and on the micro level in such common writing errors as sentence fragments, fused sentences, comma splices, and indefinite pronoun reference. These "writing problems" are more productively thought of as "symptoms" manifesting themselves in enunciation—in the *je*—of the fragmentation of the self, of the *moi*, experienced by students who are in the process of discovering that the "enunciatory strategies" they had once understood as the "truth" are "linguistic strategies inhabited by unconscious desire, by another's desire" (Schleifer 812).

E. L. felt that she was losing control of her essay and falling apart—her choice of words is suggestive of her own sense of fragmentation—just as I thought that she was glimpsing a locus from which to produce language. We wrestled with this illuminating point of resistance for almost a month. As late as 5 June, the resistance was still strongly voiced in her diary; E. L.'s need for control was as great as ever. She could still write, "One thing that I have learned is that I can't do it. I can't sit down and start writing on one thing and end up somewhere else, not unless it is an unguided freewrite or something. I have just been trained too well." She wanted to *be* in control—of her writing, of her learning, of her life—whereas I wanted her to explore her *need* for control, which was ultimately what her essay on eating disorders was about. To find a place from which she could produce rather than mimic language, E. L. had to situate herself in relation to both feminist and medical discourses on eating disorders. She wanted to resist the characterizations of eating disorders as symptoms produced by the excessive need for control because such characterizations posed a threat to her own desire for control and mastery. Yet she lacked any language to articulate that resistance until she was willing to interrogate that desire and her own relation to authority. E. L. also had to realize that her resistance was not simply psychological. It was also culturally produced. She had been "trained too well" to reproduce behavior that in other authoritarian situations had brought her success. She had been taught to desire control, a desire that enabled her to please other authoritative figures from whom she had learned. Her behavior had been adaptive, a "survival insistence."

The process of working through the resistance that her diary records led E. L. to an understanding that goes beyond specific knowledge of feminist theory or eating disorders to the ways in which learning happens, to its enunciatory framework. The entry of 6 June suggests that E. L. found not a "voice," but a place from which to produce language with its own relation to its subject:

> I still have no idea if this paper is what you were looking for. I feel better about it than I did about my exploratory essay, and you liked that. I decided a couple of days ago that because I couldn't figure out [what] was being asked of me, I would simply write for myself. What a freeing feeling.

This entry suggests that E. L.'s sense of fragmentation, her loss of identity, has been at least temporarily resolved. The process of working through her resistance to the task has enabled her once more to reassert the tenuous and fragile coherence of her own subjectivity. To be sure, her assertion that she will "write for myself" may ring a bit hollow, phrased as it is in her diary in the language of "voice" and "self" which she has internalized. But even though she may not have the language to articulate it, there is a clear sense in this entry of breaking through a block (the language of the "freeing feeling"). I would assert that E. L. found not some essential core "self' that was waiting to be freed from the inauthentic trappings of another's words; nor did she undergo some now permanent transformation or reach a new stasis. Instead she solved a problem. Both her paper and this diary entry suggest that she found a "place from which to produce (rather than merely repeat) language," a relation to particular disciplinary discourses and practices. She fashioned a subject position that enabled her to use the enunciatory strategies of feminist theory to articulate her dissatisfaction with *both* feminist and medical discourses on eating disorders rather than merely mimic their language.

Not all narratives of feminist teaching have such a happy ending. Many students remain stuck either in enunciatory strategies that limit them, as Katherine is limited in *Henry V*, to mimicking the other's language, or in a state of cognitive dissonance where the production of language itself becomes symptomatic of the gaps, holes, and scars in the illusory armor of the ego. I offer this case history not to suggest that the resistance E. L. exhibited can be avoided—or even "cured"—because, as Felman argues, it is at the heart of any pedagogy worth the name, erasing the very opposition between ignorance and learning. But E. L.'s diary—her articulation of her own resistance to *writing* feminist theory (which was not, I would add, a resistance to feminist theory itself)—may finally be less significant for what it revealed to E. L. about her relation to learning than for the insight it provided me into my own ambiguous relation to authority as a feminist teacher. Because E. L. so dutifully kept it, the diary provided a record of our communicative and enunciatory strategies. Reading the diary after the class had ended compelled me to interrogate my own position of mastery and authority in relation to the claims of feminist thinking about pedagogy, which often purports to have dispensed with mastery and authority. It forced me to look at the blind spots in what Evelyn Fox Keller and Helene Moglen have called the "romance of women's culture."

My discovery, I admit, was serendipitous, but in retrospect it makes sense that an instrument designed to enable students to speak about their relation to the discourse of theory might reveal something about the transformation of their enunciatory strategies in relation to a subject supposed to know. I offer this narrative in the hopes that other feminist teachers might find in it a means to interrogate the relations among authority, mastery, ignorance, and resistance necessary to any real knowledge. I do not pretend that it is the only pedagogical practice that could engage both students and teachers in such an analysis of transference or of the enunciatory dimension of teaching. There is no one orthodox approach to feminist pedagogy any more than there is to psychoanalysis. Feminist pedagogy and other radical pedagogies are not static practices. Rather, like feminist or psychoanalytic theory, such pedagogy is a contested ground, full of conflict and struggle, continually being renewed, recreated, and rethought in light of specific classroom practices, even in relation to such institutionalized discourses as psychoanalysis.

Works Cited

Belenky, Mary Field, Blythe McVicker Clinchy, Nancy Rule Goldberger, and Jill Mattuck Tarule. *Women's Ways of Knowing: The Development of Self, Voice, and Mind*. New York: Basic Books, 1986.

Bernheimer, Charles, and Claire Kahane, eds. *In Dora's Case: Freud—Hysteria—Feminism*. New York: Columbia UP, 1985.

Brooks, Peter. *The Melodramatic Imagination*. New Haven: Yale UP, 1976.

Davis, Robert Con. "A Manifesto for Oppositional Pedagogy: Freire, Bourdieu, Merod, and Graff."

Reorientations: Critical Theories and Pedagogies. Ed. Bruce Henrickson and Thais E. Morgan. Urbana: U of Illinois P, 1990. 248–267.

———. "Pedagogy, Lacan, and the Freudian Subject." *College English* 49 (1987): 749–755.

de Lauretis, Theresa. *Technologies of Gender.* Bloomington: Indiana UP, 1987.

Ellsworth, Elizabeth. "Why Doesn't This Feel Empowering?: Working Through the Repressive Myths of Critical Pedagogy." Paper presented at Tenth Conference on Curriculum Theory and Classroom Practice, 1988.

Emerson, Caryl. "The Outer Word and Inner Speech: Bakhtin, Vygotsky, and the Internalization of Language." *Critical Inquiry* 10 (1983): 245–264.

Feldstein, Richard, and Judith Roof, eds. *Feminism and Psychoanalysis.* Ithaca: Cornell UP, 1989.

Felman, Shoshana. "Psychoanalysis and Education: Teaching Terminable and Interminable." *Yale French Studies* 63 (1982): 21–44.

Freire, Paulo. *Pedagogy of the Oppressed.* Trans. Myra Bergman Ramos. New York: Herder and Herder, 1968.

Freud, Sigmund. *Dora: An Analysis of a Case of Hysteria.* New York: Collier Books, 1963.

———. *Jokes and Their Relation to the Unconscious.* Trans. James Strachey. New York: Norton, 1960.

Garner, Shirley Nelson, Claire Kahane, and Madelon Sprengnether, eds. *The (M)other Tongue: Essays in Feminist Psychoanalytic Interpretation.* Ithaca: Cornell UP, 1985.

Gay, Peter, ed. *The Freud Reader.* New York: Norton, 1989.

Graff, Gerald. *Professing Literature: An Institutional History.* Chicago: U of Chicago P, 1987.

Hodge, Robert, and Gunther Kress. *Social Semiotics.* Ithaca: Cornell UP, 1988.

Jay, Gregory S. "The Subject of Pedagogy: Lessons in Psychoanalysis and Politics." *College English* 49 (1987): 785–800.

Keller, Evelyn Fox, and Helene Moglen. "Competition and Feminism: Conflicts for Academic Women." *Signs* 12 (1987): 493–511.

Lacan, Jacques. "Intervention on Transference." In Juliet Mitchell and Jacqueline Rose. *Feminine Sexuality: Jacques Lacan and the école freudienne.* New York: Norton, 1982. 62–73.

Millot, Catherine. *Freud, Anti-pedagogue.* Paris: Editions du Seuil, 1979.

Nelson, Cary, ed. *Theory in the Classroom.* Urbana: U of Illinois P, 1986.

Penley, Constance. "Teaching in Your Sleep: Feminism and Psychoanalysis." Nelson 129–48.

Ragland-Sullivan, Ellie. *Jacques Lacan and the Philosophy of Psychoanalysis.* Urbana: U of Illinois P, 1987.

Robyns, Janet. "Reproductive versus Regenerative Education: The Extension of English Education through Reference to Feminism." Unpublished associateship report, University of London Institute of Education, 1977.

Rose, Jacqueline. "Where Does the Misery Come From? Psychoanalysis, Feminism, and the Event." Feldstein and Roof 25–39.

Schleifer, Ronald. "Lacan's Enunciation and the Cure of Mortality: Teaching, Transference, and Desire." *College English* 49 (1987): 801–815.

Shakespeare, William. *Henry V.* In *The Riverside Shakespeare.* Boston: Houghton Mifflin, 1974.

Smith, Paul. "Julia Kristeva et al.; or, Take Three More." Feldstein and Roof 84–104.

Tetreault, Mary Kay, and Francis Maher. "Doing Feminist Ethnography: Lessons from Feminist Classrooms." *International Journal of Qualitative Studies in Education* 6 (1993).

———. "Breaking Through Illusion: A Case Study of Feminist Teaching." Unpublished paper (1990).

Treichler, Paula A. "Teaching Feminist Theory." Nelson 57–128.

Laurie Finke is Associate Professor and Director of Women's and Gender Studies at Kenyon College. She is the author of *Feminist Theory, Women's Writing* (Cornell UP, 1992) as well as numerous articles on feminist theory. She is co-editor with Robert Con Davis of *Critical Texts: Literary Theory from the Greek to the Present* (Longman, 1989).

Chapter 40

Gender and Race in the Classroom: Teaching Way Out of Line

Lana F. Rakow

Both students and teachers have experienced and participated in relationships of domination, submission, oppression, and privilege which have helped to shape who they are and how they interpret the world. This recognition of students and teachers as historically situated subjects with conflicting gender, race, and class interests is vital to understanding the possibilities and limits of the classroom. (Weiler, 1988: 125)

Kathleen Weiler is one among a growing number of scholars interested in feminist and critical pedagogy who call our attention to the fact that classrooms are not and can never be neutral sites for the production or reproduction of knowledge. Those of us who step into classrooms as professors and as students do not shed our identities at the door with our coats. We enter those rooms as humans situated as subjects and as objects of discourses that give us the identities we claim for ourselves and that are assigned by others. We cannot set aside the social relationships of the larger world—a world in which classifications of gender, race, and class are among the most paramount—as we take up the more temporary relationship of professor and students.[1]

In the traditional classroom, these identities are hidden or may be viewed as irrelevant. In fact, the traditional academic definition of a good teacher and of a successful classroom could be described as this: a generic professor, with sufficient knowledge of and enthusiasm for his subject matter, using appropriate pedagogical techniques, incites his generic students to the impassioned mastery of the material he brings to them. But feminist, ethnic study, and other critical scholars have debunked the myth of the generic—in the English language and in the classroom (see Bisseret Moreau, 1984 for a good example). This generic professor is, as the language indicates, presumed to be a white male, and the students who successfully master his content will likely be most like him. Because the white male who enters the classroom simply adds the compatible identity of professor to his other identities, his own subject position may appear to be and may feel unproblematic. While gender, race, and class identities may seem irrelevant as a consequence, they are actually the foundational structure upon which the traditional classroom—and the academy as a whole—is built.

When women and men of color and white women enter the classroom, "there's sure to be trouble" (Schuster and Van Dyne, 1985: 162). The identity of professor is almost certainly incompatible with their gender and racial identities, since, as we have seen, the "generic" professor is white and male. They stand out as a member of a group or groups, their gender and race visible where the gender and race of the "norm" fades away. They disrupt old certainties and civilities (Schuster and Van Dyne's words, 163) because the normal discourse of the academic classroom becomes problematic. How will students position and "read" the professor and the text of the classroom and vice versa?

Even in a classroom with a traditional format and content, the professor who is the Inappropriate Other (see Ellsworth, 1989: 321) must struggle for the authority and respect that is granted automatically to a white man (see Friedman, 1985: 206). Thus this professor must engage in tiring "identity work" (McDermott and Church, 1976) in a constant relational negotiation with colleagues and students. When the professor cannot or will not take up an expected identity, conflict ensues. Susan Friedman explains that even where authority and respect is accorded, it may be granted with great resentment and even hostility, and, citing Norma Wikler, points out that students may pressure women to take up the identity of all-forgiving, nurturing mother who gives unconditional approval, perhaps one of the few identities women can successfully meld with that of professor. However, hostile challenges to their authority may come at grading time or other times when women are perceived as punitive, since this violates the expectations of the mother identity, though not of professor (Friedman, 1985: 206; see also Martin, 1984).

When the professor who is the Inappropriate Other, however, self-consciously chooses to bring a different text to the classroom, a text that challenges the traditional curriculum because it centers the theories and experiences of people of color and white women, she or he has committed a further transgression and heightens the salience of personal gender and racial identities in the classroom. The material is "volatile" (Anderson and Grubman, 1985: 221), and the classroom can become "explosive" (Culley, 1985: 209). Because gender and race are such inseparable parts of the identities of all of us, students find it difficult to acknowledge their existence. As Schuster and Van Dyne say:

> Students may be extremely fearful of relinquishing the invisible paradigms of personal definition and gender they have absorbed in their educational socialization, because these seem, quite literally, all that they know about themselves. (1985: 170)

Hence the content, as well as the instructor, may be resisted for this and other reasons, not the least of which is that, as Elizabeth Spelman puts it, "For the most part, educational institutions do not know how to reward students for learning about themselves or about others unless the others are (1) male, (2) white, and (3) dead" (Spelman 1985: 243). In addition, white women and racial minority women and men may have little interest in or appreciation for their own histories and for understanding their own experiences, particularly since this material seems to have so little relevance for their own upward mobility. The parents of racial minority students may even discourage their sons and daughters from taking courses taught by racial minority professors (Butler, 1985: 234), because they want their children to have the "right" education.

Not surprisingly, however, it is white males who most object to being decentered in the classroom. The introduction of discourses that place women and racial minorities as subjects and that permit the possibility for women and racial minorities in the classroom to speak in their own discourses is both a new experience and a threatening one for many white males. A number of feminist teachers (see Mumford, 1985 and Rothenberg, 1985) have reported aggressive and disruptive attempts on the part of white male students to bring the classroom back to the dominant sexist, racist, and homophobic discourse. While it is true that others in the classroom may also be more comfortable with a dominant discourse, it is generally white males who are accorded the powerful subject position in that discourse to act on it aggressively. If the teacher is a woman, the attempt may be made to relocate her as the sexist object of this discourse, thereby negating her authority as a professor in academic discourse. Several examples illustrate how this occurs.

Though this example does not occur in an institution of higher learning, Valerie Walkerdine (1981) reports an interaction between four-year-old British nursery school boys and their teacher, who is a woman about thirty. The boys make explicit sexual commands to the teacher ("show your knickers" and "take all your clothes off, your bra off'), delighting in their use of obscenities as well as in the power they command over her as a sexual object. As Walkerdine explains, in the classroom, the boys exist simultaneously as objects of powerlessness in the institutional discourse where the teacher has power and as subjects of patriarchal discourse where they can render the teacher the object of their sexist discourse where she signifies not as "teacher" but as "woman."

In another example, Margo Culley describes an incident that happened to her on the first day of class for the women's studies section of a course, "Man and Woman in Literature." Upon hearing which section he was in, a male student walked past her in the front of the room, made noises as if to vomit, and stopped at the door to wave to the class and say, "See you later, girls," to the nervous laughter of the rest of the class (Culley, 1985: 214). Despite any other terms on which Culley wished to present herself or the course, the dominant patriarchal discourse and this student's position of power within it could negate them.

A third example is closer to home. I teach a course called "Communication and the Human Condition," which I have structured around understanding how humans take up and are assigned identities in order to exist within a community of meaning. I emphasize gender, race, and class as the primary means by which people in this historical time period are given identities. One semester, when I introduced the section on gender, I began with a presentation summarizing scholarly research which questions the "generic" masculine in English, thinking it would be a non-threatening introduction to the topic of gender identity. Before I had gone far, a white male student burst out with an angry, "You are way out of line shoving this dogma down our throats!"

The student had successfully placed me in a double bind situation. If I responded punitively, as my professor subjectivity permitted, I was indeed "out of line" for a woman, and I would have confirmed his and probably other students' reading of me, exacerbating their antagonism. If I capitulated to his complaint and appeared apologetic or "weak," he would have successfully drawn me back as the object of sexist discourse, in which I would signify as "woman" but not as "professor." His use of male sexual imagery ("shoving this dogma done our throats") illustrates how he had collapsed the dominant academic and sexual discourse so that only a male could "rightfully" take up the subject position in either.

The only ground between those positions was to make the interaction part of the discourse of the classroom, which I did by responding, "Let's look at why it is you are able to speak to me in that way." The student, however, refused my explanation that gender was the foundation for that interaction (ironically all the more confirming it), and classroom dynamics remained unsettled and uneasy through the remainder of the semester.[2] My example illustrates that the resistance we face is as much to the material we bring to the classroom as it is to the discursive subject position we wish to take up, a position which can only be taken up if granted by the students with whom we interact. The combination of material about gender and race with the subordinate subject position of the instructor as woman and/or racial minority can mean both are dismissed by students because the instructor is seen to have a personal bone to pick with the world.

Despite such attempts to recenter themselves through the assertion of the dominant discourse, white male students are more likely to feel themselves silenced because they learn their discourse will not pass uncritiqued (as it did not in the above case). They may report on student course evaluation forms that the professor does not let students disagree or that she does not like men (or in the case of a professor of color, does not like whites or treats them unfairly) while other students may report they have felt encouraged to speak for the first time. One Hispanic woman reported in a workshop that she conducted on teaching material on women of color that a student had written on her course evaluation form, "The problem with this course is that there is no tolerance for racism and sexism." Students may feel there is too much emphasis on race and gender because it stands out in such marked contrast to the supposed neutrality of the rest of the encounter in their undergraduate careers (see Miner, 1987). They may see lecture materials and readings as "biased" or "one-sided" because the politics of writers and researchers are generally made explicit. One of my students (white and male) reported to me in my office that he did not like a reading by a white feminist because "It sounds like she wrote it on the 28th day of her month." Margo Culley offers the somewhat reassuring reminder that "If she [the feminist instructor] initiates a process challenging the world view and the view of self of her students, she will surely—if she is doing her job—become the object of some students' unexamined anger" (Culley, 1985: 213).

Of course, not all students resist the material and the instructor, and some students respond with enthusiasm, particularly those typically marginalized in the classroom. However, the presence of other, resistant discourses can present its own struggle. Despite the good intentions expressed by feminist, ethnic studies, and critical scholars, the classroom cannot become an egalitarian place where all those who are silenced and marginalized by the dominant discourse can find equal opportunity speaking rights. Elizabeth Ellsworth (1989) examines the complexity in relation to one of her own teaching experiences at the University of Wisconsin–Madison. Even in a course of students representing a wide diversity of "differences" and all committed to challenging racism, conflicting discourses and the shifting subjectivities of students and professor made the classroom a site of struggle. The injustices of race, class, and gender outside the classroom cannot be overcome in the classroom, she explains, no matter how committed the teacher and students (316). For example," . . a Chicano student had to define her voice in part through opposition to—and rejection of—definitions of 'Chicana' assumed and taken for granted by other student/professor voices in the classroom" (311). Ellsworth and her students found they had to struggle against oppressive ways of being known by others, even when those others were articulating their own experiences and self-definitions. All experience and all knowings are partial, hence, she says,

> I brought a social subjectivity that has been constructed in such a way that I have not and can never participate unproblematically in the collective process of self-definition, naming of oppression, and struggles for visibility in the face of marginalization engaged in by students whose class, race, gender, and other positions I do not share. (Ellsworth, 1989: 309–310)

Ellsworth's experience teaches us the lesson that despite what might be our own sensitivity to the marginalized positions of others, we cannot hope to achieve equality in the classroom since it does not exist *outside* the classroom. Weiler's analysis of an incident in a public school classroom (Weiler, 1985: 140–141) illustrates the problem. In a classroom discussion about Malcolm X's autobiography, a black male student attempts to interpret a passage in a discourse arriving out of his lived experience of racism. The white feminist teacher, though she was sensitive to black experience and on other occasions encouraged such discourse, persisted in reading the passage from the interpretive framework of an academic discourse about socialization. The student dropped the course.

Weiler does not criticize this teacher for her actions, but rather points out that "the classroom is always a site of conflict" whether the teacher is a traditional one or a feminist or critical one:

> This is precisely because students are agents and creators of meaning in both settings. The dominant and subordinate forms of power that Giroux [a critical education theorist] mentions are not simply the dominance of the teacher and the subordination of the student. Students also are gendered, raced, and classed; they therefore 'read' texts and classroom social relationships according to those subjectivities. (Weiler, 1988: 137)

The discourse of the classroom is not completely controlled by teachers, but teachers can open the possibility that other discourses besides the dominant sexist and racist discourse can be heard. Elizabeth Spelman (1985: 241) suggests to combat marginalization we use material that has some chance of speaking to the lives of all members of the class, if not everyone all of the time, then everyone some of the time. What happens in this kind of classroom cannot be predicted, nor can the pedagogical approach that is appropriate be learned through any kind of "cookbook" approach to teaching methods. Each classroom will be different depending upon the constellation of subjectivities that come together and are invoked in the course of the semester. As Ellsworth addresses it:

> The terms in which I can and will assert and unsettle 'difference' and unlearn my positions of privilege in future classroom practices are wholly dependent on the Others/others whose presence with their concrete experiences of privileges and subju-

gated or oppressive knowledges—I am responding to and acting with in any given classroom. My moving about between the positions of privileged speaking subject and Inappropriate/d Other cannot be predicted, prescribed, or understood beforehand by any theoretical framework or methodological practice. (Ellsworth, 1989: 323)

While those of us who enter such classrooms as teachers will no doubt continue to think of strategies and assignments and frameworks to try, hoping to derive better ways of dealing with the conflicts and resistance and of coming out the other side of the semester less bruised, our identities more intact, these are only individualistic and limited solutions. We need institutional support. The colleges and universities we teach in generally express their approval of teachers who do not take risks in the classroom, who do not rethink the content and format of their courses, who do not address the potentially explosive social relations of their classrooms, who speak and encourage the dominant discourse that silences and explains away most people of the world, including many of those represented in their own classrooms.

The University of Wisconsin System, for one, is currently advocating the value of "diversity" in hiring, student enrollment, and the curriculum. But an attention to diversity cannot be advocated without attention to the teaching situations that will be produced and the differential impact such teaching has on racial minorities and white women. We will ultimately have to convince not only administrators but our colleagues that we are up to something different in the classroom that cannot be assessed in the way that classroom teaching has traditionally been assessed. We will have to convince them that what goes on in our classrooms should be going on in their classrooms as well. They will have to learn to acknowledge and account for their own subjectivities and those of their students, a process which will unmask the "objective" curriculum and the neutral classroom.

Paula Rothenberg says it well:

The problem cannot be solved by changing either our course content or teaching skills. The majority of students will continue to resist dealing with issues of race, class, and gender as long as those issues are raised in a few isolated courses. Who can blame them? We tell them that racism and sexism are everywhere, that they pervade our past and our present and shape our future and yet these same realities go unmentioned in most of the courses these students take throughout their undergraduate career... Until this content is integrated into the entire curriculum students will continue to view it as the peculiar concern of a small group of faculty. (Rothenberg, 1987: 22)

Notes

1 See Bromley, 1989 for a discussion of the state of this position in critical educational theory.
2. This is despite the fact that l attempted to diffuse and work out students' feelings through classroom discussions. It may be some comfort to know that the same student came to my office a year later to apologize.

References

Anderson, Judith, and Stephen Grubman. 1985. "CommunicatIng Difference: Forms of Resistance." In *Women's Place in the Academy: Transforming the Liberal Arts Curriculum*, edited by Marilyn R. Schuster and Susan R. Van Dyne, 221–231. Totowa, New Jersey: Rowman & Allanheld.

Bisseret Moreau, Noelle. 1984. "Education, Ideology, and Class/Sex Identity." In *Language and Power*, edited by Cheris Kramarae, Muriel Schulz, and William M. O'Barr, 43–61. Beverly Hills: Sage.

Bromley, Hank. 1989. "Identity Politics and Critical Pedagogy." *Educational Theory* 39, no. 3: 207–223.

Butler, Johnnella E. 1985. "Toward a Pedagogy of Everywoman's Studies." In *Gendered Subjects: The Dynamics of Feminist Teaching*, edited by Margo Culley and Catherine Portuges, 230–239. Boston: Routledge & Kegan Paul.

Culley, Margo. 1985. "Anger and Authority in the Introductory Women's Studies Classroom." In *Gendered Subjects; The Dynamics of Feminist Teaching*, edited by Margo Culley and Catherine Portuges, 209–218. Boston: Routledge & Kegan Paul.

Ellsworth, Elizabeth. 1989. "Why Doesn't This Feel Empowering? Working Through the Repressive Myths of Critical Pedagogy." *Harvard Educational Review* 59, no. 3 (August): 297–324.

Friedman, Susan Stanford, 1985. "Authority in the Feminist Classroom: A Contradiction in Terms?" In *Gendered Subjects: The Dynamics of Feminist Teaching*, edited by Margo Culley and Catherine Portuges, 203–208. Boston: Routledge & Kegan Paul.

Martin, Elaine. 1984. "Power and Authority in the Classroom: Sexist Stereotypes in Teaching Evaluations." *Signs* 9, no. 3: 482–492.

McDermott, R. P., and Joseph Church. 1976. "Making Sense and Feeling Good: An Ethnography of Communication and Identity Work." *Communication* 2.

Miner, Madonne. 1987. "'Another Women's Play? Doesn't That Make Like Number 6!'" *Radical Teacher* April: 1–4.

Mumford, Laura Stempel. 1985. "'Why Do We Have to Read All This Old Stuff?' Conflict in the Feminist Theory Classroom." *Journal of Thought* 20, no. 3 (Fall): 88–96.

Rothenberg, Paula. 1987. "Integrating the Study of Race, Gender and Class: Some Preliminary Observations." Paper Presented to the National Women's Studies Association Conference, Atlanta, June.

———. 1985. "Teaching About Racism and Sexism: A Case History." *Journal of Thought* 20, no. 3 (Fall): 122–136.

Schuster, Marilyn R., and Susan R. Van Dyne. 1985. "The Changing Classroom." In *Women's Place in the Academy: Transforming the Liberal Arts Curriculum*, edited by Marilyn R. Schuster and Susan R. Van Dyne, 161–171. Totowa, New Jersey: Rowman & Allanheld.

Spelman, Elizabeth V. 1985. "Combating the Marginalization of Black Women in the Classroom." In *Gendered Subjects: The Dynamics of Feminist Teaching*, edited by Margo Culley and Catherine Portuges, 240–244. Boston: Routledge & Kegan Paul.

Walkerdine, Valerie. 1981. "Sex, Power and Pedagogy." *Screen Education* 1981: 38–51.

Weiler, Kathleen. 1988. *Women Teaching for Change; Gender, Class, & Power.* South Hadley, Mass.: Bergin & Garvey.

Lana Rakow's article originally appeared in *Teaching Forum*, a publication of the University of Wisconsin System Undergraduate Teaching Improvement Council. It is reprinted with permission of *Teaching Forum*.

CHAPTER 41

SCHOLARSHIP ON THE OTHER SIDE: POWER AND CARING IN FEMINIST EDUCATION

BECKY ROPERS-HUILMAN

In this paper, I explore the complexities of power and caring in educational settings from both a student and teacher perspective. Analyses of power and caring—two interrelated threads that are woven through feminist educational literature—are complex, yet essential to any feminist analysis of teaching and learning relationships. Through the interrogation of several educational scenarios, this analysis both constructs power and caring as useful in feminist education and problematizes our ability to ever fully understand or anticipate their effects. I conclude with what I have learned from this analysis about how to approach teaching and learning from a feminist perspective.

Time is the space between you and me.
—Lyrics from *Seal* 1994

Feminist teaching is a practice that has been well documented, problematized, and critiqued. Examinations of the intersections between feminism and higher education have produced considerable scholarship on feminist research, service, and pedagogy, all with the underlying quest to understand what it means to engage in feminist teaching and learning (Brown 1992; Bunch and Pollack 1983; Culley and Portuges 1985; Frye 1980; Gore 1993; Heald 1989; Lather 1991; Maher and Tetreault 1994).

Two interwoven threads frequently emerge in conversations about feminist teaching. These threads, often represented by the terms "power" and "caring," seem to be crucial—but not easy—concepts for feminist educators to grapple with and enact. For example, Roberta Bennett (1991) suggested that feminist teaching generally supports attempts to create nonhierarchical, egalitarian classrooms where teachers and students value each others' interpretations of their lives. Yet others wonder if a nonhierarchical class is possible or if all experiences should be (or could be) valued in the same ways (Ellsworth 1989; Luke 1996; Ropers-Huilman 1998). Jennifer Gore (1993) suggested that discussions about feminist pedagogy have often emphasized the importance of student experience and voice, along with a simultaneous empowerment for social change. Yet several scholars wonder whether empowerment is desirable or possible within the social and institutional constraints that feminist educators are generally operating (Gore 1990; Orner 1992). Carmen Luke (1996, 296) asserts, "Feminism is still fundamentally about transformation and enlightenment and, therefore, feminist educators still attempt in their teaching to give students access to 'better,' more inclusive, socially just, and non-exploitative knowledges." In this vein, feminist education continues to question how teachers can use their power to enact care for students.

Reprinted from *NWSA Journal*, Vol. 11, No. 1, 1999. Copyright© 1999 Indiana University Press.

Still, feminist teaching is not a "pure" practice. It is affected not only by participants, but also by the institutions in which it takes place. While many scholars have suggested the potential benefits of feminist approaches to teaching and learning, others have recognized the limitations of feminist teaching when it remains situated within educational institutions (Gore 1990; Middleton 1995). Magda Gere Lewis (1993, 145) reminds us, "Universities are both the site where reactionary and repressive ideologies and practices are entrenched and, at the same time, the site where progressive, transformative possibilities are born." Within those contexts, then, feminist educators have realized that certain guidelines and expectations—both implicit and explicit—affect the ways they can operate within higher education settings. Norms and expectations are interpreted in multiple ways by all who choose to participate, yet no one fully escapes the pressures and effects of standards and structures embedded in institutional climates (Damrosch 1995). While each institution undoubtedly has its own unique characteristics, feminism has been characterized as "subversive" to the commonly accepted traditions of academe (Bezucha 1985). Feminist education can be cloaked with institutional trappings, yet continue to seek "progressive and transformative possibilities."

I propose that one way feminism has subverted traditional roles of educational participants in academic climates is by reconsidering the proper or most useful roles and interactions of teachers and students, especially as they relate to power and caring. Who can or should care for whom? Nel Noddings (1992, 14) poses the questions: "What does it mean to care?" and "Can we make caring the center of our educational efforts?" These questions urge a consideration of the deliberate ways in which we, as educators, can use our positions to improve educational practices through an intense and respectful engagement with students. Yet complicating these considerations are poststructural questions about the instability of power within any position. Who really has "the power" in classrooms? How would one know? What are the ways the use of power helps and hinders learning? The student-teacher dichotomy whereby all educational participants are essentialized by their place on a designated side of the divide pervades educational literature and thought (Mayberry and Rees 1997). I suggest that feminism offers new ways of thinking about the usefulness of strict enforcement of that dichotomy and considers the complexities of moving from "one side" to the other—from student to teacher and back again.

Underlying much of the literature on feminist educational experiences is a concentrated and deliberate examination of the uses of power and caring in our teaching and learning settings. In this article, I examine the various relationships that feminists, as both students and teachers, experience in formal teaching and learning settings in higher education. Further, I consider the complexities of expanding those relationships within the structures that define higher education. Undergirding this analysis is my belief that power and caring are not dichotomous concepts. I do not try to get my power as a teacher "out of the way" so that I can care for the students with whom I work. Simultaneously, I do not try to care about students by ensuring either that they have power over others or that we exist in a powerless classroom. Contrary to common understandings, I propose to examine power and caring not as dichotomous terms, but rather as terms whose enactment lends strength to the other. Further, I hope to explore how power and caring intersect and, often, have unintended effects.

Philosophical Framework

The use of poststructural theories and approaches in feminist work has been oft considered in recent years. For various reasons, many feminist thinkers have claimed that poststructuralism could be useful for feminist purposes at this particular time in history (Gore 1991; Lather 1991; Sawicki 1991; Scott 1990). Others, though, have pointed out the potential dangers of a wholesale adoption of poststructuralism and suggested that feminists should consider what it could offer cautiously, if at all (Alcoff 1988; Nicholson 1995). As someone who is quite optimistic about what a feminist poststructuralism might offer intellectually, politically, and strategically to my life's work in and outside of academic settings, I have followed these discussions with great interest.

Feminist poststructuralism, as a theory that recognizes fluctuating power relations and situational meanings, yet acknowledges our own place as gendered actors in those relations, can be useful in understanding classroom and educational interactions. Still, one of the primary criticisms of poststructuralism has been its lack of applicability to "real world" settings (Alcoff 1988; Lather 1991). Within higher education, one scholar has suggested that the ramifications of poststructural theorizing have been decidedly absent from our professional conversations (Bloland 1995). While several pieces of feminist poststructural work deftly examined poststructural tenets in varied higher education settings (Ellsworth 1989; Gore 1993; Luke 1996; Orner 1992), those of us who are attempting to embrace and problematize poststructural and feminist offerings in our higher education settings continue to encounter much ambiguity.

One of the greatest uncertainties at this point is the use of power and caring in teaching and learning settings. If power is fluid and shifting (Foucault 1978), how can teachers and students enact it? Where can educational participants carve out places for action for themselves and others? How can teachers and students use or direct power in caring ways? Carmen Luke (1996) has pointed out the absence in the literature of discussions of those "decidedly visceral moments" when women teachers begin to feel their power and authority in educational settings (286). My task in this paper is to detail the visceral moments of my transition from feminist student to teacher and to begin a response to the question: how can feminist educational participants enact power to care about each other? I intend to do this while examining the usefulness of the power *vs.* caring dichotomy that is frequently found in feminist teaching literature (Luke 1996) and whose deconstruction is proposed by the theoretical approaches of feminist poststructuralism.

Feminist poststructuralism has much to offer a discussion on education as well as on teaching and learning processes (Ellsworth 1989; Gore 1993; Heald 1989; Lather 1991; Orner 1992). Not only does it problematize our understandings of knowledge and how those understandings have shifted over time, it also can aid in our understandings of power relations within our educational systems. As Chris Weedon (1987, 139) stated:

> From a feminist poststructural perspective the process of criticism is infinite and constantly changing. At any particular historical moment, however, there is a finite number of discourses in circulation, discourses which are in competition for meaning. It is the conflict between these discourses which creates the possibility of new ways of thinking and new forms of subjectivity.

Criticism that acknowledges and problematizes power relations in social interactions is particularly useful in considering the ways in which power is related to, and supportive of, caring practices in education.

A feminist poststructural approach to education would involve a conscious effort to recognize and utilize the positions that one embodies as a participant in feminist education, with the caveat that we cannot always know the effects of the actions that we choose. Further, since feminist education has often advanced examinations of participants as they relate to power and caring, our chosen actions should be evaluated with these concepts in mind. In this analysis, drawing on feminist poststructural philosophy led me to look closely at the ways in which power relations were enacted as I, or other teachers and students, attempted to care about others within several educational settings. I look at ways that I perceived feminism and higher education to disrupt each other, especially as these disruptions affected my attempts to engage within feminist learning environments.

Power and Caring as Student and Teacher

In August 1996, I took my first post-graduate teaching position at Louisiana State University. Having completed my doctorate at the University of Wisconsin–Madison just months before assuming my new responsibilities, I found the summer of 1996 to be filled with tension, challenges, and excitement. What would I be able to teach the graduate students with whom I was going to work? That I would learn from them was unquestioned in my mind. What if none of the students thought that I was worth listening to or working with? Why was I, who at the time identified much more with the "student" position, thought to possess certain skills that had magically changed my status from student to teacher? The barriers that I perceived between those two roles had seemed nearly insurmountable. As the fall approached, I wondered at the impermanence of those barriers through which I apparently had passed.

The approaching professorship was unsettling. I had experienced a wide range of interactions with professors in graduate school and was looking forward to the time when I determined my own path of study and developed my own timeline for following that path. In much of my previous education, I felt that my learning was determined by others in ways that were sometimes uncomfortable, offensive, and even boring. I felt that my "best interests" or educational needs were not always being respected, or cared for. How was I to ensure that my attempts to provide a structure for others' learning would not make them feel as I occasionally did? As I prepared for the new position, I realized that the institutionally sanctioned power that others used to determine the structures of my learning would now be granted to me. The gravity of this responsibility was both exhilarating and overwhelming.

My concerns were elevated by my conscious desire to hold fast to certain principles that I admired (or sorely missed) in other teachers' practices. I had recently completed my dissertation on feminist teaching and had encountered many issues in my research participants' work that seemed unresolvable (Ropers-Huilman 1996). For example, was empowerment useful, harmful, or both when talking about what teachers should do to or for students in their relationships? To what degree should we strive to nurture community and/or difference in our classrooms? When should teachers consciously try to use their power to encourage "desirable" or stifle "undesirable" student behaviors, in order to balance group dynamics in the class or individual class members? Regardless of my uncertainties, I wanted to identify as a feminist educator and, therefore, knew that I would have a bumpy road ahead of me (Middleton 1993; Frye 1980; Lewis 1993; Ropers-Huilman 1997; Weiler 1988).

Many of these unresolved concerns related to the concepts of power and caring. Primarily, I was interested in how power circulates in feminist educational environments and where and how the openings for both student and teacher agency were located and crafted. My belief is that feminist educators can be powerful, in both deliberate and spontaneous ways, while simultaneously caring for the overall purposes of the class as they relate to individual students. In this exploration, I focus on my experiences as a feminist in transition from student to teacher and consider the factors that shape my responses to these concerns and my subsequent practices. Through three teaching and learning "scenes," I examine the contradictions I encountered in attempting to enact power and caring on both sides of the student–teacher dichotomy.

Scene one: Peeking out from under the cloak of power

As a student, I saw power as ubiquitous among the faculty. Regardless of faculty members' practices, they still had an authority over students' lives in meaningful ways. Yet that authority, while apparently omnipresent in the academic area of my life, seemed entirely absent from the personal area. I was being conditioned toward individuality, separateness, and hierarchy during graduate school, the time when "habits of mind are learned and reinforced [and] . . . choices made by the profession begin to seem natural" (Damrosch 1995, 140). Yet "natural" would never have been my chosen word to describe a learning where personal lives and school lives were in conflict, where "school learning" was divorced from "real learning." I was more convinced than ever that "Who we are, to whom we are related, how we are situated all matter in what we learn, what we value, and how we approach intellectual and moral life" (Noddings 1992, xiii).

As a graduate student, I felt powerless in many arenas for the first several years of my experience. Later, I learned that my previous analysis was quite simplistic. Foucault (1978) reminds us that power is not stable or consistent. While it can be situated in certain ways within discourses, it is fluid and, therefore, always moving. Faculty and students were engaged in a dance of power that was shaped by each person's talents, hesitancies, limitations, and desires. Still, the norms of our graduate school context that dictated "proper" relations between teacher, student, and knowledge (Damrosch, 1995) circumscribed the variety of dances that might have taken place.

Considering my relation to power made me nervous. I felt sure that if I voiced my beliefs, they wouldn't make sense to anyone else and, in worrying about such an event, I was often unable to think of anything to say at all. I thought that people would hear my words, pause briefly, and then go on as if I hadn't said anything. This happens all too often to certain students (hooks 1994) and has happened to me many times. I worried that someone in a seminar, either the professor or other students would interrupt me, and I would feel obligated to stop my thoughts in mid-stream, acknowledging that my thoughts were not going to shape the ensuing discussion. I recognized my lack of power in this setting and resonated with Magda Gere Lewis' (1993, 49) words: "The potential power of a pedagogical practice, whether in the realm of the personal or that of the political, whether inside the academy or out, is its ability to bring people to a point where they care to listen." It seemed there was only a finite amount of power available—represented, in part, in speaking prominence—and faculty members and a very few students held the pot in which it was kept tightly against their bodies. Students and teachers cared to listen differently to different participants.

Caring was an elusive concept for me when I was a student. I was socialized to think I was caring about someone when I allowed them to speak over me, when their problems and concerns received prominence and when I succumbed to their wishes without burdening them with mine. In classrooms, then, caring was a bit problematic. How was I to learn to be a critical thinker if my thoughts were subsumed by others? How was I to be a participant in active learning—a hallmark, in my mind, of feminist education? I felt rude and uncaring if I interrupted others, even if it was the only way to make my voice heard. I did not expect the teachers who led my classes to "care" about me. I believed that they had better things to do and many students with much grander ambitions with whom they could work. Of course, caring is no more simple a concept than power. How could faculty members have demonstrated their care for me in a way that I would have noticed or accepted it? Nel Noddings (1992) asserts that caring is only realized when both the "carer" and "cared-for" are willing and able to enter into such a relationship. If students are resistant to such interactions with faculty members, or, in other words, are not trained or willing to see their teachers in caring roles, is there anything a teacher can do to break down students' preconceptions?

How can teachers and students broaden educational discourses to reconceptualize the intersections of power and caring in their relationships? Here we circle back to the difficulty of the relationships between care and power. Who can interrupt hierarchical and distant teacher–student interactions? In what discourses is this possible? What are the strategies through which power and caring can be disrupted and reshaped in learning and teaching relationships? More importantly, what are the assumptions underlying a desire for certain shaping? And whose desires ultimately get played out in which classrooms?

Potential responses to these questions are constantly spinning as we draw lines in the sand between and among teachers and students. Below, I describe an experience at the end of my graduate years that stands out prominently as shifting the sands of power and caring that demarcated those lines within a classroom. Through this example, I hope to show how the middle position—somewhere between student and teacher—taught me about my desires to engage in both powerful and careful educational practices.

During my last semester at the University of Wisconsin, I audited a seminar course in my major area. From the beginning, there was something different about this course for me. While I am still uncertain about the complex changes that occurred within that context, some relevant variables come to mind. First, I had worked for almost four years establishing a relationship with the teacher that existed both within and outside of the classroom. We had been in several classes together, and I felt that I knew his style fairly well. Because of the associated power linked to that knowledge, I felt comfortable attempting to care about and attend to class dynamics when I felt that the current line of conversation was not working for me or for other students in the class. Second, the professor and I had taken the time to talk about student–teacher relationships both in general and as they applied specifically to our interactions. We had learned a bit about each other's fallibility and knew that beyond being teacher and student, we were also people with strengths, weaknesses, aspirations, and disappointments. In various ways, I had the sense that I was both cared for, and worthy of expressing care, in this relationship. Third, the class was small, met in a comfortable place off-campus, and regularly encompassed a meal or snack together. In this way, we cared for our physical needs for comfort and interaction, while in some ways crossing the boundaries that are typically enforced by the traditional positioning of students sitting in rows facing a teacher behind a podium or desk. Fourth, I felt confident about my own work in a role outside that of a student. I successfully completed my dissertation during that semester and had received positive feedback from a variety of sources, both within and outside academe. I had learned a lot on my own volition and felt very "in charge" of my own learning experiences. Fifth, I was not being graded—or de-graded, as Page Smith (1990) suggests. While I completed the majority of the assigned work for the class (and additional work that I thought would add to class discussion), I regarded the teacher's feedback on my participation as *one* perspective, rather than *the* perspective. My valuing of people in this class was based on much more than student or teacher status. In my mind, I was able to more clearly see how each member of our discussion group could both contribute to and learn from our interactions. We were all powerful and, therefore, had the responsibility to care for each other.

While undoubtedly other factors played a part in making this experience different from previous ones, I believe that those listed here serve a useful purpose in exploring my transforming definitions of power and caring as I moved from student to teacher. I learned that I enjoyed power, to some extent. As a teacher/ student, I experienced a power that gave me the opportunity to care for myself and others. I read additional material, and developed unassigned summaries and critiques of texts. I brought copies of additional readings that I thought would further the class members' learning about a given issue. I liked being in control of my learning, while attempting to contribute to others'. For various reasons, power seemed to be circulating through me this time, and was finally palpable. Power was indeed alive, and I was invigorated by it.

My role as a student/teacher was complicated by various other identities, attitudes, and experiences, and was situated within a unique context. I was more than a student, just as teachers are more than teachers. As feminist teachers and students who value inclusive classrooms wherein power is used to care about, for, and with others, we have choices, opportunities, and responsibilities to recognize the strengths and challenges of our own multiple positions and those of others. It is only then that educational participants can shape practices aimed at creating an inclusive society that discovers and utilizes the potential of its actors. This goal, though, is not as simple as it seems. I turn now to the other side and to my attempts to enact these emerging feminist beliefs from the standpoint of a teacher.

Scene Two: Finding the ruptures in power and caring

It seemed I had come too late to my realizations about the various forms teaching and learning interactions could take. After more than two decades of schooling, I had finally got it. I thought I had some substantial control over my own learning. While this control was admittedly a comforting feeling, I recognized the instability of that feeling and its illusory qualities. The time had come to move on.

When I arrived at Louisiana State University to take an assistant professor position, power issues related to my newly acquired "teacher" status were immediately apparent. I remember very clearly the first time a student, who was an African American woman, walked into my office. While I was dressed quite informally and was in the middle of doing manual labor (moving boxes into my office), the student seemed to immediately acknowledge my position as a professor. I remember the unnerving feeling, more than the details, of this situation. The student asked about an upcoming class I was teaching and about my work. I wondered why she was acting so strangely, why she cared. Why was I immediately given a respect that I had to fight for with many professors as a graduate student? Was this related to the south? Our races? Our positions as teacher and student? Through her questions and interest in my work, this person cared for me as an intellectual, perhaps in an effort to get me to use a presumed power to care for her progress in her academic program. I knew at that moment, as I went to work trying to convince her that I was a "normal"[1] person, that I had, in this situation, crossed to the other side.

In the first few weeks of my graduate level class that fall, I had similar deliberations about enacting power and caring as I attempted to stretch my role to include active educational participation. After the first day of class, I wrote the following in my teaching journal:

> I realized that most people looked at me when they were introducing themselves, rather than at their other colleagues. The people in the class are so experienced and have so much to offer.... Should we always push as far as we can? Or should we place barriers in front of ourselves to limit our experiences if we don't think we can contribute?... In some sense, if I don't speak out and take an active part in this discourse, I will live and die without being heard—without making a difference. (1996a)

I started this entry concerned that students were talking primarily to me instead of to their other class colleagues. I wanted to immediately refute the idea that all students would need to respond to and craft their "answers" for me. This concern, though, quickly turned to a concern about my need or desire to participate. I wanted to enact power to care for others, but I also wanted to use that power to insist my contributions be attended to—and cared for—as well. While I didn't want to leave anyone out, my gendered role of being a nurturer, while useful and expected in some ways, threatened to push my contribution out of the conversations.

I soon learned that even if I had wanted to remain silent, students' strong expectations for teacher direction would have made that very difficult. Power and caring were both part of my responsibility as a feminist educator. I had to discover how to enact them in a way that was useful, both for students and for myself.

On the second night of this class, I reflected again on the ways in which power and caring can be manifested in educational environments:

> I hope that people are soon able to find more of a voice in arguing with each other. I hope I continue to keep learning how to do that better.... We do have some caretakers in the class. I'm one of them. We want there to be disruption, but we want others to disrupt each other within the bounds of our own normalcy. What a fiasco we've got going on here. What does the phrase, "Be nice" really mean? There's been some discussion that it means different things in different cultures (Moffatt 1989; hooks 1994). Doesn't it relate to what we think our end goal for somebody should be? If we love or care for someone, shouldn't we want an *outcome* to be the best possible for them? Therefore, maybe it's not the process, but the end that would be most important. I guess I really don't subscribe to that view, though. How could I when we're always in process? Therefore, what we're doing right now needs to be important. It can't be put off until we know more or until we feel more competent. We need to engage with Each Other, Each Time in caring ways that reflect our constructed hopes and desires. We're always operating with a working definition. (1996a)

Again, this entry demonstrated my struggles to move from a feminist student who was concerned primarily with my own interactions in the classroom, to a feminist teacher who used my power to ensure caring interactions of all involved. That change of focus, though, does not lead to clear and distinct ways of behaving in relation to power and caring. In an effort to care, can and should we enact power over others? When and how? To what degree is it our choice to do that? I was beginning to learn that power was a fluid and reciprocal relationship in educational interactions. In other words, the power to care about students was only possible when students enacted power to care about what I could offer them.

In the final example I present here, I struggled with opening class discussion so much that I minimized what I could contribute to the interchange. After the third meeting of this class, I wrote:

> In class we talked about feminism—and brainstormed words that students associated with feminism. We put them all on the board—I felt somewhat radical writing "lesbians" and "bitchy" on the board. I didn't share what I knew about feminism with

students, though. In fact, I really didn't include any of my adjectives or "thought words" on the board. I feel like I may have missed an opportunity to let them question me in terms of my experience thinking about and working within feminism. I also feel like I didn't provide any sort of "closure" whatsoever. Now, I know that's OK according to my own epistemologies and pedagogical preferences, but it sure felt uneasy—like they wanted the answer and I didn't give it to them. Maybe in class next week I'll give them an opportunity to ask me about feminism and my thoughts if they're interested. (1996a)

While I have consistently received very positive feedback on this particular class session from a variety of students, I wonder whether this was the most useful approach to our learning. The environment I helped to craft did a few things well, I think. First, it opened up the discussion in a safe way, so that even though students knew I supported feminism, they voiced both positive and derogatory views of the feminisms that they had encountered in their lived experiences. I cared about students and their perspectives on one of my primary political commitments. Second, the class provided students with an opportunity to contribute and have every contribution valued, regardless of their contradictions. Third, it provided a forum through which students could share their perspectives with each other and, in doing so, could learn from each other's experiences. On the other hand, I struggled with my participation. While admittedly I enacted power in initiating this discussion in class, my beliefs were only implicitly stated during this meeting. In trying to care about students and respect their views, I chose not to enact the "teacher role" who "taught" them historical and political information about the feminist movement. In crafting an "open" space, I relinquished my power to care about the knowledge that I might have been able to share.

Scene Three: Reconsidering power ruptures in classroom practices

As evidenced in the discussion above, I have spent much time deliberating over the desired roles of teachers and students in feminist education, or rather what I desired. Literature on feminist pedagogy, while helpful in a variety of ways, does not provide me with easy or certain answers about the enactment of various feminist principles in my classrooms. It would violate its own assertions if it attempted to do so, since an acknowledgment of the personal as political necessitates an examination of relationships as uniquely embedded in particular contexts. The challenge of engaging with/in personally and locally defined teaching and learning practices has been appealing to me as I struggle with the issues raised in and outside of various classrooms.

Recently, I inadvertently initiated an incident that provoked the many complexities of trying to utilize my power in caring ways as a teacher. In a class session focusing on teaching and learning relationships, I proposed a change in the syllabus. While I believed that I was contributing to students' learning of class material, the discussion that unfolded taught me about the effects of power and caring in educational discourse as well.

As is customary in the classes I teach, I address administrative issues at the beginning of class so that we can move onto an unencumbered dialogue about the class texts for the rest of the time. That day, I proposed to revise the syllabus by omitting several readings and replacing them with a writing assignment (with a maximum of 5 pages) reflecting on the readings that we had already covered. After I handed out my proposal, everyone was silent as they reviewed the terms. While no one immediately objected, the rousing appreciation that I expected for my flexibility did not occur. What I perceived to be an act of care on my part was apparently not being welcomed by others in the room. Instead, people started asking clarifying questions. Eventually, one student expressed her discomfort with the change and her reluctance to support it.

In my efforts to understand her hesitancy and other students' less than enthusiastic responses, I asked them if they thought the writing would take more time than their readings would have. I said that I needed to reflect, not just race through additional readings, and asked, "Aren't you feeling that, too?" I wondered why they weren't unquestioningly embracing this teacher-supported break to reflect on what they were learning through our class this semester. I told them that I wouldn't be grading their papers except to indicate that they had turned them in. I merely wanted to see the writing so that I could dialogue with each student as an individual. Without extensive discussion, we came to an "agreement" that we would have these reflection papers due in two weeks instead of one. We then moved to our readings for the day, one of which (ironically) was Elizabeth Ellsworth's (1989) piece entitled, "Why doesn't this feel empowering?: Working through the repressive myths of liberatory pedagogy."

Given these events and the complexity of the issues that Ellsworth proposes in her work, I might have anticipated that we had not yet finished the discussion about the changed syllabus. By the end of the class, students had told me in many ways that my actions in proposing this change were both useful and problematic. They often invoked themes found in Ellsworth's work to support their concern. While some students thought it would be helpful to have time to reflect without having the responsibility of additional readings, others reminded me that they had not expressed the need to reflect. I was the one who had made that determination. I was presuming to know what was best. And as Jennifer Gore (1990, 63) suggested:

> In attempts to empower others we need to acknowledge that our agency has limits, that we might "get it wrong" in assuming we know what would be empowering for others, and that no matter what our aims or how we go about "empowering," our efforts will be partial and inconsistent.

Some students believed that it might be helpful for them to have my feedback on their work as a way to improve their writing skills, especially before the final paper was to be handed in and graded. Others indicated that they felt an incredible pressure to "produce" "good" writing if I was to read it, and that it was this pressure that they were resisting. Finally, as I was trying to reassure them that this exercise was not about me grading them, but was instead about their learning and reflection, one student told me, "'We don't trust you that much." My immediate response was, "You shouldn't." With Ellsworth's caution that we can never be divested of the complexities of our identities in teaching and learning settings, I recognized the instability of my guarantees, the flexibility of my assurances, and the sound "rationale" that students were using when they distrusted my attempts to enact power and care.

While this statement will probably be eternally problematic in my mind, my initial reaction was one mired in compassion, intellectual stimulation, and respect for the classroom discourse that we had created because it had evoked such a "risky" statement. I felt trusted because this student had the courage to tell me that his trust for me only went so far. I was reminded of Patricia Hill Collins' (1991) insistence on the importance of the discussions we have about the relationship between trust and truth: "Epistemological choices about who to trust, what to believe, and why something is true are not benign academic issues. Instead, these concerns tap the fundamental question of which versions of truth will prevail and shape thought and action" (202—203). The relationship between trust and classroom interaction was emphasized as others began to voice their agreement with the student who expressed some initial hesitancy in embracing my proposed changes. They said that they had been feeling similarly, but did not feel comfortable to speak their thoughts because they did not know me well enough. The limits of our relationships were educating all of us about the complexities of feminist teaching and learning.

Throughout this discussion, I felt honored by students' forthrightness with me about their perceptions of the classroom discourses that we were struggling within. Yet, I also felt trapped by the constraints of pedagogy that attempts to enact power in efforts to empower, and care in efforts to ensure comfort, ease, and positive outcomes in learning. I attempted to "care" about others through my "flexibility" in the use of my teacher-power. But I realized that my caring had different effects for individual students and was not desired or requested by all students. As I tried to change the relationships I had with students by providing "better learning opportunities" for them, I came to see that with various power sources that I claim, *I do not know the effects that my caring will have.* Further, if I proclaim to enact care in classrooms, while simultaneously trying to reposition teacher–student dichotomies through the lenses of liberatory ideals, my caring becomes suspect. If I can never omit power from our classrooms, then my assertions that any part of our relationship can be free from that dynamic come dangerously close to lying.

Final Thoughts

> *What then are we dealing with when researchers and teachers are made to rehearse the method for so long that they forget the purpose of the rehearsal and they all begin to do the two-step and try to eliminate from the dance floor those who would do the wild interpretive dance? Is method a need to define? To critique? To remove?* (Leck 1994, 93).

I learned many things about power and caring in feminist education through these classroom interactions. First, I learned that regardless of the seemingly clear lines between teachers and students in classroom contexts, all educational participants have the ability to enact the power to care. Power and caring are interwoven to form the wire on which we perch our performances: wild and interpretive, or otherwise. The embodiment of multiple educational positions, though, dictates a balancing act that is always being modified. Learning and teaching in feminist classrooms depend on continual attention to the ways in which our power is taking effect, and the ways that our caring practices are being perceived.

Second, I relearned the importance of actively recognizing and embodying both teacher and learner positions when I interacted with others in educational environments. Even when positioned as an institutionally sanctioned "teacher," I find that what has been conceptualized as the "other side" of the teacher/student dichotomy has qualities that are far too appealing to me to give up. Learning is embedded in teaching; to tear one from the other would greatly diminish the possibilities for either. For students, though, it is risky for teachers to desire the "student side" and claim that crossing over is entirely possible and educationally useful. As students reminded me in the incident described above, our pleasure, power, and ability to care is marked and modified always by our multiple identity positions—one of which places us on one side or another of the teacher–student dichotomy—regardless of the pleasure class participants were deriving from our experiences. Carmen Luke warns, "Pedagogy without a locus of authority thus risks deceit: embodied difference and differential power access camouflaged under false pretence of allegedly equal subject positions" (1996, 297). It would be disingenuous and dangerous for me to ever mislead students to believe that we are in all ways equal; I can always retreat back to my side, a side which would not currently welcome them. It is dangerous for students if teachers forget their axes of privilege. In my current transition from student to teacher, it is most likely easier for me to remember multiple positions now than it will be after many years. I am learning that the assumptions and practices of an academy that positions us on one side or the other of a teacher–student dichotomy have already begun to restructure my thinking.

Third, our very modes of learning are deeply embedded in assumptions of which we are not always aware. For example, in the third scene above, I thought I was using my power to care by giving students the "opportunity" to "reflect." My "caring," though, had strict parameters. Students had to reflect on paper, to be handed in to a teacher, who at the end of the term assigns a grade. I would imagine that no student in the class felt free to say during this assignment, "I've already been reflecting, teacher, so I don't need to do this assignment, but thanks for the opportunity." Reflect. Present an image back. If students are reflecting for themselves, why is it necessary for a teacher to be involved with the process? At the same time, could it be helpful for a teacher to be involved? This tension, I believe, will be important to consider in future interactions.

Finally, I came to believe that it is imperative that we, as feminist educators, consciously model what we value and how we think values should take shape in educational environments. As Jo Anne Pagano believes, "To act is to theorize" (1991, 194). Our actions become statements of our beliefs, of the theories that guide us as educators. Decisions about how to interact with others are not easy, though, and require a willingness to continue movement around prescribed dichotomies in order to view situations from other locations. We need to realize the ways in which who we are as teachers are defined by the students with whom we are interacting. Further, the ways in which teachers and students can be powerful are related to the ways in which we have constructed caring relationships within our classrooms. Understandably, the struggles and choices we encounter in educational settings are not clear or predictable in their effects. Yet we have an obligation as the ones who are vested with an assumed power, even if that power is easily and regularly disrupted, to assess and address the effects that it is having on our classrooms.

The choices we make in our classrooms as we interact with students are vestiges of our beliefs about what educational experiences are supposed to be like. We need to share our struggles with students as we negotiate relationships supported and disrupted by power and caring practices. By our modeling, we teach students what we think it means to be feminist educational participants. Simultaneously, though, feminist teachers and students can model to each other the complexities of using our power to care about each other and the educational environments that we create.

Becky Ropers-Huilman is an Assistant Professor in the College of Education and Women's and Gender Studies at Louisiana State University. Her research and interests focus on feminist intersections with higher education institutions, feminist theory and methodology, higher education cultures, teaching and learning in academic environments, and critical and poststructural approaches to inquiry. She is the author of Feminist Teaching in Theory and Practice: Situating Power and Knowledge in Poststructural Classrooms. *Correspondence should be sent to Ropers-Huilman at 121C Peabody Hall, Louisiana State University, Baton Rouge, LA 70803; broper1@lsu.edu*

Note

1. I wonder as I write this: What is "normal?" Is my student status normal? Is my teacher status normal? It is troubling to me that I want again to "care" for others by diminishing the unconditional/unproven respect that my voice accords. I want to "reduce" my "power" because I have experienced the hurtful place of being on the opposite sides of those who have seemed to hoard it. Poststructural conceptions of power, then, are difficult for me here. If power supposedly circulates and acts through each of us, why do some persons feel like they are unable to find or enact their power? For example, while Sue Middleton (1993) proposes that women's silence can be a form of resistance, I struggle with knowing that my silence, my "resistance," limited my options for participation in educational environments. My shaping of my own and others' knowing was sadly lacking. I wondered about myself and others who chose silence, "What knowledge . . . do students have of college classrooms that makes the decision not to talk a 'realistic' decision?" (Karp & Yoels 1994; orig. 1976, 457). To what degree is silence a decision to resist or disengage with the acting out of power and care in classrooms?

References

Alcoff, Linda. 1988. "Cultural Feminism Versus Poststructuralism: The Identity Crisis in Feminist Theory." In *Reconstructing the Academy: Women's Education and Women's Studies*, eds. Elizabeth Minnich, Jean O'Barr, and Rachel Rosenfeld, 257–288. Chicago: University of Chicago Press.

Bennett, Roberta S. 1991. "Empowerment = Work over Time: Can There Be Feminist Pedagogy in the Sport Sciences?" *Journal of Physical Education, Recreation, and Dance* 62:62–67, 75.

Bezucha, Robert J. 1985. "Feminist Pedagogy as a Subversive Activity." In *Gendered Subjects: The Dynamics of Feminist Teaching*, eds. Margo Culley & Catherine Portuges, 81–95. Boston: Routledge & Kegan Paul.

Bloland, Harland. G. 1995. "Postmodernism and Higher Education." *Journal of Higher Education* 66(5):521–559.

Brown, Julie. 1992. "Theory or Practice—What Exactly Is Feminist Pedagogy?" *Journal of General Education* 41:51–63.

Bunch, Charlotte, and Sandra Pollack, eds. 1983. *Learning Our Way: Essays in Feminist Education*. Trumansburg, NY: Crossing.

Collins, Patricia Hill. 1991. *Black Feminist Thought: Knowledge, Consciousness, and the Politics of Empowerment*. New York: Routledge.

Culley, Margo, and Catherine Portuges, eds. 1985. *Gendered Subjects: The Dynamics of Feminist Teaching*. Boston: Routledge & Kegan Paul.

Damrosch, David. 1995. *We Scholars: Changing the Culture of the University*. Cambridge, MA: Harvard.

Ellsworth, Elizabeth. 1989. "Why Doesn't this Feel Empowering?: Working Through the Repressive Myths of Critical Pedagogy." *Harvard Educational Review* 59(3): 297–324.

Foucault, Michel. 1978. *The History of Sexuality: An Introduction*. Vol. 1. New York: Random House.

Frye, Marilyn. 1980. "On Second Thought . . ." *Radical Teacher* 17:37–38.

Gore, Jennifer. 1990. "What We Can Do for You! What Can 'We' Do for 'You'?: Struggling over Empowerment in Critical and Feminist Pedagogy." *Educational Foundations* 4(3): 5–26.

Gore, Jennifer. 1993. *The Struggle for Pedagogies: Critical and Feminist Discourses as Regimes of Truth.* New York: Routledge.

Heald, Susan. 1989. "The Madwoman out of the Attic: Feminist Teaching in the Margins." *Resources for Feminist Research* 18:22–26.

hooks, bell. 1994. *Teaching to Transgress: Education as the Practice of Freedom.* New York: Routledge.

Karp, David A., and William C. Yoels. [1976] 1994. "The College Classroom: Some Observations on the Meanings of Student Participation." In *Teaching and Learning in the College Classroom,* eds. Kenneth A. Feldman and Michael B. Paulsen, 451–464. Needham Heights, MA: Ginn.

Lather, Patti. 1991. *Getting Smart: Feminist Research and Pedagogy With/in the Postmodern.* New York: Routledge.

Leck, Glorianne M. 1994. "Queer Relations with Educational Research." In *Power and Method: Political Activism and Educational Research,* ed. Andrew Gitlin, 77–96. New York: Routledge.

Lewis, Magda Gere. 1993. *Without a Word: Teaching Beyond Women's Silence.* New York: Routledge.

Luke, Carmen. 1996. "Feminist Pedagogy Theory: Reflections on Power and Authority." *Educational Theory* 46(3):283–302.

Maher, Frances A. and Mary Kay Thompson Tetreault. 1994. *The Feminist Classroom.* New York: Basic Books.

Mayberry, Maralee and Margaret N. Rees. 1997. "Feminist Pedagogy, Interdisciplinary Praxis, and Science Education." *National Women's Studies Association Journal* 9(1):57–75.

Middleton, Sue. 1993. *Educating Feminists: Life Histories and Pedagogy.* New York: Teachers College.

———. 1995. "Doing Feminist Educational Theory: A Post-modernist Perspective." *Gender and Education* 7(1):87–100.

Moffatt, Michael. 1989. *Coming of Age in New Jersey: College and American Culture.* New Brunswick, NJ: Rutgers University.

Nicholson, Carol. 1995. "Postmodern Feminisms." In *Education and the Post-modern Condition,* ed. Michael Peters, 75–85. Westport, CT: Bergin & Garvey.

Noddings, Nel. 1992. *The Challenge to Care in Schools: An Alternative Approach to Education.* New York: Teachers College.

Orner, Mimi. 1992. "Interrupting the Calls for Student Voice in 'Liberatory' Education: A Feminist Poststructuralist Perspective." In *Feminism and Critical Pedagogy,* eds. Carmen Luke and Jennifer Gore, 74–89. New York: Routledge.

Pagano, Jo Anne. 1991. "Moral Fictions: The Dilemma of Theory and Practice." In *Stories Lives Tell: Narrative and Dialogue in Education,* eds. Carol Witherell and Nel Noddings, 193–206. Teachers College: New York.

Ropers-Huilman, Becky. 1996. "Shaping an Island of Power and Change: Creating a Feminist Poststructural Teaching Discourse." Unpublished doctoral dissertation, University of Wisconsin–Madison.

———. 1996a. Teaching Journal. Unpublished.

———. 1997. "Constructing Feminist Teachers: Complexities of Identity." *Gender and Education* 9(3):327–343.

———. 1998. *Feminist Teaching in Theory and Practice: Situating Power and Knowledge in Poststructural Classrooms.* New York: Teachers College.

Sawicki, Jana. 1991. *Disciplining Foucault: Feminism, Power, and the Body.* New York: Routledge.

Scott, Joan Wallach. 1990. "Deconstructing Equality-versus-difference: Or, the Uses of Poststructuralist Theory for Feminism." In *Conflicts in Feminism,* eds. Marianne Hirsch and Evelyn Fox Keller, 134–148. New York: Routledge.

Seal. 1994. "Prayer for the Dying." *Seal.* Wea/Warner compact disc; ASIN:B000002MMQ.

Smith, Page. 1990. *Killing the Spirit: Higher Education in America.* New York: Viking.

Weedon, Chris. 1987. *Feminist Practice and Poststructuralist Theory.* Oxford: Basil Blackwell.

Weiler, Kathleen. 1988. *Women Teaching for Change: Gender, Class and Power.* New York: Bergin & Garvey.

Part VI

Selective Bibliography

SELECTIVE BIBLIOGRAPHY

Compiled by Monisa Shackelford

Context: Historical, Social, and Institutional

Bannerji, H., Carty, L., Dehli, K., Heald, S., & McKenna, K. (1991). *Unsettling relations: The university as site of feminist struggles*. Ontario: Women's Press.

De Los Reyes, E. (1997). Narratives of possibility and impossibility: What unites us and what separates us. *Harvard Educational Review*, 67(4), 796–802.

Gordon, L.D. (1990). *Gender and higher education in the progressive era*. New Haven, CT: Yale University Press.

Griffin, G.B. (1992). *Calling: Essays on teaching in the mother tongue*. Pasadena, CA: Trilogy Books.

Marcus, J. (1997). Working lips, breaking hearts: Class acts in American feminism. *Signs*, 22(3), 715–734.

Sandler, B.R. & Shoop, R.J. (Eds.). (1997). *Sexual harassment on campus: A guide for administrators, faculty, and students*. Boston: Allyn & Bacon.

Townsend, B.K. (1993). Feminist scholarship in core higher education journals. *Review of Higher Education*, 17(1), 21–41.

Urrutia, A.M. (1994). The development of black feminism. *Human Mosaic*, 28(1), 26–35.

Theoretical and Research Perspectives

Feminist Theory

Ahmed, S. (1996). Beyond humanism and postmodernism: Theorizing a feminist practice. *Hypatia*, 11(2), 71–93.

Alfonso, D.R. & Trigilio, J. (1997). Surfing the third wave: A dialogue between two third wave feminists. *Hypatia*, 12(3), 7–16.

Alway, J. (1995). The trouble with gender: Tales of the still-missing feminist revolution in sociological theory. *Sociological Theory*, 13(3), 209–228.

Anderson, A. (1998). Debatable performances: Restaging contentious feminisms. *Social Text*, 16(1), 1–24.

Bailey, C. (1997). Making waves and drawing lines: The politics of defining the vicissitudes of feminism. *Hypatia*, 12(3), 17–28.

Bem, S.L. (1995). Dismantling gender polarization and compulsory heterosexuality: Should we turn the volume down or up? *Journal of Sex Research*, 32(4), 329–334.

Burnett, R.E. & Ewald, H.R. (1994). Rabbit trails, ephemera, and other stories: Feminist methodology and collaborative research. *Journal of Advanced Composition*, 14(1), 21–51.

Chafetz, J.S. (1997). Feminist theory and sociology: Underutilized contributions for mainstream theory. *Annual Review of Sociology*, 23, 97–120.

Code, L. (1991). *What can she know? Feminist theory and the construction of knowledge*. Ithaca: Cornell University Press.

Collins, P.H. (1991). *Black feminist thought: Knowledge, consciousness, and the politics of empowerment*. London: Routledge.

Detloff, M. (1997). Mean spirits: The politics of contempt between feminist generations. *Hypatia*, 12(3), 76–99.

Gilligan, C. (1982). *In a different voice: Psychological theory and women's development*. Cambridge and London: Harvard University Press.

Harding, S. (1991). *Whose science? Whose knowledge? Thinking from women's lives*. Ithaca: Cornell University Press.

Hartmann, H., Bravo, E., Bunch, C., Hartsock, N., Spalter-Roth, R., Williams, L., & Blanco, M. (1996). Bringing together feminist theory and practice: A collective interview. *Signs*, 21(4), 917–951.

Hekman, S. (1990). *Gender and knowledge: Elements of a postmodern feminism*. Boston: Northwestern University Press.

Hekman, S. (1987). The feminization of epistemology: Gender and the social sciences. *Women and Politics*, 7(3), 65–83.

Higgenbotham, E.B. (1992). African-American women's history and the metalanguage of race. *Signs*, 17(2), 251–274.

Homans, M. (1994). 'Women of color' writers and feminist theory. *New Literacy History*, 25(1), 73–94.

hooks, b. (1994). *Teaching to transgress: Education as the practice of freedom*. New York: Routledge.

Howard, J.A. (1987). Dilemmas in feminist theorizing: Politics and the academy. *Current Perspectives in Social Theory, 8*, 279–312.

Humm, M. (Ed.). (1992). *Modern feminisms: Political, literary, cultural*. New York: Columbia University Press.

Kensinger, L. (1997). (In)Quest of liberal feminism. *Hypatia, 12*(4), 178–197.

Kyte, R. (1996). Moral reasoning as perception: A reading of Carol Gilligan. *Hypatia, 11*(3), 97–113.

Lerum, K. (1998). A glossary of feminist theory. *Contemporary Sociology, 27*(5), 543–544.

MacKinnon, C. (1989). *Toward a feminist theory of the state*. Cambridge, MA: Harvard University Press.

McLaren, M.A. (1997). Foucault and the subject of feminism. *Social Theory and Practice, 23*(1), 109–128.

Neath, J. (1997). Social causes of impairment, disability, and abuse: A feminist perspective. *Journal of Disability Policy Studies, 8*(1–2), 195–230.

Nicholson, L. (Ed.). (1997). *The second wave: A reader in feminist theory*. New York & London: Routledge.

Oakley, A. (1998). Science, gender, and women's liberation: An argument against postmodernism. *Women's Studies International Forum, 21*(2), 133–146.

Orr, C.M. (1997). Charting the currents of the third wave. *Hypatia, 12*(3), 29–45.

Sykes, H. (1998). Turning the closets inside/out: Towards a queer-feminist theory in women's physical education. *Sociology of Sport Journal, 15*(2), 154–173.

Taylor, F.O. (1998). The continuing significance of structural Marxism for feminist social theory. *Current Perspectives in Social Theory, 18*, 101–129.

Townsend, B. (1993). Feminist scholarship and the study of women in higher education. *Initiatives, 55*(1).

Feminist Research Methods

Bird, S.E. (1995). Understanding the ethnographic encounter: The need for flexibility in feminist reception studies. *Women and Language, 18*(2), 22–26.

Chase, S.E. (1989). Social science for women: A reading of studies of women's work. *Humanity and Society, 13*(3), 246–267.

DeVault, M.L. (1996). Talking back to sociology: Distinctive contributions of feminist methodology. *Annual Review of Sociology, 22*, 29–50.

Fonow, M.M. & Cook, J.A. (1991). *Beyond methodology: Feminist scholarship as lived research*. Bloomington: Indiana University Press.

Glick, P. & Fiske, S.T. (1997). Hostile and benevolent sexism: Measuring ambivalent sexist attitudes toward women. *Psychology of Women Quarterly, 21*(1), 119–135.

Jansen, G.G. & Davis, D.R. (1998). Honoring voice and visibility: Sensitive-topic research and feminist interpretive inquiry. *Affilia, 13*(3), 289–311.

Kerr, E.A. (1998). Toward a feminist natural science: Linking theory and practice. *Women's Studies International Forum, 21*(1), 95–109.

Lieberman, L. (1997). Gender and the deconstruction of the race concept. *American Anthropologist, 99*(3), 545–558.

Madriz, E.I. (1998). Using focus groups with lower socioeconomic status Latina women. *Qualitative Inquiry, 4*(1), 114–128.

Mairs, N. (1994). *Voice lessons: On becoming a woman writer*. Boston, MA: Beacon Press.

March, C., Smyth, I., & Mukhopadhyay, M. (1999). *A guide to gender-analysis frameworks*. Oxford, UK: Oxfam.

Mathison, M.A. (1997). Complicity as epistemology: Reinscribing the historical categories of 'woman' through standpoint feminism. *Communication Theory, 7*(2), 149–161.

Neumann, A. & Peterson, P. (Eds.). (1997). *Learning from our lives: Women, research, and autobiography in education*. New York: Teacher's College Press.

Oakley, A. (1981). Interviewing women: A contradiction in terms. In H. Roberts (Ed.), *Doing feminist research*. London: Routledge & Kegan Paul.

Oreskes, N. (1996). Objectivity or heroism? On the invisibility of women in science. *Osiris, 11*, 87–113.

Reinharz, S. (1992). *Feminist methods in social research*. New York: Oxford University Press.

Richardson, L. (1997). Skirting a pleated text: De-disciplining an academic life. *Qualitative Inquiry, 3*(3), 295–303.

Ring, J. (1987). Toward a feminist epistemology. *American Journal of Political Science, 31*(4), 753–772.

Schacht, S.P. (1997). Feminist fieldwork in the misogynist setting of the rugby pitch: Temporarily becoming a sylph to survive and personally grow. *Journal of Contemporary Ethnography, 26*(3), 338–363.

Wilkinson, S. (1998). Focus groups in feminist research: Power, interaction, and the co-construction of meaning. *Women's Studies International Forum, 21*(1).

Wylie, A. (1997). The engendering of archaeology: Refiguring feminist science studies. *Osiris, 12*, 80–99.

Feminist Policy Studies

Elenes, C.A. (1997). Reclaiming the borderlands: Chicana/o identity, difference, and critical pedagogy. *Educational Theory, 47*(3), 359–375.

Fondas, N. (1995). The biological clock confronts complex organizations: Women's ambivalence about work and implications for feminist management research. *Journal of Management Inquiry, 4*(1), 57–65.

Gitlin, A. (Ed.). (1994). *Power and method: Political activism and educational research. Critical social thought series.* New York: Routledge.

Marshall, C. (Ed.). (1997). *Feminist critical policy analysis. A perspective from post-secondary education.* Vol. 2. London: Falmer Press.

Marshall, C. (Ed.). (1997). *Feminist critical policy analysis. A perspective from primary and secondary schooling.* Volume 1. London: Falmer Press.

Scott, J.W. (1996). *More than paradoxes to offer: French feminists and the rights of man.* Cambridge, MA: Harvard University Press.

Thayer-Bacon, B.J. (1992). A feminine reconceptualization of critical thinking theory. *Journal of Thought, 27*(1–2), 4–17.

Townsend, B.K. & Twombly, S. (1998). A feminist critique of organizational change in the community college. In J. Levin (Ed.) *Organizational change in the community college.* New Directions for Community Colleges, No. 102. San Francisco: Jossey-Bass.

Women in Academe: As Students, Faculty, and Academic Leaders

Women Leaders

American Council on Education. (1994). *A blueprint for leadership: How women college and university presidents can shape the future.* Washington, DC: American Council on Education.

Astin, Helen S., & Carole Leland. (1991). *Women of influence, women of vision: A cross-generational study of leaders and social change.* San Francisco: Jossey-Bass.

Blackmore, J. (1999). *Troubling women: Feminism, leadership and educational change.* Buckingham: Open University Press.

Calas, M.B. & Smircich, L. (1991). Voicing seduction to silence leadership. *Organization Studies, 12*(4), 567–602.

Chlinwiak, Luba. (1997). *Higher education leadership: Analyzing the gender gap.* ASHE-ERIC Higher Education Report Volume 25, No. 4. Washington, DC: The George Washington University, Graduate School of Education and Human Development.

David, M. (Ed.). (1998). *Negotiating the glass ceiling.* London: Taylor & Francis.

Davidson, M.J. & Burke, R.J. (Eds.) (1994). *Women in management: Current research issues.* London: Paul Chapman.

Gillett-Karam, R. (1994). Women and leadership. In G. Baker III (Ed.), *A handbook on the community college in America* (pp. 94–108). Westport, CT: Greenwood Press.

Glazer, J.S. (1991). Feminism and professionalism in teaching and educational administration. *Educational Administration Quarterly, 27*(3), 321–342.

Glazer, J.S., Bensimon, E.M., & Townsend, B.K. (Eds.). (1993). *Women in higher education: A feminist perspective.* Needham Heights, MA: Ginn Press.

Haring-Hidore, M., Freeman, S.C., Phelps, S., Spann, N.G., & Wooten, H.R. (1990). Women administrators' ways of knowing. *Education and Urban Society, 22*(2), 170–181.

Hill, M.S. & Jackson, B.W. (1995). *Women as educational leaders: Opening windows, pushing ceilings.* Thousand Oaks, CA: Corwin.

Johnsrud, L.K. (1991). Administrative promotion: The power of gender. *Journal of Higher Education, 62*(2), 119.

Johnsrud, L.K. & Heck, R.H. (1994). Administrative promotion within a university: The cumulative impact of gender. *Journal of Higher Education, 65,* 25–44.

Jones, L. (1990). The gender difference hypothesis: A synthesis of research findings. *Educational Administration Quarterly, 26*(1), 5–37.

Kolodny, Annette. (1998). *Failing the future: A dean looks at higher education in the twenty-first century.* Durham, NC: Duke University Press.

Korabik, A. (1982). Sex role orientation and leadership style. *International Journal of Women's Studies, 5,* 329–337.

Mitchell, P.T. (Ed.). (1993). *Cracking the wall: Women in higher education administration.* Washington, DC: College and University Personnel Association.

Sagaria, M.D. (Ed.). (1988). *Empowering women: Leadership development strategies on campus.* San Francisco: Jossey-Bass.

Sturnick, J.A., Milley, J.E., and Tisinger, C.A. (Eds.). (1991). *Women at the helm: Pathfinding presidents at state colleges and universities.* Washington, DC: American Association of State Colleges and Universities.

Wear, D. (1997). *Privilege in the medical academy: A feminist examines gender, race, and power.* New York: Teacher's College Press.

Wenninger, M.D. (1996). Women in Higher Education, 1996. *Women in Higher Education, 6*(1–2).

Wenninger, M.D. (1997). Women in Higher Education, 1997. *Women in Higher Education, 6*(1–2).

Women Faculty

Aisenberg, N. & Harrington, M. (1988). *Women of academe.* Amherst: University of Massachusetts Press.

Applegate, R. (1993). Deconstructing faculty status: Research and assumptions. *Journal of Academic Librarianship, 19*(3), 158–164.

Benjamin, L. (1997). *Black women in the academy: Promises and perils.* Gainesville, FL: University Press of Florida.

Chamberlain, M.K. (1991). *Women in academe: Progress and prospects.* New York: Russell Sage Foundation.

Feldman, K.A. (1993). College students' views of male and female college teachers: Evidence from students' evaluations of their classroom teachers. *Research in Higher Education, 34* (2), 151–211.

Finkel, S.K. & Olswang, S.G. (1996). Child rearing as a career impediment to women assistant professors. *Review of Higher Education, 19*(2), 123–139.

Glazer, J.S. (1997). Beyond male theory: A feminist perspective on teaching motivation. In J.L. Bess (Ed.). *Teaching well and liking it: Motivating faculty to teach effectively* (pp. 37–56). Baltimore: Johns Hopkins University Press.

Glazer-Raymo, J. (1999). *Shattering the myths: Women in academe.* Baltimore, MD: Johns Hopkins University Press.

Glazer-Raymo, J. (2000). The fragmented paradigm: Women, tenure, and schools of education. In W.G. Tierney (Ed.). *Faculty work in schools of education: Rethinking roles and rewards for the 21st century.* Albany: SUNY Press.

Hagedorn, L. (1996). Wage equity and female faculty job satisfaction: The role of wage differentials in a job satisfaction causal model. *Research in Higher Education, 37*(5), 569–598.

Hensel, N. (1991). *Realizing gender equality in higher education: The need to integrate work/family issues.* ASHE-ERIC Higher Education Report No. 3. Washington, DC: Association for the Study of Higher Education.

James, J. & Farmer, R. (Eds.). (1993). *Spirit, space, and survival: African American women in (White) academe.* New York: Routledge.

Johnsrud, L.K. & Des Jarlais, C.D. (1994). Barriers to tenure for women and minorities. *Review of Higher Education, 17*(4), 335–353.

Lomperis, A.M.T. (1990). Are women changing the nature of the academic profession? *Journal of Higher Education, 61*(6), 643–677.

McDermott, P. (1994). *Politics and scholarship: Feminist academic journals and the production of knowledge.* Champaign, IL: University of Illinois Press.

McElrath, K. (1992). Gender, career disruption, and academic rewards. *Journal of Higher Education, 63,* 269–281.

Mintz, B. & Rothblum, E. (Eds.). (1997). *Lesbians in academe.* New York: Routledge.

Richardson, L. (1998). *Fields of play: Constructing an academic life.* New Brunswick, NJ: Rutgers University Press.

Riger, S., Stokes, J., Raja, S., & Sullivan, M. (1997). Measuring perceptions of the work environment for female faculty. *Review of Higher Education, 21*(1), 63–78.

Ropers-Huilman, Becky. (1997). Constructing feminist teachers: Complexities of identity. *Gender and Education, 9*(3), 327–343.

Rosser, S.V. (1997). *Re-engineering female friendly science.* New York: Teacher's College Press.

Schwartz, R.A. (1997). Reconceptualizing the leadership roles of women in higher education: A brief history on the importance of deans of women. *Journal of Higher Education, 68*(5), 502–522.

Tokarczyk, M.M. & Fay, E.A. (Eds.). (1993). *Working-class women in the academy: Laborers in the knowledge factory.* Amherst: University of Massachusetts Press.

Townsend, B.K. (1995) Women community college faculty: On the margins or in the mainstream? In *Gender and Power in the Community College* (pp. 39–46). New Directions for Community Colleges, No. 89. San Francisco: Jossey-Bass.

Townsend, B.K. (1998). Women faculty's satisfaction with employment in the community college. *Community College Journal of Research and Practice, 22*(7), 655–661.

Thoreson, R.W., Kardash, C.M., Lewthold, D.A., & Morrow, K.A. (1990). Gender differences in the academic career. *Research in Higher Education, 31*(2), 193–209.

Welch, L.B. (Ed.) (1992). *Perspectives on minority women in higher education.* New York: Praeger.

Welch, L.B. (Ed.) (1990). *Women in higher education: Changes and challenges.* New York: Praeger.

Wisker, G. (1996). *Empowering women in higher education.* Sterling, VA: Stylus Publishing.

Wunsch, M.A. & Johnsrud, L.K. (1992). Breaking barriers: Mentoring junior faculty women for professional development and retention. *To improve the academy, 11,* 175–187.

Women Students

Boxer, M.J. (1985). Women's studies, feminist goals, and the science of women. In B.M. Solomon (Ed.), *In the company of educated women: A history of women and higher education in America.* New Haven: Yale University.

Edwards, R. (1993). *Mature women students: Separating or connecting family and education, gender, and society. Feminist perspectives on the past and present series.* Bristol, PA: Taylor and Francis.

Eisenhart, M.A. & Finkel, E. (1998). *Women's science: Learning and succeeding from the margins.* Chicago: University of Chicago Press.

Hall, R.M & Sandler, B.R. (1982). *The classroom climate: A chilly one for women.* Washington, DC: Association of American Colleges, Project on the Status and Education of Women.

Heinrich, K.T. (1991). Loving partnerships: Dealing with sexual attraction and power in doctoral advisement relationships. *Journal of Higher Education, 62*(5), 515–538.

Johnson, K.K. (1995). *Focus groups: A method of evaluation to increase retention of female engineering students*. College Park: Maryland University Press.

Johnsrud, L.K. (1991). Mentoring between academic women: The capacity for the interdependence. *Initiatives, 53*, 7–17.

Luebke, B.F. & Reilly, M.A. (1995). *Women's studies graduates: The first generation*. New York: Teacher's College Press.

Naples, N.A. (1998). Bringing everyday life to policy analysis: The case of white rural women negotiating college and welfare. *Journal of Poverty, 2*(1), 23–53.

Rittner, B. & Trudeau, P. (1997). *The women's guide to surviving graduate school*. Thousand Oaks, CA: Sage Publications.

Rosser, S.V. (1995). *Teaching the majority: Breaking the gender barrier in science, mathematics, and engineering*. New York: Teacher's College Press.

Serex, C. & Townsend, B.K. (1999). Student perceptions of chilling practices in sex-atypical majors. *Research in Higher Education, 40*(5), 527–538.

Stone, N.V., Nelson, & Neimann. (1994). Poor single-mother college students' view on the effect of some primary sociological and psychological belief factors on their academic success. *Journal of Higher Education, 65*(5), 571–584.

Suitor, J.J. (1987). Marital happiness of returning women students and their husbands: Effects of part-time and full-time enrollment. *Research in Higher Education, 27*, 311–331.

Turner, C.S.V. & Thompson, J.R. (1993). Socializing women doctoral students: Minority and majority experiences. *Review of Higher Education, 16*(3), 355–370.

Global Feminism: International and Comparative Perspectives

Barriteau, V.E. (1996). Structural adjustment policies in the Caribbean: A feminist perspective. *NSWA Journal, 8*(1), 142–156.

Biron, R.E. (1996). Feminist periodicals and political crisis in Mexico: Fem, debate feminista, and La Correa Feminista in the 1990s. *Feminist Studies, 22*(1), 151–169.

Birke, L. & Whitworth, R. (1998). Seeking knowledge: Women, science, and Islam. *Women's Studies International Forum, 21*(2), 147–159.

Blackmore, J. (1999). Globalization: A useful concept for feminists rethinking theory and strategies in education? In N.C. Burbules and C.A. Torres (Eds.). *Globalization and education: Critical perspectives*. New York & London: Routledge.

Eggins, H. (Ed.). (1997). *Women as leaders and managers in higher education*. Buckingham, England: Society for Research in Higher Education & Open University Press.

Fuchs, E. (1997). Women and Jewish studies. *National Women's Studies Association Journal, 9*(3), 163–173.

Ghorayshi, P. (1996). Women in developing countries: Methodological and theoretical considerations. *Women and Politics, 16*(3), 89–111.

Kelly, G.P. & Slaughter, S. (Eds.). (1991). *Women's Higher Education in Comparative Perspective*. Dordrecht, Netherlands: Kluwer.

Lunneborg, P.W. (1994). *OU women. Undoing educational obstacles*. Herndon, VA: Cassell.

Reay, D. (1998). Surviving in dangerous places: Working-class women, women's studies, and higher education. *Women's Studies International Forum, 21*(1), 11–19.

Reeves, J.B. (1995). Toward a sociology of the Argentine women's movement. *Quarterly Journal of Ideology, 18*(3–4), 3–12.

Robinson, F. (1997). Globalizing care: Ethics, feminist theory, and international relations. *Alternatives, 22*(1), 113–133.

Sharoni, S. (1997). Women and gender in Middle East studies: Trends, prospects, and challenges. *Middle East Report, 27*(4), 27–29.

Schor, N. (1995). French feminism is a universalism. *Differences, 7*(1), 15–47.

Feminist Pedagogy and Curriculum Transformation

Butler, J.E. & Walter, J.C. (Eds.). (1991). *Transforming the curriculum: Ethnic studies and women's studies*. Albany, NY: State University of New York.

Clough, P.T. (1994). *Feminist thought: Desire, power, and academic discourse*. Oxford and Cambridge: Blackwell.

Davis, F. & Steiger, A. (1993). *Feminist pedagogy in the physical sciences*. Montréal, Québec: Vanier College.

Eichstedt, J.L. (1996). Heterosexism and gay/lesbian/bisexual experiences: Teaching strategies and exercises. *Teaching Sociology, 24*(4), 384–388.

Gabriel, S.L. & Smithson, I. (1990). *Gender in the classroom*. Urbana, IL: University of Illinois Press.

Gore, J. (1990). What we can do for you! What *can* 'we' do for 'you'?: Struggling over empowerment in critical and feminist pedagogy. *Educational Foundations, 4*(3).

Jeffreys, S. (1994). The queer disappearance of lesbians: Sexuality in the academy. *Women's Studies International Forum, 17*(5), 459–472.

Kenny, S.J. (1995). Women, feminism, gender, and law in political science: Ruminations of a feminist academic. *Women and Politics, 15*(3), 43–69.

Kohlstedt, S.G. & Longino, H. (1997). The women, gender, and science question: What do research on women in science and research on gender and science have to do with each other? *Osiris, 12*, 3–15.

Kramarae, C. and Spender, D. (Eds.). (1992). *The knowledge explosion: Generations of feminist scholarship*. New York: Teacher's College Press.

Krouse, M.B. (1996). Reeducating emotions in a feminist classroom: Addressing emotional resistance from privileged students. *Transformations, 7*(2), 24–41.

Lather, P. (1991). *Getting smart: Feminist research and pedagogy with/in the postmodern*. New York: Routledge.

Lewis, M. (1990). Interrupting patriarchy: Politics, resistance, and transformation in the feminist classroom. *Harvard Educational Review, 60*(2), 467–488.

Luke, C. & Gore, J. (Eds.). (1992). *Feminisms and critical pedagogy*. New York: Routledge.

Lurie, S. (1992). The 'women' (in) question: Feminist and cultural studies. *Discourse, 14*(3), 89–103.

Maher, F.A. (1987). Toward a richer theory of feminist pedagogy: A comparison of 'liberation' and 'gender' models for teaching and learning. *Journal of Education, 169*, 91–100.

Maher, F.A. & Tetreault, M.K.T. (1994). *The feminist classroom*. New York: Basic Books.

Mayberry, M. & Rees, M.N. (1997). Feminist pedagogy, interdisciplinary praxis, and science education. *NWSA Journal, 9*(1), 57–75.

Michelson, E. (1996). 'Auctoritee' and 'experience': Feminist epistemology and the assessment of experiential learning. *Feminist Studies, 22*(3), 627–655.

Munson, C.E. & Hipp, J. (1998). Social work students' knowledge of feminism. *Journal of Teaching in Social Work, 16*(1–2), 57–73.

Orner, M. Interrupting the calls for student voice in 'liberatory' education: A feminist poststructuralist perspective. In C. Lankshear & P. McLaren (Eds.), *Critical literacy: Politics, praxis, and the postmodern*. Albany: SUNY Press.

Orozco, C.E. (1990). Getting started in Chicana studies. *Women's Studies Quarterly, 1&2*, 46–69.

Richmond, G., Howes, E., Kurth, L. & Hazelwood, C. (1998). Connections and critique: Feminist pedagogy and science teacher education. *Journal of Research in Science Teaching, 35*(8), 897–918.

Ropers-Huilman, B. (1998). *Feminist teaching in theory and practice: Situating power and knowledge in poststructural classrooms*. New York: Teacher's College Press.

Scully, D. (1996). Overview of women's studies: Organization and institutional status in U.S. higher education. *NWSA Journal, 8*(3), 122–128.

Thompson, A. & Gitlin, A. (1995). Creating spaces for reconstructing knowledge in feminist pedagogy. *Educational Theory, 45*(2), 125–150.

Walters, C.E. (1991). *Pedagogy and the struggle for voice: Issues of language, power, and schooling for Puerto Ricans*. South Hadley, MA: Bergin & Garvey.

Walters, S.D. (1996). From here to queer: Radical feminism, postmodernism, and the lesbian menace (or, why can't a woman be more like a fag?). *Signs, 21*(4), 830–869.

Zinn, M.B. & Dill, B.T. (1996). Theorizing difference from multiracial feminism. *Feminist Studies, 22*(2), 321–331.